HUTCHINSON
GALLUP

INFO 93

TODAY'S YEARBOOK & FACTFINDER

HUTCHINSON
GALLUP

INFO 93

Helicon

Helicon Publishing Ltd
42 Hythe Bridge Street
Oxford OX1 2EP

Set in Clearface Gothic and Trade Gothic

Data prepared on Telos

Printed and bound in England

ISBN 0 09 175397X

British Library Cataloguing in Publication Data
A catalogue record for this book is available from the
British Library

Project Editor Denise Dresner

Commissioning Editor Anne-Lucie Norton

Editors Gian Douglas Home, Sara Jenkins-Jones,
Ingrid von Essen

Copy editors Janet Browne, Lionel Browne

Researcher Anna Farkas

Design Terry Caven

Graphics Ken Brooks

Maps Swanston Graphics

Page Make-up Helen Bird, Anneset

Index Edith Harkness, Ingrid von Essen

We would like to thank Jane Anson, Ruth Barratt, and
Eric Smith for their help

Contributors Dr Owen Adikibi, Paul Bahn, Nick Beard, Tia
Cockrell, Susan Cusworth, Ian Derbyshire, Dr J D
Derbyshire, Col Michael Dewar, Dougal Dixon, Nigel
Dudley, Robert Dyer, Caroline Evans, Anna Farkas, Wendy
Grossman, Michael Hitchcock, Stuart Holroyd, Stephen
Kite, Peter Lafferty, Mike Lewis, Graham Littler, Robin
Maconie, Tom McArthur, David Munro, Joanna O'Brien,
Maureen O'Connor, Robert Paisley, Martin Palmer,
Ranchor Prime, Tim Pulleine, John Pym, Chris Rhys, Ian
Ridpath, Dr Julian Rowe, John Rowlinson, Kate Salway,
Emma Shackleton, Mark Slade, Steve Smyth, Joe Staines,
Prof Ian Stewart, Callum Storrie, Ingrid von Essen, Prof
Trevor Watkins, Imogen Stooke-Wheeler, Charles Wintour

C<u>ONTEN</u>S

THE WORLD

MISCELLANEOUS

PREFACE

INFO 93 is the second edition of a yearbook with a difference. Keeping the successful format of INFO 92, it aims to provide the reader with concise and informed coverage of the essential topics and issues of today as they affect us: from the federation of republics that replaced the USSR to the rise of the right-wing in Europe, from the latest advances in medicine to the global medium of online communications.

It has been compiled with the help of more than forty subject specialists, and written to inform and explain without pedantry or obscure technical jargon.

INFO 93 is designed for use by everyone: home, office, school and college, and library. We have made every effort to include the most up-to-date, best-informed expert opinion, together with the salient fact. It is equally for the student, the curious, and the quiz-game buff.

How it is different
Of course INFO 93 includes the major events of the year—who died (pp 31–53), what happened when (pp 11–22), even who said what (pp 3–10)—but it is more than just a yearbook. It provides a concise overview of subjects in the sciences, arts, business, and society, including dates (when was RNA discovered? p 369), facts (the latest Wimbledon champions, p 199), figures (the size of the UK national debt, p 276), and background information. And INFO 93 goes beyond this to provide analysis and insight, covering events in a European and world context—what shape will the CIS take? (p 154); how will the Social Charter affect workers in the European Community? (p 261); is air travel a major environmental hazard? (p 480); are tigers on the path to extinction? (p 540). INFO 93 also sets out to guide and explain—where do you put the apostrophe? (p 139); what are the pros and cons of genetically engineered food? (p 498); how can we contribute to a cleaner environment? (p 478). We have tried in every section not simply to include an undigested mass of figures, but to present information in a clear, easily understandable way, with illustrations, graphics, and photographs supplementing the text, as well as feature articles and topic boxes on the most current developments in a particular field.

With the aid of the extensive resources of Gallup Opinion Poll material, INFO 93 also provides statistical information on people's views on a variety of topics, ranging from the top-selling videos and CDs to surrogacy, fashion trends, and politics.

How to use INFO 93
INFO 93 can be used in two ways. Look in the contents for the five major categories—Society, Economics and Business, The Arts, Science and Technology, and The World—which are in turn divided into forty subjects, from archaeology to warfare, each one forming a compact, logically arranged outline that includes key terms, dates, and people. Or use the index, which includes over 12,500 items, for a detailed guide to individual entries. The index contains many additional references to topics in the book, enabling you to find, for instance, information on CFCs in both the Chemistry and Environment sections.

How you can help
Writing and compiling INFO 93 showed us convincingly that an encyclopedic yearbook can be fun; it can inform while being entertaining, and need not be a dull compilation of official titles and statistics. But with your help it can become much better. Please write to us and let us know what you liked, what you didn't use, and what you think should be included next time. Your letters will enable us to produce a bigger, better third edition which corresponds more closely with what you, the reader, want to know.

ACKNOWLEDGEMENTS

We would like to thank the following for photographs supplied: AFP Photo; Alfred A Kalmus Ltd; Bell Labs; British Airways; Dr Carlos Bustamante; Circa Photo Library; Format Photographs Ltd; Simon Fowler; Sergio Gurrieri; JET Joint Undertaking; The Kobal Collection; Kodak; Jane Lewis; The Marconi Company Ltd; Phillips; Photographic Library, Conservative Central Office; Photographic Services; Central Office of Information; Popperfoto; Press Association Photos; Rank Film Distributors Ltd; Rex Features; RSPCA; South American Pictures; Keith Turnbull Photography; The Wallace Collection; World Council of Churches; Yves Saint-Laurent.

Gallup

Gallup Social Surveys (Gallup Polls) Limited, have provided all the polls and surveys which appear in the book, generally at the end of each subject section. All Gallup material is based on a sample of approximately 1000 adults in the UK and all figures are percentages of people sampled unless stated otherwise.

Statistics

It should be borne in mind that official statistics take a full year or more to compile. We have provided the latest figures available at the time of going to press.

THE YEAR

QUOTES OF THE YEAR

Even Jesus Christ cannot untie the knots.
Mikhail Gorbachev *Soviet leader, on his continuing commitment to socialist ideals and a united USSR.*
June 1991.

People are not willing to be governed by those who do not speak their language.
Norman Tebbit *former UK Conservative Party chair.*
June 1991.

We do not want the faddist diet that has had removed from it the natural mix which humans are meant to eat and in which meat plays its part.
John Gummer *UK minister for agriculture, fisheries, and food.*
June 1991

I always get asked how I manage to juggle the demands of a career and a family. Nobody asks Sting how he juggles two families, a career, and the rainforests.
Kirsty McColl *singer and songwriter.*
June 1991.

If I were knocked down tomorrow by a passing train, I would be considered the most important artist ever in the history of English pop music, which today I am not considered to be.
Morrissey *singer and songwriter.*
June 1991.

This is no longer ordinary—typhoons, earthquakes, dormant volcanoes erupting. So you know, one solution to this is President Marcos should be allowed home.
Imelda Marcos *former Philippine first lady, explaining the country's recent natural disasters as divine retribution for the government's refusal to allow her late husband to be buried there.*
July 1991.

Anything you write, you must have the sneaking suspicion that you are addressing it to yourself.
Elvis Costello.
July 1991.

What is it about August, anyway?
George Bush *US president, on the way world crises keep disrupting his summer holidays.*
August 1991.

Everything is OK. No problems. We can't see why people don't go.
Ali S al-Gammoudi *Libyan tourism official, on Libya as a holiday resort.*
1991.

Negotiations with the European Community are like wrestling with a blancmange.
Austin Mitchell *Labour member of Parliament.*
1991.

It would have been better if the experiment had been conducted in some small country to make it clear that it was a utopian idea, although a beautiful idea.
Boris Yeltsin *Russian president, on communism.*
September 1991.

We will sit steadily on the fishing boat despite the waves.
Wu Jianmin *of the Chinese foreign ministry, reaffirming Beijing's commitment to communist principles in the wake of the demise of the Soviet Communist Party.*
September 1991.

No one.
Fidel Castro *Cuban leader, asked to name Cuba's closest friends.*
September 1991.

This is a circus ... it is a hi-tech lynching for uppity blacks.
Clarence Thomas *during the US Senate inquiry into accusations of sexual harassment prior to his confirmation as a Supreme Court judge.*
October 1991.

I was never attached to power or valuables. I have no attachment to worldly things.
Imelda Marcos *shortly before her return to the Philippines, where she faced arrest on charges related to the alleged plundering of $5 billion from state coffers.*
October 1991.

It always boils down to the same thing, self-interest, and you're not going to get people to abrogate their self-interest.
Sam Cummings *arms dealer.*
October 1991.

More likely, I feel myself to be a child because our democracy is in diapers, and with it our parliament and our president are also in diapers.
Vaclav Havel *president of Czechoslovakia, on whether he considers himself the father of his country.*
October 1991.

I owe a lot of who I am and what I've been and what I've done to the beatniks from the fifties and to the poetry and art and music that I've come in contact with. I feel like I'm part of a continuous line of a certain thing in American culture, of a root.
Jerry Garcia *of the Grateful Dead rock group.*
October 1991.

Some months ago, I could give a single command and 541,000 people would immediately obey it. Today I can't get a plumber to come to my house.
Norman Schwarzkopf *retired US general, on life after the Gulf War.*
November 1991.

I have come home penniless.
Imelda Marcos *after her return to the Philippines.*
November 1991.

We can safely abandon the basic doctrine of the 1980s: namely that the rich were not working because they had too little money, the poor because they had too much.
John Kenneth Galbraith *US economist.*
November 1991.

There is nothing in my past of which I am not proud.
Yitzhak Shamir *former Israeli prime minister.*
November 1991.

There's songs of mine that I get really sick of. When you consider I recorded 'Stand By Your Man' for the first time 23 years ago and I've probably sung it four or five times a week since then, you can appreciate how it gets to me.
Tammy Wynette *country singer.*
November 1991.

Groups who deal with rape try to educate women about how to defend themselves. What really needs to be done is teaching men not to rape.
Kurt Cobain *of US rock group Nirvana.*
November 1991.

The left doesn't have a monopoly on ecology. We at the National Front respect life and love animals. I myself have a white rat whom I kiss every day on the mouth.
Jean-Marie le Pen *French politician, on environmentalism.*
November 1991.

Dozens of people have seen this green monster, which has the girth of a large tree trunk and is around six or seven metres long. It swims with its head high in the air.
Tass *Soviet news agency, on the sighting of Nessie in a remote Siberian lake.*
November 1991.

This is what we fought wars about.
Norman Tebbit *after former chancellor Nigel Lawson's comment that creating a single European currency could prove the height of folly.*
November 1991.

His mission in Britain was to secure control of our islands for the rule of the pope. Jacques Delors is his natural heir.
Conservative politician Teresa Gorman *on Guy Fawkes.*
November 1991

George Bush thinks that if he feeds enough oats to the horse, some will pass through to feed the sparrows in the road.
John Kenneth Galbraith
November 1991.

This system is to open competition what Oliver North was to open government.
Frank Dobson *speaking for the Labour Party on the newly privatized UK electricity industry.*
November 1991.

Delinquents like these agitators have to be shot and we will shoot them.
Try Sutrusno *commander of Indonesia's armed forces, after the army's shooting of an alleged 180 people.*
November 1991.

I'm sure once Guns n' Roses started becoming really successful, Bush had them checked out, and found they weren't articulate enough to be a threat to anybody.
Kurt Cobain *of Nirvana.*
November 1991.

We apologize for having captured you. We recognize now that this was the wrong thing to do; holding hostages prisoner serves no useful purpose.
Terry Waite *released British hostage, quoting one of his captors.*
November 1991.

One thing I can say is the British take a long time to get things done. Terry Waite came to rescue me, and after five years he is finally taking me home.
Thomas Sutherland *US hostage, after his release from captivity in Lebanon.*
November 1991.

I was drowning my sorrows, but my sorrows they learned to swim.
U2 *Irish rock group.*
November 1991.

There are all kinds of classical music, but Mozart seems to make the best sake.
Hatsue Kodama *Sawada brewery employee, on the Japanese rage for Mozart, whose music plays at the Sawada works every day.*
December 1991.

They have no right to declare the Soviet Union nonexistent.
Mikhail Gorbachev *reacting to the formation of the CIS by Russia, Belarus, and Ukraine.*
December 1991.

It's a very balanced text. It allows all sides to say they've won.
European Community official *on the Maastricht treaty.*
December 1991.

If America does not wish to end her days in the same nursing home as Britannia she had best end this geo-babble about new world orders.
Patrick Buchanan *aspiring Republican candidate for the US presidency.*
December 1991.

Why is it that right-wing bastards always stand shoulder to shoulder in solidarity while liberals fall out among themselves?
Yevgeny Yevtushenko *Russian poet.*
December 1991.

It's quite a change to have a prime minister who hasn't got any political ideas at all.
Michael Foot *former UK Labour Party leader.*
December 1991.

It used to be that college kids were activists. Now they're driving around in big expensive cars and they're happy to tell you how intolerant they are of things like racial quotas. They're proud to be conservatives. We're marching backwards. It's embarrassing.
Mike Mills *of US rock group REM.*
December 1991.

If you are driving a car, and sitting behind you is a lady with a handbag and a man with fangs, you may feel it wiser to drive in the slow lane.
Dennis Healey *Labour politician, on John Major's European predicament.*
December 1991.

This country was going nowhere and we couldn't possibly live the way we did.
Mikhail Gorbachev *in his farewell speech.*
December 1991.

In a democracy everybody has a right to be represented, including the jerks.
Chris Patten *former UK Conservative Party chair.*
December 1991.

It's like trying to dislodge something caught in the smokestack of the *Queen Mary* by using a rowboat pushing from the stern.
William O'Neil *of the* Galileo *spacecraft project on trying to fix its malfunctioning telescope from the ground.*
December 1991.

I like pornography, but I don't like that.
Phil Collins *pop singer, on sexually explicit rap music.*
December 1991.

I'm glad that Maradona is going. If the city of Naples wants to have an idol to venerate, it should stick with its patron saint, San Gennaro: he was a better man, he was less expensive, and he didn't snort cocaine.
Luigi Compagnone *Neapolitan writer, on football.*
December 1991.

The nearest thing Ireland has to a medieval prince—with the cunning of a Machiavelli, the lifestyle of a Louis XVI and the apparent personal wealth of a Medici.
Dick Spring *Irish Labour Party leader, on former prime minister Charles Haughey.*
December 1991.

No kissing, please.
Saudi Crown Prince Abdullah *holding off an eager Yassir Arafat, who is still kept at arm's length by Riyadh for supporting Saddam Hussein in the Gulf War.*
December 1991.

I didn't know that. God almighty, why would they aim nuclear weapons at us when we're trying to pull their ox out of a ditch?
William L Dickinson *member of the US House Armed Services Committee, when informed by CIA director Robert Gates that China aims some of its missiles at the USA.*
December 1991.

Money's no reason for doing anything. See, I don't want to sell something that I would give away. And that's what playing is, you're giving that away. And if you're doing it just to make money, then you're selling it. And there's something wrong with that.
Peter Buck *of REM on why the band didn't tour in 1991.*
December 1991.

Roll me under the table until the dinner's over.
George Bush *to his personal physician after fainting at a state banquet in Tokyo.*
January 1992.

My mother has been telling me for a long time: give it all up and come home. I am going to call her today. I am sure she will tell me the same thing. She may even say: 'Thank God, now get some rest.'
Mikhail Gorbachev.
December 1991.

I think television should be abolished completely. I think it's completely destructive and there's nothing positive about it, nothing at all.
Sinead O'Connor *Irish singer and songwriter.*
January 1992.

There's only one country any more that's all white and that's Iceland. And Iceland is not enough.
David Duke *right-wing US politician.*
January 1992.

We are talking about two totally different concepts; in Europe, extramarital affairs are considered a sign of good health, a feat.
Jean-Pierre Detremmerie *Belgian politician, on the US media's treatment of Democratic presidential hopeful Bill Clinton.*
January 1992.

Am I tempted by a political job? The only thing that would make me leave my work would be to become president of the USA.
Umberto Eco *Italian writer, turning down an offer from Italy's former Communist Party to be a general election candidate.*
January 1992.

We did not leave the back of the bus only to place our children in the back of an ambulance.
David Dinkins *mayor of New York, on a spate of hate crimes against black children.*
January 1992.

My own education was ... private ... and I got a lot out of it. I was regularly beaten. I belt my own children and then it's over and forgotten.
Jeremy Irons *actor.*
January 1992.

I'm not one in a million, I'm merely expressing the feelings of millions of people ... I'm operating for all the abused children and all the women and all of the people who have been completely and utterly oppressed.
Sinead O'Connor.
January 1992.

These are not Mickey Mouse complaints.
Spokesperson *for a consortium of building contractors who claim to be owed $5 million by Eurodisney.*
January 1992.

If this was a few years ago, I would go and get pretty thoroughly drunk. Fortunately for me, the only beer that will touch my lips will be non-alcoholic.
Bob Hawke *at a press conference after his resignation as Australian prime minister.*
January 1992.

A government is not an old pair of socks that you throw out. Come to think of it, you don't throw out old pairs of socks anyway these days.
Boris Yeltsin *dismissing a call for his government to resign.*
January 1992.

I think continuity is very important. It is a job for life.
Queen Elizabeth II *reflecting on her role.*
January 1992.

If the European Community should one day become a strong political union, why shouldn't it have its own nuclear weapons?
François Mitterrand *president of France.*
January 1992.

Lloyd Webber's music is everywhere, but then so is AIDS.
Malcolm Williamson *Master of the Queen's music, on the highlight of a pageant marking the 40th anniversary of Queen Elizabeth II's accession to the UK throne.*
January 1992.

I hope he'll change his mind but if he doesn't then I'll play bass. I'll do it myself. How hard can it be?
Mick Jagger *on Bill Wyman's threat to retire from the Rolling Stones.*
January 1992.

It sounds glib and pretentious to say you want to be up there with Dostoievsky, but I do want to make art that'll live for ever, whether on record or the printed page.
Lou Reed *US singer and songwriter.*
January 1992.

Our instincts are worth more than a thousand years of guitar lessons.
Jim Reid *of the Jesus and Mary Chain rock group.*
February 1992.

We are just becoming a country with a fair number of well-off people and a lot of people who are just going to hell in a handbasket.
Bill Clinton *aspiring Democratic candidate for the US presidency.*
February 1992.

There used to be a time when the idea of heroes was important. People grew up sharing myths and legends and ideals. Now they grow up sharing McDonald's and Disneyland.
Bob Dylan.
February 1992.

If I am elected I will follow the example of my grandfather.
Alessandra Mussolini *granddaughter of Italy's fascist dictator, announcing she will stand in the general election.*
February 1992.

The two great providers of work and the developers of self-respect were two very different people—Franklin Roosevelt and Adolf Hitler.
Lord White *chair of Hanson Industries in the USA.*
February 1992.

I'm beginning to sound like a rightwing lunatic.
Lord White.
February 1992.

Only states which have experienced the Age of Enlightenment should be members of the EC. I doubt whether Ireland can stay in the Community.
Gerhardt Schmidt *German socialist MEP, after the row over abortion in Ireland.*
February 1992.

My dear, I'm always nervous about doing something for the first time.
Dame Gwen Ffrangcon-Davies *actress, referring to death, at 101.*
February 1992.

Skilled people will be liberated as the result of these cutbacks.
Michael Jack *junior minister, on British Aerospace job losses.*
February 1992.

Stereo is more democratic, mono more totalitarian.
Jean-Luc Godard *French film director, opening a cinema in Dolby stereo in Moscow.*
February 1992.

It is more a means of expression, a form of exuberance, than a form of provocation or deliberate vandalism.
Jaques Chirac *mayor of Paris, speaking out for graffiti artists.*
February 1992.

The reason why I believe in the soul is because scientists don't know why music affects people.
William Reid *of the Jesus and Mary Chain.*
February 1992.

I never thought that it wasn't the thing to admit that you'd got a Teasmade. You learn the hard way.
Norma Major *wife of the UK prime minister.*
February 1992.

Maybe a person gets to the point where they have written enough songs. Let someone else write them.
Bob Dylan.
February 1992.

Why not enjoy your misery? Even good things can be dismal.
John Lydon *former member of the Sex Pistols rock group.*
March 1992.

He was an extraordinary leader of workers. He is a terrible head of state.
Gustaw Herling *Polish writer, on President Lech Walesa.*
March 1992.

I don't think my wife would allow me to keep Lenin at home. It wouldn't go with the furniture.
James Bevill *on his $10,000 bid for the corpse of Lenin.*
March 1992.

She even has my ... shoes. I want back my shoes.
Imelda Marcos *on her successor in the Philippine presidential palace, Corazón Aquino.*
March 1992.

I don't want to be charged with child abuse.
Pat Buchanan *on why he won't attack Dan Quayle.*
March 1992.

Purity is a bogus notion. When cultures mix against one another, that's where heat and energy come from.
David Byrne *singer, songwriter, and filmmaker, former member of Talking Heads.*
March 1992.

I'd feel like a joke if I was on TV selling Coca-Cola. I think it eventually weakens the power of the music. I think it weakens the credibility of rock in general.
Tom Petty *US rock singer, on commercial sponsorship.*
March 1992.

For the first time in my life, I will be involved with a company I don't own.
Richard Branson *entrepreneur, on selling Virgin Music to Thorn EMI.*
March 1992.

Your food stamps will be stopped effective March 1992 because we received notice that you passed away. May God bless you. You may reapply if there is a change in your circumstances.
Letter sent by South Carolina's Greenville County department of social services to a local man two weeks after his death.
March 1992.

These people would have us keep quiet about the plague on the grounds that it provides jobs for undertakers.
Spokesperson *for Friends of the Earth on property developers.*
March 1992.

A lot of people use their kids as ego extensions. It justifies their dismal marriage and boring life. Right now if we wanted a kid we'd go and buy one.
John Lydon *singer.*
March 1992.

I am on a diet. I have lost eight pounds and when you see me in four weeks' time, I am going to wear a red carnation so you can recognize me.
Luciano Pavarotti *Italian tenor.*
March 1992.

It is not even well written.
Mary Whitehouse *self-appointed censor, on* Lady Chatterley's Lover, *to be screened by the BBC.*
March 1992.

Study hard and you might grow up to be president. But let's face it, even then you'll never make as much money as your dog.
George Bush *US president, whose dog Millie earned $889,176 in book royalties in 1991, to students visiting the White House.*
April 1992.

He looks even better now.
Imelda Marcos *viewing her late husband, Ferdinand, in his open-casket crypt.*
April 1992.

I don't accept the idea that all of a sudden Major is his own man.
Margaret Thatcher *on her successor.*
April 1992.

Some vegetables I am particularly fond of, but on peas I am relatively neutral.
John Major, *prime minister.*
April 1992.

The tragedy of the Labour Party is not that their aims aren't sincere, it's just that they have this absurd obsession that high earners are rich.
Andrew Lloyd Webber *a high earner.*
April 1992.

When I started out, I didn't want to change the world, I just wanted money and fame. Then I sort of changed my mind.
Bob Geldof *philanthropist and singer.*
April 1992.

I always said and believed that the British character is quite different from the characters of people on the Continent—quite different.
Margaret Thatcher.
April 1992.

Consensus is the absence of principle and the presence of expediency.
Margaret Thatcher
April 1992.

We said zero, and I think any statistician will tell you that when you're dealing with very big numbers, zero must mean plus or minus a few.
William Waldegrave *former UK health secretary, on hospital waiting lists.*
April 1992.

The only way I can describe 'alternative' any more is 'good music'. There are so many bad bands and so many bad songwriters out there that the only alternative to bad music is good music. And that's very rare.
Kurt Cobain *of Nirvana.*
April 1992.

Real socialism is inside man. It wasn't born with Marx. It was in the communes of Italy in the Middle Ages. You can't say it is finished.
Dario Fo *Italian dramatist.*
April 1992.

One has to upset some people; as long as they're not one's potential voters, in terms of election tactics, it doesn't matter too much.
Norman Tebbit *Conservative politician.*
April 1992

People who are in a fortunate position always attribute virtue to what makes them so happy.
John Kenneth Galbraith.
May 1992.

The thing that would have been more exciting would have been if we hadn't found anything.
George F Smoot *US astrophysicist, on discovering evidence of the birth of the universe.*
May 1992.

It's either the discovery of the decade or pure codswallop.
Professor Arnold Wolfendale *Astronomer Royal, on Smoot's findings.*
May 1992.

We issue declarations, but no one cares to adhere to them. We get together occasionally, sign papers and depart.
Nursultan Nazarbayev *president of Kazakhstan, on the workings of the Commonwealth of Independent States.*
May 1992.

You know, the main shortcoming of all socialist countries is that we are not clever with figures.
Kim Dal Hyon *North Korean deputy prime minister, asked how much money the country spent celebrating the 80th birthday of dictator Kim Il Sung.*
May 1992.

I wonder how one can speak of democracy in a country where there is a minority with huge fortunes and others who have nothing; what sort of equality or fraternity can exist between a beggar and a millionaire.
Fidel Castro *Cuban leader.*
May 1992.

Japan will have to take a break from being the world's sugar daddy.
Kiichi Miyazawa *prime minister of Japan, on the implications of his country's recession.*
May 1992.

I think it's just for effect that they fire from so close to us.
European Community monitor *in Sarajevo.*
May 1992.

Men are very, very simple beings. They just want approval and attention, you pat them on the head and they go off and conquer the North Pole. But they are desperate. They are exiles from the world of intimacy.
Camille Paglia *US professor.*
May 1992.

We are looking at a house in Orléans. You know Orléans? It is where Joan of Arc became famous. She was a legend. I too am a legend. Now Orléans will have two legends.
Michel Aoun *exiled Lebanese militia leader, house-hunting in France.*
May 1992.

In this country American means white. Everybody else has to hyphenate.
Toni Morrison *US author.*
June 1992

It would appear that the worst map-readers in the British Army have been sent to Northern Ireland.
Resident *of the border town of Dundalk, on British helicopter incursions.*
June 1992.

If I think I can do it better, I won't buy it.
Sylvester Stallone *US film actor, on collecting art.*
June 1992.

One day Saddam will wake up after a bad dream and decide to invade somebody. But this time I will be ready. I will have my grenades and my CNN.
Abdullah Ali Ahmad Rashed *Bedouin shepherd in Kuwait on why he keeps a generator-powered TV in his tent.*
June 1992.

Britain is not a homeless society. [Rather,] a small number of people sleep rough, rather ostentatiously, on the streets of central London.
Nicholas Ridley *former Conservative minister.*
June 1992

My fear will be that in 15 years' time Jerusalem, Bethlehem, once centres of strong Christian presence, might become a kind of Walt Disney theme park.
Archbishop of Canterbury.
June 1992.

The law is not an exact science.
Lord Donaldson *who originally tried the Maguire Seven.*
June 1992

[You showed] concern and consideration by wearing a contraceptive.
Judge Myerson *jailing a rapist for three years.*
June 1992

CHRONOLOGY

JUNE 1991

INTERNATIONAL

5   South Africa's parliament approved new legislation that repealed the Land Acts of 1913 and 1936 and the Groups Areas Act of 1966, laws that were the pillars of the apartheid system of racial separation.

5   Algerian President Chadli Benjedid declared a state of emergency in response to 12 consecutive days of violent protests in Algiers by Islamic fundamentalists.

9   King Hussein and representatives of Jordan's principal political factions signed a newly drafted national charter that legalized political parties in the kingdom, ending a 34-year ban.

12   Boris Yeltsin, campaigning as a political independent, was elected to the newly created executive presidency of the Soviet Union's Russian republic, becoming the first Russian leader to be directly elected by a popular vote.

12   The Albanian People's Assembly (parliament) confirmed a 24-member nonpartisan caretaker cabinet led by the new interim premier, Ylli Bufi. It was the country's first non-communist government in 47 years.

18–21 South Africa's parliament repealed the Population Registration Act of 1950 which had required all South Africans to record their race with the government, and approved sweeping amendments to the Internal Security Act of 1982 which had restricted political opposition.

20   Following the Congress (I) Party's victory in Indian general elections (held 20 May–15 June) President Ramaswamy Venkataraman named Congress (I) Party president P V Narasimha Rao prime minister.

23   The finance chiefs of the seven leading industrial democracies ended a meeting in London with a statement of optimism on the world economy. The G-7 economic ministers also focused on discussions on how best to encourage and aid a Soviet transition to a free-market economy.

23–28 Iraqi soldiers obstructed, and in one incident fired warning shots at, inspectors from the UN commission overseeing the destruction of Iraq's nuclear arms.

25   The republics of Slovenia and Croatia declared independence from Yugoslavia, but hedged on actual secession.

26–29 Fierce battles erupted in the disputed Krajina region of Croatia involving Croats and ethnic Serbs, leaving at least five people dead, and in Slovenia, where at least 100 Slovenes were killed or wounded on the first day alone. The breakaway Yugoslav republics of Slovenia and Croatia agreed to a three-month suspension of their independence declarations in order to halt federal military intervention on their soil.

28–29 The leaders of the 12 European Community nations met in Luxembourg. The centrepiece of the regular semi-annual summit was discussion of a draft treaty on political union.

NATIONAL

3   British security forces killed three men who the IRA later said were on an active service mission.

11   The House of Commons approved legislation putting strict curbs on the ownership of dogs bred for fighting. The legislation was rushed through the house after several recent vicious attacks on people by pit bull terriers.

14   Prime Minister John Major laid out Britain's negotiating position on the creation of a single European currency: he reiterated his stance that Britain would be 'at the heart of Europe', while opposing the imposition of a single currency.

17   Direct negotiations among the four leading Northern Ireland political parties opened at the former Stormont parliament building in Belfast. The talks, aimed at forming a regional government to replace direct rule from Britain, were the first direct negotiations among the parties in 16 years.

26   Lloyd's of London, the world's oldest insurance market, announced a record pre-tax loss of £509.7 million ($983.7 million) for 1988. The loss was Lloyd's first since 1967.

GENERAL

3   Mt Unzen, a Japanese volcano that until recently had been dormant for two centuries, erupted, taking the lives of at least 38 people.

5–14 The US space shuttle *Columbia* carried out a mission devoted to studying the biological effects of space travel on humans and other organisms.

12–13 The Mt Pinatubo volcano in the Philippines erupted in a huge mushroom cloud. The fallout from the eruption caused a total of 200 deaths, and the collapse of residences under the weight of ash reportedly left about 100,000 people homeless.

16–21 Thousands of scientists and health officials from around the world gathered in Florence, Italy , for the seventh annual international conference on AIDS.

JULY 1991

INTERNATIONAL

1   The Warsaw Pact, the last vestige of the

Cold War-era Soviet bloc, was formally disbanded.

1 The Supreme Soviet approved a law that would for the first time allow the sale of state-owned enterprises in the USSR.

1–5 Fighting erupted in southern Lebanon between the PLO and the Lebanese army. Lebanese government troops seized control of PLO-held territory in and around the port city of Sidon, effectively shutting down the PLO's long-standing principal base for operations against Israel.

2 The African National Congress, South Africa's largest anti-apartheid movement, met in Durban for its first national conference inside the country in 32 years.

4 Colombia President Cesar Gaviria Trujillo lifted a state of siege that had been in effect since 1984. The move was in honour of a new constitution that took effect 5 July.

8 Iraq admitted to the UN that it had been conducting clandestine programs to produce enriched uranium, a key element in nuclear weapons.

10 US President George Bush lifted US trade and investment sanctions against South Africa.

17 Leaders of the Group of Seven ended their 17th annual summit in London with strong commitments of technical aid and strong political support for visiting non-member Mikhail Gorbachev. At the same time Presidents Bush and Gorbachev reached a final agreement on a new Strategic Arms Reduction Treaty (START).

19 A major political scandal erupted in South Africa after the government admitted that it had made secret payments to the Zulu-based Inkatha Freedom Party.

22 As many as 20 people died in fighting between Croats and ethnic Serbs in the Yugoslav republic of Croatia. The news prompted Croatian President Franjo Trudjman to walk out of high-level talks on Yugoslavia's future which had been mandated by a truce agreement mediated by the EC 7 July.

31 At a superpower summit in Moscow Presidents Bush and Gorbachev signed the Strategic Arms Reduction Treaty (START), limiting both sides to no more than 6,000 nuclear warheads and 1,600 strategic delivery systems. The leaders also announced that the superpowers were prepared to cosponsor a Middle East peace conference in October.

NATIONAL
3 Northern Ireland secretary Peter Brooke told the House of Commons he had decided to break off the Stormont talks on Ulster's future.

4 The Labour Party retained its parliamentary seat for the Liverpool district of Walton in a by-election. The winning Labour candidate, Peter Kilfoyle, received 21,317 votes (53% of those cast).

9 Defence Secretary Tom King unveiled government plans to pare the nation's defence forces in the wake of a reduced threat of conflict in Europe. The white paper outlined the government's goal to create a smaller, but more mobile and better-equipped force.

22 Prime Minister John Major unveiled the government's 'Citizen's Charter' aimed at improving public services. The charter, outlined in a 50-page white paper, contained more than 70 legislative proposals. Labour criticized the document for providing no extra cash for the public sector.

22 A lawyer for the Bank of England told Britain's High Court that Bank of Credit and Commerce International (BCCI) had succeeded in concealing losses from regulators for years.

GENERAL
6–7 Michael Stich of Germany won the men's finals at Wimbledon; Steffi Graf of Germany won the women's singles title.

9 The International Olympic Committee lifted a 21-year-old boycott on South Africa after judging the country to have made significant advances in abolishing racial discrimination in sports.

11 A charter jet carrying Nigerian Muslims home from a pilgrimage to Saudi Arabia crashed while attempting to make an emergency landing at King Abdel-Aziz international airport in Jidda, Saudi Arabia. All 247 passengers and 14 crew members on board were killed in the accident.

12 Hitoshi Igarashi, the Japanese translator of Salman Rushdie's novel *The Satanic Verses*, was found stabbed to death outside his office at Tsukuba University, northeast of Tokyo.

29 The international scandal implicating BCCI widened further as the district attorney of the New York City borough of Manhattan unveiled a 12-count criminal indictment of the institution and four of its units.

AUGUST 1991
INTERNATIONAL
1 Israeli Prime Minister Yitzhak Shamir announced that Israel would take part in a peace conference sponsored by the USA and the Soviet Union, provided its conditions on the composition of the Palestinian delegation were met.

5–12 Turkish commandos backed by fighter planes and helicopters launched raids against what Turkey claimed were bases of the separatist Kurdish Workers Party (PKK) within the Kurdish 'safe haven' in northern Iraq.

7   A truce was decreed by Yugoslavia's collective presidency, but faltered when Serbs lobbed mortar shells into a village about 50 km/30 mi south of Zagreb, the Croatian capital.

8   Islamic Jihad, a radical Shiite Muslim faction in Lebanon, released John McCarthy, a British journalist who had been held hostage since April 1986.

8   An estimated 18,000 Albanian refugees fled to Bari, southern Italy. The Italian government's tough policy of detention and repatriation was criticized by many both inside and outside Italy.

9   Right-wing whites battled police outside a hall where South African President F W de Klerk was addressing supporters. The clash, which left three dead and 58 injured, was the first fatal battle between police and members of the Afrikaaner Resistance Movement.

10   A coalition of opposition parties launched a campaign to unseat Madagascar's president, Didier Ratsiraka. At least 51 protesters were killed when troops opened fire on a group of demonstrators outside the presidential palace.

19–21   In an attempted coup d'état, a group of top Soviet hard-liners, backed by the security forces, detained President Mikhail Gorbachev in the Crimea. An eight-man emergency committee took charge, but faced with international condemnation and the defiance of popular protests led by Russian President Yeltsin, the junta stepped down.

22   President Gorbachev returned to Moscow and disclosed that the prosecution of the conspirators was under way. Huge crowds celebrating the junta's fall in Moscow cheered Boris Yeltsin, the hero of the resistance to the coup.

22–23   Leaders throughout the West and Asia hailed the fall of the hard-line coup in the Soviet Union, welcoming the return of President Gorbachev and praising the resistance efforts of Russian President Boris Yeltsin.

24   President Gorbachev resigned as the general secretary of the Communist Party, stating that it was 'no longer possible' for him to carry out his duties as party leader. Gorbachev also issued a series of decrees curbing the party.

24–27   The Ukraine, Byelorussia, and Moldavia joined the Baltic republics in taking steps towards independence from the Soviet Union.

28   A cease-fire negotiated between Croatian President Franjo Tudjman and federal army leaders fell through less than a day after it was put into effect, as fighting broke out again throughout Croatia.

29   The Supreme Soviet voted to suspend

formally all activities of the Community Party.

NATIONAL

2   According to a report released by the House of Commons select committee on defence, development of a new class of British submarine—the *Upholder*—was behind schedule, over budget and flawed.

7   Home Secretary Kenneth Baker rejected calls from the Labour Party to resign. The calls stemmed from the 7 July escape of two Provisional IRA suspects from Brixton jail in South London.

13   A street riot in Shropshire was sparked off by the police killing of a black man who was carrying what turned out to be an unloaded airgun.

27   Prime Minister John Major set off with his family for a three-day working holiday with George Bush at the president's Kennebunkport home in Maine.

GENERAL

3–18   Cuba, the host nation for the 11th Pan American Games, won the most gold medals in the competition. The USA won the most medals overall.

12   England defeated the West Indies in the fifth Test match at the Oval, to draw the summer series 2–2. The winning runs were hit by veteran Ian Botham.

13   Prosecutors announced the discovery of one of the largest bank frauds in Japan's history, in which $2.5 billion in loans had been fraudulently obtained from some of Japan's largest banks.

18–19   Hurricane Bob, the first major hurricane of the 1991 season, tore up the eastern seaboard of North America, causing 16 deaths and more than $1 billion in property damage.

SEPTEMBER 1991
INTERNATIONAL

2   US President Bush announced full recognition of Latvia, Lithuania, and Estonia.

4   South Africa's President F W de Klerk outlined his government's proposals for a new constitution that would provide suffrage to the country's black majority for the first time in modern history. The ANC rejected the constitutional outline as it ensured that 'whites would retain the accumulated privileges of apartheid under the guise of constitutional principle'.

5   The Soviet Congress of People's Deputies approved an immediate and sweeping transfer of power to the republics from the central regime.

7   Peace talks on the Yugoslav civil war opened in The Hague, The Netherlands, under EC sponsorship.

8   Citizens of the Yugoslav republic of

Macedonia, in a referendum, voted by a significant majority to declare independence from Yugoslavia.

11 Soviet President Gorbachev announced that his country would soon begin negotiations with Cuba over a withdrawal of Soviet military forces from the island.

11 Israel released 51 Lebanese and Palestinian guerrillas from prison and returned the remains of nine others, in exchange for information confirming the deaths of two Israeli soldiers who had been missing since 1986.

14 The South African government, the ANC, and the Inkatha Freedom Party signed a peace accord aimed at ending the factional violence in the black townships. At least 125 people, mostly blacks, were killed in the period 8–14 Sept.

16 Swedish Premier Ingvar Carlsson resigned, one day after his Social Democratic Labour Party suffered its worst electoral defeat in 60 years.

17–18 Fighting continued in the breakaway republic of Croatia in spite of a new cease-fire engineered by the European Community. The Yugoslav navy began a blockade of seven port cities on the Adriatic southern coast in Dalmatia.

23 A contingent of Zairean paratroopers mutinied and went on a two-day looting spree in Kinshasa, the capital. Belgium and France dispatched troops to protect foreign residents.

24 Iraq provoked international outrage over its resistance to efforts to dismantle its arms programme when Iraqi troops blockaded 44 UN inspectors in Baghdad. Detention of the UN inspectors ended 28 Sept.

24 The Revolutionary Justice Organization, a Shiite Muslim faction in Lebanon, freed Jack Mann, a British retired airline pilot who had been kidnapped in May 1989.

24 Zviad Gamsakhurdia, the president of Soviet Georgia, declared a state of emergency in the southern republic, amid mounting popular opposition to his government and outbreaks of violence.

24 Canadian Prime Minister Brian Mulroney presented to the House of Commons a package of far-reaching constitutional reforms designed primarily to convince the province of Québec to remain part of the Canadian confederation.

25 The government and representatives of El Salvador's five main rebel groups signed a broad agreement on the country's political and economic future, marking the first step toward a cease-fire in the country's 11-year-old civil war.

26 Romanian Premier Petre Roman and his entire cabinet resigned amid three days of rioting by thousands of angry coal miners in Bucharest.

29 Haitian President Jean-Bertrand Aristide, Haiti's first freely elected president, was overthrown in a coup d'état led by Haiti's powerful military.

NATIONAL

1–6 The annual conference of the Trades Union Congress was held in Glasgow, Scotland. The Labour Party was pleased by the conference's rejection of a call for the repeal of all Tory anti-union legislation.

8–12 The Liberal Democrats held their annual conference in Bournemouth. The party outlined its distinctive centre politics, and promised better education.

9 Rioting broke out in a housing estate in North Shields, Tyneside. Confrontations between youths and police had broken out on 1 Sept on housing estates in Cardiff, Oxford, and Birmingham, and, following the Tyneside clash, in Newcastle.

25 Labour MPs Dave Nellist and Terry Fields were suspended by party leaders because of their alleged links with Militant Tendency.

GENERAL

5 The new KGB Chief, Vadim V Bakatin, pledged his agency's total cooperation in a joint Soviet-Swedish investigation of the fate of Raoul Wallenberg, a Swedish diplomat who disappeared in 1945 after helping thousands of Jews in Hungary escape Nazi persecution.

5 The US Justice Department unsealed indictments against six former officials of BCCI, charging that they were involved in money laundering.

12–18 The US space shuttle *Discovery* carried out a mission in which a satellite was deployed to study the Earth's ozone layer.

16 All Iran-Contra charges against Oliver North were dropped.

OCTOBER 1991
INTERNATIONAL

5 Soviet President Gorbachev offered a package of unilateral cuts and proposals that surpassed the broad arms control initiative presented by US President Bush a week earlier.

6 Portuguese President Anibal Cavaco Silva won re-election; his centrist Social Democratic Party won a clear majority the second time running.

8 The Organization of American States, following its unsuccessful diplomatic efforts to press for the reinstallation of ousted Haitian President Aristide, voted unanimously to embargo trade with Haiti and freeze its assets abroad.

8 The fourth cease-fire in three weeks was signed and broken in Yugoslavia. The ancient Croatian port cities of Dubrovnik and Zadar were under siege.

10 Askar Akayev, a democrat, was elected

president of the Soviet republic of Kirghizia.

10 German political leaders agreed to establish large refugee camps to protect people seeking asylum and speed up the processing of their applications. The agreement came amid continuing violence against foreigners.

11 Turkish aircraft attacked targets in the Kurdish safe haven in northern Iraq. The Turks claimed that they had targeted bases of the Kurdish Workers' Party; the Kurds said the victims were civilians.

13 The Union of Democratic Forces, the main opposition coalition, won Bulgaria's second national elections since the fall of communism.

16–21 The Commonwealth held its biennial national leaders' conference in Harare, Zimbabwe. British Prime Minister John Major announced that his government would cancel debts owed to it by the poorest developing countries. The conference ended with a call for all of its 50 members to respect human rights.

16 Two bomb blasts in Rampur, in northern India, killed 55 people and injured 100 others. The terrorism was attributed to Sikh separatists.

17 The defence ministers of NATO approved a 50% reduction in tactical nuclear bombs stockpiled in Europe for use by US and British aircraft.

20 Zairean President Mobutu fired his recently selected premier, Etienne Tshiseki. The move sparked rioting in major cities.

21 Jesse Turner, an American who had been held hostage in Lebanon for just under five years, was set free by his captors.

27 Colombia held elections for a new senate, chamber of deputies, and 27 state governors. President Cesar Gaviria's Liberal party received the most votes, but only about one-third of the electorate actually went to the polls.

27 Former Japanese Finance Minister Kiichi Miyazawa was elected leader of the Liberal Democratic Party, and so became Japan's prime minister-designate. Japanese Premier Toshiki Kaifu had unexpectedly announced 4 Oct that he would decline to seek re-election as party leader.

29 Vietnam formally approved a plan to repatriate forcibly tens of thousands of Vietnamese refugees living in camps in Hong Kong.

30 Representatives of Israel, Syria, Egypt, Lebanon, and Jordan, and Palestinians of the Israeli-occupied territories attended the opening session of the long-awaited Middle East peace conference in Madrid, Spain. The US- and Soviet-sponsored conference marked the first time that all major parties in the Middle East conflict had been gathered at one table for comprehensive talks. The PLO was not allowed to attend.

31 President Kenneth Kaunda (president of Zambia since the country gained independence from Britain in 1964) was defeated in Zambia's first pluralistic presidential balloting since 1972. The opposition Movement for Multiparty Democracy (MMD) won an overwhelming victory, and Frederick Chiluba was sworn in as the new president.

NATIONAL

3 Allen Green, the director of public prosecutions, resigned his post. He had been stopped by the police near London's King's Cross station after they had seen him talking to a prostitute.

4 The Labour Party's annual conference in Brighton ended. Party leader Neil Kinnock chided John Major for postponing the general election and sought to rally Labour towards a general election victory after 12 years in opposition.

8–11 The Conservative Party held its annual conference in Blackpool. Prime Minister John Major ended the meeting with a speech rejecting charges by the Labour Party that the Conservatives planned to privatize the National Health Service.

31 Prime Minister John Major's legislative programme for the final session of Parliament was outlined in the traditional Speech from the Throne by Queen Elizabeth II. The controversial community charge or poll tax would be replaced with a new property-based levy known as the council tax.

GENERAL

3 The Rugby Union World Cup kicked off at Twickenham, UK. The four-week competition among 16 teams, including Zimbabwe and Japan (but not South Africa), was billed as one of Britain's biggest sporting events.

14 The Nobel Peace Prize was awarded to Aung San Suu Kyi, the leader of Myanmar's opposition. It was not known whether she knew of her prize, as she has been under house arrest since July 1989.

15 After one of the most bitter and divisive confirmation battles in the history of the US Supreme Court, the Senate confirmed Judge Clarence Thomas as the court's 106th associate justice. The vote came after three days of televised Senate Judiciary Committee hearings on charges of sexual harassment made against Thomas by a former aide, Anita Hill.

NOVEMBER 1991
INTERNATIONAL

4 The Middle East peace conference in

Madrid came to a close without major concessions or peace proposals from the parties involved.

4 Between three and four million black South Africans began a two-day general strike to protest against a new value-added tax that had taken effect 30 Sept.

7–8 During their annual summit in Rome, Italy, NATO leaders set a new, post-Cold War course for the alliance, and approved a new 'strategic concept', or military strategy, for NATO.

8 EC foreign ministers, meeting in Rome, imposed an economic embargo on Yugoslavia in an effort to halt the civil war in that country.

12 Indonesian troops opened fire at a funeral in the province of East Timor, killing about 50 people. The mourners had reportedly been peacefully demonstrating against Indonesian occupation of the island when the shooting began.

14 The US Justice Department and Scottish authorities issued separate indictments against two Libyan intelligence officers believed to have engineered the Dec 1988 bombing of Pan Am flight 103 over Lockerbie, Scotland, in which 270 people died.

14 Prince Norodom Sihanouk, Cambodia's former head of state, returned to Phnom Penh after nearly 13 years in exile to head the country's interim government.

18 The Lebanese Shiite Muslim faction Islamic Jihad freed Church of England envoy Terry Waite (held since Jan 1987) and US university professor Thomas Sutherland (held since June 1985). Waite had been the last British hostage held in Lebanon.

21 The UN Security Council nominated Egyptian Deputy Prime Minister Boutros Boutros Ghali to become the sixth secretary general of the UN. The first African and the first Arab to hold the post, Ghali would replace Javier Perez de Cuellar of Peru, who planned to retire 31 Dec.

23 Croatian, Serbian, and Yugoslav army officials signed a UN-mediated cease-fire accord in which they agreed in principle to allow a multinational peace-keeping force into Yugoslavia. The accord was the 14th mediated truce to be initiated since the civil war began in June.

27 Khien Samphan, one of the Khmer Rouge's most prominent public officials, was beaten and nearly lynched by an angry mob just hours after his return to Cambodia. After treatment for injuries, he flew to Thailand.

NATIONAL

5 Robert Maxwell, the owner of Mirror Group Newspapers and Maxwell Communication Corporation, was found dead in the sea off the Canary Islands, several hours after he was reported missing off his luxury yacht, the *Lady Ghislaine*. Amid public speculation on the possibility of foul play or suicide, preliminary results of an autopsy suggested that Maxwell had died of heart failure and had fallen overboard.

6 Chancellor Norman Lamont presented the annual autumn statement on public spending plans. The plans for the 1992–1993 fiscal year included increases in spending on health, transport, and social security.

15 In the wake of increased sectarian violence in Northern Ireland, Britain called up 1,400 reserve troops from the Ulster Defence Regiment for full time active duty.

25–28 Three men found guilty in the 1985 killing of a policeman in riots in Tottenham, north London, had their convictions overturned. The Court of Appeal took the action after finding that evidence in the case had apparently been tampered with by the police.

GENERAL

2 England lost to Australia by 12–6 in the final of the World Cup rugby tournament in Twickenham.

4 Former First Lady Imelda Marcos returned to the Philippines, ending more than five years of exile in the USA. Imelda Marcos, who had arrived on a specially chartered jet and was renting the $2,000-a-night Imperial Suite in Manila's Plaza Hotel, described herself as 'penniless' and 'deprived of all things'. The government had endorsed her return so that she could be tried on corruption and tax evasion charges.

6 The last of more than 700 Kuwaiti oil wells that had been set on fire by Iraqi forces during the Gulf War was capped. It took fire-fighting teams about eight months to complete their task.

7 Area relief agencies reported that floods resulting from tropical storm Thelma had killed at least 3,400 people in the south central Philippines.

DECEMBER 1991
INTERNATIONAL

1 Voters in the Soviet republic of Ukraine overwhelmingly voted for independence from the USSR. They also elected Leonid Kravchuk, the republic's former Communist boss, as president.

2 President Moi of Kenya proposed scrapping a 1982 constitutional clause outlawing opposition parties. The decision came after Western donor nations 25–26 Nov froze aid to Kenya at 1991 levels and threatened drastic cuts unless political and economic reforms were made within six months.

4 Associated Press correspondent Terry Anderson, the longest-held Western

hostage in Lebanon (2,454 days in captivity) was freed by the Islamic Jihad faction. Anderson's release followed the 2 Dec freeing of US hostage Joseph Cicippio (held since Sept 1986) and Alan Steen (held since Jan 1987) by other factions.

4   The chief of Libyan intelligence said that the two Libyans charged by the USA and UK for the 1988 bombing of Pan Am flight 103 over Lockerbie had been arrested. The charges would be investigated, but the men would not be extradited as the British and Americans had requested.

4–18   A scheduled round of US-sponsored Middle East peace talks were held in Washington, DC. The talks were adjourned with little or no progress having been made.

8   The leaders of Russia, Byelorussia, and the Ukraine signed an agreement forming a 'Commonwealth of Independent States' to replace the USSR. President Gorbachev denounced the decision as unconstitutional.

10   The leaders of the 12 EC nations ended their two-day summit and agreed on the treaty of Maastricht, pledging closer political and economic union. A monetary union pact was also agreed upon, although Britain kept open the option of not joining the economic and monetary union (EMU).

11   A meeting of the Organization of the Islamic Conference in Dakar ended a day early in disarray. Yassir Arafat, leader of the PLO, had left stormily after the organization voted to withdraw its customary call for a jihad (holy war) against Israel.

13   The premiers of North and South Korea signed a comprehensive agreement governing nonaggression, reconciliation, trade and other issues between the two countries.

16   The UN General Assembly voted by an overwhelming margin to repeal its Nov 1975 resolution equating Zionism with racism.

17   The EC, seeking a diplomatic solution to the civil war in Yugoslavia, announced that it would recognize the independence of the Yugoslav republics of Slovenia and Croatia in Jan 1992.

19   Bob Hawke was deposed as Australia's prime minister by his parliamentary colleagues and replaced by Paul Keating.

22   Eleven of the 12 Soviet republics agreed in Alma Ata, Kazakhstan's capital, on the creation of a Commonwealth of Independent States. Georgia, preoccupied with its own power struggle, did not sign up.

25   Mikhail Gorbachev announced his resignation as Soviet president; the Soviet Union's parliament formally voted the country out of existence the following day.

30   The leaders of the Commonwealth of Independent States confirmed that the ex-Soviet strategic nuclear arsenal would continue to be under a unified command.

31   North and South Korea agreed to ban nuclear weapons from their peninsula and to allow mutual inspection of their nuclear facilities.

NATIONAL

3   Education Secretary Kenneth Clark launched an inquiry into primary school teaching.

5   The privately owned companies of the late publisher Robert Maxwell sought bankruptcy protection from their creditors. The action, taken by Maxwell's sons Ian and Kevin, came amid mounting debt problems of the companies and investigations of possible fraudulent transactions between the Maxwell private concerns and two publicly traded companies that the Maxwells controlled.

11   Prime Minister John Major's return from the Maastricht summit was greeted at the Commons with cheers from Tory backbenchers. The government's decision to opt out from a single European currency and a social charter was criticized by Labour.

16   Rail traffic in London was disrupted after the IRA exploded a bomb beside a railway line in south London; the terrorist act formed part of the IRA's pre-Christmas fire-bombing campaign.

16   Stella Rimington was appointed the first woman to head MI5, the country's counterintelligence service. It was the first time that the appointment of an MI5 chief was publicly announced.

GENERAL

1   France won its first Davis Cup tennis title in 59 years by upsetting the USA, the defending champions, at the finals in Lyons, France.

13   Terry Norris retained his World Boxing Council super-welterweight title with a unanimous decision over Jorge Castro of Argentina in Paris.

15   Nearly 500 people drowned when an Egyptian ferry sank in the Red Sea, after hitting a reef. There were close to 200 survivors.

16   The Canadian government announced that it had reached an agreement with Inuit leaders on a massive land claim settlement that would lead to the creation of a new Canadian Territory. The territory, covering an area of some 2,000,000 sq km/772,000 sq mi, was named Nunavut ('our land' in Inuit).

JANUARY 1992

INTERNATIONAL

3   More than 2,000 people turned up for a rally in Tbilisi, in support of ousted Georgian President Gamsakhurdia. Rebel opponents of the president fired point blank at the crowd, killing at least two people and wounding 25 others.

6   An unusually strong resolution condemning Israel's deportations of Palestinians from the occupied territories was unanimously passed by the UN Security Council. Pressured by hardline Jewish settlers, the Israeli government had expelled 12 Palestinians it claimed were linked to attacks on Israeli soldiers and fellow Palestinians.

7   A Yugoslav federal-force jet fighter shot down an EC helicopter over Croatia, killing all five members of an EC monitoring team on board.

8   The ANC commemorated its 80th anniversary with a demand for an interim government of national unity and elections for a constituent assembly in South Africa by the end of the year.

12 Algeria's High Security Council cancelled general elections in what Islamic fundamentalists called an army-backed constitutional coup designed to rob them of victory.

15 The EC granted diplomatic recognition to Slovenia and Croatia, essentially recognizing the dismemberment of Yugoslavia.

22 Rebel soldiers seized the national radio station in Kinshasa, Zaire's capital, and broadcast a demand for the government's resignation and the reconvening of the country's national political conference which was scrapped 20 Jan.

23 The Estonian government resigned after parliament refused to cooperate in implementing a crisis strategy to deal with shortages.

25–28 More than 150 people were killed or wounded in armed clashes between Azerbaijan forces and Armenians in the enclave of Nagorno-Karabakh.

26 Russian President Boris Yeltsin announced that his country would stop targeting US cities with nuclear weapons.

26 At least 20 people were killed in an upsurge of violence in the north Indian state of Kashmir.

27–28 About 1,000 supporters of the ousted Georgian President Zviad Gamsakhurdia marched on a prison in Tbilisi as new military clashes broke out in the sea port of Poti. While Gamsakhurdia was still in hiding, forces loyal to the ruling military council in the Georgian capital took control of Poti (under attack since 22 Jan),

one of the last centres of rebellion in the west of the republic.

27 The third round of Middle East peace talks opened in Moscow without the participation of the Palestinian delegates. The Palestinians wanted to choose their own delegation to represent them in the continuing rounds of talks.

28 Russian President Boris Yeltsin announced a plan to cut the old Soviet arsenal of long range weapons from 12,200 to a maximum of 2,500, surpassing US President Bush's proposed arms cuts.

NATIONAL

8   British Steel confirmed the closure of the Ravenscraig steel works complex in Lanarkshire by Sept, with the loss of 1,220 jobs.

10 A bomb exploded in Whitehall, 300 m from Downing Street. The IRA, which claimed responsibility for the explosion, threatened further attacks on the mainland.

17 Seven building workers were killed and seven injured when the van they were in was blown up by a massive bomb placed next to a remote country road in County Tyrone, Northern Ireland. The IRA claimed responsibility for the attack.

26 Transport Secretary Malcolm Rifkind secretly halted British Rail investment of up to £300 million in new freight schemes after a row over the privatization of the network. He also proposed to end state funding for future rail freight schemes, saying that the private sector should step in.

27 It was announced that more than £567 million plundered by the late Robert Maxwell from his companies' pension funds could be irrecoverable.

GENERAL

26 It was reported that Russian cosmonauts, once the most glamorous symbol of the former Soviet Union's superpower status, were barely earning above the poverty line and might decide to go on strike.

27 Former world boxing champion Mike Tyson went on trial for allegedly raping an 18-year-old contestant in the 1991 Miss Black America contest. He was charged with confinement and rape and, if convicted, could face up to a maximum sentence of 63 years.

31 Research findings suggested that breast-fed babies may become more intelligent children than those whose mothers bottle-fed them.

FEBRUARY 1992
INTERNATIONAL

7   Russian President Yeltsin and French President Mitterrand signed a landmark treaty in Paris declaring unprecedented political, economic, and military co-operation between Russia and France.

14   Representatives of the two warring factions in Mogadishu, the Somali capital, agreed to an immediate, UN-brokered cease-fire. However, continued fighting was reported 16–18 Feb.

16   Sheik Abbas al-Musawi, the leader of the Lebanese Shiite organization Hezbollah, was slain when Israeli helicopter gunships attacked his motorcade in southern Lebanon. Musawi's wife, son and at least four bodyguards were also killed in the raid.

17–18   Following diplomatic visits to six former Soviet republics, US Secretary of State James Baker met in Moscow with Russian leaders to discuss speeding up the disarmament of the superpowers' nuclear arsenals. During his visit, the USA, Russia and Germany agreed to set up an international science centre to employ former Soviet nuclear-weapons scientists in peace-time projects.

18   A special congress of Tanzania's governing Revolutionary Party approved a proposal to end one-party rule.

19   Yitzhak Rabin was elected leader of Israel's Labour Party. Rabin's victory meant that he would challenge Prime Minister Shamir in national elections scheduled for 23 June.

20   President F W de Klerk stunned South Africa by announcing a white-only referendum, scheduled for 17 March, on the popularity of his political reforms. He said he would resign if he failed to win significant support.

20–21   The Israeli army conducted a 24-hour raid into Lebanon, seizing and practically demolishing two villages in an attempt to halt rocket attacks on northern Israel by Hezbollah guerillas. Hezbollah had stepped up its rocket barrages after the slaying of its leader, Musawi.

21   The UN Security Council unanimously approved a resolution that could send nearly 14,400 peacekeepers to Croatia to enforce the truce in the Yugoslav civil war and to protect the ethnic minority in Croatia. It would be the first deployment of a UN peace force in Europe.

24   Arab and Israeli negotiators began their third round of direct bilateral talks in Washington, DC.

24   US Secretary of State Baker announced that the Bush administration would grant $10 billion in loan guarantees to Israel over the next five years only if Israel halted all its settlement activity in the occupied territories.

NATIONAL

3   Brian Nelson, a British army secret agent who had infiltrated the Ulster Defence Association, was sentenced to 10 years in prison for terrorist offences committed by the group.

4–5   Eight people died and at least 14 were wounded in two separate shooting attacks in Belfast.

11   Prime Minister Major met with Northern Ireland political leaders in London in an attempt to restart the suspended talks on the province's future governance.

14–17   Four of the five remaining defendants in the Blue Arrow case were convicted but then given suspended sentences. The Blue Arrow trial had lasted a year and, with an estimated cost of £35 million, was said to be the most expensive trial in British history.

16   Four suspected IRA operatives were killed and two other wounded men captured by security forces in an apparent ambush in County Tyrone.

28   A bomb exploded at London Bridge railway station during the morning rush hour, injuring about 30 persons, four seriously. The IRA claimed responsibility for the blast.

GENERAL

1   It was reported that the NASA–European Space Agency *Ulysses* probe had met Jupiter en route to the sun.

1   Several villages in the Kurdish region of southeastern Turkey were buried by avalanches. At least 170 people were killed, including 106 troops who had been sent there to fight Kurdish guerrillas.

23   The 16th Olympic Winter Games in Albertville, France concluded, after two weeks of competition. Germany, whose athletes earned a games-high 26 medals, competed as a single team for the first time since 1964.

26   A 14-year-old girl who said she had become pregnant after being raped was cleared by Ireland's Supreme Court to leave the country to obtain an abortion. An initial injunction barring the girl from travelling had reignited the abortion controversy in the country, where it had been illegal since 1861.

MARCH 1992
INTERNATIONAL

1   The citizens of the Yugoslav republic of Bosnia-Herzegovina overwhelmingly supported independence in a referendum.

2–17   At least 30 people died in fighting between Moldovan security forces and Slavic separatists in the Dniester region of Moldova.

15 In one peace effort, by Iranian Foreign Minister Velayati, Armenian and Azerbaijani officials signed a draft truce agreement in Teheran. An escalating war between the two former Soviet republics since 28 Jan had cost hundreds of lives and spurred international attempts at mediation.

17 A Palestinian from the Gaza Strip stabbed two Israelis to death and wounded 19 others during a rampage on a crowded street in Tel Aviv.

17 South African whites, voting in record numbers, overwhelmingly endorsed President de Klerk's reform policies in a referendum on whether to negotiate an end to white minority rule through talks with the black majority.

17 A powerful car bomb exploded in front of the Israeli embassy in Buenos Aires, Argentina, destroying the building and trapping dozens of staff members beneath the rubble. At least 28 people were killed and 220 wounded. Islamic Jihad, a Lebanese Shiite group, claimed responsibility for the bombing.

20 Ten of the 11 CIS presidents held a summit in the Ukraine capital of Kiev, but failed to resolve any crucial military, economic or political issues.

20 Iraq agreed to comply fully with UN Security Council demands calling for the dismantling of its weapons of mass destruction and weapons-related facilities and full disclosure of its efforts to build nuclear, chemical and biological weapons.

20–25 Fighting in Turkey between government forces and Kurdish separatists escalated. At least 75 people were killed in the fighting.

22 The Albanian Democratic Party, the largest opposition group, captured about 62% of the vote in the nation's second multiparty national elections.

25 Narong Wongwan, a wealthy businessman who had been denied entrance to the USA because of suspected links to drug trafficking, was named premier of Thailand by a coalition of five pro-army parties.

31 The UN Security Council voted to impose limited sanctions against Libya if its government failed to extradite agents suspected in the 1988 bombing of Pan Am flight 103 over Lockerbie and the 1989 bombing of UTA flight 727 over Niger.

NATIONAL

6 Home Secretary Kenneth Baker announced plans for a national lottery, to be launched in 1994. Britain was the only nation in Europe without a national lottery.

9 The House Select Committee on Social Security issued a report urging reform of Britain's pensions laws. It was released in the wake of a scandal over the apparent looting of more than £450 million from the pension funds of companies connected to the late Robert Maxwell.

11 Prime Minister John Major called a general election for 9 April. The announcement of what was expected to be Britain's closest election since 1974 came one day after the government had set out its 1992–93 budget.

16–18 The general election campaign heated up as all three major parties released their election manifestos. The Labour Party also offered an alternative 1992–93 fiscal budget that contrasted sharply with the government's budget.

GENERAL

3 More than 270 miners were killed when an explosion of natural methane gas caused the collapse of a portion of a coal mine in the Turkish town of Kozlu.

6 President Mugabe declared Zimbabwe's drought a natural disaster. It was reported that southern Africa was experiencing its worst drought of the century. Meteorologists blamed the drought on El Niño, a periodic heating of Pacific waters that disrupted weather patterns across the globe.

13, 15 A pair of earthquakes struck the mountainous region of eastern Turkey, killing several hundred people.

25 Sergei Krikalyov, a Russian cosmonaut aboard the space station *Mir* since May 1991, returned to Earth. During his ten months in orbit the Soviet Union had disintegrated and its leader, Mikhail Gorbachev, had left office. Krikalyov's republic, Russia, was now an independent country with its own president, and his home town, Leningrad, had been renamed St Petersburg.

APRIL 1992
INTERNATIONAL

22 Mar Ethnic Serb guerillas and elements of
–9 the Serb-dominated Yugoslav military opposed to Bosnia's secession fought Slavs and ethnic Croats. The fighting effectively extended the Yugoslav civil war to Bosnia.

1 US President Bush and German Chancellor Kohl separately announced a $24 billion aid package for the Russian Federation by the G7 nations.

2 Socialist Edith Cresson, France's first woman premier, resigned after less than 11 months in office; she was succeeded by finance minister Pierre Bérégovoy.

4 Sali Berisha, a 47-year-old heart surgeon, became Albania's first non-Marxist president since World War II.

4 A contingent of 1,200 UN peacekeeping

troops arrived in Croatia.

5 Peruvian President Fujimori, in what he called an attack on rebels and drug traffickers, announced decrees dissolving the National Congress, suspending parts of the constitution, and instituting press censorship.

7 The EC and the USA separately recognized as independent the Yugoslav republic of Bosnia-Herzegovina. The USA also recognized Croatia and Slovenia, which it had declined to recognize in Jan.

15 Limited international sanctions took effect against Libya, in accordance with UN Security Council Resolution 748 passed in late March.

15 The Russian Congress of People's Deputies approved a declaration of conditional support for the radical economic reforms of President Yeltsin. The move, a compromise, appeared to ease a tense standoff between the president and the legislators.

19 Abdul Rahim Hatif was named interim president of Afghanistan, three days after communist President Najibullah had abruptly resigned and gone into hiding. Hatif offered to cede control of the war-torn nation to a coalition of Muslim rebels, as competing guerrilla forces advanced to within 8 km/5 mi of Kabul.

27 The Yugoslav republics of Serbia and Montenegro proclaimed a new 'Federal Republic of Yugoslavia' in a ceremony in Belgrade. The proclamation came shortly after the Yugoslav national parliament had amended the constitution, tacitly acknowledging the independence of Slovenia, Croatia, Bosnia-Herzegovina and Macedonia.

27–30 Officials of Afghanistan's collapsed communist government relinquished power to a commission of Mujaheddin rebels headed by moderate Islamic leader Sibghatullah Mojadidi. The transfer formally ended 14 years of rule by Soviet-backed regimes in Afghanistan.

NATIONAL

9 The Conservative Party won a 21-seat majority in the House of Commons in the general election. The election victory was the fourth straight for the Conservatives, a feat unmatched in Britain since the early 19th century.

10 Three people died in a huge night-time explosion in the City of London financial district. The IRA claimed responsibility for the blast, which was described as the most powerful in Britain since World War II.

13 Neil Kinnock announced that he would step down as Labour Party leader. Deputy leader Roy Hattersley had also announced his intention to stand down.

27 Betty Boothroyd became the first woman to be elected speaker of the House of Commons. Boothroyd, the Labour MP from West Bromwich West, succeeded Bernard Weatherill.

GENERAL

2 The US space shuttle *Atlantis* landed at the Kennedy Space Center after a 9-day flight. It carried out a mission to initiate a comprehensive space-based study of the Earth's atmosphere.

20 Spain's King Juan Carlos officially opened the 1992 World's Fair in Seville.

22 At least 190 people were killed and more than 1,400 injured in Guadalajara, Mexico, when a series of violent explosions in the sewer system destroyed a 20-block area of the city.

23 McDonald Corp. opened its first outlet in China near Beijing's Tiananmen Square. The fast-food restaurant served about 400,000 people on its debut day, an international record for a single McDonald's outlet.

MAY 1992
INTERNATIONAL

4 A dawn-to-dusk curfew established 30 April in Los Angeles was lifted after five days of violence had left 58 dead, 4,000 injured, and about $1 billion in damages. Rioting had erupted after the acquittal of four white city police officers in the videotaped beating of black motorist Rodney King.

6 Lebanese Premier Omar Karami and his cabinet resigned, amid nationwide rioting spurred by skyrocketing inflation and the collapse of the country's currency.

7 A strike by Germany's public-sector workers ended when unions and government agreed to a pact with an average pay increase of about 5.4%. The 11-day national strike, which had disrupted public transportation, air travel, postal service and rubbish collection, was the first in the public sector since 1978.

7 Russian President Yeltsin issued decrees creating Russia's own armed forces and naming himself as supreme commander in chief.

13 A cease-fire in Bosnia, set to last five days, temporarily halted a bloody offensive by Serbian paramilitary forces. Hundreds of people had been killed in fighting since the beginning of the month.

15 The leaders of Russia, Kazakhstan, Byelorussia, Armenia, Turkmenistan, and Uzbekistan signed a mutual security treaty at a one-day summit in Tashkent, capital of Uzbekistan.

19 After five days of turmoil in Baku, the Azerbaijan capital, the parliament voted

to turn all legislative and executive powers over to an opposition-dominated national council for an interim period.

20   An uneasy peace returned to Nigeria after five days of ethnic clashes that claimed at least 200 lives.

22   General Suchinda Kraprayoon, Thailand's embattled prime minister, resigned from office after six days of anti-government violence in Bangkok had left over 100 dead and 700 injured. Having failed in his attempts to appease protesters, the General bowed to pro-democracy demonstrators and agreed to introduce constitutional amendments to ensure that any prime minister would be elected.

23   Giovanni Falcone, Italy's best-known anti-Mafia judge, was assassinated when a ton of explosives detonated under his motorcade on a motorway outside Palermo.

27   At least 16 people queuing for bread were killed as mortar bombs exploded among crowds in the Bosnian capital of Sarajevo. Up to 110 of the starving people who had come out on the street during the latest cease-fire were injured in the assault, which Bosnian defence officials blamed on Serbs.

29   Residents of Sarajevo suffered one of the worst nights of shelling in almost two months of siege, while the Croatian port of Dubrovnik came under sustained fire for the first time in six months.

30   UN Security Council resolution 757 was passed, imposing sanctions on the Serb-led Yugoslav state.

NATIONAL

5   The Bank of England engineered a half-percentage-point cut in commercial banks' base lending rates. The reduction, to 10%, brought interest rates to their lowest in four years.

11   Judith Ward, who had been sentenced in 1974 to 12 life terms in prison for a bombing linked to the IRA, was freed by the Court of Appeal. The court had determined that her confession to the bombing of a British army bus, killing 12 people, was unreliable.

20   The Director of Public Prosecutions announced that more than 200 officers investigated over allegations of police malpractice would not face criminal proceedings, following the close of a £1.8 million inquiry into the activities of the West Midlands serious crime squad. The inquiry had produced insufficient evidence.

GENERAL

5   A temporary stand for spectators collapsed at Furiani football stadium in Bastia, Corsica. Twelve died and more than 500 people were injured.

7–12   The US Space Shuttle *Endeavour* carried out a mission in which the crew, after two failed attempts, captured a wayward communications satellite and sent it into its proper orbit.

9   Representatives of 143 countries, meeting at UN headquarters in New York City, approved a draft treaty calling on the world's industrialized nations to reduce their emissions of 'greenhouse gases' believed to cause global warming. The treaty was to be signed by world leaders at the Earth Summit scheduled for June in Rio de Janeiro, Brazil.

ON THIS DAY

JANUARY
1 Queen Victoria was proclaimed Empress of India in Delhi. *1887*
2 Cardinal Richelieu established the Académie Française. *1635*
3 English explorer Howard Carter discovered the sarcophagus of Tutankhamun in the Valley of the Kings, near Luxor, Egypt. *1924*
4 The attack on Monte Cassino was launched by the British Fifth Army in Italy. *1944*
5 Charles the Bold was killed by the Swiss at the battle of Nancy. *1477*
6 The Committee of Inquiry on the South Sea Bubble published its findings. *1720*
7 Calais, the last English possession on mainland France, was recaptured by the French. *1558*
8 The final withdrawal of Allied troops from Gallipoli took place. *1916*
9 New York State introduced a bill to outlaw flirting in public. *1902*
10 The first meeting of the United Nations General Assembly took place in London. *1946*
11 Leonard Thompson became the first person to be successfully treated with insulin. *1922*
12 Kwang-su was made emperor of China. *1875*
13 The Independent British Labour Party was formed by Keir Hardie. *1893*
14 The king of Denmark ceded Norway to the king of Sweden. *1814*
15 President Nixon called a halt to the USA's Vietnam offensive. *1973*
16 Ivan the Terrible was crowned first Tsar of Russia. *1547*
17 Captain Cook's *Resolution* became the first ship to cross the Antarctic Circle. *1773*
18 The Versailles Peace Conference opened. *1919*
19 John Wilkes was expelled from the House of Commons for seditious libel. *1764*
20 Hong Kong was ceded by China and occupied by the British. *1841*
21 Louis XVI, King of France, was found guilty of treason and guillotined. *1793*
22 Insurgent workers were fired upon in St Petersburg, resulting in 'Bloody Sunday'. *1905*
23 The first British Labour government was formed, under Ramsey McDonald. *1924*
24 Beer in cans was first sold, in Virginia, by the Kreuger Brewing Company. *1935*
25 King Henry VIII and Ann Boleyn were secretly married. *1533*
26 Vincente Yanez Pinzon discovered Brazil and claimed it for Portugal. *1500*
27 The US Air Force carried out its first bombing raid on Germany. *1943*
28 The US Space Shuttle *Challenger* exploded shortly after liftoff from Cape Canaveral, killing five men and two women on board. *1986*
29 The first successful petrol-driven motor car, built by Karl Benz, was patented. *1886*
30 The Commonwealth of England was established upon the execution of Charles I. *1649*
31 The Soviet government expelled Leon Trotsky and he went into exile. *1929*

FEBRUARY
1 Ayatollah Khomeini returned to Iran after 14 years of exile in France. *1979*
2 Greece declared war on Turkey. *1878*
3 The first rocket-asssisted controlled landing on the moon was made by the Soviet space vehicle Luna IX. *1966*
4 Roosevelt, Churchill, and Stalin met at Yalta. *1945*
5 Glenn Miller recorded 'Tuxedo Junction' with his orchestra. *1940*
6 Britain declared war on France. *1778*
7 Edward Caernarvon (later King Edward II) became the first Prince of Wales. *1301*
8 Odessa was taken by Bolshevik forces. *1920*
9 Lieutenant Dawson's expedition in search of Dr Livingstone began. *1872*
10 Canada was ceded to Britain by the Peace of Paris. *1763*
11 The Virgin Mary is said to have appeared to three young girls in Lourdes. *1858*
12 Independence was proclaimed by Chile. *1818*
13 Britain, Prussia, Austria, Holland, Spain and Sardinia formed an alliance against France. *1793*
14 Captain Cook was stabbed to death by natives in the Sandwich Islands (now Hawaii). *1779*
15 The first shipment of frozen meat left New Zealand for England. *1882*
16 Fidel Castro became Cuban premier. *1959*
17 The British parliament voted to join the European Common Market. *1972*
18 The planet Pluto was discovered by Clyde Tombaugh at Lowell Observatory in the USA. *1930*
19 Napoleon Bonaparte established himself in the Tuileries as First Consul. *1800*
20 Austria announced that it was bankrupt. *1811*
21 The Germans launched an all-out attack on the French fortress of Verdun. *1916*
22 Florida was purchased by the United States from Spain. *1819*
23 Captains Speke and Grant announced the discovery of the source of the Nile. *1863*
24 Louis-Philippe of France abdicated. *1848*
25 Cassius Clay (later Muhammad Ali) won the world heavyweight boxing title for the first time in Miami. *1964*
26 A severe earthquake in Lisbon resulted in the loss of an estimated 20,000 lives. *1531*
27 The British were defeated by the Boers at the battle of Majuba, South Africa. *1881*
28 Albert Berry made the first parachute jump

from a plane over Missouri. *1912*

29 Hugh Heffner opened the first Playboy Club in Chicago. *1960*

MARCH

1 Mozambique, on the southeastern coast of Africa, was discovered by Vasco de Gama. *1498*

2 Nicholas II, the last Russian tsar, was forced to abdicate. *1917*

3 Beethoven's Moonlight Sonata was published. *1802*

4 The *Nautilus*, USA atomic submarine, passed under the North Pole ice cap. *1958*

5 The Nazis won almost half the seats in the German elections. *1933*

6 The Alamo fell to Mexican forces commanded by Santa Anna. *1836*

7 Alexander Graham Bell patented the first telephone capable of relaying sustained articulate speech. *1876*

8 Queen Anne acceded to the British throne. *1702*

9 The first battle of iron-clad ships took place during the American Civil War. *1862*

10 A Japanese soldier was discovered on Lubang Island in the Philippines who believed that World War II was still continuing. *1974*

11 A Maori uprising against the British in New Zealand began. *1845*

12 Mahatma Gandhi began a campaign of civil disobedience in India. *1930*

13 The planet Uranus was discovered by the German-born English astronomer William Herschel. *1781*

14 The first telephone cable was laid across the British Channel. *1891*

15 Julius Caesar was assassinated by Brutus and others in Rome. *44 BC*

16 The first liquid-fuelled rocket was launched, by Dr Robert Goddard in the USA. *1926*

17 The British were forced to evacuate Boston by George Washington. *1776*

18 Napoleon Bonaparte was proclaimed Emperor of France. *1804*

19 The USA Senate rejected the Versailles Treaty. *1920*

20 The Dutch East India Company was founded by the Netherlands government to trade with the East Indies. *1602*

21 The 'Sharpeville Massacre' took place when South African police opened fire on demonstrators, killing 56 and injuring 162. *1960*

22 The English were defeated by the Scots at Anjou. *1421*

23 The Fascist Party was founded by Benito Mussolini. *1919*

24 Greece was formally declared a republic. *1924*

25 Tuscany was occupied by French Troops. *1799*

26 The seven men accused of the £2.5 million 'Great Train Robbery' (8 Aug 1963) were found guilty in London. *1964*

27 The world's worst aviation disaster took place, when two jumbo jets collided on the ground at Tenerife airport killing 574 people. *1977*

28 The Irish parliament passed the Act of Union with England. *1800*

29 The Battle of Towton took place in north Yorkshire in a snowstorm during the War of the Roses—the bloodiest battle ever fought on British soil, in which it was said that over 28,000 died. *1461*

30 Alaska was sold by Russia to the USA for $7.2 million (approximately two cents an acre). *1867*

31 The 300 m/884 ft Eiffel Tower was completed in readiness for the Universal Exhibition in Paris. *1889*

APRIL

1 The invasion of Okinawa by USA forces began. *1945*

2 The British annexed the Punjab. *1849*

3 Stalin was appointed as General Secretary of the Communist Party. *1922*

4 Eleven countries signed the North Atlantic Treaty in Washington DC. *1949*

5 Kissing was banned on the French railways because it would cause delays. *1910*

6 Robert Peary became the first man to reach the North Pole, at his sixth attempt in 15 years. *1909*

7 The notorious highwayman Richard Turpin was hanged in York. *1739*

8 The first Home Rule for Ireland bill was introduced by WE Gladstone. *1886*

9 Confederate General Robert E Lee surrendered to General Grant at Appomattox Court House in Virginia, bringing the American Civil War to an end. *1865*

10 The Prussians defeated the Austrians at Molwitz, *1741*

11 Napoleon abdicated as Emperor, and was exiled to the island of Elba. *1814*

12 The Fourth Crusade was diverted by the Venetians to the riches of Constantinople. *1204*

13 The Anti-Semitic League was founded and a petition presented to Bismarck demanding restrictions on the liberty of Prussian Jews. *1882*

14 USA President Abraham Lincoln was assassinated in Ford's Theatre in Washington by John Wilkes Booth. *1865*

15 The SS *Titanic* sank on its maiden voyage and over 1,500 people were drowned. *1912*

16 The Senate in Rome appointed two emperors, D Caelinus Balbinus to run civil affairs, and M Clodius Pupierus Maximus to commmand the legions. *238*

17 The sea broke through the dykes at Dort in Holland and an estimated 100,000 people were drowned. *1421*

18 The first launderette was opened in Fort Worth, Texas by JF Cantrell, and called a 'Washeteria'. *1934*

19 Halley's Comet reappeared. *1910*

20 The Spanish fleet was destroyed in the harbour of Santa Cruz by the English under

Admiral Blake. *1657*

21 Over 100,000 Chinese students poured into Tiananmen Square, ignoring government warnings of severe punishment. *1989*

22 Pedro Alvarez Cabral discovered Brazil and claimed it on behalf of the King of Portugal. *1500*

23 The USA announced the discovery of the AIDS virus. *1984*

24 Captain Joshua Slocum set sail, in his sloop *Spray*, on his single-handed voyage around the world (completed 27 June 1898). *1895*

25 Work began on the construction of the 161 km/100 mi Suez Canal, under the direction of Ferdinand de Lesseps. *1859*

26 The largest underground nuclear device ever to be tested in the USA exploded in Nevada. *1968*

27 Guernica in northern Spain was destroyed in a blitz by German planes. *1937*

28 Captain Cook, Sir Joseph Banks and others landed in Australia, in what is now known as Botany Bay, and named the country New South Wales. *1770*

29 Women were first admitted to Oxford University examinations. *1885*

30 Galerius Valerius Maximianus issued an edict at Nicomedia which gave legal recognition to Christians by the Roman Empire. *311*

MAY

1 The German Army in Italy surrendered to the Allies. *1945*

2 The Emperor Haile Selassie and his family fled from the Abyssinian capital, Addis Ababa, three days before it fell to Italian forces. *1936*

3 The first duel fought from two hot air balloons took place above Paris. *1808*

4 The Geneva Conference on arms, poison gas, and related matters began. *1925*

5 The next conjunction of the Sun, Moon, Mercury, Venus, Mars, Jupiter, and Saturn will take place. *2000*

6 Manhattan Island, now a borough of New York City, was bought from the native indians by Peter Minuit for trinkets worth no more than $25. *1626*

7 A German submarine torpedoed and sank the *Lusitania* off the coast of Ireland; around 1,400 people were drowned. *1915*

8 Dr Pemberton first produced the world's top-selling soft drink, Coca-Cola, in Atlanta, Georgia. *1886*

9 Disguised as a clergyman, Colonel Thomas Blood attempted to steal the Crown Jewels from the Tower of London. *1671*

10 The Sepoy Revolt broke out in Meerat, triggering the Indian mutiny against British rule. *1857*

11 The first printed book, known as the *Diamond Sutra*, was published in China. *868*

12 The Russian blockade of Berlin, which had lasted 11 months, was lifted. *1949*

13 A state of emergency was declared in Kuala Lumpur, Malaysia, after continued fighting between Malays and Chinese. *1969*

14 Louis XIV ascended the throne of France, aged 4 years, and reigned for over 72 years. *1643*

15 Soviet troops began their evacuation from Afganistan after more than eight years of occupation. *1988*

16 The first meeting of Dr Johnson and James Boswell took place at Tom Davie's bookshop in Russell Street, London. *1763*

17 The first 'package holiday', arranged by Thomas Cook, set out from London Bridge on a six-day trip to Paris. *1861*

18 Ville Marie (Montreal) was formally founded. *1642*

19 Ann Boleyn, Henry VIII's second wife and mother of Queen Elizabeth I, was beheaded. *1536*

20 The Spanish Armada, under the command of the Duke of Medina, set sail from Lisbon in an attempt to invade England. *1588*

21 Charles Lindbergh became the first to fly the Atlantic solo, from New York to Paris in 33.5 hours. *1927*

22 Ceylon was declared a republic and changed its name to Sri Lanka. *1972*

23 Marlborough defeated the French at the battle of Ramilles in Belgium. *1706*

24 The first morse message over a telegraph line was transmitted from Washington to Baltimore by Samuel Morse, its inventor. *1844*

25 The Philadelphia Convention met under George Washington to draw up the USA constitution. *1787*

26 The last public execution in England took place, outside Newgate Prison in London. *1868*

27 Tsar Peter the Great proclaimed St Petersburg the new capital of Russia. *1703*

28 Belgian King Leopold III surrendered to Germany. *1940*

29 Constantinople fell to the Turkish army after a year's seige. *1453*

30 Joan of Arc was burned at the stake in Rouen. *1431*

31 The colonies of the Cape of Good Hope, Natal, Transvaal and the Orange River Colony became united to form the Union of South Africa. *1910*

JUNE

1 The first attack on London by Zeppelins took place. *1915*

2 The coronation of Queen Elizabeth II, the first to be televised, took place. *1953*

3 The first 'bikini' bathing suit was unveiled in Paris. *1946*

4 The evacuation of allied forces from Dunkirk, which had begun 27 May, was completed. *1940*

5 The 'Six Day War' between Israel and Egypt, Jordan, Syria, and Iraq began. *1967*

6 'Operation Overlord', the allied landings on the coast of Normandy, took place. *1944*

7 The Addled Parliament was dissolved without having passed a Bill since it first sat on

5 April—hence its name. *1614*

8 George Mallory, on his third attempt to climb Mount Everest, was last seen at a point some 244 m/800 ft below the summit. *1924*

9 Hong Kong was leased by Britain from the Chinese for 99 years. *1898*

10 The first of 19 people were hanged at Salem at the end of the hysterical witch hunt trials conducted by Judge Corwin. *1692*

11 Henry VIII married Spanish Princess Catherine of Aragon, the first of his six wives. *1509*

12 Abner Doubleday invented baseball in Cooperstown, New York. *1839*

13 The Boxer Rebellion, led by a secret society originally formed to promote boxing, began in China to end foreign domination. *1900*

14 Argentinian forces formally surrendered to the British task force in the Falkland Islands. *1982*

15 The Magna Carta was stamped with the Royal seal by King John at Runnnymede, near Windsor. *1215*

16 A Cathay Pacific's Catalina flying boat on a scheduled flight to Hong Kong was the first plane to be hijacked, by a gang of Chinese bandits. *1948*

17 Sir Francis Drake anchored the *Golden Hind* just north of what would later be named San Francisco Bay. *1579*

18 The combined forces led by the Duke of Wellington and von Blucher defeated Napoleon at the Battle of Waterloo. *1815*

19 Ethel and Julius Rosenberg were executed in New York, the first US civilians to go to the electric chair for espionage. *1953*

20 146 British subjects were imprisoned by the Nawab of Bengal in a dungeon known as the 'Black Hole of Calcutta'; only 23 survived overnight. *1756*

21 Tobruk fell to Rommel with the capture of 25,000 Allied troops. *1943*

22 The first cricket match was played at the present Lord's ground in London. *1814*

23 General Nasser became Egypt's first president, after an election in which voting was compulsory, and he was the only candidate. *1956*

24 The first Freemason Lodge was inaugurated in London. *1717*

25 General Custer led US troops against the Sioux Indians at the Little Bighorn in Montana, and he and his 264 soldiers of the 7th Cavalry were massacred. *1876*

26 The first Grand Prix took place at Le Mans, and was won by the Hungarian Ferenc Szisz, driving a Renault at an average speed of 63 mph. *1906*

27 The *Ladies' Mercury*, the first magazine for women, was published. *1693*

28 The Archduke Ferdinand of Austria and his wife were assassinated in Sarajevo, by terrorist Gavrillo Princip. *1914*

29 Tahiti was annexed by France. *1880*

30 Montezuma, the last Aztec ruler, was killed by his own subjects in Mexico City during the Spanish Conquest of Mexico under Cortes. *1520*

JULY

1 Charles Darwin, together with Alfred Russell Wallace, presented a paper to the Linnean Society in London, on his theory of the evolution of the species. *1838*

2 President Johnson signed the USA Civil Rights Bill prohibiting racial discrimination. *1964*

3 French explorer, Samuel Champlain, founded Quebec. *1608*

4 The Philippine Islands were given independence by the USA. *1946*

5 Israel annexed Gaza. *1967*

6 Sir Thomas More was beheaded in London. *1535*

7 The unseeded 17-year-old Boris Becker became the youngest ever men's singles champion at Wimbledon. *1985*

8 Vasco de Gama left Lisbon for a voyage on which he discovered the Cape route to India. *1497*

9 Argentina declared independence from Spain. *1816*

10 The Yorkists defeated the Lancastrians and captured Henry VI at the battle of Northampton. *1460*

11 America's *Skylab I* returned to earth after 34,981 orbits and six years in space. *1979*

12 President Wilson opened the Panama Canal. *1920*

13 Queen Victoria became the first sovereign to move into Buckingham Palace. *1837*

14 The Bastille was stormed by the citizens of Paris and razed to the ground as the French Revolution began. *1789*

15 Jerusalem was captured by the Crusaders with troops led by Godfrey and Robert of Flanders and Tancred of Normandy. *1099*

16 The first atomic bomb developed by Robert Oppenheimer and his team at Los Alamos was exploded in New Mexico. *1945*

17 The British royal family changed their name from 'House of Saxe-Coburg-Gotha' to 'House of Windsor'. *1917*

18 The Spanish Civil War began with an army revolt led by Francisco Franco against the Republican government. *1936*

19 At a convention in Seneca Falls, New York, female rights campaigner Amelia Bloomer introduced 'bloomers' to the world. *1848*

20 Charles Sturt became the first white man to enter Simpson's Desert in Central Australia. *1845*

21 The lunar module from *Apollo 11* landed on the Moon, and US astronauts Armstrong and Aldrin took their first exploratory walk. *1969*

22 American bank robber and 'public enemy no. 1', John Dillinger, was gunned down by an FBI squad in Chicago. *1934*

23 Dr Livingstone returned to England. *1864*

24 Admiral Sir George Rooke captured Gibraltar from the Spaniards. *1704*

25   Magarethe Geertruida Zelle, the Dutch spy known as 'Mata Hari', was sentenced to death. *1917*
26   Liberia became the first African colony to secure independence. *1847*
27   The Korean armistice was signed at Panmunjom, ending three years of war. *1953*
28   The first potato arrived in Britain, brought from Colombia by Thomas Harriot. *1786*
29   The Spanish Armada was defeated by the English fleet under Howard and Drake, off Plymouth. *1588*
30   The world's first radar station was opened, to assist shipping at the port of Liverpool. *1948*
31   The Weimar Republic was established in post-war Germany. *1919*

AUGUST
1   The first savings bank was opened, in Hamburg. *1778*
2   Iraq invaded Kuwait causing an international crisis. *1990*
3   La Scala Opera House opened in Milan. *1778*
4   Britain declared war on Germany after the Germans had violated the Treaty of London, and the First World War began. *1914*
5   The first transatlantic cable was opened when Queen Victoria exchanged greetings with US President Buchanan. *1858*
6   An atomic bomb was dropped on the Japanese city of Hiroshima from a US Boeing B29 bomber. *1945*
7   Queen Victoria chose Ottawa as the capital of the Dominion of Canada. *1858*
8   Richard Nixon became the first US president to resign from office in face of threats to impeach him for his implication in the Watergate scandal. *1974*
9   The frontier between Canada and the USA was defined by the Webster-Ashburton treaty, signed by the USA and Britain. *1842*
10   Mozart completed his popular 'Eine kleine Nachtmusik'. *1787*
11   Canton was entered by Chiang Kai-shek and his supporters. *1963*
12   The first communications satellite was launched—America's *Echo I*. *1969*
13   The Battle of Blenheim took place in southern Germany, in which the Anglo-Austrian army inflicted a decisive defeat on the French and Bavarian armies. *1704*
14   The first British troops were deployed in Northern Ireland to restore order. *1969*
15   The Tivoli Pleasure Gardens were opened in Copenhagen. *1843*
16   The Peterloo Massacre took place in Manchester when militia opened fire on a crowd gathered to hear discussion of reform, killing eleven people. *1819*
17   Gold was discovered at Bonanza Creek in Canada's Yukon Territory, leading to the great gold rush of 1898. *1896*
18   The first oral contraceptive was marketed by the Searle Drug Company in the USA. *1960*
19   France and Spain formed an alliance against Britain. *1796*
20   Russian and troops of other communist countries invaded Czechoslovakia. *1968*
21   Leonardo da Vinci's painting the *Mona Lisa* was stolen from the Louvre in Paris—it was recovered two years later. *1911*
22   The Civil War in England began, between the supporters of Charles I (Royalists or Cavaliers) and of Parliament (Roundheads), when the king raised his standard at Nottingham. *1642*
23   The Blitz began as German bombers launched an all-night raid on London. *1940*
24   The Visigoths, led by Alaric, sacked Rome. *410*
25   Daily flights between Paris and London began, starting the first scheduled international air service. *1919*
26   The French Assembly adopted the Declaration of the Rights of Man. *1789*
27   Krakatoa, a volcanic island in the Sunda Strait between Sumatra and Java, erupted with thousands killed by the resulting tidal waves. *1883*
28   Venice was taken by the Austrians after a seige. *1849*
29   The 100-ton battleship HMS *Royal George* sank off Spithead while at anchor, with the loss of 900 lives. *1782*
30   The seige of Leningrad by German forces began (ended in Jan 1943) *1941*
31   Mary Ann 'Polly' Nichols, the first victim of Jack the Ripper, was found mutilated in Buck's Row. *1888*

SEPTEMBER
1   Germany invaded Poland, starting World War II. *1939*
2   The Great Fire of London started; it destroyed 13,000 buildings in four days. *1666*
3   Britain recognized US independence with the signing of a treaty in Paris. *1783*
4   Emperor Napoleon III, Bonaparte's nephew, was deposed and the Third Republic was proclaimed. *1870*
5   The world's longest road tunnel, the St Gotthard, was opened; it ran ten miles from Goschenen to Airolo, Switzerland. *1980*
6   After three years voyaging the *Vittoria*, which had set out under the command of Ferdinand Magellan, sailed into San Lucar harbour in Spain with 17 surviving crew members having completed the first circumnavigation of the world. *1522*
7   Bishop Desmond Tutu was appointed Archbishop of Capetown, the first black head of South African Anglicans. *1986*
8   The Dutch colony of New Amsterdam was surrendered to the British who renamed it New York in 1669. *1664*
9   North Korea declared its independence. *1948*
10   Hungary opened its border to the West allowing thousands of East German refu-

gees to leave, much to the anger of the East German government. *1989*

11 A military junta, with USA support, overthrew the elected government of Chile. *1973*

12 Cleopatra's Needle, the obelisk of Thothmes II, was erected on London's Embankment. *1878*

13 *The Mousetrap* became Britain's longest-running play, reaching its 1,998th performance. *1957*

14 Miguel Primo de Riviera became dictator of Spain. *1923*

15 The civil war in Beirut began between Christians and Muslims. *1975*

16 The USA Buick and Oldsmobile car manufacturers merged to become General Motors. *1908*

17 The British airborne invasion of Arnhem, Holland began as part of 'Operation Market Garden'. *1944*

18 France abolished the use of the guillotine. *1981*

19 Led by Edward, the Black Prince, the English defeated the French at the Battle of Poitiers in the Hundred Years' War. *1356*

20 The US embassy in Beirut was attacked by a suicide bomber who drove into the compound with a lorry full of explosives and set them off killing 40 people. *1984*

21 Bonnie Prince Charles and his Jacobite army defeated the English at the Battle of Prestonpans in Scotland. *1745*

22 Idi Amin gave the 8,000 Asians in Uganda 48 hours to leave the country. *1972*

23 German astronomer Johann Galle discovered the planet Neptune. *1846*

24 The Iraqis blew up the Abadan oil refinery, turning the Iran-Iraq conflict into a full-scale war. *1980*

25 The first blood transfusion using human blood, as opposed to earlier attempts with animal blood, took place at Guy's Hospital in London. *1818*

26 The Parthenon was severely damaged by mortar bombs fired by the Venetian army which was beseiging the Turkish-held Acropolis. *1687*

27 Constantine I, King of Greece, abdicated following the Greek defeat in Turkey. *1922*

28 Pope John Paul I, pope for only 33 days, was found dead. *1978*

29 The first British monarch to abdicate, Richard II, was replaced by Bolingbroke who ascended the throne as Henry IV. *1399*

30 The first performance of Mozart's *The Magic Flute* took place in Vienna. *1791*

OCTOBER

1 The Arab forces of Emir Faisal, with British officer T E Lawrence, captured Damascus from the Turks. *1918*

2 Saladin, the Muslim sultan, captured Jerusalem after an 88-year occupation by the Franks. *1187*

3 The Kingdom of Serbs, Croats, and Slovenes was renamed Yugoslavia. *1929*

4 Orville Wright became the first to fly an aircraft for over 33 minutes. *1905*

5 Bulgaria declared its independence from Turkey. *1908*

6 One day after the 11th anniversary of his election to office, Egyptian President Anwar Sadat was assassinated by Muslim extremists. *1981*

7 The Battle of Lepanto between Christian allied naval forces and the Ottoman Turks attempting to capture Cyprus from the Venetians, took place. *1571*

8 St Mark's Cathedral in Venice was consecrated. *1085*

9 Henry VI was restored to the English throne after being deposed in 1461. *1470*

10 Mrs Emmeline Pankhurst formed the Women's Social and Political Union to fight for women's emancipation in Britain. *1903*

11 The Anglo-Boer War began. *1899*

12 President Theodore Roosevelt renamed the Executive Mansion 'The White House'. *1901*

13 Sigmund Freud's *The Interpretation of Dreams* was published. *1904*

14 The Battle of Hastings was fought on Senlac Hill, where King Harold was slain as William the Conqueror's troops routed the English army. *1066*

15 The first major ballet was staged at the request of Catherine de' Medici at the palace in Paris. *1581*

16 Nazi war criminals, including von Ribbentrop, Rosenberg and Streicher, were hanged at Nuremberg. *1946*

17 British commander General Burgoyne surrendered to General Horatio Gates at Saratoga, a victory for the American colonists. *1777*

18 Germany's anti-terrorist squad stormed a hijacked Lufthansa aircraft at Mogadishu Airport, Somalia, killing three of the four Palestinian highjackers and freeing all of the hostages. *1977*

19 The first company to manufacture internal combustion engines was formed in Florence. *1860*

20 Mao Zedong's Long March ended in Yenan, north China. *1935*

21 Mao Zedong's Long March with his 100,000 strong Communist army began, after they had fought their way out of the seige mounted by Chiang Kai-shek's Nationalist armies in Funkien. *1934*

22 The first parachute jump was made by Andre-Jacques Garnerin from a balloon 6,000 feet above the Parc Monceau, Paris. *1797*

23 The Hungarian revolt against Soviet leadership began, in which thousands of demonstrators called for the withdrawal of Soviet forces. *1956*

24 The first football club was formed by a group of Cambridge University Old Boys meeting in Sheffield. *1857*

25 Lord Cardigan led the Charge of the Light Brigade during the Battle of Balaclava in the Crimean War. *1854*

26 Sweden and Norway ended their union and Oscar II, the Norwegian king, abdicated. *1905*

27 Charles II sold Dunkirk to Louis XIV for 2,500,000 livres. *1662*

28 The Statue of Liberty, designed by Auguste Bartholdi, was presented by France to the USA to mark the hundredth anniversary of the Declaration of Independence. *1886*

29 The Wall street crash known as 'Black Tuesday' took place, leading to the Great Depression. *1929*

30 P'u-i, the boy emperor of China aged five, granted a new constitution on the advice of the regent Prince Chun, officially ending three centuries of Manchu domination over China. *1911*

31 The Battle of Britain ended. *1940*

NOVEMBER

1 An earthquake reduced two-thirds of Lisbon to rubble and resulted, according to contemporary accounts, in the death of 60,000 people. *1755*

2 The Balfour Declaration, stating British sympathies for Jewish Zionist aspirations for a homeland in Palestine and promising aid to support efforts to achieve this goal, was sent to Lord Rothschild. *1917*

3 The Russian dog, Laika, became the first in space aboard Sputnik II. *1957*

4 Iranian students stormed the US Embassy in Tehran and held over 60 staff and US marines hostage. *1979*

5 The combined British and French armies defeated the Russians at the Battle of Inkerman during the Crimean War. *1854*

6 The construction of the Kariba High Dam began on the Zambezi River between Zambia and Zimbabwe. *1956*

7 The *Marie Celeste*, the ill-fated brigantine, sailed from New York to be found mysteriously abandoned near the Azores. *1872*

8 The Louvre was opened to the public by the revolutionary government, although only part of the collection could be viewed. *1793*

9 The SS (Schutzstaffel or 'Protection Squad') was formed in Germany. *1922*

10 Bulldozers began demolishing the 28-year-old Berlin Wall, the day after the East German government had announced that it would lift the 'iron curtain' and allow free travel between East and West Germany. *1989*

11 The armistice was signed between the Allies and Germany in Compeigne. *1918*

12 Leotard, the daring young man on the flying trapeze, made his debut in Paris. *1859*

13 The first helicopter rose 2 m/6.5 ft above ground in Normandy, powered by two motor-driven propellers above the pilot. *1907*

14 Scottish explorer James Bruce discovered the source of the Blue Nile in northeastern Ethiopia, then considered the main stream of the Nile. *1770*

15 Winston Churchill was captured by the Boers while covering the war as a reporter for the *Morning Post*. *1899*

16 The USSR launched *Venus III*, an unmanned spacecraft that successfully landed on Venus. *1965*

17 The last sultan of Turkey was deposed by Kemal Ataturk. *1922*

18 St Peter's in Rome was consecrated. *1626*

19 President Lincoln delivered his famous Gettysburg address, during the American Civil War. *1863*

20 The lights of Piccadilly Circus and the Strand were switched back on after five years of blackout. *1944*

21 The discovery of the 'Piltdown Man' skull by Charles Dawson in Sussex in 1912 was finally revealed as a hoax. *1953*

22 Portuguese navigator Vasco de Gama rounded the Cape of Good Hope in his search for a route to India. *1497*

23 The first jukebox was installed in Palais Royal Saloon in San Francisco. *1889*

24 Dutch navigator Abel Tasman discovered Van Diemen's Land which he named after his captain, but it was later renamed Tasmania. *1642*

25 Evaporated milk was patented by John Mayenberg of St Louis, Missouri. *1884*

26 The Soviet forces counterattacked at Stalingrad, ending the seige and forcing General von Paulus's Sixth Army to retreat. *1942*

27 President de Gaulle rejected British entry into the Common Market. *1967*

28 The Irish political party Sinn Fein was founded by Arthur Griffith in Dublin. *1905*

29 USA admiral Richard Byrd became the first man to fly over the South Pole, with his pilot Bernt Balchen. *1929*

30 Napoleon I's remains were returned from St Helena to Paris. *1840*

DECEMBER

1 The Spanish were driven out of Portugal and the country regained its independence. *1640*

2 The rebuilt St Paul's Cathedral, work of Sir Christopher Wren, was opened. *1697*

3 At Groote Schurr Hospital, Cape Town, Dr Christaan Barnard carried out the world's first heart transplant. *1967*

4 The only Englishman to become a pope, Nicholas Breakspear, became Adrian IV. *1154*

5 The Russian fleet was almost totally destroyed by the Japanese at Port Arthur. *1904*

6 Austria became the first nation to introduce a state education system. *1774*

7 The Japanese attacked the US fleet in Pearl Harbor. *1941*

8 Pope Pius IX declared the dogma of the Im-

maculate Conception of the Blessed Virgin Mary to be an article of faith. *1854*

9 The first martyrs of the 'intifada' in the Gaza Strip were created when an Israeli patrol attacked in the Jabaliya refugee camp. *1987*

10 Cuba became independent of Spain following the Spanish-American War. *1898*

11 The first wildlife preservation society was formed in Britain, called the Society for the Preservation of Wild Fauna of the Empire. *1903*

12 Bill Haley and the Comets recorded 'See You Later Alligator' at Decca Recording Studios, New York. *1955*

13 The Metropolitan Underground railway in London went electric. *1904*

14 US *Mariner II* sent the first close-up pictures of the planet Venus back to Earth. *1962*

15 A meteorological office established in Tuscany began recording daily temperature readings. *1654*

16 The first immigrant ship, the *Charlotte Jane*, arrived at Lyttleton, New Zealand. *1850*

17 *A Christmas Carol* by Charles Dickens was published. *1843*

18 The USA officially abolished slavery with the ratification of the 13th Amendment. *1865*

19 Henry II became King of England. *1154*

20 General Noriega, Panama's former military leader, dictator and alleged drug baron, was overthrown by a US invasion force invited by the new civilian government, headed by Guillermo Endara. *1989*

21 Charles de Gualle became President of France. *1958*

22 Alfred Dreyfus, the French officer who was falsely convicted for selling military secrets, was sent to Devil's Island. *1894*

23 English architect Joseph Hansom patented his 'safety cab', better known as the Hansom cab. *1834*

24 The War of 1812 between the USA and Britain was brought to an end with the signing of the Treaty of Ghent. *1814*

25 The Nicaraguan capital Managua was devastated by an earthquake which killed over 10,000 people. *1972*

26 Marie and Pierre Curie discovered radium while experimenting with pitchblende. *1898*

27 Charles Darwin set sail in the *Beagle* on his voyage of scientific discovery. *1831*

28 An earthquake killed over 75,000 at Messina in Sicily. *1908*

29 Sun Yat Sen became the first president of a republican China following the Revolution. *1911*

30 A petition to Queen Victoria with over one million names of women appealing for public houses to be closed on Sundays was handed to the Home Secretary. *1887*

31 The first Huguenots set sail from France for the Cape of Good Hope, where they would escape religious persecution and create the South African wine industry with the vines they took with them on the voyage. *1687*

OBITUARIES

Abbott Berenice 1898–1991. US photographer who made portrait studies of artists in the 1920s, documentary studies especially of New York City, and scientific photography.

Abbott began as a studio assistant to the Surrealist photographer Man Ray in Paris and by 1926 had set up on her own, specializing in austere but penetrating portraits of the city's leading artistic personalities. Her portrait of the writer James Joyce dates from this period. Returning to New York in 1929, she spent the next ten years on a systematic study of the city which culminated in the publication of her book *Changing New York* 1939. In the 1940s and 1950s she was mainly occupied with scientific work, creating some outstanding microscopic images and producing illustrations for school textbooks. Throughout this period she taught photography on a programme which she had established at the New York New School. Her last important documentary project was a study of US Route 1, from Maine to Florida. In 1989 she was honoured with a retrospective at the Portland Museum in New York.

Akhromeyev Sergei Fedorovich 1923–1991. Soviet military leader. He directed Soviet military operations in Afghanistan 1979–89. As chief of general staff of the Soviet armed forces 1984–88, he was key military adviser to President Mikhail Gorbachev, accompanying him to the 1986 and 1987 summits. During this period he gained respect in the West as a pragmatic and trustworthy supporter of the disarmament process. However, from 1988 his views became more reactionary. Disillusioned with the collapse of the attempted anti-Gorbachev coup in August 1991, he committed suicide by hanging. He wrote in his long suicide note: 'Everything I have devoted my life to is collapsing'.

Born in central Russia, Akhromeyev trained as a naval cadet in 1939 and fought in the naval infantry in 1941, defending the Baltic base of Liepaja. He transferred to the Red Army's tank divisions, and became a platoon commander after the battle of Stalingrad in 1943. Having fought on the Ukrainian fronts, he ended the 'Great Patriotic War' as a captain. After the war he continued to concentrate on a military career. In 1974, by now a colonel-general, he was made chief of the main operations directorate of the general staff. From the late 1970s, Akhromeyev, elevated to the position of general, was given charge of reorganizing the Afghanistan conflict. In 1982 he was made a Hero of the Soviet Union and, a year later, a marshal and member of the CPSU's powerful central committee. In September 1984 he reached the pinnacle of his military career, being promoted to chief of the general staff.

Almendros Nestor 1931–1992. Spanish-born director of photography. One of the cinematographers most prominently associated with the French New Wave, Almendros worked on several films directed by François Truffaut, and later moved to the USA, establishing a reputation there after winning the Academy Award for cinematography for *Days of Heaven* 1978.

Born in Barcelona, Almendros grew up in Cuba and studied cinematography in Rome. Increasingly out of sympathy with the Castro regime, he migrated to Paris. Among the Truffaut films he worked on was *L'Enfant Sauvage* 1970, with its ambitious reproduction of the visual texture of early black-and-white cinematography. He was also a collaborator of Eric Rohmer on a succession of films including *Ma Nuit Chez Maud* 1969, and later imported a distinctively European refinement into the lighting of the US pictures on which he worked, which included *Sophie's Choice* 1982 and *Heartburn* 1986. His book *A Man With a Camera* 1985 is an eloquent autobiographical discourse on the nature of his craft.

Andronikos Manolis 1919–1992. Leading Greek archaeologist. He was professor of classical archaeology at the University of Thessaloniki, and best known for his excavations in the burial mounds of Vergina in northern Greece. Vergina proved to be the site of Aigai, capital of ancient Macedonia. It was the place where Philip II of Macedon, father of Alexander the Great, was assassinated in 336 BC.

In 1977 Andronikos uncovered a series of decorated royal tombs from the 4th century BC at Vergina. One of them is probably that of Philip himself. Andronikos found many rich treasures inside this unplundered tomb. They included two marble sarcophagi containing gold burial caskets. One had a lid bearing a 16-point star. It held cremated bones in a purple and gold cloth, and topped with a gold wreath. There were miniature ivory carvings matching descriptions of Alexander and his father. There was also a set of gilded leg armour made for a man with one leg shorter than the other. This matches descriptions of Philip. Reconstruction of the cremated bone fragments showed that the occupant of the tomb had severe eye injuries; Philip was hit in the eye by an arrow during a siege. Andronikos later uncovered more than ten other royal tombs and, in 1982, the theatre where Philip was assassinated at his daughter's wedding.

Arlott John 1914–1991. Writer and broadcaster. For more than 30 years he popularized cricket on radio with his descriptive powers and deliberate and delightful way of painting the whole picture. He was the first commentator to go outside and beyond the cricket itself. He wrote books on cricket, soccer, cheese and his other great love, wine. He was made an OBE in 1970 and an honorary life member of MCC 1980–91. He was president of the Cricketers Association 1968–91. He retired from broadcasting in 1980.

Born in Basingstoke, Hampshire, he joined the BBC in 1945 after spending 11 years with the Southampton Borough Police. He became General Instructor for the BBC staff training school in 1951 and was a Liberal candidate for Epping in the general elections of 1955 and 1959. An expansive man in life as well as on the air, he had a generous spirit and a lovely sense of humour. His voice to countless millions around the globe meant, quite simply, cricket.

Arnold Jack 1916–1992. US film director. His lasting achievement in the cinema is the making of a string of science-fiction thrillers during the 1950s that are regarded by critics as among the most effective the genre has produced. The films, which included *Creature from the Black Lagoon* 1954, *Tarantula* 1955 (about a hugely enlarged spider), and *The Incredible Shrinking Man* 1957, were made at Universal studios on modest budgets and without elaborate resources. But the result of this economy was that the almost matter-of-fact surface heightened the grotesque imagination behind the scenarios.

Arnold had been an actor and later, perhaps more significantly, worked on numerous industrial documentaries before directing his first film in 1951. In addition to his science-fiction movies, he was an efficient exponent of Westerns and melodramas, as well as of comedies such as the Bob Hope vehicle *Bachelor in Paradise* 1961. But sadly his output dwindled away after the mid-1960s into cheap exploitation films.

Asimov Isaac 1920–1992. Russian-born American science-fiction writer and popularizer of science. His rational approach to science fiction did much to rid it of its more sensational aspects and helped it to be taken seriously. His 'Three Laws of Robotics', an ethical code of behaviour for artificial intelligence, have been almost universally employed by subsequent writers.

Asimov was born in Petrovich, Russia but emigrated with his parents to New York in 1923. His father ran a candy store and reluctantly allowed his son to read the SF magazines that he sold there. His first story was published in 1938, the year he met John A Campbell, the editor of *Astounding Science Fiction* and an important influence. In the same year he got a BSc in chemistry at Columbia University and, after working at the Naval Air Experimental Station in 1945, gained a PhD in 1948. From 1951 until his death he taught biochemistry at the Boston University School of Medicine, as professor from 1979. His first important story 'Nightfall' 1941 is regarded by many as the greatest SF story ever. It poses the question: how would man react if the stars were only visible once every thousand years? It was printed in *Astounding*, as were the stories that were to make up his most famous work, the *Foundation Trilogy* 1951–53. This epic tells of the decline of a million-year empire

and the attempts to preserve its important truths or 'psychohistory'. All Asimov's writing is marked by clarity and intelligence; what it often lacks is good plots and psychological depth. He was immensely prolific, writing about a wide variety of subjects including the arts.

Babbit Art(hur) 1904–1992. US film animator. A key participant in the Walt Disney studio in the 1930s, he animated *The Country Cousin*, a Mickey Mouse cartoon that won an Academy Award 1935, and was later animation director on *Pinocchio* 1940, and an animation supervisor on *Fantasia* 1940.

Babbit was born into a farming family in Omaha, Nebraska, and began his working life as a commercial artist in New York. He joined the Terry-Toons animation studio there in 1931 and the next year was hired by Disney, though apparently the two men were never on friendly terms. In 1941, the year he was animation director on *Dumbo*, Babbit's attempt to win a salary increase for his assistant, and Disney's refusal, led to a strike by studio personnel, which severely dented its 'family' reputation. After war service as a Marine Corps intelligence officer, Babbit returned to working for Disney, but subsequently joined the rival, more modernist-inclined, UPA studio. He directed several short cartoons for UPA, but was not altogether happy with their regime. In the 1960s, he gravitated to television work for the Hanna-Barbera production company, and in the 1970s moved to London to work with the Canadian animator Richard Williams, functioning as an instructor for younger talent. Babbit retired to the USA 1987.

Bacon Francis 1909–1992. British painter whose anguished and twisted figures, usually set in an enclosed boxlike interior, are some of the most powerful and lasting images of human isolation painted this century. He created several versions of the Spanish painter Velàzquez's *Pope Innocent X*, caged in glass and endlessly screaming.

Born in Dublin to English parents, Bacon left home when he was 16 and spent two years in Berlin and in Paris, where he was impressed by the work of Picasso. In 1928 he settled in London, initially working as an interior designer before taking up painting. Apart from some advice from his friend Roy de Maistre, he was largely self-taught. Although mentioned in Herbert Read's influential book *Art Now*, Bacon was not accepted for the International Surrealists' London Exhibition in 1936 and he later destroyed most of his work from this period.

Bacon's first major work was the *Three Studies for Figures at the base of a Crucifixion* 1945. It introduced into his work a simplicity of composition with an uncompromising violence of feeling which shocked critics. *Painting 1946* presents a dark and solitary figure in front of a hanging carcass of meat, the figure's fiercely gaping mouth strangely emphasized. Photographic images and other paintings were often employed as a starting point for his work: not only the Velázquez but also Eadweard Muybridge's sequential photographs of movement and the screaming woman from Sergei Eisenstein's film *The Battleship Potemkin*. Even the portraits of Bacon's friends reveal a fascination with convulsive movement and with the richly coloured degeneration of flesh, qualities whose apparent negativity has repelled many viewers.

Bacon Francis Thomas 1904–1992. English scientist and engineer who devoted his life to the development of an energy-saving technology, the fuel cell. This device, because it is based on electrochemistry, converts fuel, for example gas or methyl alcohol, into electrical power extremely efficiently. It does so with negligible emissions, because burning of fuel is not involved. Fuel cells have operated successfully in space to provide power and drinking water—Neil Armstrong, the astronaut, has said that the *Apollo* programme would not have been possible without Bacon's work. Bacon first demonstrated a 6kW fuel cell in 1959.

Bacon was educated at Eton and Trinity College, Cambridge. Apprenticed to the electrical company C Parsons, Bacon became aware of the tremendous potential for the fuel cell in 1932. Now prototype buses and cars are being developed in a programme sponsored by the US Department of Energy, and the largest fuel-cell power station in Europe is about to come into operation. Bacon, an honorary member of the European Fuel Cell Group, was awarded the OBE in 1967, and became a Fellow

Francis Bacon

of the Royal Society in 1973. In 1991, 50 years after Bacon constructed his first fuel cell, the Royal Institution awarded him a medal struck in platinum—the metal which acts as the catalyst in a fuel cell to ensure clean and efficient generation of power.

Bakhtiar Shapur 1914–1991. Iranian politician, the last prime minister under the shah, in 1979. He was a supporter of the political leader Muhammad Mossadeq in the 1950s and active in the National Front opposition to the shah from 1960. He lived in exile after the 1979 Islamic revolution.

Educated in France, Bakhtiar returned to Iran in the 1940s to find that his father had been executed for treason by the Pahlavi regime headed by Reza Shah. Nevertheless Bakhtiar became a civil servant and eventually director of the Department of Labour in the oil-rich province of Khuzistan. He had already joined the Iran Party, which subsequently affiliated with the National Front led by Mossadeq. When Mossadeq became prime minister in 1951, Bakhtiar seemed likely to benefit, but the coup against Mossadeq in 1953 temporarily ended Bakhtiar's political career and he spent some time in prison. By 1960 the National Front had been revived as a result of the unpopularity of the shah's government, and Bakhtiar became the Front's spokesperson on student affairs. As opposition to the Pahlavi regime increased, the shah looked for support from the Front, and in 1979 Bahktiar, as a member of the executive willing to do a deal with the shah, was made prime minister. Soon afterwards, Ayatollah Khomeini came to power. Bakhtiar fled to France, where, despite protection from the French government, attempts were made on his life by Islamic zealots; in Aug 1991 he and an aide were assassinated at his home in a Paris suburb.

Begin Menachem (Wolfovitch) 1913–1992. Israeli politician and nationalist leader, cofounder of the Likud Party, and prime minister 1977–83. The Camp David peace agreement with Egypt was signed by Begin and earned him and Egyptian president Anwar Sadat the 1979 Nobel Peace Prize.

Begin was born in Brest-Litovsk, Poland. He studied law at Warsaw University and became an active Zionist while still in his teens. When Poland was invaded in 1939 he fled to Lithuania, where he was arrested and imprisoned. On his release 1941 he joined the Free Polish Army and in 1942 was sent to Palestine, then a British mandated territory. Discharged from the army a year later, he beame leader of the Irgun Zvai Leumi resistance group, fighting for an independent Israeli state. One of their terrorist actions was to blow up the King David Hotel in Jerusalem in 1946, killing more than 90 people.

As a politician in the new state of Israel, Begin helped to found the right-wing Likud Party, which in 1977, under his leadership, ousted the ruling Labour Party and allowed him to form a Likud-dominated coalition. Regarded as an uncompromising hardliner, he surprised the world by responding positively to the peace initiative of President Sadat by participating in the Egypt–Israel peace talks brokered by US president Jimmy Carter, leading to the Camp David Agreement 1979. Begin's reputation as a peacemaker was tarnished in 1982 by the Israeli invasion of S Lebanon, allegedly to evict the Palestine Liberation Organization, and by the subsequent war. He resigned the premiership 1983. A very complex person, torn between his romantic feelings for Poland and his vision for Israel, he spent his last years as a virtual recluse.

Brooks Richard 1912–1992. US novelist, screenwriter and film director. A former journalist and radio commentator, he established a reputation as a Hollywood writer in the 1940s, directed his first film in 1950 and, after several routine productions, made his name with the juvenile delinquency picture *The Blackboard Jungle* 1955. He later made a wide range of films, notable among them *Elmer Gantry* 1960 and *In Cold Blood* 1967.

Brooks's most significant work as a screenwriter was on *Brute Force* 1947 and *Key Largo* 1948, in the vein of socially conscious melodrama also mined by his first novel, *The Brick Foxhole* 1945. His subsequent work as a writer and director reflected similar preoccupations, though in contexts as wide-ranging as African colonialism (*Something of Value* 1957) and the milieu of singles bars (*Looking for Mr Goodbar* 1977). His ambitions also ran to elaborate adaptations of classic novels, including *The Brothers Karamazov* 1958 and *Lord Jim* 1965. Brooks was married for some years to the actress Jean Simmons, star of two of his films.

Brown Freddie 1910–1991. Peruvian-born cricketer. His 33-year playing career as a hard-hitting batsman and shrewd slow bowler included 22 tests for England and captaincy of Northamptonshire County Cricket Club 1949–53. He was awarded first an MBE and then a CBE.

He first emerged as a schoolboy prodigy at the Leys school, and after two years at Cambridge University he joined Surrey County Cricket Club. At 22 he was a spectacular choice for Jardine's England team for the 'bodyline' tour of Australia in 1932–33. In 1950–51 he captained England in Australia where they achieved their first postwar victory. After his retirement at the age of 43 he served as president of MCC, chairman of the Cricket Council and National Cricket Association, and president of the English Schools Cricket Association.

Crawford Jack 1908–1991. Australian lawn-tennis player who became one of the great prewar players, winning the Wimbledon, French and Australian titles in the same year, 1933. His victory at Wimbledon provided one of the greatest matches in its history—a gruelling match against Elsworth

Frank Capra

Vines, which he won 4–6, 11–9, 6–2, 2–6, 6–4. He also won seven men's doubles titles, including five Australian titles, and a mixed doubles title. Tall and well built, he always played in a long-sleeved cricket shirt. One of his quirks was to ask in a long match for a pot of tea on a tray with hot water, milk and sugar. In the changeovers he would pour himself a cup.

Capra Frank 1897–1991. US film director. As maker of such classics as *It Happened One Night* 1934, *Mr Deeds Goes to Town* 1936, and *Mr Smith Goes to Washington* 1939, Capra was one of the most celebrated directors of the 1930s, and on the strength of the populist vision that his films consistently contained, he was one of those most responsible for establishing in the public mind the notion of the film director as an individual artist.

The son of poor Sicilian immigrants, Capra had a chequered early career and entered films almost by accident. He became a 'gagman' for silent comedies, then directed several vehicles for the comedian Harry Langdon. The huge, and Oscar-laden, success of *It Happened One Night* established him as an independent force, and his progress continued unabated until World War II, during which he supervised an influential documentary series, *Why We Fight*. His first postwar picture, *It's a Wonderful Life* 1946, met popular acclaim and is frequently revived. His career subsequently faltered; his output became sporadic and his last film was made in 1961. His autobiography, *Name Above the Title* 1971, concluded on a note of unconcealed rancour at the changed climate of Hollywood filmmaking.

Chaplin Oona (born O'Neill) 1926–1991. US society hostess, daughter of the playwright Eugene O'Neill and widow of the actor Charlie Chaplin. The couple had eight children, among them the actress Geraldine Chaplin.

Oona O'Neill was born in Bermuda and educated in New York. She suffered as a girl from intense shyness, exacerbated by her parents' divorce. Yet she decided to become an actress. Chaplin saw a screen test she made at 17 and considered her for a part in an eventually unrealized film project. When they met he was a thrice-married man of 54, and their marriage infuriated Oona's father, who broke off all contact with her. But the marriage proved happy and successful, and the couple established an idyllic home in Vevey, Switzerland. Charlie Chaplin once said: 'It took me 54 years to find happiness. But it was worth waiting for.' In his later years, he could hardly bear to be parted from his wife. After his death in 1977, she found it difficult to adjust to changed circumstances, and though she continued to fulfil the role of society hostess, she made no secret of suffering from a reduced sense of purpose in life.

Clayton Buck (Wilbur Dorsey) 1911–1991. US jazz trumpeter, band leader, composer, and arranger, a member of Count Basie's band in the 1930s, Humphrey Lyttelton's in the 1960s, and several line-ups in his own name, the last being Buck Clayton's Big Swing Band from 1987.

Like so many jazz musicians, Clayton began playing in Kansas City, but moved to Los Angeles at 19 and joined a band that appeared in such Hollywood films as *42nd Street*. Becoming the band's leader 1934, he took it to Shanghai, which they left only days before the Japanese invasion 1936. As a member of Count Basie's band 1936–43, Clayton worked with the big names in jazz. The singer Billie Holiday described him as 'the prettiest cat I ever laid my eyes on'. Called up, Clayton joined an army service band until 1946. Subsequently he was based in New York but spent much time in Europe and also toured the Far East with guitarist Eddie Condon. His playing was a versatile mainstream style based on that of Louis Armstrong. Dental problems forced him to give up the trumpet 1969 but he continued composing, arranging, and lecturing, and at the age of 77 formed the big band he had always wanted. He also published an autobiography, *Buck Clayton's Jazz World* 1986.

D'Aubuisson (Arrieta) Roberto 1953–1992. El Salvadorean soldier and right-wing politician, founder of the ARENA (Republican Nationalist Alliance) party. His ruthless pursuit of political power, aided by death squads, made him reviled and feared. In 1984 he was a presidential candidate.

After receiving his education from Jesuits in San Salvador, D'Aubuisson embarked on a military career and joined the National Guard, notorious for its excesses and brutality. He returned from a period of study at the International Police Academy in Washington, DC to enter the political arena. Using the Kuomintang of Taiwan as his model, he founded ARENA, complete with its own military wing. Among other terrorist acts, he was believed to be behind the assassination of Oscar Romero, the archbishop of San Salvador, in 1980. This prompted the US Carter administration to ban him from entering the USA, but President Reagan later assisted in his rehabilitation. D'Aubuisson narrowly failed to win the presidency in 1984 and retired shortly afterwards on health grounds. His party won the presidency in 1989.

Davis Miles (Dewey) 1926–1991. US jazz trumpeter, composer, and band leader, one of the most influential and innovative figures in jazz. He pioneered bebop with saxophonist Charlie Parker 1945, cool jazz in the 1950s, and jazz-rock fusion from the late 1960s. His albums include *Birth of the Cool* 1949, *Sketches of Spain* 1959, *Bitches Brew* 1969, and *Tutu* 1985.

Davis, born in Illinois, studied briefly at the Juilliard School of Music in New York before joining Charlie Parker's group 1946–48. In 1948 he began an association with composer and arranger Gil Evans that was to last throughout his career, and from then on Davis led bands of his own. The line-up at various times included saxophonists John Coltrane, Cannonball Adderley (both can be heard on the seminal LP *Kind of Blue* 1959), and Wayne Shorter, pianists Herbie Hancock and Keith Jarrett, and guitarist John McLaughlin. Davis's 1950s work included quartet and quintet recordings that explored new ideas and directions, as well as three orchestral albums with Gil Evans, beginning with *Miles Ahead* 1957. He took improvisation even further in the 1960s, and began to make use of electronic instrumentation and rock rhythms; in the 1980s he also drew on the work of rock composers like Prince. 'I've changed music five or six times,' Davis asserted. 'People who don't change will find themselves like folk musicians, playing in museums.'

Dietrich Marlene. Adopted name of Maria Magdalena von Losch 1901–1992. German-born actress and singer. A cabaret performer and occasional film actress in Berlin in the 1920s, she was discovered by the director Josef von Sternberg to play the starring role of Lola-Lola in *The Blue Angel* 1930. The film's success, largely predicated on Dietrich's sultry eroticism, took both to Hollywood. There, Dietrich acted for von Sternberg in a succession of films, including *Morocco* 1930 and *The Scarlet Empress* 1934, usually exotic and sexually charged in tone. After they parted company professionally, Dietrich continued to act in a wide range of American films, displaying a gift for comedy in *Destry Rides Again* 1939.

Peaks of her postwar movie career included *Rancho Notorious* 1952 and *Witness for the*

Marlene Dietrich

Prosecution 1957. At the same time she established an international reputation as a singer, offering inimitable, smoky-voiced renderings of songs like 'Lili Marlene'. She continued these performances, looking imperishably glamorous, until she was over 70. Her last screen appearance was a brief role in *Just a Gigolo* 1976. In her last years she lived quietly in Paris, shunning publicity and media attention.

Dixon Willie (William James) 1915–1992. US blues musician, songwriter, producer, arranger, and singer. His main instrument was the acoustic bass. As house producer, session player, and A & R person at Chess Records in Chicago 1952–56 and 1960–70, he played a vital role in the development of urban blues, and his song credits include standards like 'Hoochie Coochie Man' 1953, 'My Babe' 1955, 'Spoonful' 1960, and 'Little Red Rooster' 1961.

Dixon was born in Mississippi and moved to Chicago 1937, where he gave up boxing for bass and played in several small groups; his first recordings were made 1946 with the Big Three Trio. He featured as backing musician on classic recordings by Muddy Waters, Howlin' Wolf, Bo Diddley, Chuck Berry, and many others, and his songs were recorded by bands like the Rolling Stones and the Doors as well as by the blues greats. About his white colleagues Dixon remarked: 'If you play them a little Chopin or *Liebestraum* first, that helps. That way you prove your abilities, and then you say, Hey, man, why don't you lay some blues on me?' Dixon toured and recorded with singer and pianist Memphis Slim, appeared at various festivals, acted as a talent scout, and had a music-publishing company. His slogan

'I am the blues' was also the title of his 1989 autobiography and a 1970 LP. His last album was *Hidden Charms* 1991.

Dupree Champion Jack (William Thomas) 1910–1992. US blues pianist, singer, and songwriter who spent much of his career in Europe. His rough and rolling New Orleans piano style influenced Fats Domino. Among his recordings is the album *Blues from the Gutter* 1958.

Dupree ran away at 14 from the same New Orleans Colored Waifs' Home that had sheltered Louis Armstrong, and learned to play from a barrelhouse pianist known as Drive 'Em Down. He also took up boxing and claimed to have taken part in 107 professional bouts before giving it up in 1940. In the 1930s he moved to Indianapolis, improving his piano style by learning from the classic blues player Leroy Carr (1905–1935), and began his long recording career in 1940 in Chicago, making the transition from the rural blues style to urban rhythm and blues with a small jump band. His lyrics were bawdy or political, generally humorous. He first toured Europe in 1959 and returned to settle the next year, initially in Switzerland, then for many years in Yorkshire, from the mid-1970s in Scandinavia, and finally in Hanover, Germany. During the British blues boom of the 1960s Dupree was based in England and appeared with such popular bands of the day as those of Chris Barber and John Mayall. 'Life ain't been too bad to me,' Dupree admitted, 'but I ain't forgotten none. I set out after them Ku Klux Klan guys and I'm still after them.'

Ferrer José. Adopted name of José Vincente Ferrer de Otero y Cintron 1912–1992. US stage and film actor and director. He played the lead in *Cyrano de Bergerac* 1950 (for which he won an Academy Award) and Toulouse-Lautrec in *Moulin Rouge* 1952. He later directed several films, of which the most significant was the media satire *The Great Man* 1957.

Puerto Rican-born, Ferrer grew up in the USA and made his Broadway acting debut in 1935. He turned to directing in 1942, and acted in his first film in 1948. His versatility as a stage actor, encompassing both farce and Shakespeare, carried over into his screen career, where he won attention for a variety of showily offbeat roles. However, his reputation was not sustained in later years. Of the several films he directed, few achieved commercial or artistic success. He was reduced to playing supporting roles in such films as *Lawrence of Arabia* 1962 and more recently figured in a disparate selection of international productions. The third of his four wives was the singer Rosemary Clooney.

Fletcher James 1919–1991. Director of the US National Aeronautics and Space Administration (NASA) 1971–77 and 1986–89. His chief achievements were the *Viking* missions to Mars in 1976 and the *Voyager* probes to the outer planets, launched 1977.

Fletcher was educated at Columbia University and in 1940 became a research physicist with the US Navy. A succession of research and teaching positions followed. In 1948 he joined the electronics division of Hughes Aircraft and played a vital role in the development of the Falcon air-to-air missile and the F-102 interceptor. In 1954 he moved to Ramo-Wooldridge corporation, and soon became head of the guided-missile division. This led to the founding of the Space Electronics Corporation which manufactured a range of sophisticated space instruments and communications equipment. In 1964 he became president of Utah University. He was the longest-serving director of NASA, where both his terms were preceded by setbacks which he overcame. In April 1970, the US space programme was in the doldrums after the failure of the *Apollo 13* mission. Fletcher soon started a vast new technical programme which resulted in the *Viking* probes that landed on Mars in 1976 and the stunning achievements of the *Voyager* 'grand tour' of the outer planets in the late 1970s and 1980s. In 1986 the explosion of the *Challenger* shuttle was the worst disaster suffered by NASA. Fletcher was called in by President Reagan to sort out the situation. He saw the shuttle successfully return to duty in 1988.

Fletcher was once described as the right balance between soft-hearted idealism and cold-blooded commercialism. It was this balance that enabled him to get quick results in the half-scientific, half-industrial world of space technology. He realized that the space programme had changed humanity's view of the environment. He said: 'You can't help but be a little concerned when you see the Earth from space. It's a beautiful place. There's nothing else like it in the solar system. It's the only one we've got and we'd better take care of it.'

Ford Tennessee Ernie (Ernest Jennings) 1919–1991. US country and gospel singer and songwriter who had two top-ten pop hits in the UK and the USA in 1955: 'The Ballad of Davy Crockett' and 'Sixteen Tons'. His deep baritone and crisp, jazzy backings made his records distinctive.

Ford, born in Tennesse, began his career as a disc jockey, presenting himself as a bashful hillbilly and greeting his audience with the catch phrase 'Howdy, pea-pickers!' In 1948 he signed with Capitol Records, and his early recordings, such as 'Smokey Mountain Boogie' 1949, 'Mule Train' 1949, and 'Shotgun Boogie' 1950, are proto-rockabilly numbers. In 1953 Ford became the first country singer to perform at the London Palladium ('Shotgun Boogie' was allegedly a favourite with the Queen); later he was to appear in the USSR. 'Davy Crockett', the theme song of a Walt Disney film, was covered by many singers and 'Sixteen Tons', about the hardships of coalminers, had been written and recorded by Merle Travis 1947, but it was Ford's versions that charted, the latter selling a million copies within three weeks. He had his own

TV show until 1961, then slowly faded from prominence, with a last country hit in 1971, though he also recorded some 20 well-received gospel-music albums.

Ford was said to look like Prince Rainier of Monaco, even when blacking out two front teeth to appear in his early Tennessee Ernie persona.

Furst Anton (Anthony Francis) 1944–1991. British film designer who won an Academy Award as set designer of the hit film *Batman* 1989.

Furst graduated from the Royal College of Art in London in 1969. He developed a holography show that became the touring light show for the rock group the Who in the mid-1970s. His London-based laser special effects firm, Holoco, worked on films including *Star Wars* 1977. Furst moved into production design, working to highly imaginative effect on films that included *Company of Wolves* 1984 and *Full Metal Jacket* 1987. He subsequently moved to Los Angeles. The success of *Batman*, in which the Gotham City sets were one of the most praised elements, led to the prospect of his directing a film for the singer Michael Jackson. But his personal life became fraught, and his death was by suicide.

Garcia Robles Alfonso 1911–1991. Mexican diplomat, a United Nations delegate from 1977 and an advocate of nuclear disarmament. Nobel Peace Prize 1982.

Originally intended for the priesthood, Garcia instead studied law in Mexico, France, and the Netherlands, then joined the Mexican foreign service, becoming undersecretary for foreign affairs 1964–71. In this role he was largely instrumental in obtaining the Treaty of Tlatelolco 1967, which sought to abolish nuclear weapons throughout Latin America. From 1977 he was the Mexican delegate on the UN Disarmament Committee. A quiet, self-effacing man, he came to world attention in 1982 when he was awarded the Nobel Peace Prize. On hearing of his death, Javier Pérez de Cuéllar, then UN secretary general, described him as 'one of the figures to whom the United Nations owes the most'.

Gertler Willie 1907–1991. Hungarian-born UK entrepreneur. Sole distributor of Levi jeans in the UK, Gertler was the first to introduce the jeans into the country in 1959, and into eastern Europe as early as 1979. He was well known for flamboyant sales gimmicks—he once built a pair of jeans with a 190 cm/75 in waist and offered a prize to the person whom they fitted.

Born in Budapest, Gertler moved to England in 1939. His first job was as a packer, but he quickly worked his way up to become managing director, before setting up his own company, Gertler & Co, in 1953, distributing rainwear. He was a lifelong fan of Fulham football club and used to kit the entire team out in the current range of raincoats. Six years later he won the Levi account, despite 80 other competitors, by borrowing Levi samples for an hour and then returning with £400 worth of orders. Under Gertler, sales for Levi soon doubled every year, and eventually formed 90% of his business. In 1972 he officially retired and wrote an autobiography, *Selling Is My Game* 1974. He continued to devote much of his energy to charitable work.

Graham Bill. Adopted name of Wolfgang Grajonca 1931–1991. US concert promoter whose Fillmore West and Fillmore East venues in San Francisco and New York were showcases for the rock bands of the late 1960s. Later he promoted tours by the Grateful Dead, Bob Dylan, the Rolling Stones, and Guns n' Roses, as well as large benefits for campaigns like Amnesty International.

Graham was born in Berlin and most of his family were killed by the Nazis; Graham escaped to the USA. Based in San Francisco from 1965, he staged there some of the earliest events of the hippie movement and in 1966 opened his first auditorium, the Fillmore. Its operations transferred in 1968 to the larger Fillmore West and its New York counterpart, both of which closed 1971. His booking policies, mixing jazz and blues performers with psychedelic rock bands, influenced the musical development of the period and he always remained associated with performers who came to prominence in the Fillmore days, many of whom (including the Grateful Dead and Neil Young) gave a free concert in his memory for 300,000 people in a San Francisco park in Nov 1991. His business sense mixed with irascible idealism made Graham a prime mover on the international rock-music scene. Just before his death he exclaimed to an interviewer: 'Wouldn't it be something if we could see the social and political changes in the nineties that we just dreamed about in the sixties?'

Grant Julius 1901–1991. English forensic scientist. The Great Train Robbery, the attempted murder of Archbishop Makarios, and the Tom Keating forgeries were settled largely thanks to Grant's forensic work, and in 1983 he exposed as fakes the alleged Hitler diaries.

Born into a poor east London family, Grant studied part-time for a degree in chemistry at Queen Mary College. In 1931 he joined the John Dickinson Paper Company and became expert in the properties of paper. His experience was put to use in a variety of projects. He devised a technique for exposing forged Hong Kong bank notes (the watermark dissolved in ether). During World War II he put cow hair into paper for ration books as an anti-forgery device—the hair smelled when burned. He invented edible papers for secret agents, special paper for prisoners of war that retained invisible writing, and a radar-deflecting foil. After the war he was involved in extending the use of recycled paper, one of the few plentiful raw materials at the time.

Grant became interested in forensic science after analysing a piece of cloth excavated from Tutankhamen's tomb. This led to a succession of famous cases. Safecracker Alfie Hinds, who was convicted on forensic evidence provided by Grant, seems to have borne him no ill will. Hinds telephoned Grant to discuss the details of his case whenever he escaped from prison. In 1983, diaries supposedly written by Adolf Hitler surfaced and after fooling many experts were placed in Grant's hands. It took him only a few minutes to demonstrate that the paper used fluoresced under ultraviolet light because it contained 'optical whiteners'. These chemicals came into use only after the war and so the diaries were fakes.

Harris Milton 1906–1991. US research chemist who held several patents in the textile field. One of his discoveries helped preserve the sperm whale: in 1975 he led studies that showed that oil extracted from the little-known North American shrub, the jojoba, could be used as a substitute for sperm-whale oil.

Educated at Oregon State University and Yale, Harris was a brilliant student. He gained his doctorate in chemistry at the age of 23 and founded his own research laboratory in Washington, DC. He joined the Gillette Corporation in 1956 as director of research and as a vice-president. After retiring from Gillette at the age of 60, he became a director of the Warner–Lambert Pharmaceutical company and chair of Sealectro Corporation. He served on many academic, scientific, and government boards and committees. He published over 200 research papers, and the American Institute of Chemists gave Harris its highest honour, the Harold DeWitt Smith Gold Medal, in 1966.

During World War II, Allied soldiers marched in greater comfort thanks to one of his discoveries—a process to decrease the shrinkage and prolong the life of woollen socks. By the end of the war, over 100 million pairs of army socks had been treated by the Harris method.

Hart Judith (Constance Mary), Lady Hart 1924–1991. British Labour politician, a member of Parliament 1959–79. She held several government posts, serving three terms as minister of overseas development.

Hart graduated from the London School of Economics with first-class honours. A lifetime Labour Party member, she entered the House of Commons, representing the Scottish constituency of Lanark, in 1959, and joined Harold Wilson's government in 1964. She reached cabinet rank, as paymaster-general, in 1968. A popular and influential left-winger, with a strong concern for the needs of Third World countries, she was minister of overseas development 1969–70, 1974–75, and 1977–79. She was made a Dame of the British Empire 1979 and a life peer 1988.

Havers Robert Michael Oldfield, Baron Havers 1923–1992. British lawyer and Conservative politician who was solicitor-general under Edward Heath and attorney-general under Margaret Thatcher. In the latter capacity he took part in the government's attempts to ban publication of Peter Wright's book *Spycatcher*. He became a life peer in 1987 and served briefly, and unhappily, as Lord Chancellor before retiring in 1988.

While at the bar, Havers defended Mick Jagger and Brian Jones of the Rolling Stones on drugs charges. After a successful legal career he became Conservative member of Parliament for Wimbledon in 1970. As attorney-general he took part in several Official Secrets Act trials and in the prosecution of Peter Sutcliffe, the Yorkshire Ripper. He declined the opportunity of pursuing firms accused of breaking sanctions against Rhodesia. His most notorious involvement was in the *Spycatcher* affair. The attempt to suppress these memoirs of a retired British intelligence officer, alleging serious misconduct in MI5, cost the UK taxpayer more than £1 million, and it could be argued that Havers helped to make the book into a worldwide bestseller. He retired from the Lord Chancellorship because of poor health after only five months, leaving Margaret Thatcher's government in some disarray.

Hayek Friedrich August von 1899–1992. Austrian-born British economist who held academic posts in London, Chicago, and Freiburg, Germany. His theories, opposing those of the economist Maynard Keynes, were often invoked by free-market enthusiasts of the 1980s. Nobel prize 1974.

Hayek was born in Vienna. After a distinguished academic career in Austria, he became Tooke professor of economic science at London University 1931–50. From London he went to Chicago and then to the University of Freiburg 1962–69. He was a prolific author, his earlier works being concerned mostly with the problems of industrial fluctuations. Subsequent books, such as *The Road to Serfdom* 1944, were strongly anti-Keynesian and provided a theoretical, if often abused, justification for what later became categorized as Thatcherism or Reaganomics. Serious students of Hayek's work would, however, dismiss this as much too simplistic; indeed, it is possible to quote him in direct opposition to these policies. In his later years his interest broadened into psychology and the history of ideas. His 1974 Nobel Prize for Economic Science was shared with the Swedish economist Gunnar Myrdal.

Heidelberger Michael 1888–1991. US chemist whose long life encompassed the scientific field he created: immunochemistry. In effect, by showing that immunity resided in a particular kind of protein, he demystified the phenomenon of immunity.

He started his research career as organic chemist at the Rockefeller Institute for Medical Research, New York (1912–27), and his major discoveries in immunology were achieved at Columbia University (1928–56). Here he perfected the first quantitative measurement of an antibody. He gained his PhD from Columbia University and did a post-doctoral year in Zurich, before returning to the city

Benny Hill

of New York which he loved. Many important results followed, and during his long 'working' retirement (he was working in his New York University office the week before he died) the detailed structure and the molecular genetics of antibodies were virtually completely worked out. Michael Heidelberger was a great teacher as well as an important scientist. His passion for music ensured that he rarely attended a scientific meeting without his clarinet.

Hill Benny 1924–1992. English comedian whose television shows combined the bawdy humour of the seaside postcard with the manic slapstick of the silent cinema, a format which in 30 years he perfected but never really changed.

Born to working-class parents in Southampton, UK, his real name was Alfred. After various jobs, including working at Woolworths and as a milkman (the inspiration for his 1971 hit song 'Ernie'), he joined the army in 1942. While still serving, he appeared as a Forces entertainer in *Stars in Battle Dress*. His first professional break came in 1948 when he became the straight man to cockney comedian Reg Varney. Over 200 radio broadcasts followed, but it was in television that he really made his mark, his first series appearing as early as 1952.

He wrote all his own scripts as well as the music to his shows but his greatest skill was in exploiting the versatile technology of television. A 1961 parody of the TV pop show *Juke Box Jury* employed a split screen and had Hill playing all the characters himself. In the early, stricter days of television his shows sometimes got into trouble for being too risqué. By the time Thames Television dropped him in 1988, his world of lusty old men and scantily dressed young women was regarded as irredeemably sexist, despite its universal popularity and the fact that many critics regarded him as the last of the great visual comics. He lived for his work and his private life was solitary and reclusive.

Honda Soichirō 1906–1991. Japanese industrialist, who founded in 1946 the firm that has become the world's largest maker of motorcycles and car engines, and Japan's third largest maker of cars. Honda products are known for their innovative nature and high quality.

At the age of 15, Honda was apprenticed to a Tokyo car-repair workshop. All his spare time was spent making racing cars. In one of these, he set a Japanese speed record which stood until 1945. His business career began in the late 1930s when he set up a factory making piston rings. At first, lacking technical knowledge or education, he was unable to turn out an acceptable product. However, a combination of hard work and a willingness to take the advice of experts triumphed. In 1945 his company was bought by Toyota. The next year, after the end of the war, Honda began making motorcycles, adapting a supply of war-surplus two-stroke engines made for electricity generators. His first factory was a shack on a bomb site. Within 20 years, Honda dominated the motorcycle world, collecting 137 Grand Prix wins and 16 world championships by 1966.

These achievements were based on a remarkable series of technical developments, particularly an efficient high-revving multivalve

Grace Hopper

engine. Over the years, Honda introduced other developments that made the motorcycle socially acceptable: electric starters, efficient silencers, lead-free fuelling, and better handling characteristics.

In 1962, Honda produced its first four-wheeled vehicles, a truck and a sports car. In 1966, a Honda engine powered the Brabham car which won almost every Formula Two race it entered. Since the mid-1980s, Honda engines have dominated Formula One racing. On the roads, too, technical developments have kept Honda ahead of the field. The Honda Civic was the first car to use a lean-burn engine that met the stringent US emissions standards. Other Honda refinements included acoustic manifolds, antilock braking, variable valve timing, and four-wheel steering. These developments were made possible by Soichirō Honda's attitude to research, which he funded lavishly, and to the freedom he allowed his employees to do their own thing in their own way. He said: 'If you hire only those people you understand, the company will never get people better then you are', and 'Always remember that you often find outstanding people among those whom you don't particularly like.' Good people, well financed and given responsibility when they were ready—this was the Honda formula for success.

Hopper Grace 1906–1992. US computer pioneer whose most significant contributions were in the field of software. She created the first compiler and helped invent the computer language COBOL. She was also the first person to isolate a computer 'bug' and successfully debug a computer.

After doing postgraduate work at Yale, Hopper returned to her original university, Vassar, as a member of the mathematics faculty. She volunteered for duty in World War II with the Naval Ordinance Computation Project. This was the beginning of a long association with the Navy, resulting in her being appointed to the rank of rear admiral in 1983. She was then the oldest officer on active duty in the US armed forces. In 1945 Hopper was ordered to Harvard University to assist Howard Aiken in building a computer. In those days, computers had to be rewired for each new task and Hopper frequently found herself entwined in the wiring of the computer. One day a breakdown of the machine was found to be due to a moth that had flown into the computer. Aiken came into the laboratory as Hopper was dealing with the insect. 'Why aren't you making numbers, Hopper?' he asked. Hopper replied: 'I am debugging the machine!' This first computer 'bug' was removed with tweezers and is preserved at the Naval Museum in Virginia in the laboratory logbook, glued beside the entry for 15.45 on 9 Sept 1945.

After the war, Hopper joined John Mauchly and Presper Eckert who had set up a firm (eventually to become the Univac division of Sperry-Rand) to manufacture a commercial

Frankie Howerd

computer. Her main contribution was to create the first computer language, together with the compiler needed to translate the instructions into a form that the computer could work with. In 1959 she was invited to join a Pentagon team attempting to create and standardize a single computer language for commercial use. This led to the development of the COBOL language, still one of the most widely used languages.

Howerd Frankie (né Francis Alex Howard) 1922–1992. English comedian and actor best known for his role as the Roman slave Lurcio in the TV series *Up Pompeii*. The trademark of his rambling monologues was the smuttily suggestive innuendo followed by aggrieved disapproval when audiences laughed. 'No . . . please! Really . . . Don't laugh' etc. Such pleas, accompanied by outraged grimaces, became like catchphrases and would inevitably reduce the audience to still further laughter.

Frankie Howerd was born in York but moved at an early age to Eltham in Kent. His desire to enter the world of showbusiness came after a childhood visit to the pantomime, but he failed to get into RADA and it was during the war, while a soldier in the Royal Artillery, that he first performed professionally as a forces entertainer. From there he went into radio, becoming a star of the BBC *Variety Bandbox* series. He was a big man whose heavy-jowled and expressive face gave him an air of wounded vulnerability. Throughout the 1950s he appeared as a stand-up comedian, in revue, films, pantomime and occasionally in the 'straight' theatre, most notably as Bottom at the Old Vic in 1957. A lull in his career in the early 1960s almost led him to give up but

in 1963 he performed in the musical *A Funny Thing Happened on the Way to the Forum*, the inspiration behind his later TV series *Up Pompeii*. He was never an ensemble actor and his appearances in several *Carry On* films were disappointing. He was at his best manipulating a live audience through a finely tuned combination of lewdness and mock indignation.

Husak Dr Gustav 1913–1991. Czech politician, leader of the Communist Party of Czechoslovakia (CPC) 1969–87 and president 1975–89. He came to power after the August 1968 Soviet invasion of Czechoslovakia, which crushed the 'Prague Spring' liberalization movement led by the reform communist Alexander Dubcek. Having presided over widespread 'normalization' political purges, he remained a reviled figure throughout his later life. He was unable to adjust to the changed realities of the post-1985 Gorbachev era. He spent his last years as a recluse, afflicted with cancer and virtually blind. On his death he received the last rites from the Roman Catholic Archbishop of Trnava.

Born in Bratislava in Slovakia, he trained as a lawyer and became a communist in 1933. During World War II, with Slovakia under Nazi rule, he became prominent within the resistance movement. He joined the group which was sent to Moscow to negotiate terms to bring Czechoslovakia within the Soviet orbit. After the war he worked for the Slovak Communist Party, but was imprisoned in 1951 on charges of 'bourgeois nationalism'. Rehabilitated in 1960, he became a vice-premier in the reformist government of Olrich Cernik in April 1968. In 1969, after the Red Army crushed the 'Prague Spring' reform movement, he was appointed party leader and directed the purge of hundreds of thousands of Czechs from their party and state posts. Loyal to the 'Moscow line' throughout the Brezhnev era, Husak found himself increasingly at odds with the programme of economic and political reform encouraged from 1985 by Mikhail Gorbachev. After his wife died in 1977, he became more withdrawn; during the later 1980s his health deteriorated greatly. In December 1987 he was removed as CPC leader. After the 'Velvet Revolution' peaceful popular uprising of 1989 overthrew communism, the former dissident Vaclav Havel replaced him as state president. In February 1990 Husak was again expelled from the CPC, this time for having taken 'erroneous political decisions' while in office.

Imai Tadashi 1912–1991. Japanese film director whose films are strongly humanist. Although highly regarded by Japanese critics, Imai has been little known in the West: of the 40 films he directed, only one (*Mon and Ino* 1976) received distribution in the UK.

Imai, the son of a priest, began his career as a screenwriter in 1934, and directed his first film in 1939. His wartime output amounted to little more than militaristic propaganda, but in the postwar period he became a communist, and several of his films were in a vein of social criticism. They included *Dokkoi ikiteru/And Yet We Live* 1951, about a family on the breadline, and the powerful melodrama *Mahiru no ankoku/Darkness at Noon* 1956, set in the Tokyo underworld.

Unlike many of his contemporaries, Imai showed a marked preference for contemporary subjects and only occasionally ventured into historical drama, though the complex period movie *Yoru no tsuzumi/Night Drum* 1959 is regarded as one of his major achievements. He had been inactive in recent years but returned to directing shortly before his death with *Senso to seishun/War and Youth* 1991, a wartime love story.

Irwin James Benson 1930–1991. US astronaut who landed on the Moon during the *Apollo 15* mission July 1971. In 1972 he started a religious cult. He also led expeditions to Mount Ararat in search of Noah's Ark.

Irwin, a test pilot with the US Air Force, was accepted as an astronaut in 1966, despite having broken both legs in a plane crash five years earlier. Irwin became the lunar module pilot on the *Apollo 15* mission, when he and mission commander David Scott landed on the Moon near a lunar valley called Hadley Rille. Theirs was the first Apollo mission to carry an electrically powered Moon car, in which they drove across the lunar surface collecting rock samples during their three-day stay.

A year after his Moon flight Irwin left the space agency NASA and set up a religious organization, the High Flight Foundation. He travelled the world to lecture on his flight and his religious beliefs, which his trip to the Moon had strengthened. In 1973 he published his autobiography, *To Rule the Night*.

Jaffa Max 1911–1991. English violinist and light-orchestra leader whose immaculate direction of popular classics made him a favourite broadcaster and entertainer.

Jaffa, born in London, began playing for silent movies at 13 and was directing orchestras at major London hotels while still in his mid-teens. After graduating from the Guildhall School of Music he led the Scottish Orchestra for a year, on the recommendation of Sir Landon Ronald, but found light music more congenial and returned to London to take up a freelance career.

He found national fame as a radio personality after the war, leading the Palm Court Orchestra in the programme *Grand Hotel*, and his popularity was secured as leader of the evergreen Max Jaffa Trio. Asked why he played a dated repertoire, he replied that it was because his repertoire was dated that people wanted to hear it. His concert appearances, including annual seasons in Scarborough from 1960 to his retirement in 1987, were marked by a combination of old-world decorum and Viennese suavity.

Kinski Klaus. Adopted name of Claus Gunther Nicklaus Nakszynski 1926–1991. German actor who made a series of films with the director Werner Herzog, including *Nosferatu*

1978 and *Fitzcarraldo* 1981. Kinski possessed a disconcerting, almost ratlike appearance, which combined with a rare capacity for portraying characters variously obsessive or driven.

Kinski grew up in great poverty in Berlin, and was taken prisoner by the British after being drafted into the German army. In postwar years he built a reputation in cabaret and poetry reading, and made his film debut in 1948. But until his association with Herzog he mainly performed in mediocre movies, rejecting more artistic offers on the grounds that they did not pay enough to finance his sybaritic lifestyle. He was a driven and difficult personality, who on at least one occasion threatened to kill Herzog during a professional disagreement.

He was three times married; the daughter of his second marriage is the successful actress Nastassja Kinski.

Krenek Ernst 1900–1991. Austrian-born US composer and teacher. Although he never quite regained the early success of his 1927 jazz opera *Jonny spielt auf*, Krenek was widely respected by fellow professionals as an artisan and intellectual able to reconcile the assurance of European tradition with the radicalism of a burgeoning younger generation of US avant-garde composers.

Born in Vienna, Krenek studied with Franz Schreker in Berlin, displaying a facility for imitation in two symphonies in Mahlerian style (1921 and 1922: he married Mahler's daughter Anna in 1922), the satirical *Zwingberg* 1923 in the Karl Kraus cabaret tradition, and a Neo-Classical *Second Piano Concerto* 1924. Serious flirtations with Schubertian romanticism and Schoenbergian abstraction

Ernst Krenek

followed, but beneath all the time-travelling lay a consistency of moral and cultural values, his eventual exile to the USA being provoked as much by the anti-establishment politics of the opera *Karl V*, for example, as by the more obvious employment of 'degenerate' jazz and atonal idioms.

His US career, less public than those of the composers Hindemith, Schoenberg, or Stravinsky, was marked nonetheless by a continuing commitment to political freedom: the opera *Pallas Athene weint* 1952 was a typically oblique condemnation of McCarthyism. Always fascinated by new ideas, Krenek rose to the challenge of permutational serialism in *Lamentatio Jeremae Prophetae* 1941–42, of chance procedures in *Sestina* 1957, and of electronic music in the cantata *Spiritus Intelligentiae Sanctus* 1956. His published books include a scholarly study of Johannes Ockeghem 1953, and the collection of essays *Exploring Music* 1966.

Kruchina Nikolai Yefimovich 1928–1991. Soviet politician. He was an orthodox *apparatchik*, specializing in party organization and funding, and adviser to Mikhail Gorbachev. He committed suicide on 26 August 1991, jumping out of his seventh floor apartment, after the collapse of the attempted anti-Gorbachev coup.

Kruchina became a member of the Communist Party in 1949. After graduating from the Azov-Black Sea Agricultural Institute in Zernograd in 1952, he spent a decade in communist youth-league work. An efficient and pragmatic administrator, he climbed the party ladder, working initially in Kazakhstan before becoming a member of the CPSU's central committee in 1976. He worked under the fast-rising Mikhail Gorbachev in the agricultural department 1978–83. When Gorbachev became party leader in 1985, Kruchina became a member of his inner circle of trusted advisers. He was a supporter of early *glasnost* and *perestroika*. However, he balked at the more radical reforms envisaged by Gorbachev from 1989 and thus sympathized with the attempted coup in August 1991. His involvement in the coup was unclear. However, as general manager of the Soviet Communist Party and its finances, he faced the prospect of arrest and trial on charges of corruption and fraud. Since 1985, up to $15 billion of money and valuables had been channelled out of the USSR into secret party bank accounts established overseas. Kruchina's predecessor as party finance chief, Georgy Pavlov, also committed suicide after the failed coup.

Lorentz Pare 1905–1992. US documentary filmmaker. Appointed in the early 1930s as film adviser to President F D Roosevelt's New Deal administration, Lorentz went on to make two films that are landmarks in the US documentary movement. *The Plow That Broke the Plains* 1936, with music by Virgil Thomson, dealt forcefully and lyrically with efforts to improve the lot of farmers in the Oklahoma dust bowl. *The River* 1937 offered a poetic impression of the Mississippi Basin and a celebration of the work of the Tennessee Valley Authority. Both were early pleas of the conservationist cause.

A third, lesser film, *Flight for Life* 1940, was concerned with the hazards of childbirth among the poor. During World War II, Lorentz made instructional films for the Office of War Information and other agencies, but in postwar years he was unable to resume his documentary career and worked as a film consultant in various capacities.

MacMurray Fred 1908–1991. US screen actor. His most famous film role, as the duplicitous insurance man caught up in murder in *Double Indemnity* 1944, ran counter to his more usual screen image as debonair bachelor or good-natured family man.

Having started out as a band musician and vocalist, MacMurray graduated to the Broadway production of *Roberta* and was signed to a Paramount contract in 1934.

He appeared in a long line of films, mainly light comedies of no great distinction, but he had a knack of underplaying and seemed to possess a natural ease. In the 1950s his career faltered, and he was consigned to secondary roles. But his fortunes revived in the TV series *My Three Sons* 1960–71 and in several films produced by Walt Disney, such as *The Absent-Minded Professor* 1961. His last film role was in *The Swarm* 1978.

Marton Andrew. Adopted name of Endre Marton 1904–1991. Hungarian-born US film director. His reputation rests on his work as a second unit director, in which capacity he was responsible for the action sequences in such blockbusters as *Cleopatra* 1963, *Fall of the Roman Empire* 1944, and, most memorably, the chariot race in *Ben-Hur* 1959.

Marton began his career as a film editor in Vienna, and later commuted between Germany and Hollywood as a director, but left Germany with the rise of Nazism and worked in Switzerland and England before settling in the USA in 1940. He worked on a wide variety of films, and later on several TV series. The films for which Marton took directorial credit were mainly routine programmers, though not surprisingly, in the light of his skill at marshalling large crowds, most were action pictures, often involving location shooting. Among the more successful were the war movie *Men of the Fighting Lady* 1954 and the science-fiction adventure *Crack in the World* 1965.

Maxwell (Ian) Robert 1923–1991. Czechoslovakian-born British publishing tycoon, Labour member of Parliament 1964–70. He built a book- and newspaper-publishing empire in the 1980s which disintegrated on his death with the discovery that his employees' pension funds had been used against financial deficits.

Self-educated, and having fled from his native country as a youth to escape the Nazi persecution of the Jews, Maxwell distinguished himself in the British army, winning the Military Cross, before turning to civilian life and a flamboyant career in publishing. He bought Pergamon Press, which specialized in scientific journals and was one of the first publishing houses to use computers, and, after widening its range, extended his business interests into filmmaking and newspaper production. In 1980 he rescued the British Printing Corporation from financial collapse and transformed it into the successful British Printing and Communications Corporation. Four years later he purchased Mirror Group Newspapers from Reed International for £113 million. A keen supporter of the Labour Party, he used his newspapers to expound the party view—a relatively small voice in the midst of the Conservative-dominated tabloid press.

Maxwell's business ambitions seemed boundless as he acquired more and more companies and more newspapers, but the news of his death, in suspicious circumstances from his yacht off the Canary Islands, in Nov 1991, sent shock tremors through his vast empire. His companies were quickly revealed to be less sound than had once been thought, with £95 million missing from the pension fund, and it was left to his family to pick up the pieces. In June 1992, his sons Kevin and Ian were arrested on charges of large-scale fraud and theft.

Mercury Freddie. Stage name of Frederick Bulsara 1946–1991. British pop singer, lead vocalist from 1971 with the group Queen, one of the world's top-selling bands. His operatic singing style and camp theatrical performances suited the stadium-sized venues that Queen were able to fill after their 1975 hit 'Bohemian Rhapsody', for which they are also credited with the first successful pop video.

Born in Zanzibar and brought up in India, Mercury lived in the UK from 1959. In addition to his career with Queen, he made a number

Freddie Mercury

of solo recordings between 1973 and 1988, and had a hit in 1981 with an old song, 'The Great Pretender'. His flamboyance and self-mocking bombast were the key to Queen's popularity and two of their albums, *A Night at the Opera* 1975 and *A Day at the Races* 1977, were named after Marx Brothers films. Their first US number-one hits came in 1980 with the rockabilly pastiche 'Crazy Little Thing Called Love' and the album *The Game*. Queen were criticized for playing to segregated audiences in South Africa in 1984, but their performance at the Live Aid benefit concert the following year was seen to make up for it. 'You listen to it, like it, discard it, then on to the next. Disposable pop,' Mercury said of his work, but his death sent 'Bohemian Rhapsody' once more into the charts.

Messiaen Olivier 1908–1992. French composer, organist, and teacher. His music tapped a French vein of visionary ecstasy, combining grandly colourful harmonies with a clockwork ingenuity of form, decorated with birdsong freely transcribed from nature. The greatest French composer since Debussy, he taught three generations of international composers at the Paris Conservatoire, and as organist at the Sainte-Trinité he revitalized a moribund organ-playing tradition, inventing new techniques and exploiting existing sonorities with a bravura anticipating electronic music.

Born in Avignon, Messiaen won a scholarship to Paris, studying organ at the Conservatoire with Marcel Dupré and composition with Paul Dukas. His earliest published works, *Le Banquet Céleste* for organ 1928 and the *Préludes* for piano 1929 marked him out as a keyboard virtuoso of unabashed high Catholic inspiration. In 1936, reacting against the dead hand of Neo-Classicism, he formed the group *La Jeune France* with the composers Jolivet, Baudrier, and Lesur. During World War II, as a prisoner in Silesia, he composed the extraordinary *Quatour pour la fin du temps* for violin, clarinet, cello, and himself on piano, drawing on a number of earlier pieces. Restored to his teaching post, he published the influential study *Technique de mon language musical* 1943, and in later years was prevailed upon by a succession of brilliant students, including the young Boulez, Stockhausen, and Xenakis, to add serialism and concrete music to a compositional repertoire already furnished with highly individual tonal and rhythmic procedures. His monumental *Turangalîla-symphonie* 1947 brought international recognition and widespread imitation by Hollywood composers, not least on account of the leading role played by the eerie Ondes Martenot, an early synthesizer.

Miles Bernard (James), Lord Miles of Blackfriars 1907–1991. English theatre manager, actor, and director, who founded the Mermaid Theatre in Puddle Dock, Blackfriars, London, 1959. During a long career in the theatre, in which he worked as a designer and setmaker, stage manager, and director, Miles appeared in music hall and films as well as in classical roles on the stage, such as Iago in *Othello* and Face in *The Alchemist*. He built his first theatre in his garden in St John's Wood, London, where such performers as the singer Kirsten Flagstad appeared. The Mermaid, a testament to the strength and warmth of his character, was created by Miles and his wife Josephine out of a warehouse on the river Thames.

Among his friends he numbered the stage designer Edward Gordon Craig and Sean O'Casey, the latter of whom visited the Mermaid when it presented a festival of his plays in 1962. The Mermaid had success with Miles's adaptations of Henry Fielding's *Rape upon Rape* into a musical called *Lock up Your Daughters*, and of R L Stevenson's *Treasure Island* with Miles himself as Long John Silver (with parrot); he also played the title role in Bertolt Brecht's *Galileo*. Apart from his adaptations for the stage, he published three books, including *Favourite Tales from Shakespeare* for children.

Mitchell Peter 1920–1992. English chemist whose discoveries in cell biology revolutionized the science of bioenergetics—the study of energy in the living cell. He showed that the transfer of energy during life processes is not random but directed. Nobel Prize for Chemistry 1978.

Earlier ideas in bioenergetics supposed that the energy absorbed by animals from food and by plants from sunlight was utilized in cells by purely chemical means. The cell was seen as a bag of enzymes in which random and directionless processes took place. Mitchell proved that, as one admirer put it, 'there was a direction to the flame of life'. Currents of protons pass through cell walls, which, instead of being simple partitions between cells, are, in fact, full of directional pathways. This discovery demonstrated the existence of a reverse kind of electricity (Mitchell called it 'proticity'), which he successfully used to run an engine.

Mitchell's findings are now compared in importance with the theory of relativity, but for 20 years the scientific community rejected and ridiculed his ideas. Most of his work was done in a private laboratory, the Glynn Research Institute, an 18th-century mansion which he restored from ruin with his own hands.

His research was funded by money inherited from his family's construction firm, Wimpey. Recognition finally came in the form of the Nobel prize 1978, and in 1981 the Royal Society, which for years had refused him admission, awarded him its highest honour, the Copley Medal. Scientists are still struggling to understand the implications of Mitchell's work; no doubt important medical advances will eventually be based on his ideas.

Monk Christopher 1921–1991. English musicologist, maker and performer of the cornet and serpent. His entertaining advocacy of musical instruments and sonorities considered obsolete survived public scepticism to assist in the trend towards authentic early music performance practice in which England now plays a leading role.

Monk combined a performer's delight in the handling and distinctive tonal qualities of early instruments with a dry wit and a scholar's conviction that they should be heard in their proper context. His reconstruction and performance in 1964 of the demanding cornet solo in Monteverdi's *Vespers* 1610 was a landmark in early music. The London Serpent Trio, formed in association with Andrew van der Beek and Alan Lumsden, toured widely abroad and attracted tributes from composers on both sides of the Atlantic.

Montand Yves. Adopted name of Yvo Livi 1921–1991. Italian-born French singer and actor, a performer who achieved iconic status in France. He became a film star in *La Salaire de la peur/The Wages of Fear* 1953 and appeared in several US films, including *Let's Make Love* 1960.

Montand grew up in poverty in Marseille, discovering his vocation as a singer by winning a talent contest. As the protegé and lover of Edith Piaf, he achieved fame as a singer in the immediate postwar era, then embarked on a second career as an actor. He returned from Hollywood to France, acting in such films as *L'Aveu* 1970, *Tout va Bien* 1972, and, almost unrecognizably aged, as the patriarch in *Jean de Florette* and *Manon des Sources* 1986.

Montand was married to the actress Simone Signoret from 1951 until her death in 1985. Both were vocal adherents of the political left, but eventually disavowed communism.

Yves Montand

Their marriage was evidently stormy, not least because of Montand's brief affair with Marilyn Monroe, his co-star in *Let's Make Love* 1960. In 1984, a poll commissioned by a French TV company showed that one in five of the French population would have been prepared to vote for Montand as president.

Morley Robert 1908–1992. English actor and writer. His fruity voice and ample girth came to exemplify a certain kind of comic Englishness—pompous and superior but somehow always endearing.

Born in Wiltshire, the son of a major, he was educated at Wellington College and was destined for a diplomatic career. Instead he studied at RADA and after several years in provincial repertory theatre (including running his own company in Cornwall) he had his first London success playing Oscar Wilde at the Gate Theatre in 1936. This was the type of larger-than-life role he was to specialize in throughout his career. The next year saw his Hollywood debut as Louis XVI in *Marie Antoinette*, a role which won him an Oscar nomination. Later films included *Major Barbara* 1940, *Young Mr Pitt* 1942, and two for director John Huston, *The African Queen* 1952, where he played Katherine Hepburn's bumbling father, and *Beat the Devil* 1954. His most successful stage play, which he wrote with Noel Langley, was *Edward My Son* 1947. It contained star roles for himself and Peggy Ashcroft. Despite his success, he was not an actor who took his work very seriously. He was increasingly undiscriminating about the parts he chose and seemed happy to go on playing scene-stealing caricatures and appearing as a lovable English eccentric on TV advertisements. He was the author of several elegantly witty books, anthologized as *The Best of Morley* in 1981.

Motherwell Robert 1915–1991. US painter, one of the leading figures of Abstract Expressionism. His paintings possess a tragic grandeur and are less violent than the more gestural work of his contemporaries Pollock and de Kooning. Strong, elemental black and white forms predominate, most famously in the series of paintings entitled *Elegy to the Spanish Republic*.

Motherwell was one of the most highly educated and intellectual of US painters. He began studying art at the age of 11 but changed to philosophy on entering Stanford University. It was his professor at Columbia, the art historian Meyer Schapiro, who encouraged him to resume painting and introduced him to other artists. New York was then a haven for émigré avant-garde artists and Motherwell's interest in psychoanalysis drew him to the Surrealists.

In 1941 a trip to Mexico with the Chilean Surrealist Matta introduced him to 'automatic' drawing and helped to loosen his style, which gradually became more spontaneous and calligraphic. The collector Peggy Guggenheim encouraged him to work in collage and in 1944 gave him a one-person show at her Art of This Century Gallery. Motherwell

was one of the founders of a short-lived art school, named the Subject of the Artist, which became a meeting place for the avant-garde and helped to consolidate the position of New York as the international centre of modern art. He wrote regularly about art and edited a series of classic texts, *The Documents of Modern Art*. In 1965 he was given a retrospective exhibition at the New York Museum of Modern Art, which subsequently travelled to five European cities.

North Alex 1910–1991. US composer best known for his haunting, jazz-inspired scores for 55 Hollywood films, including *A Streetcar Named Desire* 1950, *Death of a Salesman* 1950, *Cleopatra* 1962, *Who's Afraid of Virginia Woolf* 1966, and *Good Morning, Vietnam* 1986. His sophisticated, often lightweight scores cultivated a mood of detachment that suited the new wide-screen cinema, in sharp contrast to the fulsome Hollywood operatic style established by European émigrés Erich Korngold, Franz Waxman, and others.

Born in Philadelphia of Russian parents, North trained at the Curtis Institute and Juilliard School of Music before winning a scholarship to Moscow Conservatory in 1934. Lured back to New York by the music of Duke Ellington, he wrote dance music for Martha Graham and incidental music for some 80 plays and US government documentary films before being launched on a Hollywood career by the director Elia Kazan, with whom he had worked in theatre, notably on *Death of a Salesman*. His astringent urban idiom influenced a generation of television composers, and he achieved fame of a kind as the composer whose score Kubrick rejected for *2001: A Space Odyssey*.

Nurnberg Walter 1907–1991. German-born photographer who became the pioneering figure in the development of British industrial photography. His belief in the dignity of labour and the advantages of technological progress are reflected in his powerful images of people and machines.

Nurnberg began his career as a financier in Berlin, his birthplace, before contact with the photographer and theorist Werner Graff led him to enrol at the Reimann School of Art, where he studied photography between 1931 and 1933. Both Graff and Albert Renger-Patsch, another important influence, were leading advocates of the 'New Photography' which argued that ordinary, everyday objects were the most valid subject for a modern photographer. In 1943 Nurnberg left Germany for London, where he opened a photography and advertising practice. After World War II, during which he served in the British Army, he concentrated his abilities on recording the rapidly changing face of British manufacturing industry. His aim was to convey the reality of the industrial process in a way which emphasized its benefits and celebrated the endeavour of those involved. The dramatic, sometimes romantic pictures that he produced for such firms as ICI and English Electric were the result of meticulous preparation and the use of both natural and artificial lighting. From 1968 he was the head of photography at the Guildford School of Art (later the West Surrey College of Art and Design), retiring in 1974.

Oliver Stephen Michael Henry 1950–1992. English composer, one of a generation of literary operatic talents whose considerable output and undoubted professional success brought little public acclaim. His role as music provider for the English National Opera, the Royal Shakespeare Company, the BBC, and other media enterprises was well rewarded but largely anonymous; he himself regarded composing as on a par with writing lyrics.

Oliver was born in Liverpool, studied at Oxford under Kenneth Leighton and Robert Sherlaw Johnson, and was briefly a teacher before embarking on a full-time career as a composer, principally of operas, of which he wrote 41, and also of incidental music for stage, television, and film. Much of his music is ephemeral, and most unpublished, but he will be remembered as long as the RSC's production of *Nicholas Nickleby* and the BBC's televised Shakespearean series remain in circulation.

Paine Thomas Otten 1921–1992. US administrator (head) of the National Aeronautics and Space Administration (NASA) 1969–1970, when the first landings on the Moon took place. An engineer with General Electric, he was appointed deputy director of NASA in 1968.

He succeeded to the NASA directorship when his predecessor James Webb resigned. Paine envisaged a space shuttle, a space station, and crewed missions to Mars. But, in the wake of the Apollo successes, public interest in space dwindled and so did NASA's budget. Realizing that his ambitious plans for crewed space exploration were unlikely to be fulfilled, Paine resigned and returned to General Electric, where he became a vice president. After retiring, he was made chair of the National Commission on Space, a government advisory body.

Panufnik Andrzej 1914–1991. Polish-born British composer of enigmatic orchestral works whose musical impact never quite attains their symbolic or emotional promise. A stoical and solitary figure, he pursued a religious and humanist vision in music admired as emblematic of a wider resistance to communist totalitarianism.

Born in Warsaw, Panufnik studied composition at the State Conservatoire 1932–36, and conducting under Felix Weingartner at the State Academy of Music. After World War II, during which his early compositions were destroyed, he rose to high office as conductor of the Kraków and Warsaw Philharmonic Orchestras, and as vice president of the Polish Composers' Union 1948–54. His international debut as a composer in 1947 revealed a talent for impressionistic effects applied to traditional folk material.

Andrzej Panufnik

After his defection to the UK in 1954, Panufnik freelanced as a conductor and was musical director of the City of Birmingham Symphony Orchestra 1957–59 before finally settling in Twickenham, Greater London, becoming a naturalized British citizen in 1961. His music remained Polish at heart, in works such as the *Sinfonia Elegaica* 1957, the *Katyn Epitaph* 1966 for the Polish victims of the wartime massacre, the visionary *Sinfonia di sfere* 1974–75, and the *Sinfonia Votiva* 1981 dedicated to the Black Madonna of Częstochowa. He received a hero's welcome on his return to a free Poland in 1990. His autobiography *Composing Myself* was published in 1987.

Pao Yoe-Kong 1918–1991. Hong Kong entrepreneur who helped catapult Hong Kong to the position of wealth and influence it enjoys today. The owner of a huge corporate empire that included 40 hotels in the USA, real-estate holdings in Hong Kong, and a shipping fleet, Pao was regularly listed in *Fortune* magazine's annual list of the world's wealthiest people.

Born in the coastal city of Ningbo in Zhejiang province, China, Pao fled to Hong Kong shortly after the Communist Party seized power in 1949. The family paper mill was taken over by the communists and Pao, figuring that ships could not be seized as easily as paper mills, built up a shipping empire. He started with the purchase of a second-hand freighter when he was 37, and within 20 years had built the world's biggest shipping fleet. Sensing what the future might hold, Pao sold many of his ships and diversified into property, banking, and transport, in time to avoid the recession that hit the shipping industry in the 1970s. Knighted in 1978, Pao became known in Hong Kong as 'Sir Y K'. He held meetings with politicians and leaders around the world. Significantly, China's supreme leader Deng Xiaoping welcomed him to Beijing. Pao was appointed vice chair of the committee that drew up Hong Kong's post-1997 constitution.

Piper John 1903–1992. English painter, print-maker, and designer. He began his career as an abstract painter but is better known for his later English landscapes and studies of architecture for which he adopted a highly expressive and romantic style.

Piper was born in Epsom in Surrey. As a child he developed a passion for old churches, an interest which was later reflected in his work as a painter and as a contributor to several architectural guides. He trained briefly as a solicitor before studying at Richmond School of Art and at the Royal College. In the 1930s he was attracted by the French avant-garde, especially Picasso and Braque, and produced brightly coloured abstract paintings and constructions. However he gradually turned his attention to the English landscape via a close study of earlier English Romantic painters. During World War II, as an official war artist, he made a series of highly evocative images of bomb-damaged buildings, including the interior of Coventry Cathedral. After the war he continued his architectural surveys as painter, photographer, and writer, producing the Shell Guides to Shropshire (with John Betjemann) and to Oxfordshire.

Piper was an enormously versatile and experimental artist. He designed some of the finest stained glass of the century, including windows for Eton College Chapel (1958) and the new Coventry Cathedral (1962). He was also a notable set designer, and was closely associated with the composer Benjamin Britten, several of whose operas he designed. He was made a Companion of Honour in 1972.

Pirie Gordon 1931–1991. British middle-distance athlete who won the 10,000 metres silver medal at the 1956 Olympics and held world records at six miles, 3,000 metres and 5,000 metres.

Gordon Pirie first experienced the taste of big-time athletics in 1948. At the age of 17 he ran with his father on the relay carrying the Olympic torch to Wembley Stadium. His first victory was in the 1951 AAA six miles championship when he set a new English record. The following year he broke the British record for three miles and ran against his idol Emil Zatopek at the 1952 Olympic Games in Helsinki. Perhaps his greatest performance was a losing one. At the 1956 Melbourne Olympics he matched surges from Russia's Kuts across 21 of the 25 laps before falling back to eighth position utterly drained. He continued to race at international level for several years and competed at the 1960 Olympics. He was also a successful competitor in orienteering events and devoted much of his time to coaching other athletes.

Poiret Jean 1926–1992. French actor and playwright. A veteran actor in more than 40 films, most never seen outside France, Poiret is best known as author of the highly successful stage comedy *La Cage aux Folles*, whose original production he both directed and starred in with his long-time cabaret associate Michel Serrault. The production ran for 2,647 performances in Paris, was staged in translation in other countries, was filmed in 1978, and became the basis of a long-running Broadway musical.

As an actor, Poiret, sleek and latterly rather plump, embodied the half-vanished tradition of French boulevard theatre. To audiences outside France, however, he is probably best known for his role as the cynical detective in two thrillers by Claude Chabrol, *Poulet au Vinaigre* 1985 and *Inspecteur Lavardin* 1986. At the time of his death, he had just completed his first film as a director, *Le Zebre*.

Pugo Boris 1937–1991. Soviet communist politician. He was renowned for his hardline views and commitment to the Soviet communist ideal. He became interior minister in Dec 1990, as President Mikhail Gorbachev, concerned at the mounting anarchy within the USSR, sided temporarily with conservatives within the communist party leadership. Eight months later, the Soviet leader had returned to the path of reform, and Pugo helped organize the August 1991 'counter-perestroika' coup against Gorbachev. Pugo, seeing his life's ideals in ruins and facing imminent arrest, took his own life as the coup collapsed. He died in a Moscow hospital from self-inflicted gunshot wounds: his wife, who had attempted simultaneous suicide, survived.

Pugo was born in 1937 in Kalinin, central Russia. He devoted his career to upholding the ideals of Soviet patriotism. He became Latvia's reviled KGB chief in 1980 and its communist party leader in 1984. In December 1990 he replaced the liberal-minded Vadim Bakatin as Soviet interior minister, to fight government corruption and re-establish discipline. He persuaded President Gorbachev to intervene to restore Moscow's authority in the Baltic republics. In January 1991 Pugo masterminded an assault on the television tower in Vilnius which left 15 civilians dead and several hundred wounded. Five died in a similar clash in Riga. Throughout 1990–1991, Pugo formed part of a counter-revolutionary 'gang of four' which conspired to block economic reforms. As internal order fractured within the USSR, they advocated the imposition of a general state of emergency. They organized the attempted anti-Gorbachev coup to prevent the signing, on 20 August 1991, of a new union treaty which would have transferred power to the republics and would have been followed by the ousting of hardline communist ministers.

Ray Satyajit 1921–1992. India's leading film director and one of the international masters of humanist cinema. Ray completed his first film, *Pather Panchali*, in 1956. His work, most of which was spoken in Bengali, never

Satyajit Ray

achieved widespread popularity, or even extensive distribution, in India. But the acclaim heaped upon it by foreign critics made him an icon of Indian culture.

Pather Panchali was financed independently and was several years in production, but its success at the Cannes festival launched him on a prolific career. Over the next three decades he was to make over 30 more films. His early films were indirectly influenced by Italian Neo-Realism. Later he branched out in many directions, embracing comedy and fantasy as well as films on political themes, such as *Distant Thunder* 1973, and meditative works, like *Days and Nights in the Forest* 1970, which were perhaps most representative of his mature output. He not only wrote the screenplays of his films but also frequently composed the music scores.

Rayne Edward 1922–1992. US-born British shoemaker, chair and president of the British Fashion Council from 1960. He transformed his family's business, H & M Rayne, into an international shoemakers; in 1970 he became the first British shoemaker to open a shop in Paris since 1900. On the British Fashion Council he raised the profile of London Fashion Week to place it on a par with Milan and Paris.

Rayne was educated in England at Harrow public school. He spent the duration of World War II learning to make luxury shoes in his father's factory in London, after being barred from active service owing to poor eyesight. As a young man he became an international bridge player and was a member of the British team that won the European championships in 1948 and 1949. By the time he became chair of H

& M Rayne in 1951, customers included the Queen and the Queen Mother and actresses such as Vivien Leigh, Marlene Dietrich, and Rita Hayworth. Under Rayne, international shoe sales expanded, and he became the first retailer to sell shoes designed by the fashion designers Mary Quant and Jean Muir.

He became chair of the Incorporated Society of London Fashion Designers (the forerunner to the British Fashion Council) in 1960. There he sought greater financial backing for designers in the UK and encouraged US buyers to visit London during their trips to Paris. He was repeatedly decorated for his contribution to the fashion industry and in 1988 he was knighted for his work on behalf of the British Fashion Council.

Rée Harry 1914–1991. English teacher, professor, and campaigner for comprehensive education. He moved from schoolteaching in 1960 to become first professor of education at the University of York, where he set up an innovative teacher-training programme to prepare students to teach children of all abilities.

Rée moved ideologically from being a staunch supporter of the grammar school—he taught languages at Bradford Grammar School before World War II, and later at Watford Grammar School, where he became head in 1951—to becoming a convinced advocate of the new comprehensive schools being established in the 1960s. He ended his formal career by making an unprecedented move (for a professor of education) back to the classroom as a teacher at a north London comprehensive.

Although he later moved to a remote and beloved part of the Yorkshire Dales, Rée never gave up teaching, lecturing, inspiring a host of pressure groups, and attempting to influence policy and his many friends and former pupils in high places. He passionately espoused the cause of community schools. An untidy, much-loved figure, he was still teaching at a local high school when he died.

Rees-Davies William 1916–1992. English barrister, a Queen's Counsel, and Conservative member of Parliament 1953–83. He was a flamboyant, theatrical figure both in court and in the House of Commons.

Rees-Davies won the safe Tory seat of the Isle of Thanet in 1953 and held the same constituency throughout his political career. He represented his party on the Select Committee on Health and Social Services 1980–83. One of the most colourful members of the House of Commons, he attended wearing a black cloak lined with red silk and was known as 'Count Dracula'. He was also nicknamed 'Billy the one-armed bandit', having lost an arm during active service in 1943.

His style of advocacy was said to be the last in the great tradition of the Victorians. One story goes that when he received a note from the dock as his line of questioning was about to put in evidence his client's character, he told the judge: 'It's a billet-doux, my lord.' The judge replied: 'Maybe it's a Billy-don't.'

He was suspended from practice twice, once for unprofessional conduct when he showed witnesses a transcript of evidence after being told not to, and again when he absented himself from a case. On one occasion a judge at the Old Bailey felt so strongly about Rees-Davies's conduct that he discharged the jury on the basis that it would be wrong for him to continue trying it.

Richardson Tony (Cecil Antonio) 1928–1991. British stage and film director. A key figure in the British theatre of the 1950s, Richardson was co-founder with George Devine of the English Stage Company, which brought new realism and contemporaneity to English theatre with its productions at the Royal Court, notably of John Osborne's *Look Back in Anger* 1956 and *The Entertainer* 1957.

Richardson moved into the cinema by founding, with Osborne, Woodfall Films, for which he directed films of both the Osborne plays, in 1959 and 1960 respectively, as well as such films as *A Taste of Honey* 1961, which introduced a new quality of poetic realism to British cinema. The bawdy romp *Tom Jones* 1963 was a huge popular and critical success, and Richardson subsequently worked in the USA as well as the UK, though he never proved really at home in Hollywood filmmaking. Of his later films, the most rewarding was perhaps *The Charge of the Light Brigade* 1968, an iconoclastic and inventive panorama of social and military history. Richardson was married from 1962 to 1967 to the actress Vanessa Redgrave, and the couple's daughters are the actresses Natasha and Joely Richardson.

Rodenberry Gene 1921–1991. US television writer and producer. As creator and producer of the science-fiction series *Star Trek* 1966–68, Rodenberry was responsible for one of the greatest cults to which television has given rise. Rodenberry, the son of an army officer, began to write fiction during service in the Army Air Corps in World War II. He later became an airline pilot, but from 1953 supported himself as a TV writer, contributing to many popular series such as *Naked City* and *Dr Kildare*, and in the early 1960s graduated to being a producer. The *Star Trek* series ran for only three seasons before being cancelled by the NBC network, but in subsequent years it has been endlessly reshown. A further series was made with different personnel, while the original TV performers starred in a run of spin-off feature films, produced by Rodenberry. Addicts of the show, known as 'Trekkies', still gather for conventions in sundry parts of the world.

Ryan Jack 1926–1991. US inventor and designer, creator of the Barbie doll, which first appeared in the USA in 1959. With annual sales of over £260 million, Barbie has had more influence over girls than any other toy during the last 30 years.

Ryan, who was married five times, lastly to Zsa Zsa Gabor, was research and design vice president for the toy company Mattel during the 1960s and 1970s. The creative environment that he introduced during this period enabled the company continually to create award-winning and best-selling toys. Barbie was only one of over 1,000 patents that he held. His creations, which personified glamour, elegance, and cartoon violence, served to influence the attitudes of millions of children that grew up with his toys. Ryan later moved to the US military contractor Raytheon in Los Angeles, where he created the Sparrow and Hawk missiles.

Seuss, Dr. Pen name of Thomas Geisel 1904–1991. US illustrator, creator of a number of children's picture books in the 1950s and early 1960s, starting with *The Cat in the Hat* 1957. It was not until much later that educational research began to show that Dr Seuss's approach to early reading, using phonics and rhymes, is scientifically sound.

Geisel began his career as a humorous illustrator in his native USA and ended it as a household name. His career crossed the boundaries between the media, and he worked for a time in advertising and as a television producer, winning awards for documentary and cartoon production. International fame came following the publication, under the pen name Dr Seuss, of *The Cat in the Hat*, an inimitable combination of phonically sound, irresistibly appealing comic verse and cartoon drawing which has been translated into dozens of languages. Other favourites followed: *Yertle the Turtle* 1958 and *One Fish, Two Fish, Red Fish, Blue Fish* 1960. Dr Seuss was awarded honorary doctorates by universities all over the USA and will remain a firm favourite with children long after his death.

Smith Buster (Henry) 1904–1991. US jazz musician, composer, and arranger, an alto-saxophone player who was a member of Count Basie's first important band in the 1930s and a mentor of the bebop revolutionary Charlie Parker. His music combined blues and western-swing influences.

Smith, born in Texas, played in various travelling bands including (1925–33) the Blue Devils of Oklahoma, leading the band from 1931. The Blue Devils comprised, at various times, Hot Lips Page on trumpet, Lester Young on tenor saxophone, and Count Basie on piano. Smith was reunited with these in Kansas City in a band called the Barons of Rhythm, and is generally albeit unofficially credited with cowriting Basie's theme song 'One o'Clock Jump'. When Basie took the band to New York in 1936, Smith chose to stay behind. He backed Big Joe Turner, the mountainous blues singer, on a couple of 1939 recordings, and hired his young admirer Charlie Parker, who 'used to follow the older cats around because he wanted to learn. He stayed with my band because I had patience with him.' Unfortunately they did not record together. In fact, Smith did not make an album until 1959 (*The Legendary Buster Smith*), the year he gave up the saxophone, though continuing to play guitar, bass guitar, and piano. He can be seen in a film about the Kansas City jazz scene, *The Last of the Blue Devils*.

Stirling James 1926–1992. British architect. His capacity for radical stylistic change made him one of the most original and influential of post-war architects but a controversial and much criticized figure in his own country.

Stirling was born in Glasgow and brought up in Liverpool, where his father was a marine engineer. After serving in World War II, he began studying architecture at Liverpool University. In 1953, while working in London, he met James Gowan, with whom he set up practice three years later. Their first important work, influenced by Le Corbusier, was a group of flats on Ham Common (1955–58) in which the uncompromising raw use of brick and concrete was then thought to be particularly severe. The Leicester University Engineering Building (1959–63) was even more daring in its combination of brick and glass with a dramatically cantilevered structure. The furore which occurred when the wedge-shaped, all-glass Cambridge University History Building (1964–67) started to leak almost led to its demolition.

The bold shapes and bright colours of Runcorn New Town (1967–76) marked a new phase, but commissions were becoming less frequent and, during the 1970s, almost dried up. The Neue Staatsgalerie, Stuttgart (1980–84) is regarded as his masterpiece, its exuberant eclecticism—mixing classical references with polychrome marble surfaces and high-tech details—has led to it being labelled Post-Modern. In fact, Stirling was always more interested in enclosing spaces than in decorating exteriors. He was awarded a knighthood just 12 days before his death.

Takano Shizuo 1923–1992. Japanese business executive, vice president of the JVC electronics company from 1986, who supervised the development of the VHS home video system used in thousands of homes across the world.

Takano was put in charge of JVC's Video Product Division in 1970 and work started on the development of a video system for the home market. The project was almost killed off before the first prototype was made, but Takano allowed the development team to work in secret until a working prototype was built. Matsushita's chair, Konosuke Matsushita, was shown the first VHS prototype and decided to back it in preference to his company's VX system. JVC declined Sony's request to back their Betamax system, having obtained the backing of Matsushita, Hitachi, Sharp, and Mitsubishi. The first VHS videocassette recorder was launched in 1976. To boost sales, Takano set out on a world tour of all the major electronics companies. He was always willing to show prototypes and to discuss future VHS developments. He was also willing to sell badged equipment to companies that did

Gene Tierney

not want to develop their own expensive production equipment. These marketing methods are now studied in business schools around the world. They helped establish the VHS system as the de facto standard. Takano worked for JVC for a total of 36 years.

Tierney Gene 1920–1992. US film actress. She appeared in a wide range of roles, often in costume dramas, but achieved greatest success as the enigmatic heroine of the mystery thriller *Laura* 1944. Her last screen appearance was in *The Pleasure Seekers* 1964.

Tierney, the daughter of a prosperous New York family, had a dark, natural beauty, which brought her rapid success in Hollywood, where she was under contract to 20th Century Fox during the 1940s and early 1950s. Not an actress of wide range, she evinced physical qualities of delicacy and poise which could encompass irony (as in the comedy *The Ghost and Mrs Muir* 1947) as well as vulnerability (best exemplified as the wealthy kleptomaniac of *Whirlpool* 1949). An ill-fated romance with Prince Aly Khan led to a nervous breakdown and she lived her later years in seclusion. Her autobiography *Self Portrait* 1979 referred to a wartime liaison with John F Kennedy.

Tinguely Jean 1925–1991. Swiss sculptor whose fantastic, automated constructions of junk materials were frequently self-destructing. He was unusual, even among modern artists, in that he actively welcomed spectator involvement in his work.

Tinguely was born in Fribourg but moved with his family to Basel, where he studied at the School of Art and Crafts 1941–45. He was attracted to the most playful Dada and Surrealist artists, like Kurt Schwitters, Marcel Duchamp, and Joan Miró, particularly by their use of found objects and unorthodox materials. From 1952 he was based in Paris, where he made reliefs of moving metal rods before developing his 'meta-mechanical' reliefs which included a machine, exhibited at the First Paris Biennale, that produced 40,000 abstract paintings. In 1960 he assembled a vast, chaotic structure, *Hommage à New York*, in the garden of New York's Museum of Modern Art. It was prevented from knocking itself to pieces, as intended, by the intervention of the city's fire department, who were concerned about its safety. This was the first of a series of spectacular constructions set up in cities around the world, many of them conceived and built by Tinguely in collaboration with his partner, the sculptor Niki de Saint-Phalle. One of their most successful and popular large-scale inventions was an elaborate aquatic sculpture built outside the Pompidou Centre, Paris, 1983, entitled, simply, *Fountain*.

Tyner Rob. Stage name of Robert Derminer 1944–1991. US rock singer and songwriter, lead vocalist with the MC5 1965–72. The MC5 were a hard-rock band associated with a revolutionary group who called themselves the White Panthers. Their advocacy of sex and drugs and their loud, distorted sound quickly made them notorious and subsequently influenced punk and other aggressive styles of music.

Tyner was born in Detroit, Michigan, the 'Motor City' that gave the group its name. Their first album, *Kick Out the Jams* 1969, was recorded live there, and the MC5 were always best in live performance, where their furious energy and free-form experimentation made them exciting. *Back in the USA* 1970 and *High Time* 1971 were hard-driving but more conventional rock albums. With hindsight, Tyner claimed in 1991: 'We were Punk, before Punk. We were New Wave, before New Wave. We were Metal, before Metal. We were even MC before Hammer.' The presumed politically motivated arrest of their manager, White Panther activist John Sinclair, on drug charges, contributed to their decline. After the MC5 folded, Tyner worked as a producer, manager, and concert promoter. His only solo album was *Bloodbrothers* 1990.

Vieira da Silva Maria Helena 1908–1992. Portuguese painter who spent most of her working life in Paris. Though essentially nonfigurative, her subtly coloured and spatially complex works often suggest traces of landscape or architectural forms.

Vieira da Silva was born in Lisbon and studied art there between 1922 and 1927. From 1929 she continued her studies in Paris, initially with the sculptor Émile-Antoine Bourdelle, later with the painters Othon Friesz and Fernand Léger. Her marriage to the Hungarian Arpad Szenes, a painter of subdued but lyrical abstracts, helped her to perfect the style that gained her critical attention in the mid-1930s. Her dynamic compositions seem to subvert orthodox perspective in a dizzying criss-cross of linear and rectangular forms. The rhythmic interaction of shapes suggests the influence of music, her greatest enthusiasm after painting.

Throughout the 1930s she used her skill as a pattern-maker for the design of fabrics and in 1954 won the first prize in a tapestry competition for the University of Basel. World War II was spent in Brazil—her husband was partly Jewish—but the couple returned to Paris in 1947 and she later became a French citizen. In 1979 she was made a Chevalier of the French Legion d'Honneur and in 1988 a major retrospective of her work was mounted, first in Lisbon and then in Paris.

Walcha Helmut 1907–1991. German organist and harpsichordist, a leading teacher and exponent of Baroque keyboard music, in particular of J S Bach, from 1924 to his retirement in 1981.

Walcha, born in Leipzig, overcame blindness to become widely celebrated as a concert and recording artist. Reacting against the Romantic style of fashion, he pioneered a reserved, factual interpretation in keeping with a Modernist aesthetic, and sympathetic to the structural intricacies of Classical counterpoint. He was an important influence on Neo-Classical organ design both in Germany and in the UK.

Webb James Edwin 1906–1992. US civil servant and lawyer, administrator (head) of the National Aeronautics and Space Administration (NASA) 1961–68, during which time he guided the crewed Moon-landing programme.

Webb was director of the US Bureau of the Budget 1946–49 and undersecretary of state 1949–52 before becoming NASA's second administrator at a time when the USA was lagging behind the USSR in the space race. With the support of President Kennedy, Webb inaugurated the Apollo Moon programme, designed to counter Soviet successes. Under Webb, the USA firmly took the lead in space with the Gemini series of two-person flights, during which astronauts rehearsed techniques for the Apollo missions. In 1967 came a setback when three astronauts were killed in a fire during a practice countdown for the first Apollo flight. Crewed flights were suspended for 21 months while the spacecraft was redesigned. To ensure continued support for Apollo, Webb released details of a secret Soviet lunar landing programme. Webb left NASA when Richard Nixon was elected president, just as the Apollo flights were beginning.

Welensky Roy 1907–1991. Rhodesian right-wing politician. He was one of the architects of the Federation of Northern and Southern Rhodesia and Nyasaland 1953 and was its prime minister from 1956 until its breakup in 1963. His Federal Party was defeated by Ian Smith's Rhodesian Front in 1964.

Born in what was then Salisbury, Southern Rhodesia, the son of an impoverished Lithuanian, Welensky joined the railways at 17 and soon became an influential trade unionist. From this base he moved into politics and was elected to the legislative council of Northern Rhodesia 1938. Three years later he formed the Northern Rhodesia Labour Party, rising to become prime minister of the federation of the countries that are now Malawi, Zambia, and Zimbabwe, in 1956. The demise of the federation dismayed Welensky, who placed much of the blame on the Macmillan government in London. Welensky made a final foray into Rhodesian politics in 1964, opposing Ian Smith's Rhodesian Front and forming his own party, but enjoyed little success. This bluff, larger-than-life man, who had once been heavyweight boxing champion of the Rhodesias, spent his last years in the UK, where, if he had chosen, he could have had a safe Conservative seat in the House of Commons or a peerage.

Wick Gian Carlo 1909–1992. Italian physicist who made many contributions to nuclear and particle physics at a time when these subjects were first being explored. For example, he made an estimate of the range of nuclear forces based on the uncertainty principle, and explained the magnetic moments of nucleons in terms of their dissociation into virtual particles. Shared Nobel prize 1957.

Wick was one of the group of physicists who gathered around Enrico Fermi in Rome in the 1930s; he was Fermi's personal assistant 1932–37. Together they proved the existence of new radioactive elements produced by bombardment with neutrons, and discovered nuclear reactions produced by slow neutrons. When Fermi left for the USA in 1938, Wick took over his chair at Rome. The work now concentrated on the study of mesons, particles found in cosmic rays.

In 1946 Wick also moved to the USA, working successively at Notre Dame, Berkeley, Carnegie Tech, Brookhaven National Laboratory, and Columbia University. During his years at Brookhaven and Columbia, Wick often worked with Tsung Dao Lee, who shared the Nobel prize of 1957. In 1971 they introduced

the idea that, in quantum field theory, the vacuum could exhibit structure. This idea is typical of Wick's insights—revolutionary in its day, it now seems simple and obvious to physicists.

Wick had integrity beyond his scientific work. He was aware of the evils of fascism from the start, and in old age he became increasingly concerned with the social responsibilities of physicists. He once compared the physics community to parents who left their children alone in a log cabin, giving them a box of matches to play with. Physicists, he stressed, had a responsibility to inform and advise society about the consequences of scientific discoveries.

Wills John Spencer 1904–1991. British engineer and business executive. He was a director of British Electric Traction (BET, chiefly a road-transport company) 1946–82 and helped build up the Rediffusion commercial and cable television network from 1947.

At BET Wills was managing director 1946–73, executive chair 1966–79, and nonexecutive chair from 1979 until his retirement. When he took over as managing director, the company was chiefly involved in road-transport operations, usually bus companies in which BET had shareholdings. Wills built up BET's holdings in other fields, notably the laundry and cleaning industry.

In 1947, he acquired a large minority stake in a company, Rediffusion, that distributed BBC radio programmes over simple cable networks in a score or more UK cities. In 15 years, Rediffusion was transformed into the biggest cable TV network in the world, at the time. It also manufactured and rented TV sets, and owned and operated a number of commercial radio and TV stations. In 1955 Rediffusion won the franchise for a weekday television service in Greater London, when the service was first licensed, and Wills became the leader of the commercial television industry, as he was already leader of the road-transport industry. He was knighted in 1969.

SOCIETY

DESIGNERS OF TODAY

Armani Giorgio 1935– . Italian fashion designer. He launched his first menswear collection 1974 and the following year started designing women's clothing. His work is known for understated styles, precise tailoring, and fine fabrics. He designs for young men and women under the Emporio label.

Banks Jeff 1943– . British textile, fashion, and interior designer. He helped establish the Warehouse Utility chain 1974 and combines imaginative designs with inexpensive materials to provide stylish and affordable garments for the younger market.

Cardin Pierre 1922– . French pioneering fashion designer whose clothes are bold and fantastic. He was the first to launch menswear (1960) and ready-to-wear collections (1963) and has given his name to a perfume.

Comme des Garçons trade name of Rei Kawakubo 1942– . Japanese fashion designer whose asymmetrical, seemingly shapeless designs, which are often sombre in colour and sometimes torn and crumpled, combine Eastern and Western ideas of clothing. She became a freelance designer 1966, after working in a Japanese textile company, and formed Comme des Garçons in 1969. In the early 1980s her avant-garde designs received acclaim in Paris and were widely influential.

Conran Jasper 1959– . English fashion designer known for using quality fabrics to create comfortable garments. He launched his first collection 1978 and has rarely altered the simple, successful style he then adopted. He has also designed costumes for the stage.

Courrèges André 1923– . French fashion designer who is credited with inventing the miniskirt 1964. His 'space-age' designs—square-shaped short skirts and trousers—were copied worldwide in the 1960s.

Dolce et Gabbana Domenico Dolce 1958– and Stefano Gabbana 1963– . Italian fashion designers, established 1982, who showed their first women's collection in 1985. Their romantic and rustic clothes are inspired by Sicilian culture. They launched a menswear collection 1990 and in 1991 began designing the mainstream label, Complice, for the Milanese manufacturing company Girombelli.

Galliano John 1960– . British fashion designer whose elegant and innovative designs are often inspired by historical motifs (for example, 'Dickensian' clothing), the elements of which he redesigns to create progressive collections. He became known before graduating from St Martin's School of Art in 1984 for his technical expertise and imaginative flair. In 1990 he designed the costumes for a production of Ashley Page's ballet *Corrulao*, performed by the Ballet Rambert. In the same year he began showing his collections in Paris.

Gaultier Jean-Paul 1952– . French fashion designer who, after working for Pierre Cardin, launched his first collection in 1978, designing clothes that went against fashion trends, inspired by London's street style. Humorous and showy, his clothes are among the most influential in the French ready-to-wear market. He designed the costumes for Peter Greenaway's film *The Cook, the Thief, his Wife and her Lover* 1989 and the singer Madonna's outfits for her world tour 1990.

Hamnett Katharine 1948– . British fashion designer with her own business from 1979. An innovative designer, she is particularly popular in the UK and Italy. Her oversized T-shirts promoting peace and environmental campaigns attracted attention 1984. She produces well-cut, inexpensive designs for men and women, predominantly in natural fabrics.

Jackson Betty 1940– . British fashion designer who produced her first collection 1981 and achieved an international reputation as a designer of young, up-to-the-minute clothes. She rescales separates into larger proportions and makes them in boldly coloured fabrics. In 1991 she launched her own accessories range.

Karan Donna 1948– . US fashion designer with her own label; for many years she worked for the Anne Klein company, producing Anne Klein sportswear until 1984 when she founded her own label. As well as trendy, wearable

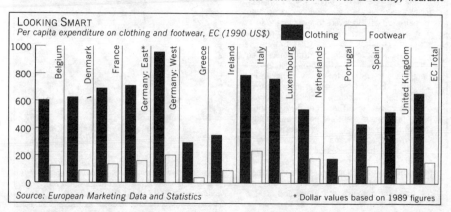

LOOKING SMART
Per capita expenditure on clothing and footwear, EC (1990 US$) ■ Clothing ☐ Footwear

Source: European Marketing Data and Statistics   * Dollar values based on 1989 figures

THE DECLINE OF HAUTE COUTURE

As sales of haute couture clothing have declined there has been much debate about the future of this traditionally exclusive line of fashion; it intensified in 1991 when Pierre Bergé, chair of Yves Saint Laurent, declared: 'Haute couture will be dead in ten years.'

In 1946 there were 200 fashion houses in France selling couture to 300,000 women. Today the number of couturiers has fallen to 21 houses competing to sell to approximately 2,000 women, who may pay up to £10,000 for an individually made dress. The high costs of creating couture collections and the restricted number of customers mean that it is not a profitable line. In 1991 the couture sector achieved sales of FFr 280 million. However, while companies such as Chanel, Dior, and Yves Saint-Laurent each turned over about FFr 50 million, smaller operators made a loss. Though they generated between FFr 3 and 6 million on average, the annual cost of staging two couture shows a year is FFr 10 million.

Despite the high costs, many designers consider couture essential. The shows are powerful publicity exercises, creating a fashion house's image. As international news items, couture collections generate sales of ready-to-wear lines, perfume, cosmetics, and licensed goods (products such as towels, shoes, bags, and watches bearing a designer's label). *The Times* reported that in 1990 couture generated ready-to-wear sales of £500 million and perfume sales of £1 billion for the fashion industry.

'Haute couture' is derived from the French *couture*, meaning sewing or needlework; thus haute couture is high-quality fashion or clothes-making. When preparing a collection a couturier will create outfits from fine linen or muslin (toiles). Garments based on the toiles are made up by cutters, tailors, and other specialists. Because haute couture relies heavily on experts for tasks such as embroidery and making trimmings and buttons for individual pieces of clothing, it is a very high-cost product.

All designs bear the mark of the Syndicat de la Couture Parisienne, the union of dress designers, founded in 1868. In the past, fashion houses have had to produce 75 garments for two shows a year, and employ 20 people in their studios. However, following calls to revitalize couture, the French industry minister set up a commission in July 1991 to examine ways of relaxing the rules to attract new talent.

Haute couture's importance has declined since ready-to-wear clothing was launched in the late 1950s; off-the-peg designer clothes are cheaper and therefore accessible to a wider range of consumers. Though couture remains highly prestigious there are now fewer young women to replace regular customers such as Catherine Deneuve, Ivana Trump, and Jerry Hall. Most fashion houses producing couture can now do so only because they have thriving ready-to-wear collections and licensing deals.

The emergence of street fashion further undermined the authority of couture and created a dialogue whereby fashion designers became influenced by what they saw on the street; notable examples are Vivienne Westwood and Jean-Paul Gaultier. Today fashion is far more plural; couturiers can no longer prescribe a look or dictate hemline lengths for a season.

The later 1980s saw fashion houses across the industry diversify further with secondary clothing lines that are even cheaper than ready-to-wear designs. The recession has knocked sales, and as ready-to-wear collections are still above most women's incomes, designers are increasingly producing 'diffusion' lines, made from less expensive fabrics and reflecting the simpler elements of a designer's style. They have proved very popular; customers can now wear designer labels for a fraction of the cost while designers have been able to keep their signatures alive by expanding to a wider market. Yves Saint-Laurent's Variation range is 40% cheaper than the Rive Gauche (ready-to-wear) main line. Valentino offers two diffusion collections: the Miss V line which is 35% cheaper than the main ready-to-wear collection and the Oliver label which is a further 30% cheaper than Miss V.

In a period of recession, with diffusion lines enabling many designers to remain in business, haute couture may seem irrelevant to the fashion world in the 1990s. But this would weaken the power of exclusive designer clothing as a brand image. When Pierre Balmain, who made losses of $100 million in 1990, did not show a couture collection in January 1991 the consequences were disastrous; the company lost its licensing contracts because the deals depended upon their couture image. Balmain began showing couture again in July of the same year.

A jacket from Yves Saint-Laurent's Variation range, the fashion house's 'diffusion' line of cheaper clothes which is used to subsidize the couture line.

The Drag Craze

In 1991–92 the 'drag' scene saw a resurgence as big as in its heyday in the early 1980s. Cross-dressing (men dressing up as women) has long been popular in the entertainment world, from Shakespeare through to cabaret and pantomime. Personalities such as Danny La Rue and Barry Humphries (otherwise known as Dame Edna Everidge) are familiar examples. However, outside the entertainment business it is often regarded as a peripheral scene.

Though cross-dressing is considered by some as a sign of sexual perversion, many see it as an art, which, in the most recent craze, has been expanded to encompass anyone, male or female, who adopts an imaginary persona. In her 1990 hit *Vogue* Madonna highlighted the glamour of Hollywood actresses such as Marlene Dietrich, Greta Garbo, and Marilyn Monroe—all ultra-feminine icons. By featuring drag artists in the video, Madonna took cross-dressing and the possibilities of self-transformation on to television screens across the world. In October 1991 cross-dressing went decidedly mainstream in fashion when drag artists appeared on the catwalks of Thierry Mugler's and Jean-Paul Gaultier's Paris shows.

In New York drag became the most exciting nightlife scene with clubs such as Copacabana regularly opening to a full house. Founded by theatrical and glamour costume designer Susanne Bartsch, Copacabana became one of the most popular clubs in the city in 1988. Bartsch also staged fundraising 'Love Balls' in 1989 and 1991 for AIDS. For £300 per ticket guests watched transvestites present designs alongside models such as Cindy Crawford and Naomi Campbell. The judging panel included Madonna and Lady Miss Kier of Deee-Lite.

In London the club Kinky Gerlinky, run by Gerlinde and Michael Kostiff, was similarly successful. Originally established in a small nightclub in Soho, it proved so popular that it had to move to the Empire Ballroom in Leicester Square.

The principle of the craze was to be glamorous and beautiful, but above all to have fun. It offered a means of self-transformation which may be understood as a parody of fashion—playing with established notions of beauty and glamour. It also provided an alternative vehicle of self-expression in which voguing (dressing convincingly as another persona) became a pose.

---

sportswear in bright colours, and tight, clingy clothes such as the bodysuit, she produces executive workwear. In 1989 she launched a ready-to-wear line, DKWY.

Kenzo trade name of Kenzo Takada 1940– . Japanese fashion designer, active in France from 1964. He opened his shop Jungle JAP 1970, and by 1972 he was well established, known initially for unconventional designs based on traditional Japanese clothing. He also produces innovative designs in knitted fabrics.

Klein Calvin (Richard) 1942– . US fashion designer whose collections are characterized by the smooth and understated. He set up his own business 1968 specializing in designing coats and suits, and expanded into sportswear in the mid-1970s. His designer jeans became a status symbol during the same period.

Klein Roland 1938– . French fashion designer, active in the UK from 1965. He opened his own-label shop 1979 and from 1991 designed menswear for the Japanese market.

Lacroix Christian 1951– . French fashion designer who opened his couture and ready-to-wear business in 1987, after working with Jean Patou 1981–87. He made headlines with his fantasy creations, including the short puffball skirt, rose prints, and low décolleté necklines.

Lagerfeld Karl (Otto) 1939– . German-born fashion designer, a leading figure on the fashion scene from the early 1970s. As design director at Chanel for both the couture and ready-to-wear collections from 1983, he updated the Chanel look. He showed his first collection under his own label 1984.

Lauren Ralph 1939– . US fashion designer, producing menswear under the Polo label from 1968, women's wear from 1971, children's wear, and home furnishings from 1983. He also designed costumes for the films *The Great Gatsby* 1973 and *Annie Hall* 1977.

Missoni knitwear fashion label established in the UK 1953 by Italian designers Rosita and Ottavio Missoni. Producing individual knitwear, characterized by bold colours and geometric patterns, Missoni has become an international business and has raised the profile of knitwear on the fashion scene.

Miyake Issey 1938– . Japanese fashion designer, active in Paris from 1965. He showed his first collection in New York and Tokyo 1971, and has been showing in Paris since 1973. His 'anti-fashion' looks combined Eastern and Western influences: a variety of textured and patterned fabrics were layered and wrapped round the body to create linear and geometric shapes. His inspired designs have had a considerable influence on the fashion scene.

Montana Claude 1949– . French fashion designer who promoted the broad-shouldered look. He established his own business and launched his first collection 1977.

Mugler Thierry 1946– . French fashion designer who launched his first collection 1971 under the label Café de Paris. By 1973 he was designing under his own label. Strongly influenced by 1940s and 1950s fashion, his designs had broad shoulders and well-defined waists. His catwalk shows are often spectacular.

Muir Jean 1933– . British fashion designer who worked for Jaeger 1956–61 and set up her own fashion house 1961. In 1991 she launched a knitwear collection. Her clothes are characterized by soft, classic, tailored shapes in leathers and soft fabrics.

Oldfield Bruce 1950– . English fashion designer who set up his own business 1975. His evening wear is worn by the British royal family, film stars, and socialites.

Ozbek Rifat 1953- . Turkish fashion designer whose opulent clothing is often inspired by different ethnic groups. He showed his first collection in London 1984, changed direction in 1990 with a collection that was entirely white, and began showing designs in Milan in 1991, with a collection inspired by native American dress.

Pollen Arabella 1961– . British fashion designer who achieved instant success in 1981 when she sold one of her first coat designs to the Princess of Wales. She has become familiar for her classic styles—tailored, sophisticated shapes in bright-coloured wool and cotton. In 1991 she launched Pollen B, a line of clothing directed at a younger market, which is simpler in design and cheaper than her main collection.

Quant Mary 1934– . British fashion designer who popularized the miniskirt in the UK. Her Chelsea boutique, Bazaar, revolutionized women's clothing and make-up in the 'swinging London' of the 1960s. In the 1970s she extended into cosmetics and textile design.

Red or Dead UK fashion design label established 1982 by Wayne Hemingway. Initially he sold clothing designed by his wife Geraldine, and customized heavy industrial footwear to make an anti-fashion statement, which was partly responsible for the trend for Doc Martens workwear boots. In 1987 he designed his own-label footwear range, and in 1988 launched clothing collections for men and women, which became popular in London's clubland.

Richmond John 1960– . British fashion designer who produces unconventional street and clubland designs. He worked in the partnership Richmond/Cornejo 1984–87, creating upmarket leather jackets and separates, before setting up his own fashion label 1987. He continued to experiment with leather, producing jackets with tattoo-printed sleeves in 1989 and covered with graffiti in 1990. In 1989 he expanded his range with the 'Destroy' line which combines the basic elements of his sig-

NATURAL COSMETICS

During the last ten years the cosmetics industry has undergone a transformation as more and more customers choose 'natural' cosmetics and toiletries. A report by Key Note Market Research has shown that today for 56% of consumers the most important consideration when buying cosmetics is that the products haven't been tested on animals; 36% expressed a preference for cosmetics made from natural ingredients. In the teenage market of 15 to 19-year-olds response to the same choice of options was more pronounced: 76% and 51% respectively.

The Bodyshop, which under the guidance of Anita Roddick has grown from one shop in 1976 to a public company with over 600 shops in 39 countries, is the most well-known toiletry company founded on ethical and ecological principles. Today Bodyshop ranks number two in the toiletry sector, and the cosmetics line 'Colourings' is one of the largest brands in the UK. The products are made from natural components where possible, and are taken from sustainable sources, such as the Brazil nut oil used in one of Bodyshop's conditioners.

However, Bodyshop is not alone; there are many companies selling natural and non-animal-tested cosmetics and toiletries, such as Beauty Without Cruelty (BWC), and Creighton's Naturally and Better World products which sell chiefly through mail order or health stores. By using natural ingredients such companies aim to enhance their goods with the attributes of organic components rather than using synthetic ingredients.

Despite the popularity of natural toiletries a clear definition of the term 'natural' has not yet been formulated. Although organic components are used as far as possible, synthetic ingredients, such as preservatives and stabilizers, still tend to be employed in the products to varying degrees when a natural substitute cannot be found. Furthermore it has been found that natural ingredients do not always make safe finished products.

The European Cosmetic Directive of 1976 states that all ingredients (natural or synthetic) introduced after this date need to pass a skin test. As a result BWC does not use any ingredient introduced after 1976; other companies follow the pressure group BUAV's (British Union for the Abolition of Vivisection) directive and do not use any constituents introduced within the last five years, or else use human volunteers for patch testing if skin tests are required.

An ethical and ecological awareness may seem strange in the toiletries and cosmetics industry but the unprecedented growth of Bodyshop (whose turnover increased by 36.8% in 1991) and the changing attitudes of customers have affected sales. The cosmetics industry is highly competitive, and therefore the changing patterns of consumption have had an influence on international beauty firms: Estée Lauder and Revlon now have their own 'green' ranges 'Origins' and 'Ecologie'. Though many of the naturally inspired cosmetics companies may not be widely known, their powers of persuasion have proved to be considerable, far outweighing their size.

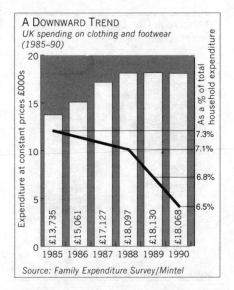

A DOWNWARD TREND
UK spending on clothing and footwear (1985–90)

Expenditure at constant prices £000s

As a % of total household expenditure

1985	1986	1987	1988	1989	1990
£13,735	£15,061	£17,127	£18,097	£18,130	£18,068

7.3%
7.1%
6.8%
6.5%

Source: Family Expenditure Survey/Mintel

nature with lower prices. He staged his first solo show in 1991.

Saint-Laurent Yves (Henri Donat Mathieu) 1936– . French fashion designer who has had an exceptional influence on fashion in the second half of the 20th century. He began working for Christian Dior 1955 and succeeded him as designer on Dior's death 1957. He established his own label 1962 and went on to create the first 'power-dressing' looks for men and women: classical, stylish city clothes.

Smith Paul 1946- . British menswear designer whose clothes are stylistically simple and practical. He opened his first shop 1970 and showed his first collection in Paris 1976. He launched a toiletry range in 1986 and a childrenswear collection 1991.

Storey Helen 1959– . British fashion designer who launched her own label 1984. She opened Boyd and Storey with fellow fashion designer Karen Boyd 1987, and in 1989 designed a range of shoes for Dr Martens UK. She staged her first solo catwalk show 1990 and launched a menswear collection 1991.

Valentino trade name of Valentino Garavani 1932– . Italian fashion designer who opened his fashion house in Rome 1959. He opened his first ready-to-wear boutique ten years later, before showing the line in Paris from 1975. He launched his menswear collection 1972. His designs are characterized by simplicity—elegantly tailored suits and coats, usually marked with a V in the seams.

Versace Gianni 1946– . Fashion designer who opened his own business and presented a menswear collection 1978. He has diversified into women's wear, accessories, perfumes, furs, and costumes for opera, theatre, and ballet. He uses simple shapes and has a strong sense of colour.

Westwood Vivienne 1941– . British fashion designer who first attracted attention in the mid-1970s as co-owner of a shop with the rock-music entrepreneur Malcolm McLaren (1946–), which became a focus for the punk movement in London. Early in the 1980s her Pirate and New Romantics looks gained her international recognition. Westwood's dramatic clothes continue to have a wide influence on the public and other designers.

Yamamoto Kansai 1944– . Japanese fashion designer who opened his own house 1971. The presentation of his catwalk shows made him famous, with dramatic clothes in an exciting atmosphere. He blends the powerful and exotic designs of traditional Japanese dress with Western sportswear to create a unique, abstract style.

RECENT CHANGES
AND AREAS OF DEBATE

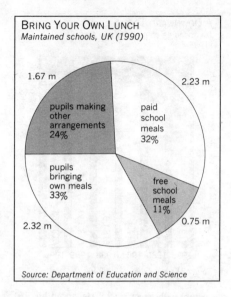

BRING YOUR OWN LUNCH
Maintained schools, UK (1990)

1.67 m

2.23 m

pupils making other arrangements
24%

paid school meals
32%

pupils bringing own meals
33%

free school meals
11%

2.32 m

0.75 m

Source: Department of Education and Science

city technology college in the UK, a new school, financed by government and industry, designed to teach technological subjects in inner cities to students aged 11-18. By 1992 only 15 schools had been approved, industry having proved reluctant to provide funding for the scheme.

CTCs have caused controversy, (a) because of government plans to operate the schools independently of local education authorities; (b) because of selection procedures; and (c) because of their emphasis on vocational training at a time when there is also a drive towards a broader curriculum. The first college opened in Sept 1987 at Solihull, West Midlands. In 1990 the Treasury announced that the scheme would not be funded beyond the originally planned 20 schools. The government now seeks to expand the scheme in cooperation with LEAs and voluntary schools.

further education college college in the UK for students over school-leaving age that provides courses of skills towards an occupation or trade, and general education at a level below that of a degree course.

GCSE (*General Certificate of Secondary Education*) in the UK, from 1988, examination for 16-year-old pupils, superseding both GCE O level and CSE, and offering qualifications for up to 60% of school leavers in any particular subject.

The GCSE includes more practical and coursework than O level. GCSE subjects are organized as part of the national curriculum.

grant-maintained school in the UK, a state school that has voluntarily withdrawn from local authority support (an action called *opting out*), and instead is maintained directly by central government. By early 1992 only 200 schools had opted out, but many more were

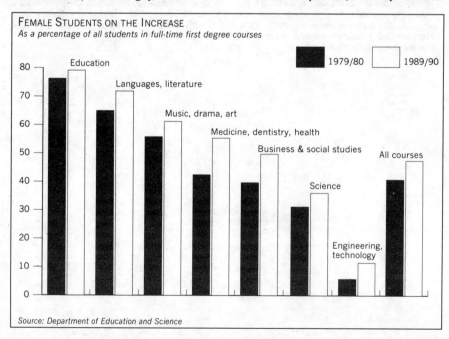

FEMALE STUDENTS ON THE INCREASE
As a percentage of all students in full-time first degree courses

1979/80   1989/90

Education
Languages, literature
Music, drama, art
Medicine, dentistry, health
Business & social studies
All courses
Science
Engineering, technology

80
70
60
50
40
30
20
10
0

Source: Department of Education and Science

LOW LITERACY—HIGH CONTROVERSY

The debate over the teaching of reading, which has rumbled on for more than a quarter of a century, flared into life again before the 1992 general election. Suggestions that the reading performance of young children had declined were fuelled by anonymous allegations by a group of educational psychologists in 1990. They based their claims on confidential local authority surveys. Government ministers were quick to blame 'trendy' or 'progressive' teaching methods but early research was of little help in apportioning blame.

Political anxiety about reading standards led to a flurry of government-inspired activity which by early 1992 had confirmed that there had been a falling away in performance since 1987. The drop in reading age was conservatively estimated at between two and five months at the age of seven.

Background—a role to play?
Evidence on the cause of the decline was more confusing. A study in Buckinghamshire was the first to link the decline in standards to poverty. Support for this interpretation was provided by the National Foundation for Educational Research which discovered that the decline in standards was concentrated more heavily in inner-city areas. Nine of the schools they surveyed in rural areas or middle-class suburbs actually showed an improvement in standards. The annual HMI report for 1991 found that while standards were poor or less than satisfactory in a third of lessons in schools overall, the proportion rose to almost half in junior schools in inner-city areas.

Are teaching methods to blame?
The research confirmed that very few teachers had adopted the 'real books' approach to the teaching of reading, one of the allegedly 'progressive' approaches condemned by ministers. Only 4% used 'real books' exclusively; two-thirds combined the use of graded reading schemes and real books. Almost all teachers used a combination of 'look and say' and phonics to teach reading skills, but the researchers suggested that some teachers were more methodical than others in their use of phonics.

National Curriculum findings
Concern was further heightened by the results of the first National Curriculum tests of seven-year-olds' performance, published at the end of 1991. These indicated that about a quarter of seven-year-olds were not yet reading independently and remained on level 1 of the National Curriculum. This was interpreted by one side in the debate as a statistically 'normal' result; level 2 is the attainment expected of the 'average' seven-year-old, and some children inevitably fall below the average. It was interpreted by others as a devastating indictment of teaching effectiveness.

Publication of more detailed analysis of the results of the tests, by researchers at the NFER and Leeds University, was delayed until after the general election. It indicated that there was a strong correlation between poor performance and schools in deprived areas and those in which large numbers of children spoke English as a second language. The results also varied between children born in the summer months—and therefore younger than average when they were tested—and those born in the winter. The amount of training teachers had received before administering the tests varied greatly, as did the rigour with which they marked the tests.

The NFER research suggested that teachers' ability to manage their classrooms effectively played a large part in effective teaching. This was a message reinforced by the Alexander report, commissioned by the government, to suggest ways of improving primary-school teaching.

One solution: individual tuition
During the early part of 1992 the argument moved away from the disputed reasons for the decline in standards towards a search for solutions. Professor Marie Clay from New Zealand, who had experienced considerable success with her Reading Recovery Programme, found herself much in demand in the UK where she had been invited by several interested local authorities to explain her methods. She claimed that by withdrawing children who were in difficulties at the age of six for one-to-one tuition outside the normal classroom she could help them make up lost ground within months.

Election promises v reality
Both the major political parties went into the general election promising to spend money on a British reading recovery scheme. The Conservatives, who were re-elected, promised £3 million. The Labour Party argued that £40 million would be needed to make an impact on the problem. The more cynical teachers pointed out that most UK local authorities had provided effective remedial reading tuition on similar lines in the 1970s, but that such expensive one-to-one help had been withdrawn in many areas as a result of public-expenditure cutbacks.

expected to follow.

national curriculum in the UK, scheme set up through the Education Reform Act 1988 to establish a single course of study in ten subjects common to all primary and secondary state schools. The national curriculum is divided into three core subjects—English, maths, and science—and seven foundation subjects: geography, history, technology, a foreign language (for secondary school pupils), art, music, and physical education. There are four key stages, on completion of which the pupil's work is assessed. The stages are for ages 5–7, 7–11, 11–14, and 14–16.

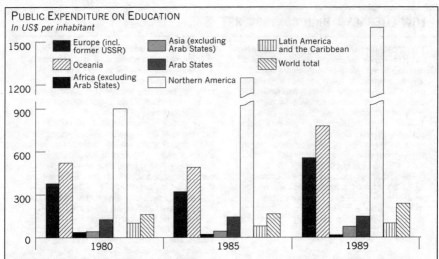

PUBLIC EXPENDITURE ON EDUCATION
In US$ per inhabitant

Note: excludes data from: Albania, Cambodia, North Korea, Laos, Lebanon, Mongolia, Mozambique, South Africa and Viet Nam. Data for the US refer to total public and private expenditure on education.
Source: Unesco

The syllabus for each subject is proposed by a working party, which after consultation with the National Curriculum Council, consisting of 14 advisers from education, industry, and commerce, proposes a final report to the secretary of state for education, who publishes regulations setting out what is to be taught. The first final report was produced June 1988. The National Curriculum is due to be fully implemented by 1997.

opting out in UK education, schools that choose to be funded directly from the Department of Education and Science are said to be opting out of local-authority control. The Education Act 1988 gave this option to all secondary schools and the larger primary schools, and in 1990 it was extended to all primary schools.

student finance payment for higher education, whether by grants, loans, parents, or the student working part time. In the UK, students in higher education have their fees paid by their local education authority and are eligible for a maintenance grant, means-tested on their parents' income. In 1990 the government introduced a system of top-up loans intended gradually to replace 50% of the grant entitlement. At the same time students were debarred from previously available welfare benefits, and the National Union of Students argued that this left many worse off.

In the USA, private organizations called loan guarantors act as intermediaries between the federal government and banks providing the money. The guarantor repays the money if the student defaults, and the government then reimburses most or all the money to the guarantor.

teacher training in the UK, teachers are trained either by means of the four-year Bachelor of Education degree, which integrates professional training and academic study, or by means of the postgraduate Certificate of Education, which offers one year of professional training to follow a degree course in a specialist subject. Most BEd students train to teach in primary schools; most PGCE students train to teach specialist subjects in secondary schools. There are plans to make teacher training more school-based.

vocational education education relevant to a specific job or career.

The term refers to medical and legal education in the universities as well as higher and further education courses in professional and craft skills. In the UK, the TVEI (Technical and Vocational Education Initiative) was intended to expand pre-vocational education in schools but was in the early 1990s being run down.

TOTAL NET EDUCATION AND RELATED
EXPENDITURE IN THE UK

Financial year	Net expenditure	
	Cash (£m)	As a % of GDP
1970–71	2,740	5.2
1975–76	7,023	6.3
1980–81	13,051	5.5
1985–86	17,288	4.8
1987–88	20,401	4.7
1988–89	22,317	4.6
1989–90*	24,102	4.6

* Provisional
Source: Dept. of Education & Science

AN ABC OF TERMS

adult education in the UK, voluntary classes and courses for adults provided mainly in further-

EDUCATION IN THE FREE MARKET

The re-election of the Conservative government will mean more of the same in terms of policy—but probably rather more quickly than before. Large swathes of the 1988 Education Act's provisions remain to be completed and will have an increasingly radical effect on both the structure and content of education. The free market in school places will become fiercer if the new government implements its pledge, so far uncosted, to allow popular schools to expand to meet demand. Further-education and sixth-form colleges will be established as free-standing institutions outside local authority control. Teacher education will move emphatically towards the schools and away from the colleges and universities.

The most dramatic change is likely to be an acceleration in the number of schools voting to 'opt out' of local authority control. The Grant Maintained Schools Trust predicted that up to 750 schools, having waited to see whether the election would end the experiment, would opt out in the six months following the Conservative victory. It is forecast that up to 2,000 will go by 1994. Financial advantages, rather than any ideological commitment, seem to be behind most schools' decision to make the change.

An unknown number of the new grant-maintained schools may also take advantage of the government's flexibility on a change of character and decide to become grammar schools, selecting pupils on the basis of their ability. The former education secretary Kenneth Clarke said that he would have no objection if one school in ten chose to become selective but before the election only one school had decided to follow this path. After the election many more might choose grammar-school status and thus the 11-plus examination, abandoned in most local authority areas 20 years ago, might become common again.

Research into the first 200 opted-out schools indicated that a third of them were already selecting pupils on the basis of interviews and a consideration of previous school reports, although this is not necessarily the only criterion being used when there are more applications than places available.

The government is also likely to pursue with increased vigour its policy for city technology schools (CTCs), looking to voluntary-aided schools in particular to take up the challenge of specialization in science and technology. Industry and commerce were originally expected to fund the CTCs generously, but in the first three years of their existence this hope was not fulfilled and the Treasury limited the original programme to 20 schools on the grounds of cost. By 1992 the programme had achieved only 15 CTCs.

The first pilot assessments for 14-year-olds took place in 1992. These were pencil-and-paper tests; teachers were complaining that they had not seen detailed specifications for them just months before they were due to be implemented. This phase will be followed by the publication of new GCSE syllabuses for the examinations to be taken in 1994, intended to bring GCSE into line with the national curriculum. Again, the final versions will have been produced at the last minute after much contention for courses which are due to commence in September 1992. The new final assessments will sharply reduce the amount of coursework which is allowed at GCSE (A-level coursework is also to be reduced later). This change is fiercely resisted by many teachers, especially those who teach English and some of the practical and creative subjects.

In primary schools, revised and less onerous standard assessment tasks for seven-year-olds were due to be implemented in the summer term. Surveys of primary teachers indicated that they still found the SATs a burden to impose and that they believed the results showed them little about children's performance that could not be gained from teacher assessment.

The last elements of the national curriculum itself—compulsory foreign languages for all up to the age of 16—are not due to fall into place until 1997, and it is still not clear exactly how much space will be left for other options, including new vocational courses, optional beyond the age of 14. There will still be much horse-trading and pressure for relaxation of the curriculum's alleged rigidity on what is appropriate for the 14-to-16 age group.

The election result held little comfort for parents and teachers concerned about dilapidated schools. The National Confederation of Parent Teacher Associations immediately called for a £3.4 billion 'rescue package', but a leak indicated that the government might cut spending on school buildings in the 1990s.

Secondary-school pupils sitting exams. Coursework will be reduced for GCSE and A level.

education colleges, adult-education institutes, and school premises. Adult education covers a range of subjects from flower arranging to electronics and can lead to examinations and qualifications. Small fees are usually charged. The Open College, Open University, and Workers' Educational Association are adult-education bodies.

comprehensive school in the UK, a secondary school which admits pupils of all abilities, and therefore without any academic selection procedure.

Most secondary education in the USA and the former Soviet republics has always been comprehensive, but most W European countries, including France and the UK, have switched from a selective to a comprehensive system within the last 20 years. In England, the 1960s and 1970s saw a slow but major reform of secondary education, in which most local authorities replaced selective grammar schools (taking only the most academic 20% of children) and secondary modern schools (for the remainder), with comprehensive schools capable of providing suitable courses for children of all abilities. By 1987, only 3% of secondary pupils were still in grammar schools. Scotland and Wales have switched completely to comprehensive education, while Northern Ireland retains a largely selective system.

conductive education specialized method of training physically disabled children suffering from conditions such as cerebral palsy. The method was pioneered at the Peto Institute in Budapest, Hungary, and has been taken up elsewhere.

curriculum in education, the range of subjects offered within an institution or course.

Until 1988, the only part of the school curriculum prescribed by law in the UK was religious education. Growing concern about the low proportion of 14- and 16-year-olds opting to study maths, science, and technology, with a markedly low take-up rate among girls, led to the government in the Education Reform Act 1988 introducing a compulsory national

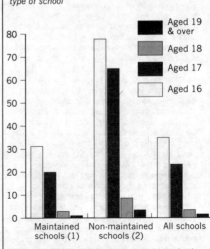

POST–16 EDUCATION IN THE UK (1990)
Percentage of all students staying on, by age and type of school

- Aged 19 & over
- Aged 18
- Aged 17
- Aged 16

Maintained schools (1)   Non-maintained schools (2)   All schools

(1) Including Grant Maintained secondary schools
(2) Including City Technology Colleges.
Source: Department of Education and Science

curriculum, which applied to all children of school age (5–16) in state schools. There are three core subjects in the curriculum: English, maths, and science, and seven foundation subjects: technology, history, geography, music, art, physical education, and a foreign language.

health education teaching and advice on healthy living, including hygiene, nutrition, sex education, and advice on alcohol and drug abuse, smoking, and other threats to health. Health education in most secondary schools is also included within a course of personal and social education, or integrated into subjects such as biology, home economics, or physical education.

higher education in most countries, education beyond the age of 18 leading to a university or college degree or similar qualification.

HIGHER EDUCATION IN THE UK

	Males				Females			
	1975 /76	1980 /81	1985 /86	1989 /90	1975 /76	1980 /81	1985 /86	1989 /90
Full-time students by origin ('000s)								
From the UK								
Universities								
– post-graduate	23.2	20.7	21.0	21.2	10.2	11.3	12.6	15.0
– first degree	130.1	145.1	134.3	143.1	73.6	96.2	99.9	115.3
Polytechnics and colleges	109.3	111.9	143.5	157.4	120.1	96.4	132.2	161.4
Total full-time UK students	262.6	277.7	298.9	337.3	203.9	203.9	244.7	291.7
From abroad	38.6	40.7	38.4	46.1	9.9	12.6	15.3	26.6
Total full-time students	301.2	318.4	337.3	367.8	213.8	216.5	260	318.3
Full-time students by age (%)								
18 years and under	11	16	15	15	14	19	17	17
19–24 years	71	67	67	66	70	66	68	65
25 years and over	19	17	18	18	16	15	15	19

Source: Social Trends 1992

THE INTERNATIONAL LEAGUE

British children compare unfavourably with some other countries in the latest international comparison of attainment in maths and science. Children in 20 countries took part in the survey. England and Scotland were marked separately, and were judged against nine other European nations, including the former USSR, plus Brazil, Canada, the USA, Israel, Jordan, China, Korea, Mozambique and Taiwan. Neither Japanese nor German children were tested. The study was coordinated by the US-based Centre for the Assessment of Educational Progress. Papers were translated and delivered in sealed bags to 6,000 classrooms all over the world.

Korean 9-year-olds outperformed the rest in maths and science. Korean 13-year-olds came top in science and second, behind China, in maths. English 9-year-olds came fifth in science and Scottish primary children were fifth in maths. At 13, the two countries shared eleventh place in maths; in science the English pupils came eleventh, and the Scots twelfth.

Those seeking easy explanations for the discrepancies in international performance will find little comfort here. America and Israel are both big spenders on education, yet the former came near the bottom in three tests out of four, while the Israelis did well. Korean and Taiwanese children, who did well, spend far more time in school than the Hungarians, whose results were also impressive. Korean children of 13 are taught in classes averaging 49, while American children of that age work in groups of 23. Spanish and Italian children do far more homework than those in Taiwan and the UK, but performed worse. The only factor which apparently relates to performance is television watching, with the successful Taiwanese and Koreans watching far less than English and Scottish 13-year-olds (10% and 7% compared to 23% watching more than five hours a day). In academically successful France, parents seem to have found a magic formula for restricting 95% of children to less than five hours a day.

AVERAGE % OF QUESTIONS ANSWERED CORRECTLY

| Country | Maths | | Science | |
	Age 9	Age 13	Age 9	Age 13
Brazil	–	37	–	53
Canada	60	62	63	69
China	–	80	–	67
England	59	61	63	69
France	–	64	–	69
Hungary	68	68	63	73
Ireland	60	61	57	63
Israel	64	63	61	70
Italy	68	64	67	70
Jordan	–	40	–	57
Korea	75	73	68	78
Mozambique	–	28	–	–
Portugal	35	48	55	63
Scotland	66	61	62	68
Slovenia	56	57	58	70
Soviet Union	66	70	62	71
Spain	62	55	62	68
Switzerland	–	71	–	74
Taiwan	68	73	67	76
USA	58	55	65	67
Average	63	58	62	67

independent school school run privately without direct assistance from the state. In the UK, just over 7% of children (1992) attend private fee-paying schools; the proportion has risen since the 1980s. The sector includes most boarding education in the UK. Although a majority of independent secondary schools operate a highly selective admissions policy for entrants at the age of 11 or 13, some specialize in the teaching of slow learners or difficult children and a few follow particular philosophies of progressive education. A group of old-established and prestigious independent schools are known as public schools. The Conservative government has encouraged state funding of selected students within certain independent schools under the Assisted Places Scheme.

PUBLIC AND PRIVATE: WHO SPENDS WHAT?

Scandal was caused before the general election when it emerged that a primary school in Surrey was asking parents for a £30-a-year 'donation' to help pay its teachers, and a Warwickshire comprehensive admitted that it had been seeking £40 a year from parents for some time. The charging of fees by maintained schools is illegal.

The general election highlighted conflicting political claims about the funding of the state education system. Both Labour and Liberal Democrats claimed that the system was seriously underfunded. The Conservatives claimed that real spending on education had increased by 50% during their term in office.

According to independent expert Tony Travers of the London School of Economics, the real rise in spending since 1979 has been 20%, but because educational inflation outstrips general inflation, this has not brought a 20% increase in services.

The evidence is that higher spending was concentrated in specific areas, particularly nursery and special education. Cuts have hit school transport and school meals hard. At the end of the day there was little change in spending in secondary schools. Costs per child in state schools vary from one local authority to another but generally lag behind private day-school fees by about one third.

Private schools normally launch major charitable appeals for new building work while the state sector has to wait—sometimes for decades—for its allocation from the arcane system of grants to local education authorities for capital projects. Capital spending in state schools fell sharply in the early 1980s and although it has now risen again the backlog for repairs has not eased.

Private schools add optional extras to the bill; state schools beg. A major survey by the National Confederation of Parent-Teacher Associations in 1990 concluded that parents were contributing £55 million from their own pockets to state education, and providing 27% of the cost of essential items in primary schools, and 7% in secondary schools.

---

literacy the ability to read and write. The level at which functional literacy is set rises as society becomes more complex, and it becomes increasingly difficult for an illiterate person to find work and cope with the other demands of everyday life.

Nearly 1,000 million adults in the world, most of them women, are unable to read or write. Africa has the world's highest illiteracy rate: 54% of the adult population. Asia has 666 million illiterates, 75% of the world total. Surveys in the USA, the UK, and France in the 1980s found far greater levels of functional illiteracy than official figures suggest, as well as revealing a lack of basic general knowledge, but no standard of measurement has been agreed.

magnet school school that specializes in a particular area of the curriculum; for example, science, sport, or the arts. Magnet schools were established in the USA from 1954 in some inner cities, with the aim of becoming centres of excellence in their special field.

Critics say that magnet schools attract talented pupils and staff away from equally deserving schools in the surrounding neighbourhood. In the UK, the idea has been discussed since 1987 but no magnet schools have been established.

nursery school or **kindergarten** semi-educational establishment for children aged three to five. The first was established in Germany 1836 by Friedrich Froebel.

Open University an institution established in the UK 1969 to enable mature students without qualifications to study to degree level without regular attendance. Open University teaching is based on a mixture of correspondence courses, TV and radio lectures and demonstrations, personal tuition organized on a regional basis, and summer schools.

Announced by Harold Wilson 1963 as a 'university of the air', it was largely created by Jennie Lee, minister for the arts, from 1965. There are now over 30 similar institutions in other countries, including Thailand and South Korea.

remedial education special classes, or teaching strategies, that aim to help children with learning difficulties to catch up with children within the normal range of achievement.

statement in UK education, the results of an assessment of the special educational needs of a child with physical or mental disabilities. Under the Education Act 1981, less able children are entitled to such an assessment by various professionals, to establish what their needs are and how they might be met. Approximately 2.4% children were in receipt of statements in 1990.

In recent years, do you think educational standards in primary schools have......?

Risen considerably	5
Risen slightly	18
Remained the same	21
Fallen slightly	28
Fallen considerably	23
Don't know	6

What do you consider the greatest obstacle to the raising of educational standards in primary schools?

Shortage of resources (i.e. books, equipment, teachers)	60
Teaching methods used by teachers	20
Lack of parental interest and encouragement	13
Some other reason	5
Don't know	3

MEDICAL TERMS

abortion the ending of a pregnancy before the fetus is developed sufficiently to survive outside the womb. Loss of a fetus at a later gestational age is termed premature stillbirth. Abortion may be accidental (miscarriage) or deliberate (termination of pregnancy).

Methods of deliberate abortion vary according to the gestational age of the fetus. Up to 12 weeks, the cervix is dilated and a suction curette passed into the uterus to remove its contents (*D and C*). Over 12 weeks, a prostaglandin pessary is introduced into the vagina, which induces labour, producing a miscarriage.

In 1989, there were 183,974 abortions performed in England and Wales (includes residents and non-residents). In April 1990 Parliament approved a measure to lower the time limit on abortions to 24 weeks from 28.

In 1991 the anti-progesterone abortion pill, mefipristone, was licensed in the UK. (See feature in this section).

allergy special sensitivity of the body that makes it react, with an exaggerated response of the natural immune defence mechanism, especially with histamines, to the introduction of an otherwise harmless foreign substance termed an ***allergen***.

amniocentesis sampling the amniotic fluid surrounding a fetus in the womb for diagnostic purposes. It is used to detect Down's syndrome and other abnormalities.

blood pressure the pressure, or tension, of the blood against the inner walls of blood vessels, especially the arteries, due to the muscular pumping activity of the heart. Abnormally high blood pressure (see hypertension) may be associated with various conditions or arise with no obvious cause; abnormally low blood pressure occurs in shock.

Caesarean section surgical operation to deliver a baby by cutting through the mother's abdominal and intrauterine walls. It may be recommended for almost any obstetric complication implying a threat to mother or baby. In the USA in 1987, 24% of all births were by Caesarean section.

cervical smear removal of a small sample of tissue from the cervix (neck of the womb) to screen for changes implying a likelihood of cancer. The procedure is also known as the *Pap test* after its originator, George Papanicolau.

chemotherapy any medical treatment with chemicals. It usually refers to treatment of cancer with cytotoxic and other drugs. The term was coined by the German bacteriologist Paul Ehrlich for the use of synthetic chemicals against infectious diseases.

contraceptive any drug, device, or technique that prevents pregnancy. The contraceptive pill (the Pill) contains female hormones that interfere with egg production or the first stage of pregnancy. The 'morning-after' pill can be taken up to 72 hours after unprotected intercourse. Barrier contraceptives include condoms (sheaths) and diaphragms, also called caps or Dutch caps; they prevent the sperm entering the cervix (neck of the womb). Intrauterine devices, also known as IUDs or coils, are inserted into the womb. By causing a slight inflammation of the lining of the womb, the IUD prevents the fertilized egg from becoming implanted. A more recent development is a spermicide-impregnated sponge that is inserted into the vagina.

Other contraceptive methods include sterilization (women) and vasectomy (men); these are usually nonreversible. 'Natural' methods include withdrawal of the penis before ejaculation (coitus interruptus), and avoidance of intercourse at the time of ovulation (rhythm method). These methods are unreliable and normally only used on religious grounds.

The effectiveness of a contraceptive method is often given as a percentage. To say that a method has 95% effectiveness means that, on average, out of 100 healthy couples using that method for a year, 95 will not conceive.

convulsion series of violent contractions of the muscles over which the patient has no control. It may be associated with loss of consciousness. Convulsions may arise from any one of a number of causes, including brain disease (such as epilepsy), injury, high fever, and poisoning.

dermatology science of the skin, its nature and diseases.

dialysis the process used to mimic the effects of the kidneys. It may be life-saving in some types of poisoning. Dialysis is usually performed to compensate for failing kidneys; there are two main methods, haemodialysis and peritoneal dialysis.

endoscopy examination of internal organs or tissues by an instrument allowing direct vision. An endoscope is equipped with an eyepiece, lenses, and its own light source to illuminate the field of vision. The endoscope that examines the alimentary canal is a flexible fibreoptic instrument swallowed by the patient.

gallstone pebblelike, insoluble accretion formed in the human gall bladder or bile ducts from cholesterol or calcium salts present in bile. Gallstones may be symptomless or they may cause pain, indigestion, or jaundice. They can be dissolved with medication or removed, along with the gall bladder, in an operation known as cholecystectomy.

geriatrics branch of medicine concerned with diseases and problems of the elderly.

gynaecology branch of medicine concerned with disorders of the female reproductive system.

haematology branch of medicine concerned with disorders of the blood.

hormone-replacement therapy (HRT) the use of oral oestrogen and progesterone to help lessen the side effects of the menopause in women. The treatment was first used in the 1970s.

hospice residential facility specializing in palliative care for terminally ill patients and their relatives.

hysterectomy surgical removal of all or part of the uterus (womb). Instead of a full hysterectomy it is sometimes possible to remove the lining of the womb, the endometrium, using either diathermy or a laser.

immunization conferring immunity to infectious disease by artificial methods. The most widely used technique is vaccination.

inflammation defensive reaction of the body tissues to disease or damage, including redness, swelling, and heat. Denoted by the suffix -*itis* (as in appendicitis), it may be acute or chronic, and may be accompanied by the formation of pus. This is an essential part of the healing process.

intrauterine device IUD or coil, a contraceptive device that is inserted into the womb (uterus). It is a tiny plastic object, sometimes containing copper. By causing a mild inflammation of the lining of the uterus it prevents fertilized eggs from becoming implanted. It has a success rate of about 98%; there is a very small risk of a pelvic infection leading to infertility.

in vitro fertilization (IVF) literally, 'fertilization in glass', that is, allowing eggs and sperm to unite in a laboratory to form embryos. The embryos produced may then either be implanted into the womb of the otherwise infertile mother (an extension of artificial insemination), or used for research. In cases where the fallopian tubes are blocked, fertilization may be carried out by *intra-vaginal culture*, in which egg and sperm are incubated (in a plastic tube) in the mother's vagina, then transferred surgically into the uterus. The first baby to be born by IVF was Louise Brown in 1978 in the UK.

mammography X-ray procedure used to detect breast cancer at an early stage, before the tumours can be seen or felt. It is recommended that women have annual mammographies after the age of 35.

nursing care of the sick, the very young, the very old and the disabled. Nurses give day-to-day care and carry out routine medical and surgical procedures under the supervision of a physician. Organized training originated 1836 in Germany, and was developed in Britain by the work of Florence Nightingale (1820–1910), who, during the Crimean War, established standards of scientific, humanitarian care in military hospitals.

In the UK there are four National Boards (England, Scotland, Wales, and Northern Ireland) for Nursing, Midwifery and Health Visiting, and the Royal College of Nursing (1916) is the professional body.

nutrition the science of food, and its effect on human and animal life, health, and disease. Nutrition is the study of the basic nutrients required to sustain life, their bioavailability in foods and overall diet, and the effects upon them of cooking and storage. *Malnutrition* can be caused by underfeeding, an imbalanced diet, and over-feeding.

obstetrics branch of medicine concerned with the management of pregnancy, childbirth, and the immediate postnatal period.

oncology branch of medicine concerned with the diagnosis and treatment of neoplasms, especially cancer.

ophthalmology branch of medicine concerned with diseases of the eye and its surrounding tissues.

orthopaedics branch of medicine concerned with the surgery of bones and joints.

pacemaker medical device implanted in a patient whose heart beats irregularly. It delivers minute electric shocks to stimulate the heart muscles and restores normal heartbeat. The latest ones are powered by radioactive isotopes for long life and weigh no more than 15 grams/ 0.5 oz. They are implanted under the skin.

paediatrics or *pediatrics* branch of medicine concerned with the care of children.

pain the sense that gives an awareness of harmful effects on or in the body. It may be triggered by stimuli such as trauma, inflammation, and heat. Pain is transmitted by specialized nerves and also has psychological components controlled by higher centres in the brain. Painkillers are also known as analgesics.

paraplegia paralysis of the lower limbs, involving loss of both movement and sensation, usually due to spinal injury.

physiotherapy treatment of injury and disease by physical means such as exercise, heat, manipulation, massage, and electrical stimulation.

poison or *toxin* any chemical substance that, when introduced into or applied to the body, is capable of injuring health or destroying life. The liver is the organ that removes some poisons from the blood.

prematurity the condition of an infant born before term. In obstetrics, an infant born after less than 37 weeks' gestation is described as premature. In hospitals with advanced technology, special-care baby units (SCBUs) can save babies born as early as 24 weeks.

prophylaxis any measure taken to prevent disease, including exercise and vaccination. Prophylactic (preventive) medicine is an aspect of public-health provision that is receiving increasing attention.

psychosomatic descriptive term for any physical symptom or disease thought to arise from emotional or mental factors. The term 'psychosomatic' has been applied to many conditions, including asthma, migraine, hypertension, and peptic ulcers. Whereas it is unlikely that these and other conditions are wholly due to psychological factors, emotional states such as anxiety or depression do have a distinct influence on the frequency and severity of illness.

radiotherapy treatment of disease by radiation from X-ray machines or radioactive sources. Radiation, which reduces the activity of dividing cells, is of special value for its effect on malignant tissues, certain nonmalignant tumours, and some diseases of the skin.

remission temporary disappearance of symptoms during the course of a disease.

resuscitation steps taken to revive anyone on

the brink of death. The most successful technique for life-threatening emergencies, such as electrocution, near-drowning, or heart attack, is mouth-to-mouth resucitation. Medical and paramedical staff are trained in cardiopulmonary resuscitation: the use of specialized equipment and techniques to attempt to restart the breathing and/or heartbeat and stabilize the patient long enough for more definitive treatment.

retrovirus any of a family (*Retroviridae*) of viruses containing the genetic material RNA rather than the more usual DNA. For the virus to express itself and multiply within an infected cell, its RNA must be converted to DNA; it does this by using a built-in enzyme known as reverse transcriptase. Retroviruses include those causing AIDS and some forms of leukemia.

screening or *health screening* the systematic search for evidence of a disease, or of conditions that may precede it, in people who are not suffering from any symptoms. The aim of screening is to try to limit ill health from diseases that are difficult to prevent and might otherwise go undetected. Examples are hypothyroidism and phenylketonuria, for which all newborn babies in Western countries are screened; breast cancer and cervical cancer; and stroke, for which high blood pressure is a known risk factor.

spastic person with cerebral palsy. The term is also applied generally to limbs with impaired movement, stiffness, and resistance to passive movement, and to any body part (such as the colon) affected with spasm.

spermicide any cream, jelly, pessary, or other preparation that kills the sperm cells in semen. Spermicides are used for contraceptive purposes, usually in combination with a condom or diaphragm. Sponges impregnated with spermicide have been developed but are not yet in widespread use. Spermicide used alone is only 75% effective in preventing pregnancy.

sterilization any surgical operation to terminate the possibility of reproduction. In women, this is normally achieved by sealing or tying off the Fallopian tubes (tubal ligation) so that fertilization can no longer take place. In men, the transmission of sperm is blocked by vasectomy (an operation in which the ducts carrying sperm from the testes are cut and tied).

tomography the obtaining of plane-section X-ray photographs, which show a 'slice' through any object. Crystal detectors and amplifiers can be used that have a sensitivity 100 times greater than X-ray film, and, in conjunction with a computer system, can detect, for example, the difference between a brain tumour and healthy brain tissue. In modern medical imaging there are several types, such as the CAT scan (computerized axial tomography).

transfusion intravenous transfer of blood or blood products (plasma, red cells) into a patient's circulation to make up for deficiencies due to disease, injury, or surgical intervention.

transplant the transfer of a tissue or organ from one human being to another or from one part of the body to another (skin grafting). In most organ transplants, the operation is for life-saving purposes, though the immune system tends to reject foreign tissue. Careful matching and immunosuppressive drugs must be used, but these are not always successful.

The 1990 Nobel Prize for Medicine and Physiology was awarded to two US surgeons, Donnall Thomas and Joseph Murray, for their pioneering work on organ transplants.

trauma a painful emotional experience or shock with lasting psychic consequences; any physical damage or injury.

tumour overproduction of cells in a specific area of the body, often leading to a swelling or lump. Tumours are classified as **benign** or **malignant**. Benign tumours are essentially harmless and can be cured by removal; a malignant tumour is cancerous.

ultrasound vibrations similar to sound waves but too rapid to be heard. Ultrasound is very useful in diagnosis, and can be used in the treatment of disease. An ultrasonic beam can be aimed at a certain depth below the skin surface and the energy of the vibrations dissipated as heat (this is used to alleviate pain in joints and muscles).

vaccine any preparation of modified viruses or bacteria that is introduced into the body, usually either orally or by a hypodermic syringe, to induce the specific antibody reaction that produces immunity against a particular disease. In the UK, children are routinely vaccinated against diphtheria, tetanus, whooping cough, polio, measles, mumps, German measles, and tuberculosis (BCG).

X-rays rays with a short wavelength that pass through most body tissues. Dense tissues such as bone prevent their passage and show up as white areas on X-ray photographs. X-rays with very short wavelengths penetrate the tissues deeply and destroy them: these are used in radiotherapy.

THE HUMAN BODY

Achilles tendon the tendon pinning the calf muscle to the heel bone. It is one of the largest in the human body.

adenoids masses of lymphoid tissue, similar to tonsils, located in the upper part of the throat, behind the nose. They are part of a child's natural defences against the entry of germs but usually shrink and disappear by the age of ten.

adrenal gland or *suprarenal gland* a gland situated on top of the kidney. The adrenals are soft and yellow, and consist of two parts: the cortex and medulla. The *cortex* (outer part) secretes various steroid hormones, controls salt and water metabolism, and regulates the use of carbohydrates, proteins, and fats. The *medulla* (inner part) secretes the hormones adrenaline

THE ABORTION PILL

In 1991 a new method of abortion became available to women in the UK, using the abortion pill mefipristone with a pessary of the prostaglandin gemeprost. The method is suitable for healthy women under 35 whose last period began less than nine weeks previously, and who smoke no more than a few cigarettes each day. By taking a combination of mefipristone and gemeprost 95% of eligible women can avoid having a suction termination of pregnancy.

Mefipristone works by blocking receptors in the lining of the womb which are normally stimulated by the hormone progesterone. Without this stimulus the womb lining or endometrium degenerates and separates from the underlying muscle, producing an abortion which resembles a spontaneous miscarriage. Gemeprost softens the cervix and encourages contractions of the womb to expel the fetus. In about 5% of cases, a surgical evacuation of the womb is necessary either because of heavy bleeding or because the pregnancy fails to abort.

The pill-based method of abortion requires four visits to the clinic, making it more time-consuming than the traditional method. At the first visit the woman is counselled about the technique, and given some time to reflect upon her decision. If she decides to go ahead, she is given a tablet of mefipristone at her second visit, and allowed home, but given a contact telephone number to ring in case of any problems. She is readmitted to the clinic 36–48 hours later, when a gemeprost pessary is given. About half of all women will have had some bleeding by this stage, and a few will abort before returning, having had mefipristone alone. A final checkup is necessary about ten days later to ensure that the process of abortion is complete and that there has been no further bleeding.

Is the abortion pill safe? The answer seems to be 'yes', given that over 100,000 abortions have now been performed using the drug in China and France. The main point of con-cern over mefipristone involves the 1 in 100 women who fail to abort using this technique. Most will then decide to go ahead with a conventional suction termination, but if they change their mind at this point and decide to continue with their pregnancy, many doctors believe their baby will be at risk of severe birth defects. Mefipristone has been shown to be a powerful cause of birth defects in rabbits, and one woman in France who had taken the drug had a baby which suffered from sirenomyelia or fusion of the legs, producing a 'mermaid' appearance, as well as having a cleft palate and deformed jaw. It is likely that women opting for the abortion pill will be asked to sign a form advising them of these risks and recommending that they proceed to suction termination if mefipristone fails. There are few side-effects of mefipristone and gemeprost. About a third of women will suffer contractions which are sufficiently powerful to require analgesics, and gemeprost can cause diarrhoea and vomiting. The principal problem with the abortion-pill method is likely to be delay in referral. A woman is unlikely to find out that she is pregnant until at least 30 days after the start of her last period, and will then have only 33 more days before the nine-week deadline. This will allow very little time for reflection and decision unless the process of referral from her doctor to the abortion clinic is rapid.

Is the abortion pill popular with women? When offered a genuine choice between mefipristone and suction, at a centre that offered both methods, about half of French women chose mefipristone, and women who had experienced both methods seemed to prefer it. The incidence of psychological problems following abortion seems to be the same with both methods. Mefipristone and gemeprost offer a safe alternative method of early abortion in healthy young women, if they can be seen early enough. Women who have taken the drug but who fail to abort and decide to continue their pregnancy are at risk of having a deformed baby.

and noradrenaline which constrict the blood vessels of the belly and skin so that more blood is available for the heart, lungs, and voluntary muscles, an emergency preparation for the stress reaction 'fight or flight'.

alimentary canal the tube through which food passes; it extends from the mouth to the anus. It is a complex organ, adapted for digestion. In human adults, it is about 9 m/30 ft long, consisting of the mouth cavity, pharynx, oesophagus, stomach, and the small and large intestines.

antibody protein molecule produced in the blood by lymphocytes in response to the presence of invading substances, or antigens, including the proteins carried on the surface of microorganisms. Antibody production is only one aspect of immunity in vertebrates. Many diseases can only be contracted once because anti-bodies remain in the blood after the infection has passed, preventing any further invasion. Vaccination boosts a person's resistance by causing the production of antibodies specific to particular infections.

aorta the chief artery, the dorsal blood vessel carrying oxygenated blood from the left ventricle of the heart. It branches to form smaller arteries, which in turn supply all body organs. Loss of elasticity in the aorta indicates atherosclerosis, which may lead to heart disease.

artery vessel that conveys blood from the heart of a vertebrate to the body tissues. The largest of the arteries is the aorta, which leads from the left ventricle of the heart, up over the heart, and down through the diaphragm into the belly. Arteries are flexible, elastic tubes, consisting of three layers, the middle of which is muscular.

blood liquid circulating in the arteries, veins, and capillaries. Blood carries nutrients and oxygen to individual cells and removes waste products, such as carbon dioxide. It is also important in the immune response and, in many animals, in the distribution of heat throughout the body.

Blood consists of a colourless, transparent liquid called *plasma*, containing microscopic cells of three main varieties. *Red cells* (erythrocytes) form nearly half the volume of the blood, with 5 billion cells per litre. *White cells* (leucocytes) include phagocytes which ingest invading bacteria and so protect the body from disease; these also help to repair injured tissues. Others (lymphocytes) produce antibodies, which help provide immunity. Blood *platelets* (thrombocytes) assist in the clotting of blood.

bone marrow substance found inside the cavity of bones. In early life it produces red blood cells but later on lipids (fat) accumulate and its colour changes from red to yellow. Bone marrow may be transplanted using immunosuppressive drugs in the recipient to prevent rejection.

brain a mass of interconnected nerve cells, contained by the skull, forming the anterior part of the central nervous system, whose activities it coordinates and controls. (See *Life Sciences* for more.)

bronchus medium-sized airway within the lung. The bronchi have cartilage within their walls, which helps to keep them open when the lung is compressed during exhalation. The respiratory epithelium lining the bronchi produces mucus, which is swept up to the throat by the beating action of the cilia, and prevents small particles in the inhaled air from reaching the lungs themselves. This mechanism is damaged by smoking.

cranium the dome-shaped area of the skull, consisting of several fused plates, that protects the brain. Fossil remains of the human cranium have aided the development of theories concerning human evolution.

ear the organ of hearing consisting of three parts: outer ear, middle ear, and inner ear. It responds to the vibrations that constitute sound, and these are translated into nerve signals and passed to the brain.

eye the organ of vision, a roughly spherical structure contained in a bony socket. Light enters it through the *cornea*, and passes through the circular opening (*pupil*) in the *iris* (the coloured part of the eye). The light is focused by the combined action of the curved cornea, the internal fluids, and the *lens* (the rounded transparent structure behind the iris). The ciliary muscles act on the lens to change its shape, so that images of objects at different distances can be focused on the *retina*. This is at the back of the eye, and is packed with light-sensitive cells (rods and cones), connected to the brain by the optic nerve.

Fallopian tube or *oviduct* one of two tubes that carry eggs from the ovary to the uterus. An egg is fertilized by sperm in the Fallopian tubes,

Joint   *hinge joint (knee)*

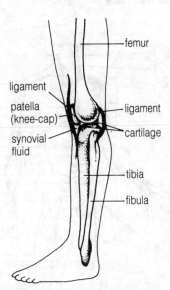

which are lined with cells whose cilia move the egg towards the uterus.

gall bladder small muscular sac attached to the underside of the liver and connected to the small intestine by the bile duct. It stores bile from the liver.

hair threadlike structure growing from the skin. Each hair grows from a pit-shaped follicle embedded in the second layer of the skin, the dermis. The hair consists of dead cells impregnated with the protein keratin. There are about a million hairs on the average person's head. Each grows at the rate of 5–10 mm per month, lengthening for about three years before being replaced by a new one.

heart a muscular organ that rhythmically contracts to force blood around the body. The beating of the heart is controlled by the autonomic nervous system and an internal control centre or pacemaker, the sinoatrial node.

joint a point of movement or articulation in the skeleton. Joints between bones are fixed (*fibrous*, for example the bones of the skull) or mobile (*synovial*). Of the latter, some allow a gliding motion (one vertebra of the spine on another), some have a hinge action (elbow and knee), and others allow motion in all directions (hip and shoulder joints), by means of a ball-and-socket arrangement. In synovial joints, the ends of the bones are covered with cartilage for greater elasticity and smoothness, and enclosed in an envelope (capsule) of tough white fibrous tissue lined with a membrane which secretes a lubricating and cushioning synovial fluid. The joint is further strengthened by ligaments, however the stability of most joints depends more on muscles than on ligaments.

kidney one of a pair of organs responsible for water regulation, excretion of waste products,

the human body

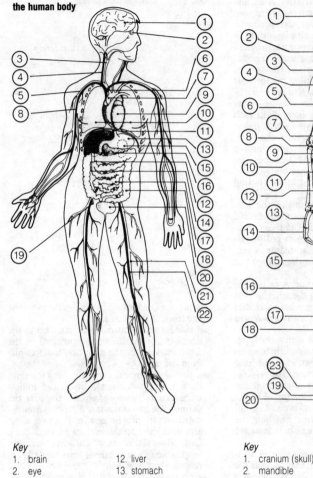
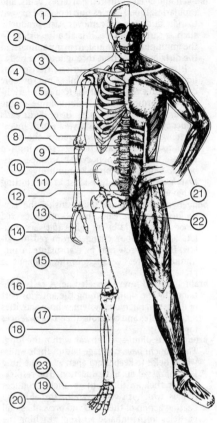

Key
1. brain
2. eye
3. carotid artery
4. jugular vein
5. subclavian artery
6. superior vena cava
7. aorta
8. subclavian vein
9. heart
10. lungs
11. diaphragm
12. liver
13. stomach
14. gall bladder
15. kidney
16. pancreas
17. small intestine
18. large intestine
19. appendix
20. bladder
21. femoral artery
22. femoral vein

Key
1. cranium (skull)
2. mandible
3. clavicle
4. scapula
5. sternum
6. rib cage
7. humerus
8. vertebra
9. ulna
10. radius
11. pelvis
12. coccyx
13. metacarpals
14. phalanges
15. femur
16. patella
17. fibula
18. tibia
19. metatarsals
20. phalanges
21. superficial (upper) layer of muscles
22. carpals
23. tarsals

and maintaining the ionic composition of the blood. It consists of a number of long tubules; the outer parts filter the aqueous components of blood, and the inner parts selectively reabsorb vital salts, leaving waste products in the remaining fluid (urine), which is passed through the ureter to the bladder.

The action of the kidneys is vital, although if one is removed, the other enlarges to take over its function. A patient with two defective kidneys may continue near-normal life with the aid of a kidney machine or continuous ambulatory peritoneal dialysis (CAPD).

liver a large organ which has many regulatory and storage functions, situated in the upper abdomen, and weighs about 2 kg/4.5 lbs. It receives the products of digestion, converts glucose to glycogen (a long-chain carbohydrate used for storage), and breaks down fats. It removes excess amino acids from the blood, converting them to urea, which is excreted by the kidneys. The liver also synthesizes vitamins, produces bile and blood-clotting factors, and removes damaged red cells and toxins such as alcohol from the blood.

lung organ of respiration, used for gas exchange.

The paired lungs are essentially sheets of thin, moist membrane that are folded so as to occupy less space, situated in the pleural cavities of the thorax (the upper part of the trunk). Lungs function by bringing inhaled air into close contact with the blood, so that oxygen can pass into the organism and waste carbon dioxide can be passed out; the oxygen is carried by haemoglobin in red blood cells. The principal diseases of the lungs are tuberculosis, pneumonia, bronchitis, emphysema, and cancer.

lymph nodes small masses of lymphatic tissue in the body that occur at various points along the major lymphatic vessels. Tonsils and adenoids are large lymph nodes. As the lymph passes through them it is filtered, and bacteria and other microorganisms are engulfed by cells known as macrophages.

muscle contractile tissue that produces locomotion and maintains the movement of body substances. Muscle is made of long cells that can contract to between one-half and one-third of their relaxed length. Muscle is the body's most abundant tissue, accounting for some two-fifths of the body weight.

An artificial muscle fibre was developed in the USA 1990. Besides replacing muscle fibre, it can be used for substitute ligaments and blood vessels and to prevent tissues sticking together after surgery. (See *Life Sciences* for more.)

nerve strand of nerve cells enclosed in a sheath of connective tissue joining the central and the autonomic nervous systems with receptor and effector organs. A single nerve may contain both motor and sensory nerve cells, but they act independently.

oesophagus the passage about 23 cm/9 in long by which food travels from mouth to stomach. Its upper end is at the bottom of the pharynx, immediately behind the windpipe.

ovary the organ that generates the ovum. The two ovaries are whitish rounded bodies about 25 mm/1 in by 35 mm/1.5 in, located in the abdomen near the ends of the Fallopian tubes. Every month, from puberty to the onset of the menopause, an ovum is released from the ovary. This is called ovulation, and forms part of the menstrual cycle.

pancreas an accessory gland of the digestive system located close to the duodenum. When stimulated by secretin, it secretes enzymes into the duodenum that digeest starches, proteins, and fats. In humans, it is about 18 cm/7 in long, and lies behind and below the stomach. It contains groups of cells called the *islets of Langerhans*, which secrete the hormones insulin and glucagon that regulate the blood sugar level.

parathyroid one of a pair of small endocrine glands located behind the thyroid gland. They secrete parathyroid hormone, which regulates the amount of calcium in the blood.

pelvis the lower area of the abdomen featuring the bones and muscles used to move the legs or hindlimbs. The *pelvic girdle* is a set of bones that allows movement of the legs in relation to the rest of the body and provides sites for the attachment of relevant muscles.

penis male reproductive organ, used for internal fertilization; it transfers sperm to the female reproductive tract. In mammals, the penis is made erect by vessels that fill with blood, and in most mammals (but not humans) is stiffened by a bone. It also contains the urethra, through which urine is passed.

pharynx the interior of the throat, the cavity at the back of the mouth. Its walls are made of muscle strengthened with a fibrous layer and lined with mucous membrane. The internal nostrils lead backwards into the pharynx, which continues downwards into the oesophagus and (through the epiglottis) into the windpipe. On each side, a Eustachian tube enters the pharynx from the middle ear cavity. The upper part (nasopharynx) is an airway, but the remainder is a passage for food. Inflammation of the pharynx is called pharyngitis.

prostate gland gland surrounding, and opening into, the urethra at the base of the bladder in male mammals. The prostate gland produces an alkaline fluid that is released during ejaculation; this fluid activates sperm, and prevents their clumping together. In humans, the prostate often enlarges and obstructs the urethra; this is treated by prostatectomy.

red blood cell or *erythrocyte* the most common type of blood cell, responsible for transporting oxygen around the body. It contains haemoglobin, which combines with oxygen from the lungs to form oxyhaemoglobin. When transported to the tissues, these cells are able to release the oxygen because the oxyhaemoglobin splits into its original constituents. Mammalian erythrocytes are disc-like with a depression in the centre and no nucleus; they are manufactured in the bone marrow and, in humans, last for only four months before being destroyed in the liver and spleen.

rib long, usually curved bone that extends laterally from the spine. Humans have 12 pairs of ribs; they protect the lungs and heart, and allow the chest to expand and contract easily. At the rear, each pair is joined to one of the vertebrae of the spine. The upper seven are joined by cartilage directly to the breast bone (sternum). The next three are joined by cartilage to the end of the rib above. The last two ('floating ribs') are not attached at the front.

skull the collection of flat and irregularly shaped bones (or cartilage) that enclose the brain and the organs of sight, hearing, and smell, and provide support for the jaws. The skull consists of 22 bones joined by sutures. The floor of the skull is pierced by a large hole for the spinal cord and a number of smaller apertures through which other nerves and blood vessels pass.

spinal cord major component of the central nervous system. It is enclosed by the bones of the spine, and links the peripheral nervous system to the brain, of which it is a continuation.

stomach the first cavity in the digestive system, between the lower end of the oesophagus and the beginning of the intestine. Food enters it from the oesophagus, is digested by the acid and enzymes secreted by the stomach lining, and then passes into the duodenum.

testis (plural *testes*) the organ that produces sperm in male (and hermaphrodite) animals. The paired testes (or testicles) descend from the body cavity during development, to hang outside the abdomen in a scrotal sac.

throat the passage that leads from the back of the nose and mouth to the trachea and oesophagus. It includes the pharynx and the larynx, the latter being at the top of the trachea; it is also used to mean the front part of the neck, both in humans and other vertebrates.

thyroid endocrine gland situated in the neck in front of the trachea. It secretes several hormones, among them thyroxin, a hormone containing iodine. This stimulates growth, metabolism, and other functions of the body. Excessive action produces Graves's disease, characterized by bulging eyeballs and an elevated metabolism, while deficient action produces myxoedema in adults and dwarfism in juveniles. *Goitre* is an enlargement of the thyroid gland, caused (in simple goitres) by lack of iodine in the diet.

tongue a muscular organ usually attached to the floor of the mouth, crucial for speech. It has a thick root attached to a U-shaped bone (hyoid), and is covered with a mucous membrane containing nerves and 'taste buds'. It directs food to the teeth and into the throat for chewing and swallowing.

trachea tube that forms an airway, also known as the *windpipe*. It runs from the larynx to the upper part of the chest; its diameter is about 1.5 cm/0.6 in and its length 10 cm/4 in. It is strong and flexible, and reinforced by rings of cartilage. In the upper chest, the trachea branches into two tubes: the left and right bronchi, which enter the lungs.

uterus (womb) hollow muscular organ in females, located between the bladder and rectum, and connected to the Fallopian tubes above and the vagina below. The embryo develops within the uterus, and is attached to it after implantation via the placenta and umbilical cord. The lining of the uterus (endometrium) is shed every month (menstruation) and replaced by a new one. During pregnancy menstruation does not occur and the endometrium remains intact. The outer wall of the uterus is composed of smooth muscle, capable of powerful contractions (induced by hormones) during childbirth.

vagina the front passage in females, linking the uterus to the exterior. It admits the penis during sexual intercourse, and is the birth canal down which the fetus passes during delivery.

PSYCHOLOGICAL DISORDERS

agoraphobia a phobia involving fear of open spaces and crowded places. The anxiety produced can be so severe that some sufferers are confined to their homes for many years.

anorexia lack of desire to eat, especially the pathological condition of *anorexia nervosa*, usually found in adolescent girls and young women, who may be obsessed with the desire to lose weight. Compulsive eating, or bulimia, often accompanies anorexia. In anorexia nervosa, the patient refuses to eat and finally becomes unable to do so. The result is severe emaciation and, in rare cases, death.

anxiety emotional state of fear or apprehension. Anxiety is a normal response to potentially dangerous situations. Abnormal anxiety can either be free-floating, experienced in a wide range of situations, or it may be phobic, when the sufferer is excessively afraid of an object or situation.

behaviour therapy the application of behavioural principles, derived from learning theories, to the treatment of clinical conditions such as phobias, obsessions, sexual and interpersonal problems. For example, in treating a phobia the person is taken into the feared situation in gradual steps. Over time, the fear typically reduces, and the problem becomes less acute.

claustrophobia a phobia involving fear of enclosed spaces.

clinical psychology discipline dealing with the understanding and treatment of health problems, particularly mental disorders. The main problems dealt with include anxiety, phobias, depression, obsessions, sexual and marital problems, drug and alcohol dependence, childhood behavioural problems, psychoses (such as schizophrenia), mental handicap, and brain damage (such as dementia).

cognitive therapy a treatment for emotional disorders such as depression and anxiety, developed by Professor Aaron T Beck in the USA. This approach encourages the client to challenge the distorted and unhelpful thinking that is characteristic of these problems. The treatment includes behaviour therapy and has been most helpful for people suffering from depression.

delusion a false belief that is unshakeably held. Delusions are a prominent feature of schizophrenia and paranoia, but may also occur in severe depression and manic depression.

depression emotional state characterized by sadness, unhappy thoughts, apathy, and dejection. Sadness is a normal response to major losses such as bereavement or unemployment.

After childbirth, postnatal depression is common. However, clinical depression, which is prolonged or unduly severe, often requires treatment, such as antidepressant medication, cognitive therapy, or, in very rare cases, electroconvulsive therapy (ECT), in which an electrical current is passed through the brain.

drug and alcohol dependence physical or psychological craving for addictive drugs such as alcohol, nicotine (in cigarettes), tranquillizers, heroin, or stimulants (for example, amphetamines). Such substances can alter mood or behaviour. When dependence is established, sudden withdrawal from the drug can cause unpleasant physical and/or psychological reactions, which may be dangerous.

dyslexia malfunction in the brain's synthesis and interpretation of sensory information, popularly 'word blindness'. It results in poor ability to read and write, though the person may otherwise excel, for example, in mathematics. A similar disability with figures is called *dyscalculia*.

electroconvulsive therapy (ECT) or *electroshock therapy* treatment for depression, given under anaesthesia and with a muscle relaxant. An electric current is passed through the brain to induce alterations in the brain's electrical activity. The treatment can cause distress and loss of concentration and memory.

hyperactivity condition of excessive activity in young children, combined with inability to concentrate and difficulty in learning. The cause is not known, although some food additives have come under suspicion. Modification of the diet may help, and in the majority of cases there is improvement at puberty.

hypnosis an artificially induced state of relaxation in which suggestibility is heightened. The subject may carry out orders after being awakened, and may be made insensitive to pain. Hypnosis is sometimes used to treat addictions to tobacco or overeating, or to assist amnesia victims.

hysteria according to the work of Freud, the conversion of a psychological conflict or anxiety feeling into a physical symptom, such as paralysis, blindness, recurrent cough, vomiting, and general malaise. The term is little used today in diagnosis.

manic depression mental disorder characterized by recurring periods of depression which may or may not alternate with periods of inappropriate elation (mania) or overactivity. Sufferers may be genetically predisposed to the condition.

mental handicap impairment of intelligence. It can be very mild, but in more severe cases, it is associated with social problems and difficulties in living independently. A person may be born with a mental handicap (for example, Down's syndrome) or may acquire it through brain damage. There are between 90 and 130 million people in the world suffering such disabilities.

nervous breakdown popular term for a reaction to overwhelming psychological stress. It has no equivalent in medicine: patients said to be suffering from a nervous breakdown may in fact be going through an episode of depression, manic depression, anxiety, or even schizophrenia.

neurosis in psychology, a general term referring to emotional disorders, such as anxiety, depression, and obsessions. The main disturbance tends to be one of mood; contact with reality is relatively unaffected, in contrast to the effects of psychosis.

obsession repetitive unwanted thought or compulsive action that is often recognized by the sufferer as being irrational, but which nevertheless causes distress. It can be associated with the irresistible urge of an individual to carry out a repetitive series of actions. For example, a person excessively troubled by fears of contamination by dirt or disease may engage in continuous handwashing.

paranoia mental disorder marked by delusions of grandeur or persecution.

phobia an excessive irrational fear of an object or situation, for example, agoraphobia (fear of open spaces and crowded places), acrophobia (fear of heights), claustrophobia (fear of enclosed places). Behaviour therapy is one form of treatment.

postnatal depression short-lived mood change occurring in many mothers four to five days after delivery, also known as 'baby blues'. Sometimes this is prolonged and the most severe form of depressive illness, puerperal psychosis, requires hospital treatment. In mild cases, antidepressant drugs and hormone treatment may help.

psychiatry the branch of medicine dealing with the diagnosis and treatment of mental disorder.

In practice there is considerable overlap between psychiatry and clinical psychology, the fundamental difference being that psychiatrists are trained medical doctors (holding an MD degree) and may therefore prescribe drugs, whereas psychologists may hold a PhD but do not need a medical qualification to practise.

psychoanalysis a theory and treatment method for neuroses, developed by Freud. The main treatment method involves the free association of ideas, and their interpretation by patient and analyst. It is typically prolonged and expensive and its effectiveness has been disputed.

psychology the systematic study of human and animal behaviour. The first psychology laboratory was founded 1879 by Wilhelm Wundt at Leipzig, Germany. The subject includes diverse areas of study and application, among them the roles of instinct, heredity, environment, and culture; the processes of sensation, perception, learning and memory; the bases of motivation and emotion; and the functioning of thought, intelligence, and language.

psychosis or *psychotic disorder* general term for a serious mental disorder where the individual commonly loses contact with reality and may experience hallucinations (seeing or hearing things that do not exist) or delusions (fixed false beliefs). For example, in a paranoid psychosis, an individual m.y believe that others are plotting against him or her. A major type of psychosis is schizophrenia (which may be biochemically induced).

psychotherapy treatment approaches for psychological problems involving talking rather than surgery or drugs. Examples include cognitive therapy and psychoanalysis.

schizophrenia mental disorder, a psychosis of unknown origin, which can lead to profound changes in personality and behaviour including paranoia and hallucinations. Modern treatment approaches include drugs, family therapy, stress reduction, and rehabilitation.

senile dementia a general term associated with old age. (See *dementia* and *Alzheimer's disease* in *Diseases*.)

stress any event or situation that makes demands on a person's mental or emotional resources. Stress can be caused by overwork, anxiety about exams, money, or job security, unemployment, bereavement, poor relationships, marriage breakdown, sexual difficulties, poor living or working conditions, and constant exposure to loud noise.

Many changes that are apparently 'for the better', such as being promoted at work, going to a new school, moving house, and getting married, are also a source of stress. Stress can cause, or aggravate, physical illnesses, among them psoriasis, eczema, asthma, stomach and mouth ulcers. Apart from removing the source of stress, acquiring some control over it and learning to relax when possible are the best treatments.

DISEASES AND DISORDERS

acne skin eruption, mainly occurring among adolescents and young adults, caused by inflammation of the sebaceous glands which secrete an oily substance (sebum), the natural lubricant of the skin. Sometimes their openings become stopped and they swell; the contents decompose and pimples form on the face, back, and chest.

AIDS (acronym for *a*cquired *i*mmune *d*eficiency *s*yndrome) the gravest of the sexually transmitted diseases, or STDs. It is caused by the human immunodeficiency virus (HIV), now known to be a retrovirus, an organism first identified 1983. HIV is transmitted in body fluids (mainly blood and sexual secretions) and endangers heterosexual men and women as well as high-risk groups, such as homosexual and bisexual men, prostitutes, intravenous drug-users sharing needles, and haemophiliacs and surgical patients treated with contaminated blood products.

Infection with HIV is not synonymous with having AIDS. The effect of the virus on those who do become ill is the devastation of the immune system, leaving the victim susceptible to (opportunistic) diseases that would not otherwise develop. Some AIDS victims die within a few months, some survive for several years. There is no cure for the disease, although the new drug zidovudine (AZT) is claimed to delay the onset of AIDS and diminish its effects. The search continues for an effective vaccine. (See feature in this section).

In the UK, 2,549 people had died of AIDS by March 1991, and between 30,000 and 50,000 people were thought to be carriers of the disease. In the USA, 90,990 cases were reported up to April 1989, with 52,435 deaths.

alcoholism dependence on alcoholic liquor. It is characterized as an illness when consumption of alcohol interferes with normal physical or emotional health. Excessive alcohol consumption may produce physical and psychological addiction and lead to nutritional and emotional disorders. The direct effect is cirrhosis of the liver, nerve damage, and heart disease, and the condition is now showing genetic predisposition.

Alzheimer's disease common cause of dementia, thought to afflict one in 20 people over 65. Attacking the brain's 'grey matter', it is a disease of mental processes rather than physical function, characterized by memory loss and progressive intellectual impairment.

The cause is unknown, although a link with high levels of aluminium in drinking water was discovered 1989. It has also been suggested that the disease may result from a defective protein circulating in the blood. There is no treatment, but recent insights into the molecular basis of the disease may aid the search for a drug to counter its effects. For example, one type of early-onset Alzheimer's disease has been shown to be related to a defective gene on chromosome 21.

anaemia condition caused by a shortage of haemoglobin, the oxygen-carrying component of red blood cells. The main symptoms are fatigue, pallor, breathlessness, palpitations, and poor resistance to infection. Treatment depends on the cause; untreated anaemia taxes the heart and may prove fatal.

angina or *angina pectoris* severe pain in the chest due to impaired blood supply to the heart muscle because a coronary artery is narrowed.

appendicitis inflammation of the appendix, a small, blind extension of the bowel in the lower right abdomen. In an acute attack, the pus-filled appendix may burst, causing a potentially lethal spread of infection. Treatment is by removal (appendectomy).

arthritis inflammation of the joints, with pain, swelling, and restricted motion. Many conditions may cause arthritis, including gout and trauma to the joint. More common in women, *rheumatoid arthritis* usually begins in middle age in the small joints of the hands and feet, causing a greater or lesser degree of deformity and painfully restricted movement. It is alleviated by drugs, and surgery may be performed to correct deformity. *Osteoarthritis*, a degenerative condition, tends to affect larger,

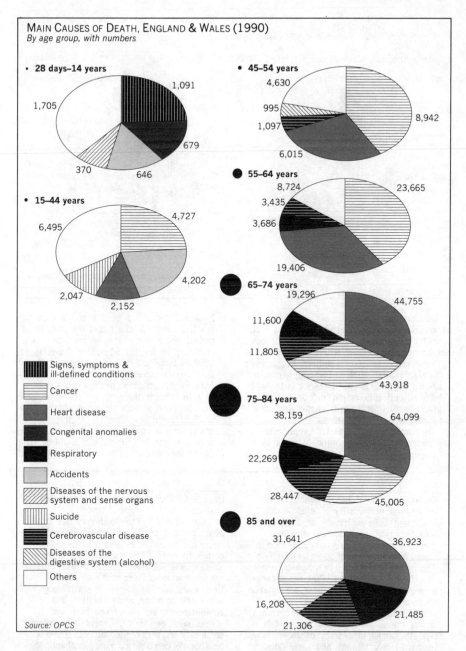

MAIN CAUSES OF DEATH, ENGLAND & WALES (1990)
By age group, with numbers

- **28 days–14 years**
  1,091
  1,705
  679
  370
  646

- **15–44 years**
  4,727
  6,495
  4,202
  2,047
  2,152

- **45–54 years**
  4,630
  995
  1,097
  8,942
  6,015

- **55–64 years**
  8,724   23,665
  3,435
  3,686
  19,406

- **65–74 years**
  19,296   44,755
  11,600
  11,805
  43,918

- **75–84 years**
  38,159   64,099
  22,269
  28,447   45,005

- **85 and over**
  31,641   36,923
  16,208
  21,306   21,485

Legend:
- Signs, symptoms & ill-defined conditions
- Cancer
- Heart disease
- Congenital anomalies
- Respiratory
- Accidents
- Diseases of the nervous system and sense organs
- Suicide
- Cerebrovascular disease
- Diseases of the digestive system (alcohol)
- Others

Source: OPCS

load-bearing joints, such as the knee and hip. It appears in later life, especially in those whose joints may have been subject to earlier stress or damage; one or more joints stiffen and may give considerable pain. Joint replacement surgery is nearly always successful.

asthma difficulty in breathing due to spasm of the bronchi (air passages) in the lungs. Attacks may be provoked by allergy, infection, stress, or emotional upset. It may also be increasing as a result of air pollution and occupational hazards. Treatment is with bronchodilators to relax the bronchial muscles and thereby ease the breathing, and with inhaled steroids that reduce inflammation of the bronchi. Asthma sufferers may monitor their own status by use of a peak-flow meter, a device that measures how rapidly air is breathed out. Peak-flow meters are available on prescription in the UK.

Although the symptoms are similar to those of bronchial asthma, *cardiac asthma* is an unrelated condition and is a symptom of heart

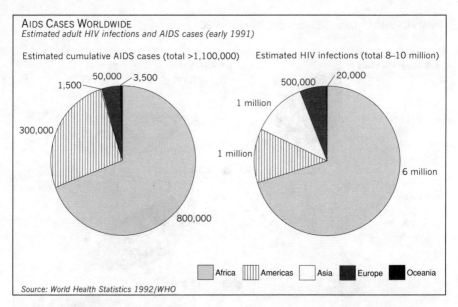

AIDS CASES WORLDWIDE
Estimated adult HIV infections and AIDS cases (early 1991)

Estimated cumulative AIDS cases (total >1,100,000)   Estimated HIV infections (total 8–10 million)

50,000 3,500
1,500

300,000

800,000

500,000 20,000

1 million

1 million

6 million

Africa Americas Asia Europe Oceania

Source: World Health Statistics 1992/WHO

deterioration.

atherosclerosis thickening and hardening of the walls of the arteries, associated with atheroma.

autoimmunity condition where the body's immune responses are mobilized not against 'foreign' matter, such as invading germs, but against the body itself. Diseases considered to be of autoimmune origin include myasthenia gravis, pernicious anaemia, rheumatoid arthritis, and lupus erythematosus.

In autoimmune diseases T-lymphocytes reproduce to excess to home in on a target (properly a foreign disease-causing molecule); however, molecules of the body's own tissue that resemble the target may also be attacked (for example insulin-producing cells, resulting in insulin-dependent diabetes). In 1990 in Israel a T-cell vaccine was produced that arrests the excessive reproduction of T-lymphocytes attacking healthy target tissues.

back pain aches in the region of the spine. Low back pain can be caused by a very wide range of medical conditions. About half of all episodes of back pain will resolve within a week, but severe back pain can be chronic and disabling. The causes include damage to muscles, a prolapsed

CANCER

Cancer is a group of diseases characterized by abnormal proliferation of cells. Cancer (malignant) cells are usually degenerate, capable only of reproducing themselves (tumour formation). Malignant cells tend to spread from their site of origin by travelling through the bloodstream or lymphatic system.

There are more than 100 types of cancer. Some, like lung or bowel cancer, are common; others are rare. The likely cause remains unexplained. Triggering agents (carcinogens) include chemicals such as those found in cigarette smoke, other forms of smoke, asbestos dust, exhaust fumes, and many industrial chemicals. Some viruses can also trigger the cancerous growth of cells, as can X-rays and radioactivity. Dietary factors are important in some cancers; for example, lack of fibre in the diet may predispose people to bowel cancer and a diet high in animal fats and low in fresh vegetables and fruit increases the risk of breast cancer. Stress may increase the risk of cancer, more so if the person concerned is not able to control the source of the stress.

In some families there is a genetic tendency towards a particular type of cancer.

Cancer is one of the leading causes of death in the industrialized world, yet it is by no means incurable, especially in the case of certain tumours, including Hodgkin's disease, acute leukaemia, and testicular cancer. Cures are sometimes achieved with specialized treatments, such as surgery, chemotherapy with cytotoxic drugs, and irradiation, or a combination of all three. Monoclonal antibodies have been used therapeutically against some cancers, with limited success. There is also hope of combining a monoclonal antibody with a drug that will kill the cancer cell to produce a highly specific magic bullet drug. In 1990 it was discovered that the presence in some patients of a particular protein, p-glycoprotein, protects the cancer cells from drugs intended to destroy them. If this action can be blocked, the cancer should become easier to treat. However, at present public health programmes are more concerned with prevention and early detection.

A VACCINE AGAINST HIV: PANACEA OR IMPOSSIBLE DREAM?

It is ten years since HIV infection and AIDS were discovered. Researchers have learned more about them than about any other human disease, but there is still no prospect of a cure. The number of people infected continues to grow rapidly. Public information campaigns have not succeeded in promoting wider use of condoms. Is an HIV vaccine the only hope?

Scientists are pursuing vaccine research intensively; there are millions of lives and billions of dollars at stake. In the USA alone there are four government bodies, 18 universities and 12 manufacturers involved. However, HIV vaccine research faces formidable problems.

Vaccines work by challenging the immune system with a dummy 'enemy'. The antigens in the vaccine cause an immune response of antibodies and killer T-lymphocytes. 'Memory' T-cells remain which can respond faster and more effectively the next time they encounter the same antigens. The vaccine may be a killed sample of the natural pathogen (e.g. in whooping cough), a live but less virulent strain (e.g. polio), or simply antigenic proteins from the surface of the pathogen (hepatitis B). The problem with HIV is that it infects the T-helper lymphocytes that coordinate the immune response. After infection HIV incorporates its genes in the host cell's DNA. It can then remain hidden, present only as a strand of DNA, for many years. Fighting HIV infection is like dealing with a 'mole' operating within the headquarters of an intelligence service. HIV can mutate rapidly, so that a vaccine that is active against one strain may not work against others. A vaccine which boosts the immune response to HIV may even destroy greater numbers of T-helper cells, suppressing immunity more than in the natural course of the disease.

These are the theoretical problems. Scientists can only solve them by testing potential vaccines experimentally. However, there is no adequate animal model for HIV infection in humans. HIV can infect chimps, but they do not get AIDS. Macaques are affected by a retrovirus, simian immunodeficiency virus (SIV), which produces an AIDS-like disease, but it is different from HIV in many ways. However, SIV is the closest approximation to HIV that scientists can study easily.

Experiments have shown that using whole, killed SIV as a vaccine can protect macaques from infection. This is too risky in humans, because a few viruses might survive the inactivation process and be injected alive into the recipient. The alternative is to use individual proteins from the viral envelope to stimulate an immune response. These could be manufactured in free form by genetic engineering methods—the approach used for hepatitis B vaccine. Alternatively, the gene coding for the envelope protein could be spliced into another, harmless organism; when injected into the body, it would replicate and continue to produce the HIV protein, generating a long-lasting immune response. HIV enters the body across the mucous membranes of the vagina, rectum or mouth, but the vaccine is injected directly into a vein. Since the mucous membranes have their own specialized immune system, the best defence against HIV may be somehow to boost this mucosal immunity, keeping the virus out.

If researchers develop a promising candidate vaccine, they will have to test it by clinical trials in humans. They will then run into the problems of selecting at-risk recipients and protecting their privacy. HIV infection is diagnosed by detecting antibodies to the virus. People who have received a successful vaccine will develop antibodies, and thus become 'HIV positive' by conventional tests. They might face difficulties in obtaining insurance or employment. There might also be difficulty if a person contracted HIV in spite of having had the vaccine, because the presence of antibodies would be unhelpful. In those parts of the third world where an HIV vaccine might be most beneficial, there are ethical issues concerning whether recipients could give truly informed consent.

In spite of the enormous challenges that HIV presents to vaccine researchers, many scientists still hope that candidate vaccines will enter trials by 1995. With 40 million people expected to be infected with the virus by the end of the decade, it won't be a moment too soon.

intervertebral disc, and vertebral collapse due to osteoporosis or cancer. Treatment methods include rest, analgesics, physiotherapy, and exercises.

blindness complete absence or impairment of sight. It may be caused by heredity, accident, disease, or deterioration with age. Aids to the blind include the use of the Braille and Moon alphabets in reading and writing, and of electronic devices now under development that convert print to recognizable mechanical speech; guide dogs; and sonic torches.

blood poisoning condition in which poisons are spread throughout the body by the bloodstream, such as those produced by pathogens.

bronchitis inflammation of the bronchi (air passages) of the lungs, usually caused initially by a viral infection, such as a cold or flu. It is aggravated by environmental pollutants, especially smoking, and results in a persistent cough, irritated mucus-secreting glands, and large amounts of sputum.

cataract eye disease in which the crystalline lens or its capsule becomes opaque, causing blindness. Fluid accumulates between the fibres of the lens and gives place to deposits of albumin. These coalesce into rounded bodies, the lens fibres break down, and areas of the lens or the lens capsule become filled with opaque products of degeneration. The condition nearly always affects both eyes, usually one more than the other. In most cases, the treatment is replacement of the lens with an artificial implant.

chickenpox or *varicella* common acute disease, caused by a virus of the herpes group and transmitted by airborne droplets. Chickenpox chiefly attacks children under ten. The incubation period is two to three weeks. One attack normally gives immunity for life.

cirrhosis any degenerative disease in an organ of the body, especially the liver, characterized by excessive development of connective tissue, causing scarring and painful swelling. Cirrhosis of the liver may be caused by an infection such as viral hepatitis, by chronic alcoholism or drug use, blood disorder, or malnutrition. If cirrhosis is diagnosed early, it can be arrested by treating the cause; otherwise it will progress to jaundice, oedema, vomiting blood, coma, and death.

coma a state of deep unconsciousness from which the subject cannot be roused and in which the subject does not respond to pain. Possible causes include head injury, liver failure, cerebral haemorrhage, and drug overdose.

cot death death of an apparently healthy baby during sleep, also known as *sudden infant death syndrome* (SIDS). It is most common in the winter months, and strikes boys more than girls. The cause is not known.

cystitis inflammation of the bladder, usually caused by bacterial infection, and resulting in frequent and painful urination. Treatment is by antibiotics and copious fluids with vitamin C.

Cystitis is more common after sexual intercourse, and it is thought that intercourse encourages bacteria, especially *Escherichia coli*, which are normally present on the skin around the anus and vagina, to enter the urethra and ascend to the bladder.

deafness lack or deficiency in the sense of hearing, either inborn or caused by injury or disease of the middle or inner ear. Of assistance are hearing aids, lip-reading, a cochlear implant in the ear in combination with a special electronic processor, sign language (signs for concepts), and 'cued speech' (manual clarification of ambiguous lip movement during speech).

dementia a progressive loss of mental abilities such as memory and orientation as a result of physical changes in the brain. It may be due to degenerative change, circulatory disease, infection, injury, or chronic poisoning. Typically a problem of old age, it can be accompanied by depression.

dermatitis inflammation of the skin, usually related to allergy. *Dermatosis* refers to any skin disorder and may be caused by contact or systemic problems.

diabetes the disease *diabetes mellitus*, in which a disorder of the islets of Langerhans in the pancreas prevents the body from producing the hormone insulin, so that sugars cannot be used properly. Treatment is by strict dietary control and tablets or injected insulin.

Glucose (sugar) builds up first in the blood of the sufferer, and is then filtered in the kidneys, where its osmotic effect leads to an excessive production of urine, causing dehydration and thirst in the sufferer. Insulin is an important means of regulation and lack of it can cause acids to build up in the blood, leading to diabetic ketoacidosis, a potentially life-threatening condition. In the long term diabetes can damage both the retina and lens of the eye, the kidneys, and the arteries by accelerating the process of atherosclerosis. It is an important cause of kidney failure and premature death from heart disease. Laser treatment and lens implants have improved the outlook in diabetic eye disease, while dialysis and renal transplants can be offered to kidney sufferers. In future it may be possible to cure diabetes by transplanting islets of Langerhans cells into diabetics. In 1989, it was estimated that 4% of the world's population had diabetes.

diarrhoea excessive action of the bowels so that the faeces are fluid or semifluid. It is caused by intestinal irritants (including some drugs and poisons), infection with harmful organisms (as in dysentery, salmonella, or cholera), or allergies.

Diarrhoea is the biggest killer of children in the world. The World Health Organization estimates that 4.5 million children die each year from dehydration as a result of diarrhoeal disease in Third World countries. It can be treated by giving an accurately measured solution of salt and glucose by mouth in large quantities. Since most diarrhoea is viral in origin, antibiotics are ineffective.

Down's syndrome condition caused by a chromosomal abnormality (the presence of an extra copy of chromosome 21) which in humans produces mental retardation; a flattened face; coarse, straight hair; and a fold of skin at the inner edge of the eye (hence the former name 'mongolism'). Those afflicted are usually born to mothers over 40 (one in 100); they are good-natured and teachable with special education. The syndrome is named after J L H Down (1828–1896), an English physician who studied it.

All people with Down's syndrome who live long enough eventually develop early-onset Alzheimer's disease, which led to the discovery in 1991 that some forms of early-onset Alzheimer's disease are caused by a gene defect on chromosome 21.

drug misuse the illegal use of drugs for nonmedicinal purposes.

Under the UK Misuse of Drugs Acts they comprise: (1) *most harmful* heroin, morphine, opium, and other narcotics; hallucinogens, such as mescalin and LSD, and injectable amphetamines, such as methedrine; (2) *less harmful* narcotics such as codeine and cannabis; stimulants of the amphetamine type, such as Benzedrine and barbiturates; (3) *least harmful* milder drugs of the amphetamine type. *Designer drugs*, for example ecstasy, are usually modifications of the amphetamine molecule, altered in order to evade the law as well as for different effects, and may be many

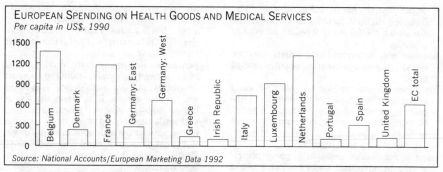

EUROPEAN SPENDING ON HEALTH GOODS AND MEDICAL SERVICES
Per capita in US$, 1990

Source: National Accounts/European Marketing Data 1992

times more powerful and dangerous. Crack, a smokable form of cocaine, became available to drug users in the 1980s. Sources of traditional drugs include the 'Golden Triangle' (where Myanmar, Laos, and Thailand meet), Mexico, Colombia, China, and the Middle East.

eczema inflammatory skin condition, a form of dermatitis, marked by dryness, rashes, itching, the formation of blisters, and the exudation of fluid. It may be allergic in origin and is sometimes complicated by infection.

endometriosis common gynaecological complaint in which patches of endometrium (the lining of the womb) are found outside the uterus. This ectopic (abnormally positioned) tissue is present most often in the ovaries, although it may invade any pelvic or abdominal site, as well as the vagina and rectum. Endometriosis may be treated with analgesics, hormone preparations, or surgery.

epilepsy medical disorder characterized by a tendency to develop fits, which are convulsions or abnormal feelings caused by abnormal electrical discharges in the cerebral hemispheres of the brain. Epilepsy can be controlled with a number of anticonvulsant drugs. Most epileptics have infrequent fits that have little impact on their daily lives. Epilepsy does not imply that the sufferer has any impairment of intellect, behaviour, or personality. Epilepsy is more common in the Third World, with up to 30 sufferers per 1,000 people in some areas; in industrialized countries the figure is 3–5 per 1,000.

food poisoning any acute illness characterized by vomiting and diarrhoea and caused by eating food contaminated with harmful bacteria (for example, listeriosis), poisonous food (for example, certain mushrooms, puffer fish), or poisoned food (for example, lead or arsenic introduced accidentally during processing). A frequent cause of food poisoning is salmonella bacteria. These come in many forms, and various strains are found in some cattle, pigs, poultry, and eggs. The most dangerous food poison is the bacillus that causes botulism. This is rare but leads to muscle paralysis and, often, death. Food irradiation is intended to prevent food poisoning.

Food poisoning has increased in the UK. In northern England there were 4,000 reported cases in 1990, up from 600 cases in 1982; East Anglia and the Mersey area reported rises of 50% of the northern region.

gastroenteritis inflammation of the stomach and intestines, giving rise to abdominal pain, vomiting, and diarrhoea. It may be caused by food or other poisoning, allergy, or infection, and is dangerous in babies.

German measles (or *rubella*) mild, communicable virus disease, usually caught by children. It is marked by a sore throat, pinkish rash, and slight fever, and has an incubation period of two to three weeks. If a woman contracts it in the first three months of pregnancy, it may cause serious damage to the unborn child.

glandular fever or *infectious mononucleosis* viral disease characterized at onset by fever and painfully swollen lymph nodes (in the neck); there may also be digestive upset, sore throat, and skin rashes. Lassitude persists for months and even years, and recovery is often very slow. It is caused by the Epstein-Barr virus.

glaucoma condition in which pressure inside the eye (intraocular pressure) is raised abnormally as excess fluid accumulates. It occurs when the normal flow of intraocular fluid out of the eye is interrupted. As pressure rises, the optic nerve suffers irreversible damage, leading to a reduction in the field of vision and, ultimately, loss of eyesight.

gout a hereditary form of arthritis, marked by an excess of uric acid crystals in the tissues, causing pain and inflammation in one or more joints (usually of the feet or hands). Acute attacks are treated with anti-inflammatories. The disease, ten times more common in men, poses a long-term threat to the blood vessels and the kidneys, so ongoing treatment may be needed to minimize the levels of uric acid in the body fluids. It is worsened by drinking alcohol.

haemophilia any of several inherited diseases in which normal blood clotting is impaired. The sufferer experiences prolonged bleeding from the slightest wound, as well as painful internal bleeding without apparent cause.

Haemophilias are nearly always sex-linked, transmitted through the female line only to male infants; it has afflicted a number of European royal households. Males affected by the most common form are unable to synthesize Factor VIII, a protein involved in the clotting of blood. Treatment is primarily with Factor VIII (now mass-produced by recombinant techniques), but the haemophiliac remains at risk from the slightest incident of bleeding. The disease is a painful one that causes deformities of joints.

haemorrhoids distended blood vessels (varicose veins) in the area of the anus, popularly called piles.

hay fever allergic reaction to pollen, causing sneezing, inflammation of the eyes, and asthmatic symptoms. Sufferers experience irritation caused by powerful body chemicals related to histamine produced at the site of entry. Treatment is by antihistamine drugs.

heart attack sudden onset of gripping central chest pain, often accompanied by sweating and vomiting, caused by death of a portion of the heart muscle following occlusion of a coronary artery by thrombosis. Half of all heart attacks result in death within the first two hours, but in the remainder survival has improved following the widespread use of streptokinase and aspirin to treat heart-attack victims.

heartburn burning sensation below the breastbone (sternum). It results from irritation of the lower oesophagus (gullet) by acid stomach contents flowing back up into the oesophagus, often because of a weak valve at the entrance to the stomach. Heartburn sometimes happens during pregnancy or in obese people.

hepatitis any inflammatory disease of the liver, usually caused by a virus. Other causes include alcohol, drugs, gallstones, lupus erythematosus, and amoebic dysentery. Symptoms include weakness, nausea, and jaundice.

The viral disease *hepatitis A* (infectious or viral hepatitis) is spread by contaminated food, often seafood, and via the oro-faecal route. Incubation is about four weeks. Temporary immunity is conferred by injections of normal immunoglobulin (gamma globulin). In 1992 a genetically engineered vaccine became available. The virus causing *hepatitis B* (serum hepatitis) was isolated in the 1960s. Contained in all body fluids, it is very easily transmitted. Some people become carriers; others may be sick for weeks or months. The illness may be mild, or may result in death from liver failure. A vaccine was developed in the late 1970s. *Hepatitis C* virus causes an illness similar to hepatitis B. About half of all cases are due to the receipt of infected blood transfusions, although it may also be transmitted by intimate contact with body fluids.

hernia or *rupture* protrusion of part of an internal organ through a weakness in the surrounding muscular wall, usually in the groin or navel. The appearance is that of a rounded soft lump or swelling.

herpes any of several infectious diseases caused by viruses of the herpes group. *Herpes simplex I* is the causative agent of a common inflammation, the cold sore. *Herpes simplex II* is responsible for genital herpes, a highly contagious, sexually transmitted disease characterized by painful blisters in the genital area. It can be transmitted in the birth canal from mother to newborn. *Herpes zoster* causes chickenpox when it first infects the body. In later life it can proliferate again, after lying dormant in the sensory nerves, to cause shingles. The Epstein–Barr virus of glandular fever also belongs to this group.

hypertension abnormally high blood pressure due to a variety of causes, leading to excessive contraction of the smooth muscle cells of the walls of the arteries. It increases the risk of kidney disease, stroke, and heart attack.

hypothermia condition in which the deep (core) temperature of the body spontaneously drops. If it is not discovered, coma and death ensue. Most at risk are the aged and babies (particularly if premature).

impotence in men, failure to achieve an erection; this may be due to illness, the effects of certain drugs, or psychological factors.

incontinence failure or inability to control evacuation of the bladder or bowel (or both in the case of double incontinence). It may arise as a result of injury, childbirth, disease, or senility.

infection invasion of the body by disease-causing organisms (pathogens, or germs) that become established, multiply, and produce symptoms.

Most pathogens enter and leave the body through the digestive or respiratory tracts. Polio, dysentery, and typhoid are examples of diseases contracted by ingestion of contaminated foods or fluids. Organisms present in the saliva or nasal mucus are spread by airborne or droplet infection; fine droplets or dried particles are inhaled by others when the affected individual talks, coughs, or sneezes. Diseases such as measles, mumps, and tuberculosis are passed on in this way. The common cold is passed from hand to hand, which then touches the eye or nose.

influenza any of various virus infections primarily affecting the air passages, accompanied by systemic effects such as fever, chills, headache, joint and muscle pains, and lassitude. Depending on the virus strain, influenza varies in virulence and duration, and there is always the risk of secondary (bacterial) infection of the lungs (pneumonia). Treatment is with bed rest and analgesic drugs such as aspirin and paracetamol. Vaccines are effective against known strains but will not give protection against newly evolving viruses.

jaundice yellow discoloration of the skin and whites of the eyes caused by an excess of bile pigment in the bloodstream. Bile pigment is normally produced by the liver from the breakdown of red blood cells, then excreted into the intestines. A build-up in the blood is due to abnormal destruction of red cells (as in some cases of anaemia), impaired liver function (as in hepatitis), or blockage in the excretory channels (as in gallstones or cirrhosis). The jaundice gradually recedes following treatment of the underlying cause.

laryngitis inflammation of the larynx, causing soreness of the throat, dry cough, and hoarseness. The acute form is due to a virus or other infection, excessive use of the voice, or inhalation of irritating smoke, and may cause the voice to be completely lost. With rest, the inflammation usually subsides in a few days.

leukaemia any one of a group of cancers of the blood cells, with widespread involvement of the bone marrow and other blood-forming tissue. The central feature is runaway production of white blood cells that are immature or in some way abnormal. These rogue cells, which lack the defensive capacity of healthy white cells, overwhelm the normal ones, leaving the victim vulnerable to infection. Abnormal functioning of the bone marrow also suppresses production of red blood cells and blood platelets, resulting in anaemia and a failure of the blood to clot.

Leukaemias are classified into acute or chronic, depending on their known rates of progression. They are also grouped according to the type of white cell involved. Treatment is with cytotoxic drugs to suppress replication of abnormal cells, or by bone-marrow transplantation.

measles acute virus disease (rubeola), spread by airborne infection. Symptoms are fever, severe catarrh, small spots inside the mouth, and a raised, blotchy red rash appearing for about a week after two weeks' incubation. Prevention is by vaccination. In industrialized countries it is not usually a serious disease, though serious complications may develop. Third World children particularly suffer a high mortality.

In the UK a vaccination programme is under way, combining measles, mumps, and rubella (German measles) vaccine; this is given to children at age 15 months. A total of 86,001 cases of measles were recorded in England and Wales in 1988.

melanoma mole or growth containing the dark pigment melanin. Malignant melanoma is a type of skin cancer, sometimes developing in association with a pre-existing mole. Unlike other skin cancers, it is associated with brief but excessive exposure to sunlight. Once rare, this disease is now frequent, owing to the increasing popularity of holidays in the sun. Most at risk are those with fair hair and light skin, and those who have had severe sunburn in childhood.

meningitis inflammation of the meninges (membranes) surrounding the brain, caused by bacterial or viral infection. The severity of the disease varies from mild to rapidly lethal, and symptoms include fever, headache, nausea, neck stiffness, delirium, and (rarely) convulsions. Many common viruses can cause the occasional case of meningitis, although not usually in its more severe form. The treatment for viral meningitis is rest. Bacterial meningitis, though treatable by antibiotics, is a much more serious threat. Diagnosis is by lumbar puncture.

migraine acute, sometimes incapacitating headache (generally only on one side), accompanied by nausea, that recurs, often with advance symptoms such as flashing lights. No cure has been discovered, but ergotamine normally relieves the symptoms. Some sufferers learn to avoid certain foods, such as chocolate, which suggests an allergic factor.

In 1990, Hammersmith Hospital in London, England, reported successful treatment with goggles that turn down beta waves in the brain (associated with stress) and stimulate alpha waves (whose effect is calming).

multiple sclerosis (MS) incurable chronic disease of the central nervous system, occurring in young or middle adulthood. It is characterized by degeneration of the myelin sheath that surrounds nerves in the brain and spinal cord. It is also known as disseminated sclerosis. Its cause is unknown.

Depending on where the demyelination occurs—which nerves are affected—the symptoms of MS can mimic almost any neurological disorder. Typically seen are blindness, unsteadiness, ataxia (loss of muscular coordination), weakness, speech difficulties, and rapid involuntary movements of the eye. The course of the disease is episodic, with frequent intervals of remission.

mumps virus infection marked by fever and swelling of the parotid salivary glands (such as those under the ears). It is usually minor in children, although meningitis is a possible complication. In adults the symptoms are severe and it may cause sterility in adult men. An effective vaccine against mumps, measles, and rubella (MMR vaccine) is now offered to children aged 15 months.

muscular dystrophy any of a group of inherited chronic muscle disorders marked by weakening of muscle. Muscle fibres degenerate, to be replaced by fatty tissue, although the nerve supply remains unimpaired. Death occurs in early life.

The commonest form, Duchenne muscular dystrophy, strikes boys, usually before the age of four. The child develops a waddling gait and an inward curvature (lordosis) of the lumbar spine. The muscles affected by dystrophy and the rate of progress vary. There is no cure, but physical treatments can minimize disability.

myalgic encephalitis (ME) a debilitating condition still not universally accepted as a genuine disease. The condition occurs after a flulike attack and has a diffuse range of symptoms. These strike and recur for years and include extreme fatigue, muscular pain, weakness, and depression.

ME, sometimes known as *postviral fatigue syndrome* or *chronic fatigue syndrome* or *yuppie flu*, is not a new phenomenon. Outbreaks have been documented worldwide for more than 50 years. Recent research suggests that ME may be the result of chronic viral infection, leaving the sufferer exhausted, debilitated, and with generally lowered resistance. There is no definitive treatment for ME, but with time the symptoms become less severe.

osteoarthritis degenerative disease of the joints in later life, sometimes resulting in disabling stiffness and wasting of muscles. Formerly thought to be due to wear and tear, it has been shown to be less common in the physically active. It appears to be linked with crystal deposits (in the form of calcium phosphate) in cartilage, a discovery that suggests hope of eventual prevention.

osteoporosis disease in which the bone substance becomes porous and brittle. It is common in older people, affecting more women than men. It may occur in women whose ovaries have been removed, unless hormone-replacement therapy is instituted. It can also be treated with calcium supplements and etidronate. Osteoporosis may occur as a side effect of long-term treatment with corticosteroids. Early menopause in women, childlessness, small body build, lack of exercise, heavy drinking, smoking, and hereditary factors may also contribute.

otitis inflammation of the ear. *Otitis externa*, occurring in the outer ear canal, is easily treated with antibiotics. Inflamed conditions of the middle ear (*otitis media*) or inner ear (*otitis interna*) may become more serious, but usually respond well to antibiotics.

Parkinson's disease or *parkinsonism* or *paralysis agitans* degenerative disease of the brain characterized by a progressive loss of mobility, muscular rigidity, tremor, and speech difficulties. The condition is mainly seen in people over the age of 50.

Parkinson's disease destroys a group of cells called the *substantia nigra* ('black substance') in the upper part of the brainstem. These cells are concerned with the production of a neurotransmitter known as dopamine, which is essential to the control of voluntary movement. The almost total loss of these cells, and of their chemical product, produces the disabling effects. The introduction of L-dopa in the 1960s seemed at first the answer to Parkinson's disease. However, it became evident that long-term use of the drug brings considerable problems. At best, it postpones the terminal phase of the disease. Brain grafts with dopamine-producing cells were pioneered in the early 1980s, and attempts to graft Parkinson's patients with fetal brain tissue have been made. In 1989 a large US study showed that the drug deprenyl may slow the rate at which disability progresses in patients with early Parkinson's disease.

pneumonia inflammation of the lungs, generally due to bacterial or viral infection but also to particulate matter or gases. It is characterized by a build-up of fluid in the alveoli, the clustered air sacs (at the end of the air passages) where oxygen exchange takes place. Symptoms include fever and pain in the chest. With widespread availability of antibiotics, infectious pneumonia is much less common than it was. However, it remains a dire threat to patients whose immune systems are suppressed (including transplant recipients and AIDS and cancer victims) and to those who are critically ill or injured.

polio (*poliomyelitis*) viral infection of the central nervous system affecting nerves that activate muscles. The disease used to be known as infantile paralysis. The World Health Organi-

zation expects that polio will be eradicated by 2000.

premenstrual tension (PMT) popular name for *premenstrual syndrome*, a medical condition caused by hormone changes and comprising a number of physical and emotional features that occur cyclically before menstruation and disappear with its onset. Symptoms include mood changes, breast tenderness, a feeling of bloatedness, and headache.

psoriasis chronic, recurring skin disease characterized by raised, red, scaly patches, usually on the scalp, back, arms, and/or legs. It is a common disease, affecting 2% of the UK population. Tar preparations, steroid creams, and ultraviolet light are used to treat it, and sometimes it disappears spontaneously. Psoriasis may be accompanied by a form of arthritis.

puerperal fever infection of the genital tract of the mother after childbirth, due to lack of aseptic conditions. Formerly often fatal, it is now rare and treated with antibiotics.

rabies or *hydrophobia* disease of the central nervous system that can afflict all warm-blooded creatures. It is almost invariably fatal once symptoms have developed (fever, muscle spasm, delirium). Its transmission to humans is generally by a bite from a rabid dog. Injections of rabies vaccine and antiserum may save those bitten by a rabid animal from developing the disease.

rheumatic fever or *acute rheumatism* acute or chronic illness characterized by fever and painful swelling of joints. Some victims also experience involuntary movements of the limbs and head, a form of chorea. Rheumatic fever, which strikes mainly children and young adults, is always preceded by a streptococcal infection such as scarlet fever or a severe sore throat. It is treated with bed rest, antibiotics, and painkillers. The most important complication of rheumatic fever is damage to the heart valve, producing rheumatic heart disease, which may lead to disability and death. It is now very rare in the industrialized world.

rubella technical term for German measles.

scabies contagious infection of the skin caused by the parasitic itch mite *Sarcoptes scaboi*, which burrows under the skin to deposit eggs. Treatment is by antiparasitic creams and lotions.

sciatica persistent pain in the leg, along the sciatic nerve and its branches. Causes of sciatica include inflammation of the nerve or pressure on, or inflammation of, a nerve root leading out of the lower spine.

septicaemia technical term for blood poisoning.

shingles common name for herpes zoster, a disease characterized by infection of sensory nerves, with pain and eruption of blisters along the course of the affected nerves.

shock in medicine, circulatory failure marked by a sudden fall of blood pressure and resulting in pallor, sweating, fast (but weak) pulse, and sometimes complete collapse. Causes include disease, injury, and psychological trauma. In shock, the blood pressure falls below that necessary to supply the tissues of the body,

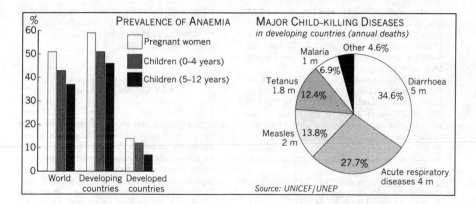

Source: UNICEF/UNEP

especially the brain. Treatment depends on the cause. Rest is needed, and, in the case of severe blood loss, restoration of the normal circulating volume.

sickle-cell disease hereditary chronic blood disorder common among people of black African descent; also found in the E Mediterranean, parts of the Gulf, and in NE India. It is characterized by distortion and fragility of the red blood cells, which are lost too rapidly from the circulation. This often results in anaemia.

sinusitis painful inflammation of one of the sinuses, or air spaces, that surround the nasal passages. Most cases clear with antibiotics and nasal decongestants, but some require surgical drainage.

spina bifida congenital defect in which part of the spinal cord and its membranes are exposed, due to incomplete development of the spine (vertebral column).

Spina bifida, usually present in the lower back, varies in severity. The most seriously affected babies may be paralysed below the waist. There is also a risk of mental retardation and death from hydrocephalus, which is often associated. Surgery is performed to close the spinal lesion shortly after birth, but this does not usually cure the disabilities caused by the condition.

stroke a sudden interruption of the blood supply to the brain. It is also termed a cerebrovascular accident or apoplexy. Strokes are caused by a sudden bleed in the brain (cerebral haemhorrhage) or interruption of the blood supply to part of the brain due to embolism or thrombosis. They vary in severity from producing almost no symptoms to proving rapidly fatal. In between are those (often recurring) that leave a wide range of impaired function, depending on the size and location of the event.

The disease of the arteries that predisposes to stroke is atherosclerosis. High blood pressure (hypertension) is also a precipitating factor. Strokes can sometimes be prevented by surgery (as in the case of some aneurysms), or by use of anticoagulant drugs or daily aspirin to minimize the risk of stroke due to blood clots.

syphilis venereal disease caused by the spiral-

shaped bacterium (spirochete) *Treponema pallidum*. Untreated, it runs its course in three stages over many years, often starting with a painless hard sore, or chancre, developing within a month on the area of infection (usually the genitals). The second stage, months later, is a rash with arthritis, hepatitis, and/or meningitis. The third stage, years later, leads eventually to paralysis, blindness, insanity, and death.

With widespread availability of antibiotics, syphilis is now increasingly cured in the industrialized world, at least to the extent that the final stage of the disease is rare. The risk remains that the disease may go undiagnosed or that it may be transmitted by a pregnant woman to her fetus.

tetanus or *lockjaw* acute disease caused by the toxin of the bacillus *Clostridium tetani*, which usually enters the body through a wound. The bacterium is chiefly found in richly manured soil. Untreated, in seven to ten days tetanus produces muscular spasm and rigidity of the jaw spreading to the other muscles, convulsions, and death. There is a vaccine, and the disease may be treatable with tetanus antitoxin and antibiotics.

thrombosis condition in which a blood clot forms in a vein or artery, causing loss of circulation to the area served by the vessel. If it breaks away, it often travels to the lungs, causing pulmonary embolism. Thrombosis in veins of the legs is often seen in association with phlebitis, and in arteries with atheroma. Thrombosis increases the risk of heart attack (myocardial infarct) and stroke. It is treated by surgery and/or anticoagulant drugs.

thrush infection usually of the mouth (particularly in infants), but also sometimes of the vagina, caused by a yeastlike fungus (genus *Candida*). It is seen as white patches on the mucous membranes.

Thrush, also known as *candidiasis*, may be caused by antibiotics removing natural antifungal agents from the body. It is treated with a further antibiotic.

tonsillitis inflammation of the tonsils.

toxic shock syndrome condition marked by rapid

onset of fever, vomiting, and low blood pressure. It is caused by a toxin of the bacterium *Staphylococcus aureus* which may accumulate, for example, if a tampon used by a woman during a period remains unchanged beyond four to six hours.

travel sickness nausea and vomiting caused by the motion of cars, boats, or other forms of transport. Constant vibration and movement may stimulate changes in the fluids of the semicircular canals (responsible for balance) of the inner ear, to which the individual fails to adapt, and to which are added visual and psychological factors. Some proprietary cures contain antihistamine drugs.

tropical disease the most important tropical diseases worldwide are malaria, schistosomiasis, leprosy, and river blindness. Malaria kills about 1.5 million people each year, and produces chronic anaemia and tiredness in one hundred times as many, while schistosomiasis is responsible for one million deaths annually.

All the main tropical diseases are potentially curable, but the facilities for diagnosis and treatment are rarely adequate in the countries where they occur. There is evidence that malaria, which was eliminated from Norfolk, England only last century, will spread into more temperate regions as global warming develops.

tuberculosis (TB) formerly known as *consumption* or *phthisis* infectious disease caused by the bacillus *Mycobacterium tuberculosis*. It takes several forms, of which pulmonary tuberculosis is by far the most common.

In pulmonary TB, a patch of inflammation develops in the lung, with formation of an abscess. Often, this heals spontaneously, leaving only scar tissue. The dangers are of rapid spread through both lungs (what used to be called 'galloping consumption') or the development of miliary tuberculosis (spreading in the bloodstream to other sites) or tuberculous meningitis. The first antituberculosis drug, streptomycin, was developed in 1944. In England and Wales 478 people died of TB in 1988 out of 5,164 recorded cases.

varicose veins or *varicosis* condition where the veins become swollen and twisted. The veins of the legs are most often affected, although other vulnerable sites include the rectum (haemorrhoids) and testes.

vomiting the expulsion of the contents of the stomach through the mouth. It may have numerous causes, including direct irritation of the stomach, severe pain, dizziness, and emotion. Sustained or repeated vomiting is always a serious symptom, because it may indicate serious disease, and because dangerous loss of water, salt, and acid may result (as in bulimia).

whooping cough or *pertussis* acute infectious disease, seen mainly in children, caused by colonization of the air passages by the bacterium *Bordetella pertussis*. There may be catarrh, mild fever, and loss of appetite, but the main symptom is violent coughing, associated with the sharp intake of breath that is the characteristic 'whoop', and often followed by vomiting and severe nose bleeds. The cough may persist for weeks.

TYPES OF DRUGS

anaesthetic drug that produces loss of sensation or consciousness; the resulting state is *anaesthesia*, in which the patient is insensitive to stimuli. Anaesthesia may also happen as a result of nerve disorder.

analgesic agent for relieving pain. Opiates alter the perception or appreciation of pain and are effective in controlling 'deep' visceral (internal) pain. Non-opiates, such as aspirin, paracetamol, and NSAIDs, relieve musculoskeletal pain and reduce inflammation in soft tissues.

Temporary or permanent analgesia may be achieved by injection of an anaesthetic agent into, or the severing of, a nerve. Implanted devices enable patients to deliver controlled electrical stimulation to block pain impulses. Production of the body's natural opiates, endorphins, can be manipulated by techniques such as relaxation and biofeedback. For the severe pain of, for example, terminal cancer, however, opiate analgesics are required.

antibiotic drug that kills or inhibits the growth of bacteria and fungi. It is derived from living organisms such as fungi or other bacteria, which distinguishes it from synthetic antimicrobials.

The earliest antibiotics, the penicillins, came into use from 1941 and were quickly joined by chloramphenicol, the cephalosporins, erythromycins, tetracyclines, and aminoglycosides. A range of broad-spectrum antibiotics, the 4-quinolones, was developed 1989, of which ciprofloxacin was the first. Each class and individual antibiotic acts in a different way and may be effective against either a broad spectrum or a specific type of disease-causing agent. Use of antibiotics has become more selective as side effects, such as toxicity, allergy, and resistance, have become better understood. Bacteria have the ability to develop immunity following repeated or subclinical (insufficient) doses, so more advanced and synthetic antimicrobials are continually required to overcome them.

antidepressant any drug used to relieve symptoms in depressive illness. The two main groups are the tricyclic antidepressants (TCADs) and the monoamine oxidase inhibitors (MAOIs), which act by altering chemicals available to the central nervous system. Both may produce serious side effects and are restricted.

anti-inflammatory a substance that reduces swelling in soft tissues. Antihistamines relieve allergic reactions; aspirin and NSAIDs are effective in joint and musculoskeletal conditions; rubefacients (counterirritant liniments) ease painful joints, tendons, and muscles; steroids, because of the severe side effects, are only prescribed if other therapy is ineffective, or if a condition is

NEW DRUGS FOR AIDS

In 1991 zidovudine was the only drug licensed for use in the UK against HIV infection. It is an analogue of thymidine, a building block of DNA, and can become incorporated into a strand of DNA in its place. Once in position it exerts its anti-HIV effect by blocking the action of reverse transcriptase. This is a viral enzyme which transcribes the genes of the virus (made from RNA) into DNA, ready for incorporation into the host cell's DNA. Zidovudine's success in improving the survival of AIDS sufferers has led to the development of several other nucleoside analogues. One is dideoxyinosine (ddI), which was licensed in the USA early in 1992. Trials are now assessing the possibility that ddI and zidovudine together are effective against strains of HIV that have become resistant to zidovudine alone. Another nucleoside, dideoxycytidine, should be available for clinical trials soon.

Drugs that use a different mechanism of action may be more successful against resistant strains of HIV. A new family of drugs, the protease inhibitors, is currently on trial. They work by preventing the proteins synthesized from HIV genes from being separated into their active components.

---

life-threatening. A corticosteroid injection into the affected joint usually gives long-term relief from inflammation.

antiseptic any substance that kills or inhibits the growth of microorganisms. The use of antiseptics was pioneered by Joseph Lister. He used carbolic acid (phenol), which is a weak antiseptic; substances such as TCP are derived from this.

antiviral any drug that acts against viruses, usually preventing them from multiplying. Most viral infections are not susceptible to antibiotics. Antivirals have been difficult drugs to develop, and do not necessarily cure viral diseases.

aspirin acetylsalicylic acid, a popular analgesic developed in the early 20th century for headaches and arthritis. It inhibits prostaglandins, and is derived from the white willow tree *Salix alba*.

beta-blocker any of a class of drugs that block impulses that stimulate certain nerve endings (beta receptors) serving the heart muscles. This reduces the heart rate and the force of contraction, which in turn reduces the amount of oxygen (and therefore the blood supply) required by the heart. Beta-blockers are banned from use in competitive sports. They may be useful in the treatment of angina, arrhythmia, and raised blood pressure, and following myocardial infarctions. They must be withdrawn from use gradually.

codeine opium derivative that provides analgesia in mild to moderate pain. It also suppresses the cough centre of the brain. It is an alkaloid $C_{18}H_{21}NO_3$, derived from morphine but less toxic and addictive.

corticosteroid any of several steroid hormones secreted by the cortex of the adrenal glands; also synthetic forms with similar properties. Corticosteroids have anti-inflammatory and immunosuppressive effects and may be used to treat a number of conditions including rheumatoid arthritis, severe allergies, asthma, some skin diseases, and some cancers. Side effects can be serious, and therapy must be withdrawn very gradually.

insulin protein hormone, produced by specialized cells in the islets of Langerhans in the pancreas, that regulates the metabolism (rate of activity) of glucose, fats, and proteins. Insulin was discovered by Canadian physician Frederick Banting, who pioneered its use in treating diabetes.

L-dopa chemical, normally produced by the body, which is converted by an enzyme to dopamine in the brain. It is essential for integrated movement of individual muscle groups.

L-dopa is a left-handed isomer of an amino acid $C_9H_{11}NO_2$. As a treatment, it relieves the rigidity of Parkinson's disease but may have significant side effects, such as extreme mood changes, hallucinations, and uncontrolled writhing movements. It is often given in combination with other drugs to improve its effectiveness at lower doses.

mefipristone abortion pill (previously known as RU 486), licensed in the UK in 1991. It is administered in conjunction with a prostaglandin to induce termination of pregnancy, which occurs within 48 hours.

The pill was introduced in France in 1989, and trials there showed that it was effective in 94% of patients up to 10 weeks pregnant. Up to March 1991, 60,000 abortions were carried out in France by this method. (See feature in this section).

oxytocin hormone that stimulates the uterus in late pregnancy to initiate and sustain labour. After birth, it stimulates the uterine muscles to contract, reducing bleeding at the site where the placenta was attached.

paracetamol analgesic, particularly effective for musculoskeletal pain. It is as effective as aspirin in reducing fever, and less irritating to the stomach, but has little anti-inflammatory action (as for joint pain). An overdose can cause severe, often irreversible, liver and kidney damage.

penicillin any of a group of antibiotic compounds obtained from filtrates of moulds of the genus *Penicillium* (especially *P. notatum*) or produced synthetically. Penicillin was the first antibiotic to be discovered (by Alexander Fleming), and it kills a broad spectrum of bacteria, many of which cause disease in humans.

The use of the original type of penicillin is limited by the increasing resistance of pathogens and by allergic reactions in patients. Since 1941, numerous other antibiotics of the penicillin family have been discovered, which are more selective against, or resistant to, specific microorganisms.

placebo any harmless substance, often called a 'sugar pill', that has no chemotherapeutic value and yet produces physiological changes.

Its use in medicine is limited to drug trials, where it is given alongside the substance being tested, to compare effects. The 'placebo effect', first named in 1945, demonstrates the control 'mind' exerts over 'matter', including causing changes in blood pressure, perceived pain, and rates of healing. Recent research finds the release of certain neurotransmitting substances in the production of the placebo effect.

premedication combination of drugs given before surgery to prepare a patient for general anaesthesia.

steroid any of a group of cyclic, unsaturated alcohols (lipids without fatty acid components), which, like sterols, have a complex molecular structure consisting of four carbon rings. Steroids include the sex hormones, such as testosterone, the corticosteroid hormones produced by the adrenal gland, bile acids, and cholesterol.

An **anabolic steroid** is any hormone of the steroid group of organic compounds that stimulates tissue growth. Its use in medicine is limited to the treatment of some anaemias and breast cancers; it may help to break up blood clots. Side effects include aggressive behaviour, masculinization. In 1988 the Canadian sprinter Ben Johnson was stripped of an Olympic gold medal for taking anabolic steroids.

warfarin poison that induces fatal internal bleeding in rats; neutralized with sodium hydroxide, it is used in medicine as an anticoagulant: it prevents blood clotting by inhibiting the action of vitamin K. It can be taken orally and begins to act several days after the initial dose.

Warfarin is a crystalline powder, $C_{19}H_{16}O_4$. Heparin may be given in treatment at the same time and discontinued when warfarin takes effect. It is often given as a preventive measure, to reduce the risk of thrombosis or embolism after major surgery.

zidovudine formerly *AZT* antiviral drug used in the treatment of AIDS. Developed in the mid-1980s and approved for use by 1987, it is not a cure for AIDS but is effective in suppressing the causative virus (HIV) for as long as it is being administered. Taken every four hours, night and day, it reduces the risk of opportunistic infection and relieves many neurological complications. However, frequent blood monitoring is required to control anaemia, a potentially life-threatening side effect of zidovudine. Blood transfusions are often necessary, and the drug must be withdrawn if bone-marrow function is severely affected.

ALTERNATIVE MEDICINE

acupuncture ancient Chinese medical art based on a theory of physiology that posits a network of life-energy pathways or 'meridians' in the human body and some 800 'acupuncture points' where metal needles may be inserted to affect the energy flow for purposes of preventive or remedial therapy or to produce a local anaesthetic effect. Numerous studies and surveys have attested the efficacy of the method, which is widely conceded by orthodox practitioners despite the lack of an acceptable scientific explanation.

Alexander technique a method of correcting established bad habits of posture, breathing, and muscular tension which Australian therapist F M Alexander (1869–1955) maintained cause many ailments. Back troubles, migraine, asthma, hypertension, and some gastric and gynaecological disorders are among the conditions said to be alleviated by the technique, which is also effective in preventing disorders, particularly those of later life, and conferring a general health benefit, promoting relaxation and enhancing vitality.

applied kinesiology an extension of chiropractic developed in the USA in the 1960s and '70s, principally by US practitioner Dr George Goodheart. Relating to the science of kinesiology, or muscle testing, the Chinese principle that there exist energy pathways in the body and that disease results from local energy blockages or imbalances, Goodheart developed both diagnostic and therapeutic techniques, working on the body's musculature, which have proved particularly effective with stress-related ailments.

aromatherapy the medicinal use of oils and essences derived from plants, flowers, and wood resins. Bactericidal properties and beneficial effects upon physiological functions are attributed to the oils, which are sometimes ingested but generally massaged into the skin. Aromatherapy was practised in the ancient world and revived in the 1960s in France, where today it is an optional component of some courses available to postgraduate medical students.

astrological diagnosis the casting of a horoscope to ascertain a person's susceptibility to specific kinds of disease. From statistical evidence that offspring tend to have the same planetary positions in their charts as a parent, astrologers infer that there is a significant correlation between genetic and planetary influences, and that medical horoscopes, by pinpointing pathological tendencies, can be a useful tool of preventative medicine.

aura diagnosis ascertaining a person's state of health from the colour and luminosity of the aura, the 'energy envelope' of the physical body commonly claimed to be seen by psychics. A recent Charing Cross Hospital Medical School

ARTIFICIAL BLOOD

Blood transfusions are the oldest and most important of all tissue transplants. If an artificial blood substitute could be developed that would replace some or all of the donated blood that is currently required, it would be one of the medical breakthroughs of the century. The pursuit of this goal has been given added impetus by the rise of blood-borne diseases, particularly HIV. Although all donated blood is now tested for antibodies to the virus, there is still a small risk that HIV-infected blood could be donated by someone who has contracted the virus but not had time to develop antibodies.

Artificial blood would have several other benefits: it could be manufactured to meet demand, have a long shelf life, and would not require labour-intensive cross-matching. It would not wholly eliminate the need for natural blood, which is a complex tissue containing cells, antibodies, clotting factors, and transport proteins. In emergencies, however, the function which it is essential to restore by transfusion is the oxygen-carrying capacity of the blood. Artificial blood would be most useful in replacing short-term blood loss, of the type that occurs following surgery or in emergencies. Over half the 2.5 million pints of blood that are donated each year in the UK are used for this purpose.

Red blood cells carry oxygen from the lungs to the rest of the body, using a transport protein, haemoglobin, which is made up of four protein subunits bound to an iron atom. Two approaches have been tried in the pursuit of a blood substitute, using either artificial fluids in which oxygen dissolves easily, or solutions of haemoglobin itself. There are problems, however, with both methods. In 1966 in Birmingham, Alabama, Leland C Clark discovered that mice could survive for prolonged periods submerged in oxygenated solutions of a perfluorocarbon, a biologically inert substance which can dissolve large amounts of oxygen. Although perfluorocarbons are insoluble in water, they can be given into the bloodstream by forming an emulsion. One perfluorocarbon, Fluosol DA20, has been used to treat patients suffering from severe blood loss who, for religious reasons, have been unable to accept transfusions. Unfortunately,

it did not improve survival rates in humans, although promising experiments showed that it could keep alive animals effectively depleted of natural blood. Oxygenated Fluosol DA20 has proved successful, however, in improving the supply of oxygen to the heart muscle in patients undergoing angioplasty of their coronary arteries. In spite of the disappointing track record of these chemicals, there remains hope that they may one day prove successful. A new perfluorocarbon, perfluoroctobromide, can carry five times as much oxygen as Fluosol DA20, and the results of clinical trials are eagerly awaited.

Haemoglobin solutions might be considered a more natural approach to artificial blood. Oxygen carriage would be similar to that in normal red cells, but the separation of the haemoglobin from the rest of the red cell would mean that the substitute would not require cross-matching. Early attempts to produce artificial blood by this method used haemoglobin that had been extracted from fragmented red cells, but unfortunately there were major problems. The haemoglobin, once outside its normal red-cell environment, quickly split into two separate pieces, each of which was then small enough to pass through the blood filter of the kidneys and into the urine, so that the solution only remained in the circulation for a few hours. Both the red cell fragments and the haemoglobin subunits were found to be very toxic to the kidneys. Human haemoglobin made by these methods has in any case always been scarce because only out-of-date blood transfusions could be spared to prepare it.

Recently, however, the haemoglobin approach has taken a leap forward. In 1991 Dr Kiyoshi Nagai, of the Medical Research Council laboratories in Cambridge, used bacteria to produce a modified haemoglobin that remains fully assembled in the circulation, and has improved oxygen-carrying characteristics. Clinical trials are underway to assess its safety. If these are successful it has been suggested that a working blood substitute might be available within five years, to meet a market worth tens of billions of dollars worldwide.

study confirmed that the aura can be viewed by high frequency electrophotography techniques and is broadly indicative of states of health, but concluded that aura diagnosis cannot identify specific abnormalities.

autogenics a system developed in the 1900s by German physician Johannes Schultz, designed to facilitate mental control of biological and physiological functions generally considered to be involuntary. Effective in inducing relaxation, assisting healing processes and relieving psychosomatic disorders, autogenics is regarded as a precursor of biofeedback.

Ayurveda a basically naturopathic system of medicine widely practised in India and based on principles derived from the ancient Hindu

scriptures, the Vedas. Hospital treatments and remedial prescriptions tend to be non-specific and to co-ordinate holistic therapies for body, mind, and spirit.

Bach flower healing an essentially homoeopathic system of therapy developed in the 1920s by English physician Edward Bach. Based on the healing properties of wild flowers, it seeks to alleviate mental and emotional causes of disease rather than their physical symptoms.

Bates eyesight training a method developed by US ophthalmologist William Bates (1860–1931) to enable people to correct problems of vision without wearing glasses. The method is of proven effectiveness in relieving all refractive conditions, correcting squints, lazy eyes, and similar problems, but does not claim to treat eye disease.

biochemic tissue salts therapy the correction of imbalances or deficiencies in the body's resources of essential mineral salts. There are 12 tissue salts in the body and the healthy functioning of cells depends on their correct balance, but there is scant evidence that disease is due to their imbalance and can be cured by supplements, as claimed by German physician W H Schuessler in the 1870s, though many people profess to benefit from the 'Schuessler remedies'.

bioenergetics an extension of Reichian therapy principles developed in the 1960s by US physician Alexander Lowen, and designed to promote, by breathing, physical exercise, and the elimination of muscular blockages, the free flow of energy in the body and thus restore optimum health and vitality.

biofeedback the use of electrophysiological monitoring devices to 'feed back' information about internal processes and thus facilitate conscious control. Developed in the USA in the 1960s, independently by neurophysiologist Barbara Brown and neuropsychiatrist Joseph Kamiya, the technique is particularly effective in alleviating hypertension and preventing associated organic and physiological dysfunctions.

chiropractic a technique of manipulation of the joints of the body, particularly the spine, based on the principle that pathology originates in disordered physiology attributable to aberrations in the functioning of the nervous system, which manipulation can correct.

clinical ecology a recent development in medical science which specializes in ascertaining environmental factors involved in illnesses, particularly those manifesting non-specific symptoms such as fatigue, depression, allergic reactions and immune system malfunctions, and in prescribing means of avoiding or minimizing these effects.

colour therapy the application of light of appropriate wavelength to alleviate ailments or facilitate healing.

crystal therapy the application of crystals to diseased or disordered physical structures or processes to effect healing or stabilizing.

cupping an ancient 'folk medicine' method of drawing blood to the surface of the body by applying cups or glasses in which a vacuum has been created, found to be effective in alleviating (though not curing) rheumatism, lumbago, arthritis, asthma, and bronchitis.

dietetics the prescription of dietary regimens to promote health or healing. Although no one quarrels with the general principle that diet affects health, the preventative or curative effects of specific diets, such as the 'grape cure' or raw vegetable diets sometimes prescribed for cancer patients, are disputed by orthodox medicine.

electrocrystal diagnosis a technique recently developed by British biologist Harry Oldfield, based on the finding that stimulated electromagnetic fields of the human body resonate at a particular frequency which varies with individuals, and that actual or incipient disease can be pinpointed by a scanning device responsive to local deviations from the person's norm.

endogenous endocrinotherapy the fostering of hormonal balance in the body by regulating the activities of the endocrine glands without recourse to introduced stimulants, suppressants or supplements.

fasting total abstinence from food for a limited period is prescribed by some naturopaths to eliminate body toxins or make available for recuperative purposes the energy normally used by the digestive system.

Gerson therapy a radical nutritional therapy for degenerative diseases, particularly cancer, developed by German-born US physician Max Gerson (1881–1959).

hair analysis a diagnostic technique for ascertaining deficiencies or excesses of mineral resources in the body, using a sophisticated analytic procedure called atomic-emission spectroscopy.

hand healing a form of *spiritual healing* in which apparently energy emanating from the healer's hands cures or alleviates a condition suffered by the healee.

herbalism the prescription and use of plants and their derivatives for medication.

holistic medicine umbrella term for an approach that virtually all alternative therapies profess, which considers the overall health and lifestyle profile of a patient, and treats specific ailments not primarily as conditions to be alleviated but rather as symptoms of more fundamental dis-ease.

homoeopathy system of medicine based on the principle that symptoms of disease are part of the body's self-healing processes, and on the practice of administering extremely diluted doses of natural substances found to produce in a healthy person the symptoms manifest in the illness being treated. Developed by German physician Samuel Hahnemann (1755–1843), the system is widely practised today as an alternative to allopathic medicine, and many controlled tests and achieved cures testify to its efficacy.

hydrotherapy the use of water, externally or internally, for health or healing.

hypnotherapy the use of hypnotic trance and post-hypnotic suggestions to relieve stress-related conditions such as insomnia and hypertension, or to break health-inimical habits or addictions.

ionization therapy enhancement of the atmosphere of an environment by instrumentally boosting the negative ion content of the air.

iridology a diagnostic technique based on correspondences between specific areas of the iris and bodily functions and organs, discovered over a century ago independently by a Hungarian and a Swedish physician, and later refined and developed in the USA by Dr Bernard Jensen.

magnet therapy the use of applied magnetic fields to regulate potentially pathogenic disorders in the electrical charges of body cells and structures.

megavitamin therapy the administration of large doses of vitamins to combat conditions considered wholly or in part due to their deficiency.

music therapy the use of music as an adjunct to relaxation healing, or in psychotherapy to elicit expressions of suppressed emotions by prompting patients to dance, shout, laugh, cry or whatever, in response.

naturopathy the facilitating of the natural self-healing processes of the body. Naturopaths are the GPs of alternative medicine and often refer clients to other specialists, particularly in manipulative therapies, to complement their own work of seeking, through diet, the prescription of natural medicines and supplements, and lifestyle counselling, to restore or augment the vitality of the body and thereby its optimum health.

osteopathy a therapy developed over a century ago by US physician Andrew Taylor Still, who maintained that most ailments can be prevented or cured by techniques of spinal manipulation. Osteopaths are generally consulted to treat problems of the musculo-skeletal structure such as back pain, and many doctors refer patients to them for such treatments, but the wider applicability of their skills is not generally recognized.

psionic medicine a system of medical diagnosis and therapy developed by British physician George Lawrence in the 1930s and subsequently. Diagnosis is effected by dowsing a small blood sample with the aid of a pendulum to ascertain deficiencies or imbalances affecting the body's vitality, and treatment by the administration of homoeopathic remedies to combat illness and restore the vital balance.

pulsed high frequency (PHF) the instrumental application of high frequency radio waves in short bursts to damaged tissue to relieve pain, reduce bruising and swelling, and speed healing.

radionics occult healing method said to work on the 'subtle energy' level of the organism, and

the alternative therapy that the orthodox love to deride as of exemplary crankiness. Critics regard the radionic 'black box'—invented early in the century by US physician Albert Adams and later modified by his follower Ruth Drown—as a fraudulent quasi-scientific instrument, though practitioners maintain that it is an enabling device to effect psychic healing at a distance and can adduce numerous successes, both diagnostic and curative.

reflexology manipulation and massage of the feet to ascertain and treat disease or dysfunction elsewhere in the body.

Reichian therapy a general term for a group of body-therapies based on the theory propounded in the 1930s by Austrian/US psychiatrist Wilhelm Reich, that many functional and organic illnesses are attributable to constriction of the flow of vital energies in the body by tensions that become locked into the musculature. Bioenergetics and Rolfing are related approaches.

relaxation therapy entrainment in regular and conscious control of physiological processes and their related emotional and mental states, and of muscular tensions in the body, to avert or alleviate ailments attributable to such stresses. Meditation, hypnotherapy, autogenics, and biofeedback are techniques commonly employed.

Rolfing a technique of deep muscular manipulation developed in the 1960s and '70s by US physiologist Ira Rolf. Also known as 'structural integration', the technique is designed to correct gravitational imbalance in body postures and movements, and to relieve muscular rigidities and inflexibilities, thus enhancing general health and vitality.

shiatsu a Japanese method of massage derived from acupuncture and sometimes referred to as 'acupressure', which treats organic or physiological dysfunctions by applying finger or palm-of-the-hand pressure to parts of the body remote from the affected part.

sound therapy a therapy based on the finding that human blood cells respond to sound

---

THE FEMALE CONDOM

In 1992 the first effective, over-the-counter contraceptive for women became available in the UK. The female condom is a thin polyurethane pouch which fits inside the vagina. It is too early to say whether this condom will be acceptable to consumers, but it is an important advance in contraceptive choice for women.

Why has the female condom been developed? More and more women over 35 wish to remain sexually active. Their doctors advise them against continuing with the contraceptive pill, but they do not want to be sterilized. For such women the only choice has been the intra-uterine device (IUD) or the diaphragm. These are only available from a GP or family-planning clinic. Many women dislike IUDs. There have been fears

of an increased risk of infection and ectopic pregnancy with these devices. They are also associated with heavier periods and occasional discomfort.

The female condom is the only barrier contraceptive that protects women adequately against HIV and other sexually transmitted diseases. This is an important advantage for women of all ages. A woman has always had the option of persuading her partner to wear a conventional condom, but the new device provides extra independence for her.

Chartex, the manufacturer of the new condom, reports that up to 50% of women may prefer the device to the male equivalent. If scientists can develop an effective male contraceptive pill, the symmetry in contraception will be complete.

frequencies by changing colour and shape, and the hypothesis that therefore sick or rogue cells can be healed or harmonized by sound. Currently being developed and researched by French musician and acupuncturist Fabien Maman and US physicist Joel Sternheimer. It is claimed that sound frequencies applied to acupuncture points are as effective as needles.

spiritual healing (or *psychic healing*) the transmission of energy from or through a healer, who may practise hand healing or absent healing through prayer or meditation.

thanatology the study of the psychological aspects of the experiences of death and dying and its application in counselling and assisting the terminally ill. Pioneered by US psychiatrist Elizabeth Kübler-Ross in the 1970s.

visualization the use of guided mental imagery to activate and focus the body's natural self-healing processes. A component of integrated multi-method complementary techniques for the treatment of cancer patients to which some remarkable remissions have been attributed.

vitalistic medicine a generic term for a range of therapies that base their practice on the theory that disease is engendered by energy deficiency in the organism as a whole or dynamic dysfunction in the affected part. Such deficiencies or dysfunctions are regarded as antecedent to the biochemical effects in which disease becomes manifest and upon which orthodox medicine focuses. Acupuncture, crystal therapy, homoeopathy, magnet therapy, naturopathy, radionics, and Reichian therapy are all basically vitalistic.

zone therapy an alternative name for reflexology.

Both the Prime Minister, and the health secretary have recently promised that they will not privatize the health service. Do you believe them or not?

Yes	30
No	57
Don't know	13

INTERNATIONAL ORGANIZATIONS

(excluding United Nations and European Community)

Amazon Pact treaty signed in 1978 by Bolivia, Brazil, Colombia, Ecuador, Guyana, Peru, Surinam, and Venezuela to protect and control the industrial or commercial development of the Amazon River.

Andean Group (Spanish *Grupo Andino*) South American organization aimed at economic and social cooperation between member states. It was established under the Treaty of Cartagena 1969, by Bolivia, Chile, Colombia, Ecuador, and Peru; Venezuela joined 1973, but Chile withdrew 1976. The organization is based in Lima, Peru.

Antarctic Treaty international agreement aiming to promote scientific research and keep Antarctica free from conflict. The agreement was signed 1959 between 12 nations with an interest in Antarctica (including Britain), and came into force 1961 for a 30-year period; by 1990 a total of 35 countries were party to it. In 1980 the treaty was extended to conserve marine resources within the larger area bordered by the Antarctic Convergence. In 1991 a 50-year ban on mining activity was secured.

Arab League organization of Arab states established in Cairo 1945 to promote Arab unity, primarily in opposition to Israel. The original members were Egypt, Syria, Iraq, Lebanon, Transjordan (Jordan 1949), Saudi Arabia, and Yemen. In 1979 Egypt was suspended and the league's headquarters transferred to Tunis in protest against the Egypt-Israeli peace, but Egypt was readmitted as a full member May 1989, and in March 1990 its headquarters returned to Cairo.

Arab Maghreb Union (AMU) association formed 1989 by Algeria, Libya, Morocco, and Tunisia to formulate common policies on military, economic, international, and cultural issues. The AMU issued proposals for ending the Gulf conflict 1990–91.

Asian and Pacific Council (ASPAC) organization established 1966 to encourage cultural and economic cooperation in Oceania and Asia. Its members include Australia, Japan, South Korea, Malaysia, New Zealand, the Philippines, Taiwan, and Thailand.

Asia-Pacific Economic Cooperation Conference (APEC) trade group comprising 12 Pacific Asian countries, formed Nov 1898 to promote multilateral trade and economic cooperation between member states. Its members are the USA, Canada, Japan, Australia, New Zealand, South Korea, Brunei, Indonesia, Malaysia, the Philippines, Singapore, and Thailand.

Association of South East Asian Nations (ASEAN) regional alliance formed in Bangkok 1967; it took over the nonmilitary role of the Southeast Asia Treaty Organization 1975. Its members are Indonesia, Malaysia, the Philippines, Singapore, Thailand, and (from 1984) Brunei; its headquarters are in Jakarta, Indonesia. The six member states signed an agreement 1992 to establish an ASEAN free trade area (AFTA) by the beginning of 2008.

Benelux (acronym from *Bel*gium, the *Net*herlands, and *Lux*embourg) customs union agreed by Belgium, the Netherlands, and Luxembourg 1944, fully effective 1960. It was the precursor of the European Community.

Caribbean Community and Common Market (CARICOM) organization for economic and foreign policy coordination in the Caribbean region, established by the Treaty of Chaguaramas 1973 to replace the former Caribbean Free Trade Association. Its members are Antigua and Barbuda, Bahamas, Barbados, Belize, Dominica, Grenada, Guyana, Jamaica, Montserrat, St Christopher–Nevis, St Lucia, St Vincent and the Grenadines, and Trinidad and Tobago. The British Virgin Islands and the Turks and Caicos Islands are associate members, and the Dominican Republic, Haiti, Mexico, Puerto Rico, Surinam, and Venezuela are observers. CARICOM headquarters are in Kingston, Jamaica.

CERN nuclear research organization founded 1954 as a cooperative enterprise among European governments. It has laboratories at Meyrin, near Geneva, Switzerland. It was originally known as the *Conseil Européen pour la Recherche Nucléaire* but subsequently renamed *Organisation Européenne pour la Recherche Nucléaire*, although still familiarly known as CERN. It houses the world's largest particle accelerator, the Large Electron–Positron Collider (LEP), with which notable advances have been made in particle physics.

Commonwealth of Independent States (CIS) successor body to the Union of Soviet Socialist Republics, established Jan 1992 by 11 out of the 12 former constituent republics of the USSR (Georgia did not join). It has no real, formal political institutions and its role is uncertain. Its headquarters are in Mensk (Minsk), Belarus.

Conference on Security and Cooperation in Europe (CSCE) international forum attempting to reach agreement in security, economics, science, technology, and human rights. The CSCE first met at the Helsinki Conference in Finland 1975. By the end of March 1992, having admitted the former republics of the USSR, as well as Croatia and Slovenia, its membership had risen to 51 states.

A second conference in Paris Nov 1990 was hailed as marking the formal end of the Cold War. Reversing a long-standing policy of noninterference in members' internal affairs, the CSCE agreed in 1991 that fact-finding teams could be sent to investigate alleged human-rights abuses in any of the member countries.

A ministerial bureaucracy, an Office for Democratic Institutions, and a Conflict Prevention Centre were established 1992. Bosnia and Macedonia applied for admission 1992.

Council of Europe body constituted 1949 in Strasbourg, France (still its headquarters), to secure 'a greater measure of unity between the European countries'. The widest association of European states, it has a *Committee* of foreign ministers, a *Parliamentary Assembly* (with members from national parliaments), and a *European Commission* investigating violations of human rights.

The first session of the *Consultative Assembly* opened Aug 1949, the members then being the UK, France, Italy, Belgium, the Netherlands, Sweden, Denmark, Norway, the Republic of Ireland, Luxembourg, Greece, and Turkey; Iceland, Germany, Austria, Cyprus, Switzerland, Malta, Portugal, Spain, Liechtenstein, Finland, and San Marino joined subsequently. With the collapse of communism in E Europe, the Council acquired a new role in assisting the establishment of Western-style democratic and accountable political systems in the region, and several countries applied for membership. Hungary joined 1990, Czechoslovakia and Poland 1991; Romania and Yugoslavia applied for membership 1991 and Albania for observer status.

Council of the Entente (CE, Conseil de l'Entente) organization of W African states for strengthening economic links and promoting industrial development. It was set up 1959 by Benin, Burkina Faso, Ivory Coast, and Niger; Togo joined 1966 when a Mutual Aid and Loan Guarantee Fund was established. The headquarters of the CE are in Abidja'n, Côte d'Ivoire.

Danube Commission organization that ensures the freedom of navigation on the river Danube, from Ulm in Germany to the Black Sea, to people, shipping, and merchandise of all states, in conformity with the Danube Convention 1948. The commission comprises representatives of all the states through which the Danube flows: Germany, Austria, Czechoslovakia, Hungary, Bulgaria, and Romania. Its headquarters are in Budapest, Hungary.

Economic Community of Central African States (CEEAC, Communauté Economique des Etats de l'Afrique Centrale) organization formed 1983 to foster economic cooperation between member states, which include Burundi, Cameroon, Central African Republic, Chad, Congo, Equatorial Guinea, Gabon, Rwanda, São Tomé and Principe, and Zaire. Angola has observer status.

Economic Community of West African States (ECOWAS, Communauté Economique des Etats de l'Afrique de l'Ouest) organization for the promotion of economic cooperation and development, established 1975 by the Treaty of Lagos. Its members include Benin, Burkina Faso, Cape Verde, Gambia, Ghana, Guinea, Guinea-Bissau, Ivory Coast, Liberia, Mali Mauritania, Niger, Nigeria, Senegal, Sierra Leone, and Togo. Its headquarters are in Lagos, Nigeria.

Economic Cooperation Organization (ECO) Islamic regional grouping formed 1985 by Iran, Pakistan, and Turkey to reduce customs tariffs and promote commerce, with the aim of eventual customs union. In 1992 the newly independent former Soviet republics of Azerbaijan, Turkmenistan, and Uzbekistan were admitted into the ECO.

European Free Trade Association (EFTA) organization established 1960 consisting of Austria, Finland, Iceland, Norway, Sweden, Switzerland, and (from 1991) Liechtenstein, previously a nonvoting associate member. There are no import duties between members.

Of the original members, Britain and Denmark left (1972) to join the European Community, as did Portugal (1985). A pact signed Oct 1991 between the EC and EFTA provided for a European Economic Area (EEA) to be set up, allowing EFTA greater access to the EC market by ending many of the restrictions currently imposed. The area would span 19 nations and 380 million people. Subject to ratification by the European Parliament, the provisions are expected to take effect from Jan 1993.

European Space Agency (ESA) an organization of European countries (Austria, Belgium, Denmark, France, Germany, Ireland, Italy, the Netherlands, Norway, Spain, Sweden, Switzerland, and the UK) that engages in space research and technology. It was founded 1975, with headquarters in Paris.

G7 or *Group of Seven* the seven wealthiest nations in the world: the USA, Japan, Germany, France, the UK, Italy, and Canada. Since 1975 their heads of government have met once a year to discuss economic and, increasingly, political matters. The eighteenth meeting was held in Munich July 1992. As at the 1991 London summit, when Mikhail Gorbachev still held office, President Yeltsin of Russia was invited to a final session, presaging a possible eventual expansion of G7 into G8.

Gulf Cooperation Council (GCC) Arab organization for promoting peace in the Persian Gulf area, established 1981. Its declared purpose is 'to bring about integration, coordination, and cooperation in economic, social, defence, and political affairs among Arab Gulf states'. Its members include Bahrain, Kuwait, Oman, Qatar, Saudi Arabia, and the United Arab Emirates; its headquarters are in Riyadh, Saudi Arabia.

Inter-American Development Bank (IADB) bank founded 1959, at the instigation of the Organization of American States, to finance economic and social development, particularly in the less wealthy regions of the Americas. Its membership includes Austria, Belgium, Canada, Denmark, Finland, France, Germany, Israel, Italy, Japan, the Netherlands, Spain, Sweden, Switzerland, and the UK, as well as the states of Central and Southern America, the Caribbean, and the USA. Its headquarters are in Washington DC.

Islamic Conference Organization (ICO) association of 44 states in the Middle East, Africa, and Asia, established 1971 to promote Islamic solidarity between member countries, and to consolidate economic, social, cultural, and scientific cooperation. Its headquarters are in Niger.

Latin American Economic System (Sistema Economico Latino-Americana LAES/SELA) international organization for economic, technological, and scientific cooperation in Latin America, aiming to create and promote multinational enterprises in the region and provide markets. Founded in 1975 as the successor to the Latin American Economic Coordination Commission, it has 26 members in Central and South America and parts of the Caribbean, with headquarters in Caracas, Venezuela.

Latin American Integration Association (Asociacion Latino-Americana de Integration ALADI) organization aiming to create a common market in Latin America; to promote trade it applies tariff reductions preferentially on the basis of the different stages of economic development that individual member countries have reached. Formed in 1980 to replace the Latin American Free Trade Association, it has 11 member countries, all in South America except Mexico. Its headquarters are in Montevideo, Uruguay.

Lomé Convention convention in 1975 that established economic cooperation between the European Community and African, Caribbean, and Pacific countries. It was renewed 1979 and 1985.

North Atlantic Treaty Organization (NATO) association set up 1949 to provide for the collective defence of the major W European and North American states against the perceived threat from the USSR. Its chief body is the Council of Foreign Ministers (who have representatives in permanent session), and there is an international secretariat in Brussels, Belgium, and also the Military Committee consisting of the Chiefs of Staff. The military headquarters SHAPE (Supreme Headquarters Allied Powers, Europe) is in Chièvres, near Mons, Belgium. After the E European Warsaw Pact was disbanded 1991, an adjunct to NATO, the *North Atlantic Cooperation Council*, was established, including all the former Soviet republics, with the aim of building greater security in Europe.

Organisation Commune Africaine et Mauricienne (OCAM; French 'Joint African and Mauritian Organization') organization founded 1965 to strengthen the solidarity and close ties between member states, raise living standards, and coordinate economic policies. The membership includes Benin, Burkina Faso, Central African Republic, Ivory Coast, Niger, Rwanda, Senegal, and Togo. Through the organization, members share an airline, a merchant fleet, and a common postal and communications system. The headquarters of OCAM are in Bangui in the Central African Republic.

Organization for Economic Cooperation and Development (OECD) international organization of 24 industrialized countries that provides a forum for discussion and coordination of member states' economic and social policies. Founded 1961, with its headquarters in Paris, the OECD superseded the Organization for European Economic Cooperation, which had been established 1948 to implement the Marshall Plan.

Organization of African Unity (OAU) association established 1963 to eradicate colonialism and improve economic, cultural, and political cooperation in Africa; headquarters Addis Ababa, Ethiopia. Its membership expanded to 51 countries when Namibia joined after independence 1990. The secretary general is Salim Ahmed Salim of Tanzania.

Organization of American States (OAS) association founded 1948 by a charter signed by representatives of 30 North, Central, and South American states. It aims to maintain peace and solidarity within the hemisphere, and is also concerned with the social and economic development of Latin America.

The OAS is based on the International Union of American Republics 1890–1910 and Pan-American Union 1910–48, set up to encourage friendly relations between countries of North and South America. Cuba became suspended from membership 1962. Canada held observer status from 1972 and became a full member 1990. Belize and Guyana were admitted 1991, by which time OAS membership had expanded to 35. Its headquarters are in Washington DC.

Organization of Arab Petroleum Exporting Countries (OAPEC) body established 1968 to safeguard the interests of its members and encourage cooperation in economic activity within the petroleum industry. Its members are Algeria, Bahrain, Egypt, Iraq, Kuwait, Libya, Qatar, Saudi Arabia, Syria, and the United Arab Emirates; its headquarters are in Kuwait.

Organization of Central American States ODECA (Organización de Estados Centroamericanos) international association promoting common economic, political, educational, and military aims in Central America. Its members are Costa Rica, El Salvador, Guatemala, Honduras, and Nicaragua, provision being made for Panama to join at a later date. The first organization, established 1951, was superseded 1962. ODECA comprises executive, legislative, and economic councils and the Central American Court of Justice; it was responsible for establishing the Central American Common Market 1960. Its permanent headquarters are in Guatemala City.

Organization of Petroleum-Exporting Countries (OPEC) body established 1960 to coordinate price and supply policies of oil-producing states, and also to improve the position of Third World states by forcing Western states to open their markets to the resultant products. Its concerted action in raising prices in the 1970s triggered worldwide recession but also lessened demand so that the influence of OPEC was markedly reduced by the mid-1980s.

OPEC members in 1991 were: Algeria, Ecuador, Gabon, Indonesia, Iran, Iraq, Kuwait, Libya, Nigeria, Qatar, Saudi Arabia, the United Arab Emirates, and Venezuela.

Preferential Trade Area for Eastern and Southern African States (PTA) organization established 1981 with the object of increasing economic and commercial cooperation between member states, harmonizing tariffs, and reducing trade barriers, with the eventual aim of creating a common market. Members include (1992) Angola, Burundi, Comoros, Djibouti, Ethiopia, Kenya, Lesotho, Malawi, Mauritius, Mozambique, Rwanda, Somalia, Sudan, Swaziland, Tanzania, Uganda, Zaire, Zambia, and Zimbabwe. The headquarters of the PTA are in Lusaka, Zambia.

Rarotonga Treaty agreement that formally declares the South Pacific a nuclear-free zone. The treaty was signed 1987 by Australia, Fiji, Indonesia, New Zealand, and the USSR.

Southeast Asia Treaty Organization (SEATO) collective defence system 1954–77 established by Australia, France, New Zealand, Pakistan, the Philippines, Thailand, the UK, and the USA, with Vietnam, Cambodia, and Laos as protocol states. After the Vietnam War, SEATO was phased out.

Southern African Development Coordination Conference (SADCC) organization of countries in the region working together to reduce their economic dependence on South Africa. It was established 1980 and focuses on transport and communications, energy, mining, and industrial production. The member states are Angola, Botswana, Lesotho, Malawi, Mozambique, Namibia, Swaziland, Tanzania, Zambia, and Zimbabwe; its headquarters are in Gaborone, Botswana.

South Pacific Bureau for Economic Cooperation (SPEC) organization founded 1973 for the purpose of stimulating economic cooperation and the development of trade in the region. The headquarters of SPEC are in Suva, Fiji.

South Pacific Commission (SPC) organization to promote economic and social cooperation in the region, established 1947. Its members include most of the sovereign and dependent states in the South Pacific, plus France, the UK, and the USA; headquarters in Nouméa, New Caledonia.

South Pacific Forum (SPF) association of states in the region to discuss common interests and develop common policies, created 1971 as an offshoot of the South Pacific Commission. Member countries include (1992) Australia, Cook Islands, Fiji, Kiribati, Marshall Islands, the Federated States of Micronesia, Nauru, New Zealand, Niue, Papua New Guinea, Solomon Islands, Tonga, Tuvalu, Vanuatu, and Western Samoa. In 1985 the forum adopted a treaty for creating a nuclear-free zone in the Pacific.

Unrepresented Nations' and Peoples' Organization (UNPO) international association founded 1991 to represent ethnic and minority groups (unrecognized by the United Nations) and to defend the right to self-determination of oppressed peoples around the world. The founding charter was signed by representatives of Tibet, the Kurds, Turkestan, Armenia, Estonia, Georgia, the Volga region, the Crimea, the Greek minority in Albania, North American Indians, Australian Aborigines, West Irians, West Papuans, the minorities of the Cordillera in the Philippines, and the non-Chinese in Taiwan.

Warsaw Pact or *Eastern European Mutual Assistance Pact* military alliance 1955–91 between the USSR and East European communist states, originally established as a response to the admission of West Germany into NATO. Its military structures and agreements were dismantled early in 1991; a political organization remained until the alliance was officially dissolved July 1991.

Western European Union (WEU) organization established 1955 as a consultative forum for military issues among the W European governments: Belgium, France, the Netherlands, Italy, Luxembourg, the UK, Germany, and (from 1988) Spain and Portugal.

World Council of Churches (WCC) international organization aiming to bring together diverse movements within the Christian church. Established 1945, it had by 1988 a membership of more than 100 countries and more than 300 churches; its headquarters are in Geneva, Switzerland.

THE EUROPEAN COMMUNITY (EC)

Member states

1957: (founder members) Belgium, France, West Germany, Italy, Luxembourg, Netherlands. 1973: Denmark, Ireland, UK. 1981: Greece. 1986: Portugal and Spain.

Background

Following World War II, those countries that had experienced the war first hand—France, Belgium, Luxembourg, Netherlands, West Germany, and Italy—took steps to set up institutions which would make another war in Europe virtually impossible. The first such institution to be established was the European Steel and Coal Community (ESC) in 1952, based on the premise that if the leading European nations shared coal and steel-making facilities (seen as the basic raw materials of war) future conflicts would be avoided. 1957 saw the momentous signing of treaties in Rome which established the European Economic Community (EEC) and the European Atomic Energy Community (Euratom).

Other Western European countries remained aloof, resisting the prospect of eventual political integration, and, led by the UK, formed a purely economic association, the European Free Trade Association (EFTA). The EEC grew in strength and influence, while EFTA declined, leading the UK eventually to apply for membership. After two attempts at entry in 1963 and 1967, blocked largely by France, the UK became a full member in 1973, along with Denmark, Ireland, and Norway. Norway withdrew soon afterwards, but membership continued to grow. In 1990 the former East Germany was admitted as part of unified Germany. In 1991 association agreements were signed with Czechoslovakia, Hungary, and Poland, providing for free trade within ten years and the possibility of eventual full EC membership.

Aims

The establishment of a closer union among European peoples; the improvement of their working and living conditions; the progressive abolition of trading restrictions between them; and the encouragement of free movement of capital and labour within the community.

EC institutions and policies collectively constitute an economic, social, and potentially political system which is still developing and which could become, if all member states eventually agree, a single European state. Steps towards monetary union have already been taken in the form of the EMS and the European currency unit (ECU), but the community remains divided over the question of political unity, the UK in particular resisting any move which may weaken national sovereignty and decision-making powers.

Throughout 1991, following a summit meeting in Rome in December 1990, a series of intergovernmental conferences on European political union (EPU) and European monetary union (EMU) were held, culminating in a crucial summit at Maastricht in December 1991. This summit secured agreement by the 12 heads of government on a treaty framework for European union, including political and monetary union, with a timetable for implementation, and for a new system of security and military EC cooperation. A European Charter of Social Rights was also approved at Maastricht by all members except the UK. All members are committed to the establishment of a single market with free movement of goods and capital from Jan 1993.

Almost 60% of the EC's budget in 1990 was spent on supporting farmers; of this, £4 billion a year went to dairy farmers, because the dairy quotas, which were introduced 1984, were 14% greater than EC consumption. 30 million tonnes of excess grain were exported annually at a subsidized price. Altogether it cost member countries' taxpayers almost 9 billion in 1989–90 to maintain the international competitiveness of the EC's overpriced produce under CAP. A major reform of CAP, agreed 1992 by EC ministers, aimed to lower support costs and reduce prices of agricultural products.

Constituent institutions and policies

Common Agricultural Policy
(CAP)
established 1962
purpose to ensure reasonable standards of living for farmers in member states by controlling outputs, giving financial grants, and supporting prices to even out fluctuations
base Brussels

European Atomic Energy Commission
(EURATOM)
established 1957
purpose the cooperation of member states in nuclear research and the development of large-scale nonmilitary nuclear energy
base Brussels

European Coal and Steel Community
(ECS)
established 1952
purpose the creation of a single European market for coal, iron ore, and steel by the abolition of customs duties and quantitative restrictions
base Brussels

European Court of Justice
established 1957
purpose to ensure the treaties that established the Community are observed and to adjudicate on disputes between members on the interpretation and application of the laws of the Community
base Luxembourg

European Economic Community
(EEC), popularly called the Common Market
established 1957
purpose the creation of a single European market for the products of member states by the abolition of tariffs and other restrictions on trade
base Brussels

European Investment Bank
(EIB)
established 1958
purpose to finance capital investment that will assist the steady development of the Community
base Brussels

European Monetary System
(EMS)
established 1979
purpose to bring financial cooperation and monetary stability to the Community. Central to the EMS is the Exchange Rate Mechanism (ERM), which is a voluntary arrangement whereby members agree to their currencies being fixed within certain limits. The value of each currency is related to the European Currency Unit (ECU), which, it is anticipated, will eventually become the single currency for all member states. If the currency of any one member state moves outside the agreed limits, its government must buy or sell to avert the trend

THE EUROPEAN COMMUNITY: WHICH WAY FORWARD?

When the heads of government of the European Community came to an agreement at Maastricht on 11 Dec 1991, advocates of closer political and economic union saw it as a triumph. Anti-Community critics saw it as surrendering national sovereignty to the unelected Brussels bureaucrats.

The Maastricht agreement set out a timetable leading to full European Monetary Union (EMU) (see table). By the end of the century, Community members would have a single currency under a European central bank, and common foreign and defence policies. The next phase would be a federal Europe, with an enhanced role for the European Parliament and a recast role for the European Commission. Europhiles would welcome this as a democratization of the Community. Eurosceptics would see it as the end of national identities.

This timetable assumed that all 12 member states would ratify the Maastricht agreement. In June 1992 the Danish electorate rejected a treaty based on it. This threw the timetable into doubt, and forced the Commission and ministers to review and reconstruct it. Members of the Commission and most heads of government saw the Danish vote as a major obstacle to achieving Maastricht's aims. Eurosceptics saw it as vindicating their opposition to the creation of a federal system.

There is increasing opposition to greater integration. Supporters of Maastricht have pointed to the important idea of 'subsidiarity' which is inherent in the agreement. This means that the Community will act at the lowest level possible—regional, national, or local—and reserve supranational action for only a few decisions.

The electorate of Denmark either failed to understand what Maastricht was really about or, if they did, disliked what they saw. They felt that their bigger neighbours were overpowering them—notably Germany. The original motivation for creating the Community was to bring Germany into the European fold, and so ensure that another European war could not occur. Apparently the Danes did not believe that a reunited Germany outside the Community posed a greater threat than within it. What persuaded them to say no? Perhaps it was the failure of the Danish political leaders to explain the issues, or perhaps it was the overenthusiastic pronouncements of the European Commission's president, Jacques Delors. Meanwhile, there is a queue of new Community applicants. It includes Austria, Cyprus, Finland, Malta, Norway, Sweden, Switzerland, and Turkey. Will the Danish rejection of Maastricht affect their enthusiasm for membership? That remains to be seen.

The founder members of the Community see greater integration as more important than enlargement—as do the Commission. But not all the later members share this view. While member states were still considering ratifying the Maastricht agreement, the UK's John Major was advocating the eventual inclusion of the newly liberated eastern European states. This may have come from a genuine desire to help the democratization of Eastern Europe—or it may have been a subtle way of slowing integration by a process of dilution.

Closer membership of the Community means integrating political, social, and defence policies, not just operating a free trade area. Wider membership like that envisaged by John Major and others makes this look impracticable. The Community began after the war as a noble vision. It could now deteriorate into a squalid squabble about national interests. The Community still has great potential for creating permanent peace and prosperity for Europe. It requires a leader with sufficient courage and stature to rekindle the original vision and realize that potential.

POST–MAASTRICHT TIMETABLE TOWARDS EUROPEAN UNION

March 1992	Signature of treaties on political, economic and monetary union.
June 1992	Lisbon summit to agree future financing of EC.
January 1993	Single internal market implemented.
Early 1993	Earliest date for negotiations with new applicants for EC membership.
December 1993	Decision on whether asylum policy should be dealt with on a Community basis.
January 1994	Start of second stage of EMU; European Monetary Institute (EMI) set up.
June 1994	Elections to the European Parliament (EP).
1996	Conference to review Community foreign and defence policy.
December 1996	Decision on move to stage three of EMU, if member states can converge their economies sufficiently. Deadline for the UK to notify its intention, or not, to move to stage three.
July 1998	Deadline for setting up European central bank and European system of central banks.
December 1998	Expiry of Brussels treaty establishing Western European Union (WEU).
January 1999	Latest date for stage three of EMU and introduction of single currency.

Central organs and methods of working of the Community

European Commission

membership 17: two each from France, Germany, Italy, Spain, and the UK; and one each from Belgium, Denmark, Greece, Ireland, Luxembourg, the Netherlands, and Portugal. The members are pledged to independence of national interests, and are nominated by each state for a four-year, renewable term of office. One member is chosen as president for a two-year, renewable term. The post of president is a mixture of head of government and head of the European civil service

operational methods the commissioners are drawn proportionally from member states, and each takes an oath on appointment not to promote national interests. They head a comparatively large bureaucracy, with 20 directorates-general, each responsible for a particular department

base Brussels

Council of Ministers

membership one minister from each of the 12 member countries

operational methods it is the supreme decision-taking body of the Community. The representatives vary according to the subject matter under discussion. If it is economic policy, it will be the finance ministers; if it is agricultural policy, the agriculture ministers. It is the foreign ministers, however, who tend to be the most active. The presidency of the Council changes hands at six-monthly intervals, each member state taking its turn

base Brussels

Committee of Permanent Representatives (COREPER)

membership a subsidiary body of officials, often called 'ambassadors', who act on behalf of the Council. The members of COREPER are senior civil servants who have been temporarily released by member states to work for the Community

operational methods COREPER receives proposals from the Council of Ministers for consideration in detail before the Council decides on action

base Brussels

Economic and Social Committee

membership representatives from member countries covering a wide range of interests, including employers, trade unionists, professional people, and farmers

operational methods a consultative body advisin the Council of Ministers and the Commission

base Brussels

European Parliament

membership determined by the populations of member states. The total number of seats is 518, of which France, Germany, Italy, and the UK have 81 each, Spain has 60, the Netherlands 25, Belgium, Greece, and Portugal 24 each, Denmark 16, Ireland 15, and Luxembourg 6. Members are elected for five-year terms in large Euro-constituencies. Voting is by a system of proportional representation in all countries except the UK

role and powers mainly consultative, but it does have power to reject the Community budget and to dismiss the Commission if it has good grounds for doing so. It debates Community present and future policies and its powers will undoubtedly grow as the political nature of the Community becomes clearer

base Luxembourg and Strasbourg

UNITED NATIONS

The UN is an association of states for international peace, security, and cooperation, with its headquarters in New York. The UN was established 1945 as a successor to the League of Nations, and has played a role in many areas, such as refugee aid and resettlement, development assistance, disaster relief, and cultural cooperation.

Its total budget for 1992/93 was $2,006 million. Boutros Boutros Ghali succeeded Javier Pérez de Cuellar as secretary-general in 1992.

Members contribute financially according to their resources, an apportionment being made by the General Assembly, with the addition of voluntary contributions from some governments to the funds of the UN. These finance the programme of assistance carried out by the UN intergovernmental agencies, the **United Nations Children's Fund** (UNICEF), the UN refugee organizations, and the **United Nations Special Fund** for developing countries. Javier Pérez de Cuellar, the former outgoing secretary-general, reported in December 1991 that total unpaid contributions approximating $988 million had brought the UN to the brink of insolvency. Fewer than half the members had paid their full contributions.

There are six official working languages used within the UN: English, French, Russian, Spanish, Chinese, and Arabic.

Background

The UN charter was drawn up at the San Francisco Conference 1945, based on proposals drafted at the Dumbarton Oaks conference held in Washington DC in 1944 between the World War II allies—the USSR, the UK, and the USA. The original intention was that the UN's Security Council would preserve this alliance (with France and China also permanent members) in order to maintain the peace. This never happened because of the outbreak of the Cold War between the two superpowers, the USSR and the USA.

The influence in the UN, originally with the Allied states of World War II, is now more widely spread. Although part of the value of the UN lies in the recognition of member states as sovereign and equal, the rapid increase in membership of minor—in some cases minute—states was causing concern by 1980 (154 members) as lessening the weight of voting decisions. Taiwan, formerly a permanent member of the Security Council, was expelled 1971 on the admission of

UN MEMBERSHIP

country	year of admission	contribution to UN budget (%)	country	year of admission	contribution to UN budget (%)
Afghanistan	1946	0.01	Haiti †	1945	0.01
Albania	1955	0.01	Honduras †	1945	0.01
Algeria	1962	0.16	Hungary	1955	0.18
Angola	1976	0.01	Iceland	1946	0.03
Antigua & Barbuda	1981	0.01	India †	1945	0.36
Argentina †	1945	0.57	Indonesia	1950	0.16
Australia †	1945	1.51	Iran †	1945	0.77
Austria	1955	0.75	Iraq †	1945	0.13
Bahamas	1973	0.02	Ireland	1955	0.18
Bahrain	1971	0.03	Israel	1949	0.23
Bangladesh	1974	0.01	Italy	1955	4.29
Barbados	1966	0.01	Ivory Coast	1960	0.02
Belarus †	1945	0.31	Jamaica	1962	0.01
Belgium †	1945	1.06	Japan	1956	12.45
Belize	1981	0.01	Jordan	1955	0.01
Benin	1960	0.01	Kenya	1963	0.01
Bhutan	1971	0.01	Kuwait	1963	0.25
Bolivia †	1945	0.01	Laos	1955	0.01
Botswana	1966	0.01	Latvia	1991	***
Brazil †	1945	1.59	Lebanon †	1945	0.01
Brunei	1984	0.03	Lesotho	1966	0.01
Bulgaria	1955	0.13	Liberia †	1945	0.01
Burkina Faso	1960	0.01	Libya	1955	0.24
Burundi	1962	0.01	Liechtenstein	1990	0.01
Cambodia	1955	0.01	Lithuania	1991	***
Cameroon	1960	0.01	Luxembourg †	1945	0.06
Canada †	1945	3.11	Madagascar	1960	0.01
Cape Verde	1975	0.01	Malawi	1964	0.01
Central African Republic	1960	0.01	Malaysia	1957	0.12
Chad	1960	0.01	Maldives	1965	0.01
Chile †	1945	0.08	Mali	1960	0.01
China †	1945	0.77	Malta	1964	0.01
Colombia †	1945	0.13	Marshall Islands	1991	0.01
Comoros	1975	0.01	Mauritania	1961	0.01
Congo	1960	0.01	Mauritius	1968	0.01
Costa Rica †	1945	0.01	Mexico †	1945	0.88
Cuba †	1945	0.09	Micronesia	1991	0.01
Cyprus	1960	0.02	Mongolia	1961	0.01
Czechoslovakia †	1945	0.55	Morocco	1956	0.03
Denmark †	1945	0.65	Mozambique	1975	0.01
Djibouti	1977	0.01	Myanmar (Burma)	1948	0.01
Dominica	1978	0.01	Namibia	1990	0.01
Dominican Republic †	1945	0.02	Nepal	1955	0.01
Ecuador †	1945	0.03	Netherlands †	1945	1.50
Egypt †	1945	0.07	New Zealand †	1945	0.24
El Salvador †	1945	0.01	Nicaragua †	1945	0.01
Equatorial Guinea	1968	0.01	Niger	1960	0.01
Estonia	1991	***	Nigeria	1960	0.20
Ethiopia †	1945	0.01	North Korea	1991	0.05
Fiji	1970	0.01	Norway †	1945	0.55
Finland	1955	0.57	Oman	1971	0.03
France †	1945	6.00	Pakistan	1947	0.06
Gabon	1960	0.02	Panama †	1945	0.02
Gambia	1965	0.01	Papua New Guinea	1975	0.01
Germany **	1973/1990	8.93	Paraguay †	1945	0.03
Ghana	1957	0.01	Peru †	1945	0.06
Greece †	1945	0.35	Philippines †	1945	0.07
Grenada	1974	0.01	Poland †	1945	0.47
Guatemala †	1945	0.02	Portugal	1955	0.20
Guinea	1958	0.01	Qatar	1971	0.05
Guinea-Bissau	1974	0.01	Romania	1955	0.17
Guyana	1966	0.01	Russian Federation *	1991	9.41

UN MEMBERSHIP (cont.)

country	year of admission	contribution to UN budget (%)	country	year of admission	contribution to UN budget (%)
Rwanda	1962	0.01	Tanzania	1961	0.01
St Christopher & Nevis	1983	0.01	Thailand	1946	0.11
St Lucia	1979	0.01	Togo	1960	0.01
St Vincent & Grenadines	1980	0.01	Trinidad & Tobago	1962	0.05
São Tomé e Principe	1975	0.01	Tunisia	1956	0.03
Saudi Arabia †	1945	0.96	Turkey †	1945	0.27
Senegal	1960	0.01	Uganda	1962	0.01
Seychelles	1976	0.01	Ukraine †	1945	1.18
Sierra Leone	1961	0.01	United Arab Emirates	1971	0.21
Singapore	1965	0.12	United Kingdom †	1945	5.02
Solomon Isles	1978	0.01	United States of America †	1945	25.00
Somalia	1960	0.01	Uruguay †	1945	0.04
South Africa †	1945	0.41	Vanuatu	1981	0.01
South Korea	1991	0.69	Venezuela †	1945	0.49
Spain	1955	1.98	Vietnam	1977	0.01
Sri Lanka	1955	0.01	Western Samoa	1976	0.01
Sudan	1956	0.01	Yemen **	1947	0.01
Surinam	1975	0.01	Yugoslavia †	1945	0.42
Swaziland	1968	0.01	Zaire	1960	0.01
Sweden	1946	1.11	Zambia	1964	0.01
Syria †	1945	0.04	Zimbabwe	1980	0.02

† founder members   * Became a separate member upon the demise of the USSR which was a founder member 1945   ** represented by two countries until unification in 1990   *** contributions to be determined

China. The break up of the USSR and the increasing recognition of independent states throughout the world resulted in a significant increase in UN membership between 1990 and 1992. In particular, the major role formerly played by the USSR fell to the Russian Federation, led by Boris Yeltsin. The USA regularly (often alone or nearly so) votes against General Assembly resolutions on aggression, international law, human-rights abuses, and disarmament, and has exercised its veto on the Security Council more times than any other member (the UK is second, France a distant third).

The UN suffers from a lack of adequate and independent funds and forces (the latter having been employed with varying success, for example in Korea, Cyprus, and Sinai), and, until recently, from the political polarization resulting from the Cold War, which divided members into adherents of the East or West and the uncommitted. However, during his period of office as UN secretary general, Javier Pérez de Cuellar was responsible for several successful peace initiatives, including the ending of the Iran–Iraq war.

The UN also responded promptly to the Iraqi invasion of Kuwait but was less successful in its efforts to establish a permanent peace in the troubled republics of Yugoslavia.

The principal UN institutions (all based in New York except the International Court of Justice in The Hague) are:

General Assembly the General Assembly is the UN parliament of which all nations are members, each having one vote. Representatives from each of 175 member states meet annually for a session generally lasting from late Sept to the end of the year; it can be summoned at any time for an emergency session. Decisions are made by simple majority voting, but on certain important issues, such as the condemnation of an act by one of its members, a two-thirds majority is needed;

Security Council five permanent members (China, France, UK, USA, the Russian Federation, with the power of veto, so their support is requisite for all decisions), plus ten others, elected for two-year terms by a two-thirds vote of the General Assembly; retiring members are not eligible for re-election. Any UN member may be invited to participate in the Security Council's discussions (though not to vote) if they bear on its interests. The council may undertake investigations into disputes and make recommendations to the parties concerned and may call on all members to take economic or military measures to enforce its decisions; it has at its disposal a Military Staff Committee, composed of the chiefs of staff of the permanent member countries. The presidency of the Security Council is held for a month at a time by a representative of a member state, in English-language alphabetical order;

Economic and Social Council 54 members elected for three years, one-third retiring in rotation; presidency rotating on same system as Security Council. It initiates studies of international economic, social, cultural, educational, health, and related matters, and may make recommendations to the General Assembly. It operates largely through specialized commissions of international experts on economics, transport and communications, human rights, status of women, and so on,

THE UNITED NATIONS: PEACEKEEPER OR PEACEMAKER?

According to the charter of the United Nations, one of its main aims is to maintain international peace and security. It does this through the Security Council. The five permanent and ten rotating members of the Council can require or allow the governments of member states to take action to maintain peace. For example, on 29 Nov 1990 UN resolution 678 authorized governments to use 'all necessary means' to ensure that Iraq withdrew completely from occupied Kuwait. This was the first resolution authorizing the use of force since June 1950, when the Korean War began.

The UN could not have embarked on the Korean War or the Gulf conflict without the interest of the major powers, and particularly the USA. In such situations it has always been the major powers, led by the USA, that have provided the necessary weapons and troops. Does this mean that the world's one remaining military superpower only ever acts out of self-interest, using the UN as a front for its national objectives? Opinions differ.

However, even without USA involvement, the UN has become an important international peacekeeper through the deployment of troops, supplied by member states but all under UN command and all wearing the famous blue beret. Since 1991 the UN has stationed over 400,000 extra personnel in some of the world's crucial trouble spots (see table).

Why has there been this growth? One obvious reason is the increase in tension in many parts of the world, particularly eastern Europe. Also, the ending of actual fighting in some regional conflicts has at last allowed the UN to adopt a peacekeeping role. The break up of the USSR and the end of the Cold War have allowed the major powers, led by the USA, to concentrate on securing peace without the constant worry of a potential Soviet threat. Finally, former UN secretary-general, Javier Perez de Cuellar, brought a new dynamism to the peace process.

Should the UN be a peacemaker as well as a peacekeeper? Up to now, the UN has seen itself mainly as a peacekeeper. It has kept out of active conflicts, preferring to wait until hostilities have clearly ended before it gets involved. UN representatives have often said that they cannot get into peacekeeping until there is peace to keep. However, the last summit meeting of the Security Council in January 1992 issued a declaration stressing 'the importance of strengthening and improving the UN to increase its effectiveness'. It invited the secretary-general to recommend ways of rendering 'more efficient . . the capacity of the UN for preventive diplomacy, for peacemaking and for peacekeeping'.

We have all seen the reports and pictures of the senseless loss of life and destruction of property in what was once Yugoslavia. Many ordinary people throughout the world feel that the UN should not just sit on the sidelines waiting for peace to break out. They want to see it mount an operation as it did in the Gulf to enforce peace by military means. This feeling is likely to grow, with calls for active intervention in other conflict regions, such as Palestine.

But if the UN does take on a peacemaking role, who will pay for it? The USA is meant to provide 30% of the UN peacekeeping budget, but in March 1992 its contributions were $141 million in arrears. Other wealthy nations, such as Japan have provided substantial amounts; but neither Japan nor Germany (the wealthiest country in Europe) has a permanent seat in the Security Council.

Under the leadership of the new secretary-general, Boutros Boutros Ghali, the UN may well soon rethink its peacekeeping and peacemaking role. This could include revised membership of the Security Council, the nucleus of a permanent international force, and a recast security budget.

---

as well as regional commissions and hundreds of nongovernmental agencies that have been granted consultative status. It coordinates the activities of the *Food and Agriculture Organization* (FAO);

Trusteeship Council responsible for overseeing the administration of the UN trust territories. Its members are China, France, the Russian Federation, the UK, and the USA. It holds one regular session a year and can meet in special sessions if required;

International Court of Justice 15 independent judges, elected by the Security Council and the General Assembly on the basis of their competence in international law and irrespective of their nationalities, except that no two judges can be nationals of the same state. They serve for nine years and may be immediately re-elected. The president and vice president are elected by the court for three-year terms. Decisions are by majority vote of the judges

present, and the president has a casting vote. Only states, not individuals, can be parties to cases before the court. There is no appeal;

Secretariat the chief administrator of the UN is the secretary-general, who has under- and assistant secretaries-general and a large international staff. The secretary-general is appointed by the General Assembly for a renewable five-year term.

UN SPECIALIZED AGENCIES

(More information on financial agencies below can be found in the International Economics section.)

Food and Agriculture Organization
(FAO)

established 1945
responsibilities to raise levels of nutrition and standards of living, to improve the production and distribution of food and agricultural products particularly for the less developed parts of the world, and to sponsor relief in emergency situations
headquarters Rome

General Agreement on Tariffs and Trade (GATT)
established 1948
responsibilities a multilateral treaty which lays down a common code of conduct in international trade, providing a forum for discussion of trade problems, with the object of reducing trade barriers
headquarters Geneva

International Atomic Energy Agency (IAEA)
established 1957
responsibilities to accelerate and enlarge the contribution of atomic energy to peace, health and prosperity throughout the world and to prevent its diversion from peaceful purposes to military ends
headquarters Vienna

International Bank for Reconstruction and Development—(*World Bank*) (IRBD)
established 1945
responsibilities to provide funds and technical assistance to help the economies of the poorer nations of the world
headquarters Washington DC

International Civil Aviation Organization (ICAO)
established 1947
responsibilities to establish technical standards for safety and efficiency in air navigation, to develop regioinal plans for ground facilities and services for civil aviation, and generally provide advice to airline operators
headquarters Montréal

International Development Association (IDA)
established 1960
responsibilities as an agency of the World Bank, to provide financial and technical help to the poorest nations

headquarters Washington DC

International Finance Corporation (IFC)
established 1956
responsibilities as an affiliate of the World Bank, to make investments in companies, to assist their development, or provide loans
headquarters Washington DC

International Fund for Agricultural Development (IFAD)
established 1977
responsibilities to mobilize funds for agricultural and rural development
headquarters Rome

International Labour Organization (ILO)
established 1919, becoming part of the UN in 1946
responsibilities to improve labour conditions, raise living standards and promote productive employment through international cooperation
headquarters International Labour Conference, ILO's supreme deliberative body, meets annually in Geneva; International Labour Office and International Institute for Labour Studies, both based permanently in Geneva; a training institution, particularly concerned with the needs of developing countries, based in Turin

International Maritime Organization (IMO)
established 1948
responsibilities to promote cooperation between governments on technical matters affecting merchant shipping, with the object of improving safety at sea
headquarters London

International Monetary Fund (IMF)
established 1945
responsibilities to promote international monetary cooperation and to help remedy any serious disequilibrium in a country's balance of payments by allowing it to draw on the resources of the Fund while it takes measures to correct the imbalance
headquarters Washington DC

UN Peacekeeping Operations 1992

location	year of establishment	number of personnel	annual cost $m
Angola	1991	440	72
Cambodia	1992	22,000	1,500
Cyprus	1964	2,200	31
El Salvador	1991	1,000	52
Golan Heights	1974	1,300	42
India/Pakistan	1949	40	5
Iraq-Kuwait	1991	540	65
Lebanon	1978	5,900	157
Palestine/Israel	1948	300	31
Western Sahara	1991	2,700	177
Yugoslavia	1991	14,000	600
TOTALS		50,420	2,732

International Telecommunication Union
(ITU)
established 1932
responsibilities to maintain and extend international cooperation in improving telecommunications of all kinds by promoting the development of technical skills and services and harmonizing national activities
headquarters Geneva

United Nations Centre for Human Settlements
(UNCHS; Habitat)
established 1978
responsibilities to service the intergovernmental Commission on Human Settlements by providing planning, construction, land development, and finance
headquarters Nairobi

United Nations Children's Emergency Fund
(UNICEF)
established 1953
responsibilities to meet the emergency needs of children in developing countries
headquarters New York

United Nations Conference on Trade and Development
(UNCTAD)
established 1964
responsibilities to promote international trade, particularly in developing countries
headquarters Geneva

United Nations Development Programme
(UNDP)
established 1965
responsibilities to promote higher standards of living in the poorer nations and to try to remedy the economic imbalance between industrialized and developing countries
headquarters New York

United Nations Disaster Relief Coordinator
(UNDRO)
established 1972
responsibilities to provide a 24-hour service for monitoring natural disasters and emergencies; to promote disaster prevention; and to coordinate preparedness and relief
headquarters Geneva

United Nations Educational, Scientific and Cultural Organization
(UNESCO)
established 1946
responsibilities to promote peace by encouraging international collaboration in education, science, and culture
headquarters Paris

United Nations Environment Programme
(UNEP)
established 1972
responsibilities to monitor the state of the environment and to promote environmentally sound developments throughout the world
headquarters Nairobi

United Nations Fund for Population Activities
(UNFPA)
established 1972
responsibilities to provide finance for projects in the areas of family planning, education, and research into population trends and the needs of particular age groups
headquarters New York

United Nations High Commission for Refugees
(UNHCR)
established 1951
responsibilities to provide international protection for refugees and to find solutions to their problems
headquarters Geneva

United Nations Institute for Training and Research
(UNITAR)
established 1965
responsibilities to improve the effectiveness of the UN through training and research
headquarters New York

World Food Programme
(WFP)
established 1963
responsibilities to improve economic and social development through food aid and to provide emergency relief
headquarters Rome

THE BRITISH COMMONWEALTH

The British Commonwealth is a voluntary association of 50 countries and their dependencies, which once formed part of the British Empire and are now independent sovereign states. They are all regarded as 'full members' of the Commonwealth. Additionally, there are some 20 other territories that are not completely sovereign and remain dependencies of the United Kingdom or another of the other fully-sovereign members, but are regarded as 'Commonwealth countries'. Heads of government, apart from those of Nauru and Tuvalu, meet every two years in different capitals in the Commonwealth. Nauru and Tuvalu enjoy special membership in that they have the right to participate in all functional activities but are not represented at the heads of government biennial summits. The Commonwealth has no charter, treaty, or constitution, and is founded more on tradition and sentiment than political or economic factors.

As the successor to the British Empire, the Commonwealth was initially based on allegiance to a common Crown. However in 1949 India chose to become a republic and from that date the modern Commonwealth was born, based now on the concept of the British monarch being a symbol, rather than a legal entity; Queen Elizabeth II is thus the formal head but not the ruler of member states. Presently, 16 of the 50 sovereign member states accept the Queen as their head of state, 29 are republics, and five have their own local monarchs. Heads of government of Commonwealth countries meet every two years to discuss international affairs and areas of cooperation. Finance ministers meet annually, and other ministers meet as and when the need arises.

THE BRITISH COMMONWEALTH

country	capital	date joined	area in sq km	constitutional status
IN AFRICA				
Botswana	Gaborone	1966	582,000	sovereign republic
British Indian Ocean Territory	Victoria	1965	60	British dependent territory
Gambia	Banjul	1965	10,700	sovereign republic
Ghana	Accra	1957	238,300	sovereign republic
Kenya	Nairobi	1963	582,600	sovereign republic
Lesotho	Maseru	1966	30,400	sovereign constitutional monarchy
Malawi	Zomba	1964	118,000	sovereign republic
Mauritius	Port Louis	1968	2,000	sovereign republic
Namibia	Windhoek	1990	824,000	sovereign republic
Nigeria	Lagos	1960	924,000	sovereign republic
St Helena	Jamestown	1931	100	British dependent territory
Seychelles	Victoria	1976	450	sovereign republic
Sierra Leone	Freetown	1961	73,000	sovereign republic
Swaziland	Mbabane	1968	17,400	sovereign republic
Tanzania	Dodoma	1961	945,000	sovereign republic
Uganda	Kampala	1962	236,900	sovereign republic
Zambia	Lusaka	1964	752,600	sovereign republic
Zimbabwe	Harare	1980	390,300	sovereign republic
IN THE AMERICAS				
Anguilla	The Valley	1931	155	British dependent territory
Antigua and Barbuda	St John's	1981	400	sovereign constitutional monarchy*
Bahamas	Nassau	1973	13,900	sovereign constitutional monarchy*
Barbados	Bridgetown	1966	400	sovereign constitutional monarchy*
Belize	Belmopan	1982	23,000	sovereign constitutional monarchy*
Bermuda	Hamilton	1931	54	British dependent territory
British Virgin Islands	Road Town	1931	153	British dependent territory
Canada	Ottawa	1931	9,958,400	sovereign constitutional monarchy*
Cayman Islands	Georgetown	1931	300	British dependent territory
Dominica	Roseau	1978	700	sovereign republic
Falkland Islands	Port Stanley	1931	12,100	British dependent territory
Grenada	St George's	1974	300	sovereign constitutional monarchy*
Guyana	Georgetown	1966	215,000	sovereign republic
Jamaica	Kingston	1962	11,400	sovereign constitutional monarchy*
Montserrat	Plymouth	1931	100	British dependent territory
St Christopher–Nevis	Basseterre Charlestown	1983	300	sovereign constitutional monarchy*
St Lucia	Castries	1979	600	sovereign constitutional monarchy*
St Vincent and the Grenadines	Kingstown	1979	400	sovereign constitutional monarchy*
Trinidad and Tobago	Port of Spain	1962	5,100	sovereign republic
Turks and Caicos Islands	Grand Turk	1931	400	British dependent territory
IN THE ANTARCTIC				
Australian Antarctic Territory	uninhabited	1936	5,403,000	Australian external territory
British Antarctic Territory	uninhabited	1931	390,000	British dependent territory
Falkland Islands Dependencies	uninhabited	1931	1,600	British dependent territories
Ross Dependency	uninhabited	1931	453,000	New Zealand associated territory
IN ASIA				
Bangladesh	Dhaka	1972	144,000	sovereign republic
Brunei	Bandar Seri Begawan	1984	5,800	sovereign monarchy
Hong Kong	Victoria	1931	1,100	British crown colony
India	Delhi	1947	3,166,800	sovereign republic
Malaysia	Kuala Lumpur	1957	329,800	sovereign constitutional monarchy
Maldives	Malé	1982	300	sovereign republic
Pakistan	Islamabad	1947†	803,900	sovereign republic
Singapore	Singapore	1965	600	sovereign republic
Sri Lanka	Colombo	1948	66,000	sovereign republic

THE BRITISH COMMONWEALTH (cont.)

country	capital	date joined	area in sq km	constitutional status
IN AUSTRALASIA AND THE PACIFIC				
Australia	Canberra	1931	7,682,300	sovereign constitutional monarchy*
Cook Islands	Avarua	1931	300	New Zealand associated territory
Norfolk Island	Kingston	1931	34	Australian external territory
Kiribati	Tawawa	1979	700	sovereign republic
Nauru	Yaren	1968	21	sovereign republic
New Zealand	Wellington	1931	268,000	sovereign constitutional monarchy*
Niue	Alofi	1931	300	New Zealand associated territory
Papua New Guinea	Port Moresby	1975	462,800	sovereign constitutional monarchy*
Pitcairn Islands	Adamstown	1931	5	British dependent territory
Solomon Islands	Honiara	1978	27,600	sovereign constitutional monarchy*
Tokelau	Nukunonu	1931	10	New Zealand associated territory
Tonga	Nuku'alofa	1970	700	sovereign monarchy
Tuvalu	Funafuti	1978	24	sovereign constitutional monarchy*
Vanuatu	Villa	1980	15,000	sovereign republic
Western Samoa	Apia	1970	2,800	sovereign republic
IN EUROPE				
Channel Islands		1931	200	UK crown dependencies
Guernsey	St Peter Port			
Jersey	St Helier			
Cyprus	Nicosia	1961	9,000	sovereign republic
Gibraltar	Gibraltar	1931	6	British dependent territory
Malta	Valletta	1964	300	sovereign republic
Isle of Man	Douglas	1931	600	UK crown dependency
United Kingdom	London	1931	244,100	sovereign constitutional monarchy*
England	London			
Northern Ireland	Belfast			
Scotland	Edinburgh			
Wales	Cardiff			
TOTAL			33,089,900	

* Queen Elizabeth II constitutional monarch and head of state   † left 1972 and rejoined 1989

The Commonwealth is not a mutual defence organization and most member countries are committed to regional treaties.

The Commonwealth secretariat, headed from Oct 1989 by Secretary-General Chief Emeka Anyaoko of Nigeria, is based in London. The secretariat's staff come from a number of member countries; these members also pay the secretariat's operating costs.

ENVIRONMENTAL AND HUMAN RIGHTS GROUPS

ActionAid
established 1972
objectives to help children, families, and communities in the world's poorest countries to overcome poverty, and to secure lasting improvements in the quality of their lives
areas of operation 18 countries in Africa, Asia, and Latin America
membership over 110,000 sponsors and supporters
annual budget (1990) £10,216,000
current projects long-term integrated rural development in the areas of water, health, agriculture, education, and income generation
headquarters London

Amnesty International
established 1961
objectives to free all prisoners of conscience; to ensure fair and prompt trials for political prisoners; to abolish the death penalty, torture, and other cruel treatment of prisoners; to end extrajudicial executions and 'disappearances'. Amnesty International also opposes similar abuses by opposition groups. Politically unaligned
areas of operation organized sections in 47 countries (24 in Latin America, Asia, Africa, Middle East)
membership more than 6,000 volunteer groups active in more than 70 countries and 1,100,000 individual members, subscribers, and regular donors in more than 150 countries and territories
annual budget (1991) £12.9 million
headquarters international secretariat, London

Campaign for Nuclear Disarmament (CND)
established 1958
objectives to campaign for the dismantling of

nuclear weapons, bases, and alliances; also campaigns against nuclear power. Politically unaligned
areas of operation mainly the UK
membership 60,000 plus affiliated organizations
annual budget (1990) £842,000 and £477,000 (publications wing)
current projects campaigning against international arms trade and nuclear proliferation, especially for the implementation of UN Security Council policy for general and complete disarmament under effective international control
headquarters London

Friends of the Earth
(FoE)
established 1971
objectives to conserve the planet's resources and reduce pollution; campaigns, among other things, for recycling and renewable energy, and against the destruction of wildlife and habitat
areas of operation 44 countries worldwide
membership 38 groups internationally; 250 local groups in the UK
annual budget (1990) £6m
current projects participation in forthcoming international conference in Rio de Janeiro, Brazil
headquarters Amsterdam

Greenpeace
established 1971
objectives to persuade governments to protect and improve the environment; campaigns against pollution, whaling, nuclear power, and on many other issues, with a policy of nonviolent direct action backed by scientific research
areas of operation 28 countries worldwide
membership 5 million
current projects protection of wildlife; disposal of toxics; civil nuclear energy; atmosphere and energy
headquarters Amsterdam

Human Rights Watch
established 1978
objectives to monitor and publicize human-rights abuses by governments, especially attacks on those who defend human rights in their own countries
areas of operation separate committees focus on one area each:
Africa Watch, *Americas Watch*, *Asia Watch*, *Middle East Watch*, *Helsinki Watch* monitors compliance with the 1975 Helsinki accords by the 35 signatory countries
annual budget does not accept financial support from governments or government-funded agencies
current projects more than 100 investigative missions every year to some 60 countries around the world
headquarters New York

Minority Rights Group
established 1965
objectives to promote human rights and increase awareness of minority issues

areas of operation Europe, Australia, North America, India
membership non-membership organization
current projects publishing reports on minority groups worldwide; producing educational material for schools; making representations at the United Nations
headquarters London

Oxfam
(Oxford Committee for Famine Relief)
established 1942
objectives to relieve poverty, distress, and suffering in any part of the world
areas of operation worldwide, particularly in developing countries
membership not a membership organization
annual budget (1990) £62m
current projects 50th anniversary year, 'working for a fairer world'
headquarters Oxford

The Red Cross
established 1864 by the Geneva Convention; the Muslim equivalent is the Red Crescent
objectives to assist the wounded and prisoners in war, and war-related victims such as refugees and the disabled; to aid victims of natural disasters—floods, earthquakes, epidemics, famine, and accidents—and to organize emergency relief operations worldwide
membership non-membership organization
annual budget (1991) £64 million
areas of operation worldwide
headquarters Geneva, Switzerland

Save the Children Fund
established 1919
objectives to promote the rights of children to care, good health, material welfare, and moral, spiritual, and educational development, throughout the world
areas of operation more than 50 Third World countries and the UK
membership over 850 branches in the UK
annual budget (1990) 52m
current projects assistance in famine-affected areas; provision of health care, education, community development, and emergency relief
headquarters London

Survival International
established 1969
objectives to support tribal peoples and their right to decide their own future, and to help them protect their lands, environment, and way of life
areas of operation more than 60 countries
membership 12,000
annual budget (1990) 530,000
current projects lobbying against rainforest logging, huge dams, and industrial activity that displaces tribal people, and for the return of confiscated lands; emergency medical aid; protests against killing and intimidation of tribal people
headquarters London

Voluntary Service Overseas
(VSO)
established 1958

objectives to help Third World development by providing opportunities for people with skills to make a practical contribution as volunteers
areas of operation 40 developing countries worldwide
membership 45 local groups
annual budget (1990) £15.7m
headquarters London

War on Want
established 1952
objectives to support development work in developing countries and to campaign in Europe on world poverty
areas of operation Bangladesh, Cambodia, Vietnam, Sri Lanka, India, Philippines, South Africa, Namibia, Ethiopia, Eritrea, West Bank and Gaza Strip, Brazil, Chile, Nicaragua, El Salvador, Guatemala, Jamaica
membership (1992) 1,400 individual members and trade-union affiliations
annual budget (1992) 990,000
current projects Chile, urban development and women's textile workshops; Nicaragua, peasant cooperative shops, women's employment fund, Miskito community development; Cambodia, clinic for prosthetic limbs; West Bank, dental clinic; Bangladesh, urban literacy; Vietnam, film equipment
headquarters London

World Conservation Monitoring Centre

established 1983
objectives to support international programmes for conservation and sustainable development through the provision of information on the world's biological diversity
areas of operation provides information to the World Wide Fund for Nature, the World Conservation Union (IUCN), and the United Nations Environment Programme (UNEP) (*not* direct to the general public)
membership non-membership
annual income (1989–90) £1,307,179
current projects managing information holdings on threatened species, important habitats, national parks, wildlife trade, and conservation bibliography
headquarters Cambridge, England

World Wide Fund for Nature (WWF)
established 1961
objectives to protect endangered species and to tackle all environmental problems that threaten any form of life
areas of operation worldwide
membership 28 offices in 23 countries
annual budget (1990) £12m
current projects tropical rainforests; marine conservation; wetlands; pollution within EC member countries
headquarters Gland, Switzerland; UK office, Godalming, Surrey

---

What form would you like to see the European Community take in the future?

	Young people	General public
A fully integrated Europe, with most major decisions taken by a European government	17	13
A Europe more integrated than now, but with decisions that mainly affect Britain staying in British hands	34	51
The situation much as it is now, with Britain retaining control over major policy changes it does not like	26	17
Complete British withdrawal from the European Community	7	13
Don't know	15	7

Over the next five years do you think that the UK's membership of the European Community will generally make things better for you and your family, make them worse, or will it make no difference? And what impact do you think the UK's membership of the European Community will have on you and your family over the next 10 years? What impact do you think the UK's membership will have over the next 15 years?

	5 years	10 years	15 years
Better	33	43	44
Worse	16	13	13
No difference	42	29	23
Don't know	9	15	20

LEGAL TERMS

accessory a party to a crime that is actually committed by someone else.

accomplice a person who acts with another in the commission or attempted commission of a crime, either as a principal or as an accessory.

acquittal the setting free of someone charged with a crime after a trial.

action any proceeding in a civil court of law, including an ecclesiastical court. Actions in the High Court are commenced by the plaintiff issuing a writ, which will usually include a concise statement about the nature of the claim and the damages which are being sought from the defendant.

Act of Parliament in Britain, a change in the law originating in Parliament and called a statute. Before an act receives the royal assent and becomes law it is a *bill*. The US equivalent is an act of Congress.

An Act of Parliament may be either public (of general effect), local, or private. The body of English statute law comprises all the acts passed by Parliament: the existing list opens with the Statute of Merton, passed in 1235. An Act (unless it is stated to be for a definite period and then to come to an end) remains on the statute book until it is repealed.

How an act of Parliament becomes law:

1 first reading of the bill The title is read out in the House of Commons (H of C) and a minister names a day for the second reading.

2 The bill is officially printed.

3 second reading A debate on the whole bill in the H of C followed by a vote on whether or not the bill should go on to the next stage.

4 committee stage A committee of MPs considers the bill in detail and makes amendments.

5 report stage The bill is referred back to the H of C which may make further amendments.

6 third reading The H of C votes whether the bill should be sent on to the House of Lords.

7 House of Lords The bill passes through much the same stages in the Lords as in the H of C. (Bills may be introduced in the Lords, in which case the H of C considers them at this stage.)

8 last amendments The H of C considers any Lords' amendments, and may make further amendments which must usually be agreed by the Lords.

9 royal assent The Queen gives her formal assent.

10 The bill becomes an act of Parliament at royal assent, although it may not come into force until a day appointed in the act.

adjournment the postponement of the hearing of a case for later consideration. If a hearing is adjourned *sine die* (without day) it is postponed for an indefinite period. If a party requests an adjournment the court may find the costs of the adjournment have been unnecessarily incurred and make an order for costs against that party.

adoption the permanent legal transfer of parental rights and duties in respect of a child from one person to another.

adultery voluntary sexual intercourse between a married person and someone other than his or her legal partner. It is one factor that may prove 'irretrievable breakdown' of marriage in actions for judicial separation or divorce in Britain.

advocate (Latin *advocatus*, one summoned to one's aid, especially in a lawcourt) pleader in a court of justice. A more common term for a professional advocate is barrister or counsel. In many tribunals lay persons may appear as advocates.

affidavit legal document, used in court applications and proceedings, in which a person swears that certain facts are true.

alibi a provable assertion that the accused was elsewhere when a crime was committed.

amnesty the release of political prisoners under a general pardon, or a person or group of people from criminal liability for a particular action; for example, the occasional amnesties in Britain for those who surrender firearms that they hold illegally.

appeal an application for the judicial examination of the decision of a lower court by a higher court. In the UK, summary trials (involving minor offences) are heard in the magistrate's court and appeals against conviction and/or sentence are heard in the Crown Court. The appeal in the Crown Court takes the form of a full retrial but no jury is present. Appeals against conviction and/or sentence in the Crown Court are heard by the Criminal Division of the Court of Appeal.

The number of cases heard by a full court of the Court of Appeal criminal division increased from 2,528 in 1979 to 3,627 in 1990, an increase of 43%.

arrest the apprehension and detention of a person suspected of a crime classified as sufficiently serious (an 'arrestable' offence).

arson the malicious and wilful setting fire to property. A capital offence in the UK until 1971, it still carries a maximum sentence of life imprisonment.

assault intentional act or threat of physical violence against a person. In English law it is both a crime and a tort (a civil wrong). The kinds of criminal assault are common (ordinary); aggravated (more serious, such as causing actual bodily harm); or indecent (of a sexual nature).

Attorney General in England, principal law officer of the Crown and head of the English Bar. The consent of the Attorney General is required for bringing certain criminal proceedings where offences against the state of public order are at issue, for example incitement to racial hatred. Under the Criminal Justice Act 1988, cases can be referred to the Court of Appeal by the Attorney General if it appears to him that the sentencing of a person convicted of a serious offence (e.g. murder, rape, robbery) has been unduly lenient.

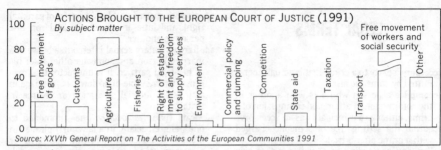

ACTIONS BROUGHT TO THE EUROPEAN COURT OF JUSTICE (1991)
By subject matter

Source: XXVth General Report on The Activities of the European Communities 1991

bail the setting at liberty of a person in legal custody on an undertaking, (usually backed by some security, given either by that person or by someone else), to attend a legal proceeding at a stated time and place. If the person does not attend, the bail may be forfeited.

barrister in the UK, a lawyer qualified by study at the Inns of Court to plead for a client in court. In Scotland they are called advocates. Barristers also undertake the writing of opinions on the prospects of a case before trial. They act for clients through the intermediary of solicitors. In the highest courts, only barristers can represent litigants but this distinction between barristers and solicitors seems likely to change in the 1990s. In the USA an attorney (lawyer) may serve both functions. When pupil barristers complete their training they are 'called to the bar': this is the name of the ceremony in which they are admitted as members of the profession. A Queen's Counsel (silk) is a senior barrister appointed on the recommendation of the Lord Chancellor.

bigamy the offence of marrying a person while already lawfully married to another. In some countries marriage to more than one wife or husband is lawful.

blackmail criminal offence of extorting money with menaces or threats of detrimental action, such as exposure of some misconduct on the part of the victim.

blasphemy written or spoken insult directed against religious belief or sacred things with deliberate intent to outrage believers.

breathalyzer an instrument for on-the-spot checking by police of the amount of alcohol consumed by a suspect driver. The driver breathes into a plastic bag connected to a tube containing a chemical that changes colour. Another method is to use a gas chromatograph, again from a breath sample.

Approximately 500,000 breath tests are carried out each year. Alcohol-related road traffic accidents result in 22,000 casualties each year; 50% of those injured are victims of drunk drivers.

brief the written instructions sent by a solicitor to a barrister before a hearing.

burden of proof in court proceedings, the duty of a party to produce sufficient evidence to prove that his or her case is true. In English and American law a higher standard of proof is required in criminal cases (beyond all reasonable

doubt), than in civil cases (on the balance of probabilities).

capital punishment punishment by death; methods of execution include electrocution, lethal gas, hanging, shooting, lethal injection, garrotting, and decapitation. 44 countries have abolished the death penalty for all offences, and 17 (including the UK) have done so for all but exceptional crimes such as wartime crimes. 25 countries can be considered abolitionist *de facto*, that is they retain the death penalty in law but have not carried out any executions for the past ten years or more. Capital punishment is retained and used in 92 countries, including the USA (37 states), China, and the ex-Soviet republics.

In 1990, a record-breaking number of countries abolished the death penalty—Namibia, the Czech and Slovak Federative Republic, Ireland, Andorra, São Tomé and Príncipe, Mozambique, and Hungary abolished the death penalty for all offences; Nepal abolished the death penalty for ordinary offences.

The International Covenant on Civil and Political Rights 1977 ruled out imposition of the death penalty on those under the age of 18. The covenant was signed by President Carter on behalf of the USA, but in 1989 the US Supreme Court decided that it could be imposed from the age of 16 for murder, and that the mentally retarded could also face the death penalty. In 1990 there were over 2,000 prisoners on death row (awaiting execution).

care order in Britain, a court order that places a child in the care of a local authority; this may be with foster parents or in a community home.

child abuse the molesting of children by parents and other adults. It can give rise to various criminal charges and has become a growing concern since the early 1980s. A local authority can take abused children away from their parents by obtaining a care order from a juvenile court under the Children's and Young Persons Act 1969 (replaced by the Children's Act 1989). Controversial methods of diagnosing sexual abuse led to a public inquiry in Cleveland, England 1988, which severely criticized the handling of such cases. The standard of proof required for criminal proceedings is greater than that required for a local authority to take children into care. This has led to highly publicized cases where children have been taken into care but prosecutions have eventually not

COUNTRIES WHICH HAVE ABOLISHED THE DEATH PENALTY SINCE 1976

1976	Portugal*; Canada **
1978	Denmark*; Spain **
1979	Luxembourg, Nicaragua, Norway*; Brazil (1), Fiji, Peru**
1981	France*
1982	The Netherlands*
1983	Cyprus, El Salvador**
1984	Argentina (2), Australia**
1985	Australia*
1987	The Philippines, Haiti, Liechtenstein, German Democratic Republic*
1989	Cambodia, New Zealand, Romania*
1990	Andorra, Czech and Slovak Federative Republic, Hungary, Ireland, Mozambique, Namibia, São Tomé and Príncipe*; Nepal** (3)
1992	!Switzerland

* for all offences ** for ordinary offences

1. Brazil had abolished the death penalty in 1882 but reintroduced it in 1969 while under military rule. 2. Argentina had abolished the death penalty for all offences in 1921 and again in 1972 but reintroduced it 1976 following a military coup. 3. Nepal had abolished the death penalty for murder in 1946 but reintroduced it in 1985 after bomb explosions killed several people.

been brought, as in Rochdale, Lancashire, and the Orkneys, Scotland in 1990.

civil disobedience the deliberate breaking of laws considered unjust, a form of nonviolent direct action; the term was coined by the US writer Thoreau in an essay of that name 1849. It was advocated by Mahatma Gandhi to prompt peaceful withdrawal of British power from India. Civil disobedience has since been employed by, for instance, the US civil-rights movement in the 1960s and the peace movement in the 1980s.

civil law the legal system based on Roman law. It is one of the two main European legal systems, English (common) law being the other. Civil law may also mean the law relating to matters other than criminal law, such as contract and tort. Inside the Commonwealth, Roman law forms the basis of the legal systems of Scotland and Québec and is also the basis of that of South Africa.

commissioner for oaths in English law, a person appointed by the Lord Chancellor with power to administer oaths or take affidavits. All practising solicitors have these powers but must not use them in proceedings in which they are acting for any of the parties or in which they have an interest.

common law that part of the English law not embodied in legislation. It consists of rules of law based on common custom and usage and on judicial decisions. English common law became the basis of law in the USA and many other English-speaking countries.

compulsory purchase in the UK the right of the state and authorized bodies to buy land required for public purposes even against the wishes of the owner. Under the Land Compensation Act 1973, fair recompense is payable.

consumer protection laws and measures designed to ensure fair trading for buyers. Responsibility for checking goods and services for quality, safety, and suitability has in the past few years moved increasingly away from the consumer to the producer.

contempt of court behaviour that shows contempt for the authority of a court, such as disobeying a court order, breach of an injunction, or improper use of legal documents. Behaviour that disrupts, prejudices, or interferes with court proceedings either inside or outside the courtroom may also be contempt. The court may punish contempt with a fine or imprisonment.

contract of employment the legal basis of an agreement between an employer and an employee.

copyright law applying to literary, musical, and artistic works (including plays, recordings, films, photographs, radio and television broadcasts, and, in the USA and Britain, computer programs), which prevents the reproduction of the work, in whole or in part, without the author's consent.

coroner official who investigates the deaths of persons who have died suddenly by acts of violence, or under suspicious circumstances, by holding an inquest or ordering a postmortem examination.

The coroner's court aims not to establish liability but to find out how, where, and why the death occurred. A coroner must be a barrister, solicitor, or medical practitioner with at least five years' professional service. In Scotland similar duties are performed by the procurator-fiscal. The coroner alone decides which witnesses should be called, and legal aid is not available for representation in a coroner's court. Nor may any of the parties make a closing speech to the jury.

corporal punishment physical punishment of wrongdoers, for example, by whipping. It is still used as a punishment for criminals in many countries, especially under Islamic law. It was abolished as a punishment for criminals in Britain 1967 but only became illegal for punishing schoolchildren in state schools 1986. Corporal punishment of children by parents is illegal in some countries, including Sweden, Finland, Denmark, and Norway.

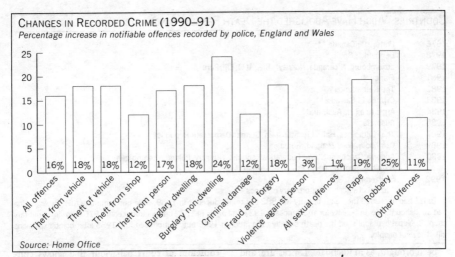

CHANGES IN RECORDED CRIME (1990–91)
Percentage increase in notifiable offences recorded by police, England and Wales

All offences	16%
Theft from vehicle	18%
Theft of vehicle	18%
Theft from shop	12%
Theft from person	17%
Burglary dwelling	18%
Burglary non-dwelling	24%
Criminal damage	12%
Fraud and forgery	18%
Violence against person	3%
All sexual offences	1%
Rape	19%
Robbery	25%
Other offences	11%

Source: Home Office

court martial court convened for the trial of persons subject to military discipline who are accused of violations of military laws.

criminal law the body of law that defines the public wrongs (crimes) that are punishable by the state and establishes methods of prosecution and punishment. It is distinct from civil law, which deals with legal relationships between individuals (including organizations), such as contract law.

In England and Wales crimes are either: *indictable offences* (serious offences triable by judge and jury in the crown court); *summary offences* dealt with in magistrates' courts; or *hybrid offences* tried in either kind of court according to the seriousness of the case and the wishes of the defendant. The crown court has power to punish those found guilty more severely than a magistrates' court. Punishments include imprisonment, fines, suspended terms of imprisonment (which only come into operation if the offender is guilty of further offences during a specified period), probation, and community service. Overcrowding in prisons and the cost of imprisonment have led to recent experiments with noncustodial sentences such as electronic tags fixed to the body to reinforce curfew orders on convicted criminals in the community.

The total cost of criminal justice services for England and Wales was £7 billion in 1990, an increase of 77% in real terms from 1980.

custody the state of being held by the police or prison authorities in confinement. Following an arrest, a person may either be kept in custody or released on bail. Custody is also the legal guardianship of a child; a parent, guardian, or authority who has custody of a child usually exercises all parental rights.

damages compensation for a tort (such as personal injuries caused by negligence) or breach of contract. Damages for personal injuries include compensation for loss of earnings, as well as for the injury itself. The court might reduce the damages if the claimant was partly to blame. In the majority of cases, the parties involved reach an out-of-court settlement (a compromise without going to court).

decree nisi conditional order of divorce. A *decree absolute* is normally granted six weeks after the decree nisi, and from the date of the decree absolute the parties cease to be husband and wife.

deed legal document that passes an interest in property or binds a person to perform or abstain from some action. Deeds are of two kinds: indenture and deed poll. *Indentures* bind two or more parties in mutual obligations.
A *deed poll* is made by one party only, such as when a person changes his or her name.

defamation an attack on a person's reputation by libel or slander.

defendant a person against whom court proceedings are brought.

defence the defendant and his or her legal advisors and representatives are collectively known as the defence. The defence is also the case made in answer to the action or claim being made against the defendant.

Director of Public Prosecutions (DPP) in the UK, the head of the Crown Prosecution Service (established 1985), responsible for the conduct of all criminal prosecutions in England and Wales. The DPP was formerly responsible only for the prosecution of certain serious crimes, such as murder.

divorce the legal dissolution of a lawful marriage. It is distinct from an annulment, which is a legal declaration that the marriage was invalid. The ease with which a divorce can be obtained in different countries varies considerably and is also affected by different religious practices.

easement rights that a person may have over the land of another. A common example is a right of way; others are the right to bring water over another's land and the right to a sufficient quantity of light.

ecclesiastical law church law. In England, the Church of England has special ecclesiastical courts to administer church law. Each diocese has a consistory court with a right of appeal to the Court of Arches (in the archbishop of Canterbury's jurisdiction) or the Chancery Court of York (in the archbishop of York's jurisdiction). They deal with the constitution of the Church of England, church property, the clergy, services, doctrine, and practice. These courts have no influence on churches of other denominations, which are governed by the usual laws of contract and trust.

employment law law covering the rights and duties of employers and employees. During the 20th century, statute law has increasingly been used to give new rights to both employers and employees. Industrial tribunals are statutory bodies that adjudicate in disputes between employers and employees or trade unions and include complaints concerning unfair dismissal, sex or race discrimination, and equal pay. Discrimination against employees on the ground of their sex or race is illegal under the Sex Discrimination Act 1975 and the Race Relations Act 1976. '

English law one of the major European legal systems, Roman law being the other. English law has spread to many other countries, including former English colonies such as the USA, Canada, Australia, and New Zealand.

equal opportunities the right to be employed or considered for employment without discrimination on the grounds of race, gender, physical or mental handicap.

equity system of law supplementing the ordinary rules of law where the application of these would operate harshly in a particular case; sometimes it is regarded as an attempt to achieve 'natural justice'. So understood, equity appears as an element in most legal systems, and in a number of legal codes judges are instructed to apply both the rules of strict law and the principles of equity in reaching their decisions.

escrow a document sealed and delivered to a third party and not released or coming into effect until some condition has been fulfilled or performed, whereupon the document takes full effect.

executor a person appointed in a will to carry out the instructions of the deceased. A person so named has the right to refuse to act. The executor also has a duty to bury the deceased, prove the will, and obtain a grant of probate (that is, establish that the will is genuine and obtain official approval of his or her actions).

extradition the surrender, by one state or country to another, of a person accused of a criminal offence in the state or country to which that person is extradited.

foreclosure the transfer of title of a mortgaged property from the mortgagor (borrower, usually a home owner) to the mortgagee (loaner, for example a bank) if the mortgagor is in breach of the mortgage agreement, usually by failing to make a number of payments on the mortgage (loan).

forgery the making of a fake document, painting, or object with deliberate intention to deceive or

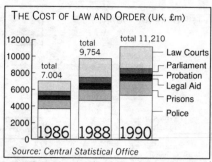

THE COST OF LAW AND ORDER (UK, £m)

Source: Central Statistical Office

defraud. The most common forgeries involve financial instruments such as cheques or credit-card transactions, or money (counterfeiting). There are also literary forgeries, forged coins, and forged antiques.

fraud an act of deception resulting in injury to another. To establish fraud it has to be demonstrated that (1) a false representation (for example, a factually untrue statement) has been made, with the intention that it should be acted upon; (2) the person making the representation knows it is false or does not attempt to find out whether it is true or not; and (3) the person to whom the representation is made acts upon it to his or her detriment.

A contract based on fraud can be declared void, and the injured party can sue for damages.

freehold in England and Wales, ownership of land which is for an indefinite period. It is contrasted with a leasehold, which is always for a fixed period. In practical effect, a freehold is absolute ownership.

grievous bodily harm (GBH) in English law, very serious physical harm suffered by the victim of a crime. The courts have said that judges should not try to define grievous bodily harm but leave it to the jury to decide.

hearsay evidence evidence given by a witness based on information passed to that person by others rather than evidence experienced at first-hand by the witness. It is usually not admissable in criminal proceedings.

homicide the killing of a human being. This may be unlawful or lawful, depending on the circumstances. Unlawful homicides include murder, manslaughter, infanticide, and causing death by dangerous driving. Lawful homicide occurs where, for example, a police officer is justified in killing a criminal in the course of apprehension or when a person is killed in self-defence or defence of others.

illegitimacy the status of a child born to a mother who is not legally married; since the Family Law Reform Act 1987, illegitimate children have the same rights as those born within marriage, and legal references to children's legitimacy have been abolished. The child's nationality is usually that of the mother.

indemnity an undertaking to compensate another for damage, loss, trouble, or expenses, or the money paid by way of such compensation, as under insurance agreements.

THE CRIMINAL COURTS

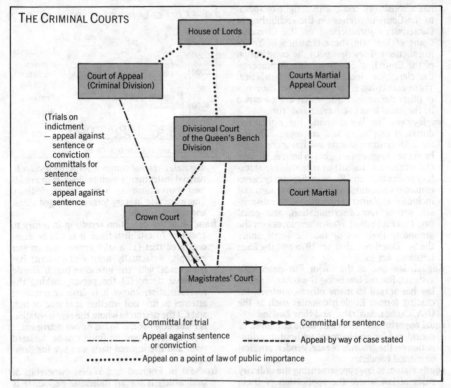

(Trials on indictment
— appeal against
sentence or
conviction
Committals for
sentence
— sentence
appeal against
sentence

——————— Committal for trial

▶▶▶▶▶▶▶ Committal for sentence

————— Appeal against sentence
or conviction

----------- Appeal by way of case stated

•••••••••• Appeal on a point of law of public importance

injunction court order that forbids a person from doing something, or orders him or her to take certain action. Breach of an injunction is contempt of court.

inquest inquiry held by a coroner into an unexplained death. At an inquest, a coroner is assisted by a jury of between 7 and 11 people. Evidence is on oath, and medical and other witnesses may be summoned.

international law body of rules generally accepted as governing the relations between countries, pioneered by Hugo Grotius, especially in matters of human rights, territory, and war. The scope of the law is now extended to space – for example, the 1967 treaty that (among other things) banned nuclear weapons from space. *The Genocide Convention* 1948 declares that acts of killing, causing serious bodily harm, prevention of births, forcible transfer of children, the deliberate infliction of conditions of life calculated to bring about the physical destruction of a group, if those acts are 'committed with intent to destroy, in whole or in part, a national, ethnical, racial or religious group', are international crimes. *The Geneva Convention* is a series of international conventions on the laws of war. The Geneva Protocol of 1925 prohibits the use of gas and bacteriological warfare. The 1949 conventions include provision for the protection of sick and wounded soldiers, prisoners of war and certain groups of civilians; a Protocol of 1977 extends such protection and further regulates the law

of bombing. Some of the Geneva conventions have been extended to cover civil wars and wars of national liberation.

judge a person invested with power to hear and determine legal disputes.

judicial review in English law, action in the High Court to review the decisions of lower courts, tribunals, and administrative bodies. Various court orders can be made: *certiorari* (which quashes the decision); *mandamus* (which commands a duty to be performed); *prohibition* (which commands that an action should not be performed because it is unauthorized); a *declaration* (which sets out the legal rights or obligations); or an *injunction*.

jurisprudence the science of law in the abstract – that is, not the study of any particular laws or legal system, but of the principles upon which legal systems are founded.

jury body of lay people (usually 12) sworn to decide the facts of a case and reach a verdict in a court of law. Juries, used mainly in English-speaking countries, are implemented primarily in criminal cases, but also sometimes in civil cases; for example, inquests and libel trials.

In July 1991 a jury at the Old Bailey acquitted Michael Randle and Pat Pottle of helping the Soviet agent George Blake escape from prison in 1966. The two defendants were prosecuted 25 years after the escape following publication of a book in which they admitted to their part in the escape. The judge told the

ASYLUM WITHIN EUROPE

Of the 17.5 million refugees which the UN Commission on Human Rights says are scattered worldwide, less than 100,000 have obtained refuge in Europe. Of the European applications, 60% are made to Germany (latterly in 1991 averaging about 30,000 month) and 20–25% are filed in France. Britain is at the lower end of the European league although 1992 is expected to produce a record number of asylum-seekers in the UK. In 1991, applications were seven times the level of 1988 at an estimated 50,000.

The increased anxiety about the scale of immigration to Europe as well as the tough stance taken by many governments towards asylum-seekers and illegal immigrants is thought to be a response not only to the increased numbers but also to the end of the Cold War. Mass movements from the East as well as the South are now feared. In recent years several European countries, including the UK, have announced laws on immigration and asylum. Administrative procedures have been changed, appeals limited, and the definition of access frequently narrowed. Rightwing groups throughout Europe have made political capital by playing on fears of a flood of bogus asylum-seekers and economic refugees.

The European Commission has not yet adopted a common criterion for deciding who is a refugee and who is not. The UK defines an immigrant as someone who has lived abroad for at least one year and who declares an intention to stay in the UK for at least a year, whereas a refugee seeks asylum as a means of protection. In the UK, a person may apply for asylum on the grounds that, if he or she were required to leave, it would be to a country where there was a real prospect of persecution for reasons of race, religion, nationality, membership of a particular social group, or political opinion. Irregular immigrants are people who enter the UK without presenting themselves to an immigration officer, as well as those who enter with forged documents. They are automatically sent back to the country they came from unless they are refugees who ask for asylum and are able to show that they have a well-founded fear of persecution. A person who has been granted asylum and recognized as a refugee enjoys rights conferred by the 1951 UN convention relating to the status of refugees.

About 10% of asylum seekers are refused leave to remain in Britain. A further 25% are given full political asylum and the remaining 65% are given 'exceptional leave to remain' on humanitarian grounds.

The Asylum Bill, introduced by the Conservative government in 1991, sought to accelerate and simplify decision-making in asylum cases. The bill introduced a new right of appeal, powers to cut short the stay of those refused right of abode, fingerprinting of all applicants, and limited the duties of local authorities to provide permanent homes for those seeking refugee status. The provisions were designed to supplement existing legislation such as the Carriers Liability Act, which introduced fines of £1,000 and the requirement to return any arriving passenger who was subsequently not admitted. However, the home secretary's suggestion that existing legal aid facilities be withdrawn and the UK Immigration Advisory Service become the monopoly supplier of legal aid to asylum seekers met fierce opposition and was withdrawn. Automatic fingerprinting of applicants, to prevent multiple applications from the same person, has been criticized by the Law Society and other groups because it would confer a stigma of criminality on asylum seekers.

In September 1991 there was a backlog of 60,000 outstanding applications for asylum. Each one takes an average of 18 months to two years before a decision is reached. The Home Office put the cost of supporting refugees in 1990 at £200 million. Apart from the cost, long delays allow refugees to argue that their cases have taken so long to be processed that they have put down roots in Britain. There is then a case for claiming 'exceptional leave to remain' on humanitarian grounds. Amnesty International has called for an independent body to be set up to hear asylum cases, run by experts familiar with human rights problems and the law relating to refugees.

In November 1991, Kenneth Baker, the home secretary, was found guilty of contempt over the deportation of an asylum seeker. It was the first time a minister has been found guilty of contempt of court.

Demonstration in London against a Home Office decision on asylum seekers.

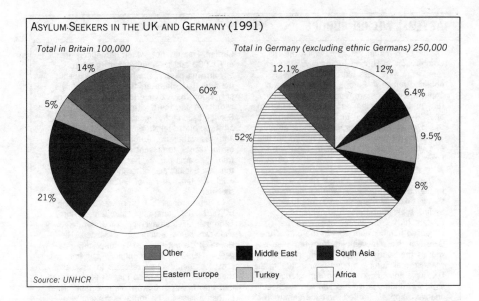

Asylum-Seekers in the UK and Germany (1991)

Total in Britain 100,000

Total in Germany (excluding ethnic Germans) 250,000

Source: UNHCR

Legend: Other, Middle East, South Asia, Eastern Europe, Turkey, Africa

jury that the two men had no defence in law. However, in an instance of reaching a 'perverse judgment', the jury adopted a common-sense rather than strict letter-of-the-law approach and disobeyed the judge, acquitting both defendants. The case strengthened support for maintaining the jury system, in the face of abolitionist arguments.

juvenile offender term for young persons who commit offences. Young people under age 17 are commonly referred to by the law as juveniles, although for some purposes a distinction is made between children (aged under 14) and 'young persons' (14–16). Most legal proceedings in respect of juveniles are brought in specially constituted magistrates' courts known as juvenile courts, where the procedure is simpler and less formal than in an adult magistrates' court. Members of the public are not admitted to juvenile courts and the name of the juvenile may not be disclosed in any report of the proceedings. A juvenile under the age of ten may not be found guilty of an offence.

King's Counsel in England, a barrister of senior rank; the term is used when a king is on the throne and Queen's Counsel when the monarch is a queen.

law lords in England, the ten Lords of Appeal in Ordinary who, together with the Lord Chancellor and other peers, make up the House of Lords in its judicial capacity. The House of Lords is the final court of appeal in both criminal and civil cases. Law lords rank as life peers.

leasehold land or property held by a tenant (lessee) for a specified period, (unlike freehold, outright ownership) usually at a rent from the landlord (lessor).

legacy a gift of personal property made by a testator in a will and transferred on the testator's

death to the legatee. **Specific legacies** are definite named objects; a **general legacy** is a sum of money or item not specially identified; a **residuary legacy** is all the remainder of the deceased's personal estate after debts have been paid and the other legacies have been distributed.

legal aid public assistance with legal costs. In Britain it is given only to those below certain thresholds of income and unable to meet the costs. There are separate provisions for civil and criminal cases. Since 1989 legal aid is administered by the Legal Aid Board.

libel defamation published in a permanent form, such as in a newspaper, book, or broadcast.

licensing laws laws governing the sale of alcoholic drinks. Most countries have some restrictions on the sale of alcoholic drinks, if not an outright ban, as in the case of Islamic countries.

lien the right to retain goods owned by another until the owner has satisfied a claim against him by the person in possession of the goods. For example, the goods may have been provided as security for a debt.

Lord Advocate chief law officer of the Crown in Scotland who has ultimate responsibility for criminal prosecutions in Scotland. The Lord Advocate does not usually act in inferior courts where prosecution is carried out by proscurators-fiscal acting under the Lord Advocate's instructions.

Lord Chancellor UK state official, originally the royal secretary, today a member of the cabinet, whose office ends with a change of government. The Lord Chancellor acts as speaker of the House of Lords, may preside over the court of appeal, and is head of the judiciary.

magistrate in English law, a person who presides in a magistrates' court: either a justice of the

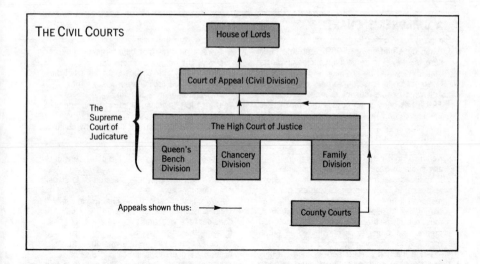

THE CIVIL COURTS

House of Lords

Court of Appeal (Civil Division)

The Supreme Court of Judicature

The High Court of Justice

Queen's Bench Division

Chancery Division

Family Division

County Courts

Appeals shown thus: ⟶

peace (with no legal qualifications, and unpaid) or a stipendiary magistrate. Stipendiary magistrates are paid, qualified lawyers largely used in London and major cities.

maintenance payments to support children or a spouse, under the terms of an agreement, or by a court order. In Britain, financial provision orders are made on divorce, but a court action can also be brought for maintenance without divorce proceedings. Applications for maintenance of illegitimate children are now treated in the same way as for legitimate children.

malpractice in US law, negligence by a professional person, usually a doctor, that may lead to an action for damages by the client. Such legal actions result in doctors having high insurance costs that are reflected in higher fees charged to their patients.

manslaughter the unlawful killing of a human being in circumstances less culpable than murder—for example, when the killer suffers extreme provocation, is in some way mentally ill (diminished responsibility), did not intend to kill but did so accidentally in the course of another crime or by behaving with criminal recklessness, or is the survivor of a genuine suicide pact that involved killing the other person.

maritime law that part of the law dealing with the sea: in particular, fishing areas, ships, and navigation. Seas are divided into *internal waters* governed by a state's internal laws (such as harbours, inlets); *territorial waters* (the area of sea adjoining the coast over which a state claims rights); the *continental shelf* (the seabed and subsoil that the coastal state is entitled to exploit beyond the territorial waters); and the *high seas*, where international law applies.

martial law the replacement of civilian by military authorities in the maintenance of order.

minor the legal term for those under the age of majority, which varies from country to country but is usually between 18 and 21. In the USA

(from 1971 for voting, and in some states for nearly all other purposes) and certain European countries (in Britain since 1970) the age of majority is 18. Most civic and legal rights and duties only accrue at the age of majority; for example, the rights to vote, to make a will, and (usually) to make a fully binding contract, and the duty to act as a juror.

motoring law the law affecting the use of vehicles on public roads. It covers the licensing of vehicles and drivers, and the criminal offences that can be committed by the owners and drivers of vehicles.

murder unlawful killing of one person by another. In the USA, first-degree murder requires proof of premeditation; second-degree murder falls between first-degree murder and manslaughter.

negligence negligence consists in doing some act that a 'prudent and reasonable' person would not do, or omitting to do some act that such a person would do. Negligence may arise in respect of a person's duty towards an individual or towards other people in general. Breach of the duty of care that results in reasonably foreseeable damage is a tort. *Contributory negligence* is a defence sometimes raised where the defendant to an action for negligence claims that the plaintiff by his or her own negligence contributed to the cause of the action.

neighbourhood watch local crime-prevention schemes. Under the supervision of police, groups of residents agree to increase watchfulness in order to prevent crimes such as burglary and vandalism in their area.

oath a solemn promise to tell the truth or perform some duty, combined with an appeal to a deity or something held sacred.

obscenity law law prohibiting the publishing of any material that tends to deprave or corrupt.

parole the conditional release of a prisoner from jail. The prisoner remains on licence until the date release would have been granted,

A CHILDREN'S CHARTER

When the Children Act 1989 came into force, Lord Mackay, the Lord Chancellor, announced that there would be no more 'winners and losers' of children when parents separate. The Act, which came into force on 14 October 1991, has been described as the most comprehensive and far-reaching reform of child law ever.

Tne Act covers virtually all law relating to children. The key principle is that the child's welfare is the paramount consideration in any decision about his or her upbringing. It introduces the important new concept 'parental responsibility': all the rights, duties, powers, responsibilities and authority which by law a parent has in relation to the child. Parents must recognize their responsibilities, and children are no longer to be considered as simply part of a divorce package.

While married parents and all mothers have parental responsibility automatically, as under the old law, the new Act allows unmarried fathers to acquire parental responsibility by court order. The father is then on the same footing in relation to the child as if married to the mother. An unmarried father may also enter into a shared parental responsibility agreement with the mother and this agreement, once recorded, may only be brought to an end by the court.

If resort to the court is necessary the first hurdle an unmarried father may face is to satisfy the court that he is the child's biological father; paternity testing may be required. Case law since implementation of the Act suggests that an unmarried father must also satisfy the court of a mutual attachment with the child, sufficient parental responsibility, and adequate reasons for making the application. Parental responsibility is not only retained on separation or divorce but also when a child is taken into care. It is only lost when a child is adopted.

The court recognizes that the family is the best place for a child to be brought up, even if the family is not perfect. Therefore the state, in the form of the court or local authority, should not intervene unless necessary to safeguard the child's welfare.

The Act requires that before making any decision, the court must consider:
—the ascertainable wishes and feelings of the child concerned (considered in the light of his/her age and understanding);
—the child's physical, emotional and educational needs;
—the likely effect on the child of any change in circumstances;
—the age, sex, background and any characteristics of the child which the court considers relevant;
—any harm the child has suffered or is at risk of suffering;
—how capable each of the parents, and any other person in relation to whom the court considers the question to be relevant, is of meeting the child's needs.

The Act creates a system whereby all courts in family proceedings will have the same remedies available to them. These include four new types of court order all granted under section 8 of the Act:

Contact order: this replaces the old access order and requires the person with whom the child lives to allow the child to visit or stay with the person named in the order.

Residence order: this replaces the old custody order and settles the arrangements about which person a child is to live with. A residence order can be made in favour of more than one person even though they don't live together: for example, a child might spend weekends with one parent and weekdays with another.

Prohibited steps order: this order prohibits certain actions, such as removal of the child from the UK, when abduction is feared.

Specific issue order: this gives directions for determining a specific question about which there is a dispute, for example, which school the child will attend. Depending on the type of proceedings, section 8 orders may be applied for by any genuinely concerned person, including a local authority, with the leave of the court. Children can also go to court themselves to apply for an order.

In general, court orders should be made only if they safeguard or promote the child's welfare. Undue delays are to be avoided under the new scheme.

and may be recalled if the authorities deem it necessary.

Under the Criminal Justice Act 1991 parole will be automatic for sentences under 4 years. and may be recalled if the authorities deem it necessary.

party a person who takes part in legal proceedings. Parties to a civil action may include one or more plaintiffs or defendants. In a criminal trial the parties include the Crown (as prosecutor) and one or more defendants.

patent or **letters patent** documents conferring the exclusive right to make, use, and sell an invention for a limited period. Ideas are not eligible; neither is anything not new.

In 1987 the US began issuing patents for new animal forms (new types of livestock and assorted organisms) being created by gene splitting. The payment of $909.5 million by Eastman Kodak to Polaroid 1990 was a record sum for infringement of patent.

perjury the offence of deliberately making a false statement on oath (or affirmation) when appearing as a witness in legal proceedings, on a point material to the question at issue. In Britain and the USA it is punishable by a fine, imprisonment, or both.

perverting the course of justice the criminal offence of acting in such a way as to prevent justice being done. Examples are tampering with evidence, misleading the police or a court, and threatening witnesses or jurors.

picketing gathering of workers and their trade-union representatives to try to persuade others to support them in an industrial dispute. Secondary picketing (picketing somewhere other than one's workplace) has been 'outlawed' since enactment of the Employment Act 1980. This allows for employers or other persons picketed to sue pickets who are not at their own workplace, and who are attempting to persuade other workers to break their contracts.

plaintiff a person who brings a civil action in a court of law seeking relief (for example, damages).

poaching illegal hunting of game and fish on someone elses property.

power of attorney legal authority to act on behalf of another, for a specific transaction, or for a particular period.

precedent the common law principle that, in deciding a particular case, judges are bound to follow any applicable principles of law laid down by superior courts in earlier reported cases.

probate formal proof of a will. In the UK, if its validity is unquestioned, it is proven in 'common form'; the executor, in the absence of other interested parties, obtains at a probate registry a grant upon their own oath. Otherwise, it must be proved in 'solemn form': its validity established at a probate court (in the Chancery Division of the High Court), those concerned being made parties to the action.

probation the placing of offenders under supervision of probation officers in the community, as an alternative to prison.

procurator fiscal officer of a Scottish sheriff's court who (combining the role of public prosecutor and coroner) inquires into suspicious deaths and carries out the preliminary questioning of witnesses to crime.

prosecution the party by whom criminal proceedings are instituted. In the UK, the prosecution is begun by bringing the accused (defendant) before a magistrate, either by warrant or summons, or by arrest without warrant. Most criminal prosecutions are conducted by the Crown Prosecution Service although other government departments may also prosecute some cases, for example the Department of Inland Revenue. An individual may bring a private prosecution, usually for assault.

provost chief magistrate of a Scottish burgh, approximate equivalent of an English mayor.

proxy a person authorized to stand in another's place; also the document conferring this right. The term usually refers to voting at meetings, but there may be marriages by proxy.

public inquiry in English law, a legal investigation where witnesses are called and evidence is produced in a similar fashion to a court of law. Inquiries may be held as part of legal procedure, or into a matter of public concern.

Queen's Counsel (QC) in England, a barrister appointed to senior rank by the Lord Chancellor. When the monarch is a king the term is *King's Counsel (KC)*.

rape sexual intercourse without the consent of the subject. Most cases of rape are of women by men. A new ruling in 1991 made rape within marriage an offence; in the first prosecution of such a case a London man was found guilty of raping his wife and jailed for five years.

receiver a person appointed by a court to collect and manage the assets of an individual, company, or partnership in serious financial difficulties. In the case of bankruptcy, the assets may be sold and distributed by a receiver to creditors.

redundancy rights in English law, the rights of employees to a payment (linked to the length of their employment) if they lose their jobs because they are no longer needed. The statutory right was introduced in 1965, but payments are often made in excess of the statutory scheme.

remand the committing of an accused but not convicted person into custody or release on bail pending a court hearing.

reply, right of right of a member of the public to respond to a media statement. A statutory right of reply, enforceable by a Press Commission, as exists in many Western European countries, failed to reach the statute book in the UK in 1989. There is no legal provision in the UK that any correction should receive the same prominence as the original statement and legal aid is not available in defamation cases, so that only the wealthy are able to sue. However, the major newspapers signed a Code of Practice in 1989 that promised some public protection.

reprieve legal temporary suspension of the execution of a sentence of a criminal court. It is usually associated with the death penalty. It is distinct from a pardon (extinguishing the sentence) and commutation (alteration) of a sentence (for example, from death to life imprisonment).

rule of law doctrine that no individual, however powerful, is above the law. The principle had a significant influence on attempts to restrain the arbitrary use of power by rulers and on the growth of legally enforceable human rights in many Western countries. It is often used as a justification for separating legislative from judicial power.

Scots law the legal system of Scotland. Owing to its separate development, Scotland has a system differing from the rest of the UK, being based on civil law. Its continued separate existence was guaranteed by the Act of Union with England in 1707.

settlement out of court a compromise reached between the parties to a legal dispute. Most civil legal actions are settled out of court, reducing legal costs, and avoiding the uncertainty of the outcome of a trial.

sheriff in England and Wales, the crown's chief executive officer in a county for ceremonial purposes; in Scotland, the equivalent of the English county-court judge, but also dealing with criminal cases; and in the USA the popularly elected head law-enforcement officer of a county, combining judicial authority with administrative duties.

show trial public and well-reported trials of peo-

EC LEGISLATION FROM START TO FINISH (DIRECTIVES AND REGULATIONS)

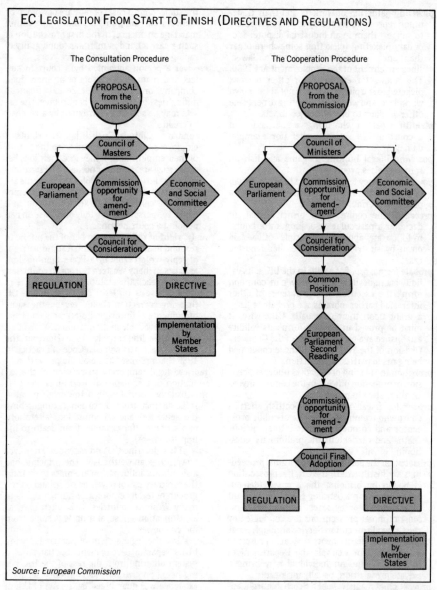

Source: European Commission

ple accused of crimes against the state. In the USSR in the 1930s and 1940s, Stalin carried out show trials against economic saboteurs, Communist Party members, army officers, and even members of the Bolshevik leadership.

slander spoken defamatory statement, although if broadcast on radio or television it constitutes libel.

solicitor in the UK, a member of one of the two branches of the English legal profession, the other being a barrister. A solicitor is a lawyer who provides all-round legal services (making wills, winding up estates, conveyancing, divorce, and litigation). A solicitor cannot appear at High Court level, but must brief a barrister

on behalf of his or her client. Solicitors may become circuit judges and recorders. In the USA the general term is lawyer or attorney.

subpoena an order requiring someone who might not otherwise come forward of his or her own volition to give evidence before a court or judicial official at a specific time and place. A witness who fails to comply with a subpoena is in contempt of court.

summons a court order officially delivered, requiring someone to appear in court on a certain date.

tagging, electronic long-distance monitoring of the movements of people charged with or convicted of a crime, thus enabling them to be

Changing Faces

LORD CHIEF JUSTICE

On 26 April 1992 Sir Peter Taylor became Lord Chief Justice. Lord Taylor, previously a Lord Justice of Appeal, is aged 61. He first came to the attention of the public at the time of his report on the Hillsborough football club disaster.

Aware of the need to restore public confidence in, and improve aspects of, the criminal justice system, Lord Taylor said on his appointment that 'Judges need to be made more accountable and user-friendly'. Issues expected to concern the new Lord Chief Justice include the increase of advocacy rights, judicial appointments (there is only one female Lord Justice of Appeal and only 4 out of 84 High Court judges are women), the televising of criminal trials, libel damages, and the role of the Court of Appeal when a wrongful conviction has been alleged.

Lord Lane, who had been Lord Chief Justice since 1980, could have continued in office until July 1993 (his 75th birthday). His resignation had been widely expected following the quashing of the convictions of the Guildford Four, the Birmingham Six, and the Tottenham Three. Lord Lane had dismissed the latter two cases before they were referred back to the Court of Appeal by the Home Secretary.

The Lord Chancellor, Lord Mackay, is planning to cut the retirement age of judges from 75 to 70 following widespread criticism of the judiciary as old and out of touch with mainstream opinion.

DIRECTOR OF PUBLIC PROSECUTIONS

In February 1992 Barbara Mills QC was appointed Director of Public Prosecutions (DPP). The former director of the Serious Fraud Office (SFO), a post she held from September 1990, she was called to the Bar in 1963 and was junior crown prosecutor at the Old Bailey from 1981 to 1986. She became a QC in 1986 and represented Winston Silcott in the Blakelock murder trial and prosecuted in the Guinness trial. During her time in office at the SFO, well-publicized trials included the Barlow Clowes, Polly Peck, BCCI, and Maxwell cases. In the Blue Arrow trial, the judge ordered the jury to dismiss the case because of the flimsiness of the evidence against the defendants. The case ran up legal fees of £50 million and led to widespread criticism of the SFO's handling of the case. Issues expected to concern the new DPP are rights of audience of solicitors and other advocates in the Crown Prosecution Service, the length of trials and the relationship of the service to the police and courts. While Barbara Mills is the first woman to be appointed DPP, her successor at the SFO, George Staple, is the first solicitor to be appointed to that office.

The former Director of Public Prosecutions, Sir Allan Green QC, resigned in October 1991 after being stopped by the police for allegedly kerb crawling in the Kings Cross area of North London. Sir Allan has since returned to the Bar to concentrate on criminal defence cases.

---

detained in their homes rather than in prison. In the UK, the system was being tested in Nottingham from Aug 1989. The system is in use in the USA.

telephone tapping method of listening in on a telephone conversation; in the UK and the USA it is a criminal offence if done without a warrant or the consent of the person concerned.

In 1990 the Home Office carried out an estimated 35,000 telephone taps, and issued 539 warrants.

tort a wrongful act for which someone can be sued for damages in a civil court. It includes such acts as libel, trespass, injury done to someone (whether intentionally or by negligence), and inducement to break a contract (although breach of contract itself is not a tort).

In general a tort is distinguished from a crime in that it affects the interests of an individual rather than of society at large, but some crimes can also be torts (for example, assault).

treason act of betrayal, in particular against the sovereign or the state to which the offender owes allegiance. Treason is punishable in Britain by death.

treasure trove in England, any gold or silver, plate or bullion found concealed in a house or the ground, the owner being unknown. Normally, treasure originally hidden, and not abandoned, belongs to the crown, but if the treasure was casually lost or intentionally abandoned, the first finder is entitled to it against all but the true owner. Objects buried with no intention of recovering them, for example in a burial mound, do not rank as treasure trove, and belong to the owner of the ground.

trespass going on to the land of another without authority. A landowner has the right to eject a trespasser by the use of reasonable force and can sue for any damage caused. A trespasser who refuses to leave when requested may, in certain circumstances, be committing a criminal offence under the Public Order Act 1986 (designed to combat convoys of caravans trespassing on farm land).

trial the determination of an accused person's innocence or guilt by means of the judicial examination of the issues of the case in accordance with the law of the land. The two parties in a trial, the defendant and plaintiff, or their counsel, put forward their cases and question the witnesses; on the basis of this evidence the jury or other tribunal body will decide on the innocence or guilt of the defendant.

tribunal strictly, a court of justice, but used in English law for a body appointed by the government to arbitrate in disputes, or investigate certain matters. Tribunals usually consist of a lawyer as chair, sitting with two lay assessors.

trust arrangement whereby a person or group of people holds property for the benefit of others entitled to the beneficial interest.

verdict a jury's decision, usually a finding of 'guilty' or 'not guilty'.

ward of court in the UK, a child whose guardian is the High Court. Any person may, by issuing proceedings, make the High Court guardian of any child within its jurisdiction. No important step in the child's life can then be taken without the court's leave.

will declaration of how a person wishes his or her property to be disposed of after death. It also appoints administrators of the estate (executors) and may contain wishes on other matters, such as place of burial or use of organs for transplant. Wills must comply with formal legal requirements.

witness a person who was present at some event (such as an accident, a crime, or the signing of a document) or has relevant special knowledge (such as a medical expert) and can be called on to give evidence in a court of law.

writ a document issued by a court requiring performance of certain actions.

LEGAL AND PENAL INSTITUTIONS

Bar to be called to the Bar is to become a barrister. Prospective barristers must complete a course of study in law and be admitted to one of the four Inns of Court before they can be 'called'. The General Council of the Bar and of the Inns of Court (known as the Bar Council) is the professional governing body of the Bar.

borstal institutions in the UK, formerly places of detention for offenders aged 15–21. The name was taken from Borstal prison near Rochester, Kent, where the system was first introduced in 1908. From 1983 they were officially known as youth custody centres, and have now been replaced by *young offender institutions*.

Citizens Advice Bureau (CAB) UK organization established 1939 to provide information and advice to the public on any subject, such as personal problems, financial, house purchase, or consumer rights. If required, the bureau will act on behalf of citizens, drawing on its own sources of legal and other experts. There are more than 600 bureaux located all over the UK.

Court of Appeal UK court comprising two divisions: a Civil Division and a Criminal Division set up under the Criminal Appeals Act 1968. The Court of Appeal consists of 16 Lord Justices of Appeal and a number of ex-officio judges, for example, the Lord Chancellor, the Master of the Rolls, and the President of the Family Division. Usually, three judges sit, but where a case raises new or important issues, up to seven judges may form the court. The Criminal Division of the Court of Appeal has the power to revise sentences or quash a conviction on the grounds that in all the circumstances of the case the verdict is unsafe or unsatisfactory, or that the judgement of the original trial judge was wrong in law, or that there was a material irregularity during the course of the trial.

The Court of Appeal in 1991 had a backlog of appeals by people charged and prosecuted by the West Midlands Serious Crime Squad, which was disbanded due to corruption.

Court of Protection in English law, a department of the High Court that deals with the estates of people who are incapable, by reason of mental disorder, of managing their own property and affairs.

Criminal Injuries Compensation Board UK board established 1964 to administer financial compensation by the state for victims of crimes of violence. Victims can claim compensation for their injuries, but not for damage to property. The compensation awarded is similar to the amount that would be obtained by a court in damages for personal injury.

Criminal Investigation Department (CID) detective branch of the London Metropolitan Police, established 1878 and comprising a force of about 4,000 men and women, recruited entirely from the uniformed police and controlled by an assistant commissioner. Branches are now also found in the regional police forces.

Crown Prosecution Service body established by the Prosecution of Offences Act 1985, responsible for prosecuting all criminal offences in England and Wales. It is headed by the Director of Public Prosecutions (DPP), and brings England and Wales in line with Scotland (which has a procurator fiscal) in having a prosecution service independent of the police.

European Court of Human Rights court that hears cases referred from the European Commission of Human Rights, if the Commission has failed to negotiate a friendly settlement in a case where individuals' rights have been violated by a member state. The Court sits in Strasbourg, and comprises one judge for every state that is a party to the 1950 convention. Court rulings have forced the Republic of Ireland to drop its constitutional ban on homosexuality, and Germany to cease to exclude political left- and right-wingers from the civil service.

European Court of Justice the court of the European Community (EC), which is responsible for interpreting Community law and ruling on breaches by member states and others of such law. It sits in Luxembourg with judges from the member states.

Inns of Court four private societies in London, England: Lincoln's Inn, Gray's Inn, Inner Temple, and Middle Temple. All barristers must belong to one of the Inns of Court. The

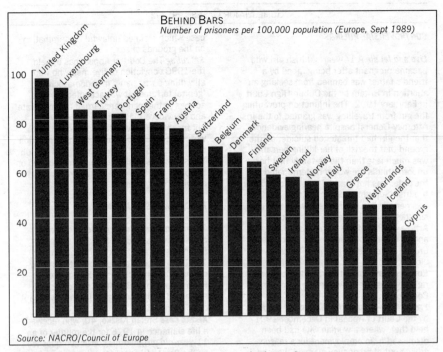

BEHIND BARS
Number of prisoners per 100,000 population (Europe, Sept 1989)

Source: NACRO/Council of Europe

main function of each Inn is the education, government, and protection of its members. Each is under the administration of a body of Benchers (judges and senior barristers).

International Court of Justice the main judicial organ of the United Nations, at The Hague, the Netherlands.

Interpol (acronym for *Inter*national Criminal *Pol*ice Organization) agency founded following the Second International Judicial Police Conference 1923 with its headquarters in Vienna, and reconstituted after World War II with its headquarters in Paris. It has an international criminal register, fingerprint file, and methods index.

Land Registry, HM official body set up 1925 to register legal rights to land in England and Wales. There has been a gradual introduction, since 1925, of compulsory registration of land in different areas of the country. This requires the purchaser of land to register details of his or her title and all other rights (such as mortgages and easements) relating to the land. Once registered, the title to the land is guaranteed by the Land Registry, subject to those interests that cannot be registered; this makes the buying and selling of land easier and cheaper. The records are open to public inspection (since Dec 1990).

Law Commission in Britain, either of two statutory bodies established 1965 (one for England and Wales and one for Scotland) which consider proposals for law reform and publish their findings. They also keep British law under constant review, systematically developing and reforming it by, for example, the repeal of obsolete and unnecessary enactments.

law courts the bodies that adjudicate in legal disputes. Civil and criminal cases are usually dealt with by separate courts. In many countries there is a hierarchy of courts that provide an appeal system.

In England and Wales the court system was reorganized under the Courts Act 1971. The higher courts are: the *House of Lords* (the highest court for the whole of Britain), which deals with both civil and criminal appeals; the *Court of Appeal*, which is divided between criminal and civil appeal courts; the *High Court of Justice* dealing with important civil cases; *crown courts*, which handle criminal cases; and *county courts*, which deal with civil matters. *Magistrates' courts* deal with minor criminal cases and are served by justices of the peace or stipendiary (paid) magistrates; and *juvenile courts* are presided over by specially qualified justices. There are also special courts, such as the Restrictive Practices Court and the Employment Appeal Tribunal.

The courts are organized in six circuits. The towns of each circuit are first-tier (High Court and circuit judges dealing with both criminal and civil cases), second-tier (High Court and circuit judges dealing with criminal cases only), or third-tier (circuit judges dealing with criminal cases only). Cases are allotted according to gravity among High Court and circuit judges and recorders (part-time judges with the same jurisdiction as circuit judges). From 1971, solicitors were allowed for the first time to appear in

SOME MAJOR CASES 1991–92

CONTROVERSIAL RULINGS

Live and let die A 14-year-old Irish girl who became pregnant after being raped by a friend's father was banned from seeking an abortion in Britain by the Dublin High Court in February 1992. The injunction preventing the girl from travelling was granted to the Irish Attorney-General despite hearing evidence that the girl had threatened suicide, on the ground that the risk of her killing herself was much less than the certainty that her unborn child's life would be terminated if the order was not made. However, on appeal the Irish Supreme Court ruled that abortion was permissible where there was a real and substantial risk to the life of the mother. Article 40.3.3 of the Irish constitution guarantees equal protection to the life of the unborn child and its mother. The case was closely watched by international lawyers as European law currently protects a citizen's right to travel freely within the European Community.

Pregnancy—grounds for dismissal A decision by the Court of Appeal in December 1991 held that, where a woman who had been dismissed from employment for a reason arising out of pregnancy claimed that she had been unlawfully discriminated against, it was necessary to establish whether a man with a condition as nearly comparable as possible, and which had the same practical effect upon his ability to do the job, would or would not have been dismissed. The case, the first of its kind, involved the dismissal of a woman replacing another woman about to take maternity leave but who found herself to be pregnant as well. The applicant lost her case which claimed unlawful discrimination on the grounds of sex.

SM ruling The Court of Appeal has upheld the 1990 conviction of five men who were all willing participants in sadomasochistic 'genital tortures'. It was accepted that the actions of the men were carried out in private and the videos that had been made were not for sale. However, the court ruled that a victim's consent to wounding or the infliction of injury could not negate a charge of assault. The sentences of all five men were reduced on the basis that they were not aware that their activities were criminal.

MISCARRIAGES OF JUSTICE

Tottenham Three Winston Silcott had his conviction quashed 25 Nov 1991, as did Engin Raghip and Mark Braithwaite 5 Dec 1991. All three had been convicted of murdering PC Blakelock on the Broadwater Farm Estate in 1985. The Court of Appeal expressed 'profound regret' for their wrongful conviction.

Kiszko case Stefan Kiszko, 40, who received a life sentence in 1976 for the murder of an 11-year-old girl, had his conviction quashed by the Court of Appeal after disclosure that fresh evidence showed that he could not have been the killer.

Judith Ward case Judith Ward was freed May 1992, following the Court of Appeal's ruling that her conviction was 'unsafe and unsatisfactory'. She was jailed for life in 1974 for allegedly killing 12 people in the M62 bombing case. Convicted on the basis of an uncorroborated confession, she was later acknowledged to be prone to fantasy.

---

and conduct cases at the level of the crown courts, and solicitors as well as barristers of ten years' standing became eligible for appointment as recorders, who after five years become eligible as circuit judges. In 1989 a Green Paper proposed (1) omitting the Bar's monopoly of higher courts, removing demarcation between barristers and solicitors; (2) cases to be taken on a 'no-win, no-fee' basis (as already happens in Scotland). In the UK 1989 there were 5,500 barristers and 47,000 solicitors.

In Scotland, the supreme civil court is the **Court of Session**, with appeal to the House of Lords; the highest criminal court is the **High Court of Justiciary**, with no appeal to the House of Lords.

magistrates' court in England and Wales, a local law court that mainly deals with minor criminal cases, but also decides, in committal proceedings, whether more serious criminal cases should be referred to the crown court. It deals with some civil matters, too, such as licensing, certain domestic and matrimonial proceedings, and may include a juvenile court. A magistrates' court consists of between two and seven lay justices of the peace (who are advised on the law by a clerk to the justices), or a single paid lawyer called a stipendiary magistrate.

Old Bailey popular name for the Central Criminal Court in London, situated in a street of that name in the City of London, off Ludgate Hill.

Police Complaints Authority in the UK, an independent group of a dozen people set up under the Police and Criminal Evidence Act 1984 to supervise the investigation of serious complaints against the police by members of the public.

prison place of confinement for those convicted of contravening the laws of the state; most countries claim to aim at rehabilitation. The average number of people in prison in the UK (1990) was 45,500; 1,775 were women (less than 4%). About 9,400 were on remand (awaiting trial or sentence), and, due to overcrowding in prisons, over 1,000 prisoners were held in police cells. It costs 30 times more per

Drug Offences in the UK

Numbers

	1976	1981	1986	1990
Unlawful production	785	1,603	944	629
Unlawful supply	836	1,000	1,876	2,151
Possession with intent to supply unlawfully	496	699	1,858	2,751
Unlawful possession	11,097	14,850	20,052	39,350
Unlawful import or export	366	1,357	1,525	2,478
All drug offences	12,754	17,921	23,905	44,922

Source: Social Trends 1992

year to keep a prisoner in custody than it would for 100 hours' community service.

Experiments have been made in Britain and elsewhere in 'open prisons' without bars, which included releasing prisoners in the final stages of their sentence to work in ordinary jobs outside the prison, and the provision of aftercare on release. Attempts to deal with the increasing number of young offenders include, from 1982, accommodation in community homes in the case of minor offences, with (in more serious cases) 'short, sharp shock' treatment in detention centres

(although the latter was subsequently found to have little effect on reconviction rates).

In 1990 there was widespread rioting in several prisons in Britain, notably the 25-day siege at Strangeways Prison in Manchester; this was the longest ever prison seige in the UK, during which several prisoners died and extensive damage was caused.

In April 1992, The Wolds, the first privatised prison, opened. Situated near Hull, it has a capacity of 320 and will confine only prisoners on remand.

Writers to the Signet society of Scottish solicitors. Their predecessors were originally clerks in the secretary of state's office entrusted with the preparation of documents requiring the signet, or seal. Scottish solicitors may be members of other societies, such as the Royal Faculty of Procurators in Glasgow.

Young Offender Institution in England, institution of detention for young offenders, both juveniles (aged under 17) and young adults (17–21). The period of detention depends both on the seriousness of the offence and on the age and sex of the offender. A number of statutory requirements support the principle that a custodial sentence in a young offender institution should only be used as a last resort for young offenders. The institution was introduced by the Criminal Justice Act 1988.

ETHNIC GROUPS AND LANGUAGES

Abkhazi member of a Muslim minority in Georgia. Abkhazia was a Georgian kingdom from the 4th century, and converted from Christianity to Islam in the 17th century. By the 1980s some 17% of the population were Muslims and two-thirds were of Georgian origin.

Afrikaans language an official language (with English) of the Republic of South Africa and Namibia. Spoken mainly by the Afrikaners—descendants of Dutch and other 17th-century colonists—it is a variety of the Dutch language, modified by circumstance and the influence of German, French, and other immigrant as well as local languages. It became a standardized written language about 1875.

Afro-Asiatic languages (formerly *Hamito-Semitic languages)* family of languages spoken throughout the world. It has two main branches: the *Hamitic* languages of N Africa and the *Semitic* languages originating in Syria, Mesopotamia, Palestine, and Arabia, but now found from Morocco in the west to the Persian Gulf in the east.

Ainu aboriginal people of Japan, driven north in the 4th century AD by ancestors of the Japanese. They now number about 25,000, inhabiting Japanese and Russian territory on Sakhalin, Hokkaido, and the Kuril Islands. Their language has no written form, and is unrelated to any other.

Algonquin member of a North American Indian hunting and fishing people formerly living around the Ottawa River in E Canada. Many now live on reservations in NE USA, E Ontario, and W Québec; others have chosen to live among the general populations of Canada and the USA.

Amhara member of an ethnic group comprising approximately 25% of the population of Ethiopia; 13,000,000 (1987). The Amhara are traditionally farmers. They speak Amharic, a language of the Semitic branch of the Afro-Asiatic family. Most are members of the Ethiopian Christian Church.

Annamese or *Vietnamese* or *Nguoi Kinh* member of the majority ethnic group in Vietnam, comprising 90% of the population. The Annamese (Vietnamese) language belongs to the Viet-Muong group of the Austro-Asiatic family. Their religious beliefs embrace Buddhism, Confucianism, and Taoism, and to a certain extent Christianity. Some Annamese subscribe to Cao Dai, a syncretist religion embracing Eastern and Western elements.

Arab member of a Semitic people native to the Arabian peninsula but now settled throughout N Africa and the nations of the Middle East. Arabic is the main Semitic language of the Afro-Asiatic family of W Asia and N Africa, originating among the Arabs of the Arabian peninsula. It is spoken by about 120 million people (1991). Arabic script is written from right to left.

Armenian member of the largest ethnic group inhabiting Armenia. There are Armenian minorities in Azerbaijan, as well as in Turkey and Iran. Christianity was introduced to the ancient Armenian kingdom in the 3rd century. There are 4-5 million speakers of Armenian, which belongs to the Indo-European family of languages.

Asante or *Ashanti* person of Asante culture from central Ghana, west of Lake Volta. The Asante language belongs to the Kwa branch of the Niger-Congo family.

Australian Aborigine any of the 500 groups of indigenous inhabitants of the continent of Australia, who migrated to this region from S Asia about 40,000 years ago. They were hunters and gatherers, living throughout the continent in small kin-based groups before European settlement. Several hundred different languages developed, the most important being Aranda (Arunta), spoken in central Australia, and Murngin, spoken in Arnhem Land. In recent years there has been a movement for the recognition of Aborigine rights and campaigning against racial discrimination.

Aymara member of an American Indian people of Bolivia and Peru, builders of a great culture, who were conquered first by the Incas and then by the Spaniards. Today 1.4 million Aymara farm and herd llamas and alpacas in the highlands; their language, belonging to the Andean-Equatorial language family, survives and their Roman Catholicism incorporates elements of their old beliefs.

Azerbaijani or *Azeri* native of the Azerbaijan region of Iran (population 5,500,000) or of the Republic of Azerbaijan (formerly a Soviet republic) (population 7,145,600). Azerbaijani is a Turkic language belonging to the Altaic family. Of the total population of Azerbaijanis, 70% are Shi'ite Muslims, 30% Sunni Muslims.

Bashkir member of the majority ethnic group of the autonomous republic of Bashkir in Russia. The Bashkirs have been Muslims since the 13th century. The Bashkir language belongs to the Turkic branch of the Altaic family, and has about 1 million speakers.

Basque member of a people who occupy the Basque Country of central N Spain and the extreme SW of France. The Basques are a pre-Indo-European people who largely maintained their independence until the 19th century. During the Spanish Civil War 1936-39, they were on the republican side defeated by Franco. Their language (Euskara) is unrelated to any other language. The Basque separatist movement ETA (Euskadi ta Askatasuna 'Basque Nation and Liberty') and the French organization Iparretarrak ('ETA fighters from the North Side') have engaged in guerrilla activity from 1968 in an attempt to secure a united Basque state.

Bengali person of Bengali culture from Bangladesh and India (W Bengal, Tripura). There are 80–150 million speakers of Bengali, an Indo-Iranian language belonging to the Indo-European family. It is the official language of Bangladesh and of the state of Bengal, and is also used by emigrant Bangladeshi and Bengali communities in such countries as the UK and the USA. Bengalis in Bangladesh are predominantly Muslim, whereas those in India are mainly Hindu.

Bhil member of a semi-nomadic people of Dravidian origin, living in NW India and numbering about 4 million. They are hunter-gatherers and also practise shifting cultivation. The Bhili language belongs to the Indo-European family, as does Gujarati, which is also spoken by the Bhil. Their religion is Hinduism.

Bihari member of a N Indian people, also living in Bangladesh, Nepal, and Pakistan, and numbering over 40 million. The Bihari are mainly Muslim. The Bihari language is related to Hindi and has several widely varying dialects. It belongs to the Indic branch of the Indo-European family. Many Bihari were massacred during the formation of Bangladesh, which they opposed.

Burman member of the largest ethnic group in Myanmar (formerly Burma). The Burmans, speakers of a Sino-Tibetan language, migrated from the hills of Tibet, settling in the areas around Mandalay by the 11th century AD.

Bushman former name for the Kung, San, and other hunter-gatherer groups (for example, the Gikwe, Heikom, and Sekhoin) living in and around the Kalahari Desert in southern Africa. They number approximately 50,000 and speak San and other languages of the Khoisan family. They are characteristically small-statured.

Byelorussian or **Belorussian** 'White Russian' native of Belarus. Byelorussian, a Balto-Slavic language belonging to the Indo-European family, is spoken by about 10 million people, including some in Poland. It is written in the Cyrillic script. Byelorussian literature dates to the 11th century AD.

Celtic languages branch of the Indo-European family, divided into two groups: the **Brythonic** or **P-Celtic** (Welsh, Cornish, Breton, and Gaulish) and the **Goidelic** or **Q-Celtic** (Irish, Scottish, and Manx Gaelic). Celtic languages once stretched from the Black Sea to Britain, but have been in decline for centuries, limited to the so-called 'Celtic fringe' of western Europe.

Chinese native to or an inhabitant of China and Taiwan, or a person of Chinese descent. The Chinese comprise more than 25% of the world's population, and the Chinese language (Mandarin) is the largest member of the Sino-Tibetan family.

Chuvash member of the majority ethnic group inhabiting the autonomous republic of Chuvash, Russia. The Chuvash have lived in the middle Volga region since the 8th century.

Their language belongs to the Altaic family, although whether it is a member of the Turkic branch or constitutes a branch on its own is not certain.

Copt descendant of those ancient Egyptians who adopted Christianity in the 1st century and refused to convert to Islam after the Arab conquest. They now form a small minority (about 5%) of Egypt's population. Coptic is a member of the Afro-Asiatic language family. It is descended from the language of the ancient Egyptians and is the ritual language of the Coptic Christian Church. It is written in the Greek alphabet with some additional characters derived from demotic script.

creole language any pidgin language that has ceased to be simply a trade jargon in ports and markets and has become the mother tongue of a particular community. Many creoles have developed into distinct languages with literatures of their own; for example, Jamaican Creole, Haitian Creole, Krio in Sierra Leone, and Tok Pisin, now the official language of Papua New Guinea.

Croat member of the majority ethnic group in Croatia; there is also a Croatian minority in Bosnia-Herzegovina. Their language is generally considered to be identical to that of the Serbs, hence its name Serbo-Croatian. The Croats are predominantly Roman Catholics.

Dariganga member of a Mongolian people numbering only 30,000. Their language is a dialect of Khalka, the official language of Mongolia. In the past, the Dariganga were nomads, and lived by breeding camels for use in the Chinese imperial army. With the rise of the Communist regime in China, they supported the new Mongolian state, and have become sedentary farmers.

Dinka member of a Nilotic minority group in S Sudan, numbering 1–2 million (1991). Primarily cattle herders, they inhabit the lands around the river system that flows into the White Nile. Their language belongs to the Nilo-Saharan family. The Dinka's traditional beliefs conflict with those of Islam, the official state religion; this has caused clashes between the Dinka and the Sudanese army.

Dogon member of the W African Dogon culture from E Mali and NW Burkina Faso. The Dogon number approximately 250,000 and their language belongs to the Voltaic (Gur) branch of the Niger-Congo family.

Dongxiang member of a minority ethnic group mainly living in Gansu Province, China, numbering around 279,000 (1992). They are Muslims and their language belongs to the Altaic family. The Dongxiang are farmers and cultivate potatoes, peaches, and apricots. They are known for their narrative poems and folk songs.

Estonian member of the largest ethnic group in Estonia. There are 1 million speakers of the Estonian language, a member of the Finno-Ugric branch of the Uralic family. Most live in Estonia.

Ewe member of a group of people inhabiting Ghana and Togo, numbering about 25 million (1991). The Ewe live by fishing and farming, and retain many traditional beliefs. Their language belongs to the Kwa branch of the Niger-Congo family.

Fang member of a W African people living in the rainforests of Cameroon, Equatorial Guinea, and NW Gabon, numbering about 2.5 million. They live by farming, as well as by hunting and fishing. In the colonial period the Fang were involved in trading, and used coins made of copper and iron. The Fang language belongs to the Bantu branch of the Niger-Congo family.

Farsi or **Persian** language belonging to the Indo-Iranian branch of the Indo-European family, and the official language of Iran (formerly Persia). It is also spoken in Afghanistan, Iraq, and Tajikistan.

Finno-Ugric group of more than 20 languages belonging to the Uralic family and spoken by some 22 million people (1991) in scattered communities from Norway in the northwest to Siberia in the east and the Carpathian Mountains in the south. Members of the family include Finnish, Saami, and Hungarian.

Fon member of a people living mainly in Benin, and also in Nigeria, numbering about 2.5 million. The Fon language belongs to the Kwa branch of the Niger-Congo family. The Fon founded a kingdom which became powerful in the 18th and 19th centuries through the slave trade, and the region became known as the Slave Coast.

Fulani member of a W African culture from the southern Sahara and Sahel. Traditionally nomadic pastoralists and traders, Fulani groups are found in Senegal, Guinea, Mali, Burkina Faso, Niger, Nigeria, Chad, and Cameroon. The Fulani language is divided into four dialects and belongs to the W Atlantic branch of the Niger-Congo family; it has more than 10 million speakers.

Galla or **Oromo** nomadic pastoralists inhabiting S Ethiopia and NW Kenya. Galla is an Afro-Asiatic language, and is spoken by about 12 million people.

Ganda member of the Baganda people, the majority ethnic group in Uganda; the Baganda also live in Kenya. Until the 19th century they formed an independent kingdom, the largest in E Africa. It was a British protectorate 1894–1962, and the monarchy was officially overthrown in 1966. Their language, Luganda, belongs to the Niger-Congo language family and has about 3 million speakers.

Georgian or **Grazinian** member of any of a number of related groups which make up the largest ethnic group in Georgia and the surrounding area. There are 3-4 million speakers of Georgian, a member of the Caucasian language family.

Germanic languages branch of the Indo-European language family, divided into **East Germanic** (Gothic, now extinct), **North Germanic** (Danish, Faroese, Icelandic, Norwegian, Swedish), and **West Germanic** (Afrikaans, Dutch, English, Flemish, Frisian, German, Yiddish).

Gond member of a heterogenous people of central India, about half of whom speak unwritten languages belonging to the Dravidian family. The rest speak Indo-European languages. There are over 4 million Gonds, most of whom live in Madhya Pradesh, E Maharashtra, and N Andra Pradesh, although some live in Orissa. Traditionally, many Gonds practised shifting cultivation; agriculture and livestock remain the basis of the economy.

Guaraní member of a South American Indian people who formerly inhabited the area that is now Paraguay, S Brazil, and Bolivia. The Guaraní live mainly in reserves; few retain the traditional ways of hunting in the tropical forest, cultivation, and ritual warfare. About 1 million speak Guaraní, a member of the Tupian language group.

Gujarati inhabitant of Gujarat on the NW coast of India. The Gujaratis number approximately 30 million and speak their own Indo-European language, Gujarati, which has a long literary tradition. They are predominantly Hindu (90%), with Muslim (8%) and Jain (2%) minorities.

Hamito-Semitic languages former name for the Afro-Asiatic family of languages.

Han member of the majority ethnic group in China, numbering about 990 million. The Hans speak a wide variety of dialects of the same monosyllabic language, a member of the Sino-Tibetan family. Their religion combines Buddhism, Taoism, Confucianism, and ancestor worship.

Hausa member of an agricultural Muslim people of NW Nigeria, numbering 9 million. The Hausa language belongs to the Chadic sub-family of the Afro-Asiatic language group. It is used as a trade language throughout W Africa.

Hindi language member of the Indo-Iranian branch of the Indo-European language family, the official language of the Republic of India, although resisted as such by the Dravidian-speaking states of the south. Hindi proper is used by some 30% of Indians, in such northern states as Uttar Pradesh and Madhya Pradesh.

Hmong member of a SE Asian highland people. They are predominantly hill farmers, rearing pigs and cultivating rice and grain, and many are involved in growing the opium poppy. Estimates of the size of the Hmong population vary between 1.5 million and 5 million, the greatest number being in China. Although traditional beliefs remain important, many have adopted Christianity. Their language belongs to the Sino-Tibetan family. The names **Meo** or **Miao**, sometimes used to refer to the Hmong, are considered derogatory.

Hui member of one of the largest minority groups in China, numbering around 7,219,000 (1992). Most live in the Ningxia autonomous region; the remainder are scattered over Gansu, Qinghai, and Xinjiang Uygur. They are Muslims and many are said to be the descendants of Arabs and Persians who came to trade

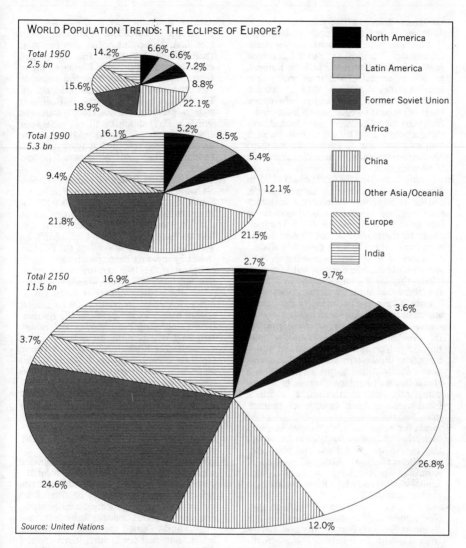

WORLD POPULATION TRENDS: THE ECLIPSE OF EUROPE?

Total 1950
2.5 bn

14.2%   6.6% 6.6%
                 7.2%
15.6%   8.8%
18.9%   22.1%

Total 1990
5.3 bn

16.1%   5.2% 8.5%
                5.4%
9.4%   12.1%
21.8%   21.5%

Total 2150
11.5 bn

2.7%   9.7%
16.9%
                3.6%
3.7%
                26.8%
24.6%
            12.0%

North America

Latin America

Former Soviet Union

Africa

China

Other Asia/Oceania

Europe

India

Source: United Nations

in China from the 7th century onwards. The Hui later became mixed with the Han Chinese, Uigurs, and Mongols.

Hutu member of the majority ethnic group of both Burundi and Rwanda. The Hutu tend to live as peasant farmers, while the ruling minority, the Tutsi, are town dwellers. There is a long history of violent conflict between the two groups. The Hutu language belongs to the Bantu branch of the Niger-Congo family.

Iban or *Sea Dyak* member of a Dyak people of central Borneo. Approximately 250,000 Iban live in the interior uplands of Sarawak, while another 10,000 live in the border area of W Kalimantan. Traditionally the Iban live in long houses divided into separate family units, and practise shifting cultivation. Their languages belong to the Austronesian family.

Ibo or *Igbo* member of the W African Ibo culture group occupying SE Nigeria and numbering

about 18,000,000. Primarily cultivators, they inhabit the richly forested tableland, bounded by the river Niger to the west and the river Cross to the east. They are divided into five main groups, and their languages belong to the Kwa branch of the Niger-Congo family.

Ifugao member of an indigenous people of N Luzon in the Philippines, numbering approximately 70,000. In addition to practising shifting cultivation on highland slopes, they build elaborate terraced rice fields. Their language belongs to the Austronesian family.

Indian languages traditionally, the languages of the subcontinent of India; since 1947, the languages of the Republic of India. These number some 200, depending on whether a variety is classified as a language or a dialect. They fall into five main groups, the two most widespread of which are the Indo-European languages (mainly in the north) and the Dravidian languages (mainly in the south).

Indo-European languages family of languages that includes some of the world's major classical languages (Sanskrit and Pali in India, Zend Avestan in Iran, Greek and Latin in Europe), as well as several of the most widely spoken languages (English worldwide; Spanish in Iberia, Latin America, and elsewhere; and the Hindi group of languages in N India). Indo-European languages were once located only along a geographical band from India through Iran into NW Asia, E Europe, the northern Mediterranean lands, N and W Europe and the British Isles.

Inuit people inhabiting the Arctic coasts of North America, the E islands of the Canadian Arctic, and the ice-free coasts of Greenland. Inuktitut, their language, has about 60,000 speakers; it belongs to the Eskimo-Aleut group. The Inuit object to the name Eskimos ('eaters of raw meat') given them by the Algonquin Indians.

Jat member of an ethnic group living in Pakistan and N India, numbering about 11 million (1991); they are the largest group in N India. The Jat are predominantly farmers. They speak Punjabi, a language belonging to the Iranian branch of the Indo-European family.

Javanese member of the largest ethnic group in the Republic of Indonesia. There are more than 50 million speakers of Javanese, which belongs to the western branch of the Austronesian family. Although the Javanese have a Hindu-Buddhist heritage, they are today predominantly Muslim, practising a branch of Islam known as *Islam Jawa*, which contains many Sufi features.

Kannada (or Kanarese) a language spoken in S India, the official state language of Karnataka; also spoken in Tamil Nadu and Maharashtra. There are over 20,000,000 speakers of Kannada, which belongs to the Dravidian family. Written records in Kannada date from the 5th century AD.

Karen member of a group of SE Asian peoples, numbering 1.9 million. They live in E Myanmar (formerly Burma), Thailand, and the Irrawaddy delta. Their language belongs to the Thai division of the Sino-Tibetan family. In 1984 the Burmese government began a large-scale military campaign against the Karen National Liberation Army (KNLA), the armed wing of the Karen National Union (KNU).

Kazakh or *Kazak* member of a pastoral Kirghiz people of Kazakhstan. Kazakhs also live in China (Xinjiang Uygur, Gansu, and Qinghai), Mongolia, and Afghanistan. There are 5-7 million speakers of Kazakh, a Turkic language belonging to the Altaic family. They are predominantly Sunni Muslim, although pre-Islamic customs have survived. Kazakhs herd horses and make use of camels; they also keep cattle. Traditionally the Kazakhs lived in tents and embarked on seasonal migrations in search of fresh pastures. Collectivized herds were established in the 1920s and 1930s, but Soviet programmes had to adapt to local circumstances.

Khmer or *Kmer* member of the largest ethnic group in Cambodia, numbering about 7 million. Khmer minorities also live in E Thailand and S Vietnam. The Khmer language belongs to the Mon-Khmer family of Austro-Asiatic languages. They live mainly in agricultural and fishing villages under a chief. The Khmers practise Theravāda Buddhism and trace descent through both male and female lines. Traditionally, Khmer society was divided into six groups: the royal family, the Brahmans (who officiated at royal festivals), Buddhist monks, officials, commoners, and slaves.

Khoikhoi (formerly *Hottentot*) member of a people living in Namibia and the Cape Province of South Africa, numbering about 30,000 (1991). Their language is related to San (spoken by the Kung) and belongs to the Khoisan family. Like the Kung, the Khoikhoi once inhabited a wider area, but were driven into the Kalahari Desert by invading Bantu peoples and Dutch colonists in the 18th century. They live as nomadic hunter-gatherers, in family groups.

Khoisan the smallest group of languages in Africa. It includes fewer than 50 languages, spoken mainly by the people of the Kalahari Desert (including the Khoikhoi and Kung). Two languages from this group are spoken in Tanzania. The Khoisan languages are known for their click consonants (clicking sounds made with the tongue, which function as consonants).

Kikuyu member of Kenya's dominant ethnic group, numbering about 3 million. The Kikuyu are primarily cultivators, although many are highly educated and have entered the professions. Their language belongs to the Bantu branch of the Niger-Congo family.

Kirghiz member of a pastoral people numbering approximately 1.5 million. They inhabit the central Asian region bounded by the Hindu Kush, the Himalayas, and the Tian Shan mountains. The Kirghiz are Sunni Muslims, and their Turkic language belongs to the Altaic family. During the winter the Kirghiz live in individual family yurts (tents made of felt). In summer they come together in larger settlements of up to 20 yurts. They herd sheep, goats, and yaks, and use Bactrian camels for transporting their possessions.

Kung (formerly *Bushman*) member of a small group of hunter-gatherer peoples of the NE Kalahari, southern Africa, still living to some extent nomadically. Their language belongs to the Khoisan family.

Kurd member of the Kurdish culture, living mostly in the Taurus and Sagros mountains of W Iran and N Iraq in the region called Kurdistan. Although divided among more powerful states, the Kurds have nationalist aspirations; there are some 8 million in Turkey (where they suffer from discriminatory legislation), 5 million in Iran, 4 million in Iraq, 500,000 in Syria, and 100,000 in Azerbaijan and Armenia. The Kurdish language is a member of the Indo-Iranian branch of the

Indo-European family and the Kurds are a non-Arab, non-Turkic ethnic group. They are predominantly Sunni Muslims, although there are some Shi'ites in Iran. Some 1 million Kurds were made homeless and 25,000 killed as a result of chemical-weapon attacks by Iraq 1984–89, and in 1991 more than 1 million were forced to flee their homes in N Iraq.

Lahnda language spoken by 15–20 million people in Pakistan and N India. It is closely related to Punjabi and Romany, and belongs to the Indo-Iranian branch of the Indo-European language family.

Latvian (or **Lett**) member of the majority ethnic group living in Latvia. The region has been Christian since the 13th century. The Latvian language is also known as **Lettish**; with Lithuanian, it is one of the two surviving members of the Baltic branch of the Indo-European family.

Lithuanian member of the majority ethnic group living in Lithuania, comprising 80% of the population. The Lithuanian language belongs to the Baltic branch of the Indo-European family and is closely related to Latvian. It acquired a written form in the 16th century, using the Latin alphabet, and is currently spoken by about 3-4 million people.

Makua member of a people living to the north of the Zambezi River in Mozambique. With the Lomwe people, they make up the country's largest ethnic group. The Makua are mainly farmers, living in villages ruled by chiefs. The Makua language belongs to the Niger-Congo family, and has about 5 million speakers.

Malagasy inhabitant of or native to Madagascar. The Malagasy language has about 9 million speakers; it belongs to the Austronesian family.

Malayalam southern Indian language, the official language of the state of Kerala. Malayalam is closely related to Tamil, also a member of the Dravidian language family; it is spoken by about 20 million people. Written records in Malayalam date from the 9th century AD.

Maori member of the indigenous Polynesian people of New Zealand, numbering 294,200 (1986), about 10% of the total population. Maori is a member of the Polynesian branch of the Austronesian language family. Only one-third use the language today, but efforts are being made to strengthen it after a long period of decline and official indifference. The Maoris claim 70% of the country's land; they have secured a ruling that the fishing grounds of the far north belong solely to local Maori people.

Maratha or **Mahratta** member of a people living mainly in Maharashtra, W India. There are about 40 million speakers of Marathi, a language belonging to the Indo-European family. The Maratha are mostly farmers, and practise Hinduism.

Masai member of an E African people whose territory is divided between Tanzania and Kenya, and who number about 250,000. They were originally warriors and nomads, breeding humped zebu cattle, but some have adopted a more settled life. Their cooperation is being sought by the Kenyan authorities to help in wildlife conservation. They speak a Nilotic language belonging to the Nilo-Saharan family.

Mende member of a W African people living in the rainforests of central east Sierra Leone and W Liberia. They number approximately 1 million. The Mende are farmers as well as hunter-gatherers, and each of their villages is led by a chief and a group of elders. The Mende language belongs to the Niger-Congo family.

Moldavian member of the majority ethnic group living in Moldova, comprising almost two-thirds of the population; also, an inhabitant of the Romanian province of Moldavia. The Moldavian language is a dialect of Romanian, and belongs to the Romance group of the Indo-European family.

Mon or **Talaing** member of a minority ethnic group living in Myanmar (Burma) and Thailand. The Mon established kingdoms in the area as early as the 7th century. Much of their culture was absorbed by the Khmer and Thai invaders who conquered them. The Mon language belongs to the Mon-Khmer branch of the Austro-Asiatic family. The Mon are Buddhists.

Mordvin Finnish people inhabiting the middle Volga valley in W Asia. They are known to have lived in the region since the 1st century AD. There are 1 million speakers of Mordvin in W Russia, about one-third of whom live in the autonomous republic of Mordvinia. Mordvin is a Finno-Ugric language belonging to the Uralic family.

Mossi member of the majority ethnic group living in Burkina Faso. Their social structure, based on a monarchy and aristocracy, was established in the 11th century. The Mossi have been prominent traders, using cowrie shells as currency. There are about 4 million speakers of Mossi, a language belonging to the Gur branch of the Niger-Congo family.

Munda member of any of several groups of people living in NE and central India, and numbering about 5 million (1983). Their most widely spoken languages are Santali and Mundari, languages of the Munda group, an isolated branch of the Austro-Asiatic family. The Mundas were formerly nomadic hunter-gatherers, but now practise shifting cultivation. They are Hindus but retain local beliefs.

Naga member of any of the various peoples who inhabit the highland region near the Indian-Myanmar border; they number approximately 800,000. These peoples do not possess a common name; some of the main groups are Ao, Konyak, Sangtam, Lhota, Sema, Rengma, Chang, and Angami. They live by farming, hunting, and fishing. Their languages belong to the Sino-Tibetan family.

Nahuatl member of any of a group of Mesoamerican Indian peoples (Mexico and Central America), of which the best-known

EUROPE'S CULTURAL HERITAGE AT RISK?

Europe is in danger of losing 15 of its 50 languages within the next few decades unless urgent action is taken. Among those threatened with extinction are: Aromanian, Corsican, Friulian, Galician, Ladin, Occitan, Provençal, Sard, and Sorbian. Language is closely associated with culture and the death of these languages could mean the extinction of many distinct ethnic identities. Both linguists and politicians are aware of the dangers, not least because some 50 million Europeans speak minority languages.

European leaders are increasingly beginning to recognize the cultural benefits of linguistic diversity and some languages may achieve special status in the new Europe. Basque, Catalan, and Galician have already benefited through the introduction of special education schemes.

The European Bureau of Lesser Used Languages, which is based in Dublin, is to open an information bureau in Brussels to help protect dying languages. The term 'lesser used languages' was originally devised by the Irish when the European Community began to appreciate the significance of these languages. To date, 31 European languages have been placed in this category.

The expression 'lesser used' is often preferred to 'minority' because some of these languages have national status. Irish, for example, is spoken by fewer than 100,000 people, though it is the first official language of the Republic of Ireland. In some cases the state language of one country may be the lesser-used language of another, as is the case with Greek in south-east Italy and Dutch in northern France.

The bureau uses four criteria to decide whether or not a language is dying. If speakers of a language cannot be educated, judged, administered, or informed in their language, then it is threatened. In practice, however, the costs of catering for these linguistic needs may prove prohibitively expensive. Small communities cannot often afford to pay for special schools, a system of justice, a media service, and a system of administration. But when these services are provided by the state, speakers of mainstream languages may argue that they are being asked unfairly to subsidize minority interests. Other minorities, especially religious ones, may demand similar privileges, thereby adding to the overall costs.

The provision of cultural and linguistic facilities within an existing state structure may not satisfy the aspirations of linguistic minorities who favour full nationhood. There are, for example, around 500,000 speakers of Euskara (Basque) in north-west Spain, a substantial proportion of whom support outright independence as opposed to the regional autonomy they currently enjoy. This poses problems for the European Community because it was founded on treaties signed by its member states. Not only would new agreements have to be drawn up to accommodate the separatists, but the question of representation in the European Parliament would have to be re-examined.

Although many western European politicians remain wary of the demands of separatists and prefer to work within existing structures, eastern European leaders have followed a markedly different course since the collapse of communism. The popular revolts of 1989–90 led to the re-emergence of countries which had long been submerged beneath larger political entities. Yugoslavia, for example, split apart along ethno-linguistic lines as the Slovenes and Croats tried to shake off what they saw as Serbian domination. Likewise the break up of the Soviet Union gave birth to an array of nations and a host of inter-ethnic problems. These changes had far-reaching linguistic implications since languages such as Estonian, Lithuanian, and Latvian, which had long been overshadowed by Russian, became the national languages of independent states.

The eastern European experience has shown that the status of languages can be enhanced through independence. But probably the greatest threat to lesser-used languages today comes not from national domination, but from modern communications. The young often opt for the language of the media instead of their mother tongue and may question whether or not it is worthwhile speaking their own language any more. Some specialists are concerned that even widely spoken languages like Dutch are under threat because of the growing popularity of English, which is spoken fluently in much of Holland. Attempts to reverse this trend through the use of minority languages in broadcasting are not invariably successful, especially when the channels are privately owned and fail to attract sufficient advertising revenue. It remains to be seen whether or not the resurgence of language and ethnicity in eastern Europe will withstand the onslaught of media-led popular culture.

group were the Aztecs. The Nahuatl are the largest ethnic group in Mexico, and their languages, which belong to the Uto-Aztecan (Aztec-Tanoan) family, are spoken by over 1 million people today.

Natchez member of a North American Indian people of the Mississippi area, one of the Moundbuilder group of peoples. They had a highly developed caste system unusual in North America, headed by a ruler priest (the 'Great Sun'). Members of the highest caste always married members of the lowest caste. The system lasted until French settlers colonized the area 1731. Only a few Natchez now survive in Oklahoma. Their Muskogean language is extinct.

Navajo or **Navaho** (Tena **Navahu** 'large planted field') member of a North American Indian people related to the Apache, and numbering about 200,000, mostly in Arizona. They speak an Athabaskan language, belonging to the Na-Dené family. The Navajo were traditionally cultivators; many now herd sheep and earn an income from tourism, making and selling rugs, blankets, and silver and turquoise jewellery. The Navajo refer to themselves as *Dineh*, 'people'.

Niger-Congo languages the largest group of languages in Africa. It includes about 1,000 languages and covers a vast area south of the Sahara desert, from the west coast to the east, and down the east coast as far as South Africa. It is divided into groups and subgroups; the most widely spoken Niger-Congo languages are Swahili (spoken on the east coast), the members of the Bantu group (southern Africa), and Yoruba (Nigeria).

Nuba member of a minority ethnic group living in S Sudan. The Nuba farm terraced fields in the Nuba mountains, to the west of the White Nile. They speak related dialects of Nubian, which belongs to the Chari-Nile family.

Nyanja member of a central African people living mainly in Malawi, and numbering about 400,000 (1984). The Nyanja are predominantly farmers, living in villages under a hereditary monarchy. They speak a Bantu language belonging to the Niger-Congo family.

Oriya member of the majority ethnic group living in the Indian state of Orissa. Oriya is Orissa's official language; it belongs to the Eastern group of the Indo-Iranian branch of the Indo-European family.

Oromo member of a group of E African peoples, especially of S Ethiopia, who speak an Afro-Asiatic language.

Palikur member of a South American Indian people living in N Brazil and numbering about 1 million (1980). Formerly a warlike people, they occupied a vast area between the Amazon and Orinoco rivers.

Pathan member of a people of NW Pakistan and Afghanistan, numbering about 14 million (1984). The majority are Sunni Muslims. The Pathans speak Pashto, a member of the Indo-Iranian branch of the Indo-European family. Some live as nomads with herds of goats and camels; while others are farmers. Formerly a constant threat to the British Raj, the Pakistani Pathans are now claiming independence, with the Afghani Pathans, in their own state of Pakhtoonistan, although this has not yet been recognized.

pidgin language any of various trade jargons, contact languages, or lingua francas arising in ports and markets where people of different linguistic backgrounds meet for commercial and other purposes.

Potiguara member of a group of South American Indians living in NW Brazil, and numbering about 1 million (1983). Their language belongs to the Tupi-Guarani family. Their religion is centred around a shaman, who mediates between the people and the spirit world.

Punjabi member of the majority ethnic group living in the Punjab. Approximately 37 million live in the Pakistan half of Punjab, while another 14 million live on the Indian side of the border. In addition to Sikhs, there are Raj-

puts in Punjab, some of whom have adopted Islam. The Punjabi language belongs to the Indo-Iranian branch of the Indo-European family. It is considered by some to be a variety of Hindi, by others to be a distinct language.

Pygmy (sometimes *Negrillo*) member of any of several groups of small-statured peoples of the rainforests of equatorial Africa. They were probably the aboriginal inhabitants of the region, before the arrival of farming peoples from elsewhere. They live nomadically in small groups, as hunter-gatherers; they also trade with other, settled people in the area.

Quechua or *Quichua* or *Kechua* member of the largest group of South American Indians. The Quechua live in the Andean region. Their ancestors included the Inca, who established the Quechua language in the region. Quechua is the second official language of Peru and is widely spoken as a lingua franca in Ecuador, Bolivia, Columbia, Argentina, and Chile; it belongs to the Andean-Equatorial family.

Romance languages branch of Indo-European languages descended from the Latin of the Roman Empire ('popular' or 'vulgar' as opposed to 'classical' Latin). The present-day Romance languages with national status are French, Italian, Portuguese, Romanian, and Spanish.

Romany member of a mainly nomadic people, also called *Gypsy* (a corruption of 'Egyptian', since they were erroneously thought to come from Egypt). They are now believed to have originated in NW India, and live throughout the world. The Romany language, spoken in several different dialects, belongs to the Indic branch of the Indo-European family.

Russian member of the majority ethnic group living in Russia. Russians are also often the largest minority in neighbouring republics. Russian is a member of the East Slavonic branch of the Indo-European language family and was the official language of the USSR, with 130-150 million speakers. It is written in the Cyrillic alphabet. The ancestors of the Russians migrated from central Europe between the 6th and 8th centuries AD.

Saami or *Lapp* member of a group of herding people living in N Scandinavia and the Kola Peninsula, and numbering about 46,000 (1983). Some are nomadic, others lead a more settled life. They live by herding reindeer, hunting, fishing, and producing handicrafts. Their language belongs to the Finno-Ugric branch of the Uralic family. The different dialect groups agreed on a standard written form in the 1980s, and there has been increased official support for keeping the language and customs alive in Sweden, Norway, and Finland. The Saami are Christian, but some groups retain pre-Christian customs.

Serb member of Yugoslavia's largest ethnic group, found mainly in Serbia; there are also Serbian minorities in neighbouring Bosnia-Herzegovina and Croatia. Their language is generally considered to be identical to that of the Croats, hence its name Serbo-Croatian. The Serbs belong to the Christian Orthodox Church.

Serbo-Croatian or *Serbo-Croat* the most widely spoken language in Yugoslavia; it is also spoken in neighbouring Croatia and Bosnia-Herzegovina. It is a member of the Southern Slavonic branch of the Indo-European family and has more than 17 million speakers. The different dialects of Serbo-Croatian tend to be written by the Greek Orthodox Serbs in the Cyrillic script, and by the Roman Catholic Croats in the Latin script.

Shona member of a Bantu-speaking people of southern Africa, comprising approximately 80% of the population of Zimbabwe. They also occupy the land between the Save and Pungure rivers in Mozambique, and smaller groups are found in South Africa, Botswana, and Zambia. The Shona are mainly farmers, living in scattered villages. The Shona language belongs to the Niger-Congo family.

Sindhi member of the majority ethnic group living in the Pakistani province of Sind. The Sindhi language is spoken by about 15 million people. Since the partition of India and Pakistan 1947, large numbers of Urdu-speaking refugees have moved into the region from India, especially into the capital, Karachi.

Sinhalese member of the majority ethnic group of Sri Lanka (70% of the population). Sinhalese is the official language of Sri Lanka; it belongs to the Indo-Iranian branch of the Indo-European family, and is written in a script derived from the Indian Pali form. The Sinhalese are Buddhists. Since 1971 they have been involved in a violent struggle with the Tamil minority, who are seeking independence.

Sino-Tibetan languages group of languages spoken in E and SE Asia. This group covers a large area and includes Chinese and Burmese, both of which have numerous dialects. Some classifications include the Tai group of languages (including Thai and Lao) in the Sino-Tibetan family; other systems place the Tai languages with the Tai-Kadai family.

Slav member of an Indo-European people in central and E Europe, the Balkans, and parts of N Asia, speaking closely related Slavonic languages. The ancestors of the Slavs are believed to have included the Sarmatians and Scythians. Moving west from Central Asia, they settled in E and SE Europe during the 2nd and 3rd millennia BC.

Slavonic languages (or *Slavic languages*) branch of the Indo-European language family spoken in central and E Europe, the Balkans, and parts of N Asia. The family comprises the *southern group* (Slovene, Serbo-Croatian, Macedonian, and Bulgarian); the *western group* (Czech and Slovak, Sorbian in Germany, and Polish and its related dialects); and the *eastern group* (Russian, Ukrainian, and Byelorussian).

Slovene member of the Slavic people of Slovenia and parts of the Austrian Alpine provinces of Styria and Carinthia. There are 1.5-2 million speakers of Slovene, a language belonging to the South Slavonic branch of the Indo-European family. The Slovenes use the Roman alphabet and the majority belong to the Roman Catholic Church.

Sotho member of a large ethnic group in southern Africa, numbering about 7 million (1987) and living mainly in Botswana, Lesotho, and South Africa. The Sotho are predominantly farmers, living in small village groups. They speak a variety of closely related languages belonging to the Bantu branch of the Niger-Congo family. With English, Sotho is the official language of Lesotho.

Sundanese member of the second largest ethnic group in the Republic of Indonesia. There are more than 20 million speakers of Sundanese, a member of the western branch of the Austronesian family. Like their neighbours, the Javanese, the Sundanese are predominantly Muslim. They are known for their performing arts, especially *jaipongan* dance traditions, and distinctive batik fabrics.

Swahili language belonging to the Bantu branch of the Niger-Congo family, widely used in east and central Africa. Swahili originated on the E African coast as a *lingua franca* used among traders, and contains many Arabic loan words. It is an official language in Kenya and Tanzania.

The name Swahili is also used for a member of an African people using the language, especially someone living in Zanzibar and adjoining coastal areas of Kenya and Tanzania. The Swahili are not an isolated group, but are part of a mixed coastal society engaged in fishing and trading.

Tagalog member of the majority ethnic group living around Manila on the island of Luzon in the Philippines, and numbering about 10 million (1988). In its standardized form, known as Pilipino, Tagalog is the official language of the Philippines and belongs to the Western branch of the Austronesian family. Luzon is a predominantly Christian island.

Tajik or *Tadzhik* member of the majority ethnic group in Tajikistan; Tajiks also live in Afghanistan and parts of Pakistan and W China. The Tajiki language belongs to the West Iranian subbranch of the Indo-European family, and is similar to Farsi; it is written in the Cyrillic script. The Tajiks have long been associated with neighbouring Turkic peoples and their language contains Altaic loan words. The majority of the Tajik people are Sunni Muslims; there is a Shi'ite minority in Afghanistan. During the Soviet period, the Tajiks adopted skills introduced by the Russians, while retaining their cultural identity. Today, there are both textile and mining industries in Tajikistan, as well as sheep farming.

Tamil member of the majority ethnic group living in the Indian state of Tamil Nadu (formerly Madras). Tamils also live in S India, N Sri Lanka, Malaysia, Singapore, and South Africa, totalling 35-55 million worldwide. The 3 million Tamils in Sri Lanka are predominantly

Hindu, although some are Muslims, unlike the Sinhalese majority, who are mainly Buddhist. Tamil belongs to the Dravidian family of languages; written records in Tamil date from the 3rd century BC. The **Tamil Tigers**, most prominent of the various Tamil groupings, are attempting to create a separate homeland in N Sri Lanka through both political and military means.

Tatar or **Tartar** member of a Turkic people, the descendants of the mixed Mongol and Turkic followers of Genghis Khan, called the Golden Horde because of the wealth they gained by plunder. The vast Tatar state was conquered by Russia 1552. The Tatars now live mainly in the Russian autonomous republic of Tatarstan, W Siberia, Turkmenistan, and Uzbekistan (where they were deported from the Crimea 1944). There are over 5 million speakers of the Tatar language, which belongs to the Turkic branch of the Altaic family. The Tatar people are mainly Muslim, although some have converted to the Orthodox Church.

Telugu language spoken in SE India. It is the official language of Andhra Pradesh, and is also spoken in Malaysia, giving a total number of speakers of around 50 million. Written records in Telugu date from the 7th century AD. Telugu belongs to the Dravidian family.

Thai member of the majority ethnic group living in Thailand and N Myanmar (Burma). Thai peoples also live in SW China, Laos, and N Vietnam. They speak Tai languages, all of which belong to the Tai-Kadai family. There are more than 60 million speakers (1991), most of whom live in Thailand. Most Thais are Buddhists, but the traditional belief in spirits, *phi*, remains.

Tigré group of people living in N Ethiopia. The Tigré language is spoken by about 2.5 million people; it belongs to the SE Semitic branch of the Afro-Asiatic family. *Tigrinya* is a closely related language spoken slightly to the south.

Tswana member of the majority ethnic group living in Botswana. The Tswana are divided into four subgroups: the Bakwena, the Bamangwato, the Bangwaketse, and the Batawana. Traditionally they are rural-dwelling farmers, though many now leave their homes to work as migrant labourers in South African industries. The Tswana language belongs to the Bantu branch of the Niger-Congo family.

Tuareg nomadic stockbreeders from west and central Sahara and Sahel (Algeria, Libya, Mali, Niger, and Burkina Faso). The eight Tuareg groups refer to themselves by their own names. Their language, Tamashek, belongs to the Berber branch of the Afro-Asiatic family and is spoken by 500,000–850,000 people. It is written in a noncursive script known as *tifinagh*, derived from ancient Numidian. Tuareg men wear dark-blue robes, turbans, and veils.

Turkoman or **Turkman** member of the majority ethnic group in Turkmenistan. They live to the E of the Caspian Sea, around the Kara Kum desert, and along the borders of Afghanistan and Iran. Traditionally the Turkomen were tent-dwelling pastoral nomads, though the majority are now sedentary farmers. Their language belongs to the Turkic branch of the Altaic family. They are predominantly Sunni Muslims.

Tutsi member of a minority ethnic group living in Rwanda and Burundi. Although fewer in number, they have traditionally been politically dominant over the Hutu majority and the Twa. The Tutsi are traditionally farmers; they also hold virtually all positions of importance in Burundi's government and army. They have carried out massacres in response to Hutu rebellions, notably in 1972 and 1988. In Rwanda the balance of power is more even.

Twa member of an ethnic group comprising 1% of the populations of Burundi and Rwanda. The Twa are the aboriginal inhabitants of the region. They are a pygmoid people, and live as nomadic hunter-gatherers in the forests.

Uigur or **Uygur** member of a Turkic people living in NW China and Kazakhstan; they form about 80% of the population of the Chinese province of Xinjiang Uygur. There are about 5 million speakers of Uigur, a language belonging to the Turkic branch of the Altaic family; it is the official language of the province.

Ukrainian member of the majority ethnic group living in Ukraine; there are minorities in Siberian Russia, Kazakhstan, Poland, Czechoslovakia, and Romania. There are 40–45 million speakers of Ukrainian, a member of the East Slavonic branch of the Indo-European family, closely related to Russian. It is sometimes referred to by Russians as Little Russian, although this is a description that Ukrainians generally do not find appropriate. Ukrainian-speaking communities are also found in Canada and the USA.

Urdu language member of the Indo-Iranian branch of the Indo-European language family, related to Hindi and written not in Devanagari but in Arabic script. Urdu is strongly influenced by Farsi (Persian) and Arabic. It is the official language of Pakistan and a language used by Muslims in India.

Uzbek member of the majority ethnic group (almost 70%) living in Uzbekistan; minorities live in Turkmenistan, Tajikistan, Kazakhstan, and Afghanistan. There are 10–14 million speakers of the Uzbek language, which belongs to the Turkic branch of the Altaic family. Uzbeks are predominantly Sunni Muslims.

Vedda member of the aboriginal peoples of Sri Lanka, who occupied the island before the arrival of the Aryans c. 550 BC. They live mainly in the central highlands, and many practise shifting cultivation. Formerly cave-

Indo-European Languages

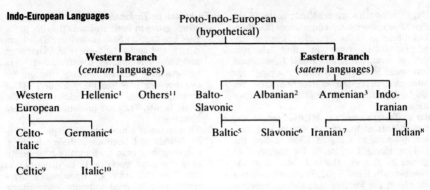

The Indo-European languages An outline diagram of the historical relationships among the Indo-European languages, followed by lists of languages in each branch of the family tree. Extinct languages are marked with an asterisk (*).

1 Hellenic: Greek (including *Ancient, *Archaic, *Classical, *Koine, *Byzantine and the modern forms *Demotiki* and *Katharevousa*)

2 Albanian: Albanian

3 Armenian: Armenian

4 Germanic: Afrikaans, *Anglo-Saxon, (Old English), Bavarian, Danish, Dutch/Flemish, English/Scots, Faroese, Frisian, German (Low, High, Swiss, etc), *Gothic, Icelandic, Luxemburgish, *Old Norse, *Old High German, Norwegian, Swedish, Yiddish

5 Baltic: Latvian, Lithuanian, *Old Prussian

6 Slavonic: Bulgarian, Byelorussian, Croatian, Czech, Kashubian, Macedonian, Polish,
(or Slavic) Pomeranian, Russian, Serbian, Slovak, Slovene, Sorbian, Ukrainian

7 Iranian: *Avestan (Zend or Zand), *Bactrian, Baluchi, Kurdish, *Median, Ossetic, *Pahlavi, *Parthian, Pashto, Persian (Farsi), Tadzhik

8 Indian: Assamese, Bengali, Bhili, Bihari, Gujarati, Hindi, Kashmiri, Konkani, Marathi, Oriya, Pahari, *Pali, Punjabi, Rajasthani, *Sanskrit, Sindhi, Sinhalese, Urdu

9 Celtic: Breton, *Brythonic, *Cornish, Gaelic (Irish, *Manx and Scottish), *Gaulish, *Goidelic, Welsh

10 Italic: (1) *Latin, *Oscan, *Umbrian
(2) Romance: Catalan, French, Gallego (Galician), Italian, Portuguese, Provençal, Romanian (Rumanian), Romansh, Spanish (Castilian)

11 others *Anatolian (including Hittite), *Tocharian

dwelling hunter-gatherers, they have now almost died out or merged with the rest of the population. They speak a Sinhalese language, belonging to the Indo-European family.

Wolof member of the majority ethnic group living in Senegal. There is also a Wolof minority in Gambia. There are about 2 million speakers of Wolof, a language belonging to the Niger-Congo family. The Wolof are Muslims.

Xhosa member of a Bantu people of southern Africa, living mainly in the Black National State of Transkei. Traditionally, the Xhosa were farmers and pastoralists, with a social structure based on a monarchy. Many are now town-dwellers, and provide much of the unskilled labour in South African mines and factories. Their Bantu language belongs to the Niger-Congo family.

Yanamamo or **Yanomamo** (plural **Yanamami**) member of a semi-nomadic South Ameri-

can Indian people, numbering approximately 15,000, who live in S Venezuela and N Brazil. The Yanamamo language belongs to the Macro-Chibcha family, and is divided into several dialects, although there is a common ritual language. Together with other Amazonian peoples, the Yanamamo have been involved in trying to conserve the rainforest where they live. In Brazil gold prospectors on their territory have spread disease and environmental damage.

Yao member of a people living in S China, N Vietnam, N Laos, Thailand, and Myanmar (Burma), and numbering about 4 million (1984). The Yao are generally hill-dwelling farmers practising shifting cultivation, growing rice, vegetables, and opium poppies. The Yao language belongs to the Miao-Yao branch of the Sino-Tibetan family. The Yao are predominantly Taoist and are known for their religious paintings.

Yi or **Lolo** or **Hei-I** or **Hei Ku T'ou** member of a S Chinese minority living in Sichuan, Yunnan, and Guizhou provinces, as well as in the Guangxi autonomous region, numbering around 5,453,000 (1992); there are small Yi populations in Laos and Vietnam. The Yi are mainly engaged in highland agriculture, supplemented by animal husbandry. Their arts and crafts include lacquerwork, embroidery, jewellery, sculpture, and painting. There is a Yi calendar and a number of books on history and medicine have been written in the old Yi language, a member of the Sino-Tibetan family.

Yoruba member of the majority ethnic group living in SW Nigeria; there is a Yoruba minority in E Benin. They number approximately 20 million in all, and their language belongs to the Kwa branch of the Niger-Congo family. The Yoruba established powerful city states in the 15th century, known for their advanced culture which includes sculpture, art, and music.

Zhuang or **Chuang** member of the largest ethnic minority in China, numbering about 13,378,000 (1992) and living mainly in Guangxi autonomous region and Yunnan and Guangdong provinces. A written form of their language, a member of the Tai-Kadai family, was created in the 1950s. The Zhuang are mainly engaged in wet rice agriculture. They retain elements of traditional beliefs.

Zulu member of a group of southern African peoples mainly from Natal, South Africa. Their present homeland, KwaZulu, represents the nucleus of the once extensive and militaristic Zulu kingdom. Today many Zulus work in the industrial centres around Johannesburg and Durban. The Zulu language, closely related to Xhosa, belongs to the Bantu branch of the Niger-Congo family.

GRAMMAR AND USAGE

adjective grammatical part of speech for words that describe nouns (for example, *new* and *beautiful*, as in 'a new hat' and 'a beautiful day'). Adjectives generally have three degrees (grades or levels for the description of relationships): the positive degree (*new*, *beautiful*) the comparative degree (*newer*, *more beautiful*), and the superlative degree (*newest*, *most beautiful*).

Some adjectives do not normally need comparative and superlative forms; one person cannot be 'more asleep' than someone else, a lone action is unlikely to be 'the most single-handed action ever seen', and many people dislike the expression 'most unique' or 'almost unique', because something unique is supposed to be the only one that exists. For purposes of emphasis or style these conventions may be set aside ('I don't know who

is more unique; they are both remarkable people'). Double comparatives such as 'more bigger' are not grammatical in Standard English, but Shakespeare used a double superlative ('the most unkindest cut of all'). Some adjectives may have both the comparative and superlative forms (*commoner* and *more common*; *commonest* and *most common*), usually shorter words take on the suffixes -*er*/-*est* but occasionally they may be given the *more*/*most* forms for emphasis or other reasons ('Which of them is the *most clear*?').

When an adjective comes before a noun it is attributive; when it comes after noun and verb (for example, 'It looks *good*') it is predicative. Some adjectives can only be used predicatively ('The child was asleep', but not 'the asleep child'). The participles of verbs are regularly used adjectivally ('a *sleeping* child', '*boiled* milk'), often in compound forms ('a *quick-acting* medicine', 'a *glass-making* factory'; 'a *hard-boiled* egg', '*well-trained* teachers'). Adjectives are often formed by adding suffixes to nouns (sand: sand*y*; nation: nation*al*).

adverb grammatical part of speech for words that modify or describe verbs ('She ran *quickly*'), adjectives ('a *beautifully* clear day'), and adverbs ('They did it *really* well'). Most adverbs are formed from adjectives or past participles by adding -*ly* (*quick*: *quickly*) or -*ally* (*automatic*: *automatically*).

Sometimes adverbs are formed by adding -*wise* (*likewise* and *clockwise*, as in 'moving *clockwise*'; in 'a *clockwise* direction', *clockwise* is an adjective). Some adverbs have a distinct form from their partnering adjective; for example, *good*/*well* ('It was *good* work; they did it *well*'). Others do not derive from adjectives (*very*, in '*very* nice'; *tomorrow*, in 'I'll do it *tomorrow*'); and some are unadapted adjectives (*pretty*, as in 'It's *pretty* good'). Sentence adverbs modify whole sentences or phrases: '*Generally*, it rains a lot here'; '*Usually*, the town is busy at this time of year.' Sometimes there is controversy in such matters. *Hopefully* is universally accepted in sentences like 'He looked at them *hopefully*' (= in a hopeful way), but some people dislike it in '*Hopefully*, we'll see you again next year' (= We hope that we'll see you again next year).

apostrophe mark (') used in written English and some other languages. In English it serves primarily to indicate either a missing letter (*mustn't* for *must not*) or number ('*47* for *1947*), or grammatical possession ('*John's* camera', '*women's* dresses'). It is often omitted in proper names (Publishers Association, Actors Studio, *Collins Dictionary*). Many people otherwise competent in writing have great difficulty with the apostrophe, which has never been stable at any point in its history.

An apostrophe may precede the plural *s* used with numbers and abbreviations (*the 1970's*, *a group of P.O.W.'s*) but is equally often omitted (*the 1970s*, *a group of POWs*). For possessives of certain words ending with *s*, usage is split, as between *James's book* and *James' book*.

Names and dates used adjectivally are not usually followed by an apostrophe ('a *1950s* car', 'a *Beatles* record'). The use of an apostrophe to help indicate a plural (as in a shopkeeper's *Apple's* and *Tomato's*, followed by their prices) is regarded by many as semiliterate.

article grammatical part of speech. There are two articles in English: the *definite article the*, which serves to specify or identify a noun (as in 'This is *the* book I need'), and the *indefinite article a* or (before vowels) *an*, which indicates a single unidentified noun ('They gave me *a* piece of paper and *an* envelope').

Some people use the form 'an' before *h* ('an historic building'); this practice dates from the 17th century, when an initial *h* was often not pronounced (as in '*h*onour'), and is nowadays widely considered rather pompous.

asterisk starlike punctuation mark (*) used to link the asterisked word with a note at the bottom of a page, and to indicate that certain letters are missing from a word (especially a taboo word such as 'f**k').

An asterisk is also used to indicate that a word or usage is nonexistent, for example, 'In English we say three boys and not three *boy'.

colon punctuation mark (:) intended to direct the reader's attention forward, usually because what follows explains or develops what has just been written (for example, *The farmer owned the following varieties of dogs: a spaniel, a pointer, a terrier, a border collie, and three mongrels*).

comma punctuation mark (,) intended to provide breaks or pauses within a sentence; commas may come at the end of a clause, to set off a phrase, or in lists (for example, *apples, pears, plums, and pineapples*).

Some writers, uncertain where sentences properly end, use a comma instead of a period (or full stop), writing *We saw John last night, it was good to see him again*, rather than *We saw John last night. It was good to see him again*. The meaning is entirely clear in both cases. One solution in such situations is to use a *semicolon* (;), which bridges the gap between the close association of the comma and the sharp separation of the period. For parenthetical commas, see parenthesis.

conjunction grammatical part of speech that serves to connect words, phrases, and clauses; for example *and* in 'apples and pears' and *but* in 'we're going but they aren't'.

exclamation mark or *exclamation point* punctuation mark (!) used to indicate emphasis or strong emotion ('That's terrible!'). It is appropriate after interjections ('Rats!'), emphatic greetings ('Yo!'), and orders ('Shut up!'), as well as those sentences beginning *How* or *What* that are not questions ('How embarrassing!', 'What a surprise!').

The exclamation mark is most often seen in dialogue. Its use is kept to a minimum in narrative prose and technical writing. Within a quotation an exclamation mark may be placed in square brackets to indicate that the writer or editor is surprised by something. The convention that all sentences in comic books end with an exclamation mark is on the wane.

grammar the rules of combining words into phrases, clauses, sentences, and paragraphs. Emphasis on the standardizing impact of print has meant that spoken or colloquial language is often perceived as less grammatical than written language, but all forms of a language, standard or otherwise, have their own grammatical systems of differing complexity. People often acquire several overlapping grammatical systems within one language; for example, one formal system for writing and standard communication and one less formal system for everyday and peer-group communication. Originally 'grammar' was an analytical approach to writing, intended to improve the understanding and the skills of scribes, philosophers, and writers. When compared with Latin, English has been widely regarded as having less grammar or at least a simpler grammar; it would be truer, however, to say that English and Latin have different grammars, each complex in its own way. In linguistics (the contemporary study of language) grammar, or syntax, refers to the arrangement of the elements in a language for the purposes of acceptable communication in speech, writing, and print.

All forms of a language, standard or otherwise, have their grammars or grammatical systems, which children acquire through use; a child may acquire several overlapping systems within one language (especially a nonstandard form for everyday life and a standard form linked with writing, school, and national life). Not even the most comprehensive grammar book (or grammar) of a language like English, French, Arabic, or Japanese completely covers or fixes the implicit grammatical system that people use in their daily lives. The rules and tendencies of natural grammar operate largely in nonconscious ways but can, for many social and professional purposes, be studied and developed for conscious as well as inherent skills.

hyphen punctuation mark (-) with two functions: to join words, parts of words, syllables, and so on, for particular purposes; and to mark a word break at the end of a line. Adjectival compounds (see adjective) are hyphenated because they modify the noun jointly rather than separately ('a small-town boy' is a boy from a small town; 'a small town boy' is a small boy from a town). The use of hyphens with adverbs is redundant unless an identical adjective exists (*well, late, long*): 'late-blooming plant' but 'brightly blooming plant'.

Phrasal verbs are not hyphenated ('things *turned out* well', 'it *washed up* on the beach') unless used adjectivally ('a well-*turned-out* crowd', 'a *washed-up* athlete'). Nouns formed from phrasal verbs are hyphenated or joined together ('a good *turnout* tonight', 'please do the *washing-up*'). In the use of certain prefixes, modern style is moving towards omitting the hyphen (*noncooperation*).

The hyphenation of compound nouns in English is by no means clear cut; the same person may inadvertently in one article write, for example, *world view*, *worldview* and *world-view*.

Here, conventional hyphenation is a first stage in bringing two words together; if their close association is then generally agreed, the two words are written or printed as one (*teapot*, as opposed to *tea-pot* or *tea pot*), or are kept apart for visual and aesthetic reasons (*coffee pot* rather than *coffee-pot* or *coffeepot*). Practice does, however, vary greatly.

inflection or **inflexion** in grammatical analysis, an ending or other element in a word that indicates its grammatical function (whether plural or singular, masculine or feminine, subject or object, and so on).

In a highly inflected language like Latin, nouns, verbs, and adjectives have many inflectional endings (for example, in the word *amabunt* the base *am* means 'love' and the complex *abunt* indicates the kind of verb, the future tense, indicative mood, active voice, third person, and plurality). English has few inflections: for example, the *s* for plural forms (as in *the books*) and for the third person singular of verbs (as in *He runs*).

noun grammatical part of speech that names a person, animal, object, quality, idea, or time. Nouns can refer to objects such as *house, tree* (**concrete nouns**); specific persons and places such as *John Alden*, the *White House* (**proper nouns**); ideas such as *love, anger* (**abstract nouns**). In English many simple words are both noun and verb (*jump, reign, rain*). Adjectives are sometimes used as nouns ('a *local* man', 'one of the *locals*').

A common noun does not begin with a capital letter (*child, cat*), whereas a proper noun does, because it is the name of a particular person, animal, or place (*Jane, Rover, Norfolk*). A concrete noun refers to things that can be sensed (*dog, box*), whereas an abstract noun relates to generalizations abstracted from life as we observe it (*fear, condition, truth*). A **countable noun** can have a plural form (*book: books*), while an **uncountable noun** or mass noun cannot (*dough*). Many English nouns can be used both countably and uncountably (*wine*: 'Have some *wine*; it's one of our best *wines*'). A **collective noun** is singular in form but refers to a group (*flock, group, committee*), and a **compound noun** is made up of two or more nouns (*teapot, baseball team, car-factory strike committee*). A **verbal noun** is formed from a verb as a gerund or otherwise (*build: building; regulate: regulation*).

participle in grammar, a form of the verb, in English either a **present participle** ending in *-ing* (for example, 'work*ing*' in 'They were work*ing*', 'work*ing* men', and 'a hard-*working* team') or a **past participle** ending in *-ed* in regular verbs (for example, 'train*ed*' in 'They have been *trained* well', '*trained* soldiers', and

'a well-*trained* team').

In irregular verbs the past participle has a special form (for example, drive/*driven*; light/*lit*, burn/*burned, burnt*). The participle is used to open such constructions as '*Coming* down the stairs, she paused and ...' and '*Angered* by the news, he ...'. Such constructions, when not logically formed, may have irritating or ambiguous results. '*Driving* along a country road, a stone broke my windscreen' suggests that the stone was driving along the road. This illogical usage is a **misplaced participle**. A **dangling** or **hanging participle** has nothing at all to relate to: 'While *driving* along a country road there was a loud noise under the car.' Such sentences need to be completely re-expressed, except in some well-established usages where the participle can stand alone (for example, '*Taking* all things into consideration, your actions were justified').

part of speech the grammatical function of a word, described in the grammatical tradition of the Western world, based on Greek and Latin. The four major parts of speech are the noun, verb, adjective, and adverb; the minor parts of speech vary according to schools of grammatical theory, but include the article, conjunction, preposition, and pronoun.

In languages like Greek and Latin, the part of speech of a word tends to be invariable (usually marked by an ending, or inflection); in English, it is much harder to recognize the function of a word simply by its form. Some English words may have only one function (for example, *and* as a conjunction). Others may have several functions (for example, *fancy*, which is a noun in the phrase 'flights of *fancy*', a verb in '*Fancy* that!', and an adjective in 'a *fancy* hat').

period punctuation mark (.). The term 'period' is universally understood in English and is the preferred usage in North America; **full stop** is the preferred term in the UK. The period has two functions: to mark the end of a sentence and to indicate that a word has been abbreviated. It is also used in mathematics to indicate decimals and is then called a **point**.

Such abbreviations as acronyms are unlikely to have periods (NATO rather than N.A.T.O.), and contractions (incorporating the last letter of the word, for example Dr for 'doctor') may or may not have periods. In such contexts as fictional dialogue and advertising, periods sometimes follow incomplete sentences in an effort to represent speech more faithfully or for purposes of emphasis.

preposition in grammar, a part of speech coming before a noun or a pronoun to show a location (*in, on*), time (*during*), or some other relationship (for example, figurative relationships in phrases like '*by* heart' or '*on* time').

In the sentence 'Put the book *on* the table', *on* is a preposition governing the noun 'table' and relates the verb 'put' to the phrase 'the table', indicating where the book should go. Some words of English that are often prepositional in function may, however, be used adverbially, as in the sentences, 'He picked the book *up*' and 'He picked *up* the book', in which the ordering is different but the meaning the same. In such cases *up* is called an *adverbial particle* and the form *pick up* is a *phrasal verb*.

pronoun in grammar, a part of speech that is used in place of a noun, usually to save repetition of the noun (for example 'The people arrived around nine o'clock. *They* behaved as though we were expecting *them*').

They, *them*, *he*, and *she* are **personal pronouns** (representing people); *this/these*, and *that/those* are **demonstrative pronouns** (demonstrating or pointing to something: '*this* book and not *that* book'. Words like *that* and *who* can be **relative pronouns** in sentences like 'She said *that* she was coming' and 'Tell me *who* did it' relating one clause to another), and *myself* and *himself* are **reflexive pronouns** (reflecting back to a person, as in 'He did it *himself*').

punctuation the system of conventional signs (punctuation marks) and spaces by means of which written and printed language is organ-ized in order to be as readable, clear, and logical as possible.

It contributes to the effective layout of visual language; if a work is not adequately punctuated, there may be problems of ambiguity and unclear association among words. Conventions of punctuation differ from language to language, and there are preferred styles in the punctuation of a language like English. Some people prefer a fuller use of punctuation, while others punctuate lightly; comparably, the use of punctuation will vary according to the kind of passage being produced: a personal letter, a newspaper article, and a technical report are all laid out and punctuated in distinctive ways.

Standard punctuation marks and conventions include the period (full stop or point), comma, colon, semicolon, exclamation mark (or point), question mark, apostrophe, asterisk, hyphen, and parenthesis (including dashes, brackets, and the use of parenthetical commas).

question mark punctuation mark (?) used to indicate enquiry or doubt. When indicating enquiry, it is placed at the end of a *direct question* ('Who is coming?') but never at the end of an *indirect question* ('He asked us who

COMMON ROOTS

similarities of six words in Indo-European languages contrast with their differences in other language groups

English	month	mother	new	night	nose	three
Welsh	mis	mam	newydd	nos	trwyn	tri
Gaelic	mí	máthair	nua	oíche	srón	trí
French	mois	mère	nouveau	nuit	nez	trois
Spanish	mes	madre	nuevo	noche	nariz	tres
Portuguese	mês	mãe	novo	noite	nariz	três
Italian	mese	madre	nuovo	notte	naso	tre
Latin	mensis	mater	novus	nox	nasus	tres
German	Monat	Mutter	neu	Nacht	Nase	drei
Dutch	maand	moeder	nieuw	nacht	neus	drie
Icelandic	mánudur	módir	nýr	nótt	nef	brír
Swedish	månad	moder	ny	natt	näsa	tre
Polish	miesiąc	matka	nowy	noc	nos	trzy
Czech	měsíc	matka	nový	noc	nos	tři
Rumanian	lună	mamă	nou	noapte	nas	trei
Albanian	muaj	nënë	iri	natë	hundë	tre,tri
Greek	men	meter	neos	nux	rhïs	treis
Russian	mesyats	mat'	novy	noch'	nos	tri
Lithuanian	menuo	motina	naujas	naktis	nosis	trys
Armenian	amis	mayr	nor	kisher	kit	yerek
Persian	mäh	mädar	nau	shab	bini	se
Sanskrit	mäs	matar	nava	nakt	näs	trayas

NON-INDO-EUROPEAN LANGUAGES

	(month)	(mother)	(new)	(night)	(nose)	(three)
Basque	hilabethe	ama	berri	gai	sūdūr	hirur
Finnish	kuukausi	äiti	uusi	yö	nenä	kolme
Hungarian	hónap	anya	új	éjszaka	orr	három
Turkish	ay	anne	yeni	gece	burun	úç

Source: Katzner, Kenneth/The Languages of the World/Routledge & Kegan Paul London 1986

GENETIC FINGERPRINTING PROVIDES NEW CLUES

Anthropologists have long refuted the idea championed by Thor Heyerdahl, who sailed his raft *Kon-Tiki* from South America to Polynesia, that the Pacific was colonized from east to west. The peoples of Polynesia—the name given to the vast group of islands scattered between Hawaii, New Zealand, and Easter Island—speak languages belonging to the Austronesian family. This major family embraces the languages of Micronesia, parts of Melanesia, Indonesia, and Madagascar and, though their origins remain obscure, linguistic evidence links them to the Asia-Pacific region. The ancestors of the Polynesians probably colonized the far-flung Pacific islands in outrigger canoes loaded with coconuts, yams, breadfruits, and pigs.

The material, cultural, botanical, and linguistic information suggests a west/east pattern of migration beginning around 3,000 BC. Although this evidence in itself is not conclusive, recent medical research strongly supports the contention that the Pacific was settled from west to east. The discovery of a rare mutant gene by Oxford's Institute of Molecular Medicine corroborates the work of anthropologists and linguists and finally puts paid to Heyerdahl's *Kon-Tiki* hypothesis. The research also helps to clarify the nature of Polynesian colonization and the relationship between these seafarers and other Pacific islanders, namely the Melanesians. By using these research methods scientists are pioneering a new human geography which will help reconstruct human population movements around the world.

The history of Oxford's involvement in genetic research in the Pacific goes back to 1978 when Don Bowden, the chief medical officer for Vanuatu, noticed that a large number of these Melanesian islanders suffered from anaemia. Other doctors attributed the condition to a combination of hookworm and poor diets and advised Dr Bowden to prescribe iron supplements. But the treatment proved to be unsatisfactory, so Bowden contacted the scientists in Oxford and sent them samples of his patients' blood. Much to their surprise the scientists found that 50% of the patients carried alpha-thalassaemia, an inherited condition linked to the presence of malaria. Moreover, the Vanuatu samples were intriguing because the donors appeared to be afflicted with only one type of the disorder. This provided the scientists with the opportunity to examine the connection between thalassaemia and malaria. Research on the condition in other parts of the world had been hampered because sufferers were usually afflicted with several varieties of the condition; in Vanuatu, however, the scientists seemed to be dealing with a specific type which had arisen because of a rare genetic disorder. They embarked, therefore, on a survey of around 2,500 people from islands throughout the Melanesian region. The number of people afflicted with alpha-thalassaemia was compared with medical records kept since the colonial period showing the incidence of malaria.

The researchers found that 90% of the people of coastal Papua New Guinea either carried or suffered from alpha-thalassaemia, whereas in New Caledonia only 5% of the population were affected. The results correlated with the incidence of malaria, which was high in coastal New Guinea but gradually declined towards New Caledonia. The evidence indicated a causal link between thalassaemia and malaria and the scientists concluded that the condition provided some protection against the disease. But when scientists began to examine the Pacific islands further to the east they were surprised to find that there was still a significant frequency of alpha-thalassaemia even when there was no malaria. In Tahiti, for example, the researchers found that not only had the island always been free of malaria, but that the thalassaemia was of the same type found in Vanuatu.

The scientists suggested that the condition had arisen in Melanesia, where it provided protection from malaria, and had then been acquired by the ancestors of the Polynesians who took the mutant gene to the malaria-free eastern Pacific. The Melanesians may have already been well established in their islands by the time the proto-Polynesians passed through and the research indicates that there must have been some interbreeding. The other possibility is that the Melanesians followed the Polynesians into the Pacific as far as Fiji and that the two groups mixed at a later date. In order to resolve these questions the Oxford scientists are now using a method known as polymerase chain reaction to analyse the genetic composition of ancient Polynesian and Melanesian bones. The technique enables researchers to create genetic samples which are large enough to study from minute pieces of information. The use of genetic fingerprinting will undoubtedly help solve the anthropological questions of the Pacific and provide a test case for the study of other regions.

was coming'). When indicating doubt, it usually appears between brackets, to show that a writer or editor is puzzled or uncertain about quoted text.

semicolon punctuation mark (;) with a function halfway between the separation of sentence from sentence by means of a period, or full stop, and the gentler separation provided by a comma. It also helps separate items in a complex list: 'pens, pencils, and paper; staples, such as rice and beans; tools, various; and rope'.

Rather than the abrupt 'We saw Mark last night. It was good to see him again', and the casual (and often condemned) 'We saw Mark last night, it was good to see him again', the semicolon reflects a link in a two-part statement and is considered good style: *We saw Mark last night; it was good to see him again*. In such cases an alternative is to use a comma followed by *and* or *but*.

verb the grammatical part of speech for what someone or something does (*to go*), experiences (*to live*), or is (*to be*). Verbs involve the grammatical categories known as number (singular or plural: 'He *runs*; they *run*'), voice (active or passive: 'She *writes* books; it *is written*'), mood (statements, questions, orders, emphasis, necessity, condition), aspect (completed or continuing action: 'She *danced*; she *was dancing*'), and tense (variation according to time: simple present tense, present progressive tense, simple past tense, and so on).

Many verbs are formed from nouns and adjectives by adding affixes (prison: *imprison*; light: *enlighten*; fresh: *freshen up*; pure: *purify*). Some words function as both nouns and verbs (*crack, run*), both adjectives and verbs (*clean; ready*), and as nouns, adjectives, and verbs (*fancy*). In the sentences 'They *saw* the accident', 'She *is working* today', and 'He *should have been trying to meet* them', the words in italics are verbs (and, in the last case) two verb groups together; these sentences show just how complex the verbs of English can be.

types of verb

A *transitive* verb takes a direct object ('He *saw* the house').

An *intransitive* verb has no object ('She *laughed*').

An *auxiliary or helping* verb is used to express tense and/or mood ('He *was* seen'; 'They *may* come').

A *modal* verb or *modal auxiliary* generally shows only mood; common modals are *may/might, will/would, can/could, shall/should, must*.

The *infinitive* of the verb usually includes *to* (*to go, to run* and so on), but may be a bare infinitive (for example, after modals, as in 'She may *go*').

A *regular* verb forms tenses in the normal way (*I walk: I walked: I have walked*); irregular verbs do not (*swim: swam: swum; put: put: put*; and so on). Because of their conventional nature, regular verbs are also known as weak verbs, while some irregular verbs are strong verbs with special vowel changes across tenses, as in *swim: swam: swum* and *ride: rode: ridden*.

A *phrasal verb* is a construction in which a particle attaches to a usually single-syllable verb (for example, *put* becoming *put up*, as in 'He put up some money for the project', and *put up with*, as in 'I can't put up with this nonsense any longer').

POLITICAL IDEOLOGIES

absolutism or *absolute monarchy* system of government in which the ruler or rulers have unlimited power. The principle of an absolute monarch, given a right to rule by God, was extensively used in Europe during the 17th and 18th centuries. Absolute monarchy is contrasted with limited or constitutional monarchy, in which the sovereign's powers are defined or limited.

anarchism political belief that society should have no government, laws, police, or other authority, but should be a free association of all its members. It does not mean 'without order'; most theories of anarchism imply an order of a very strict and symmetrical kind, but they maintain that such order can be achieved by cooperation. Anarchism must not be confused with nihilism (a purely negative and destructive activity directed against society); anarchism is essentially a pacifist movement.

authoritarianism rule of a country by a dominant elite who repress opponents and the press to maintain their own wealth and power. They are frequently indifferent to activities not affecting their security, and rival power centres, such as trade unions and political parties, are often allowed to exist, although under tight control. An extreme form is totalitarianism.

collectivism a position in which the collective (such as the state) has priority over its individual members. It is the opposite of individualism, which is itself a variant of anarchy.

communism revolutionary socialism based on the theories of the political philosophers Marx and Engels, emphasizing common ownership of the means of production and a planned economy. The principle held is that each should work according to their capacity and receive according to their needs. Politically, it seeks the overthrow of capitalism through a proletarian revolution. The first communist state was the USSR after the revolution of 1917.

Revolutionary socialist parties and groups united to form communist parties in other countries (in the UK 1920). After World War II, communism was enforced in those countries that came under Soviet occupation. China emerged after 1961 as a rival to the USSR in world communist leadership, and other countries attempted to adapt communism to their own needs.

The late 1980s saw a movement for more individual freedoms in many communist countries, culminating in the abolition or overthrow of communist rule in eastern European countries and Mongolia, and further state repression in China. The failed hardline coup in the USSR against Mikhail Gorbachev 1991 resulted in the effective abandonment of communism there.

conservatism approach to government favouring the maintenance of existing institutions and identified with a number of Western political parties, such as the British Conservative, German Christian Democratic, and Australian Liberal parties. It tends to be explicitly nondoctrinaire and pragmatic but generally emphasizes free-enterprise capitalism, minimal government intervention in the economy, rigid law and order, and the importance of national traditions.

democracy government by the people, usually through elected representatives. In the modern world, democracy has developed from the American and French revolutions.

In *direct democracy* the whole people meets for the making of laws or the direction of executive officers (for example in Athens in the 5th century BC, and allegedly in modern Libya). Today it is represented mainly by the use of the referendum, as in the UK, France, Switzerland, and certain states of the USA.

The two concepts underlying *liberal democracy* are the right to representative government and the right to enjoy individual freedom. In practice, the principal features of a liberal democratic system include representative institutions based on majority rule, through free elections and a choice of political parties; accountability of the government to the electorate; freedom of expression, assembly, and the individual, guaranteed by an independent judiciary; limitations on the power of government.

It is estimated that approximately a third (1.6 billion) of the world's total population live within political systems founded on liberal democracy. While it is an ideology that has been successfully implemented in all parts of the world, this type of political system tends to flourish best in high-income, 'First World' states.

Social democracy is founded on the belief in the gradual evolution of a democratic socialism within existing political structures. The earliest was the German *Sozialdemokratische Partei* (SPD), today one of the two major German parties, created in 1875. Parties along the lines of the German model were founded in the last two decades of the 19th century in a number of countries including Austria, Belgium, Holland, Hungary, Poland, and Russia. The British Labour Party is in the social democratic tradition.

egalitarianism the belief that all citizens in a state should have equal rights and privileges. Interpretations of this can vary, from the notion of equality of opportunity to equality in material welfare and political decision-taking. Some states clearly reject any thought of egalitarianism; most accept the concept of equal opportunities but recognize that people's abilities vary widely. Even those states which claim to be socialist find it necessary to have hierarchical structures in the political, social, and economic spheres. Egalitarianism was one of the principles of the French Revolution.

THE DEMOCRATIZATION OF AFRICA AND THE MIDDLE EAST

In 1990 only four of the 19 African and Middle Eastern states north of the Sahara could claim to have governments based on multiparty democracy. They were Egypt, Israel, Morocco, and Tunisia. By 1992, Lebanon had moved into the democratic arena. Algeria, too, had introduced a multiparty system, but retreated after Islamic fundamentalists won the first round of elections Dec 1991.

In sub-Saharan Africa the changes have been more dramatic. In 1990 only four states were practising some form of genuine pluralistic politics: Botswana, Gambia, Mauritius, and Uganda. This represented less than 9% of the total of 45 in the region. By 1992 the number that had moved, were moving, or had promised to move, towards the Western liberal democratic model had grown to 36, or 80%.

The most striking example of this is Benin. From 1975, Benin's unquestioned leader, General Mathieu Kerekou had committed it to the path of 'scientific socialism'. In 1989, with the economy in tatters and the government unable to pay its own civil servants, Kerekou had to seek advice from his country's leading figures. They persuaded him to abandon Marxist–Leninist policies and introduce a pluralist political system. Two years later, in the first free elections for 21 years, Kerekou was defeated by a former World Bank executive director, Nicephore Soglo.

South Africa provides a very different example of how the political landscape is changing. Here skin colour has always determined the enjoyment of what the West calls liberal democracy. The changes now under way will extend democratic government from a privileged minority to the whole population.

Why has all this happened in so short a time? Political factors have been at work, but economic forces have dominated.

The political 'reeducation' of Black Africa is linked to the changes in the former USSR and the rest of eastern Europe. The USSR showed the poorer countries of the world how a state could provide a basic standard of living for all whatever their background or ability, through its political and social system. Marx and Lenin's teachings provided the ideological foundations. When Mikhail Gorbachev started to undermine this seemingly indestructible edifice it fell apart at a pace no one could have foreseen. There was now no clear sociopolitical model for the African nations to copy.

While this philosophical base was disappearing, the massive Soviet support for the underdeveloped world was ending. The former communist superpower was struggling with its own economic problems. Additionally, in recent years the West has increasingly made its provision of aid dependent on the willingness of countries to democratize their political systems.

The change in Benin was peaceful. There is no guarantee that other states will follow this example; the advanced countries of the West should not expect a swift and painless transition throughout Africa. The removal of autocratic leadership in parts of eastern Europe has unleashed passionate ethnic rivalries. In the same way the attempt to create liberal regimes in Africa could reveal the deep tribal divisions which still exist. The West needs to be patient and tolerant. It needs to recognize that generosity of spirit and generosity of material help will, in the long term, benefit the people of the West as much as the people of Africa.

MILESTONES ON THE ROAD TO DEMOCRACY

NORTH OF THE SAHARA

country	multiparty system operates	multiparty system promised	absolutist state	one-party state
*Algeria	+			
Bahrain			+	
Djibouti				+
Egypt	+			
Iran				+
Iraq				+
Israel	+			
Jordan			+	
Kuwait			+	
Lebanon	+			
Libya				+
Morocco	+			
Oman			+	
Qatar			+	
Saudi Arabia			+	
Syria				+
Tunisia		+		
United Arab Emirates			+	
Yemen		+		

*restrictions placed on fundamentalist parties

MILESTONES ON THE ROAD TO DEMOCRACY (cont.)

SOUTH OF THE SAHARA

country	multiparty system operates	multiparty system promised	absolutist state	one-party state
Angola		+		
Benin	+			
Botswana	+			
Burkina Faso	+			
Burundi		+		
Cameroon	+			
Cape Verde	+			
Central African Republic				+
Chad		+		
Comoros		+		
Congo	+			
Equatorial Guinea				+
Ethiopia				+
Gabon	+			
Gambia	+			
Ghana		+		
Guinea				+
Guinea-Bissau		+		
Ivory Coast	+			
Kenya		+		
Lesotho		+		
Liberia		+		
Madagascar		+		
Malawi				+
Mali	+			
Mauritania	+			
Mauritius	+			
Mozambique		+		
Namibia	+			
Niger		+		
Nigeria		+		
Rwanda		+		
São Tomé e Príncipé	+			
Senegal	+			
Seychelles		+		
Sierra Leone		+		
*Somalia		+		
**South Africa		+		
Sudan				+
Swaziland			+	
Tanzania		+		
Togo		+		
Uganda		+		
Zaire				+
Zambia	+			
***Zimbabwe	+			

*democracy threatened by civil war   **black majority disenfranchised   ***effectively a one-party state

fascism ideology that denies all rights to individuals in their relations with the state; specifically, the totalitarian nationalist movement founded in Italy 1919 by Mussolini and followed by Hitler's Germany 1933.

imperialism the policy of extending the power and rule of a government beyond its own boundaries. A country may attempt to dominate others by direct rule or by less obvious means such as control of markets for goods or raw materials. The latter is often called neo-colonialism.

individualism a view in which the individual takes precedence over the collective, the opposite of collectivism. The term *possessive individualism* has been applied to the writings of Locke and Bentham, describing society as comprised of individuals interacting through market relations.

liberalism political and social theory that favours representative government, freedom of the press, speech, and worship, the abolition of class privileges, the use of state resources to protect the welfare of the individual, and international free trade. It is historically associated with the Liberal Party in the UK and the Democratic Party in the USA.

Maoism form of communism based on the ideas and teachings of the Chinese communist leader Mao Zedong. It involves an adaptation of Marxism to suit conditions in China and apportions a much greater role to agriculture and the peasantry in the building of socialism, thus effectively bypassing the capitalist (industrial) stage envisaged by Marx.

Marxism philosophical system, developed by the 19th-century German social theorists Marx and Engels, also known as *dialectical materialism*, under which matter gives rise to mind (materialism) and all is subject to change. As applied to history, it supposes that the succession of feudalism, capitalism, socialism, and finally the classless society is inevitable. The stubborn resistance of any existing system to change necessitates its complete overthrow in the *class struggle*—in the case of capitalism, by the proletariat—rather than gradual modification.

nationalism a movement that consciously aims to unify a nation, create a state, or liberate it from foreign rule. Nationalist movements became a potent factor in European politics during the 19th century; since 1900 nationalism has become a strong force in Asia and Africa and in the late 1980s revived strongly in E Europe.

pluralism in political science, the view that decision-making in contemporary liberal democracies is the outcome of competition among several interest groups in a political system characterized by free elections, representative institutions, and open access to the organs of power. This concept is opposed by corporatism and other approaches that perceive power to be centralized in the state and its principal elites.

socialism movement aiming at the establishment of a classless society through the substitution of common for private ownership of the means of production, distribution and exchange. The term is used both to cover all movements with this aim, such as communism and anarchism, and more narrowly for evolutionary socialism or democracy. In general the tendency since 1917 has been for a clear distinction, if not opposition, to exist between parties governed by Marx's revolutionary, 'scientific' socialism and the gradualist, reforming approach of the British Labour Party and Western European Social Democratic Parties.

Thatcherism a political outlook associated with Margaret Thatcher but stemming from an individualist view found in Britain's 19th-century Liberal and 20th-century Conservative parties. Thatcherism is an ideology no longer confined to Britain and comprises a belief in the efficacy of market forces, the need for strong central government, and a conviction that self-help is preferable to reliance on the state, combined with a strong element of nationalism.

theocracy a political system run by priests, as was once found in Tibet. In practical terms it means a system where religious values determine political decisions. The clearest modern example was Iran during the period when Ayatollah Khomeini was its religious leader, 1979–89. The term was coined by the 1st century AD historian Josephus.

totalitarianism government control of all activities within a country, overtly political or otherwise, as in fascist or communist dictatorships. Examples of totalitarian regimes are Italy under Benito Mussolini 1922–45; Germany under Adolf Hitler 1933–45; the USSR under Joseph Stalin from 1930s until his death in 1953; more recently Romania under Nicolae Ceausescu 1974–89.

Trotskyism form of Marxism advocated by Leon Trotsky. Its central concept is that of *permanent revolution*. In his view a proletarian revolution, leading to a socialist society, could not be achieved in isolation, so it would be necessary to spark off further revolutions throughout Europe and ultimately worldwide. This was in direct opposition to the Stalinist view that socialism should be built and consolidated within individual countries.

POLITICAL TERMS

affirmative action in the USA, a government-endorsed policy of positive discrimination that favours members of minority ethnic groups and women in such areas as employment and education, designed to counter the effects of long-term discrimination against them. The policy has been controversial, and has prompted lawsuits by white males who have been denied jobs or education as a result.

Positive discrimination in favour of ethnic-minority construction companies by local government was outlawed in the UK in Jan 1989.

alliance agreement between two or more states to come to each other's assistance in the event of war. Alliances were criticized after World War I as having contributed to the outbreak of war but NATO and until 1991 the Warsaw Pact have been major parts of the post-1945 structure of international relations.

ambassador officer of the highest rank in the diplomatic service, who represents the head of one sovereign state at the court or capital of another.

apartheid the racial-segregation policy of the government of South Africa that began 1948, when it was legislated by the Afrikaner National Party that had gained power; in 1990, apartheid legislation began to be repealed by President de Klerk and a new constitution promised. Also in 1990, Nelson Mandela, the current vice-president of the African National Congress, was finally released.

The term has also been applied to similar movements and other forms of racial separation, for example social or educational, in other parts of the world.

arms control attempts to limit the arms race between the superpowers by reaching agreements to restrict the production of certain weapons, as in the Strategic Arms Limitation talks (SALT) of the 1970s and the Strategic Arms Reductions Talks (START) of the 1980s-90s.

autonomy political self-government.

ballot the process of voting in an election. In political elections in democracies ballots are usually secret: voters indicate their choice of candidate on a voting slip which is placed in a sealed ballot box. *Ballot rigging* is the fraudulent interference with the voting process or the counting of votes.

blockade the cutting-off of a place by hostile forces by land, sea, or air so as to prevent any movement to or fro, in order to compel a surrender without attack. For example, in 1990 a United Nations resolution stated the determination of the member countries to implement a blockade in an attempt to force Iraq, under the leadership of President Saddam Hussein, to withdraw from the invaded territory of Kuwait.

cabinet the group of ministers holding a country's highest executive offices who decide government policy. In Britain the cabinet system originated under the Stuarts. Under William III it became customary for the king to select his ministers from the party with a parliamentary majority. The US cabinet, unlike the British, does not initiate legislation, and its members, appointed by the president, must not be members of Congress.

citizenship status as a member of a state. In most countries citizenship may be acquired either by birth or by naturalization. The status confers rights such as voting and the protection of the law and also imposes responsibilities such as military service, in some countries.

civil service body of administrative staff appointed to carry out the policy of a government. Members of the UK civil service may not take an active part in, and do not change with, the government.

coalition association of political groups, usually for some limited or short-term purpose, such as fighting an election or forming a government when one party has failed to secure a majority in a legislature.

constitution the fundamental laws of a state, laying down the system of government and defining the relations of the legislature, executive, and judiciary to each other and to the citizens. Since the French Revolution almost all countries (the UK is one exception) have adopted written constitutions; that of the USA (1787) is the oldest.

council in local government in England and Wales, a popularly elected local assembly charged with the government of the area within its boundaries. Under the Local Government Act of 1972, there are three types: county councils, district councils, and parish councils.

coup d'état or *coup* forcible takeover of the government of a country by elements from within that country, generally carried out by violent or illegal means. It differs from a revolution in typically being carried out by a small group (for example, of army officers or opposition politicians) to install its leader as head of government, rather than being a mass uprising by the people. Recent coups include the military seizure of power in Surinam in Dec 1990 and the short-lived removal of Mikhail Gorbachev from power in the USSR by hardline communists 19-22 Aug 1991.

détente (French) a reduction of political tension and the easing of strained relations between nations; for example, the ending of the Cold War 1989-90.

dictatorship the term or office of an absolute ruler, overriding the constitution. Although dictatorships were common in Latin America during the 19th century, the only European example during this period was the rule of Napoleon III. The crises following World War I produced many dictatorships, including the regimes of Atatürk and Pilsudski (nationalist); Mussolini, Hitler, Primo de Rivera, Franco, and Salazar (all right-wing); and Stalin (communist).

diplomacy process by which states attempt to settle their differences through peaceful means such as negotiation or arbitration.

dissident in one-party states, a person intellectually dissenting from the official line. Dissidents have been sent into exile, prison, labour camps, and mental institutions, or deprived of their jobs. In the USSR the number of imprisoned dissidents declined from more than 600 in 1986 to fewer than 100 in 1990, of whom the majority were ethnic nationalists. In China the number of prisoners of conscience increased after the 1989 Tiananmen Square massacre, and in South Africa, despite the release of Nelson Mandela in 1990, numerous political dissidents remained in jail.

federalism system of government where two or more separate states unite under a common central government while retaining a considerable degree of local autonomy. A federation should be distinguished from a *confederation*, a looser union of states for mutual assistance. Switzerland, the USA, Canada, Australia, and Malaysia are all examples of federal government, and many supporters of the European Community see such a system as the forerunner of a federal Europe.

glasnost former Soviet leader Mikhail Gorbachev's policy of liberalizing various aspects of Soviet life, such as introducing greater freedom of expression and information and opening up relations with the West. It was introduced and adopted by the Soviet government 1986.

Glasnost has involved the lifting of bans on books, plays, and films, the release of political dissidents, the tolerance of religious worship, a reappraisal of Soviet history (destalinization), the encouragement of investigative journalism to uncover political corruption, and the sanctioning of greater candour in the reporting of social problems and disasters (such as Chernobyl).

Under legislation introduced 1990, censorship of mass media was abolished; however, publication of state secrets, calls for the overthrow of the state by force, incitement of national or religious hatred, and state interference in people's private lives were prohibited. Journalists' rights to access were enshrined, and the right of reply instituted. Citizens gained the right to receive information from abroad.

high commissioner representative of one independent Commonwealth country in the capital of another, ranking with ambassador.

judiciary in constitutional terms, the system of courts and body of judges in a country. The independence of the judiciary from other branches of the central authority is generally considered to be an essential feature of a democratic political system. This independence is often written into a nation's constitution and is protected from abuse by politicians.

left wing the progressive, radical, or socialist faction of the political spectrum. The term originated in the French National Assembly 1789 where the nobles sat in the place of honour to the right of the president, and the commons sat to the left. It is also usual to speak of the right, left, and centre, when referring to the different elements composing a single party.

lobby individual or pressure group that sets out to influence government action. The lobby is prevalent in the USA, where the term originated in the 1830s from the practice of those wishing to influence state policy waiting for elected representatives in the lobby of the Capitol.

local government that part of government dealing mainly with matters concerning the inhabitants of a particular area or town, usually financed at least in part by local taxes. In the USA and UK local government has had comparatively large powers and responsibilities.

mandate in general, any official command; in politics also the right (given by the electors) of an elected government to carry out its programme of policies.

Historically, mandate referred to a territory whose administration was entrusted to Allied states by the League of Nations under the Treaty of Versailles after World War I. Mandated territories were former German and Turkish possessions (including Iraq, Syria, Lebanon, and Palestine). When the United Nations replaced the League of Nations in 1945, mandates that had not achieved independence became known as trust territories.

manifesto the published prospectus of a political party, setting out the policies that the party will pursue if elected to govern. When elected to power a party will often claim that the contents of its manifesto constitute a mandate to introduce legislation to bring these policies into effect.

militia a body of civilian soldiers, usually with some military training, who are on call in emergencies, distinct from professional soldiers. In Switzerland, the militia is the national defence force, and every able-bodied man is liable for service in it. In the UK the *Territorial Army* and in the USA the *National Guard* have supplanted earlier voluntary militias.

nationalization policy of bringing a country's essential services and industries under public ownership. It was pursued, for example, by the UK Labour government 1945–51. In recent years the trend towards nationalization has slowed and in many countries (the UK, France, and Japan) reversed (privatization). Assets in the hands of foreign governments or companies may also be nationalized; for example, Iran's oil industry, the Suez Canal, and US-owned fruit plantations in Guatemala, all in the 1950s.

parliament the legislative body of a country. The world's oldest parliament is the Icelandic Althing from about 930. The UK parliament is usually dated from 1265.

In the UK, Parliament is the supreme legislature, comprising the House of Commons and the House of Lords. The origins of parliament are in the 13th century, but its powers were not established until the late 17th century. The powers of the Lords were curtailed 1911, and the duration of parliaments was fixed at five years, but any parliament may extend its own life, as happened during both world wars. It meets in the Palace of Westminster, London.

perestroika in Soviet politics, the wide-ranging economic and political reforms initiated during Mikhail Gorbachev's leadership of the Soviet state.

The term was first proposed at the 26th Party Congress in 1979 and actively promoted by Gorbachev from 1985. Originally, in the economic sphere, perestroika was conceived as involving the 'switching onto a track of intensive development' by automation and improved labour efficiency. It evolved to attend increasingly to market indicators and incentives ('market socialism') and the gradual dismantling of the Stalinist central-planning system, with decision-taking authority being devolved to self-financing enterprises.

president usual title of the head of state in a republic; the power of the office may range from the equivalent of a constitutional monarch to the actual head of the government.

prime minister or *premier* head of a parliamentary government, usually the leader of the largest party.

In some countries, such as Australia, a distinction is drawn between the prime minister of the whole country and the premier of an individual state. In countries with an executive president, the prime minister is of lesser standing, whereas in those with dual executives, such as France, power is shared with the president.

privatization reconversion of nationalized services and industries to private ownership, as under the Conservative governments in the UK after 1953, especially the Thatcher government 1979–90, and in France since 1986.

propaganda the systematic spreading (propagation) of information or disinformation, usually to promote a religious or political doctrine with the intention of instilling particular attitudes or responses.

purge the removal (for example from a political party) of suspected opponents or persons regarded as undesirable. In 1934 the Nazis carried out a purge of their party and a number of party leaders were executed for an alleged plot against Hitler. During the 1930s purges were conducted in the USSR under Joseph Stalin, carried out by the secret police against political opponents, communist party members, minorities, civil servants, and large sections of the armed forces' officer corps. Some 10 million people were executed or deported to labour camps from 1934 to 1938. Later purges include communist purges in Hungary 1949, Czechoslovakia 1951, and China 1955.

radical anyone with opinions more extreme than the main current of a country's major political party or parties. It is more often applied to those with left-wing opinions.

rainbow coalition or *rainbow alliance* from the mid-1980s, a loose, left-of-centre grouping of disparate elements, encompassing sections of society that are traditionally politically underrepresented, such as nonwhite ethnic groups. Its aims include promoting minority rights and equal opportunities.

referendum procedure whereby a decision on proposed legislation is referred to the electorate for settlement by direct vote of all the people.

It is most frequently employed in Switzerland, the first country to use it, but has also been used in Australia, New Zealand, Québec, and certain states of the USA. It was used in the UK for the first time 1975 on the issue of membership of the European Community. Critics argue that referenda undermine parliamentary authority, but they do allow the elector to participate directly in decision-making. A similar device is the *recall*, whereby voters are given the opportunity of demanding the dismissal from office of officials.

refugee a person fleeing from oppressive or dangerous conditions—such as political, religious, or military persecution—to a foreign country. They come from every race and religion, and few areas of the world have been spared the tragedy of refugees. Their numbers grow every year: in 1970 they numbered 2.5 million; in 1985, 10 million; in 1987, 12 million; in 1990, 15 million; in June 1991, 17 million, most of them women and children.

Refugees are the responsibility of the United Nations High Commission for Refugees (UNHCR), which was created by the UN General Assembly in 1945. Originally set up for a period of three years, as the numbers of refugees grew, its mandate has been repeatedly

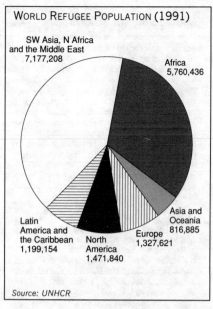

WORLD REFUGEE POPULATION (1991)

SW Asia, N Africa and the Middle East 7,177,208

Africa 5,760,436

Asia and Oceania 816,885

Europe 1,327,621

North America 1,471,840

Latin America and the Caribbean 1,199,154

Source: UNHCR

renewed. Its funds come chiefly from government contributions, and its main functions are to protect refugees, to find durable solutions for them, and to provide them with the necessary assistance until solutions can be found.

right wing the more conservative or reactionary section of a political party or spectrum. It originated in the French National Assembly 1789, where the nobles sat in the place of honour on the president's right, whereas the commons were on his left (hence left wing).

sanction economic or military measure taken by a state or number of states to enforce international law. Examples of the recent use of sanctions are the attempted economic boycott of Rhodesia, after its unilateral declaration of independence 1965, by the United Nations; the call for measures against South Africa on human-rights grounds by the United Nations and other organizations from 1985; the economic boycott of Iraq (1990) in protest over its invasion of Kuwait, following resolutions passed by the United Nations.

secretary of state in the UK, a title held by a number of ministers, for example, the secretary of state for foreign and commonwealth affairs. In the USA the secretary of state deals with foreign affairs.

shuttle diplomacy form of international diplomacy prominent in the 1970s where an independent mediator would travel between belligerent parties in order to try and achieve a compromise solution.

In 1990–91 it was practised by US Secretary of State, James Baker, in the period leading up to, and following, the Gulf War.

sovereignty absolute authority within a given territory. The possession of sovereignty is taken to be the distinguishing feature of the state, as against other forms of community. The term

MAJOR'S APRIL SURPRISE

Across continental Europe there was considerable voter restlessness in the spring of 1992. In the April elections in Italy, the ruling four-party coalition, dominated by the Christian Democrats, lost its majority though a surge in support for the regionalist Lombardy League. In France and Germany, in March and April, environmentalist and far-right fringe parties received strong support in regional and local contests. This volatility was reflected in Germany by increasing labour unrest. Its main cause was the economic recession. Another influence was the uncertainty following the abrupt ending of the Cold War and the accelerating process of European Community federalization.

UK voters bucked the trend to vote for change. The April general election took place during the longest, deepest recession in the postwar era. Unemployment was up by 1.1 million from 1990 to 2.7 million: 9.4% of the labour force. Nevertheless the Conservative Party, led by John Major, won a record fourth successive election. Its parliamentary majority was reduced to 21 seats, and in Scotland it received the support of only a quarter of all voters, but its share of the vote remained solid at 43%. This gave it a comfortable eight-point lead over its chief rival, the Labour Party.

The date of the election was announced on 11 March, immediately after the unveiling of a tax-cutting budget. National opinion polls showed the Conservatives trailing Labour by between one and three points. Labour held their lead throughout the five-week campaign. The Conservative campaign was liberally funded, but the party's strategy seemed uncertain. Supporters and opponents criticized it for being too negative. The final opinion surveys before the election all suggested that the most likely

John Major and Chris Patten about to announce the Conservative Party manifesto March 1992.

outcome would be a hung parliament—with Labour support standing at 39% and Conservative at 38%, no single party would hold a majority.

However, once the first counts had been announced, this prediction was obviously very wrong. There had been a late surge towards the Conservatives among millions of voters. During the campaign they had either remained undecided or had been 'soft' in their support for the opposition parties. Perhaps some electors had simply lied in their interviews with polling organizations. The apparent decency and quiet competence of John Major—a definitively classless figure—had drawn in considerable support. So had self-interest among the nation's 'comfortable majority': electors who had remained in employment and had benefited from increasing pay packets and mortgage-rate reductions during 1991–92. They were clearly worried about the financial consequences of the election of a Labour government.

Many electors were tired of the decade-long 'Thatcher experiment' upheavals, and were looking for a change in political direction. For them, a new order was already in place. The decisive shift had occurred during 1990–91, with the departure of Margaret Thatcher and the scrapping of the unpopular 'poll tax'. They now believed it was time to give John Major his own mandate.

The Labour Party ran a professional campaign; it received an extra 44 parliamentary seats and a 3% increase in its share of the vote. But set against their expectations, the result of 9 April was a devastating blow. Within days, the party's leader, Neil Kinnock, announced his resignation.

Labour's initial reactions to their defeat centred on the distorting excesses of the Tory-dominated tabloid press. Considered reflection suggested that the party's problems were more deep-seated. The Labour party had remodelled its policy on social democratic lines since 1987, but changes in employment and housing patterns were eroding its base of support. With revisions of constituency boundaries set to lead to additional Labour seat losses, the party faced a huge task to achieve victory in 1996 or 1997.

Some Labour members suggested that the way forward would be to form a broad centre-left progressive front including the Liberal Democrats and, possibly, realistic Greens. It would put forward a 'new politics' programme that embraced constitutional and electoral reform and greater environmental awareness. Faced with the longest period of unbroken single-party government since the beginning of the 19th century, political analysts began to suggest that without such a realignment of the centre left, Britain was set to become politically the 'Japan of the Western world'—a country so dominated by one party that policy changes would be determined by factional manoeuvrings rather than by the ballot box.

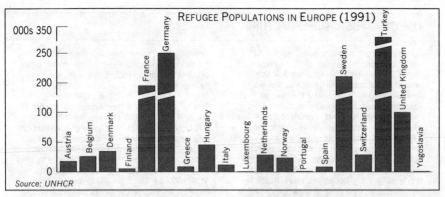

REFUGEE POPULATIONS IN EUROPE (1991)

000s

Source: UNHCR

has an internal aspect, in that it refers to the ultimate source of authority within a state, such as a parliament or monarch, and an external aspect, where it denotes the independence of the state from any outside authority. In the latter sense, the preservation of national sovereignty is a major factor in the UK conservative government's opposition to certain aspects of EC plans for European integration (such as a single currency and a single foreign policy).

state territory that forms its own domestic and foreign policy, acting through laws that are typically decided by a government and carried out, by force if necessary, by agents of that government. It can be argued that growth of regional international bodies such as the European Community means that states no longer enjoy absolute sovereignty.

summit or **summit conference** meeting of heads of government to discuss common interests, especially the US–Soviet summits 1959-90, of which there were 15. The term was first used during World War II, and the Yalta Conference and Potsdam Conference 1945 were summits that did much to determine the political structure of the postwar world. Later summits have been of varying importance, partly as public-relations exercises.

terrorism systematic violence in the furtherance of political aims, often by small guerrilla groups, such as the Fatah Revolutionary Council led by Abu Nidal, a splinter group that split from the Palestine Liberation Organization in 1973.

trade union organization of employed workers formed to undertake collective bargaining with employers and to try to achieve improved working conditions for its members. Attitudes of government to unions and of unions to management vary greatly from country to country. Probably the most effective trade-union system is that of Sweden, and the most internationally known is the Polish Solidarity.

The *Trades Union Congress* in the UK is a voluntary organization of trade unions, founded in 1868. Delegates of affiliated unions meet annually to consider matters affecting their members. In 1991 there were 78 affiliated unions, with an aggregate membership of 10.4 million. Its headquarters are in London.

unilateralism support for *unilateral nuclear disarmament*: scrapping a country's nuclear weapons without waiting for other countries to agree to do so at the same time.

veto (Latin 'I forbid') exercise by a sovereign, branch of legislature, or other political power, of the right to prevent the enactment or operation of a law, or the taking of some course of action.

vote expression of opinion by ballot, show of hands, or other means. In systems that employ direct vote, the plebiscite and referendum are fundamental mechanisms. In parliamentary elections the results can be calculated in a number of ways. The main electoral systems are:

simple plurality or *first past the post*, with single-member constituencies (USA, UK, India, Canada);

absolute majority, achieved for example by the *alternative vote*, where the voter, in single-member constituencies, chooses a candidate by marking preferences (Australia), or by the *second ballot*, where, if a clear decision is not reached immediately, a second ballot is held (France, Egypt);

proportional representation, achieved for example by the *party list* system (Israel, most countries of Western Europe, and several in South America), the *additional member* system (Germany), the *single transferable vote* (Ireland and Malta), and the *limited vote* (Japan).

All British subjects over 18, except peers, the insane, and felons, are entitled to vote in UK local government and parliamentary elections. A register is prepared annually, and since 1872 voting has been by secret ballot. The voting system is by a simple majority in single-member constituencies.

Voter registration and turnout in the USA remains the lowest in the industrialized world. In 1988, 37% of potential voters failed to register and barely 50% bothered to vote in the presidential election, so that George Bush became president with the support of only 27% of the people.

welfare state political system under which the state (rather than the individual or the private sector) has responsibility for the welfare

THE CIS—FUSION OR FRACTURE

Conservative communists launched the anti-Gorbachev coup of August 1991 to preserve the USSR as a Moscow-dominated federation. Instead, it hastened the destruction of an already fractured Union. The Communist Party was discredited and forced into dissolution. The Union's titular head, President Gorbachev, returned to Moscow but was unable to recognize and adjust to the changed situation. He consequently lost residual political authority, as well as popular sympathy gained from the coup. The Ukrainian electors' vote for independence in early December 1991 frustrated his remaining hope of creating a looser Union of Sovereign States. It was left to Boris Yeltsin, president of the giant Russian Federation, to assume Gorbachev's power-broking mantle and salvage something from the wreckage. In mid-December he negotiated the formation of a new Commonwealth of Independent States (CIS).

The CIS was conceived as a confederation of Slav states, but by late December 1991 it had broadened to incorporate eight other former USSR republics. Only Georgia and the three Baltic republics stayed outside. Nevertheless, it was clear that the CIS would differ greatly from the USSR. It aimed to provide order and stability while the ex-Soviet republics struggled to achieve independent statehood, market economics, and democratic politics. It was held together by voluntary ties. It had no permanent political institutions or secretariat; it reached *ad hoc* decisions at summits held in state capitals.

The republics most committed to the CIS's success were the Russian Federation, Belarus, and Kazakhstan. They hoped it would forestall dangerous boundary disputes and coordinate foreign and defence policies. By maintaining a 'single economic space' and coordinating market reform and price liberalization, it could avert damaging trade, price, and currency wars.

During spring 1992 the CIS averted military conflict between member states, except for the continuing disputes between Armenia and Azerbaijan. However, by early summer splits were showing: only six state leaderships attended the May 1992 summit in Tashkent. With Azerbaijan and Ukraine threatening to withdraw and Moldova likely to merge with Romania, commentators began writing the CIS's obituary.

The CIS may well survive as an east European hybrid of the UK Commonwealth and the early European Economic Community—a debating forum and free-trade zone. The real centres of power, however, are the newly independent republics, each faced with managing its own economic and political transitions.

GDP fell by a fifth in the USSR during 1991. The republics face similar contractions during 1992, as they undergo the 'shock therapy' of price liberalization and privatization, putting at risk their weak democratic institutions. Equally threatening are potentially bitter inter-ethnic conflicts from the Caucasus to Tatarstan. A new federative treaty signed in April 1992 by 18 of the 20 republics within the Russian Federation marks one hopeful step forward.

For the outside world the collapse of the USSR and its replacement by the noncommunist CIS has marked the end of the Cold War. The world now has only one true military superpower, the USA. Nevertheless, the CIS states have inherited a vast military arsenal whose future has caused considerable international concern.

The Soviet Army was the USSR's last surviving pan-republican institution. Initially, the CIS members pledged to maintain it as the nucleus of a new Commonwealth army. However, by spring 1992 they had abandoned this plan. The republics, including Russia, had decided to establish national armies. They would maintain joint 'dual key' control over the arsenal of 12,000 long-range nuclear weapons in Russia, Belarus, Ukraine, and Kazakhstan, which would be subject to the provisions of the START treaty. Meanwhile, the 15,000 shorter-range tactical weapons scattered across the CIS republics were collected within the Russian Federation to be gradually destroyed with Western assistance.

More pressing has been the problem of dividing the Soviet Army's conventional assets, concentrated in Belarus and Ukraine under Soviet control. Another complication has been the complex quota arrangements of the CFE (conventional forces in Europe) treaty, by which all the republics are to reduce their conventional forces rapidly and nationalize/republicanize them. This is bound to cause problems of resettlement and re-employment, particularly in the Central Asian Republics, which supplied almost half the Soviet Army's recruits in 1991. The poorer states, suffering the loss of financial aid from Moscow, have been courted since independence by neighbouring Iran and Turkey. Some have joined the Economic Cooperation Organization, an Islamic regional economic grouping, thus weakening their commitment to the CIS.

of its citizens. Services such as unemployment and sickness benefits, family allowances and incomes supplements, pensions, medical care, and education may be provided and financed through state insurance schemes and taxation.

Internationally, the aim of creating a welfare state has been adopted in several countries, particularly in Scandinavia, but, again, often more as an ideal than a reality. The welfare state concept was built into the political structures of communist states, led by the Soviet Union, but even here economic realities tempered its practical implementation.

Ten Largest Unions 1992

	trade union	membership
1	Transport & General Workers (TGW)	1,223,891
2	General Municipal Boilermakers (GMB)	933,425
3	National and Local Government Officers Association (NALGO)	744,453
4	Amalgamated Engineering Union (AEU)	702,228
5	Manufacturing Science Finance (MSF)	653,000
6	National Union of Public Employees (NUPE)	578,992
7	Union of Shop, Distributive and Allied Workers (USDAW)	361,789
8	Graphical, Paper and Media Union	288,469
9	Union of Construction, Allied Trades & Technicians (UCATT)	207,232
10	Confederation of Health Services Employees (COHSE)	203,311

Ten Smallest Unions 1992

1	Sheffield Wool Shear Workers Union	17
2	Society of Shuttlemakers	29
3	Military and Orchestral Music Instrument-Makers Trade Society	42
4	Scottish Union of Power-loom Overlookers	70
5	Card Setting Machine Tenters' Association	75
6	Amalgamated Association of Beamers, Twisters and Drawers (Hand and Machine)	403
7	Engineering and Fastener Trade Union	430
8	Yorkshire Association of Power-loom Overlookers	519
9	General Union of Associations of Loom Overlookers	680
10	Northern Carpets Trade Union	770

Source: TUC

UK CENTRAL GOVERNMENT

Central government in the UK is currently based on 16 major departments of state, each headed by a minister who is a member of the cabinet, and 16 minor or subdepartments.

Major departments

Ministry of Agriculture, Fisheries and Food
Ministry of Defence
Department of Education
Department of Employment
Department of the Environment
Foreign and Commonwealth Office
Department of Health
Department for National Heritage
Home Office
Northern Ireland Office
Scottish Office
Department of Social Security
Department of Trade and Industry
Department of Transport
Treasury *
Welsh Office
* The Treasury is the one department with two cabinet representatives, the chancellor of the Exchequer and the chief secretary to the Treasury, and, since the prime minister is formally also First Lord of the Treasury, it can be argued that the cabinet representation is threefold.

Minor departments

Board of Inland Revenue
Central Office of Information
Department of National Savings
Export Credits Guarantee Department
H M Customs and Excise Department
Her Majesty's Household
Her Majesty's Stationery Office
Law Officers' Department
Lord Advocate's Department
Lord Chancellor's Department *
Office of Arts and Libraries
Office of the Minister for the Civil Service
Overseas Development Administration
Parliamentary Counsel's Office
Paymaster General's Office
Privy Council Office *
* Direct representation in the cabinet.

Nondepartmental cabinet members

Apart from the prime minister, there are three members of the cabinet without specific departmental responsibilities: Lord President of the Council, who is Leader of the House of Commons; Lord Privy Seal, who is Leader of the House of Lords; and Chancellor of the Duchy of Lancaster, who is responsible for the implementation of the Citizen's Charter, science, and civil-service reform.

Ministerial gradings

The top-ranking ministers are members of the cabinet. Most cabinet ministers heading departments are now styled *secretary of state*. The exceptions are the minister of Agriculture, Fisheries, and Food, the Lord Chancellor, the chancellor of the Exchequer, and the President of the Board of Trade.

The other ministers, in descending order of rank, are:

minister of state who may be of cabinet rank (may sometimes be styled minister of state and sometimes minister) *undersecretary of state* (may sometimes be styled minister)

parliamentary undersecretary (in the case of Agriculture, Fisheries, and Food, and the Treasury, styled parliamentary secretary).

When the minister heading a major department is styled secretary of state, junior ministers in that department are styled parliamentary undersecretaries. In other cases they are styled parliamentary secretaries.

Civil-service gradings

The three most senior grades in the home civil service, found in all major departments, are: permanent secretary, deputy secretary, undersecretary.

Typical structure of a department

All departments have specific, distinctive features but most conform to the following pattern: (political head) secretary of state, supported by one or more ministers of state and junior ministers; (nonpolitical head) permanent secretary, supported by administrative, executive, and clerical staff.

Major departments

Ministry of Agriculture, Fisheries, and Food
established 1955, through combination of existing agriculture, fisheries, and food ministries
responsibilities agriculture, horticulture, fisheries, and food policies
ministerial team minister, one minister of state, two parliamentary secretaries
head John Selwyn Gummer
permanent staff 10,400
administrative headquarters Whitehall Place, London SW1.

Ministry of Defence
established 1964, when Admiralty, War Office, and Air Defence were brought together in one ministry
responsibilities national defence, including overall control of the Royal Navy, Army, and Royal Air Force, and arms procurement
ministerial team secretary of state, two ministers of state, one parliamentary undersecretary
head Malcolm Rifkind
permanent staff 98,000, including Royal Ordnance factories
administrative headquarters Whitehall, London SW1.

Department of Education
established 1944, as the Ministry of Education
responsibilities education and scientific research policies
ministerial team secretary of state, one minister of state, one parliamentary undersecretary
head John Patten
permanent staff 2,600
administrative headquarters York Road, London SE1.

Department of Employment
established 1970 in its present form. The original Ministry of Labour was formed in 1917
responsibilities employment and training policies

ministerial team secretary of state, one minister of state, two parliamentary undersecretaries
head Gillian Shephard
permanent staff 53,700
administrative headquarters Tothill Street, London SW1.

Department of the Environment
established 1970, bringing together ministries of Housing and Local Government, Transport, and Building and Works. Transport returned to an independent status in 1975
responsibilities housing, construction, local government, sport and recreation policies, and preservation of the environment
ministerial team secretary of state, three ministers of state, one parliamentary undersecretary
head Michael Howard
permanent staff 19,400
administrative headquarters Marsham Street, London SW1.

Foreign and Commonwealth Office
established 1782, as the Foreign Office
responsibilities conduct of foreign policy, representation of British interests abroad, relations with other members of the Commonwealth, overseas aid policy and administration
ministerial team secretary of state, four ministers of state, one parliamentary undersecretary
head Douglas Hurd
permanent staff 8,300
administrative headquarters Downing Street, London SW1.

Department of Health
established 1988, following the division of the Department of Health and Social Security into two separate departments. Ministry of Health formed in 1919
responsibilities operation of the national health service and overall policies on health
ministerial team secretary of state, one minister of state, three parliamentary undersecretaries
head Virginia Bottomley
permanent staff 11,400, excluding NHS staff
administrative headquarters Whitehall, London SW1.

Department for National Heritage
established 1992
responsibilities broadcasting and the media, the arts, sport and recreation, the national lottery
ministerial team secretary of state, one minister of state
head David Mellor
permanent staff not yet known
administrative headquarters Whitehall, London SW1.

Home Office
established 1782
responsibilities administration of justice, penal system (including the prison and probation services), police, fire, civil defence, licensing (including marriage, liquor, theatres, and cinemas), radio and television broadcasting, immigration and nationality policies

ministerial team secretary of state, two ministers of state, two parliamentary undersecretaries
head Kenneth Clarke
permanent staff 45,000
administrative headquarters Queen Anne's Gate, London SW1.

Northern Ireland Office
established 1972
responsibilities direct government of Northern Ireland, including administration of security, law and order, and economic, industrial, and social policies
ministerial team secretary of state, one minister of state, one parliamentary undersecretary
head Patrick Mayhew
permanent staff 29,500
administrative headquarters Whitehall, London SW1, and Belfast.

Scottish Office
established 1707 in England, 1938 in Scotland
responsibilities administration for Scotland of policies on agriculture and fisheries, education, industrial development, law and order, and health
ministerial team secretary of state, two ministers of state, two parliamentary undersecretaries
head Ian Lang
permanent staff 13,000
administrative headquarters Whitehall, London SW1, and Edinburgh.

Department of Social Security
established 1988, after being part of the Department of Health and Social Security
responsibilities administration of social-service policies, including pensions, unemployment, income support, and disability benefits
ministerial team secretary of state, one minister of state, three parliamentary undersecretaries
head Peter Lilley
permanent staff 78,000
administrative headquarters Whitehall, London SW1.

Department of Trade and Industry
established 1970, bringing together the Board of Trade, founded in 1786, and the Ministry of Technology, formed in 1964; took over the responsibilities of the Department of Energy in 1992
responsibilities administration of policies on international trade, industry, competition, industrial research and assistance to exporters
ministerial team President of the Board of Trade (secretary of state), three ministers of state, three parliamentary undersecretaries
head Michael Heseltine
permanent staff 12,500
administrative headquarters Victoria Street, London SW1.

Department of Transport
established 1975, in its present form
responsibilities land, sea, and air transport policies, including sponsorship of British Rail, and construction and maintenance of motorways and trunk roads

ministerial team secretary of state, two ministers of state, two parliamentary undersecretaries
head John MacGregor
permanent staff 16,000
administrative headquarters Marsham Street, London SW1.

Treasury
established 1612
responsibilities control of public expenditure, national economic policy, including monetary and fiscal measures, efficiency in the public sector, international finance, and oversight of the financial system
ministerial team chancellor of the Exchequer, chief secretary (of cabinet rank), three ministers of state rank (paymaster general, financial secretary, and economic secretary), one parliamentary secretary
chancellor Norman Lamont
chief secretary Michael Portillo
permanent staff 3,200
administrative headquarters Parliament Street, London SW1.

Welsh Office
established 1951
responsibilities administration for Wales of policies on agriculture, education, health and social services, local government, planning, sport, and tourism. It is also responsible for promoting the Welsh language and culture
ministerial team secretary of state, one minister of state, one parliamentary undersecretary
head David Hunt
permanent staff 2,300
administrative headquarters Whitehall, London SW1, and Cardiff.

Minor departments

Board of Inland Revenue
parent department Treasury
responsibilities collection of central government taxes, other than VAT and customs and excise duties, throughout the UK.

Cabinet Office
parent department Cabinet
responsibilities services the cabinet and all its committees and subcommittees; it organizes meetings; prepares and distributes agendas and cabinet papers, including minutes; and decides, with the prime minister, which issues should go to the full cabinet and which to one of its committees or subcommittees.

Central Office of Information (COI)
parent department Treasury
resposibilities operation of government information services.

Customs and Excise Department
parent department Treasury
responsibilities collection of customs and excise duties, including VAT.

Department of National Savings
parent department Treasury
responsibilities management of government savings schemes.

Exports Credits Guarantee Department
parent department Department of Trade and

EUROPE'S NEOFASCISTS GAIN GROUND

During 1991–92 voters throughout western Europe transferred their support from the mainstream political parties of the centre right and centre left to an array of fringe parties. There were election successes for regionalists in Catalonia, Flanders, Lombardy, and Scotland; for environmentalists, notably in France; and for the extreme right.

The most successful far-right party was Jean-Marie Le Pen's Front National in France. In the March 1992 regional elections it captured a seventh of the national vote and in nine of the country's 22 regions it received more votes than the ruling socialist party. Extremist parties also received strong support in state and national elections in Belgium, Germany, and Italy. They ranged from the Vlaams Blok and Northern League regionalists to the neofascist DVU, Die Republikaner, and the MSI (see table).

There was a surge in support for parties led by charismatic and autocratic strongmen propounding simplistic, racist policy programmes. It reflected deepening disillusionment with the existing party system. This was particularly true among marginal groups, faced with economic austerity and rising levels of unemployment, drug trafficking, and crime. The trend also reflected concern about the loss of national sovereignty to Brussels as the process of EC 'deepening' gathered pace, and worries about refugee inflows from eastern Europe and the south. There was also a general loss of ideological identity and a sense of political flux as the Cold War came to an abrupt end.

The most worrying trend in 1991–92 was in Germany's eastern *Länder* (states). Neofascist organizations were attracting violent and eager young recruits as the region made the painful transition from socialist planning to a capitalist 'social market' economy. Further east, beyond the Elbe, the problems of adjustment were even more severe. Party identities and democratic structures were dangerously weak in central and eastern Europe. There was the real possibility of a lurch towards rightist autocracy, feeding on ethnic and religious rivalries, as already seen in the Balkans and Caucasus.

The challenge facing Europe's politicians during the 1990s is to solve economic problems through moderate and gradualist policies rather than succumb to the simple, superficially attractive alternative of strong, autocratic leadership. This is true not just in the newly restored democracies, but also in those with long and well-established liberal traditions. The dictators of the 1930s came to power on a wave of social and economic disillusionment, similar to the loss of faith experienced by many Europeans today. Will today's politicians learn from history and come up with viable alternatives before it is too late?

THE SWING TO THE RIGHT

country	party	leader	share of vote
Austria	Freedom Party	Jorg Haider	23%*
Belgium	Vlaams Blok+	Karel Dillen	6%**
France	Front National	Jean-Marie Le Pen	14%***
Germany	Die Republikaner	Franz Schonhuber	11%****
Germany	Deutsche Volksunion (DVU)	Gerhard Frey	6%****
Italy	Italian Social Movement (MSI)	Pino Rauti	5%**
Italy	Northern League+	Umberto Bossi	9%**

+a party combining regionalism and xenophobia
*in Vienna local elections   **in national elections   ***in regional elections   ****in state elections

Industry
responsibilities management of government scheme to underwrite finance for exporters.
Her Majesty's Household
   parent department Lord Chamberlain
   responsibilities management of the affairs of the royal household.
Her Majesty's Stationery Office (HMSO)
   parent department Treasury
   responsibilities production and sale of government publications.
Law Officers' Department
   parent department freestanding, under Attorney General
   responsibilities legal advice to the government and representation of the Crown in court.
Lord Advocate's Department
   parent department freestanding

responsibilities administration of law in Scotland.
Lord Chancellor's Department
   parent department freestanding, under Lord Chancellor
   responsibilities administration of civil law in England and Wales, including the appointment of the judiciary in lower courts and advice on appointments in the higher courts.
   The Lord Chancellor also presides over sittings in the House of Lords.
Office of Arts and Libraries
   parent department Privy Council Office, under Lord President of the Council
   responsibilities promotion of the arts.
Office of the Minister for the Civil Service
   parent department prime minister
   responsibilities management of the home civil

service.

Overseas Development Administration (ODA)
parent department Foreign and Commonwealth
Office
responsibilities administration of development
assistance to overseas countries.

Parliamentary Counsel's Office
parent department freestanding
responsibilities drafting of parliamentary legislation.

Paymaster General's Office
parent department Treasury
responsibilities administration of payment of
government financial liabilities.

Privy Council Office
parent department freestanding, under Lord
President of the Council
responsibilities a miscellany of duties, including management of the civil service and promotion of the arts.

What political party in the UK do you think has the most positive attitude towards Europe?

Conservative	40
Labour	19
Liberal Democrats	11
Nationalist	3
Green Party	1
All the same	7
Don't know	20

What degree of influence does a Party's policy towards Europe have on your decision to vote for it?
And what degree of influence does a Party's policy on the economy have on your decision to vote for it?

	Europe	Economy
A great deal	10	37
A fair amount	33	36
Not very much	32	13
None at all	20	10
Don't know	5	5

When governments deal with political opponents, what is better—sticking firmly to one's beliefs or trying to meet them half-way?

	Today	Dec 1989	Apr 1989	May 1987	Sep 1986
Sticking to beliefs	42	37	35	45	41
Meeting them halfway	6	57	56	48	51
Don't know	52	6	9	7	8

In difficult economic times, what is better—for the government to be caring or for it to be tough?

	Today	Dec 1989	Apr 1989	May 1987	Sep 1986
Caring	47	50	51	50	48
Tough	40	39	36	36	39
Don't know	13	11	13	14	12

When governments make decisions about the economy, what is better—to involve major interests like trade unions and business, or to keep them at arms length?

	Today	Dec 1989	Apr 1989	May 1987	Sep 1986
Involve interests	66	67	70	68	68
Keep at arms length	24	25	23	23	23
Don't know	9	8	7	10	9

It is sometimes said that no government of any party can in fact do much to create economic prosperity; that is up to people themselves. Do you agree or disagree?

	Today	Dec 1989	Apr 1989	May 1987	Sep 1986
Agree	43	43	39	39	42
Disagree	46	46	51	48	44
Don't know	11	10	10	13	15

In its relations with the rest of world, what is better—for Britain to stick resolutely to its own position, or for Britain to meet other countries halfway?

	Today	Dec 1989	Apr 1989	May 1987	Sep 1986
Stick to own position	29	23	28	28	27
Meet them halfway	64	70	65	63	63
Don't know	7	7	7	9	10

RELIGIOUS TRADITIONS

BCE/CE before the common era (BCE) and common era (CE) are abbreviations used in this section to replace, respectively, before Christ (BC) and anno Domini (AD).

African religions there is a wide variety of belief and practice in African religion. Most indigenous African religions are basically polytheistic (believing in a number of gods), but there is often a concept of one High God, generally a creator who has withdrawn from interaction with the world. There are also many spirits, which are present in all natural objects: water is seen as a particularly powerful force. Dead ancestors are very important in African religions, and are consulted before major undertakings. If offended, they can cause natural disasters and sterility, so they must be placated with offerings. In society, healers are highly regarded, as they deal with supernatural powers, as do diviners, but the most powerful human figure is the chief-king, who is surrounded by prohibitions because he is so dangerous: he is the life of the tribe incarnate, though because of this he may be required to sacrifice himself to preserve the health of his people.

Australian aboriginal religion the creation story of the Australian Aborigines is recorded in the *Dreamtime* stories. These reveal how giant human and other animals sprang from the earth, sea, and sky and criss-crossed the empty continent of Australia on a journey known as Dreamtime. At the end of their journey they returned into the earth where it is believed their spirits still exist. The places where they travelled or sank back into the land became mountain ranges, rocks, and sites full of sacred meaning.

Every sacred site has its own Dreamtime story that is part of the sacred law and must be re-enacted at certain times of the year in order to maintain the life of the land and the Dreamtime. Each Australian Aborigine has their own particular Dreamtime Ancestor although they are related to many other ancestors through kinship. When hunting, Aborigi-

LEADING ORGANIZED RELIGIONS OF THE WORLD (1991)

Religion	Followers
Christianity	1,382,000,000
Islam	819,000,000
Hinduism	653,000,000
Buddhism	300,000,000
Judaism	18,000,000
Sikhism	16,500,000
Confucianism	5,750,000
Baha'ism	4,500,000
Jainism	4,000,000
Shintoism	3,200,000

Source: Icorec.

nes are careful never to trap, maim, or kill the animals who are associated with their kinship ancestors.

Buddhism one of the great world religions, which originated in India about 500 BC. It derives from the teaching of Buddha, who is regarded as one of a series of such enlightened beings; there are no gods. The chief doctrine is that of *karma*, good or evil deeds meeting an appropriate reward or punishment either in this life or (through reincarnation) a long succession of lives. The main divisions in Buddhism are *Theravāda* (or Hīnayāna) in SE Asia and *Mahāyāna* in N Asia; *Lamaism* in Tibet and *Zen* in Japan are among the many Mahāyāna sects. Its symbol is the lotus. There are approximately 300 million (1990) Buddhists worldwide.

scriptures The only complete canon of the Buddhist scriptures is that of the Sinhalese (Sri Lanka) Buddhists, in Pāli, but other schools have essentially the same canon in Sanskrit. The scriptures, known as *pitaka*s (baskets), date from the 2nd to 6th centuries CE. There are three divisions: *vinaya* (discipline), listing offences and rules of life; the *sūtras* (discourse) or *dharma* (doctrine), the exposition of Buddhism by Buddha and his disciples; and *abhidharma* (further doctrine), later discussions on doctrine.

beliefs The self is not regarded as permanent, as it is subject to change and decay. It is attachment to the things that are essentially impermanent that cause delusion, suffering, greed, and aversion, the origin of karma, and they in turn create further karma and the sense of self is reinforced. Actions which incline towards selflessness are called 'skilful karma' and they are on the path leading to enlightenment. In the *Four Noble Truths* the Buddha acknowledged the existence and source of suffering, and showed the way of deliverance from it through the *Eightfold Path*. The aim of following the Eightfold Path is to break the chain of karma and achieve dissociation from the body by attaining *nirvana* ('blowing out')—the eradication of all desires, either in annihilation or by absorption of the self in the infinite. Supreme reverence is accorded to the historical Buddha (Śākyamuni, or, when referred to by his clan name, Gautama), who is seen as one in a long and ongoing line of Buddhas, the next one (Maitreya) being due c. CE 3000.

divisions: Theravāda Buddhism, the School of the Elders, also known as *Hīnayāna* or Lesser Vehicle, prevails in SE Asia (Sri Lanka, Thailand, and Burma), and emphasizes the mendicant, meditative life as the way to break the cycle of *samsāra*, or death and rebirth. Its three alternative goals are *arahat*: one who has gained insight into the true nature of things; *Paccekabuddha*, an enlightened one who lives alone and does not teach; and fully awakened *Buddha*. Its scriptures are written in *Pāli*, an Indo-Aryan language with its roots in N India. In India itself Buddhism had virtually died out by the 13th century, and was replaced by Hinduism. However, it has 5 million devotees in the 20th century and is still growing.

Mahāyāna, or Greater Vehicle arose at the beginning of the Christian era. This tradition emphasized the eternal, formless principle of the Buddha as the essence of all things. It exhorts the individual not merely to attain personal nirvana, but to become a trainee Buddha, or *bodhisattva*, and so save others; this meant the faithful could be brought to enlightenment by a bodhisattva without following the austerities of Theravāda, and the cults of various Buddhas and bodhisattvas arose. Mahāyāna Buddhism also emphasises *shunyata*, or the experiential understanding of the emptiness of all things, even Buddhist doctrine.

Mahāyāna Buddhism prevails in N Asia (China, Korea, Japan, and Tibet). In the 6th century CE Mahāyāna spread to China with the teachings of Bodhidharma and formed Ch'an, which became established in Japan from the 12th century as *Zen Buddhism*. Zen emphasises silent meditation with sudden interruptions from a master to encourage awakening of the mind. Japan also has the lay organization *Sōka Gakkai* (Value Creation Society), founded 1930, which equates absolute faith with immediate material benefit; by the 1980s it was followed by more than 7 million households.

Esoteric, Tantric, or Diamond Buddhism became popular in Tibet and Japan, and holds that enlightenment is already within the disciple and with the proper guidance (that is privately passed on by a master), can be realized.

Christianity world religion derived from the teaching of Jesus in the first third of the 1st century, with a present-day membership of about 1 billion. It is divided into different groups or denominations which differ in some areas of belief and practice. Its main divisions are the Roman Catholic, Eastern Orthodox, and Protestant churches. There are approximately 1,382 million (1990) Christian believers worldwide.

beliefs Christianity is based on the belief that the man Jesus, born about 2,000 years ago, is 'the Christ', the Son of God, and that his death and resurrection broke down the barrier that human sinfulness put between humanity and God. Christians believe in one God with three aspects or persons: God the Father, God the Son (Jesus), and God the Holy Spirit, who is the power of God working in the world. Christians believe in God the Creator, who came to Earth as Jesus, was crucified, resurrected three days after his death, appeared to his disciples, and then ascended into heaven.

Christians believe that Jesus is alive and present in the world as the Holy Spirit. The main commandments are to love God and to love one's neighbour as oneself, which, if followed successfully, lead to an afterlife in heaven.

divisions: Orthodox Church or Eastern Orthodox Church or Greek Orthodox Church a federation of self-governing Christian churches mainly found in E and SE Europe, Russia, and parts of Asia. The centre of worship is the Eucharist. There is a married clergy, except for bishops; the Immaculate Conception is not accepted. The highest rank in the church is that of the Ecumenical Patriarch, or Bishop of Istanbul. There are approximately 135 million (1990) adherents.

The church's teaching is based on the Bible, and the Nicene Creed (as modified by the Council of Constantinople 381) is the only confession of faith used. The celebration of the Eucharist has changed little since the 6th century. The ritual is elaborate, and accompanied by singing in which both men and women take part, but no instrumental music is used. Besides the seven sacraments, the prayer book contains many other services for daily life. During the marriage service, the bride and groom are crowned.

Its adherents include Greeks, Russians, Romanians, Serbians, Bulgarians, Georgians, and Albanians. In the last 200 years the Orthodox Church has spread into China, Korea, Japan, and the USA, as well as among the people of Siberia and central Asia. Some of the churches were founded by the apostles and their disciples; all conduct services in their own languages and follow their own customs and traditions, but are in full communion with one another. There are many monasteries, for example Mount Athos in Greece, which has flourished since the 10th century. The senior church of Eastern Christendom is that of Constantinople (Istanbul).

Protestantism one of the main divisions of Christianity, which emerged from Roman Catholicism at the Reformation. The chief denominations are the Anglican Communion (Episcopalian in the USA), Baptists, Lutherans, Methodists, Pentecostals, and Presbyterians, with a total membership of about 327 million (1990).

Protestantism takes its name from the protest of Luther and his supporters at the Diet of Spires 1529 against the decision to reaffirm the edict of the Diet of Worms against the Reformation. The first conscious statement of Protestantism as a distinct movement was the Confession of Augsbury 1530. The chief characteristics of original Protestantism are the acceptance of the Bible as the only source of truth, the universal priesthood of all believers, and forgiveness of sins solely through faith in Jesus Christ. The Protestant church minimises the liturgical aspects of Christianity and emphasizes the preaching and hearing of the word of God before sacramental faith and practice. The many interpretations of doctrine and practice are reflected in the various denominations. The ecumenical movement of the 20th century has unsuccessfully attempted to reunite various Protestant denominations and, to some extent, the Protestant churches and the Catholic church. During the last 20 years there has been a worldwide upsurge in Christianity taking place largely outside the established church.

Roman Catholicism one of the main divi-

AFTER COMMUNISM: OLD FAITHS, NEW CONFLICTS

With the dramatic collapse of the USSR and its satellite countries of eastern Europe, the lid has been prised off an explosive mixture of suppressed but simmering national, ethnic, and religious rivalries. To understand the forces at work in conflicts such as those in Croatia, Bosnia, and Serbia, or in the warfare between Armenia and Azerbaijan, some appreciation of the religious dimension is needed. Likewise, religion plays a role in the sense of renewal and hope felt by the people of Russia or the Turkish peoples of the former central Asian states of the USSR.

There are three major religious blocks at play in eastern Europe and the former USSR. The most powerful is probably the various independent—autocephalous—Orthodox churches of Russia, Georgia, Serbia, and Armenia. In each case, national identity is closely connected to the national church and has been sustained in terms of language, culture, and tradition during the long winter of Communist rule. In Ukraine, the desire to have one's own religious identity has meant that the dissolved Ukrainian Orthodox Church (which was absorbed into the Russian Orthodox Church this century) has reappeared and the senior leadership of the church is now pushing for autonomy from Moscow. The Russian Orthodox Church looks likely to agree, but relationships between the churches are badly strained. This struggle reflects the wider struggle of Ukraine in trying to assert its identity over against Russia.

Ukraine is also a tense area for Orthodox–Roman Catholic relations. Alongside the Ukrainian Orthodox and Roman Catholic churches, there is also the Uniate Church. Orthodox in practice, it is allied with Rome and was suppressed by Communism and officially absorbed into the Orthodox Church after World War II. It has now resurfaced and has seized back churches which it once owned, and is being aided by Roman Catholic missions which are designed to ensure the revitalization of this hybrid church.

In the former states of Yugoslavia, the Orthodox–Roman Catholic split is at the heart of the struggles there. The Serbians and Macedonians are Orthodox, while the Croatians are Roman Catholic. Here, where the old boundary between the empires of the West and East once ran, the divisions are deep-rooted.

The other major faith in the picture is Islam. In Bosnia Herzegovina, just over 50% of the population are Muslims. They are also Slavs and share a common ethnic background with the Orthodox. They now find themselves caught between Serbian nationalism and Croatian/Roman Catholic opposition. There is also fear within some quarters in western Europe that Bosnia will become the first fully European Muslim state.

In the central Asian republics such as Kazakhstan, Islam is proving to be an important force for identity. But there are two models on Islam of offer. The first is Iranian,

fundamentalist and out to create a fully Islamic state. The second model is Turkish. Turkey is a secular Islamic state, where the secular has power over the religious. With the strong links between the Turkish-speaking people and the economic record of Turkey, it seems likely that the second model is the one to be favoured, but there are powerful forces working for a more fundamentalist model.

On a more positive note, religion is offering people significant hope and an alternative order after the collapse of Communism. The role of the Roman Catholic Church in Poland, Slovenia, and Croatia is critical in offering intellectual, ethical, moral, and practical assistance to the recovery of the various countries. Likewise, Orthodoxy has come to be seen as a pillar upon which the new order can begin to build in Russia, Georgia, Armenia, and Serbia/Macedonia. The social, moral, educational, and cultural forces which the church represents in such states is vital in the reconstruction. The Orthodox churches in particular see the need to steer a path between the rejection of Communism and the wholesale adoption of capitalism.

The Protestant churches, especially the Lutherans, played a key role in bringing down the political system in East Germany and in aiding the change in Hungary. But in neither country have they continued to exercise anything like the power of the other churches. This is linked to the Lutheran teaching that church and state should be separate.

Primates of the eastern churches celebrating the triumph of Orthodoxy at a 1992 summit.

sions of the Christian religion, separate from the Eastern Orthodox Church from 1054, and headed by the pope. For history and beliefs, see Christianity. Membership is about 920 million worldwide (1990), concentrated in S Europe, Latin America, and the Philippines.

The Protestant churches separated from the Catholic with the Reformation in the 16th century, to which the Counter-Reformation was a response. An attempt to update Catholic doctrines in the late 19th century was condemned by Pope Pius X in 1907, and more recent moves have been rejected by John Paul II.

doctrine The focus of liturgical life is the Mass or Eucharist, and attendance is obligatory on Sundays and Feasts of Obligation such as Christmas or Easter. The Roman Catholic differs from the other Christian churches in that it acknowledges the supreme jurisdiction of the pope, infallible when he speaks *ex cathedra* ('from the throne'); in the doctrine of the Immaculate Conception (which states that the Virgin Mary, the mother of Jesus, was conceived without the original sin with which all other human beings are born); and in according a special place to the Virgin Mary.

organization Since the Second Vatican Council 1962–66, major changes have taken place. They include the use of vernacular or everyday language instead of Latin in the liturgy, and increased freedom amongst the religious and lay orders. The pope has an episcopal synod of 200 bishops elected by local hierarchies to collaborate in the government of the church. The priesthood is celibate and there is a strong emphasis on the monastic orders.

Confucianism the body of beliefs and practices that are based on the Chinese classics and supported by the authority of the philosopher Confucius (Kong Zi). The origin of things is seen in the union of *yin* and *yang*, the passive and active principles. Human relationships follow the patriarchal pattern. For more than 2,000 years Chinese political government, social organization, and individual conduct was shaped by Confucian principles. In 1912, Confucian philosophy, as a basis for government, was dropped by the state. There are approximately 5.75 million Confucian believers (1990) worldwide.

The writings on which Confucianism is based include the ideas of a group of traditional books edited by Confucius, as well as his own works, such as the *Analects*, and those of some of his pupils. The *I Ching* is included among the Confucianist texts.

doctrine Until 1912 the emperor of China was regarded as the father of his people, appointed by heaven to rule. The Superior Man was the ideal human and filial piety was the chief virtue. Accompanying a high morality was a kind of ancestor worship.

practices Under the emperor, sacrifices were offered to heaven and earth, the heavenly bodies, the imperial ancestors, various nature gods, and Confucius himself. These were abolished at the Revolution in 1912, but ancestor worship (better expressed as reverence and remembrance) remained a regular practice in the home.

Under communism Confucianism continued. The defence minister Lin Biao was associated with the religion, and although the communist leader Mao Zedong undertook an anti-Confucius campaign 1974–76, this was not pursued by the succeeding regime.

Hinduism religion originating in N India about 4,000 years ago, which is superficially and in some of its forms polytheistic, but has a concept of the supreme spirit, Brahman, above the many divine manifestations. These include the triad of chief gods (the Trimurti): Brahma, Vishnu, and Siva (creator, preserver, and destroyer). Central to Hinduism are the beliefs in reincarnation and karma; the oldest scriptures are the *Vedas*. Temple worship is almost universally observed and there are many festivals.

There are over 653 million (1990) Hindus worldwide. Women are not regarded as the equals of men but should be treated with kindness and respect. Muslim influence in N India led to the veiling of women and the restriction of their movements from about the end of the 12th century.

roots Hindu beliefs originated in the Indus Valley civilization dating from about 4,500 years ago. Much of the tradition that is now associated with Hinduism stems from the ritual and religion of the Aryans who invaded N India about 3,000 years ago.

scriptures The *Veda* collection of hymns, compiled by the Aryans, was followed by the philosophical *Upanishads*, centring on the doctrine of Brahman, and the epics *Rāmāyana* and *Mahābhārata* (which includes the *Bhagavad-Gītā*), all from before the Christian era.

beliefs Hindu belief and ritual can vary greatly even between neighbouring villages. Some deities achieve widespread popularity such as Krishna, Hanuman, Lakshmi, and Durga; others, more localized and specialized, are referred to particularly in times of sickness or need. Some deities manifest themselves in different incarnations or avatars such as Rama or Krishna: both avatars of the god Vishnu.

Underlying this multi-faceted worship is the creative strength of Brahman, the Supreme Being. Hindus believe that all living things are part of Brahman: they are sparks of atman or divine life that transmute from one body to another, sometimes descending into the form of a plant or an insect, sometimes the body of a human. This is all according to its karma or past actions which are the cause of its sufferings or joy as it rises and falls in *samsara* (the endless cycle of birth and death). Humans have the opportunity, through knowledge and devotion, to break the karmic chain and achieve final liberation or moksha. The atman is then free to return to Brahman. The creative force of the universe is recognized in the god Brahma, once he has brought the cosmos into being it is sustained by Vishnu

RELIGIONS ON THE RISE

In the 1960s sociologists and many clergy were foretelling the early demise of the religious within Western society. Falling church attendance, secularism, teenage cults, rock and roll, communism, and free sex were all signs that the hold of the religious and the quest for the spiritual were declining in the heat of technology and progress. The 1990s have been heralded as the decade when the spiritual agenda will dominate many spheres of life worldwide. What has happened over these 30 years, and is this religious revival taking place within or without the major churches?

In most countries in the West, except the USA, Ireland, and Poland, formal religious observance is still falling or has levelled out. The mainstream Christian churches of the USA and the UK all show a continued decline in attendance. However, the newer churches—house churches, evangelical groups, independent churches, and the like—are growing. In the UK, the evangelical independent churches have experienced a 67% increase in members over the period 1980–90. The same is true for virtually all Western societies. There has also been an increase in members of other religious communities. Except for Judaism, all major faiths (Buddhists, Hindus, Muslims, Sikhs, and Baha'is) have grown, partly through migration and partly by conversion.

Alongside the major religions, newer movements have also grown. They are often small, but still impact strongly on the religious scene in many countries. They include the Unification Church, claiming to be a branch of Christianity while actually teaching a form of dualism; the Church of Scientology with its psychological and science-fiction angles; and the various groups originating in Hinduism, focusing upon a guru or leader. Then there is the wider community of people seeking a spiritual path, but wary of formal religious structures. This shows in various ways, from the rapid growth in interest in spiritual retreats to the profusion of books on spiritual issues, many taking either an 'ancient wisdom' stance such as shamanism or Native American spirituality, or adopting a psychoanalytic angle.

'New Age' is often used to cover many such directions, but this is a misleading term. It includes ideas and pathways which are frequently contradictory, and has become a catchbag for numerous fraudulent and foolish teachings which obscure the more important frontier writers and thinkers or the recovery of ancient teachings in modern form. A 1991 survey of religious attitudes and commitments in the USA found that, while many people enjoyed reading New Age books and exploring their ideas, less than 0.01% described themselves as New Age. Many people use New Age ideas within a much wider framework often supplied by more traditional religious teachings or structures.

Increasingly, people are looking to construct their own faith and lifestyle, based only partially on any one tradition. For many,

Ancient Chinese sage P'an Ku holding the symbol of yin and yang.

involvement in issues such as the environment, aid, the arts, self-discovery, analysis, or feminism, is as important spiritually as membership of a religious organization. Many people explore religious ideas, teachings, and even practices without belonging formally to any faith. The sale of religious or spiritual books, ranging from Eastern classics such as the *Tao Te Ching* or *Bhagavad Gita* to modern books on the healing powers of crystals, illustrates the interest in something beyond everyday experience.

In the 1960s science seemed to be close to explaining everything and controlling most things. The collapse of that myth and the recognition of science's reductionist model of the world and our place within it has also fuelled the quest for the spiritual, setting off a search for alternative sources of meaning and authority. For some this has meant a reversion to fundamentalism—Christian, Hindu, Muslim, Sikh, and even Marxist. Here no questions exist unanswered and certainty is the key. For others, the collapse of religious and scientific certainty has been challenging and liberating, leaving them free to explore and to experience.

This exploration is beginning to give new shape to the churches and to certain of the other major faiths. But the tussle is still on between those for whom belonging to a church or faith means following the teachings of that faith, and the majority of people for whom a church or faith is a foundation or launching pad for the confidence and sense of direction to pursue their spiritual quest, well beyond the confines of what would have been considered acceptable 50 years ago.

and then annihilated by the god Shiva, only to be created once more by Brahma. Vishnu and Shiva are, respectively, the forces of light and darkness, preservation and destruction, with Brahma as the balancing force that enables the existence and interaction of life. The cosmos is seen as both real and an illusion (*maya*), since its reality is not lasting; the cosmos is itself personified as the goddess Maya.

practice Hinduism has a complex of rites and ceremonies performed within the framework of the *jati* or caste system under the supervision of the Brahman priests and teachers. In India, caste is traditionally derived from the four classes of early Hindu society: brahmans (priests), kshatriyas (nobles and warriors), vaisyas (traders and cultivators), and sudras (servants). A fifth class, the untouchables, regarded as polluting in its origins, remained (and still largely remains) on the edge of Hindu society. The Indian Constituent Assembly 1947 made discrimination against the Scheduled Castes or Depressed Classes illegal, but strong prejudice continues.

Western influence The International Society for Krishna Consciousness (ISKON), the western organization of the Hare Krishna movement, was introduced to the west by Swami Prabhupada (1896–1977). Members are expected to lead ascetic lives. It is based on devotion to Krishna which includes study of the *Bhagavad-Gita*, temple and home ritual, and the chanting of the name Hare (saviour) Krishna. Members are expected to avoid meat, eggs, alcohol, tea, coffee, drugs, and gambling. Sexual relationships should be for procreation within the bonds of marriage.

Islam religion founded in the Arabian peninsula in the early 7th century CE. It emphasizes the oneness of God, his omnipotence, benificence, and inscrutability. The sacred book is the *Koran* or *Quran* of the prophet Muhammad, the Prophet or Messenger of Allah. There are two main Muslim sects: *Sunni* and *Shi'ite*. Other schools include *Sufism*, a mystical movement originating in the 8th century. There are over 819 million Muslims (1990) worldwide.

beliefs The fundamental beliefs of Islam are contained in the Adhan: 'I bear witness that there is no God but Allah and Muhammad is the Prophet of Allah.' Creation, Fall of Adam, angels and jinns, heaven and hell, Day of Judgment, God's predestination of good and evil, and the succession of scriptures revealed to the prophets, including Moses and Jesus, but of which the perfect, final form is the *Koran*, divided into 114 *suras* or chapters, said to have been divinely revealed to Muhammad; the original is said to be preserved beside the throne of Allah in heaven.

Islamic law Islam embodies a secular law (the *Shari'a* or 'Highway'), which is clarified for Shi'ites by reference to their own version of the *sunna*, 'practice' of the Prophet as transmitted by his companions and embodied in the Hadith; the Sunni sect also take into account *ijma'*, the endorsement by universal consent of practices and beliefs among the faithful. For the Sufi, the *Sharia*, is the starting point on the 'Sufi Path' to self-enlightenment. A *mufti* is a legal expert who guides the courts in their interpretation. (In Turkey until the establishment of the republic 1924 the mufti had supreme spiritual authority.)

organization There is no organized church or priesthood, although Muhammad's descendants (the Hashim family) and popularly recognized holy men, mullahs, and ayatollahs are accorded respect.

observances The Shari'a includes the observances known as 'The Five Pillars of the Faith', which are binding on all adult believers. The observances include: *shahada* or profession of the faith; *salat* or worship five times a day facing the holy city of Mecca (the call to prayer is given by a muezzin, usually from the minaret or tower of a mosque); *zakat* or obligatory almsgiving; *saum* or fasting dawn to sunset through Ramadan (ninth month of the year, which varies with the calendar); and the *hajj* or pilgrimage to Mecca at least once in a lifetime.

history Islam began as a militant and missionary religion, and between 711 and 1492 spread east into India, west over N Africa, then north across Gibraltar into the Iberian peninsula. During the Middle Ages, Islamic scholars preserved ancient Greco-Roman learning, while the Dark Ages prevailed in Christian Europe. Islam was seen as an enemy of Christianity by European countries during the Crusades, and Christian states united against a Muslim nation as late as the Battle of Lepanto 1571. Driven from Europe, Islam remained established in N Africa and the Middle East.

Islam is a major force in the Arab world and is a focus for nationalism among the peoples of the Central Asian Republics. It is also a significant factor in Pakistan, Indonesia, Malaysia, and parts of Africa. It is the second largest religion in the UK. Since World War II there has been a resurgence of fundamentalist Islam in Iran, Libya, Afghanistan, and elsewhere. In the UK 1987 the manifesto *The Muslim Voice* demanded rights for Muslim views on education (such as single-sex teaching) and on the avoidance of dancing, mixed bathing, and sex education.

divisions: Shi'ite or *Shiah* member of a sect of Islam who believe that Ali was Muhammad's first true successor. The term Shi'ite originally referred to shi'a ('the partisans') of Ali. They are doctrinally opposed to the Sunni Muslims. They developed their own law differing only in minor directions, such as inheritance and the status of women. Holy men have greater authority in the Shi'ite sect than in the Sunni sect. They are prominent in Iran, the Lebanon, and Indo-Pakistan, and are also found in Iraq, Bahrain, and the eastern province of Saudi Arabia. In the aftermath of the Gulf War 1991, many thousands of Shi'ites in Iraq were forced to take refuge in the marshes of S Iraq, after unsuccessfully rebelling against

Saddam Hussein. Shi'ite sacred shrines were desecrated and atrocities committed by the armed forces on civilians. There are approximately 129 million Shi'ites (1990) worldwide.

Breakaway sub-sects include the *Alawite* sect, to which the ruling party in Syria belongs; the *Ismaili* sect, with the Aga Khan IV (1936–) as its spiritual head; and the Baha'i religion founded from a Muslim splinter group.

Sufism a mystical movement of Islam which originated in the 8th century. Sufis believe that deep intuition is the only real guide to knowledge. The movement has a strong strain of asceticism. The name derives from the *suf*, a rough woollen robe worn as an indication of disregard for material things. There are a number of groups or brotherhoods within Sufism, each with its own method of meditative practice, one of which is the whirling dance of the dervishes.

Sunni a member of the larger of the two main sects of Islam. Sunni Muslims believe that the first three caliphs were all legitimate successors of the prophet Muhammad, and that guidance on belief and life should come from the Koran and the Hadith, and from the Shari'a, not from a human authority or spiritual leader. Imams in Sunni Islam are educated lay teachers of the faith and prayer leaders. The name derives from the *Sunna*, Arabic 'code of behaviour', the body of traditional law evolved from the teaching and acts of Muhammad. There are approximately 690 million (1990) Sunni Muslims worldwide.

Jainism ancient Indian religion, sometimes regarded as an offshoot of Hinduism. Jains believe that non-injury to living beings is the highest religion, and their code of ethics is based on sympathy and compassion for all forms of life. They also believe in karma. In Jainism there is no deity and, like Buddhism, it is a monastic, ascetic religion. There are two main sects: the Digambaras and the Swetambaras. Jainism practises the most extreme form of non-violence (*ahimsā*) of all Indian sects, and influenced the philosophy of Mahātmā Gāndhī. Jains number approximately 4 million (1990); there are Jain communities throughout the world but the majority live in India.

Jainism's sacred books record the teachings of Mahavira (c. 540–468 BCE), the last in a line of 24 great masters called Tirthankaras (or *jinas*, 'those who overcome'). Mahavira was born in Vessali (now Bihar), E India. He became an ascetic at the age of 30, achieved enlightenment at 42, and preached for 30 years.

During the 3rd century BCE two divisions arose regarding the extent of austerities. The Digambaras ('sky-clad') believe that enlightenment can only occur when all possessions have been given up, including clothes, and that it can only be achieved when a soul is born into a human male body. Monks of this sect go naked on the final stages of their spiritual path. The Swetambaras ('white-clad') believe that both human sexes can achieve enlightenment and

that nakedness is not a prerequisite.

Judaism the religion of the ancient Hebrews and their descendents the Jews, based, according to the Old Testament, on a covenant between God and Abraham about 2000 BCE, and the renewal of the covenant with Moses about 1200 BCE. It rests on the concept of one eternal invisible God, whose will is revealed in the *Torah* and who has a special relationship with the Jewish people. The Torah comprises the first five books of the Bible (the Pentateuch), which contains the history, laws, and guide to life for correct behaviour. Besides those living in Israel, there are large Jewish populations today in the USA, USSR, the UK and Commonwealth nations, and in Jewish communities throughout the world. There are approximately 18 million Jews (1990), with about 9 million in the Americas, 5 million in Europe, and 4 million in Asia, Africa, and the Pacific.

scriptures The *Talmud* combines the *Mishna*, rabbinical commentary on the law handed down orally from CE 70 and put in writing about 200, and the *Gemara*, legal discussions in the schools of Palestine and Babylon from the 3rd and 4th centuries. The *Haggadah* is a part of the Talmud dealing with stories of heroes. The *Midrash* is a collection of commentaries on the scriptures written 400–1200, mainly in Palestine. Along with the *Torah* they are regarded as authoritative sources of Jewish ritual, worship, and practice.

observances The *synagogue* (in US non-Orthodox usage *temple*) is the local building for congregational worship (originally simply the place where the Torah was read and expounded); its characteristic feature is the Ark, the enclosure where the Torah scrolls are kept. *Rabbis* are ordained teachers schooled in the Jewish law and ritual who act as spiritual leaders and pastors of their communities; some devote themselves to study. Religious practices include: circumcision, daily services in Hebrew, observance of the *Sabbath* (sunset on Friday to sunset Saturday) as a day of rest, and, among Orthodox Jews, strict dietary laws. High Holy days include *Rosh Hashanah* marking the Jewish New Year (first new moon after the autumn equinox) and, a week later, the religious fast *Yom Kippur* (Day of Atonement). Other holidays are celebrated throughout the year to commemorate various events of Biblical history.

history In the late Middle Ages when Europe and Western Asia were divided into Christian and Islamic countries, the Jewish people also found itself divided into two main groups. Jews in central and eastern Europe, namely in Germany and Poland, were called *Ashkenazi*. Sefardic Jews can trace their tradition back to the Mediterranean countries, particularly Spain and Portugal under Muslim rule. When they were expelled in 1492 they settled in north Africa, the Levant, the Far East and northern Europe. The two traditions differ in a number of ritual and cultural ways but their theology and basic Jewish practice is the same. The Hassidic sects of eastern Europe and some north African and Oriental countries also differ from other groups in their rites but they, too, maintain the concept of divine authority.

divisions In the 19th and early 20th centuries there was a move by some Jewish groups away from traditional or orthodox observances. This trend gave rise to a number of groups within Judaism. *Orthodox Jews*, who form the majority, assert the supreme authority of the Torah, adhere to all the traditions of Judaism, including the strict dietary laws and the segregation of women in the synagogue. *Reform Judaism* rejects the idea that Jews are the chosen people, has a liberal interpretation of the dietary laws, and takes a critical attitude towards the Torah. *Conservative Judaism* is a compromise between Orthodox and Reform in its acceptance of the traditional law, making some allowances for modern conditions, although its services and ceremonies are closer to Orthodox than to Reform. *Liberal Judaism*, or *Reconstructionism*, goes further than Reform in attempting to adapt Judaism to the needs of the modern world and to interpret the Torah in the light of current scholarship. In all the groups except Orthodox, women are not segregated in the synagogue, and there are female rabbis in both Reform and Liberal Judaism. In the 20th century many people who call themselves Jews prefer to identify Judaism with a historical and cultural tradition rather than with strict religious observance, and a contemporary debate (complicated by the history of non-Jewish attitudes towards Jews) centres on the question of how to define a Jew. As in other religions, fundamentalist movements have emerged, for example, Gush Emunim.

North American indigenous religions these form a wide variety, but have some features in common, especially a belief that everything in nature is alive and contains powerful forces which can be helpful or harmful to humans. If the forces are to be helpful, they must be treated with respect, and so hunting and other activities require ritual and preparation. Certain people are believed to be in contact with or possessed by the spirit world and so to have special powers; but each individual can also seek power and vision through ordeals and fasting.

Shinto the indigenous religion of Japan. It combines an empathetic oneness with natural forces and loyalty to the reigning dynasty as descendants of the Sun goddess, Amaterasu-Omikami. Traditional Shinto followers stressed obedience and devotion to the emperor, and an aggressive nationalistic aspect was developed by the Meiji rulers. Today Shinto has discarded these aspects. There are about 3.2 million (1990) adherents worldwide.

Shinto is the Chinese transliteration of the Japanese *Kami-no-Michi*. Shinto ceremonies appeal to the Kami, the mysterious forces of nature manifest in topographical features such as mountains, trees, stones, springs, and caves. Shinto focuses on purity, devotion, and sincerity; aberrations can be cleansed through purification rituals. In addition, purification procedures make the worshipper presentable and acceptable when making requests before the Kami.

Shinto's holiest shrine is at Ise, near Kyoto, where in the temple of the Sun Goddess is preserved the mirror that she is supposed to have given to Jimmu, the first emperor, in the 7th century BCE. Sectarian Shinto consists of 130 sects; the sects are officially recognized but not state-supported (as was state Shinto until its disestablishment after World War II and Emperor Hirohito's disavowal of his divinity 1946).

There is no Shinto philosophical literature although there are texts on mythologies, ceremonial and administrative procedures, religious laws, and chronicles of ruling families and temple construction.

Sikhism religion professed by 14 million Indians, living mainly in the Punjab. Sikhism was founded by Nanak (1469–c. 1539). Sikhs believe in a single God who is the immortal creator of the universe and who has never been incarnate in any form, and in the equality of all human beings; Sikhism is strongly opposed to caste divisions. There are approximately 16.5 million (1990) adherents worldwide.

Their holy book is the *Guru Granth Sahib*. Guru Gobind Singh (1666–1708) instituted the Khanda-di-Pahul, the Baptism of the Sword, and established the *Khalsa* ('pure'), the company of the faithful. The Khalsa wear the five Ks: *kes*, long hair; *kangha*, a comb; *kirpan*, a sword; *kachh*, short trousers; and *kara*, a steel bracelet. Sikh men take the last name 'Singh' ('lion') and women 'Kaur' ('princess').

beliefs Human beings can make themselves ready to find God by prayer and meditation but can achieve closeness to God only as a result of God's *nadar* (grace). Sikhs believe in reincarnation and that the ten human gurus were teachers through whom the spirit of Guru Nanak was passed on to live today in the *Guru Granth Sahib* and the Khalsa.

practice Sikhs do not have a specific holy day, but hold their main services on the day of rest of the country in which they are living. Daily prayer is important in Sikhism, and the gurdwara (the Sikh place for worship) functions as a social as well as religious centre; it contains a kitchen, the *langar*, where all, male and female, Sikh and non-Sikh, may eat together as equals. Sikh women take the same role as men in religious observances, for example, in reading from the *Guru Granth Sahib* at the gurdwara. Festivals in honour of the ten human gurus include a complete reading of the *Guru Granth Sahib*; Sikhs also celebrate at the time of some of the major Hindu festivals, but their emphasis is on aspects of Sikh belief and the example of the gurus. Sikhs avoid the use of all nonmedicinal drugs and, in particular, tobacco.

history On Nanak's death he was followed as guru by a succession of leaders who converted the Sikhs (the word means 'disciple') into a military confraternity which established itself as a political power. Gobind Singh was assassinated by a Muslim 1708, and since then the *Guru Granth Sahib* has taken the place of a leader.

Upon the partition of India many Sikhs migrated from W to E Punjab, and in 1966 the efforts of Sant Fateh Singh (*c.* 1911–72) led to the creation of a Sikh state within India by partition of the Punjab. However, the Akali separatist movement agitates for a completely independent Sikh state, Khalistan, and a revival of fundamentalist belief and was headed from 1978 by Sant Jarnail Singh Bhindranwale (1947–84), killed in the siege of the Golden Temple, Amritsar. In retaliation for this, the Indian prime minister Indira Gandhi was assassinated in Oct of the same year by her Sikh bodyguards. Heavy rioting followed, in which 1,000 Sikhs were killed. Mrs Gandhi's successor, Rajiv Gandhi, reached an agreement for the election of a popular government in the Punjab and for state representatives to the Indian parliament with the moderate Sikh leader Sant Harchand Singh Longowal, who was himself killed 1985 by Sikh extremists.

South American indigenous religions religious beliefs and practice are diverse and since early Indian contact with whites there has been some reconciliation between Christian and local belief, and also the emergence of new religious movements. Many of the local religions have the concept of a supreme religious force or god, but this force is often so remote or great that it is not worshipped directly. There are many powerful spirits, including souls of the ancestors, that inhabit and influence the natural environment and the lives of humans. To maintain harmony with the forest, rivers, or animals these spirits are respected and frequently associated with creation myths or as the harbingers of fortune or suffering, and they are not hunted, for example, the anaconda snake amongst the Sarema people of the Amazonian rainforest.

Taoism Chinese philosophical system, traditionally founded by the Chinese philosopher Lao Zi 6th century BCE. He is also attributed authorship of the scriptures, *Tao Te Ching*, which were apparently compiled later in the 3rd century BCE. The 'tao' or 'way' denotes the hidden principle of the universe, and less stress is laid on good deeds than on harmonious interaction with the environment, which automatically ensures right behaviour. The second major work is that of Zhuangzi (*c.* 389–286 BCE), *The Way of Zhuangzi*. The magical side of Taoism is illustrated by the *I Ching* or *Book of Changes*, a book of divination. There are approximately 190 million (1990) Taoists worldwide.

beliefs The universe is believed to be kept in balance by the opposing forces of yin and yang that operate in dynamic tension between themselves. Yin is female and watery: the force in the moon and rain which reached its peak in the winter; yang is masculine and solid: the

force in the sun and earth which reaches its peak in the summer. The interaction of yin and yang is believed to shape all life.

This magical, ritualistic aspect of Taoism developed from the 2nd century CE and was largely responsible for its popular growth; it stresses physical immortality, and this was attempted by means ranging from dietary regulation and fasting to alchemy. By the 3rd century, worship of gods had begun to appear, including that of the stove god Tsao Chun. From the 4th century, rivalry between Taoists and Mahāyāna Buddhists was strong in China, leading to persecution of one religion by the other; this was resolved by mutual assimilation, and Taoism developed monastic communities similar to those of the Buddhists.

Taoist texts record the tradition of mental and physical discipline, and methods to use in healing, exorcism, and the quest for immortality.

Zoroastrianism pre-Islamic Persian religion founded by the Persian prophet Zarathustra or Zoroaster (Greek), and still practised by the Parsees in India. The *Zendavesta* are the sacred scriptures of the faith. The theology is dualistic, **Ahura Mazda** or **Ormuzd** (the good God) being perpetually in conflict with **Ahriman** (the evil God), but the former is assured of eventual victory. There are approximately 150,000 (1990) adherents worldwide.

beliefs Humanity has been given free will to choose between the two powers, thus rendering believers responsible for their fate after death in heaven or hell. Moral and physical purity is central to all aspects of Zoroastrianism *yasna* or worship: since life and work are part of worship, there should be purity of action. Fire is considered sacred, and Ahura Mazda believed to be present when the ritual flame is worshipped at home or in the temple. It is believed that there will be a second universal judgement at *Frashokereti*, a time when the dead will be raised and the world cleansed of unnatural impurity.

The Parsee community in Bombay is now the main centre of Zoroastrianism, but since conversion is generally considered impossible, the numbers in India have been steadily decreasing at the rate of 10% per decade since 1947. Parsee groups, mainly in Delhi and outside India, have been pushing for the acceptance of converts, but the concern of the majority in Bombay is that their religious and cultural heritage will be lost.

RELIGIOUS MOVEMENTS

Baha'i movement founded in 19th-century Persia by a Muslim splinter group, the Babis. It evolved into the Baha'i religion under the leadership of Baha'ullah. His message in essence was that all great religious leaders are manifestations of the unknowable God and all scriptures are sacred. There is no priesthood: all Baha'is are expected to teach, and to work towards unification. There are about 4.5 million (1990) Baha'is worldwide.

Jehovah's Witness member of a religious organization originating in the USA 1872 under Charles Taze Russell (1852–1916). Jehovah's Witnesses attach great importance to Christ's Second Coming, which Russell predicted would occur 1914, and which Witnesses still believe is imminent. All Witnesses are expected to take part in house-to-house preaching; there are no clergy. There are approximately 6.75 million (1990) adherents worldwide.

Mormon or **Latter-day Saint** member of a Christian sect, the **Church of Jesus Christ of Latter-day Saints**, founded at Fayette, New York, in 1830 by Joseph Smith. According to Smith, Mormon was an ancient prophet in North America whose *Book of Mormon*, of which Smith claimed divine revelation, is accepted by Mormons as part of the Christian scriptures. In the 19th century the faction led by Brigham Young was polygamous. It is a missionary church with headquarters in Utah and a worldwide membership of about 5 million.

Rajneesh meditation meditation based on the teachings of the Indian Shree Rajneesh (born Chaadra Mohan Jain), established in the early 1970s. Until 1989 he called himself **Bhagwan** (Hindi 'God'). His followers, who number about half a million worldwide, regard themselves as Sannyas, or Hindu ascetics; they wear orange robes and carry a string of prayer beads. They are not expected to observe any specific prohibitions but to be guided by their instincts.

Rastafarianism religion originating in the West Indies, based on the ideas of Marcus Garvey, who called on black people to return to Africa and set up a black-governed country there. When Haile Selassie (**Ras Tafari**, 'Lion of Judah') was crowned emperor of Ethiopia 1930, this was seen as a fulfilment of prophecy and Rastafarians acknowledged him as the Messiah, the incarnation of God (**Jah**). The use of ganja (marijuana) is a sacrament. There are no churches. There were about one million Rastafarians by 1990.

Scientology (Latin *scire* 'to know' and Greek *logos* 'branch of learning') an 'applied religious philosophy' based on dianetics, founded in California in 1954 by L Ron Hubbard as the **Church of Scientology**. Through a form of psychotherapy it claims to 'increase man's spiritual awareness', but its methods of recruiting and retaining converts have met criticism. Its headquarters from 1959 have been in Sussex, England.

Seventh Day Adventist often called an **Adventist** member of the Protestant religious sect of the same name. It originated in the USA in the fervent expectation of Christ's Second Coming, or advent, that swept across New York State following William Miller's prophecy that Christ would return on 22 Oct, 1844. When this failed to come to pass, a number of Millerites, as his

followers were called, reinterpreted his prophetic speculations and continued to maintain that the millennium was imminent. Adventists observe Saturday as the Sabbath and emphasize healing, temperance, and diet; many are vegetarians. The sect has about 500,000 members in the USA.

transcendental meditation (TM) technique of focusing the mind, based in part on Hindu meditation. Meditators are given a *mantra* (a special word or phrase) to repeat over and over to themselves; such meditation is believed to benefit the practitioner by relieving stress and inducing a feeling of well-being and relaxation. It was introduced to the West by Maharishi Mahesh Yogi and popularized by the Beatles in the late 1960s.

Unification Church or **Moonies** church founded in Korea 1954 by the Reverend Sun Myung Moon. The theology unites Christian and Taoist ideas and is based on Moon's book *Divine Principle*, which teaches that the original purpose of creation was to set up a perfect family, in a perfect relationship with God. The church has met with criticism over its recruiting methods and use of finances. The number of members (often called 'moonies') is about 200,000 worldwide.

Unitarianism a Christian denomination that rejects the orthodox doctrine of the Trinity and gives a preeminent position to Jesus as a religious teacher, while denying his deity. Unitarians believe in individual conscience and reason as a guide to right action, rejecting the doctrines of original sin, the atonement, and eternal punishment. There are approximately 750,000 adherents (1990) worldwide.

RITES OF PASSAGES

Most religions mark certain important stages in a person's life, such as birth, initiation, marriage, and death, by special ceremonies or rites of passage. These rituals provide a way of publicly recognizing a change of status; they are also a time for the whole community to reaffirm its faith.

Birth rites Birth is often a time of rejoicing, but it is also a time of new responsibility. The rituals associated with birth mark the child's entrance into a new community and the adult's commitment to that child.

Hindu birth rites begin with the choice of a suitable day for conception, and continue through pregnancy; the mother-to-be must avoid certain foods and recite verses from the Hindu holy books. When the baby is born, there are a number of further ceremonies including naming the child, the calculation of a horoscope, and the inscription of the word 'aum' (the elemental sound of the universe) in honey on the child's tongue. The last of these ceremonies, the shaving of the child's hair, may take place up to two years after the birth.

NEW LIGHT ON ANCIENT TEXTS

In 1991, the press displayed renewed interest in the Dead Sea Scrolls. The long academic silence about their contents was shattered by the decision of scholars and academic centres to make microfilms of the scrolls available to general scholarship. Previously, they had been given exclusively to a small, very secretive team of primarily Roman Catholic scholars. Widened accessibility again raised questions of why so little had been published and what, if anything, was being hidden.

The scrolls were first discovered in 1947 in caves beside the Dead Sea. Over 600 manuscripts have been recovered in ten complete scrolls and masses of fragments. About a quarter are biblical texts, including the earliest known texts of books or chapters of the Hebrew Bible. Of greatest importance are those which illustrate the social and religious milieu from which Jesus's teachings arose—particularly the teaching of the community at Qumran, the religious site below the caves where the scrolls were found. Books such as the *Manual of Discipline* and the *Rule for the War* explore the beliefs and eschatological hopes of the remote, austere religious communities of the period *c.* 135 BC–AD 70 who wrote the scrolls. The key figure is the enigmatic Righteous Teacher. Parallels with Jesus have been made, and some have even said that this figure is Jesus and that he lived 100 years earlier than the Gospels claim. However, most of this is unfounded.

What emerges from the little that has been translated of the Dead Sea Scrolls is that in Jesus' time there were many religious reformers, teachers, and bands of followers, and that a good deal of what he said was not so much new, as original in its presentation and conclusions. The scrolls show how much Jesus was a person of his time. The fact that his teachings and life have created the world's largest religion shows that whatever it was he shared with others of his time, his message and life struck chords which none of his contemporaries could match. The Dead Sea Scrolls reveal how Jewish religious thought and especially apocalyptic thought developed after the last books in the Old Testament were written—roughly 400 BC. They illustrate a world filled with fears for the future mixed with hopes of the Messiah. Great teachers gathered groups around them, many of whom shunned contemporary society and sought purity and thus salvation in rigid adherence to rules. Such groups saw themselves as playing a vital role in a cosmic struggle between good and evil, notions which had come into Judaism through the Zoroastrian faith encountered in exile in Babylon. Without these texts we would have a much poorer understanding of how Judaism was developing around the time of Jesus.

The Dead Sea Scrolls are not the only recent finds to illuminate the origins of Christianity and our understanding of Jesus. In 1945–46, 13 books containing 52 primarily Gnostic scriptures were discovered in Upper Egypt

Codex II of the Gnostic library found at Nag-Hammadi, Upper Egypt; it is opened to the title page of the Gospel of Thomas.

at a site known as Nag-Hammadi. They were probably buried some time before AD 400 when the authoritative canon of the New Testament had been established and unauthorized gospels were banned, including those of the Gnostics (who believed there was a hidden knowledge open to a few initiates), and those of Thomas, of the Truth, and of Philip as well as texts such as the Apocalypse of Peter. In these texts, many of which appear to date from the end of the 1st to middle 2nd century AD, Jesus speaks and acts in a way both familiar from the New Testament and at times challengingly new. The struggles, debates, and concerns of these gospels are with an expression of Christianity which stresses Christ's humanity while revelling in secret knowledge (gnosis) which Jesus passed to a select few. The Gospel of Thomas has attracted particular interest as possibly being the original text upon which Matthew, Mark, and Luke drew for their materials. Could Thomas be this long-lost source? The issue is hotly debated.

The Nag-Hammadi texts are not a threat to Christianity but a very important source for understanding how the early church defined itself and what other versions of Christianity were circulating at the time. There is always the fascination of hearing new words credited to Jesus, some of which speak with a ring of authority, while others show how from its very earliest days, Christianity and the figure of Christ have attracted many and varied theories and beliefs—some of which may be now of greater relevance than when they were first mooted.

Hindus believe that these ceremonies will help the child towards a better rebirth.

Sikh birth rites Sikhs believe that the first words a child should hear are those of the Mool Mantra, the beginning of the Sikh holy book, and so, as soon as the baby is born, it is washed and the words of the Mool Mantra whispered into its ear. A few weeks later the child is taken to the gurdwara, the Sikh place of worship, to be named. The initial of the name is chosen by opening the *Guru Granth Sahib* at random and choosing the first letter of the hymn on the left hand page.

Muslim birth rites the first words which a Muslim baby will hear are those of the call to prayer, which is used to call Muslims to the mosque or place of worship each day; these words, which contain the basic beliefs of Islam, are whispered into its ears. Seven days later, the child is named. This ceremony involves the shaving of the baby's head. If the child is a boy, he will also be circumcised at this time, to recall Abraham and his son Ismail.

Jewish birth rites the surgical operation of *circumcision* consists of the removal of a small part of the foreskin. All Jewish boys must be circumcised on the eighth day after birth, as long as health permits. During circumcision a prayer is said which recalls the covenant or agreement God made with Abraham and the ceremony marks the boy's entry into this covenant. If the child is a girl, her name is announced in the synagogue (the Jewish place of worship) by the father on the first Sabbath after her birth.

Christian birth rites universal in the Christian Church from its beginning has been the religious initiation rite of **baptism** (Greek 'to dip'), involving immersion in or sprinkling with water. In the baptismal ceremony, sponsors or godparents make vows on behalf of the child which are renewed by the child at confirmation. Baptism was originally administered to adults by immersion, and infant baptism has been common only since the 6th century. In some of the Protestant churches, adults are still baptized by immersion in a pool of water. The immersion symbolizes death and new life.

Chinese birth rites Chinese babies are not named until the first month after birth; then the Full Month ceremony is held, with special foods, including red eggs which are symbols of luck and new life. The name given to the baby is a nickname designed to convince any malevolent spirits that the child is not worth stealing.

Initiation rites Initiation is a passage into full membership of a group, whether religious or social. It gives the individual both rights and responsibilities.

Sikh initiation rites the tenth guru of Sikhism, Guru Gobind Singh, set up a brotherhood of dedicated Sikhs, the Khalsa; any sufficiently mature and dedicated Sikh may apply to join the Khalsa. The ceremony is conducted by five members of the Khalsa in the presence of the *Guru Granth Sahib*, the Sikh holy book; it involves special prayers, the sharing of karah

parshad (a sweet mixture) to symbolize the equality of Sikhs, and the drinking and sprinkling of amrit (sugar and water). Those initiated in the Khalsa should always wear five things known as the Five K's: uncut hair; a steel bracelet; a short sword; a comb and *kaccha*, a type of shorts.

Jewish initiation is marked by the **bar mitzvah** (Hebrew 'son of the commandment'), initiation of a boy at the age of 14 into the adult Jewish community; less common is the bat mitzvah for girls. In the synagogue, the boy says a special bar mitzvah prayer promising to keep God's commandments, and accept responsibility for his actions before God; he then reads a passage from the Torah in the synagogue on the Sabbath. After this, he is regarded as a full member of the congregation.

Christian initation is marked by **confirmation**, a rite by which a previously baptized person is admitted to full membership of the Christian Church. It consists in the laying on of hands by a bishop, in order that the confirmed person may receive the gift of the Holy Spirit, the third aspect of the Trinity. Among Anglicans, the rite is deferred until the child is able to comprehend the fundamental beliefs of Christian doctrine.

Marriage rites Marriage involves not only a change in status for the two people concerned, but also a new set of relationships for their families and the probability of children. In many cultures the choice of marriage partner is made by the parents, though the participants usually have some say in the matter.

Hindu marriage rites Hindu weddings may take place at the bride's home, or in a temple. The bride usually wears a red sari, and her hands and feet are painted with patterns in henna, an orange dye. Offerings are made before a sacred fire and prayers said; the bride and groom take seven steps around the fire, which symbolize food, strength, wealth, good fortune, children, the seasons, and everlasting friendship.

Sikh wedding rites a Sikh wedding may be held anywhere, as long as the *Guru Granth Sahib* is present. During the ceremony, the couple show their assent to the marriage by bowing to the holy book. The couple walk together round the *Guru Granth Sahib* four times as a hymn written by the fourth Guru is sung: this hymn contains all the basic teachings of Sikhism.

Jewish wedding rites the ceremony usually takes place in the synagogue, the place of worship. The bride and groom, with their parents, stand under a canopy or chupah. Blessings are recited by the rabbi, the religious leader, and the groom gives the bride a ring. The couple are now legally married and the *ketubah* or marriage contract, is read out. At the end of the ceremony the groom steps on and shatters a glass as a reminder, amidst the happiness, of the destruction of the Temple at Jerusalem.

Christian marriage rites Christian marriages are usually celebrated at the place of worship (church or chapel). The groom is accompanied by a helper, or best man, while the bride is escorted by her father, who officially 'gives' her to her new husband, and by attendants (bridesmaids). The couple make promises to love, honour and care for each other and exchange rings.

Muslim marriage rites Muslim weddings may take place in the bride's home or in the place of worship, the mosque. The bride and groom are normally in separate rooms throughout the short ceremony. There is often a reading from the Koran, and a talk on the duties of marriage. The couple must both consent to the marriage and rings are sometimes exchanged.

Chinese wedding rites in Chinese weddings, the concept of yin and yang, the two complementary forces which make up the universe, plays a prominent part; among their other attributes yin is seen as female and yang as male. There is a series of rituals leading up to the wedding, including the giving of gifts, an exchange of horoscopes (a prediction of a person's fortune) and a payment to the bride's family. The ceremony itself involves offerings and prayers to the bridegroom's ancestors and the household gods.

Death rites Death rites fulfil three main purposes: to comfort and strengthen the dying person, to comfort those left behind, and to ensure the best possible outcome for the deceased person in the next world or next birth. In several religions, such as Sikhism, Judaism, and Islam, people are encouraged to speak a declaration of faith before death, and Sikhs and Muslims read from their holy books to the dying person. Some religions discourage mourning, because they feel that death should not be regarded as a tragedy for the individual, especially after a long life, while others such as Judaism, set time aside for the family to grieve. There are many ways in which religions try to help the deceased in the afterlife. The Chinese offer practical help: since the afterlife may have resemblances to this life, replicas of useful goods, cars, washing machines, and money, are burnt at the funeral for the use of the deceased who will, with the other ancestors, now watch over the family.

HOLY BOOKS

Many religions have a book or books which are regarded as holy or as providing especial wisdom. These books are treated with great reverence and copies may be kept in a place particularly set aside or have specific ceremonies associated with them. Such books are sometimes referred to as scriptures.

Buddhist Buddhist literature is divided into two groups, the teachings and discourses of the Buddha himself, and the teachings of saints, sages, and scholars. Since Buddhism was transmitted by word of mouth for about five hundred years after the death of the Buddha, it is difficult to say which of these writings contain the original word of the Buddha and which are later additions. One of the fundamental differences between the Hinayana and Mahayana schools is the attribution of the Buddha's word to the various texts. The Buddha's words are assembled in the *Tipitaka* or *Tripitaka* (three baskets) containing sutra (discourses), vinaya (rules of discipline), abhidharma (further knowledge). Important texts in this group include the commentaries on the Buddha's word by Buddhagosa in the Theravada tradition and Nagarjuna and Asanga in the early Indian Mahayana tradition.

Chinese Since Chinese religion is a mixture of Buddhism, Confucianism and Taoism, the Chinese generally respect the writings of all three. The main text of Taoism is the Tao Te Ching, attributed to the traditional founder of Taoism, Lao Tzu, although its date and authorship are obscure. Confucianism's main writings are those of Confucius himself, especially the Analects or 'selected sayings'. Confucius is traditionally the author of the Five Classics: *Su Ching, Shi Ching, Li Chi, I Ching*, and the annals of *Lu*.

Buddhist literature that emerged from China developed a practical approach that appealed to the Chinese sense of balance and the preference for direct, intuitive practice is reflected in the Ch'an school with such writing as Seng Chao's *On the Immutability of Phenomena*; and Tu Shun's *Meditation upon the Dharmadhadhatu*.

Christian The Christian *Bible* (Greek *ta biblia* 'the books') consists of the *Old Testament*, the first five books of the Hebrew Bible, and the *New Testament*, originally written in Greek, containing the Gospels, Acts of the Apostles, Letters and Revelation. It is believed that the books of the New Testament were written within a hundred years of the death of Christ, and from the 4th century were recognized by the Christian church as canonical. Early church history is recorded in the *Acts of the Apostles*, the life of Jesus Christ in the four *Gospels*, the epistles are the letters of St Paul and other Christian leaders to fellow Christians, and the New Testament closes with the *Book of Revelation* which records St John's vision of the end of time and Christ's second coming.

Hindu *Veda* (Sanskrit, divine knowledge). The most sacred of the Hindu scriptures, hymns written in an old form of Sanskrit; the oldest may date from 1500 or 2000 BCE. The four main collections are: the Rigveda (hymns and praises); Yajurveda (prayers and sacrificial formulae); Sâmaveda (hymns); and Atharvaveda, (spells, charms, and chants).

Rāmāyana Hindu epic of 24,000 stanzas written in Sanskrit. It was assembled in its received form between the 1st century BCE and 1st century CE. The story reveals how Rama, an incarnation of the god Vishnu, and his friend Hanuman (the monkey chieftain) strive to recover Rama's wife, Sita, abducted by the

PRINERMS (PRIMAL NEW RELIGIOUS MOVEMENTS)

The acronym PRINERMS was coined during the late 1980s to cover the whole field of new religious movements among primal or tribal people. Such movements, which began almost 500 years ago as a result of European peoples' expansion into other parts of the world, are numerically significant worldwide, and expanding. In Africa alone there are approximately 10,000 distinct movements with as many as 20 million adherents.

While new religious movements (NRMs) in the West have received a great deal of publicity, the phenomenon in non-Western societies is not widely known and has received little systematic study. There is ample evidence of the proliferation of new movements in the continents of Africa ('Prophetic' or 'Zionist' churches), South America (Amerindian, Afro-Brazilian groups, folk Catholicism, Western-influenced fundamentalist or neo-pentecostal movements), Asia (mostly in Japan, India, Korea), and in such regions as Melanesia (from cargo cults to recent Holy Spirit movements) and the Caribbean ('Spiritual Baptists', Rastafarians).

Although widely diverse, these movements have many common traits—principally the way in which they originated. PRINERMS have arisen from interactions between a primal or tribal religion and one or more of the universal traditions, usually the Christian faith. Emerging as new synthesist movements, they contain elements of both the old and the new and are distinguished by the special interaction within which they arose, and the dynamics of the relations between the primal and universal religions in question.

1. Neo-primal movements, concerned primarily with remodelling or revitalizing traditional religion. These include many of the cargo cults of Melanesia, and many native American movements, such as the Ghost Dance.

2. Synthesist movements, drawing on both the old and new traditions to create a religious synthesis. Vodon (voodoo) in Haiti is perhaps the best-known example of this type. Many movements in Central and South America and the Caribbean, characterized by a complex mix-ture of traditional beliefs, Western Christianity, and African religion, fall in this category.

3. Hebraist movements, influenced heavily by the Bible, particularly the Old Testament, and viewing themselves as the 'new people of God'. These include the Rastafarians of Jamaica, with their emphasis on Jah and belief in themselves as the true Israelites, and the lesser known Israelites of the New Covenant in Peru, who celebrate the Passover, offer blood sacrifices, and believe the New Jerusalem will be in Peru.

4. Independent churches, substantially accepting traditional Christianity and giving prominence to the Bible, Jesus Christ and the Holy Spirit, but interpreting these teachings in a way which would be more relevant and meaningful to indigenous converts. These include many of the African independent churches, such as the Kimbanguist Church in Zaire and the Zion Christian Church in South Africa, as well as the Christian Fellowship Church in the Solomon Islands. Such groups are often led by highly charismatic figures who may come to be seen as prophets, or even new Messiahs, by their followers.

Unlike NRMs (Hare Krishna, Baha'i, Children of God), PRINERMS are not missionary-based. However, there are cases of migration into Western societies. The A'Dura-type churches from West Africa appear in the UK and several continental cities; Jamaican Rastafari appear in various parts of the English-speaking world and as far afield as New Zealand; and the Unification Church (arriving amid Korean folk 'shamanism') appears almost all over the world.

When PRINERMS first developed during the colonial period they were often regarded by the ruling authorities with a high degree of suspicion bordering on paranoia, and were treated harshly. Many new governments of the immediate post-colonial period were also suspicious of the movements, which they saw as examples of proto-nationalism. Today, such movements are still generally misunderstood and even persecuted by governments in many parts of the world.

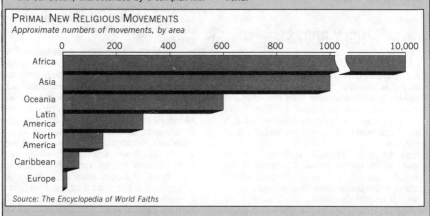

PRIMAL NEW RELIGIOUS MOVEMENTS
Approximate numbers of movements, by area

	0	200	400	600	800	1000	10,000
Africa							
Asia							
Oceania							
Latin America							
North America							
Caribbean							
Europe							

Source: The Encyclopedia of World Faiths

POPES OF THE LAST 500 YEARS

1492–1503	Alexander VI	1676–89	Innocent XI
1503	Pius III	1689–91	Alexander VIII
1503–13	Julius II	1691–1700	Innocent XII
1513–21	Leo X	1700–21	Clement XI
1522–23	Hadrian VI	1721–24	Innocent XIII
1523–34	Clement VII	1724–30	Benedict XIII
1534–49	Paul III	1730–40	Clement XII
1550–55	Julius III	1740–58	Benedict XIV
1555	Marcellus II	1758–69	Clement XIII
1555–59	Paul IV	1769–74	Clement XIV
1559–65	Pius IV	1775–99	Pius VI
1566-72	Pius V	1800–23	Pius VII
1572–85	Gregory XIII	1823–29	Leo XII
1585–90	Sixtus V	1829–30	Pius VIII
1590	Urban VII	1831–46	Gregory XVI
1590–91	Gregory XIV	1846–78	Pius IX
1591	Innocent IX	1878–1903	Leo XIII
1592–1605	Clement VIII	1903–14	Pius X
1605	Leo XI	1914–22	Benedict XV
1605–21	Paul V	1922–39	Pius XI
1621–23	Gregory XV	1939–58	Pius XII
1623–44	Urban VIII	1958–63	John XXIII
1644–55	Innocent X	1963–78	Paul VI
1655–67	Alexander VII	1978	John Paul I
1667–69	Clement IX	1978–	John Paul II
1670–76	Clement X		

demon king Ravana. It upholds the Hindu ideal of a relationship between a man and woman.

Mahābhārata Sanskrit ('great poem of the Bharatas') Hindu epic of 90,000 stanzas probably written between the 2nd century BCE and the end of the 1st century CE. With the *Rāmāyana*, it forms the two great epics of Hindu literature. The story is set on the Upper Ganges plain and deals with the fortunes of two rival families, the Kauravas and the Pandavas. It reveals the ethical values of ancient Hindu society and individual responsibility in particular. The central and most popular part is the *Bhagavad-Gītā* or *Song of the Blessed One*, a religious and philosophical poem delivered by Krishna to the hero Arjuna. The *Bhagavad Gītā* is regarded as one of the essential Hindu religious texts.

Jain The Swetabaras' canon is the *Siddhanta* assembled in the 5th century CE which includes accounts of the monastic discipline and teachings of Mahavira. The Digambaras' canon is made of two early Pakrit texts (Indian vernacular language) supplemented by commentaries from later scholars. There is also a large body of literature, dating from the 8th century CE, including narratives, commentaries, and cosmologies on existing texts. This later material is generally accepted by both Jain groups.

Jewish The *Torah* contains the first five books of the Hebrew Bible and it is given absolute religious authority by orthodox Jews. As well as referring to the first five books of Moses the *Torah* is sometimes used as a term for the whole Hebrew Bible. The First Five Books of Moses contain 613 laws covering social and religious customs, and histories of the early patriarchs

of the Jewish nation. The Hebrew Bible contains two further sections, the Prophets, and the Writings.

The Oral Law, traditionally revealed to Moses on Mount Sinai alongside the Written Law, is codified in the Mishna which was compiled after the destruction of the Temple CE 70. Further debates and interpretations by rabbis on the Torah's law and guidance are recorded in the Gemara and Midrash. The combined texts of the Mishna, Gemara, and Midrash, together with later rabbinical commentaries, are recorded in the *Talmud* the main compilation of traditional Jewish thought.

Muslim *Koran* more properly, Quran, though both are transliterations; the sacred book of Islam. Written in the purest Arabic, it contains 114 suras or chapters, and is stated to have been divinely revealed to the prophet Muhammad from Allah through the angel Jibra'el; the original is supposed to be preserved beside the throne of Allah in heaven.

Sikh The Sikh holy book is the *Guru Granth Sahib*, also known as the *Adi Granth* or 'first book'. It is a collection of hymns by the Sikh gurus or teachers, as well as by Muslim and Hindu writers, which was compiled largely by the fifth guru, Guru Arjan, and completed by the tenth guru, Guru Gobind Singh. On the death of the tenth guru, the *Guru Granth Sahib* took over the role of teacher and leader of the Sikhs. Guidance is sought by opening the holy book at random and reading verses. Any copy of the *Guru Granth Sahib* must have a special room to itself; people entering the room must cover their heads and remove their shoes. All copies of the holy book are idential, having 1,430 pages, and written in Gurmukhi, the written form of Punjabi.

RELIGIOUS FIGURES

Abraham *c.*2300 BCE. In the Old Testament, founder of the Jewish nation. Jehovah promised him heirs and land for his people in Canaan (Israel), renamed him Abraham ('father of many nations') and tested his faith by a command (later retracted) to sacrifice his son Isaac. Jehovah's promise to Abraham was fulfilled when the descendants of Abraham's grandson, Jacob, were led out of Egypt by Moses.

Abu Bakr or *Abu-Bekr* 573–634. 'Father of the virgin', name used by Abd-el-Ka'aba from about 618 when the prophet Muhammad married his daughter Ayesha. He was a close adviser to Muhammad in the period 622–32. On the prophet's death, he became the first caliph adding Mesopotamia to the Muslim world and instigating expansion into Iraq and Syria.

Ali *c.* 598–660. 4th caliph of Islam. He was born in Mecca, the son of Abu Talib, uncle to the prophet Muhammad, who gave him his daughter Fatima in marriage. On Muhammad's death

Religious Festivals

Date	Festival	Religion	Commemorating
6 Jan	Epiphany	Western Christian	coming of the Magi
6–7 Jan	Christmas	Orthodox Christian	birth of Jesus
18–19 Jan	Epiphany	Orthodox Christian	coming of the Magi
Jan–Feb	New Year	Chinese	Return of Kitchen god to heaven
Feb–Mar	Shrove Tuesday	Christian	day before Lent
	Ash Wednesday	Christian	first day of Lent
	Purim	Jewish	story of Esther
	Mahashivaratri	Hindu	Siva
Mar–Apr	Palm Sunday	Western Christian	Jesus's entry into Jerusalem
	Good Friday	Western Christian	crucifixion of Jesus
	Easter Sunday	Western Christian	resurrection of Jesus
	Passover	Jewish	escape from slavery in Egypt
	Holi	Hindu	Krishna
	Holi Mohalla	Sikh	(coincides with Holi)
	Rama Naumi	Hindu	birth of Rama
	Ching Ming	Chinese	remembrance of the dead
13 Apr	Baisakhi	Sikh	founding of the Kalsa
Apr–May	Easter	Orthodox Christian	death and resurrection of Jesus
	Lailut ul Isra wal Mi'raj	Muslim	Prophet Muhammad's journey Jerusalem and then up to Heaven
	Lailat ul-Bara'h	Muslim	forgiveness before Ramadan
May–Jun	Shavuot	Jewish	giving of ten Comandments to Moses
	Lailat ul-Qadr	Muslim	revelation of the Qur'an to Muhammad
	Eid ul-Fitr	Muslim	end of Ramadan
	Pentecost (Whitsun)	Christian	Jesus's followers receiving the Holy Spirit
	Wesak	Buddhist	day of Buddha's birth, enlightenment and death
	Martyrdom of Guru Arjan	Sikh	death of fifth guru of Sikhism
June	Dragon Boat Festival	Chinese	Chinese martyr
Jul	Dhammacakka	Buddhist	preaching of Buddha's first sermon
	Eid ul-Adha	Muslim	Ibrahim's willingness to sacrifice his son
Aug	Raksha Bandhan	Hindu	family
Aug–Sept	Janmashtami	Hindu	birthday of Khrishna
Sept	Moon Festival	Chinese	Chinese hero
Sept–Oct	Rosh Hashana	Jewish	start of Jewish New Year
	Yom Kippur	Jewish	day of atonement
	Succot	Jewish	Israelites' time in the wilderness
Oct	Dusshera	Hindu	goddess Devi
Oct–Nov	Divali	Hindu	goddess Lakshmi
	Divali	Sikh	release of Guru Hargobind from prison
Nov	Guru Nanak's Birthday	Sikh	founder of Sikhism
1 Nov	All Saint's Day	Christian	deceased Christian saints and holy people
2 Nov	All Soul's Day	Christian	Christian deceased
	Bodhi Day	Buddhist (Mahāyāna)	Buddha's enlightenment
Dec	Hanukkah	Jewish	recapture of Temple of Jerusalem
	Winter Festival	Chinese	time of feasting
25 Dec	Christmas	Western Christian	birth of Christ
Dec–Jan	Birthday of Guru Gobind Sind	Sikh	last (tenth) human guru of Sikhism
	Martyrdom of Guru Tegh Bahadur	Sikh	ninth guru of Sikhism

632, Ali had a claim to succeed him, but this was not conceded until 656. After a stormy reign, he was assassinated. Around Ali's name the controversy has raged between the Sunni and the Shi'ites, the former denying his right to the caliphate and the latter supporting it.

Asoka *c.*273–238 BCE. Indian emperor, and Buddhist convert from Hinduism. He issued edicts, carved on pillars and rock faces throughout his dominions, promoting wise government and the cultivation of moral virtues according to Buddhist teachings. Many still survive, and are amongst the oldest deciphered texts in India. In Patna there are the remains of a hall built by him.

Augustine, St first archbishop of Canterbury, England. He was sent from Rome to convert England to Christianity by Pope Gregory I. He landed at Ebbsfleet in Kent 597, and soon after baptized Ethelbert, King of Kent, along with many of his subjects. He was consecrated bishop of the English at Arles in the same year, and appointed archbishop 601, establishing his see at Canterbury. Feast day 26 May.

Bodhidharma 6th century CE. Indian Buddhist and teacher. He entered China from S India about 520, and was the founder of the Ch'an school (Zen is the Japanese derivation). Ch'an focuses on contemplation leading to intuitive meditation, a direct pointing to and stilling of the human mind. In the 20th century, Zen has attracted many followers in the west.

Buddha 'enlightened one', title of Prince *Gautama Siddhārtha* c.563–483 BCE. Religious leader, founder of Buddhism, born at Lumbini in Nepál. At the age of 29, he left his wife and son and a life of luxury, to escape from the material burdens of existence. After six years of austerity he realized that asceticism, like overindulgence, was futile, and chose the middle way of meditation. He became enlightened under a bo or bodhi tree in Bihar, India. He began teaching at Varanasi, and founded the Sangha, an order of monks. He spent the rest of his life travelling around N India, and died at Kusinagara in Uttar Pradesh.

Confucius Latinized form of *K'ung Tzu*, 'Kong the master' 551–479 BCE. Chinese sage whose name is given to Confucianism. He devoted his life to relieving suffering among the poor through governmental and administrative reform. His emphasis on tradition and ethics attracted a growing number of pupils during his lifetime. *The Analects of Confucius*, a compilation of his teachings, was published after his death. Within three hundred years of the death of Confucius his teaching was adopted by the Chinese state, and remained so until 1912.

Ghazzali, al- 1058–1111. Muslim philosopher and one of the most celebrated Sufis (Muslim mystics). He was responsible for easing the conflict between the Sufi and the Ulema, a body of Muslim religious and legal scholars.

Gobind Singh 1666–1708. Indian religious leader, the tenth and last guru (teacher) of Sikhism, 1675–1708, and founder of the Sikh brotherhood known as the Khalsa. On his death, the Sikh holy book, the *Guru Granth Sahib*, replaced the line of human gurus as the teacher and guide of the Sikh community.

Jesus c.4 BCE–CE 29 or 30. Hebrew preacher on whose teachings Christianity was founded. According to the accounts of his life in the four Gospels, he was born in Bethlehem, Palestine, son of God and the Virgin Mary, and brought up by Mary and her husband Joseph as a carpenter in Nazareth. After adult baptism, he gathered 12 disciples, but his preaching antagonized the Roman authorities and he was executed by crucifixion. Three days later there came reports of his resurrection and, later, his ascension to heaven.

Lao Zi or Lao Tzu c.604–531 BCE. Chinese philosopher, commonly regarded as the founder of Taoism, with its emphasis on the Tao, the inevitable and harmonious way of the universe. Nothing certain is known of his life, and he is variously said to have lived in the 6th or the 4th century BCE. The *Tao Tê Ching*, the Taoist scripture, is attributed to him but apparently dates from the 3rd century BCE.

Luther Martin 1483–1546. German Christian reformer, a founder of Protestantism. While he was a priest at the University of Wittenberg, he wrote an attack on the sale of indulgences (remissions of punishment for sin) in 95 theses which he nailed to a church door 1517, in defiance of papal condemnation. The Holy Roman Emperor Charles V summoned him to the Diet of Worms 1521, where he refused to retract his objections. Originally intending reform, his protest led to schism, with the emergence, following the Augsburg Confession 1530, of a new Protestant Church. Luther is regarded as the instigator of the Protestant revolution, and Lutheranism is now the major religion of many north-European countries including Germany, Sweden, and Denmark.

Mahavira c.540–468 BCE. Indian teacher and scholar. He was born into the warrior-king caste in Vessili (now Bihar). He became an ascetic at 30, achieved enlightenment at 42, and preached for 30 years. He was last in a line of 24 Jain masters called *Tirthankaras* or jinas ('those who overcome').

Maimonides Moses (Moses Ben Maimon) 1135–1204. Jewish rabbi and philosopher, born in Córdoba, Spain. Known as one of the greatest Hebrew scholars, he attempted to reconcile faith and reason. He was author of the *Thirteen Principles of Faith*.

Moses c. 13th century BCE. Hebrew lawgiver and judge who led the Israelites out of Egypt to the promised land of Canaan. On Mount Sinai he claimed to have received from Jehovah the oral and written Law, including the **Ten Commandments** engraved on tablets of stone. The first five books of the Old Testament—in Judaism, the *Torah*—are ascribed to him.

Muhammad or *Mohammed, Mahomet* c. 570–632. Prophet of Islam, born in Mecca on the Arabian peninsula. He began his prophetic mission c. 610 CE when it is believed he began to receive the revelations of the *Koran*, revealed to him by God (it was later written down by his followers), through the angel Jibra'el. He fled from persecution to the town now known as Medina in 622: the flight, **Hegira**, marks the beginning of the Islamic era.

Nanak 1469–c. 1539. Indian guru and founder of Sikhism, a religion based on the unity of God and the equality of all human beings. He was strongly opposed to caste divisions. He was the first of ten human gurus in the Sikh faith.

Paul, St c.3– c.AD 68. Christian missionary and martyr; in the New Testament, one of the apostles and author of 13 epistles. He is said to have been converted by a vision on the road to Damascus. His emblems are a sword and a book; feast day 29 June.

Shankara 799–833. Hindu philosopher who wrote commentaries on some of the major Hindu scriptures, as well as hymns and essays on religious ideas. Shankara was responsible for the final form of the Advaita

Vedanta school of Hindu philosophy, which teaches that Brahman, the supreme being, is all that exists in the universe, everything else is illusion. Shankara was fiercely opposed to Buddhism and may have influenced its decline in India.

Zoroaster or *Zarathushtra* 6th century or 16th century BCE. Persian prophet and religious teacher, founder of Zoroastrianism. Zoroaster believed that he had seen God, Ahura Mazda, in a vision. His first vision came at the age of 30 and, after initial rejection and violent attack, he converted King Vishtaspa. Subsequently, his teachings spread rapidly, becoming the official religion of the kingdom. Zoroastrianism was a dualistic theology: the god of absolute purity and goodness, Ahura Mazda, being opposed by the twin spirit of violence and death, Angra Mainyu. According to tradition, Zoroaster was murdered at the age of 70 while praying at the altar.

HOLY PLACES

The concept of *pilgrimage*, a journey to sacred places inspired by religious devotion, is common to many religions. For Hindus the holy places include Benares and the purifying Ganges; for Buddhists, Bodhgaya, the site of the Buddha's enlightenment, the Tooth of the Buddha in Sri Lanka, and numerous temples and sacred mountains throughout China and south-east Asia; for the ancient Greeks the shrines at Delphi, Ephesus, among others; for the Jews, the Western Wall at Jerusalem; and for Muslims, Mecca. Among Christians, pilgrimages were common by the second century, and as a direct result of the established necessity of making pilgrimages there arose the numerous hospices catering for pilgrims, the religious orders of knighthood, and the Crusades. The great centres of Christian pilgrimages have been, or are, Jerusalem, Rome, the tomb of St James of Compostella in Spain, the shrine of Becket at Canterbury, and the holy places at La Salette and Lourdes in France.

Amritsar city in the Punjab, India, founded 1577. It is the religious centre of the Sikhs and contains the Golden Temple and Guru Nanak University 1969, named after the first Sikh Guru.

Jerusalem ancient city of Palestine, which is a holy place for Jews, Christians and Muslims. It was divided in 1948 between the new republic of Israel and Jordan. In 1950 the western New City was proclaimed as the Israeli capital, and following the Israeli capture of the eastern Old City in 1967 from the Jordanians, it was affirmed in 1980 that the united city was the country's capital, but the United Nations does not recognize the claim.

history by 1400 BCE Jerusalem was ruled by a king subject to Egypt, but *c.* 1000 BCE David, the second king of Israel, made it the capital of a united Jewish kingdom. It

was captured by Nebuchadnezzar 586 BCE, who deported its population. Later conquerors include Alexander the Great and Pompey (63 BCE), and it was under Roman rule that Jesus Christ was executed. In 70 CE a Jewish revolt led to its complete destruction by Titus. It was first conquered by Islam in 637; was captured by Crusaders, Christians who were fighting the Muslims in Israel, 1099, and recaptured by Saladin 1187, to remain under almost unbroken Islamic rule until the British occupation of Palestine in 1917.

Notable buildings include the Church of the Holy Sepulchre (built 335), and the mosque of the Dome of the Rock. The latter was built on the site of Solomon's Temple, and the Western ('wailing') Wall, held sacred by Jews, is part of the walled platform on which the Temple once stood.

Temple the centre of Jewish national worship at Jerusalem. Three temples occupied the site: Solomon's Temple, which was destroyed by Nebuchadnezzar; Zerubbabel's Temple, built after the return from Babylon; and Herod's Temple, which was destroyed by the Romans in 70 CE. The Mosque of Omar occupies the site. The Wailing Wall is the surviving part of the western wall of the platform of the enclosure of the Temple of Herod, so-called by tourists because of the chanting style of the Jews in their prayers there. Under Jordanian rule Jews had no access to the place, but Israel took this part of the city in the 1967 campaign.

Mecca city of Saudi Arabia, the holiest city of the Muslim world, where the Prophet was born. It stands in the desert, in a valley about 72 km/45 mi east of Jidda, its port on the Red Sea, with which it is linked by an asphalted road, and long before the time of Muhammad was a commercial centre, caravan junction, and place of pilgrimage. In the centre of Mecca is the Great Mosque, in whose courtyard is the Kaaba; it also contains the well Zam-Zam, associated by tradition with Ishmael, the son of Abraham, and his mother Hagar, and the Maqām Ibrāhīm, a holy stone believed to bear the imprint of Abraham's foot.

kaaba the oblong building in the quadrangle of the Great Mosque at Mecca into the south-east corner of which is built the black stone declared by Muhammad to have been given to Abraham by Gabriel, and devoutly revered by Muslim pilgrims. The name means chamber.

Medina city in Saudi Arabia, about 355 km/220 mi north of Mecca. To Muslims it is a holy city second only to Mecca, since Muhammad lived here for many years after he fled from Mecca, and died here. The Mosque of the Prophet is believed to contain Muhammad's tomb, and those of the caliphs or Muslim leaders Abu Bakr, Omar, and Fatima, Muhammad's daughter.

Varanasi or **Benares** Indian city on the sacred Ganges river in Uttar Pradesh. It is holy to Hindus with a 5 km/3 mi frontage of stairways (ghats), leading up from the river to innumerable streets, temples, and the 1,500 golden shrines. The ritual of purification is practised daily by thousands of devout Hindus, who bathe from the ghats in the sacred river. At the burning ghats, the ashes, following cremation, are scattered on the river, a ritual followed to ensure a favourable reincarnation.

FESTIVALS

Buddhist festivals

Wesak the day of the Buddha's birth, enlightenment and death. A large act of worship is held and gifts given to monks; captive animals may be freed.

Dhammacakka celebrates the preaching of the Buddha's first sermon. Visits are made to monasteries and gifts are given to the monks.

Bodhi Day Mahayana Buddhist celebration of the Buddha's enlightenment.

Chinese festivals

New Year time when the Kitchen God, whose picture is in every home, returns to heaven to report on the family's behaviour during the year. There are elaborate lion dances and fireworks, and vegetarian feasts are eaten.

Ching Ming a time for visiting ancestral tombs, making offerings and remembering the dead.

Dragon Boat Festival celebrates the story of a brave official who persuaded a harsh emperor to relent over his crippling taxation of the people by drowning himself. Races are held between boats carved to resemble dragons, in memory of the boat chase to save the official's body from being eaten by dragons and demons.

Moon Festival commemorates the story of a brave woman who defied her husband, a wicked king, to stop him obtaining immortality, and was carried off by the gods to live on the moon. The festival is held at the harvest full moon and the moon is greeted with incense, lanterns and feasting.

Winter Festival time of feasting to build up strength for the winter ahead.

Christian festivals

Epiphany annual festival (6 Jan) of the Christian Church, celebrating the coming of the Magi or wise men to Bethlehem with gifts for the infant Christ, and symbolizing the manifestation of Christ to the world. It is the twelfth day after Christmas, and marks the end of the Christmas festivities. In many countries the night before, called *Twelfth Night*, is marked by the giving of gifts.

Shrove Tuesday the day before Ash Wednesday. The name comes from the Anglo-Saxon *scrifan*, to shrive, and in former times it was the time for confession before Lent. Another name for it is Pancake Tuesday; the pancakes are a survival of merry-making in anticipation of Lenten abstinence.

Ash Wednesday first day of Lent, the period in the Christian calendar leading up to Easter; in the Catholic Church the foreheads of the congregation are marked with a cross in ash, as a sign of penitence.

Lent in the Christian Church, the forty days' period of fasting which precedes Easter, beginning on Ash Wednesday, but omitting Sundays.

Palm Sunday the Sunday before Easter, and first day of Holy Week; so-called to commemorate Christ's entry into Jerusalem, when the crowd strewed palm leaves in his path.

Good Friday (probably a corruption of God's Friday). In the Christian Church, the Friday before Easter, which is kept in memory of the Crucifixion (the death of Jesus).

Easter feast of the Christian Church, commemorating the Resurrection of Christ. It usually falls around the time of the Jewish Passover since Christ's crucifixion coincided with the time of this festival. The English name derives from Eostre, Anglo-Saxon goddess of spring, who was honoured in Apr. Eggs are given at this time as a symbol of new life.

Whitsun celebrates the filling of the followers of Jesus with the Holy Spirit, which Christians believe to be the third aspect of God, after Jesus had returned to heaven. As the disciples went out and told everyone about Jesus, so at Whitsun many Christians go on processions around the parish boundaries.

Advent the time leading up to Christmas; a time of preparation for Christians.

Christmas day on which the birth of Christ is celebrated by Christians. Although the actual birth date is unknown, the choice of a date near the winter solstice owned much to missionary desire to facilitate conversion of pagans, for example in Britain 25 Dec had been kept as a festival long before the introduction of Christianity. Many of its customs also have a non-Christian origin.

Hindu festivals

Mahashivaratri Festival of Siva, who is celebrated as lord of the dance, dancing on the demon of ignorance.

Holi a harvest time festival in honour of Krishna, when bonfires are lit; people throw coloured water at each other and play games and tricks as a reminder of Krishna's mischievous behaviour.

Rama Naumi celebration of the Birth of Rama. An eight-day fast during which the *Rāmāyana* is recited; the fast is broken on the ninth day with fruit and nuts, and offerings are made to Rama.

Raksha Bandhan a family festival in which sisters present their brothers with a bracelet of thread to protect them from harm, in return for which the brothers promise to look after their sisters.

Janmashtami celebration of the birthday of Krishna. Children act out stories of Krishna, and a statue of the young Krishna is used in the celebrations.

Dusshera a festival (also known as Durga Puja) which lasts ten days; the great goddess Devi is worshipped in her many forms.

Divali a new year festival which honours

Lakshmi, goddess of fortune. Lights are lit in every window.

Jewish festivals

Purim celebrates the story of Esther, a Jewish woman who risked her life to save her people from treacherous slaughter. The story is read from a scroll in the synagogue, and the congregation boo and hiss when the villain's name is read out. It is a time for noisy parties and merriment.

Passover (Pesach) festival which commemorates the escape from slavery in Egypt. A special meal, the seder meal, is eaten and the story of how the Jews were saved by God from this bondage is told.

Shavuot or *Pentecost* commemorates the giving of the ten commandments to Moses.

Rosh Hashanah the two-day festival at the start of the Jewish New Year (first new moon after the autumn equinox), a time for repentence and forgiveness. This reflective period is brought to a close nine days later at Yom Kippur. Rosh Hashanah begins on the first day of the month of Tishri (Sept–Oct), the seventh month of the Jewish year.

Yom Kippur (Day of Atonement) day of Jewish religious fast held on the tenth day of Tishri. Final forgiveness is sought for past deeds and the Kol Nidrei is sung in the synagogue to end the old vows of the past year and to prepare for the demands of the coming year. The festival ends with the blowing of the shofar, the ram's horn.

Succot the feast of Tabernacles (tents), a reminder of the time the Israelites spent wandering in the wilderness. Temporary homes of branches are built at the synagogue and sometimes at home.

Hanukkah celebrates the recapture and rededication of the Temple of Jerusalem by Judah Maccabee in 165 BCE. The festival lasts eight days; each day, a new candle is lit on a special candlestick or menorah.

Muslim festivals

The Muslim calendar is lunar, and correspondences with the Western calendar cannot be given; festivals fall 11–12 days earlier each year.

Lailat ul-Isra Wal Mi'raj celebrates Muhammad's night journey by horse to Jerusalem and up to heaven.

Lailat ul-Barah the night of forgiveness; a time to prepare for Ramadan.

Ramadan the ninth month of the Muslim year, throughout which a strict fast is observed during the hours of daylight.

Lailat ul-Qadr commemorates the night the Koran was first revealed to Muhammad.

Eid ul-Fitr the end of the fast of Ramadan. Gifts are given to charity, new clothes are worn and sweets are given.

Eid ul-Adha celebrates the faith of the prophet Abraham, who was prepared to sacrifice his son Ismail when Allah asked him to. Lamb is eaten and shared with the poor, as a reminder of the sheep which Allah provided as a sacrifice instead of Ismail.

Day of Hirja commemorates the journey of Muhammad from Mecca to Medina.

Sikh festivals

Hola Mohalla a three-day festival held at the time of the Hindu festival Holi. Sporting competitions and other tests of skill take place.

Baisakhi originally a harvest festival, it now celebrates the founding of the Khalsa, the Sikh brotherhood, and commemorates those Sikhs killed by British troops in Amritsar on Baisakhi, 1919.

Martyrdom of Guru Arjan commemorates the death of the fifth guru, Guru Arjan, who built the Golden Temple at Amritsar and compiled the main part of the Sikh holy book.

Divali celebrates the release from prison of the sixth guru, Guru Hargobind, who also managed to secure the release of 51 Hindu princes who were imprisoned with him.

Guru Nanak's birthday celebrates the birth of the founder of the first guru of Sikhism.

Martyrdom of Guru Tegh Bahadur the ninth guru, martyred for the faith.

Birthday of Guru Gobind Singh The tenth and last human guru of Sikhism, and the founder of the Khalsa.

EVENTS AND RECORDS

angling fishing with rod and line. *Freshwater fishing* embraces game fishing, in which members of the salmon family, such as salmon and trout, are taken by spinners (revolving lures) and flies (imitations of adult or larval insects); and coarse fishing, in which members of the carp family, pike, perch, and eels are taken by baits or lures, and (in the UK) are returned to the water virtually unharmed. In *sea fishing* the catch includes flatfish, bass, and mackerel; big-game fishes include shark, tuna or tunny, marlin, and swordfish. World championships take place for most branches of the sport.

WORLD FRESHWATER CHAMPIONSHIP
first held 1957
individual
1982 Kevin Ashurst *(England)*
1983 Wolf-Rüdiger Kremkus *(West Germany)*
1984 Bobby Smithers *(England)*
1985 Dave Roper *(England)*
1986 Lud Wever *(Holland)*
1987 Clive Branson *(Wales)*
1988 Jean-Pierre Fouquet *(France)*
1989 Tom Pickering *(England)*
1990 Bob Nudd *(England)*
1991 Bob Nudd *(England)*
team
1982 Holland
1983 Belgium
1984 Luxembourg
1985 England
1986 Italy
1987 England
1988 England
1989 Wales
1990 France
1991 England

---

archery shooting with a bow and arrow at a circular target made up of ten concentric scoring zones. The highest score (10 points) is obtained by hitting the central, gold-coloured zone. Competitions usually take the form of Double FITA (Fédération Internationale de Tir à l'Arc) rounds—that is, 72 arrows are fired at each of four targets from distances of 90, 70, 50, and 30 m (70, 60, 50, and 30 m for women). The highest possible score is 2,880.

WORLD CHAMPIONSHIP
first held 1931; now contested every two years
men—individual
1983 Richard McKinney *(USA)*
1985 Richard McKinney *(USA)*
1987 Vladimir Asheyer *(USSR)*
1989 Stanislav Zabrodsky *(USSR)*
1991 Simon Fairweather *(Australia)*

men—team
1983 USA
1985 South Korea
1987 South Korea
1989 USSR
1991 South Korea
women—individual
1983 Jin-Ho Kim *(South Korea)*
1985 Irina Soldatova *(USSR)*
1987 Ma Xiagjuan *(China)*
1989 Soo Nyung-Kim *(South Korea)*
1991 Soo Nyung-Kim (South Korea)
women—team
1983 South Korea
1985 USSR
1987 China
1989 South Korea
1991 South Korea

---

athletics competitive track and field events consisting of running, throwing, and jumping disciplines. *Running events* range from sprint races (100 metres) and hurdles to the marathon (26 miles 385 yards). *Jumping events* are the high jump and long jump, and, for men only, the triple jump and pole vault. *Throwing events* are javelin, discus, shot put, and hammer throw (men only).

WORLD RECORDS
at 1 June 1992
men
100 metres: 9.86 sec Carl Lewis *(USA)*
200 metres: 19.72 sec Pietro Mennea *(Italy)*
400 metres: 43.29 sec Butch Reynolds *(USA)*
800 metres: 1 min 41.73 sec Sebastian Coe *(UK)*
1,000 metres: 2 min 12.18 sec Sebastian Coe *(UK)*
1,500 metres: 3 min 29.46 sec Said Aouita *(Morocco)*
mile 3 min 46.32 sec Steve Cram *(UK)*
2,000 metres: 4 min 50.81 sec Said Aouita *(Morocco)*
3,000 metres: 7 min 29.45 sec Said Aouita *(Morocco)*
5,000 metres: 12 min 58.39 sec Said Aouita *(Morocco)*
10,000 metres: 27 min 08.23 sec Arturo Barrios *(Mexico)*
20,000 metres: 56 min 55.6 sec Arturo Barrios *(Mexico)*
20,994 metres: 1 hr Jos Hermans *(Holland)*
25,000 metres: 1 hr 13 min 55.8 sec Toshihiko Seko *(Japan)*
30,000 metres: 1 hr 29 min 18.8 sec Toshihiko Seko *(Japan)*
110 metres hurdles: 12.92 sec Roger Kingdom *(USA)*
400 metres hurdles: 47.02 sec Edwin Moses *(USA)*
3,000 metres steeplechase: 8 min 5.35 sec Peter Koech *(Kenya)*
4 × 100 metres relay: 37.50 sec USA
4 × 400 metres relay: 2 min 56.16 sec USA
4 × 800 metres relay: 7 min 03.89 sec UK
4 × 1,500 metres relay: 14 min 38.8 sec West Germany
high jump: 2.44 metres Javier Sotomayor *(Cuba)*
pole vault: 6.10 metres Sergey Bubka *(USSR)*
long jump: 8.95 metres Mike Powell *(USA)*

triple jump: 17.97 metres Willie Banks *(USA)*
shot: 23.12 metres Randy Barnes *(USA)*
discus: 74.08 metres Jurgen Schult *(East Germany)*
hammer: 86.74 metres Yuriy Sedykh *(USSR)*
javelin: 91.46 metres Steve Backley *(UK)*
decathlon: 8,847 points Daley Thompson *(UK)*
marathon: 2 hr 6 min 50 sec Belayneh Dinsamo *(Ethiopia)*
women
100 metres: 10.49 sec Florence Griffith-Joyner *(USA)*
200 metres: 21.34 sec Florence Griffith-Joyner *(USA)*
400 metres: 47.60 sec Marita Koch *(East Germany)*
800 metres: 1 min 53.28 sec Jarmila Kratochvilova *(Czechoslovakia)*
1,500 metres: 3 min 52.47 sec Tatyana Kazankina *(USSR)*
mile: 4 min 15.61 sec Paula Ivan *(Romania)*
2,000 metres: 5 min 28.69 sec Maricica Puica *(Romania)*
3,000 metres: 8 min 22.62 sec Tatyana Kazankini *(USSR)*
5,000 metres: 14 min 37.33 sec Ingrid Kristiansen *(Norway)*
WORLD CROSS-COUNTRY CHAMPIONSHIP
men—individual
1988 John Ngugi *(Kenya)*
1989 John Ngugi *(Kenya)*
1990 Khaled Skah *(Morocco)*
1991 Khaled Skah *(Morocco)*
1992 John Ngugi *(Kenya)*
women—individual
1988 Ingrid Kristiansen *(Norway)*
1989 Annette Sergant *(France)*
1990 Lynn Jennings *(USA)*
1991 Lynn Jennings *(USA)*
1992 Lynn Jennings *(USA)*
men—team
1988 Kenya
1989 Kenya
1990 Kenya
1991 Kenya
1992 Kenya
women—team
1988 USSR
1989 USSR
1990 USSR
1991 Kenya/Ethiopia
1992 Kenya

badminton indoor racket game, similar to lawn tennis but played with a shuttlecock (a half sphere of cork or plastic with a feather or nylon skirt) instead of a ball. It may be played by two or four players. The game takes place on a court 13.4 m/44 ft long and 5.2 m/17 ft wide (6.1 m/20 ft wide for doubles), with a raised net across the middle. The object of the game is to prevent the opponent from being able to return the shuttlecock.

WORLD CHAMPIONSHIP
first held 1977; now contested every two years
men

1983 Icuk Sugiarto *(Indonesia)*
1985 Han Jian *(China)*
1987 Yang Yang *(China)*
1989 Yang Yang *(China)*
1991 Zao Zinhua *(China)*
women
1983 Li Lingwei *(China)*
1985 Han Aiping *(China)*
1987 Han Aiping *(China)*
1989 Li Lingwei *(China)*
1991 Tang Jiu Hong *(China)*
THOMAS CUP
men's team championship, first held 1949
1970 Indonesia
1973 Indonesia
1976 Indonesia
1979 Indonesia
1982 China
1984 Indonesia
1986 China
1988 China
1990 China
1992 Malaysia
UBER CUP
women's team championship, first held 1957
1969 Japan
1972 Japan
1975 Indonesia
1978 Japan
1981 Japan
1984 China
1986 China
1988 China
1990 China
1992 China

baseball national summer game of the USA, derived in the 19th century from the English game of rounders. Baseball is a bat-and-ball game played between two teams, each of nine players. The field is marked out in the form of a diamond, with a base at each corner. The ball is struck with a cylindrical bat, and the players try to score ('make a run') by circuiting the bases. A 'home run' is a circuit on one hit.

WORLD SERIES
first held 1903 as an end-of-season game between the winners of the two professional leagues, the National League and the American League, and established as a series of seven games 1905
1982 St Louis Cardinals
1983 Baltimore Orioles
1984 Detroit Tigers
1985 Kansas City Royals
1986 New York Mets
1987 Minnesota Twins
1988 Los Angeles Dodgers
1989 Oakland Athletics
1990 Cincinatti Reds
1991 Minnesota Twins

basketball ball game between two teams of five players on a rectangular enclosed court. The object is to throw the large inflated ball through a circular hoop and net positioned at each end of the court, 3.05 m/10 ft above the ground. Players move the ball by passing it or by dribbling it (bouncing it on the floor) while running.

WORLD CHAMPIONSHIP
first held 1950 for men, 1953 for women; contested every four years
men
1954 USA
1959 Brazil
1963 Brazil
1967 USSR
1970 Yugoslavia
1974 USSR
1978 Yugoslavia
1982 USSR
1986 USA
1990 Yugoslavia
women
1957 USA
1959 USSR
1964 USSR
1967 USSR
1971 USSR
1975 USSR
1979 USA
1983 USSR
1986 USA
1990 USA

NBA (NATIONAL BASKETBALL ASSOCIATION) CHAMPIONSHIP
US end-of-season contest, first held 1947, between the top teams of the two professional leagues, the Western Conference and the Eastern Conference
1982 Los Angeles Lakers
1983 Philadelphia 76ers
1984 Boston Celtics
1985 Los Angeles Lakers
1986 Boston Celtics
1987 Los Angeles Lakers
1988 Los Angeles Lakers
1989 Detroit Pistons
1990 Detroit Pistons
1991 Chicago Bulls

billiards indoor game played, normally by two players, with tapered poles (cues) and composition balls (one red, two white) on a rectangular table covered with a green feltlike cloth (baize). The table has six pockets, one at each corner and in each of the long sides at the middle. Scoring strokes are made by potting the red ball, potting the opponent's ball, or potting another ball off one of these two. The cannon (when the cue ball hits the two other balls on the table) is another scoring stroke.

WORLD PROFESSIONAL CHAMPIONSHIP
instituted 1870, on a challenge basis, and restored as an annual tournament 1980

1982 Rex Williams *(England)*
1983 Rex Williams *(England)*
1984 Mark Wildman *(England)*
1985 Ray Edmonds *(England)*
1986 Robert Foldvari *(Australia)*
1987 Norman Dagley *(England)*
1988 Norman Dagley *(England)*
1989 Mike Russell *(England)*
1990 Mike Russell *(England)*
1991 Mike Russell *(England)*

bobsleighing or **bobsledding** racing steel-bodied, steerable toboggans, crewed by two or four people, down mountain ice-chutes at speeds of up to 130 kph/80 mph.

WORLD CHAMPIONSHIP
four-crew championship introduced 1924, two-crew 1931; in Olympic years winners automatically become world champions
two-person/four-person
1983 Switzerland/Switzerland
1984 East Germany/East Germany
1985 East Germany/East Germany
1986 East Germany/Switzerland
1987 Switzerland/Switzerland
1988 USSR/Switzerland
1989 East Germany/Switzerland
1990 Switzerland/Switzerland
1991 Germany/Germany
1992 Switzerland/Switzerland

bowls outdoor and indoor game popular in Commonwealth countries. The outdoor game is played on a finely cut grassed area called a rink, with biased bowls 13 cm/5 in in diameter. It is played as either singles, pairs, triples, or fours. The object is to position one's bowl (or bowls) as near as possible to the jack (target). **Lawn bowls** is played on a flat surface; **crown green bowls** is played on a rink with undulations and a crown at the centre of the green.

WORLD OUTDOOR CHAMPIONSHIP
first held 1966 for men, and 1969 for women
men: singles
1972 Maldwyn Evans *(Wales)*
1976 Doug Watson *(South Africa)*
1980 David Bryant *(England)*
1984 Peter Bellis *(New Zealand)*
1988 David Bryant *(England)*
women: singles
1973 Elsie Wilke *(New Zealand)*
1977 Elsie Wilke *(New Zealand)*
1981 Norma Shaw *(England)*
1985 Merle Richardson *(Australia)*
1988 Janet Ackland *(Wales)*
1992 Margaret Johnston *(Ireland)*
WORLD INDOOR CHAMPIONSHIP
first held 1979 for men, 1988 for women
men: singles
1988 Hugh Duff *(Scotland)*

1989 Richard Corsie *(Scotland)*
1990 John Price *(Wales)*
1991 Richard Corsie *(Scotland)*
1992 Ian Schubacic *(Australia)*
women: singles
1988 Margaret Johnston *(Ireland)*
1989 Margaret Johnston *(Ireland)*
1991 Mary Price *(England)*
WATERLOO HANDICAP
crown green tournament first held 1907
1982 Dennis Mercer
1983 Stan Frith
1984 Steve Ellis
1985 Tommy Johnstone
1986 Brian Duncan
1987 Brian Duncan
1988 Ingham Gregory
1989 Brian Duncan
1990 John Bancroft
1991 John Eccles

boxing fighting with gloved fists, almost entirely a male sport. Contests take place in a square, roped ring 4.3–6.1 m/14–20 ft square. All rounds last 3 minutes. Amateur bouts last three rounds and professional championship bouts for as many as 12 or 15 rounds. Boxers are classified according to weight and may not fight in a division lighter than their own. The weight divisions in professional boxing range from straw-weight (also known as paperweight and mini-flyweight), under 49 kg/108 lb, to heavyweight, over 88 kg/195 lb.

WORLD CHAMPIONSHIP
(WBC = World Boxing Council; WBA = World Boxing Association; IBF = International Boxing Federation; WBO = World Boxing Organization)
heavyweight
1986 Tim Witherspoon *(USA, WBA)*
1986 Trevor Berbick *(Canada, WBC)*
1986 Mike Tyson *(USA, WBC)*
1986 James Smith *(USA, WBA)*
1987 Mike Tyson *(USA, WBA)*
1987 Tony Tucker *(USA, IBF)*
1987 Mike Tyson *(USA, undisputed)*
1989 Francesco Damiani *(Italy, WBO)*
1990 James Douglas *(USA, undisputed)*
1990 Evander Holyfield *(USA, undisputed)*
great heavyweight champions include:
John L Sullivan (bare-knuckle champion) 1882–92
Jim Corbett (first Marquess of Queensberry champion) 1892–97
Jack Dempsey 1919–26
Joe Louis 1937–49
Rocky Marciano 1952–56
Muhammad Ali 1964–67, 1974–78, 1978–79
Larry Holmes 1978–85
Mike Tyson 1986–1990

cricket bat-and-ball game between two teams of 11 players each. It is played with a small solid ball and long flat-sided wooden bats, on a round or oval field, at the centre of which is a finely mown pitch, 20 m/22 yd long. At each end of the pitch is a wicket made up of three upright wooden sticks (stumps), surmounted by two smaller sticks (bails). The object of the game is to score more runs than the opposing team. A run is normally scored by the batsman's striking the ball and exchanging ends with his or her partner until the ball is returned by a fielder, or by hitting the ball to the boundary line for an automatic four or six runs.

COUNTY CHAMPIONSHIP
first held officially 1890
1982 Middlesex
1983 Essex
1984 Essex
1985 Middlesex
1986 Essex
1987 Nottinghamshire
1988 Worcestershire
1989 Worcestershire
1990 Middlesex
1991 Essex
REFUGE ASSURANCE LEAGUE
(formerly John Player League), first held 1969
1982 Sussex
1983 Yorkshire
1984 Essex
1985 Essex
1986 Hampshire
1987 Worcestershire
1988 Worcestershire
1989 Lancashire
1990 Derbyshire
1991 Nottinghamshire
NATWEST TROPHY
(formerly the Gillette Cup), first held 1963
1982 Surrey
1983 Somerset
1984 Middlesex
1985 Essex
1986 Sussex
1987 Nottinghamshire
1988 Middlesex
1989 Warwickshire
1990 Lancashire
1991 Hampshire
BENSON AND HEDGES CUP
first held 1972
1982 Somerset
1983 Middlesex
1984 Lancashire
1985 Leicestershire
1986 Middlesex
1987 Yorkshire
1988 Hampshire
1989 Nottinghamshire
1990 Lancashire
1991 Worcestershire
1992 Hampshire
WORLD CUP
first held 1975, contested every four years
1975 West Indies
1979 West Indies
1983 India

1987 Australia
1992 Pakistan

curling game resembling bowls that is played on ice, between two teams of four players each. Each player has two disclike stones, of equal size, fitted with a handle. The object of the game is to slide the stones across the ice so that they are positioned as near as possible to a target object (the tee), those nearest scoring. The stone may be curled in one direction or another according to the twist given as it leaves the hand. The match is played for an agreed number of heads or shots, or by time.

WORLD CHAMPIONSHIP
first held 1959 for men, 1979 for women
men
1988 Norway
1989 Canada
1990 Canada
1991 Scotland
1992 Switzerland
women
1988 West Germany
1989 Canada
1990 Norway
1991 Norway
1992 Sweden

cycling cycle racing can take place on oval artificial tracks, on the road,or across country (cyclo-cross). *Stage races* are run over gruelling terrain and can last anything from three to five days up to three and a half weeks, as in the Tour de France, Tour of Italy, and Tour of Spain. *Criteriums* are fast, action-packed races around the closed streets of town or city centres. *Road races* are run over a prescribed circuit, which the riders will lap several times. Such a race will normally cover a distance of approximately 100 mi/160 km. *Track racing* takes place on a concrete or wooden banked circuit, either indoors or outdoors. In *time trialling* each rider races against the clock, with all the competitors starting at different intervals.

TOUR DE FRANCE
first held 1903
1982 Bernard Hinault (France)
1983 Laurent Fignon (France)
1984 Laurent Fignon (France)
1985 Bernard Hinault (France)
1986 Greg LeMond (USA)
1987 Stephen Roche (Ireland)
1988 Pedro Delgado (Spain)
1989 Greg LeMond (USA)
1990 Greg LeMond (USA)
1991 Miguel Indurain (Spain)
TOUR OF BRITAIN
(formerly the Milk Race), first held 1951
1982 Yuri Kashirin (USSR)

1983 Matt Eaton (USA)
1984 Oleg Czougeda (USSR)
1985 Erik van Lancker (Belgium)
1986 Joey McLoughlin (UK)
1987 Malcolm Elliott (UK)
1988 Vasily Zhdanov (USSR)
1989 Brian Walton (Canada)
1990 Shane Sutton (Australia)
1991 Chris Walker (UK)
WORLD PROFESSIONAL ROAD RACE CHAMPIONS
first held 1927
1982 Giuseppe Saroni (Italy)
1983 Greg LeMond (USA)
1984 Claude Criquielon (Belgium)
1985 Joop Zoetemelk (Holland)
1986 Moreno Argentin (Italy)
1987 Stephen Roche (Ireland)
1988 Maurizio Fondriest (Italy)
1989 Greg LeMond (USA)
1990 Rudy Dhaenens (Belgium)
1991 Gianni Bugno (Italy)

darts indoor game played on a circular board. Darts about 13 cm/5 in long are thrown at segmented targets, and score points according to their landing place.

WORLD CHAMPIONSHIP
first held 1978
1983 Keith Deller (England)
1984 Eric Bristow (England)
1985 Eric Bristow (England)
1986 Eric Bristow (England)
1987 John Lowe (England)
1988 Bob Anderson (England)
1989 Jocky Wilson (Scotland)
1990 Phil Taylor (England)
1991 Dennis Priestley (England)
1992 Phil Taylor (England)

diving sport of entering water either from a springboard (3 m/10 ft) above the water, or from a platform, or highboard, (10 m/33 ft) above the water. Various starts are adopted, and twists and somersaults may be performed in midair. Points are awarded and the level of difficulty of each dive is used as a multiplying factor.

OLYMPIC GAMES
springboard diving
men
1980 Aleksandr Portnov (USSR)
1984 Greg Louganis (USA)
1988 Greg Louganis (USA)
women
1980 Irina Kalinina (USSR)
1984 Sylvie Bernier (Canada)
1988 Gao Min (China)
highboard diving
men
1980 Falk Hoffmann (East Germany)
1984 Greg Louganis (USA)

1988 Greg Louganis *(USA)*
women
1980 Martina Jäschke *(East Germany)*
1984 Zhou Jihong *(China)*
1988 Xu Yanmei *(China)*

---

equestrianism skill in horse riding, as practised under International Equestrian Federation rules. *Showjumping* is horse-jumping over a course of fences. The winner is usually the competitor with fewest 'faults' (penalty marks given for knocking down or refusing fences), but in timed competitions it is the competitor completing the course most quickly, additional seconds being added for mistakes. *Dressage* tests the horse's obedience skills, and the rider's control. Tests consist of a series of movements at walk, trot, canter, with each movement marked by judges who look for suppleness, balance and the special harmony between rider and horse. *Three-Day Eventing* tests the all-round abilities of a horse and rider in dressage, cross-country, and showjumping.

WORLD CHAMPIONSHIP
show jumping; first held 1953 for men, 1965 for women; since 1978 men and women have competed together
men
1953 Francisco Goyoago *(Spain)*
1954 Hans-Günter Winkler *(West Germany)*
1955 Hans-Günter Winkler *(West Germany)*
1956 Raimondo D'Inzeo *(Italy)*
960 Raimondo D'Inzeo *(Italy)*
1966 Pierre d'Oriola *(France)*
1970 David Broome *(UK)*
1974 Hartwig Steenken *(West Germany)*
women
1965 Marion Coakes *(UK)*
1970 Janou Lefebvre *(France)*
1974 Janou Tissot (born Lefebvre) *(France)*
mixed
1978 Gerd Wiltfang *(West Germany)*
1982 Norbert Koof *(West Germany)*
1986 Gail Greenough *(Canada)*
1990 Eric Navet *(France)*
EUROPEAN CHAMPIONSHIP
show jumping; first held 1957 with men and women competing separately; since 1975 they have competed together
1977 Johan Heins *(Holland)*
1979 Gerd Wiltfang *(West Germany)*
1981 Paul Schockemöhle *(West Germany)*
1983 Paul Schockemöhle *(West Germany)*
1985 Paul Schockemöhle *(West Germany)*
1987 Pierre Durand *(France)*
1989 John Whitaker *(UK)*
1991 Eric Navet *(France)*
BRITISH SHOWJUMPING DERBY
first held 1961
1982 Paul Schockemöhle *(West Germany)*
1983 John Whitaker *(UK)*
1984 John Ledingham *(Ireland)*
1985 Paul Schockemöhle *(West Germany)*
1986 Paul Schockemöhle *(West Germany)*

1987 Nick Skelton *(UK)*
1988 Nick Skelton *(UK)*
1989 Nick Skelton *(UK)*
1990 Joe Turi *(UK)*
1991 Michael Whitaker *(UK)*
THREE-DAY EVENTING WORLD CHAMPIONSHIP
1974 Bruce Davidson *(USA)*
1978 Bruce Davidson *(USA)*
1982 Lucinda Green (born Prior-Palmer) *(UK)*
1986 Virginia Leng (born Holgate) *(UK)*
1990 Blyth Tait *(New Zealand)*
BADMINTON HORSE TRIALS
three-day eventing; first held 1949
1983 Lucinda Green *(UK)*
1984 Lucinda Green *(UK)*
1985 Virginia Holgate *(UK)*
1986 Ian Stark *(UK)*
1987 cancelled
1988 Ian Stark *(UK)*
1989 Virginia Leng *(UK)*
1990 Nicola McIrvine *(UK)*
1991 Rodney Powell *(UK)*
1992 Mary Thompson *(UK)*

---

fencing sport of fighting with swords including the *foil*, derived from the light weapon used in practice duels; the *épée*, a heavier weapon derived from the duelling sword proper; and the *sabre*, with a curved handle and narrow V-shaped blade. In sabre fighting, cuts count as well as thrusts. Masks and protective jackets are worn, and hits are registered electronically in competitions.

WORLD CHAMPIONSHIP
first held 1921; Olympic winners automatically become world champions
foil—men
1982 Aleksandr Romankov *(USSR)*
1983 Aleksandr Romankov *(USSR)*
1984 Mauro Numa *(Italy)*
1985 Mauro Numa *(Italy)*
1986 Andrea Borella *(Italy)*
1987 Mathias Gey *(West Germany)*
1988 Stefano Cerioni *(Italy)*
1989 Alexandr Koch *(West Germany)*
1990 Philippe Onnes *(France)*
1991 Ingo Weissenborn *(Italy)*
foil—women
1982 Naila Giliazova *(USSR)*
1983 Dorina Vaccaroni *(Italy)*
1984 Jujie Luan *(China)*
1985 Cornelia Hanisch *(West Germany)*
1986 Anja Fichtel *(West Germany)*
1987 Elisabeta Tufan *(Romania)*
1988 Anja Fichtel *(West Germany)*
1989 Olga Velichko *(USSR)*
1990 Anja Fichtel *(Germany)*
1991 Giovann Trillini *(Italy)*
épée—men
1982 Jenö Pap *(Hungary)*
1983 Ellmar Bormann *(West Germany)*
1984 Philippe Boisse *(France)*
1985 Philippe Boisse *(France)*
1986 Philippe Riboud *(France)*

1987 Volker Fischer *(West Germany)*
1988 Arnd Schmitt *(West Germany)*
1989 Manuel Pereira *(Spain)*
1990 Thomas Gerull *(Germany)*
1991 Andrei Chouvalov *(USSR)*

épée—women

1989 Anja Straub *(Switzerland)*
1990 Taimi Chappe *(Cuba)*
1991 Mariann Horvath *(Hungary)*

sabre—men

1982 Viktor Krovopuskov *(USSR)*
1983 Vasiliy Etropolski *(Bulgaria)*
1984 Jean-Francois Lamour *(France)*
1985 György Nebald *(Hungary)*
1986 Sergey Mindirgassov *(USSR)*
1987 Jean-François Lamour *(France)*
1988 Jean-François Lamour *(France)*
1989 Grigoriy Kirienko *(USSR)*
1990 Gyorgy Nebald *(Hungary)*
1991 Grigoriy Kirienko *(USSR)*

football, American contact sport played between two teams of 11 players, with an inflated oval ball. Players are well padded for protection and wear protective helmets. The game is played on a field 91.4 m/100 yd long and 48.8 m/ 53.3 yd wide, marked out with a series of parallel lines giving a gridiron effect. There is a goalpost at each end of the field, and beyond this an endzone 9 m/10 yd long. Points are scored by running or passing the ball across the goal line (touchdown); by kicking it over the goal's crossbar after a touchdown (conversion or point after touchdown), or from the field during regular play (field goal); or by tackling an offensive player who has the ball in the end zone, or blocking an offensive team's kick so it goes out of bounds from the end zone (safety). A touchdown counts 6 points, a field goal 3, a safety 2, and a conversion 1. Games are divided into four quarters of 15 minutes each.

SUPER BOWL
first held 1967
1983 Washington Redskins
1984 Los Angeles Raiders
1985 San Francisco 49ers
1986 Chicago Bears
1987 New York Giants
1988 Washington Redskins
1989 San Francisco 49ers
1990 San Francisco 49ers
1991 New York Giants
1992 Washington Redskins

football, association or *soccer* form of football originating in the UK, popular in Europe and Latin America. It is played between two teams each of 11 players, on a field 90–120 m/ 100–130 yd long and 45–90 m/ 50–100 yd wide, with an inflated spherical ball. The object of the game is to kick or head the ball into the opponents' goal, an area 7.31 m/8 yd wide and

2.44 m/8 ft high. Games are divided into two halves of 45 minutes each, the teams changing ends at half-time.

In the UK the game is played according to the rules laid down by the Football Association, founded 1863. Slight amendments to the rules take effect in certain competitions and overseas matches as laid down by the sport's world governing body, Fédération Internationale de Football Association (FIFA, 1904).

WORLD CUP
first held 1930; contested every four years
1954 West Germany
1958 Brazil
1962 Brazil
1966 England
1970 Brazil
1974 West Germany
1978 Argentina
1982 Italy
1986 Argentina
1990 West Germany
EUROPEAN CHAMPIONSHIP
instituted 1958, first final 1960; contested every four years
1960 USSR
1964 Spain
1968 Italy
1972 West Germany
1976 Czechoslovakia
1980 West Germany
1984 France
1988 Holland
1992 Denmark
EUROPEAN CHAMPIONS CUP
first held 1955
1983 SV Hamburg *(West Germany)*
1984 Liverpool *(England)*
1985 Juventus *(Italy)*
1986 Steaua Bucharest *(Romania)*
1987 FC Porto *(Portugal)*
1988 PSV Eindhoven *(Holland)*
1989 AC Milan *(Italy)*
1990 AC Milan *(Italy)*
1991 Red Star Belgrade *(Yugoslavia)*
1992 Barcelona *(Spain)*
EUROPEAN CUP WINNERS' CUP
first held 1960
1983 Aberdeen *(Scotland)*
1984 Juventus *(Italy)*
1985 Everton *(England)*
1986 Dinamo Kiev *(USSR)*
1987 Ajax *(Holland)*
1988 Mechelen *(Belgium)*
1989 Barcelona *(Spain)*
1990 Sampdoria *(Italy)*
1991 Manchester United *(England)*
1992 Werder Bremen *(Germany)*
UEFA CUP
(formerly Inter Cities Fairs Cup) first held 1955
1983 Anderlecht *(Belgium)*
1984 Tottenham Hotspur *(England)*
1985 Real Madrid *(Spain)*
1986 Real Madrid *(Spain)*

1987 IFK Gothenburg *(Sweden)*
1988 Bayer Leverkusen *(West Germany)*
1989 Napoli *(Italy)*
1990 Juventus *(Italy)*
1991 Internazionale Milan *(Italy)*
1992 Ajax *(Holland)*

UK CHAMPIONSHIPS

FA CUP
a knockout club competition, first held 1872
1983 Manchester United
1984 Everton
1985 Manchester United
1986 Liverpool
1987 Coventry City
1988 Wimbledon
1989 Liverpool
1990 Manchester United
1991 Tottenham Hotspur
1992 Liverpool

FOOTBALL LEAGUE CUP
(currently known as the Rumbelows Cup, formerly the
Milk Cup and the Littlewoods Cup) first final 1961 in
two stages, now a single game
1983 Liverpool
1984 Liverpool
1985 Norwich City
1986 Oxford United
1987 Arsenal
1988 Luton Town
1989 Nottingham Forest
1990 Nottingham Forest
1991 Sheffield Wednesday
1992 Manchester United

DIVISION ONE CHAMPIONS
Football League founded 1888–89
1982–83 Liverpool
1983–84 Liverpool
1984–85 Everton
1985–86 Liverpool
1986–87 Everton
1987–88 Liverpool
1988–89 Arsenal
1989–90 Liverpool
1990–91 Arsenal
1991–92 Leeds United

SCOTTISH PREMIER DIVISION CHAMPIONS
Scottish League formed 1899–91, reformed into
three divisions 1975–76
1982–83 Dundee United
1983–84 Aberdeen
1984–85 Aberdeen
1985–86 Celtic
1986–87 Rangers
1987–88 Celtic
1988–89 Rangers
1989–90 Rangers
1990–91 Rangers
1991–92 Rangers

SCOTTISH FA CUP
first final held 1874
1983 Aberdeen
1984 Aberdeen
1985 Celtic
1986 Aberdeen
1987 St Mirren
1988 Celtic
1989 Celtic

1990 Aberdeen
1991 Motherwell
1992 Rangers

football, Australian Rules game that combines
aspects of Gaelic football, rugby, and association football; it is played between two
teams of 18 players, with an inflated oval ball.
It is unique to Australia. The game is played
on an oval pitch, 164.4 m/180 yd long and
137 m/150 yd wide, with a pair of goalposts,
6 m/19 ft high, at each end. On either side of
each pair of goalposts is a smaller post. Each
team is placed in five lines of three persons
each, and three players follow the ball all
the time. Points are scored by kicking the
ball between the goalposts, without its being
touched on the way (goal, 6 points), or by
passing the ball between a goalpast and one
of the smaller posts, or causing it to hit a post
(behind, 1 point).

VICTORIA FOOTBALL LEAGUE PREMIERSHIP
TROPHY
first contested 1897
1982 Carlton
1983 Hawthorn
1984 Essendon
1985 Essendon
1986 Hawthorn
1987 Carlton
1988 Hawthorn
1989 Hawthorn
1990 Collingwood
1991 Hawthorn

football, Gaelic kicking and catching game
played mainly in Ireland, between two teams
of 15 players each. It is played with an inflated
spherical ball, on a field 76–91 m/ 84–100 yd
long and 128–146 m/140–160 yd wide. At
each end is a set of goalposts 4.88 m/16 ft
high, with a crossbar 2.44 m/8 ft above the
ground, and a net across its lower half. Goals
are scored by kicking the ball into the net (3
points) or over the crossbar (1 point).

ALL-IRELAND CHAMPIONSHIP
first played 1887
1982 Offaly
1983 Dublin
1984 Kerry
1985 Kerry
1986 Kerry
1987 Meath
1988 Meath
1989 Cork
1990 Cork
1991 Down

golf outdoor game in which a small rubber-cored
ball is hit with a wooden- or iron-faced club. Its

object of is to sink the ball in a hole than can be anywhere between 90 m/100 yd and 457 m/500 yd away, using the least number of strokes. The faces of the clubs have varying angles and are styled for different types of shot.

Most golf courses consist of 18 holes and are approximately 5,500 m/6,000 yd in length. Each hole is made up of distinct areas: the *tee*, from where plays start at each hole; the *green*, a finely manicured area where the hole is located; the *fairway*, the grassed area between the tee and the green, not cut as finely as the green; and the *rough*, the perimeter of the fairway, which is left to grow naturally. Natural hazards such as trees, bushes, and streams make play more difficult, and there are additional artificial hazards in the form of sand-filled bunkers.

BRITISH OPEN
first held 1860
1983 Tom Watson *(USA)*
1984 Severiano Ballesteros *(Spain)*
1985 Sandy Lyle *(UK)*
1986 Greg Norman *(Australia)*
1987 Nick Faldo *(UK)*
1988 Severiano Ballesteros *(Spain)*
1989 Mark Calcavecchia *(USA)*
1990 Nick Faldo *(UK)*
1991 Ian Baker-Finch *(Australia)*
1992 Nick Faldo *(UK)*
UNITED STATES OPEN
first held 1895
1983 Larry Nelson *(USA)*
1984 Fuzzy Zoeller *(USA)*
1985 Andy North *(USA)*
1986 Ray Floyd *USA)*
1987 Scott Simpson *(USA)*
1988 Curtis Strange *(USA)*
1989 Curtis Strange *(USA)*
1990 Hale Irwin *(USA)*
1991 Payne Stewart *(USA)*
1992 Tom Kite *(USA)*
MASTERS
first held 1934
1983 Severiano Ballesteros *(Spain)*
1984 Ben Crenshaw *(USA)*
1985 Bernhard Langer *(West Germany)*
1986 Jack Nicklaus *(USA)*
1987 Larry Mize *(USA)*
1988 Sandy Lyle *(UK)*
1989 Nick Faldo *(UK)*
1990 Nick Faldo *(UK)*
1991 Ian Woosnam *(UK)*
1992 Fred Couples *(USA)*
UNITED STATES PGA
first held 1916
1982 Ray Floyd *(USA)*
1983 Hal Sutton *(USA)*
1984 Lee Trevino *(USA)*
1985 Hubert Green *(USA)*
1986 Ray Floyd *(USA)*
1987 Larry Nelson *(USA)*
1988 Jeff Sluman *(USA)*
1989 Payne Stewart *(USA)*
1990 Wayne Grady *(Australia)*

1991 John Daly *(USA)*

greyhound racing spectator sport, invented in 1919 in the USA, that has a number of greyhounds pursuing a mechanical hare around a circular or oval track. It is popular in the UK and Australia, attracting much on- and off-course betting.

GREYHOUND DERBY
UK, first held 1927
1983 I'm Slippy
1984 Whisper Wishes
1985 Pagan Swallow
1986 Tico
1987 Signal Park
1988 Hit the Lid
1989 Lartigue Note
1990 Slippy Blue
1991 Ballinderry Ash
1992 Farloe Melody

gymnastics competitive physical exercises. *Men's gymnastics* includes exercises on apparatus such as the horizontal bar, parallel bars, horse vault, pommel horse, and rings, and on an area of floor 12 m/13 yd square. *Women's gymnastics* includes work on the asymmetric bars, side horse vault, and beam, and floor exercises. Each exercise is marked out of ten by a set of judges, who look for suppleness, balance, control, and innovation. *Rhythmic gymnastics*, is choreographed to music and performed by individuals or six-woman teams, with small hand apparatus such as a ribbon, ball, or hoop.

WORLD CHAMPIONSHIP
first held 1903 for men, 1934 for women; contested every two years; Olympic champions automatically become world champions
men: individual/team
1970 Eizo Kenmotsu *(Japan)*/Japan
1974 Shigeru Kasamatsu *(Japan)*/Japan
1978 Nikolai Adrianov *(USSR)*/Japan
1979 Aleksandr Ditiatin *(USSR)*/USSR
1981 Yuri Korolev *(USSR)*/USSR
1983 Dimitri Belozertchev *(USSR)*/China
1985 Yuri Korolev *(USSR)*/USSR
1987 Dimitri Belozertchev *(USSR)*/USSR
1989 Igor Korobichensky *(USSR)*/USSR
1991 Vitaly Scherbo *(USSR)*/USSR
women: individual/team
1970 Ludmila Tourischeva *(USSR)*/USSR
1974 Ludmila Tourischeva *(USSR)*/USSR
1978 Elena Mukhina *(USSR)*/USSR
1979 Nelli Kim *(USSR)*/Romania
1981 Olga Bitcherova *(USSR)*/USSR
1983 Natalia Yurchenko *(USSR)*/USSR
1985 Elena Shoushounova *(USSR)* and Oksana Omeliantchik *(USSR)*/USSR
1987 Aurelia Dobre *(Romania)*/Romania
1989 Svetlana Boginskaya *(USSR)*/USSR

SHOULD THE OLYMPICS BE ENDED?

The original Olympic games were held in Olympia, ancient Greece, every four years during a sacred truce. They were finally abolished in AD 394. Centuries later, Baron Pierre de Coubertin, the French sports minister of the day, had the idea of resurrecting the dormant Olympic movement. He suggested that young athletes could meet in a series of sports events under the old Olympic ideal that to take part was better than to win.

Athens staged the first Games in 1896. Paris—Coubertin's home—hosted the second in 1900. St Louis, USA was next in 1904, followed by London in 1908 and Stockholm in 1912. The number of participants grew from 311 in 1896 to 2,000 by 1908 and 2,500 in 1912.

In the early days of the Olympic Games, Coubertin's ideals flourished. Until 1956 the Olympics were held either in Europe or the USA, but as transport facilities improved and finance became more readily available, they moved outside this environment to the other continents. In more recent times Melbourne, Tokyo, Mexico and Seoul have hosted the Games. However, in recent years the Olympic movement has increasingly come under fire from those who suggest, with some justification, that the Games have become too unwieldy, too costly, too political, and too open to threats of terrorism.

Critics were at pains to suggest that the Games were too vast: the number of participants, press, media, and coaches was approaching the size of the population of an English market town. Typical of the mood of doom and gloom were questions like: Why have football in the Olympics when that sport has the World Cup? Why restore tennis to the Games when Wimbledon and the other Grand Slam events are the obvious yardsticks of ability? Why have boxing when the world champions (68 at the last count) are not eligible? And do not other major backbone Olympic sports such as swimming, weightlifting, gymnastics, rowing and equestrianism have their own credible world championships?

The doubters were vindicated in the 12-year period from 1972 to 1984. The 1972 Munich Games witnessed the terrifying raid on the Olympic village, with 13 deaths. The 1976 Games left the host city, Montréal, saddled with debts which its citizens are still paying for in taxes a generation later. The Moscow Games of 1980 were a skeleton event, since most countries boycotted the event as a result of the Soviet invasion of Afghanistan. The 1984 celebration at Los Angeles became a tit-for-tat affair with the Soviets and their Iron Curtain colleagues boycotting a US-staged Games as a direct result of what had happened at Moscow.

Surrounded by this air of uncertainty, and the feeling that the Olympic movement has run headlong out of control, most sporting authorities have long since decided to hold their own world championships. When athletics, the fulcrum of the Olympic Games, staged its own inaugural World Championships in Helsinki in 1983, free from politics and boycotts, there were those ready to wrap the veil over Coubertin's old amateur ethics.

With all the sniping and anti-Olympic depth of feeling, the Games seem, surprisingly, to be weathering the storm. Seoul, the first boycott-free Olympics since 1968, was an outstanding success. It needed to be. Baron de Coubertin's beliefs in fair play and sporting competition shone through; but the era of the amateur is gone for ever. And there were other problems. Drugs—the bane of sport—had revealed the winner of one of the Blue Riband events, the men's 100 metres, as a cheat. Ben Johnson had been caught; others began to duck the Games, fearful of being caught and branded in the same way.

Despite such problems, after Seoul the youth of the world once more had a goal to aim at. Third World countries could learn from others (and beat them). Trade and commercial interests—if managed properly—could be beneficial to the hosts. But it was the view of one of Britain's former Olympic gold medallists, the 1980 800 metres champion Steve Ovett, who spoke for those who matter most—the competitors. 'You can have as many world titles as you like; you can break as many world records as you want' he said, 'but the only thing that really matters to an athlete is an Olympic gold medal—you can forget the rest.'

1991 Kim Zmeskai *(USA)*/USSR

---

handball game resembling football, but played with the hands instead of the feet. The indoor game has seven players in a team; the outdoor version (field handball) has 11. The indoor court is 40 m/43.8 yd long and 20 m/21.9 yd wide, with goals 2 m/6.6 ft high and 3 m/9.8 ft wide.

OLYMPIC GAMES
indoor event introduced 1972 for men, 1976 for women

men
1972 Yugoslavia
1976 USSR
1980 East Germany
1984 Yugoslavia
1988 USSR
women
1976 USSR
1980 USSR
1984 Yugoslavia
1988 South Korea

---

hockey or *field hockey* stick-and-ball game played by two teams of 11 players each. Its object is to strike the solid white ball, by means of a hooked stick, into the opposing team's goal. The game is played on a pitch 91.5 m/100 yd long and 54.9 m/60 yd wide, with a goal, 2.13 m/7 ft high and 3.65 m/4 yd wide, at each end. All shots at goal must be made from within a striking 'circle', a semicircle of 14.64 m/16 yd radius in front of each goal. The game is divided into two 35-minute periods.

WORLD CUP
men's tournament first held 1971 and contested every four years; women's tournament first held 1974 and contested every four years
men
1971 Pakistan
1973 Holland
1975 India
1978 Pakistan
1982 Pakistan
1986 Australia
1990 Holland
women
1974 Holland
1976 West Germany
1978 Holland
1981 West Germany
1983 Holland
1986 Holland
1990 Holland

---

horse racing the sport of racing mounted or driven horses. Two popular forms in Britain are *flat racing*, for thoroughbred horses over a flat course, and *National Hunt racing*, in which the horses have to clear obstacles. Forms of National Hunt racing include *steeplechasing*, a development of foxhunting, in which horses jump over fixed fences 0.9–1.2 m/3–4 ft high (the amateur version is point-to-point), and *hurdling*, in which the horses negotiate less taxing, and movable, fences. *Harness racing* is popular in North America. It is for standard-bred horses pulling a two-wheeled 'sulky' on which the driver sits. Leading races include The Hambletonian and Little Brown Jug.

DERBY
first held 1780; 1 mi 4 furlongs long
horse/jockey
1983 Teenoso/Lester Piggott
1984 Secreto/Christy Roche
1985 Slip Anchor/Steve Cauthen
1986 Shahrastani/Walter Swinburn
1987 Reference Point/Steve Cauthen
1988 Kahyasi/Ray Cochrane
1989 Nashwan/Willie Carson
1990 Quest for Fame/Pat Eddery
1991 Generous/Alan Munro
1992 Dr Devious/John Reid
OAKS
first held 1779; 1 mi 4 furlongs long
horse/jockey
1982 Time Charter/Billy Newnes
1983 Sun Princess/Willie Carson

1984 Circus Plume/Lester Piggott
1985 Oh So Sharp/Steve Cauthen
1986 Midway Lady/Ray Cochrane
1987 Unite/Walter Swinburn
1988 Diminuendo/Steve Cauthen
1989 Aliysa/Walter Swinburn
1990 Salsabil/Willie Carson
1991 Jet Ski Lady/Christy Roche
1,000 GUINEAS
first held 1814; 1 mi long
horse/jockey
1983 Ma Biche/Freddy Head
1984 Pebbles/Philip Robinson
1985 Oh So Sharp/Steve Cauthen
1986 Midway Lady/Ray Cochrane
1987 Miesque/Freddy Head
1988 Ravinella/Gary Moore
1989 Musical Bliss/Walter Swinburn
1990 Salsabil/Willie Carson
1991 Shadayid/Willie Carson
1992 Hatoof/Walter Swinburn
2,000 GUINEAS
first held 1809; 1 mi long
horse/jockey
1983 Lomond/Pat Eddery
1984 El Gran Senor/Pat Eddery
1985 Shadeed/Lester Piggott
1986 Dancing Brave/Greville Starkey
1987 Don't Forget Me/Willie Carson
1988 Doyoun/Walter Swinburn
1989 Nashwan/Walter Swinburn
1990 Tirol/Michael Kinane
1991 Mystiko/Michael Roberts
1992 Rodrigo de Triano/Lester Piggott
ST LEGER
the oldest English classic, first held 1776; 1 mi 6 furlongs 127 yd long
horse/jockey
1982 Touching Wood/Paul Cook
1983 Sun Princess/Willie Carson
1984 Commanche Run/Lester Piggott
1985 Oh So Sharp/Steve Cauthen
1986 Moon Madness/Pat Eddery
1987 Reference Point/Steve Cauthen
1988 Minster Son/Willie Carson
1989 Michelozza/Steve Cauthen
1990 Snurge/Richard Quinn
1991 Toulou/Pat Eddery
GRAND NATIONAL
steeplechase; first held 1847; 4 mi 4 furlongs long
horse/jockey (amateurs are shown as Mr)
1983 Corbiere/Ben De Haan
1984 Hallo Dandy/Neale Doughty
1985 Last Suspect/Hywel Davies
1986 West Tip/Richard Dunwoody
1987 Maori Venture/Steve Knight
1988 Rhyme N'Reason/Brendan Powell
1989 Little Polveir/Jimmy Frost
1990 Mr Frisk/Marcus Armytage
1991 Seagram/Nigel Hawke
1992 Party Politics/Carl Llewellyn
PRIX DE L'ARC DE TRIOMPHE
first held 1920; 2,400 m long
horse/jockey
1982 Akiyda/Yves Saint-Martin
1983 All Along/Walter Swinburn
1984 Sagace/Yves Saint-Martin

1985 Rainbow Quest/Pat Eddery
1986 Dancing Brave/Pat Eddery
1986 Lieutenant's Lark/Robbie Davis
1987 Trempolino/Pat Eddery
1988 Tony Bin/John Reid
1989 Caroll House/Michael Kinane
1990 Saumarez/Gerald Mosse
1991 Suave Dancer/Cash Asmussen

hurling or **hurley** stick-and-ball game played between two teams of 15 players each, popular in Ireland. Its object is to hit the ball, by means of a curved stick, into the opposing team's goal. If the ball passes under the goal's crossbar 3 points are scored; if it passes above the crossbar 1 point is scored.

ALL-IRELAND CHAMPIONSHIP
first held 1887
1982 Kilkenny
1983 Kilkenny
1984 Cork
1985 Offaly
1986 Cork
1987 Galway
1988 Galway
1989 Tipperary
1990 Cork
1991 Tipperary

ice hockey game played on ice between two teams of six, developed in Canada from hockey. A rubber disc (puck) is used in place of a ball. Players wear skates and protective clothing.

OLYMPIC GAMES
event introduced 1920
1952 Canada
1956 USSR
1960 United States
1964 USSR
1968 USSR
1972 USSR
1976 USSR
1980 United States
1984 USSR
1988 USSR
STANLEY CUP
end-of-season playoff tournament conducted between the top teams of the Canadian and US National Hockey League conferences
1983 New York Islanders
1984 Edmonton Oilers
1985 Edmonton Oilers
1986 Montréal Canadiens
1987 Edmonton Oilers
1988 Edmonton Oilers
1989 Calgary Flames
1990 Edmonton Oilers
1991 Pittsburgh Penguins
1992 Pittsburgh Penguins

judo form of wrestling of Japanese origin. The two combatants wear loose-fitting, belted jackets and trousers to facilitate holds, and falls are broken by a square mat; when one has established a painful hold that the other cannot break, the latter signifies surrender by slapping the ground with a free hand. Degrees of proficiency are indicated by the colour of the belt: for novices, white; after examination, brown (three degrees); and finally, black (nine degrees).

WORLD CHAMPIONSHIP
first held 1956 for men, 1980 for women; contested every two years
men: open class
1983 Angelo Parisi *(France)*
1985 Yoshimi Masaki *(Japan)*
1987 Noayo Ogawa *(Japan)*
1989 Noayo Ogawa *(Japan)*
1991 Noayo Ogawa *(Japan)*
women: open class
1984 Ingrid Berghmans *(Belgium)*
1986 Ingrid Berghmans *(Belgium)*
1987 Fengliang Gao *(China)*
1989 Estela Rodriguez *(Cuba)*
1991 Y Zhaung *(China)*

lacrosse Canadian ball game, adopted from the North American Indians, and named from a fancied resemblance of the lacrosse stick (crosse) to a bishop's crosier. Thongs across the curved end of the crosse form a pocket to carry the small rubber ball. The field is approximately 100 m/110 yd long and a minimum 55 m/60 yd wide in the men's game, which is played with ten players per side; the women's field is larger, and there are twelve players per side. The goals are just under 2 m/6 ft square, with loose nets.

WORLD CHAMPIONSHIP
first held 1967 for men, 1969 for women
men
1967 USA
1974 USA
1978 Canada
1982 USA
1986 USA
1990 USA
women
1969 UK
1974 USA
1978 Canada
1982 USA
1986 Australia
1989 USA

motorcycle racing speed contests on motor-cycles. It has many different forms: **road racing** over open roads; **circuit racing** over purpose-built tracks; **speedway** over oval-shaped dirt tracks; **motocross** (or **scrambling**) over natural terrain, incorporating hill climbs; and *trials*, also over natural terrain, but with the addition of artificial hazards. For finely tuned production machines, there exists a season-long world championship Grand Prix series with various categories for machines with engine sizes 125–500 cc.

WORLD CHAMPIONSHIP
Grand Prix racing; first held 1949
500cc class
rider/manufacturer
1982 Franco Uncini/Suzuki *(Italy)*
1983 Freddie Spencer/Honda *(USA)*
1984 Eddie Lawson/Yamaha *(USA)*
1985 Freddie Spencer/Honda *(USA)*
1986 Eddie Lawson/Yamaha *(USA)*
1987 Wayne Gardner/Honda *(Australia)*
1988 Eddie Lawson/Yamaha *(USA)*
1989 Eddie Lawson/Honda *(USA)*
1990 Wayne Rainey/Yamaha *(USA)*
1991 Wayne Rainey/Yamaha *(USA)*
ISLE OF MAN TOURIST TROPHY
road race; first held 1907
Senior TT
rider/manufacturer
1983 Rob McElnea/Suzuki *(UK)*
1984 Rob McElnea/Suzuki *(UK)*
1985 Joey Dunlop/Honda *(Ireland)*
1986 Roger Burnett/Honda *(UK)*
1987 Joey Dunlop/Honda *(Ireland)*
1988 Joey Dunlop/Honda *(Ireland)*
1989 Steve Hislop/Honda *(UK)*
1990 Carl Fogarty/Honda *(UK)*
1991 Steve Hislop/Honda *(UK)*
1992 Steve Hislop/Norton *(UK)*

WORLD CHAMPIONSHIP
speedway; first held 1936
individual
1982 Bruce Penhall *(USA)*
1983 Egon Müller *(West Germany)*
1984 Erik Gundersen *(Denmark)*
1985 Erik Gundersen *(Denmark)*
1986 Hans Nielsen *(Denmark)*
1987 Hans Nielsen *(Denmark)*
1988 Erik Gundersen *(Denmark)*
1989 Hans Nielsen *(Denmark)*
1990 Per Jonsson *(Sweden)*
1991 Jan Pedersen *(Denmark)*
pairs
event introduced 1970
1982 Dennis Sigalos and Bobby Schwartz *USA)*
1983 Kenny Carter and Peter Collins *(England)*
1984 Peter Collins and Chris Morton *England)*
1985 Erik Gundersen and Tommy Knudsen *Denmark)*
1986 Erik Gundersen and Hans Nielsen *(Denmark)*
1987 Erik Gundersen and Hans Nielsen *(Denmark)*
1988 Erik Gundersen and Hans Nielsen *(Denmark)*
1989 Erik Gundersen and Hans Nielsen *(Denmark)*
1990 Hans Nielsen and Jan Pedersen *(Denmark)*
1991 Hans Nielsen, Jan Pedersen and Tommy Knudsen *(Denmark)*
team
event introduced 1960

1982 USA
1983 Denmark
1984 Denmark
1985 Denmark
1986 Denmark
1987 Denmark
1988 Denmark
1989 England
1990 USA
1991 Denmark
WORLD CHAMPIONSHIP
motocross; first held 1957
500cc class
rider/manufacturer
1982 Brad Lackey/Suzuki *(USA)* 1983 Håkan Carlqvist/Yamaha *(Sweden)*
1984 André Malherbe/Honda *(Belgium)*
1985 Dave Thorpe/Honda *(UK)*
1986 Dave Thorpe/Honda *(UK)*
1987 Georges Jobé/Honda *(Belgium)*
1988 Eric Geboers/Honda *(Belgium)*
1989 Dave Thorpe/Honda *(UK)*
1990 Eric Geboers *(Belgium)*
1991 Georges Jobé *(Belgium)*

---

motor racing competitive racing of motor vehicles. It has forms as diverse as hill-climbing, stock-car racing, rallying, sports-car racing, and Formula One Grand Prix racing. The first organized race was from Paris to Rouen 1894.

WORLD DRIVER'S CHAMPIONSHIP
Formula One Grand Prix racing; instituted 1950
driver/manufacturer
1982 Keke Rosberg/Ferrari *(Finland)*
1983 Nelson Piquet/Ferrari *(Brazil)*
1984 Niki Lauda/McLaren *(Austria)*
1985 Alain Prost/McLaren *(France)*
1986 Alain Prost/Williams *(France)*
1987 Nelson Piquet/Williams *(Brazil)*
1988 Ayrton Senna/McLaren *(Brazil)*
1989 Alain Prost/McLaren *(France)*
1990 Ayrton Senna *(Brazil)*
1991 Ayrton Senna *(Brazil)*
LE MANS GRAND PRIX D'ENDURANCE
(Le Mans 24-Hour Race) first held 1923
1983 Vern Schuppan *(Austria)*/Al Holbert *(USA)*/Hurley Haywood *(USA)*
1984 Klaus Ludwig *(West Germany)*/Henri Pescarolo *(France)*
1985 Klaus Ludwig *(West Germany)*/'John Winter' *(West Germany)*/Paolo Barilla *(Italy)*
1986 Hans Stuck *(West Germany)*/Derek Bell *(UK)*/Al Holbert *(USA)*
1987 Hans Stuck *(West Germany)*/Derek Bell *(UK)*/Al Holbert *(USA)*
1988 Jan Lammers *(Holland)*/Johnny Dumfries *(UK)*/Andy Wallace *(UK)*
1989 Jochen Mass *(West Germany)*/Manuel Reuter *(West Germany)*/Stanley Dickens *(Sweden)*
1990 John Nielsen *(Denmark)*/Price Cobb *(USA)*/Martin Brundle *(UK)*
1991 Volker Weidler *(Germany)*/John Herbert *(UK)*/Bertrand Gachot *(Belgium)*

1992 Derek Warwick (UK)/Yannick Dalmas *(France)*/
Mark Blundell *(UK)*
INDIANAPOLIS 500
first held 1911
driver/manufacturer
1983 Tom Sneva/March—Cosworth *(USA)*
1984 Rick Mears/March—Cosworth *(USA)*
1985 Danny Sullivan/March—Cosworth *(USA)*
1986 Bobby Rahal/March—Cosworth *(USA)*
1987 Al Unser/March—Cosworth *(USA)*
1988 Rick Mears/Penske—Chevrolet *(USA)*
1989 Emerson Fittipaldi/Penske—Chevrolet *(Brazil)*.
1990 Arie Luyendyk/Lola—Chevrolet *(Holland)*
1991 Rick Mears/Penske—Chevrolet *(USA)*
1992 Al Unser, Jr/Galmer—Chevy *(USA)*
MONTE CARLO RALLY
1983 Walter Röhrl *(West Germany)*
1984 Walter Röhrl *(West Germany)*
1985 Ari Vatanen *(Finland)*
1986 Henri Toivonen *(Finland)*
1987 Mikki Biasion *(Italy)*
1988 Bruno Saby *(France)*
1989 Mikki Biasion *(Italy)*
1990 Didier Auriol *(France)*
1991 Carlos Sainz *(Spain)*
1992 Didier Auriol *(France)*
LOMBARD—RAC RALLY
(formerly RAC International Rally of Great Britain) first
held 1927
1982 Hannu Mikkola *(Finland)*
1983 Stig Blomqvist *(Sweden)*
1984 Ari Vatanen *(Finland)*
1985 Henri Toivonen *(Finland)*
1986 Timo Salonen *(Finland)*
1987 Juha Kankkunen *(Finland)*
1988 Markku Alén *(Finland)*
1989 Pentti Arikkala *(Finland)*
1990 Carlos Sainz *(Spain)*
1991 Juha Kankkunen *(Finland)*

netball a women's game, developed from basketball, played by two teams of seven players each. It is played on a hard court 30.5 m/100 ft long and 15.25 m/50 ft wide. At each end is a goal, consisting of a post 3.05 m/10 ft high, at the top of which is attached a circular hoop and net. The object of the game is to pass an inflated spherical ball through the opposing team's net. The ball is thrown from player to player; no contact is allowed between players, and no one may run with the ball.

WORLD CHAMPIONSHIP
first held 1963; contested every four years
1963 Australia
1967 New Zealand
1971 Australia
1975 Australia
1979 Australia, New Zealand, and Trinidad and
Tobago
1983 Australia
1987 New Zealand
1991 Australia

orienteering sport of cross-country running and route-finding. Competitors set off at one-minute intervals and have to find their way, using map and compass, to various checkpoints (approximately 0.8 km/0.5 mi apart), where their control cards are marked.

WORLD CHAMPIONSHIP
first held 1966
individual (men/women)
1983 Morten Berglia *(Norway)*/Annichen Kringstad
(Norway)
1985 Kari Sallinen *(Finland)*/Annichen Kringstad
(Norway)
1987 Kent Olsson *(Sweden)*/Arja Hannus *(Sweden)*
1989 Peter Thoresen *(Norway)*/Marita Skogum *(Sweden)*
1991 Jorgen Martensson *(Sweden)*/Katarina Olch
(Hungary)
relay (men/women)
1983 Norway/Sweden
1985 Norway/Sweden
1987 Norway/Norway
1989 Norway/Sweden
1991 Switzerland/Sweden

polo stick-and-ball game played between two teams of four on horseback. It is played on the largest pitch of any game, measuring up to 274m/300yd by 182 m/200yd. A small solid ball is struck with the side of a long-handled mallet through goals at each end of the pitch. A typical match lasts about an hour, and is divided into 'chukkas' of 71/2 minutes each. No pony is expected to play more than two chukkas in the course of a day.

COWDRAY PARK GOLD CUP
British Open Championship; first held 1956
1982 Southfield
1983 Falcons
1984 Southfield
1985 Maple Leafs
1986 Tramontana
1987 Tramontana
1988 Tramontana
1989 Tramontana
1990 Hildon
1991 Tramontana

rowing propulsion of a boat by oars, either by one rower with two oars (sculling) or by crews (two, four, or eight persons) with one oar each, often with a coxswain.

WORLD CHAMPIONSHIP
first held 1962 for men, 1974 for women
men—single sculls
1982 Rudiger Reiche *(East Germany)*
1983 Peter-Michael Kolbe *(West Germany)*
1985 Pertti Karppinen *(Finland)*
1986 Peter-Michael Kolbe *(West Germany)*

1987 Thomas Lange *(East Germany)*
1989 Thomas Lange *(East Germany)*
1990 Uri Janson *(USSR)*
1991 Thomas Lange *(Germany)*
women—single sculls
1982 Irina Fetisova *(USSR)*
1983 Jutta Hampe *(East Germany)*
1985 Cornelia Linse *(East Germany)*
1986 Jutta Hampe *(East Germany)*
1987 Magdalena Georgeyeva *(Bulgaria)*
1989 Elisabeta Lipa *(Romania)*
1990 Birgit Peter *(East Germany)*
1991 Silke Laumann *(Canada)*
THE BOAT RACE
first held 1829; rowed annually by crews from Oxford
and Cambridge Universities, between Putney and
Mortlake on the river Thames
1986 Cambridge
1987 Oxford
1988 Oxford
1989 Oxford
1990 Oxford
1991 Oxford
1992 Oxford
wins
Cambridge 69
Oxford 68

rugby league the professional form of rugby football founded in England 1895 as the Northern
Union when a dispute about pay caused northern clubs to break away from the Rugby
Football Union. The game is similar to rugby
union, but the number of players is reduced
from 15 to 13, and other rule changes have
made the game more open and fast-moving.

CHALLENGE CUP
first held 1897
1983 Featherstone Rovers
1984 Widnes
1985 Wigan
1986 Castleford
1987 Halifax
1988 Wigan
1989 Wigan
1990 Wigan
1991 Wigan
1992 Wigan
PREMIERSHIP TROPHY
introduced at the end of the 1974–75 season; a
knockout competition involving the top eight clubs
in the first division
1983 Widnes
1984 Hull Kingston Rovers
1985 St Helens
1986 Warrington
1987 Wigan
1988 Widnes
1989 Widnes
1990 Widnes
1991 Hull
1992 Wigan

rugby union the amateur form of rugby football
in which there are 15 players on each side. It
is played with an inflated oval ball, on a field
69 m/75 yd long and 100 m/110 yd wide. At
each end of the field is an H-shaped set of
goalposts 5.6 m/18.5 ft wide, with a crossbar
3 m/10 ft above the ground. Points are scored
by 'touching down', or grounding, the ball
beyond the goal line (try, 4 points), or by
kicking it over the goal's crossbar after a
touchdown (conversion, 2 points), from the
field during regular play (dropped goal, 3
points), or in response to a penalty against
the opposing team (3 points).

WORLD CUP
William Webb Ellis Trophy; first held 1987
1987 New Zealand
1991 Australia
INTERNATIONAL CHAMPIONSHIP
instituted 1884, now a tournament between England,
France, Ireland, Scotland, and Wales
1983 France and Ireland
1984 Scotland
1985 Ireland
1986 France
1987 France
1988 France and Wales
1989 France
1990 Scotland
1991 England
1992 England
COUNTY CHAMPIONSHIP
first held 1889
1983 Gloucestershire
1984 Gloucestershire
1985 Middlesex
1986 Warwickshire
1987 Yorkshire
1988 Lancashire
1989 Durham
1990 Lancashire
1991 Cornwall
1992 Lancashire
PILKINGTON CUP
formerly the John Player Special Cup, the English club
knockout tournament, first held 1971–72
1983 Bristol
1984 Bath
1985 Bath
1986 Bath
1987 Bath
1988 Harlequins
1989 Bath
1990 Bath
1991 Harlequins
1992 Bath
SCOTTISH CLUB CHAMPIONSHIP
first held 1974
Division One
1982 Hawick
1983 Gala
1984 Hawick
1985 Hawick
1986 Hawick
1987 Hawick

1988 Kelso
1989 Kelso
1990 Melrose
1991 Boroughmuir
1992 Melrose
SCHWEPPES WELSH CUP
the Welsh club knockout tournament, first held
1971–72
1983 Pontypool
1984 Cardiff
1985 Llanelli
1986 Cardiff
1987 Cardiff
1988 Llanelli
1989 Neath
1990 Neath
1991 Llanelli
1992 Llanelli

---

shinty (Gaelic *camanachd*) stick-and-ball game, resembling hurling, popular in the Scottish Highlands. It is played between two teams of 12 players each, on a field 132–183 m/144–200 yd long and 64–91 m/70–99 yd wide. A curved stick (caman) is used to propel a leather-covered cork-and-worsted ball into the opposing team's goal (hail).

CAMANACHD CUP
instituted 1896
1983 Kyles Athletic
1984 Kingussie
1985 Newtonmore
1986 Newtonmore
1987 Kingussie
1988 Kingussie
1989 Kingussie
1990 Skye
1991 Kingussie
1992 Fort William

---

skating self-propulsion on ice by means of bladed skates, or on other surfaces by skates with small rollers. The chief competitive ice-skating events are figure skating, for singles or pairs, ice-dancing, and simple speed skating.

WORLD CHAMPIONSHIP
ice-skating; first held 1896
men
1988 Brian Boitano *(USA)*
1989 Kurt Browning *(Canada)*
1990 Kurt Browning *(Canada)*
1991 Kurt Browning *(Canada)*
1992 Viktor Petrenko *(USSR)*
women
1988 Katarina Witt *(East Germany)*
1989 Midoria Ito *(Japan)*
1990 Jill Trenary *(USA)*
1991 Kristi Yamaguchi *(USA)*
1992 Kristi Yamaguchi *(USA)*
pairs
1988 Oleg Vasilyev and Yelena Valova *(USSR)*

1989 Sergey Grinkov and Ekaterina Gordeeva *(USSR)*
1990 Sergey Grinkov and Ekaterina Gordeeva *(USSR)*
1991 Artur Dmitriev and Natalya Mishkuteniok *(USSR)*
1992 Artur Dmitriev and Natalya Mishkuteniok *(USSR)*
ice dance
1988 Andrei Bukin and Natalia Bestemianova *(USSR)*
1989 Sergey Ponomarenko and Marina Klimova *(USSR)*
1990 Sergey Ponomarenko and Marina Klimova *(USSR)*
1991 Paul Duchesnay and Isabelle Duchesnay *(France)*
1992 Sergey Ponomarenko and Marina Klimova *(USSR)*

---

skiing self-propulsion on snow by means of elongated runners (skis) for the feet, slightly bent upward at the tip. Events include downhill; slalom, in which a series of turns between flags have to be negotiated; cross-country racing; and ski jumping, when jumps of over 150 m/490 ft are achieved from ramps up to 90 m/295 ft high. Speed-skiing uses skis approximately 1/3 longer and wider than normal, with which speeds of up to 200 kph/125 mph have been recorded.

OLYMPIC GAMES
events introduced 1936
men –downhill
1976 Franz Klammer *(Austria)*
1980 Leonhard Stock *(Austria)*
1984 William Johnson *(USA)*
1988 Pirmin Zurbriggen *(Switzerland)*
1992 Gustavo Ortleib *(Austria)*
men–slalom
1976 Piero Gros *(Italy)*
1980 Ingemar Stenmark *(Sweden)*
1984 Phil Mahre *(USA)*
1988 Alberto Tomba *(Italy)*
1992 Christian Jagge *(Norway)*
women—downhill
1976 Rosi Mittermaier *(West Germany)*
1980 Annemarie Moser-Proll *(Austria)*
1984 Michela Figini *(Switzerland)*
1988 Marina Kiehl *(Germany)*
1992 Kerrin Lee-Gartner *(Canada)*
women—slalom
1976 Rosi Mittermaier *(West Germany)*
1980 Hanni Wenzel *(Liechtenstein)*
1984 Paoletta Magoni *(Italy)*
1988 Vreni Schneider *(Switzerland)*
1992 Petra Krönberger *(Austria)*
ALPINE WORLD CUP
first held 1967
men—overall
1983 Phil Mahre *(USA)*
1984 Pirmin Zurbriggen *(Switzerland)*
1985 Marc Girardelli *(Luxembourg)*
1986 Marc Girardelli *(Luxembourg)*
1987 Pirmin Zurbriggen *(Switzerland)*
1988 Pirmin Zurbriggen *(Switzerland)*
1989 Marc Girardelli *(Luxembourg)*
1990 Pirmin Zurbriggen *(Switzerland)*
1991 Marc Girardelli *(Luxembourg)*

1992 Paul Accola *(Switzerland)*
women—overall
1983 Tamara McKinney *(USA)*
1984 Erika Hess *(Switzerland)*
1985 Michela Figini *(Switzerland)*
1986 Maria Walliser *(Switzerland)*
1987 Maria Walliser *(Switzerland)*
1988 Michela Figini *(Switzerland)*
1989 Vreni Schneider *(Switzerland)*
1990 Petra Krönberger *(Austria)*
1991 Petra Krönberger *(Austria)*
1992 Petra Kro4nberger *(Austria)*

1976 Canada, New Zealand, and USA
1980 USA
1984 New Zealand
1988 USA
1992 Canada
women
1965 Australia
1970 Japan
1974 USA
1978 USA
1982 New Zealand
1986 USA
1990 USA

snooker indoor game derived from billiards. It is played with 22 balls: 15 red, one each of yellow, green, brown, blue, pink, and black, and one white cueball. Red balls are worth one point when sunk, while the coloured balls have ascending values from two points for the yellow to seven points for the black.

WORLD PROFESSIONAL CHAMPIONSHIP
first held 1927
1983 Steve Davis *(England)*
1984 Steve Davis *(England)*
1985 Dennis Taylor *(Northern Ireland)*
1986 Joe Johnson *(England)*
1987 Steve Davis *(England)*
1988 Steve Davis *(England)*
1989 Steve Davis *(England)*
1990 Stephen Hendry *(Scotland)*
1991 John Parrott *(England)*
1992 Stephen Hendry *(Scotland)*
WORLD AMATEUR CHAMPIONSHIP
first held 1963
1978 Cliff Wilson *(Wales)*
1980 Jimmy White *(England)*
1982 Terry Parsons *(Wales)*
1984 O B Agrawal *(India)*
1985 Paul Mifsud *(Malta)*
1986 Paul Mifsud *(Malta)*
1987 Darren Morgan *(Wales)*
1988 James Wattana *(Thailand)*
1989 Ken Doherty *(Ireland)*
1990 Anthony O'Connor *(Ireland)*
1991 Noppadon Noppachom *(Thailand)*

softball a form of baseball played with similar equipment. The two main differences are the distances between the bases (18.29 m/60 ft) and that the ball is pitched underhand in softball. There are two forms of the game, *fast pitch* and *slow pitch*; in the latter the ball must be delivered to home plate in an arc that must not be less than 2.4 m/8 ft at its height.

WORLD CHAMPIONSHIP
fast pitch; introduced 1965 for women, 1966 for men; now contested every four years
men
1966 USA
1968 USA
1972 Canada

squash or **squash rackets** racket-and-ball game usually played by two people on an enclosed court. Each player hits the small rubber ball against the front wall of the court alternately. The object is to win points by playing shots the opponent cannot return to the wall. There are two forms of the game: the American form, which is played in North and some South American countries, and the English, which is played mainly in Europe, Pakistan, and Commonwealth countries such as Australia and New Zealand. In English singles, the court is 6.4 m/21 ft wide and 10 m/32 ft long. Doubles squash is played on a larger court.

WORLD OPEN CHAMPIONSHIP
first held 1975
men
1982 Jahangir Khan *(Pakistan)*
1983 Jahangir Khan *(Pakistan)*
1984 Jahangir Khan *(Pakistan)*
1985 Jahangir Khan *(Pakistan*
1986 Ross Norman *(New Zealand)*
1987 Jansher Khan *(Pakistan)*
1988 Jahangir Khan *(Pakistan)*
1989 Jansher Khan *(Pakistan)*
1990 Jansher Khan *(Pakistan)*
1991 Rodney Martin *(Australia)*
women
1981 Rhonda Thorne *(Australia)*
1983 Vicky Cardwell *(Australia)*
1985 Sue Devoy *(New Zealand)*
1987 Sue Devoy *(New Zealand)*
1989 Martine Le Moignan *(UK)*
1990 Sue Devoy *(New Zealand)*
1991 Sue Devoy *(New Zealand)*

surfing riding on the crest of large waves while standing on a narrow, keeled surfboard, usually of a light synthetic material such as fibreglass, about 1.8 m/6 ft long (or 2.4–7 m/8–9 ft known as the Malibu), as first developed in Hawaii and Australia.

WORLD PROFESSIONAL CHAMPIONSHIP
first held 1970
men
1986 Tommy Curren *(USA)*
1987 Damien Hardman *(Australia)*

1988 Barton Lynch *(Australia)*
1989 Martin Potter *(UK)*
1990 Tommy Curren *(USA)*
1991 Damien Hardman *(Australia)*
women
1986 Frieda Zamba *(USA)*
1987 Wendy Botha *(South Africa)*
1988 Frieda Zamba *(USA)*
1989 Wendy Botha *(South Africa)*
1990 Pam Burridge *(Australia)*
1991 Wendy Botha *(South Africa)*
WORLD AMATEUR CHAMPIONSHIP
first held 1964
men
1982 Tommy Curren *(USA)*
1984 Scott Farnsworth *(USA)*
1986 Mark Sainsbury *(Australia)*
1988 Fabio Gouveia *(Brazil)*
1990 Heifara Tahutini *(Tahiti)*
women
1982 Jenny Gill *(Australia)*
1984 Janice Aragon *(USA)*
1986 Connie Nixon *(Australia)*
1988 Pauline Menczer *(Australia)*
1990 Kathy Newman *(Australia)*

---

swimming self-propulsion of the body through water. There are four strokes in competitive swimming: *freestyle* (or *front crawl*), the fastest stroke; *breaststroke*, the slowest stroke; *backstroke*; and *butterfly*, the newest stroke, developed in the USA from breaststroke. Swimmers enter the water with a 'racing plunge' (a form of dive) with the exception of the backstroke, when competitors start in the water. Distances of races vary between 50 m/54.7 yd and 1,500 m/1,641 yd. Olympic-size pools are 50 m/55 yd long and have eight lanes. *Synchronized swimming* is a form of 'ballet' performed in and under water.

OLYMPIC GAMES
event introduced 1896 for men, 1912 for women
most gold medals
9 Mark Spitz *(USA)* 1968, 1972
6 Kirstin Otto *(East Germany)* 1988
5 Charles Daniels *(USA)* 1904, 1908
5 Johnny Weissmuller *(USA)* 1924, 1928
5 Don Schollander *(USA)* 1964, 1968
5 Matt Bondi *(USA)* 1984, 1988
4 Henry Taylor *(UK)* 1906, 1908
4 Murray Rose *(Australia)* 1956, 1960
4 Dawn Fraser *(Australia)* 1956, 1960, 1964
4 Roland Matthes *(East Germany)* 1968, 1972
4 John Naber *(USA)* 1976
4 Kornelia Ender *(East Germany)* 1976
4 Vladimir Salnikov *(USSR)* 1980, 1988
most medals
11 Mark Spitz *(USA)* 1968, 1972
8 Charles Daniels *(USA)* 1904, 1908
8 Roland Matthes *(East Germany)* 1968, 1972
8 Henry Taylor *(UK)* 1906, 1908, 1912, 1920
8 Dawn Fraser *(Australia)* 1956, 1960, 1964
8 Kornelia Ender *(East Germany)* 1972, 1976
8 Shirley Babashoff *(USA)* 1972, 1976

WORLD CHAMPIONSHIP
introduced 1973, next held 1975, 1978, and every four years since
most gold medals
8 Kornelia Ender *(East Germany)* 1973, 1975
7 Kristin Otto *(East Germany)* 1982, 1986
6 Jim Montgomery *(USA)* 1973, 1975
5 Rowdy Gaines *(USA)* 1978, 1982
most medals
10 Kornelia Ender *(East Germany)* 1973, 1975
9 Kristin Otto *(East Germany)* 1982, 1986
9 Mary Meagher *(USA)* 1978, 1982
8 Rowdy Gaines *(USA)* 1978, 1982

---

table tennis or *ping pong* indoor game played on a rectangular table by two or four players. Play takes place on a table measuring 2.74 m/9 ft long by 1.52 m/5 ft wide. Across the middle is a 15.25 cm/6 in high net over which the ball must be hit. The players use small, wooden paddles covered in sponge or rubber. Points are scored by forcing the opponent(s) into an error. The first to score 21 wins the game. A match may consist of three or five games. Volleying is not allowed. In doubles play, the players must hit the ball in strict rotation.

WORLD CHAMPIONSHIP
first held 1926, now contested every two years
men's team
1983 China
1985 China
1987 China
1989 Sweden
1991 Sweden
women's team
1983 China
1985 China
1987 China
1989 China
1991 Korea
men's singles
1983 Guo Yue-Hua *(China)*
1985 Jiang Jialiang *(China)*
1987 Jiang Jialiang *(China)*
1989 Jan-Ove Waldner *(Sweden)*
1991 Jorgen Persson *(Sweden)*
women's singles
1983 Cao Yan-Hua *(China)*
1985 Cao Yan-Hua *(China)*
1987 He Zhili *(China)*
1989 Qiuo Hong *(China)*
1991 Deng Yalping *(China)*

---

tennis, lawn racket-and-ball game for two or four players, invented towards the end of the 19th century. It may be played on a grass, wood, shale, clay, or concrete surface. The object of the game is to strike the ball into the prescribed area of the court, with oval-headed rackets (strung with gut or nylon), in such a way that it cannot be returned. The game is won by those first winning four points (called 15, 30, 40, game), unless both sides reach

40 (deuce), when two consecutive points are needed to win. A set is won by winning six games with a margin of two over opponents, though a tie-break system operates, that is at six games to each side (or in some cases eight) except in the final set.

The Grand Slam events are the Wimbledon Championship, the United States Open, French Open, and Australian Open.

WIMBLEDON CHAMPIONSHIPS
All-England Lawn Tennis Club championships; first held 1877; grass surface
men's singles
1983 John McEnroe *(USA)*
1984 John McEnroe *(USA)*
1985 Boris Becker *(West Germany)*
1986 Boris Becker *(West Germany)*
1987 Pat Cash *(Australia)*
1988 Stefan Edberg *(Sweden)*
1989 Boris Becker *(West Germany)*
1990 Stefan Edberg *(Sweden)*
1991 Michael Stich *(Germany)*
1992 Andre Agassi *(USA)*
women's singles
1983 Martina Navratilova *(USA)*
1984 Martina Navratilova *(USA)*
1985 Martina Navratilova *(USA)*
1986 Martina Navratilova *(USA)*
1987 Martina Navratilova *(USA)*
1988 Steffi Graf *(West Germany)*
1989 Steffi Graf *(West Germany)*
1990 Martina Navratilova *(USA)*
1991 Steffi Graf *(Germany)*
1992 Steffi Graf *(Germany)*
UNITED STATES OPEN
first held 1881 as the United States Championship; became the United States Open 1968; concrete surface
men's singles
1983 Jimmy Connors *(USA)*
1984 John McEnroe *(USA)*
1985 Ivan Lendl *(Czechoslovakia)*
1986 Ivan Lendl *(Czechoslovakia)*
1987 Ivan Lendl *(Czechoslovakia)*
1988 Mats Wilander *(Sweden)*
1989 Boris Becker *(West Germany)*
1990 Pete Sampras *(USA)*
1991 Stefan Edberg *(Sweden)*
1992 Stefan Edberg *(Sweden)*
women's singles
1983 Martina Navratilova *(USA)*
1984 Martina Navratilova *(USA)*
1985 Hana Mandlikova *(Czechoslovakia)*
1986 Martina Navratilova *(USA)*
1987 Martina Navratilova *(USA)*
1988 Steffi Graf *(West Germany)*
1989 Steffi Graf *(West Germany)*
1990 Gabriela Sabatini *(Argentina)*
1991 Monica Seles *(Yugoslavia)*
1992 Monica Seles *(Yugoslavia)*
FRENCH OPEN
first held 1891 (a national championship until 1924); clay surface
men's singles
1983 Yannick Noah *(France)*
1984 Ivan Lendl *(Czechoslovakia)*
1985 Mats Wilander *(Sweden)*
1986 Ivan Lendl *(Czechoslovakia)*
1987 Ivan Lendl *(Czechoslovakia)*
1988 Mats Wilander *(Sweden)*
1989 Michael Craig *(USA)*
1990 Andres Gomez *(Ecuador)*
1991 Jim Courier *(USA)*
1992 Jim Courier *(USA)*
women's singles
1983 Chris Evert-Lloyd *(USA)*
1984 Martina Navratilova *(USA)*
1985 Chris Evert-Lloyd *(USA)*
1986 Chris Evert-Lloyd *(USA)*
1987 Steffi Graf *(West Germany)*
1988 Steffi Graf *(West Germany)*
1989 Arantxa Sanchez Vicario *(Spain)*
1990 Monica Seles *(Yugoslavia)*
1991 Monica Seles *(Yugoslavia)*
1992 Monica Seles *(Yugoslavia)*
AUSTRALIAN OPEN
first held 1905 (a national championship until 1925); clay surface
men's singles
1983 Mats Wilander *(Sweden)*
1984 Mats Wilander *(Sweden)*
1985 Stefan Edberg *(Sweden)*
1987 Stefan Edberg *(Sweden)*
1988 Mats Wilander *(Sweden)*
1989 Ivan Lendl *(Czechoslovakia)*
1990 Ivan Lendl *(Czechoslovakia)*
1991 Boris Becker *(Germany)*
1992 Jim Courier *(USA)*
women's singles
1983 Martina Navratilova *(USA)*
1984 Chris Evert-Lloyd *(USA)*
1985 Martina Navratilova *(USA)*
1987 Hana Mandlikova *(Czechoslovakia*
1988 Steffi Graf *(West Germany)*
1989 Steffi Graf *(West Germany)*
1990 Steffi Graf *(West Germany)*
1991 Monica Seles *(Yugoslavia)*
1992 Monica Seles *(Yugoslavia)*
DAVIS CUP
first contested 1900
1982 USA
1983 Australia
1984 Sweden
1985 Sweden
1986 Australia
1987 Sweden
1988 West Germany
1989 West Germany
1990 USA
1991 France

---

trampolining gymnastics performed on a sprung canvas sheet that allows the performer to reach great heights before landing again. Marks are gained for carrying out difficult manoeuvres. Synchronized trampolining and tumbling are also popular forms of the sport.

WORLD CHAMPIONSHIP
first held 1964

men
1974 Richard Tisson *(France)*
1976 Richard Tisson *(France)* and Evgeni Janes *(USSR)*
1978 Evgeni Janes *(USSR)*
1980 Stewart Matthews *(UK)*
1982 Carl Furrer *(UK)*
1984 Lionel Pioline *(France)*
1986 Lionel Pioline *(France)*
1988 Vadim Krasonchapka *(USSR)*
1990 Alexandr Moskalenko *(USSR)*
1991 Dimitri Polyarush *(USSR)*
women
1974 Alexandra Nicholson *(USA)*
1976 Svetlana Levina *(USSR)*
1978 Tatyana Anisimova *(USSR)*
1980 Ruth Keller *(Switzerland)*
1982 Ruth Keller *(Switzerland)*
1984 Sue Shotton *(UK)*
1986 Tatyana Lushina *(USSR)*
1988 Khoperla Rusudum *(USSR)*
1990 Elena Merkulova *(USSR)*
1991 Andrea Holmes *(UK)*

volleyball an indoor and outdoor game played between two teams of six players each. The court measures 18 m/59 ft by 9 m/29 ft 6 in, and has a raised net drawn across its centre. Players hit an inflated spherical ball over the net with their hands or arms, the aim being to ground the ball in the opponents' court. The ball may not be hit more than three times on one team's side of the net.

WORLD CHAMPIONSHIP
first held 1949 for men, 1952 for women
men
1972 Japan
1974 Poland
1976 Poland
1978 USSR
1980 USSR
1982 USSR
1984 USA
1986 USA
1988 USA
1990 Italy
women
1972 USSR
1974 Japan
1976 Japan
1978 Cuba
1980 USSR
1982 China
1984 China
1986 USA
1988 USSR
1990 USSR

water polo (formerly *football-in-water*) sport played in a swimming pool, between two teams of seven players each. An inflated ball is passed among the players, who must swim around the pool without touching the bottom. Goals are scored when the ball is thrown past the opposing team's goalkeeper and into a net.

WORLD CHAMPIONSHIP
first held 1973; contested every four years since 1978
1973 Hungary
1975 USSR
1978 Italy
1982 USSR
1986 Yugoslavia
1990/91 Yugoslavia

water skiing sport in which a person is towed across water on a ski or skis, by means of a rope (23 m/75 ft long) attached to a speedboat. Competitions are held for overall performances, slalom, tricks, and jumping.

WORLD CHAMPIONSHIP
first held 1949; contested every two years
men—overall
1973 George Athans *(Canada)*
1975 Carlos Suarez *(Venezuela)*
1977 Mike Hazelwood *(UK)*
1979 Joel McClintock *(Canada)*
1981 Sammy Duvall *(USA)*
1983 Sammy Duvall *(USA)*
1985 Sammy Duvall *(USA)*
1987 Sammy Duvall *(USA)*
1989 Patrice Martin *(France)*
1991 Patrice Mastin *(France)*
women—overall
1973 Lisa St John *(USA)*
1975 Liz Allan-Shetter *(USA)*
1977 Cindy Todd *(USA)*
1979 Cindy Todd *(USA)*
1981 Karin Roberge *(USA)*
1983 Ana-Maria Carrasco *(Venezuela)*
1985 Karen Neville *(Australia)*
1987 Deena Brush *(USA)*
1989 Deena Mapple (née Brush) *(USA)*
1991 Karen Neville *(Australia)*

weightlifting the sport of lifting the heaviest possible weight above one's head to the satisfaction of judges. In international competitions there are two standard lifts: snatch and jerk. In the **snatch**, the bar and weights are lifted from the floor to a position with the arms outstretched and above the head in one continuous movement. The arms must be locked for two seconds for the lift to be good. The **jerk** is a two-movement lift: from the floor to the chest, and from the chest to the outstretched position. The aggregate weight of the two lifts counts.

OLYMPIC GAMES
24th Olympics 1988
52 kg Sevdalin Marinov *(Bulgaria)*
56 kg Oxen Mirzoian *(USSR)*
60 kg Naim Suleymanoglu *(Turkey)*

67.5 kg Joachim Kunz *(East Germany)*
75 kg Borislav Guidikov *(Bulgaria)*
82.5 kg Israil Arsanmakov *(USSR)*
90 kg Anatoliy Khrapati *(USSR)*
100 kg Pavel Kouznetsov *(USSR)*
110 kg Yuriy Zacharovich *(USSR)*
110+ kg Aleksandr Kurlovich *(USSR)*

wrestling fighting without the use of fists. The two main modern international styles are **Greco-Roman**, concentrating on above-waist holds, and *freestyle*, which allows the legs to be used to hold or trip; in both the aim is to throw the opponent to the ground. Competitors are categorized according to weight: there are ten weight divisions in each style of wrestling, ranging from light-flyweight (under 48 kg) to super-heavyweight (over 100 kg). The professional form of the sport has become popular, partly due to television coverage, but is regarded by purists as an extension of show-business. Many countries have their own forms of wrestling. **Glima** is unique to Iceland; **kushti** is the national style practised in Iran; **schwingen** has been practised in Switzerland for hundreds of years; and **sumo** is the national sport of Japan.

WORLD CHAMPIONSHIP
in Olympic years Olympic champions automatically become world champions
Greco-Roman
first held 1921
super-heavyweight
1982 Nikolai Dinev *(Bulgaria)*
1983 Yevgeniy Artioshin *(USSR)*
1984 Jeffrey Blatnick *(USA)*
1985 Igor Rostozotskiy *(USSR)*
1986 Tomas Johansson *(Sweden)*
1987 Igor Rostozotskiy *(USSR)*
1988 Aleksandr Karelin *(USSR)*
1989 Aleksandr Karelin *(USSR)*
1990 Aleksandr Karelin *(USSR)*
1991 Aleksandr Karelin *(USSR)*
freestyle
first held 1951
super-heavyweight
1982 Salman Khasimikov *(USSR)*
1983 Salman Khasimikov *(USSR)*
1984 Bruce Baumgartner *(USA)*
1985 David Gobedzhishvilli *(USSR)*
1986 Bruce Baumgartner *(USA)*
1987 Aslan Khadartzev *(USSR)*
1988 David Gobedzhishvilli *(USSR)*
1989 Ali Reza Soleimani *(Iran)*
1990 David Gobedzhishvilli *(USSR)*
1991 Andreas Schroder *(Germany)*

yachting racing a small, light sailing vessel. At the Olympic Games, seven categories exist: Soling, Flying Dutchman, Star, Finn, Tornado, 470, and Windglider (or windsurfing/boardsailing), which was introduced at the 1984 Los Angeles games. The Finn and Windglider are solo events; the Soling class is for three-person crews; all other classes are for crews of two.

AMERICA'S CUP
first held 1870; now contested approximately every four years; all winners have been US boats, except for
Australia II 1983
1962 *Weatherly*
1964 *Constellation*
1967 *Intrepid*
1970 *Intrepid*
1974 *Courageous*
1977 *Courageous*
1980 *Freedom*
1983 *Australia II*
1987 *Stars and Stripes*
1988 *Stars and Stripes*
ADMIRAL'S CUP
first held 1957; national teams consisting of three boats compete over three inshore courses and two offshore courses; contested every two years
1973 West Germany
1975 UK
1977 UK
1979 Australia
1981 UK
1983 West Germany
1985 West Germany
1987 New Zealand
1989 UK
1991 France

BIOGRAPHIES

Agostini Giacomo 1943– . Italian motorcyclist who won a record 122 grand prix and 15 world titles. His world titles were at 350cc and 500cc and he was five times a dual champion. In addition he was ten times winner of the Isle of Man Tourist Trophy (TT) races; a figure only bettered by Mike Hailwood and Joey Dunlop.

CAREER HIGHLIGHTS
world titles
350cc: 1968–73 (MV Agusta), 1974 (Yamaha)
500cc: 1966–72 (MV Agusta), 1975 (Yamaha)
Isle of Man TT wins
Junior TT: 1966, 1968–70, 1972 (all MV Agusta)
Senior TT: 1968–72 (all MV Agusta)

Alexeev Vasiliy 1942– . Soviet weightlifter who broke 80 world records 1970–77, a record for any sport. He was Olympic super-heavyweight champion twice, world champion seven times, and European champion on eight occasions. At one time the most decorated man in the USSR, he was regarded as the strongest man in the world. He carried the Soviet flag at the 1980 Moscow Olympics opening ceremony, but retired shortly afterwards.

CAREER HIGHLIGHTS
Olympic champion: 1972, 1976
world champion: 1970–71, 1973–75, 1977
European champion: 1970–78

Ali Muhammad. Adopted name of Cassius Marcellus Clay, Jr 1942– . US boxer. Olympic light-heavyweight champion 1960, he went on to become world professional heavyweight champion 1964, and was the only man to regain the title twice. Ali had his title stripped from him 1967 for refusing to be drafted into the US Army. He was known for his fast footwork and extrovert nature.

CAREER HIGHLIGHTS
fights: 61
wins: 56 (37 knockouts)
draws: 0
defeats: 5
first professional fight: 29 Oct 1960 v. Tunny Hunsaker (*USA*)
last professional fight: 11 Dec 1981 v. Trevor Berbick (*Canada*)

Aouita Said 1960– . Moroccan runner. Outstanding at middle and long distances, he won the 1984 Olympic and 1987 World Championship 5,000-metres title. In 1985 he held world records at both 1,500 and 5,000 metres, the first person for 30 years to hold both. He has since broken the 2 miles, 3,000 metres, and 2,000 metres world records.

CAREER HIGHLIGHTS
Olympic Games
1984: gold 5,000 metres
world records
1985: 1,500 metres, 5,000 metres
1987: 2,000 metres, 3,000 metres, 5,000 metres
1989: 3,000 metres
world championships
1987: gold 5,000 metres
world best
2 miles: 1987

Ashe Arthur Robert, Jr 1943– . US tennis player and coach, renowned for his exceptionally strong serve. He won the US national men's singles title at Forest Hills and the first US Open 1968. He won the Australian men's title 1970 and Wimbledon 1975. Cardiac problems ended his playing career 1979, but he continued his involvement with the sport as captain of the US Davis Cup team.

Ballesteros Seve(riano) 1957– . Spanish golfer who came to prominence 1976 and has won several leading tournaments in the USA, including the Masters Tournament 1980 and 1983. He has also won the British Open three times: in 1979, 1984, and 1988.

CAREER HIGHLIGHTS
British Open: 1979, 1984, 1988
Ryder Cup (individual): 1979, 1983, 1985, 1987, 1989, 1991
Ryder Cup (team): 1985,1987, tie 1989
US PGA Championship: 1983, 1991
US Masters: 1980, 1983
World Match-Play Championship: 1981–82, 1984–85, 1991

Bannister Roger Gilbert 1929– . English track and field athlete, the first person to run a mile in under four minutes. He achieved this feat at Oxford, England, on 6 May 1954 in a time of 3 min 59.4 sec. Bannister also broke the four-minute barrier at the 1954 Commonwealth Games in Vancouver, Canada.

Beckenbauer Franz 1945– . German football player who made a record 103 appearances for his country. He captained West Germany to the 1972 European Championship and the 1974 World Cup, and was twice European Footballer of the Year. After retiring as a player, he became West Germany's team manager, taking them to the runners-up spot in the 1986 World Cup and victory in the 1990 World Cup. He is the only person both to captain and manage a winning World Cup team.

CAREER HIGHLIGHTS
as player
World Cup: 1974
European Championship: 1972
European Cup: 1974–76
European Footballer of the Year: 1972, 1976
as manager
World Cup: 1990

Becker Boris 1967– . German tennis player. In 1985 he became the youngest winner of a singles title at Wimbledon at the age of 17. He has won the title three times and helped West Germany to win the Davis Cup 1988 and 1989. He also won the US Open 1989.

CAREER HIGHLIGHTS
Wimbledon
singles: 1985, 1986, 1989
US Open
singles: 1989
Australian Open
singles: 1991
Grand Prix Masters
1988

Best George 1946– . Irish footballer. He won two League championship medals and was a member of the Manchester United side that won the European Cup in 1968. Best joined Manchester United as a youth and made his debut at 17; seven months later he made his international debut for Northern Ireland. Trouble with managers, fellow players, and the media led to his early retirement.

CAREER HIGHLIGHTS
Football League
appearances: 411
goals: 147
League championship: 1965, 1967
Footballer of the Year: 1968
internationals
appearances: 37
goals: 9
European Cup: 1968
European Footballer of the Year: 1968

Blanco Serge 1958– . French rugby union player, renowned for his pace, skill, and ingenuity on the field. Blanco played a world-record 93 internationals before his retirement in 1991, scoring 38 tries of which 34 were from full back—another world record. He was instrumental in France's Grand Slam wins of 1981 and 1987.

Borg Bjorn 1956– . Swedish tennis player who won the men's singles title at Wimbledon five times 1976–80, a record since the abolition of the challenge system 1922. He also won six French Open singles titles. In 1990 Borg announced plans to return to professional tennis, but he enjoyed little competitive success 1991–92.

CAREER HIGHLIGHTS
Wimbledon
singles: 1976–80
French Open
singles: 1974–75, 1978–81
Davis Cup
1975 (member of winning Sweden team)
Grand Prix Masters
1980–81
WCT Champion
1976
ITF World Champion
1978–80

Botham Ian (Terrence) 1955– : English cricketer whose test record places him among the world's greatest all-rounders. He has played county cricket for Somerset, Worcestershire, and Durham as well as playing in Australia. He played for England 1977-89 and returned to the England side 1991. Botham has raised money for leukaemia research with much-publicized walks from John o'Groats to Land's End in the UK, and across the Alps in the style of Hannibal.

CAREER HIGHLIGHTS
all first-class matches (to start of 1992 season)
runs: 18,254
average: 34.44
best: 228 (Somerset v. Gloucestershire 1980)
wickets: 1,128
average: 26.70
best: 8 for 34 (England v. Pakistan 1978)
test cricket
appearances: 99
runs: 5,176
average: 34.27
best: 208 (England v. India 1982)
wickets: 380
average: 28.26
best: 8 for 34 (England v. Pakistan 1978)
catches: 117

Boycott Geoffrey 1940– . English cricketer born in Yorkshire, England's most prolific run-maker with 8,114 runs in test cricket until overtaken by David Gower in 1992. He played in 108 test matches and in 1981 overtook Gary Sobers' world record total of test runs. Twice, in 1971 and 1979, his average was over 100 runs in an English season. Boycott was banned as a test player in 1982 for taking part in matches against South Africa. He was released by Yorkshire after a dispute in 1986 and has not played first-class cricket since.

CAREER HIGHLIGHTS
all first-class matches
runs: 48,426
average: 56.83
best: 261 not out (MCC v. WIBC President's XI 1973–74)
test cricket
runs: 8,114
average: 47.72
best: 246 not out (England v. India 1967)

Bradman Don (Donald George) 1908– . Australian test cricketer with the highest average in test history. From 52 test matches he averaged 99.94 runs per innings. He only needed four runs from his final test innings to average 100 but was dismissed at second ball. Bradman played for Australia for 20 years and was captain 1936–48. He twice scored triple centuries against England and in 1930 scored 452 not out for New South Wales against Queensland, the highest first-class innings until 1959.

CAREER HIGHLIGHTS
all first-class matches
runs: 28,067
average: 95.14
best: 452 not out (New South Wales v. Queensland 1930)
test cricket
runs: 6,996

average: 99.94
best: 334 (Australia v. England 1930)

Bristow Eric 1957– . English darts player nicknamed 'the Crafty Cockney'. He has won all the game's major titles, including the world professional title a record five times between 1980 and 1986.

CAREER HIGHLIGHTS
world professional champion: 1980–81, 1984–86
World Masters: 1977, 1979, 1981, 1983–84
World Cup (individual): 1983, 1985, 1987, 1989
World Cup (team): 1979, 1981, 1983, 1985, 1987, 1989
British Open: 1978, 1981, 1983, 1985–86
News of the World: 1983–84
World Pairs: 1987 (with Peter Locke)

Bryant David 1931– . English flat-green (lawn) bowls player. He has won every honour the game has offered, including four outdoor world titles (three singles and one triples) 1966–88 and three indoor titles 1979–81.

CAREER HIGHLIGHTS
world outdoor champion: 1966, 1980, 1988
world indoor champion: 1979–81
Commonwealth Games
singles: 1962, 1970, 1974, 1978
fours: 1962
English Bowling Association titles
singles: 1960, 1966, 1971–73, 1975
pairs: 1965, 1969, 1974
triples: 1966, 1977
fours: 1957, 1968–69, 1971

Budge Donald 1915– . US tennis player. He was the first to perform the Grand Slam when he won the Wimbledon, French, US, and Australian championships all in 1938. He won 14 Grand Slam events in all, including Wimbledon singles twice.

CAREER HIGHLIGHTS
Wimbledon
singles: 1937–38
doubles: 1937–38
mixed: 1937–38
US Open
singles: 1937–38
doubles: 1936, 1938
mixed: 1937–38
French Open
singles: 1938
Australian Open
singles: 1938

Campese David– . 1962 Australian rugby union player, one of the outstanding entertainers of

the game. He holds the world record for the most tries scored in international rugby (46 international tries by 1 May 1992). Australia's most capped player, he was a key element in their 1991 World Cup victory.

Carson Willie (William Hunter) 1942– . Scottish jockey who has ridden three Epsom Derby winners as well as the winners of most major races worldwide. The top flat-race jockey on five occasions, Carson has had over 3,000 wins in Britain. For many years he has ridden for the royal trainer, Major Dick Hern.

CAREER HIGHLIGHTS
Champion Jockey
1972–73, 1978, 1980, 1983
Derby
1979 (Troy)
1980 (Henbit)
1989 (Nashwan)

Caslavska Vera 1943– . Czechoslovak gymnast, the first of the great present-day stylists. She won a record 21 world, Olympic, and European gold medals 1959-68; she also won eight silver and three bronze medals.

CAREER HIGHLIGHTS
Olympic champion
overall individual: 1964, 1968
beam: 1964, 1968
vault: 1964, 1968
floor exercise: 1968
world champion
overall individual: 1966
vault: 1962, 1966

Charlton Bobby (Robert) 1937– . English footballer, younger brother of Jack Charlton, who scored a record 49 goals in 106 appearances. An elegant midfield player who specialized in fierce long-range shots, Charlton spent most of his playing career with Manchester United. On retiring he had an unsuccessful spell as manager of Preston North End. He later became a director of Manchester United.

CAREER HIGHLIGHTS
Football League appearances: 644; goals: 206
international appearances: 106; goals: 49
World Cup: 1966
Football League championship: 1965, 1967
FA Cup: 1963
European Cup: 1968
Footballer of the Year: 1966
European Footballer of the Year: 1966

Christie Linford 1960– . Jamaican-born English sprinter. In 1986, Christie won the European 100-metres championship and finished second to Ben Johnson in the Commonwealth

Games. At the 1988 Seoul Olympics, he won two silver medals in the 100 metres and 4 × 100 metres relay. In 1990 he won gold medals in the Commonwealth Games for the 100 metres and 4 × 100 metres relay.

CAREER HIGHLIGHTS
Olympic games
1988: silver 100 metres; silver 4 × 100 metres relay
Commonwealth games
1990 gold 100 metres; gold 4 × 100 metres relay
European championships
1986 gold 100 metres
1990 gold 100 metres
World Cup
1989 gold 100 metres

Clark Jim (James) 1936–1968. Scottish-born motor-racing driver who was twice world champion 1963 and 1965. He spent all his Formula One career with Lotus. Clark won 25 Formula One Grand Prix races, a record at the time, before losing his life at Hockenheim, West Germany, in April 1968 during a Formula Two race.

CAREER HIGHLIGHTS
world champion
1963 (Lotus)
1965 (Lotus)
Formula One Grand Prix
races: 72
wins: 25

Cobb Ty(rus Raymond), nicknamed 'the Georgia Peach' 1886–1961. US baseball player, one of the greatest batters and base runners of all time. He played for Detroit and Philadelphia 1905–28, and won the American League batting average championship 12 times. He holds the record for runs scored (2,254) and batting average (0.367). He had 4,191 hits in his career—a record that stood for almost 60 years.

Coe Sebastian 1956– . English middle-distance runner, Olympic 1,500-metre champion 1980 and 1984. Coe became Britain's most prolific world-record breaker with eight outdoor world records and three indoor world records 1979–81. After his retirement in 1990 he pursued a political career with the Conservative party, and in 1992 was elected member of parliament for Falmouth and Camborne in Cornwall.

CAREER HIGHLIGHTS
Olympic Games
1980: gold 1,500 metres, silver 800 metres
1984: gold 1,500 metres, silver 800 metres

world records
1979: 800 metres, one mile, 1,500 metres
1980: 1,000 metres
1981: 800 metres, 1,000 metres, one mile (twice)
1982: 4 × 800 metres relay

Comaneci Nadia 1961– . Romanian gymnast. She won three gold medals at the 1976 Olympics at the age of 14, and was the first gymnast to record a perfect score of 10 in international competition. Upon retirement she became a coach of the Romanian team, but defected to Canada 1989.

CAREER HIGHLIGHTS
Olympic Games
1976: gold beam, vault, floor exercise
1980: gold beam, parallel bars

Connolly Maureen 1934–1969. US tennis player, nicknamed 'Little Mo' because she was just 157 cm/5 ft 2 in tall. In 1953 she became the first woman to complete the Grand Slam by winning all four major tournaments. All her singles titles (at nine major championships) and her Grand Slam titles were won between 1951 and 1954. Her career ended 1954 after a riding accident.

CAREER HIGHLIGHTS
Wimbledon
singles: 1952–54
US Open
singles: 1951–53
French Open
singles: 1953–54
doubles: 1954
mixed: 1954
Australian Open
singles: 1953
doubles: 1953

Connors Jimmy 1952– . US tennis player who won the Wimbledon title 1974, and subsequently won ten Grand Slam events. He was one of the first players to popularize the two-handed backhand.

CAREER HIGHLIGHTS
Wimbledon
singles: 1974, 1982
doubles: 1973
US Open
singles: 1974, 1976, 1978, 1982–83
doubles: 1975
Australian Open
singles: 1974
Grand Prix Masters
1978

A SPORTING REVIEW OF 1893

A look back at the sporting highlights of 1893, one century ago, reveals some almost incredible stories of heroism and versatility. Remember that in 1893 much travel was limited to the horse and carriage; road and rail were in their embryo stages, and air travel was many decades away. It was an era when facilities were spartan and basic. Thoughts of anything more than healthy exercise would be mightily discouraged.

1893 introduced one of sport's legendary characters to the world's attention. Charles Burgess Fry broke the world long-jump record with a leap of 7.16 m/23 ft 6 in. Fry was then an Oxford undergraduate. He took up cricket, and became one of the heaviest run scorers in the history of the game, amassing 30,000 runs at an average of 50 and with 94 centuries. He played for England on 26 occasions. In the winter he was good enough at football to play for England twice, and to play for Southampton in the 1902 FA Cup final. He played rugby for the Barbarians and was injured in the University match when in the winning Oxford XV. In later life Fry was offered the job as king of Albania. Unfortunately for that country, he declined in favour of the rather less well known King Zog.

Lottie Dod was the female equivalent of C B Fry. In 1893 she won her third successive Wimbledon singles title and her fifth in all. Lottie Dod was another with a wide range of sporting talents: in 1904, she became women's golf champion.

Tommy Loates was the jockey who could have put the bookies out of business. Loates won the Derby, the 1,000 Guineas, the 2,000 Guineas and the St Leger in 1893, riding all except the 1,000 Guineas on the same horse, Isinglass. Not surprisingly he was leading jockey with 222 winners, one of the select band who have ridden 200 winners in a season.

Boxing in 1893 was not governed by a maximum of 12 rounds of three minutes each round. World champions were the first to wear gloves and to move on from the bare knuckle era. Largely uncontrolled and ungoverned, boxing matches tended to drag on. Andy Bowen and Jack Burke fought in New York over 110 rounds; the fight lasted 7 hours and 19 minutes. The referee was unimpressed; he declared the bout a draw.

There was an unusual cricketing hat trick in 1893. At Cheltenham, the Gloucestershire bowler C L Townsend took a hat trick against Somerset. All three batsmen were dismissed in the same manner, stumped by C L Bain.

The groundwork was being laid for international competition. The US amateur golf championship (no professionals yet) was instituted; Victoria won the inaugural Sheffield Shield cricket title in Australia; the Argentinian Football Association was formed; America's famous Stanley Cup—ice hockey's blue riband event—first saw the light of day; Rosslyn Park became the first rugby union tourists to France; and the first European rowing championships were held.

But some of the sporting results of 1893 make one wonder whether if it could ever happen again. British tennis players actually won Wimbledon. Not only did Lottie Dod win the ladies singles, but Joshua Pim was the men's champion. Pim was also in the winning men's doubles team. The old soccer favourites Sunderland and Wolves won the League and the FA Cups. That great cricketing county, Yorkshire, won the fourth of their record 31 cricket championships—and the England cricket team regained the Ashes. Who would be prepared to bet that such results would recur in 1993?

Court Margaret (born Smith) 1942– . Australian tennis player. The most prolific winner in the women's game, she won a record 64 Grand Slam titles, including 25 at singles. Court was the first from her country to win the ladies title at Wimbledon 1963, and the second woman after Maureen Connolly to complete the Grand Slam 1970.

CAREER HIGHLIGHTS
Wimbledon
singles: 1963, 1965, 1970
doubles: 1964, 1969
mixed: 1963, 1965–66, 1968, 1975
US Open
singles: 1962, 1965, 1968–70, 1973
doubles: 1963, 1968–70, 1973, 1975
mixed: 1961–65, 1969–70, 1972

French Open
singles: 1962, 1964, 1969–70, 1973
doubles: 1964–66, 1973
mixed: 1963–65, 1969
Australian Open
singles: 1960–66, 1969–71, 1973
doubles: 1961–63, 1965, 1969–71, 1973
mixed: 1963–64

Cruyff Johan 1947– . Dutch football player, an outstanding European player in the 1970s. He was capped 48 times by his country, scoring 33 goals. He spent most of his career playing with Ajax and Barcelona and was named European Footballer of the Year on three occasions. As a coach he took both clubs to domestic and European honours.

CAREER HIGHLIGHTS
as player:
European Cup
1971–73 (with Ajax)
as coach:
European Cup Winners Cup
1987 (with Ajax)
1989 (with Barcelona)
European Cup
1992 (with Barcelona)
European Footballer of the Year
1971, 1973, 1974
World Club Champions
1972 (with Ajax)

Davis Steve 1957– . English snooker player, who has won every major honour in the game since turning professional 1978. Davis won his first major title 1980 when he won the Coral UK Championship. He has been world champion six times, and has also won world titles at pairs and with the England team.

CAREER HIGHLIGHTS
World Professional Champion
1981, 1983–84, 1987–89
World Pairs Championship (with Tony Meo)
1982–83, 1985–86
World Team Championship
1981, 1983, 1988–89

Dempsey Jack 1895–1983. US heavyweight boxing champion, nicknamed 'the Manassa Mauler'. He beat Jess Willard 1919 to win the title and held it until 1926, when he lost it to Gene Tunney. In a re-match the following year (the 'Battle of the Long Count') Dempsey narrowly lost his chance to regain the title, when after knocking out Tunney in the seventh round he failed to return to a neutral corner, and thereby obliged the referee to delay the start of the count.

CAREER HIGHLIGHTS
fights: 79
wins: 64
draws: 9
defeats: 6

DiMaggio Joe 1914– . US baseball player with the New York Yankees 1936–51. In 1941 he set a record by getting hits in 56 consecutive games. He was an outstanding fielder, played centre field, hit 361 home runs, and had a career average of 0.325. He was once married to the actress Marilyn Monroe.

Edberg Stefan 1966– . Swedish tennis player and twice winner of Wimbledon 1988, 1990. He won the junior Grand Slam 1983 and his first senior Grand Slam title, the Australian Open 1985, and three more Grand Slam events

by the end of 1991. At Wimbledon in 1987, he became the first male player in 40 years to win a match without conceding a game.

CAREER HIGHLIGHTS
Wimbledon
singles: 1988, 1990
Australian Open
singles: 1985, 1987
doubles: 1987
US Open
singles: 1991, 1992
doubles: 1987
Grand Prix Masters
1989

Edwards Gareth 1947– . Welsh rugby union player. He was appointed captain of his country when only 20 years old. Edwards appeared in seven championship winning teams, five Triple Crown winning teams, and two Grand Slam winning teams. In 53 international matches he scored a record 20 tries.

CAREER HIGHLIGHTS
international championship: 1969, 1970*, 1971, 1975–76, 1978
Triple Crown: 1969, 1971, 1976–78
Grand Slam: 1971, 1976, 1978
British Lions tours: 1968 to South Africa, 1971 to New Zealand, 1974 to South Africa
(* denotes title shared)

Evert Chris(tine) 1954– . US tennis player renowned for her outstanding two-handed backhand and baseline technique. She won her first Wimbledon title 1974, and has since won 21 Grand Slam titles. From 1974–89 she never failed to reach the quarter-finals at Wimbledon. She became the first woman tennis player to win $1 million in prize money.

CAREER HIGHLIGHTS
Wimbledon
singles: 1974, 1976, 1981
doubles: 1976
US Open
singles: 1975–78, 1980, 1982
French Open
singles: 1974–75, 1979–80, 1983, 1985–86
doubles: 1974–75
Australian Open
singles: 1982, 1984

Faldo Nick 1957– . English golfer who was the first Briton in 40 years to win two British Open titles, and the only person after Jack Nicklaus to win two successive US Masters titles (1989 and 1990). He is one of only six golfers to win the Masters and British Open in the same year.

CAREER HIGHLIGHTS
British Open: 1987, 1989
US Masters: 1989, 1990
US PGA Championship: 1978, 1980-81, 1989
Ryder Cup winning team: 1985, 1987, tie 1989
World Match-Play Championship: 1989

Ferrari Enzo 1898–1988. Italian founder of the Ferrari car manufacturing company, which specializes in Grand Prix racing cars and high-quality sports cars. He was a racing driver for Alfa Romeo in the 1920s, went on to become one of their designers and in 1929 took over their racing division. In 1947 the first 'true' Ferrari was seen. The Ferrari car has won more world championship Grands Prix than any other car.

Finney Tom (Thomas) 1922– . English footballer, known as the 'Preston Plumber'. His only Football League club was his home-town team, Preston North End. He played for England 76 times, in every forward position. He was celebrated for his ball control and goal-scoring skills, and was the first person to win the Footballer of the Year award twice.

CAREER HIGHLIGHTS
Football League appearances: 433; goals: 187
international appearances: 76; goals: 30
FA Cup (runners-up medal): 1954
Footballer of the Year: 1954, 1957

Francome John 1952– . English jockey who holds the record for the most National Hunt winners (over hurdles or fences). Between 1970 and 1985 he rode 1,138 winners from 5,061 mounts—the second person (after Stan Mellor) to ride 1,000 winners. He took up training after retiring from riding.

CAREER HIGHLIGHTS
Champion Jockey: 1979, 1981–85 (shared title 1982)
Cheltenham Gold Cup: 1978
Champion Hurdle: 1981
Hennessy Cognac Gold Cup: 1983–84
King George VI Chase: 1982

Gascoigne Paul ('Gazza') 1967– . English footballer who has played for Tottenham Hotspur since July 1988. At the 1989 World Cup semifinal against West Germany, he committed a foul for which he was booked (cautioned by the referee), meaning that he would be unable to play in the final, should England win. His tearful response drew public sympathy, and he was subsequently lionized by the British press.

Gavaskar Sunil Manohar 1949– . Indian cricketer. Between 1971 and 1987 he scored a record 10,122 test runs in a record 125 matches (including 106 consecutive tests).

CAREER HIGHLIGHTS
all first-class matches
runs: 25,834
average: 51.46
best: 340 (Bombay v. Bengal, 1981–82)
test cricket
runs: 10,122
average: 51.12
best: 236 not out (India v. West Indies, 1983–84)

Gooch Graham Alan 1953– . English cricketer who plays for Essex county and England. He made his first-class cricket debut in 1973, and was first capped for England two years later. Banned for three years for captaining a team for a tour of South Africa in 1982, he was later re-instated as England captain in 1989. He scored a world record 456 runs in a test match against India in 1990.

CAREER HIGHLIGHTS
all first-class matches (to start of 1992 season)
runs: 33,897
average: 47.40
best: 333 (England v. India 1990)
wickets: 219
average: 34.90
best: 7-14 (Essex v. Worcestershire 1982)
test cricket
appearances: 91
runs: 7,028
average: 43.92
best: 333 (England v. India 1990)
wickets: 17
average: 47.05
best: 2-12 (England v. India 1981–82)

Gower David 1957– . English left-handed cricketer who played for Leicestershire 1975–89 and for Hampshire from 1990. In 1992, during the third test against Pakistan, he became England's highest-scoring batsman in test cricket, surpassing Geoffrey Boycott's record of 8,114 runs.

CAREER HIGHLIGHTS
all first-class matches (to start of 1992 season)
runs: 23,978
average: 39.69
best: 228 (Leicestershire v. Glamorgan 1989)
test cricket
appearances (to April 1991): 114
runs: 8,081
average: 44.15
best: 215 (England v. Australia 1985)

Grace W(illiam) G(ilbert) 1848–1915. English cricketer. By profession a doctor, he became the best batsman in England. He began playing first-class cricket at the age of 16, scored 152 runs in his first test match, and scored the first triple century 1876. Throughout his career, which lasted nearly 45 years, he scored more than 54,000 runs.

CAREER HIGHLIGHTS
all first-class matches
runs: 54,896
average: 39.55
best: 344 MCC v. Kent, 1876
wickets: 2,876
average: 17.92
best: 10-49 MCC v. Oxford University, 1886
test cricket
runs: 1,098
average: 32.29
best: 170 v. Australia, 1886
wickets: 9
average: 26.22
best: 2-12 v Australia, 1890

Graf Steffi 1969– . German tennis player who brought Martina Navratilova's long reign as the world's number-one female player to an end. Graf reached the semifinal of the US Open 1985 at the age of 16, and won five consecutive Grand Slam singles titles 1988–89.

CAREER HIGHLIGHTS
Wimbledon
singles: 1988–89, 1991, 1992
doubles: 1988
US Open
singles: 1988–89
French Open
singles: 1987–88
Australian Open
singles: 1988–90
Olympics
gold: 1988

Green Lucinda (born Prior-Palmer) 1953– . English three-day eventer. She has won the Badminton Horse Trials a record six times 1973–84 and was world individual champion 1982.

Gretzky Wayne 1961– . Canadian ice-hockey player, probably the best in the history of the National Hockey League (NHL). Gretsky played with the Edmonton Oilers 1979–88 and with the Los Angeles Kings from 1988. He took just 11 years to break the NHL scoring record of 1,850 goals (accumulated by Gordie Howe over 26 years) and won the Hart Memorial Trophy as the NHL's most valuable player of the season a record nine times (1980–87, 1989).

CAREER HIGHLIGHTS
Stanley Cup: 1984, 1985, 1987, 1988
Hart Memorial Trophy (NHL's most valuable player): 1980–87, 1989
Ross Trophy (most points in regular season): 1981–90

Griffith-Joyner (born Griffith) Delorez Florence 1959– . US track athlete, nicknamed 'Flo-Jo', who won three gold medals at the 1988 Seoul Olympics, the 100 and 200 metres and the sprint relay. Her time in the 200 metres was a world record 21.34 seconds.

Hadlee Richard John 1951– . New Zealand cricketer. In 1987 he surpassed Ian Botham's world record of 373 wickets in test cricket and went on to set the record at 431 wickets. He played for Canterbury and Nottinghamshire in England, and retired from international cricket 1990.

CAREER HIGHLIGHTS
all first-class matches
runs: 12,052
average: 31.78
best: 210 not out (Nottinghamshire v. Middlesex 1984)
wickets: 1,490
average: 18.11
best: 9 for 52 (New Zealand v. Australia 1985–86)
test cricket
appearances: 86
runs: 3,124
average: 27.16
best: 151 not out (New Zealand v. Sri Lanka 1986–87)
wickets: 431
average: 22.29
best: 9 for 52 (New Zealand v. Australia 1985–86)

Hanley Ellery 1965– . English rugby league player, a regular member of the Great Britain team since 1984 and the inspiration behind Wigan's domination of the sport in the 1980s. Hanley started his career in 1981 with Bradford Northern before his transfer to Wigan 1985 for a then world record £85,000. He has since won all the top honours of the game in Britain as well as earning a reputation in Australia, the world's top rugby league nation. He joined Leeds in 1991.

CAREER HIGHLIGHTS
Challenge Cup: 1985, 1988–91
Division One Championship: 1987, 1990–91
Regal Trophy: 1986–87, 1989–90
Lancashire County Cup: 1986–89
Premiership Trophy: 1987

Hendry Stephen 1970– . Scottish snooker player. Hendry was the youngest winner ever of a professional tournament when he claimed the 1986 Scottish professional title, and won his first ranking event in the 1987 Rothmans Grand Prix. During the 1989–90 season he replaced Steve Davis as the top-ranking player, and became the youngest world champion ever.

CAREER HIGHLIGHTS
Embassy World Professional Championship: 1990
Rothmans Grand Prix: 1987, 1990
MIM/Pearl Assurance British Open: 1988, 1991
Benson and Hedges Masters: 1989–91
Stormseal UK Open: 1989–91
555 Asian Open: 1989, 1990
Dubai Duty Free Classic: 1989, 1990

Hick Graeme 1966– . Rhodesian-born cricketer who became Zimbabwe's youngest professional cricketer at the age of 17. A prolific batsman, he joined Worcestershire, England, in 1984. He achieved the highest score in England in the 20th century in 1988 against Somerset with 405 not out. He made his test debut for England in 1991 after a seven-year qualification period.

CAREER HIGHLIGHTS
all first-class cricket (to start of 1992 season)
runs: 17,184
average: 59.46
best: 405 (Worcestershire v. Somerset 1988)

Hill Graham 1929–1975. English motor-racing driver. He won the Dutch Grand Prix in 1962, progressing to the world driver's title in 1962 and 1968. In 1972 he became the first world driver's champion to win the Le Mans Grand Prix d'Endurance (Le Mans 24-Hour Race). Hill started his Formula One career with Lotus 1958, went to BRM 1960–66, returned to Lotus 1967–69, moved to Brabham 1970–72, and formed his own team, Embassy Shadow, 1973–75. He was killed in an air crash.

CAREER HIGHLIGHTS
world champion
1962 BRM
1968 Lotus
Formula One Grand Prix
races: 176
wins: 14
Le Mans Grand Prix d'Endurance
1972 Matra-Simca
Indianapolis 500
1966 Lola Ford

Hobbs Jack (John Berry) 1882–1963. English cricketer who represented his country 61 times. In first-class cricket he scored a world record 61,237 runs, including a record 197 centuries, in a career that lasted nearly 30 years.

CAREER HIGHLIGHTS
all first-class matches
runs: 61,237
average: 50.65

test cricket
runs: 5,410
average: 56.94
best: 211 v. South Africa, 1924

Howe Gordie 1926– . Canadian ice-hockey player who played for the Detroit Red Wings (National Hockey League) 1946–71 and then the New England Whalers (World Hockey Association). In the NHL, he scored more goals (801), assists (1,049), and points (1,850) than any other player in ice-hockey history until beaten by Wayne Gretsky. Howe played professional hockey until he was over 50.

Hutton Len (Leonard) 1916–1990. English cricketer. He captained England in 23 test matches 1952–56 and was England's first professional captain. In 1938 at the Oval he scored 364 against Australia, a world record test score until beaten by Gary Sobers 1958.

CAREER HIGHLIGHTS
all first-class matches
runs: 40,140
average: 55.51
best: 364 England v. Australia, 1938
test cricket
runs: 6,971
average: 55.51
best: 364 (England v. Australia, 1938)

Johnson Ben 1961– . Canadian sprinter. In 1987, he broke the world record for the 100 metres, running it in 9.83 seconds. At the Olympic Games 1988, he again broke the record, but was disqualified and suspended for using anabolic steroids to enhance his performance.

Johnson Jack 1878–1968. US heavyweight boxer. He overcame severe racial prejudice to become the first black heavyweight champion of the world 1908 when he travelled to Australia to challenge Tommy Burns. The US authorities wanted Johnson 'dethroned' because of his colour but could not find suitable challengers until 1915, when he lost the title in a dubious fight decision to the giant Jess Willard.

CAREER HIGHLIGHTS
fights: 107
wins: 86
draws: 11
defeats: 10

Jones Bobby (Robert Tyre) 1902–1971. US golfer who was the game's greatest amateur player. He never turned professional but won 13 major amateur and professional tournaments, including the Grand Slam of the amateur and professional opens of both the USA and Britain 1930. Jones finished playing competitive golf 1930, but maintained his contacts with the sport and was largely responsible for inaugurating the US Masters.

CAREER HIGHLIGHTS
British Open: 1926–27, 1930
US Open: 1923, 1926, 1929–30
British Amateur: 1930
US Amateur: 1924–25, 1927–28, 1930
US Walker Cup (team): 1922, 1924, 1926, 1928*, 1930*
* indicates playing captain

Khan Imran 1952– . Pakistani cricketer. He played county cricket for Worcestershire and Sussex in the UK, and made his test debut for Pakistan 1971, subsequently playing for his country 82 times. In first-class cricket he has scored over 16,000 runs and taken over 1,200 wickets. He captained Pakistan to victory in 1992.

CAREER HIGHLIGHTS
test cricket (to start of 1992 season)
appearances: 85
runs: 3,692
average: 37.29
best: 136 (Pakistan v. Australia 1989–90)
wickets: 362
average: 22.76
best: 8–58 (Pakistan v. Sri Lanka 1981–82)

Khan Jahangir 1963– . Pakistani squash player who won the world open championship a record six times 1981–85 and 1988. He was ten times British Open champion 1982–911, and World Amateur champion 1979, 1983, and 1985. After losing to Geoff Hunt of Australia in the final of the 1981 British Open he did not lose again until Nov 1986 when he lost to Ross Norman of New Zealand in the World Open final.

King Billie Jean (born Moffitt) 1943– . US tennis player. She won a record 20 Wimbledon titles between 1961 and 1979 (including six singles titles), and her 39 Grand Slam events at singles and doubles are third only to Navratilova and Margaret Court.

CAREER HIGHLIGHTS
Wimbledon
singles: 1966–68, 1972–73, 1975
doubles: 1961–62, 1965, 1967–68, 1970–73, 1979
mixed: 1967, 1971, 1973–74
US Open
singles: 1967, 1971–72, 1974
doubles: 1964, 1967, 1974, 1978, 1980
mixed: 1967, 1971, 1973, 1976
French Open
singles: 1972
doubles: 1972
mixed: 1967, 1970

Australian Open
singles: 1968
mixed: 1968

Klammer Franz 1953– . Austrian skier who won a record 35 World Cup downhill races between 1974 and 1985. He was the combined world champion 1974, Olympic gold medallist 1976, and the World Cup downhill champion 1975–78 and 1983.

Korbut Olga 1955– . Soviet gymnast who attracted world attention at the 1972 Olympic Games with her lively floor routine. She won gold medals for the beam and floor exercises, a silver for the parallel bars, and another gold as member of the winning Soviet team.

CAREER HIGHLIGHTS
Olympic Games
1972: gold beam, floor exercise, team
1976: team

Kristiansen Ingrid 1956– . Norwegian athlete, an outstanding long-distance runner of 5,000 metres, 10,000 metres, marathon, and cross-country races. She has won all the world's leading marathons. In 1986 she knocked 45.68 seconds off the world 10,000 metres record. She was the world cross-country champion 1988 and won the London marathon 1984–85 and 1987–88.

Latynina Larissa Semyonovna 1935– . Soviet gymnast, winner of more Olympic medals than any person in any sport. She won 18 between 1956 and 1964, including nine gold medals. During her career she won a total of 12 individual Olympic and world championship gold medals.

CAREER HIGHLIGHTS
Olympic champion
team: 1956, 1960, 1964
overall individual: 1956, 1960
floor exercise: 1956*, 1960, 1964
vault: 1956
world championship
team: 1958, 1962
overall individual: 1958, 1962
vault: 1958
beam: 1958
floor exercise: 1962
asymmetric bars: 1958
* denotes shared title

Lauda Niki 1949– . Austrian motor racing driver who won the world championship in 1975, 1977 and 1984. He was also runner-up in 1976 just six weeks after a serious accident at Nurburgring, Germany, which left him badly burned. Lauda was Formula Two champion in 1972, and drove for March, BRM, Ferrari, and Brabham before his retirement in 1978.

He returned to the sport in 1984 and won his third world title in a McLaren before eventually retiring in 1985 to concentrate on his airline business, Lauda-Air.

CAREER HIGHLIGHTS
world champion
1975 Ferrari
1977 Ferrari
1984 McLaren
Formula One Grand Prix
races: 171
wins: 25

Laver Rod(ney George) 1938– . Australian tennis player. He was one of the greatest left-handed players, and the only player to perform the Grand Slam twice (1962 and 1969). He won four Wimbledon singles titles, the Australian title three times, the US Open twice, and the French Open twice. He turned professional after winning Wimbledon in 1962 but returned when the championships were opened to professionals in 1968.

CAREER HIGHLIGHTS
Wimbledon
singles: 1961–62, 1968–69
doubles: 1971
mixed: 1959–60
US Open
singles: 1962, 1969
French Open
singles: 1962, 1969
doubles: 1961
mixed: 1961
Australian Open
singles: 1960, 1962, 1969
doubles: 1959–61, 1969

Leonard Sugar Ray 1956– . US boxer. In 1988 he became the first man to have won world titles at five officially recognized weights. He was Olympic light-welterweight champion 1976, and won his first professional title in 1979 when he beat Wilfred Benitez for the WBC welterweight title. He later won titles at junior middleweight (WBA version) 1981, middleweight (WBC) 1987, light-heavyweight (WBC) 1988, and super-middleweight (WBC) 1988. In 1989 he drew with Thomas Hearns.

Lewis Carl (Frederick Carleton) 1961– . US track and field athlete. At the 1984 Olympic Games he equalled the performance of Jesse Owens, winning gold medals in the 100 and 200 metres, sprint relay, and long jump. In the 1988 Olympics, he repeated his golds in the 100 metres and long jump, and won a silver in the 200 metres.

CAREER HIGHLIGHTS
Olympic Games
1984: gold 100 metres, 200 metres, 4 × 100 metres relay, long jump
1988: gold 100 metres, long jump; silver 200 metres

Lillee Dennis 1949– . Australian cricketer regarded as the best fast bowler of his generation. He made his test debut in the 1970–71 season and subsequently played for his country 70 times. Lillee was the first to take 300 wickets in test cricket. He played Sheffield Shield cricket for Western Australia and at the end of his career made a comeback with Tasmania.

CAREER HIGHLIGHTS
test cricket (to the beginning of the 1992 season)
appearances: 70
wickets: 355
average: 23.92

Lineker Gary 1960– . English footballer who scored over 250 goals in 550 games for Leicester, Everton, Barcelona, and Tottenham. With 48 goals in 75 internationals to the end of the 1991–2 English season, he needed just two goals to beat Bobby Charlton's record of 49 goals for England. Lineker was elected Footballer of the Year in 1986 and 1992 and was leading scorer at the 1986 World Cup finals.

CAREER HIGHLIGHTS
FA Cup: 1991 (with Tottenham)
European Cup Winners Cup: 1989 (with Barcelona)
Footballer of the Year: 1986, 1992

Lopez Nancy 1957– . US golfer who turned professional in 1977 and in 1979 became the first woman to win $200,000 in a season. She has won the US LPGA title three times 1978, 1985, and 1989, and has won over 35 tour events, and $3 million in prize money.

Louis Joe. Assumed name of Joseph Louis Barrow 1914–1981. US boxer, nicknamed 'the Brown Bomber'. He was world heavyweight champion between 1937 and 1949 and made a record 25 successful defences (a record for any weight). Louis was the longest-reigning world heavyweight champion at 11 years and 252 days before announcing his retirement in 1949. He made a comeback and lost to Ezzard Charles in a world title fight in 1950.

CAREER HIGHLIGHTS
professional fights: 66
wins: 63
knockouts: 49
defeats: 3
1st professional fight: 4 July 1934 v. Jack Kracken

last professional fight: 26 Oct 1951 v. Rocky Marciano

McBride Willie John 1940– . Irish rugby union player. He was capped 63 times by Ireland, and won a record 17 British Lions caps. He played on five Lions tours 1962, 1966, 1968, 1971, and in 1974 as captain when they returned from South Africa undefeated.

CAREER HIGHLIGHTS
British Lions tours
1962 South Africa
1966 Australia and New Zealand
1968 South Africa
1971 Australia and New Zealand
1974 South Africa (captain)
1983 New Zealand (manager)

McEnroe John Patrick 1959– . US tennis player whose brash behaviour and fiery temper on court dominated the men's game in the early 1980s. He was three times winner of the Wimbledon men's title 1981, 1983, and 1984. He also won three successive US Open titles 1979–81 and again in 1984. A fine doubles player, McEnroe also won ten Grand Slam doubles titles, seven in partnership with Peter Fleming.

CAREER HIGHLIGHTS
Wimbledon
singles: 1981, 1983, 1984
doubles: 1979, 1981, 1983, 1984, 1992
US Open
singles: 1979–81, 1984
doubles: 1979, 1981, 1983, 1989
French Open
mixed doubles: 1977
Grand Prix Masters
singles: 1979, 1984, 1985
doubles: 1979–85

Mansell Nigel 1954– . English motor-racing driver. Runner-up in the world championship on two occasions, he has won over 28 Grand Prix races—more than any other British driver. Mansell started his Formula One career with Lotus 1980 and won the European Grand Prix 1985. He drove for the Williams team 1985–88, then for Ferrari 1989–90, before returning to Williams shortly after announcing his 'retirement'.

Mantle Mickey (Charles) 1931– . US baseball player. Signed by the New York Yankees, he broke into the major leagues 1951. A powerful switch-hitter (able to bat with either hand), he also excelled as a centre-fielder. In 1956 he won baseball's Triple Crown, leading the American League in batting average, home runs, and runs batted in. He retired 1969 after 18 years with the Yankees and seven World Series championships.

Maradona Diego 1960– . Argentine footballer who was voted the best player of the 1980s by the world's press. He has won 79 international caps, and helped his country to two successive World Cup finals. Maradona played for Argentinos Juniors and Boca Juniors before leaving South America for Barcelona, Spain, 1982 for a transfer fee of approximately £5 million. He moved to Napoli, Italy, for £6.9 million 1984, and contributed to their first Italian League title.

CAREER HIGHLIGHTS
World Cup: 1986
UEFA Cup: 1989
Italian League: 1987, 1990
Italian Cup: 1987
Spanish Cup: 1983
South American footballer of the year: 1979, 1980

Marciano Rocky (Rocco Francis Marchegiano) 1923–1969. US boxer, world heavyweight champion 1952–56. He retired after 49 professional fights, the only heavyweight champion to retire undefeated. He was killed in a plane crash.

CAREER HIGHLIGHTS
professional fights: 49
wins: 49
knockouts: 43
defeats: 0
1st professional fight: 17 March 1947 v. Lee Epperson (*USA*)
last professional fight: 21 Sept 1955 v. Archie Moore (*USA*)

Matthews Stanley 1915– . English footballer who played for Stoke City, Blackpool, and England. An outstanding right-winger, he won the nickname 'the Wizard of the Dribble' because of his ball control. Matthews played nearly 700 Football League games, and won 54 international caps. He continued to play first-division football after the age of 50. He was the first European Footballer of the Year 1956.

CAREER HIGHLIGHTS
Football League appearances: 698, goals: 71
international appearances: 54, goals: 11
FA Cup: 1953
Footballer of the Year: 1948, 1963
European Footballer of the Year: 1956

Merckx Eddie 1945– . Belgian cyclist, known as 'the Cannibal', who won the Tour de France a joint record five times 1969–74. Merckx turned professional 1966 and won his first classic race, the Milan–San Remo, the same year. He went on to win 24 classics as well as the three major tours (of Italy, Spain, and France) a total of 11 times. He was world professional road-race champion three times and in 1971 won a record 54 races in the season. He rode 50 winners in a season four times. He retired in 1977.

CAREER HIGHLIGHTS
Tour de France: 1969–72, 1974
Tour of Italy: 1968, 1970, 1972–74
Tour of Spain: 1973
world professional champion: 1967, 1971, 1974
world amateur champion: 1964

Miandad Javed 1957– . Pakistani test cricketer, his country's leading run-maker. He scored a century on his test debut in 1976 and has since become one of a handful of players to make 100 test appearances. He has captained his country and helped Pakistan to win the 1992 World Cup. His highest score of 311 was made when he was aged 17.

CAREER HIGHLIGHTS
test cricket
appearances: 109
runs: 3,692
average: 37.29
best: 280 not out v. India 1982–83

Montana Joe 1956– . US football player who has appeared in four winning Super Bowls as quarterback for the San Francisco 49ers 1982, 1985, 1989, and 1990, winning the Most Valuable Player award in 1982, 1985, and 1990. He had a record five touchdown passes in the 1990 Super Bowl.

Namath Joe (Joseph William) 1943– . US football player. In 1965 Namath signed with the New York Jets of the newly established American Football League. In 1969 Namath led the Jets to a historic upset victory over the Baltimore Colts in the Super Bowl. After leaving the Jets 1977, Namath joined the Los Angeles Rams; however, knee injuries forced his retirement as a player the following year. He later became a sports broadcaster and actor.

Navratilova Martina 1956– . Czech tennis player who became a naturalized US citizen 1981. The most outstanding woman player of the 1980s, she had 55 Grand Slam victories by 1991, including 18 singles titles. She has won the Wimbledon singles title a record nine times, including six in succession 1982–87.

CAREER HIGHLIGHTS
Wimbledon
singles: 1978–79, 1982–87, 1990
doubles: 1976, 1979, 1981–84, 1986
mixed: 1985
US Open
singles: 1983–84, 1986–87
doubles: 1977–78, 1980, 1983–84, 1986–90
mixed: 1985, 1987

French Open
singles: 1982, 1984
doubles: 1975, 1982, 1984–88
mixed: 1974, 1985
Australian Open
singles: 1981, 1983, 1985
doubles: 1980, 1982–85, 1987–89

Nicklaus Jack (William) 1940– . US golfer, nicknamed 'the Golden Bear'. He won a record 20 major titles, including 18 professional majors between 1962 and 1986. When he won the Masters for a record sixth time 1986 he was the oldest winner at the age of 48 years and 82 days. Nicklaus played for the US Ryder Cup team six times 1969–81 and was nonplaying captain 1983 and 1987 when the event was played over the course he designed at Muirfield Village, Ohio. In 1988 he was voted Golfer of the Century.

CAREER HIGHLIGHTS
US Amateur: 1959, 1961
US Open: 1962, 1967, 1972, 1980
British Open: 1966, 1970, 1978
US Masters: 1963, 1965–66, 1972, 1975, 1986
US PGA Championship: 1963, 1971, 1973, 1975, 1980
US Ryder Cup (team): 1969, 1971, 1973, 1975, 1977

Owens Jesse (James Cleveland) 1913–1980. US track and field athlete who excelled in the sprints, hurdles, and the long jump. At the 1936 Berlin Olympics he won four gold medals, and the Nazi leader Hitler is said to have stormed out of the stadium in disgust at the black man's triumph. Owens held the world long-jump record for 25 years 1935–60. At Ann Arbor, Michigan, on 25 May 1935, he broke six world records in less than an hour.

CAREER HIGHLIGHTS
Olympic Games
1936: gold 100 metres, 200 metres, 4 × 100 metres relay, long jump
world records:
1935: 100 yards, 200 metres, 220 yards, 200 metre hurdles, 220 yards hurdles, long jump
1936: 100 metres, 100 yards, 4 × 100 metres relay (US National team)

Palmer Arnold (Daniel) 1929– . US golfer who helped to popularize the professional sport in the USA in the 1950s and 1960s. He won the US amateur title 1954, and went on to win all the world major professional trophies except the US PGA Championship. In the 1980s he enjoyed a successful career on the US Seniors Tour.

CAREER HIGHLIGHTS
US Open: 1960
British Open: 1961–62
Masters: 1958, 1960, 1962, 1964
World Match-Play: 1964, 1967
US Ryder Cup: 1961, 1963*, 1965, 1967, 1971, 1973, 1975**
* playing captain; ** nonplaying captain

Pelé Adopted name of Edson Arantes do Nascimento 1940– . Brazilian soccer player who was celebrated as one of the finest inside-forwards in the history of the game. A prolific goal scorer, he appeared in four World Cup competitions 1958–70 and led Brazil to three championships 1958, 1962, and 1970. He spent most of his playing career with the Brazilian team Santos, before ending it with the New York Cosmos in the USA.

Piggott Lester 1935– . English jockey. He has adopted a unique high riding style and is renowned as a brilliant tactician. A champion jockey 11 times between 1960 and 1982, he has ridden a record nine Derby winners. He retired from riding 1985 and took up training. In 1987 he was imprisoned for tax evasion. He returned to racing in 1990.

CAREER HIGHLIGHTS
Champion Jockey: 1960, 1964–71, 1981–82
Derby: 1954, 1957, 1960, 1968, 1970, 1972, 1976–77, 1983
Oaks: 1957, 1959, 1966, 1975, 1981, 1984
St Leger: 1960–61, 1967–68, 1970–72, 1984
1,000 Guineas: 1970, 1981
2,000 Guineas: 1957, 1968, 1970, 1985, 1992
Irish 2,000 Guineas: 1992

Platini Michel 1955– . French football player who was the inspiration of the French team that won the 1984 European Championship. He represented his country on 72 occasions, scoring a record 41 goals and playing in three World Cups, and was the first to be elected European Footballer of the Year on three successive years 1983–85. He became manager of the French national team in 1988.

CAREER HIGHLIGHTS
European Championship: 1984
French Cup: 1978 (with Nancy)
French Championship: 1981 (with St Etienne)
Italian Championship: 1984, 1986 (with Juventus)
European Cup: 1985 (with Juventus)
European Cup Winners Cup: 1984 (with Juventus)
European Footballer of the Year: 1983–85

Prost Alain 1955– . French motor-racing driver who was world champion 1985, 1986, and 1989, the first French world drivers' champion. He raced in Formula One events from 1980 and had his first Grand Prix win 1981, driving a Renault. In 1984 he began driving for the McLaren team. To the start of 1991 he had won a record 44 Grands Prix from 169 starts.

CAREER HIGHLIGHTS
world champion
1985 Marlboro–McLaren
1986 Marlboro–McLaren
1989 Marlboro–Honda
Formula One Grand Prix
races: 168
wins: 44 (record)

Rhodes Wilfred 1877–1973. English cricketer who took more wickets than anyone else in the game—4,187 wickets from 1898 to 1930—and also scored 39,802 first-class runs. Playing for Yorkshire, Rhodes made a record 763 appearances in the county championship. He took 100 wickets in a season 23 times and completed the 'double' of 1,000 runs and 100 wickets in a season 16 times (both records). He played his 58th and final game for England, against the West Indies 1930, when he was 52 years old, the oldest ever test cricketer.

CAREER HIGHLIGHTS
all first-class matches
runs: 39,802
average: 30.83
best: 267 not out Yorkshire v. Leicestershire, 1921
wickets: 4,187
average: 16.71
best: 9-24 C I Thornton's XI v. Australians, 1899
test cricket
runs: 2,325
average: 30.19
best: 179 v. Australia, 1911-12
wickets: 127
average: 26.96
best: 8-68 v. Australia, 1903-04

Richards Gordon 1905–1986. English jockey and trainer who was champion on the flat a record 26 times between 1925 and 1953. He started riding 1920 and rode 4,870 winners from 21,834 mounts before retiring 1954 and taking up training. He rode the winners of all the classic races but only once won the Derby (on Pinza 1953). In 1947 he rode a record 269 winners in a season.

CAREER HIGHLIGHTS
Champion Jockey: 1925, 1927-29, 1931-40, 1942-53
Derby: 1953
Oaks: 1930, 1942
St Leger: 1930, 1937, 1940, 1942, 1944
1,000 Guineas: 1942, 1948, 1951
2,000 Guineas: 1938, 1942, 1947

Richards Viv (Isaac Vivian Alexander) 1952– .
West Indian cricketer, captain of the West
Indies team 1986–91. He has played for the
Leeward Islands and, in the UK, for Somerset and Glamorgan. A prolific run-scorer, he
holds the record for the greatest number of
runs made in test cricket in one calendar year
(1,710 runs in 1976). He retired from international cricket after the West Indies tour of
England in 1991.

CAREER HIGHLIGHTS
all first-class cricket (to start of 1992 season)
runs: 34,255
average: 50.00
best: 322 (Somerset v. Warwickshire 1985)
wickets: 219
average: 44.75
best: 5 for 88 (West Indies v. Queensland 1981-82)
test cricket
appearances: 121
runs: 8,540
average: 50.23
best: 291 (v. England 1976)
wickets: 32
average: 61.37
best: 2 for 17 (v. Pakistan 1988)

Rodnina Irina 1949– . Soviet ice skater.
Between 1969 and 1980 she won 23 world,
Olympic, and European gold medals in pairs
competitions. Her partners were Alexei Ulanov
and then Alexsandr Zaitsev.

CAREER HIGHLIGHTS
Olympic champion: 1972, 1976, 1980
world champion: 1969-78
European champion: 1969-78

Ruth Babe (George Herman) 1895–1948. US
baseball player, regarded by many as the greatest of all time. He played in ten World Series
and hit 714 home runs, a record that stood
from 1935 to 1974 and led to the nickname
'Sultan of Swat'. He is still the holder of the
record for most bases in a season: 457 in 1921.
Yankee Stadium is known as 'the house that
Ruth built' because of the money he brought
into the club.

CAREER HIGHLIGHTS
games: 2,503
runs: 2,174
home runs: 714
average: .342
World Series wins: 1915–16, 1918, 1923, 1927–28,
1932

Sawchuk Terry (Terrance Gordon) 1929–1970.
Canadian ice-hockey player, often considered
the greatest goaltender of all time. He played

for Detroit, Boston, Toronto, Los Angeles,
and New York Rangers 1950–67, and holds
the National Hockey League record of 103
shut-outs (games in which he did not concede
a goal).

Scudamore Peter 1958– . English National
Hunt jockey who was champion jockey 1982
(shared with John Francome) and from 1986
to 1991. In 1988–89 he rode a record 221 winners, and after the 1990–91 season his total of
winners stood at a world record 1,374.

Seles Monica 1973– . Yugoslavian tennis player
who won her first Grand Slam title, the French
Open, at the age of 16. She dominated the
major events in 1991 but withdrew from Wimbledon and consequently missed the chance
to achieve the Grand Slam. In the same year
she became the youngest woman player ever
to achieve number-one ranking.

CAREER HIGHLIGHTS
US Open
singles: 1991, 1992
French Open
singles: 1990–92
Australian Open
singles: 1991, 1992

Senna Ayrton 1960– . Brazilian motor-racing
driver. He had his first Grand Prix win in the
1985 Portuguese Grand Prix, and progressed
to the world driver's title in 1988, 1990, and
1991. By the beginning of the 1991 season he
had 26 wins in 100 starts, which he improved
early on in the season with a record four consecutive victories.

Shilton Peter 1949– . English international
footballer, an outstanding goalkeeper, who has
set records for the highest number of Football
League appearances (over 900) and England
caps (125). First capped by England 1970 he
announced his retirement from international
football in 1990, after the England–West Germany World Cup semifinal. In 1992 he became
manager of Plymouth Argyle.

Shoemaker Willie (William Lee) 1931– . US
jockey whose career, from 1949 to 1990, was
outstandingly successful. He rode 8,833 winners from 40,351 mounts and his earnings
exceeded $123 million. He retired Feb 1990
after finishing fourth on Patchy Groundfog at
Santa Anita, California.

CAREER HIGHLIGHTS
Kentucky Derby: 1955, 1959, 1965, 1986
Preakness Stakes: 1963, 1967
Belmont Stakes: 1957, 1959, 1962, 1967, 1975
leading US money winner: 1951, 1953–54, 1958–64

Sobers Gary (Garfield St Aubrun) 1936– . West
Indian test cricketer. One of the game's great
all-rounders, he holds the record for the highest test innings (365 not out). Sobers played

English county cricket with Nottinghamshire and while playing for them against Glamorgan at Swansea in 1968, he established a world record by scoring six 6s in one over. He played for the West Indies 93 times.

CAREER HIGHLIGHTS
all first-class cricket
runs: 28,315
average: 54.87
best: 365 not out West Indies v. Pakistan 1957–58
wickets: 1,043
average: 27.74
best: 9-49 West Indies v. Kent 1966
test cricket
runs: 8,032
average: 57.78
best: 365 not out v. Pakistan 1957–58
wickets: 235
average: 34.03
best: 6-73 v. Australia 1968–69

Spitz Mark Andrew 1950– . US swimmer. He won a record seven gold medals at the 1972 Olympic Games, all in world record times. He won 11 Olympic medals in total (four in 1968) and set 26 world records between 1967 and 1972. After retiring in 1972 he became a movie actor, two of his films being elected candidates for 'The Worst of Hollywood'.

CAREER HIGHLIGHTS
Olympic medals
1968: gold—4 × 100 metres freestyle relay, 4 × 200 metres freestyle relay; silver—100 metres butterfly; bronze—100 metres freestyle
1972: gold—100 metres freestyle, 200 metres freestyle, 100 metres butterfly, 200 metres butterfly, 4 × 100 metres freestyle relay, 4 × 200 metres freestyle relay, 4 × 100 metres medley relay

Stewart Jackie (John Young) 1939– . Scottish motor-racing driver. Until surpassed by Alain Prost in 1987, Stewart held the record for the most Formula One Grand Prix wins (27). With manufacturer Ken Tyrrell, Stewart built up one of the sport's great partnerships. His last race was the 1973 Canadian Grand Prix. He pulled out of the next race (which would have been his 100th) because of the death of his team-mate Francois Cevert. He is now a motor-racing commentator.

CAREER HIGHLIGHTS
world champion
1969 Matra
1971 Tyrrell
1973 Tyrrell
Formula One Grand Prix

races: 99
wins: 27
first: 1965 (South African Grand Prix; BRM)
last: 1973 (Canadian Grand Prix; Tyrrell)

Thompson Daley (Francis Morgan) 1958– . English decathlete who has broken the world record four times since winning the Commonwealth Games decathlon title 1978. He has won two more Commonwealth titles (1982, 1986), two Olympic gold medals (1980, 1984), three European medals (silver 1978; gold 1982, 1986), and a world title (1983).

Torvill and Dean English ice-dance champions Jayne Torvill (1957–) and Christopher Dean (1959–). They won the world title four times 1981–84 and were the 1984 Olympic champions. They turned professional upon ending their amateur careers.

Tyson Mike (Michael Gerald) 1966– . US heavyweight boxer, undisputed world champion from Aug 1987 to Feb 1990 (when he was defeated by James 'Buster' Douglas). He won the World Boxing Council heavyweight title 1986 when he beat Trevor Berbick to become the youngest world heavyweight champion ever. He beat James 'Bonecrusher' Smith for the World Boxing Association title 1987 and later that year became the first undisputed champion since 1978 when he beat Tony Tucker for the International Boxing Federation title. Of Tyson's first 25 opponents, 15 were knocked out in the first round. In 1992 he was imprisoned for rape.

Witt Katarina 1965– . German ice-skater. She was 1984 Olympic champion (representing East Germany) and by 1990 had won four world titles (1984–85, 1987–88) and six consecutive European titles (1983–88).

Woosnam Ian 1958– . Welsh golfer who, in 1987, became the first UK player to win the World Match-Play Championship. He has since won many tournaments, including the World Cup 1987, World Match-Play 1990, and US Masters 1991. Woosnam was Europe's leading money-winner in 1987 (as a result of winning the $1 million Sun City Open in South Africa) and again in 1990. He was ranked Number One in the world for 50 weeks in 1991–92.

CAREER HIGHLIGHTS
Ryder Cup (individual): 1983, 1985, 1987, 1989, 1991
Ryder Cup (team): 1985, 1987, tie 1989
US Masters: 1991
World Match-Play Championship: 1987, 1990
World Cup (individual): 1987, 1991
World Cup (team): 1987 (Wales)

Governing bodies of Olympic sports affiliated to the British Olympic Association

archery: Grand National Archery Society, Seventh Street, National Agricultural Centre, Stoneleigh, Kenilworth, Warwickshire CV8 2LG Tel: (0203) 696631

athletics: British Athletic Federation, Edgbaston House, 3 Duchess Place, Hagley Road, Edgbaston, Birmingham B16 8NM Tel: 021-456 4050

badminton: British Badminton Olympic Committee, 2 Broadstrood, Loughton, Essex IG10 2SE Tel: 081-508 7218

baseball: British Baseball Federation, 19 Troutsdale Grove, Southcoates Lane, Hull HU9 3SD Tel: (0482) 792337

basketball: British and Irish Basketball Federation, The Carnegie National Sports Development Centre, Beckett Park, Leeds LS6 3QS Tel: (0532) 832600 x 3574

bobsleigh: British Bobsleigh Association, Springfield House, Woodstock Road, Couldsdon, Surrey CR5 3HS Tel: (0737) 555152

boxing: British Amateur Boxing Association, Francis House, Francis Street, London SW1P 1DE Tel: 071-828 8568

canoeing: British Canoe Union, John Dudderidge House, Adbolton Lane, West Bridgford, Nottingham NG2 5AS Tel: (0602) 821100

cycling: British Cycling Federation, 36 Rockingham Road, Kettering, Northamptonshire NN16 8HG Tel: (0536) 412211

equestrianism: British Equestrian Federation, British Equestrian Centre, Stoneleigh, Kenilworth, Warwickshire CV8 2LR Tel: (0203) 696697

fencing: Amateur Fencing Association, 1 Barons Gate, 33–35 Rothschild Road, London W4 5HT Tel: 081-742 3032

football, association: Football Association, 16 Lancaster Gate, London W2 3LW Tel: 071-262 4542

gymnastics: British Amateur Gymnastics Association, Ford Hall, Lilleshall National Sports Centre, Newport, Shropshire TF10 9ND Tel: (0952) 820330

handball: British Handball Association, 60 Church Street, Radcliffe, Manchester M26 8SQ Tel: 061-724 9656

hockey: Great Britain Olympic Hockey Board, Coventry Farmhouse, Hankins Lane, London NW7 3AJ Tel: 081-959 2339

ice hockey: British Ice Hockey Association, 517 Christchurch Road, Boscombe, Bournemouth, Dorset Tel: (0202) 303946

judo: British Judo Association, 7A Rutland Street, Leicester LE1 1RB Tel: (0533) 559669

luge: Great Britain Luge Association, 1 Highfield House, Hampton Bishop, Hereford HR1 4JN Tel: (0432) 353920

pentathlon, modern: Modern Pentathlon Association of Great Britain, Wessex House, Silchester Road, Tadley, Basingstoke, Hampshire Tel: (0734) 810111

rowing: Amateur Rowing Association, The Priory, 6 Lower Mall, London W6 9DJ Tel: 081-748 3632

shooting: Great Britain Target Shooting Federation, Lord Roberts House, Bisley Camp, Brookwood, Woking, Surrey GU24 0NP Tel: (0483) 476969

skating: National Skating Association of Great Britain, 15–27 Gee Street, London EC1V 3RE Tel: 071-253 3824

skiing: British Ski Federation, 258 Main Street, East Calder, Livingston, West Lothian EH53 0EE Tel: (0506) 884343

swimming: Amateur Swimming Federation of Great Britain, Harold Fern House, Derby Square, Loughborough, Leicestershire LE11 0AL Tel: (0509) 230431

table tennis: British Olympic Table Tennis Committee, Third Floor, Queensbury House, Havelock Road, Hastings, East Sussex TN34 1HF Tel: (0424) 722525

tennis, lawn: Lawn Tennis Association, Queens Club, Barons Court, West Kensington, London W14 9EG Tel: 071-385 2366

volleyball: British Volleyball Association, 27 South Road, West Bridgford, Nottingham Tel: (0602) 816324

weightlifting: British Amateur Weightlifters' Association, 3 Iffley Turn, Oxford OX4 4DU Tel: (0865) 778319

wrestling: British Amateur Wrestling Association, 41 Great Clowes Street, Salford, Lancashire M7 9RQ Tel: 061-832 9209

yachting: Royal Yachting Association, RYA House, Romsey Road, Eastleigh, Hampshire SO5 4YA Tel: (0703) 629962

Other sporting bodies affiliated to the British Olympic Association

athletics: Scottish Amateur Athletic Association, Caledonia House, South Gyle, Edinburgh EH12 9DQ Tel: 031-317 7320

Universities Athletic Union, Suite 36, London Fruit Exchange, Brushfield Street, London E1 6EU Tel: 071-247 3066

Welsh Amateur Athletic Association, Morfa Stadium, Landore, Swansea, West Glamorgan SA1 7DF Tel: (0792) 456237

Women's Amateur Athletic Association, Francis House, Francis Street, London SW1P 1DE Tel: 071-828 4731

boxing: Scottish Amateur Boxing Association, 96 High Street, Lochee, Dundee, Tayside Tel: (0382) 611412

Welsh Amateur Boxing Association, 8 Erw Wen, Rhiwbina, Cardiff, South Glamorgan Tel: (0222) 623506

clay pigeon shooting: Clay Pigeon Shooting Association, 107 Epping New Road, Buckhurst Hill, Essex IG9 5TQ Tel: 081-505 6221

cross-country running: Welsh Cross Country Association, Harries Haunt, 40 Twyni-Teg, Killay, Swansea SA2 7NS

karate: British Karate Federation, Smalldrink, Parsonage Lane, Begelly, Kilgetty, Dyfed SA68 0YL Tel: (0834) 813776

lacrosse: English Lacrosse Union, Winton House, Winton Road, Bowdon, Altrincham, Cheshire WA14 Tel: 061-928 9600

netball: All England Netball Association, Netball House, 9 Paynes Park, Hitchin, Hertfordshire SG5 1EH Tel: (0462) 442344

orienteering: British Orienteering Federation, Riversdale, Dale Road North, Darley Dale, Matlock, Derbyshire DE4 2HX Tel: (0629) 734042

race walking: Race Walking Association, Hustlers, Herds Lane, Shenfield, Brentwood, Essex CM15 0SH

swimming: Scottish Amateur Swimming Association, Holmhills Farm, Greenlees Road, Cambusleng, Glasgow G72 8DT Tel: 041-641 8818

Welsh Amateur Swimming Association, Wales Empire Pool, Wood Street, Cardiff, South Glamorgan Tel: (0222) 342201

taekwondo: British Taekwondo Control Board (WTF), 53 Geary Road, London NW10 1HJ Tel: 081-450 3818

tenpin bowling: British Tenpin Bowling Association, 114 Balfour Road, Ilford, Essex IG1 4JD Tel: 081-478 1745

water skiing: British Water Ski Federation, 390 City Road, London EC1V 2QA Tel: 071-833 2855

Army Sport Control Board Ministry of Defence, Clayton Barracks, Thornhill Road, Aldershot, Hampshire GU11 2BG Tel: (0252) 348569

British Association of Sport and Medicine c/o The National Sports Medicine Institute, Medical College of St Bartholomew's Hospital,

Charterhouse Square, London EC1M 6BQ Tel: 071-253 3244

Central Council of Physical Recreation Francis House, Francis Street, London SW1P 1DE Tel: 071-828 3163

Civil Service Sports Council 7–8 Buckingham Place, Bellfield House, High Wycombe, Buckinghamshire Tel: (0494) 461800

Royal Air Force Sports Board Room 334, Ministry of Defence, Adastral House, Theobalds Road, London WC1X 8RU Tel: 071-430 7265

Royal Navy & Royal Marines Sports Control Board HMS Temeraire, Burnaby Road, Portsmouth, Hampshire PO1 2HB Tel: (0705) 822351 x 23994

Which of these different sports would you dare to do?	
Parachuting	57
Hang gliding	46
Bob sleighing	46
Mountain climbing	43
Paragliding	43
White water rafting	35
Potholing	29
Bungee jumping	24
Wing walking	15
High wire walking	13
None of these	15

AIR TRANSPORT

People first took to the air in balloons and began powered flight in airships but the history of flying is dominated by the aeroplane. The aeroplane is a development of the model glider, first flown by George Cayley in 1804. Not until the invention of the petrol engine did powered flight become feasible. The Wright brothers in the USA first achieved success, when they flew their biplane *Flyer* on 17 Dec 1903. In Europe, France led in aeroplane design (Voisin brothers) and Louis Ble1riot brought aviation much publicity by crossing the Channel in 1909. The first powered flight in the UK was made by S F Cody in 1908. In 1912 Sopwith and Bristol both built small biplanes.

The stimulus of World War I (1914–18) and the rapid development of the petrol engine led to increased power, and speeds rose to 320 kph/200 mph. Streamlining the body of planes became imperative: the body, wings, and exposed parts were reshaped to reduce drag. Eventually the biplane was superseded by the internally braced monoplane structure—for example, the Hawker Hurricane and Supermarine Spitfire fighters and the Avro Lancaster and Boeing Flying Fortress bombers of World War II (1939–45).

The German Heinkel 178, built 1939, ushered in a new era in aviation. It was the first jet plane, driven, not as all planes before it with a propeller, but by a jet of hot gases. The first British jet aircraft, the Gloster E.28/39 flew from Cranwell, Lincolnshire, on 15 May 1941, powered by a jet engine invented by Frank Whittle. Twin-jet Meteor fighters were in use by the end of the war. The rapid development of the jet plane led to enormous increases in power and speed until air-compressability effects were felt near the speed of sound, which at first seemed to be a flight speed limit (the sound barrier). To exceed supersonic speed, mere streamlining of the aircraft body became insufficient: wings were swept back, engines buried in wings and tail units, and bodies were even eliminated in all-wing delta designs.

In the 1950s the first jet airliners, such as the Comet, were introduced into service. Today jet planes dominate both military and civilian aviation, although many light planes still use piston engines and propellers. The late 1960s saw the introduction of the jumbo jet, and in 1976 the Anglo-French Concorde, which makes a transatlantic crossing in under three hours, came into commercial service.

During the 1950s and 1960s research was done on V/STOL (vertical and/or short take-off) aircraft. The British Harrier jet fighter has been the only VTOL aircraft to achieve commercial success, but STOL technology has fed into subsequent generations of aircraft. The 1960s and 1970s also saw the development of variable geometry ('swing-wing') aircraft, whose wings can be swept back in flight to achieve higher speeds. In the 1980s much progress has been made in 'fly-by-wire' aircraft with computer-aided controls.

International partnerships have developed both civilian and military aircraft. The Panavia Tornado is a joint project of British, German, and Italian aircraft companies. It is an advanced swing-wing craft of multiple roles—interception, strike, ground support, and reconnaissance. The Airbus is a wide-bodied airliner built jointly by companies from France, Germany, the UK, the Netherlands, and Spain.

FINDING THE WAY BY SATELLITE

Eighty-five nations have agreed to take part in trials of a new aircraft-navigation system which makes use of surplus military space technology left over from the Cold War. The new system, known as FANS or Future Air Navigation System, will make use of the 24 Russian Glonass satellites and the 24 US global positioning system satellites. Small low-cost computers will be gradually fitted to civil aircraft to process the signals from the satellites, allowing aircraft to navigate with pinpoint accuracy anywhere in the world. The signals from at least three satellites will guide the craft to within a few metres' accuracy. The system will also enable aircraft to fly closer together. At present over oceans and deserts, where there is no direct radar contact, aircraft must remain at least 8 km/5 mi apart to allow for navigational errors and unforeseen drift. FANS will be used in conjunction with four Inmarsat satellites to provide worldwide communications between pilots and air traffic controllers.

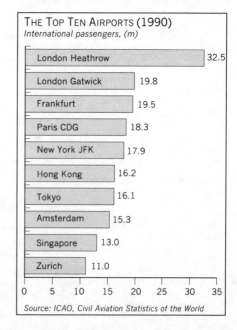

THE TOP TEN AIRPORTS (1990)
International passengers, (m)

Airport	Passengers (m)
London Heathrow	32.5
London Gatwick	19.8
Frankfurt	19.5
Paris CDG	18.3
New York JFK	17.9
Hong Kong	16.2
Tokyo	16.1
Amsterdam	15.3
Singapore	13.0
Zurich	11.0

Source: ICAO, Civil Aviation Statistics of the World

from France, Germany, the UK, the Netherlands, and Spain.

aeroplane heavier-than-air craft supported in flight by fixed wings: it may be unpowered (a glider) or powered, when it is propelled by the thrust of a jet engine or propeller. It must be designed aerodynamically, since streamlining ensures maximum flight efficiency. The shape of a plane depends on its use and operating speed—aircraft operating at well below the speed of sound need not be as streamlined as supersonic aircraft.

Efficient streamlining prevents the formation of shock waves over the body surface and wings, which would cause instability and power loss. The wing of an aeroplane has the cross-sectional shape of an aerofoil, being broad and curved at the front, flat underneath, curved on top, and tapered to a sharp point at the rear. The wings are so shaped that air passing above them is speeded up, reducing pressure below atmospheric pressure, while that above is slowed. This results in a force acting vertically upwards, called lift, which counters the aircraft's weight. In level flight, lift equals weight. The wings develop sufficient lift to support the plane when they move quickly through the air. The thrust that causes propulsion comes from the reaction to the air stream accelerated backwards by the propeller or the gases shooting backwards from the jet exhaust. In flight the engine thrust must overcome the air resistance, or drag. Drag depends on frontal area (large in the case of an airliner; small in the case of a fighter plane) and shape (drag coefficient); in level flight, drag equals thrust. The drag is reduced by streamlining the plane, resulting in higher speed and reduced fuel consumption for a given power. Less fuel need be carried for a given distance of travel, so a larger payload (cargo or passengers) can be carried.

Planes are constructed using light but strong aluminium alloys such as duralumin (with copper, magnesium, and so on). For supersonic planes special stainless steel and titanium may be used in areas subjected to high heat loads. The structure of the plane, or the airframe (wings, fuselage, and so on) consists of a surface skin of alloy sheets supported at intervals by struts known as ribs and stringers.

The structure is bonded together by riveting or by powerful adhesives such as epoxy resins. In certain critical areas, which have to withstand very high stresses (such as the wing roots), body panels are machined from solid metal for extra strength.

Fastest aeroplane—the Lockheed SR-71, holder of the world air-speed record of 3,529 kph/2,193 mph (over Mach 3.3).

Fastest airliner—Concorde, which can cruise at up to Mach 2.2 (2,333 kph/1,450 mph).

Largest airliner—Boeing 747, with a wingspan of 59.6 m/195.7 ft and a length of 70.7 m/231.8 ft.

Largest volume aeroplane—the Guppy-201, with a usable volume of 1,104 cu m/39,000 cu ft.

airship a power-driven balloon. All airships have streamlined envelopes or hulls, which contain the inflation gas, and are either non-rigid, semi-rigid, or rigid. Count Ferdinand von Zeppelin (1838–1917) pioneered the rigid type, named after him, and used for bombing raids on the UK in World War I. The destruction by fire of the British R101 in 1930 halted airship building in Britain, but the Germans continued and built the 248 m/812 ft long *Hindenburg*. However, this airship exploded at Lakehurst, New Jersey 1937, marking the effective end of airship travel. The early airships were vulnerable because they used hydrogen for inflation. It is the lightest gas, but highly flammable. After World War II, interest grew in airships using the nonflammable gas helium. They cause minimum noise, can lift enormous loads, and are economical on fuel. Britain's Airship Industries received large orders in 1987 from the US Navy for airships to be used for coastguard patrols, and the Advanced Airship Corporation on the Isle of Man was reported in 1989 to be constructing the fastest passenger airship ever built (80 knots), powered by twin-propeller turbine engines.

balloon bag or envelope of impermeable fabric that rises from the ground when filled with a gas lighter than the surrounding air. In 1783, the first successful human ascent was piloted by Pilâtre de Rozier in Paris, in a hot-air balloon designed by the Montgolfier brothers. During the French Revolution balloons were used for observation; in World War II they were used to defend London against low-flying aircraft. Balloons continue in use for sport, as a low-cost means of meteorological, infrared, gamma-ray, and ultraviolet observation. The first transatlantic crossing by gas balloon (from Presque Isle, Maine to Miserey, France) was made 11-17 Aug 1978 by a US team.

helicopter an aircraft that achieves both lift and propulsion by means of a rotary wing, or rotor, on top of the fuselage. It can take off and land vertically, move in any direction, or remain stationary in the air. Igor Sikorsky built the first practical single rotor craft, in the USA 1939. The rotor of a helicopter has two or more blades, which are of aerofoil cross-section, like an aeroplane's wings. Lift and propulsion are achieved by angling the blades as they rotate. A single-rotor helicopter must also have a small tail rotor to counter the tendency of the body to spin in the opposite direction to the main rotor. Twin-rotor helicopters, like the Boeing Chinook, have their rotors turning in opposite directions, and this prevents the body from spinning.

Helicopters are now widely used in passenger service, rescue missions on land and sea, police pursuits and traffic control, firefighting, and agriculture. In war they carry troops and equipment into difficult terrain, make aerial reconnaissance and attacks, and carry wounded to aid stations. Helicopters are increasingly being associated with naval aircraft carriers, as many as 30 helicopters being used on larger

AIR TRANSPORT: CHRONOLOGY

1783	First human flight, by Jean F Pilâtre de Rozier and the Marquis d'Arlandes, in Paris, using a hot-air balloon made by Joseph and Etienne Montgolfier; first ascent in a hydrogen-filled balloon by Jacques Charles and M N Robert in Paris.
1785	Jean-Pierre Blanchard and John J Jeffries made the first balloon crossing of the English Channel.
1804	George Cayley flew the first true aeroplane, a model glider 1.5 m/5 ft long.
1852	Henri Giffard flew the first steam-powered airship over Paris.
1891–96	Otto Lilienthal piloted a glider in flight.
1903	First powered and controlled flight of a heavier-than-air machine by Orville Wright, at Kitty Hawk, North Carolina, USA.
1909	Louis Bleriot flew across the English Channel in 36 minutes.
1919	First transatlantic flight by Albert C Read, using a flying boat; first non-stop trans-atlantic flight by John William Alcock and Arthur Whitten Brown in 16 hours 27 minutes; first flight from the UK to Australia by Ross Smith and Keith Smith.
1923	Juan de la Cieva flew the first autogyro with a rotating wing.
1927	Charles Lindbergh made the first solo nonstop flight across the Atlantic.
1928	First trans-Pacific flight, from San Francisco to Brisbane, by Charles Kinsford Smith and C T P Ulm.
1930	Frank Whittle patented the jet engine; Amy Johnson became the first woman to fly solo from England to Australia.
1937	The first fully pressurized aircraft, the Lockheed XC-35, came into service.
1939	Erich Warsitz flew the first jet aeroplane, in Germany; Igor Sikorsky designed the first modern helicopter, with a large main rotor and a smaller tail rotor.
1947	A rocket-powered plane, the Bell X-1, was the first aircraft to fly faster than the speed of sound.
1949	The de Havilland Comet, the first jet airliner, entered service; James Gallagher made the first nonstop round-the-world flight, in a Boeing Superfortress.
1953	The first vertical takeoff aircraft, the Rolls-Royce 'Flying Bedstead', was tested.
1968	The world's first supersonic airliner, the Soviet TU-144, flew for the first time.
1969	First flight of the BAC/Aérospatiale supersonic airliner Concorde.
1976	A Lockheed SR-17A, piloted by Eldon W Joersz and George T Morgan, set the world air-speed record of 3,529.56 kph/2,193.167 mph over Beale Air Force Base, California, USA.
1978	US team made the first transatlantic crossing by balloon, in the helium-filled *Double Eagle II*.
1979	First crossing of the English Channel by a human-powered aircraft, *Gossamer Albatross*, piloted by Bryan Allen.
1981	The solar-powered *Solar Challenger* flew across the English Channel, from Paris to Kent, taking 5 hours for the 262 km/162.8 mi journey.
1986	Dick Rutan and Jeana Yeager made the first nonstop flight around the world without refuelling, piloting *Voyager*, in 9 days 3 minutes 44 seconds.
1987	Richard Branson and Per Linstrand made the first transatlantic crossing by hot-air balloon, *Virgin Atlantic Challenger*, in 31 hours 41 minutes.
1988	*Daedelus*, a human-powered craft piloted by Kanellos Kanellopoulos, flew 118 m/74 mi across the Aegean Sea.
1991	Richard Branson and Per Lindstrand crossed the Pacific Ocean in the hot-air balloon *Virgin Otsuka Pacific Flyer* from the southern tip of Japan to NW Canada in 46 hours 15 minutes.

carriers, in combination with V/STOL aircraft, such as Harriers. The helicopter may possess depth charges and homing torpedoes guided to submarine or surface targets beyond the carrier's attack range. It may also use dunking sonar to find targets beyond the carrier's own radar horizon.

jet propulsion a method of propulsion in which an object is propelled in one direction by a jet, or stream of gases, moving in the other. This follows from Newton's celebrated third law of motion 'to every action, there is an equal and opposite reaction'. The most wide-spread application of the jet principle is in the jet engine, the commonest kind of aero-engine.

The jet engine is a type of gas turbine. Air, after passing through a forward-facing intake, is compressed by a compressor, or fan, and fed into a combustion chamber. Fuel (usually kerosene) is sprayed in and ignited. The hot gas produced expands rapidly rearwards, spinning a turbine that drives the compressor before being finally ejected from a rearward-facing tail pipe, or nozzle, at very high speed. Reaction to the jet of gases streaming backwards produces a propulsive thrust forwards, which acts on the aircraft through its engine-mountings, not from any pushing of the hot gas stream against the static air.

rocket a projectile driven by the reaction of gases produced by a fast-burning fuel. Unlike the jet

PAYING FOR ROAD CONGESTION

Every day motorists face the grind of commuting into city centres: overcrowded roads, snarl-ups, and even 'gridlock', when traffic comes to a halt over a wide area. The congestion on city roads dissipates enormous amounts of time and money—and emotional energy. However, the problem is at last receiving the attention it deserves.

One approach is road pricing—charging motorists to drive in congested city centres. The idea started in Singapore in 1975. Motorists had to buy and display a daily licence to drive into the city. The scheme was judged a success by an OECD report which stated that by 1983 fewer than one in four commuters were driving to work, compared to one in two eight years earlier. The problem with the scheme is that it is costly and bureaucratic. Now Singapore is thinking about going electronic.

There are several electronic versions of road pricing. The world's first system was tested in Hong Kong from 1983 to 1985. Roadside beacons transmitting microwaves were used to identify vehicles fitted with transponders as they drove past. The information gathered was fed to a central computer, and motorists were sent a monthly bill calculated on the basis of where they had driven. The scheme was stopped because of worries about civil liberties; the bills could be used to check the movements of individuals.

Similar systems were introduced in the Norwegian cities of Bergen and Oslo in 1990, and in Trondheim during 1991, but elsewhere progress has been slow. The Dutch have abandoned plans for countrywide road pricing on motorways and freeways. Sweden's schemes are bogging down in political controversy. In the UK, the Department of Transport is now showing interest after a period of opposition to the idea, and plans to spend £3 million over the next three years to review the technology for possible use in London.

There are two road-pricing schemes under development which should provide useful experience. The first, Timezone, is being developed by GEC-Marconi. Under the scheme, cars are fitted with meters which communicate by radio with beacons erected at strategic points within defined zones. The beacons transmit information to indicate which zone a car is in and what charge is being made. The meter is pre-paid with a smart card, similar to a phonecard, whose credits are consumed as the motorist drives through the zones.

Motorists are charged at rates depending on the zone, time, and length of journey. The highest rates might be charged for driving through central areas at peak times. Driving at weekends or in outer areas would be cheaper or free. Local residents could be charged different rates or could travel free. The meter shows how much credit is available. When the credit runs out, the driver has to buy another card, available at a variety of outlets including shops and garages. If credit runs out during

The Timezone road-pricing meter keeps track of the variable rates charged.

a journey, the meter transmits radio signals which activate roadside TV cameras to photograph the car so that a bill can be sent to the owner. The cameras also photograph cars without meters. Signs around the perimeter of the zones warn visiting motorists to purchase daily permits. The technology for Timezone has already been developed and the system will be tested in Richmond in southwest London in 1992.

The second scheme centres on Cambridge, a city with increasing congestion problems. However, the congestion there varies from day to day, as well as by district. The University of Newcastle upon Tyne is helping Cambridge develop an unusual pricing scheme, in which motorists pay when they cause congestion rather than when they pass through a zone. Each car will have a meter, fed by a pre-paid smart card, which will be switched on by a roadside beacon when the car enters Cambridge along main roads and switched off when it leaves. Inside the city, when the car is moving freely, the meter will not register a charge. However, when the car encounters a jam and stops, the meter clocks up a charge. The threshold for charging has not yet been decided—it might be four stops in 500 m/500 yd, for example. If the motorist runs out of credit, the meter continues to register a charge until the car stops. When the engine is switched off for more than, say, 30 seconds, the car is immobilized and the motorist has to buy a new card to get going again. Field tests of the equipment should begin in 1994, with a large-scale trial around 1995.

RAIL TRANSPORT: CHRONOLOGY

1500s	Tramways—wooden tracks along which trolleys ran—were in use in mines.
1804	Richard Trevithick built the first steam locomotive and ran it on a track at the Pen-y-darren ironworks in South Wales.
1825	British engineer George Stephenson built the first public railway to carry steam trains — the Stockton and Darlington line.
1829	Stephenson designed his locomotive *Rocket*, which trounced its rivals at the Rainhill trials.
1830	Stephenson completed the Liverpool and Manchester Railway, the first steam passenger line; the first US-built locomotive, *Best Friend of Charleston*, went into service on the South Carolina Railroad.
1835	Germany pioneered steam railways in Europe, using *Der Adler*, a locomotive built by Stephenson.
1863	Robert Fairlie, a Scot, patented a locomotive with pivoting driving bogies, allowing tight curves in the track (this was later applied in the Garratt locomotives); London opened the world's first underground railway, powered by steam.
1869	The first US transcontinental railway was completed at Promontory, Utah, when the Union Pacific and the Central Pacific railroads met; George Westinghouse of the USA invented the compressed-air brake.
1879	Werner von Siemens demonstrated an electric train in Germany; Volk's Electric Railway along the Brighton seafront was the world's first public electric railway.
1883	Charles Lartique built the first monorail, in Ireland.
1890	The first electric underground railway opened in London.
1901	The world's most successful monorail, the Wuppertal Schwebebahn, went into service.
1912	The first diesel locomotive took to the rails in Germany.
1938	The British steam locomotive *Mallard* set a steam-rail speed record of 201 kph/125 mph.
1941	Swiss Federal Railways introduced a gas-turbine locomotive.
1964	Japan National Railways inaugurated the 512 km/320 mi New Tokaido line between Osaka and Tokyo, on which run the 210 kph/130 mph 'bullet' trains.
1973	British Rail's High Speed Train (HST) set a diesel rail speed record of 22 kph/143 mph.
1981	France's TGV superfast trains began operation between Paris and Lyons, regularly attaining a peak speed of 270 kph/168 mph.
1987	British Rail set a new diesel-traction speed record of 238.9kph/148.5 mph, on a test run between Darlington and York; France and the UK began work on the Channel Tunnel, a railway link running beneath the English Channel; Japanese maglev MLV-001 test train reaches speed with passengers of 400 kph/249 mph.
1988	The West German Intercity Experimental train reached 405 kph/252 mph on test run between Würzburg amd Fulda.
1990	A new rail-speed record of 515 kph/320 mph was established by a French TGV train, on a stretch of line between Tours and Paris.
1991	British and French twin tunnels meet 23 km/14 mi out to sea to form the Channel Tunnel.
1992	Trams return to the streets of Manchester, England, after an absence of 40 years; towns in France and the USA follow suit.

---

engine, which is also a reaction engine, the rocket engine carries its own oxygen supply to burn its fuel and is totally independent of any surrounding atmosphere. As rockets are the only form of propulsion available that can function in a vacuum, they are essential to the exploration of outer space.

RAIL TRANSPORT

Tracks to carry goods waggons were in use at collieries in the 18th century, but the first practical public passenger service was that between Stockton and Darlington in 1825, under the power of Stephenson's engine 'Locomotion'. A railway boom ensued, and railways were the major form of land transport for passengers and goods until after World War II when the private car, coach services, internal air services, and road haulage door-to-door, destroyed their monopoly. In the UK the railways (known as British Rail from 1965) were nationalized in 1948, and the network increasingly shrank. In the USA and Canada railways made the 19th-century exploitation of the central and western territories possible, and in the USA underpinned the victory of the north in the Civil War, the 'Railway War'.

In countries with less developed road systems and large areas of difficult terrain, the railway is still important as in India, China, South Amer-

COMPUTERS WITH WINGS

An oft-repeated joke in the aviation industry runs like this: today's aircraft only require a pilot and a dog to fly them. Why? The dog is there to bite the pilot if he tries to touch the controls. The pilot's job is to feed the dog. The joke may be stale, but there is a serious point behind it. Today's aircraft are becoming increasingly computerized, making some pilots feel they are almost redundant.

The pace of aircraft automation has quickened recently. Until the 1980s, aircraft technology was based on mechanical controls and hydraulic systems to move the flight surfaces on the wing. Autopilots enabled planes to fly straight and level through dense cloud, but the pilot was still very much in charge.

Then came the microprocessor. Engineers incorporated the 'computer on a chip' into aircraft such as the Boeing 757 and 767, and the European Airbus A310. However, these planes still used hydraulic and mechanical control systems. In 1988, the designers of the Airbus A320 took another step towards complete automation by introducing 'fly by wire'—a system in which electrical signals along a network of wire activate the flight surfaces without input from the pilot.

The cockpit of the Airbus 320 is a product of the computer age. It is filled with computer screens and input devices, dispensing with the plethora of analogue dials and gauges of earlier aircraft. By displaying information in a more concise form, the computer screens simplify the pilot's task. A keyboard between the pilot and the first officer provides the input to the flight management system. This contains

The flight deck of the European Airbus A320. Its makers claim the plane will fail only once in a billion flights, because it has no fewer than five separate control computers. Some experts argue, however, that computerizing the aircraft's controls completely may not be as risk-free as supposed.

several dozen microprocessors which assume many of the routine tasks once undertaken by the crew.

If the pilot attempts a manoeuvre beyond the capabilities of the aircraft, it will be overridden by the control computer. This feature irritates pilots, who feel that they should have freedom of action. If a plane is heading for the side of a mountain, they argue, they should be able to pull up sharply, even if the plane is stressed beyond normal tolerances. However, aircraft makers argue that the new planes are safer. Boeing's 757 and 767 aircraft, among the most automated, have had only one accident in nearly 4 million flights; this compares with one accident in 200,000 flights for the Boeing 707, a 1950s model.

The Airbus A320 has an estimated design failure rate of one failure every billion flights, say the makers, Airbus Industrie. To achieve these levels of reliability, the aircraft has five separate control computers. Only one is required at any one time; the rest are held in reserve in case of failure. The failure rate of each computer is estimated as one failure in 100,000 flight-hours. The odds against all five computers failing at the same time are calculated by multiplying the odds of separate failures: hence the extremely low failure rate estimated by the makers. However, these estimates have been criticized. Computer systems have a tendency to fail under similar conditions so that, if one fails, the others are likely to fail too.

A comparable doubt hangs over the control computer software. The chance of an error occurring in a computer program rises as the program gets longer. The average programmer can write tiny programs, say 20 lines of code long, without making mistakes, but such programs are trivial compared to the programs airline passengers entrust their lives to, which often contain hundreds of thousands of lines of code. As yet no one has devised a way of assessing software reliability for very large programs. Sloppy programming is sometimes found by spot checks and routine testing of programs. But errors do get through; aircraft deliveries have been delayed when cockpit displays gave incorrect readings.

Two Airbuses have crashed since the aircraft took to the skies: one in 1987 at an air show at Habsheim in France, and the other at Bangalore, India, in 1990. In both cases, pilot error was blamed, but the pilot at Habsheim reported that the plane failed to respond to his commands. Computer error is therefore a possibility.

Some experts feel that the aircraft industry is moving too fast. The human pilot, although fallible, has often survived against near-impossible odds by quick thinking and fine judgement. If it is impossible to guarantee the reliability, and hence safety, of the computerized plane, manufacturers may have to fall back on tried and tested mechanical methods of control.

ica, and Russia. Electrification, or the use of diesel electric engines, has superseded the steam engine in most countries, and there has been some revival in the popularity of the train for longer distance 'inter-city' services.

The 1970s saw diesel high-speed trains (HSTs) introduced in the UK, followed by super-fast networks in Japan and France.

monorail a railway that runs on a single (mono) rail. It was invented in 1882 to carry light loads, and when run by electricity was called a *telpher*. The most successful monorail, the Wuppertal Schwebebahn, has been running in Germany since 1901. It is a suspension monorail, where the passenger cars hang from an arm fixed to a trolley that runs along the rail. Today most monorails are of the straddle type, where the passenger cars run on top of the rail. They are used to transport passengers between terminals at some airports—as at Birmingham, where the monorail works on the *maglev* (magnetic levitation) principle.

tramway a transport system for use in cities, by which wheeled vehicles run along parallel rails. It originated in collieries in the 18th century. The earliest passenger system was established in 1832, in New York, and by the 1860s horse-drawn trams plied in London and Liverpool. Trams are now powered either by electric conductor rails below ground, or conductor arms connected to overhead wires, but their use on public roads is very limited because of their lack of manoeuvrability. Greater flexibility is achieved with the *trolleybus*, similarly powered by conductor arms overhead but without tracks. In the 1980s both trams and trolleybuses were being revived in some areas. Both vehicles have the advantage of being nonpolluting to the local environment.

ROAD TRANSPORT

Specially constructed, reinforced tracks became necessary with the invention of wheeled vehicles in about 3000 BC and most ancient civilizations had some form of road network. The Romans developed engineering techniques that were not equalled for another 1,400 years. Until the late 18th century most European roads were haphazardly maintained, making winter travel difficult. In the UK the turnpike system of collecting tolls created some improvement. The Scottish engineers Thomas Telford and John McAdam introduced sophisticated construction methods in the early 19th century. Recent developments have included durable surface compounds and machinery for rapid ground preparation.

bicycle a pedal-driven two-wheeled vehicle. It consists of a metal frame mounted on two large wire-spoked wheels, with handlebars in front and a seat between the front and back wheels. The first pedal-bicycle was invented by Kirkpatrick Macmillan, a Scot, in about 1840, pneumatic tyres being added from 1846, and by

1888 these had been improved by J B Dunlop to boost the cycling craze of the turn of the century. Design changes were then minor until the small-wheeled Moulton bicycle appeared after World War II. The bicycle is an energy-efficient, nonpolluting form of transport and is used throughout the world.

car a small self-propelled vehicle able to be run and be steered on normal roads. Most are four-wheeled and have water-cooled, piston-type internal-combustion engines fuelled by petrol or diesel.

Although it is recorded that in 1479 one Gilles de Dom was paid 25 livres by the treasurer of Antwerp, for supplying such a vehicle, the forerunner of the automobile is generally agreed to be Nicolas-Joseph Cugnot's cumbrous steam carriage 1769, still preserved in Paris. Another Parisian, Étienne Lenoir, made the first gas engine in 1860, and in 1885 Benz built and ran the first petrol-driven motor car. Panhard 1890 (front radiator, engine under the bonnet, sliding-pinion gearbox, wooden ladder-chassis) and Mercédès 1901 (honeycomb radiator, in-line four-cylinder engine, gate-change gearbox, pressed-steel chassis) set the pattern for the modern car.

A typical modern medium-sized saloon car has a semi-monocoque construction in which

---

ON YOUR ZIKE

The latest offering from British inventor Clive Sinclair is an electric bicycle called the Zike. The Zike is as light as a racing bake at 11 kg/24 lb. The frame is made of light aircraft-grade aluminium alloy, and ultra-strong composites—in this case 'Verton', a material invented and manufactured by ICI which combines long glass fibres and nylon. The nickel—cadmium batteries, held inside the central strut of the frame, are half the weight of the equivalent lead—acid battery. They can be charged in an hour, rather than the usual eight hours. Over 2000 recharges are possible, at a cost of around 1p per charge. The electric motor, also in the central strut, uses a new form of 'rare earth' magnets made of neodymium, iron and boron, which are less than one-third the weight of conventional ferrite magnets. The result of the weight-saving is a vehicle that can reach a speed of 19 kph/12 mph, low enough to avoid the need for a licence, tax or insurance in Britain.

The Zike can operate in three modes, selected by a switch on the handlebars. In the first mode, under electric power, Zike does all the work without pedalling and runs for between 30 minutes and 1 hour depending upon wind and terrain. It will carry a passenger up the steepest normal hill. The second mode—motor and light pedalling—extends the range to around $1\frac{1}{2}$ hours. In the third mode, the rider does most of the pedalling with some assistance from the motor. The range is extended to 2–3 hours.

CAR: CHRONOLOGY

1769	Nicholas-Joseph Cugnot in France built a steam tractor.
1860	Jean Etienne Lenoir built a gas-fuelled internal-combustion engine.
1831	The British government passed the 'Red Flag' Act, requiring a man to precede a 'horseless carriage' with a red flag.
1876	Nikolaus August Otto improved the gas engine, making it a practical power source.
1885	Gottlieb Daimler developed a successful lightweight petrol engine and fitted it to a bicycle to create the prototype of the modern motorbike; Karl Benz fitted his lightweight petrol engine to a three-wheeled carriage to pioneer the motor car.
1886	Gottlieb Daimler fitted his engine to a four-wheeled carriage to produce a four-wheeled motor car.
1891	René Panhard and Emile Levassor established the modern design of cars by putting the engine in front.
1896	Frederick Lanchester introduced epicyclic gearing, which foreshadowed automatic transmission.
1901	The first Mercedes took to the roads. It was the direct ancestor of the modern car; Ransome Olds in the USA introduced mass production on an assembly line.
1906	Rolls-Royce introduced the legendary Silver Ghost, which established their reputation for superlatively engineered cars.
1908	Henry Ford used assembly-line production to manufacture his famous Model T, nicknamed the Tin Lizzie because lightweight steel sheets were used for the body, which looked 'tinny'.
1911	Cadillac introduced the electric starter and dynamo lighting.
1913	Ford introduced the moving conveyor belt to the assembly line, further accelerating production of the Model T.
1920	Duesenberg began fitting four-wheel hydraulic brakes.
1922	The Lancia Lambda featured unitary (all-in-one) construction and independent front suspension.
1928	Cadillac introduced the synchromesh gearbox, greatly facilitating gear changing.
1934	Citroën pioneered front-wheel drive in their 2CV model.
1936	Fiat introduced their baby car, the Topolino, 500 cc.
1938	Germany produced their 'people's car', the Volkswagen 'beetle'.
1948	Jaguar launched the XK120 sports car; Michelin introduced the radial-ply tyre; Goodrich produced the tubeless tyre.
1950	Dunlop announced the disc brake.
1951	Buick and Chrysler in the USA introduced power steering.
1952	Rover's gas-turbine car set a speed record of 243 kph/152 mph.
1954	Bosch introduced fuel-injection for cars.
1955	Citroën produced the DS-19 'shark-front' car with hydropneumatic suspension.
1957	Felix Wankel built his first rotary petrol engine.
1959	BMC (now Rover) introduced the Issigonis-designed Mini, with front-wheel drive, transverse engine, and independent rubber suspension.
1966	California introduced legislation regarding air pollution by cars.
1972	Dunlop introduced safety tyres, which sealed themselves after a burst.
1979	American Sam Barrett exceeded the speed of sound in the rocket-engined *Budweiser Rocket*, reaching 1,190.377 kph/739.666 mph, a speed not officially recognized as a record because of timing difficulties.
1980	The first mass-produced car with four-wheel drive, the Audi Quattro, was introduced; Japanese car production overtook that of the USA.
1981	BMW introduced the on-board computer, which monitored engine performance and indicated to the driver when a service was required.
1983	British driver Richard Noble set an official speed record in the jet-engined *Thrust 2* of 1,019.4 kph/ 633.468 mph; Austin Rover introduced the Maestro, the first car with a 'talking dashboard' that alerted the driver to problems.
1987	The solar-powered *SunRaycer* travelled 3,000 km/1,864 mi from Darwin to Adelaide, Australia, in six days.
1990	Fiat of Italy, and Peugeot of France launched electric passenger cars on the market; the solar-powered *Spirit of Biel-Bienne* won a 3,000 km/1,864 mi race, travelling from Darwin to Adelaide, Australia, in six days.
1991	European Parliament voted to adopt stringent controls of car emissions.

the body panels, suitably reinforced, support the road loads through independent front and rear sprung suspension, with seats located within the wheelbase for comfort. It is usually powered by a petrol engine using a carburettor to mix petrol and air for feeding to the engine cylinders (typically four or six). The engine is usually water cooled. From the engine, power is transmitted through a clutch to a four-or five-speed gearbox and thence, in a

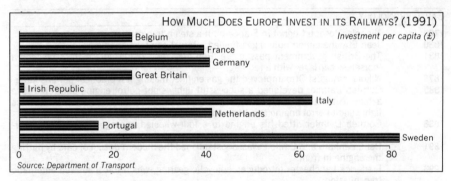

How Much Does Europe Invest in its Railways? (1991)

Investment per capita (£)

Belgium
France
Germany
Great Britain
Irish Republic
Italy
Netherlands
Portugal
Sweden

0   20   40   60   80

Source: Department of Transport

front-engine rear-drive car, through a drive (propeller) shaft to a differential gear, which drives the rear wheels. In a front-engine front-wheel drive car, clutch, gearbox, and final drive are incorporated with the engine unit. An increasing number of high-performance cars are being offered with four-wheel drive. This gives vastly superior roadholding in wet and icy conditions.

internal-combustion engine a heat engine in which fuel is burned inside the engine, contrasting with an external-combustion engine (such as the steam engine) in which fuel is burned in a separate unit. The petrol and diesel engines are both internal-combustion engines. They are reciprocating piston engines in which pistons move up and down in cylinders to effect the engine operating cycle. This may be a four-stroke cycle or a two-stroke cycle. Gas turbines and jet and rocket engines are sometimes also considered to be internal-combustion engines because they burn their fuel inside their combustion chambers.

motorcycle or ***motorbike*** a two-wheeled vehicle propelled by a petrol engine. Daimler created the first motorcycle when he installed his lightweight petrol engine in a bicycle frame in 1885. The first really successful two-wheel design was devised by Michael and Eugene Werner in France 1901. They adopted the classic motorcycle layout with the engine low down between the wheels. Harley Davidson in the USA and Triumph in the UK began manufacture 1903. Road races like the Isle of Man TT (Tourist Trophy), established in 1907, helped improve motorcycle design and it soon evolved into more or less its present form. Today Japanese motorcycles, such as Honda, Suzuki, Yamaha, and Kawasaki, dominate the world market. They make a wide variety of machines, from mopeds (lightweights with pedal assistance) to streamlined superbikes capable of speeds up to 250 kph/160 mph.

SEA TRANSPORT

People have travelled on and across the seas, for various purposes, throughout history. The Greeks and Phoenicians built wooden ships, propelled by oar or sail, to transport themselves and their goods across the sea. The Romans and Carthaginians built war galleys equipped with rams and several tiers of oars. The oak ships of the Vikings were designed for rough seas, and propelled by oar and sail. The Crusader fleet of Richard the Lionheart was largely of sail. By 1840 iron had largely replaced wood, but fast-sailing clippers survived, built with wooden planks on iron frames. The USA and the UK experimented with steam propulsion as the 19th century opened. The paddle-wheel-propelled *Comet* appeared 1812, the Canadian *Royal William* crossed the Atlantic 1833, and the English *Great Western* steamed from Bristol to New York 1838. Pettit Smith first used the screw propeller in the *Archimedes* 1839, and after 1850 the paddle-wheel became largely obsolete, its use being confined to the inland waterways, particularly the great American rivers. The introduction of the internal-combustion engine and turbine completed the revolution in propulsion until the advent of nuclear-powered vessels after World War II, chiefly submarines.

More recently hovercraft and wave-piercing catamarans have been developed for specialized purposes, particularly as short-distance fer-

---

THE ELECTROMAGNETIC SHIP

The world's first electromagnetically powered ship was launched in 1992. The prototype, called *Yamato 1*, can reach a modest 4 m per sec/8 knots, but the Japanese builders feel that such ships could reach 185 kph/100 knots. *Yamato 1* weighs 280,000 kg/617,000 lb, is 30 m/100 ft long, and carries seven passengers and three crew. It is propelled by a novel system using electromagnetic forces. Water enters ducts that run along the length of the ship below the water line. An electric current passes horizontally through the water, and interacts with a vertical magnetic field produced by superconducting magnets cooled by liquid helium. The water is propelled out of the rear of the ship, pushing it forward. Although the system is too costly for commercial use, it has possible applications in submarines and military ships where quietness and lack of vibration are at a premium.

Sᴇᴀ Tʀᴀɴsᴘᴏʀᴛ Cʜʀᴏɴᴏʟᴏɢʏ

BC

8000–7000	Reed boats developed in Mesopotamia and Egypt; dug-out canoes used in NW Europe.
4000–3000	Egyptians used single-masted square-rigged ships on Nile.
1200	Phoenicians built keeled boats with hulls of wooden planks.
1st century BC	Chinese invented the rudder.
AD 200	Chinese built ships with several masts.
200–300	Arabs and Romans developed fore-and-aft rigging that allowed boats to sail across the direction of wind.
800–900	Square-rigged Viking longboats crossed the North Sea to Britain, the Faroe Islands, and Iceland.
1090	Chinese invented the magnetic compass.
1400–1500	Three-masted ships developed in western Europe, stimulating voyages of exploration.
1620	Dutch engineer Cornelius Drebbel invented the submarine.
1776	US engineer David Bushnell built a handpowered submarine, *Turtle*, with buoyancy tanks.
1777	The first boat with an iron hull built in Yorkshire, England.
1783	French engineer Jouffroy d'Abbans built the first paddle-driven steam boat.
1802	Scottish engineer William Symington launched the first stern paddle-wheel steamer *Charlotte Dundas*.
1836	The screw propeller was patented, by Francis Pettit Smith in the UK.
1838	British engineer Isambard Kingdom Brunel's *Great Western*, the first steamship built for crossing the Atlantic, sailed from Bristol to New York in 15 days.
1845	*Great Britain*, also built by Isambard Kingdom Brunel, became the first propeller-driven iron ship to cross the Atlantic.
1845	The first clipper ship, *Rainbow*, was launched in the USA.
1863	*Plongeur*, the first submarine powered by an air-driven engine was launched in France.
1866	The British clippers *Taeping* and *Ariel* sailed, laden with tea, from China to London in 99 days.
1886	German engineer Gottlieb Daimler built the first boat powered by an internal-combustion engine.
1897	English engineer Charles Parson fitted a steam turbine to *Turbinia*, making it the fastest boat of the time.
1900	Irish-American John Philip Holland designed the first modern submarine *Holland VI*, fitted with an electric motor for underwater sailing and an internal-combustion engine for surface travel; E Forlanini of Italy built the first hydrofoil.
1902	The French ship *Petit-Pierre* became the first diesel-powered boat.
1955	The first nuclear-powered submarine, *Nautilus*, was built; the hovercraft was patented by British inventor Christopher Cockerell.
1959	The first nuclear-powered ship, the Soviet ice-breaker *Lenin*, was commissioned; the US *Savannah* became the first nuclear-powered merchant (passenger and cargo) ship.
1980	Launch of the first wind-assisted commercial ship for half a century, the Japanese tanker *Shin-Aitoku-Maru*.
1983	German engineer Ortwin Fries invented a hinged ship designed to bend into a V-shape in order to scoop up oil spillages in its jaws.
1989	*Gentry Eagle* set a record for the fastest crossing of the Atlantic by a power vessel, taking 2 days, 14 hours, and 7 minutes.
1990	*Hoverspeed Great Britain*, a wave-piercing catamaran, crossed the Atlantic in 3 days, 7 hours, and 52 minutes, setting a record for the fastest crossing by a passenger vessel; the world's largest car and passenger ferry, the *Silja Serenade*, entered service between Stockholm and Helsinki, carrying 2,500 passengers and 450 cars.

ries—for example, the catarmarans introduced 1991 by Hoverspeed cross the English Channel from Dover to Calais in 35 minutes, cruising at a speed of 35 knots (84.5 kph/52.5 mph). Sailing ships in automated form for cargo purposes, and maglev (magnetic-levitation) ships, are in development.

Largest ship—the oil tanker *Happy Giant*, which is 458 m/1,505 ft long, with a beam of 69 m/226 ft. Of 564,739 tonnes/555,816 tons deadweight, it was launched in 1979.

Longest and largest passenger liner – the *Norway*, launched in 1961 as the *France*. It weighs 70,292 tonnes/69,093 tons, and measures 316 m/1,035 ft long.

hovercraft a vehicle that rides on a cushion of high-pressure air, free from all contact with the surface beneath, invented by British engineer Christopher Cockerell 1959. Hovercraft need a smooth terrain when operating over-

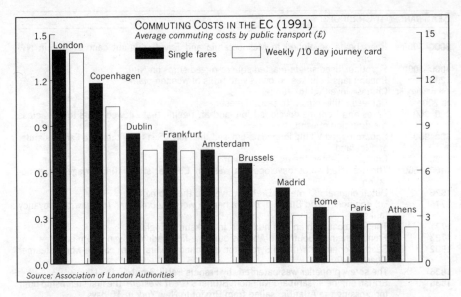

COMMUTING COSTS IN THE EC (1991)
Average commuting costs by public transport (£)

■ Single fares   □ Weekly /10 day journey card

London · Copenhagen · Dublin · Frankfurt · Amsterdam · Brussels · Madrid · Rome · Paris · Athens

Source: Association of London Authorities

land, and are best adapted to use on lakes, sheltered coastal waters, river estuaries and swamps. They are useful in places where harbours have not been established. Large hovercraft (SR-N4) operate a swift car-ferry service across the English Channel, taking only about 35 minutes between Dover and Calais.

hydrofoil boat a boat whose hull rises out of the water when it travels at speed. The boat gets its lift from a set of hydrofoils, underwater wings that develop lift in the water in much the same way that an aeroplane wing develops lift in the air.

jetfoil an advanced type of hydrofoil boat built by Boeing, propelled by water jets. It features horizontal, fully submerged hydrofoils fore and aft, and has a sophisticated computerized control system to maintain its stability in all waters. Jetfoils have been in service worldwide since 1975. A jetfoil service currently operates between Dover and Ostend, with a passage time of 1 hr 40 min.

submarine an underwater ship, especially a warship. The first underwater boat was constructed for King James I of England by the Dutch scientist Cornelius van Drebbel 1620. A century and a half later, David Bushness in the USA designed a submarine called *Turtle* for attacking British ships. In both world wars submarines, from the oceangoing to the midget type, played a vital role. The conventional submarine of this period was driven by diesel engine on the surface and by battery-powered electric motors underwater. The diesel engine also drove a generator that produced electricity

to charge the batteries.

In 1955 the USA launched the first nuclear-powered submarine, *Nautilus*. The US nuclear submarine *Ohio*, USA, in service from 1981, is 170 m/560 ft long and carries 24 Trident missiles, each with 12 independently targetable nuclear warheads. The nuclear warheads on US submarines have a range that is being extended to 11,000 km/6.750 mi. Operating depth is usually up to 300 m/1,000 ft, and nuclear power speeds of 30 knots (i.e. 55 kph/34 mph) are reached. As in all nuclear submarines, propulsion is by steam turbine driving a propellor. The steam is raised using the heat given off by the nuclear reactor.

In most countries of the world, motorists drive on the right hand side of the road. Would you like to see us do the same or do you think we should stay as we are?

Do the same	16
Stay as we are	80
Don't know	3

Suppose you had the choice of using local public transport, with low fares and frequent buses, or using your own car, which would you choose?

Public transport	40
Own car	59
Don't know	1

MILITARY TERMS

ABM abbreviation for *anti-ballistic missile* (see *nuclear warfare* in this section).

air force a nation's fighting aircraft and the organization that maintains them.

history The emergence of the aeroplane at first brought only limited recognition of its potential value as a means of waging war. Like the balloon, used since the American Civil War, it was considered a way of extending the vision of ground forces. A unified air force was established in the UK 1918, Italy 1923, France 1928, Germany 1935 (after repudiating the arms limitations of the Versailles treaty), and the USA 1947 (it began as the Aeronautical Division of the Army Signal Corps in 1907, and evolved into the Army's Air Service Division by 1918; by 1926 it was the Air Corps and in World War II the Army Air Force). The main specialized groupings formed during World War I—such as *combat*, *bombing*, *reconnaissance*, and *transport*—were adapted and modified in World War II; activity was extended, with self-contained tactical air forces to meet the needs of ground commanders in the main theatres of land operations and for the attack on and defence of shipping over narrow seas.

During the period 1945–60 the piston engine was superseded by the jet engine, which propelled aircraft at supersonic speeds; extremely precise electronic guidance systems made both missiles and aircraft equally reliable delivery systems; and flights of much longer duration became possible with air-to-air refuelling. The US Strategic Air Command's bombers can patrol 24 hours a day armed with thermonuclear weapons. It was briefly anticipated that the pilot might become redundant, but the continuation of conventional warfare and the evolution of tactical nuclear weapons have led in the 1970s and 1980s to the development of advanced combat aircraft able to fly supersonically beneath an enemy's radar on strike and reconnaissance missions, as well as so-called stealth aircraft that cannot be detected by radar.

Allied Mobile Force (AMF) permanent multinational military force established 1960 to move immediately to any NATO country under threat of attack. Its headquarters are in Heidelberg, Germany.

Allies, the in World War I, the 23 countries allied against the Central Powers (Germany, Austria-Hungary, Turkey and Bulgaria), including France, Italy, Russia, Great Britain and Commonwealth, and, in the latter part of the war, the USA; and in World War II, the 49 countries allied against the Axis powers (Germany, Italy and Japan), including France, Great Britain and Commonwealth, the USA, and the USSR. In the 1991 Gulf War, there were 28 countries in the Allied coalition.

Armistice Day anniversary of the armistice signed 11 Nov 1918, ending World War I.

armour body protection worn in battle. Body armour is depicted in Greek and Roman art. Chain mail was developed in the Middle Ages but the craft of the armourer in Europe reached its height in design in the 15th century, when knights were completely encased in plate armour that still allowed freedom of movement. Medieval Japanese armour was articulated, made of iron, gilded metal, leather, and silk. Contemporary bulletproof vests and riot gear are forms of armour. The term is used in a modern context to refer to a mechanized armoured vehicle, such as a tank.

arms trade the sale of arms from a manufacturing country to another nation. Nearly 50% of the world's arms exports end up in the Middle East, and most of the rest in Third World countries. Iraq, for instance, was armed in the years leading up to the 1991 Gulf War mainly by the USSR but also by France, Brazil, and South Africa.

The proportion of global arms spending accounted for by Third World countries was 24% in the late 1980s (up from 6% in 1965). Arms exports are known in the trade as 'arms transfers'.

In the UK, the Defence Export Services, a department of the Ministry of Defence, is responsible for British arms exports. Its annual budget is about £10 million.

army organized military force for fighting on land. A national army is used to further a political policy by force either within the state or on the territory of another state. Most countries have a national army, maintained at the expense of the state, raised either by conscription (compulsory military service) or voluntarily (paid professionals). Private armies may be employed by individuals and groups. As a result of the ending of the Cold War, the US, former Soviet and European armies were to be substantially cut between 1991 and 1995. The UK army will be cut from 155,000 to 116,000.

artillery collective term for military firearms too heavy to be carried. Artillery can be mounted on ships or aeroplanes and includes cannons and missile launchers.

ASAT acronym for *antisatellite weapon*.

AWACS acronym for *Airborne Warning and Control System*. The system incorporates a long-range surveillance and detection radar mounted on a Boeing E-3 sentry aircraft. The system was used with great success in the 1991 Gulf War.

battalion or *unit* the basic personnel unit in the military system, usually consisting of four or five companies and about 500–600 soldiers. A battalion is commanded by a lieutenant colonel. Several battalions form a brigade.

battleship class of large warships with the biggest guns and heaviest armour. In 1991, four US battleships were in active service.

biological warfare use of living organisms, or of infectious material derived from them, to bring about death or disease in humans, animals, or plants. It was condemned by the Geneva

THE WORLD'S LEADING ARMS EXPORTERS (*US$m)

	1986	1990
USSR	12,796	11,652
USA	8,800	10,755
France	3,970	2,732
UK	1,699	1,620
China	1,088	779
Germany	1,025	780
Czechoslovakia	497	546
Italy	646	149
Sweden	163	323
Netherlands	88	631

Source: SIPRI Yearbook 1991
* at constant 1986 prices

Convention 1925, to which the United Nations has urged all states to adhere. Nevertheless research in this area continues; the Biological Weapons Convention permits research for defence purposes but does not define how this differs from offensive weapons development. In 1990 the US Department of Defense allocated $60 million to research, develop and test defence systems. Advances in genetic engineering make the development of new, potentially offensive biological weapons more likely. At least ten countries have this capability.

bomb container filled with explosive or chemical material and generally used in warfare. There are also incendiary bombs and nuclear bombs and missiles (see nuclear warfare). Any object designed to cause damage by explosion can be called a bomb (car bombs, letter bombs). Initially dropped from aeroplanes (from World War I), bombs were in World War II also launched by rocket (V1, V2). The 1960s saw the development of missiles that could be launched from aircraft, land sites, or submarines. Although high explosive is increasingly delivered by means of missiles, free fall and so-called 'smart' or laser-guided munitions are still widely used.

The rapid development of *laser guidance systems* in the 1970s meant that precise destruction of small but vital targets could be more effectively achieved with standard 450 kg/1,000 lb high-explosive bombs. The laser beam may be directed at the target by the army from the ground, but additional flexibility is gained by coupling ground-directed beams with those of guidance carried in high-performance aircraft accompanying the bombers, for example, the Laser Ranging Marker Target System (LRMTS). These systems' effectiveness was demonstrated during the Gulf War of 1991.

brigade military formation consisting of a minimum of two battalions, but more usually three or more, as well as supporting arms. There are typically about 5,000 soldiers in a brigade, which is commanded by a brigadier. Two or more brigades form a division.

carrier warfare naval warfare involving aircraft carriers. Carrier warfare was conducted during World War II in the battle of the Coral Sea May 1942, which stopped the Japanese advance in the South Pacific, and in the battle of Midway Islands June 1942, which weakened the Japanese navy through the loss of four aircraft carriers. The US Navy deployed six aircraft carriers during the Gulf War 1991.

Central Command US military strike force consisting of units from the army, navy, and air force, which operates in the Middle East and North Africa. Its headquarters are in Fort McDill, Florida. It was established 1979, following the Iranian hostage crisis and the Soviet invasion of Afghanistan, and was known as the Rapid Deployment Force until 1983. It commanded coalition forces in the Gulf War 1991.

chemical warfare use in war of gaseous, liquid, or solid substances intended to have a toxic or lethal effect on humans, animals, or plants. Together with biological warfare, it was banned 1925 by the Geneva Convention, although this has not always been observed. In 1989, when the 149-nation Conference on Chemical Weapons unanimously voted to outlaw chemical weapons, the total US stockpile was estimated at 30,000 tonnes and the Soviet stockpile variously at 30,000 and 300,000 tonnes.

In a deal with the USA, the USSR offered to eliminate its stocks; the USA began replacing its stocks with new 'binary' nerve-gas weapons. In 1990 President Bush offered to destroy all US chemical weapons if the convention to outlaw them were ratified in 1992. Some 20 nations currently hold chemical weapons, including Iraq, Iran, Israel, Syria, Libya, South Africa, and China.

civil defence or *civil protection* organized activities by the civilian population of a state to mitigate the effects of enemy attack on them. The threat of nuclear weapons in the post-World War II period led to the building of fallout shelters in the USA, the USSR, and elsewhere. China has networks of tunnels in the cities that are meant to enable the population to escape nuclear fallout and reach the countryside, but which do not protect against the actual blast. Sweden and Switzerland have highly developed civil-defence systems.

A new structure of 'Home Defence' was introduced in the early 1980s in Britain, in which the voluntary services, local authorities, the Home Service Force, and the Territorial Army would cooperate. Regulations came into force in 1983 compelling local authorities to take part in civil-defence exercises. Councils have to provide blast-proof bunkers and communication links, train staff, and take part in the exercises. In July 1991 it was announced that much of the Home Defence infrastructure would be severely cut back since the Cold War had ended.

COIN acronym for *counter insurgency*, the suppression by a state's armed forces of uprisings against the state. Also called internal security (IS) operations of counter-revolutionary warfare (CRW). The British army has been engaged in COIN operations in Northern Ireland since 1969.

commando member of a specially trained, highly mobile military unit. The term originated in South Africa in the 19th century, where it referred to Boer military reprisal raids against Africans and, in the South African Wars, against the British. Commando units have often carried out operations behind enemy lines.

company in the army, a subunit of a battalion. It consists of about 120 soldiers, and is commanded by a major in the British army, a captain or major in the US army. Four or five companies make a battalion.

corps a military formation consisting of 2–5 divisions. Its strength is between 50,000 and 120,000 men. All branches of the army are represented. A corps is commanded by a lieutenant general or, in the USA, a three-star general. Two or more corps form an army group.

deception in warfare, the use of dummies, decoys, and electronics to trick the enemy into believing in and preparing to defend against armies that do not exist.

The Allied ground offensive in the 1991 Gulf War was launched 160 km/100 mi west of where the Iraqi army was led to believe it would take place—a deception technique which completely wrong-footed the Iraqi forces.

Delta Force US antiguerrilla force, based at Fort Bragg, North Carolina, and modelled on the British Special Air Service.

destroyer small, fast warship designed for antisubmarine work. They played a critical role in the convoy system in World War II. Modern destroyers often carry guided missiles and displace 3,700–5,650 tonnes.

disarmament the reduction of a country's weapons of war. Most disarmament talks since World War II have been concerned with nuclear-arms verification, but biological, chemical, and conventional weapons have also come under discussion at the United Nations and in other forums.

division military formation consisting of two or more brigades. A major general at divisional headquarters commands the brigades and also additional artillery, engineers, attack helicopters, and other logistic support. There are 10,000 or more soldiers in a division. Two or more divisions form a corps.

early warning in war, advance notice of incoming attack, often associated with nuclear attack. There are early-warning radar systems in the UK (Flyingdales), Alaska, and Greenland. *Airborne early warning* (AEW) aircraft supplement the ground stations.

The most efficient AEW system, which NATO uses, is the Boeing Sentry AWACS (airborne warning and control system), capable of covering a wide area. Carrier battle groups also need AEW. During the 1982 Falklands War the British Royal Navy was not equipped with an adequate over-the-horizon surveillance capability, and some ships were sunk by Exocet surface-to-surface missiles as a result.

explosive any material capable of a sudden release of energy and the rapid formation of a large volume of gas, leading when compressed to the development of a high-pressure wave (blast). Examples include gelignite, dynamite, nitroglycerin, nitrobenzene, TNT (trinitrotoluene), and RDX (Research Department Explosive).

fallout harmful radioactive material released into the atmosphere in the debris of a nuclear explosion and descending to the surface. Such material can enter the food chain.

field marshal the highest rank in many European armies. A British field marshal is equivalent to a 5-star US general.

firearm weapon from which projectiles are discharged by the combustion of an explosive. Firearms are generally divided into two main sections: *artillery* (ordnance or cannon), with a bore greater than 2.54 cm/1 in, and *small arms*, with a bore of less than 2.54 cm/1 in. Although gunpowder was known in Europe 60 years previously, the invention of guns dates from 1300–25, and is attributed to Berthold Schwartz, a German monk.

flag piece of cloth used as an emblem or symbol for nationalistic, religious, or military displays, or as a means of signalling. Flags have been used since ancient times.

frigate warship, an escort vessel smaller than a destroyer. Before 1975 the term referred to a warship larger than a destroyer but smaller than a light cruiser. In the 18th and 19th centuries a frigate was a small, fast sailing warship.

general senior military rank, the ascending grades being major general, lieutenant general, and general. The US rank of general of the army, or 5-star general, is equivalent to the British field marshal.

guerrilla irregular soldier fighting in a small unofficial unit, typically against an established or occupying power, and engaging in sabotage, ambush, and the like, rather than pitched battles against an opposing army. Guerrilla tactics have been used both by resistance armies in wartime (for example, the Vietnam War) and in peacetime by national liberation groups and militant political extremists (for example the PLO; Tamil Tigers).

Political activists who resort to violence, particularly *urban guerrillas*, tend to be called 'freedom fighters' by those who support their cause, 'terrorists' by those who oppose it.

Efforts by governments to put a stop to their activities have had only sporadic success. The Council of Europe has set up the European Convention on the Suppression of Terrorism, to which many governments are signatories. In the UK the Prevention of Terrorism Act 1984 is aimed particularly at the IRA. The Institute for the Study of Terrorism was founded in London 1986.

Gurkha a people living in the mountains of Nepal, whose young men have been recruited since 1815 for the British and Indian armies. There are currently five battalions of Gurkhas in the British Army (though the cuts of July 1991 will reduce these to two by 1996). There

YUGOSLAVIA: A EUROPEAN BATTLEGROUND

1991 was the year in which Yugoslavia died. The Cold War had kept the lid on ethnic, religious, and nationalist tensions in Yugoslavia for 40 years. The iron hand of communism in the Balkans in general, and of Tito's special brand of communism in Yugoslavia in particular, conspired to postpone a conflagration that was waiting to happen.

The first of the Yugoslav republics to become restless was Slovenia. Slovenia had always been different from the rest of the republics: it is geographically the most far removed from Belgrade, being the northernmost of the constituent parts of Yugoslavia. Like its neighbour Italy, it is European and Catholic. Slovenia had always looked northwards. Thus Belgrade was prepared to let Slovenia go without too much of a fight. It was only when the Croatian crisis came to a head in January 1991 that the cohesiveness of Yugoslavia was seriously threatened. On 21 February Croatia invalidated all federal laws within its territory, and it finally declared independence on 25 June. While Belgrade had been prepared to accept Slovenian defection, it was not prepared to abandon Serbian minorities in Croatia.

The remainder of 1991 saw vicious fighting throughout Croatia with the Yugoslav federal army and Serbian militias gaining large tracts of territory within Croatia. EC-brokered peace talks led by Lord Carrington failed in November and continued into 1992. Germany recognized Slovenian and Croatian independence on 23 December 1991. Most of the rest of the world followed suit in early 1992. Meanwhile Croatia appealed to the UN to deploy a peacekeeping force. Although the first monitors arrived in Zagreb on 26 December 1991, the bulk of the peacekeeping force was not in place until May 1992. These troops may be able to prevent further fighting between the new Croatian army and Serbian militias, but the border issue remains unresolved. Croatia claims its original borders; Serbia requires some sort of autonomy—at the very least—for the Serbian minorities within Croatia.

It was probably only a matter of time before conflict erupted in Bosnia–Herzegovina. Not only is there an ethnic mix between Bosnians, Croats, and Serbs in the republic, there is also the complication of a Catholic/Orthodox/Muslim divide. Fighting in Bosnia was as vicious throughout the spring of 1992 as it had been in Croatia the previous summer and autumn. By May 1992 Serbian irregulars had seized large parts of Bosnia, which had by this stage declared its independence. The UN force headquartered in Sarajevo had its troops deployed in Croatia. In the meantime Bosnians were being slaughtered in the vicinity of Sarajevo where UN troops did not have a mandate—nor the means to intervene.

Outright civil war ensued and by June Serbs were in control of roughly two thirds of the republic and Croats the remaining third. With Bosnia-Herzegovina's independence awarded official recognition the same month by the EC and USA, the decision was taken to draft in Canadian/French UN forces in an attempt to relieve the three-month Serbian siege of the capital, Sarajevo. The initial success of the UN relief effort was, however, largely overshadowed by the failure of the latest of several cease-fires.

Meanwhile Kosovo, populated largely by ethnic Albanians, simmered in the south. Macedonia, which had stated its intention to achieve independence, awaited the right moment to break loose. That it will do so is not in doubt. The main stumbling block remains what it will call itself. 'Macedonia' is not acceptable to Greece lest it be confused with that part of northern Greece commonly called Macedonia.

The future of the three newly independent republics will be uncertain for a long time to come, with their economic viability remaining in doubt. Moreover there could be tensions with Albania over Kosovo, and with Hungary over the Vojvodina, where there is a sizeable Hungarian minority.

The potential for continuing chaos is immense. The main way in which the West can hope to influence the situation is by using economic levers. The use of military force by outside powers, whilst not inconceivable as an emotional response to the dismemberment of Bosnia by Serbia, for instance, would be a massive undertaking and might not necessarily produce a solution. The Wermacht learned this lesson to its cost using half a million troops in 1943 and 1944.

A Serbian soldier on the alert during clashes with Muslims in northern Bosnia-Herzegovina.

are many more Gurkhas in the Indian army.

home service force (HSF) military unit established in the UK 1982, linked to the Territorial Army and recruited from volunteers of ages 18–60 with previous army (TA or Regular) experience. It was introduced to guard key points and installations likely to be the target of enemy 'special forces' and saboteurs, so releasing other units for mobile defence roles.

ICBM abbreviation for *intercontinental ballistic missile* (see nuclear warfare in this section).

Luftwaffe German air force. In World War I and, as reorganized by the Nazi leader Goering 1933, in World War II, it also covered anti-aircraft defence and the launching of the flying bombs V1, V2.

manoeuvre in warfare, to move around the battlefield so as to gain an advantage over the enemy. It implies rapid movement, shock action, and surprise. Bold manoeuvre warfare can be synonymous with blitzkrieg or a swift military campaign. An example of manoeuvre warfare was the wide-ranging encirclement of the Iraqi army by coalition forces in the 1991 Gulf War.

marines fighting force that operates both on land and at sea. The *US Marine Corps* (1775) is constituted as an arm of the US Navy. It is made up of infantry and air support units trained and equipped for amphibious landings under fire. The *Royal Marines* founded by Charles II 1664 is the British equivalent, numbering approximately 7,000 (1992), and is part of the Royal Navy.

mercenary soldier hired by the army of another country or by a private army. Mercenary military service originated in the 14th century, when cash payment on a regular basis was the only means of guaranteeing soldiers' loyalty. In the 20th century mercenaries have been common in wars and guerrilla activity in Asia, Africa, and Latin America.

Article 47 of the 1977 Additional Protocols to the Geneva Convention stipulates that 'a mercenary shall not have the right to be a combatant or a prisoner of war' but leaves a party to the Protocols the freedom to grant such status if so wished.

minesweeper small naval vessel for locating and destroying mines at sea. A typical minesweeper weighs about 725 tonnes, and is built of reinforced plastic (immune to magnetic and acoustic mines). Remote-controlled miniature submarines may be used to lay charges next to the mines and destroy them.

mobilization the preparation of armed forces (land, sea, air) for active service.

MRBM abbreviation for *medium-range ballistic missile* such as the French M-5 ballistic missile.

navy fleet of ships, usually a nation's warships, and the organization to maintain them. In the early 1990s, the UK had a force of small carriers, destroyers, frigates, and submarines. In the light of the 1991 Armed Forces reductions, the Royal Navy is to be reduced from around 50 to 40 destroyers and frigates, and the submarine fleet to be cut by 50%.

NBC abbreviation for nuclear, biological and chemical warfare, a term used to describe the form of warfare fought with weapons of mass destruction. The only case of nuclear warfare to date was the dropping of two nuclear weapons on Hiroshima and Nagasaki by the US Air Force in 1945, with the purpose of forcing Japan to surrender in World War II. Biological warfare is a weapon that is difficult to use in the field of battle but which could be used as a strategic weapon to poison water supplies or cause epidemics. Chemical weapons were first used during World War I in the form of mustard gas, and they have been used since in Vietnam, Afghanistan, and during the Iran–Iraq war by the Iraqis.

North Atlantic Treaty Organization (NATO) association set up 1949 to provide for the collective defence of the major W European and North American states against the perceived threat from the USSR. Its chief body is the Council of Foreign Ministers (who have representatives in permanent session), and there is an international secretariat in Brussels, Belgium, and also the Military Committee consisting of the Chiefs of Staff. The military headquarters SHAPE (Supreme Headquarters Allied Powers, Europe) is in Chièvres, near Mons, Belgium. In 1990, after a meeting in London, NATO declared that nuclear weapons were 'weapons of last resort' rather than 'flexible response', and offered to withdraw all nuclear artillery shells from Europe if the USSR did the same. With the ending of the Cold War, the role of NATO was reassessed to provide a flexible Atlantic security structure in an uncertain and fast changing world. A *North Atlantic Cooperation Council*, including all former Soviet republics, was established Dec 1991. For post-Cold War contingencies, a 100,000 strong, UK-commanded 'rapid-reaction corps' (RRC) was to be operational from late 1994.

nuclear warfare war involving the use of nuclear weapons. Nuclear-weapons research began in Britain 1940, but was transferred to the USA after it entered World War II. The research programme, known as the Manhattan Project, was directed by J Robert Oppenheimer. The first atom bomb relied on the use of a chemical explosion to trigger a chain reaction. The first test explosion was at Alamogordo, New Mexico, 16 July 1945; the first use in war was by the USA against Japan 6 Aug 1945 at Hiroshima and three days later at Nagasaki. The worldwide total of nuclear weapons in 1990 was about 50,000, and the number of countries possessing nuclear weapons stood officially at five—USA, USSR, UK, France, and China—although some other nations were thought to have a usable stockpile of these weapons (Israel), the ability to produce them quickly (India, Pakistan, North Korea), or develop them in the longer term (Iran, Iraq).

atom bomb The original weapon relied on use of a chemical explosion to trigger a chain reaction.

hydrogen bomb A much more powerful weapon

than the atom bomb, it relies on the release of thermonuclear energy by the condensation of hydrogen nuclei to helium nuclei (as happens in the Sun). The first detonation was at Eniwetok Atoll, Pacific Ocean, 1952 by the USA.

neutron bomb or enhanced radiation weapon (ERW) is a very small hydrogen bomb that has relatively high radiation but relatively low blast, designed to kill (in up to six days) by a brief neutron radiation that leaves buildings and weaponry intact.

nuclear methods of attack now include aircraft bombs, missiles (long- or short-range, surface to surface, air to surface, and surface to air), depth charges, and high-powered landmines ('atomic demolition munitions') to destroy bridges and roads.

Major subjects of disarmament negotiations are:

intercontinental ballistic missiles (ICBMs), which have from 1968 been equipped with clusters of warheads (which can be directed to individual targets) and are known as multiple independently targetable re-entry vehicles (MIRVs). The 1980s US-designed MX (Peacekeeper) carries up to ten warheads in each missile. In 1989, the UK decision to purchase submarine-launched Trident missiles from the USA was confirmed. Each warhead has eight independently targetable re-entry vehicles (each nuclear-armed) with a range of about 6,400 km/4,000 mi to eight separate targets within about 240 km/150 mi of the central aiming point. The Trident system is scheduled to enter service within the Royal Navy in the mid-1990s.

nuclear methods of defence include:

antiballistic missile (ABM) is an earth-based system with two types of missile, one short-range with high acceleration, and one comparatively long-range for interception above the atmosphere.

Strategic Defense Initiative (announced by the USA 1983 to be operative from 2000; popularly known as the 'Star Wars' programme).

The danger of nuclear weapons increases with the number of nations possessing them (USA 1945, USSR 1949, UK 1952, France 1960, China 1964), and nuclear-arms verification has been complicated by the ban on aboveground testing. Testing grounds include Lop Nor (China); Mururoa Atoll in the S Pacific (France); Nevada Desert, Amchitka Islands in the Aleutians (USA); Semipalatinsk in Kazakhstan, Novaya Zemlya Islands in Russia.

platoon in the army, the smallest infantry unit. It contains 30–40 soldiers and is commanded by a lieutenant or second lieutenant. There are three or four platoons in a company.

prisoner of war (POW) person captured in war, who has fallen into the hands of, or surrendered to, an opponent. Such captives may be held in prisoner-of-war camps. The treatment of POWs is governed by the Geneva Convention.

Rapid Reaction Force or *(RRF)* any military unit that is maintained at a high state of readiness to react to an emergency. Specifically it is the corps-sized unit, the formation of which was announced by NATO in May 1991 to meet threats anywhere in its area of responsibility.

reconnaissance the gathering of information about a military objective. This can be carried out by a reconnaissance (or 'recce') patrol, or by using a small, fast-moving recce vehicle or an aircraft configured for the recce role, or a remotely piloted vehicle (RPV). The SAS (Special Air Service) carried out invaluable reconnaissance work in the 1991 Gulf War. Less precise information was provided by satellites.

Red Army name of the army of the former USSR until 1946, when it was officially renamed the *Soviet Army*. It grew out of the Red Guards, volunteers who carried out the Bolshevik revolution, and took its name from the red flag under which it fought. The Chinese revolutionary army was also called the Red Army.

regiment military formation equivalent to a battalion in parts of the British army, and to a brigade in the armies of many countries.

In the British infantry, a regiment may encompass more than one battalion, and soldiers belong to the same regiment throughout their career.

Royal Air Force (RAF) the air force of Britain. The RAF was formed 1918 by the merger of the Royal Naval Air Service and the Royal Flying Corps. It numbers approximately 85,000 (1991), with some 48 front line squadrons of aircraft out of approximately 600 aircraft. The 1991 defence cuts will reduce this by 15 squadrons.

Royal British Legion full name of the British Legion, a nonpolitical body promoting the welfare of war veterans and their dependants.

Royal Marines British military force trained for amphibious warfare. See marine.

services, armed the air, sea, and land forces of a country; also called the armed forces.

SHAPE abbreviation for *Supreme Headquarters Allied Powers Europe*, situated near Mons, Belgium, and the headquarters of NATO's Supreme Allied Commander Europe (SACEUR).

SLBM abbreviation for *submarine-launched ballistic missile.*

Special Air Service (SAS) specialist British regiment recruited from regiments throughout the army. It has served in Malaysia, Oman, Yemen, the Falklands, Northern Ireland, and during the 1991 Gulf War, as well as against international terrorists, as in the siege of the Iranian embassy in London 1980.

Strategic Defense Initiative (SDI) also called *Star Wars* attempt by the USA to develop a defence system, using advanced laser and particle-beam technology (and based in part outside the Earth's atmosphere) against incoming nuclear missiles. It was announced by President Reagan in March 1983, and the research had by 1990 cost over $16.5 billion. In 1988, the joint Chiefs of Staff announced that they expected to be able to intercept no more than 30% of incoming missiles.

HOPE FOR PEACE IN THE MIDDLE EAST?

The Middle East is arguably the world's most unstable region. There are numerous instabilities and tensions. Islam, supposedly a unifying force, is split between Sunni and Shi'ite. There is the divide between the oil-rich Gulf states and the more populous, less prosperous states further north and west—Syria, Jordan, Egypt, and Algeria. There are ethnic tensions between Arabs and Kurds in Iraq, between Arabs and Africans in Sudan, and between Arabs and Iranians. There are border disputes throughout the region, and tensions and suspicions over the control of a vital resource: water. Superimposed over everything is the Israeli-Palestinian conflict.

Four wars have been fought between Israel and its neighbours. The first Arab-Israeli war (Oct 1948–March 1949) ended with a victorious Israel annexing three-quarters of what had been Palestine under British mandate. The second Arab-Israeli war (29 Oct–4 Nov 1956) occurred after Egypt had seized the Suez Canal and blockaded the Straits of Tiran. Israel, with French and British support, invaded and captured the Sinai Peninsula and Gaza Strip. The third Arab-Israeli war—the Six-Day War—took place 5–10 June 1967. The Israelis captured the Sinai Peninsula as far as the Suez Canal, plus the Golan Heights from Syria and the eastern half of Jerusalem and the west bank of the Jordan river from Jordan. The fourth Arab-Israeli war—the Yom Kippur War—occupied three weeks of Oct 1973. Israel was attacked by Syria in the Golan Heights and Egypt across the Suez Canal. Despite initial gains by its enemies, Israel stabilized the position on both fronts.

Over 40 years of conflict have left a legacy of mistrust, bigotry, and hatred on both sides. The 1991 Gulf War presented a brief opportunity. James Baker, the US secretary of state, initiated shuttle diplomacy which resulted in the Madrid peace conference in Oct/Nov 1991. The process continued fitfully and painfully into 1992. The combination of a new, tougher US attitude to Israel, linking loan guarantees to undertakings to stop building settlements on the West Bank, and the more realistic attitude of the Palestinian delegation to the peace talks, has created some potential for progress.

The Intifada—the uprising by Palestinians on the West Bank against the Israeli authorities—has gradually modified worldwide attitudes from sympathy for Israelis fighting against all odds, to antagonism against an overbearing Israeli security apparatus and expansionist regime. Even the US Jewish lobby has been placated. Thus a land-for-peace deal may eventually emerge, granting partial autonomy to Palestinians on the West Bank. The Golan Heights and Gaza Strip present more complicated problems, but there may be scope for a demilitarized zone in the Golan Heights and for extending to the Gaza Strip any arrangements made for the West Bank.

Especially with Israeli Prime Minister Yitzhak Rabin's immediate peace initiatives, beginning with a state visit to Egypt's President Hosni Mubarak nine days after taking office, the prospects for progress in the Israeli-Palestinian dispute are probably better than ever.

The Middle East can conveniently be divided into four sub-regions: the Levant, the Horn of Africa, the Maghreb, and the Gulf. The peace process started in Madrid is providing the best opportunity for peace and progress in the Levant since the end of World War II. Even Lebanon seems to be finding a way out of the chaos and killing of the 1970s and 1980s. Syria appears to want to join the real world. The Horn of Africa, however, remains in a state of continuing and depressing instability. Sudan is crippled by civil war, Somalia is in anarchy, and Ethiopia is emerging groggily from an era of imposed Marxist-Leninism. Egypt, between the Levant and the Horn, despite the threat of Islamic fundamentalism, remains a secular and relatively stable state. The Maghreb states remain unpredictable. Libya's leader, Moamer al-Khaddhafi, continues to ensure that Libya is branded a pariah state. And Algeria's 1991 brush with Islamic fundamentalism has increased the uncertainty about that country's future. In the Gulf, the Gulf Cooperation Council has managed to provide some cohesion among its six members. However, it is the bilateral security arrangements made by most of its members with the USA, the UK, and France that provide the real security guarantees. Iraq cannot project military force outside its borders for the foreseeable future. Meanwhile Iran appears to be taking an increasingly moderate line, but is not beyond opportunistic destabilization of its ideologically errant neighbours.

Thus for the moment, the Middle East is more stable than it has been for a long time. The next conflict, though, could be over water and who controls it.

Picking celery on the West Bank. Water is a vital resource in the region.

Israel, Japan, and the UK are among the nations assisting in research and development. In 1987 Gorbachev acknowledged that the USSR was developing a similar defence. system. The SDI programme was subsequently scaled down dramatically, and it is unlikely that the original concept will ever be deployed. The scaled-down version is known as Global Protection Against Limited Strikes (GPALS).

tank armoured fighting vehicle that runs on tracks and is fitted with weapons systems capable of defeating other tanks and destroying other targets. The term was originally a code name for the first effective tracked and armoured fighting vehicle, invented by the British soldier and scholar Ernest Swinton, and used in the battle of the Somme 1916.

A tank consists of a body or hull of thick steel or other composite, on which are mounted machine guns and a larger gun. The hull contains the crew (usually consisting of a commander, driver, and one or two soldiers), engine, radio, fuel tanks, and ammunition. The tank travels on caterpillar tracks that enable it to cross rough ground and debris. It is known as an MBT (main battle tank).

Territorial Army British force of volunteer soldiers, created from volunteer regiments (incorporated 1872) as the *Territorial Force* 1908. It was raised and administered by county associations, and intended primarily for home defence. It was renamed Territorial Army 1922. Merged with the Regular Army in World War II, it was revived 1947, and replaced by a smaller, more highly trained Territorial and Army Volunteer Reserve, again renamed Territorial Army 1979.

war act of force, usually on behalf of the state, intended to compel a declared enemy to obey the will of the other. The aim is to render the opponent incapable of further resistance by destroying its capability and will to bear arms in pursuit of its own aims. War is therefore a continuation of politics carried on with violent and destructive means, as an instrument of policy.

The estimated figure for loss of life in Third World wars since 1945 is 17 million. The conduct of war is generally divided into **strategy**, the planning and conduct of a war, and **tactics**, the deployment of forces in battle. Types of war include:

guerrilla war the waging of low-level conflict by irregular forces against an occupying army or against the rear of an enemy force. Examples include Mao Zedong's campaign against the Nationalist Chinese and T E Lawrence's Arab revolt against the Turks;

low-intensity conflict US term for its interventions in the Third World (stepped up in the 1980s), ranging from drug-running to funding and training guerrillas, and fought with political, economic, and cultural weapons as well as by military means;

civil war the waging of war by opposing parties, or members of different regions, within a state. The American Civil War 1861–65, the English Civil War of the 1600s, and the Spanish Civil War 1936-39 are examples;

limited war the concept that a war may be limited in both geographical extent and levels of force exerted and have aims that stop short of achieving the destruction of the enemy. The Korean War 1950-53 and the Falklands War 1982 fall within this category;

total war the waging of war against both combatants and noncombatants, taking the view that no distinction should be made between them. The Spanish Civil War marked the beginning of this type of warfare, in which bombing from the air included both civilian and military targets;

absolute war the view that there should be no limitations, such as law, compassion, or prudence, in the application of force, the sole aim being to achieve the complete annihilation of one's opponent. Such a concept contradicts the notion, formulated by Clausewitz, of war as an instrument of political dialogue since it implies that no dialogue is actually intended. It has been claimed that nuclear warfare would assume such proportions and would be in accordance with the doctrine of mutually assured destruction (MAD).

warship fighting ship armed and crewed for war. The supremacy of the battleship at the beginning of the 20th century was rivalled during World War I by the development of submarine attack, and was rendered obsolescent in World War II with the advent of long-range air attack. Today the largest and most important surface warships are the aircraft carriers.

aircraft carriers The large-scale aircraft carrier was temporarily out of favour, as too vulnerable, until the resumption of building, especially by the USA, in the late 1970s and 1980s. The *Carl Vinson* USA 1982 weighs 81,600 tonnes.

Some countries, such as the UK, have opted for **mini-carriers** with vertical takeoff aircraft and long-range helicopters. Mini-carriers evolved in the early 1970s and have been advocated by US military reformers.

submarines The first nuclear-powered submarine was the US *Nautilus* 1955; the first Polaris was the *George Washington* 1960. Submarines fall into two classes: the specially designed, almost silent **attack submarine**, intended to release its fast torpedoes and missiles at comparatively close range, and the **ballistic-missile submarine** with guided missiles of such long range that the submarine itself is virtually undetectable to the enemy. For the USA these submarines form one leg of the strategic 'triad' of land-based missiles, crewed bombers, and submarine-launched missiles.

battleships The US Navy has recommissioned and modernized several World War II battleships for shore bombardment and force projection purposes. These were used with great effect during the 1991 Gulf War.

withdrawal in a military action, an orderly

CURRENT REGIONAL CONFLICTS

Europe
Northern Ireland (vs IRA)
Spain (vs Basque separatist organization, ETA)
Croatia (vs Serbian irregulars and Yugoslav Army)
Bosnia-Herzegovina (vs Serbian irregulars and Yugoslav Army)

Middle East
Iran (vs Kurdish irregulars)
Iraq (vs Kurdish irregulars and Shi'ite Muslim irregulars)
Lebanon (Southern Lebanon a battleground for Israeli–Palestinian conflict)
Turkey (vs Kurdish irregulars)

Former USSR
Georgia (civil war)
Armenia (vs Azerbaijan)
Azerbaijan (vs Armenians in Nagorno-Karabakh)

South Asia
Afghanistan (civil war)
Bangladesh (antigovernment insurgency)
India (Hindu–Muslim clashes)
India–Pakistan (over Kashmir)
Myanmar (Sha, Kachin, Karen secessionists, and prodemocracy rebellions)
Sri Lanka (antigovernment insurgency by Tamil Tigers)

Pacific Asia
Cambodia (fragile ceasefire between four Cambodian factions maintained by
    newly introduced UN peacekeeping force)
Indonesia (continuing resistance to government in East Timor, and Aceh
    independence movement in northern Sumatra)
Philippines (armed communist and Muslim insurgencies)
Spratly Islands (contested by China, Vietnam, Brunei, Malaysia, Taiwan and the
    Philippines; some islands occupied by Chinese and Vietnamese troops; clashes have occurred)
Korea (spasmodic incidents on N Korea/S Korea border; 1.4 million troops
    facing each other across demilitarized zone)

Africa
Algeria (suppression of fundamentalist rebellion)
Chad (antigovernment insurgency)
Zaire (antigovernment insurgency and French and Belgian military
    intervention to evacuate nationals)
Morocco/Western Sahara (to establish independence for Western Sahara)
Liberia (civil war)
Somalia (civil war)
South Africa (Inkatha–ANC violence and antigovernment insurgency)
Sudan (civil war)
Sierra Leone (antigovernment rebellion)
Uganda (sporadic violence)

Central and South America
Columbia (narco-terrorism)
El Salvador (newly introduced UN peacekeeping force maintaining
    fragile peace between FMLN and government forces)
Guatemala (antigovernment insurgency)
Nicaragua (former Contra soldiers staging occasional violence)
Peru (antigovernment insurgency by Shining Path terrorists)

movement of forces in a rearward direction in order to occupy more favourable ground. It is voluntary and controlled, unlike a retreat.

women's services the organized military use of women on a large scale, a 20th-century development. First, women replaced men in factories, on farms, and in noncombat tasks during wartime; they are now found in combat units in many countries, including the USA, Cuba, the UK, Russia, and Israel.

TREATIES AND CONFERENCES

Georgetown, Declaration of call in 1972, at a conference in Guyana of nonaligned countries, for a multipolar system to replace the two world power blocs, and for the Mediterranean Sea and Indian Ocean to be neutral.

Helsinki Conference international conference 1975 at which 35 countries, including the USSR and the USA, attempted to reach agreement on cooperation in security, economics, science, technology, and human rights.

INF abbreviation for *intermediate nuclear forces*, as in the Intermediate Nuclear Forces Treaty.

Intermediate Nuclear Forces Treaty agreement signed 8 Dec 1987 between the USA and the USSR to eliminate all ground-based nuclear missiles in Europe that were capable of hitting only European targets (including European Russia). It reduced the countries' nuclear arsenals by some 2,000 (4% of the total). The treaty included provisions for each country to inspect the other's bases. A total of 1,269 weapons (945 Soviet, 234 US) was destroyed in the first year of the treaty.

Paris, Treaty of any of various peace treaties signed in Paris.

SALT abbreviation for *Strategic Arms Limitation Talks*, a series of US–Soviet negotiations 1969–79.

START abbreviation for *Strategic Arms Reduction Talks*.

Strategic Arms Limitation Talks (SALT) series of US–Soviet discussions aimed at reducing the rate of nuclear-arms build-up. The talks, delayed by the Soviet invasion of Czechoslovakia 1968, began in 1969 between the US President Lyndon Johnson and the

Soviet leader Brezhnev. Neither the SALT I accord (effective 1972–77) nor SALT II called for reductions in nuclear weaponry, merely a limit on the expansion of these forces. SALT II was mainly negotiated by US President Ford before 1976 and signed by Soviet leader Brezhnev and President Carter in Vienna in 1979. It was never fully ratified because of the Soviet occupation of Afghanistan, although the terms of the accord were respected by both sides until President Reagan exceeded its limitations during his second term 1985–89. SALT talks were superseded by START (Strategic Arms Reduction Talks) negotiations under Reagan, and the first significant reductions began under Soviet President Gorbachev.

Strategic Arms Reduction Talks (START) disarmament talks, which began in Geneva 1983 and lead to the signing of the Intermediate Nuclear Forces (INF) treaty 1987. In 1989 proposals for reductions in strategic nuclear weapons systems were added to the agenda. In Aug 1991 Presidents Bush and Gorbachev signed the START treaty, cutting strategic nuclear warheads (land-based ballistic missiles, sea-launched ballistic missiles, and strategic bombers) by approximately one third to an official limit of 6,000 for both sides. In Sept 1991 Bush and Gorbachev proposed additional unilateral cuts.

Versailles, Treaty of peace treaty after World War I between the Allies and Germany, signed 28 June 1919. It established the League of Nations. Germany surrendered Alsace-Lorraine to France, and large areas in the east to Poland, and made smaller cessions to Czechoslovakia, Lithuania, Belgium, and Denmark. The Rhineland was demilitarized, German rearmament was restricted, and Germany agreed to pay reparations for war damage. The treaty was never ratified by the USA, which made a separate peace with Germany and Austria 1921.

Western European Union (WEU) organization established 1955 as a consultative forum for military issues among the W European governments: Belgium, France, Holland, Italy, Luxembourg, the UK, West Germany, and (from 1988) Spain and Portugal.

Yalta Conference in 1945, a meeting at which the Allied leaders Churchill (UK), Roosevelt (USA), and Stalin (USSR) completed plans for the defeat of Germany in World War II and the foundation of the United Nations. It took place in Yalta, a Soviet holiday resort in the Crimea.

TREATIES OF PARIS

1919–20	The conference preparing the Treaty of Versailles at the end of World War I was held in Paris.
1946	After World War II the peace treaties between the Allies and Italy, Romania, Hungary, Bulgaria, and Finland.
1951	Treaty signed by France, West Germany, Italy, Belgium, Netherlands and Luxemburg, embodying the Schuman Plan to set up a single coal and steel authority.
1973	Ending US participation in the Vietnam War.

WARS AND LEADERS

Alamein, El, Battles of in World War II, two decisive battles in the western desert, N Egypt. In the *First Battle of El Alamein* 1–27 Jul 1942 the British 8th Army under Auchinleck held the German and Italian forces under Rommel. In the *Second Battle of El Alamein* 23 Oct–4 Nov 1942 Montgomery defeated Rommel.

Arab-Israeli Wars a series of wars between Israel and various Arab states in the Middle East since the founding of the state of Israel 1948.

First Arab-Israeli War 14 Oct 1948–13 Jan/24 Mar 1949. As soon as the independent state of Israel had been proclaimed by the Jews in Palestine, it was invaded by combined Arab forces. The Israelis defeated them and went on to annex territory until they controlled 75% of what had been Palestine under British mandate.

Second Arab-Israeli War or *Suez War* 29 Oct–4 Nov 1956. After Egypt had taken control of the Suez Canal and blockaded the Straits of Tiran, Israel, with British and French support, invaded and captured Sinai and the Gaza Strip, from which it withdrew under heavy US pressure after the entry of a UN force.

Third Arab-Israeli War 5–10 June 1967, the *Six Day War*. It resulted in the Israeli capture of the Golan Heights from Syria; the E half of Jerusalem and the West Bank from Jordan; and, in the south, the Gaza Strip and Sinai Peninsula as far as the Suez Canal.

Fourth Arab-Israeli War 2–22/24 Oct 1973, the '*October War*' or *Yom Kippur War*, so called because the Israeli forces were taken by surprise on the Day of Atonement. It started with the recrossing of the Suez Canal by Egyptian forces who made initial gains, as did the Syrians in the Golan Heights area. However, the Israelis stabilized the position in both cases.

Fifth Arab-Israeli War From 1978 the presence of Palestinian guerrillas in Lebanon led to Arab raids on Israel and Israeli retaliatory incursions, but on 6 June 1982 Israel launched a full-scale invasion. By 14 June Beirut was encircled, and Palestine Liberation Organization (PLO) and Syrian forces were evacuated (mainly to Syria) 21–31 Aug, but in Feb 1985 there was a unilateral Israeli withdrawal from the country without any gain for losses incurred. Israel maintains a 'security zone' in S Lebanon and supports the South Lebanese Army militia as a buffer against Palestinian guerrilla incursions.

Arnhem, Battle of in World War II, airborne operation by the Allies, 17–26 Sept 1944, to secure a bridgehead over the Rhine, thereby opening the way for a thrust towards the Ruhr and a possible early end to the war. It was only partially successful, with 7,600 casualties. Arnhem is a city in the Netherlands, on the Rhine SE of Utrecht; population (1988) 297,000. It produces salt, chemicals, and pharmaceuticals.

Arras, Battle of battle of World War I, April–May 1917. It was an effective but costly British attack on German forces in support of a French offensive, which was only partially successful, on the Siegfried Line. British casualties totalled 84,000 as compared to 75,000 German casualties.

Atlantic, Battle of the continuous battle fought in the Atlantic Ocean throughout World War II (1939–45) by the sea and air forces of the Allies and Germany, to control the supply routes to Britain. The number of U-boats destroyed by the Allies during the war was nearly 800. At least 2,200 convoys of 75,000 merchant ships crossed the Atlantic, protected by US naval forces. Before the US entry into the war 1941, destroyers were supplied to the British under the Lend-Lease Act 1941.

Bataan peninsula in Luzon, the Philippines, which was defended against the Japanese in World War II by US and Filipino troops under General MacArthur 1 Jan–9 Apr 1942. MacArthur was evacuated, but some 67,000 Allied prisoners died on the *Bataan Death March* to camps in the interior.

Bradley Omar Nelson 1893–1981. US general in World War II. In 1943 he commanded the 2nd US Corps in their victories in Tunisia and Sicily, leading to the surrender of 250,000 Axis troops, and in 1944 led the US troops in the invasion of France. His command, as the 12th Army Group, grew to 1.3 million troops, the largest US force ever assembled.

Britain, Battle of World War II air battle between German and British air forces over Britain lasting 10 Jul–31 Oct 1940.

At the outset the Germans had the advantage because they had seized airfields in the Netherlands, Belgium, and France, which were basically safe from attack and from which SE England was within easy range. On 1 Aug 1940 the Luftwaffe had about 4,500 aircraft of all kinds, compared to about 3,000 for the RAF. The Battle of Britain had been intended as a preliminary to the German invasion plan *Seelöwe* (Sea Lion), which Hitler indefinitely postponed 17 Sept and abandoned 10 Oct, choosing instead to invade the USSR.

Bulge, Battle of the or *Ardennes offensive* in World War II, Hitler's plan, code-named 'Watch on the Rhine', for a breakthrough by his field marshal Rundstedt aimed at the US line in Ardennes 16 Dec 1944–28 Jan 1945. There were 77,000 Allied casualties and 130,000 German, including Hitler's last powerful reserve, his Panzer elite. Although US troops were encircled for some weeks at Bastogne, the German counteroffensive failed.

Caporetto former name of Kobarid, Slovenia (see entry).

Cassino town in S Italy, 80 km/50 mi NW of Naples; at the foot of Monte Cassino; population (1981) 31,139. It was the scene of heavy fighting during World War II in 1944, when most of the town was destroyed. It was rebuilt 1.5 km/1 mi to the N. The abbey on the sum-

THE DISINTEGRATION OF THE SOVIET ARMY

The disintegration of the Soviet army began when the Berlin Wall came down in November 1989. Within months Mikhail Gorbachev had reluctantly accepted the inevitability of German reunification; as a result, the Soviet forces in Germany would have to be disbanded and withdrawn. That withdrawal is due to be completed in 1994. A small military presence is likely to remain in Poland until then. Soviet forces were also withdrawn from Czechoslovakia and Hungary in 1990 and 1991.This withdrawal from central Europe (and from Afghanistan, Cuba, Iraq, and Cam Rahn Bay in Vietnam) sees the end of the imperial role of the former Soviet army, and has undoubtedly contributed to the process of its disintegration.

However, it is the disintegration of the USSR itself that has really changed the nature of its armed forces. After the Commonwealth of Independent States (CIS) was created in December 1991, there was a brave but futile attempt to create a common security system for the 15 republics of the former USSR. It was accepted from the outset that the Baltic republics would insist on being responsible for their own security, but it was hoped that the other republics, particularly Ukraine, would cooperate. That hope is now dead. As soon as Ukraine and Kazakhstan insisted on the right to establish their own armed forces, the possibility of maintaining integrated CIS forces

A Soviet army soldier in Czechoslovakia about to board a train taking him home. The newly independent republics of the CIS opted for their own national forces rather than a common security system.

was dealt a fatal blow. One by one the states of the former USSR insisted on going their own way. For example, Ukraine has set up an independent army, navy, and air force totalling some 50,000 personnel.

The shape of these independent forces will probably become clearer during 1992, when some outstanding issues should be resolved, notably the ownership of the Black Sea fleet and the nationality of aircraft stationed on Ukrainian soil. A compromise is likely to emerge with Russia keeping most of the major surface combatants and Ukraine inheriting the smaller craft in order to build a coastal navy. However, Ukraine is likely to inherit many advanced combat aircraft, including several squadrons of the highly capable Blackjack bomber. It has also inherited many ethnic Russians, particularly officers, who anticipate a more secure future in Ukraine than in Russia.

The Russian army will emerge as the successor to the Soviet army. But it will probably be much smaller and not rely so much on conscripts; the disintegration of the former Soviet army was partly caused by the increasing unwillingness of conscripts to report for duty in 1991 and 1992. The army that emerges will be more efficient, less politicized, and much more inward-looking—and therefore much less of a threat to the West. Boris Yeltsin has talked about armed forces totalling 2 million persons and deploying 3,500 combat aircraft, 180 submarines, 5,000–6,000 main battle tanks, and 2,500 nuclear warheads. The intention is that armed forces of this size should cost the equivalent of 5% of GNP, but this is probably optimistic; most objective analysis indicates a cost nearer 10%. Thus these forces are unlikely to be sustainable and further reduction/disintegration is probably unavoidable.

The one area of continuing cooperation throughout the former USSR is the command and control of nuclear weapons. The West has insisted on this, fearing nuclear proliferation or unauthorized use in the event of internal conflict. In early 1992, Belarus, Kazakhstan, and Ukraine agreed to return all tactical nuclear warheads to Russia for destruction by July 1992 and to decommission all strategic systems by 1994. Despite contradictory statements by President Kravchuk of Ukraine and President Nazarbayev of Kazakhstan, this process is likely to continue. Thus central (or Russian) control over nuclear weapons has been maintained.

Every state of the former USSR is busy creating its own independent armed forces. In the short term there could be chaos in the Caucasus, where the lines of communication from the Moscow general staff to local field commanders have broken down. These units could even resort to theft and looting as food and supplies run out, and local warlords may arise. The short-term picture is not encouraging. However, in the longer term, relatively stable national forces are likely to emerge in the larger republics.

mit of Monte Cassino, founded by St Benedict in 529, was rebuilt in 1956.

Clausewitz Karl von 1780–1831. Prussian officer and writer on war, born near Magdeburg. His book *Vom Kriege/On War* 1833, translated into English 1873, gave a new philosophical foundation to the art of war and put forward a concept of strategy that was influential until World War I.

D-day 6 June 1944, the day of the Allied invasion of Normandy under the command of General Eisenhower, with the aim of liberating Western Europe from German occupation. The Anglo-American invasion fleet landed on the Normandy beaches on the stretch of coast between the Orne River and St Marcouf. Artificial harbours known as 'Mulberries' were constructed and towed across the Channel so that equipment and armaments could be unloaded on to the beaches. After overcoming fierce resistance the Allies broke through the German defences; Paris was liberated on 25 Aug, and Brussels on 2 Sept.

de Gaulle Charles André Joseph Marie 1890–1970. French general and first president of the Fifth Republic 1959–69. He organized the Free French troops fighting the Nazis 1940–44, was head of the provisional French government 1944–46, and leader of his own Gaullist party. In 1958 the national assembly asked him to form a government during France's economic recovery and to solve the crisis in Algeria. He became president at the end of 1958, having changed the constitution to provide for a presidential system, and served until 1969.

Desert Storm, Operation codename of the military action to eject the Iraqi army from Kuwait in 1991. The build-up phase was codenamed *Operation Desert Shield* and lasted from Aug 1990, when Kuwait was first invaded by Iraq, to Jan 1991 when Operation Desert Storm was unleashed, starting the Gulf War. Desert Storm ended with the defeat of the Iraqi army in the Kuwaiti theatre of operations in late Feb 1991.

Dönitz Karl 1891–1980. German admiral, originator of the wolf-pack submarine technique, which sank 15 million tonnes of Allied shipping in World War II. He succeeded Hitler in 1945, capitulated, and was imprisoned 1946–56.

Dunkirk (French *Dunkerque*) seaport on the N coast of France, in Nord *département*, on the Strait of Dover; population (1983) 83,760, conurbation 196,000.

It was close to the front line during much of World War I, and in World War II, 337,131 Allied troops (including about 110,000 French) were evacuated from the beaches as German forces approached.

Falklands War 1982 war between Argentina and the UK. Some 30,000 Argentine troops invaded and occupied the British colony/dependency of the Falklands in the South Atlantic, renamed them Las Malvinas and declared them a sovereign part of Argentina. A British task force of about 15,000 soldiers, sailors, and airmen was assembled over a period of months and

an amphibious landing took place on 20 May at San Carlos Bay in the Sound between East and West Falkland. Shortly thereafter British troops marched on Darwin and Port Stanley. Finally, on 12 June, British troops launched a surprise attack on Argentine positions outside Port Stanley, capturing 400 troops and isolating the town. Two days later all Argentine forces on the island surrendered. The most significant event of the war at sea was the sinking of the Argentine cruiser *Belgrano*, by the British nuclear attack submarine HMS *Conqueror* when some 300 Argentines lost their lives. There were approximately 500 UK casualties, and 1,500 Argentine casualties during the hostilities. The war cost £1.6 billion.

Fuchs Klaus (Emil Julius) 1911–1988. German spy who worked on atom-bomb research in the UK in World War II. He was imprisoned 1950–59 for passing information to the USSR and resettled in East Germany.

Fuller John Frederick Charles 1878–1966. British major general and military theorist who propounded the concept of armoured warfare which, when interpreted by the Germans, became *blitzkrieg* in 1940.

Gallipoli port in European Turkey, giving its name to the peninsula (ancient name *Chersonesus*) on which it stands. In World War I, at the instigation of Winston Churchill, an unsuccessful attempt was made Feb 1915–Jan 1916 by Allied troops to force their way through the Dardanelles and link up with Russia. The campaign was fought mainly by Australian and New Zealand (ANZAC) forces, who suffered heavy losses. An estimated 36,000 Commonwealth troops died during the nine-month campaign.

Galtieri Leopoldo 1926– . Argentinian general, leading member of the right-wing military junta that ordered the seizure 1982 of the Falkland Islands (Malvinas), a British colony in the SW Atlantic claimed by Argentina. He and his fellow junta members were tried for abuse of human rights and court-martialled for their conduct of the war; he was sentenced to 12 years in prison in 1986.

Georgetown, Declaration of call in 1972, at a conference in Guyana of nonaligned countries, for a multipolar system to replace the two world power blocs, and for the Mediterranean Sea and Indian Ocean to be neutral.

Gulf War 16 Jan–28 Feb 1991 war between Iraq and a coalition of 28 nations led by the USA. The invasion and annexation of Kuwait by Iraq on 2 Aug 1990 provoked a build-up of US troops in Saudi Arabia, eventually totalling over 500,000. The UK subsequently deployed 42,000 troops, France 15,000, Egypt 20,000, and other nations smaller contingents. An air offensive lasting six weeks, in which 'smart' weapons came of age, destroyed perhaps one-third of Iraqi equipment and inflicted massive casualties. A 100-hour ground war followed, which effectively destroyed the remnants of the 500,000-strong Iraqi army in or near Kuwait. The cost of the war is estimated to be $60–70 billion. A sum approximating $54.5 billion was donated by the Japanese, Germans, and Saudi Arabians towards the cost of conducting the war.

Hiroshima industrial city and port on the S coast of Honshu, Japan, destroyed by the first wartime use of an atomic bomb 6 Aug 1945. The city has largely been rebuilt since the war; population (1987) 1,034,000.

Towards the end of World War II the city was utterly devastated by the US atom bomb. More than 10 sq km/4 sq mi was obliterated, with very heavy damage outside that area. Casualties totalled at least 137,000 out of a population of 343,000: 78,150 were found dead, others died later.

Iwo Jima largest of the Japanese Volcano Islands in the W Pacific Ocean, 1,222 km/760 mi S of Tokyo; area 21 sq km/8 sq mi. Annexed by Japan 1891, it was captured by the USA 1945 after fierce fighting. It was returned to Japan 1968.

Jutland, Battle of naval battle of World War I, fought between England and Germany on 31 May 1916, off the W coast of Jutland. Its outcome was indecisive, but the German fleet remained in port for the rest of the war.

Khe Sanh in the Vietnam War, US Marine outpost near the Laotian border and just south of the demilitarized zone between North and South Vietnam. Garrisoned by 4,000 Marines, it was attacked unsuccessfully by 20,000 North Vietnamese troops 21 Jan–7 Apr 1968.

Kobarid formerly *Caporetto* village on the Isonzo river in Slovenia. Originally in Hungary, it was in Italy from 1918, and in 1947 became part of Yugoslavia as Kobarid. During World War I, German-Austrian troops defeated Italian forces there 1917.

Liddell Hart Basil 1895–1970. British military strategist. He was an exponent of mechanized warfare, and his ideas were adopted in Germany 1935 in creating the 1st Panzer Division, combining motorized infantry and tanks. From 1937 he advised the UK War Office on army reorganization.

Marne, Battles of the in World War I, two unsuccessful German offensives: *First Battle* 6–9 Sept 1914, von Moltke's advance was halted by the British Expeditionary Force and the French under Foch; *Second Battle* 15 July–4 Aug 1918, Ludendorff's advance was defeated by British, French, and US troops under the French general Pétain, and German morale crumbled.

Mons (Flemish *Bergen*) industrial city (coalmining, textiles, sugar) and capital of the province of Hainaut, Belgium; population (1985) 90,500. The military headquarters of NATO is at nearby Chièvres-Casteau.

Montgomery Bernard Law, 1st Viscount Montgomery of Alamein 1887–1976. British field marshal. In World War II he commanded the 8th Army in N Africa in the Second Battle of El Alamein 1942. As commander of British troops in N Europe from 1944, he received the German surrender on 1945.

Okinawa largest of the Japanese Ryukyu Islands

in the W Pacific; area 2,250 sq km/869 sq mi; population (1986) 1,190,000. It was captured by the USA in the *Battle of Okinawa* 1 Apr–21 June 1945, with 47,000 US casualties (12,000 dead) and 60,000 Japanese (only a few hundred survived as prisoners); the island was returned to Japan 1972.

Passchendaele village in W Flanders, Belgium, near Ypres. The Passchendaele ridge before Ypres was the object of a costly and unsuccessful British offensive in World War I, between July and Nov 1917; British casualties numbered nearly 400,000.

Patton George (Smith) 1885–1945. US general in World War II, known as 'Blood and Guts'. He commanded the 2nd Armoured Division 1940, and in 1942 led the Western Task Force that landed at Casablanca, Morocco. After commanding the 7th Army, he led the 3rd Army across France and into Germany, and in 1945 took over the 15th Army.

Pearl Harbor an inlet of the Pacific Ocean where the US naval base is situated in Hawaii on Oahu Island. It was the scene of a Japanese surprise air attack on 7 Dec 1941, that brought the US into World War II. It took place while Japanese envoys were holding so-called peace talks in Washington. The local commanders Admiral Kummel and Lieutenant General Short were relieved of their posts and held responsible for the fact that the base, despite warnings, was totally unprepared at the time of the attack. About 3,300 US military personnel were killed, 4 battleships were lost, and a large part of the US Pacific fleet was destroyed or damaged. The Japanese, angered by US embargoes of oil and other war materiel and convinced that US entry into the war was inevitable, opted to strike a major blow in hopes of forcing US concessions. Instead, it galvanized public opinion and raised anti-Japanese sentiment to a fever pitch, with war declared thereafter.

Rommel Erwin 1891–1944. German field marshal. He served in World War I, and in World War II he played an important part in the invasions of central Europe and France. He was commander of the N African offensive from 1941 (when he was nicknamed 'Desert Fox') until defeated in the Battles of El Alamein. He was commander in chief for a short time against the Allies in Europe 1944 but (as a sympathizer with the Stauffenberg plot against Hitler) was forced to commit suicide.

Russo-Japanese War war between Russia and Japan 1904–05, which arose from conflicting ambitions in Korea and Manchuria, specifically, the Russian occupation of Port Arthur (modern Lüda) 1896 and of the Amur province 1900. Japan successfully besieged Port Arthur May 1904–Jan 1905, took Mukden 29 Feb–10 Mar, and on 27 May defeated the Russian Baltic fleet, which had sailed halfway around the world to Tsushima Strait. A peace was signed in Portsmouth, New Hampshire, USA, 23 Aug 1905. Russia surrendered its lease on Port Arthur, ceded S Sakhalin to Japan, evacuated

Manchuria, and recognized Japan's interests in Korea.

Schwarzkopf H Norman 1934– . US general in the Gulf War. A considered, calculating approach belies his 'Stormin' Norman' image. A graduate from the military academy of West Point, he obtained a masters degree in guided missile engineering. He became an infantryman and later a paratrooper. He was a battalion commander during the Vietnam War, earning two Purple Hearts and three Silver Stars for his two tours of service there. As Supreme Commander of the Allied Forces in the Gulf, he planned and executed a blitzkrieg campaign, termed 'Desert Storm' which sustained remarkably few casualties, whilst crushing the enemy. His diplomatic skills were extended to the full in maintaining a 28-member Arab–Western anti-Iraqi military coalition. With victory secured, he emerged in March 1991 with a national approval rating in excess of 90%.

Sevastopol or **Sebastopol** port, resort, and fortress in the Crimea, Ukraine; population (1987) 350,000. It is the base of the (former Soviet) Black Sea fleet and also has shipyards and a wine-making industry. Founded by Catherine II 1784, it was successfully besieged by the English and French in the Crimean War (Oct 1854–Sept 1855), and in World War II by the Germans (Nov 1941–July 1942), but was retaken by the Soviets 1944.

Sinai Egyptian peninsula, at the head of the Red Sea; area 65,000 sq km/25,000 sq mi. Resources include oil, natural gas, manganese, and coal; irrigation water from the river Nile is carried under the Suez Canal.

Sinai was occupied by Israel 1967–82. After the Battle of Sinai 1973, Israel began a gradual withdrawal from the area, under the disengagement agreement 1975, and the Camp David peace treaty 1979 and restored the whole of Sinai to Egyptian control by Apr 1982.

Sino-Japanese Wars wars waged by Japan against China to expand to the mainland.
First Sino-Japanese War 1894–95. Under the treaty of Shimonoseki, Japan secured the 'independence' of Korea, cession of Taiwan and the nearby Pescadores Islands, and the Liaodong peninsula (for a naval base). France, Germany, and Russia pressured Japan into returning the last-named, which Russia occupied 1896 to establish Port Arthur (now Lüda); this led to the Russo-Japanese War 1904–05.
Second Sino-Japanese War 1931–45. The Japanese occupied Manchuria, turning it into a puppet state of Manchukuo; they also attacked Shanghai and moved into NE China. In 1941 the Japanese attacked Pearl Harbor, leading to the extension of lend-lease aid to China and US entry into war against Japan and its allies. In Sep 1945, the Chinese received the Japanese surrender at Nanjing, after the Allies had concluded World War II.

Somme river in N France, on which Amiens and Abbeville stand; length 240 km/150 mi. It rises in Aisne *département* and flows W through Somme *département* to the English Channel.

Stalingrad former name (1925–61) of the Russian city of Volgograd.

Tirpitz Alfred von 1849–1930. German admiral. As secretary for the navy 1897–1916, he created the German navy and planned the World War I U-boat campaign.

Tonkin Gulf Incident clash that triggered US entry into the Vietnam War in Aug 1964. Two US destroyers (USS *C Turner Joy* and USS *Maddox*) reported that they were fired on by North Vietnamese torpedo boats. It is unclear whether hostile shots were actually fired, but the reported attack was taken as a pretext for retaliatory air raids against North Vietnam. On 7 Aug the US Congress passed the **Tonkin Resolution**, which allowed President Johnson 'to take all necessary steps, including the use of armed forces' to help SEATO (South-East Asia Treaty Organization) members 'defend their freedom'. This resolution formed the basis for the considerable increase in US military involvement in the Vietnam War; it was repealed 1970.

Verdun fortress town in NE France on the Meuse. During World War I it became the symbol of French resistance, withstanding a German onslaught in 1916.

Vietnam War 1954–75. War between communist North Vietnam and US-backed South Vietnam. 200,000 South Vietnamese soldiers, 1 million North Vietnamese soldiers, and 500,000 civilians were killed. 56,555 US soldiers were killed 1961–75, a fifth of them by their own troops. The war destroyed 50% of the country's forest cover and 20% of agricultural land. Cambodia, a neutral neighbour, was bombed by the US 1969–75, with 1 million killed or wounded.

Volgograd formerly (until 1925) *Tsaritsyn*, and 1925-61 *Stalingrad* industrial city in SW Russia, on the river Volga; population (1987) 988,000. Its successful defence 1942-43 against Germany was a turning point for the Allied forces in World War II. The German 6th army under field marshal Friedrich Paulus, captured Stalingrad 1943, but was forced to surrender to the Soviets under marshal Georgi Zhukov. After intense fighting, the Germans lost 70,000 men.

World War I 1914–18. War between the Central European Powers (Germany, Austria-Hungary, and allies) on one side and the Triple Entente (Britain and the British Empire, France, and Russia) and their allies, including the USA (which entered 1917), on the other side. An estimated 10 million lives were lost and twice that number were wounded.

World War II 1939–45. war between Germany, Italy, and Japan (the Axis powers) on one side, and Britain, the Commonwealth, France, the USA, the USSR, and China (the Allied powers) on the other. An estimated 55 million lives were lost, 20 million of them citizens of the USSR.

Ypres (Flemish *Ieper*) Belgian town in W Flanders, 40 km/25 mi S of Ostend, a site of three major battles 1914–17 fought in World War I. In Oct–Nov 1914 the Germans launched an assault on British defensive positions and captured the Messines Ridge, but failed to take Ypres. In Apr–May 1915, the Germans launched a renewed attack using poison gas and chlorine (the first recorded use in war), in an unsuccessful attempt to break the British line. In July–Nov 1917 (known also as Passchendaele), an allied offensive, including British, Canadian, and Australian troops, was launched under British commander-in-chief Douglas Haig, in an attempt to capture ports on the Belgian coast held by Germans. The long and bitter battle, fought in appalling conditions of driving rain and waterlogged ground, achieved an advance of only 8 km/5 mi of territory that was of no strategic significance. The allied attack cost over 300,000 casualties.

Zhukov Georgi Konstantinovich 1896–1974. Marshal of the USSR in World War II and minister of defence 1955–57. As chief of staff from 1941, he defended Moscow 1941, counterattacked at Stalingrad in 1942, organized the relief of Leningrad 1943, and led the offensive from the Ukraine Mar 1944 which ended in the fall of Berlin. He subsequently commanded the Soviet occupation forces in Germany.

WEAPONS AND EQUIPMENT

aircraft carrier sea-going base for military aircraft. After World War II the cost and vulnerability of such large vessels were thought to have outweighed their advantages. However, by 1980 the desire to have a means of destroying enemy aircraft beyond the range of a ship's own weapons, especially on convoy duty, led to a widespread revival of aircraft carriers of 20,000–30,000 tonnes. Aircraft carriers are equipped with combinations of fixed-wing aircraft, helicopters, missile launchers, and anti-aircraft guns.

armoured personnel carrier (APC) wheeled or tracked military vehicle designed to transport up to ten people. Armoured to withstand small-arms fire and shell splinters, it is used on battlefields.

assault ship naval vessel designed to land and support troops and vehicles under hostile conditions.

bayonet short sword attached to the muzzle of a firearm. The new British Army rifle, the SA-80, is fitted with a bayonet; its predecessor, the SLR, was similarly equipped and used, with its bayonet, during the 1982 Falklands conflict.

binary weapon in chemical warfare, weapon consisting of two substances that in isolation are harmless but when mixed together form a poisonous nerve gas. They are loaded into the delivery system separately and combine after launch.

enhanced radiation weapon another name for the neutron bomb.

fuel-air explosive warhead containing a highly flammable petroleum and oxygen mixture; when released over a target, this mixes with the oxygen in the atmosphere and produces a vapour which, when ignited, causes a blast approximately five times more powerful than conventional high explosives. Fuel-air explosives were used by the US Air Force in the 1991 Gulf War to flatten Iraqi defensive positions.

Harrier the only truly successful vertical takeoff and landing fixed-wing aircraft, often called the *jump jet*. Built in Britain, it made its first flight 1966. It has a single jet engine and a set of swivelling nozzles. These deflect the jet exhaust vertically downwards for takeoff and landing, and to the rear for normal flight. Designed to fly from confined spaces with little ground support, it can refuel in midair.

incendiary bomb a bomb containing inflammable matter. Usually dropped by aircraft, incendiary bombs were used in World War I, and were a major weapon in attacks on cities in World War II. To hinder firefighters, delayed-action high-explosive bombs were usually dropped with them. In the Vietnam War, the USA used napalm in incendiary bombs.

machine gun rapid-firing automatic gun. The forerunner of the modern machine gun was the Gatling, perfected in the USA in 1860 and used in the Civil War. The Maxim of 1884 was recoil-operated, but some later types have been gas-operated (Bren) or recoil assisted by gas (some versions of the Browning). The *submachine-gun*, exploited by Chicago gangsters in the 1920s, was widely used in World War II; for instance, the Thompson, often called the Tommy gun.

mechanized infantry combat vehicle (MICV) tracked military vehicle designed to fight as part of an armoured battle group; that is, with tanks. It is armed with a quick-firing cannon and one or more machine guns. MICVs have replaced armoured personnel carriers.

mine explosive charge on land or sea, or in the atmosphere, designed to be detonated by contact, vibration (for example from an enemy engine), magnetic influence, or a timing device. Countermeasures include metal detectors (useless for plastic types), specially equipped helicopters, and (at sea) minesweepers.

missile rocket-propelled weapon, which may be nuclear-armed. Modern missiles are classified according to range into *intercontinental ballistic missiles* (ICBMs, capable of reaching targets over 5,500 km/3,400 mi), *intermediate-range* (1,100 km/680 mi–2,750 km/1,700mi), and *short-range* (under 1,100 km/680 mi) missiles. They are also categorized as *surface to surface, surface to air, air to air,* or *air to surface.*

A *ballistic missile* is one whose trajectory is governed by gravity once the power is shut off. The first long-range ballistic missile used in warfare was the V2 launched by Germany against Britain in World War II. Outside the industrialized countries, 22 states had active ballistic-missile programmes by 1989, and

MISSILE SYSTEMS (EXCLUDING BALLISTIC MISSILES)

	Range (miles)	Country
Cruise Missiles		
Tomahawk		
ground (GLCM) and sea (SLCM) launched	1550	US
Boeing AGM-86B ALCM (air launched)	1865	US
Air Launched Missiles		
Short Range Attack Missile (SRAM)	40	US
ASMP (Air-Sol Moyen Portée)	52	France
AS-15	approx. 1500	Russia
Air-to-Air Missiles		
AIM-9 Sidewinder	11	US
AA-2 Atoll	5	Russia
AA-7 Apex	12	Russia
AA-6 Acrid	15	Russia
Matra Magic	6	France
Skyflash (radar homing)	62	UK
Anti-Ship Missiles/Air to Surface Missiles		
AS-4 Kitchen	500	Russia
Harpoon	75	US
Sea Skua	12	UK
Sea Eagle	62	UK
Exocet	43	France
Maverick	approx. 15	US
Fleet Air Defence		
Sea Dart	20	UK
Seawolf	5	UK
Standard SM-1MR	approx. 35	US
Crotale	8	France
SA-SS-1 Goa	15	Russia
Anti-Tank Missiles (ground launched) range 3000–5000 metres		
Tow		US
Sagger		Russia
Swing fire		UK
Dragon		US
Milan		France/Germany
Surface to Air Missiles (SAM) (range 6.5–25 miles)		
SA-6 Gainful		Russia
SA-8 Gecho		Russia
Crotale		France
Rapier		UK
Hawk		US
Patriot		US
Man Portable SAM (range 3–5 miles)		
Blowpipe		UK
Javelin		UK
Stinger		US
SA-7 Grail		Russia
Bofors RBS-70		Sweden
Anti-Radar Missiles (range approx. 10 miles)		
ALARM		UK
HARM		US

17 had deployed these weapons: Afghanistan, Argentina, Brazil, Cuba, Egypt, India, Iran, Iraq, Israel, North Korea, South Korea, Libya, Pakistan, Saudi Arabia, South Africa, Syria, and Taiwan. Non-nuclear short-range missiles were used during the Iran–Iraq War 1980–88 against Iraqi cities.

A *cruise missile* is in effect a pilotless, computer-guided aircraft. It can be sea-launched from submarines or surface ships, or launched from the air or the ground. Tomahawk cruise missiles launched from both US submarines and battleships lying offshore were devastatingly effective and accurate against targets deep within Iraq during the 1991 Gulf War.

Battlefield missiles used in the 1991 Gulf War include anti-tank missiles and short-range attack missiles. NATO announced in 1990 that it was phasing out ground-launched nuclear battlefield missiles, and these are being replaced by types of tactical air-to-surface missile (TASM), also with nuclear warheads.

mortar method of projecting a bomb via a high trajectory at a target up to 6–7 km/3–4 mi away. A mortar bomb is stabilized in flight by means of tail fins. The high trajectory results in a high angle of attack and makes mortar more suitable than artillery for use in built-up areas or mountains; mortars are not, however, as accurate. Artillery also differs in firing a projectile through a rifled barrel, thus creating greater muzzle velocity.

napalm fuel used in flamethrowers and incendiary bombs. Produced from jellied petrol, it is a mixture of *na*phthenic and *palm*itic acids. Napalm causes extensive burns because it sticks to the skin even when aflame. It was widely used by the US Army during the Vietnam War.

Patriot a ground-to-air medium-range missile system used in the air defence role. It has high-altitude coverage, electronic jamming capability, and excellent mobility. It was tested in battle against SCUD missiles fired by the Iraqis in the 1991 Gulf War.

periscope optical instrument designed for observation from a concealed position such as from a submerged submarine. In its basic form it consists of a tube with parallel mirrors at each end, inclined at 45° to its axis. The periscope attained prominence in naval and military operations of World War I.

remotely piloted vehicle (RPV) crewless mini-aircraft used for military surveillance and to select targets in battle. RPVs barely show up on radar, so they can fly over a battlefield without being shot down, and they are equipped to transmit TV images to an operator on the ground.

RPVs were used by Israeli forces in 1982 in Lebanon and by the Allies in the 1991 Gulf War. The US system is called Aquila and the British system Phoenix.

rifle firearm that has spiral grooves (rifling) in its barrel. When a bullet is fired, the rifling makes it spin, thereby improving accuracy. Rifles were first introduced in the late 18th century.

Scud surface-to-surface missile designed and produced in the USSR, which can be armed with a nuclear, chemical, or conventional warhead. The *Scud-B*, deployed on a mobile launcher, was the version most commonly used by the Iraqi army in the Gulf War 1991. It is a relatively inaccurate weapon.

Semtex plastic explosive, manufactured in Czechoslovakia. It is safe to handle (it can only be ignited by a detonator), and difficult to trace, since it has no smell. It has been used by extremist groups in the Middle East and by the IRA in Northern Ireland.

0.5 kg of Semtex is thought to have been the cause of an explosion that destroyed a Pan-American Boeing 747 in flight over Lockerbie, Scotland, in Dec 1988, killing 270 people.

small arms one of the two main divisions of firearms, guns that can be carried by hand. The first small arms were portable handguns in use in the late 14th century, supported on the ground and ignited by hand. Today's small arms range from breech-loading single shot rifles and shotguns to sophisticated automatic and semiautomatic weapons. In 1980, there were 11,522 deaths in the USA caused by hand-held guns; in the UK, there were 8.

smart weapons programmable missiles which can be guided to their target by either laser technology, TV homing technology, or TERCOM (terrain contour matching). A smart bomb or missile relies on its pinpoint accuracy to destroy a target rather than the size of its warhead. Examples include: the cruise missile (Tomahawk) , laser-guided artillery shells (Copperhead), laser-guided bombs and short-range TV guided missiles such as SLAM. Smart weapons were first used on the battlefield in the Gulf War, but only 3% of all the bombs dropped or missiles fired were 'smart'. Of that 3%, it is estimated that 50–70% of those fired hit their targets, which is a high accuracy rate.

stealth technology methods used to make an aircraft as invisible as possible, primarily to radar detection but also to detection by visual means and heat sensors. This is achieved by a combination of aircraft-design elements: smoothing off all radar-reflecting sharp edges; covering the aircraft with radar-absorbent materials; fitting engine coverings that hide the exhaust and heat signatures of the aircraft; and other, secret technologies.

The US F-117A stealth fighter-bomber was used successfully during the 1991 Gulf War to attack targets in Baghdad completely undetected. The B-2 bomber, a larger stealth aircraft, is being put into limited production.

TASM abbreviation for *tactical air-to-surface missile*, a missile with a range of under 500 km/300 mi and a nuclear warhead. TASMs are being developed independently by the USA and France to replace the surface-to-surface missiles being phased out by NATO from 1990.

torpedo self-propelled underwater missile, invented 1866 by British engineer Robert

Whitehead. Modern torpedoes are homing missiles; some resemble mines in that they lie on the seabed until activated by the acoustic signal of a passing ship. A television camera enables them to be remotely controlled, and in the final stage of attack they lock on to the radar or sonar signals of the target ship.

U-2 a US military reconnaissance aeroplane, used in secret flights over the USSR from 1956 to photograph military installations. In 1960 a U-2 was shot down over the USSR and the pilot, Gary Powers, was captured and imprisoned. He was exchanged for a US-held Soviet agent two years later.

U-boat German submarine. The title was used in both world wars.

vertical takeoff and landing craft (VTOL) aircraft that can take off and land vertically. Helicopters, airships, and balloons can do this, as can a few fixed-wing aeroplanes.

ECONOMICS

BUSINESS TERMS

added value or **value added** the sales revenue from selling a firm's products less the cost of the materials or purchases used in those products. It is an increasingly used indicator of relative efficiency within and between firms, although in the latter case open to distortion where mark-up varies between standard and premium-priced segments of a market.

adverse variance difference between actual and budgeted spending or income that results in the organization having less money than planned.

alpha share a share in any of the companies most commonly traded on the London Stock Exchange—the 100 or so largest.

amortization the ending of a debt by paying it off gradually, over a period of time. The term is used to describe either the paying off of a cash debt or the accounting procedure by which the value of an asset is progressively reduced (depreciated) over a number of years.

annual accounts summary of the records of a company's financial activities, prepared by an accountant and in most countries made available for public inspection. Annual accounts include a balance sheet and profit/loss or income/expenditure account.

annual general meeting (AGM) yearly meeting of the shareholders of a company or the members of an organization, at which business including consideration of the annual report and accounts, the election of officers, and the appointment of auditors is normally carried out. UK company law requires an AGM to be called by the board of directors.

annual percentage rate (APR) the charge (including interest) for granting consumer credit, expressed as an equivalent once-a-year percentage figure of the amount of the credit granted. In the UK, lenders are legally required to state the APR when advertising loans.

arbitrageur a person who buys securities (such as currency or commodities) in one country or market for immediate resale in another market, to take advantage of different prices. Arbitrage became widespread during the 1970s and 1980s with the increasing deregulation of financial markets.

articles of association in the UK, the rules governing the relationship between a registered company, its members (shareholders), and its directors. The articles of association are deposited with the registrar of companies. In the USA they are called **by-laws**.

asset the land or property of a company or individual, payments due from bills, investments, and anything else owned that can be turned into cash. On a company's balance sheet, total assets must be equal to liabilities (money and services owed). A **fixed asset** is normally not for sale and is intended for use within a business; for example, machinery, land, buildings, plant, and equipment. A **liquid asset** refers to cash or any asset that can easily be converted into cash, for example, stock-exchange investments.

asset stripping sale, or exploitation by other means, of assets of a business often taken over for the purpose. The parts of the business may be potentially more valuable separately than together. Asset stripping is a major force for the more efficient use of assets, but it has been criticised for not taking into account the welfare of employees.

audit the official inspection of a company's accounts by a qualified accountant as required each year by law to ensure that the company balance sheet reflects the true state of its affairs. An **internal audit** is an independent in-house inspection of accounts. By reviewing controls in the organization, and by analysing, counselling, and making recommendations concerning the activities appraised, an internal audit may lead to greater efficiency and effectiveness.

balance sheet a statement of the financial position of a company or individual on a specific date, showing both assets, liabilities, and capital.

bankruptcy the process by which the property of a person (in legal terms, an individual or corporation) unable to pay debts is taken away under a court order and divided fairly among the person's creditors, after preferential payments such as taxes and wages. Proceedings may be instituted either by the debtor (voluntary bankruptcy) or by any creditor for a substantial sum (involuntary bankruptcy). Until discharged, a bankrupt is severely restricted in financial activities.

base lending rate the rate of interest to which most bank lending is linked, the actual rate depending on the status of the borrower. A prestigious company might command a rate only 1% above base rate while an individual would be charged several points above.

bear a speculator who sells stocks or shares on the stock exchange expecting a fall in the price in order to buy them back at a profit, the opposite of a bull. In a bear market, prices fall, and bears prosper.

beta share a share traded less actively on the stock exchange than an alpha share.

bill of exchange a form of commercial credit instrument, or IOU, used in international trade. In Britain, a bill of exchange is defined by the Bills of Exchange Act 1882 as an unconditional order in writing addressed by one person to another, signed by the person giving it, requiring the person to whom it is addressed to pay on demand or at a fixed or determinable future time a certain sum in money to, or to the order of, a specified person, or to the bearer. US practice is governed by the Uniform Negotiable Instruments Law, drafted on the same lines as the British, and accepted by all states by 1927.

bill of lading document giving proof of particular goods having been loaded on a ship. The

OUT OF BUSINESS

America's 10 biggest bankruptcies (1991)

	Date of bankruptcy	Assets before bankruptcy, US$ (bn)
First Executive *insurance*	May 13th	15.19
First Capital Holdings *insurance & financial services*	May 30th	9.68
Maxwell Communications *print & electrical publishing*	Dec 16th	6.35
Columbia Gas Systems *gas & energy production*	July 31st	6.20
Enstar Group *holding company*	Jan 4th	5.59
Pan Am Group *airline*	Jan 4th	2.44
Farley *textiles, clothing & metals*	Sept 24th	2.41
Landmark Land Co *banking & property*	Oct 11th	2.40
Carter Hawley Hale Stores *retailing*	Feb 11th	2.05
Statewide Bancorp *bank holding company*	May 22nd	1.98

Source: The Economist

person to whom the goods are being sent normally needs to show the bill of lading in order to obtain the release of the goods. For air freight, there is an *air waybill*.

blue chip a stock that is considered strong and reliable in terms of the dividend yield and capital value. Blue chip companies are favoured by stock market investors more interested in security than risk taking.

bond a security issued by a government, local authority, company, bank, or other institution on fixed interest. Usually a long-term security, a bond may be irredeemable, secured or unsecured. Property bonds are non-fixed securities with the yield fixed to property investment. See also Eurobond.

brand leader branded product that has the largest share of the market for all products of that type.

breakeven point situation where income equals expenditure so that neither a profit nor a loss is made.

broker intermediary who arranges the sale of financial products (shares, insurance, mortgages, and so on) to the public for a commission or brokerage fee.

budget complete financial plan for an organization, usually drawn up for a future 12-month period. A *capital budget* is a financial plan for tangible items whose benefits and/or costs may extend over a period longer than one year. A *cash budget* or *cash-flow projection* is a statement drawn up to show the net inflows and outflows of cash, with the resulting balance identified at the end of each period. Its purpose is to identify when surpluses or deficits of cash are expected.

bull a speculator who buys stocks or shares on the stock exchange expecting a rise in the price in order to sell them later at a profit, the opposite of a bear. In a bull market, prices rise and bulls profit.

business plan document that analyses the activities of a business in detail and predicts its objectives for at least the coming year. It is usually presented to the bank in support of a request for a loan and/or overdraft facilities.

call a demand for money, usually instalments of part-paid securities.

capital employed total assets (excluding intangibles, such as goodwill) less current liabilities (including overdrafts, short-term loans, trade and other creditors).

capital expenditure spending on fixed assets such as plant and equipment, trade investments, or the purchase of other businesses.

capital flight transfer of funds from a particular national economy or out of a particular currency in anticipation of less attractive investment conditions.

cartel (German *Kartell*, a group) association of firms that remain independent but which enter into agreement to set mutually acceptable prices for their products. A cartel may restrict output or raise prices in order to prevent entrants to the market and increase member profits.

cash flow the input of cash required to cover all expenses of a business, whether revenue or capital. Alternatively, the actual or prospective balance between the various outgoing and incoming movements, which is designated negative or positive according to whether outflow or inflow is greater.

commodity something produced for sale. Commodities may be consumer goods, such as radios, or producer goods, such as copper bars. *Commodity markets* deal in raw or semi-raw materials that are amenable to grading and that can be stored for considerable periods without deterioration.

company a number of people grouped together as a business enterprise. Types of company include public limited companies, partnerships, joint ventures, sole proprietorships, and branches of foreign companies. Most companies are private limited companies and, unlike public companies, cannot offer their shares to the general public.

convertible loan stock stock or bond (paying a fixed interest) that may be converted into a stated number of shares at a specific date.

corporate strategy the way an organization intends to meet its objectives. This may be set out in a document of its principles, its situation, and the environment in which it expects to operate.

cost-benefit analysis technique used in business decision-making that assesses all relevant costs and compares them with estimated returns. It is often used to take into account factors that are difficult to quantify and therefore might be overlooked.

cost of sales cost incurred directly in making sales. This could include the cost of raw materials or goods bought for resale and labour costs incurred in producing goods. It does not include overhead costs.

critical path analysis procedure used in the management of complex business projects, which indicates the project's minimum duration and those subprojects critical to reduction in execution time, by identifying the duration and the relationship between them.

cumulative preference share preference share whose entitlement to dividend is carried forward to a subsequent year whenever a dividend is not paid.

current asset or *circulating* or *floating asset* any asset of a business that could be turned into cash in a limited period of time, generally less than a year. Current assets include stocks, accounts receivable or billings, short-term investments, and cash.

current liability any debt of a business that falls due within one year. Current liabilities include creditors (including employees), bank overdrafts, and interest.

current ratio in a company, the ratio of current assets to current liabilities. It is a general indication of the adequacy of an organization's working capital and its ability to meet day-to-day calls upon it.

debenture loan raised by a company using its assets as security for repayment.

decision theory mathematical technique for analysing decision-making problems, especially over unpredictable factors, seeking to minimize error; it includes game theory, risk analysis, and utility theory.

deferred share a share that typically warrants a dividend only after a specified dividend has been paid on the ordinary shares; it may, however, be entitled to a dividend on all the profits after that point.

depreciation a fall in value of an asset (such as factory machinery) resulting from age, wear and tear, or other circumstances. It is a factor in assessing company profit.

director person appointed to participate in decisions relating to the running of a company, who may or may not have executive powers. A director is usually elected by the shareholders of a company. A *board of directors* (comprising all of the directors of a company) meets regularly to decide company policy and may elect one of its members to act as *managing director*, with responsibility for the overall running of the company.

diversification a corporate strategy of entering distinctly new products or markets as opposed to simply adding to an existing product range. A company may diversify in order to spread its risks or because its original area of operation is becoming less profitable.

dividend the amount of money that company directors decide should be taken out of profits for distribution to shareholders. It is usually declared as a percentage or fixed amount per share. Most companies pay dividends once or twice a year.

economies of scale increase in production capacity at a financial cost that is more than compensated for by the greater volume of output. In a dress factory, for example, a reduction in the unit cost may be possible only by the addition of new machinery, which would be

THE TOP 20 EUROPEAN COMPANIES (1991)

Company	Country	Turnover US$ (m)
Royal Dutch Shell	Netherlands/UK	86,943.3
British Petroleum	UK	47,049.2
Daimler-Benz	Germany	44,936.4
Nikko Securities (Europe)	UK	42,358.7
Volkswagen	Germany	38,442.3
IRI	Italy	37,066.1
Siemens	Germany	35,957.5
Fiat	Italy	34,888.1
Unilever NV	Netherlands	34,523.4
Nestlé	Switzerland	31,192.2
Sharps Pixley	UK	30,401.5
Philips	Netherlands	29,804.1
Veba	Germany	28,945.7
Hoescht	Germany	26,998.8
Peugeot	France	26,417.1
ENI	Italy	25,969.3
Elf Aquitaine	France	25,872.5
BASF	Germany	25,804.7
EDF	France	25,235.4

Source: ELC International

MORTGAGE ARREARS AND HOME REPOSSESSION: UK, 1987–1991

Mortgage arrears and home repossessions have shown a steady upward trend since the second half of 1988, culminating in an all-time high in 1991. The number of homes repossessed by mortgage lenders because their owners could not keep up with monthly payments reached 75,540 in 1991, a staggering 72% increase on the 1990 figures. The high rate of repossession is matched by the increasing number of borrowers in arrears. At the end of 1991, the number of borrowers with more than six months' arrears was 275,530, while borrowers with more than twelve months' arrears totalled 91,740 compared with 59,690 halfway through 1991.

Far from the recent optimistic prediction by the Council for Mortgage Lenders of a declining trend of repossession, these figures suggest that repossessions will remain at high levels in 1992 and 1993. The response of the mortgage lenders has been, understandably, an agreement with the government in December 1991 on a package of measures aimed at stabilizing the housing market. These measures include the direct payment to lenders of social security payments for mortgage interest and the provision of £1 billion for mortgage rescue schemes.

Building societies and banks (most notably National Westminster Bank) came up with their respective rescue packages. The Leeds Permanent, the sixth largest building society, launched its rescue package on 13 February 1992. The package included a £100 million scheme in which the society will take a share in the value of a house and provide the borrower with a reduced mortgage payment. In addition, the interest rate for such borrowers was frozen at 9.9% for the next five years from 1992. National Westminster Bank was the only high street clearing bank so far to put up a rescue scheme, worth £30 million.

These measures are expected, in the short term, to result in 40,000 homes being saved from repossession. Already, the Council for Mortgage Lenders has reported a decline in the number of new arrears cases and in eviction rates. In the long term, full recovery is contingent upon a quick recovery from the current economic recession. The number of repossessed homes for sale is expected to continue to depress the housing market for some months given the backlog of repossessed homes which, at the end of 1991, stood at 67,370 after sales of more than 47,000 properties.

---

worthwhile only if the volume of dresses produced were increased and there was sufficient market demand for them.

electronic funds transfer at point of sale (EFTPOS) the transfer of funds from one bank account to another by electronic means. For example, a bank customer inserts a plastic card in a point-of-sale computer terminal in a supermarket, and telephone lines are used to make an automatic debit from the customer's bank account to settle the bill.

end-use certificate in shipping, a document intended to assure authorities of the eventual application (generally also the final customer and destination) of an actual or intended shipment. End-use certificates are needed in cases where there are political controls on exports.

equal-opportunity policy plan of action that spells out what constitutes unfair discrimination in order to guide employment practices and to ensure that the organization is working within the legislation on equal pay, sex, and race discrimination.

equity a company's assets, less its liabilities, which are the property of the owner or shareholders. Popularly, equities are stocks and shares which, unlike debentures and preference shares, do not pay interest at fixed rates but pay dividends based on the company's performance. The value of equities tends to rise over the long term, but in the short term they are a risk investment because of fluctuating values.

Eurobond a bond underwritten by an international syndicate and sold in countries other than the country of the currency in which

the issue is denominated. They provide longer-term financing than is possible with loans in Eurodollars.

executive director company director who is also an employee of the company.

experience curve the observed effect of improved performance of individuals and organizations as experience of a repeated task increases.

factoring lending money to a company on the security of their accounts receivable; this is often done on the basis of collecting those accounts. Factoring also means acting as a commission agent for the sale of goods.

favourable variance difference between actual and budgeted spending or income that results in the organization having more money than planned.

Financial Times indices scales for measuring aspects of the stock market, published by the *Financial Times* of London. They are: FT ordinary, FT-SE 100, FT-Actuaries All Share, FT Government Securities, FT Fixed Interest, FT-SE Eurotrack 200, FT-Actuaries World Index and Indices of National and Regional Markets.

financial year any year relating to finance, such as the accounting year of a business. It need not correspond with the calendar year.

fixed costs or *indirect costs* or *overheads* the costs of a business that do not vary in proportion to changes in sales or output; for example, rent, rates, and administrative expenses.

Fordism type of mass production characterized by a high degree of job specialization, as typified by Ford motor company's early use of assembly lines. *Post-Fordism* management theory and practice emphasizes flexibility and autonomy of decision-making for nonmanagerial staff. It is concerned more with facilitating and coordinating tasks than with control.

Mass-production techniques were influenced by US management consultant F W Taylor's book *Scientific Management*, which emphasized work study, work specialization, and managerial control.

franchise the right to use the name of another company and to market its products and/or services in exchange for a royalty. The franchisee agrees to abide by the conditions set out in the franchise agreement.

future a contract to buy or sell a specific quantity of a particular commodity or currency (or even a purely notional sum, such as the value of a particular stock index) at a particular date in the future. There is usually no physical exchange between buyer and seller. It is only the difference between the ground value and the market value that changes hands. The *futures market* trades in financial futures (for example, LIFFE, the London International Financial Futures Exchange).

gearing, financial the relationship between fixed-interest debt and shareholders' equity used to finance a company. The additional profit made by borrowing at fixed interest and earning a greater return on those funds than the interest payable accrues to the shareholders. A high proportion of fixed-interest funding, known as 'high gearing', can leave the firm more vulnerable in poorer trading conditions.

GmbH abbreviation for *Gesellshaft mit beschrankter Haftung* (German 'limited liability company').

golden share a share, often with overriding voting powers, issued by governments to control privatized companies.

greenmail payment made by a target company to avoid a bid—for example, buying back a stake in its own shares (where permitted) from a potential predator at an inflated price.

grey market dealing in shares using methods that are legal but perhaps officially frowned upon—for example, before issue and flotation.

gross of a particular figure or price, calculated before the deduction of specific items such as commission, discounts, interest, and taxes. The opposite is net.

human-resource management or *personnel management* recruitment, selection, and training of staff, and efforts to involve them in the company. Japanese firms, in particular, invest heavily in human-resource management.

industrial tribunal independent judicial body whose principal role is to deal with individual employment rights in cases such as unfair dismissal. Industrial tribunals are more flexible and less formal and expensive than ordinary courts of law.

inflation accounting a method of accounting that allows for the changing purchasing power of money due to inflation.

insider trading or *insider dealing* illegal use of privileged information in dealing on the stock exchanges, for example when a company takeover bid is imminent. Insider trading is in theory detected by the Securities and Exchange Commission (SEC) in the USA, and by the Securities and Investment Board (SIB) in the UK. Neither agency, however, has any legal powers other than public disclosure nor do they bring prosecution themselves.

insolvent unable to pay debts.

investment trust public company that makes investments in other companies on behalf of its shareholders. It may issue shares to raise capital and issue fixed interest securities.

issued capital the nominal value of those shares in a company that have been allotted. The issued capital is equivalent to the amount invested, provided the issue has not been at a premium price.

job enrichment the vertical loading of a job by adding responsibility. The horizontal loading of a job— adding more of the same thing—is termed *job enlargement*. Both are supposed to improve employee performance by increasing the worker's motivation.

joint venture an undertaking in which an individual or legal entity of one company or country forms a company with those of another, with risks being shared.

junk bond derogatory term for a security, officially rated as 'below investment grade'. It is issued in order to raise capital quickly, typically to finance a takeover to be paid for by the sale of assets once the company is acquired. Junk bonds have a high yield, but are a high-risk investment.

just-in-time (JIT) production management practice requiring that incoming supplies arrive at the time when they are needed by the customer, most typically in a manufacturer's assembly operations. JIT requires considerable cooperation between supplier and customer, but can reduce expenses and improve efficiency.

key-results analysis management procedure involving the identification of performance components critical to a particular process or event, the necessary level of performance required from them, and the methods of monitoring to be used.

learning curve graphical representation of the improvement in performance of a person executing a new task.

leveraged buyout the purchase of a controlling proportion of the shares of a company by its own management, financed almost exclusively by borrowing. It is so called because the ratio of a company's long-term debt to its equity (capital assets) is known as its 'leverage'.

lien in law, the right to retain goods owned by another until the owner has satisfied a claim against him by the person in possession of the goods. For example, the goods may have been provided as security for a debt.

limited company or *joint stock company* the usual type of company formation in the UK.

It has its origins in the trading companies that began to proliferate in the 16th century. The capital of a limited company is divided into small units, and profits are distributed according to shareholding.

liquidation the termination of a company by converting all its assets into money to pay off its liabilities.

management buyout purchase of control of a company by its management, generally with debt funding, making it a leveraged buyout.

management information system computer system for converting company data from internal and external sources into appropriate information and communicating it to managers at all levels, enabling them to carry out their work.

market capitalization the market value of a company, based on the market price of all its issued securities—a price that would be unlikely to apply, however, if a bid were actually made for control of them.

marketing mix the blending of the four key elements of all marketing activity—product or service, price, promotion, and distribution—in such a way that the combination is likely to prove attractive to chosen sectors of the customer market.

market maker in the UK, a stockbroker entitled to deal directly on the stock exchange. The role was created in Oct 1986, when the jobber (intermediary) disappeared from the stock exchange. Market makers trade in the dual capacity of broker and jobber.

market segment portion of a market characterized by such similarity of customers, their requirements, and/or buying behaviour that those who sell the products or services bought by these customers can aim their marketing effort specifically at this segment.

market share the percentage of total market sales in a given period that is attributable to one business.

memorandum of association document that defines the purpose of a company and the amount and different classes of share capital. In the UK, the memorandum is drawn up on formation of the company, together with the articles of association.

merger the linking of two or more companies, either by creating a new organization by consolidating the original companies or by absorption by one of the others. Unlike a takeover, which is not always a voluntary fusion of the parties, a merger is the result of an agreement.

minority interest an item in the consolidated accounts of a holding company that represents the value of any shares in its subsidiaries that it does not itself own.

multinational corporation company or enterprise operating in several countries, usually defined as one that has 25% or more of its output capacity located outside its country of origin.

net of a particular figure or price, calculated after the deduction of specific items such as commission, discounts, interest, and taxes. The opposite is gross.

net assets either the total assets of a company less its current liabilities (that is, the capital employed) or the total assets less current liabilities, debt capital, long-term loans and provisions, which would form the amount available to ordinary shareholders if the company were to be wound up.

net worth the total assets of a company less its total liabilities, equivalent to the interest of the ordinary shareholders in the company.

nonexecutive director member of the board of a company who is not an employee of the company. A nonexecutive director can provide a wider perspective to the outlook of the board, but may be limited by not having access to informal sources of information.

nonvoting share ordinary share in a company that is without entitlement to vote at shareholders' meetings. Shares are often distinguished as A-shares (voting) and B-shares (nonvoting).

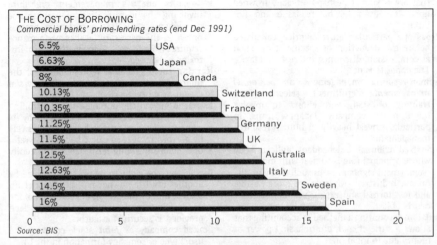

THE COST OF BORROWING
Commercial banks' prime-lending rates (end Dec 1991)

6.5%	USA
6.63%	Japan
8%	Canada
10.13%	Switzerland
10.35%	France
11.25%	Germany
11.5%	UK
12.5%	Australia
12.63%	Italy
14.5%	Sweden
16%	Spain

Source: BIS

option a contract giving the owner the right (as opposed to the obligation, as with futures contracts) to buy or sell a specific quantity of a particular commodity or currency at a future date and at an agreed price, in return for a premium. The buyer or seller can decide not to exercise the option if it would prove disadvantageous.

overhead fixed costs in a business that do not vary in the short term. These might include property rental, heating and lighting, insurance, and administration costs.

patent document granting an inventor the exclusive legal right to make and sell an invention for a limited period. Ideas are not eligible; neither is anything not new.

PAYE (abbreviation for *pay as you earn*) in the UK, a system of tax collection in which income tax is deducted on a regular basis by the employer before wages are paid. PAYE tax deductions are calculated so that when added up they will approximately equal the total amount of tax likely to be due in that year. The system was introduced in the UK in 1944. In the USA, it is called *withholding tax*.

performance-related pay element of a wage or salary that is linked to the working performance of an individual or working group, according to a prior arrangement.

piggy-back export scheme a firm already established in the export field making its services available without charge to a small firm just entering the market. The small firm thus obtains the assistance of the large firm's good will, experience, and know-how, and is saved the trouble and expense of setting up its own export department.

poison pill a tactic to avoid hostile takeover by making the target unattractive. For example, a company may give a certain class of shareholders the right to have their shares redeemed at a very good price in the event of the company being taken over, thus involving the potential predator in considerable extra cost.

preference share a share in a company with rights in various ways superior to those of ordinary shares; for example, priority to a fixed dividend and priority over ordinary shares in the event of the company being wound up.

premium price difference between the current market price of a security and its issue price (where the current price is the greater).

price/earnings ratio or *p/e ratio* a company's share price divided by its earnings per share after tax.

prime rate the rate charged by commercial banks to their best customers. It is the base rate on which other rates are calculated according to the risk involved. Only borrowers who have the highest credit rating qualify for the prime rate.

profit-sharing scheme in a company, arrangements for some or all the employees to receive cash or shares on a basis generally related to the performance of the company.

public relations deliberate, planned, and sustained effort of an organization to establish and maintain mutual understanding between itself and its employees, customers, shareholders, relevant trade unions, and local communities.

put option the right to sell a specific number of shares at a specific price on or before a specific date.

quality circle small group of production workers concerned with problems relating to the quality, safety, and efficiency of their product. Key characteristics of quality circles are size (8–12 members); voluntary membership; natural work groups, rather than artificially created ones; autonomy in setting their own agenda; access to senior managers; and a relatively permanent existence. Quality circles were popularized in Japan.

quality control inspection of a product at various stages of completion. It usually involves an *input stage* when components and materials purchased from suppliers are inspected; a *process stage* when production processes are observed; and an *output stage* when the finished product is checked against the design specification. Typically, although not universally, quality control involves the use of sampling.

rate of return the income from an investment expressed as a percentage of the cost of that investment.

receiver a person appointed by a court to collect and manage the assets of an individual, company, or partnership in serious financial difficulties. In the case of bankruptcy, the assets may be sold and distributed by a receiver to creditors.

redeemable preference share a share in a company that the company has a right to buy back at a specific price.

reverse takeover a takeover where a company sells itself to another to avoid being itself the target of a purchase by an unwelcome predator.

rights issue new shares offered to existing shareholders to raise new capital. Shareholders receive a discount on the market price while the company benefits from not having the costs of a re-launch of the new issue.

risk capital or *venture capital* finance provided by venture capital companies, individuals, and merchant banks for medium- or long-term business ventures that are not their own and in which there is a strong element of risk.

sales promotion any marketing activity intended to sell a product or service, especially activities that exclude advertising and public relations. Examples of sales promotion are free samples, price reductions, competitions, point-of-sale displays, exhibitions, and sponsorship of sporting events.

scrip issue or *subscription certificate* a free issue of new shares to existing shareholders based on their holdings. It does not involve the raising of new capital as in a rights issue.

Securities and Exchange Commission (SEC) official US agency created in 1934 to ensure full disclosure to the investing public and protection against malpractice in the securities (stocks and shares) and financial markets (such as insider trading).

Securities and Investment Board (SIB) official UK body with the overall responsibility for policing financial dealings in the City of London. Introduced in 1987 following the deregulation process of the so-called Big Bang, it acts as an umbrella organization to such self-regulating bodies as the Stock Exchange.

sequestrator person or organization appointed by a court of law to control the assets of another person or organization within the jurisdiction of that court.

spreadsheet matrix format on a computer that can provide a basis for numerical manipulation; it is used in financial planning. Software packages include Lotus 1-2-3 and Supercalc.

stag a subscriber for new share issues who expects to profit from a premium price on early trading in the shares.

stakeholder any person or group that has a stake in an organization: primarily shareholders, employees, management, customers, and suppliers.

Standard and Poor's Stock Price Index or *S & P 500* index of the US stock market covering 500 stocks broken down into sectors.

stock exchange institution for the buying and selling of stocks and shares (securities).

stocks and shares investment holdings (securities) in private or public undertakings. Although distinctions have become blurred, in the UK stock usually means fixed-interest securities (such as those issued by central and local government), while shares represent a stake in the ownership of a trading company which, if they are ordinary shares, yield to the owner dividends reflecting the success of the company. In the USA the term stock generally signifies what in the UK are ordinary shares.

SWOT analysis breakdown of an organization into its *s*trengths and *w*eaknesses (the internal analysis), with an assessment of the *o*pportunities open to it and the *t*hreats confronting it. SWOT analysis is commonly used in marketing and strategic studies.

takeover the acquisition by one company of a sufficient number of shares in another company to have effective control of that company—usually 51%, although a controlling stake may be as little as 30%. Takeovers may be agreed or contested; methods employed include the dawn raid, and methods of avoiding an unwelcome takeover include reverse takeover, poison pills, or inviting a white knight to make a takeover bid.

TESSA (acronym from *t*ax-*e*xempt *s*pecial *s*avings *a*ccount) UK scheme, introduced 1991, to encourage longer-term savings by making interest tax-free on deposits of up to £9,000 over five years.

trading account summary of a company's sales for a period, usually a year, together with the cost of sale for the same period, showing the resulting gross profit or loss.

unit trust a company that invests its clients' funds in other companies. The units it issues represent holdings of shares, which means unit shareholders have a wider spread of capital than if they bought shares on the stock market.

venture capital or *risk capital* money put up by investors such as merchant banks to fund the setting up of a new company or expansion of an established company. The organization providing the money receives a share of the company's equity and seeks to make a profit by rapid growth in the value of its stake, as a result of expansion by the start-up company or 'venture'.

white knight a company invited by the target of a takeover bid to make a rival bid. The company invited to bid is usually one that is already on good terms with the target company.

working capital the capital required to finance the short-term activities of a business, principally the investment in stock and debtors.

yield the annual percentage return from an investment; on ordinary shares it is the dividend expressed as a percentage.

zero-based budgeting management technique requiring that no resources for a new period of a programme are approved and/or released unless their justification can be demonstrated against alternative options.

CORPORATE WINNERS AND LOSERS

US companies (1991)
HIGHEST PROFITS

Company	Sales rank*	Profits US$ m
Exxon	2	5,600.0
Philip Morris	7	3,006.0
General Electric	5	2,636.0
Merck	59	2,121.7
Bristol-Myers Squibb	40	2,056.0
Mobil	6	1,920.0
Proctor & Gamble	13	1,773.0
Coca-Cola	37	1,618.0
Boeing	12	1,567.0
Amoco	14	1,484.0

BIGGEST LOSSES

Company	Sales rank*	Loss US$ m
General Motors	1	4,452.8
IBM	4	2,827.0
Ford Motor	3	2,258.0
UNISYS	58	1,393.3
Westinghouse Electric	30	1,086.0
United Technologies	16	1,021.0
Chrysler	11	795.0
Bethlehem Steel	115	767.0
Owens-Corning Fiberglass	164	742.0
Tenneco	27	732.0

* The Fortune 500 1991 Sales Rank
Source: Fortune

THE COMMUNITY CHARTER: PROVIDING FOR SOCIAL RIGHTS OF WORKERS

Following the acceptance of the Single European Act in 1987, the European Community, under its new Belgian Presidency, attempted to steer away from deregulation and labour market flexibility (advocated by the UK during its 1986 presidency) towards a community-wide agreement on social and employment rights. This approach was aimed at re-establishing the political basis for an active Community role in social policy and at defining the Community's approach to employment law harmonization.

Later, under the French Commission President, Jacques Delors, the first draft of the Community Charter of the Fundamental Social Rights of Workers (the 'Social Charter') was issued in May 1989. It was to have no formal status under the Treaty of Rome, but was to be implemented by a variety of EC measures, individual member state measures, and collective agreements. Furthermore, contrary to the earlier approach, the principle of subsidiarity was established. This meant that no action was to taken at Community level unless it could not be achieved by the member states themselves. At this time, the main concern was so-called social dumping occurring as a result of the increased competition and economic union that the single market of 1992 would bring. Social dumping is any downward pressure on the levels of social protection through employers' desires to remain competitive, whether through investing in low-cost countries or by importing cheaper labour.

The Social Charter stressed that the social aspects of the large 1992 market would be as important as the economic aspects, and that the social dimension was essential for ensuring sustained economic growth. The preamble to the Social Charter states: 'The solemn proclamation of fundamental social rights at EC level may not, when implemented, provide grounds for any retrogression compared with the situation currently existing in each member State'. This statement was designed to quash the fears of social dumping.

The final text of the Social Charter, adopted 8/9 Dec 1989 by the European Council—with the exception of the UK members—was substantially diluted compared with the initial proposals. It received a further setback at the Maastricht Summit on 9/10 Dec 1991. Following the UK's steadfast refusal to sign the Economic Treaty if social policy were also included, the charter now takes the form of a social protocol to which the other 11 member states will adhere. In practice this means that should the UK approve certain proposed EC social laws then the commission would proceed as in the past. However, should the UK be opposed to other social laws, the Commission would propose them only to the other 11 states. This led to much comment, the resurgence of fears about social dumping, and the accusation that the UK will now become the 'sweat shop of Europe'.

As it now stands, the charter sets out 12 basic principles listed below. Implementation of these principles is to be carried out by the adoption of 47 initiatives contained in the Social Action Programme. However, this is posing the EC member states a major problem since the Single European Act introduced majority voting for most harmonization measures but left the founding EC principle of unanimity unchanged for social legislation. As a result, certain items of legislation, such as health and safety, can be voted in by a qualified majority, whilst others must still adhere to the unanimity rule. Of the 47 initiatives in the Social Programme, 17 are legally binding directives on all member states; the remainder are recommendations, communications, and programmes, which seek to encourage a greater convergence of labour employment practices within the member states without recourse to statutory involvement.

The Social Charter's 12 basic principles

1. The right to work in the EC country of one's choice.

2. The right to a fair wage.

3. The right to improved living and working conditions.

4. The right to social protection under prevailing national systems.

5. The right to freedom of association and collective bargaining.

6. The right to vocational training.

7. The right of men and women to equal treatment.

8. The right of workers to information, consultation, and participation.

9. The right to health protection and safety at work.

10. The protection of children and adolescents.

11. The guarantee of minimum living standards for the elderly.

12. Improved social and professional integration for the disabled.

Source: Office for Official Publications of the European Community (1991)

NEWS

ALLIANCES, BIDS, BUYOUTS, AND MERGERS

The battle for Midland

The battle for the control of Midland Bank, typified by the bids and counter-bids between the Hong Kong and Shanghai Bank (HSBC) and Lloyds Bank, seemed to be drawing to an end in June 1992. HSBC launched an increased and final offer valuing Midland Bank at £3.9 billion or around 470p a share, an improvement on its previous £3.4 billion offer. Lloyds failed to make a counter-bid and withdrew from the fight.

The move by HSBC was well timed: the closing date for the bid was 7 July and the outcome of the investigation into Lloyd's bid by the Monopolies and Mergers Commission would not be known until 25 August. Furthermore, HSBC had all the regulatory approvals it needed, following the rejection by the US Federal Reserve of an attempt by Lloyds Bank to use the UK banking laws to block HSBC's bid. HSBC was already in possession of 15% of Midland shares and had picked up a few more in the market after the announcement of its final offer.

BBA Group expands US interests

BBA, the British automotive, engineering, and aviation services group, has bought Butler Aviation International, a Dallas-based company, which operates corporate aircraft terminals and airline support facilities. The purchase was made through Page Avjet Airport Services, BBA's US subsidiary. It will lift Page Avjet's facilities in the USA from 20 operations at 18 airports to 42 operations at 38 airports.

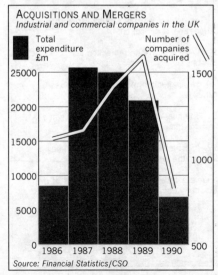

ACQUISITIONS AND MERGERS
Industrial and commercial companies in the UK

■ Total expenditure £m

Number of companies acquired

Source: Financial Statistics/CSO

British Airways buys stake in US Air

In July 1992 British Airways (BA) took a major step towards its goal of creating a global airline by agreeing to take a $750 million (£402 million) stake in US Air, America's fourth largest carrier. The link-up gives BA access to the US air-travel market, which accounts for some 40% of global air traffic. It also creates the world's biggest airline alliance, with 80 million passengers, a fleet of 670 aircraft, and a combined turnover of £96 billion.

The investment gives BA access to a carrier that has 8% of the US market, serves 210 domestic destinations, and is the biggest airline at nine US airports, operating 2,750 flights daily, and carrying 55.6 million passengers per year. This will enable the British company to channel US Air's domestic passengers on to its transatlantic flights, while US Air will gain access to one of the world's largest intercontinental airlines. BA estimates the partnership will generate savings of at least £80 million in the short term, rising to about £200 million.

Cadbury Schweppes acquires a foothold in the German confectionery market

In May 1992, Cadbury Schweppes made a cash purchase of 70% of Piasten Schokoladenfabrik Hoffmann, a privately owned Bavarian chocolate and sweets manufacturer. Piasten is currently the leader in the German boxed-chocolate-assortment market, with sales of DM126.1 million in 1991. Cadbury's holding has a net book value of DM3.5 million (£1.23 billion) and should contribute 2p per share to its earnings by 1993. The deal will enable Cadbury to introduce some of its confectionery products to Germany and also provide low-risk access to central and eastern European markets, particularly Poland. Piasten's products may now be sold through Cadbury's operations in other parts of Europe. The deal gives Cadbury an option to buy the remaining shares in Piasten.

Hanson sells Beazer Australian Construction and Property interests

Hanson sold the Beazer Australian Construction and Property interests for A$32.5 million (£14 million) to B&B Asia, a Hong Kong–quoted company, controlled by the German construction firm Bilfinger und Berger Bau AG. The interests are primarily in New South Wales and Queensland, and Beazer is to receive A$8 million from the sales of some of the developments by the new owner.

London Futures Exchange and Options Market merge

The London International Financial Futures Exchange (LIFFE) merged with the London Traded Options Market (LTOM), moving from their respective premises at Royal Exchange and the Stock Exchange to new premises in the Cannon Bridge development. For the time being, the colourful 'open outcry' pit trading will continue, but computerized dealing is being discussed.

INTERNATIONAL STRATEGIC ALLIANCES

When the single European market takes effect towards the end of this year, it will pose several challenges for indigenous European companies.

The possible threat from Japanese and US companies has meant a re-orientation of the marketing strategy of European companies. The emphasis is now on outward-looking strategies. The expansion of markets to reap economies of scale and the effective competition with US and Japanese firms are two such strategies. Hence the objective hinges on survival while the policy is that of rationalizing current operations in terms of increasing investment on research and development (R&D). The cost of such strategies would be a problem for financially stretched European companies, who have therefore embraced alliances, both amongst themselves and with outside companies. This is especially the case with Europe's ailing electronics manufacturers.

In March 1992, Philips, the Dutch electronics group and Grundig, the German consumer electronics company, agreed to combine their video and cordless telephone operations. In the same month, Olivetti, the Italian computers and office equipment group, announced an alliance with Canon, the Japanese camera and electronics group, to produce bubble ink-jet printers. Philips still plans to look for a partner to invest in a plant to manufacture liquid crystal displays, a product of increasing strategic importance.

These alliances offer manufacturers the chance to pool resources and rationalize operations, at a time of spiralling costs and stagnant growth of key domestic markets. However, meeting the challenge of increasing the competitiveness of European manufacturers in the future would necessitate much more than alliances between European manufacturers. European companies will have to look to US and Japanese companies for the key technologies necessary to remain competitive and profitable.

The recognition of this factor is evidenced in similar alliances which have taken place over the past year between European, US and Japanese companies. In the early part of 1992, Groupe Bull of France, the computer group, announced a link with IBM of the USA to develop advanced semiconductor chips. Siemens recently announced ventures in chip development with both IBM and Toshiba of Japan. Philips, again, announced it was joining forces with Motorola, the US group, to design and develop semiconductor chips for Compact Disk Interactive, a new CD-based medium combining graphics, data, CD audio and video. Olivetti has set up a division specifically to look for possible technological cooperation.

Because of the growing need to gain competitive advantage in the European market, the race among European companies to forge alliances is far from over. The single European market will only serve to intensify the process.

Lufthansa–Lauda Air alliance
In July 1992, the Lufthansa Group board approved a 26.5% stake investment in Niki Lauda's airline, Lauda Air, as part of a strategic alliance aimed at joint exploitation of the expanding tourist travel market in Europe and America. The deal, worth about £4.5 million, resulted from an increase in the capitalization of Lauda Air from about £12.5 million to £17 million. Niki Lauda and his Austrian partner, the ITAS group, remain the majority shareholders in the company.

The Lufthansa–Lauda alliance intends to concentrate on charter flights, but will expand into schedule flights as well. The alliance will place the Lufthansa Group in a strategic position in Austria and southern and eastern European markets, while providing Lauda Air with a much-needed base for expansion. The alliance's inaugural joint flight from Vienna to Miami via Munich is planned for Nov 1992.

Coupled with the deal is the purchase of a 25% stake in ITAS by Condour, the charter-flight subsidiary of the Lufthansa Group. Within an enlarged European market, this alliance is expected to both strengthen and expand the operations of Condour in Austria and eastern Europe.

Nestlé wins fight for Perrier
Nestlé, the Swiss food group, announced in April 1992 its takeover of Perrier, the French mineral-water company, after fighting a fiercely contested takeover bid of £15.46 billion French francs ($2.76 billion).

Redland takes over Steetley
On 26 March 1992, Redland, Europe's leading building-materials group, won a four-month battle to take over Steetley, its main UK rival, valued at £613 million. The expected turnover of £2 billion effectively makes the group the second largest in bricks in the UK and the world's largest in roofing tiles.

Takeover bid for Pacific Horizon concluded
In an all-share deal, Pacific Horizon, an investment trust launched 1989, was taken over in April 1992 by Martin Currie Pacific, a fellow investment trust. The takeover took account of the uncertain element of Pacific Horizon's portfolio: about 11% of the portfolio, consisting of investments in illiquid closed-end funds, had been excluded from the terms of offer. These holdings were to be sold and the proceeds distributed to Pacific Horizon shareholders. Shares

were offered at 92% of the formula asset value of the rest of Pacific Horizon's portfolio.

LTU buys Thomas Cook
Midland Bank announced the sale for £200 million of Thomas Cook to Germany's third biggest package-tour operator, LTU. Thomas Cook, one of the oldest names in the travel industry and the inventor of the traveller's cheque, runs 1,600 outlets in more than 100 countries. Midland bought Thomas Cook from British Rail in 1972 for £20 million and expects a net gain of £99 million; the proceeds will be used to develop core businesses. LTU and its 34% shareholder, Westdeutsche Landesbank, will acquire 90% and 10% of Thomas Cook respectively.

Rolls-Royce links up with Westinghouse
Rolls-Royce has agreed to form a 15-year partnership with Westinghouse of the USA after successfully jointly bidding for the $160-million (£300-million) US-government contract to develop a new gas-turbine engine for the US Navy in January 1992.

The deal, which will also link Rolls-Royce to Westinghouse partners such as Mitsubishi Heavy Industries of Japan and Fiat Avio of Italy, will pitch the UK group against General Electric, its American arch-rival in the aero-engine business and the power-generation world-market leader. Westinghouse's power business had total sales of $2.6 billion (£1.44 billion) in 1991 and made an operating profit of $283 million (£530 million).

Yorkshire and Tyne Tees Television merge
Yorkshire Television and Tyne Tees Television, two northern England companies that won independent television franchises in 1991, have agreed to merge, creating the third largest independent TV company in the industry, after Thames and Central. A recommended offer from Yorkshire Television values the Tyne Tees share capital at £30.4 million and the deal has been approved by the Independent Television Commission.

PROGRESS AND ENTERPRISE

BICC
BICC, the UK-based cables and construction group, agreed to a £55 million deal which should double its share of the power-cable market in North America. BICC Cables, the group's North American subsidiary, agreed to buy the electrical division of Reynolds Metals, a leading maker of transmission and distribution cables in the USA and Canada.

Brent Walker
Giant Canadian brewer Labatt has spent more than £100 million setting up a joint-venture pubs operation with Brent Walker. It is the first time that a major foreign group has moved into the British pubs market in force. The deal provides Labatt with a large ready-made distribution network, which will eventually comprise 2,000 pubs. All the funding is provided by Labatt, whose lagers were formerly brewed under licence by Brent Walker at the Camerons Brewery in Hartlepool. Day-to-day running of the new business will rest with Brent's Pubmaster operation.

British Airways
British Airways (BA) has demonstrated its ability to manage itself effectively, after experiencing a severe downturn in 1990, by revealing a set of remarkable figures for the year ending in March 1992. Pre-tax profits stood at £285 million against £130 million in March 1990. Sales increased to £5,224 million from £4,937 million in 1990. Passenger revenue per kilometre rose by 3% in the year. This success was attributed largely to BA's promotion strategy.

Forte
Forte, the UK hotels group, has reached agreement with ENI, the Italian state-owned energy and chemicals concern, on a joint venture to take management control of ENI's motorway hotels in Italy. No value has been placed on the deal, which involves 18 hotels and motels owned by ENI's Agip and Snam subsidiaries. The deal will raise some £200 billion for the Forte group, whose June 1992 records showed a fall in pre-tax profits from £187 million in 1991 to £70 million in 1992.

General Electric
In June 1992, General Electric of the USA won a contract worth more than $150 million (£382 million) to equip the new Medway electricity-generating power plant at the Isle of Grain in Kent with gas and steam turbines. The company will supply two gas and one steam turbine generator for the 660 mW plant owned by Medway Power, a joint venture between Seeboard and Southern Electricity. The plant is due to start operation in 1995.

Hewlett-Packard
Hewlett-Packard, the computer and electronics group, unveiled the smallest hard-disk drive yet available, targeted at portable electronic products. The 1.3-in drive will be used initially in hand-held computers.

The new drive was developed through a joint effort with AT & T Microelectronics, a unit of American Telephone and Telegraph, and Citizen Watch of Japan, which will manufacture the product.

IBM
IBM has set up independent wholly owned subsidiaries in the UK and Canada to sell low-cost personal computers that will compete directly with cheap clones. The new UK company, Industrial Computer Products International, will

market a range of PCs under the Ambra brand name with the aim of targetting the low end of the European market.

Through this new unit, IBM aims to gain entry to highly price-sensitive segments of the PC market in which its own brand-name products cannot compete.

Manweb
Manweb, the Chester-based regional electricity company, reported a pre-tax profit of £94.7 million for the year to March 1992, up 60.5% from £58.9 million the previous year. The company's core distribution business increased its profits by 83% to £106.3 million.

Mercury
A planned expansion of Mercury's domestic telephone service was unveiled after the company reported a 34% increase in trading profit to £155 million from £116 million in 1991 and a 30% increase in turnover from £702 million in 1991 to £915 million in 1992. Links with cable television companies and mobile telephone networks are planned in order to accelerate growth. Cable and Wireless, Mercury's parent company, has invested £1.66 million in Mercury to achieve this objective.

Microsoft and Bill Gates
From its initial success in the 1980s with MS-DOS software, Microsoft has gone from strength to strength, producing the highly successful Windows program, and more recently Multimedia, a computer-driven learning and entertainment program using television and graphics. The phenomenal success of Microsoft's software is attributable to its founder and owner, Bill Gates, who, at 37, is the richest man in the USA, with a net personal worth of $6.4 billion (£3.4 billion). He founded the company in 1975, when he was only 19, with his schoolmate Paul Allen. In 1980 he bought an existing operating system (86-DOS) for $50,000, re-wrote it, and licensed it to IBM under the name MS-DOS.

National Power
National Power, the UK electricity generator, reported pre-tax profits up 18% to £514 million for the year to 31 March 1992, the first full year since it was privatized. A sharp rise in electricity prices and cost savings accounted for the increase in operating profits.

Sainsbury's
Sainsbury's presented its annual results on 13 May 1992. They showed profits creeping ahead of Marks & Spencer for the first time since 1969. Sainsbury's pre-tax profits which stood at £628 million revealed a phenomenal 28% compound growth in profits over the last 20 years. Sales were 11% up (£8,695 million) on 1991 figures of £7,813 million. The increase in productivity was the highest in four years and the increase in selling space was the highest ever.

Smithkline Beecham
Smithkline Beecham, the Anglo-American pharmaceuticals group, completed two deals aimed at positioning itself as a significant force in the world vaccine market. The first deal, with the State of Michigan's department of public health, gave Smithkline exclusive rights to distribute vaccines for diphtheria, tetanus, whole-cell pertussis, and rabies in the USA outside Michigan. The second deal, with Pasteur Merieux Serum et Vaccins and Connaught Laboratories, both subsidiaries of Institut Merieux, gave Smithkline the US marketing rights for an influenza vaccine designed for children. The two agreements make Smithkline the second largest company in the market after Merck of the USA.

Southern Electric and Phillips Petroleum
Southern Electric and Phillips Petroleum Company UK have agreed to enter into a 50/50 joint venture to acquire and market gas. Initially, this will be gas released by tender from British Gas, but over time it is expected that the joint venture will market gas from other sources, including fields in which Phillips has an interest.

United Biscuits
United Biscuits is to set up a sales company to distribute its McVitie's, Carr's, and Ortiz products in Spain. The company will be jointly owned with Royal Brands, a Spanish food group, and will also handle that company's brands. The operation is due to start in January 1993. McVitie's is the largest UK biscuit-maker with sales of £787 million in 1991. Royal Brands is owned by Tabacalera, the leading Spanish tobacco group, and is the market leader in the Spanish biscuit market.

Woolworth
Woolworth, the US retail group, revealed plans to expand in Europe by opening at least 890 Foot Locker athlete footwear and apparel stores in the next eight years. The company currently has 110 Foot Locker stores in seven European countries, including England. Sixty new stores were to be opened by the end of 1992.

TROUBLES

Belling
Belling, the electric cooker manufacturer, went into receivership in May 1992 after 82 years in business. The company had incurred losses for three years and had debts of around £25 million. More than 1,000 employees were to lose their jobs.

British Aerospace
After putting its troubled Space and Communications Systems Division up for sale, British Aerospace announced in May 1992 the cut of nearly 740 jobs, most of them (640) in its satellite-making operation at Stevenage, Hertfordshire. British Aerospace had failed to win orders. Recently, in May 1992, the group lost out

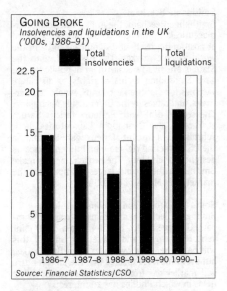

GOING BROKE
Insolvencies and liquidations in the UK
('000s, 1986–91)

Total insolvencies / Total liquidations

Source: Financial Statistics/CSO

to US firm Hughes in a bid for a Japanese satellite project.

Canary Wharf
Canary Wharf, the London Docklands development owned by debt-ridden Canadian property company Olympia and York (O&Y), was placed into administration in the UK in May 1992. O&Y needed an extra £350 million to complete the Canary Wharf project but failed to elicit financial support from the banks, who were owed billions of dollars by O&Y. The company's debts were $14.3 billion (£25.7 billion), plus a further $3 billion (£5.4 billion) which was owed through other companies. The Canary Wharf project alone cost O&Y $85 million (£155 million) a month in debt payments and other expenses. The Jubilee Line extension to the London Underground, the key to the success of O&Y's Canary Wharf project, could be abandoned. Tenders for the extension project began to expire in June 1992 and no firm commitment to the project was expected from either the Department of Transport or O&Y.

Heron
Gerald Ronson's Heron International property-to-motor-dealing empire is on the brink of collapse. Heron, which owes banks and bond holders £1.3 billion, only has assets of £1.1 billion. According to the firm's interim report (June 1992) the properties in the UK, USA, and continental Europe have fallen in value to £1 billion. As the fallout from the collapse of the Canadian property company, Olympia and York, continues, there is every prospect they will drop still further.

Equally worrying is the disastrous downturn in Heron's trading performance. The group made an operating loss of £124 million to 31 March 1992. In the 12 months to 31 March 1991, it made an operating profit of £59.9 million, down from £125.1 million the previous year. The com-

pany's US operations have lost more than £200 million over the past four years.

Llva
Europe's third biggest producer of Steel, Llva announced a loss of £498 billion on 2 June 1992. Like its big European counterparts, Llva has been hit by weak demand and depressed prices, just as competition from low-cost eastern Europe and developing country producers is surging.

The Maxwell Empire
Revelations of a string of malpractices within the Maxwell media empire came hard on the heels of the death of its founder, Robert Maxwell, on 5 Nov 1991. The catalyst was the public revelation of the theft of assets totalling more than £450 million from his companies' pension funds. Around 5,000 pensioners stood to lose their main retirement income entirely or see it cut by 70%, forcing the government to announce emergency grants of £2.5 million in June 1992 to assist those worst affected by the theft.

Porsche
Porsche, Germany's fading star of the luxury sports car business, shed 950 jobs in the year up to July 1992. This followed a 25% drop in international sales to DM2.5 billion. Pre-tax earnings in the first half-year slumped 97% to DM2 billion on sales of DM1.1 billion. The USA, which once imported 30,000 Porsches a year, took just 4,000 this year, after 6,100 in 1990. In Britain, the figure was around 1,200 in 1992, compared with 2,000 in 1990.

Saatchi & Saatchi
In a move to reduce group debt, Saatchi and Saatchi sold its wholly owned subsidiary, Yankelovich Skelly White/Clancy Shulman of the USA, to an investor group led by Wand Partners. The sale consisted of an immediate cash payment of $4.6 million (£2.52 million) and a $4.5 million (£2.46 million) interest-bearing note repayable in tranches up to the end of 1997. Saatchi will also receive non-complete payments, totalling $1.5 million (£2.74 million).

Seiko
Watchmaker Seiko Corporation made a 2.27 billion yen (£9.5 million) loss in the year ending March 1992, the worst performance recorded for any of the internationally known Japanese companies. High operating costs and the recession were blamed for the poor performance.

Which of the following factors do you think have encouraged organizations to take action to improve customer service?

As a result of the recession, organizations are becoming more competitive	61
British people are complaining more	48
Consumer magazines and TV programmes	40
Britain is becoming more influenced by other countries	39
The government is pressurising companies to try harder e.g. Citizen's Charter	15

INSTITUTIONS AND ORGANIZATIONS

Arab Common Market organization founded 1965, providing for the abolition of customs duties on agricultural products, and reductions on other items, between the member states: Egypt, Iraq, Jordan, and Syria.

Arab Monetary Fund (AMF) money reserve established 1976 by 20 Arab states plus the Palestine Liberation Organization to provide a mechanism for promoting greater stability in exchange rates and to coordinate Arab economic and monetary policies. It operates mainly by regulating petrodollars within the Arab community to make member countries less dependent on the West for the handling of their surplus money. The fund's headquarters are in Abu Dhabi in the United Arab Emirates.

Asian Development Bank (ADB) a bank founded 1966 to stimulate growth in Asia and the Far East by administering direct loans and technical assistance. Members include 30 countries within the region and 14 countries of W Europe and North America. The headquarters are in Manila, Philippines.

Bank for International Settlements (BIS) organization whose function is to promote co-operation between central banks and to facilitate international financial settlements, including transactions in European Currency Units (ECUs). Central banks of the main trading states are members, each providing a director to the board, which meets at least ten times a year. BIS was founded 1930, originally to coordinate war reparations, and is based in Basel, Switzerland.

Bank of England UK central bank founded by Act of Parliament in 1694. It was entrusted with the note issue in 1844 and nationalized in 1946. It is banker to the clearing banks and the UK government. As the government's bank, it manages and arranges the financing of the public-sector borrowing requirement and the national debt, implements monetary policy and exchange-rate policy through intervention in foreign-exchange markets, and supervises the UK banking system.

Central American Common Market ODECA (*Organización de Estados Centro-americanos*) economic alliance established in 1960 by El Salvador, Guatemala, Honduras (seceded 1970), and Nicaragua; Costa Rica joined in 1962. Its headquarters are in San Salvador.

Colombo Plan plan for cooperative economic development in S and SE Asia, established 1951. The member countries meet annually to discuss economic and development plans such as irrigation, hydroelectric schemes, and technical training. The plan has no central fund but technical assistance and financing of development projects are arranged through individual governments or the International Bank for Re-construction and Development.

Comecon (*Council for Mutual Economic Assistance*, or CMEA) economic organization established 1949 and prompted by the Marshall Plan, linking the USSR with Bulgaria, Czechoslovakia, Hungary, Poland, Romania, East Germany (from 1950), Mongolia (from 1962), Cuba (from 1972), and Vietnam (from 1978), with Yugoslavia as an associated member. Albania also belonged 1949–61.

The secretariat is based in Moscow and regular annual meetings are held in the member countries. It was agreed in 1987 that official relations should be established with the European Community, and a free-market approach to trading was adopted 1990. In Jan 1991 it was agreed that Comecon should be effectively disbanded and replaced by a new body, the Organization for International Economic Co-operation (OIEC), probably to be based in Budapest. The OIEC would act as a 'clearing house' for mutual East European trade and to co-ordinate East European policy towards the European Community. From Jan 1991, trade between Comecon members was switched from the transferable rouble to a hard currency basis, with adverse consequences for East European importers of Soviet oil and gas.

European Free Trade Association (EFTA) organization established 1960 and as of 1988 consisting of Austria, Finland, Iceland, Norway, Sweden, and Switzerland. There are no import duties between members. Of the origi-

WORLD'S TOP 20 COMPANIES
Ranked by sales in US$m (July 1991)

Sales	Company
125,126	General Motors US
107,204	Royal Dutch/Shell Group UK/Neth
105,885	Exxon US
98,274.7	Ford Motor US
69,018	IBM US
64,516.1	Toyota Motor Japan
61,433	IRI Italy
59,540.5	British Petroleum UK
58,770	Mobil US
58,414	General Electric US
54,259	Daimler-Benz Germany
50,685.8	Hitachi Japan
47,751.6	Fiat Italy
45,042	Samsung S Korea
44,323	Philip Morris US
43,710.2	Volkswagen Germany
43,516.1	Matsushita Japan
41,761.9	ENI Italy
41,235	Texaco US
40,217.1	Nissan Motor Japan

0   30,000   60,000 90,000 120,000 150,000

Source: Fortune

A WORLD RECESSION?

A feature of the 1992 election campaign in the UK was the debate over the extent to which its economic difficulties were part of a worldwide phenomenon. This article looks at the nature of the world economy and international economic comparisons, and the validity of the claim that there has been a worldwide recession.

The world economy is generally divided into industrialized countries and developing countries. For the purposes of economic analysis, the UK is usually compared to the other 'G7' countries, the group of the seven largest industrialized economies in the OECD (Organization for Economic Cooperation and Development), that is, the seven countries with the greatest national income and output. Table

GDP (gross domestic product) is the value of the output of all goods and services produced within a nation's borders. It is also equal to the total income generated within that nation's borders, because all production of goods and services generates income in the form of wages, salaries, rent, interest, and profits. GDP is therefore an indicator of national income. It can be seen from Table 1 that the national output and income generated by the UK economy in 1990 was approximately 542 billion. In terms of output and income, the UK economy is the fifth largest in the OECD. The G7's combined output is over 60% of total world output, and 80% of the industrialized countries' output.

To obtain an indicator of standard of living in each country, national income and population have both to be taken into account. This is shown in the calculation of GDP per head. Table 1 shows that the largest economies do not necessarily produce the highest standards of living: for example, Canada has the seventh largest output but the second highest standard of living measured in terms of GDP per head.

Table 1 gives us a snapshot of the relative living standards in the G7 economies in 1990. However, to analyse the state of the world economy in terms of past performance we need to look at the rates of change of output, and in particular the economic growth of each economy, which is measured as the rate of increase in GDP in real terms (after taking inflation into account) from one year to the next. Table 2 shows comparative growth rates for the G7 countries.

Table 2 shows that in 1991 the world economy was in a depressed state, in the sense that the G7 average growth rate was less

than 1%, well below the historical average of 3.7%. Compared to the last peak in G7 growth of 4.3% in 1988, there has been a significant slow-down. But is it a recession? Economists generally define a recession as a fall in national output of six months or more. Only three of the G7 countries were actually in recession in 1991. In the UK, GDP fell by 2.5% in 1991, which was much sharper than the US or Canadian recessions, and much sharper than expected.

So while there was certainly a world slow-down in 1991, it could hardly be described as a recession, neither does Britain's performance seem to have been typical. 1992 generally shows a recovery in the world economy, although Germany's growth rate is slipping back further as part of the adjustment costs of unification (the data for 1960–90 are for West Germany only).

NATIONAL INCOME AND POPULATION OF THE G7 COUNTRIES (1990)

Country	GDP (£ bn)	GDP per head (£ 000)	Population (m)
USA	340	313.5	251.4
Japan	134	610.9	123.5
Germany	638	10.1	63.1
France	55	59.8	56.4
UK	54	29.4	57.4
Italy	53	69.3	57.6
Canada	337	12.6	26.6

Source: OECD Main Economic Indicators

COMPARATIVE GROWTH RATES OF G7 COUNTRIES (% CHANGE IN REAL GDP)

Country	Annual average 1960–90	1991	1992 (Forecast)
USA	3.2	0.5	1.5
Japan	6.4	4.5	2.0
Germany	3.1	3.2	1.6
France	3.7	1.4	1.9
UK	2.4	2.5	0.7
Italy	3.9	1.0	1.5
Canada	4.2	1.1	2.3
G7	3.7	0.9	1.6

Source: OECD Economic Indicators and Economic Outlook

nal members, Britain and Denmark left (1972) to join the European Community, as subsequently did Portugal (1985).

European Monetary System (EMS) attempt by the European Community to bring financial cooperation and monetary stability to Europe. It was established 1979 in the wake of the 1974 oil crisis, which brought growing economic disruption to European economies because of

floating exchange rates. Central to the EMS is the *Exchange Rate Mechanism* (ERM), a voluntary system of semi-fixed exchange rates based on the European Currency Unit (ECU).

The UK entered the ERM in Oct 1990. In 1990 and 1991, Sterling's central rate with the ECU within the ERM was £1=1.43ECU. There are also central rates with other ERM currencies; Sterling's central rate with the

Deutschmark was £1=DM2.95 in 1990 and 1991.

Federal Reserve System ('Fed') US central banking system and note-issue authority, established 1913 to regulate the country's credit and monetary affairs. The Fed consists of the 12 federal reserve banks and their 25 branches and other facilities throughout the country; it is headed by a board of governors in Washington, appointed by the US president with Senate approval.

The Fed, which is independent in its decisions, plays a major role in the formulation and implementation of US monetary policy. Inflation, interest rates, and overall economic activity can be governed by the Fed's decision to expand or restrict the supply of money to the economy.

General Agreement on Tariffs and Trade (GATT) organization within the United Nations founded 1948 with the aim of encouraging free trade between nations through low tariffs, abolitions of quotas, and curbs on subsidies.

During the latest round of talks, begun 1986 in Uruguay and ending 1990 in Geneva, the USA opposed EC restrictions on agricultural imports, but argued to maintain restrictions on textile imports to the USA. The talks reached a deadlock Dec 1990 after negotiators failed to agree on a plan to reduce farm subsidies.

International Monetary Fund (IMF) specialized agency of the United Nations, headquarters Washington DC, established under the 1944 Bretton Woods agreement and operational since 1947. It seeks to promote international monetary cooperation and the growth of world trade, and to smooth multilateral payment arrangements among member states. IMF stand-by loans are available to members in balance of payments difficulties (the amount being governed by the member's quota), usually on the basis of acceptance of instruction on stipulated corrective measures.

The Fund also operates other drawing facilities, including several designed to provide preferential credit to developing countries with liquidity problems. Having previously operated in US dollars linked to gold, the IMF has used since 1972 the special drawing right (SDR) as its standard unit of account, valued in terms of a weighted 'basket' of major currencies. Since the 1971 Smithsonian agreement permitting wider fluctuations from specified currency parities, IMF rules have been progressively adapted to the increasing prevalence of fully floating exchange rates.

LIFFE acronym for *London International Financial Futures Exchange*, one of the exchanges in London where futures contracts are traded. Established in 1982, it provides a worldwide exchange for futures dealers and investors, and began options trading in 1985. All transactions pass through a clearing house which serves as a financially independent guarantor and regulator of the exchange; the Bank of England also supervises the exchange. LIFFE

was a forerunner of the Big Bang in bringing US-style 'open-house' dealing (as opposed to telephone dealing) to the UK.

Monopolies and Mergers Commission (MMC) UK government body re-established in 1973 under the Fair Trading Act and, since 1980, embracing the Competition Act. Its role is to investigate and report when there is a risk of creating a monopoly following a company merger or takeover, or when a newspaper or newspaper assets are transferred. It also investigates companies, nationalized industries, or local authorities that are suspected of operating in a noncompetitive way. The US equivalent is the *Federal Trade Commission* (FTC).

Organization for Economic Cooperation and Development (OECD) Paris-based international organization of 24 industrialized countries, which coordinates member states' economic policy strategies. The OECD's subsidiary bodies include the International Energy Agency 1974, set up in the face of a world oil crisis.

It superseded the Organization for European Economic Cooperation (established 1948 to promote European recovery under the Marshall Plan) 1961, when the USA and Canada became members and its scope was extended to include development aid. The OECD members are: Australia, Austria, Belgium, Canada, Denmark, Finland, France, Germany, Greece, Iceland, Ireland, Italy, Japan, Luxembourg, Netherlands, New Zealand, Norway, Portugal, Spain, Sweden, Switzerland, Turkey, UK, and USA.

Organization of Petroleum Exporting Countries (OPEC) body established in 1960 to coordinate the price and supply policies of certain oil-producing countries, and also to improve the position of Third World states by forcing Western states to open their markets to the resultant products. Its concerted action in raising prices in the 1970s triggered worldwide recession but also lessened demand so that its influence was reduced by the mid-1980s. OPEC members in 1991 were: Algeria, Ecuador, Gabon, Indonesia, Iran, Iraq, Kuwait, Libya, Nigeria, Qatar, Saudi Arabia, the United Arab Emirates, and Venezuela.

OPEC's importance in the world market was reflected in its ability to implement oil price increases from $3 a barrel in 1973 to $30 a barrel in 1980. In the 1980s, OPEC's dominant position was undermined by reduced demand for oil in industrialized countries, increased non-OPEC oil supplies, and production of alternative energy. These factors contributed to the dramatic fall in world oil prices to $10 a barrel in July 1986 from $28 at the beginning of the year. OPEC's efforts to stabilize oil prices through mandatory reduced production have been resisted by various members.

Securities and Exchange Commission (SEC) official US agency created 1934 to ensure full disclosure to the investing public and protection against malpractice in the securities (stocks and shares) and financial mar-

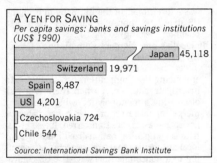

A YEN FOR SAVING
Per capita savings: banks and savings institutions (US$ 1990)

Japan 45,118
Switzerland 19,971
Spain 8,487
US 4,201
Czechoslovakia 724
Chile 544

Source: International Savings Bank Institute

kets. The SEC is also an impartial advisor to federal courts in bankruptcy cases involving publicly held corporations. Since 1988, it has been authorized to pay bounties for information leading to conviction of inside traders.

Securities and Investment Board UK body with overall responsibility for policing financial dealings in the City of London. Introduced in 1987 following the deregulation process of the so-called Big Bang, it acts as an umbrella organization to such self-regulating bodies as the Stock Exchange.

World Bank popular name for the *International Bank for Reconstruction and Development*, established 1945 under the 1944 Bretton Woods agreement, which also created the International Monetary Fund. The World Bank is a specialized agency of the United Nations that borrows in the commercial market and lends on commercial terms. The *International Development Association* is an arm of the World Bank.

The World Bank now earns almost as much money from interest and loan repayments as it hands out in new loans every year. Over 60% of the bank's loans goes to suppliers outside the borrower countries for such things as consultancy services, oil, and machinery. Control of the bank is vested in a board of executives representing national governments, whose votes are apportioned according to the amount they have funded the bank. Thus the USA has nearly 20% of the vote and always appoints the board's president.

In 1990 the World Bank made a net transfer of $46.7 million to developing countries.

TERMS

aid, development money given or lent on concessional terms to developing countries or spent on maintaining agencies for this purpose. In the late 1980s official aid from governments of richer nations amounted to $45–60 billion annually whereas voluntary organizations in the West received about $2.4 billion a year for the Third World. The World Bank is the largest dispenser of aid. All industrialized United Nations (UN) member countries devote a proportion of their gross

national product to aid, ranging from 0.20% of GNP (Ireland) to 1.10% (Norway) (1988 figures). Each country spends more than half this contribution on direct bilateral assistance to countries with which it has historical or military links or hopes to encourage trade. The rest goes to international organizations such as UN and World Bank agencies, which distribute aid multilaterally.

The UK development aid budget in 1990 was 0.31% of GNP, with India and Kenya among the principal beneficiaries. The European Development Fund (an arm of the European Community) and the International Development Association (an arm of the World Bank) receive approximately 5% and 8% respectively of the UK development-aid budget. The Overseas Development Administration is the department of the Foreign Office that handles bilateral aid.

The combined overseas development aid of all EC member countries is less than the sum ($20 billion) the EC spends every year on storing surplus food produced by European farmers.

In 1990 the US development-aid budget was 0.15% of GDP, with Israel and Egypt among the principal beneficiaries; Turkey, Pakistan, and the Philippines are also major beneficiaries. The United States Agency for International Development (USAID) is the State Department body responsible for bilateral aid. The USA is the largest contributor to, and thus the most powerful member of, the International Development Association.

annual percentage rate (APR) rate of interest on credit sales or borrowing that reflects the fact that the proportion of the amount outstanding paid in interest rises as the repayments are made. It is usually approximately double the flat rate of interest, or simple interest.

balance of payments a tabular account of a country's debit and credit transactions with other countries. Items are divided into the *current account*, which includes both visible trade (imports and exports) and invisible trade (such as transport, tourism, interest, and dividends), and the *capital account*, which includes investment in and out of the country, international grants, and loans. Deficits or surpluses on these accounts are brought into balance by buying and selling reserves of foreign currencies.

A *balance of payments crisis* arises when a country's current account deteriorates because the cost of imports exceeds income from exports. In developing countries persistent trade deficits often result in heavy government borrowing overseas, which in turn leads to a debt crisis.

bank financial institution that uses funds deposited with it to lend money to companies or individuals, and which also provides financial services to its customers.

A *central bank* (in the UK, the Bank of England) issues currency for the government, in order to provide cash for circulation and ex-

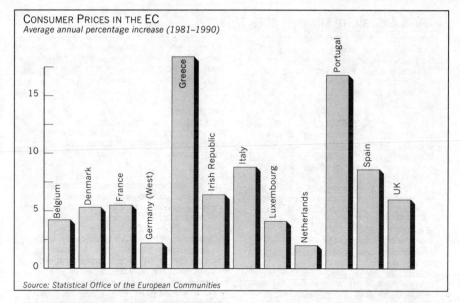

CONSUMER PRICES IN THE EC
Average annual percentage increase (1981–1990)

Source: Statistical Office of the European Communities

change. In terms of assets, seven of the world's top ten banks were Japanese in 1990.

Big Bang popular term for the major changes instituted in late 1986 to the organization and practices of the City of London as Britain's financial centre, ensuring that London retained its place as a leading world financial centre. Facilitated in part by computerization and on-line communications, the changes included the liberalization of the London Stock Exchange. This involved merging the functions of jobber (dealer in stocks and shares) and broker (who mediates between the jobber and the public), introducing negotiated commission rates, and allowing foreign banks and financial companies to own British brokers/jobbers, or themselves to join the London Stock Exchange.

capital accumulated or inherited wealth held in the form of assets (such as stocks and shares, property, and bank deposits). In stricter terms, capital is defined as the stock of goods used in the production of other goods, and may be *fixed capital* (such as buildings, plant, and machinery) that is durable, or *circulating capital* (raw materials and components) that is used up quickly.

collective bargaining the process whereby management, representing an employer, and a trade union, representing employees, agree to negotiate jointly terms and conditions of employment. Agreements can be company-based or industry-wide.

comparative advantage law of international trade first elaborated by David Ricardo showing that trade becomes advantageous if the cost of production of particular items differs between one country and another.

At a simple level, if wine is cheaper to produce in country A than in country B, and the reverse is true of cheese, A can specialize in wine and B in cheese and they can trade to mutual benefit.

consumption the purchase of goods and services for final use, as opposed to spending by firms on capital goods, known as capital formation.

cost of living the cost of goods and services needed for an average standard of living. In Britain the cost-of-living index was introduced 1914 and based on the expenditure of a working-class family of man, woman, and three children; the standard is 100. Known from 1947 as the Retail Price Index (RPI), it is revised to allow for inflation.

Supplementary to the RPI are the Consumer's Expenditure Deflator (formerly Consumer Price Index) and the Tax and Price Index (TPI), introduced in 1979. Comprehensive indexation has been advocated as a means of controlling inflation by linking all forms of income (such as wages and investment), contractual debts and tax scales, to the RPI. Index-linked savings schemes were introduced in the UK in 1975.

credit means by which goods or services are obtained without immediate payment, usually by agreeing to pay interest. The three main forms are *consumer credit* (usually extended to individuals by retailers), *bank credit* (such as overdrafts or personal loans) and *trade credit* (common in the commercial world both within countries and internationally). Consumer credit is increasingly used to pay for goods. In the USA in 1990 it amounted to $713 billion, with about 18% of disposable income expended on hire-purchase and credit-card payments.

In the UK in 1991, new credit advanced to consumers amounted to approximately £40 billion.

crowding out a hypothetical situation in which an increase in government expenditure results

THE MAASTRICHT SUMMIT: STEP BY STEP

At the Maastricht Summit in December 1991, the heads of government of the European Community member states met to agree a treaty whose main elements include economic and monetary union (EMU), social policy, and political union.

The part of the treaty concerning EMU complies with the three-stage plan laid down by a committee of the European Commission chaired by EC President Jacques Delors. In *stage one*, greater convergence of economic performance and policies should be brought about by the completion of the single European market (SEM) by the end of 1992, and the participation of all member currencies in the exchange rate mechanism (ERM) of the European monetary system. The completion of the SEM involves lifting all barriers to goods, services, and labour, and adopting common standards and regulations across the Community.

Stage one also involves lifting controls on the movement of capital and increasing the independence from central government of the central banks—those that are responsible for interest rates and reserves of foreign currency. Greater independence of the Bank of England from the UK government would mean that interest rates could be managed in such a way as to maintain the exchange rate of the pound with less regard to political factors. Since the pound is already relatively fixed in relation to other EC currencies in the ERM, an independent central bank would help pave the way for full EMU and a single currency. The treaty calls for the completion of stage one by the end of 1993.

Stage two involves the formulation of a common monetary (interest rate) policy, through the creation of the European Monetary Institute (EMI), comprising representatives of EC central banks.

In *stage three*, exchange rates will be permanently fixed, and ultimately national currencies will be replaced by a single European currency. To promote the 'convergence of economic performance' laid down by the Delors plan, the summit laid down specific criteria for convergence and entry into stage three:

(1) inflation rates to be no more than 1.5% above the average of the three EC countries with the lowest inflation rates;

(2) long-term interest rates to be no more than 2% above the average of the three countries with the lowest rates;

(3) government budget deficits to be less than 3% of gross domestic product (GDP);

(4) national debts to be less than 60% of GDP;

(5) participation in the narrow band of the ERM (within 2.25% of the central rate with other EC currencies) for at least two years and no devaluation of the currency's central rate during the same period.

In 1996, a conference of EC states is to determine which members meet the criteria for stage three. If at least seven member states meet all the criteria, they will then set a date for monetary union. Those states that meet the criteria for stage three by 1998 will automatically adopt a common currency in 1999, except possibly the UK, which negotiated the right to opt out of the adoption of the single currency, if the UK parliament voted against it. This reflects the continuing debate within the UK about the desirability of a single European currency. Those against, such as former Conservative MP Norman Tebbit, suggest that the criteria for stage three and the loss of a national currency would severely limit a national government's ability to pursue an independent economic policy. Those in favour, such as the Liberal Democrat leader, Paddy Ashdown, suggest that a common currency will further stimulate trade with other EC countries, increase the stability of the UK economy, and prevent economic isolation.

The 'social charter' of the proposed treaty included the right of all workers to be consulted by their employers about certain decisions, the extension of the rights of full-time workers to part-time workers, and the setting of certain minimum standards for wages and working conditions. It was rejected by the UK government, who claimed that its implementation would reduce the cost-competitiveness of UK industry, run counter to some of their trade-union reforms, and discourage inward investment. Thus the charter was left out of the final treaty, with the other 11 members agreeing to it separately. Opposition parties in the UK are generally in favour of the charter, saying that it would reduce poverty, improve working conditions, and promote more informed, committed, and cooperative workforces.

In accordance with the Maastricht agreement, the treaty must be ratified by each country before it can come into force. Unexpectedly, it was the Danish electorate who put a spanner in the works, voting decisively in a referendum in June 1992 to reject the treaty as it then stood. It now seems likely that the treaty will be modified slightly to limit some of its centralizing policies and encourage 'subsidiarity', thereby allaying fears expressed in the Danish referendum. These might also calm the fears of some British Conservatives, who are sceptical about the value of European union. However, French proponents of the union consider that any concessions would encourage the Danes and others to dilute the Maastricht agreement and weaken the cohesion of the Community.

The outcome of the Maastricht Summit can be seen as a triumph for John Major, in negotiating a solution that contributed to party unity among the Conservatives and hence to their victory in the 1992 general election, or as further evidence of British detachment from the 'fast track' towards closer integration within the European Community.

in a fall in private-sector investment, either because it causes inflation or a rise in interest rates (as a result of increased government borrowing) or because it reduces the efficiency of production as a result of government intervention. Crowding out has been used in recent years as a justification of supply-side economics such as the privatization of state-owned industries and services.

currency the type of money in use in a country, for example the US dollar, the UK pound sterling, the German Deutschmark and the Japanese yen.

debt crisis any situation in which an individual, company, or country owes more to others than it can repay or pay interest on; more specifically, the massive indebtedness of many Third World countries that became acute in the 1980s, threatening the stability of the international banking system as many debtor countries became unable to service their debts.

deficit financing planned excess of expenditure over income, dictated by government policy, creating a shortfall of public revenue that is then met by borrowing. The decision to create a deficit is taken in order to stimulate an economy by increasing consumer purchasing and to create more jobs.

depreciation decline of a currency's value in relation to other currencies. Depreciation also describes the fall in value of an asset (such as factory machinery) resulting from age, wear and tear, or other circumstances. It is an important factor in assessing company profit.

deregulation action to abolish or reduce government controls and supervision over private economic activities, with the aim of improving competitiveness. In some areas, however, increased competition has had the effect of driving smaller companies out of business. An example is the deregulation of the US airline industry 1978, after which 14 new companies began flying; by 1991, only one was left. In Britain, the major changes in the City of London 1986 (the Big Bang) were in part deregulation.

devaluation lowering of the official value of a currency against other currencies, so that exports become cheaper and imports more expensive. Used when a country is badly in deficit in its balance of trade, it results in the goods the country produces being cheaper abroad, so that the economy is stimulated by increased foreign demand.

The increased cost of imported food, raw materials, and manufactured goods as a consequence of devaluation may, however, stimulate an acceleration in inflation, especially when commodities are rising in price because of increased world demand. *Revaluation* is the opposite process.

Devaluations of important currencies upset the balance of the world's money markets and encourage speculation. Significant devaluations include that of the German mark in the 1920s and Britain's devaluation of sterling in the 1960s. To promote greater stability, many countries have allowed the value of their currencies to 'float', that is, to fluctuate in value.

disinvestment the withdrawal of investments in a country for political reasons. The term is also used to describe non-replacement of stock as it wears out.

It is generally applied to the removal of funds from South Africa in the 1970s and 1980s by such multinational companies as General Motors and to the withdrawal of private investment funds (by universities, pension funds, and other organizations) from portfolios doing business in South Africa. Disinvestment may be motivated by fear of loss of business in the home market caused by adverse publicity or by fear of loss of foreign resources if the local government changes.

Dow Jones Index (*Dow Jones Industrial 30 Share Index*) scale for measuring the average share price and percentage change of 30 major US industrial companies.

economic growth the rate of growth of output of all goods and services produced within an economy. It is usually measured as the percentage increase in gross domestic product from one year to the next. It is regarded as an indicator of the rate of increase or decrease in the standard of living. Economic growth rises in a recovery, falls in a slow-down, and is negative in a recession—as it was in the UK in 1991, when economic growth was –2.5%.

electronic funds transfer (EFT) method of transferring funds automatically from one account to another by electronic means, for example *electronic funds transfer at point of sale* (EFTPOS), which provides for the automatic transfer of money from buyer to seller at the time of sale. In the UK the system is not yet widely used (Barclay's Connect card is the only vehicle widely promoted for the purpose).

exchange rate the price at which one currency is bought or sold in terms of other currencies, gold, or accounting units such as the special drawing right (SDR) of the International Monetary Fund. Exchange rates may be fixed by international agreement or by government policy; or they may be wholly or partly allowed to 'float' (that is, find their own level) in world currency markets, as with most major currencies since the 1970s.

Central banks, as large holders of foreign currency, often intervene to buy or sell particular currencies in an effort to maintain some stability in exchange rates.

export goods or service produced in one country and sold to another. Exports may be visible (goods physically exported) or invisible (services provided in the exporting country but paid for by residents of another country).

Financial Times Index (FT Index) an indicator measuring the daily movement of 30 major industrial share prices on the London Stock Exchange (1935 = 100), issued by the UK *Financial Times* newspaper. Other FT indices cover government securities, fixed-interest securities, goldmine shares, and Stock Exchange activity.

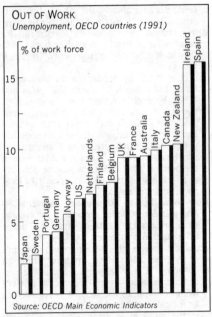

OUT OF WORK
Unemployment, OECD countries (1991)

% of work force

Source: OECD Main Economic Indicators

fiscal policy that part of government policy devoted to achieving the desired level of revenue, notably through taxation, and deciding the priorities and purposes governing expenditure.

gilt-edged securities stocks and shares issued and guaranteed by the British government to raise funds and traded on the Stock Exchange. A relatively risk-free investment, gilts bear fixed interest and are usually redeemable on a specified date. According to the redemption date, they are described as short (up to five years), medium, or long (15 years or more).

gross domestic product (GDP) the value of the output of all goods and services produced within a nation's borders, normally given as a total for the year. It thus includes the production of foreign-owned firms within the country, but excludes the income of domestically owned firms located abroad.

Since output is derived from expenditure on goods and services by firms, consumers, and government net of imports; and income (in the form of wages, salaries, interest, rent, and profits) is derived from the production of goods and services, GDP can be measured either by the sum of total output or expenditure or incomes. However, in practice there is usually a slight discrepancy between the three because of the highly complex calculations involved. GDP fluctuates in relation to the trade cycle and standard of living.

In the UK, the percentage increase in GDP from one year to the next is the standard measure of economic growth.

gross national product (GNP) the most commonly used measurement of the wealth of a country. GNP is defined as the total value of all goods and services produced by firms owned by the country concerned. It is measured as the gross domestic product plus income from abroad, minus income earned during the same period by foreign investors within the country.

The national income of a country is the GNP minus whatever sum of money needs to be set aside to replace ageing capital stock.

hyperinflation rapid and uncontrolled inflation, or increases in prices, usually associated with political and/or social instability (as in Germany in the 1920s and Latin America in the 1970s and 1980s).

import product or service that one country purchases from another for domestic consumption, or for processing and re-exporting (Hong Kong, for example, is heavily dependent on imports for its export business). Imports may be visible (goods) or invisible (services). If an importing country does not have a counterbalancing value of exports, it may experience balance-of-payments difficulties and accordingly consider restricting imports by some form of protectionism (such as an import tariff or imposing import quotas).

incomes policy government-initiated exercise to curb inflation by restraining rises in incomes, on either a voluntary or a compulsory basis; often linked with action to control prices, in which case it becomes a prices and incomes policy.

In Britain incomes policies have been applied at different times since the 1950s, with limited success. An alternative to incomes policy, employed by the post-1979 Conservative government in Britain, is monetary policy, which attempts to manage the economy by controlling the quantity of money in circulation (money supply).

income tax a direct tax levied on personal income, mainly wages and salaries, but which may include the value of receipts other than in cash. It is one of the main instruments for achieving a government's income redistribution objectives. In contrast, *indirect taxes* are duties payable whenever a specific product is purchased; examples include VAT and customs duties.

Most countries impose income taxes on company (corporation) profits and on individuals (personal), although the rates and systems differ widely from country to country. In the case of companies in particular, income tax returns are prepared by an accountant, who will take advantage of the various exemptions, deductions, and allowances available. Personal income taxes are usually progressive so that the poorest members of society pay little or no tax, while the rich make much larger contributions.

inflation a rise in the general level of prices. The many causes include *cost-push inflation* that occurred in 1974 as a result of the world price increase in oil, thus increasing production costs. *Demand-pull inflation* results when overall demand exceeds supply. Suppressed inflation occurs in controlled economies and is reflected in rationing, shortages, and black market prices. Deflation, a fall in the general level of prices, is the reverse of inflation.

interest a sum of money paid by a borrower to a lender in return for the loan, usually expressed as a percentage per annum.

Simple interest is interest calculated as a straight percentage of the amount loaned or invested. In *compound interest*, the interest earned over a period of time (for example, per annum) is added to the investment, so that at the end of the next period interest is paid on that total.

investment the purchase of any asset with the potential to yield future financial benefit to the purchaser (such as a house, a work of art, stocks and shares, or even a private education).

laissez faire theory that the state should not intervene in economic affairs, except to break up a monopoly.

The 20th century has seen an increasing degree of state intervention to promote social benefits, which after World War II in Europe was extended into the field of nationalization of leading industries and services. However, from the 1970s *laissez-faire* policies were again pursued in the UK and the USA.

market forces the forces of demand (a want backed by the ability to pay) and supply (the willingness and ability to supply).

Some economists argue that resources are allocated most efficiently when producers are able to respond to consumer demand without intervention from 'distortions' such as governments and trade unions, and that profits and competition between firms and individuals provide sufficient incentives to produce efficiently (monetarism). Critics of this view suggest that market forces alone may not be efficient because they fail to consider social costs and benefits, and may also fail to provide for the needs of the less well-off, since private firms aiming to make a profit respond to the ability to pay.

monetarism economic policy, advocated by the economist Milton Friedman and the Chicago school of economists, that proposes control of a country's money supply to keep it in step with the country's ability to produce goods, with the aim of curbing inflation. Cutting government spending is advocated, and the long-term aim is to return as much of the economy as possible to the private sector, allegedly in the interests of efficiency.

Central banks—in the USA, the Federal Reserve Bank—use the discount rate and other tools to restrict or expand the supply of money to the economy. Unemployment may result from some efforts to withdraw government 'safety nets,' but monetarists claim it is less than eventually occurs if the more interventionist methods of Keynesian economics are adopted. Monetarist policies were widely adopted in the 1980s in response to the inflation problems caused by spiraling oil prices in 1979.

Additionally, credit is restricted by high interest rates, and industry is not cushioned against internal market forces or overseas competition (with the aim of preventing 'overmanning', 'restrictive' union practices, and 'excessive' wage demands).

monetary policy economic policy aimed at controlling the amount of money in circulation, usually through controlling the level of lending or credit. Increasing interest rates is an example of a contractionary monetary policy, which aims to reduce inflation by reducing the rate of growth of spending in the economy.

money any common medium of exchange acceptable in payment for goods or services or for the settlement of debts. Money is usually coinage (invented by the Chinese in the second millennium BC) and paper notes (used by the Chinese from about AD 800). Recent developments such as the cheque and credit card fulfil many of the traditional functions of money.

money supply the quantity of money in circulation in an economy at any given time. It can include notes, coins, and clearing-bank and other deposits used for everyday payments. Changes in the quantity of lending are a major determinant of changes in the money supply. One of the main principles of monetarism is that increases in the money supply in excess of the rate of economic growth are the major cause of inflation.

In the UK there are several definitions of money supply. M0 was defined as notes and coins in circulation, together with the operational balance of clearing banks with the Bank of England. The M1 definition encompasses M0 plus current account deposits; M2, now rarely used, covers the M1 items plus deposit accounts; M3 covers M2 items plus all other deposits held by UK citizens and companies in the UK banking sector. In May 1987 the Bank of England introduced new terms including M4 (M3 plus building society deposits) and M5 (M4 plus Treasury bills and local authority deposits).

monopoly the domination of a market for a particular product or service by a single company, which can therefore restrict competition and keep prices high. In practice, a company can be said to have a monopoly when it controls a significant proportion of the market (technically an oligopoly).

In the UK, monopoly was originally a royal grant of the sole right to manufacture or sell a certain article. The Fair Trading Act of 1973 defines a monopoly supplier as one having 'a quarter of the market', and the Monopolies and Mergers Commission controls any attempt to reach this position; in the USA 'antitrust laws' are similarly used. In communist systems the state itself has the overall monopoly; in capitalist ones some services such as transport or electricity supply may be state monopolies, but in the UK the Competition Act of 1980 covers both private monopolies and possible abuses in the public sector. A *monopsony* is a situation in which there is only one buyer, for example, most governments are the only legal purchasers of military equipment inside

UK UNEMPLOYMENT 1974–1991

	Workforce in employment (m)	Unemployed (000's)
1974	25,676	599.3
1975	25,894	902.8
1976	26,110	1,298.9
1977	26,224	1,413.6
1978	26,358	1,410.5
1979	26,627	1,312.1
1980	26,839	1,611.2
1981	26,741	2,481.8
1982	26,677	2,904.1
1983	26,610	3,127.4
1984	27,265	3,158.3
1985	27,714	3,281.4
1986	27,791	3,312.4
1987	27,979	2,993.0
1988	28,260	2,425.7
1989	28,504	1,841.3
1990	26,918	1,622.7
1991	26,018	2,287.4

Source: Economic Trends 1991, Annual Supplement

their countries.

multiplier the theoretical concept, formulated by John Maynard Keynes, of the effect on national income or employment of an adjustment in overall demand. For example, investment by a company in a new plant will stimulate new income and expenditure, which will in turn generate new investment, and so on, so that the actual increase in national income may be several times greater than the original investment.

national debt debt incurred by the central government of a country to its own people and institutions and also to overseas creditors. If it does not wish to raise taxes to finance its activities, a government can borrow from the public by means of selling interest-bearing bonds, for example, or from abroad. Traditionally, a major cause of incurring national debt was the cost of war but in recent decades governments have borrowed heavily in order to finance development or nationalization, to

support an ailing currency, or to avoid raising taxation.

On 31 March 1992 the UK national debt was approximately £92 billion. This represented a rise in the national debt since 1991, caused by a budget deficit, or public-sector borrowing requirement (PSBR), of £14 billion in the financial year 1991–92.

national insurance in the UK, state social security scheme which provides child allowances, maternity benefits, and payments to the unemployed, sick, and retired, and also covers medical treatment. It is paid for by weekly contributions from employees and employers.

newly industrialized country (NIC) country that has in recent decades experienced a breakthrough into manufacturing and rapid export-led economic growth. The prime examples are Taiwan, Hong Kong, Singapore, and South Korea. Their economic development during the 1970s and 1980s was partly due to a rapid increase of manufactured goods in their exports.

oligopoly a situation in which a few companies control the major part of a particular market and concert their actions to perpetuate such control. This may include an agreement to fix prices (a cartel).

poll tax tax levied on every individual, without reference to his or her income or property. Being simple to administer, it was among the earliest sorts of tax (introduced in England 1377), but because of its indiscriminate nature (it is a regressive tax, in that it falls proportionately more heavily on poorer people) it has often proved unpopular.

privatization the policy or process of selling or transferring state-owned or public assets and services (nationalized industries) to private investors. Privatization of services takes place by the contracting out to private firms of the rendering of services previously supplied by public authorities. The proponents of privatization argue for the public benefit from its theoretically greater efficiency in a competitive market, and the release of resources for more appropriate use by government. Those against privatization believe that it removes a country's assets from all the people to a minority, whereas public utilities such as gas and water become private monopolies, and that a profit-making state-owned company raises revenue for the government.

In many cases the trend towards privatization was prompted by dissatisfaction with the high level of subsidies being given to often inefficient state enterprise. The term 'privatization' is used even when the state retains a majority share of an enterprise.

The policy has been pursued by the post-1979 Conservative administration in Britain, and by recent governments in France, Japan (Nippon Telegraph and Telephone Corporation 1985, Japan Railways 1987, Japan Air Lines 1987), Italy, and elsewhere. By 1988 the practice had spread worldwide with communist countries such as China and Cuba selling off

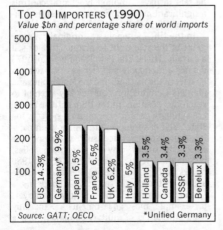

TOP 10 IMPORTERS (1990)
Value $bn and percentage share of world imports

- US 14.3%
- Germany* 9.9%
- Japan 6.5%
- France 6.5%
- UK 6.2%
- Italy 5%
- Holland 3.5%
- Canada 3.4%
- USSR 3.3%
- Benelux 3.3%

Source: GATT; OECD   *Unified Germany

housing to private tenants.

productivity the output produced by a given quantity of labour, usually measured as output per person employed in the firm, industry, sector, or economy concerned. Productivity is determined by the quality and quantity of the fixed capital used by labour, and the effort of the workers concerned. The level of productivity is a major determinant of cost-efficiency: higher productivity tends to reduce average costs of production. Increases in productivity in a whole economy are a major determinant of economic growth.

It is important to distinguish between the rate of growth of productivity and the level of productivity, since at lower levels of productivity, higher rates of productivity growth may be achieved.

profit-sharing system whereby an employer pays the workers a fixed share of the company's profits. It originated in France in the early 19th century and was widely practised for a time within the cooperative movement.

public-sector borrowing requirement (PSBR) amount of money needed by a government to cover any deficit in financing its own activities, including loans to local authorities and public corporations, and also the funds raised by local authorities and public corporations from other sources.

The PSBR is financed chiefly by sales of debt to the public outside the banking system (gilt-edged securities, national savings, and local-authority stocks and bonds), by external transactions with other countries, and by borrowing from the banking system. In the UK, after the 1986 budget this measure was changed to the *Public Sector Financial Deficit (PSFD)*, which is net of the asset sales due to privatization thought to distort the PSBR.

public-sector debt repayment (PSDR) the amount left over when government expenditure (public spending) is subtracted from government receipts. This occurs only when government spending is less than government receipts. A PSDR enables a government to repay some of the national debt.

quantity theory of money economic theory claiming that an increase in the amount of money in circulation causes a proportionate increase in prices.

The theory dates from the 17th century and was elaborated by the US economist Irving Fisher (1867–1947). Supported and developed by Milton Friedman, it forms the theoretical basis of monetarism.

recession a fall in business activity lasting more than a few months, causing stagnation in a country's output. A serious recession is called a *slump*.

reserve currency a country's holding of internationally acceptable means of payment (major foreign currencies or gold); central banks also hold the ultimate reserve of money for their domestic banking sector. On the asset side of company balance sheets, undistributed profits are listed as reserves.

retail price index (RPI) indicator of variations in the cost of living, superseded in the USA by the consumer price index.

savings unspent income, after deduction of tax. In economics a distinction is made between investment, involving the purchase of capital goods, such as buying a house, and saving (where capital goods are not directly purchased, for example, buying shares).

Say's law the 'law of markets' formulated by Jean-Baptiste Say (1767–1832) to the effect that supply creates its own demand and that resources can never be under-used. Widely accepted by classical economists, the 'law' was regarded as erroneous by J M Keynes in his analysis of the depression in Britain during the 1920s and 1930s.

social costs and benefits the costs and benefits to society as a whole that result from economic decisions. These include private costs (the financial cost of production incurred by firms) and benefits (the profits made by firms and the value to people of consuming goods and services) and external costs and benefits (affecting those not directly involved in production or consumption); pollution is one of the external costs.

For example, a chemical plant installs machinery that increases output and reduces employment. The private costs of the extra output are the price of the new machinery. The private benefits are the increases in the chemical firm's profits and in consumption. The external costs include the effects of any increased pollution as a result of the increased output, and the effects of increased unemployment, such as higher expenditure on unemployment benefits. The external benefits include any improvements in technology that other firms can benefit from.

stagflation economic condition (experienced in Europe in the 1970s) in which rapid inflation is accompanied by stagnating, even declining, output and by increasing unemployment. Its cause is often sharp increases in costs of raw materials and/or labour.

stock exchange institution for the buying and selling of stocks and shares (securities). The world's largest stock exchanges are London, New York (Wall Street), and Tokyo. The former division on the London Stock Exchange between brokers (who bought shares from jobbers to sell to the public) and jobbers (who sold them only to brokers on commission, the 'jobbers' turn') was abolished in 1986.

trade cycle or *business cycle* period of time that includes a peak and trough of economic activity, as measured by a country's national income. In Keynesian economics (those of the economist John Maynard Keynes), one of the main roles of the government is to smooth out the peaks and troughs of the trade cycle by intervening in the economy, thus minimizing 'overheating' and 'stagnation'. This is accomplished by regulating interest rates and government spending to maintain a proper balance of economic activity.

Treasury bill in Britain, borrowing by the government in the form of a promissory note to repay the bearer 91 days from the date of issue; such bills represent a flexible and relatively cheap way for the government to borrow money for immediate needs.

unemployment lack of paid employment. The unemployed are usually defined as those out of work who are available for and actively seeking work. Unemployment is measured either as a total or as a percentage of those who are available for work, known as the working population or labour force. Unemployment is generally subdivided into *frictional unemployment*, the inevitable temporary unemployment of those moving from one job to another; *cyclical unemployment*, caused by a downswing in the business cycle; *seasonal unemployment*, in an area where there is high demand only during holiday periods, for example; and *structural unemployment*, where changing technology or other long-term change in the economy results in large numbers without work. Periods of widespread unemployment in Europe and the USA in the 20th century include 1929–1930s, and the years since the mid-1970s.

In Britain deflationary economic measures tended to exacerbate the unemployment trend that began in the mid-1970s, and in the mid-1980s the rate had risen to 14% (although the basis on which it is calculated has in recent years been changed several times and many commentators argue that the real rate is higher). Since Sept 1988 it has been measured as the total or percentage of the working population unemployed and claiming benefit. This only includes people aged 18 or over, since the under-18s are assumed to be in full-time education or training. As the British economy experienced significant economic growth between 1986 and 1989, the rate of unemployment fell to a low of 5.6% in April 1990 (using the post-1988 definition) but rose again during the 1990–92 recession, standing at 9.5% in April 1992.

Many Third World countries suffer from severe unemployment and underemployment; the problem is exacerbated by rapid growth of population and lack of skills. In industrialized countries unemployment has been a phenomenon since the mid-1970s, when the rise in world oil prices caused a downturn in economic activity, and greater use of high technology improved output without creating more jobs. The average unemployment rate in industrialized countries (the members of the Organization for Economic Cooperation and Development) rose to 11% in 1987 compared with only 3% in 1970, with some countries, such as Spain and Ireland, suffering around 20%. In the USA the unemployment rate was 7.5% in 1992. In China, nearly a quarter of the urban labour force is unemployed.

unlisted securities markets markets for shares of companies not included in the official list for the main market of the stock exchange. These lower-tier markets where unlisted shares are traded are less stringently regulated and provide an important intermediate step to the main markets.

What would you say is the most urgent problem facing the country at the present time (March 1992)?

Unemployment	40
Cost of living	15
Other economic issues	14
Health	12
Housing	4
Poll tax	2
Education	3
Law and order	2
Pensions	2
Environment	1
Immigrants	0
International affairs	0
Defence	0
Strikes	0
Other	3
Don't know	2

It is now generally agreed that Britain's economy is in recession. Who or what do you think is most to blame for the recession: the worldwide economic recession, the Thatcher government's policies, or the Major government's policies?

Worldwide recession	48
Thatcher government	43
Major government	4
Other	2
Don't know	3

THE ARTS

HISTORY

architecture the art of designing structures. The term covers design of the visual appearance of structures; their internal arrangements of space; selection of external and internal building materials; design or selection of natural and artificial lighting systems, as well as mechanical, electrical, and plumbing systems; and design or selection of decorations and furnishings. Architectural style may emerge from evolution of techniques and styles particular to a culture in a given time period with or without identifiable individuals as architects or may be attributed to specific individuals or groups of architects working together on a project.

early architecture little remains of the earliest forms of architecture, but archaeologists have examined remains of prehistoric sites and documented Stone Age villages of wooden post buildings with above-ground construction of organic materials such as mud or wattle and daub from the Upper Paleolithic, Mesolithic, and Neolithic periods in Asia, the Middle East, Europe, and the Americas. More extensive remains of stone-built structures have given clues to later Neolithic farming communities as well as habitations, storehouses, and religious and civic structures of early civilizations. The best documented are those of ancient Egypt, where exhaustive work in the 19th and 20th centuries revealed much about ordinary buildings, the monumental structures such as the pyramid tombs near modern Cairo, and the temple and tomb complexes concentrated at Luxor and Thebes.

Classical this architecture evolved its basic forms in Greece between the 16th and 2nd centuries BC. Its hallmark characteristic is its post-and-lintel construction of temples and public structures, classified into the Doric, Ionic, and Corinthian orders, defined by simple, scrolled, and acanthus-leaf capitals for support columns, respectively. The Romans copied and expanded on Greek Classical forms, notably introducing bricks and concrete and inventing the vault, arch, and dome for public buildings and aqueducts.

Byzantine this architecture developed primarily in the E Roman Empire from the 4th century, with its centre at Byzantium (later named Constantinople, currently known as Istanbul). Its most notable feature was construction of churches, some very large, based on the Greek cross plan (Hagia Sophia, Istanbul; St Mark's, Venice), with formalized painted and mosaic decoration.

Islamic this architecture developed from the 8th century, when the Islamic religion spread from its centre in the Middle East W to Spain and E to China and parts of the Philippine Islands. Notable features are the development of the tower with dome and the pointed arch. Islamic architecture, particularly through Spanish examples such as the Great Mosque at Córdoba and the Alhambra in Granada, profoundly influenced Christian church architecture – for example, by adoption of the pointed arch into the Gothic arch.

Romanesque this architecture in W European Christianity developed from the 8th to the 12th centuries. It is marked by churches with massive walls for structural integrity, rounded arches, small windows, and resulting dark volumes of interior space. In England this style is generally referred to as Norman architecture (Durham Cathedral). The style enjoyed a renewal of interest in Europe and the USA in the late 19th and early 20th centuries.

Gothic this architecture emerged out of Romanesque, since the pointed arch and flying buttress made it possible to change from thick supporting walls to lighter curtain walls with extensive expansion of window areas (and stained-glass artwork) and resulting increases in interior light. Gothic architecture was developed particularly in France from the 12th to 16th centuries. The style is divided into Early Gothic (Sens Cathedral), High Gothic (Chartres Cathedral), and Late or Flamboyant Gothic. In England the corresponding divisions are Early English (Salisbury Cathedral), Decorated (Wells Cathedral), and Perpendicular (Kings College Chapel, Cambridge). Gothic was also developed extensively in Germany and neighbouring countries and in Italy.

Renaissance this architecture of 15th- and 16th-century Europe saw the rebirth of Classical form and motifs in the Italian Neo-Classical movement. A major source of inspiration was the work of the 1st-century BC Roman engineer Vitruvius for Palladio, Alberti, Brunelleschi, Bramante, and Michelangelo, the major Renaissance architects. The Palladian style was extensively used later in England by Inigo Jones and the Classical idiom by Christopher Wren. Classical or Neo-Classical style and its elements have been popular in the USA from the 18th century, as evident in much of the civic and commercial architecture since the time of the early republic (the US Capitol and Supreme Court buildings in Washington; many state capitols).

Baroque European architecture of the 17th and 18th centuries elaborated on Classical models with exuberant and extravagant decoration. In large-scale public buildings, the style is best seen in the innovative work of Giovanni Bernini and Francesco Borromini in Italy and later by John Vanbrugh, Nicholas Hawksmoor, and Christopher Wren in England. There were numerous practitioners in France and the German-speaking countries; Vienna is rich in Baroque work.

Rococo this architecture extends the Baroque style with an even greater extravagance of design motifs, using a new lightness of detail and naturalistic elements, such as shells, flowers, and trees.

Neo-Classical European architecture of the 18th and 19th centuries again focused on the more severe Classical idiom (inspired by archaeological finds), producing, for example, the large-scale rebuilding of London by Robert Adam and John Nash and later of Paris by Georges Haussman.

Neo-Gothic the later part of the 19th century saw a Gothic revival, most evident in churches and public buildings (Houses of Parliament, London, Charles Barry).

Art Nouveau was a new movement arising at the end of the 19th century, characterized by sinuous, flowing shapes, informal room plans, and particular attention to interior as well as architectural design. The style is best seen in England in the work of Charles Rennie Mackintosh (Glasgow Art School), in Paris at the entrances to the Metro and in Spain by that of Antonio Gaudí.

Modernism an increasing emphasis on rationalism and reduction of ornament led to Modernism (also known as Functionalism or International Style) in the 1930s. Seeking to exclude everything that did not have a purpose, the latest technological advances in glass, steel, and concrete were used to full advantage. Major architects included Frank Lloyd Wright, Mies van der Rohe, Le Corbusier, and Alvar Aalto.

Town planning also emerged as a discipline in its own right and whole new cities were planned, such as Le Corbusier's Chandigarh in India and Brasilia in Brazil.

Brutalism architectural style of the 1950s and 1960s that evolved from the work of Le Corbusier and Mies van der Rohe. It stressed functionalism and honesty to materials; steel and concrete were favoured. In the UK the style was developed by Alison and Peter Smithson.

Neo-Vernacular by the 1970s a reversion from this movement showed itself in a renewed enthusiasm for vernacular architecture (traditional local styles), to be seen in the work of, for instance, the British firm Darbourne and Darke.

Post-Modernism in the 1980s a Post-Modernist movement emerged, which split into two camps: **high tech**, represented in Britain by architects such as Norman Foster, Richard Rogers, and James Stirling (Hong Kong and Shanghai Bank, Hong Kong, Lloyd's, London, *Staatsgalerie Stuttgart* respectively); and architects using elements from the architecture of previous times, either following certain tenets of the Classical orders – Neo-Classicism yet again – such as Quinlan Terry, or using such elements at whim, such as Michael Graves.

Deconstruction a style that fragments forms and space by taking the usual building elements of floors, walls, and ceilings and sliding them apart to create a sense of disorientation and movement. Its proponents include Zaha Hadid (1950–) in the UK, Frank Gehry (1929–)

and Peter Eisenman (1932–) in the USA, and Co-op Himmelbau in Austria.

BIOGRAPHIES

Aalto Alvar 1898–1976. Finnish architect and designer. One of Finland's first Modernists, his architectural style was unique, characterized by asymmetry, curved walls, and contrast of natural materials. His buildings include the Hall of Residence at the Massachusetts Institute of Technology, Cambridge, Massachusetts 1947–49; Technical High School, Otaniemi 1962–65; and Finlandia Hall, Helsinki 1972. He invented a new form of laminated bent plywood furniture in 1932 and won many design awards for household and industrial items.

Adam family of Scottish architects and designers. *William Adam* (1689–1748) was the leading Scottish architect of his day, and his son *Robert Adam* (1728–1792) is considered one of the greatest British architects of the late 18th century, who transformed the prevailing Palladian fashion in architecture to a Neo-Classical style. He designed interiors for many great country houses and earned a considerable reputation as a furniture designer.

Alberti Leon Battista 1404–1472. Italian Renaissance architect and theorist who recognized the principles of Classical architecture and their modification for Renaissance practice in *On Architecture* 1452.

Archigram London-based group of English architects in the 1960s including Peter Cook (1936–), Dennis Crompton (1935–), and Mike Webb (1937–). Their work was experimental and polemical; architecture was to be technological and flexible.

Barry Charles 1795–1860. English architect of the Neo-Gothic Houses of Parliament at Westminster, London, 1840–60, in collaboration with Pugin.

Berlage Hendrikus 1856–1934. Dutch architect of the Amsterdam Stock Exchange 1897–1903, whose individualist style marked a move away from 19th-century historicism and towards Dutch Expressionism.

Bernini Giovanni Lorenzo 1598–1680. Italian sculptor, architect, and painter, a leading figure in the development of the Baroque style. His work in Rome includes the colonnaded piazza in front of St Peter's Basilica (1656), fountains (as in the Piazza Navona), and papal monuments. His sculpture includes *The Ecstasy of St Theresa* 1645–52 (Sta Maria della Vittoria, Rome) and numerous portrait busts.

Borromini Francesco 1599–1667. Italian Baroque architect, one of the two most important (with Bernini) in 17th-century Rome. Whereas Bernini designed in a florid, expansive style, his pupil Borromini developed a highly idiosyncratic and austere use of the classical language of architecture. The churches of San

Carlo alle Quattro Fontane and San Ivo in Rome demonstrate his revolutionary disregard for convention.

Bramante Donato c. 1444–1514. Italian Renaissance architect and artist. He spent the first part of his life mostly in Milan where he built the Tempietto of San Pietro, Rome c. 1502. Inspired by Classical designs, he was employed by Pope Julius II in rebuilding part of the Vatican and St Peter's in Rome. His work exercised a profound effect upon the development of Renaissance architecture in Italy.

Breuer Marcel 1902–1981. Hungarian-born architect and designer, who studied and taught at the Bauhaus school in Germany. His tubular steel chair 1925 was the first of its kind. He moved to England, then to the USA, where he was in partnership with Walter Gropius 1937–40. His buildings show an affinity with natural materials; the best known is the Bijenkorf, Rotterdam (with Elzas) 1953.

Brunelleschi Filippo 1377–1446. Italian Renaissance architect. One of the earliest and greatest Renaissance architects, he pioneered the scientific use of perspective. He was responsible for the construction of the dome of Florence Cathedral (completed 1438), a feat deemed impossible by many of his contemporaries.

Burlington Richard Boyle, 3rd Earl of 1694--1753. English architectural patron and architect; one of the premier exponents of the Palladian style in Britain. His buildings, such as Chiswick House in London (1725–29), are characterized by absolute adherence to the Classical rules. His major protégé was William Kent.

Butterfield William 1814–1900. English architect. His work is Gothic Revival characterized by vigorous, aggressive forms and multicoloured striped and patterned brickwork, as in the church of All Saints, Margaret Street, London, and Keble College, Oxford.

Chambers William 1726–1796. English architect and popularizer of Chinese influence (for example, the pagoda in Kew Gardens, London) and designer of Somerset House, London.

Coates Nigel 1949– . English architect. While teaching at the Architectural Association in London in the early 1980s, Coates and a group of students founded NATO (Narrative Architecture Today) and produced an influential series of manifestoes and drawings on the theme of the imaginative regeneration of derelict areas of London.

Eyck Aldo van 1918– . Dutch architect with a strong commitment to social architecture. His works include an Orphans' Home 1957–60 and a refugee for single mothers, Mothers' House 1978, both in Amsterdam.

Farrell Terry 1938– . English architect working in a Post-Modern idiom, largely for corporate clients seeking an alternative to the rigours of High Tech or Modernist office blocks. His Embankment Place scheme 1991 sits theatrically on the north bank of the Thames in London and has been likened to a giant jukebox.

Foster Norman 1935– . English architect of the High Tech school. His works include the Willis Faber office, Ipswich, 1978, the Sainsbury Centre for Visual Arts at the University of East Anglia 1979, the headquarters of the Hongkong and Shanghai Bank, Hong Kong, 1986, and Stansted Airport, Essex, 1991.

Fuller (Richard) Buckminster 1895–1983. US architect and engineer. In 1947 he invented the lightweight *geodesic dome*, a half-sphere of triangular components independent of buttress or vault. It combined the maximum strength with the minimum structure. Within 30 years over 50,000 had been built.

Gaudí Antonio 1852–1926. Spanish architect distinguished for his flamboyant Art Nouveau style. He designed both domestic and industrial buildings. His spectacular Church of the Holy Family, Barcelona, begun 1883, is still under construction.

Gehry Frank 1929– . US architect, based in Los Angeles. His architecture approaches abstract art in its use of collage and montage techniques.

Gibbs James 1682–1754. Scottish Neo-Classical architect whose works include St Martin-in-the-Fields, London 1722–26, Radcliffe Camera, Oxford 1737–49, and Bank Hall, Warrington, Cheshire 1750.

Gilbert Cass 1859–1934. US architect, major developer of the skyscraper. His most notable work is the Woolworth Building, New York 1913, the highest building in America (265 m/ 868 ft) when built and famous for its use of Gothic decorative detail. He was also architect of the US Supreme Court building in Washington DC, the Minnesota state capitol in St Paul, and the US Customs House in New York City.

Gropius Walter Adolf 1883–1969. German architect who lived in the USA from 1937. A founder-director of the Bauhaus school in Weimar 1919–28, he was an advocate of team architecture and artistic standards in industrial production. He was an early proponent of the international modern style defined by glass curtain walls, cubic blocks, and unsupported corners. His works include the Fagus-Werke (a shoe factory in Prussia), the Model Factory at the 1914 Werkbund exhibition in Cologne, and the Harvard Graduate Center 1949–50.

Hardouin-Mansart 1646–1708. French architect to Louis XIV from 1675. He designed the lavish Baroque extensions to the palace of Versailles (from 1678) and Grand Trianon. Other works include the Invalides Chapel in Paris 1680–91, the Place de Vendôme, and the Place des Victoires, in Paris.

Haussmann Georges Eugène, Baron Haussmann 1809–1891. French administrator who re-planned medieval Paris 1853–70 with wide boulevards and parks. The cost of his scheme and his authoritarianism caused opposition, and he was made to resign.

Hawksmoor Nicholas 1661–1736. English archi-

IMAGINE TOMORROW, BUILD TODAY

In April 1992 King Juan Carlos of Spain opened Expo '92 in Seville. About two weeks earlier EuroDisney, outside Paris, had its opening-night party, which was televised live around the world with Tina Turner as the star attraction.

Expo '92 was designed to run for six months before undergoing a transformation into a European communications and business park. Its theme, 'discovery', was chosen to celebrate the now controversial achievements of Christopher Columbus. As if to echo this controversy, the construction of Expo was dogged by problems. Not only was there the usual anxiety over completing on time, but a series of mishaps culminated in the destruction of the main theme pavilion in a fire caused by a stray spark from a welder's torch.

The British government decided that this year, unlike the case at other recent Expos, the country should be represented by a high-profile pavilion. To this end, an architectural competition was held, with Nicholas Grimshaw and Partners coming out on top. There then followed a lengthy process of choosing designers for the interior. After much speculation in the design press, this came down to RSCG Conran.

The building, with its simple rectangular plan, exploited the need for climate control. Its face was a full-height glass wall reminiscent of Grimshaw's *Financial Times* printing works in London, but here the sculptor William Pye designed an extra skin in the form of a sheet waterfall to help cool the interior. The roofline was dominated by elegant louvres that controlled heat gain.

Amid the hullaballoo of the opening, it became clear that the British pavilion had made its mark architecturally. Only two other pavilions—Japan's, designed by Tadao Ando, and Hungary's, designed by Imre Makowecz—elicited as much response. The former was a blend of timber and concrete, traditional and modern, that left no doubt about Japan's confidence in its place in the world. Hungary's pavilion was a post-Modern evocation of the country's religious architecture, seen through the eyes of a designer deeply influenced by natural forms. This building, with its great sweeping roof and seven spires, was probably the single most striking image of Expo.

The various theme pavilions and those designed for the Spanish regions made little impact. The exception to this was the Pavilion of the Future by Martorell, Bohigas and Mackay, one of Barcelona's leading practices. Outside the Expo site, another two of Spain's world-renowned designers made bold statements: the engineer Santiago Calatrava with his Alamillo Bridge and the architect Rafael Moneo, best known for the museum in Mérida, with Seville's new international airport.

Perhaps the most surprising aspect of this roll-call of architects was the lack of an original American contribution. To the disappointment of the Expo authorities, the US government decided at the last moment to cancel its purpose-built pavilion in favour of reused geodesic domes left over from another, lesser, world's fair. Therefore no eminent contemporary US architects represented their own country at Expo.

Three American architects were, however, employed elsewhere in Europe by that most famous American institution, the Disney Corporation. They were Robert Stern, Michael Graves, and Frank Gehry, and the project was EuroDisney.

The Disney theme parks have a tradition of a special kind of visionary city planning. Walt Disney himself often employed architects in other capacities and he was personally responsible for the setting up of the Epcot Center at Disney World in Florida, a kind of utopia for communal living. Many have complained that Epcot was hijacked for the purposes of commercialism. It is disappointing that when the organization began once more to employ architects in a big way, their work was confined to the periphery of the theme park. Stern and Graves were each given the job of designing hotels. Stern designed two, the Newport Bay Club and the Cheyenne Hotel, while Graves worked on the New York Hotel. The Disney attitude to marketing suggests that when the architects were briefed on these projects the names were already attached. Not surprisingly, each of the finished buildings is a pastiche of its given theme. The Newport Bay Club echoes the hotels of America's east coast around the turn of the century; the Cheyenne is Western style; and the New York is a kind of Art Deco skyscraper laid low.

Only Gehry has built something that cannot be easily pigeonholed. He was given the brief to design, as he said, 'a place to catch the last half-buck of the weary traveller'—in other words, a shopping street. What he has made is a deconstructionist Wild West town with fairy lights. Even the copywriters seemed unable to cope with this; in brochures it is called merely the 'Disney Entertainment Center'.

The five lands of EuroDisney itself are, like its predecessors in the USA and Japan, entirely the work of Disney's 'imagineers'. Many of the attractions, like Main Street USA and Big Thunder Mountain, have been lifted straight from these projects. No wonder there was so much alarm in French cultural circles at the arrival of this huge American import.

Despite the obvious differences between Expo '92 and EuroDisney—temporary against permanent, realistic against fantastic, and so on—their similarities are striking. Both are 'instant cities'; both present possibilities of new kinds of recreation and even learning. However, it might be possible to draw some conclusions from the architecture of each. In EuroDisney, the buildings come as part of a package dedicated, in the end, to the selling of one commodity, the Disney ideal: Mickey Mouse. Expo, saturated with nationalism, competition, and collective doubt over its reason for existence, has given birth to some wonderful buildings.

tect, assistant to Christopher Wren in designing London churches and St Paul's Cathedral; joint architect with Vanbrugh of Castle Howard and Blenheim Palace. His genius is displayed in a quirky and uncompromising style incorporating elements from both Gothic and Classical sources.

Howard Ebenezer 1850–1928. English town planner and founder of the ideal of the garden city, through his book *Tomorrow* 1898 (republished as *Garden Cities of Tomorrow* 1902).

Isozaki Arata 1931– . Japanese architect. One of Kenzo Tange's team 1954–63, his Post-Modernist works include Ochanomizu Square, Tokyo (retaining the existing facades), and buildings for the 1992 Barcelona Olympics.

Jencks Charles 1939– . US architectural theorist and furniture designer. He coined the term 'Post-Modern Architecture' and wrote *The Language of Post-Modern Architecture* 1984.

Johnson Philip (Cortelyou) 1906– . US architect who coined the term 'international style'. Originally designing in the style of Mies van der Rohe, he later became an exponent of Post-Modernism. He designed the giant AT&T building in New York 1978, a pink skyscraper with a Chippendale-style cabinet top.

Jones Inigo 1573–c. 1652. English architect. Born in London, he studied in Italy and was influenced by the works of Palladio. He was employed by James I to design scenery for Ben Jonson's masques. In 1619 he designed his English Renaissance masterpiece, the banqueting room at Whitehall, London.

Kahn Louis 1901–1974. US architect, born in Estonia. He developed a classically romantic style, in which functional 'servant' areas, such as stairwells and air ducts, featured prominently, often as tower-like structures surrounding the main living and working, or 'served', areas. His projects are characterized by an imaginative use of concrete and brick and include the Salk Institute for Biological Studies, La Jolla, California, and the British Art Center at Yale University.

Lasdun Denys 1914– . English architect. He designed the Royal College of Surgeons in Regent's Park, London 1960–64, some of the buildings at the University of East Anglia, Norwich, and the National Theatre 1976–77 on London's South Bank.

Le Corbusier Assumed name of Charles-Édouard Jeanneret 1887–1965. Swiss architect. His functionalist approach to town planning in industrial society was based on the interrelationship between machine forms and the techniques of modern architecture. His concept, *La Ville Radieuse*, developed in Marseille, France (1945–50) and Chandigarh, India, placed buildings and open spaces with related functions in a circular formation, with buildings based on standard-sized units mathematically calculated according to the proportions of the human figure.

Ledoux Claude-Nicolas 1736–1806. French Neo-Classical architect, stylistically comparable to E-L Boullée in his use of austere, geometric forms, exemplified in his toll houses for Paris; for instance, the Barrière de la Villette in the Place de Stalingrad.

Lethaby William Richard 1857–1931. English architect. An assistant to Richard Norman Shaw, he embraced the principles of William Morris and Philip Webb in the Arts and Crafts movement, and was cofounder and first director of the Central School of Arts and Crafts from 1894. He wrote a collection of essays entitled *Form in Civilization* 1922.

Lutyens Edwin Landseer 1869–1944. English architect. His designs ranged from picturesque to Renaissance style country houses and ultimately evolved into a Classical style as in the Cenotaph, London, and the Viceroy's House, New Delhi.

Mackintosh Charles Rennie 1868–1928. Scottish architect, designer, and painter, whose chief work includes the Glasgow School of Art 1896, various Glasgow tea rooms 1897–c. 1911, and Hill House, Helensburgh, 1902–03. His early work is Art Nouveau; he subsequently developed a unique style, both rational and expressive.

Mansart Jules Hardouin 1646–1708. see Hardouin-Mansart, Jules.

Meier Richard 1934– . US architect whose white designs spring from the poetic modernism of the Le Corbusier villas of the 1920s. His abstract style is at its most mature in the Museum für Kunsthandwerk (Museum of Arts and Crafts), Frankfurt, West Germany, which was completed 1984.

Mendelsohn Erich 1887–1953. German Expressionist architect who designed the Einstein Tower, Potsdam, 1919–20. His later work fused Modernist and Expressionist styles; in Britain he built the de la Warr Pavilion 1935–36 in Bexhill-on-Sea, East Sussex. In 1941 he settled in the USA, where he built the Maimonides Hospital, San Francisco, 1946–50.

Michelangelo Buonarroti 1475–1564. Italian sculptor, painter, architect, and poet, active in his native Florence and in Rome. His giant talent dominated the High Renaissance. Michelangelo became the architect and sculptor of the Medici funerary chapel 1520–34 in San Lorenzo, he also designed San Lorenzo's library. In his last years he took over the completion of St Peter's basilica, Rome, and designed its great dome. Michelangelo had a lasting influence, with the Mannerist school of architecture copying his decorative details and motifs.

Mies van der Rohe Ludwig 1886–1969. German architect who practised in the USA from 1937. He succeeded Gropius as director of the Bauhaus 1929–33. He became professor at the Illinois Technical Institute 1938–58, for which he designed new buildings on characteristically functional lines from 1941. He also designed the bronze-and-glass Seagram building in New York City 1956–59 and numerous apartment blocks. He designed the National Gallery,

Berlin 1963–68.

Moore Charles 1925– . US architect with an eclectic approach to design. He was an early exponent of Post-Modernism in, for example, his students' housing for Kresage College, University of California at Santa Cruz, 1972--74, and the Piazza d'Italia in New Orleans, 1979.

Nash John 1752–1835. English architect. He laid out Regent's Park, London, and its approaches. Between 1813 and 1820 he planned Regent Street (later rebuilt), repaired and enlarged Buckingham Palace (for which he designed Marble Arch), and rebuilt Brighton Pavilion in flamboyant oriental style.

Nervi Pier Luigi 1891–1979. Italian architect who used soft steel mesh within concrete to give it flowing form. For example, the Turin exhibition hall 1949; the UNESCO building in Paris 1952; and the cathedral at New Norcia, near Perth, Australia 1960.

Neutra Richard Joseph 1892–1970. Austrian-born architect, who became a US citizen 1929. His works, often in impressive landscape settings, include Lovell Health House, Los Angeles (1929), and Mathematics Park, Princeton, New Jersey.

Niemeyer Oscar 1907– . Brazilian architect, joint designer of the United Nations headquarters in New York, and of many buildings in Brasília.

Olbrich Joseph Maria 1867–1908. Viennese architect who worked under Otto Wagner and was opposed to the overornamentation of Art Nouveau. His major buildings, however, remain Art Nouveau in spirit: the Vienna Sezession 1897–98, the Hochzeitsturm 1907, and the Tietz department store in Düsseldorf, Germany.

Palladio Andrea 1518–1580. Italian Renaissance architect noted for his harmonious and balanced Classical structures. He designed numerous country houses in and around Vicenza, Italy, making use of Roman Classical forms, symmetry, and proportion. He also designed churches in Venice and published his studies of Classical form in several illustrated books. His ideas were revived in England in the early 17th century by Inigo Jones and in the 18th century by Lord Burlington and later by architects in Italy, Holland, Germany, Russia, and the US.

Paxton Joseph 1801–1865. English architect, garden superintendent to the Duke of Devonshire from 1826 and designer of the Great Exhibition building 1851 (Crystal Palace), revolutionary in its structural use of glass and iron.

Piranesi Giambattista 1720–1778. Italian architect, most significant for his powerful etchings of Roman antiquities and as a theorist of architecture, advocating imaginative use of Roman models. Only one of his designs was built, Sta Maria del Priorato, Rome.

Pugin Augustus Welby Northmore 1812–1852. English architect, collaborator with Barry in the detailed design of the Houses of Parliament.

He did much to revive Gothic architecture in England.

Rogers Richard 1933– . English architect. His works include the Centre Pompidou in Paris 1977 (jointly with Renzo Piano) and the Lloyd's building in London 1986.

Rossi Aldo 1931– . Italian architect and theorist. Rossi is strongly influenced by rationalist thought and Neo-Classicism. His works include the Gallaratese II apartment complex in Milan, 1970; the Modena cemetery, 1973, and the Teatro del Mondo/Floating Theatre in Venice, 1979. He won the Pritzker prize 1990.

Saarinen Eero 1910–1961. Finnish-born US architect distinguished for a wide range of innovative modern designs using a variety of creative shapes for buildings. His works include the US embassy, London, the TWA terminal, New York, and Dulles Airport, Washington DC. He collaborated on a number of projects with his father, Eliel Saarinen.

Saarinen Eliel 1873–1950. Finnish architect and town planner, founder of the Finnish Romantic school. In 1923 he emigrated to the USA, where he contributed to US skyscraper design by his work in Chicago, and later turned to functionalism.

Sant'Elia Antonio 1888–1916. Italian architect. His drawings convey a Futurist vision of a metropolis with skyscrapers, traffic lanes, and streamlined factories.

Schinkel Karl Friedrich 1781–1841. Prussian Neo-Classical architect. Major works include the Old Museum, Berlin, 1823–30, the Nikolaikirche in Potsdam 1830–37, and the Roman Bath 1833 in the park of Potsdam.

Scott (George) Gilbert 1811–1878. English architect. As the leading practical architect in the mid-19th-century Gothic revival in England, Scott was responsible for the building or restoration of many public buildings, including the Albert Memorial, the Foreign Office, and St Pancras Station, all in London.

Serlio Sebastiano 1475–1554. Italian architect and painter, author of *L'Architettura* 1537–51, which set down practical rules for the use of the Classical orders, and was used by architects of the Neo-Classical style throughout Europe.

Shaw (Richard) Norman 1831–1912. English architect. He was the leader of the trend away from Gothic and Tudor styles back to Georgian lines. His buildings include Swan House, Chelsea, 1876.

Sinan 1489–1588. Ottoman architect, chief architect from 1538 to Suleiman the Magnificent. Among the hundreds of buildings he designed are the Suleimaniye in Istanbul, a mosque complex, and the Topkapi Saray, palace of the sultan (now a museum).

Smirke Robert 1780–1867. English Classical architect, designer of the British Museum, London (1823–47).

Smithson Alison (1928–) and Peter (1923–) English architects, teachers, and theorists, best known for their development in the 1950s and 1960s of the style known as Brutalism, for example in Hunstanton School, Norfolk, 1954; the Economist Building, London, 1964; and Robin Hood Gardens, London, 1968–72.

Soane John 1753–1837. English architect, whose individual Neo-Classical designs anticipated contemporary taste. He designed his own house in Lincoln's Inn Fields, London, now the Soane Museum. Little remains of his extensive work at the Bank of England, London.

Speer Albert 1905–1981. German architect and minister in the Nazi government during World War II. Commissioned by Hitler, Speer, like his counterparts in Fascist Italy, chose an overblown Classicism to glorify the state, as, for example, in his plan for the Berlin and Nuremberg Party Congress Grounds 1934.

Stirling James 1926– . English architect, associated with collegiate and museum architecture. His works include the engineering building at Leicester University, and the Clore Gallery (the extension to house the Turner collection) at the Tate Gallery, London, opened in 1987.

Sullivan Louis Henry 1856–1924. US architect who worked in Chicago and designed early skyscrapers such as the Wainwright Building, St Louis, 1890 and the Guaranty Building, Buffalo, 1894. He was influential in the anti-ornament movement. Frank Lloyd Wright was his pupil.

Tange Kenzo 1913– . Japanese architect. His works include the National Gymnasium, Tokyo, for the 1964 Olympics, and the city of Abuja, planned to replace Lagos as the capital of Nigeria.

Terry (John) Quinlan 1937– . English Neo-Classical architect. His work includes country houses, for example Merks Hall, Great Dunmow, Essex, 1982, and the larger-scale Richmond, London, riverside project, commissioned 1984.

Vanbrugh John 1664–1726. English Baroque architect and dramatist. He designed Blenheim Palace, Oxfordshire, and Castle Howard, Yorkshire, and wrote the comic dramas *The Relapse* 1696 and *The Provok'd Wife* 1697.

van Eyck Aldo Dutch architect; see Eyck, Aldo van.

Venturi Robert 1925– . US architect. He pioneered Post-Modernism through his books, *Complexity and Contradiction in Architecture* 1967 and *Learning from Las Vegas* 1972. In 1986 he was commissioned to design an extension to the National Gallery, London.

Vitruvius (Marcus Vitruvius Pollio) 1st century BC. Roman architect, whose ten-volume interpretation of Roman architecture *De architectura* influenced Alberti and Palladio.

Voysey Charles Francis Annesley 1857–1941. English architect and designer. He designed country houses which were characteristically asymmetrical with massive buttresses, long sloping roofs, and rough-cast walls. He also designed textiles and wallpaper.

Wagner Otto 1841–1918. Viennese architect. Initially designing in the Art Nouveau style, for example Vienna Stadtbahn 1894–97, he later rejected ornament for rationalism, as in the Post Office Savings Bank, Vienna, 1904–06. He influenced Viennese architects such as Josef Hoffmann, Adolf Loos, and Joseph Olbrich.

Waterhouse Alfred 1830–1905. English architect. He was a leading exponent of Victorian Neo-Gothic using, typically, multicoloured tiles and bricks. His works include the Natural History Museum in London 1868.

Webb Philip (Speakman) 1831–1915. English architect. He mostly designed private houses, including the Red House, Bexley Heath, Sussex, for William Morris, and was one of the leading figures, with Richard Norman Shaw and C F A Voysey, in the revival of domestic English architecture in the late 19th century.

Wren Christopher 1632–1723. English architect, designer of St Paul's Cathedral, London, built 1675–1710; many London churches including St Bride's, Fleet Street, and St Mary-le-Bow, Cheapside; the Royal Exchange; Marlborough House; and the Sheldonian Theatre, Oxford.

Wright Frank Lloyd 1869–1959. US architect, who, as a student of Louis Sullivan 1888–93, rejected Neo-Classicist styles for 'organic architecture' in which buildings reflected their natural surroundings. Among his buildings are the Robie house 1909 in Chicago; his Spring Green home, Wisconsin, Taliesin East 1925; Falling Water, near Pittsburgh, Pennsylvania, 1936, a house built straddling a waterfall; the Johnson Wax Company Administration building, Racine, Wisconsin, 1938, and the company's Laboratory Tower 1949; the high-rise Price Company Tower, Bartlesville, Oklahoma, 1953; and the Guggenheim Museum, New York, 1959.

TERMS

adobe building constructed of sun-dried mud bricks commonly found in Spain, Latin America, and New Mexico.

arch curved structure of masonry that supports the weight of material over an open space, as in a bridge or doorway. It originally consisted of several wedge-shaped stones supported by their mutual pressure. The term is also applied to any curved structure that is an arch in form only.

atrium an inner, open courtyard. Originally the central court or main room of an ancient Roman house, open to the sky, often with a shallow pool to catch water.

bailey open space or court of a stone-built castle.

basilica type of Roman public building; a large roofed hall flanked by columns, generally with an aisle on each side, used for judicial or other public business. The earliest known basilica, at Pompeii, dates from the 2nd century BC. This architectural form was adopted by the early Christians for their churches.

brick common building material, rectangular in shape, made of clay that has been fired in a

LONDON: TOWARDS THE MILLENNIUM

Was it just the coming and going of a general election and the effects of recession on boom town, or is every year until 2001 going to be like this? In 1992, while office space emptied, Canary Wharf faltered, and rents dropped, speculation about London's future soared.

The year began with an exhibition at the Architecture Foundation documenting London's lost opportunities. On show was a mixture of alternative designs for famous sites and great visionary schemes proposed but rejected in favour of, at best, architectural infill and, at worst, piecemeal development.

In political mood, the architect Richard Rogers cooperated with Mark Fisher, the shadow arts minister, and the Labour Party in proposing 'A New London'. In this, the Thames would become an urban resource rather than a north–south divide, public transport would be revitalized, and stultifying planning procedures would be overhauled. The models for this were Europe's strong, locally governed cities such as Frankfurt, Nîmes, and Barcelona. The recommendations were very much in tune with the high-tech style for which Rogers has become known.

Publication of the book *A New London* came at the same time as the news of the financial predicament of Canary Wharf's developers Olympia and York. Rogers's criticism of the Docklands Enterprise Zone seemed, at least temporarily, to hit its target. It coincided with public criticism of the viability both of Docklands as an alternative financial centre and of its spin-offs, such as the privately subsidized extension to the Underground system. Others, however, had no time for gloomy predictions. Peter Hall, sometime ministerial planning adviser and author of the influential books *London 2000* and *London 2001*, argued that Docklands would recover and that the City would retain its supremacy as London's 'nerve centre'. In his words, he did not believe in the 'dinosaur-city' argument.

Another exhibition, 'City Changes,' again instigated by the Architecture Foundation, seemed to back Hall's view. This display of new and refurbished buildings under construction or recently given planning permission invited comparison with Paris's architecture centre, where the public is invited to view and comment on new developments in their city.

'City Changes' was centred on a huge-scale model of the Square Mile, giving the visitor the helicopter pilot's view. The effect of this was to make the City into a perfect set piece with St Paul's Cathedral and the chosen schemes picked out in detail. Needless to say, there was no sense of the congestion of traffic, the noise pollution, or the disruption caused by large construction projects. What the model and the exhibition did show, however, was the consideration given to the impact of these new buildings by both clients and architects. There were schemes from Norman Foster and James Stirling, as newcomers to the City, and new projects from Richard Rogers and Terry Farrell, among others. All this could be read as a reassertion of the City as 'nerve centre'. The speculative buildings of the preceding three decades were still there, disguised in the uniform finishes of the model, but added to these were new, responsive, and, to a large extent, architecturally distinguished schemes.

in his book *The 100-Mile City*, the critic Deyan Sudjic looked not only at London but also at other First World post-industrial metropolises—Paris, New York, Los Angeles, and Tokyo. He differed from Hall's view in arguing that we can no longer consider the city as a hierarchy of centre, hinterland, and suburb. Further, he claimed that even the idea of 'neighbourhood' is outmoded and hopelessly nostalgic in these cities. The new 'force field' or '100-mile' city is based on mobility, allowing easy access equally to shopping mall, theme park, historic city 'centre', and workplace. This suggests that everything is almost all right in the way that London is evolving as long as it can sustain its 'force field'. However, Sudjic asked: What happens when the energy to power this urban matrix runs out or when it suffers from terminal gridlock?

Of course there is no easy answer to this question. It is impossible to imagine that architects will be able to solve problems that are geopolitical. However, it is interesting to return here to the visionary view. The architect Nigel Coates has stirred a certain amount of controversy over the last few years in manifestoes for what his group call 'narrative architecture'. As a partner in Branson Coates, he has worked on a number of imaginative and eclectic projects in the UK and Japan. So far, his work here has been confined to the design of exhibitions and shop interiors, but in 1992 he returned to the polemical style of earlier work in the exhibition 'Ecstacity' at the Architectural Association. Focusing on an axis running from Buckingham Palace to St Paul's and the parallel route of the Embankment, he referred to a place that was 'no longer a museum, the city is both living history and living future'. Often obscure, and with references to computer games and cyberpunk science fiction, Coates still managed to conjure up a view of London where technology is benign and there are hints throughout of a city that might be easier to live in than at present. He talked of 'membranes that fill the gaps between buildings with their organic sensor mechanisms' and '52 islands that form a plankton spread from Westminster to Canary Wharf'. This was a vision where the architect worked with the existing environment while proposing a radical re-evaluation of how it is used. It was, in some ways, close to the Friends of the Earth slogan 'Think globally, act locally'.

All this has echoes of 'A New London', but who is to say whether London will be 'Ecstacity', 'force-field city', or 'dinosaur city' come the 21st century?

kiln. Bricks are made by kneading a mixture of crushed clay and other materials into a stiff mud and extruding it into a ribbon. The ribbon is cut into individual bricks, which are fired at a temperature of up to about 1,000°C/1,800°F. Bricks may alternatively be pressed into shape in moulds.

buttress reinforcement in brick or masonry, built against a wall to give it strength. A *flying buttress* is an arc transmitting the force of the wall to be supported to an outer buttress, common in Gothic architecture.

cantilever beam or structure that is fixed at one end only, though it may be supported at some point along its length; for example, a diving board. The cantilever principle, widely used in construction engineering, eliminates the need for a second main support at the free end of the beam, allowing for more elegant structures and reducing the amount of materials required. Many large-span bridges have been built on the cantilever principle.

caryatid building support or pillar in the shape of a woman, the name deriving from the Karyatides who were priestesses at the temple of Artemis at Karyai; a male figure is a *telamon* or *atlas*.

castle the private fortress of a king or noble during the Middle Ages. At first a building on a mound surrounded by a wooden fence, this was later copied in stone. The earliest castles in Britain were built following the Norman Conquest, and the art of castle building reached a peak in Europe during the 13th century. By the 15th century, the need for castles for domestic defence had largely disappeared, and the advent of gunpowder had made them largely useless against attack.

cement any bonding agent used to unite particles in a single mass or to cause one surface to adhere to another. *Portland cement* is a powder obtained from burning together a mixture of lime (or chalk) and clay, and when mixed with water and sand or gravel, turns into mortar or concrete. In geology, a chemically precipitated material such as carbonate that occupies the interstices of clastic rocks is called cement.

château term originally applied to a French medieval castle, but now used to describe a country house or important residence in France. The château was first used as a domestic building in the late 15th century; by the reign of Louis XIII (1610–43) fortifications such as moats and keeps were no longer used for defensive purposes, but merely as decorative features. The Loire valley contains some fine examples of châteaux.

cladding thin layer of external covering on a building; for example, tiles, wood, stone, concrete.

cloister a covered walk within a convent or monastery, often opening onto a courtyard.

colonnade row of columns supporting arches or an entablature.

column a structure, round or polygonal in plan, erected vertically as a support for some part of a building. Cretan paintings reveal the existence of wooden columns in Aegean architecture, about 1500 BC. The Hittites, Assyrians, and Egyptians also used wooden columns, and they are a feature of the monumental architecture of China and Japan. In Classical architecture there are five principal types of column; see *order*.

community architecture movement enabling people to work directly with architects in the design and building of their own homes and neighbourhoods. It is an approach strongly encouraged by the Prince of Wales.

concrete building material composed of cement, stone, sand, and water. It has been used since Roman and Egyptian times. During the 20th century, it has been increasingly employed as an economical alternative to materials such as brick and wood.

conservation, architectural attempts to maintain the character of buildings and historical areas. In England this is subject to a growing body of legislation that has designated more listed buildings. There are now over 6,000 conservation areas throughout England alone.

Corinthian in Classical architecture, one of the five types of column; see *order*.

curtain wall in buildings, a light-weight wall of glass or aluminium that is not load-bearing and is hung from a metal frame rather than built up from the ground like a brick wall. Curtain walls are typically used in high-rise blocks.

Doric in Classical architecture, one of the five types of column; see *order*.

garden city a town built in a rural area and designed to combine town and country advantages, with its own industries, controlled developments, private and public gardens, and cultural centre. The idea was proposed by Ebenezer Howard (1850–1928) who, in 1899 founded the Garden City Association, which established the first garden city, Letchworth (in Hertfordshire).

gargoyle spout projecting from the roof gutter of a building with the purpose of directing water away from the wall. The term is usually applied to the ornamental forms found in Gothic architecture; these were carved in stone in the form of fantastic animals, angels, or human heads.

green belt area surrounding a large city, officially designated not to be built on but preserved as open space (for agricultural and recreational use).

ha-ha in landscape gardening, a sunken boundary wall permitting an unobstructed view beyond a garden; a device much used by Capability Brown in the 18th century.

Ionic in Classical architecture, one of the five types of column; see *order*.

keep or *dungeon* or *donjon* the main tower of a castle, containing enough accommodation to serve as living-quarters under siege conditions.

listed building a building officially recognized as having historical or architectural interest and therefore legally protected from alteration or demolition. In England the listing is drawn up by the Secretary of State for the Environment under the advice of the English Heritage organization, which provides various resources for architectural conservation.

mezzanine architectural term for a storey with a lower ceiling placed between two main storeys, usually between the ground and first floors of a building.

minaret slender turret or tower attached to a Muslim mosque or to buildings designed in that style. It has one or more balconies, from which the *muezzin* calls the people to prayer five times a day.

misericord or *miserere* in church architecture, a projection on the underside of a hinged seat of the choir stalls, used as a rest for a priest when standing during long services. Misericords are often decorated with carvings.

module in construction, a standard or unit that governs the form of the rest: for example, Japanese room sizes are traditionally governed by multiples of standard tatami floor mats; today prefabricated buildings are mass-produced in a similar way. The components of a spacecraft are designed in coordination; for example, for the Apollo Moon landings the craft comprised a command module (for working, eating, sleeping), service module (electricity generators, oxygen supplies, manoeuvring rocket), and lunar module (to land and return the astronauts).

obelisk tall, tapering column of stone, much used in ancient Egyptian as well as Roman architecture.

order in Classical architecture, the column (including capital, shaft, and base) and the entablature, considered as an architectural whole. The five orders are Doric, Ionic, Corinthian, Tuscan, and Composite.

pantheon originally a temple for worshipping all the gods, such as that in ancient Rome, rebuilt by Hadrian and still used as a church. In more recent times, it is a building where famous people are buried (Panthéon, Paris).

pediment the triangular part crowning the fronts of buildings in classic styles. The pediment was a distinctive feature of Greek temples.

peristyle range of columns surrounding a building or open courtyard.

piano nobile the main floor of a house, containing the main reception room.

portico porch with a pediment and columns.

prestressed concrete reinforced concrete in which ducts enclose mechanically tensioned steel cables. This allows the most efficient use of the tensile strength of steel with the compressive strength of concrete.

pylon steel lattice tower that supports high-tension electrical cables. In ancient Egyptian architecture, a pylon is one of a pair of inward-sloping towers that flank an entrance.

pyramid four-sided building with triangular sides used in ancient Egypt to enclose a royal tomb; for example, the Great Pyramid of Khufu/Cheops at Giza, near Cairo; 230 m/ 755 ft square and 147 m/481 ft high. In Babylon and Assyria broadly stepped pyramids (ziggurats) were used as the base for a shrine to

architectural orders

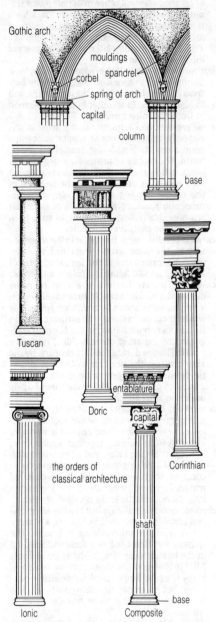

Gothic arch

mouldings

spandrel

corbel

spring of arch

capital

column

base

Tuscan

entablature

Doric

capital

the orders of classical architecture

Corinthian

shaft

base

Ionic

Composite

a god: the Tower of Babel was probably one of these.

RIBA abbreviation for *Royal Institute of British Architects*.

satellite town new town planned and built to serve a particular local industry, or as a dormitory or overspill town for people who work in a nearby metropolis. New towns in Britain include Port Sunlight near Birkenhead (Cheshire), built to house workers at Lever

Brothers soap factories. More recent examples include Welwyn Garden City (1948), Cumbernauld (1955), and Milton Keynes (1967).

sick building syndrome malaise diagnosed in the early 1980s among office workers and thought to be caused by such pollutants as formaldehyde (from furniture and insulating materials), benzene (from paint), and the solvent trichloroethylene, concentrated in air-conditioned buildings. Symptoms include headache, sore throat, tiredness, colds, and flu. Studies have found that it can cause a 40% drop in productivity and a 30% rise in absenteeism.

skyscraper building so tall that it appears to 'scrape the sky', developed 1868 in New York, USA, where land prices were high and the geology adapted to such methods of construction. Skyscrapers are now found in cities throughout the world. The world's tallest free-standing structure is the CN (Canadian National) Tower, Toronto, 555 m/1,821 ft.

town planning the design of buildings or groups of buildings in a physical and social context, concentrating on the relationship between various buildings and their environment, as well as on their uses. See also garden city; new town.

Tuscan in Classical architecture, one of the five types of column; see *order*.

urban renewal the adaptation of existing buildings in towns and cities to meet changes in economic, social, and environmental requirements, rather than demolishing them.

vault arched ceiling or roof built mainly of stone or bricks.

vernacular the domestic or peasant building tradition of different localities, not designed by trained architects; for example, thatched cottages in England, stone in Scotland, adobe huts in Mexico, wooden buildings in the Nordic countries.

HISTORY OF WESTERN ART

In the visual arts of Western civilization, painting and sculpture have been the dominant forms for many centuries. This has not always been the case in other cultures. Islamic art, for example, is one of ornament, as artists were forbidden to portray living creatures. In some cultures masks, tattoos, pottery, and metalwork have been the main forms of visual art. In the recent past technology has made new art forms possible, such as photography and cinema, and today electronic media—computer graphics, computer-aided animation and 'painting', and other imaging techniques—have led to entirely new ways of creating and presenting visual images.

ANCIENT ART

prehistoric art 25,000–1000 BC. The history of the fine arts, painting and sculpture, begins about 21,000 BC in the Paleolithic, or Old Stone Age. Vivid, lifelike images of animals and humans have been found incised, painted or sculpted on the walls deep inside the caves where our ancestors sheltered, mostly in Spain and in southwestern France, but also in Portugal, Sicily, and Russia. The images of reindeer, mammoth, horses and bison are most common, varying from very small to almost lifesize. It is thought that they served as part of a 'magic' ritual to ensure a successful hunt. Paintings such as those at the caves of *Lascaux* in France show great skill in drawing, with vigorous and sweepingly graceful outlines. Stone Age people also used flint tools to carve small figurines in bone, horn, or stone. The most famous of these is the so-called *Venus of Willendorf*, a limestone statuette 11 cm/4.5 in high, found in lower Austria and dating from about 21,000 BC. Her exaggeratedly bulbous form makes clear her magic significance as a fertility figure.

art of early civilizations 14,000–300 BC. Architecture became the new art form when people began to settle in communities as farmers rather than as hunters. They decorated their buildings with sculpture, imposing a sense of pattern and order on them, although Stonehenge in Britain (1800–1400 BC) had not achieved this sophistication. In Europe, *Celtic art* ornamented tombs, crosses, metalwork and pottery with stylized animal and plant forms in swirling curvilinear patterns. Pottery had reached Europe from the Near East where it began as early as 5500 BC in Mesopotamia, where sign pictures also grew into cuneiform (wedge-shaped) writing. The Near and Middle East produced many highly developed urban civilizations, including the *Sumerian* (4000 BC), and the *Persian* (550 BC). In these cultures, sculptures and reliefs of people, gods, and animals decorated palaces, temples, and tombs telling stories or praising their gods and rulers. A fine example is the grand stairway of the *Persian royal palace*, Persepolis, from 518–516 BC. Outstanding examples of precious metalwork, glassware, and pottery also survive, of which there are splendid collections in the British Museum and the Louvre.

Egyptian art 3000–200 BC. The *Great Sphinx at Giza* (2680–2565 BC), a gigantic human-headed lion carved from an outcropping of natural rock, is the supreme example of Egyptian sculpture. 56 m/185 ft long and 19 m/63 ft high, it was meant to guard for eternity the god-king's pyramid tomb nearby. Most Egyptian art is funerary, largely consisting of sculptured relief panels painted in bright, lifelike colours covering the walls of tombs and temples. They depend on strong, simple outlines, the main aim being clarity: to portray the dead in their idealized prime, their servants and families, and the objects, animals, foods and activities they enjoyed in life, so that these could be magically transported into the afterworld to be enjoyed forever.

Human forms are composed almost diagrammatically to show the whole of a person, face and legs in profile, upper torso in front view, hips three-quarters and with the eye magnified. If anything needed further description a hieroglyphic label would be added. Statues, whether of wood or stone, were also generally painted. They retain a strong cubic sense of the block from which they were hewn, with the figures facing straight ahead, the arms in a single unit with the body. The serene vision of eternity found in all Egyptian art is epitomized in the beautiful portrait head of *Queen Nefertiti* in the Staatlich Museum, Berlin, dating from about 1360 BC.

art of Aegean civilizations 2800–100 BC. The *Minoan* and *Mycenean* civilizations flourished in the area of the Aegean Sea from about 2800 BC. Based on the island of Crete, Minoan society was pleasure-loving and open, and its major monument, the new *palace at Knossos* 1700 BC, was decorated with cheerful frescoes of scenes from daily life, plants, birds, and leaping fish and dolphins. Their pottery was painted in the same fresh, spontaneous style with plant and animal motifs curving to suit the form of the vases. In 1400 BC they were conquered by the Myceneans from the Peloponnese, whose art reflected their more warlike society. Instead of airy palaces, they constructed fortified citadels such as Mycenae itself, which was entered through the *Lion Gate* 1330 BC, named for the remarkable monumental sculpture that adorns it. In the nearby Cyclades Islands a unique art form emerged about 2800 BC: the small marble *Cycladic figures* much admired today, which represent the Great Mother Goddess in such streamlined simplicity that her face is simply an elongated oval with a triangular nose.

Many of the ideas and art forms of these early sea-faring civilizations were to be adapted by the Greeks who came from Central Asia between 2000–1000 BC to establish their own splendid culture that was to dominate Western taste and thought for many centuries.

CLASSICAL ART

Greek art 1000–400 BC. Greek temples are almost sculptures in themselves, designed not to be entered but to be looked at. The sculptured reliefs which decorated them, such as the *Elgin Marbles* (now in the British Museum) which came from the Parthenon in Athens, show perfectly the Greek artistic ideal: the human form at its most beautiful.

The major periods of Greek art can be divided into the Archaic (late 8th century–480 BC), Classical (480–323 BC), and Hellenistic (323–27 BC). No large-scale painting survives, although colour was very important, and even the white marble sculptures we admire today were originally brightly painted.

In the **Archaic** period the statues of naked standing men (*kouroi*) and draped females (*korai*) show an Egyptian influence in their rigid frontality. By about 500 BC the figure was allowed to relax its weight onto one leg and immediately seemed to come alive. The archaic smile which gave these early figures a certain cheerful sameness vanished in the **Classical** period when expressions assumed a dignified serenity. Further movement was introduced in new poses such as in Myron's bronze *Diskobolus/The Discus Thrower* 460–50 BC, and in the rhythmic Parthenon reliefs of men and horses supervised by Phidias. Artists were no longer anonymous and among sculptors whose work is known are **Praxiteles**, **Scopas**, **Lysippus**, and **Polykleitos**, whose *Doryphoros/The Spear Carrier* 450–440 BC was of such harmony and poise that it set a standard for beautiful proportions which is still in use today. Praxiteles introduced the female nude into the sculptural repertory with the graceful *Aphrodite of Knidos*, c. 350 BC. It was easier to express movement in bronze, hollow-cast by the lost wax method, but few bronze sculptures survive and many are known only through Roman copies in marble.

The **Hellenistic** period, when the Greek Empire under Alexander the Great spread to Egypt and beyond Iraq, produced such sculptures as the *Winged Victory of Samothrace* with its dramatic drapery, the expressive *Dying Gaul* and the tortured *Laocoon*, which explored the effects of movement and of deeply-felt emotion.

Vase painting is the one form of Greek painting which has survived the centuries. Good, even great, artists worked as both potters and painters until the 5th century BC and the works they signed were exported throughout the Empire. Made in several standard shapes and sizes, the pottery served as functional containers for wine, water, and oil. The first decoration took the form of simple lines and circles, from which the *'Geometric style'* emerged near Athens in the 10th century BC. It consisted of precisely drawn patterns, the most charac-

teristic being the key meander. Gradually the bands of decoration multiplied and the human figure, geometrically stylized, was added.

About 700 BC the potters of Corinth invented the **black figure** technique in which the unglazed red clay was painted in black with mythological scenes, gods and battles in a narrative frieze. About 530 BC Athenian potters reversed the process and developed the more sophisticated **red figure** pottery, which allowed for more detailed and elaborate painting of the figures in red against a black background. This grew increasingly naturalistic, with lively scenes of daily life. The finest examples date from the mid-6th century to mid-5th century BC at Athens. Later painters tried to follow major art trends and represent spatial depth, dissipating the unique quality of their fine linear technique.

The ancient Greeks excelled in carving gems and cameos, and in jewellery and metalwork. They also invented the pictorial mosaic and from the 5th century BC onwards floors were paved with coloured pebbles depicting mythological subjects. Later, specially cut cubes of stone and glass called *tesserae* were used, and Greek craftsmen working for the Romans reproduced famous paintings such as that of *Alexander at the Battle of Issus* from Pompeii, giving us some idea of these lost masterpieces.

Roman art 753 BC–AD 410. During the 8th century BC the Etruscans appeared as the first native Italian civilization, north and west of the river Tiber. Their art shows influences of archaic Greece and the Near East. Their coffins (*sarcophagi*), carved with reliefs and topped with portraits of the dead, reclining on one elbow as if at an eternal banquet, were to influence the later Romans and early Christians.

Under Julius Caesar's successor Augustus (27 BC–AD 14) the Roman Empire was established. Art and architecture played an important role in unifying the European nations under Roman rule. The Romans greatly admired Greek art and became the first collectors, importing vast quantities of marbles and bronzes, and even Greek craftsmen to make copies. Realistic portrait sculpture was an important original development by the Romans. A cult of heroes began and in public places official statues were erected of generals, rulers and philosophers. The portrait bust developed as a new art form from about 75 BC; these were serious, factual portraits of a rugged race of patriarchs to whose wisdom and authority their subject nations should reasonably submit.

Narrative relief sculpture also flourished in Rome, again linked to the need to commemorate publicly the glorious victories of their heroes. These appeared on monumental altars, triumphal arches and giant columns such as *Trajan's Column* AD 106–113 which records his historic battles like a strip cartoon, winding its way around the column for 200 m/656 ft. Strict realism in portraiture gave way to a certain amount of Greek-style idealization in the

TEN HIGHEST PRICES EVER PAID FOR WORKS OF ART AT AUCTION

Artist	Title of work	Auction house/date of sale	Auction price $m
Van Gogh	Portrait of Dr Gachet	Christie's, May 1990	82.5
Renoir	Au Moulin de la Galette	Sotheby's, May 1990	78.1
Van Gogh	Irises	Sotheby's, Nov 1987	53.9
Picasso	Les Noces de Pierette	Binoche et Godeau, Nov 1989	51.9
Picasso	Self portrait—Yo Picasso	Sotheby's, May 1989	47.8
Picasso	Au Lapine Agile	Sotheby's, Nov 1989	40.7
Van Gogh	Sunflowers	Christie's, Mar 1987	40.3
Picasso	Acrobate et Jeune Arlequin	Christie's, May 1989	38.9
Pontormo	Portrait of Duke Cosimo I de Medici	Christie's, Nov 1988	35.2
Manet	Rue Mosnier decorated with flags	Christie's, Nov 1989	26.4

Source: Cultural Trends 1990

propaganda statues of the emperors, befitting their semi-divine status. Gods and allegorical figures feature with Rome's heroes on such narrative relief sculptures as those on Augustus's giant altar to peace, the *Ara Pacis* 13–9 BC.

Very little **Roman painting** has survived, and much of what has is due to the volcanic eruption of Mount Vesuvius in AD 79 which buried the southern Italian seaside towns of Pompeii and Herculaneum under ash, thus preserving the lively and impressionistic wall paintings (frescoes) which decorated the holiday villas of an art-loving elite. Favourite motifs were illusionistic and still-life. A type of interior decoration known as *Grotesque*, rediscovered in Rome during the Renaissance, combined swirling plant motifs, strange animals and tiny fanciful scenes. Grotesque was much used in later decorative schemes whenever it was fashionable to quote the Classical period.

The art of *mosaic* was universally popular throughout the Roman Empire. It was introduced from Greece and used for floors as well as walls and vaults, in *trompe l'oeil* effects, geometric patterns and scenes from daily life and mythology.

MEDIEVAL ART

early Christian and Byzantine art AD 330–1453. In 312 the Emperor Constantine was converted to Christianity and made it one of the official religions of the Roman State. Churches were built, and artistic traditions adapted to the portrayal of the new Christian saints and symbols. Roman burial chests *(sarcophagi)* were adopted by the Christians and their imagery of pagan myths gradually changed into biblical themes.

Byzantine style developed in the East in Constantinople which in 330 became the headquarters of the Roman Empire, and an Eastern Christian tradition was maintained there until 1453 when Constantinople was conquered by the Turks. The use of mosaic came to be associated with both Byzantine art and early Christian church decoration in the West. Ravenna became the Western imperial capital in the 5th century, and the ecclesiastical buildings there, built in the 5th and 6th centuries, are a glorious tribute to the art of mosaic, presenting powerful religious images on walls and vaults in brilliant, glittering colour. Byzantine art moved away from the natural portrayal of people and became highly stylized, symbolizing the divine. Ornament became flattened into intricate lacework patterns. Oriental, highly decorative, and unchanging, the Byzantine style can be seen in the icons—often thought to be capable of working miracles—which have remained for centuries the main religious art of Greece and Russia.

art of the Dark Ages AD 400–800. The 400 years between the fall of the Roman Empire and the establishment of Charlemagne's new Holy Roman Empire in 800 are traditionally known as the Dark Ages, and the art of that period as belonging to the **Migration Period**. Through a time of turmoil and invasion, with the northern 'barbarians' overrunning the old Mediterranean civilizations, the Christian church maintained its stability and the interchange of artistic traditions fostered creativity.

The art of the migrant peoples consisted mainly of portable objects, articles of personal use or adornment. They excelled in metalwork and jewellery, often in gold with garnet or enamel inlays and ornamented with highly stylized, animal-based interlace patterns. This type of ornament was translated into manuscript illumination such as the decorated pages of the *Lindisfarne Gospel* (in the British Museum) which dates from the 7th century, or the 8th century *Book of Kells* (in Trinity College, Dublin). With Charlemagne's Christian Empire modelled on that of ancient Rome, a cultural renaissance ensued, drawing its inspiration from the late Classical artistic traditions of the early Christians. At Charlemagne's capital, Aachen, the human figure was reintroduced into art and continuous narrative was rediscovered in the *Tours Bibles* produced there. They in turn influenced the sculptured reliefs on the bronze doors at St Michael's Church, Hildesheim in Germany, dating from 1015, the first doors cast in one piece in the West since Roman times.

art of the Middle Ages AD 800–1300. Under the unifying force of the Latin Church, a new civilization spread across Europe which during the 10th century produced a style in art called **Romanesque**, and, in England, **Norman**. Chiefly evident in relief sculpture surrounding church portals, on capitals and corbels, it translated manuscript illuminations into stone, combining naturalistic elements from the antique Roman style with the fantastic, poetical, and pattern-loving Celtic and Germanic tradition. Imaginary beasts, monsters, saints, and sinners mingle with humour and innocence in an enchanted world of biblical themes. Fine examples remain in Burgundy and southwest France, extending down into Spain on the pilgrimage route to Santiago de Compostela.

Gothic during the late 12th and 13th centuries European cities began to raise great cathedrals, and sculptural decoration became more monumental. The cathedrals of Chartres and Reims in France had such extensive sculptural programmes that many artists came from far afield to work and learn there. A new interest in the natural world is shown in such examples as the strikingly life-like founder figures of Naumberg Cathedral, East Germany, (*c.* 1245) or in the naturalistic foliage on the capitals at Southwell in England.

With the increased height of the cathedrals, stained glass windows became their new glory. Chartres, where an entire set of stained glass is preserved, awesomely illustrates the magical effect of coloured light seemingly suspended within its dark interior. Both windows and sculpture, by depicting the lives of the saints and texts from the bible, gave the faithful an encyclopedic view of the Christian history of the world.

Art patronage, although still mainly concerned with religious imagery, now burgeoned in the many small courts of Europe and under this influence art became more stylized, delicate and refined. Even the Virgin Mary was portrayed as an elegant young queen. In her most characteristic pose, holding the Christ child in her arms, her weight shifts gracefully onto one hip causing her body to form an S-curve and her drapery to fall into elegant folds. This figure stance, the 'Gothic sway', became a hallmark of the period. Court patronage produced exquisite small ivories, precious goldsmith's work, devotional books illustrated with miniatures, and tapestries which warmed cold castle walls, depicting romantic tales or the joys of springtime.

In Italy, the monumentality of the antique Roman past subdued the spread of northern Gothic ideas. A type of *Gothic Classicism* was developed by the sculptors Nicola and Giovanni **Pisano** (working 1258–1314) whose four great pulpits carved in relief (at Siena, Pistoia, and two at Pisa) show the influence of antique sarcophagi but also that of French Gothic in the dramatic expressiveness of their figures.

An innovative group of painters brought the art of *fresco painting*, always important in Italy, to a new height. Giotto's cycle of the lives of Mary and Christ in the Arena Chapel, Padua (*c.* 1300) set a new standard for figural naturalism, seen as proto-Renaissance, and in the Town Hall of Siena Ambrogio **Lorenzetti**

illustrated the effects of *Good and Bad Government* (1337) in panoramic townscapes and landscapes.

Panel painting, in jewel-like colours on a gold background, developed from Byzantine models, and the Sienese painter **Duccio**'s *Maestá* for the High Altar of Siena Cathedral (1308–11) achieved a peak of expressive power of line and colour. Simone **Martini** developed this into courtly refinement in both frescoes (for example Assisi, Siena) and panel paintings, and became a major influence on the *International Gothic* style which in the years around 1400 achieved the perfect mix of French courtliness and the Italian command of form, together with a delight in the observed details of nature. A magnificent example of this moment in art can be seen in the miniatures painted for the devotional book, the *Très Riches Heures du Duc de Berry*, by the Flemish **Limbourg** brothers in about 1415.

THE ITALIAN RENAISSANCE

Florence the rebirth or 'Renaissance' of Classical art and learning began in Florence in the early 15th century. The self-made men of Florence, merchants and bankers, saw themselves as direct descendants of the great men of ancient Rome and, led by the Medici family, vied with each other in patronage of all the arts, building palaces and churches filled with sculptured and painted monuments to themselves. In this new age of humanism, people—and the aesthetic delights of the world they lived in—were suddenly important.

The most far-reaching artistic innovation of the period, which was one of continual discovery and rediscovery, was that of scientific *perspective* by Filippo **Brunelleschi** 1377–1446, the architect who later built the dome of Florence Cathedral. Perspective allowed artists to create an authentic three-dimensional space, correctly sized to the figures within their paintings. **Masaccio** 1401–28 used this new style to superb effect in his frescoes in the Brancacci Chapel, Santa Maria del Carmine, in which the apostles look like Roman gods. The sculptor **Donatello** *c.* 1386–1466 used perspective in his relief sculptures. His bronze statues like the youthful *David* 1430–2, the first free-standing nude since antiquity, or his equestrian statue of the mercenary General Gattamelata (Padua, 1443) look back to Classical prototypes but have the alert liveliness of all early Renaissance art. In his later work, such as his wood-carving of the aged Mary Magdalene 1445, he sought dramatic expression through distortion, even ugliness. His only real rival was the goldsmith and bronze sculptor Lorenzo **Ghiberti** 1378–1455, who only gradually adapted his graceful *International Gothic* style to Renaissance ideals in such works as the gilt-bronze Baptistery doors which Michelangelo called 'The Gates of Paradise'.

Paolo **Uccello**'s (1397–1475) decorative

WHEN IS A REMBRANDT NOT A REMBRANDT?

Thirteen years ago the catalogue of London's Wallace Collection listed six of its paintings as being by Rembrandt. Today it lays claim to only one, the *Portrait of the artist's son Titus*. What has befallen the collection is not a disastrous lapse in security but the eagle-eyed attention of the Rembrandt Research Project, a group of experts funded by the Dutch government to decide which of the hundreds of paintings ascribed to the master are actually from his hand. Five out of the six Wallace Rembrandts have simply been downgraded. Similar dramatic reattributions of works have occurred all over the world. In New York the Frick Collection possesses, in *The Polish Rider*, one of the most famous and best-loved of all Rembrandt's paintings. It too is heading for demotion—an opinion that, though as yet unpublished, has already caused great controversy and has met with much resistance.

Why is it so difficult to establish the authenticity of a work of art and why is it necessary to do so in the first place? In Rembrandt's case, some of the problems stem from his success as an artist and his subsequent success as an entrepreneur. Within a few years of setting up as an independent painter Rembrandt began to take on pupils and as his fame grew so did the number of young artists wishing to train under him. Part of their training included the copying, either of details or in full, of works by the master. (*The Good Samaritan* in the Wallace Collection is probably such a copy and is now ascribed to Govert Flinck who attended Rembrandt's workshop around 1633.)

Given that it was also common practice for the more advanced apprentices to assist the master in the creation of his own works, there are three categories of painting that Rembrandt could have put his name to: copies of his work, works in which he had assistance, and works entirely in his own hand—plenty of scope for confusion, both at the time and in the years to come.

The Rembrandt Research Project is the latest in a series of attempts to establish the true Rembrandt from the false. What distinguishes it from earlier efforts is that a committee of scholars, rather than just one scholar, now makes the decisions. Does this mean that its judgements are any more authoritative or are they simply more intimidating for those who disagree? The Project insists that its findings are not 'carved in granite' but so far their investigations have taken 23 years and have produced three closely argued volumes covering paintings up to the year 1642, less than halfway through Rembrandt's career.

At the start their method of analysis tried to be comprehensive: they examined the documentary, stylistic, material, and iconographic evidence in order to reach their conclusions. Where necessary science assisted them: tree rings were counted by the University of Hamburg; signatures scrutinized at the Dutch ministry of justice; threads of canvas counted to find out which bolt of material a canvas

The Good Samaritan *(Wallace Collection, London), previously attributed to Rembrandt, is now thought to be by Govert Flinck, one of his pupils.*

came from. All the paraphernalia of modern detection have been employed. And yet, increasingly, critics of the project suggest that it is style—an artist's unique 'handwriting'—that has become the dominant analytical tool. Ernst van de Wetering, the Project's leader, has reattributed *The Polish Rider* to Willem Drost entirely on stylistic grounds, arguing, among other things, that the figure is not substantial enough and the drapery too detailed for a Rembrandt of that period—valid enough reasons but still essentially vague and subjective.

Why has Rembrandt been singled out for such exhaustive analysis? Since the 19th century the myth surrounding him has grown, and he has come to be regarded as a universal genius whose humanity speaks to everybody—rivalled only by Shakespeare and Mozart. Ironically it is this special cultural status that fuels the scholarly machinery which now presents us with a new Rembrandt, no longer an isolated figure but at the centre of a large and complicated art business. The Rembrandt Research Project, by rejecting so much once thought to be by Rembrandt, has pushed into the spotlight several workshop artists, like Flinck and Drost, who have been too long in the shadows. *The Polish Rider* is no less great a painting for having a new artist ascribed to it. Museum directors may resort to counter-attacking the Project's findings with scholarly opinions of their own, and private owners of Rembrandts may quake at the thought of their property being drastically devalued, but the debate has encouraged both scholar and lay person to look more carefully at the work itself.

CONFESSIONS OF AN ART FORGER

Curators swooned and reputations collapsed when Eric Hebborn's autobiography was published in Nov 1991. The British artist revealed that he was the author of a thousand or so forgeries—mostly old-master drawings—many of which were handled by Christie's, Sotheby's, and Conalghi. Hebborn has claimed authorship of many works that appear in the world's greatest museums, including Van Dyck's *The Crowning with Thorns* in the British Museum and Jan Brueghel the Younger's *Temple of Venus and Diana at Baia* in New York's Metropolitan Museum.

A scholar at the Royal Academy Schools during the 1950s, Hebborn has spent 30 years forging away and taking pleasure in watching his products authenticated. He decided to come clean because no Hebborns were included in the British Museum's 1990 show 'Fake? The Art of Deception'—the artist was offended by the exclusion. Hebborn claims that his homage to the masters has been genuine and that 'there is no such thing as a fake drawing or painting, only drawings and paintings'.

Various interested parties have begun to question Hebborn's attribution of some works to himself. After all, how easily can one believe a character who confesses that he is an inveterate manipulator of the truth?

---

paintings reflect an obsessive interest in mathematical perspective. **Fra Angelico** *c.* 1400–55 used delicate colours and a simple style to express his religious feeling. Andrea **Del Castagno**'s style was fiercely linear. The antithesis of his violent suffering figures are Piero **della Francesca**'s strangely silent ones. Solidly rounded in pale light, immobile within perfect perspective spaces, they express an enigmatic timelessness. His mastery of geometry, proportion, form, and colour is breathtakingly evident in his frescoes of *The Legend of the True Cross* in San Francesco in Arezzo 1452–66.

Many sculptors produced public statues, grandiose tombs, Roman-style portrait busts and innumerable versions of the Madonna and Child. The Florentines enjoyed seeing themselves in religious paintings and they appear in crowd scenes in many magnificent frescoes in the churches of their city, such as those by Domenico del **Ghirlandaio**. He was the most popular painter in Florence in the latter part of the 15th century, respected for his honesty, which is epitomized in his portrait of *An Old Man with a Child c.* 1480 in the Louvre. His contemporaries included **Pollaiuolo**, whose interest centres on the nude in action; **Verrocchio**, famous for the equestrian statue of Bartolomeo Colleoni in Venice 1481–96; and **Botticelli** 1445–1510, whose poetic, gracefully linear paintings of Madonnas and mythological subjects such as *The Birth of Venus* 1482 show the Florentine ideal of female beauty. Almost every art work produced included some reference to antiquity, either in form or content.

Leonardo da Vinci 1452–1519. Through his genius, the art of the early 16th century became the *High Renaissance*, attaining a grandeur that appealed particularly to the popes, who now became the leading art patrons in their attempt to build the 'New Rome'. Leonardo's enquiring scientific mind led him to investigate every aspect of the natural world from anatomy to aerodynamics. His notebooks and drawings remain his finest legacy, but his experiments also revolutionized painting style. Instead of a white background, he used a dark one to allow the overlying colour a more three-dimensional existence. He invented 'aerial perspective' whereby the misty atmosphere (*sfumato*) blurs and changes the colours of the landscape as it dissolves into the distance. His principle of grouping figures within an imaginary pyramid, linked by their gestures and emotions, became a High Renaissance compositional rule. His *Madonna of the Rocks* (Louvre) exemplifies all these ideas.

Michelangelo Buonarroti 1475–1564. His giant talent dominated the High Renaissance and led his contemporaries to label him 'Divine'. No other artist could escape his influence. He said of his stone carvings, such as the monumental *David* in Florence (1501–4) that he was simply revealing the figure hidden within the block. His massive figure style was translated into paint in the *Sistine Chapel frescoes* (Vatican,

---

IN BROAD DAYLIGHT

In Dec 1991 a study for *The Death of Chatterton* by Henry Wallis was stolen from Birmingham Museum and Art Gallery, UK, by a man who was so blindingly obvious, and so blind drunk, that police could not understand how he got away with it. Unsteady on his feet, the man removed the painting from the gallery wall and put it under his coat. Although another visitor saw him and alerted security staff, the inebriated art thief managed to escape and make his getaway on a number 62 bus, where he offered to sell the art work for £200.

The oil painting, dating from the 1850s and worth £750,000, was part of a Pre-Raphaelite collection at the Birmingham Museum. Its theft from the building's public section was the first since it opened in 1885. Greatly embarrassed by the theft, museum officials admitted that a security man had not been at his post. The building had recently been fitted with electronic security devices costing several hundred thousand pounds, but designed chiefly to prevent night-time burglaries.

Following a tip-off, police recovered the painting from the loft of a house in Birmingham five days after its theft. It was returned to the museum in good condition and a man was later due to appear before magistrates.

Rome) covering the ceiling with human figures, mostly nude, all grandly Classical, telling the Old Testament story from Genesis to the Deluge (1508–11) and finishing on the altar wall with a titanic *Last Judgement* 1541.

Raphael (Raffaello Sanzio) 1483–1520. He quickly mastered the innovations of Leonardo and Michelangelo and in 1509 was commissioned to fresco the *Stanza della Segnature* in the Vatican, where his classicist *School of Athens* is his masterpiece. Immensely prolific and popular, he combined both delicacy and grandeur in his work.

Mannerism Giulio **Romano**, Raphael's principal follower, exaggerated his style into an individual one of his own, heralding the next major art movement, Mannerism. This flouted the 'rules' of Renaissance order and harmony by striving for idiosyncratic, sometimes alarming, effects. The Florentine Andrea **del Sarto** 1486–1531 and his assistants **Pontormo** and Rosso **Fiorentino** each pursued self-consciously mannered styles, as did Giorgio **Vasari**, who is chiefly remembered for his book *The Lives of the Most Excellent Architects, Painters and Sculptors* 1550, in which he coined the term 'Mannerist' and laid down the chronology of the history of art which is still in use today. Mannerism appealed particularly to courtly patrons and it became increasingly effete. The Medici, now grand dukes, employed such artists as the sculptor Benvenuto **Cellini** (1500–71), as famous for his racy autobiography as for the gilt salt cellar he made for the King of France; Agnolo **Bronzino**, whose patrician portraits display a stony hauteur; and Giovanni **Bologna**, whose elegant small bronze statuettes were widely reproduced.

Venice the Venetian Renaissance was slow in coming because of the city's traditional links with the East. Two non-Venetians were influential: Antonello **da Messina** (*c*. 1430–79), who in 1475 brought to Venice the new Flemish technique of oil painting, and Andrea **Mantegna** (*c*. 1431–1506), an archaeologically-minded painter whose figures looked like antique sculptures. Giovanni **Bellini** (*c*. 1430–1516) specialized in devotional pictures of the Madonna, but his sensitive appreciation of light and colour introduced that element of sensuality to Venetian talent which later made **Titian** (Tiziano Vecellio) (1487–1576) the preferred painter of Emperor Charles V and his son Philip II of Spain. His fellow-painter **Giorgione** (*c*. 1478–1510) died young, leaving only a few securely attributed works, but who nevertheless made an innovative mark with his small, intimate, easel paintings and a new treatment of figures in a landscape. **Veronese** (*c*. 1528–88) and Jacopo **Tintoretto** (1518–94) worked on a much larger scale, Veronese excelling in sumptuous *trompe l'oeil* interior decorations and Tintoretto in dramatic religious paintings, spectacularly lit and composed with daring foreshortening. His paintings for the Venetian Scuola di San Rocco 1566–88

foreshadow, in their exciting exuberance, the next major movement, the *Baroque*.

THE 15TH AND 16TH CENTURIES

Northern European artists took their inspiration from Gothic sources, but shared with the Italians an insatiable interest in realistic portrayals of themselves and their world.

Netherlands one of the first examples of the new *humanism* was the work of Claus **Sluter** (*c*. 1380–1406). His mourning figures on the tomb of Philip the Bold, Duke of Burgundy, their faces hidden by the hoods of their robes, are poignantly mute but solidly real people.

In Flanders where the patrons were wealthy merchants, Robert **Campin** (1378–1444) put his *Madonna and Child before a Firescreen* (1420–30, National Gallery, London) into an ordinary living room and through its open window showed a Flemish town. Mary's halo is replaced by the circular firescreen behind her, an example of disguised symbolism, making the supernatural seem real.

Among Campin's followers, all marvellous draughtsmen, was Jan **van Eyck** (d.1441) whose strength lay in his detailed analysis of the beauty of the world around him. His innovative recipe for oil painting makes his colours glow like precious jewels. In his *Arnolfini Wedding* (1434, National Gallery, London) the bride and groom appear in a domestic interior crammed with disguised symbols, in a kind of pictorial marriage certificate. Flemish realism reached Italy with the Portinari Altarpiece, an *Adoration of the Shepherds* by Hugo **van der Goes** (d. 1481). Commissioned by the Medici agent in Bruges, it was sent to Florence where it had a considerable effect on Italian artists. The quietly contemplative portraits of Hans **Memlinc** (d. 1481) sum up the achievement of 15th-century Netherlands painters.

Individual styles proliferated in the 16th century. Hieronymous **Bosch** (*c*. 1450–1516) painted nightmarish scenes filled with diminutive human figures caught in a surrealist demonic world. Pieter **Bruegel** the Elder (1525/30–69) treated biblical subjects as contemporary events, viewing with compassion a miserable humanity. In his paintings of the seasons 1565 he brilliantly evokes both winter's icy silence and the golden warmth of summer.

Germany the giant among German artists was Albrecht **Dürer** (1471–1528). His intellectual powers put him in line with the great Italian masters and their influence introduced a new solidity of form into his basically Gothic style. Particularly important as a graphic artist, he was widely influential through woodcuts and engravings. Mathias **Grünewald** (*c*. 1460–1528), a tragic visionary, used colour symbolically in the *Isenheim Altar* (1512–15, Colmar), painted for hospital patients to see the crucified Christ, covered with festering wounds, sharing their suffering. Lucas **Cranach** the Elder (1473–1538) painted self-conscious courtly nudes, and Albrecht **Altdorfer** (*c*.1489–1538) painted landscapes in which tiny human figures are dwarfed by nature's immensity.

Spain Philip II did not care for the work of **El Greco** (1541–1614), the painter who really established Spain as an artistic centre. Trained in Venice, and particularly influenced by Tintoretto, he developed his hallucinatory style in Toledo, where his patrons were ecclesiastics and the intelligentsia. In his *Burial of Count Orgaz* 1586 the flame-like figures and unearthly colours blend mystic vision and reality.

England Renaissance ideas arrived with the German Hans **Holbein** the Younger (1497–1543), who was by 1536 court painter to Henry VIII. His piercing portraits of the king and his wives, and his delicate portrait drawings, give a superb pictorial record of the Tudor court. The court of Elizabeth I comes to life for us through the art of the miniature. Nicholas **Hilliard** (*c.* 1547–1619) developed an unparalleled technique, delicate, refined and often lyrically poetic as in his *Young Man amid Roses* (*c.* 1590, Victoria and Albert Museum, London).

France Jean **Fouquet** (*c.* 1420–81) painted miniatures as well as altarpieces in which Italian influences take tangible shape. Jean **Clouet** (d. 1541) and his son François (d. 1572) were court painters to King Francis I. Jean's portrait of the king splendidly expresses the king's concern with elegance and decoration, and François' half-nude portrait of Diane de Poitiers, *The Lady in Her Bath*, is a piece of refined eroticism. His style reflects Italian Mannerist ideas as developed by the so-called *School of Fontainebleau* founded by Giovanni Battista **Rosso** (also called Rosso Fiorentino) and Francesco **Primaticcio** who came to decorate the royal hunting lodge in the 1530s. They devised a unique type of stucco decoration combining figures in high relief with decorative swags, cartouches and strapwork. These Mannerist motifs were copied all over northern Europe, where they were called 'Renaissance'.

THE 17TH CENTURY

Italy in Rome, the Counter-Reformation of the Catholic church against Protestantism launched an exciting, emotionally appealing new style, the *Baroque*. The sculptor and architect Gianlorenzo **Bernini** (1598–1680) was its principal exponent, revitalizing Rome with his exuberantly dramatic masterpieces. His *Ecstasy of St Teresa* at Santa Maria della Vittoria is a theatrical set-piece in which supernatural light pours from a hidden window to illuminate the rapturous saint, whose body seems to shudder as an angel prepares to pierce her heart with the arrow of divine love.

Large-scale illusionistic fresco painting transformed ceilings into heavens, thronged with flying saints and angels. A spectacular example is Pietro **da Cortona**'s colossal *Allegory of Divine Providence* 1629–37 in the Barberini Palace, glorifying the pope and his family.

Hundreds of figures are drawn upwards toward God's golden light, aswarm with bees, the Barberini family emblem.

Balancing this flamboyant artistic stream were the *Classicists*, who even in religious commissions looked back to the concepts of harmony and order of antiquity. Annibale **Carracci** (1560–1609) in the years around 1600 decorated Cardinal Farnese's gallery of antique sculpture in the Farnese Palace, turning the walls and ceiling into a *trompe l'oeil* classical picture gallery. He also introduced the landscape as a new category of art with his *Flight into Egypt* 1603, which has as its real subject an idealized vision of the classical Roman countryside, harmonious and calm.

Among Carracci's assistants who became famous in their own right were the consistently classicizing **Domenichino** (1581–1641) and Guido **Reni** (1575–1642) who often succumbed to popular taste with emotive paintings of repentant sinners rolling tearful eyes toward heaven.

The work of Michelangelo Merisi da **Caravaggio** (1573–1619) introduced something totally different and unique, a harsh realism in which ordinary folk with dirty feet appear as saints and apostles, lit by a raking spotlight as if God's piercing eye had picked them out from the surrounding blackness of sin. One of his most striking followers was Georges **de la Tour** (1593–1652), a French artist whose simplified figures assume a spiritual purity, modelled by God's light in the form of a single candle shining in the darkness.

France art was used to establish the splendour of Louis XIV's centralized authority and divine kingship. Although grandiose in the extreme, the decorative schemes, portraits, and history paintings produced by the members of the new artists' Academy (formed 1648) were based on Classical rules, rigidly controlled by Charles **Lebrun** (1619–90), who was appointed First Painter to the King in 1662. He was the first Director of the Academy and of the Gobelins Manufactory, which employed its members to produce the art, tapestries, and furnishings for Louis's new Palace of Versailles.

The two major French artists of the century lived in Rome, escaping the constricting grip of the Academy. Claude **Lorrain** (1600–82) was the first painter to specialize entirely in landscapes, reducing the story-telling elements to small foreground figures. The romantic suggestiveness of the Classical past appealed to him, and he created an enchanting idyllic world, luminous and poetic. The intellectual Nicolas **Poussin** (1594–1665) composed his classical landscapes with mathematical precision but his people remained important, noble and heroic. Not even his religious works escape the pervasive influence of antiquity. In his *Last Supper* (1647, Edinburgh) Christ and the disciples lounge on couches as if at a Roman banquet.

Spain as in Rome, art in Spain aimed to excite Counter-Reformation zeal. José **Ribera**

SELLING THE FAMILY SILVER?

In 1991 a remarkable piece of furniture, the Badminton cabinet, left the shores of Britain where it had been since 1732, for a new home in the USA. It left, even though expert opinion regarded it as an outstanding, unique piece—the finest of the Baroque cabinets from the Medici workshops in Florence. It left, despite an appeal by the National Art Collections Fund which only managed to raise about a third of the £8.7 million that Barbara Johnson, baby-powder heiress, had paid for it.

Was it such a loss? If funds could not be raised to save it, did not that indicate a lack of sufficient public interest? Arguments at the time suggested that individual generosity should not be responsible for preserving the national heritage and that the government had failed in its duties as well as its commitments in letting the cabinet go. Criticism was particularly strong since an export licence had just permitted the departure of Antonio Canova's *The Three Graces* (though in the end the sculpture finished up in storage where it still languishes).

There are provisions to prevent the export of culturally significant objects following their sale. All archaeological items need an export licence but for anything else this depends on its age and on its value. If an expert in the public services wishes to challenge the granting of a licence, then a body of independent experts will review the case. A decision is made by reference to the Waverley criteria: is the object of outstanding artistic merit; is it of great importance to the study of its subject, or of great importance to the history of the nation? If the answer to any of these is 'yes' then the licence can be withheld, usually for six months, to allow a public institution or an individual to purchase the object at the sale price. All public museums and galleries have had their purchasing grants frozen since the mid 1980s and so must rely on financial back-up from such bodies as the government-funded National Heritage Memorial Fund or the charitable National Art Collections Fund. Even with such help many irreplaceable objects have got away over the years.

What once seemed an efficient and flexible system has gradually fallen into disrepute. Criticism has also been directed at the original owners of important art works and at those who advise them to sell on the open market. Selling at auction may seem an attractive prospect but there are hidden costs: the auction house's 10% commission; the possible fee for the negotiating agent; and, biggest by far, the capital gains tax to be paid after sale. All this can reduce profits by up to 70%. Then there is the delay to the whole procedure if an export licence is not granted straight away. By making a deal with a public institution—a private treaty sale—prospective owners can cut out the middlemen, reduce tax costs, and even increase their profits as well as their public status.

The system's recent spectacular failures have fuelled rumours that the government is planning to draw up a list of outstanding works of art that would be prevented from ever leaving the country. A similar list operates in France and Germany. Ironically, if the government had been prepared to use emergency funds in order to retain exceptional pieces, such a list would not be necessary. The rumoured list has apparently caused consternation among those aristocrats who still possess significant works of art, to the extent that several have rushed to the sale room.

At the beginning of 1992 Christie's organized an old-master sale which was to include three outstanding paintings. Rembrandt's *Daniel and Cyrus before the Idol of Bel* was from the collection of the Earl of St Germans, Canaletto's *The Old Horse Guards, London, from St James's Park* belonged to Lord Malmesbury, and Holbein's *Portrait of a Lady with a Squirrel* was put up for sale by the Marquis of Cholmondeley. In the end the outcome was rather more satisfactory for the nation than for the auction house. After much adverse publicity Lord Cholmondeley withdrew his picture and sold it privately to the National Gallery; the Rembrandt failed to reach its reserve and remained unsold; while the Canaletto was bought for £10.12 million by Andrew Lloyd Webber who immediately lent it to the Tate Gallery (who had tried to buy it earlier) for an indefinite period. A happy ending this time, but clearly a review of the export procedures is long overdue.

(1591–1652) carried a Caravaggesque style to brutal extremes to shock people into identifying with the sufferings inherent in Christian history. Francisco **Zurbarán** (1598–1664) expressed religious feeling in the opposite way, with solemn, silent monks and saints lost in a private world of meditation. Bartolomé Esteban **Murillo** (1617–82) painted sentimental *Holy Families* and sugar-sweet *Madonnas* fluently, cheerfully, and with a feather-light touch and lovely colours.

Diego Rodriguez de Silva **Velazquez** (1599–1660) was the giant of Spanish painting, reflecting many aspects of the 17th-century Spanish world. By 1623 he was court painter to Philip IV in Madrid, where he was influenced by Philip's collection of 16th century Venetian paintings. The most fascinating of his lifelike portraits of the Spanish court is *Las Meninas/The Ladies-in-Waiting* 1655 (Prado, Madrid), a complex group portrait which includes Velazquez himself at his easel, and the king and queen as pale reflections in a mirror.

Netherlands Peter-Paul **Rubens** (1577–1640)

brought the sensual exuberance of the Italian Baroque to the Netherlands. A many-sided genius, artist, scholar and diplomat, he used his powerful pictorial imagination to create, with an army of assistants, innumerable religious and allegorical paintings for the churches and palaces of Catholic Europe. His largest commission was the cycle of 21 enormous canvases allegorizing the life of Marie de Medici, Queen of France (Louvre, Paris). His sheer delight in life can be seen in his magnificent colours, opulent nudes, and expansive landscapes.

Rubens' Grand Baroque style did not suit the Protestant merchants of the new Dutch Republic, who wanted small paintings reflecting their own lives and interests. Among the artists who responded to this demand, the towering genius was **Rembrandt** van Rijn (1606–69), all of whose paintings hint at some inner drama. In his portraits and biblical scenes he saw light as a spiritual mystery which momentarily allows his characters to loom out of the surrounding shadows. His self-portraits (nearly 100 in number) touchingly trace the drama of his own passage through life and even the large group portrait, *The Night Watch* 1642, becomes a suspense story. A master draughtsman and printmaker, over 1,000 of his drawings survive.

The greatest of the straightforward portraitists was Frans **Hals**, whose free brushstrokes caught fleeting moments brilliantly in such paintings as the so-called *Laughing Cavalier* 1624 (Wallace Collection, London).

Genre pictures, scenes of daily life, merrymakers and peasants—often uncouth, comic, or satirical—were the speciality of such painters as Jan **Steen** (1626–79), in whose anecdotal scenes of traditional festivals or slovenly households the pleasures of drink, gluttony, and wantonness hold sway.

During the 1650s genre painters took a different view of their society. Instead of depicting boisterous low-life, painters like Pieter de **Hooch** (1629–84) chose scenes of domestic virtue, well-ordered households where families live in harmony in quiet sunlit rooms. Jan **Vermeer** (1632–75) was the greatest master of these scenes of peaceful prosperity, arranging domestic interiors as if they were abstract forms and enclosing his characters within an enamelled world of pearly light. *A Young Woman Standing at a Virginal* (National Gallery, London) is a superb example of the small group of paintings he produced, each one a masterpiece.

The Dutch specialities of seascape and landscape made giant strides during the century, based on low horizons with emphasis on a great expanse of sky. Experts in this were Aelbert **Cuyp** (1620–91) who bathed his views in a golden light, and Jacob van **Ruisdael** (1638/9–1709), who painted in many moods, responding to the shifting patterns of light and shade in nature.

Still-life painting also burgeoned: fruit, flowers, fish, banquets, breakfasts, groaning boards of every kind, in which the artist displayed skill in painting inanimate objects, often with a hidden religious significance.

England Charles I had employed Rubens to paint the ceiling of the Banqueting House at Whitehall 1629–30. Rubens's assistant Anthony **van Dyck** became Court Painter in 1632 and created magnificent portraits of the aristocracy, cool and elegant in shimmering silks. The German Peter **Lely** succeeded him under the Restoration to depict a society that exudes an air of well-fed decadence. By contrast, the English-born Samuel **Cooper** (1609–72), painter to the Parliamentarians and most famous for his portraits of Oliver Cromwell ('warts and all'), was a miniaturist whose serious, objective portraits raised the status of his art to that of oil painting.

THE 18TH CENTURY

France the beginning of the 18th century saw the start of a frivolous new style in art, the *Rococo*. Jean-Antoine **Watteau** (1684–1721) devised for his aristocratic patrons the *Fête Gallante*, a type of painting in which amorous couples in poetic landscapes contemplate the transience of life and love.

The more overtly sensual work of François **Boucher** (1703–70), First Painter to Louis XV, included voluptuous scenes of naked gods and goddesses. Painting at the same time, but completely against the mainstream, was Jean-Baptiste-Siméon **Chardin** (1699–1779), whose still-lifes and genre scenes have a masterful dignity. Jean-Honoré **Fragonard** (1732–1806) continued with the Rococo theme under Louis XVI, light-heartedly reflecting the licentiousness of courtly life. But all this changed with the Revolution and in 1789 Neo-Classicism became the dominant style under the Republic. Its artistic dictator, Jacques-Louis **David** (1748–1825) in his *Death of Marat* turned a political murder into a classical tragedy. Later, under Napoleon's Empire, David painted heroic portraits and scenes celebrating its glory.

Italy Antonio **Canova** (1757–1822), the sculptor, also exalted Napoleon and his family in classicizing portraits, and the vogue for this style dominated most English and European sculpture right through the Victorian era. Rococo illusionistic fresco-painting in Italy was the special province of Giovanni-Battista **Tiepolo** (1696–1770), a Venetian who decorated palaces and churches there and elsewhere in Europe. His painted ceilings became vast, airy regions whose delicate colour shadings made the sky seem endless.

The *vedutisti* (view-painters) produced souvenir views for young English gentlemen making the Grand Tour to complete their education with first-hand viewing of Renaissance and Classical art. In Venice, Francesco **Guardi** (1712–93) painted atmospheric visions of the floating city, pulsating with life. The views of (Giovanni) Antonio **Canaletto** (1697–1768),

Major Western Artists

period	painters	sculptors
classical		Myron 5th century BC
		Phidias 5th century BC
		Polykleitos 5th century BC
		Praxiteles 4th century BC
		Lysippus 4th century BC
medieval	Limbourg brothers early 15th century	Nicola and Giovanni Pisano working c. 1258–1314
	Duccio c. 1255/60–c. 1318	Claus Sluter c. 1380–1406
	Giotto c. 1266–1337	
	Lorenzetti 1306–1345	
Italian Renaissance	Masaccio 1401–1428	Ghiberti 1378– 1455
	Leonardo da Vinci 1425–1519	Donatello 1386–1466
	Bellini c. 1430–1516	Michaelangelo 1475–1564
	Mantegna c. 1431–1506	
	Raphael 1483–1520	
	Titian 1487–1576	
Mannerism	Rosso Fiorentino 1494–1540	Cellini 1500–1571
	Pontormo 1494–1556	Giambologna 1529–1608
	Giulio Romano 1499–1546	
	Bronzino 1503–1572	
	Vasari 1511–1574	
15th and 16th centuries outside Italy	van Eyck died 1441	
	Bosch 1450–1516	
	Dürer 1471–1528	
	Brueghel 1525/30–1569	
	Holbein 1497–1543	
	El Greco 1541–1614	
17th century	Carracci 1560–1609	Bernini 1598–1680
	Caravaggio 1573–1619	
	Rubens 1577–1640	
	Poussin 1594–1665	
	Velázquez 1599–1660	
	Claude 1600–1682	
	Rembrandt 1606–1669	
18th century	Watteau 1684–1721	Canova 1757–1822
	Tiepolo 1696–1770	
	Gainsborough 1727–1788	
	Goya 1746–1828	
	David 1748–1825	
19th century	Friedrich 1774–1840	Rodin 1840–1917
	Turner 1775–1851	
	Ingres 1780–1867	
	Delacroix 1798–1863	
	Courbet 1819–1877	
	Manet 1832–1883	
	Monet 1840–1926	
	Cézanne 1839–1906	
	van Gogh 1853–1890	
20th century	Kandinsky 1866–1944	Brancusi 1876–1957
	Matisse 1869–1954	Giacometti 1901–1966
	Mondrian 1872–1944	Moore 1898–1986
	Picasso 1881–1973	Smith, David 1906–1965
	Malevich 1878–1935	Hepworth 1903–1975
	Duchamp 1887–1968	Calder, Alexander 1898–1976
	Pollock 1912–1956	Gabo 1890–1977
	Warhol 1928–1987	
	Bacon 1910–1992	
	Braque 1882–1963	
	Klee 1879–1940	
	Rothko 1903–1970	

though faithfully observed, are static in comparison.

In Rome, Giovanni Battista **Piranesi** (1720–78) produced etchings inspired by his feelings for the evocative quality of ruins. His most original work, however, was a series which turned the ruins into images of terrifying imaginary prisons, fantasies of architectural madness.

Spain produced one artist of enormous talent and versatility, Francisco de **Goya** y Lucientes (1746–1828), whose work expresses a wide range of feeling and emotion and explores a variety of themes. Court Painter to Charles IV and later to Joseph Bonaparte under the French occupation of Spain, his portraits were acutely perceptive, his war scenes savagely dramatic, his religious paintings believable and his strange late fantasies powerfully imaginative. He is often seen as the source of 20th century art.

England produced a memorable group of fine artists, each expressing the varied interests of the age. Joseph **Wright** of Derby (1734–97), scientifically-minded, painted such scenes as *Experiment with an Air Pump* 1768. George **Stubbs** (1724–1806) specialized in horse paintings, based on painstaking scientific investigation. Joshua **Reynolds** (1723–92), first President of the Royal Academy (founded 1768) wanted to introduce the European Grand Manner into English painting with history paintings on exalted themes of heroism, but the demand was for portraits; his were confident but lacking in spontaneity, based more on theory than on inspiration.

Thomas **Gainsborough** (1727–88) was also a popular portraitist, although he would have preferred to paint landscapes and made much of them in the backgrounds of his pictures. William **Hogarth** (1697–1764) is best known through engravings of his satirical series of paintings, such as *The Rake's Progress*.

Reacting against the academic theorizing of Reynolds, the poet William **Blake** (1757–1827) illustrated his writings with mystical visions, and the imaginative Henry **Fuseli** (1741–1825) plumbed the depths of his subconscious for grotesque and fantastic dream images in such paintings as *The Nightmare*.

THE 19TH CENTURY

France vast historical, religious, and mythological pictures were no longer greatly in demand, and after the fall of Napoleon in 1814 French artists trained in the Academic Grand Manner had to seek new dramatic themes. They looked to the world around them; Theodore **Géricault** (1791–1824) found his subject in the gruesome sufferings of the survivors of a recent shipwreck, which he portrayed in his huge *Raft of the Medusa* (1816, Louvre, Paris). His desire to express and evoke emotion put Géricault among the *Romantics*, whose art sought to speak passionately to the heart in contrast to the *Classicists* who appealed to the intellect. These two opposing approaches dominated much of the art of the century.

Eugène **Delacroix** (1798–1863) became the best-known Romantic painter. His *Massacre of Chios* (1824, Louvre) shows Greeks enslaved by wild Turkish horsemen, a contemporary atrocity. Admired as a colourist, he used a technique of divided brushwork—adjacent brush marks of contrasting colour which the eye mixes as it scans—that anticipates the Impressionists. He learned this from seeing Constable's *Hay Wain* when it was exhibited in Paris in 1824.

By contrast, the brushwork is invisible in the enamelled paintings of Jean-Auguste-Dominique **Ingres** (1780–1867), the leading exponent of French Neo-Classicism. Drawing was the foundation of his style, emphasizing line and control at the expense of colour and expression.

Gustave **Courbet** (1819–77), reacting against both Classicists and Romantics, set out to establish a new *Realism*, based solely on direct observation of the things around him. His *Burial at Ornans* 1850 showed ordinary working people gathered round a village grave, and shocked the Establishment art world with its 'vulgarity' and 'coarseness'. Another Realist was Honoré **Daumier** (1808–79) whose lithographs of the 1830s dissected Parisian society with a surgeon's scalpel.

Throughout Europe, 19th-century artists found their ideal subject matter in the landscape. In France, Jean-Baptiste-Camille **Corot** (1796–1875) made it acceptable by recomposing his open-air studies into a harmonious, classical whole, although a romantic mood pervades his later misty confections. Theodore **Rousseau** (1812–67) led a group of artists who in 1844 sought refuge from the Industrial Revolution in the woods of Barbizon near Paris. Their close observation of nature produced a new awareness of its changing moods. Jean-François **Millet** (1814–75) also settled at Barbizon but his romantic landscapes, such as *The Angelus* (1857–9, Louvre), introduce idealized peasants who manage to commune with nature while toiling to wrest from it their daily bread.

Germany a different, more melancholy Romantic sensibility invaded the landscapes of a small group of painters working in Germany. Seeking to express the mystery of God in nature and people's oneness with it, the evocative paintings of Caspar David **Friedrich** (1774–1840) usually include a small poetic figure contemplating distant mountain peaks or moonlit seashores.

England the two greatest artists of the century were landscapists—Joseph Mallord William **Turner** (1775–1851) and John **Constable** (1776–1837), both finding inspiration in the thriving English watercolour school. Turner was the master painter of English Romanticism. Not concerned with the human figure, it was always through nature itself that he could express human feeling, as in the poignant last voyage of the ship *The Fighting Téméraire*

(1839, Tate Gallery, London). His increasing obsession with light and its deep emotional significance turned his late pictures into misty abstract visions. Reputedly his dying words were 'The sun is God'.

Constable too was fascinated with the effects of light. He made innumerable painted sketches of the changing windy sky and in his *Hay Wain* of 1821 used white marks like snowflakes to express the way light gave the landscape its freshness and sparkle.

Although primarily interested in romantic literary or biblical themes, the **Pre-Raphaelites** led by Dante Gabriel **Rossetti** (1828–82) in the 1840s and 1850s took a detailed look at nature, in their claim to a realistic vision; from this influence the medievalist designer-artist William **Morris** (1834–96) developed his stylized patterns of leaves and flowers for fabrics and wallpapers.

The opposition to the Pre-Raphaelites was led by two Establishment artists, Frederic, Lord **Leighton** (1830–96) and Lawrence **Alma-Tadema** (1836–1912), whose equally romantic view pretended to Classicism by centring on pseudo-genre scenes of daily life in ancient Greece and Rome. This pleased their educated patrons enough to earn knighthoods for them both.

Impressionism in the second half of the century France took an innovative look at nature. A direct precursor was Edouard **Manet** (1832–83), who carried on Courbet's scientific spirit of realism, making the eye the sole judge of reality. Stylistically, he gave up modelling forms in volume in favour of *suggesting* them by juxtaposed colours and gradations of tones, and, like Courbet, the subject matter of his pictures was always modern life. His *Déjeuner sur l'herbe/Luncheon on the Grass* (Louvre) updated a Renaissance prototype to 1862.

The Impressionists delighted in painting real life but the scenes and objects they painted became increasingly less important than the way they were affected by the ever-changing play of light. Evolving in the 1860s, the Impressionist group painted out of doors, capturing the immediacy and freshness of light on rippling water or on moving leaves. To catch these fleeting moments they broke up the forms they painted into fragments of pure colour laid side by side directly on the canvas, rather than mixing them on a palette. The members of the group were Alfred **Sisley** (1839–99), Camille **Pissarro** (1831–1903), Clau le **Monet** (1840–1926) whose *Impression, sunrise* of 1872 (Musée Marmottan, Paris) gave the movement its name, Pierre-Auguste **Renoir** (1841–1919), and Edgar **Degas** (1834–1917). By the late 1870s they had each gone on to pursue individual interests, and the acceptance of a common purpose had had its day. Sisley and Pissarro continued painting landscapes, but Renoir became more interested in the female nude and Degas in 'snapshot' studies of dancers and jockeys. Degas hardly ever painted landscapes but instead concentrated on the spectacle of the racetrack and the ballet in oddly angled compositions influenced by snapshot photography. Monet remained obsessed with the optical effects of light on colour and carried his original fragmented technique to the final extreme in series of paintings such as those of the façade of Rouen Cathedral 1894 or his famous water lilies, showing the changing colour effects at different times of day. With these variations on a theme the actual subject did not matter at all, and in this he anticipated the abstract art of the 20th century.

Post-Impressionism other artists of the same generation who used the innovations of the Impressionists as a basis for developing their own styles are called the Post-Impressionists. They include Paul **Cézanne** (1839–1906), who infused something more permanent into their spontaneous vision by using geometrical shapes to form a solid scaffolding for his pictorial compositions; and Georges **Seurat** (1859–91), who achieved greater structure in his landscapes through the technique of *pointillism* (also known as Neo-Impressionism) which turns the Impressionist's separate brush-strokes into minute points of pure colour. The eye then mixes these for itself. Green grass, for instance, is made up of closely packed points of blue and yellow. In this painstaking method any idea of spontaneity vanishes, and the effect is stable and serene.

Henri de **Toulouse-Lautrec** (1864–1901) portrayed the low-life of Parisian bars and music halls without sentiment or judgement. Like Degas, he recorded contemporary life in informal poses from odd angles and his bold, colourful posters show the influence of Japanese colour prints.

The great Dutch individualist Vincent **van Gogh** (1853–90) longed to give visible form to every emotion and used violent rhythmic brushwork and brilliant unnatural colours to express his inner passions, even in something as simple as a pot of sunflowers. Paul **Gauguin** (1848–1903) also went beyond the Impressionists' notion of reality, seeking a more direct experience of life in the magical rites of so-called primitive peoples in his colourful works from the South Seas.

Symbolism was a movement initiated by poets as a reaction to materialist values, and their 1886 Manifesto sought to re-establish the imagination in art. Their most admired painter was Gustave **Moreau** (1826–98) whose paintings of biblical and mythological subjects contain psychological overtones expressed through exotic settings, strange colours and eerie light. Odilon **Redon** (1840–1916) translated dreams into bizarre and striking visual images. In the paintings of the Norwegian Edvard **Munch** (1863–1944), a particularly northern sense of fear and alienation is given extreme expression in such paintings as *The Scream* (1893).

The Nabis (from Hebrew 'prophet') were followers of Gauguin who used simple forms and flat colours as he did for emotional effect, in a new style called *synthetisme*. Among the Nabis, Pierre **Bonnard** (1867–1947) and Edouard **Vuillard** (1868–1940) were less concerned with mystical ideas and found that with contemporary domestic interiors they could develop their interest in sumptuously coloured and patterned surfaces. Their work was dubbed *intimisme*.

sculpture the work of the Parisian Auguste **Rodin** (1840–1917) shows an extraordinary technical facility and a deep understanding of the human form. A romantic realist who infused his forms with passion, such famous sculptures as *The Thinker* and *The Kiss* were originally designed for a never-completed giant set of bronze doors, *The Gates of Hell*, with themes taken from Dante's *Divine Comedy*. The Musée Rodin in Paris houses many examples of his work and their preparatory drawings.

THE 20TH CENTURY

The 20th century has been an age of experimentation, with the boundaries of art being continually stretched by a succession of avant-garde movements. The anti-naturalism of the Symbolists and the Post-Impressionists, which attempted to reveal the essential reality behind the mere appearance of things, was continued in the first decade by Picasso, Matisse, and other artists before finally developing into complete abstraction.

Fauvism, a short-lived movement, began in France around 1905 and ended just three years later. The painters were nicknamed *Les Fauves* ('wild beasts') because of the extreme brilliance of the colours, which were often applied in jarring combinations to heighten the emotional impact. Henri **Matisse** (1869–1954), the major figure of the movement, spent his life refining this expressive use of pure colour partially influenced by the pattern-making of North African decorative art. André **Derain** (1880–1954) at this time enlarged the brushstrokes of Neo-Impressionism to produce a vibrant mosaic of colour, whereas Maurice **de Vlaminck** (1876–1958) was more influenced by the violent intensity of van Gogh. Georges **Rouault** (1871–1958), though associated with the group, employed more sombre colours enclosed by thick dark outlines reminiscent of stained glass.

Cubism was invented by Pablo **Picasso** (1881–1973) and the former Fauvist Georges **Braque** (1882–1963).

By fragmenting the objects they depicted, then reconstructing them as a series of almost geometric facets that overlap and interlock with each other, they attempted to explode the harmonious and unified perspective of the Renaissance. In its place is an image of multiple viewpoints seen simultaneously. Initially the work grew out of Picasso's fascination with African sculpture as in his *Les Demoiselles d'Avignon* (1907, Museum of Modern Art, New York). The influence of Cézanne can also be found in the simplification of forms and the

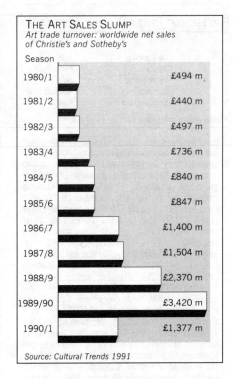

THE ART SALES SLUMP
Art trade turnover: worldwide net sales of Christie's and Sotheby's

Season	
1980/1	£494 m
1981/2	£440 m
1982/3	£497 m
1983/4	£736 m
1984/5	£840 m
1985/6	£847 m
1986/7	£1,400 m
1987/8	£1,504 m
1988/9	£2,370 m
1989/90	£3,420 m
1990/1	£1,377 m

Source: Cultural Trends 1991

ambiguity of the picture space. Emotion and narrative were avoided, colours were muted, and anti-illusionistic devices such as stencilled writing and collage were introduced. The two artists worked closely together from 1907 to 1914 but neither believed in theorizing about their work. This was done by later followers Juan Gris, Albert Gleizes, Jean Metzinger, Fernand Léger, and Robert **Delaunay**, the last named forming his own, more sensual and poetic variant of Cubism known as *Orphism*.

Futurism The Italian poet Filippo **Marinetti** (1876–1944) published the *Futurist Manifesto* in 1909, which demanded a new art to celebrate the age of the machine. He called for the destruction of the museums and eulogized the modern world and the 'beauty of speed and energy'. The most talented of the artists inspired by his ideas was the painter and sculptor Umberto **Boccioni** (1882–1916), who wrote his own *Technical Manifesto of Painting* the following year. But it was not until a trip to Paris and contact with Cubism that the Futurist artists managed to create a sufficiently dynamic style to match their rhetoric. Giacomo **Balla** (1871–1958) produced the painting *Dog on a Leash* which attempted to convey sequential movement in the manner of the photographers Muybridge and Marey. Gino **Severini** painted a topsy-turvy landscape as if seen from the moving window of a *Suburban Train Arriving at Paris* 1915 (Tate Gallery, London). Boccioni's sculpture *Unique Forms of Continuity in Space* 1913 (Tate Gallery) shows

FIVE HIGHEST PRICES PAID FOR WORKS BY LIVING ARTISTS AT AUCTION (1988-90)

	Artist	Title of work	Auction house/Year of sale	Auction price $m
1	de Kooning	Interchange*	Sotheby's, 1989	20.68
2	Johns	False Start	Sotheby's, 1988	17.05
3	de Kooning	July	Christie's, 1990	8.8
4	Lichtenstein	Torpedo Los!	Christie's, 1990	6.8
5	Lichtenstein	Kiss II	Christie's, 1990	6.05

* holds record price for a work by a living artist.

the dynamic interaction between a striding figure and its surrounding space.

Expressionism Germany was the scene of two successive Expressionist groups. In 1905 a group of artists in Dresden, with obvious parallels to the Fauves, founded *Die Brücke* ('the bridge'). Led by Ernst Ludwig **Kirchner** (1880–1938), they sought to express their 'inner convictions ... with spontaneity and sincerity'. This raw subjectivity is best seen in Kirchner's vivid scenes of the Berlin streets and in the prints of Karl **Schmidt-Rotluff** (1884–1976). The woodcut was a favourite medium of the group because of its primitive simplicity. In Munich *Der Blaue Reiter* ('the blue rider') group was set up in 1911 by Wassily **Kandinsky** (1866–1944). Influenced by the spiritual ideas of the Theosophists, Kandinsky believed that precise emotional and spiritual ideas could be conveyed by form and colour. He evolved a highly subjective style which finally became purely abstract. His colleague Franc **Marc** (1880–1916), partially inspired by Orphism, produced pantheistic celebrations of nature in which animals, particularly horses, dominate.

Suprematism After working in a manner that fused Cubism and Futurism with Russian folk styles, Kasimir **Malevich** (1878–1935) developed an abstract language of simple geometrical forms which he called Suprematism. In 1913, he painted a black square on a white ground as a rejection of 'ordinary objective life'. A white square on a white ground represented the ultimate in spiritual enlightenment, uniting the viewer with the infinite.

Constructivism was another Russian movement that also employed a nonobjective visual language, but in the service of the Revolution rather than the spiritual. *Beat the Whites with the Red Wedge* 1919 by **El Lissitsky** (1890–1941) (a student of Malevich) has an easily understandable and overtly political message. Vladimir **Tatlin** (1885–1953) designed a *Monument to the Third International* as a vast, skeletal, rotating tower, symbolic of technical endeavour and aspiration – it was never built. Naum **Gabo** (1890–1977) was less political than Tatlin but as important in pioneering the new 'constructed' architectural sculpture that employed materials like plastic to reveal the structural logic of the form. Stalin denounced these artists as bourgeois formalists and instead favoured a highly academic, official style known as Socialist Realism.

Neo-Plasticism Dutch painter Piet **Mondrian** (1872–1944), like Malevich, tried to express the 'truths of the universe' through pure aesthetics. Using primary colours, black, white, and grey, he painted parallel horizontal lines that intersected vertical ones. The perfection described by the parallel lines, the right-angle intersections, and the rectangles of pure colour were meant to mirror the ultimate perfection of the universe. In 1917 he headed a group called *De Stijl* ('the style') which included Theo **van Doesburg** (1883–1931) and the furniture designer Gerrit **Rietveld** (1888–1964). Like the Constructivists, with whom they had links, they believed in the artist as 'designer' with responsibilities to enhance every aspect of modern life by their work.

Many of the ideas of these seemingly disparate Modern groups were propagated at the *Bauhaus*, an influential German school of art and design, where several major artists, including Kandinsky, taught.

Dada, so called for its infantile associations, was considerably less positive and utopian in its aims. Born at the Cabaret Voltaire, Zürich, Switzerland, in 1916, it was an anarchic series of gestures that aimed to shock by undermining the sanctity of art with all its rules and values. Tristan **Tzara** 'created' poems by tearing out words from newspapers, then drawing them out of a hat. Similarly, Hans **Arp** (1887–1966) made collages by randomly dropping pieces of paper, then fixing them where they landed. Chance was more valid than choice. At the same time in New York, Marcel **Duchamp** (1887–1968) exhibited 'ready-made' art works: a snow shovel bought in a hardware store, a bicycle wheel mounted on a stool, a urinal.

Surrealism succeeded Dada. In 1922 the French writer André **Breton** made it a coherent and organized group, precisely what Dada rejected. Freud's investigations into the unconscious were an inspiration, as were the strange empty townscapes of the Italian painter Giorgio **de Chirico** (1888–1978). Some Surrealist artists, like André **Masson** (1896–) and Joan **Miro** (1893–1983), attempted to connect with the unconscious through automatic drawing. Others, like Salvador **Dali** (1904–1989) and René **Magritte** (1898–1967), used a more realistic style to create an imagery of dreams. In both cases, thought and creativity were liberated by the absence of reason. Even Picasso was regarded as a Surrealist by Breton and certainly his work of the late 1920s and the 1930s explored the destructive human impulses. This is most dramatically seen in *Guernica* 1936 (Prado, Madrid), in which his horrified reaction to the German Luftwaffe's bombing of a Basque town during the Spanish Civil War has the quality of an epic nightmare.

The impact of Surrealism was widespread. In Britain the landscapes of Paul **Nash** (1889–1946) became even more haunted and mysterious. The Swiss painter Paul **Klee** painted quirky semiabstract pictures and Marc **Chagall** (1881–1955) evoked the memories of his Jewish-Russian childhood. Both artists delved into the imagination for their visions in a way that paralleled Surrealism.

Abstract Expressionism Many European artists moved to the USA in the years around World War II. New York became the centre of world art and Abstract Expressionism its first major movement. Influenced by Mondrian as well as by Surrealism, US avant-garde painting divided into two groups: the Gesture painters (or Action painters) and the Colour Field painters. Jackson **Pollock** (1912–1956) led the Gesture painters. By putting his canvas on the floor and swirling paint on it, he created a complex web of multicoloured trails which spectators could retrace with their eyes, thereby reliving the artist's dynamic act of creation. The Colour Field painter Mark **Rothko** 1903–1970 filled large canvases with shimmering blocks of solid colour, the contemplation of which offered the spectator a transcendent experience.

Pop art was to some extent a reaction against the anguished soul-searching of Abstract Expressionism as well as being a celebration of consumerism and popular culture. Pop artists plundered the mass media, employing the imagery of advertising, comic strips, and the movies. Jasper **Johns** (1930–) gave us paintings of targets and the American flag in endless permutations. Andy **Warhol** (1928–1987), through the medium of the screen print, transformed celebrities and events, from Marilyn Monroe to the electric chair, into contemporary icons. Roy **Lichtenstein** (1923–), in paintings like *Whaam!* 1963 (Tate Gallery, London) presents a comic-strip moment in a wittily depersonalized parody of its original style. In the UK, artists like Richard **Hamilton** and Eduoardo **Paolozzi** had a similar disregard for the division between high and low culture. In Paolozzi's case this meant using almost any material that came to hand, making his collages and sculptures almost archaeological concentrates of the late 20th century.

Op art The paintings of Victor **Vasarely** (1908–) and Bridget **Riley** (1931–) use abstraction to create optical illusions, confusing the spectator's eye with coloured lines and dots that appear to jump, blend, and waver.

In sculpture the influence of Rodin dominated the early years of the century. Matisse, **Bourdelle**, and the Cubist sculptors extended Rodin's liberated attitude to the human form as a complex and dynamic surface. The raw directness of African sculpture affected the work of Jacob **Epstein**, Henri **Gaudier-Brzeska**, and **Modigliani**, while in Germany Ernst **Barlach** derived similar inspiration from late Gothic sculpture. Constantin **Brancusi** (1876–1957) in his carvings gradually refined and simplified his work into pure, almost abstract forms, like the ovoid *Prometheus* of 1911. Henry **Moore** (1898–1957) created a more rugged reduction of the human form which reflects the full and flowing contours of nature. At the other extreme, the elongated and emaciated figures of Alberto **Giacometti** (1901–1966) emit a sense of spiritual and existential isolation. Both Dada and Cubist collage encouraged a more varied and untraditional choice and use of materials, evident in the work of the Russian Constructivists. In the 1930s Picasso and Julio **Gonzalez** (1876–1972) made highly linear 'drawings in space' by welding sheets and strips of metal together. This direction was pursued in a more dramatic and monumental way by David **Smith** (1906–1965) and his fellow American Alexander **Calder** (1898–1976), who invented mobiles, flat shapes attached in patterns to rods that hang from the ceiling and move gently in the air. More recently Jean **Tinguely** (1925–) has employed electricity to create movement in his elaborate, whimsical machine constructions.

contemporary trends Since the freethinking 1960s, a bewildering number of new trends and movements have appeared, many of which stress the intellectual and material processes behind an art work's creation.

Minimalism reacted to the promiscuity of Pop art by reducing the art object to a bare and essential purity, devoid of any exterior reference or meaning. *Equivalent VIII* 1966 by Carl **Andre**, two layers of bricks laid on the floor, caused great controversy when purchased by the Tate Gallery, London.

Super Realism or *Photo Realism* imitates reality through exact, illusionistic copies of colour photographs in the work of Richard **Estes** and waxworklike sculptures in the work of Duane **Hanson**. Meaning and intention are obscured by the clinical detachment of the execution and the banality of the subject matter.

Conceptualism Here the actual art object is challenged and sometimes replaced by the ideas behind it. Documentation in the form of statements and photographs may be presented on gallery walls.

Performance art is the staging of events by artists. It may be theatrical but it differs from theatre in its emphasis on visual complexity rather than on a text. In *Body art* the artist uses his or her own body as a vehicle for often confrontational ideas.

Land art or *Earth art* involves the direct interaction of the artist with the environment. It is usually ephemeral and so preserved only in documentation. **Christo** (1935–) has wrapped up part of the Australian coastline 1979, erected a curtain in a Colorado valley 1981, and a long running fence across California 1986. Richard **Long** maps and photographs his landscape journeys, displaying them in galleries with works made from natural materials collected en route.

Although these developments undermined the conventional notion of the art work as permanent and unique, traditional forms like figurative oil painting have, even so, continued to thrive since World War II, albeit in increasingly extreme manifestations. In the work of the painter Francis **Bacon** (1910–), scenes of horror and brutality are presented as the typical condition of modern humans. Since the 1970s, other painters, the so-called *Neo-Expressionists* or *Bad painters*, like Julian Schnabel, Anselm Kiefer, Georg Baselitz, and Francesco Clemente, have created an equally direct and lurid visual language in order to explore issues of personal and national history and mythology.

EASTERN ART

Islamic art is one of ornament, for under the Muslim religion artists could not usurp the divine right of creation by portraying living creatures. Intricate, interlacing patterns based on geometry, Arabic calligraphy, and stylized plant motifs (including the swirling 'Arabesque') swarm over surfaces, structured by a rigid sense of symmetry. Lustreware pottery, ceramic tiles, and carpets were primary art forms. In Islamic Persia miniature painting illustrating literary or historical scenes, often in a lovingly detailed Paradise Garden setting, flourished during the Safavid period (1502–1736) and after 1526 under the Moghul Empire in India.

Chinese art manifested itself in pottery as early as 4000 BC, and its porcelains and jade and ivory carvings, are major art forms. Painting was influenced by calligraphy; the ideographic script, which used the same brush, ink, and paper, called for the same dexterity, and produced the same spontaneous impression. Whether as hanging scrolls or hand-scrolls that unrolled to provide a continuous picture, paintings on silk and paper included calligraphy, often a poem. Traditional subjects were a bamboo branch, sprig of blossom, or snowy mountain landscape. Seen from a birds-eye view, the space within a landscape was as meaningful as the subject.

Indian art influenced all of South-East Asia. From Buddha's death (485 BC) it centred on the religion which revered him as 'The Incarnation of the Truth'. Images of the Buddha followed a symbolic pattern: his plumpness signified well-being, his posture relaxation, his expression tranquillity. Hinduism also flourished and both Buddhist and Hindu temples were covered in high-relief sculpture. By the 13th century Hinduism became the major religion. The figures of its many exotic deities are rounded and sensuous, their poses based on religious dance movements. Eroticism enters with exuberantly amorous couples symbolizing the unity of the divine. Miniature painting, beginning in the 11th century, reached its peak under the Moghuls (16th–17th centuries).

Japanese art mastered all the Chinese and Buddhist traditions, adding its own interest in surface texture, bright colours, and dramatic compositions. Its most original contribution to world art was the *ukiyo-e* colour print. Originating in genre paintings of 16th–17th century theatre scenes, actors, and geishas, it developed into the woodcut, and after 1740 the true colour print, while its subject matter expanded beyond the amusements of daily life to include flowers, birds, animals, and landscapes. Their brilliant combination of flat decorative colour and expressive pattern influenced 19th-century European art. Masters included Utamaro (1753–1806) and Hokusai (1760–1849). Distinguished artists also worked in miniature sculpture, producing tiny carved *netsuke* figures, later widely collected in the West.

THE GREATEST ART FORGERS OF THE 20TH CENTURY

Dossena, Alceo 1878–1937 To this day referred to as the 'king of forgers', Italian Alceo Dossena was able to assimilate and evoke a wide range of period and personal styles, never actually copying but successfully suggesting work ranging from ancient Greek to Renaissance. Once established in a Roman studio, Dossena was employed by two unscrupulous dealers and their contacts to execute sculpture according to their orders for a piece 'in the manner of' this or that master. When Dossena eventually understood that he had been badly exploited and underpaid (he had been robbed of millions), he revealed himself to the public through court action against his dealers. A vast body of work scattered throughout Europe and the USA was then identified as Dossena's. After a short period of celebrity, his reputation declined and he died a pauper, condemned for having been an unwitting forger.

van Meegeren Henricus Antonius 1889–1947 The Dutch van Meegeren had embarked on his career as a forger by 1923, when a Frans Hals forgery of his was bought and later denounced as a fake. He is best known for the series of fake 'Vermeers' and 'de Hooghs' he produced between 1937 and 1943, many of which were eagerly bought up by the Dutch government and museums. Much to his chagrin, the leading Nazi Hermann Goering succeeded in buying one of his forgeries, *Christ and the Adulteress*, in 1942. After the end of the German occupation of the Netherlands in 1945, van Meegeren was arrested on the charge of collaboration with the Nazi government through the sale of what was considered a Dutch national treasure. Confronted with this serious charge, he confessed to his 'Vermeer' forgeries and was charged instead with fraud. Having caused the embarrassment of the nation's art historians, museum directors and curators, restorers and technical experts, as well as some of the most prominent dealers and collectors, van Meegeren, who had becomer a national hero of sorts, was sentenced to one year's imprisonment, but died before serving his sentence.

de Hory Elmyr 20th century In a secret studio on the Mediterranean island of Ibiza, the Hungarian de Hory created forgeries of paintings and drawings by practically every modern artist of any economic repute. At first, de Hory faked and sold works to many European and US galleries and even a few museums, almost always on the pretext of having financial reasons to part with family treasures. Between 1961 and 1967, however, under the guidance of his two dealers, de Hory apparently forged some $60 million worth of paintings and drawings which were sold to millionaires, art dealers, and museums. Some $250,000 worth of 'Derains', 'Dufys', and 'Modiglianis' were acquired by the Japanese National Museum of Modern Art in Tokyo. According to his biographer and fellow forger, during this period de Hory produced perhaps 1,000 items, 75–90% of which remain in collections or museums, unrecognized or undisclosed as fakes. Because of the threat to the reputations of his victims posed by publicity, de Hory has never been prosecuted for forgery.

Keating Tom 1917–1984 The English painter Keating was probably the most prolific and versatile art forger to be exposed in Britain this century. According to his own account, between the 1950s and 1970s he produced some 2,000 fakes of about a hundred different artists, including Samuel Palmer. He claimed that his outright forgery was a form of protest against the exploitation of artists by dealers. The uncovering of Keating's forgeries began in March 1976, and by Aug of that year he made a general confession at a press conference. His revelations caused a sensation in the country and consternation in the London art market, turning him into a popular hero. He was arrested in 1977, but all charges were later dropped because of his poor health. A posthumous sale of his work brought in £274,000—about seven times the estimate.

'Maestro del Ricciolo' (Master of the Curl) Numerous forgeries of Old Master drawings by this skilful perpetrator infested the art market during the late 1980s. His productions are mostly drawn imitations of the 18th-century Venetians Antonio Canaletto (1697–1768) and Francesco Guardi (1712–1793). These fakes are invariably drawn on old paper, often with a prominent watermark.

GREAT WRITERS

Abú Nuwás Hasan ibn Háni 762–*c.* 815. Arab poet celebrated for the freedom, eroticism and ironic lightness of touch he brought to traditional forms.

Andersen Hans Christian 1805–1875. Danish writer. His fairy tales such as 'The Ugly Duckling', 'The Emperor's New Clothes', and 'The Snow Queen', gained him international fame and have been translated into many languages.

Ariosto Ludovico 1474–1533. Italian poet, born in Reggio. He wrote Latin poems and comedies along Classical lines, including the poem *Orlando Furioso* 1516, 1532, an epic treatment of the *Roland* story, and considered to be the perfect poetic expression of the Italian Renaissance.

Machado de Assis Joaquim Maria 1839–1908. Brazilian writer and poet. He is regarded as the greatest Brazilian novelist. His sceptical, ironic wit is well displayed in his 30 volumes of novels and short stories, including *Epitaph for a Small Winner* 1880 and *Dom Casmurro* 1900.

Asturias Miguel Ángel 1899–1974. Guatemalan author and diplomat. He published poetry, Guatemalan legends, and novels, such as *El Señor Presidente/The President* 1946, *Men of Corn* 1949, and *Strong Wind* 1950, attacking Latin-American dictatorships and 'Yankee imperialism'. Nobel Prize for Literature 1967.

Atwood Margaret (Eleanor) 1939– . Canadian novelist, short-story writer, and poet. Her novels, which often treat feminist themes with wit and irony, include *The Edible Woman* 1969, *Life Before Man* 1979, *Bodily Harm* 1981, *The Handmaid's Tale* 1986, and *Cat's Eye* 1989.

Austen Jane 1775–1817. English novelist whose books are set within the confines of middle-class provincial society, and show her skill at drawing characters and situations with delicate irony. Her principal works are *Sense and Sensibility* 1811 (like its successors, published anonymously), *Pride and Prejudice* 1813, *Mansfield Park* 1814, *Emma* 1816, *Persuasion* 1818, and *Northanger Abbey* 1818. She died at Winchester and is buried in the cathedral.

Baldwin James 1924–1987. US writer, born in New York City, who portrayed the condition of black Americans in contemporary society. His works include the novels *Go Tell It on the Mountain* 1953, *Another Country* 1962, and *Just Above My Head* 1979; the play *The Amen Corner* 1955; and the autobiographical essays *Notes of a Native Son* 1955 and *The Fire Next Time* 1963. He was active in the civil rights movement.

Balzac Honoré de 1799–1850. French novelist. His first success was *Les Chouans/The Chouans* and *La Physiologie du mariage/The Physiology of Marriage* 1829, inspired by Scott. This was the beginning of the long series of novels *La Comédie humaine/The Human Comedy* (planned as 143 volumes, of which 80 were completed), depicting vice and folly in contemporary French society. He also wrote the Rabelaisian *Contes drolatiques/Ribald Tales* 1833.

Bashō Pen name of Matsuo Munefusa 1644–1694. Japanese poet who was a master of the *haiku*, a 17-syllable poetic form with lines of 5, 7, and 5 syllables, which he infused with subtle allusiveness and made the accepted form of poetic expression in Japan. His most famous work is *Oku-no-hosomichi/The Narrow Road to the Deep North* 1694, an account of a visit to northern Japan, which consists of haikus interspersed with prose passages.

Baudelaire Charles Pierre 1821–1867. French poet, whose work combined rhythmical and musical perfection with a morbid romanticism and eroticism, finding beauty in decadence and evil. His first book of verse, *Les Fleurs du mal/Flowers of Evil* 1857, was condemned by the censor as endangering public morals, but was enormously influential, paving the way for Arthur Rimbaud, Paul Verlaine, and the symbolist school.

Bellow Saul 1915– . Canadian-born US novelist of Russian descent, whose finely styled works and skilled characterizations of life, especially contemporary Jewish-American life, won him the Nobel Prize for Literature 1976. His works usually portray an individual's frustrating relationship with the ongoing events of an indifferent society, and include the picaresque *The Adventures of Augie March* 1953, the philosophically speculative *Herzog* 1964, *Humboldt's Gift* 1975, *The Dean's December* 1982, and *The Bellarosa Connection* 1989.

Blake William 1757–1827. English poet, painter, and mystic, a leading figure in the Romantic period. His visionary, symbolic poems include *Songs of Innocence* 1789 and *Songs of Experience* 1794. He engraved the text and illustrations for his works and hand-coloured them, mostly in watercolour. He also illustrated works by John Milton and William Shakespeare.

Boccaccio Giovanni 1313–1375. Italian poet, chiefly known for the collection of tales called the *Decameron* 1348–53. The bawdiness and exuberance of this work, as well as its narrative skill and characterization, made the work enormously popular and influential, inspiring Chaucer, Shakespeare, Dryden, and Keats among many others.

Böll Heinrich 1917–1985. West German novelist. A radical Catholic and anti-Nazi, he attacked Germany's political past and the materialism of its contemporary society. His many publications include poems, short stories, and novels which satirize German society, for example *Billard um Halbzehn/Billiards at Half-Past Nine* 1959 and *Gruppenbild mit Dame/Group Portrait with Lady* 1971. Nobel Prize for Literature 1972.

Borges Jorge Luis 1899–1986. Argentinian poet and short-story writer. In 1961 he became director of the National Library, Buenos Aires,

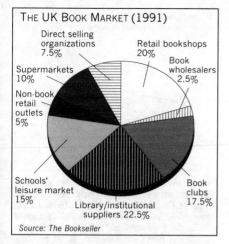

THE UK BOOK MARKET (1991)

Direct selling organizations 7.5%
Retail bookshops 20%
Book wholesalers 2.5%
Supermarkets 10%
Non-book retail outlets 5%
Schools' leisure market 15%
Library/institutional suppliers 22.5%
Book clubs 17.5%

Source: The Bookseller

and was professor of English literature at the university there. He is known for his fantastic and paradoxical work *Ficciones/Fictions* 1944.

Brontë family of English writers, including the three sisters **Charlotte** (1816–55), **Emily Jane** (1818–48) and **Anne** (1820–49), and their brother **Patrick Branwell** (1817–48). Their most enduring works are Charlotte Brontë's *Jane Eyre* 1847 and Emily Brontë's *Wuthering Heights* 1847. Later works include Anne's *The Tenant of Wildfell Hall* 1848 and Charlotte's *Shirley* 1849 and *Villette* 1853.

Burns Robert 1759–1796. Scottish poet who used the Scots dialect at a time when it was not considered suitably 'elevated' for literature. Burns's first volume, *Poems, Chiefly in the Scottish Dialect*, appeared in 1786. In addition to his poetry Burns wrote or adapted many songs, including 'Auld Lang Syne'.

Byron George Gordon, 6th Baron Byron 1788–1824. English poet who became the symbol of Romanticism and political liberalism throughout Europe in the 19th century. His reputation was established with the first two cantos of *Childe Harold* 1812. Later works include *The Prisoner of Chillon* 1816, *Beppo* 1818, *Mazeppa* 1819, and, most notably, *Don Juan* 1819–24. He left England in 1816, spending most of his later life in Italy. In 1823 he sailed for Greece to further the Greek struggle for independence, but died of fever at Missolonghi.

Camoëns or **Camões**, Luís Vaz de 1524–1580. Portuguese poet and soldier. He went on various military expeditions, and was shipwrecked in 1558. His poem, *Os Lusiades/The Lusiads*, published 1572, tells the story of the explorer Vasco da Gama and incorporates much Portuguese history; it has become the country's national epic. His posthumously published lyric poetry is also now valued.

Camus Albert 1913–1960. Algerian-born French writer. A journalist in France, he was active in the Resistance during World War II. His novels, which owe much to existentialism, include *L'Etranger/The Outsider* 1942, *La Peste/The Plague* 1948, and *L'Homme Révolté/The Rebel* 1952. He was awarded the Nobel Prize for Literature 1957.

Cao Chan or **Ts'ao Chan** 1719–1763. Chinese novelist. His tragic love story *Hung Lou Meng/The Dream of the Red Chamber* published 1792, involves the downfall of a Manchu family and is semi-autobiographical.

Carroll Lewis. Pen name of Charles Lutwidge Dodgson 1832–1898. English mathematician and writer of children's books, including the classics *Alice's Adventures in Wonderland* 1865 and its sequel *Through the Looking Glass* 1872. He also published mathematics books under his own name.

Cervantes Saavedra, Miguel de 1547–1616. Spanish novelist, playwright, and poet, whose masterpiece, *Don Quixote* (in full *El ingenioso hidalgo Don Quixote de la Mancha*) was published 1605. In 1613, his *Novelas Ejemplares/Exemplary Novels* appeared, followed by *Viaje del Parnaso/The Voyage to Parnassus* 1614. A spurious second part of *Don Quixote* prompted Cervantes to bring out his own second part in 1615, often considered superior to the first in construction and characterization.

Chaucer Geoffrey *c.* 1340–1400. English poet, the greatest and most influential English poet of the Middle Ages. In his masterpiece, *The Canterbury Tales* (*c.* 1387), a collection of tales told by pilgrims on their way to the shrine of Thomas à Becket, he showed his genius for metre and characterization. His other work includes the French-influenced *Romance of the Rose* and an adaptation of Boccaccio's *Troilus and Criseyde*. The great popularity of his work assured the dominance of the southern English dialect in literature.

Conrad Joseph 1857–1924. English novelist of Polish parentage, born Teodor Jozef Konrad Korzeniowski in the Ukraine. His novels include *Almayer's Folly* 1895, *Lord Jim* 1900, *Heart of Darkness* 1902, *Nostromo* 1904, *The Secret Agent* 1907, and *Under Western Eyes* 1911. His works vividly evoke the mysteries of sea life and exotic foreign settings and explore the psychological isolation of the 'outsider'.

Dante Alighieri 1265–1321. Italian poet. His masterpiece *La Divina Commedia/The Divine Comedy* 1307–21, the greatest poem of the Middle Ages, is an epic account in three parts of his journey through Hell, Purgatory, and Paradise, during which he is guided part of the way by the poet Virgil; on a metaphorical level the journey is also one of Dante's own spiritual development. Other works include the philosophical prose treatise *Convivio/The Banquet* 1306–08, the first major work of its kind to be written in Italian rather than Latin; *Monarchia/On World Government* 1310–13, expounding his political theories; *De vulgari eloquentia/Concerning the Vulgar Tongue* 1304–06, an original Latin work on Italian, its dialects, and kindred languages; and *Canzoniere/Lyrics*, containing his scattered lyrics.

Darío Rubén. Pen name of Félix Rubén García Sarmiento 1867–1916. Nicaraguan poet. His first major work *Azul/Azure* 1888, a collection of prose and verse influenced by French Symbolism, created a sensation. He went on to establish *modernismo*, the Spanish-American modernist literary movement, distinguished by an idiosyncratic and deliberately frivolous style that broke away from the prevailing Spanish provincialism and adapted French poetic models. His vitality and eclecticism influenced every poet writing in Spanish after him, both in the New World and in Spain.

Defoe Daniel 1660–1731. English novelist and journalist. His best-known work, *Robinson Crusoe* 1719, was greatly influential in the development of the novel. An active pamphleteer and political critic, he was imprisoned 1702–04 following publication of the ironic *The Shortest Way With Dissenters*. Fictional works include *Moll Flanders* 1722 and *A Journal of the Plague Year* 1724. Altogether he produced over 500 books, pamphlets, and journals.

Dickens Charles 1812–1870. English novelist, popular for his memorable characters and his portrayal of the social evils of Victorian England. In 1836 he published the first number of the *Pickwick Papers*, followed by *Oliver Twist* 1838, the first of his 'reforming' novels; *Nicholas Nickleby* 1839; *Barnaby Rudge* 1840; *The Old Curiosity Shop* 1841; and *David Copperfield* 1849. Among his later books are *Hard Times* 1854; *Little Dorritt* 1857; *A Tale of Two Cities* 1859 and *Great Expectations* 1861.

Donne John 1571–1631. English metaphysical poet whose work is characterized by subtle imagery and figurative language. In 1615 Donne took orders in the Church of England and as dean of St Paul's Cathedral, London, was noted for his sermons. His poetry includes the sonnets 'Batter my heart, three person'd God' and 'Death be not proud', elegies, and satires.

Dos Passos John 1896–1970. US author. He made his reputation with the war novels *One Man's Initiation* 1919 and *Three Soldiers* 1921. His major work is the trilogy *U.S.A.* 1930–36, which gives a panoramic view of US life through the device of placing fictitious characters against the setting of real newspaper headlines and contemporary events.

Dostoievsky Fyodor Mikhailovich 1821–1881. Russian novelist. Remarkable for their profound psychological insight, Dostoievsky's novels have greatly influenced Russian writers, and since the beginning of the 20th century have been increasingly influential abroad. In 1849 he was sentenced to four years' hard labour in Siberia, followed by army service, for printing socialist propaganda. *The House of the Dead* 1861 recalls his prison experiences, followed by his major works *Crime and Punishment* 1866, *The Idiot* 1868–69, and *The Brothers Karamazov* 1880.

Duras Marguerite 1914– . French writer. Her works include short stories (*Des Journées entières dans les arbres*), plays (*La Musica*), film scripts (*Hiroshima mon amour* 1960),

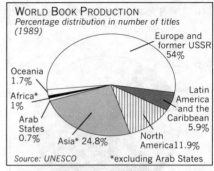

WORLD BOOK PRODUCTION
Percentage distribution in number of titles (1989)

Europe and former USSR 54%
Oceania 1.7%
Africa* 1%
Arab States 0.7%
Asia* 24.8%
North America 11.9%
Latin America and the Caribbean 5.9%

Source: UNESCO   *excluding Arab States

and novels such as *Le Vice-Consul* 1966, evoking an existentialist world from the setting of Calcutta, and *Emily L.* 1989. *La vie materielle* (published in France 1987) appeared in England as *Practicalities* 1990. Her autobiographical novel, *La Douleur*, is set in Paris in 1945.

Eliot George. Pen name of Mary Ann Evans 1819–1880. English novelist who portrayed Victorian society, including its intellectual hypocrisy, with realism and irony. In 1857 she published the story 'Amos Barton', the first of the *Scenes of Clerical Life*. This was followed by the novels *Adam Bede* 1859, *The Mill on the Floss* 1860, and *Silas Marner* 1861. *Middlemarch* 1872 is now considered one of the greatest novels of the 19th century. Her final book *Daniel Deronda* 1876 was concerned with anti-Semitism. She also wrote poetry.

Eliot T(homas) S(tearns) 1888–1965. US poet, playwright, and critic who lived in London from 1915. His first volume of poetry, *Prufrock and Other Observations* 1917, introduced new verse forms and rhythms, and expressed the disillusionment of the generation affected by World War I; further collections include *The Waste Land* 1922, which established his central position in modern poetry; *The Hollow Men* 1925, and *Old Possum's Book of Practical Cats* 1939. *Four Quartets* 1943 revealed his religious vision. His plays include *Murder in the Cathedral* 1935 and *The Cocktail Party* 1949. He was also an influential literary critic, and helped to re-assess the importance of Donne. He was awarded the Nobel Prize for Literature in 1948.

Faulkner William 1897–1962. US novelist who wrote in an experimental stream-of-consciousness style. His works include *The Sound and the Fury* 1929, dealing with a Southern US family in decline; *As I Lay Dying* 1930; *Light in August* 1932, a study of segregation; *The Unvanquished* 1938, stories of the Civil War; and *The Hamlet* 1940, *The Town* 1957, and *The Mansion* 1959, a trilogy covering the rise of the materialist Snopes family. He was awarded the Nobel Prize for Literature in 1949.

Fielding Henry 1707–1754. English novelist whose narrative power influenced the form and technique of the novel and helped to make it the most popular form of literature in England. In 1742 he parodied Richardson's novel *Pamela*

GREAT LIBRARIES OF THE WORLD

		date founded
Ambrosian Library	Milan	1605
Biblioteca Nacional	Madrid	1712
Biblioteca Nazionale Centrale	Rome	1876
Bibliotheque Nationale	Paris	1480
Bodleian Library	Oxford University	1602
British Museum Library	London	1753
Deutsche Bibliothek	Frankfurt/M	1946
Deutsche Staatsbibliothek	Berlin	1661
Harvard University Library	Cambridge, Mass.	1638
Klementinum State Library	Prague	1348
Kunrgliga Bibliotekat	Stockholm	in XVII century
Lenin Library	Moscow	1917–1925
Library of Congress	Washington DC	1800
National Diet Library	Tokyo	1948
New York Public Library	New York	1895

Source: UN

in his *Joseph Andrews*, which was followed by *Jonathan Wild the Great* 1743; his masterpiece *Tom Jones* 1749, which he described as a 'comic epic in prose'; and *Amelia* 1751.

Firdawsi Mansûr Abu'l-Qâsim *c.* 935–*c.* 1020. Persian poet, the greatest epic poet of Persia. His *Shahnama/The Book of Kings* relates the history of Persia in 60,000 verses, and included the legend of Sohrab and Rustum, in which the father unknowingly kills the son in battle.

Fitzgerald F(rancis) Scott (Key) 1896–1940. US novelist and short-story writer. His early autobiographical novel *This Side of Paradise* 1920 made him known in the postwar society of the East Coast, and *The Great Gatsby* 1925 epitomizes the Jazz Age.

Flaubert Gustave 1821–1880. French novelist, one of the greatest of the 19th century. His masterpiece, noted for its psychological realism, is *Madame Bovary* 1857. He entered Paris literary circles 1840, but in 1846 moved to Rouen, where he remained for the rest of his life. *Salammbô* 1862 earned him the Legion of Honour 1866, and was followed by *L'Education sentimentale/Sentimental Education* 1869, and *La Tentation de Saint Antoine/The Temptation of St Anthony* 1874. Flaubert also wrote the short stories *Trois contes/Three Tales* 1877.

García Márquez Gabriel 1928– . Colombian novelist. His sweeping novel *Cien años de soledad/One Hundred Years of Solitude* 1967 (which tells the story of a family over a period of six generations) is an example of magic realism, a technique used to heighten the intensity of realistic portrayal of social and political issues by introducing grotesque or fanciful material. His other books include *El amor en los tiempos del cólera/Love in the Time of Cholera* 1985. Nobel Prize for Literature 1982.

Gide André 1869–1951. French novelist, born in Paris. His work is largely autobiographical and concerned with the dual themes of self-fulfilment and renunciation. It includes *L'Immoraliste/The Immoralist* 1902, *La Porte étroite/Strait Is the Gate* 1909, *Les Caves du Vatican/The Vatican Cellars* 1914, and *Les Faux-monnayeurs/The Counterfeiters* 1926; and an almost lifelong *Journal*. Nobel Prize for Literature 1947.

Goethe Johann Wolfgang von 1749–1832. German poet, novelist, and dramatist, generally considered the founder of modern German literature, and leader of the Romantic *Sturm und Drang* movement. His works include the autobiographical *Die Leiden des Jungen Werthers/The Sorrows of the Young Werther* 1774 and *Faust* 1808, his masterpiece. A visit to Italy 1786–88 inspired the classical dramas *Iphigenie auf Tauris/Iphigenia in Tauris* 1787 and *Tasso* 1790.

Gogol Nikolai Vasilyevich 1809–1852. Russian writer. His first success was a collection of stories, *Evenings on a Farm near Dikanka* 1831–32, followed by *Mirgorod* 1835. Later works include *Arabesques* 1835, the comedy play *The Inspector General* 1836, and the picaresque novel *Dead Souls* 1842, which satirizes Russian provincial society.

Grass Günter 1927– . German writer. Born in Danzig, he studied at the art academies of Düsseldorf and Berlin, worked as a writer and sculptor (first in Paris and later in Berlin), and in 1958 won the coveted 'Group 47' prize. The grotesque humour and socialist feeling of his novels *Die Blechtrommel/The Tin Drum* 1959 and *Der Butt/The Flounder* 1977 are also characteristic of many of his poems.

Greene (Henry) Graham 1904–1991. English writer, whose novels of guilt, despair, and penitence, include *The Man Within* 1929, *Brighton Rock* 1938, *The Power and the Glory* 1940, *The Heart of the Matter* 1948, *The Third Man* 1950, *The Honorary Consul* 1973, *Monsignor Quixote* 1982, and *The Captain and the Enemy* 1988.

Hâfiz Shams al-Din Muhammad *c.* 1326–1390. Persian lyric poet, who was born in Shiraz and taught in a Dervish college there. His *Diwan*, a collection of short odes, extols the pleasures of life and satirizes his fellow Dervishes.

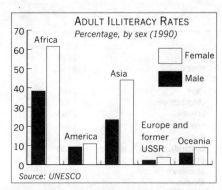

ADULT ILLITERACY RATES
Percentage, by sex (1990)

Africa · Female · Asia · Male · America · Europe and former USSR · Oceania

Source: UNESCO

Hardy Thomas 1840–1928. English novelist and poet. His novels, set in rural 'Wessex' (his native West Country), portray intense human relationships played out in a harshly indifferent natural world. They include *Far From the Madding Crowd* 1874, *The Return of the Native* 1878, *The Mayor of Casterbridge* 1886, *The Woodlanders* 1887, *Tess of the D'Urbervilles* 1891, and *Jude the Obscure* 1895. The latter, portraying social attitudes towards education, marriage, divorce, and suicide, aroused great antagonism, which reinforced his decision to confine himself to verse. His poetry includes the *Wessex Poems* 1898, and several volumes of lyrics.

Heine Heinrich 1797–1856. German romantic poet and journalist, who wrote *Reisebilder* 1826 and *Buch der Lieder/Book of Songs* 1827. From 1831 he lived mainly in Paris, working as a correspondent for German newspapers. Schubert and Schumann set many of his lyrics to music.

Hemingway Ernest 1899–1961. US writer. War, bullfighting, and fishing were used symbolically in his writings to represent honour, dignity, and primitivism—prominent themes in his short stories and novels, which included *A Farewell to Arms* 1929, *For Whom the Bell Tolls* 1940, and *The Old Man and the Sea* 1952. His deceptively simple writing styles attracted many imitators. He received the Nobel Prize for Literature in 1954.

Homer lived *c.* 8th century BC. Legendary Greek epic poet. According to tradition he was a blind minstrel and the author of the *Iliad* and the *Odyssey*, which are probably based on much older stories, passed on orally, concerning war with Troy in the 12th century BC.

Horace 65–8 BC. Roman lyric poet and satirist. He became a leading poet under the patronage of Emperor Augustus. His works include *Satires* 35–30 BC; the four books of *Odes* about 25–24 BC; *Epistles*, a series of verse letters; and a critical work, *Ars poetica*.

Hugo Victor (Marie) 1802–1885. French poet, novelist, and dramatist. The *Odes et poésies diverses* appeared 1822, and his verse play *Hernani* 1830 established him as the leader of French Romanticism. More volumes of verse followed between his series of dramatic novels, which included *The Hunchback of Notre Dame* 1831 and *Les Misérables* 1862.

Huxley Aldous (Leonard) 1894–1963. English writer. The satirical disillusionment of his first novel, *Crome Yellow* 1921, continued throughout *Antic Hay* 1923, *Those Barren Leaves* 1925, *Point Counter Point* 1928, and *Brave New World* 1932, in which human beings are mass produced in the laboratory under the control of the omnipotent state.

Iqbāl Muhammad 1875–1938. Islamic poet and thinker. His literary works, in Urdu and Persian, were mostly verse in the classical style, suitable for public recitation. He sought through his writings to arouse Muslims to take their place in the modern world.

Ishiguro Kazuo 1954– . Japanese-born British novelist. His novel *An Artist of the Floating World* won the 1986 Whitbread Prize, and *The Remains of the Day* won the 1989 Booker Prize.

James Henry 1843–1916. US novelist, who lived in Europe from 1875 and became a naturalized British subject 1915. His novels deal with the impact of sophisticated European culture on the innocent American. They include *The Portrait of a Lady* 1881, *Washington Square* 1881, *The Bostonians* 1886, *The Ambassadors* 1903, and *The Golden Bowl* 1904. He also wrote more than a hundred shorter works of fiction, notably the supernatural tale *The Turn of the Screw* 1898.

Johnson Samuel, known as 'Dr Johnson', 1709–1784. English lexicographer, author, and critic, also a brilliant conversationalist and the dominant figure in 18th-century London literary society. His *Dictionary*, published 1755, remained authoritative for over a century, and is still remarkable for the vigour of its definitions. In 1764 he founded the 'Literary Club', whose members included Joshua Reynolds, Edmund Burke, Oliver Goldsmith, David Garrick, and James Boswell, Johnson's biographer.

Joyce James (Augustine Aloysius) 1882–1941. Irish writer, born in Dublin, who revolutionized the form of the English novel with his 'stream of consciousness' technique. His works include *Dubliners* 1914 (short stories), *Portrait of the Artist as a Young Man* 1916, *Ulysses* 1922, and *Finnegan's Wake* 1939.

Kafka Franz 1883–1924. Czech novelist, born in Prague, who wrote in German. His three unfinished allegorical novels *Der Prozess/The Trial* 1925, *Der Schloss/The Castle* 1926, and *Amerika/America* 1927 were posthumously published despite his instructions that they should be destroyed. His short stories include 'Die Verwandlung/The Metamorphosis' 1915, in which a man turns into a huge insect.

Kālidāsa lived 5th century AD. Indian epic poet and dramatist. His works, in Sanskrit, include the classic drama *Sakuntala*, the love story of King Dushyanta and the nymph Sakuntala.

Keats John 1795–1821. English poet, a leading figure of the Romantic movement. He published his first volume of poetry 1817; this was followed by *Endymion, Isabella,* and *Hyperion* 1818, 'The Eve of St Agnes', his odes 'To Autumn', 'On a Grecian Urn', and 'To a Nightingale', and 'Lamia' 1819. His final volume of poems appeared in 1820.

Kerouac Jack 1923–1969. US novelist who named and epitomized the Beat Generation of the 1950s. His books, all autobiographical, include *On the Road* 1957, *Big Sur* 1963, and *Desolation Angel* 1965.

Kipling (Joseph) Rudyard 1865–1936. English writer, born in India. His stories for children include the *Jungle Books* 1894–1895, *Stalky and Co* 1899, and the *Just So Stories* 1902. Other works include the novel *Kim* 1901, the short story 'His Gift', poetry, and the unfinished autobiography *Something of Myself* 1937. In his heyday he enjoyed enormous popularity, and although subsequently denigrated for alleged 'jingoist imperialism', his work is increasingly valued for its complex characterization and subtle moral viewpoints. Nobel Prize for Literature 1907.

La Fontaine Jean de 1621–1695. French poet. He was born at Château-Thierry, and from 1656 lived largely in Paris, the friend of Molière, Jean Racine, and Nicolas Boileau. His works include *Fables* 1668–94 and *Contes* 1665–74, a series of witty and bawdy tales in verse.

Lawrence D(avid) H(erbert) 1885–1930. English writer whose work expresses his belief in emotion and the sexual impulse as creative and true to human nature. His novels include *Sons and Lovers* 1913, *The Rainbow* 1915, *Women in Love* 1921, and *Lady Chatterley's Lover* 1928 (the latter was banned as obscene in the UK until 1960). Lawrence also wrote short stories (for example 'The Woman Who Rode Away') and poetry.

Leopardi Giacomo, Count Leopardi 1798–1837. Italian romantic poet. The first collection of his uniquely pessimistic poems, *I Versi/Verses*, appeared in 1824, and was followed by his philosophical *Operette morali/Minor Moral Works* 1827, in prose, and *I Canti/Lyrics* 1831.

Levi Primo 1919–1987. Italian novelist. He joined the anti-Fascist resistance during World War II, was captured, and sent to the concentration camp at Auschwitz. He wrote of these experiences in *Se questo è un uomo/If This Is a Man* 1947.

Lewis (Harry) Sinclair 1885–1951. US novelist. He made a reputation with satirical novels: *Main Street* 1920, depicting American small-town life; *Babbitt* 1922, the story of a real-estate dealer of the Midwest caught in the conventions of his milieu; *Arrowsmith* 1925, a study of the pettiness in medical science; and *Elmer Gantry* 1927, a satiric portrayal of evangelical religion. *Dodsworth*, a gentler novel of a US industrialist, was published 1929. He was the first American to be awarded the Nobel Prize for Literature 1930.

Li Po 705–762. Chinese poet. He used traditional literary forms, but his exuberance, the boldness of his imagination, and the intensity of his feeling have won him recognition as perhaps the greatest of all Chinese poets. Although he was mostly concerned with higher themes, he is also remembered for his celebratory verses on drinking.

London Jack (John Griffith) 1876–1916. US novelist, author of the adventure stories *The Call of the Wild* 1903, *The Sea Wolf* 1904, and *White Fang* 1906.

Lorca Federico García 1898–1936. Spanish poet and playwright, born in Granada. *Romancero gitano/Gipsy Ballad-book* 1928 shows the influence of the Andalusian songs of the area. In 1929–30 Lorca visited New York, and his experiences are reflected in *Poeta en Nueva York/Poet in New York* 1940. His poems include *Lament*, written for the bullfighter Mejías. He was shot by the Falangists during the Spanish Civil War.

Machado de Assis Joaquim Maria 1839–1908. Brazilian writer and poet. He is regarded as the greatest Brazilian novelist. His sceptical, ironic wit is well displayed in his 30 volumes of novels and short stories, including *Epitaph for a Small Winner* 1880 and *Dom Casmurro* 1900.

Mann Thomas 1875–1955. German novelist and critic, concerned with the theme of the artist's relation to society. His first novel was *Buddenbrooks* 1901, which, followed by *Der Zauberberg/The Magic Mountain* 1924, led to a Nobel Prize for Literature 1929. Later works include *Dr Faustus* 1947 and *Die Bekenntnisse des Hochstaplers Felix Krull/Confessions of Felix Krull* 1954. Notable among his works of short fiction is *Der Tod in Venedig/Death in Venice* 1913.

Manzoni Alessandro, Count Manzoni 1785–1873. Italian poet and novelist, author of the historical romance, *I promessi sposi/The Betrothed* 1825–27, set in Spanish-occupied Milan during the 17th century. Verdi's *Requiem* commemorates him.

Maupassant Guy de 1850–1893. French author who established a reputation with the short story 'Boule de Suif/Ball of Fat' 1880 and wrote some 300 short stories in all. His novels include *Une Vie/A Woman's Life* 1883 and *Bel-Ami* 1885. He was encouraged as a writer by Gustave Flaubert.

Melville Herman 1819–1891. US writer, whose *Moby-Dick* 1851 was inspired by his whaling experiences in the South Seas. These experiences were also the basis for earlier fiction, such as *Typee* 1846 and *Omoo* 1847. He published several volumes of verse, as well as short stories (*The Piazza Tales* 1856). *Billy Budd* was completed just before his death and published 1924. Although most of his works were unappreciated during his lifetime, today he is one of the most highly regarded of US authors.

Milton John 1608–1674. English poet. His early poems include the pastoral *L'allegro* and *Il penseroso* 1632, the masque *Comus* 1633, and the elegy *Lycidas* 1637. His middle years were devoted to the Puritan cause and pamphleteering, including one advocating divorce, and another (*Areopagitica*) freedom of the

Prix Goncourt for fiction (French)

1981	Lucien Bodard *Anne Marie*
1982	Dominique Fernandez *Dans la Main de l'ange*
1983	Frederick Tristan *Les Égares*
1984	Marguerite Duras *L'Amant*
1985	Yann Queffelec *Les Noces barbares*
1986	Michel Host *Valet de Nuit*
1987	Tahir Ben Jelloun *La Nuit Sacrée*
1988	Erik Orsenna *L'Exposition Coloniale*
1989	Jean Vautrin *Un Grand Pas Vers le Bon Dieu*
1990	Jean Rouault *Les Champs d'Honneur*
1991	Pierre Combescot *Les Filles du Calvaire*

Pulitzer Prize for Fiction (American)

1981	John Kennedy Toole *A Confederacy of Dunces*
1982	John Updike *Rabbit is Rich*
1983	Alice Walker *The Color Purple*
1984	William Kennedy *Ironweed*
1985	Alison Lurie *Foreign Affairs*
1986	Larry McMurtry *Lonesome Dove*
1987	Peter Taylor *A Summer to Memphis*
1988	Toni Morrison *Beloved*
1989	Anne Tyler *Breathing Lessons*
1990	Oscar Hijelos *The Mambo Kings Play Songs of Love*
1991	John Updike *Rabbit at Rest*
1992	Jane Smiley *A Thousand Acres*

Booker Prize for Fiction (British)

1981	Salman Rushdie *Midnight's Children*
1982	Thomas Keneally *Schindler's Ark*
1983	J M Coetzee *Life and Times of Michael K*
1984	Anita Brookner *Hotel du Lac*
1985	Keri Hulme *The Bone People*
1986	Kingsley Amis *The Old Devils*
1987	Penelope Lively *Moon Tiger*
1988	Peter Carey *Oscar and Lucinda*
1989	Kazuo Ishiguro *Remains of the Day*
1990	A S Byatt *Possession*
1991	Ben Okri *The Famished Road*

Nobel Prize for Literature (International)

1981	Elias Canetti (Bulgarian-British)
1982	Gabriel García Márquez (Columbian-Mexican)
1983	William Golding (British)
1984	Jaroslav Seifert (Czechoslovakian)
1985	Claude Simon (French)
1986	Wole Soyinka (Nigerian)
1987	Joseph Brodsky (Soviet)
1988	Naguib Mahfouz (Egyptian)
1989	Camilo Jose Cela (Spanish)
1990	Octavio Paz (Mexican)
1991	Nadine Gordimer (South African)

Nabokov Vladimir 1899–1977. US writer who left his native Russia 1917 and began writing in English in the 1940s. His most widely known book is *Lolita* 1955, the story of the middle-aged Humbert Humbert's infatuation with a precocious child of 12. His other books include *Laughter in the Dark* 1938, *The Real Life of Sebastian Knight* 1945, *Pnin* 1957, and his memoirs *Speak, Memory* 1947.

Naipaul V(idiadhar) S(urajprasad) 1932– . British writer, born in Trinidad of Hindu parents. His novels include *A House for Mr Biswas* 1961, *The Mimic Men* 1967, *A Bend in the River* 1979, and *Finding the Centre* 1984. His brother **Shiva(dhar) Naipaul** (1940–85) was also a novelist (*Fireflies* 1970) and journalist.

Neruda Pablo. Pen name of Neftalí Ricardo Reyes y Basualto 1904–1973. Chilean poet and diplomat. His work includes lyrics and the epic poem of the American continent *Canto General* 1950. He served as consul and ambassador to many countries. Nobel Prize for Literature 1971.

Orwell George. Pen name of Eric Arthur Blair 1903–1950. English author. His books include the satire *Animal Farm* 1945, which included such sayings as 'All animals are equal, but some are more equal than others', and the prophetic *Nineteen Eighty-Four* 1949, portraying the dangers of excessive state control over the individual. Other works include *Down and Out in Paris and London* 1933 and *Homage to Catalonia* 1938.

Ovid (Publius Ovidius Naso) 43 BC–AD 17. Roman poet. His poetry deals mainly with the themes of love (*Amores* 20 BC, *Ars amatoria* 1 BC,

press. From 1649 he was (Latin) secretary to the Council of State, his assistants (as his sight failed) including Andrew Marvell. The masterpieces of his old age are his epic poems on biblical themes, *Paradise Lost* 1667, *Paradise Regained* 1677, and the classic drama *Samson Agonistes* 1677.

Mishima Yukio 1925–1970. Japanese novelist whose work often deals with sexual desire and perversion, as in *Confessions of a Mask* 1949 and *The Temple of the Golden Pavilion* 1956. He committed hara-kiri (ritual suicide) as a protest against what he saw as the corruption of the nation and the loss of the samurai warrior tradition.

Montaigne Michel Eyquem de 1533–1592. French writer, regarded as the creator of the essay form. In 1580 he published the first two volumes of his *Essais*, the third volume appeared in 1588. Montaigne deals with all aspects of life from an urbanely sceptical viewpoint. Through the translation by John Florio in 1603, he influenced Shakespeare and other English writers.

Musil Robert 1880–1942. Austrian novelist, author of the unfinished *Der Mann ohne Eigenschaften/The Man without Qualities* (three volumes, 1930–43). Its hero shares the author's background of philosophical study and scientific and military training, and is preoccupied with the problems of the self viewed from a mystic but agnostic viewpoint.

mythology (*Metamorphoses* AD 2), and exile (*Tristia* AD 9–12).

Pasternak Boris Leonidovich 1890–1960. Russian poet and novelist. His novel *Dr Zhivago* 1957 was banned in the USSR as a 'hostile act', and followed by a Nobel prize (which he declined). *Dr Zhivago* has since been unbanned and Pasternak posthumously rehabilitated.

Paz Octavio 1914– . Mexican poet and essayist. His works reflect many influences, including Marxism, surrealism, and Aztec mythology. His celebrated poem *Piedra del sol/Sun Stone* 1957 uses contrasting images, centring upon the Aztec Calendar Stone (representing the Aztec universe), to symbolize the loneliness of individuals and their search for union with others. Nobel Prize for Literature 1990.

Perrault Charles 1628–1703. French author of the fairy tales *Contes de ma mère l'oye/Mother Goose's Fairy Tales* 1697, which include 'Sleeping Beauty', 'Little Red Riding Hood', 'Blue Beard', 'Puss in Boots', and 'Cinderella'.

Pessoa Fernando 1888–1935. Portuguese poet. Born in Lisbon, he was brought up in South Africa and was bilingual in English and Portuguese. His verse is considered to be the finest written in Portuguese this century. He wrote under three assumed names, which he called 'heteronyms'—Alvaro de Campos, Ricardo Reis, and Alberto Caeiro—for each of which he invented a biography.

Petrarch (Italian **Petrarca**) Francesco 1304–1374. Italian poet, born in Arezzo, a devotee of the Classical tradition. His *Il Canzoniere* is composed of sonnets in praise of his idealized love 'Laura', whom he first saw 1327 (she was a married woman and refused to become his mistress). His 14-line sonnets, in a form which was given the name Petrarchan, were influential for centuries.

Poe Edgar Allan 1809–1849. US writer and poet. His short stories are renowned for their horrific atmosphere as in *The Fall of the House of Usher* 1839) and acute reasoning (for example, *The Gold Bug* 1843 and *The Murders in the Rue Morgue* 1841, in which the investigators Legrand and Dupin anticipate Arthur Conan Doyle's Sherlock Holmes). His most famous poem is 'The Raven' 1844.

Pope Alexander 1688–1744. English poet and satirist. He established his reputation with the precocious *Pastorals* 1709 and *Essay on Criticism* 1711, which were followed by a parody of the heroic epic *The Rape of the Lock* 1712–14 and 'Eloisa to Abelard' 1717. Other works include a highly Neo-Classical translation of Homer's *Iliad* and *Odyssey* 1715–26.

Pound Ezra 1885–1972. US poet who lived in London from 1908. His *Personae* and *Exultations* 1909 established the principles of the Imagist movement. His largest work was the series of *Cantos* 1925–1969 (intended to number 100), which attempted a massive reappraisal of history.

Proust Marcel 1871–1922. French novelist and critic. His immense autobiographical work *À la recherche du temps perdu/Remembrance of Things Past* 1913–27, consisting of a series of novels, is the expression of his childhood memories coaxed from his subconscious; it is also a precise reflection of life in provincial France at the end of the 19th century.

Pushkin Aleksandr 1799–1837. Russian poet and writer. He was exiled 1820 for his political verse and in 1824 in trouble for his atheistic opinions. He wrote ballads such as *The Gypsies* 1827, and the novel in verse *Eugene Onegin* 1823–31. Other works include the tragic drama *Boris Godunov* 1825, and the prose pieces *The Captain's Daughter* 1836 and *The Queen of Spades* 1834. Pushkin's range was wide, and his willingness to experiment freed later Russian writers from many of the archaic conventions of the literature of his time.

Pynchon Thomas 1937– . US novelist who created a bizarre, labyrinthine world in his books, the first of which was *V* 1963. *Gravity's Rainbow* 1973 represents a major achievement in 20th-century literature, with its fantastic imagery and esoteric language, drawn from mathematics and science.

Rabelais François 1495–1553. French satirist, monk, and physician, whose name has become synonymous with bawdy humour. He was educated in the Renaissance humanist tradition and was the author of satirical allegories, including *La Vie inestimable de Gargantua/The Inestimable Life of Gargantua* 1535 and *Faits et dits héroïques du grand Pantagruel/Deeds and Sayings of the Great Pantagruel* 1533, about two giants (father and son) Gargantua and Pantagruel.

Richardson Samuel 1689–1761. English novelist, one of the founders of the modern novel. *Pamela* 1740–41, written in the form of a series of letters and containing much dramatic conversation, was sensationally popular all across Europe, and was followed by *Clarissa* 1747–48 and *Sir Charles Grandison* 1753–54.

Rilke Rainer Maria 1875–1926. Austrian writer, born in Prague. His prose works include the semi-autobiographical *Die Aufzeichnungen des Malte Laurids Brigge/Notebook of Malte Laurids Brigge* 1910, and his poetical works include *Die Sonnette an Orpheus/Sonnets to Orpheus* 1923 and *Duisener Elegien/Duino Elegies* 1923. His verse is characterized by a form of mystic pantheism that seeks to achieve a state of ecstasy in which existence can be apprehended as a whole.

Rimbaud (Jean Nicolas) Arthur 1854–1891. French Symbolist poet. His verse was chiefly written before the age of 20, notably *Les Illuminations* published 1886. From 1871 he lived with Verlaine.

Rousseau Jean-Jacques 1712–1778. French social philosopher and writer, born in Geneva, Switzerland. *Discourses on the Origins of Inequality* 1754 made his name: he denounced civilized society and postulated the paradox of the superiority of the 'noble savage'. *Social Contract* 1762 emphasized the rights of the people over those of the government, and stated that a government could be legitimately overthrown if it failed to express the general will of the people. It was a significant influence on the French Revolution. In the novel *Emile* 1762 he outlined a new theory of education, based on natural development and the power of example, to elicit the unspoiled nature and abilities of children. *Confessions*, published posthumously 1782, was a frank account of his occasionally immoral life and was a founding work of autobiography.

Salinger J(erome) D(avid) 1919– . US writer, author of the classic novel of mid-20th-century adolescence *The Catcher in the Rye* 1951. He also wrote short stories about a Jewish family named Glass, including *Franny and Zooey* 1961.

Sartre Jean-Paul 1905–1980. French author and philosopher, a leading proponent of existentialism in postwar philosophy. He published his first novel, *La Nausée/Nausea*, 1937, followed by the trilogy *Les Chemins de la Liberté/Roads to Freedom* 1944–45 and many plays, including *Huis Clos/In Camera* 1944.

Scott Walter 1771–1832. Scottish novelist and poet. His first works were translations of German ballads, followed by poems such as 'The Lady of the Lake' 1810 and 'Lord of the Isles' 1815. He gained a European reputation for his historical novels such as *Heart of Midlothian* 1818, *Ivanhoe* 1819, and *The Fair Maid of Perth* 1828. His last years were marked by frantic writing to pay off his debts, after the bankruptcy of his publishing company in 1826.

Shakespeare William 1564–1616. English dramatist and poet, the greatest English playwright; he also wrote numerous sonnets. (See *Theatre* for more.)

Shelley Percy Bysshe 1792–1822. English lyric poet, a leading figure in the Romantic movement. Expelled from Oxford university for atheism, he fought all his life against religion and for political freedom. This is reflected in his early poems such as *Queen Mab* 1813. He later wrote tragedies including *The Cenci* 1818, lyric dramas such as *Prometheus Unbound* 1820, and lyrical poems such as 'Ode to the West Wind'. He drowned while sailing in Italy.

Singer Isaac Bashevis 1904–1991. Polish-born US novelist and short-story writer. His works, written in Yiddish, then translated into English, often portray traditional Jewish life in Poland and the USA, and the loneliness of old age. They include *Gimpel the Fool* 1957, *The Slave* 1960, *Shosha* 1978, *Old Love* 1979, *Lost in America* 1981, *The Image and Other Stories* 1985, and *The Death of Methuselah* 1988. He has also written plays and books for children. In 1978 he was awarded the Nobel Prize for Literature.

Solzhenitsyn Alexander (Isayevich) 1918– . Soviet novelist, a US citizen from 1974. After military service, he was in prison and exile 1945–57 for anti-Stalinist comments. Much of his writing is semi-autobiographical and highly critical of the system, including *One Day in the Life of Ivan Denisovich* 1962 which deals with the labour camps under Stalin, and

The Gulag Archipelago 1973, an exposé of the whole Soviet labour camp network. This led to his expulsion from the USSR 1974.

Soyinka Wole 1934– . Nigerian author who was a political prisoner in Nigeria 1967–69. His works include the play *The Lion and the Jewel* 1963; his prison memoirs *The Man Died* 1972; *Aké, The Years of Childhood* 1982, an autobiography, and *Isara*, a fictionalized memoir 1989. He was the first African to receive the Nobel Prize for Literature, in 1986.

Spenser Edmund c. 1552–1599. English poet, who has been called the 'poet's poet' because of his rich imagery and command of versification. He is known for his moral allegory *The Faerie Queene*, of which six books survive (three published 1590 and three 1596). Other books include *The Shepheard's Calendar* 1579, *Astrophel* 1586, the love sonnets *Amoretti* and the *Epithalamion* 1595.

Steinbeck John (Ernst) 1902–1968. US novelist. His realist novels, such as *In Dubious Battle* 1936, *Of Mice and Men* 1937, and *The Grapes of Wrath* 1939 (Pulitzer prize 1940), portray agricultural life in his native California, where migrant farm labourers from the Oklahoma dust bowl struggled to survive. He received the Nobel Prize for Literature in 1962.

Stendhal pen name of Marie Henri Beyle 1783–1842. French novelist. His novels *Le Rouge et le noir/The Red and the Black* 1830 and *La Chartreuse de Parme/The Charterhouse of Parme* 1839 were pioneering works in their treatment of disguise and hypocrisy; a review of the latter by Balzac in 1840 furthered Stendhal's reputation.

Sterne Laurence 1713–1768. Irish writer, creator of the comic anti-hero Tristram Shandy. *The Life and Opinions of Tristram Shandy, Gent* 1760–67, an eccentrically whimsical and bawdy novel, foreshadowed many of the techniques and devices of 20th-century novelists, including James Joyce. His other works include *A Sentimental Journey through France and Italy* 1768.

Stevenson Robert Louis 1850–1894. Scottish novelist and poet, author of the adventure novel *Treasure Island* 1883. Later works included the novels *Kidnapped* 1886, *The Master of Ballantrae* 1889, *Dr Jekyll and Mr Hyde* 1886, and the anthology *A Child's Garden of Verses* 1885.

Swift Jonathan 1667–1745. Irish satirist and Anglican cleric, author of *Gulliver's Travels* 1726, an allegory describing travel to lands inhabited by giants, miniature people, and intelligent horses. Other works include *The Tale of a Tub* 1704, attacking corruption in religion and learning; contributions to the Tory paper *The Examiner*, of which he was editor 1710–11; the satirical *A Modest Proposal* 1729, which suggested that children of the poor should be eaten; and many essays and pamphlets.

Tagore Rabindranath 1861–1941. Bengali Indian writer, born in Calcutta, who translated into

English his own verse *Gitanjali* ('song offerings') 1912 and his verse play *Chitra* 1896. Nobel Prize for Literature 1913.

Tennyson Alfred, 1st Baron Tennyson 1809–1892. English poet, poet laureate 1850–96, whose verse has a majestic, musical quality. His works include 'The Lady of Shalott', 'The Lotus Eaters', 'Ulysses', 'Break, Break, Break', 'The Charge of the Light Brigade'; the longer narratives *Locksley Hall* 1832 and *Maud* 1855; the elegy *In Memoriam* 1850; and a long series of poems on the Arthurian legends *The Idylls of the King* 1857–85.

Thackeray William Makepeace 1811–1863. English novelist and essayist, born in Calcutta, India. He was a regular contributor to *Fraser's Magazine* and *Punch*. *Vanity Fair* 1847–48 was his first novel, followed by *Pendennis* 1848, *Henry Esmond* 1852 (and its sequel *The Virginians* 1857–59), and *The Newcomes* 1853–55, in which Thackeray's tendency to sentimentality is most marked.

Tolstoy Leo Nikolaievich 1828–1910. Russian novelist who wrote *Tales from Sebastopol* 1856, *War and Peace* 1863–69, and *Anna Karenina* 1873–77. From 1880 Tolstoy underwent a profound spiritual crisis and took up various moral positions, including passive resistance to evil, rejection of authority (religious or civil) and private ownership, and a return to basic mystical Christianity. He was excommunicated by the Orthodox Church, and his later works were banned.

Turgenev Ivan Sergeievich 1818–1883. Russian writer, notable for poetic realism, pessimism, and skill in characterization. His works include the play *A Month in the Country* 1849, and the novels *A Nest of Gentlefolk* 1858, *Fathers and Sons* 1862, and *Virgin Soil* 1877. His series *A Sportsman's Sketches* 1852 criticized serfdom.

Twain Mark. Pen name of Samuel Langhorne Clemens 1835–1910. US writer. He established his reputation with the comic masterpiece *The Innocents Abroad* 1869 and two classic American novels, in dialect, *The Adventures of Tom Sawyer* 1876 and *The Adventures of Huckleberry Finn* 1885. He also wrote satire, as in *A Connecticut Yankee at King Arthur's Court* 1889.

Verlaine Paul 1844–1896. French lyric poet who was influenced by the poets Baudelaire and Rimbaud. His volumes of verse include *Poèmes saturniens/Saturnine Poems* 1866, *Fêtes galantes/Amorous Entertainments* 1869 and *Romances sans paroles/Songs without Words* 1874. In 1873 he was imprisoned for attempting to shoot Rimbaud. His later works reflect his attempts to lead a reformed life. He was acknowledged as leader of the Symbolist poets.

Villon François 1431–c. 1465. French poet who used satiric humour, pathos, and lyric power in works written in *argot* (slang) of the time. Very little of his work survives, but it includes the *Ballade des dames du temps jadis/Ballad of the Ladies of Former Times*, *Petit Testament* 1456, and *Grand Testament* 1461.

Virgil (Publius Vergilius Maro) 70–19 BC. Roman poet who wrote the *Eclogues* 37 BC, a series of pastoral poems; the *Georgics* 30 B, four books on the art of farming; and his epic masterpiece, the *Aeneid*.

Voltaire Pen name of François-Marie Arouet 1694–1778. French writer who believed in deism, and devoted himself to tolerance, justice, and humanity. He was threatened with arrest for *Lettres philosophiques sur les anglais/Philosophical Letters on the English* 1733 (essays in favour of English ways, thought, and political practice) and had to take refuge. Other writings include *Le Siècle de Louis XIV/The Age of Louis XIV* 1751; *Candide* 1759, a parody on Leibniz's 'best of all possible worlds'; and *Dictionnaire philosophique* 1764.

Walker Alice 1944– . US poet, novelist, critic, and essay writer. She was active in the US civil-rights movement in the 1960s and, as a black woman, wrote about the double burden of racist and sexist oppression that such women bear. Her novel *The Color Purple* 1983 (film, 1985) won the Pulitzer Prize.

Wharton Edith (born Jones) 1862–1937. US novelist. Her work, known for its subtlety and form and influenced by her friend Henry James, was mostly set in New York society. It includes *The House of Mirth* 1905, which made her reputation; the grim, uncharacteristic novel of New England *Ethan Frome* 1911; *The Custom of the Country* 1913, and *The Age of Innocence* 1920.

Whitman Walt(er) 1819–1892. US poet who published *Leaves of Grass* 1855, which contains the symbolic 'Song of Myself'. It used unconventional free verse (with no rhyme or regular rhythm) and scandalized the public by its frank celebration of sexuality.

Woolf Virginia (née Virginia Stephen) 1882–1941. English novelist and critic. Her first novel, *The Voyage Out* 1915, explored the tensions experienced by women who want marriage and a career. In *Mrs Dalloway* 1925 she perfected her 'stream of consciousness' technique. Among her later books are *To the Lighthouse* 1927, *Orlando* 1928, and *The Years* 1937, which considers the importance of economic independence for women.

Wordsworth William 1770–1850. English Romantic poet. In 1797 he moved with his sister Dorothy to Somerset to be near Samuel Taylor Coleridge, collaborating with him on *Lyrical Ballads* 1798 (which included 'Tintern Abbey'). From 1799 he lived in the Lake District, and later works include *Poems* 1807 (including 'Intimations of Immortality') and *The Prelude* (written by 1805, published 1850). He was appointed poet laureate in 1843.

Yeats W(illiam) (B)utler 1865–1939. Irish poet. He was a leader of the Celtic revival and a founder of the Abbey Theatre in Dublin. His early work was romantic and lyrical, as in the poem 'The Lake Isle of Innisfree' and plays *The Countess Cathleen* 1892 and *The Land of Heart's Desire* 1894. His later books of poetry include *The Wild Swans at Coole* 1917 and

The Winding Stair 1929. He was a senator of the Irish Free State 1922–28. Nobel Prize for Literature 1923.

Zola Émile Edouard Charles Antoine 1840–1902. French novelist and social reformer. With *La Fortune des Rougon/The Fortune of the Rougons* 1867 he began a series of some 20 naturalistic novels, portraying the fortunes of a French family under the Second Empire. They include *Le Ventre de Paris/The Underbelly of Paris* 1873, *Nana* 1880, and *La Débâcle/The Debacle* 1892. In 1898 he published *J'accuse/I Accuse*, a pamphlet indicting the persecutors of Alfred Dreyfus, for which he was prosecuted for libel but later pardoned.

What are your reading habits?

	Yes	No	Don't know
Reading romantic novels	48	35	17
Reading Westerns	10	59	31
Reading detective novels	41	35	24
Children's comics	56	25	19
Doing crosswords	70	18	12
Using public libraries	62	23	14

GREAT DIRECTORS

Allen Woody. Adopted name of Allen Stewart Konigsberg 1935- . US film writer, director, and actor, known for his cynical, witty, often self-deprecating parody and offbeat humor.

His films include *Sleeper* 1973, *Annie Hall* 1977 (for which he won three Academy Awards), *Manhattan* 1979, and *Hannah and Her Sisters* 1986, all of which he directed, wrote, and appeared in. From the late 1970s, Allen has mixed his output of comedies with straight dramas, such as *Interiors* 1978 and *Another Woman* 1988, but *Crimes and Misdemeanors* 1990 broke with tradition by combining humour and straight drama.

Other films include *Take the Money and Run* 1969, *Sleeper* 1973, *Love and Death* 1975, *Stardust Memories* 1982, *Zelig* 1983, *Purple Rose of Cairo* 1985, and *Night and Fog* 1991.

Altman Robert 1925- . US maverick film director. His antiwar comedy *M.A.S.H.* 1970 was a critical and commercial success; subsequent films include *McCabe and Mrs Miller* 1971, *The Long Goodbye* 1973, *Nashville* 1975, and *Popeye* 1980.

Antonioni Michelangelo 1912- . Italian film director, whose work evinces both formal innovation and an acute power to analyse the effects of affluence and technology on contemporary sensibility. He began as a maker of documentaries and directed his first feature film, *Cronaca di un Amore* in 1950, gradually developing the elliptical approach to narrative seen in *L'Avventura* 1960 and its successors. His other films include *Blow Up* 1966, filmed in England, the US-made *Zabriskie Point* 1970, *The Passenger* 1974, and *Identification of a Woman* 1982.

Bergman Ingmar 1918- . Swedish stage producer (from the 1930s) and film director (from the 1950s). His work deals with complex moral, psychological, and metaphysical problems and is tinged with pessimism. His films include *Wild Strawberries* 1957, *The Seventh Seal* 1957, *Persona* 1966, *Cries and Whispers* 1972, *The Serpent's Egg* and *Autumn Sonata* both 1978, and *Fanny and Alexander* 1982. He is one of the greatest directors of acting performances.

Buñuel Luis 1900–1983. Spanish Surrealist film director. He collaborated with Salvador Dali on *Un Chien andalou* 1928 and *L'Age d'or*/*The Golden Age* 1930, and established his solo career in Mexico with *Los olvidados*/*The Young and the Damned* 1950. His works are often anticlerical, with black humour and erotic imagery.

Later, he worked in France with higher budgets on such films as *Le Charme discret de la bourgeoisie*/*The Discreet Charm of the Bourgeoisie* 1972 (Academy Award winner) and *Cet Obscur Objet du désir*/*That Obscure Object of Desire* 1977.

Capra Frank 1897–1991. Italian-born US film director. His satirical, populist comedies, which often have idealistic heroes, were hugely successful in the 1930s, and he won Academy Awards for *It Happened One Night* 1934, *Mr Deeds Goes to Town* 1936, and *Mr Smith Goes to Washington* 1939.

Capra began as a gagman for silent comedies, then directed several films with Harry Langdon (1884-1944). An instinctive craftsman, his popular success continued after World War II with the sentimental and imaginative *It's a Wonderful Life* 1946, but subsequently waned. His later work included *A Hole in the Head* 1959 and *A Pocketful of Miracles* 1961.

Carné Marcel 1909- . French director known for the romantic fatalism of such films as *Drôle de Drame* 1936, *Hôtel du Nord* 1938, *Le Quai des brumes*/*Port of Shadows* 1938, and *Le Jour se lève*/*Daybreak* 1939. His masterpiece, *Les*

AWARDS FOR BEST FILM FROM FOUR TOP FESTIVALS

Cannes Film Festival
Palme d'Or for Best Film

1985	*When Father Was Away on Business* (Yug)
1986	*The Mission* (UK)
1987	*Under the Sun of Satan* (Fr)
1988	*Pelle the Conqueror* (Den)
1989	*Sex, Lies and Videotape* (USA)
1990	*Wild at Heart* (USA)
1991	*Barton Fink* (USA)
1992	*The Best Intentions* (Swe)

Venice Film Festival
Golden Lion for Best Film

1985	*Sans toit ni loi aka Vagabonde* (Fr)
1986	*Le Rayon Vert* (Fr)
1987	*Au Revoir les Enfants* (Fr)
1988	*La Leggenda del Santo Bevitore (The Legend of the Holy Drinker)* (It)
1989	*Beiqing Chengshi (City of Sadness)* (Taiwan)
1990	*Rosencrantz and Guildenstern are Dead* (UK)
1991	*Urga* (Russia)

Berlin Film Festival
Golden Bear for Best Film

1985	*Wetherby* (UK); *Die Frau und der Fremde* (FRG)
1986	*Stammheim* (FRG)
1987	*The Theme* (USSR)
1988	*Red Shorghum* (China)
1989	*Rain Man* (USA)
1990	*Skylarks on a String* (Czech); *Music Box* (USA)
1991	*La Casa del Sorriso (House of Smiles)* (It)
1992	*Grand Canyon* (USA)

British Academy of Film and Television Arts (BAFTA)
Best Film Awards

1985	*The Killing Fields* (UK)
1986	*The Purple Rose of Cairo* (USA)
1987	*A Room with a View* (UK)
1988	*Jean de Florette* (Fr)
1989	*The Last Emperor* (USA)
1990	*Dead Poets Society* (USA)
1991	*Goodfellas* (USA)
1992	*The Commitments* (UK)

Enfants du paradis/The Children of Paradise 1943–45, was made with his longtime collaborator, the poet and screenwriter Jacques Prévert (1900-1977).

Chaplin Charlie (Charles Spencer) 1889–1977. English film actor and director. He made his reputation as a tramp with a smudge moustache, bowler hat, and twirling cane in silent comedies from the mid-1910s, including *The Rink* 1916, *The Kid* 1920, and *The Gold Rush* 1925. His work often contrasts buffoonery with pathos, and his later films combine dialogue with mime and music, as in *The Great Dictator* 1940 and *Limelight* 1952 (the latter won an Oscar for Chaplin's musical theme). His other films include *City Lights* 1931, *Modern Times* 1936, and *Monsieur Verdoux* 1947. He was one of cinema's most popular and greatest stars, and his 'Little Tramp' character became recognized and loved the world over.

Chaplin was born in south London and first appeared on the stage at the age of five. In 1913 he joined Mack Sennett's Keystone Company in Los Angeles, and from 1915 he took artistic control of all his films. When accused of communist sympathies during the McCarthy witchhunt, he left the USA 1952 and moved to Switzerland. He received special Oscars 1928 and 1972.

Coppola Francis Ford 1939– . US film director and screenwriter. He directed *The Godfather* 1972, which became one of the biggest money-making films of all time, and its sequels *The Godfather Part II* 1974, which received seven Academy Awards, and *The Godfather Part III* 1990. His other films include *Apocalypse Now* 1979, *One From the Heart* 1982, *Rumblefish* 1983, *The Outsiders* 1983, and *Tucker: The Man and His Dream* 1988.

After working on horror B-films, his first successes were *Finian's Rainbow* 1968 and *Patton* 1969, for which his screenplay won an Academy Award. Among his other films are *The Conversation* 1972, *The Cotton Club* 1984, and *Gardens of Stone* 1987.

De Mille Cecil B(lount) 1881–1959. US film director and producer. He entered films 1913 with Jesse L Lasky (with whom he later established Paramount Pictures), and was one of the founders of Hollywood. He specialized in biblical epics, such as *The Sign of the Cross* 1932 and *The Ten Commandments* 1923; remade 1956. He also made the 1952 Academy Award-winning circus movie *The Greatest Show on Earth*.

De Sica Vittorio 1902–1974. Italian director and actor. He won his first Oscar with *Bicycle Thieves* 1948, a film of subtle realism. Later films included *Umberto D* 1952, *Two Women* 1960, and *The Garden of the Finzi-Continis* 1971. His considerable acting credits include *Madame de ...* 1953 and *The Millionaires* 1960.

Disney Walt(er Elias) 1901–1966. US filmmaker and animator, a pioneer of family entertainment. He established his own studio in Hollywood 1923, and his first Mickey Mouse cartoons (*Plane Crazy*, which was silent, and *Steamboat Willie*, which had sound) appeared 1928. In addition to short cartoons, the studio made feature-length animated films, including *Snow White and the Seven Dwarfs* 1938, *Pinocchio* 1940, *Fantasia* 1940, *Dumbo* 1941, *Bambi* 1942, *Cinderella* 1950, *Alice in Wonderland* 1952, and *Peter Pan* 1953. Disney's cartoon figures also appeared in comic books, magazines, books, and records, which helped make his animated characters loved throughout the world.

The Disney studio also made nature-study films such as *The Living Desert* 1953, which have been criticized for their fictionalization of nature: wild animals were placed in unnatural situations to create 'drama'. Feature films with human casts were made from 1946, such as *Davy Crockett* 1955, *The Swiss Family Robinson* 1960, and *Mary Poppins* 1964.

Disney produced the first television series in colour in 1961. He also conceived the idea of theme parks, of which Disneyland, California was the first (1955). Walt Disney World, near Orlando, Florida, 1971, included the Epcot (Experimental Prototype Community of Tomorrow) Center 1982, a cross between a science museum and a theme park. There is also a park in Tokyo, Japan, and—opened in 1992—the EuroDisney park in Paris, France.

BOX OFFICE HIGHS AND LOWS

For the US film industry, 1991 was not a year to remember. For the first time in 15 years, box-office admissions fell below 1 billion. Moreover, the year's end was marked by the filing for bankruptcy of Orion Pictures, ironically the maker of *Silence of the Lambs*, the year's third biggest money-maker with a $130 million domestic gross. But while industry earnings were down by some 6%, they were not exactly negligible at $4.6 billion. And although the estimated average budget for a major studio movie in 1992 fell fractionally to $19.5 million, compared with $19.8 million in 1990, the 'big risk' strategy was vindicated by the fact that the costliest film ever, *Terminator 2*, with a budget of nearly $100 million, had by the end of 1991 returned double that, amid predictions of an eventual worldwide gross of $500 million.

In Britain, where local production fell to an all-time low of 12 features, cinema attendance in 1991 totalled 93 million, a strong contrast with the 54 million recorded in 1984. It is, significantly, since then that multiscreen complexes (long taken for granted in the USA) have proliferated in the UK. But the upturn is unlikely to bring much cheer to the Hollywood moguls: the British market contribution to international earnings of American films is estimated at 4%.

VIOLENCE ON THE SCREEN

When *The Silence of the Lambs* won no fewer than five awards at the 1992 Oscars ceremony, including that for best picture, there were expressions of surprise and open censure. It was suggested that to honour what was deemed to be a violent horror film in this way was tacitly to accept that anything goes in the pursuit of audiences and profit.

Such reactions, however, mistake the film itself for the reputation it has achieved. *Silence* is not, properly speaking, a horror film at all; rather, it is a detective story, involving the tracking down of a serial murderer by the FBI, and in some respects (location shooting, use of dateline captions) it mimics the condition of a documentary. The film's modernity, and arguably the cause of its having tapped so deeply into the public consciousness, lies as much in its post-feminist view of the FBI agent (Jodie Foster) who is the chief protagonist, as in acknowledging the gruesome nature of the murderer's activities, an acknowledgement which mirrors the growing frankness over recent years in media reporting of comparable cases in real life.

Nonetheless, it is the figure of the psychopathic Hannibal 'the Cannibal' Lecter (Anthony Hopkins), though he is properly speaking an incidental character, which has dominated the publicity for the film and its coverage in the media. The one visually explicit act of violence in the film, in fact, occurs during Lecter's escape from incarceration, a sequence which in dramatic terms is somewhat redundant. Here, though not elsewhere, the filmmakers are guilty of giving the public the gory frisson that they are deemed to expect.

Rather the same feeling applies to another highly successful recent film, *Cape Fear*. Here again, the explicit violence—in the attack by the psychopathic jailbird (Robert De Niro) on the woman he has picked up, and in the elaborations of the shipboard finale—is essen-

tially irrelevant to the central themes of the story, which concern family tensions and the limitations of social order. Arguably, though, it is exactly the gratuitous nature of the violence which lends *Cape Fear* its distinctive modernity.

But it is worth recalling that *Cape Fear* is a loosely-based remake of a 1962 film of the same name, which at the time was attacked, and in the UK heavily censored, on the strength of its almost wholly implied violence. The difference between the two versions is that the earlier film is the more disturbing because its violence, while not explicit, is not gratuitous either, but is intrinsic to the dramatic situation.

Shortly before the first *Cape Fear*, Alfred Hitchcock's *Psycho*, made in 1960 (and to which, incidentally, the climax of *Silence of the Lambs* is recognizably indebted), conclusively pushed back the frontiers of what was deemed acceptable in mainstream filmmaking. Three decades later, there is no suggestion of any let-up in the further exploration of the terrain thus opened up. There is no great surprise when a 'family' film such as *Robin Hood—Prince of Thieves* can regale its audience with scenes of hand-lopping in a Moorish dungeon. As the filmgoing audience has become more youthful and more fragmented, novelty is increasingly a key weapon in the marketing arsenal, and violence has come to be regarded as one of the areas in which novelty can most readily be supplied.

But what is perhaps more worrying about films like *Silence of the Lambs* and *Cape Fear* is not that they contain episodes of simulated mutilation, which are not in fact especially graphic, but rather that these make what are otherwise adult and intelligent entertainments less frightening, and less satisfying, than they might otherwise have been, by forfeiting the power of suggestion.

Adult entertainment? Jodie Foster outside the serial killer's dungeon in The Silence of the Lambs.

STAR PURRFORMANCE

The sequels keep coming … No sooner had *Lethal Weapon 3* broken box-office records than *Batman Returns* came along to break them again—$47.7 million on its first weekend of US release. If the ace card in the hand of the first Batman movie was Jack Nicholson's fiendish Joker, that of the sequel is perhaps the feline villainess Catwoman.

In the duels, literal and otherwise, between Michelle Pfeiffer's Catwoman and Michael Keaton's Batman, the film provides, in the words of one American critic, a meeting of *Fatal Attraction* and *Beauty and the Beast*. And for Pfeiffer, the role sets a seal on the superstar status that was intimated by her Oscar-nominated performances as the club singer of *The Fabulous Baker Boys* and as Mme de Tournel in *Dangerous Liaisons*, and which no doubt will be consolidated by her forthcoming appearance in Martin Scorsese's *Age of Innocence*.

Certainly Catwoman—in a get-up which the film's costume designer Mary Vogt likens to 'wearing black glass'—represents a considerable stride forward for an actress who 10 years before found fame in a rather less prestigious sequel, the teenage musical *Grease 2*. No wonder that her response to a reporter's question as to how she felt about getting the role was just: 'Meow'.

Dreyer Carl Theodor 1889–1968. Danish film director. His wide range of films include the austere silent classic *La Passion de Jeanne d'Arc/The Passion of Joan of Arc* 1928 and the Expressionist horror film *Vampyr* 1932, after the failure of which Dreyer made no full-length films until *Vredens Dag/Day of Wrath* 1943. His two late masterpieces are *Ordet/The Word* 1955 and *Gertrud* 1964.

Eisenstein Sergei Mikhailovich 1898–1948. Latvian film director who pioneered film theory and introduced the use of montage (the juxtaposition of shots to create a particular effect) as a means of propaganda, as in *The Battleship Potemkin* 1925.

The Soviet dictator Stalin banned the second part of Eisenstein's projected trilogy *Ivan the Terrible* 1944–46. The last part was never made. His other films include *Strike* 1925, *October* 1928, *Que Viva Mexico!* 1931–32, and *Alexander Nevsky* 1938.

Fellini Federico 1920– . Italian film director whose films combine dream and fantasy sequences with satire and autobiographical details. His films include *I vitelloni/The Young and the Passionate* 1953, *La Strada* 1954 (Academy Award 1956), *Le notti di Cabiria/The Nights of Cabiria* 1956, *La dolce vita* 1960, *Otto e mezzo/8½* 1963, *Giulietta degli spiriti/Juliet of the Spirits* 1965, *Satyricon* 1969, *Roma/Fellini's Roma* 1972, *Amarcord* 1974, *Casanova* 1976, and *La città delle donne/City of Women* 1980.

Ford John. Adopted name of Sean O'Feeney 1895–1973. US film director. Active from the silent film era, he was one of the early creators of the 'Western', directing *The Iron Horse* 1924; *Stagecoach* 1939 became his masterpiece. But he also worked in many other genres, and won Academy Awards for *The Informer* 1935, *The Grapes of Wrath* 1940, *How Green Was My Valley* 1941, and *The Quiet Man* 1952.

Other films include *They Were Expendable* 1945, *She Wore a Yellow Ribbon* 1949, *Rio Grande* 1950, *The Last Hurrah* 1958, and *The Man Who Shot Liberty Valance* 1962.

Gance Abel 1889–1981. French film director who was one of the great innovators of the French silent cinema. His romantic epic *Napoléon* 1927 (restored in 1980 and subsequently widely shown) was the high point of his career. One of the most ambitious silent epic films, it features colour and triple-screen sequences, as well as multiple-exposure shots.

An actor in films from 1909 and a director from 1912, Gance showed his inclination for experiment in films such as *J'Accuse* 1919 and *La Roue* 1922. The process culminated in *Napoléon*, with its extravagant use of hand-held cameras, rapid cutting, and superimpositions. The arrival of sound seemed to stifle his creative output, though he continued to work, mainly on historical films, until the 1960s. Later films included *Lucreze Borgia* 1935 and *Austerlitz* 1960.

Godard Jean-Luc 1930– . French film director, one of the leaders of New Wave cinema. His works are often characterized by experimental techniques and an unconventional dramatic form, as well as by political allusions. His films include *A bout de souffle* 1959, *Vivre sa Vie* 1962, *Pierrot le fou* 1965, *Weekend* 1968, and *Je vous salue, Marie* 1985.

Griffith D(avid) W(ark) 1875–1948. US film director, one of the most influential figures in the development of cinema as an art. He made hundreds of 'one-reelers' 1908–13, in which he pioneered the techniques of masking, fade-out, flashback, crosscut, close-up, and long shot. After much experimentation, his masterpiece as a director emerged, *The Birth of a Nation* 1915, about the aftermath of the Civil War, later criticized as degrading to blacks.

Other films include the epic *Intolerance* 1916, *Broken Blossoms* 1919, *Way Down East* 1920, *Orphans of the Storm* 1921, and *The Struggle* 1931. He was a cofounder of United Artists 1919. With the advent of sound, his reputation was eclipsed, and he lived forgotten in Hollywood until his death.

Hawks Howard 1896–1977. US director and producer. In a career spanning over four decades, Hawks worked in virtually all the popular American genres—westerns, thrillers, screwball comedies, among others—and brought to them a skill and professionalism that made him the arch-exponent of Hollywood film-making.

Hawks had been an aviator and racing driver

before entering the cinema, and films as varied as *Scarface* 1932, *The Big Sleep* 1946, and *Rio Bravo* 1959 are concerned with both danger and the need for functional expertise. At the same time, uniquely fast-talking comedies like *His Girl Friday* 1940 turned the preoccupations of his action movies on their head by dramatising the lure of irresponsibility. His other films include *Bringing Up Baby* 1938 and *Gentlemen Prefer Blondes* 1953. His final film was *Rio Lobo* 1970.

Hitchcock Alfred 1899–1980. British film director who became a US citizen in 1955. A master of the suspense thriller, he was noted for his meticulously drawn storyboards that determined his camera angles and for his cameo 'walk-ons' in his own films. His *Blackmail* 1929 was the first successful British talking film; *The Thirty-Nine Steps* 1935 and *The Lady Vanishes* 1939 are British suspense classics.

He went to Hollywood 1940, where his films included *Rebecca* 1940, *Notorious* 1946, *Strangers on a Train* 1951, *Rear Window* 1954, *Vertigo* 1958, *Psycho* 1960, and *The Birds* 1963. His last film was *Family Plot* 1976. He also hosted two US television mystery series, *Alfred Hitchcock Presents* 1955-62 and *The Alfred Hitchcock Hour* 1963-65.

Huston John 1906–1987. US film director, screenwriter, and actor. An impulsive and individualistic film maker, he often dealt with the themes of greed, treachery in human relationships, and the loner. His works as a director include *The Maltese Falcon* 1941 (his debut), *The Treasure of the Sierra Madre* 1948 (in which his father Walter Huston starred and for which both won Academy Awards), *Key Largo* 1948, *The African Queen* 1951, *Moby Dick* 1956, *The Misfits* 1961, *Fat City* 1972, *Prizzi's Honor* 1984, and his last, *The Dead* 1987. His daughter is the actress Anjelica Huston.

Jennings Humphrey 1907–1950. British documentary filmmaker who introduced a poetic tone and subjectivity to factually based material. He was active in the General Post Office Film Unit from 1934 and his wartime films vividly portrayed London in the Blitz: *London Can Take It* 1940,

This Is England 1941, and *Fires Were Started* 1943.

Kubrick Stanley 1928– . US director and producer. His films include *Paths of Glory* 1957, *Dr Strangelove* 1964, *2001: A Space Odyssey* 1968, *A Clockwork Orange* 1971, and *The Shining* 1979.

A former photographer for *Life* magazine, he forged an early reputation with several low-budget features, notably *The Killing* 1956, and subsequently relocated to England. More than any of his American contemporaries, he achieved complete artistic control over his projects, which have been eclectic in subject matter and ambitious in scale and technique. His other films include *Lolita* 1962, and *Full Metal Jacket* 1987.

Kurosawa Akira 1929– . Japanese director whose film *Rashomon* 1950 introduced Western audiences to Japanese cinema. Epics such as *Shichinin no samurai/Seven Samurai* 1954 combine spectacle with intimate human drama. His other films include *Drunken Angel* 1948, *Yojimbo* 1961, *Kagemusha* 1981, and *Ran* 1985.

Lang Fritz 1890–1976. Austrian film director whose films are characterized by a strong sense of fatalism and moral inquiry. His German films include *Metropolis* 1927, *M* 1931, in which Peter Lorre starred as a child-killer, and the series of Dr Mabuse films, after which he fled from the Nazis to Hollywood in 1936. His US films include *Fury* 1936, *You Only Live Once* 1937, *Scarlet Street* 1945, *Rancho Notorious* 1952, and *The Big Heat* 1953. He returned to Germany and directed a third picture in the Dr Mabuse series in 1960.

Lean David 1908–1991. British film director. His films, noted for their storytelling flair and atmospheric quality, include early work codirected with Noël Coward. *Brief Encounter* 1946 established Lean as a leading talent. Among his later films are such accomplished epics as *The Bridge on the River Kwai* 1957 (Academy Award), *Lawrence of Arabia* 1962 (Academy Award), and *Dr Zhivago* 1965. The critics' antipathy to *Ryan's Daughter* 1970 caused him to withdraw from filmmaking for over a decade, but *A Passage to India* 1984

MULTIPLE-X CHOICE

	Annual attendance (m)	Total no. of screens	No. of multiplex sites/ no. of screens		multiplex sites: % of all UK cinemas
1984	54	1,246	-	–	–
1985	71	1,251	1	10	1
1986	73	1,229	2	18	1
1987	75	1,215	5	44	4
1988	78	1,250	14	137	11
1989	88	1,424	29	285	20
1990	89	1,552	41	387	25
1991	93	1,642	57	510	31

Source: Cinema Advertising Association

represented a return to form.

Méliès Georges 1861–1938. French film pioneer. From 1896 to 1912 he made over 1,000 films, many of them imaginative fantasies (*Le Voyage dans la Lune/A Trip to the Moon* 1902). He developed trick effects, slow motion, double exposure, and dissolves, and in 1897 built Europe's first film studio at Montreuil.

Born in Paris, Méliès started out as a stage magician. His interest in cinema was sparked by the Lumière brothers' *cinématographe*, premiered 1895. He constructed a camera and founded a production company, Star Film. Méliès failed to develop as a filmmaker and he went bankrupt 1913.

Ophuls Max. Adopted name of Max Oppenheimer 1902–1957. German film director, initially in the theatre, whose style is characterized by a bitter-sweet tone and intricate camera movement. He worked in Europe and the USA, attracting much critical praise for such films as *Letter from an Unknown Woman* 1948, *La Ronde* 1950, and *Lola Montes* 1955. His son is the documentary filmmaker Marcel Ophuls (1927–).

Ozu Yasujiro 1903–1963. One of Japan's leading film director who became known in the West only in his last years. *Tokyo Monogatari/Tokyo Story* 1953 illustrates his typical low camera angles and his predominant theme of middle- class family life. Other major films include *Late Spring* 1949 and *Autumn Afternoon* 1962.

Pasolini Pier Paolo 1922–1975. Italian director, poet, and novelist. His early work is coloured by his experience of life in the poor districts of Rome, where he lived from 1950, and illustrates the decadence and inequality of society from a Marxist viewpoint. Among his films are *Accattone!* 1961, *Mamma Roma* 1962, *Il vangelo secondo Mateo/The Gospel According to St Matthew* 1964, *Decameron* 1970, *I racconti de Canterbury/The Canterbury Tales* 1972, and *Salò/The 120 Days of Sodom* 1975.

Porter Edwin Stanton 1869–1941. US director, a pioneer of film narrative. His 1903 film *The Great Train Robbery* lasted 12 minutes—then an unusually long time for a film—and contained an early use of the close-up. More concerned with the technical than the artistic side of his films, which include *The Teddy Bears* 1907 and *The Final Pardon* 1912, Porter abandoned filmmaking 1916.

Powell Michael 1905–1990. English film director and producer. Some of his most memorable films were made in collaboration with Hungarian screenwriter Emeric Pressburger, with whom he formed a company, the Archers, in 1942. They produced a succession of ambitious and richly imaginative films, including *The Life and Death of Colonel Blimp* 1943, *A Matter of Life and Death* 1946, *Black Narcissus* 1947, *The Red Shoes* 1948, and the opera movie *The Tales of Hoffman* 1951. On his own, Powell later made *Peeping Tom* 1960, a horror film which attracted widespread criticism.

CASABLANCA

Casablanca celebrated its half-centenary in 1992, and to mark the occasion Warner Brothers re-released newly struck prints in the US and abroad.

But what has in the intervening years become the most celebrated and quoted of all Hollywood movies did not have an auspicious inauguration. For one thing, the original casting proposal for the roles played by Humphrey Bogart, Ingrid Bergman and Paul Henreid was the considerably less charismatic trio of Ronald Reagan, Ann Sheridan and Dennis Morgan. For another, the screenplay (from a play dubbed at the time as 'one of the world's worst') was written by Julius and Philip Epstein and Howard Koch at breakneck speed, while the film was already in production, with the script being fed to the actors from day to day, and with nobody knowing how the story would end.

Nor did the film have much to do with wartime reality. Julius Epstein said recently: 'We had no idea of conditions in Casablanca in 1942. Later we learned there were no Germans there at all.' And, of course, nobody actually speaks the words, 'Play it again, Sam'.

Pressburger Emeric 1902–1988. Hungarian-born director, producer, and screenwriter, known for his partnership in British films with Michael Powell. (See above.)

Ray Satyajit 1921–1992. Indian film director, internationally known for his trilogy of life in his native Bengal: *Pather Panchali*, *Unvanquished*, and *The World of Apu* 1955–59. Later films include *The Music Room* 1958, *Charulata* 1964, *The Chess Players* 1977, and *The Home and the World* 1984. (See **Obituaries** for more.)

Reed Carol 1906–1976. British film producer and director, an influential figure in the British film industry of the 1940s. His films include *Odd Man Out* 1947, *The Fallen Idol* and *The Third Man* both 1950 (both written by Graham Greene), and *Our Man in Havana* 1959. His later films included the Academy Award-winning *Oliver!* 1968.

Renoir Jean 1894–1979. French director whose films, characterized by their humanism and naturalistic technique, include *Boudu sauvé des eaux/Boudu Saved from Drowning* 1932, *La Grande Illusion* 1937, and *La Règle du Jeu/The Rules of the Game* 1939. In 1975 he received an honorary Academy Award for his life's work. He was the son of the painter Pierre-Auguste Renoir.

Rossellini Roberto 1906–1977. Italian film director. His World War II trilogy, *Roma città aperta/Rome, Open City* 1945, *Paisà/Paisan* 1946, and *Germania anno zero/Germany Year Zero* 1947, had a quality of direct realism which made it a landmark of European cinema.

In 1949 he made *Stromboli*, followed by other films in which his wife Ingrid Bergman appeared. After their divorce he made *General della Rovere* 1959 and embarked on television work including a feature-length film for French TV *La Prise de Pouvoir par Louis XIV/The Rise of Louis XIV* 1966. He and Ingrid Bergman were the parents of actress Isabella Rossellini (1952–).

Scorsese Martin 1942– . US director whose films concentrate on complex characterization and the themes of alienation and guilt. His influential and forceful work includes *Mean Streets* 1973, *Taxi Driver* 1976, *Raging Bull* 1980, *The Color of Money* 1986, *After Hours* 1987, *The Last Temptation of Christ* 1988, and *Cape Fear* 1991.

Spielberg Steven 1947– . US director, writer, and producer of such films as *Jaws* 1975, *Close Encounters of the Third Kind* 1977, *Raiders of the Lost Ark* 1981, and *ET* 1982. Immensely successful, his films usually combine cliff-hanging suspense with heartfelt sentimentality. He also directed *Indiana Jones and the Temple of Doom* 1984, *The Color Purple* 1985, *Empire of the Sun* 1987, and *Indiana Jones and the Last Crusade* 1989.

Sternberg Josef von 1894–1969. Austrian film director, in the USA from childhood. He is best remembered for his seven films with Marlene Dietrich, including *The Blue Angel/Der blaue Engel* 1930, *Blonde Venus* 1932, and *The Devil Is a Woman* 1935, all of which are marked by his expressive use of light and shadow. His subsequent career was sporadic, culminating in the Japanese-made *Saga of Anatahan* 1953.

Stroheim Erich von. Assumed name of Erich Oswald Stroheim 1885–1957. Austrian actor and director, in Hollywood from 1914. He was successful as an actor in villainous roles, then embarked on a career as a director. Such films as *Foolish Wives* 1922 won widespread praise, but his progress foundered on his extravagance (*Greed* 1923), and he returned to acting in such international films as *La Grande Illusion* 1937 and *Sunset Boulevard* 1950.

Sturges Preston. Adopted name of Edmond Biden 1898–1959. US film director and writer who enjoyed great success with a series of satirical comedies in the early 1940s, including *Sullivan's Travels* 1941, *The Palm Beach Story* 1942, and *The Miracle of Morgan's Creek* 1943. His last film *Diary of Major Thompson* 1955 was made in France.

Tarkovsky Andrei 1932–1986. Soviet film director whose work is characterized by an epic style combined with intense personal spirituality. His films include *Solaris* 1972, *Mirror* 1975, *Stalker* 1979, and *The Sacrifice* 1986. The last was made in Sweden, following his exile from the USSR in 1984.

Tati Jacques. Stage name of Jacques Tatischeff 1908–1982. French comic actor, director, and writer. He portrayed Monsieur Hulot, the embodiment of polite opposition to modern mechanization, in a series of films starting with *Les Vacances de M Hulot/Monsieur*

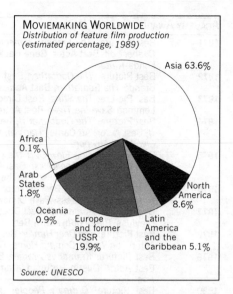

MOVIEMAKING WORLDWIDE
Distribution of feature film production (estimated percentage, 1989)

Asia 63.6%

Africa 0.1%

Arab States 1.8%

North America 8.6%

Oceania 0.9%

Europe and former USSR 19.9%

Latin America and the Caribbean 5.1%

Source: UNESCO

Hulot's Holiday 1953, and including *Mon Oncle/My Uncle* 1959 and *Playtime* 1968.

Truffaut François 1932–1984. French New Wave film director and actor, formerly a critic. A popular, romantic, and intensely humane filmmaker, he wrote and directed a series of semi-autobiographical films starring Jean-Pierre Léaud, beginning with *Les Quatre Cent Coups/The 400 Blows* 1959. His other films include *Jules et Jim* 1961, *Fahrenheit 451* 1966, *L'Enfant sauvage/The Wild Child* 1970, and *La Nuit américaine/Day for Night* 1973 (Academy Award).

His love of cinema led to a job as film critic for *Cahiers du Cinema* during the 1950s before embarking on his career as director. His later work includes *The Story of Adèle H* 1975 and *The Last Metro* 1980. He was influenced by Alfred Hitchcock, and also by French comic traditions.

Vigo Jean. Adopted name of Jean Almereida 1905–1934. French director of intensely lyrical and semi-surrealist films. He made only two shorts, *A Propos de Nice* 1930 and *Taris Champion de Natation* 1934; and two feature films, *Zéro de conduite/Nothing for Conduct* 1933 and *L'Atalante* 1934. His promising career was tragically cut short by leukemia.

Visconti Luchino 1906–1976. Italian film, opera, and theatre director. The film *Ossessione* 1942 pioneered neorealist cinema despite being subject to censorship problems from the fascist government; later works include *Rocco and His Brothers* 1960, *The Leopard* 1963, *The Damned* 1969, and *Death in Venice* 1971. His powerful social commentary led to clashes with the Italian government and Roman Catholic Church.

Wajda Andrzej 1926– . Polish film and theatre director, one of the major figures in postwar European cinema. His films are often concerned with the predicament and disillu-

ACADEMY AWARDS: RECENT WINNERS

1971	Best Picture: *The French Connection*; Best Director: William Friedkin *The French Connection*; Best Actor: Gene Hackman *The French Connection*; Best Actress: Jane Fonda *Klute*
1972	Best Picture: *The Godfather*; Best Director: Bob Fosse *Cabaret*; Best Actor: Marlon Brando *The Godfather*; Best Actress: Liza Minnelli *Cabaret*
1973	Best Picture: *The Sting*; Best Director: George Roy Hill *The Sting*; Best Actor: Jack Lemmon *Save the Tiger*; Best Actress: Glenda Jackson *A Touch of Class*
1974	Best Picture: *The Godfather II*; Best Director: Francis Ford Coppola *The Godfather II*; Best Actor: Art Carney *Harry and Tonto*; Best Actress: Ellen Burstyn *Alice Doesn't Live Here Anymore*
1975	Best Picture: *One Flew Over the Cuckoo's Nest*; Best Director: Milos Forman *One Flew Over the Cuckoo's Nest*; Best Actor: Jack Nicholson *One Flew Over the Cuckoo's Nest*; Best Actress: Louise Fletcher *One Flew Over the Cuckoo's Nest*
1976	Best Picture: *Rocky*; Best Director: John G Avildsen *Rocky*; Best Actor: Peter Finch *Network*; Best Actress: Faye Dunaway *Network*
1977	Best Picture: *Annie Hall*; Best Director: Woody Allen *Annie Hall*; Best Actor: Richard Dreyfuss *The Goodbye Girl*; Best Actress: Diane Keaton *Annie Hall*
1978	Best Picture: *The Deer Hunter*; Best Director: Michael Cimino *The Deer Hunter*; Best Actor: Jon Voight *Coming Home*; Best Actress: Jane Fonda *Coming Home*
1979	Best Picture: *Kramer vs Kramer*; Best Director: Robert Benton *Kramer vs Kramer*; Best Actor: Dustin Hoffman *Kramer vs Kramer*; Best Actress: Sally Field *Norma Rae*
1980	Best Picture: *Ordinary People*; Best Director: Robert Redford *Ordinary People*; Best Actor: Robert De Niro *Raging Bull*; Best Actress: Sissy Spacek *Coal Miner's Daughter*
1981	Best Picture: *Chariots of Fire*; Best Director: Warren Beatty *Reds*; Best Actor: Henry Fonda *On Golden Pond*; Best Actress: Katharine Hepburn *On Golden Pond*
1982	Best Picture: *Gandhi*; Best Director: Richard Attenborough *Gandhi*; Best Actor: Ben Kingsley *Gandhi*; Best Actress: Meryl Streep *Sophie's Choice*
1983	Best Picture: *Terms of Endearment*; Best Director: James L Brooks *Terms of Endearment*; Best Actor: Robert Duvall *Tender Mercies*; Best Actress: Shirley MacLaine *Terms of Endearment*
1984	Best Picture: *Amadeus*; Best Director: Milos Forman *Amadeus*; Best Actor: F Murray Abraham *Amadeus*; Best Actress: Sally Field *Places in the Heart*
1985	Best Picture: *Out of Africa*; Best Director: Sidney Pollack *Out of Africa*; Best Actor: William Hurt *Kiss of the Spiderwoman*; Best Actress: Geraldine Page *The Trip to Bountiful*
1986	Best Picture: *Platoon*; Best Director: Oliver Stone *Platoon*; Best Actor: Paul Newman *The Color of Money*; Best Actress: Marlee Matlin *Children of a Lesser God*
1987	Best Picture: *The Last Emperor*; Best Director: Bernardo Bertolucci *The Last Emperor*; Best Actor: Michael Douglas *Wall Street*; Best Actress: Cher *Moonstruck*
1988	Best Picture: *Rain Man*; Best Director: Barry Levinson *Rain Man*; Best Actor: Dustin Hoffman *Rain Man*; Best Actress: Jodie Foster *The Accused*
1989	Best Picture: *Driving Miss Daisy*; Best Director: Oliver Stone *Born on the 4th of July*; Best Actor: Daniel Day-Lewis *My Left Foot*; Best Actress: Jessica Tandy *Driving Miss Daisy*
1990	Best Picture: *Dances with Wolves*; Best Director: Kevin Costner *Dances with Wolves*; Best Actor: Jeremy Irons *Reversal of Fortune*; Best Actress: Kathy Bates *Misery*
1991	Best Picture: *The Silence of the Lambs*; Best Director: Jonathan Demme *The Silence of the Lambs*; Best Actor: Anthony Hopkins *The Silence of the Lambs*; Best Actress: Jodie Foster *The Silence of the Lambs*

sionment of individuals caught up in political events. His works include *Ashes and Diamonds* 1958, *Man of Marble* 1977, *Man of Iron* 1981, *Danton* 1982, and *Korczak* 1990. He has also worked in television and theatre. He made a television film version of Joseph Conrad's *The Shadow Line* 1976.

Welles (George) Orson 1915–1985. US actor and film and theatre director, whose first film was *Citizen Kane* 1941, which he produced, directed, and starred in. Using innovative lighting, camera angles and movements, he made it a landmark in the history of cinema, yet he directed very few films subsequently in Hollywood, and later worked mostly in Europe. His performances as an actor include the character of Harry Lime in *The Third Man* 1949.

In 1937 he founded the Mercury Theater, New York, with John Houseman, where their repertory productions included a modern-dress version of *Julius Caesar*. Welles's real-

CINEMA: CHRONOLOGY

1826–34	Various machines invented to show moving images: the stroboscope, zoetrope, and thaumatrope.
1872	Eadweard Muybridge demonstrated movement of horses' legs by using 24 cameras.
1877	Invention of Praxinoscope; developed as a projector of successive images on screen in 1879 in France.
1878–95	Marey, a French physiologist, developed various types of camera for recording human and animal movements.
1887	Augustin le Prince produced the first series of images on a perforated film; Thomas Edison, having developed the phonograph, took the first steps in developing a motion-picture recording and reproducing device to accompany recorded sound.
1888	William Friese-Greene showed the first celluloid film and patented a movie camera.
1889	Edison invented 35mm film.
1890–94	Edison, using perforated film, developed his Kinetograph camera and Kinetoscope individual viewer; developed commercially in New York, London, and Paris.
1895	The Lumière brothers, Auguste (1862–1954) and Louis (1864–1948), projected, to a paying audience, a film of an oncoming train arriving at a station. Some of the audience fled in terror.
1896	Pathé introduced the Berliner gramophone, using discs in synchronization with film. Lack of amplification, however, made the performances ineffective.
1899	Edison tried to improve amplification by using banks of phonographs.
1900	Attempts to synchronize film and disc were made by Gaumont in France and Goldschmidt in Germany, leading later to the Vitaphone system of the USA.
1902	Georges Méliès (1861–1938) made *Le Voyage dans la Lune/A Trip to the Moon*.
1903	The first Western was made in the USA: *The Great Train Robbery* by Edwin S Porter.
1906	The earliest colour film (Kinemacolor) was patented in Britain by George Albert Smith.
1908–11	In France, Emile Cohl experimented with film animation.
1910	With the influence of US Studios, film actors and actresses began to be recognized as international stars.
1912	In Britain, Eugene Lauste designed experimental 'sound on film' systems.
1914–18	Full newsreel coverage of World War I.
1915	*The Birth of a Nation*, D W Griffith's epic on the American Civil War, was released in the USA.
1917	35mm was officially adopted as the standard format for motion picture film by the Society of Motion Picture Engineers of America.
1918–19	A sound system called Tri-Ergon was developed in Germany, which led to sound being recorded on film photographically. The photography of sound was also developed by Lee De Forrest in his Phonofilm system.
1923	First sound film (as Phonofilm) demonstrated.
1926	*Don Juan*, a silent film with a synchronized music score, was released.
1927	Release of the first major sound film, *The Jazz Singer*, consisting of some songs and a few moments of dialogue, by Warner Brothers, New York City. The first Academy Awards (Oscars).
1928	Walt Disney released his first Mickey Mouse cartoon, *Steamboat Willie*. The first all-talking film, *Lights of New York*, was released.
1930	*The Big Trail*, a Western filmed and shown in 70mm rather than the standard 35mm format, was released. 70mm is still used, but usually only for big-budget epics such as *Lawrence of Arabia*.
1932	Technicolor (three-colour) process introduced and used for a Walt Disney cartoon film.
1935	*Becky Sharp*, the first film in three-colour Technicolor (a process now abandoned), was released.
1937	Walt Disney released the first feature-length (82 minutes) cartoon, *Snow White and the Seven Dwarfs*.
1939	*Gone With the Wind*, regarded as one of Hollywood's greatest achievements, was released.
1952	Cinerama, a wide-screen presentation using three cameras and three projectors, was introduced in New York.
1953	Commercial 3-D (three-dimensional) cinema and wide-screen CinemaScope were launched in the USA. CinemaScope used a single camera and projector to produce a wide-screen effect by using an anamorphic lens. The cameras were clumsy and the audiences disliked wearing the obligatory glasses. The new wide-screen cinema was accompanied by the introduction of Stereographic sound, which eventually became standard.

CINEMA: CHRONOLOGY: Cont.

1959	The first film in Smell-O-Vision, *The Scent of Mystery*, was released. The process did not catch on.
1970	Most major films were released in Dolby stereo.
1981	Designated 'the Year of Colour Film' by director Martin Scorsese in a campaign to draw attention to, and arrest, the deterioration of colour film shot since 1950 on unstable Eastman Kodak stock.
1982	One of the first and most effective attempts at feature-length, computer-generated animation was *Tron*, Walt Disney's $20-million bid to break into the booming fantasy market. 3-D made a brief comeback; some of the films released that used the process, such as *Jaws 3-D* and *Friday the 13th Part 3*, were commercial successes, but the revival was short-lived.
1987	US House Judiciary Committee petitioned by leading Hollywood filmmakers to protect their work from electronic 'colorization', the new process by which black-and-white films were tinted for television transmission.

---

istic radio broadcast of H G Wells's *The War of the Worlds* 1938 caused panic and fear of Martian invasion in the USA. He directed the films *The Magnificent Ambersons* 1942, *The Lady from Shanghai* 1948 with his wife Rita Hayworth, *Touch of Evil* 1958, and *Chimes at Midnight* 1967, a Shakespeare adaptation. As his career declined he became a familiar voice and face in US television commercials, and made guest appearances on TV shows.

MODERN DANCE

Modern dance is a 20th-century dance idiom that evolved in opposition to ballet by those seeking a freer and more immediate means of dance expression. In the USA, Martha Graham and Merce Cunningham were leading exponents of modern dance.

It was pioneered by American women seeking individual freedom and release from Victorian restrictions. Isadora Duncan and Loie Fuller worked mainly in Europe, but it is from Ruth St Denis, who founded the Denishawn School in Los Angeles 1915 with her partner Ted Shawn, that the first generation of modern dance proper—Martha Graham, Doris Humphrey, and Charles Weidman—emerged.

Doris Humphrey opened a school and performing group in New York 1928. The Humphrey-Weidman technique was based on the kinetic theory of **fall and recovery**. Humphrey's most famous protégé was José Limón.

Martha Graham's distinctive technique is based on **contraction and release**. From her company and School of Contemporary Dance, opened 1927 in New York, a long line of dancers and choreographers continues to

MODERN DANCE: CHRONOLOGY

1900–02	Isadora Duncan triumphed in London, Paris, Budapest, Vienna, Munich, Berlin. Much admired by Fokine and Diaghilev, she abandoned corsets, dancing barefoot in a simple, flowing Greek tunic; a great contribution to dance was her insistence on using great music.
1915	Denishawn School founded in Los Angeles by Ruth St Denis and her husband and partner Ted Shawn. The first platform for Modern Dance in America, Graham, Humphrey and Weidman all began their careers at Denishawn.
1927	Martha Graham opened her School of Contemporary Dance in New York City evolving and teaching the (now world-famous) Graham Technique based on 'contraction and release', and forming her company.
1928	Doris Humphrey and Charles Weidman open the Humphrey–Weidman School, teaching their method based on the principles of 'Fall and Recovery'.
1932	Ted Shawn opened his summer theatre at Jacob's Pillow, Mass., forming the all-male troupe Ted Shawn and His Men, which did much to raise the status of male dancers, touring the US.
1941	The first Jacob's Pillow Dance Festival established with Ted Shawn as director. Ted Shawn Theatre built.
1944	Graham's most memorable work, *Appalachian Spring* premiered in New York City with a specially commissioned score by Aaron Copland.
1952	Merce Cunningham formed his own company appointing composer, and longterm collaborator, John Cage as musical director.
1954	Paul Taylor Dance Company formed. A former Cunningham and Graham dancer, Taylor's generous, free and athletic style of choreography—in works ranging from witty and lyrical to bleak satire—often used atypical dancers.
1958	Alvin Ailey American Dance Theater (later A A City Center Dance Theater) formed, New York City. A multi-racial company, Ailey's works depict life in urban and rural Black America.
1960	*Revelations*, Ailey's 'signature-piece' premiered in New York City, set to traditional spirituals and Gospel music.
1962	Judson Dance Theater, a collective of choreographers exploring Cunningham's theories (at his Judson St. Studio) went further, abandoning formal dance technique and concentrating on every day movement: the leading names were Trisha Brown, Lucinda Childs, Steve Paxton, Yvonne Rainer, and later, Laura Dean and Kei Takei.
1966	Norman Morrice returned to Ballet Rambert after two years in New York City studying with Graham, and the company shifted to Modern Dance, abandoning the classics.
1967	Robert Cohan, former longterm Graham dancer, invited to England to direct the newly formed London Contemporary Dance Theatre.
1968	Lar Lubovitch Dance Company formed in New York City. Collaborating with minimalist composers Steve Reich and Philip Glass he evolved a parallel form of choreography.
1969	'The Place' opened in London, new home for London Contemporary Dance Theatre providing its own theatre, and studios for the School.
1971	Twyla Tharp's *Eight Jelly Rolls*, to the New Orleans piano music of Jelly Roll Morton, premiered in New York City. Hiding serious technique behind free-style carefree movement and off-beat humour she was immediately popular.
1981	First showing Kei Takei's *Light*, an 11-hour work in 15 parts.
1987	Rambert Dance Company became the new name for Ballet Rambert.
1990	*Maple Leaf Rag* Martha Graham's final work premiered in New York City.

Avant-garde Dance Repertory

date	title	choreographer	place
1969	*Moving Earth*	Kei Takei	New York
1970	*Walking on the Wall*	Trisha Brown	New York
1971	*Education of the Girlchild*	Meredith Monk	New York
1978	*Café Müller*	Pina Bausch	Essen
1986	*The Watteau Duet*	Karole Armitage	New York
1988	*I Am Curious Orange*	Michael Clark	Amsterdam

emerge. Among them, Erick Hawkins, Merce Cunningham, Glenn Tetley, Paul Taylor, and Dan Waggoner have each evolved his own style.

In the UK, the London Contemporary Dance Theatre and school was set up 1967 by Robert Cohan, a long-time Graham dancer. It is the only European institute authorized to teach Graham Technique. Richard Alston, Siobhan Davies, and Robert North studied, performed, and choreographed there.

In Germany, the originators of a modernist movement known as Central European dance were Jacques Dalcroze and Rudolph Laban. The leading exponents, Mary Wigman, Harald Kreutzberg, and Kurt Joss, had some influence on modern dance through their visits to the USA and through Hanya Holm, a former Wigman dancer who settled and taught in New York, and with whom Alwyn Nikolais was originally associated.

AVANT-GARDE DANCE

Avant-garde dance is an experimental form of dance that rejects the conventions of modern dance. It is often performed in informal

Modern Dance Repertory

Date	Dance	Composer	Choreographer	Place
1906	Radha	Delibes	Ruth St Denis	Los Angeles
1930	The Shakers	Lawrence	Doris Humphrey	New York City
1931	Primitive Mysteries	Horst	Martha Graham	New York City
1935	Kinetic Molpai	Meeker	Ted Shawn	Los Angeles
1937	Trend	Varèse	Hanya Holm	Bennington College, NY
1944	Appalachian Spring	Copland	Martha Graham	New York City
1949	The Moor's Pavane	Purcell	José Limón	Connecticut College, CT
1955	Rooms	Hopkins	Anna Sokolow	New York City
1958	Clytemnestra	El-Dabh	Martha Graham	New York City
1958	Blues Suite	Trad/Blues	Alvin Ailey	New York City
1958	Summerspace	Feldman	Merce Cunningham	Connecticut College, CT
1960	Acrobats of God	Surinach	Martha Graham	New York City
1960	Revelations	Trad/Spirituals	Alvin Ailey	New York City
1960	8 Clear Places	Dlugozewski	Erick Hawkins	New York City
1962	Aureole	Hayden	Paul Taylor	New York City
1967	Harbinger	Prokofiev	Eliot Feld	New York City
1969	Moving Earth		Kei Takei	New York City
1969	Transitions	Webern	John Butler	Cologne
1970	Walking On The Wall		Trisha Brown	New York City
1971	Education Of The Girlchild	Meredith Monk	Meredith Monk	New York City
1971	Eight Jelly Rolls	Jelly Roll Morton	Twyla Tharp	New York City
1972	The Lark Ascending	Vaughn Williams	Alvin Ailey	New York City
1973	Deuce Coupe	Beach Boys	Twyla Tharp	New York City
1974	Troy Game	Downes/Batacuda	Robert North	London
1975	Esplanade	J S Bach	Paul Taylor	New York City
1976	Push Comes To Shove	Hayden/Jos Lamb	Twyla Tharp	New York City
1977	Marimba	Steve Reich	Lar Lubovitch	New York City
1978	Café Müller		Pina Bausch	Essen
1978	North Star	Philip Glass	Lar Lubovitch	New York City
1980	Bell High	Maxwell Davies	Richard Alston	London
1983	Midsummer	Tippet	Richard Alston	London
1986	The Watteau Duet		Karole Armitage	New York City
1988	I Am Curious Orange		Michael Clark	Amsterdam
1988	Space	Steve Reich	Laura Dean	New York City
1988	Drink To Me Only With Thine Eyes	Virgil Thompson	Mark Morris	New York City
1990	Maple Leaf Rag	Scott Joplin	Martha Graham	New York City

THE BALLET REPERTORY

date	ballet	composer	choreographer	place
1670	Le Bourgeois Gentil homme	Lully	Beauchamp	Chambord
1761	Don Juan	Gluck	Angiolini	Vienna
1778	Les Petits Riens	Mozart	Noverre	Paris
1828	La Fille Mal Gardée	Hérold	Aumer	Paris
1832	La Sylphide	Schneitzhoeffer	F. Taglioni	Paris
1841	Giselle	Adam	Coralli/Perrot	Paris
1844	La Esmeralda	Pugni	Perrot	London
1869	Don Quixote	Minkus	M. Petipa	Moscow
1877	La Bayadère	Minkus	M. Petipa	St Petersburg
1877	Swan Lake	Tchaikovsky	Reisinger	Moscow
1890	The Sleeping Beauty	Tchaikovsky	M. Petipa	St Petersburg
1892	Nutcracker	Tchaikovsky	M. Petipa/Ivanov	St Petersburg
1898	Raymonda	Glazunov	M.Petipa	St Petersburg
1905	The Dying Swan	Saint-Saëns	Fokine	St Petersburg
1907	Les Sylphides	Chopin	Fokine	St Petersburg
1910	Le Carnaval	Schumann	Fokine	St Petersburg
1910	The Firebird	Stravinsky	Fokine	Paris
1911	Petrushka	Stravinsky	Fokine	Paris
1911	Le Spectre de la Rose	Weber	Fokine	Monte Carlo
1912	L'Après-midi d'un Faune	Debussy	Nijinsky	Paris
1912	Daphnis and Chloë	Ravel	Fokine	Paris
1913	Jeux	Debussy	Nijinsky	Paris
1913	The Rite of Spring	Stravinsky	Nijinsky	Paris
1915	El Amor Brujo	Falla	Imperio	Madrid
1923	Les Noces	Stravinsky	Nijinska	Paris
1924	Les Biches	Poulenc	Nijinska	Monte Carlo
1928	Le Baiser de la Fée	Tchaikovsky	Nijinska	Paris
1928	Bolero	Ravel	Nijinska	Paris
1929	The Prodigal Son	Prokofiev	Balanchine	Paris
1931	Bacchus and Ariadne	Roussel	Lifar	Paris
1931	Job	Vaughan Williams	de Valois	London
1934	Serenade	Tchaikovsky	Balanchine	New York
1937	Les Patineurs	Meyerbeer/Lambert	Ashton	London
1938	Billy the Kid	Copland	Loring	Chicago
1938	Romeo and Juliet	Prokofiev	Psota	Brno, Moravia
1942	The Miraculous Mandarin	Bartók	Milloss	Milan
1942	Rodeo	Copland	de Mille	New York
1942	Gayaneh	Khachaturian	Anisimova	Molotov-Perm
1944	Appalachian Spring	Copland	Graham	Washington
1944	Fancy Free	Bernstein	Robbins	New York
1945	Cinderella	Prokofiev	Zakharov	Moscow
1949	Carmen	Bizet	Petit	London
1953	Afternoon of a Faun	Debussy	Robbins	New York
1956	Spartacus	Khachaturian	Jacobson	Leningrad
1957	Agon	Stravinsky	Balanchine	New York
1959	Episodes	Webern	Balanchine	New York
1962	A Midsummer Night's Dream	Mendelssohn	Balanchine	New York
1964	The Dream	Mendelssohn/Lanchbery	Ashton	London
1965	The Song of the Earth	Mahler	MacMillan	Stuttgart
1967	Anastasia	Martinu	MacMillan	New York
1968	Enigma Variations	Elgar	Ashton	London
1969	Dancers at a Gathering	Chopin	Robbins	New York
1969	The Taming of the Shrew	Stolze/Scarlatti	Cranko	Stuttgart
1972	Duo Concertante	Stravinsky	Balanchine	New York
1974	Elite Syncopations	Joplin, etc	MacMillan	London
1976	A Month in the Country	Chopin/Lanchbery	Ashton	London
1978	Mayerling	Liszt/Lanchbery	MacMillan	London
1978	Symphony of Psalms	Stravinsky	Kylian	Scheveningen
1980	Gloria	Poulenc	MacMillan	London
1980	Rhapsody	Rachmaninov	Ashton	London

spaces—museums, rooftops, even scaling walls. Dance that is today avant-garde usually enters mainstream dance eventually in some form.

In the USA, avant-garde dance stemmed mainly from Merce Cunningham in New York and the exploration of his ideas by musician Robert Dunn in a series of choreographer's workshops which eventually became the Judson Dance Theater. While retaining technique and rhythm, Cunningham deleted the role of choreographer, giving dancers a new freedom. Steps and directions were random choices arrived at by lottery or a tossed coin, and he rejected both dramatic and romantic content, concentrating on form. The Judson collective went further, denying even the necessity for technique and concentrating on the use of everyday movement—walking, spinning, jumping. Karole Armitage, Trisha Brown, Lucinda Childs, and Steve Paxton, followed by Laura Dean and Keitakei, are the leading names in this movement.

In the UK, Rosemary Butcher and Michael Clark (both of whom worked with Post-Modernists in New York) are the leading avant-garde names. Clark's work often involves the use of zany props and outrageous costumes.

In Essen, Germany, Pina Bausch with her Wuppertal Tanztheater (dance theatre) is the most compelling influence in European dance since Diaghilev. Her works, often several hours long, blend elements of dance, music, dialogue, gesture, psychology, comedy, and stark fear, and may be performed on floors covered with churned earth, rose petals, or water.

Dancing

Can you dance?

Yes	48
Yes, but not very well	20
No	32

Have you ever paid for dancing lessons?

Yes	25
No	75

PRESS AND TV MEDIA

ABC American Broadcasting Company, absorbed 1986 into Capital Cities/ABC (see below).

Agence France-Presse the world's oldest and third largest news agency, founded in 1835. It is based in Paris and by 1992 had six 24-hour news wires in six languages, 200 bureaux, and 2,000 correspondents worldwide.

Associated Press (AP) the world's largest news service. It is a nonprofit cooperative wire news service, founded in 1848. AP has (1992) 16,200 print and broadcast subscribers in 110 countries; it is also available to individuals through on-line information services. It has 229 bureaux and more than 3,000 correspondents worldwide; headquarters in New York City.

British Broadcasting Corporation (BBC) UK state-owned broadcasting network, established as a private company 1922 and converted to a public body 1927. It operates television and national and local radio stations, and is financed solely by the sale of television viewing licences; it is not allowed to carry advertisements. Overseas radio broadcasts (World Service) have a government subsidy.

BSkyB (British Sky Broadcasting) British group of satellite TV channels, formed 1990 by a merger between Sky Television and British Satellite Broadcasting. In 1992 BSkyB operated six channels from the Astra satellite: Sky News, Sky One, Sky Movies Plus, the Movie Channel, the Comedy Channel, and Sky Sports. Rupert Murdoch's News Corporation holds a 50% interest.

Cable News Network (CNN) international television news channel; the 24-hour service was founded 1980 by US entrepreneur Ted Turner and has its headquarters in Atlanta, Georgia. It established its global reputation 1991 with eyewitness accounts from Baghdad

WATCHING THE BOX

(average hours of viewing per individual, 1985 and 1991)

	1985	1991
All BBC	1.74	1.62
All ITV	2.04	1.78
All TV	3.77	3.40

Source: BARB

of the beginning of the Gulf War.

Capital Cities/ABC US television and radio network, one of the three biggest in the country. The company owns eight TV and 21 radio stations, three cable TV channels, nine daily newspapers, plus weekly papers, shopping guides, and magazines; its 1991 turnover was $5,381.9 million. ABC was founded 1943 when NBC was forced to sell off one of its two networks. It was taken over by Capital Cities in 1986.

CBC (Canadian Broadcasting Corporation, or Société Radio-Canada) the national radio and television service of Canada. CBC was set up in 1936. It is primarily government-funded; the rest (about 30%) comes from advertising. It was the first system to use a geostationary satellite.

CBS (Columbia Broadcasting System) US television and radio network. Founded in 1927 as a rival radio network to NBC, CBS set up its first TV station in New York in 1931. It owns seven TV stations, 21 radio stations, and in 1991 acquired Midwest Communications, which included TV, radio stations, and a sports cable channel. It had an annual turnover of $3,035 million in 1991.

European Broadcasting Union (EBU) organization of W European public and national broadcasters, set up in 1950. The EBU manages Eurovision, founded 1954, a network for the exchange of programmes and news, and

REACHING CONSUMERS: EUROPEAN ADVERTISING (1990)

	expenditure per head of population (ecu)	Distribution by media (percentage)			
		Press	TV	Radio	Other
Belgium	91.3	55.8	27.5	1.2	15.6
Denmark	273.1	87.9	9.6	0.8	1.7
France	130.1	56.1	24.8	6.6	12.5
Germany	158.7	73.9	15.8	5.1	5.1
Greece	49.2	54.2	35.3	5.7	4.8
Ireland	97.6	69.2	19.6	6.2	5.1
Italy	92.4	51.9	43.2	1.4	3.6
Netherlands	140.9	78.2	9.0	2.2	10.6
Portugal	37.2	46.8	37.1	6.7	9.5
Spain	155.0	53.0	31.3	10.3	5.5
Switzerland	269.4	77.9	6.7	1.7	13.7
UK	159.6	63.4	30.5	2.2	3.9

Source: NTC

ON-LINE: THE WORLD AT YOUR FINGERTIPS

Electronic mail is only the beginning of what you can do with a computer, a modem, a telephone line, and a communications program. Armed with those simple tools, you can dial over the telephone lines into some of the finest reference libraries in the world, chat with people from all countries with interests similar to yours, and even go shopping. What you dial into when your modem picks up the phone is another, 'host', computer, with files stored on it; you access these as if they were stored on your own computer. There are several types of systems. A bulletin-board system (BBS), usually free of charge, is typically run from someone's house, with an ordinary personal computer (PC) serving as the host.

BBSs are friendly places: the people who dial in ('log on') leave messages for others to read, send ('upload') files that other people may like to use, or get ('download') files they themselves would like to use. These could be anything from a utility program someone has written to a text file explaining how to make tea.

A conference from your living room
A conferencing system is more elaborate. London's Compulink Information Exchange (CIX), for example, runs on three networked computers, two of them minicomputers and one a PC, with 7 to 8 gigabytes of hard-disc storage. CIX's 7,000 users have set up hundreds of conferences—literally, discussions—on topics from Michael Caine and astrology to technical support for the latest products. Users log on, read the messages in the conferences they are interested in, comment on what they have read or leave messages on new topics, and log off again. The whole effect is of a lively pub discussion, but one where the people can join in when it is convenient for them, rather than having to be there at a particular time.

Information networks
If BBSs and conferencing systems have a lot in common with the local pub, an on-line information system is more like a huge network of libraries that include a number of rooms where public discussions take place. The oldest such commercial system is CompuServe, which was founded in 1978 and in 1992 boasted nearly a million users worldwide. It takes 45 computers, most of them mainframes, to run CompuServe. Other such services include British Telecom's Telecom Gold service, which links to its Dialcom network, and the US-based services Genie and Prodigy. BT also runs Prestel, an older-style viewdata service.

Services like these act as retailers for other, more specialized systems, like the Dow Jones News Service, Knight-Ridder's Knowledge Index, Associated Press Online, the *Financial Times*'s Profile database of UK newspaper articles, Reuters' Textline, and Maxwell On-line's collection of specialized medical and legal databases. Still others, like Justis, the European legal database, are available both on-line

and on CD-ROM, updated regularly. Direct subscriptions to these services can work out to be expensive; accessing them through the more comprehensive services is more economical for a user at home who only occasionally needs specialist information.

Europe catches up
On-line information systems have developed, like much of computer technology, much faster in the USA. This has only partly to do with lower prices and the ready availability of computer equipment and a large, homogeneous mass market. More important has been the proprietary attitude of European national telephone networks, which have required expensive state approval of all telecommunications equipment. In Britain, it wasn't until 1985 that modems were available from suppliers other than BT, and even in 1992 the requirement for BABT (British Approvals Board for Telecommunications) approval made modems easily twice as expensive in Britain as in the USA.

Many European countries have, however, some form of national on-line service. In 1984 France inaugurated its Minitel service by distributing terminals to telephone subscribers. The French national telephone directories, plus a wealth of other financial, business, and travel information, is available on the system. Similar systems exist in other countries, such as Switzerland.

Mega-network
One of the earliest, though noncommercial, communications networks was ARPANET, developed under contract to the US Defense Advanced Research Projects Agency (DARPA) in 1969. With similar projects underway in other countries, including the UK's Joint Academic Network (JANET), DARPA began looking at ways to connect the networks. The result is the largest network in the world, known as the Internet; this connects some 7,000 networks worldwide. In 1992, the newly founded Internet Society estimated that there were some 4 million users of the Internet in 107 countries.

In Nov 1988, a Cornell University graduate student named Robert Morris, Jr, released a 'worm' program into the Internet. Intended to replicate itself onto each computer linked to the network, it replicated much faster than Morris had anticipated, and paralyzed some 6,000 computers at sites like NASA's Ames Center and Massachusetts Institute of Technology. The result has been a backlash of legislation attempting to control computer networking and the founding of the Electronic Frontier Foundation, which promotes public education about technology and civil liberties on the world's computer networks.

Euroradio, founded 1989.

Independent Television Commission (ITC) (formerly the Independent Broadcasting Authority) UK corporate body established by legislation to provide commercially funded television (ITV from 1955) and local radio (ILR from 1973) services. In the 1980s, services expanded to include the launching of Channel 4 (1982) and the provision of satellite television: services broadcast directly by satellite into homes (DBS).

ITAR-TASS (Information Telegraph Agency of Russia) Russian news service. Formerly TASS (the official Soviet news agency, founded in St Petersburg in 1925), ITAR-TASS supplies information in seven languages, and has bureaux in approximately 100 countries.

Maxwell Communications UK media group, broken up in 1991 after Robert Maxwell's death. Heavily debt-ridden, Maxwell Communications was the fifth largest European media group in 1991; by 1992 it was gone. Of its subsidiaries, Pergamon Press was sold to Elsevier, Maxwell Business Publishing was sold to EMAP, and the Mirror Group was floated on the London Stock Exchange as an independent company.

NBC (National Broadcasting Company) US television and radio network. NBC, founded 1926, is a wholly owned subsidiary of RCA (Radio Corporation of America), which was bought in 1985 by General Electric, which also owns the Financial News Network. Besides its broadcast network, NBC also has a 24-hour news channel, CNBC.

PBS (Public Broadcasting System) US public TV network of more than 300 stations. PBS and NPR (National Public Radio) were created by the Corporation for Public Broadcasting, which was set up by President Lyndon Johnson in 1967, to distribute programmes to educational TV and radio. Both are financed by a mix of government funding and public donations.

Reuters news and financial information service with (1992) 177 bureaux in 79 countries. It was founded 1851 by Baron Paul Julius von Reuter (1816-1899), and is based in London. Reuters is the largest shareholder in the television news service Visnews. Its 1991 turnover was £1,466.6 million.

RTE (Radio Telefis Eireann) the national radio and television service of the Republic of Ireland. Radio broadcasting began in Dublin 1926 and in Cork 1927. Television broadcast-

ADULT READERSHIP OF UK NATIONAL NEWSPAPERS (1991)

Title	Total circulation ('000)	Readers per copy	Adult readership ('000)	%	By sex Men	Women
National dailies						
Daily Express	1,541,680	2.4	3,643	8.1	8.3	7.8
Daily Mail	1,701,794	2.5	4,303	9.5	10.2	8.9
Daily Mirror	2,918,947	2.8	8,035	17.8	20.4	15.3
Daily Record	760,955	2.7	2,021	4.5	4.8	4.1
Daily Star	858,296	3.1	2,628	5.8	7.7	4.1
The Sun	3,678,897	2.7	9,857	21.8	24.7	19.1
Today	474,835	3.0	1,408	3.1	3.7	2.5
The Daily Telegraph	1,066,331	2.3	2,492	5.5	6.3	4.8
Financial Times (UK)	182,913	3.7	668	1.5	2.2	0.8
The Guardian	420,542	2.9	1,214	2.7	3.0	2.4
The Independent	383,339	2.8	1,083	2.4	3.0	1.8
The Times	396,755	2.6	1,035	2.3	2.8	1.8
National Sundays						
The Mail On Sunday	1,949,531	2.9	5,677	12.6	13.0	12.2
News of the World	4,811,770	2.7	12,807	28.3	30.6	26.2
Sunday Express	1,637,753	2.8	4,580	10.1	10.1	10.2
Sunday Mirror	2,811,420	3.2	9,130	20.2	21.7	18.8
Sunday Sport	367,365	3.9	1,419	3.1	4.7	1.7
The People	2,276,740	2.9	6,581	14.6	15.5	13.7
Observer	563,675	3.3	1,839	4.1	4.4	3.8
Sunday Telegraph	571,968	3.0	1,734	3.8	4.3	3.4
Sunday Times	1,162,142	3.1	3,568	7.9	9.1	6.8
Independent on Sunday	379,565	3.5	1,332	2.9	3.5	2.4
Weekend Colour Supplements						
Sunday (News of the World)	-	-	12,058	26.7	28.2	25.2
Sunday Express Mag	-	-	4,468	9.9	9.7	10.1
Sunday Mirror Mag	-	-	8,754	19.4	20.5	18.3
You (Mail on Sunday)	-	-	5,708	12.6	12.7	12.6
The Independent Mag	-	-	1,528	3.4	4.1	2.7
Observer Mag	-	-	1,820	4.0	4.4	3.7
The Sunday Times Mag	-	-	3,606	8.0	9.0	7.0
The Telegraph Weekend	-	-	2,963	6.6	6.8	6.3

Source: JICNARS Jan–Dec 1991

THE TV FRANCHISES: WHO WON AND WHO LOST

Undoubtedly the biggest media story of 1991 was the October auction of the franchises for ITV regions under the 1990 Broadcasting Act. The franchise auction is just one of many changes brought in by the Broadcasting Act, meant to open Britain's television industry to free-market forces. Other franchises to be auctioned in 1992 were TV teletext and Channel 5, and the regional franchisees themselves are open to takeovers by foreign media companies after 1994.

The October auction, in which companies submitted sealed bids, was managed by the Independent Television Commission (ITC). There are 16 ITV regions (see table opposite). All the existing franchise holders had to bid to keep their regions. Bidders had to meet a 'quality threshold'; some were rejected on this ground. Financial viability was a criterion, too. The highest bidders, therefore, did not always win. Four companies lost their franchises: TSW, TVS, TV-am, and Thames.

Cross-ownership is growing in television, as in the print media, and this is apparent in the consortia that bid for franchises. Thames's majority shareholder is Thorn EMI, which has a stake in the Astra satellite that broadcasts the BSkyB channels. Carlton, successful bidder for London weekday, owns 20% of Central. Central in turn is a shareholder in Meridian, which beat TVS. Carlton was not the only shareholder in its successful bid; the consortium comprises Carlton (90%), the *Daily Telegraph* (5%), and Italy's RCS (5%).

Carlton, a £1 billion conglomerate, was involved in two other two bids: for breakfast television (Daybreak) and south and southeast England (RCS took a share in this too). About a month after the auction, Carlton announced that it would be taking a 20% stake in Sunrise, the winning bidder for breakfast television. Other shareholders in Sunrise (since renamed GMTV) are Disney (25%), Scottish Television (20%), LWT (20%), and *The Guardian* and *Manchester Evening News* (15%), which also have a small stake in Anglia TV.

Losing franchisee TSW also backed one of

the unsuccessful Wales bidders, C3WW, and Ireland's RTE backed another unsuccessful Wales bidder, Channel 3 Wales and West. American TV and cable companies got into the act: HBO, itself owned by Time Warner, would have been a 26% shareholder in TVS had its bid been successful, and United Artists Cable owns 20% of C3W.

Associated Newspapers, which publishes a number of newspapers in southwest England, has a 20% stake in Westcountry TV, which won the area's licence. The *Daily Telegraph* was part of the Daybreak consortium. The *Daily Mail* and General Trust had a stake in Merlin TV's unsuccessful bid for Wales and West, as well as its existing 5% stake in franchise loser TVS, struggling after its takeover of the US production company MTM. Trinity International Holdings, which publishes the *Liverpool Echo*, was one of North West's backers; the *Newcastle Chronicle and Journal* backed North East; Thomson Regional Newspapers backed TUNI; and the White Rose consortium included the *Barnsley Chronicle*, the *Huddersfield Examiner*, and the *Halifax Courier*.

Thames, the largest ITV company, had held the London weekday licence for 23 years and had provided 40% of the network's weekday programmes, plus such well-known series as *Minder* and *The Bill*. Thames announced that it would become an independent production company and would rely, in part, on sales from its extensive programme library. TVS, bidding jointly with Virgin (which had led unsuccessful CPV-TV bids for south and southeast England and London weekday), won the second independent national radio licence.

The financial imbalance among the successful bids attracted criticism and concern for the stability of the network. Central, for example, knowing it was likely to be unopposed, bid £2,000 a year; Yorkshire, challenged for its smaller area, bid £37.7 million. The ITC estimates the extra revenue to the Treasury at £40 million.

---

ing started 1961. Both are financed by a mix of licence fees and advertising revenues.

United Press International (UPI) wire news service based in Washington DC. Originally founded in 1907 by publisher E W Scripps as United Press, it became UPI in 1958 after a merger with William Randolph Hearst's International News Service. In August 1991 it filed for bankruptcy; in May 1992 US TV evangelist Pat Robertson bid $6 million for the service.

Visnews TV news agency. Visnews, founded 1957 and based in London, has 35 bureaux worldwide, and provides international news to CBS, Fox, and NBC, which has a 37.5% stake in the company. Its other shareholders are Reuters, which is the majority shareholder, and the BBC. In late 1991, Visnews became the first international news agency from a

noncommunist country to be approved to set up a bureau in Havana, Cuba.

Worldwide Television News TV news agency that supplies international news to CNN, PBS, ABC, and CBS, among others. It was founded in 1956, and is jointly owned by Capital Cities/ABC (80%), Nine Network Australia (10%), and Britain's Independent Television News (10%).

EUROPE'S TOP TEN MEDIA CONGLOMERATES

Fininvest Italian media conglomerate, Europe's largest. Owned by Sivio Berlusconi, Fininvest owns Italy's three largest commercial television channels, a group of Italian magazines, and has interests in television in Germany and Spain; it also owns a substantial chunk of the

ITV region	existing franchise holder	result after auction
Borders and the Isle of Man	Border	Border (£52,000) unopposed
Central Scotland	Scottish	Scottish (£2,000) unopposed
Channel Islands	Channel	Channel (£1,000) beat C13 Group (£102,000)
East of England	Anglia	Anglia (£17.804m) beat CPV-TV (£10.125m) and Three East (£14.078m)
London weekday	Thames	Carlton (£43.17m) beat CPV-TV (£45.32m) and Thames (£32.7m)
London weekend	LWT	LWT (£7.85m) beat London Independent Broadcasting (£35.4m)
Midlands	Central	Central (£2,000) unopposed
National breakfast-time	TV-am	Sunrise, now GMTV (£17.4m) beat Daybreak (£33.2m) and TV-am (£14.12m)
North of Scotland	Grampian	Grampian (£720,000) beat C3 Caledonian (£1.1m) and North of Scotland (£2.7m)
Northeast England	Tyne Tees	Tyne Tees (£15m) beat North East (£5.01m)
Northwest England	Granada	Granada (£9m) beat North-West (£35.3m)
Northern Ireland	Ulster	Ulster (£1.03m) beat Lagan (£2.71m) and TVNI (£3.1m)
South and southeast England	TVS	Meridian (£36.52m) beat Carlton (£18m), CPV-TV (£22.1m), and TVS (£59.76m)
Southwest England	TSW	Westcountry (£7.8m) beat Telewest (£7.3m) and TSW (£16.1m)
Wales and West	HTV	HTV (£20.53m) beat C3W (£17.7m), Channel 3 Wales and West (£18.29m) and Merlin (£19.3m)
Yorkshire	Yorkshire	Yorkshire (£37.7m) beat Viking (£30.12m) and White Rose (£17.4m)

Mondadori publishing company. Its overall revenue for 1991 was $6,311 million, $2,666 million of it from its media interests.

Reed International UK-based media conglomerate, Europe's second largest. Reed's turnover for 1991 was $2,822 million, $2,184 million of it from publishing and information services. It owns IPC, Britain's largest magazine publisher, whose titles include *New Scientist* and *TV Times*, a group of regional newspapers, and publishes a variety of business magazines in the USA and the UK.

Bertelsmann German-based international media conglomerate. With an annual turnover 1991 of $8,891 million (media: $1,918 million), Bertelsmann has a 39.9% stake in the German satellite TV station RTL-Plus; it also owns German magazine publisher Grüner & Jahr and, in the USA, Doubleday, Bantam, Dell, and RCA Records. In the UK it owns Transworld Publishing.

Hachette French media conglomerate. With a turnover 1991 of $5,518 million (media: $1,874 million), Hachette is a major French

book publisher, and owns *Elle* and French TV magazines, and the US publisher Grolier.

Axel Springer German media conglomerate. It owns the Auto Bild car magazines and stakes in the TV channels Sat 1, RTL-Plus, and Tele 5. It is also a major book publisher, and owns a variety of magazines and newspapers in E Europe. Its annual turnover 1991 was $2,187 million (media: $1,814 million).

RCS Editore Italian media group. With a turnover 1991 of $2,003 million (media: $1,576 million), RCS Editori controls about 30% of the Italian press; it also has interests in book publishing and women's magazines. Its US arm is RCS Rizzoli, which owns the Rizzoli bookstores and is expanding into magazines.

Hersant French media conglomerate. The Hersant family owns a number of French newspapers, including *Le Figaro*, and has interests in TV and local radio. Its annual turnover 1991 was $1,561 million (all media).

Heinrich Bauer German media conglomerate. It publishes newspapers and women's magazines, including the UK's *Take a Break* and *Bella*. Its annual turnover 1991 was $1,547 million (media: $1,465 million).

RTVE State-owned Spanish TV and radio network. Financed heavily by advertising, RTVE is losing revenue to the newer private and regional channels such as Tele 5. In 1991, its annual turnover was $1,455 million (media: $1,424 million).

United Newspapers British newspaper group. It owns the *Daily Express* and the *Daily Star* in Britain, and a variety of other newspapers in the USA and the UK. In 1991 its annual turnover was $1,480 million (media: $1,372 million).

TOP 10 VIDEOS (1991)

1	*Fantasia*
2	*The Little Mermaid*
3	*Ghost*
4	*The Rescuers*
5	*Home Alone*
6	*The Amazing Adventures of Mr Bean*
7	*Rosemary Conley's Whole Body Programme*
8	*Pretty Woman*
9	*Greatest Flix II—Queen*
10	*The Lovers' Guide*

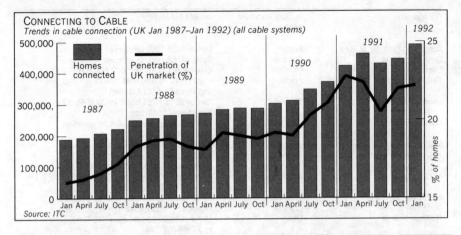

CONNECTING TO CABLE
Trends in cable connection (UK Jan 1987–Jan 1992) (all cable systems)

Homes connected

Penetration of UK market (%)

Source: ITC

NON-EUROPEAN GROUPS

Dow Jones US media and financial services group. Based in New York, Dow Jones owns the *Wall Street Journal* and *Barron's* (weekly financial newspaper), and supplies financial news around the world in affiliation with Associated Press. Its annual turnover in 1991 was $1,725 million.

Gannett US media group. Gannett owns the USA's largest newspaper chain plus *USA Today*, Harris polls, and a host of local TV and radio stations. Its annual turnover in 1991 was $3,382 million.

News International/News Corporation one of the largest international media conglomerates, owned by Rupert Murdoch. Based in Australia, News Corporation owns 67% of the Australian press; *The Times* and *The Sun* in the UK; and *TV Guide* in the USA. It also owns the US Fox network and has 50% of Britain's BSkyB satellite-channel group, plus the publisher Harper Collins. Its annual turnover in 1991 was $8,682 million.

Pearson UK-based media group. Pearson owns publishers Pearson Longman, Pitman, Penguin, Addison Wesley, and Elsevier; it also owns the UK's *Financial Times*, 50% of *The Economist*, and the Profile electronic newspaper database service, plus 20% of Yorkshire Television.

Time-Warner the world's biggest media conglomerate, formed by the 1989 merger between Time-Life and Warner Brothers. With an annual turnover 1991 of $12,021 million, Time-Warner owns the US magazines *Time*, *People*, *Sports Illustrated*, and *Fortune*, and the USA's second biggest cable TV operator, the satellite subscription service Home Box Office (HBO). It also has a 10% stake in Turner Broadcasting System, owner of CNN.

UK MEDIA WATCHDOGS

Advertising Standards Authority (ASA) organization founded by the UK advertising industry 1962 to promote higher standards of advertising in the media (excluding television and radio, which have their own authority). It is financed by the advertisers, who pay 0.1% supplement on the cost of advertisements. It recommends to the media that advertisements which might breach the British Code of Advertising Practice are not published, but has no statutory power.

Broadcasting Complaints Commission UK body responsible for dealing with complaints of invasion of privacy or unjust treatment on television or radio. It is a statutory body, formed 1981.

Broadcasting Standards Council UK body concerned with handling complaints on treatment of sex and violence. It was established 1988 and is responsible for drawing up a code on standards of taste and decency in TV and radio.

Press Complaints Commission (PCC) UK organization that replaced the Press Council (founded 1953) in 1991. It serves to preserve the freedom of the press, maintain standards, consider complaints, and report on monopoly developments.

In July 1992 it made a landmark ruling in favour of the right of the press to disclose information on public figures' personal lives, deeming such information to be in the public interest. The issue of whether or not to introduce privacy legislation was brought to the fore by press revelations of an alleged affair between David Mellor, Secretary of State for National Heritage, and actress Antonia de Sancha.

GREAT COMPOSERS

Bach Johann Sebastian 1685–1750. German composer. His appointments included positions at the courts of Weimar and Anhalt-Köthen, and from 1723 until his death, he was musical director at St Thomas's choir school in Leipzig. Bach was a master of counterpoint (combining different forms of an original melody), and his music epitomizes the Baroque polyphonic style. His orchestral music includes the six *Brandenburg Concertos*, other concertos for keyboard instrument and violin, and four orchestral suites. Bach's keyboard music, for clavier and organ, his fugues, and his choral music are of equal importance. He also wrote chamber music and songs.

Bartók Béla 1881–1945. Hungarian composer. Regarded as a child prodigy, he studied music at the Budapest Conservatory, later working with Hungarian composer Zoltán Kodály in recording and transcribing local folk music for a government project. This led him to develop a personal musical language combining folk elements with mathematical concepts of tone and rhythmic proportion. His large output includes six string quartets, a ballet *The Miraculous Mandarin* 1919, which was banned because of its subject matter (it was set in a brothel), concertos, an opera, and graded teaching pieces for piano.

Beethoven Ludwig van 1770–1827. German composer and pianist, whose mastery of musical expression in every genre made him the dominant influence on 19th-century music. Beethoven's repertoire includes concert overtures; the opera *Fidelio*; five piano concertos and two for violin (one unfinished); 32 piano sonatas, including the *Moonlight* and *Appassionata*; 17 string quartets; the *Mass in D*; and nine symphonies. He played his own piano pieces and conducted his orchestral works until he was hampered by deafness 1801; nevertheless he continued to compose.

Berg Alban 1885–1935. Austrian composer. He studied under Schoenberg and was associated with him as one of the leaders of the serial, or 12-tone, school of composition. His output includes orchestral, chamber, and vocal music as well as two operas, *Wozzeck* 1925 and the unfinished *Lulu* 1929–35.

Berlioz (Louis) Hector 1803–1869. French Romantic composer and the founder of modern orchestration. Much of his music was inspired by drama and literature and has a theatrical quality. He wrote symphonic works, such as *Symphonie fantastique*; dramatic cantatas including *La Damnation de Faust*; sacred music; and three operas, *Béatrice et Bénédict*, *Benvenuto Cellini*, and *Les Troyens*.

Brahms Johannes 1833–1897. German composer, pianist, and conductor. Considered one of the greatest composers of symphonic music and of songs, his works include four sympho-nies; lieder (songs); concertos for piano and for violin; chamber music; sonatas; and the choral *A German Requiem* 1868. He performed and conducted his own works.

Britten (Edward) Benjamin, 1913–1976. English composer. He often wrote for the individual voice; for example, the role in the opera *Peter Grimes* 1945, based on verses by Crabbe, was created for English tenor Peter Pears. Among his many works are the *Young Person's Guide* to the Orchestra 1946; *Billy Budd* 1951; *A Midsummer Night's Dream* 1960; and *Death in Venice* 1973.

Bruckner (Joseph) Anton 1824–1896. Austrian Romantic composer. He was cathedral organist at Linz 1856–68, and from 1868 he was professor at the Vienna Conservatoire. His works include many choral pieces and 11 symphonies, the last unfinished. His compositions were influenced by Richard Wagner and Beethoven.

Chopin Frédéric (François) 1810–1849. Polish composer and pianist. He made his debut as a pianist at the age of eight. As a performer, Chopin revolutionized the technique of pianoforte-playing, turning the hands outwards and favouring a light, responsive touch. His compositions for piano, which include two concertos and other works with orchestra, are characterized by great volatility of mood and rhythmic fluidity.

Debussy (Achille-) Claude 1862–1918. French composer. He broke with the dominant tradition of German Romanticism and introduced new qualities of melody and harmony based on the whole-tone scale, evoking oriental music. He is considered to be the originator of musical Impressionism. His work includes *Prélude à l'après-midi d'un faune* 1894 and the opera *Pelléas et Mélisande* 1902.

Dvořák Antonin (Leopold) 1841–1904. Czech composer. International recognition came with his series of Slavonic Dances 1877–86, and he was director of the National Conservatory, New York, 1892–95. Works such as his *New World Symphony* 1893 reflect his interest in American folk themes, including black and

	Top 10 Classical Albums (1991)	
1	*Essential Opera*	Various
2	*The Essential Mozart*	Various
3	*Vivaldi Four Seasons*	Nigel Kennedy/ECO
4	*Brahms Violin Concerto*	N Kennedy/LPO/ K Tennstedt
5	*Mendelssohn/Bruch/ Schubert*	N Kennedy/Jeffrey Tate/ ECO
6	Paul McCartney *Liverpool Oratorio*	Carl Davies/RLPO/ Various
7	*Orchestra!*	Sir Georg Solti & Dudley Moore
8	Holst *The Planets*	Herbert Von Karajan/ BPO
9	Elgar *Cello Concerto/ Sea Pictures*	Barbirolli/LSO/Baker/ J Du Pré
10	Elgar *Cello Concerto/ Enigma Variations*	D Barenboim/PDO/ J Du Pré

Source: CIN

Classical Music Using Unusual Instruments

accordion	Gerhard Nonet, *Metamorphoses*
antique cymbals	Debussy, *L'Après-midi d'un faune*
anvils	Wagner, *Das Rheingold*; Verdi, *Il Trovatore*; Varèse, *Ionisation*
basset horn (tenor clarinet)	Mozart, *Masonic Funeral Music*; Stockhausen, *Donnerstag aus LICHT*
bass tuba	Vaughan Williams, *Concerto in F minor*
bell plates	Boulez, *Rituel in Memoriam Maderna*
brake drums	John Cage, *First Construction in Metal*
castanets	Manuel de Falla, *The Three-Cornered Hat*; Ravel, *Alborada del Gracioso*
celesta	Tchaikovsky, *Nutcracker Suite*; Bartók, *Music for Strings, Percussion and Celesta*
cimbalom	Kodály, *Háry János*; Stravinsky, *Renard*
concertina	Regondi, *Concerto in D*
cowbell	Richard Strauss, *Alpen Symphony*; Mahler, Symphonies No 6 and 7
electric guitar	Martin, *Trois Poèmes de Villon*
flexatone	Schoenberg, *Variations Opus 31 for Orchestra*
glass armonica	Mozart, Beethoven (attributed)
guero	Stravinsky, *Rite of Spring*
harmonium	Schoenberg, *Herzgewächse*; Saint-Saëns, *L'Assassination du Duc de Guise*
heckelphone (baritone oboe)	Richard Strauss, *Salome*
Japanese tuned bowls (*rin*)	Stockhausen, *Inori*
Jew's harp	Albrechtsberger, concerto
lion roar (cord or friction drum)	Varèse, *Ionisation*
marimbula	H W Henze, *El Cimarrón*
mouth organ	Vaughan Williams, *Romanza in D flat*; concertos by Benjamin, Darius Milhaud
musical saw	George Crumb, *Ancient Voices of Children*
musical top	Stockhausen, *Zodiac*
musical toys (trumpet, drum, rattle, cuckoo, bird warbler, and so on)	Leopold Mozart, *'Toy' Symphony*
ondes Martenot	Messiaen, *Turangalîla Symphony*
panpipes	Mozart, *The Magic Flute*
prepared piano	John Cage, *Sonatas and Interludes*; Ravel, *L'Enfant et les Sortilèges*
piano roll	Stravinsky, *Les Noces 1917*; Conlon Nancarrow
ratchet	Beethoven, *Wellington's Victory*; Schoenberg, *Gurrelieder*
sarrusaphone (contrabass oboe)	Stravinsky, *Threni*
saxophone	Richard Strauss, *'Domestic' Symphony*; Webern, *Quartet Opus 22*
slapstick (whip)	Britten, *The Burning Fiery Furnace*
Swanee whistle	Ravel, *L'Enfant et les sortilèges*

Native American. He wrote nine symphonies; tone poems; operas; including *Rusalka* 1901; large-scale choral works; the *Carnival* and other overtures; violin and cello concertos; chamber music; piano pieces; and songs. His Romantic music extends the classical tradition of Beethoven and Brahms and displays the influence of Czech folk music.

Elgar Edward (William) 1857–1934. English composer. His *Enigma Variations* appeared 1899, and although his celebrated choral work, the oratorio setting of Newman's *The Dream of Gerontius*, was initially a failure, it was well received at Düsseldorf in 1902. Many of his earlier works were then performed, including the *Pomp and Circumstance* marches.

Franck César Auguste 1822–1890. Belgian composer. His music, mainly religious and Romantic in style, includes the Symphony in D minor 1866–68, *Symphonic Variations* 1885 for piano and orchestra, the Violin Sonata 1886, the oratorio *Les Béatitudes/The Beatitudes* 1879, and many organ pieces.

Grieg Edvard Hagerup 1843–1907. Norwegian composer. Much of his music is small scale, particularly his songs, dances, sonatas, and pi-

ano works. Among his orchestral works are the *Piano Concerto* 1869 and the incidental music for Ibsen's *Peer Gynt* 1876.

Handel Georg Frideric 1685–1759. German composer, who became a British subject 1726. His first opera, *Almira*, was performed in Hamburg 1705. In 1710 he was appointed Kapellmeister to the elector of Hanover (the future George I of England). In 1712 he settled in England, where he established his popularity with works such as the *Water Music* 1717 (written for George I). His great choral works include the *Messiah* 1742 and the later oratorios *Samson* 1743, *Belshazzar* 1745, *Judas Maccabaeus* 1747, and *Jephtha* 1752.

Haydn Franz Joseph 1732–1809. Austrian composer. A teacher of Mozart and Beethoven, he was a major exponent of the classical sonata form in his numerous chamber and orchestral works (he wrote more than 100 symphonies). He also composed choral music, including the oratorios *The Creation* 1798 and *The Seasons* 1801. He was the first great master of the string quartet.

Janáček Leoš 1854–1928. Czech composer. He became director of the Conservatoire at Brno

GREAT COMPOSERS

Giovanni Palestrina	c.1525–1594	Italian	motets, masses
Claudio Monteverdi	1567–1643	Italian	operas, vocal music
Henry Purcell	1659–1695	English	vocal music, operas
Antonio Vivaldi	1678–1741	Italian	concertos, chamber music
Georg Friedrich Handel	1685–1759	German	oratorios, operas, orchestra
Johann Sebastian Bach	1685–1750	German	keyboard choral music, concertos
Joseph Haydn	1732–1809	Austrian	symphonies, oratorios, chamber music
Wolfgang Mozart	1756–1791	Austrian	symphonies, operas, chamber music
Ludwig van Beethoven	1770–1827	German	symphonies, chamber music
Carl Maria von Weber	1786–1826	German	operas, concertos
Gioacchino Rossini	1792–1868	Italian	operas
Franz Schubert	1797–1828	Austrian	songs, symphonies, chamber music
Hector Berlioz	1803–1869	French	operas, symphonies
Felix Mendelssohn	1809–1847	German	symphonies, concertos
Frederik Chopin	1810–1849	Polish	piano music
Robert Schumann	1810–1856	German	piano, vocal music, concertos
Franz Liszt	1811–1886	Hungarian	piano, orchestral music
Richard Wagner	1813–1883	German	operas
Giuseppe Verdi	1813–1901	Italian	operas
César Franck	1822–1890	Belgian	symphony, organ works
Bedrich Smetana	1824–1884	Czech	symphonies, operas
Anton Bruckner	1824–1896	Austrian	symphonies
Johann Strauss II	1825–1899	Austrian	waltzes, operettas
Johannes Brahms	1833–1897	German	symphonies, concertos
Camille Saint Saëns	1835–1921	French	symphonies, concertos, operas
Modest Mussorgsky	1839–1881	Russian	operas, orchestral music
Peter Tchaikovsky	1840–1893	Russian	ballet music, symphonies
Antonin Dvořák	1841–1904	Czech	symphonies, operas
Edvard Grieg	1843–1907	Norwegian	concertos, orchestra music
Nikolai Rimsky-Korsakov	1844–1908	Russian	operas, orchestral music
Leos Janáček	1854–1928	Czech	operas, chamber music
Edward Elgar	1857–1934	English	orchestral music
Giacomo Puccini	1858–1924	Italian	operas
Gustav Mahler	1860–1911	Czech	symphonies
Claude Debussy	1862–1918	French	operas, orchestral music
Richard Strauss	1864–1949	German	operas, orchestral music
Carl Nielsen	1865–1931	Danish	symphonies
Jean Sibelius	1865–1957	Finnish	symphonies, orchestral music
Sergei Rachmaninov	1873–1943	Russian	symphonies, concertos
Arnold Schoenberg	1874–1951	Austrian	concertos, vocal, orchestral, and chamber music
Maurice Ravel	1875–1937	French	orchestral, piano, chamber music
Béla Bartók	1881–1945	Hungarian	operas, concertos, chamber music
Igor Stravinsky	1882–1971	Russian	ballets, operas, orchestral, chamber music
Anton Webern	1883–1945	Austrian	chamber, vocal music
Alban Berg	1885–1935	Austrian	operas, chamber music
Sergei Prokofiev	1891–1953	Russian	symphonies, operas, ballets, piano music
George Gershwin	1898–1937	American	musicals, operas
Dmitri Shostakovich	1906–1975	Russian	symphonies, chamber music
Oliver Messiaen	1908–1992	French	piano, organ, orchestral music
Benjamin Britten	1913–1976	English	vocal music, opera
Karlheinz Stockhausen	1928–	German	electronic, chamber music, music theatre

in 1919 and professor at the Prague Conservatoire in 1920. His music, highly original and influenced by Moravian folk music, includes arrangements of folk songs, operas (*Jenufa* 1904, *The Cunning Little Vixen* 1924), and the choral *Glagolitic Mass* 1927.

Liszt Franz 1811–1886. Hungarian composer and pianist. An outstanding virtuoso of the piano, he was an established concert artist by the age of 12. His expressive, romantic, and frequently chromatic works include piano music (*Transcendental Studies* 1851), symphonies, piano concertos, and organ music. Much of his music

is programmatic; he also originated the symphonic poem.

Mahler Gustav 1860–1911. Austrian composer and conductor. His ten symphonies, the moving *Das Lied von der Erde/Song of the Earth* 1909, and his song cycles display a synthesis of Romanticism and new uses of chromatic harmonies and musical forms.

Mendelssohn (-Bartholdy) (Jakob Ludwig) Felix 1809–1847. German composer, also a pianist and conductor. As a child he composed and performed with his own orchestra and as an adult was helpful to Schumann's career.

Major Operas and Their First Performances

Date	Opera	Composer	Librettist	Place
1607	Orfeo	Monteverdi	Striggio	Mantua
1642	The Coronation of Poppea	Monteverdi	Busenello	Venice
1689	Dido and Aeneas	Purcell	Tate	London
1724	Julius Caesar in Egypt	Handel	Haym	London
1762	Orpheus and Eurydice	Gluck	Calzabigi	Vienna
1786	The Marriage of Figaro	Mozart	Da Ponte	Vienna
1787	Don Giovanni	Mozart	Da Ponte	Prague
1790	Così fan tutte	Mozart	Da Ponte	Vienna
1791	The Magic Flute	Mozart	Schikaneder	Vienna
1805	Fidelio	Beethoven	Sonnleithner	Vienna
1816	The Barber of Seville	Rossini	Sterbini	Rome
1821	Der Freischütz	Weber	Kind	Berlin
1831	Norma	Bellini	Romani	Milan
1835	Lucia di Lammermoor	Donizetti	Cammarano	Naples
1850	Lohengrin	Wagner	Wagner	Weimar
1851	Rigoletto	Verdi	Piave	Venice
1853	Il Trovatore	Verdi	Cammarano	Rome
1853	La Traviata	Verdi	Piave	Venice
1859	Faust	Gounod	Barbier/Carré	Paris
1865	Tristan and Isolde	Wagner	Wagner	Munich
1866	The Bartered Bride	Smetana	Sabina	Prague
1868	Die Meistersinger	Wagner	Wagner	Munich
1871	Aida	Verdi	Ghislanzoni	Cairo
1874	Boris Godunov	Mussorgsky	Mussorgsky	St Petersburg
1874	Die Fledermaus	Johann Strauss II	Haffner/Genée	Vienna
1875	Carmen	Bizet	Meilhac/Halévy	Paris
1876	The Ring of the Nibelung	Wagner	Wagner	Bayreuth
1879	Eugene Onegin	Tchaikovsky	Tchaikovsky/Shilovsky	Moscow
1881	The Tales of Hoffman	Offenbach	Barbier	Paris
1882	Parsifal	Wagner	Wagner	Bayreuth
1885	The Mikado	Sullivan	Gilbert	London
1887	Otello	Verdi	Boito	Milan
1890	Cavalleria Rusticana	Mascagni	Menasci/Targioni-Tozzetti	Rome
1890	Prince Igor	Borodin	Borodin	St Petersburg
1892	Pagliacci	Leoncavallo	Leocavallo	Milan
1892	Werther	Massenet	Blau/Milliet/Hartmann	Vienna
1896	La Bohème	Puccini	Giacosa/Illica	Turin
1900	Tosca	Puccini	Giacosa/Illica	Rome
1902	Pelléas et Mélisande	Debussy	Maeterlinck	Paris
1904	Jenufa	Janáček	Janáček	Brno
1904	Madame Butterfly	Puccini	Giacosa/Illica	Milan
1905	Salome	Richard Strauss	Wilde/Lachmann	Dresden
1909	The Golden Cockerel	Rimsky-Korsakov	Byelsky	Moscow
1911	Der Rosenkavalier	Richard Strauss	Hofmannsthal	Dresden
1918	Duke Bluebeard's Castle	Bartók	Balázs	Budapest
1925	Wozzeck	Berg	Berg	Berlin
1935	Porgy and Bess	Gershwin	Ira Gershwin/Heyward	Boston
1937	Lulu	Berg	Berg	Zürich
1945	Peter Grimes	Britten	Slater	London
1946	War and Peace	Prokofiev	Prokiev/Mendelson	Leningrad
1951	The Rake's Progress	Stravinsky	Auden/Kallman	Venice
1978	Paradise Lost	Penderecki	Fry	Chicago
1984	Akhnaten	Glass	Glass	Stuttgart
1986	The Mask of Orpheus	Birtwistle	Zinovieff	London
1989	New Year	Tippett	Tippett	Houston
1992	Dienstag aus LICHT	Stockhausen	Stockhausen	Lisbon

Among his best-known works are *A Midsummer Night's Dream* 1827; the *Fingal's Cave* overture 1832; and five symphonies, which include the Reformation 1830, the Italian 1833, and the Scottish 1842.

Messiaen Olivier 1908–1992. French composer and organist. His music is mystical in char-

acter, vividly coloured, and incorporates transcriptions of birdsong. Among his works are the *Quartet for the End of Time* 1941, the large-scale *Turangalîla Symphony* 1949, and solo organ and piano pieces. His theories of melody, harmony, and rhythm, drawing on medieval and oriental music, have inspired contemporary composers such as Boulez and Stockhausen.

Monteverdi Claudio (Giovanni Antonio) 1567–1643. Italian composer. His pioneering early operas include *Orfeo* 1607 and *The Coronation of Poppea* 1642. He also wrote madrigals, motets, and sacred music, notably the *Vespers* 1610.

Mozart Wolfgang Amadeus 1756–1791. Austrian composer and performer who showed astonishing precocity as a child and was an adult virtuoso. He was trained by his father, *Leopold Mozart* (1719–1787). From an early age he composed prolifically, his works including 27 piano concertos, 23 string quartets, 35 violin sonatas, and more than 50 symphonies. His operas include *Idomeneo* 1781, *Le Nozze di Figaro/The Marriage of Figaro* 1786, *Don Giovanni* 1787, *Così fan tutte/Thus Do All Women* 1790, and *Die Zauberflöte/The Magic Flute* 1791. Strongly influenced by Haydn, Mozart's music marks the height of the Classical age in its purity of melody and form.

Mussorgsky Modest Petrovich 1839–1881. Russian composer, who was largely self-taught. His opera *Boris Godunov* was completed in 1869, although not produced in St Petersburg until 1874. Some of his works were 'revised' by Rimsky-Korsakov, and only recently has their harsh original beauty been recognized.

Nielsen Carl (August) 1865–1931. Danish composer. His works show a progressive tonality, as in his opera *Saul and David* 1902 and six symphonies.

Palestrina Giovanni Pierluigi da 1525–1594. Italian composer of secular and sacred choral music. Apart from motets and madrigals, he also wrote 105 masses, including *Missa Papae Marcelli*.

Prokofiev Sergey (Sergeyevich) 1891–1953. Soviet composer. His music includes operas such as *The Love of Three Oranges* 1921; ballets for Russian ballet manager Sergei Diaghilev, including *Romeo and Juliet* 1935; seven symphonies including the *Classical Symphony* 1916–17; music for films; piano and violin concertos; songs and cantatas (for example, that composed for the 30th anniversary of the October Revolution); and *Peter and the Wolf* 1936.

Puccini Giacomo (Antonio Domenico Michele Secondo Maria) 1858–1924. Italian opera composer whose music shows a strong gift for melody and dramatic effect. His realist works include *Manon Lescaut* 1893, *La Bohème* 1896, *Tosca* 1900, *Madame Butterfly* 1904, and the unfinished *Turandot* 1926.

Purcell Henry 1659–1695. English Baroque composer. His work can be highly expressive, for example, the opera *Dido and Aeneas* 1689 and music for Dryden's *King Arthur* 1691 and for *The Fairy Queen* 1692. He wrote more than 500 works, ranging from secular operas and incidental music for plays to cantatas and church music.

Rachmaninov Sergei (Vasilevich) 1873–1943. Russian composer, conductor, and pianist. After the 1917 Revolution he lived in the USA. His dramatically emotional Romantic music has a strong melodic basis and includes operas, such as *Francesca da Rimini* 1906, three symphonies, four piano concertos, piano pieces, and songs. Among his other works are the *Prelude in C Sharp Minor* 1882 for piano and *Rhapsody on a Theme of Paganini* 1934 for piano and orchestra.

Ravel (Joseph) Maurice 1875–1937. French composer. His work is characterized by its sensuousness, unresolved dissonances, and 'tone colour'. Examples are the piano pieces *Pavane pour une infante défunte* 1899 and *Jeux d'eau* 1901, and the ballets *Daphnis et Chloë* 1912 and *Boléro* 1928.

Rimsky-Korsakov Nikolay Andreyevich 1844–1908. Russian composer. He used Russian folk idiom and rhythms in his Romantic compositions and published a text on orchestration. His operas include *The Maid of Pskov* 1873, *The Snow Maiden* 1882, *Mozart and Salieri* 1898, and *The Golden Cockerel* 1907, a satirical attack on despotism that was banned until 1909.

Rossini Gioachino (Antonio) 1792–1868. Italian composer. His first success was the opera *Tancredi* 1813. In 1816 his 'opera buffa' *Il barbiere di Siviglia/The Barber of Seville* was produced in Rome. During his fertile composition period 1815–23 he produced 20 operas, and created (with Gaetano Donizetti and Vincenzo Bellini) the 19th-century Italian operatic style. After *Guillaume Tell/William Tell* 1829 he gave up writing opera and his later years were spent in Bologna and Paris.

Saint-Saëns (Charles) Camille 1835–1921. French composer, pianist, and organist. Among his many lyrical Romantic pieces are concertos, the symphonic poem *Danse macabre* 1875, the opera *Samson et Dalila* 1877, and the orchestral *Carnaval des animaux/Carnival of the Animals* 1886.

Schoenberg Arnold (Franz Walter) 1874–1951. Austro-Hungarian composer, a US citizen from 1941. After Romantic early works such as *Verklärte Nacht/Transfigured Night* 1899 and the *Gurrelieder/Songs of Gurra* 1900–11, he experimented with atonality (absence of key), producing works such as *Pierrot Lunaire* 1912 for chamber ensemble and voice, before developing the 12-tone system of musical composition. This was further developed by his pupils Alban Berg and Anton Webern.

Schubert Franz (Peter) 1797–1828. Austrian composer. He was only 31 when he died, but his musical output was prodigious. His ten symphonies include the incomplete eighth in B minor (the 'Unfinished') and the 'Great' in C major. He wrote chamber and piano music, including the 'Trout Quintet', and over 600 lieder (songs) combining the Romantic expression of emotion with pure melody. They include the cycles *Die schöne Müllerin/The Beautiful Maid of the Mill* 1823 and *Die Winterreise/The Winter Journey* 1827.

Schumann Robert Alexander 1810–1856. German composer. His Romantic songs and short

THE CLASSICAL BOOM

The decision to cease trading in vinyl recordings announced in January 1992 by high-street retailers W H Smith signalled the end of an era dominated by the 12-inch LP and 7-inch single, which now go the way of the shellac 78 and the EP. With the transition to CD comes a recognition that the market has also changed. Classical music on CD is increasingly targeted at an affluent working class disaffected with pop music, a change reflected in the appearance of new CD magazines and labels aiming to sell classical music in a breezy, uncomplicated style.

Far from having peaked, the market for classical music on CD continues to expand and segment into special interest areas such as historic performances, budget classics, novelties and avant-garde. If anything, it is the standard virtuoso-based repertoire that is now being squeezed, and where advertising and marketing skills are most obviously exercised. Sex and glamour are used to sell cellist Ofra Harnoy and singers Ute Lemper, Kiri Te Kanawa, and Cecilia Bartoli; and coloured lighting and amplification to bring excitement to stage appearances of the London Classical Orchestra, building on the successful Solti–Dudley Moore series *Orchestra!* on Channel 4. The clash of old and new marketing values came to a head with BBC chief John Drummond's widely reported verbal assault on Nigel Kennedy's dress style, which omitted to acknowledge the violinist's success in attracting Essex youth to a BBC Symphony Orchestra 60th-anniversary concert featuring a powerful performance of a difficult 20th-century classic.

Elsewhere the Mozart bicentenary stakes were comfortably won by Philips, whose 180-CD complete edition appropriately entered the *Guinness Book of Records* and incorporated, in addition to the familiar works, some 200 sketches and fragments including a board version of the *Musical Dice Game* for composing minuets. Scholarship and authenticity seized the imagination of reviewers and public alike as listeners caught on to the excitement of Roger Norrington's high-speed Beethoven and brighter-than-new Berlioz, and players discov-

ered the attractions of 19th-century *portamento* and expression.

Re-issues of historic recordings continue to expand apace as the CD demonstrates its worth as a reproducer of the original sound, from classic Tetrazzini 78s to early stereo. Even allowing for spin-off from the video, the successful release on double CD of the restored Stokowski music track for Disney's classic *Fantasia* is as much a tribute to the attractions of Fantasound, the film's unique 50-year-old surround-sound technology, as to the choice of music or conductor. The BBC announced plans to release classic live recordings from its archives once royalty matters were agreed, having been pipped at the post by a critically acclaimed release of Louis Krasner's 1936 British premiere of the Berg violin concerto, with the BBC Symphony Orchestra, conducted by Anton Webern, a recording not preserved in the BBC archives but recorded off-air and only recently rediscovered in Krasner's effects.

A refreshingly open attitude to contemporary music is now a feature of many new labels such as Collins and Virgin, unencumbered by traditional conservatism and keen to capitalize on the wealth of underexposed talent available. EMI's acquisition of Virgin Classical in 1992 now makes it a leading promoter of living British composers.

On the technical side Philips announced a new generation of CD recorders to be marketed in Britain in late 1992, selling at about £1,500, with blank discs costing about £13. CD recorders use a more powerful laser to record, and a less powerful second laser for playback of both CD-R and commercial CD recordings. Error-correction technology is said to guarantee CD-R copies that will be quieter and clearer than the original recordings. Competition for orthodox CDs is expected from the digital compact cassette (DCC), another Philips development in association with Panasonic, to be launched in summer 1992, with pre-recorded cassettes selling at around £14. With media pressure to lower the UK retail price of CDs from a present average of around £10, DCC may find it difficult to establish a hold at the higher price.

The Philips digital compact cassette recorder, another nail in the coffin of vinyl records.

piano pieces show simplicity combined with an ability to portray mood and emotion. Among his compositions are four symphonies, a violin concerto, a piano concerto, sonatas, and song cycles, such as *Dichterliebe/Poet's Love* 1840. Mendelssohn championed many of his works.

Shostakovich Dmitry (Dmitriyevich) 1906–1975. Soviet composer. His music is tonal, expressive, and sometimes highly dramatic; it has not always been to official Soviet taste. He wrote 15 symphonies, chamber music, ballets, and operas, the latter including *Lady Macbeth of Mtsensk* 1934, which was suppressed as 'too divorced from the proletariat', but revived as *Katerina Izmaylova* 1963.

Sibelius Jean (Christian) 1865–1957. Finnish composer. His works include nationalistic symphonic poems such as *En Saga* 1893 and *Finlandia* 1900, a violin concerto 1904, and seven symphonies.

Smetana Bedřich 1824–1884. Czech composer, whose music has a distinct national character, as in for example the operas *The Bartered Bride* 1866, *Dalibor* 1868, and the symphonic suite *My Country* 1875–80. He conducted the National Theatre of Prague 1866–74.

Stockhausen Karlheinz 1928– . German composer of avant-garde music, who has continued to explore new musical sounds and compositional techniques since the 1950s. His major works include *Gesang der Junglinge* 1956 and *Kontakte* 1960 (electronic music); *Klavierstücke I–XIV* 1952–85; *Momente* 1961–64, *Mikrophonie I* 1964, and *Sirius* 1977. Since 1977 all his works have been part of *Licht*, a cycle of seven musical ceremonies intended for performance on the evenings of a week. He has completed *Donnerstag* 1980, *Samstag* 1984, and *Montag* 1988.

Strauss Johann (Baptist) 1825–1899. Austrian conductor and composer, the son of Johann Strauss (1804–49). In 1872 he gave up conducting and wrote operettas, such as *Die Fledermaus* 1874, and numerous waltzes, such as *The Blue Danube* and *Tales from the Vienna Woods*, which gained him the title 'The Waltz King'.

Strauss Richard (Georg) 1864–1949. German composer and conductor. He followed the German Romantic tradition but had a strongly personal style, characterized by his bold, colourful orchestration. He first wrote tone poems such as *Don Juan* 1889, *Till Eulenspiegel's Merry Pranks* 1895, and *Also sprach Zarathustra* 1896. He then moved on to opera with *Salome* 1905, and *Elektra* 1909, both of which have elements of polytonality. He reverted to a more traditional style with *Der Rosenkavalier* 1911.

Stravinsky Igor 1882–1971. Russian composer, later of French (1934) and US (1945) nationality. He studied under Rimsky-Korsakov and wrote the music for the Diaghilev ballets *The Firebird* 1910, *Petrushka* 1911, and *The Rite of Spring* 1913 (controversial at the time for their unorthodox rhythms and harmonies). His versatile work ranges from his Neo-Classical ballet *Pulcinella* 1920, to the choral-orchestral *Symphony of Psalms* 1930. He later made use of serial techniques in works such as the *Canticum Sacrum* 1955 and the ballet *Agon* 1953–57.

Tchaikovsky Pyotr Il'yich 1840–1893. Russian composer. His strong sense of melody, personal expression, and brilliant orchestration are clear throughout his many Romantic works, which include six symphonies, three piano concertos and a violin concerto, operas (for example, *Eugene Onegin* 1879), ballets (for example *The Nutcracker* 1892), orchestral fantasies (for example *Romeo and Juliet* 1870), and chamber and vocal music.

Varèse Edgard 1885–1965. French composer, who settled in New York 1916 where he founded the New Symphony Orchestra 1919 to further the cause of modern music. His work is experimental and often dissonant, combining electronic sounds with orchestral instruments, and includes *Hyperprism* 1923, *Intégrales* 1931, and *Poème Electronique* 1958.

Verdi Giuseppe (Fortunino Francesco) 1813–1901. Italian opera composer of the Romantic period who took his native operatic style to new heights of dramatic expression. In 1842 he wrote the opera *Nabucco*, followed by *Ernani* 1844 and *Rigoletto* 1851. Other works include *Il Trovatore* and *La Traviata* both 1853, *Aïda* 1871, and the masterpieces of his old age, *Otello* 1887 and *Falstaff* 1893. His *Requiem* 1874 commemorates Alessandro Manzoni.

Vivaldi Antonio (Lucio) 1678–1741. Italian Baroque composer, violinist, and conductor. He wrote 23 symphonies, 75 sonatas, over 400 concertos, including the *Four Seasons* (about 1725) for violin and orchestra, over 40 operas, and much sacred music. His work was largely neglected until the 1930s.

Wagner Richard 1813–1883. Greman opera composer. He revolutionized the 19th-century conception of opera, envisaging it as a wholly new art form in which musical, poetic, and scenic elements should be unified through such devices as the *leitmotif*. His operas include *Tannhäuser* 1845, *Lohengrin* 1850, and *Tristan und Isolde* 1865. In 1872 he founded the Festival Theatre in Bayreuth; his masterpiece *Der Ring des Nibelungen/The Ring of the Nibelung*, a sequence of four operas, was first performed there in 1876. His last work, *Parsifal*, was produced in 1882.

POPULAR MUSIC

Armstrong Louis ('Satchmo') 1901–1971. US jazz cornet and trumpet player and singer, born in New Orleans. His Chicago recordings in the 1920s with the Hot Five and Hot Seven brought him recognition for his warm and pure trumpet tone, his skill at improvisation, and his quirky, gravelly voice. From the 1930s he also appeared in films.

Beach Boys, the US pop group formed 1961.

They began as exponents of vocal-harmony surf music with Chuck Berry guitar riffs (their hits include 'Surfin' USA' 1963 and 'Help Me, Rhonda' 1965) but the compositions, arrangements, and production by Brian Wilson (1942–) became highly complex under the influence of psychedelic rock, peaking with 'Good Vibrations' 1966. Wilson spent most of the next 20 years in retirement but returned with a solo album 1988.

Beatles, the English pop group 1960–70. The members, all born in Liverpool, were John Lennon (1940–80, rhythm guitar, vocals), Paul McCartney (1942– , bass, vocals), George Harrison (1943– , lead guitar, vocals), and Ringo Starr (formerly Richard Starkey, 1940– , drums). Using songs written largely by Lennon and McCartney, the Beatles dominated rock music and pop culture in the 1960s.

beat music pop music that evolved in the UK in the early 1960s, known in its purest form as Mersey beat, and as British Invasion in the USA. The beat groups characteristically had a simple, guitar-dominated line-up, vocal harmonies, and catchy tunes. They included the Beatles (1960–70), the Hollies (1962–), and the Zombies (1962–67).

bebop or **bop** hot jazz style, rhythmically complex, virtuosic, and highly improvisational, developed in New York 1945–55 by Charlie Parker, Dizzy Gillespie, Thelonius Monk, and other black musicians disaffected with dance bands and racism and determined to create music that would be too difficult for white people to play.

Berry Chuck (Charles Edward) 1926– . US rock-and-roll singer, prolific songwriter, and guitarist. His characteristic guitar riffs became staples of rock music, and his humorous storytelling lyrics were also emulated. He had a string of hits in the 1950s and 1960s beginning with 'Maybellene' 1955 and enjoyed a resurgence of popularity in the 1980s.

bhangra pop music evolved in the UK in the late 1970s from traditional Punjabi music, combining electronic instruments and ethnic drums.

big-band jazz swing music created in the late 1930s and 1940s by bands of 13 or more players, such as those of Duke Ellington and Benny Goodman. Big-band jazz relied on fixed arrangements rather than improvisation.

blues African-American music that originated in the rural South in the late 19th century, characterized by a 12-bar construction and often melancholy lyrics. Blues guitar and vocal styles have played a vital part in the development of jazz and pop music in general.

1920s–1930s The *rural* or *delta blues* was usually performed solo with guitar or harmonica, by artists such as Robert Johnson (1911–1938) and Bukka White (1906–1977), but the earliest recorded style, *classic blues*, by musicians such as W C Handy (1873–1958) and Bessie Smith (1894–1937), was sung with a small band.

1940s–1950s Urban blues, using electric amplification, emerged in the northern cities, chiefly Chicago. As exemplified by Howlin' Wolf (adopted name of Chester Burnett, 1910–1976), Muddy Waters (adopted name of McKinley Morganfield, 1915–1983), and John Lee Hooker (1917–), urban blues became *rhythm and blues*.

1960s The jazz-influenced guitar style of B B King (1925–) inspired many musicians of the *British blues boom*, including Eric Clapton (1945–).

1980s The 'blues *noir*' of Robert Cray (1953–) found a wide audience.

boogie-woogie jazz played on the piano, using a repeated motif for the left hand. It was common in the USA from around 1900 to the 1950s. Boogie-woogie players included Pinetop Smith (1904–1929), Meade 'Lux' Lewis (1905–1964), and Jimmy Yancey (1898–1951). Rock-and-roll pianists like Jerry Lee Lewis adapted the style.

Bowie David. Stage name of David Jones 1947– . British pop singer, songwriter, and actor. He became a glam-rock star with the release of the album *The Rise and Fall of Ziggy Stardust and the Spiders from Mars* 1972, and collaborated in the mid-1970s with the electronic virtuoso Brian Eno (1948–) and Iggy Pop. He has also acted in plays and films, including Nicolas Roeg's *The Man Who Fell to Earth* 1976.

Byrds, the US pioneering folk-rock group 1964–73. Emulated for their 12-string guitar sound, as on the hits 'Mr Tambourine Man' (a 1965 version of Bob Dylan's song) and 'Eight Miles High' 1966, they moved towards country rock in the late 1960s.

Cajun member of a French-speaking community of Louisiana, USA, descended from French-Canadians who, in the 18th century, were driven there from Nova Scotia (then known as Acadia, from which the name Cajun comes). *Cajun music* has a lively rhythm and features steel guitar, fiddle, and accordion.

calypso West Indian satirical ballad with a syncopated beat. Calypso is a traditional song form of Trinidad, a feature of its annual carnival, with roots in W African praise singing. It was first popularized in the USA by Harry Belafonte (1927–) in 1956. Mighty Sparrow (1935–) is Trinidad's best-known calypso singer.

Charles Ray 1930– . US singer, songwriter, and pianist, whose first hits were 'I've Got A Woman' 1955, 'What'd I Say' 1959, and 'Georgia on My Mind' 1960. He has recorded gospel, blues, rock, soul, country, and rhythm and blues.

Clapton Eric 1945– . English blues and rock guitarist, singer, and composer, member of the Yardbirds 1963–65 and Cream 1966–68. Originally a blues purist, then one of the pioneers of heavy rock with Cream and on the album *Layla* 1970 (released under the name of Derek and the Dominos), he later adopted a more laid-back style in his solo career, as on *Journeyman* 1989.

Coleman Ornette 1930– . US alto saxophonist and jazz composer. In the late 1950s he rejected the established structural principles of jazz for free avant-garde improvisation. He has worked with small and large groups, ethnic musicians of different traditions, and symphony orchestras.

Coltrane John (William) 1926–1967. US jazz saxophonist who first came to prominence in 1955 with the Miles Davis quintet, later playing with Thelonious Monk 1957. He was a powerful and individual artist, whose performances featured much experimentation. His 1960s quartet was highly regarded for its innovations in melody and harmony.

Costello Elvis. Stage name of Declan McManus 1954– . English rock singer, songwriter, and guitarist, whose intricate yet impassioned lyrics made him one of Britain's foremost songwriters. The great stylistic range of his work was evident from his 1977 debut *My Aim Is True*. His backing group 1978–86 was the Attractions.

country and western or *country music* popular music of the white US South and West; it evolved from the folk music of the English, Irish, and Scottish settlers and has a strong blues influence. Characteristic instruments are slide guitar, mandolin, and fiddle. Lyrics typically extol family values and traditional sex roles, and often have a strong narrative element. Country music encompasses a variety of regional styles, and ranges from mournful ballads to fast and intricate dance music.

1920s Jimmie Rodgers (1897–1933) wrote a series of 'Blue Yodel' songs that made him the first country-music recording star.

1930s Nashville, Tennessee, became a centre for the country-music industry, with the Grand Ole Opry a showcase for performers. The Carter Family arranged and recorded hundreds of traditional songs. Hollywood invented the singing cowboy.

1940s Hank Williams (1923–1953) emerged as the most significant singer and songwriter; *western swing* spread from Texas.

1950s The *honky-tonk* sound; Kentucky *bluegrass*; ballad singers included Jim Reeves (1923–1964) and Patsy Cline (1932–1963).

1960s Songs of the Bakersfield, California, school, dominated by Buck Owens (1929–) and Merle Haggard (1937–), contrasted with lush Nashville productions of singers such as George Jones (1931–) and Tammy Wynette (1942–).

1970s Dolly Parton (1946–) and Emmylou Harris (1947–); the Austin, Texas, *outlaws* Willie Nelson (1933–) and Waylon Jennings (1937–); *country rock* pioneered by Gram Parsons (1946–1973).

1980s Neotraditionalist *new country* represented by Randy Travis (1963–), Dwight Yoakam (1957–), and Nanci Griffith (1954–).

Crosby Bing (Harry Lillis) 1904–1977. US film actor and singer who achieved world success with his distinctive style of crooning in such songs as 'Pennies from Heaven' 1936 (featured in a film of the same name) and 'White Christmas' 1942. He won an acting Oscar for *Going My*

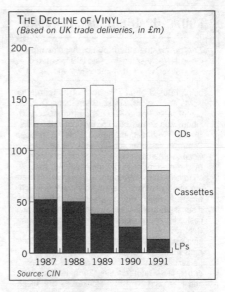

THE DECLINE OF VINYL
(Based on UK trade deliveries, in £m)

Source: CIN

Way 1944, and made a series of film comedies with Dorothy Lamour and Bob Hope, the last being *Road to Hong Kong* 1962.

Davis Miles (Dewey, Jr) 1926–1991. US jazz trumpeter, composer, and bandleader. He recorded bebop with Charlie Parker 1945, pioneered cool jazz in the 1950s and jazz-rock fusion beginning in the late 1960s. His significant albums include *Birth of the Cool* 1957 (recorded 1949 and 1950), *Sketches of Spain* 1959, and *Bitches' Brew* 1970.

Dixieland jazz jazz style that originated in New Orleans, USA, in the early 20th century, dominated by cornet, trombone, and clarinet. The trumpeter Louis Armstrong emerged from this style. The *trad jazz* movement in the UK in the 1940s–50s was a Dixieland revival.

Doors, the US psychedelic rock group formed 1965 in Los Angeles by Jim Morrison (1943–1971, vocals), Ray Manzarek (1935– , keyboards), Robby Krieger (1946– , guitar), and John Densmore (1944– , drums). Their first hit was 'Light My Fire' from their debut album *The Doors* 1967. They were noted for Morrison's poetic lyrics and flamboyant performance.

Dylan Bob. Adopted name of Robert Allen Zimmerman 1941– . US singer and songwriter whose increasingly obscure lyrics provided catchphrases for a generation and influenced innumerable songwriters. He began in the folk-music tradition but from 1965 worked in an individualistic rock style, as on the albums *Highway 61 Revisited* 1965 and *Blonde on Blonde* 1966.

Ellington Duke (Edward Kennedy) 1899–1974. US pianist who had an outstanding career as a composer and arranger of jazz. He wrote numerous pieces for his own jazz orchestra, accentuating the strengths of individual virtuoso instrumentalists, and became one of the leading figures in jazz over a 55-year

ROUND UP THE USUAL CENSORS

Efil4zaggin, the album by Los Angeles rap group NWA released in May 1991, entered the US pop chart at number two and sold a million copies in the first two weeks, despite being refused airplay because of its four-letter words and violent, sexist exhortations. The UK parent label Island Records' entire stock of the album was seized in June by Scotland Yard's Obscene Publications Squad. The International Centre Against Censorship said the seizure violated international law, and the decision by the director of public prosecutions to charge Island's distributors, Polygram, caused anxiety throughout the record industry, which turned to relief when magistrates in September dismissed charges, ordering the police to pay costs. Polygram were defended in court by Geoffrey Robertson QC, a veteran of several civil-liberties trials, who said: 'No one in their right minds or indeed their wrong minds could be sexually aroused by this record.' He described NWA numbers like 'Findum, Fuck 'em and Flee' and 'To Kill a Hooker' as the 'black equivalent to our rugby songs' and 'street journalism'. 'The stories told are in street language which is ironic, bitter, sarcastic, rude, and crude ... vivid, disturbing, and shocking, but a million miles away from pornography.'

The NWA case was the first censorship trial in the music business since 1984, when a London record store was acquitted on appeal for stocking allegedly obscene records by the punk bands Dead Kennedys and Crass. It was not, however, the first time NWA had problems with the law: in 1989 their record 'Fuck tha Police' attracted the attention of the Federal Bureau of Investigation.

A former member of NWA, Ice Cube, ran into trouble in the USA with his 1991 album *Death Certificate*, released in October. In particular, a track called 'Black Korea' was perceived as calling for the burning of grocery shops owned by ethnic Koreans in black neighbourhoods, where racial tensions between African-Americans and Koreans were already causing problems. Three thousand grocers responded by refusing to stock an alcoholic drink advertised on television and radio by Ice Cube, and one record retail chain boycotted the LP under 'community pressure'. A less than apologetic Ice Cube explained: 'All I'm saying on "Black Korea" is that if you don't like the community, move out. If you won't move out, we'll help you pack.' Elsewhere on the album, Ice Cube advocates castration for white men who have sex with black women, and calls for the murder of NWA's manager ('Cos you can't be the nigger for life crew / With a white Jew tellin' you what to do').

Four-letter words in rap records were also deemed unacceptable for Londoners by Capital Radio's head of music, even though their weekly rap show is broadcast after midnight. After the Radio Authority upheld a listener's complaint in February 1992, the disc jockey in charge was ordered to bleep out such passages or play them backwards.

Pictures rather than words upset US distributors in the case of new albums by U2 and David Bowie's outfit Tin Machine. The latter featured a full-frontal view of a classical Greek sculpture of a naked man, repeated four times on the sleeve. The artwork had to be redesigned for the US market with the offending piece of anatomy chipped off, otherwise 60% of retailers would have refused to handle the album. 'The geeks ban the Greeks,' Bowie commented, and an official statement by the band elaborated: 'This is the first time that a piece of academically classical art has been banned from the US public. We find the new "acceptable" version deeply disturbing, and the fact that it is acceptable says more about the confused morality in the States at the moment than a thousand words.'

The male organ was again censored on the sleeve of the Irish band U2's *Achtung Baby*, where a nude photo of one of the band members had to have stickers affixed to it in the strategical position for US distribution. The dominant motif of the album and tour, however, was the German Trabant car, famous for its polluting emissions but clean in the eyes of the music industry.

---

span. Some of his most popular compositions include 'Mood Indigo', 'Sophisticated Lady', 'Solitude', and 'Black and Tan Fantasy'. He was one of the founders of big-band jazz.

Fitzgerald Ella 1918– . US jazz singer, recognized as one of the finest, most lyrical voices in jazz, both in solo work and with big bands. She is celebrated for her smooth interpretations of Gershwin and Cole Porter songs.

funk dance music of black US origin, relying on heavy percussion in polyrhythmic patterns. Leading exponents include James Brown (1928–) and George Clinton (1940–).

Gershwin George 1898–1937. US composer who wrote both 'serious' music, such as the tone poem *Rhapsody in Blue* 1924 and *An American in Paris* 1928, and popular musicals and songs, many with lyrics by his brother **Ira Gershwin** (1896–1983), including 'I Got Rhythm', ''S Wonderful', and 'Embraceable You'. His opera *Porgy and Bess*, an ambitious work that incorporated jazz rhythms and popular song styles in an operatic format, was his masterpiece.

Gillespie Dizzy (John Birks) 1917– . US jazz trumpeter who, with Charlie Parker, was the chief creator and exponent of the bebop style.

Goodman Benny (Benjamin David) 1909–1986. US clarinetist, nicknamed the 'King of Swing' for the new jazz idiom he introduced with arranger Fletcher Henderson (1897–1952). Leader of his own swing band 1934–40, and again later, he is associated with numbers such as 'Blue Skies' and 'Let's Dance'.

gospel music vocal music developed in the 1920s in the black Baptist churches of the US South from spirituals, which were 18th- and 19th-century hymns joined to the old African pentatonic (five-note) scale. Outstanding among the early gospel singers was Mahalia Jackson (1911–1972), but from the 1930s to the mid-1950s male harmony groups predominated, among them the Dixie Hummingbirds, the Swan Silvertones, and the Five Blind Boys of Mississippi.

Guthrie Woody (Woodrow Wilson) 1912–1967. US folk singer and songwriter whose left-wing protest songs, 'dustbowl ballads', and 'talking blues' influenced, among others, Bob Dylan; they include 'Deportees', 'Hard Travelin", and 'This Land Is Your Land'.

Hammer, MC Stage name of Stanley Kirk Burrell 1963– . US rap vocalist and songwriter. His pop-oriented rap style and exuberant dancing gave him a wide appeal, especially in the video-based market, and his second LP, *Please Hammer Don't Hurt 'Em* 1990, sold 13 million copies in one year.

hardcore strident rock music that evolved from punk. It entails playing (guitars and drums) as fast as possible with loud, angry shouting. Tracks lasting only five seconds consisting of a loud 'Aaarrgh!' encapsulate the form. *Thrash metal* and *death metal* are very similar but developed from heavy metal. *Artcore* uses noise for artistic as well as shock effect.

Hawkins Coleman (Randolph) 1904–1969. US virtuoso tenor saxophonist. He was, until 1934, a soloist in the swing band led by Fletcher Henderson (1898–1952), and was an influential figure in bringing the jazz saxophone to prominence as a solo instrument.

heavy metal a style of rock characterized by loudness, sex-and-violence imagery, and guitar solos. Heavy metal developed out of the hard rock of the late 1960s and early 1970s, was performed by such groups as Led Zeppelin and Deep Purple, and enjoyed a resurgence in the late 1980s. Bands include Van Halen (formed 1974), Def Leppard (formed 1977), and Guns 'n' Roses (formed 1987).

Hendrix Jimi (James Marshall) 1942–1970. US rock guitarist, songwriter, and singer, legendary for his virtuoso experimental technique and flamboyance. *Are You Experienced?* 1967 was his first album. He greatly expanded the vocabulary of the electric guitar and influenced both rock and jazz musicians.

hip-hop popular music originating in New York in the early 1980s. It uses scratching (a percussive effect obtained by manually rotating a vinyl record) and heavily accented electronic drums behind a rap vocal. The term 'hip-hop' also comprises break dancing and graffiti.

Holiday Billie. Stage name of Eleanora Gough McKay 1915–1959. US jazz singer, also known as 'Lady Day'. She made her debut in Harlem clubs and became known for her emotionally charged delivery and idiosyncratic phrasing; she brought a blues feel to performances with swing bands. Songs she made her own include 'Strange Fruit' and 'I Cover the Waterfront'.

Holly Buddy. Stage name of Charles Hardin Holley 1936–1959. US rock-and-roll singer, guitarist, and songwriter, born in Lubbock, Texas. Holly had a distinctive, hiccuping vocal style and was an early experimenter with recording techniques. Many of his hits with his band, the Crickets, such as 'That'll Be the Day' 1957, 'Peggy Sue' 1957, and 'Maybe Baby' 1958, have become classics. He died in a plane crash.

house music dance music of the 1980s originating in the inner-city clubs of Chicago, USA, combining funk with European high-tech pop, and using dub, digital sampling, and cross-fading. *Acid house* has minimal vocals and melody, instead surrounding the mechanically emphasized 4/4 beat with found noises, stripped-down synthesizer riffs, and a wandering bass line. Other variants include *hip-house*, with rap elements, and *acid jazz*.

indie or *independent* in music, a record label that is neither owned nor distributed by one of the large conglomerates ('majors') that dominate the industry. Without a corporate bureaucratic structure, the independent labels are often quicker to respond to new trends and more idealistic in their aims. What has become loosely known as *indie music* therefore tends to be experimental, amateurish, or at the cutting edge of street fashion.

Jackson Michael 1958– . US rock singer and songwriter whose videos and live performances are meticulously choreographed. He began his career as the youngest member of *the Jackson Five*, but soon surpassed his brothers in popularity as a solo performer. His first solo hit was 'Got to Be There' 1971; his worldwide popularity peaked with the albums *Thriller* 1982 (which sold 41 million copies, a world record) and *Bad* 1987.

jazz polyphonic, syncopated music characterized by solo virtuosic improvisation, which developed in the USA at the turn of the 20th century. It had its roots in black American and other popular music and evolved various distinct vocal and instrumental forms.

1880–1900 Originated chiefly in New Orleans from ragtime.

1920s During Prohibition, the centre of jazz moved to Chicago (Louis Armstrong, Bix Beiderbecke) and St Louis. By the end of the decade the focus had shifted to New York City (Art Tatum, Fletcher Henderson).

1930s The *swing* bands used call-and-response arrangements with improvised solos (Paul Whiteman, Benny Goodman).

1940s swing grew into the *big band* era with jazz composed as well as arranged (Glenn Miller, Duke Ellington); rise of *West Coast* jazz (Stan Kenton) and rhythmically complex, highly improvisational *bebop* (Charlie Parker, Dizzy Gillespie, Thelonius Monk).

1950s Jazz had ceased to be dance music; *cool jazz* (Stan Getz, Miles Davis, Lionel Hampton, Modern Jazz Quartet) developed in reaction to the insistent, 'hot' bebop and *hard bop*.

1960s *Free-form* or *free jazz* (Ornette Coleman, John Coltrane).

1970s Jazz rock (US group Weather Report, formed 1970; British guitarist John McLaughlin, 1942–); jazz funk (US saxophonist Grover Washington Jr, 1943–); more eclectic free jazz (US pianist Keith Jarrett, 1945–).

1980s Resurgence of tradition (US trumpeter Wynton Marsalis, 1962– ; British saxophonist Courtney Pine, 1965–) and avant-garde (US chamber-music Kronos Quartet, formed 1978; anarchic UK group Loose Tubes, formed 1983).

karaoke amateur singing in public to prerecorded backing tapes. Karaoke originated in Japan and spread to other parts of the world in the 1980s. In Japan, karaoke machines—jukeboxes of backing tracks to well-known songs, usually with a microphone attached–have been installed not only in bars but also in taxis.

Lennon John 1940–1980. UK rock singer, songwriter, and guitarist. While still a member of the Beatles, he collaborated intermittently with his wife *Yoko Ono* (1933–). 'Give Peace a Chance', a hit 1969, became an anthem of the peace movement. His solo work alternated between the confessional and the political, as on *Imagine* 1971. He was shot dead by a fan.

Madonna stage name of Madonna Louise Ciccone 1958– . US pop singer and actress who presents herself on stage and in videos with exaggerated sexuality and Catholic trappings. Her first hit was 'Like a Virgin' 1984; others include 'Material Girl' 1985 and 'Like a Prayer' 1989. Her films include *Desperately Seeking Susan* 1985 and *Dick Tracy* 1990.

Marley Bob (Robert Nesta) 1945–1981. Jamaican reggae singer, a Rastafarian whose songs, many of which were topical and political, popularized reggae worldwide in the 1970s. One of his greatest hit songs is 'No Woman No Cry'; his albums include *Natty Dread* 1975 and *Exodus* 1977.

Miller Glenn 1904–1944. US trombonist and, as bandleader, exponent of the big-band swing sound from 1938. He composed his signature tune 'Moonlight Serenade' (a hit 1939). Miller became leader of the US Army Air Force Band in Europe 1942, made broadcasts to troops throughout the world during World War II, and disappeared without trace on a flight between England and France.

TOP 10 MUSIC VIDEOS (BOUGHT, 1991)

1	*Greatest Flix II*	Queen
2	*Pavarotti in Hyde Park*	Luciano Pavarotti
3	*In Concert*	Carreras/Domingo/ Pavarotti
4	*The Immaculate Collection*	Madonna
5	*Box of Flix*	Queen
6	*We Will Rock You*	Queen
7	*Simply The Best*	Tina Turner
8	*Pavarotti*	Luciano Pavarotti
9	*Souvenirs And Memories*	Foster & Allen
10	*Greatest Hits*	Eurythmics

Source: CIN

TOP 10 CDS (1991)

1	*Stars*	Simply Red
2	*Greatest Hits*	Eurythmics
3	*Greatest Hits II*	Queen
4	*Simply The Best*	Tina Turner
5	*Out Of Time*	REM
6	*We Can't Dance*	Genesis
7	*On Every Street*	Dire Straits
8	*Dangerous*	Michael Jackson
9	*The Immaculate Collection*	Madonna
10	*Love Hurts*	Cher

Source: CIN

Mingus Charles 1922–1979. US jazz bassist and composer. His experimentation with atonality and dissonant effects opened the way for the new style of free collective jazz improvisation of the 1960s.

Monk Thelonious (Sphere) 1917–1982. US jazz pianist and composer who took part in the development of bebop. He had a highly idiosyncratic style, but numbers such as 'Round Midnight' and 'Blue Monk' have become standards.

Morrison Van (George Ivan) 1945– . Northern Irish singer and songwriter whose jazz-inflected Celtic soul style was already in evidence on *Astral Weeks* 1968 and has been highly influential. Among other albums are *Veedon Fleece* 1974 and *Avalon Sunset* 1989.

New Age instrumental or ambient music of the 1980s, often semi-acoustic or electronic; less insistent than rock.

New Wave in pop music, a style that evolved parallel to punk in the second half of the 1970s. It shared the urban aggressive spirit of punk but was musically and lyrically more sophisticated; examples are the early work of Elvis Costello and Talking Heads.

Parker Charlie (Charles Christopher 'Bird', 'Yardbird') 1920–1955. US alto saxophonist and jazz composer, associated with the trumpeter Dizzy Gillespie in developing the bebop style. His mastery of improvisation inspired performers on all jazz instruments.

pop music short for *popular music*, umbrella term for contemporary music not classifiable as jazz or classical. Pop became distinct from folk music with the advent of sound-recording techniques, and has incorporated blues, country and western, and music-hall elements; electronic amplification and other technological innovations have played a large part in the creation of new styles. The traditional format is a song of roughly three minutes with verse, chorus, and middle eight bars.

1910s Al Jolson was one of the first recording stars. Ragtime was still popular.

1920s In the USA Paul Whiteman and his orchestra played danceable jazz, the country singer Jimmie Rodgers (1897–1933) reached a new record-buying public, the blues was burgeoning; in the UK popular singers included Al Bowlly (1899–1941, born in Mozambique).

1930s Crooner Bing Crosby and vocal groups such as the Andrews Sisters were the alternatives to swing bands.

1940s rhythm and blues evolved in the USA while Frank Sinatra was a teen idol and Glenn Miller played dance music; the UK preferred singers such as Vera Lynn.

1950s In the USA *doo-wop* (a vocal group style based on *a cappella* street-corner singing) preceded *rockabilly* and the rise of *rock and roll* (Elvis Presley, Chuck Berry). British pop records were often cover versions of US originals.

1960s The Beatles and the *Mersey beat* transcended UK borders, followed by the Rolling Stones, *hard rock* (the Who, Led Zeppelin), *art rock* (Genesis, Yes). In the USA *surf music* (group harmony vocals or fast, loud, guitar-based instrumentals) preceded *Motown*, *folk rock* (the Byrds, Bob Dylan), and *blues rock* (Jimi Hendrix, Janis Joplin). *Psychedelic rock* evolved from 1966 on both sides of the Atlantic (the Doors, Pink Floyd, Jefferson Airplane).

1970s The first half of the decade produced *glitter rock* (David Bowie), *heavy metal*, and *disco* (dance music with a very emphatic, mechanical beat); in the UK also *pub rock* (a return to basics, focusing on live performance); *reggae* spread from Jamaica. From 1976 *punk* was ascendant; the US term *New Wave* encompassed bands not entirely within the punk idiom (Talking Heads, Elvis Costello).

1980s Punk continued as *hardcore* or mutated into *gothic*; dance music developed regional US variants: *hip-hop* (New York), *go-go* (Washington DC), and *house* (Chicago). Live audiences grew, leading to anthemic *stadium rock* (U2, Bruce Springsteen) and increasingly elaborate stage performances (Michael Jackson, Prince, Madonna). An interest in *world music* sparked new fusions.

1990s Rap and heavy metal predominated in the USA at the start of the decade; on the UK *indie* scene, dance music (Happy Mondays, Inspiral Carpets) and a new wave of guitar groups (Ride, Lush) drew on the psychedelic era.

Porter Cole (Albert) 1892–1964. US composer and lyricist, mainly of musical comedies. His witty, sophisticated songs like 'Let's Do It' 1928, 'I Get a Kick Out of You' 1934, and 'Don't Fence Me In' 1944 have been widely recorded and admired. His shows, many of which were made into films, include *The Gay Divorcee* 1932 and *Kiss Me Kate* 1948.

Presley Elvis (Aaron) 1935–1977. US singer and guitarist, the most influential performer of the rock-and-roll era. With his recordings for Sun Records in Memphis, Tennessee, 1954–55 and early hits such as 'Heartbreak Hotel' 1956, 'Hound Dog' 1956, and 'Love Me Tender' 1956, he created an individual vocal style, influenced by Southern blues, gospel music, country music, and rhythm and blues.

Prince stage name of Prince Rogers Nelson 1960– . US pop musician who composes, arranges, and produces his own records and often plays all the instruments. His albums, including *1999* 1982 and *Purple Rain* 1984, contain elements of rock, funk, and jazz.

psychedelic rock or **acid rock** pop music that usually involves advanced electronic equipment for both light and sound. The free-form improvisations and light shows that appeared about 1966, attempting to suggest or improve on mind-altering drug experiences, had by the 1980s evolved into stadium performances with lasers and other special effects. Bands included the Doors, Pink Floyd, and Jefferson Airplane.

punk movement of disaffected youth of the late 1970s, manifesting itself in fashions and music designed to shock or intimidate. *Punk rock* began in the UK and stressed aggressive performance within a three-chord, three-minute format, as exemplified by the Sex Pistols.

ragtime syncopated music ('ragged time') in 2/4 rhythm, usually played on piano. It developed in the USA among black musicians in the late 19th century; it was influenced by folk tradition, minstrel shows, and marching bands, and later was incorporated into jazz. Scott Joplin was a leading writer of ragtime pieces ('rags').

rap music rapid, rhythmic chant over a prerecorded repetitive backing track. Rap emerged in New York 1979 as part of the hip-hop culture, although the macho, swaggering lyrics that initially predominated have roots in ritual boasts and insults. Different styles were flourishing by the 1990s: jazz rap, funk rap, reggae rap, and so on.

Reed Lou 1942– . US rock singer and songwriter, member (1965–70) of the New York avant-garde group *the Velvet Underground*, perhaps the most influential band of the period. His solo work deals largely with urban alienation and angst, and includes the albums *Berlin* 1973, *Street Hassle* 1978, and *New York* 1989.

reggae predominant form of West Indian popular music of the 1970s and 1980s, characterized by a heavily accented offbeat and a thick bass line. The lyrics often refer to Rastafarianism. Musicians include Bob Marley, Lee 'Scratch' Perry (1940– , performer and producer), and the group Black Uhuru (1974–). Reggae is also played in the UK, South Africa, and elsewhere.

TOP 10 SINGLES (1991)

1	*(Everything I Do) I Do It For You*	Bryan Adams
2	*Bohemian Rhapsody/ The Days Of Our Lives*	Queen
3	*The Shoop Shoop Song*	Cher
4	*I'm Too Sexy*	Right Said Fred
5	*Do The Bartman*	Simpsons
6	*Any Dream Will Do*	Jason Donovan
7	*The One And Only*	Chesney Hawkes
8	*Dizzy*	Vic Reeves & The Wonder Stuff
9	*Insanity*	Oceanic
10	*I Wanna Sex You Up*	Color Me Badd

Source: CIN

Whose Voice is it Anyway?

Remember when the Monkees were panned for not playing the instruments on their records? Since the sixties, borrowing has become a feature of Post-Modernism, but that has not kept it out of the courts. For example, pop duo Milli Vanilli were convicted of consumer fraud in the USA in September 1991 for not singing on their own album, and dissatisfied customers were awarded refunds. Singer Loleatta Holloway successfully sued Black Box for sampling her voice as the lead vocal on one of their dance hits, while Paula Abdul has been sued by a backup singer, Yvette Martin, who alleges that her voice was used instead of Abdul's, either alone or in a studio-created composite, on two LPs.

Madonna, on the other hand, came under fire for resorting to prerecorded tapes at live shows, in order to save her breath for her exhausting dance routines. This practice is becoming common, and some performers make a point of announcing the fact that they are *not* using prerecorded tape on stage.

Elsewhere, the public thronged to see certified imitations. In the cinemas, Oliver Stone's film *The Doors* built on the legend surrounding the hippie-era rock group; stage musicals were created around the work of Eddie Cochran, Louis Jordan, and other stars of yesteryear; and in the clubs, most bizarrely, appeared so-called tribute bands. Some of these offer affectionate parodies—the best known is Bjorn Again, a band that performs songs by the defunct Swedish pop group Abba—while others try earnestly to sound like their heroes. Elton Jack, the Australian Doors Show, and the Bleach Boys are all from down under; in the UK, World of Twist had a hit with a faithful cover of the Rolling Stones' 1967 song 'She's a Rainbow'. Why not the Who's 'Substitute', we ask ourselves?

remix in pop music, the studio practice of reassembling a recording from all or some of its individual components, often with the addition of new elements. Issuing a recording in several different remixes ensures additional sales to collectors and increases airplay; remixes can be geared specifically to radio, dance clubs, and so on. The practice accompanied the rise of the 12-inch single in the 1980s. Some record producers specialize in remixing. In 1987 Madonna became the first artist in the USA to release an album consisting entirely of remixes (*You Can Dance*).

rhythm and blues (R & B) US popular music of the 1940s–60s, which drew on swing and jump-jazz rhythms and blues vocals and was a progenitor of rock and roll. It diversified into soul, funk, and other styles. R & B artists include Bo Diddley (1928–   ), Jackie Wilson (1934–84), and Etta James (*c.* 1938–   ).

Robinson Smokey (William) 1940–   . US singer, songwriter, and record producer, associated with Motown records from its conception. He was lead singer of the Miracles 1957–72 (hits include 'Shop Around' 1961, 'The Tears of a Clown' 1970) and his solo hits include 'Cruisin'' 1979 and 'Being With You' 1981. His light tenor voice and wordplay characterize his work.

rock and roll pop music born of a fusion of rhythm and blues and country and western and based on electric guitar and drums. In the mid-1950s, with the advent of Elvis Presley, it became the heartbeat of teenage rebellion in the West and also had considerable impact on other parts of the world. It found perhaps its purest form in late-1950s *rockabilly*; the blanket term 'rock' later came to comprise a multitude of styles.

Rolling Stones, the British band formed 1962, once notorious as the 'bad boys' of rock. Original members were Mick Jagger (1943–   ), Keith Richards (1943–   ), Brian Jones (1942–1969), Bill Wyman (1936–   ), Charlie Watts (1941–   ), and the pianist Ian Stewart (1938–1985).

salsa Latin big-band dance music popularized by Puerto Ricans in New York City in the 1980s and by, among others, the Panamanian singer Rubén Blades (1948–   ).

Simon Paul 1942–   . US pop singer and songwriter. In a folk-rock duo with Art Garfunkel (1942–   ), he had such hits as 'Mrs Robinson' 1968 and 'Bridge Over Troubled Water' 1970. Simon's solo work includes the critically acclaimed album *Graceland* 1986, for which he drew on Cajun and African music.

Sinatra Frank (Francis Albert) 1915–   . US singer and film actor. Celebrated for his phrasing and emotion, especially on love ballads, he is particularly associated with the song 'My Way'.

Smiths, the English four-piece rock group (1982–87) from Manchester. Their songs, with lyrics by singer Morrissey (1959–   ) and tunes by guitarist Johnny Marr (1964–   ), drew on diverse sources such as rockabilly, Mersey beat, and the Byrds, with confessional humour and images of urban desolation. They were Britain's main cult band in the 1980s.

Sondheim Stephen (Joshua) 1930–   . US composer and lyricist. He wrote the lyrics of Leonard Bernstein's *West Side Story* 1957 and composed witty and sophisticated musicals, including *A Little Night Music* 1973, *Pacific Overtures* 1976, *Sweeney Todd* 1979, *Into the Woods* 1987, and *Sunday in the Park with George* 1989.

soul music emotionally intense style of rhythm and blues sung by, among others, Sam Cooke (1931–1964), Aretha Franklin (1942–   ), and Al Green (1946–   ). A synthesis of blues, gospel music, and jazz, it emerged in the 1950s. By the late 1980s, it had become associated with bland bedroom ballads.

Spector Phil 1940–   . US record producer,

known for the 'wall of sound', created using a large orchestra, distinguishing his work in the early 1960s with vocal groups such as the Crystals and the Ronettes. He withdrew into semi-retirement in 1966 but his influence can still be heard.

Springsteen Bruce 1949– . US rock singer, songwriter, and guitarist, born in New Jersey. His music combines melodies in traditional rock idiom and reflective lyrics about working-class life on albums such as *Born to Run* 1975 and *Born in the USA* 1984.

steel band musical ensemble common in the West Indies, consisting mostly of percussion instruments made from oil drums that give a sweet, metallic ringing tone.

Supremes, the US vocal group, pioneers of the Motown sound, formed 1959 in Detroit. Beginning in 1962, the group was a trio comprising, initially, Diana Ross (1944–), Mary Wilson (1944–), and Florence Ballard (1943–1976). The most successful female group of the 1960s, they had a string of pop hits beginning with 'Where Did Our Love Go?' 1964 and 'Baby Love' 1964. Diana Ross left to pursue a solo career 1969.

swing music jazz style popular in the 1930s–40s. A big-band sound with a simple harmonic base of varying tempo from the rhythm section (percussion, guitar, piano), harmonic brass and woodwind sections (sometimes strings), and superimposed solo melodic line from, for example, trumpet, clarinet, or saxophone. Exponents included Benny Goodman, Duke Ellington, and Glenn Miller, who introduced jazz to a mass white audience.

syncopation the deliberate upsetting of rhythm by shifting the accent to a beat that is normally unaccented.

U2 Irish rock group formed 1977 by singer Bono Vox (born Paul Hewson, 1960–), guitarist Dave 'The Edge' Evans (1961–), bassist Adam Clayton (1960–), and drummer Larry Mullen (1961–). Committed Christians, they play socially concerned stadium rock, and their albums include *The Unforgettable Fire* 1984, *The Joshua Tree* 1987, and the soundtrack from their documentary film *Rattle and Hum* 1988.

world music or *roots music* any music whose regional character has not been lost in the melting pot of the pop industry. Examples are W African *mbalax*, E African *soukous*, S African *mbaqanga*, French Antillean *zouk*, Javanese gamelan, Latin American salsa and lambada, Cajun music, European folk music, and rural blues, as well as combinations of these (flamenco guitar and kora; dub polka).

Young Neil 1945– . Canadian rock guitarist, singer, and songwriter, in the USA from 1966. His high, plaintive voice and loud, abrasive guitar make his work instantly recognizable despite abrupt changes of style throughout his career. *Rust Never Sleeps* 1979 and *Ragged Glory* 1990 (both with the group Crazy Horse) are among his best work.

zydeco dance music originating in Louisiana, USA, similar to Cajun but more heavily influenced by blues and West Indian music.

MUSICAL TERMS

acoustics in general, the experimental and theoretical science of sound and its transmission; in particular, that branch of the science that has to do with the phenomena of sound in a particular space such as a room or theatre.

alto (1) low-register female voice, also called *contralto*; (2) high adult male voice, also known as counter tenor; (3) (French) viola.

anthem a short, usually elaborate, religious choral composition, sometimes accompanied by the organ; also a song of loyalty and devotion.

aria solo vocal piece in an opera or oratorio, often in three sections, the third repeating the first after a contrasting central section.

atonality music in which there is an apparent absence of key; often associated with an expressionist style.

bagatelle a short character piece, often for piano.

bar a modular unit of rhythm, shown in notation by vertical 'barring' of the musical continuum into sections of usually constant duration and rhythmic content. The alternative term is 'measure'.

baritone lower-range male voice between bass and tenor.

bass (1) lowest range of male voice; (2) lower regions of musical pitch; (3) a double bass.

bel canto an 18th-century Italian style of singing with emphasis on perfect technique and beautiful tone. The style reached its peak in the operas of Rossini, Donizetti, and Bellini.

cadence termination of a musical line or phrase, expressed rhythmically and harmonically.

cadenza an unaccompanied bravura passage (requiring elaborate, virtuoso execution) in the style of an improvisation for the soloist during a concerto.

canon an echo form for two or more parts repeating and following a leading melody at regular time intervals to achieve a harmonious effect. It is often found in classical music, for example Vivaldi and J S Bach.

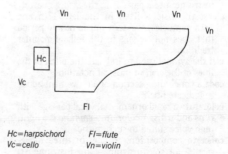

Hc=harpsichord   Fl=flute
Vc=cello   Vn=violin

Orchestra: Frederick the Great gives a concert, c. 1760. He plays solo flute. All players face inward.

Some Musical Expressions

accelerando	gradually faster	presto, prestissimo	at speed, at high speed
adagio, adagietto	easy-going	quasi	sort of, rather
agitato	agitated	ripieno	the accompanying ensemble
alla breve	four beat as two to the bar	ritardando	gradually coming to a stop
allargando	spreading out in tempo	ritenuto	pulling back
allegro, allegretto	with lightness of action	ritornello	refrain
andante, andantino	with movement	rubato	borrowed (time)
brio, con	with spirit	secco	with a dry tone
calando	winding down, slower and softer	segno	cue sign
cantabile	singing	segue	follow on
capo (da)	from the top (beginning)	sempre	always
concerto	the solo (group): cf ripieno	sforzata, sforzando	with a force tone
crescendo	gradually louder	smorzando	smothering, stifling the tone
deciso	firmly	sotto voce	in an undertone
diminuendo	gradually softer	spiccato	bounced (of the bow off the string)
divisi a 2, 3, etc.	divided in 2, 3, etc. parts	staccato, -issimo	short, very short
dolce, dolcissimo	soft and sweetly	subito	sudden, suddenly
doloroso	mournfully	Takt	(German) beat, metre, bar (measure)
espressivo	with expression	tema	theme
flatterzunge	(German) fluttertongue	tenuto	holding back
fuoco, con	with fire	tessitura	range of instrument or voice
giocoso	with fun	tranquillo	calmly
grave	with gravity	tanto	so much
largo, larghetto	expansively	troppo	too much
legato	smoothly	via	remove (e.g. mute)
lento	slowly	veloce	at speed
l'istesso (tempo)	the same (tempo)	vivo, vivace	with life
loco	in (its usual) place	voce, voci	voice, voices
lungo, lunga	long	volante	as though flying
misterioso	mysteriously	wieder	(German) again
molto	much, very	Zeitmass	(German) tempo
pesante	weightily	zingaresca	gipsy
poco, pochissimo	a little, very little	zu 2	(German) 1. for 2 players; 2. in 2 parts
portamento	lifting (note to note)		

cantata an extended work for voices, from the Italian, meaning 'sung', as opposed to sonata ('sounded') for instruments. A cantata can be sacred or secular, sometimes uses solo voices, and usually has orchestral accompaniment. The first printed collection of sacred cantata texts dates from 1670.

capriccio a short instrumental piece, often humorous or whimsical in character.

chamber music music suitable for performance in a small room or chamber, rather than in the concert hall, and usually written for instrumental combinations, played with one instrument to a part, as in the string quartet.

classical music written in the late 17th and 18th centuries; Western music of any period that does not belong to the folk or popular traditions.

clef the symbol used to indicate the pitch of the lines of the staff in musical notation.

coda a concluding section of a movement added to indicate finality.

coloratura a rapid ornamental vocal passage with runs and trills. A *coloratura soprano* is a light, high voice suited to such music.

concerto composition, usually in three movements, for solo instrument (or instruments) and orchestra. It developed during the 18th century from the *concerto grosso* form for string orchestra, in which a group of solo instruments is contrasted with a full orchestra.

contralto a low-registered female voice; also called an *alto*.

counterpoint the art of combining different forms of an original melody with apparent freedom and yet to harmonious effect. Palestrina and J S Bach were masters of counterpoint.

diatonic a scale consisting of the seven notes of any major or minor key.

encore (French 'again') an unprogrammed extra item, usually short and well-known, played at the end of a concert to please an enthusiastic audience.

étude a musical exercise designed to develop technique.

finale the last movement or section of a composition, by implication resolute in character.

fret an inlaid ridge of ivory or metal, or circlets of nylon, marking positions in the fingerboard of a plucked or bowed string instrument indicating changes of pitch.

fugue a contrapuntal form (with two or more melodies) for a number of parts or 'voices', which enter successively in imitation of each other. It was raised to a high art by J S Bach.

gamelan Indonesian orchestra employing tuned gongs, xylophones, metallophones (with bars of metal), cymbals, drums, flutes, and fiddles, the music of which has inspired such Western composers as Debussy, Colin McPhee, John

Cage, Benjamin Britten, and Philip Glass.

Gregorian chant any of a body of plainsong choral chants associated with Pope Gregory the Great (540–604), which became standard in the Roman Catholic Church.

harmonics a series of partial vibrations that combine to form a musical tone. The number and relative prominence of harmonics produced determines an instrument's tone colour (timbre). An oboe is rich in harmonics, the flute has few. Harmonics conform to successive divisions of the sounding air column or string: their pitches are harmonious.

impromptu a short instrumental piece that suggests spontaneity. Composers of piano impromptus include Schubert and Chopin.

intermezzo a short orchestral interlude often used between the acts of an opera to denote the passage of time; by extension, a short piece for an instrument to be played between other more substantial works.

key the diatonic scale around which a piece of music is written; for example, a passage in the key of C major will mainly use the notes of the C major scale. The term is also used for the lever activated by a keyboard player, such as a piano key.

libretto the text of an opera or other dramatic vocal work, or the scenario of a ballet.

madrigal a form of secular song in four or five parts, usually sung without instrumental accompaniment. It originated in 14th-century Italy. Madrigal composers include Andrea Gabrieli, Claudio Monteverdi, Thomas Morley, and Orlando Gibbons.

melody a sequence of notes forming a theme or tune.

metre accentuation pattern characteristic of a musical line; the regularity underlying musical rhythm.

mezzo-soprano female singing voice halfway between soprano and contralto.

middle C the C in mid-keyboard, so-called because it also marks the meeting-point of bass and treble clefs in keyboard notation.

minuet European courtly dance of the 17th century, later used with the trio as the third movement in a Classical symphony.

modulation movement from one key to another.

movement a section of a large work, such as a symphony, which is often complete in itself.

Muzak proprietary name for 'piped music' recorded to strict psychological criteria for transmission in a variety of work environments in order to improve occupier or customer morale.

nocturne a lyrical, dreamy piece, often for piano, introduced by John Field (1782–1837) and adopted by Chopin.

opera dramatic musical work in which singing takes the place of speech. In opera the music accompanying the action has paramount importance, although dancing and spectacular staging may also play their parts. Opera originated in late 16th-century Florence when the musical declamation, lyrical monologues, and choruses of Classical Greek drama were reproduced in current forms.

operetta a short amusing musical play, which may use spoken dialogue.

opus a term, used with a figure, to indicate the numbering of a composer's works, usually in chronological order.

oratorio musical setting of religious texts, scored for orchestra, chorus, and solo voices, on a scale more dramatic and larger than that of a cantata.

orchestration the scoring of a composition for orchestra; the choice of instruments of a score expanded for orchestra (often by another

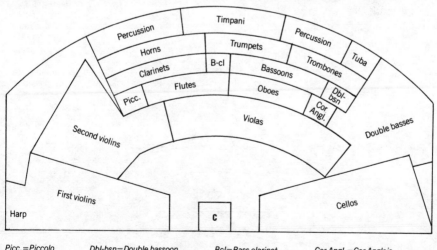

Picc.=Piccolo   Dbl-bsn=Double bassoon   Bcl=Bass clarinet   Cor Angl.=Cor Anglais
C=conductor

Orchestra: Setting most usual today. It is unbalanced — the bass instruments tend to the right, treble instruments to the left.

hand). A work may be written for piano, and then transferred to an orchestral score.

overture a piece of instrumental music, usually preceding an opera. There are also overtures to suites and plays, ballets, and 'concert' overtures, such as Elgar's *Cockaigne* and John Ireland's descriptive *London Overture*.

prelude a composition intended as the preface to further music, to set a mood for a stage work, as in Wagner's *Lohengrin*; as used by Chopin, a short piano work.

requiem in the Roman Catholic church, a mass for the dead. Musical settings include those by Palestrina, Mozart, Berlioz, and Verdi.

rhapsody instrumental fantasia, often based on folk melodies, such as Lizst's *Hungarian Rhapsodies* 1853–54.

rhythm the patterning of music in movement; a recurring unit of long and short time values.

rondo or *rondeau* form of instrumental music in which the principal section returns like a refrain. Rondo form is often used for the last movement of a sonata or concerto.

scale a sequence of pitches that establishes a key, and in some respects the character of a composition. A scale is defined by its starting note and may be *major* or *minor* depending on the order of intervals. A *chromatic* scale is the full range of 12 notes: it has no key because there is no fixed starting point. A *whole-tone* scale is a six-note scale and is also indeterminate in key: only two are possible. A *diatonic* scale has seven notes, a *pentatonic* scale has five.

scherzo a lively piece, usually in rapid triple (3/4) time; often used for the third movement of a symphony, sonata, or quartet.

serenade a musical piece for chamber orchestra or wind instruments in several movements, originally intended for evening entertainment, such as Mozart's *Eine kleine Nachtmusik/A Little Night Music*.

sonata a piece of instrumental music written for a soloist or a small ensemble and consisting of a series of related movements.

soprano the highest range of the female voice.

suite formerly a grouping of old dance forms; later the term came to be used to describe a set of instrumental pieces, sometimes assembled from a stage work, such as Tchaikovsky's *Nutcracker Suite* 1891–92.

symphonic poem a term originated by Liszt for his 13 one-movement orchestral works that interpret a story from literature or history, also used by many other composers. Richard Strauss preferred the title *tone poem*.

symphony a musical composition for orchestra, traditionally in four separate but closely related movements. It developed from the smaller sonata form, the Italian overture, and the dance suite of the 18th century.

syncopation the deliberate upsetting of rhythm by shifting the accent to a beat that is normally unaccented.

tempo the speed at which a piece is played.

tenor the highest range of adult male voice when not using falsetto (a male voice singing in the female register).

timbre the tone colour of an instrument.

tonality the observance of a key structure; that is, the recognition of the importance of a tonic or key note and of the diatonic scale built upon it.

vibrato a slight but rapid fluctuation of intensity in voice or instrument.

KEY NAMES

Abbott Berenice 1898–1991. US photographer who made portrait studies of artists in the 1920s and a comprehensive documentation of New York City in the 1930s. The latter work culminated in the publication of *Changing New York* 1939. Her straightforward style was partially influenced by French photographer Eugène Atget, whose work she rescued from obscurity.

Adams Ansel 1902–1984. US photographer best known for his printed images of dramatic landscapes and organic forms of the American West. He was associated with the zone system of exposure estimation.

Adams worked to establish photography as a fine art. He founded the first museum collection of photography, at New York City's Museum of Modern Art 1937.

Arbus Diane 1923–1971. US photographer who examined the fringes of society, the misfits, the eccentrics, and the bizarre. Her work has been attacked as cruel and voyeuristic but is essentially sympathetic in its curiosity. Initially, she practised as a fashion photographer for 20 years. A limited edition of her work was published in 1970, called *A Box of Ten Photographs*.

Atget Eugène 1857–1927. French photographer. He took up photography at the age of 40, and for 30 years documented urban Paris, leaving some 10,000 photos.

Avedon Richard 1923– . US photographer. A fashion photographer with *Harper's Bazaar* magazine in New York in the mid-1940s, he later became one of the highest-paid commercial photographers.

Bailey David 1938– . English fashion photographer, chiefly associated with *Vogue* magazine from the 1960s. He has published several books of his work, exhibited widely, and also made films.

Beaton Cecil 1904–1980. English portrait and fashion photographer, designer, illustrator, diarist, and conversationalist. He produced portrait studies and also designed scenery and costumes for ballets, and sets for plays and films.

Bourke-White Margaret 1906–1971. US photographer. As an editor of *Fortune* magazine 1929–33, she travelled extensively in the USSR, publishing several collections of photographs. Later, with her husband, the writer Erskine Caldwell, she published photo collections of American and European subjects. On the staff of *Life* magazine from 1936, she covered combat in World War II and documented India's postwar struggle for independence.

Brady Matthew B *c.* 1823–1896. US photographer. Famed for his skill in photographic portraiture, he published *The Gallery of Illustrious Americans* 1850. With the outbreak of the US Civil War 1861, Brady and his staff became the foremost photographers of battle scenes and military life. Although his war photos were widely reproduced, Brady later suffered a series of financial reverses and died in poverty.

Brandt Bill 1904–1983 English photographer. He studied with Man Ray in Paris in 1929; during the 1930s he made a series of social records contrasting the lives of the rich and the poor, and during World War II documented conditions in London in the Blitz. His outstanding creative work was his treatment of the nude, published in *Perspective of Nudes* 1966 and *Shadows of Light* 1966.

Brassäi Adopted name of Gyula Halesz 1899–1986. French photographer of Hungarian origin. From the early 1930s on he documented, mainly by flash, the nightlife of Paris, before turning to more abstract work.

Cameron Julia Margaret 1815–1879. English photographer. She made lively, revealing portraits of the Victorian intelligentsia using a large camera, five-minute exposures, and wet plates. Her subjects included Charles Darwin and Alfred Tennyson.

Cartier-Bresson Henri 1908– . French photographer, one of the greatest photographic artists. His documentary work was shot in black and white, using a small format camera. His work is remarkable for its tightly structured composition and his ability to capture the decisive moment.

Cunningham Imogen 1883–1976. US photographer. Her early work was romantic but she gradually rejected pictorialism, producing clear and detailed plant studies between 1922 and 1929. With US photographers Ansel Adams and Edward Weston she was a founder member of the f/64 group, which advocated precise definition. From the mid-1930s she concentrated on portraiture.

Daguerre Louis Jacques Mande 1789–1851. French pioneer of photography. Together with Niépce, he is credited with the invention of photography (though others were reaching the same point simultaneously). In 1838 he invented the daguerreotype, a single image process, superseded ten years later by Talbot's negative/positive process.

Evans Walker 1903–1975. US photographer best known for his documentary photographs of people in the rural American South during the Great Depression of the 1930s. Many of his photographs appeared in James Agee's book *Let Us Now Praise Famous Men* 1941. Throughout his career, he devoted much attention to photographing architecture. He also produced a renowned series of photographs of people in the New York City subways.

Fenton Roger 1819–1869. English photographer. The world's first war photographer, he went to the Crimea 1855; he also founded the Royal Photographic Society in London.

Hill David Octavius 1802–1870. Scottish photographer who, in collaboration with Robert Adamson (1821–1848), made extensive use of the calotype process in their large collection of portraits taken in Edinburgh 1843–48.

Hine Lewis 1874–1940. US photographer. His dramatic photographs of child labour conditions in American factories at the beginning of the 20th century led to changes in state and local labour laws.

Hine began to document social conditions by photographing the immigrants arriving at New York's Ellis Island 1904–08, as well as their tenement homes and the sweatshops in which they worked. His publication of those photos 1908 is considered the first 'photo story'. In later years, Hine photographed various government projects and the construction of the Empire State Building, published 1930 in his *Men at Work*.

Hosking Eric (John) 1909–1990. English wildlife photographer best known for his documentation of British birds, especially owls. Beginning at the age of eight and still photographing in Africa at 80, he covered all aspects of bird life and illustrated thousands of books.

Kertész André 1894–1986. Hungarian-born US photographer. A master of the 35-mm format camera, he recorded his immediate environment with wit and style. He lived in Paris 1925–36, where he befriended and photographed many avant-garde artists and writers, and in New York City 1936–86, where he did commercial photography for major US magazines as well as creative photography.

Land Edwin Herbert 1909–1991. US inventor of the Polaroid Land camera 1947, which developed the film in one minute inside the camera and produced an 'instant' photograph. Land established the Polaroid Corporation 1937–80. His research also led to a process for 3-D pictures, 'instant' colour film, 'instant' motion pictures, and a new theory of colour perception, the 'retinex' theory 1977.

Lange Dorothea 1895–1965. US photographer. After establishing a private studio in San Francisco, she was hired in 1935 by the federal Farm Security Administration to document the westward migration of farm families from the Dust Bowl of the southern-central USA. She won national acclaim for the gritty realism of her photographs, which were widely exhibited and subsequently published as *An American Exodus: A Record of Human Erosion* 1939.

Man Ray adopted name of Emmanuel Rudnitsky 1890–1977. US photographer, painter, and sculptor, active mainly in France; associated with the Dada movement. His pictures often showed Surrealist images like the photograph *Le Violon d'Ingres* 1924.

In 1922 he invented the **rayograph**, a black and white image obtained without a camera by placing objects on sensitized photographic paper and exposing them to light; he also used the technique of solarization (partly reversing the tones on a photograph). His photographs include portraits of many artists and writers.

Mapplethorpe Robert 1946–1989. US art photographer known for his use of racial and homoerotic imagery chiefly in fine platinum prints. He developed a style of polished el-

egance in his gallery art works.

McCullin Donald 1935– . British war photographer. He began as a freelance photojournalist for Sunday newspapers and went on to cover hostilities in the Congo, Vietnam, Cambodia, Biafra, India, Pakistan, and Northern Ireland. He has published several books of his work and held many exhibitions.

Moholy-Nagy Laszlo 1895–1946. US photographer, born in Hungary. He lived in Germany 1923–29, where he was a member of the Bauhaus school, and fled from the Nazis in 1935. Through the publication of his illuminating theories and practical experiments, he had great influence on 20th-century photography and design.

Muybridge Eadweard. Adopted name of Edward James Muggeridge 1830–1904. English-born US photographer. He made a series of animal locomotion photographs in the USA in the 1870s and proved that, when a horse trots, there are times when all its feet are off the ground. He also explored motion in birds and humans, publishing the results in *Animal Locomotion* 1899.

Nadar adopted name of Gaspard-Félix Tournachon 1820–1910. French portrait photographer and caricaturist. He took the first aerial photographs (from a balloon 1858) and was the first to take flash photographs (using magnesium bulbs).

Namuth Hans 1915–1990. German-born US photographer who specialized in portraits and documentary work. He began as a photojournalist in Europe in the 1930s and opened a portrait studio in New York in 1950. His work includes documentation of the Guatemalan Mam Indians (published as *Los Todos Santeros*

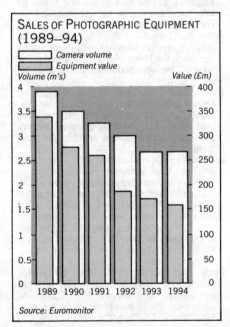

SALES OF PHOTOGRAPHIC EQUIPMENT (1989–94)

☐ Camera volume
▨ Equipment value

Source: Euromonitor

PHOTOGRAPHY CHRONOLOGY

1515	Leonardo da Vinci described the camera obscura.
1750	The Italian painter Canaletto used a camera obscura as an aid to his painting in Venice.
1790	Thomas Wedgwood in England made photograms—placing objects on leather, sensitized using silver nitrate.
1826	Nicephore Niépce (1765–1833), a French doctor, produced the world's first photograph from nature on pewter plates with a camera obscura and an eight-hour exposure.
1835	Niépce and Louis Daguerre produced the first Daguerreotype camera photograph.
1839	Daguerre was awarded an annuity by the French government and his process given to the world. The term 'photography' was coined by English astronomer John Herschel.
1840	Invention of Petzval lens, which reduced exposure time by 90%.
1841	Fox Talbot's Calotype process was patented—the first multi-copy method of photography using a negative/positive process, sensitized with silver iodide.
1844	Fox Talbot published the first photographic book, *The Pencil of Nature*.
1845	Hill and Adamson began to use Calotypes for portraits in Edinburgh.
1851	Fox Talbot used a one-thousandth of a second exposure to demonstrate high-speed photography. Invention of the wet-collodion-on-glass process and the waxed-paper negative. Photographs displayed at the Great Exhibition in London.
1852	The London Society of Arts exhibited 779 photographs.
1855	Roger Fenton made documentary photographs of the Crimean war from a specially constructed caravan with portable darkroom.
1859	Nadar in Paris made photographs underground using battery powered arc lights.
1860	Queen Victoria was photographed by Mayall. Abraham Lincoln was photographed by Matthew Brady for political campaigning.
1861	Single-lens reflex plate camera patented by Thomas Sutton. Principles of three-colour photography demonstrated by J C Maxwell.
1862	Nadar took aerial photographs over Paris.
1870	Julia Margaret Cameron used long lenses for her distinctive portraits.
1871	Gelatine-silver bromide developed.
1878	In the USA Eadweard Muybridge analyzed the movements of animals through sequential photographs, using a series of cameras.
1879	Photogravure process invented.
1880	A silver bromide emulsion was fixed with hypo. Photographs were first reproduced in newspapers in New York using the half-tone engraving process. The first twin-lens reflex camera was produced in London.
1880	Gelatine-silver chloride paper introduced.
1884	George Eastman produced flexible negative film.
1889	Eastman Company in the USA produced the Kodak No 1 camera and roll film, facilitating universal, hand-held snapshots.
1891	First telephoto lens. Interference process of colour photography developed by French doctor Gabriel Lippmann.
1897	First issue of Alfred Stieglitz's *Camera Notes* in the USA.
1902	In Germany Deckel invented a prototype leaf shutter and Zeiss introduced the Tessar lens.
1904	The autochrome colour process was patented by the Lumière brothers.
1905	Stieglitz opened the gallery '291' in New York promoting photography. Lewis Hine used photography to expose the exploitation of children in American factories, causing protective laws to be passed.
1907	The autochrome process began to be factory-produced.
1914	Oskar Barnack designed a prototype Leica camera for Leitz in Germany.
1924	Leitz launched the first 35mm camera, the Leica, delayed because of World War I. It became very popular with photojournalists because it was quiet, small, dependable, and had a range of lenses and accessories.
1929	Rolleiflex produced a twin-lens reflex camera in Germany.
1935	In the USA, Mannes and Godowsky invented Kodachrome transparency film, which produced sharp images and rich colour quality. Electronic flash was invented in the USA.
1936	*Life* magazine, significant for its photojournalism, was first published in the USA.
1938	*Picture Post* magazine was introduced in the UK.
1940	Multigrade enlarging paper by Ilford was made available in the UK.
1942	Kodacolor negative film introduced.
1945	The zone system of exposure estimation published in the book *Exposure Record* by Ansel Adams.

PHOTOGRAPHY CHRONOLOGY (cont.)

1947	Polaroid black and white instant process film invented by Dr Edwin Land, who set up the Polaroid corporation in Boston, Massachusetts. Principles of holography demonstrated in England by Dennis Gabor.
1955	Kodak introduced Tri-X, a black and white 200 ASA film.
1959	The zoom lens invented in Germany by Voigtlander.
1960	Laser invented in the USA, making holography possible. Polacolor, a self-processing colour film, introduced by Polaroid, using a 60-second colour film and dye diffusion technique.
1963	Cibachrome, paper and chemicals for printing directly from transparencies, was made available by Ciba-Geigy of Switzerland; one of the most permanent processes.
1966	International Center of Photography established in New York.
1969	Photographs taken on the Moon by US astronauts.
1970	Charge-coupled device invented at Bell Laboratories in New Jersey, USA, to record very faint images (for example in astronomy). *Rencontres Internationales de la Photographie*, annual summer festival of photography with workshops founded in Arles, France.
1971	Opening of the Photographers' Gallery, London, and the Photo Archive of the Biblioteque Nationale, Paris.
1972	SX70 system, a single-lens reflex camera with instant prints, produced by Polaroid.
1975	Center for Creative Photography established at the University of Arizona.
1980	Ansel Adams sold an original print, *Moonrise: Hernandez*, for $45,000, a record price, in the USA. *Voyager 1* sent photographs of Saturn back to Earth across space.
1983	National Museum of Photography, Film and Television opened in Bradford, England.
1985	Minolta Corporation in Japan introduced the Minolta 7000—the world's first body-integral autofocus single-lens reflex camera.
1988	Electronic camera, which stores pictures on magnetic disc instead of on film, introduced in Japan.
1990	Kodak introduced PhotoCD which converts 35mm camera pictures (on film) into digital form and stores them on compact disc (CD) for viewing on TV.

1989) and of US artists from the 1950s (published as *Artists 1950–1981*). He also carried out assignments for magazines.

Parkinson Norman (adopted name of Ronald William Parkinson Smith) 1913–1990. English fashion and portrait photographer who caught the essential glamour of each decade from the 1930s to the 1980s. Chiefly associated with the magazines *Vogue* and *Queen*, he was best known for his colour work, and from the late 1960s took many official portraits of the UK royal family.

Penn Irving 1917– . US fashion, advertising, portrait, editorial, and fine art photographer. In 1948 he took the first of many journeys to Africa and the Far East, resulting in a series of portrait photographs of local people, avoiding sophisticated technique. He was associated for many years with *Vogue* magazine in the USA.

Siskind Aaron 1903–1991. US art photographer who began as a documentary photographer and in 1940 made a radical change towards a poetic exploration of forms and planes, inspired by the Abstract Expressionist painters.

Steichen Edward 1897–1973. Luxembourg-born US photographer, who with Alfred Stieglitz helped to establish photography as an art form. His style evolved during his career from painterly impressionism to realism.

During World War I he helped to develop aerial photography, and in World War II he directed US naval-combat photography. He turned to fashion and advertising 1923–38, working mainly for *Vogue* and *Vanity Fair* magazines. He was in charge of the Museum of Modern Art's photography collection 1947–62, where in 1955 he organized the renowned 'Family of Man' exhibition.

Stieglitz Alfred 1864–1946. US photographer. After forming the Photo Secession group in 1903, he began the magazine *Camera Work*. Through exhibitions at his gallery '291' in New York he helped to establish photography as an art form. His works include 'Winter, Fifth Avenue' 1893 and 'Steerage' 1907. In 1924 he married the painter Georgia O'Keeffe, who was the model in many of his photographs.

Strand Paul 1890–1976. US photographer who used large-format cameras for his strong, clear, close-up photographs of natural objects.

Talbot William Henry Fox 1800–1877. English pioneer of photography. He invented the paper-based calotype process, the first negative/positive method. Talbot made photograms several years before Daguerre's invention was announced.

Weston Edward 1886–1958. US photographer. A founding member of the 'f/64' group (after the smallest lens opening), a school of photography advocating sharp definition. He is noted for the technical mastery, composition, and clarity in his California landscapes, clouds, gourds, cacti, and nude studies.

In his photography, Weston aimed for realism. He never used artificial light and seldom enlarged, cropped, or retouched his negatives.

IS PHOTOGRAPHY LOSING THE IMAGE WAR?

When the Gulf War finally started it became clear that the American military was determined not to repeat the experiences of Vietnam. This was particularly true of the press coverage of Operation Desert Storm, which was to be kept on an extremely tight rein. In Vietnam, journalists and photographers had relatively easy access to combat. But the steady flow of images produced came to be regarded by the authorities as counterproductive in the propaganda war, contributing to the gradual erosion of confidence that the American people felt for the US involvement in southeast Asia.

There was to be no such freedom in the Gulf. Instead, journalists and photographers nominated by five major news groups formed a 'pool' which would share images and information. Their movements and access to action were more or less exclusive but limited. Any journalists trying to work outside the pool were intimidated, and one was arrested as a spy. The result of all these restrictions was the scarcity of any powerful still images able to convey the reality of the war. Photographers were unable to compete with the on-the-spot, as-it-happened authority of the television news coverage. In several cases frustrated newspaper editors resorted to using stills of television footage; in Britain the most notorious example were the pictures of the RAF officer captured by the Iraqis.

This background goes some way to explaining the heated ethical debate that followed the *Observer*'s decision to publish one of the most memorable images of the war, Ken Jarecke's photograph of the charred remains of an Iraqi soldier at the wheel of his truck. Nobody else in the UK or the USA used the picture but its publication, with other pictures of the burnt-out trucks on the road to Basra, did something to dent the prevailing view of the war as being a clean and efficient triumph of technology.

The implication of the Gulf War for the media was that television had marginalized the significance of photojournalism, robbing it of the power of immediacy. This view seemed to be confirmed by the Russian coup and counter-coup of 1991, the live television coverage of which meant that the rest of the world was better informed of events in Moscow than most of the inhabitants of that city. The suggestion seems to be that the still photograph as a vital tool of the news media has had its day. A contrary argument might suggest that the sheer profligate abundance of news film and its monotonous presentation have blunted its capacity to make an impression and that viewers have become immune to the images of horror pumped every day into their living-rooms. In such a climate the still photograph, by the very nature of its stillness and its refusal to go away, can encapsulate an issue in a way that moving pictures are unable to.

An example of this is the image of the lone Chinese man confronting a column of tanks in Beijing in June 1989. This heroic individual act was witnessed by the world. Television recorded the whole sequence of events: his remonstrations with the tank commander and his final riding away on a bicycle. It made vivid and dramatic television. What the still images did was to turn it into a symbolic icon of the whole Beijing uprising. The unarmed youth confronting the oppressive juggernaut of the Chinese military came to represent for the world the plight of the Chinese people. It might have simplified the issues but in media terms it made the event durable.

The news photograph's power to communicate has recently been subverted by the highly sophisticated but bizarre advertising campaign of the Italian clothes company Benetton. On billboards around Europe the company presented disturbing images of modern-day tragedies. A guerrilla holding a machine gun and a human bone, an AIDS victim surrounded by his grieving family and, displayed in Northern Ireland just 50 yards from where the event took place, a burnt-out car from which two soldiers had been pulled and lynched.

The campaign caused, presumably as intended, enormous outrage and controversy. What was shocking was not simply the images but their change of context and their association with the selling of an unrelated commodity rather than, say, an appeal for charity. By replacing the usual wish-fulfilment fantasy world of advertising with a cruel picture of the real world, Benetton both confirmed the news image's power to shock and undermined its ability to do so by making it more than ever dependent on its context.

A Beijing citizen stands passively in front of a convoy of tanks on the Avenue of Eternal Peace during the popular uprising in June 1989.

His aesthetic principles dominated American photography for many years.

Wolcott Marion Post 1910–1990. US documentary photographer best known for her work for the Farm Security Administration (with Walker Evans and Dorothea Lange), showing the conditions of poor farmers in the late 1930s in Kentucky and the deep South.

TERMS

aperture an opening in the camera that allows light to pass through the lens to strike the film. Controlled by shutter speed and the iris diaphragm, it can be set mechanically or electronically at various diameters.

ASA a numbering system for rating the speed of films, devised by the American Standards Association. It has now been superseded by *ISO*, the International Standards Organization.

camera optical device used in photography for recording on film still or, in the case of a movie or video camera, moving images. There are small-, medium-, and large-format cameras; the format refers to the size of recorded image and the dimensions of the print obtained.

The simplest camera is a light-proof box with, at one end, a lens in front of a hole of variable size. The size of the hole is termed the aperture, and it can be changed by adjusting the diaphragm, or disc. At the opposite side of the camera is the light-sensitive film. A shutter situated between the lens and the film stops light reaching the film until a picture is taken, at which point an upsidedown image of the scene in front of the camera is formed on the film. The image is not visible until the film is treated by developing and fixing.

A simple camera has a fixed shutter speed and aperture, chosen so that on a sunny day the correct amount of light is admitted. More complex cameras allow the shutter speed and aperture to be adjusted; most have a built-in exposure meter to help choose the correct combination of shutter speed and aperture for the ambient conditions and subject matter. The most versatile camera is the single lens reflex (SLR) which allows the lens to be removed and special lenses attached.

Cibachrome a process of printing directly from transparencies. Distinguished by rich, saturated colours, it can be home-processed and the colours are highly resistant to fading. It was introduced 1963.

daguerreotype a single-image process using mercury vapour and an iodine-sensitized silvered plate; discovered by Daguerre in 1838.

developing the process that produces a visible image on exposed photographic film.

Developing involves treating the exposed film with a chemical developer, a reducing agent that changes the light-altered silver salts in the film into dark metallic silver. The developed image is made permanent with a fixer,

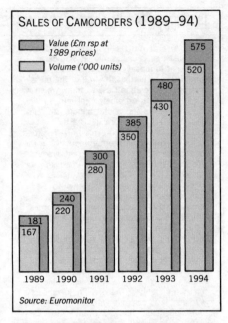

SALES OF CAMCORDERS (1989–94)

■ Value (£m rsp at 1989 prices)
□ Volume ('000 units)

Year	Value	Volume
1989	181	167
1990	240	220
1991	300	280
1992	385	350
1993	480	430
1994	575	520

Source: Euromonitor

which dissolves away any silver salts which were not affected by light. The developed image is a negative, or reverse image: darkest where the strongest light hit the film, lightest where the least light fell. To produce a positive image, the negative is itself photographed, and the development process reverses the shading, producing the final print.

dye-transfer print a print made by a relatively permanent colour process that uses red, yellow, and blue separation negatives printed together.

f-number measure of the relative aperture of a telescope or camera lens; it indicates the light-gathering power of the lens. Each successive *f* number represents a halving of exposure speed.

focus the distance that a lens must be moved in order to obtain a sharp image on the light-sensitive film at the back of the camera. The lens is moved away from the film to focus the image of closer objects. The focusing distance is often marked on a scale around the lens; however, many cameras now have an automatic focusing (*autofocus*) mechanism that uses an electric motor to move the lens.

hypo a term for sodium thiosulphate, discovered 1819 by John Herschel, and used as a fixative for photographic images since 1837.

ISO a numbering system for rating the speed of films, devised by the International Standards Organization.

lens a piece of glass (or other transparent material) with two polished surfaces—one concave or convex, and the other plane, concave, or convex—that converges or diverges rays of light and forms optical images. It is an essential component of cameras, microscopes, telescopes, and almost all optical instruments.

A *telephoto lens* is of longer focal length than normal and takes a very narrow view and gives a large image through a combination of telescopic and ordinary photographic lenses. A *wide-angle lens* is of shorter focal length than normal, taking in a wider angle of view. A *zoom lens*, by variation of focal length, allows speedy transition from long shots to close-ups.

negative/positive a reverse image, which when printed is again reversed, restoring the original scene. It was invented by Talbot about 1834.

photography process for reproducing images on sensitized materials by various forms of radiant energy, including visible light, ultraviolet, infrared, X-rays, atomic radiations and electron beams.

The most familiar photographic process depends upon the fact that certain silver compounds (called halides) are sensitive to light. A photographic film is coated with these compounds and, in a camera, is exposed to light. An image, or picture, of the scene before the camera is formed on the film because the silver halides become activated (light-altered) where light falls but not where light does not fall. The image is made visible by the process of developing, made permanent by fixing, and, finally, is usually printed on paper. Motion-picture photography uses a camera which exposes a roll of film to a rapid succession of views which, when developed, are projected in rapid succession to provide a moving image.

rangefinder instrument for determining the range or distance of an object from the observer; used to focus a camera or to sight a gun accurately. A *rangefinder camera* has a rotating mirror or prism that alters the image seen through the viewfinder, which is quite separate from the lens and coupled to the focusing mechanism.

reflex camera camera that uses a mirror and prisms to reflect light passing through the lens into the viewfinder, showing the photographer the exact scene that is being shot. When the shutter button is released the mirror springs out of the way, allowing light to reach the film. The most common type is the single-lens reflex (SLR) camera. The twin-lens reflex (TLR) camera has two lenses: one has a mirror for viewing, the other is used for exposing the film.

SLR abbreviation for *single-lens reflex*, a type of camera in which the image can be seen through the lens before a picture is taken. A small mirror directs light entering the lens to the viewfinder. When a picture is taken the mirror moves rapidly aside to allow the light to reach the film. The SLR allows different lenses, such as close-up or zoom lenses, to be used as the photographer can see exactly what is being focused on.

TLR camera twin-lens reflex camera that has a viewing lens of the same angle of view and focal length mounted above and parallel to the taking lens.

transparency a picture on slide film. This captures the original in a positive image (direct reversal) and can be used for projection or printing on positive-to-positive print material, for example by the Cibachrome or Kodak R-type process. Slide film is usually colour but can be obtained in black and white.

zone system a system of exposure estimation invented by Ansel Adams that groups infinite tonal gradations into ten zones, zone 0 being black and zone 10 white. An f-stop change in exposure is required from zone to zone.

Happy snaps

Some people like to have their photographs taken, some people don't mind and some people dislike it. What would you say about having your photograph taken?

Like a lot	4
Like a little	5
Don't mind	50
Dislike a little	19
Dislike a lot	23

Do you carry a photograph of your husband/wife or children in your wallet/handbag, or do you have one at work?

Yes, wallet/handbag	27
Yes, at work	4
No, neither	53
Not applicable	16

GENRES

Absurd, Theatre of the avant-garde drama originating with a group of playwrights in the 1950s and 1960s, including Beckett, Ionesco, Genet, and Pinter. Their work expressed the belief that in a godless universe, human existence has no meaning or purpose and therefore all communication breaks down. Logical construction and argument gives way to irrational and illogical speech and to its ultimate conclusion, silence. The plays emerge as dramatized poetic images of the human predicament.

burlesque in the 17th and 18th centuries, a form of satirical comedy parodying a particular play or dramatic genre. For example, John Gay's *The Beggar's Opera* 1728 is a burlesque of 18th century opera, and Sheridan's *The Critic* 1779 satirizes the sentimentality in the drama of this time. In the USA, the term was used for a sex-and-comedy show, consisting of a variety of acts, including acrobats, chorus, and comedy numbers. During the 1920s the striptease was introduced to counteract the growing popularity of the cinema, and Gypsy Rose Lee became its most famous artiste. Burlesque was frequeuently banned in the USA.

circus an entertainment, often held in a large tent ('big top'), involving acrobats, clowns, and sometimes performing animals. In 1897, the US showman P T Barnum created the 'Greatest Show on Earth', which included a circus, menagerie, and 'freaks', all transported in 100 rail cars. From the 1970s there was increasing protest against the inclusion of animal acts.

comedy in the simplest terms, a drama with a happy ending, as opposed to tragedy. The comic tradition developed in Ancient Greece, in the farcical satires of Aristophanes. The Vices and Devil of the medieval morality plays developed into the stock comic characters of the Renaissance Comedy of Humours with such notable villains as Jonson's Mosca in *Volpone*. The timeless comedies of Shakespeare and Molière were followed in England during the 17th century by the witty and often licentious comedy of manners of Restoration writers such as Etherege, Wycherley, and Congreve. Sentimental comedy dominated most of the 19th century, though little of it is remembered in the late 20th century, which prefers the realistic tradition of Shaw and the elegant social comedies of Wilde. The polished comedies of Coward and Rattigan from the 1920s to the 1940s were eclipsed during the late 1950s and 60s by a trend towards satire and a more cynical humour as seen in the works of Joe Orton and Peter Nichols. From the 1970s the dark comedies of Alan Ayckbourn have dominated the English stage.

commedia dell'arte popular form of Italian improvised drama in the 16th and 17th centuries, performed by trained troupes of actors and involving stock characters and situations. It exerted considerable influence on writers such as Molière and on the genres of pantomime, harlequinade, and the Punch and Judy show. It laid the foundation for the mime tradition, particularly in France.

Cruelty, Theatre of performance that aims to shock the audience into an awareness of basic, primitive human nature, through the release of feelings usually repressed by conventional behaviour. The spectators should suffer a change through their shared experience with the actors. The theory was first advanced by Antonin Artaud in his book *Le Théâtre et son double* 1938 and adopted by a number of writers and directors.

farce broad form of comedy involving stereotyped characters in complex, often improbable situations frequently revolving around extramarital relationships (hence the term 'bedroom farce'). The farce usually depicts a world where order has collapsed into anarchy. Representatives of authority are powerless to control a spiralling momentum of madness. Originating from the physical knockabout comedy of Greek satyr plays and the broad humour developed from medieval religious drama, the farce was developed and perfected during the 19th century by Labiche and Feydeau in France, and Pinero in England. In modern times two notable English series have been the Aldwych farces of Ben Travers in the 1920s and 1930s and the Whitehall farces produced by Brian Rix during the 1950s and 1960s.

fringe theatre plays that are anti-establishment or experimental, and performed in informal venues, in contrast to mainstream commercial theatre. In the UK, the term originated in the 1960s from the activities held on the 'fringe' of the Edinburgh Festival. The US equivalent is off-off-Broadway (off-Broadway is mainstream theatre that is not on Broadway).

kabuki drama originating in late 16th-century Japan, drawing on the more aristocratic Nō tradition, and incorporating acting, dance, and evocative vocal and/or instrumental music used to enhance dramatic situations. Plays are long, episodic, and based mainly on legendary themes; content is secondary to the display of elaborate costumes, staging, and virtuoso ability of the actors, who are all male.

masque spectacular and essentially aristocratic entertainment with a fantastic or mythological theme in which music, dance, and extravagant costumes and scenic design figured larger than the plot. Originating in Italy, it reached its height of popularity at the English court between 1600 to 1640, with the collaboration of Ben Jonson as writer and Inigo Jones as stage designer. The masque had great influence on the development of ballet and opera, and the elaborate frame in which it was performed developed into the proscenium arch.

melodrama a play with romantic and sensational plot elements, often unsubtly acted. Originally it meant a play accompanied by music. The early melodramas used extravagant theatrical effects to heighten violent emotions, and

THEATRE CHRONOLOGY

c 3200 BC	Beginnings of Egyptian religious drama, essentially ritualistic.
c 600	Choral performances (dithyrambs) in honour of Dionysus form beginnings of Greek tragedy, according to Aristotle.
c 534 BC	First festival of tragedy held in Athens and won by Thespis.
500–300 BC	Great age of Greek drama, which included tragedy, comedy, and satyr plays (grotesque farce).
468 BC	Sophocles' first victory at Athens festival. His use of a third actor altered the course of the tragic form.
458 BC	Aeschylus' *Oresteia* first performed.
c 425–388 BC	Comedies of Aristophanes, including *The Birds* 414, *Lysistrata* 411, and *The Frogs* 405. In tragedy the importance of the chorus diminished under Euripedes, author of *The Bacchae* 405.
c 350 BC	Menander's 'New Comedy' of social manners developed.
c 330 BC	Aristotle's *Poetics* analysed the nature of tragedy. Theatre of Dionysus in Athens built.
c 240–AD 500	Emergence of Roman drama, adapted from Greek originals under Plautus, Terence and Seneca. All were to have great influence on Elizabethan writers.
c AD 375	Kâlidâsa's *Sakuntalâ marked the height of Sanskrit drama in India.*
c 970	Earliest example of Christian liturgical drama, written by Ethelwold, bishop of Winchester
1210	Priests were forbidden to appear on public stage. This led to secularization of drama in the vernacular.
c 1250–1500	European mystery (or miracle) plays flourished, first in the churches, later in market places, and performed in England by town guilds.
c 1375	Nōor Noh drama developed in Japan.
c 1495	*Everyman*, the best known of all the morality plays, first performed.
1500–1600	Italian commedia dell'arte troupes performed popular, improvised comedies; they were to have a large influence on Molière and on English Harlequinade and Pantomime.
c 1551	Nicholas Udall's *Ralph Roister Doister* written, the first English comedy.
c 1576	First English playhouse, The Theatre, built by James Burbage in Shoreditch, London.
1587	Marlowe's *Tamburlaine the Great* marked an important advance in the use of blank verse and the beginning of the great age of Elizabethan and Jacobean drama in England.
c 1589	Kyd's *Spanish Tragedy*—the first of the 'revenge' tragedies.
1594	Lord Chamberlain's Men formed; a theatre company to which Shakespeare was attached as actor and writer from 1595.
1599	The Globe Theatre built on Bankside, Southwark, London.
c 1590–1612	Shakespeare's greatest plays, including *Hamlet* and *King Lear*, were written.
1604	Inigo Jones designed *The Masque of Blackness* for James I, written by Ben Jonson. Masques were the height of fashion at the English court around this time.
1613	The Globe Theatre burned down (rebuilt 1614; demolished 1644).
1614	Lope de Vega's *Fuenteovejuna/The Sheep Wall* marked Spanish renaissance in drama.
1637	Corneille's *Le Cid* established classical tragedy in France.
1642	Act of Parliament closed all English theatres.
1660	With the restoration of Charles II to the English throne, dramatic performances recommenced. The first professional actress appeared as Desdemona in Shakespeare's *Othello*.
1664	Molière's *Tartuffe* was banned for three years by religious factions.
1667	Racine's first success, *Andromaque*.
1680	Comédie-Française formed by Louis XIV.
1700	Congreve, the greatest exponent of Restoration comedy, wrote *The Way of the World* .
1716	First known American theatre built in Williamsburg.
1728	Gay's *The Beggar's Opera* first performed.
1737	Stage Licensing Act required all plays to be licensed and approved by the Lord Chamberlain before performance in Britain.
1747	Garrick became manager of Drury Lane Theatre, London.
1767–8	In Germany, Lessing's *Minna von Barnhelm* and publication of *Hamburgische Dramaturgie*.

THEATRE CHRONOLOGY: CONT.

1773	In England, Goldsmith's *She Stoops to Conquer* and Sheridan's *The Rivals* 1775 established the 'comedy of manners'. Goethe's *Götz von Berlichingen* is the first 'Sturm und Drang' play (literally storm and stress); this German Romantic movement, depicting extravagant emotions, was influential throughout Europe at this time and led to the rise of English melodrama.
1775	Sarah Siddons, English tragedy actress, made her debut at the Drury Lane Theatre.
1781	Schiller's *Die Raüber/The Robbers*
1784	Beaumarchais' *Le Mariage de Figaro* , (written 1778) finally performed after difficulties with censorship because of its alleged revolutionary tendencies.
1802	Holcroft's *A Tale of Mystery* marked the rise of melodrama in England.
1814	Edmund Kean's London debut as Shylock in Shakespeare's *The Merchant of Venice*.
1815	Gas lighting installed at Covent Garden, London.
1830	Hugo's *Hernani* caused riots in Paris. His work marked the beginning of a new Romantic drama, changing the course of French theatre.
1836	Gogol's *The Government Inspector*—a social satire—initially passed the Russian censors.
1838	Debut of the French tragic actress Rachel at the Comédie-Française.
1843	The Theatres Act further strengthened the powers of the Lord Chamberlain to censor plays.
1869	Sarah Bernhardt's first success, in *Le Passant* in Paris.
1878	Henry Irving became actor-manager of the Lyceum with Ellen Terry as leading lady.
1879	Ibsen's *A Doll's House*—an example of Ibsen's hugely influential plays, which marked the beginning of realism in European theatre.
1888	Strindberg's *Miss Julie*.
1893	Shaw wrote *Mrs Warren's Profession* (banned until 1902 because it deals with prostitution). Shaw's works bring the new realistic drama to Britain and introduce social and political issues as subjects for the theatre.
1895	Wilde's *The Importance of Being Earnest*.
1896	The first performance of Chekhov's *The Seagull* failed.
1899	Abbey Theatre, Dublin, founded by W B Yeats and Lady Gregory, marked the beginning of an Irish dramatic revival.
1904	Chekhov's *The Cherry Orchard* . Founding of Royal Academy of Dramatic Art (RADA) to train young actors, by Beerbohm Tree in London.
1904–07	Granville Barker and J E Vedrenne were managers of the Royal Court Theatre and directed works by Shaw, Yeats, Ibsen, and Galsworthy.
1919	Theatre Guild founded in US to perform less commercial new plays.
1923	Shaw's *St Joan*. O'Casey's first play, *The Shadow of a Gunman*.
1925	Coward's *Hay Fever* . Travers' *A Cuckoo in the Nest*, the first of the Aldwych farces.
1928	Brecht's *Die Dreigroschenoper/The Threepenny Opera* with score by Kurt Weill. In the USA, Jerome Kern's *Show Boat* with Paul Robeson, one example of the success of musical comedies. Others by Cole Porter, Irving Berlin, and George Gershwin became popular.
1930	Gielgud's first performance as Hamlet.
1935	T S Eliot's *Murder in the Cathedral*.
1943	The first of the musicals, *Oklahoma!*, opened.
1947	First Edinburgh Festival with fringe theatre events. Tennessee Williams's *A Streetcar Named Desire*.
1953	Arthur Miller's *The Crucible* opened during the period of witch-hunting of communists in USA under McCarthy. *Waiting for Godot* by Beckett exemplified the Theatre of the Absurd.
1956	English Stage Company formed at the Royal Court Theatre to provide a platform for new dramatists. Osborne's *Look Back in Anger* included in its first season.
1957	Bernstein's *West Side Story* opened in New York.
1960	Pinter's *The Caretaker*.
1961	Royal Shakespeare Company formed under directorship of Peter Hall, based at Stratford and the Aldwych, London.
1963–4	National Theatre Company formed at the Old Vic under the directorship of Laurence Olivier.
1965	Edward Bond's *Saved* initially banned by the Lord Chamberlain.
1967	Stoppard's *Rosencrantz and Guildenstern are Dead*. Success in USA of *Hair* - first of the 'rock' musicals.
1968	Abolition of theatre censorship in UK.
1970	Peter Brook's production of *A Midsummer Night's Dream*.

Theatre Chronology: Cont.

1976	National Theatre opened a new theatre complex on the South Bank, London.
1980	Howard Brenton's *The Romans in Britain* led to a private prosecution of the director for obscenity.
1982	Royal Shakespeare Company opened at the Barbican Centre, London.
1982–83	Trevor Nunn's production *Nicholas Nickleby* won Tony award, marking its success in UK and USA.
1986	*The Phantom of the Opera* opened in London, the latest in a series of successful Lloyd Webber musicals.
1987	The Theatre Museum opened in Covent Garden, London. Planning permission granted for the building of a replica of the Globe Theatre on the original site.
1989	Remains of the Rose Theatre, where Shakespeare's plays were first performed, were discovered at Southwark, South London.
1990	The Royal Shakespeare Company suspended its work at the Barbican Centre, London for six months, pleading lack of funds.
1991	Agatha Christie's *The Mousetrap* entered its 39th year, the longest-running play in the world.

overblown characters, often emphasizing one trait at the expense of others. By the end of the 19th century, melodrama had become a popular genre of stage play.

mime a type of acting in which meaning is conveyed by precise gestures, movements of the whole body, and facial expressions. It is an essential element in the training of actors. Mime has developed as a form of theatre, particularly in France, where Marcel Marceau and Jean Louis Barrault have continued the traditions established in the 19th century by Deburau and the practices of the commedia dell'arte in Italy. In ancient Greece, mime was a crude, realistic comedy with dialogue and exaggerated gesture.

morality play didactic medieval verse drama, which differs from the mystery play in that it dramatizes Everyman's journey from birth to death rather than the events of the Bible. Human characters are replaced by personified virtues and vices, the limited humorous elements being provided by the Devil. Morality plays exerted an influence on the course of Elizabethan drama.

music hall light entertainment, in which singers, dancers, comedians, and acrobats perform in 'turns', and presided over by a flamboyant master of ceremonies. It reached its heyday in the late 19th century, by which time special ornate theatres had been built in most English towns to accommodate what had originally been barroom entertainment. Famous music hall performers included Albert Chevalier, Marie Lloyd, Harry Lauder, and George Formby. Many had their special character trademark, such as Vesta Tilley's immaculate masculine outfit as Burlington Bertie. With the introduction of radio and television, music hall declined but has had something of a revival in the informal entertainment of the pub–the place of its origin. The US equivalent is known as 'vaudeville'.

musical 20th-century form of theatre, combining elements of song, dance, and the spoken word, often characterized by lavish staging and large casts. It developed from the operettas and musical comedies of the 19th century.

The **operetta** is a light-hearted entertainment with extensive musical content: Jaques Offenbach, Johann Strauss, Franz Lehár, and Gilbert and Sullivan all composed operettas. The **musical comedy** is an anglicization of the French *opéra bouffe*, of which the first was *A Gaiety Girl* 1893, mounted by George Edwardes (1852–1915) at the Gaiety Theatre, London. Typical of the 1920s were *The Student Prince* 1924 and *The Desert Song* 1926 by Sigmund Romberg. The genre reached a more sophisticated expression in the USA during the 1930s and 1940s with the work of George Gershwin, Cole Porter, Irving Berlin, and Jerome Kern. The word 'comedy' was dropped and the era of the 'musical' arrived in 1943 with *Oklahoma!* by Rodgers and Hammerstein II. Plot and character were now given more serious attention. Two great successes of the mid-1950s were Lerner and Loewe's *My Fair Lady* 1956 (based on Shaw's *Pygmalion*) and Bernstein's *West Side Story* 1957 (based on Shakespeare's *Romeo and Juliet*). Sandy Wilson's *The Boy Friend* 1953 revived the British musical and was followed by hits such as Lionel Bart's *Oliver!* 1960. Musicals began to branch into religious and political themes with *Oh What a Lovely War!* 1963, produced by Joan Littlewood and Charles Chiltern, and the Andrew Lloyd Webber musicals *Jesus Christ Superstar* 1970 and *Evita* 1978. In the 1980s 19th-century melodrama was popular, for example *Phantom of the Opera* 1986 and *Les Misérables* 1987. In recent years the American musical has declined in output owing to high production costs. Nevertheless, Stephen Sondheim has written and composed an outstanding number of musicals of originality, wit, and beauty in staging and score. These include *Sunday in the Park with George* 1989 and *Into the Woods* 1990.

mystery play or **miracle play** medieval religious drama based on stories from the Bible. Mystery plays were performed around the time of church festivals, reaching their height in Europe during the 15th and 16th centuries. A whole cycle running from the Creation to the Last Judgement was performed in separate scenes on mobile wagons by various town

RECENT AWARD WINNERS

American Theater Wing Antoinette Perry (Tony) Awards, 1986–1992 (Best Play, Best Musical, and Best Revival production)

1986	*I'm Not Rappaport, The Mystery of Edwin Drood, Sweet Charity*
1987	*Fences, Les Miserables, All My Sons*
1988	*M. Butterfly, The Phantom of the Opera, Anything Goes*
1989	*The Heidi Chronicles, Jerome Robbins' Broadway, Our Town*
1990	*The Grapes of Wrath, City of Angels, Gypsy*
1991	*Lost in Yonkers, The Will Rogers Follies, Fiddler on the Roof*
1992	*Dancing at Lughnasa, Crazy for You, Guys and Dolls*

The Laurence Olivier Awards, presented by The Society of West End Theatre (best play, best musical, and best comedy)

1986	*Les Liaisons Dangereuses, The Phantom of the Opera, When We Are Married*
1987	*Serious Money, Follies, Three Men on a Horse*
1988	*Our Country's Good, Candide, Shirley Valentine*
1989/90	*Racing Demon, Return to the Forbidden Planet, Single Spies*
1991	*Dancing at Lughnasa, Sunday in the Park with George, Out of Order*
1992	*Death and the Maiden, Carmen Jones, La Bête*

Evening Standard Drama Awards (best play, best musical, and best comedy)

1986	*Les Liaisons Dangereuses, The Phantom of the Opera, A Month of Sundays*
1987	*A Small Family Business, Follies, Serious Money*
1988	*Aristocrats,* award for best musical was not presented, *Lettice and Lovage*
1989	*Ghetto, Miss Saigon, Henceforward*
1990	*Shadowlands, Into the Woods, Man of the Moment* and *Jeffrey Bernard is Unwell* (joint award)
1991	*Dancing at Lughnasa, Carmen Jones, Kvetch*

guilds. Four English cycles survive: those of Chester, Coventry, Wakefield (or Townley). Versions are still performed, notably the York cycle at York. The German equivalent of the mystery play, the *Mysterienspiel*, survives today as the *Passion Play* . It is essentially concerned with the Crucifixion of Christ and the most famous takes place every ten years at Oberammergau.

Nó or **Noh** classical, aristocratic Japanese drama, which developed from the 14th to the 16th centuries, and is still performed. It is based on a narrative of impermanence. The pine tree that always decorates the rear panel of the stage is a symbol of constancy against which all themes of impermanence are played. There is a repertory of some 250 pieces, of which five, one from each of the several classes devoted to different subjects, may be put on in a performance lasting a whole day. Dance, mime, music, and chanting develop the mythical or historical themes. All the actors are men, some of whom wear masks and elaborate costumes; scenery is limited. Nó influenced kabuki drama.

pageant originally the wagon on which medieval plays were performed; the term was later applied to the street procession of songs, dances, and historical tableaux that became fashionable during the 1920s, and which exists today in forms such as the Lord Mayor's Show in London. Related to the pageant is the open-air entertainment *son et lumière*, in which the history of the venue is performed in a series of episodes accompanied by sound and projected lighting effects.

pantomime in the British theatre, a traditional Christmas entertainment with its origins in the harlequin spectacles of the 18th century and burlesque of the 19th century, which gave rise to the tradition of the principal boy being played by an actress and the dame by an actor. The harlequin's role diminished altogether as themes developed on folktales such as *The Sleeping Beauty* and *Cinderella*, and with the introduction of additional material such as popular songs, topical comedy, and audience participation. The term 'pantomime' was also applied to Roman dumbshows performed by a masked actor, to 18th-century ballets with mythical themes, and, in 19th-century France, to the wordless Pierrot plays from which modern mime developed.

puppet theatre drama acted by puppets manipulated by usually unseen operators. By the 16th and 17th centuries refined versions of the travelling puppet shows became popular with the aristocracy, and puppets were extensively used as vehicles for caricature and satire until the 19th century. There has been a revival of interest in the 20th century, partly stimulated by the influence of the *jōruri* tradition in Japan, with its large, intricate puppets, and by leading exponents of rod puppets such as Obraztsov and his Moscow Puppet Theatre, and most recently by Fluck and Law, whose satirical *Spitting Image* puppets, caricaturing public figures, have appeared on British television.

revue stage presentation involving short satirical and topical items in the form of songs, sketches, and monologues; it originated in the late 19th century. The first revue in the UK seems to have been *Under the Clock* 1893 by Seymour Hicks and Charles Brookfield. The 1920s revues were spectacular entertainments, but the 'intimate revue' became increasingly popular, employing writers such as Noel Coward. During the 1960s the satirical revue took off with the Cambridge Footlights' production *Beyond the Fringe* 1961, firmly establishing the revue tradition among the young and at fringe theatrical events.

tragedy in general, a play dealing with a serious theme, traditionally one in which the leading character meets disaster either as a result of personal failings or circumstances beyond his or her control. In classical tragedy the protagonist is faced with an impossible choice. This Greek view of tragedy, expressed in the work of Aeschylus, Sophocles, and Euripides, and later defined by Aristotle, has been predominant in the western tradition. In the 20th century tragedies in the narrow Greek sense of dealing with exalted personages in an elevated manner has virtually died out. Tragedy has been replaced by dramas with 'tragic' implications or overtones, as in the work of Ibsen, O'Neill, Tennessee Williams, Pinter, and Osborne, for example, or by the hybrid tragicomedy.

GREAT DRAMATISTS

Aeschylus c 525–456 BC. Greek dramatist, widely regarded as the founder of European tragedy. By the introduction of a second actor he made true dialogue and dramatic action possible. Aeschylus wrote some 90 plays between 499 and 458, of which seven survive. These are *The Suppliant Women*, performed about 490; *The Persians* 472; *Seven Against Thebes* 467; *Prometheus Bound*, about 460; and the *Oresteia* trilogy 458, dealing with the curse on the house of Atreus.

Anouilh Jean 1910–1987. French playwright whose plays dramatize his concerns with the contrasts between innocence and experience, poverty in a world of riches, and the role of memory. His plays include *Antigone* 1943, *L'Invitation au château/Ring Round the Moon* 1947, *La Répétition ou l'amour puni/The Rehearsal* 1950, and *Becket* 1959, about Thomas Becket and Henry II.

Aristophanes c 445–385 BC. Greek comedic dramatist. Of his 11 extant plays, the early comedies are remarkable for the violent satire with which he ridiculed the democratic war leaders. He also satirized contemporary issues such as the new learning of Socrates in *The Clouds* 423 and the power of women in *Lysistrata* 411. The chorus plays a prominent role, frequently giving the play its title, as in *The Birds* 414, *The Wasps* 422, and *The Frogs* 405.

Ashcroft Peggy 1907–1991. English actress. Her many leading roles included Desdemona in *Othello* (with Paul Robeson), Juliet in *Romeo and Juliet* 1935 (with Laurence Olivier and John Gielgud), Hedda Gabler 1954, and appearances in the television play *Caught on a Train* 1980 (BAFTA award), the series *The Jewel in the Crown* 1984 and the film *A Passage to India* 1985.

Ayckbourn Alan 1939– . English dramatist, and director of the Stephen Joseph Theatre in the Round, Scarborough, from 1959. His prolific output, characterized by comic dialogue and experiments in dramatic structure, includes the trilogy *The Norman Conquests* 1974, in which each play presents the events of a single weekend from a different vantage point; *A Woman in Mind* 1986; *Henceforward* 1987; and *Man of the Moment* 1988.

Beckett Samuel 1906–1990. Irish novelist and dramatist who wrote in French and English. His *En attendant Godot/Waiting for Godot* 1953, in which two tramps wait endlessly for the enigmatic 'Godot', brought the Theatre of the Absurd to public attention, portraying the 'absurdity' of the human condition in an irrational universe. This predicament is explored to further extremes in *Fin de Partie/Endgame* 1957 and *Happy Days* 1961. Nobel Prize for Literature 1969.

Bond Edward 1935– . English dramatist. His work often makes use of historical settings to expose modern injustices. Bond's early plays aroused controversy because of the savagery of some of his imagery—for example, the brutal stoning of a baby by bored youths in *Saved* 1965. Other works include *Early Morning* 1968, the last play to be banned in the

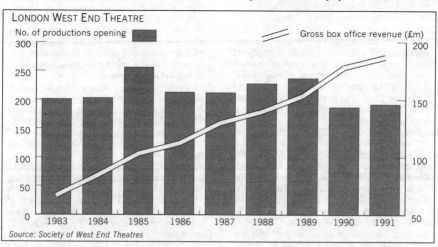

LONDON WEST END THEATRE

No. of productions opening ▮ Gross box office revenue (£m)

Source: Society of West End Theatres

UK by the Lord Chamberlain; *Lear* 1972, a reworking of Shakespeare's play; *Bingo* 1973, an account of Shakespeare's last days; and *The War Plays* 1985.

Branagh Kenneth 1960– . English actor and director. He founded, with David Parfitt, the Renaissance Theatre Company 1987, was a notable Hamlet and Touchstone in 1988, and in 1989 directed and starred in a film of Shakespeare's *Henry V.*

Brecht Bertolt 1898–1956. German dramatist and poet who aimed to destroy the 'suspension of disbelief' usual in the theatre and to express Marxist ideas. His work includes *Die Dreigoschenoper/The Threepenny Opera* 1928 (an adaptation of John Gay's *The Beggar's Opera*, with music by Kurt Weill); *Mutter Courage/Mother Courage* 1941, set during the Thirty Years' War; *and Der kaukasische Kreidekreis/The Caucasian Chalk Circle* 1949. In 1949 he established the Berliner Ensemble theatre group in East Germany.

Brook Peter (Stephen Paul) 1925– . English director. His experimental work with the Royal Shakespeare Company included a production of *A Midsummer Night's Dream* 1970, set in a white gymnasium and combining elements of circus and commedia dell'arte. In 1970 he established Le Centre International de Créations Théâtrales (International Centre for Theatre Research) in Paris. His later productions with the Théâtre Bouffes du Nord transcend Western theatre conventions and include *The Conference of the Birds* 1973, based on a Persian story; *The Ik* 1975, and *The Mahabarata* 1985/88, a cycle of three plays lasting ten hours, based on the Hindu epic.

Chekhov Anton Pavlovich 1860–1904. Russian dramatist and writer. His plays concentrate on the creation of atmosphere and the delineation of internal development, rather than external action. His first play, *Ivanov* 1887, was a failure, as was *The Seagull* 1896 until revived by Stanislavsky 1898 at the Moscow Arts Theatre, for which Chekhov went on to write his major plays *Uncle Vanya* 1899, *The Three Sisters* 1901, and *The Cherry Orchard* 1904.

Churchill Caryl 1938– . English playwright, whose predominantly radical and feminist works include *Top Girls* 1982, a study of the hazards encountered by 'career' women throughout history; *Serious Money* 1987, which satirized the world of the brash young brokers of the City of London; and *Mad Forest* 1990, set in Romania during the overthrow of the Ceaușescu regime.

Congreve William 1670–1729. English dramatist and poet. His first success was the comedy *The Old Bachelor* 1693, followed by *The Double Dealer* 1694, *Love for Love* 1695, the tragedy *The Mourning Bride* 1697, and *The Way of the World* 1700. His plays, which satirize the social affectations of the time, are characterized by elegant wit and wordplay.

Corneille Pierre 1606–1684. French dramatist. His many tragedies, such as *Oedipe* 1659, glorify the strength of will governed by reason,

and established the French classical dramatic tradition for the next two centuries. His first play, *Mélite*, was performed 1629, followed by others that gained him a brief period of favour with Cardinal Richelieu. *Le Cid* 1636 was attacked by the Academicians, although it received public acclaim. Later plays were based on Aristotle's unities of time, place, and action.

Coward Noël 1899–1973. English playwright, actor, producer, director, and composer, who epitomized the witty and sophisticated man of the theatre. From his first success with *The Young Idea* 1923, he wrote and appeared in plays and comedies on both sides of the Atlantic such as *Hay Fever* 1925, *Private Lives* 1930 with Gertrude Lawrence, *Design for Living* 1933, and *Blithe Spirit* 1941.

Craig Edward Gordon 1872–1966. English director and stage designer. His innovations and theories on stage design and lighting effects, expounded in *On the Art of the Theatre* 1911, had a profound influence on stage production in Europe and the USA.

Dench Judi (Judith Olivia) 1934– . English actress who made her professional debut as Ophelia in *Hamlet* 1957 with the Old Vic Company. Her Shakespearean roles include Portia in *Twelfth Night*, Lady Macbeth, and Cleopatra. She is also a versatile comedy actress and has appeared in musicals, notably as Sally Bowles in *Cabaret* 1968.

Donellan Declan 1953– . British theatre director, cofounder of **Cheek by Jowl** theatre company 1981, and associate director of the National Theatre from 1989. His irreverent and audacious productions include many classics, such as Racine's *Andromaque* 1985, Corneille's *Le Cid* 1987, and Ibsen's *Peer Gynt* 1990.

Euripides c 484–407 BC. Greek dramatist whose plays dealt with social issues and the emotions and reactions of ordinary people rather than with the deities and grandiose themes of his contemporaries. He wrote more than 80 plays, of which 18 survive, including *Alcestis* 438, *Medea* 431, *Andromache* 426, *The Trojan Women* 415, *Electra* 413, *Iphigenia in Tauris* 413, and *The Bacchae* 405 BC. His influence on later drama was probably greater than that of either of the other two great tragedians, Aeschylus and Sophocles.

Eyre Richard (Charles Hastings) 1943– . English stage and film director who succeeded Peter Hall as artistic director of the National Theatre, London, 1988. His productions include *Guys and Dolls* 1982, *Bartholomew Fair* 1988, *Hamlet* 1989, and *Richard III* 1990, set in 1930s Britain.

Fo Dario 1926– . Italian playwright. His plays are predominantly political satires combining black humour with slapstick. They include *Morte accidentale di un anarchico/Accidental Death of an Anarchist* 1970, and *Non si paga non si paga/Can't Pay? Won't Pay!* 1975/1981.

Garrick David 1717–79. English actor and theatre manager. From 1747 he became joint licensee of the Drury Lane theatre with his own company, and instituted a number of significant theatrical conventions, including concealed stage lighting, banishing spectators from the stage, and naturalistic painted backdrops. Garrick was also responsible for changing the acting style of his time, by replacing the traditional declamatory delivery with a naturalness of manner.

Genet Jean 1910–1986. French dramatist, novelist, and poet, an exponent of the Theatre of Cruelty. His turbulent life and early years spent in prison are reflected in his drama, characterized by ritual, role-play, and illusion, in which his characters come to act out their bizarre and violent fantasies. His plays include *Les bonnes/The Maids* 1947, *Le balcon/The Balcony* 1957, and two plays dealing with the Algerian situation: *Les nègres/The Blacks* 1959, and *Les paravents/The Screens* 1961.

Gielgud John 1904– . English actor and director, renowned as one of the greatest Shakespearean actors of his time. He made his debut at the Old Vic in 1921, and his numerous stage appearances range from works by Chekhov and Sheridan to those of Alan Bennett, Harold Pinter, and David Storey.

Goethe Johann Wolfgang von 1749–1832. German poet and dramatist. His play *Götz von Berlichingen* 1773, inspired by the work of Shakespeare, became the cornerstone of the Romantic *Sturm und Drang* ('storm and stress') movement. His masterpiece, the poetic play *Faust*, was published in two parts: Part I in 1808, Part II posthumously in 1833. Its length and sheer scale present enormous staging difficulties; producers have often resorted to using *Urfaust*, an earlier draft, not discovered until 1886.

Granville-Barker Harley 1877–1946. English theatre director and author. He was director and manager with J E Vedrenne at the Royal Court Theatre, London, 1904–18, producing plays by Shaw, Yeats, Ibsen, Galsworthy, and Masefield. Granville- Barker's plays include *Waste* 1907, *The Voysey Inheritance* 1905, and *The Madras House* 1910. His series of *Prefaces to Shakespeare* 1927–47 influenced the staging of Shakespeare for many years.

Hall Peter (Reginald Frederick) 1930– . English theatre, opera, and film director. He was director of the Royal Shakespeare Theatre at Stratford 1960–68 and developed the Royal Shakespeare Company 1968–73 until appointed director of the National Theatre 1973–88, succeeding Laurence Olivier. His productions include *Waiting for Godot* 1955, *The Wars of the Roses* 1963, *The Homecoming* stage 1967 and film 1973, and *The Oresteia* 1981. In 1988 he founded the Peter Hall Company, which opened with Tennessee Williams' *Orpheus Descending*.

Ibsen Henrik 1828–1906. Norwegian dramatist whose work, characterized by its poetic realism, revolutionized European theatre. His two great verse dramas, *Brand* 1866 and *Peer Gynt* 1867, were followed by realistic plays dealing with social issues, including *Pillars of Society* 1877, *A Doll's House* 1879, *Ghosts* 1881, *An Enemy of the People* 1882, *The Wild Duck* 1884, *Rosmersholm* 1886, *The Lady from the Sea* 1888 and *Hedda Gabler* 1890. His later plays, moving towards symbolism, include *Little Eyolf* 1894 and *When We Dead Awaken* 1899.

Ionesco Eugène 1912– . Romanian-born French dramatist, a leading exponent of the Theatre of the Absurd. Most of his plays are in one act and express his concern with the futility of language as a means of communication. These include *La Cantatrice chauve/The Bald Prima Donna* 1950 and *La Leçon/The Lesson* 1951. Later full-length plays include *Rhinocéros* 1959 and *Le Roi se meurt/Exit the King* 1962.

Irving Henry. Stage name of John Brodribb 1838–1905. English actor and manager. He established his reputation from 1871, chiefly at the Lyceum Theatre in London, where he became manager 1878. He staged a series of successful Shakespearean productions there, including *Romeo and Juliet* 1882, with himself and Ellen Terry playing the leading roles. He was the first actor to be knighted, in 1895.

Jonson Ben 1572–1637. English dramatist, poet, and critic. *Every Man in His Humour* 1598 established the English 'comedy of humours', in which each character embodies a 'humour', or vice, such as greed, lust, or avarice. His first extant tragedy is *Sejanus* 1603, which included Shakespeare as a member of the original cast. The plays of his middle years include *Volpone, or the Fox* 1606, *The Alchemist* 1610, and *Bartholomew Fair* 1614.

Leigh Mike 1943– . English playwright and filmmaker, noted for his sharp social satires. He directs his own plays, which evolve through improvisation before they are scripted; they include the comedies *Goose Pimples* 1981 and *Home Sweet Home* 1982. Leigh's work for television includes *Nuts in May* 1976 and *Abigail's Party* 1977; his films *High Hopes* 1989 and *Life Is Sweet* 1991.

Lorca Federico García 1898–1936. Spanish poet and dramatist. His plays include the three powerful and intense 'Spanish Earth' tragedies *Bodas de sangre/Blood Wedding* 1933, a savage story of feuding families; *Yerma* 1934; and *La Casa de Bernarda Alba/The House of Bernarda Alba* 1936. He was killed by fascist Falangists in the Spanish Civil War.

McKellen Ian Murray 1939– . English actor acclaimed as the leading Shakespearean player of his generation. His major stage roles include Macbeth 1977; Max in Martin Sherman's *Bent* 1979; Platonov in Chekhov's *Wild Honey* 1986, Iago in *Othello* 1989, and Richard III 1990. His films include *Priest of Love* 1982 and *Plenty* 1985.

Mamet David 1947– . US playwright. His plays, with their vivid, freewheeling language and sense of ordinary US life, include *American Buffalo* 1977, *Sexual Perversity in Chicago* 1978, *Glengarry Glen Ross* 1984, and *Speed-*

THE FINAL CURTAIN?

Who goes to the theatre these days? Hardly anybody, if one was to judge from the cries of doom echoing around London's West End in the summer of 1992. With shows closing at regular intervals, producers seemed convinced that British theatre was yet again approaching crisis point. Blame was laid at the door of the recession, the hot summer, the lack of tourists. Closer analysis suggests that the crisis, if it exists at all, has more complex causes than just these.

Twenty-five years ago commercial theatre faced considerably less competition. The two major subsidised companies, the Royal Shakespeare Company and the Royal National Theatre, were in their infancy. Today their joint grants, totalling some £18 million, enable them to present about 45 productions per year in London. In the past, these were mainly of the classics, but this has now been supplemented by new writing and even occasionally by musicals. The prestige of these companies means that they are able to attract the cream of the theatrical profession. The same period has also seen the proliferation of small, alternative venues, known collectively as the Fringe, whose more intimate and relaxed atmosphere has attracted a substantial young audience. Then there is television, which has grown from one channel to four and now includes the extended choice presented by cable and satellite TV. Cinema attendance is also up, and has managed to counter any loss of revenue by video sales.

People no longer need to go out to be entertained. If they do gamble on a live show, what should they hope to expect? Firstly, to pay a substantial amount of money—average prices in the West End in 1990 were £15.70

per ticket, compared with £7.50 in 1983, an increase well above the level of inflation and one which cannot simply be explained by the increase in Value Added Tax. Secondly, many of the West End's theatres are old Edwardian buildings with areas of restricted visibility and without the air-conditioning that visitors, especially Americans, have come to take for granted in other leisure facilities. Quite apart from these practical considerations, there is the question of the quality of the entertainment itself. If the critics are to be believed, fewer and fewer good, serious plays are to be found in the West End. Producers are no longer prepared to risk such plays unless they are written by an established author, or feature a well-known name, preferably from television. Even then, this is no guarantee of success, as witnessed by Ronald Harwood's latest play *Reflected Glory* which, although it starred Albert Finney and had reasonably good reviews, closed after only a few weeks. The two most successful new plays of the last few years both originated in the subsidised theatre—Ariel Dorfman's *Death and the Maiden* transferred from the Royal Court, Brian Friel's *Dancing at Lughnasa* from the Abbey Theatre Dublin via the Royal National Theatre.

In fact, people *are* still going to the theatre. What really frightens critics is the thought that the West End might be following the path of Broadway towards a theatre dominated by musicals and star-studded revivals. When *Death and the Maiden* opened on Broadway, the production was attacked by British critics for being a watered-down version of the original. What they had seen in London as a painful political exposé had apparently become an emotional and psychological vehicle for its three Hollywood stars. The message seemed to be that if there was no room on Broadway for plays with intellectual substance or uncomfortable ideas, how long before the West End would end up in a similar plight? Certainly, it is musicals that seem to draw the crowds on both sides of the Atlantic. Of the 33 West End theatres open in the summer of 1992, 18 were showing musicals (five by Sir Andrew Lloyd Webber), two of which were on the verge of closing but with two more about to replace them. *Grand Hotel*, a new show imported from Broadway, opened at the newly refurbished Dominion Theatre after advance ticket sales of nearly £1 million.

Perhaps there is no crisis after all. There are certainly many success stories in the West End. If there has been, as it seems, a shift towards more populist, spectacular entertainment, is this necessarily a bad thing? Good new writing has continued to emerge through the subsidised theatre and the more enterprising Fringe venues. Commercial theatre has always been a gamble, and distress is a natural reaction when you get your fingers burnt—but the sound of mourning at the West End's impending demise does seem, at this point, a little premature.

Queuing for tickets for London's Royal Opera House in Covent Garden.

the-Plow 1987.

Marlowe Christopher 1564–93. English poet and dramatist, a contemporary of Shakespeare, and a strong influence on the course of Elizabethan drama. His work includes the blank-verse plays *Tamburlaine the Great* about 1587, *The Jew of Malta* about 1590, and *Edward II* and *The Tragical History of Doctor Faustus* both about 1592. He was murdered in a Deptford tavern, allegedly in a dispute over the bill, but it may have been a political killing.

Miller Arthur 1915– . American playwright. His plays deal with family relationships and contemporary American values, and include *All My Sons* 1947, a condemnation of war profiteering; *Death of a Salesman* 1949; *The Crucible* 1953, based on the Salem witch trials of the 17th century but reflecting the communist witch-hunts of Senator Joe McCarthy in the 1950s; and *After the Fall* 1964, in which the character of Maggie is allegedly based on the actress Marilyn Monroe, to whom Miller was married 1956–61. His prolific output still continues: *Danger: Memory!* appeared in 1987.

Molière pen name of Jean-Baptiste Poquelin 1622–1673. French comic dramatist and actor who founded and acted in the Illustre-Théâtre in Paris from 1643. After failure and prison he formed a successful touring company and returned to Paris in 1658. He established his reputation with *Les Précieuses ridicules/The Affected Wives* 1660. This was followed by his great satiric masterpieces, which include: *L'Ecole des femmes/The School for Wives* 1662; *Le Tartuffe/Tartuffe* 1664, banned until 1669 for attacking the hypocrisy of the clergy; *Le Misanthrope/The Misanthrope* 1666; *L'Avare/The Miser* 1668; *Le Bourgeois gentilhomme/The Would-be Gentleman* 1670; and *Le Malade imaginaire/The Hypochondriac* 1673.

O'Casey Sean. Adopted name of John Casey 1884–1964. Irish dramatist. His early plays are tragicomedies, blending realism with symbolism and poetic with vernacular speech: *The Shadow of a Gunman* 1922, *Juno and the Paycock* 1925, and *The Plough and the Stars* 1926. Later plays include *Red Roses for Me* 1946 and *The Drums of Father Ned* 1960.

Olivier Laurence Kerr, Baron Olivier 1907–1989. English actor and director. He established his reputation at the Old Vic, particularly in *Hamlet* 1937. His other major stage roles include Henry V, Richard III, and Archie Rice in John Osborne's *The Entertainer*, which were all filmed. He was director of the Chichester Festival Theatre from 1961–65 and first director of the National Theatre Company 1962–73. He was one of the finest English actors in the history of the theatre.

O'Neill Eugene Gladstone 1888–1953. US dramatist. His first full-length play, *Beyond the Horizon* 1920, won a Pulitzer Prize. His best plays are characterized by a down-to-earth quality even when he is experimenting with expressionism, symbolism, or stream of consciousness, and include *The Emperor Jones* 1921, *Desire under the Elms* 1924, *Mourning Becomes Electra* 1931 (a version of Aeschylus' *Oresteia*) and *The Iceman Cometh* 1946. His masterpiece, *Long Day's Journey into Night*, written in 1941, was first performed posthumously in 1956. He was awarded a Nobel Prize for Literature 1936.

Orton Joe 1933–1967. English dramatist in whose black comedies surreal and violent action takes place in genteel and unlikely settings. Plays include *Entertaining Mr Sloane* 1964, *Loot* 1966, and *What the Butler Saw* 1968. He was murdered by his lover Kenneth Halliwell.

Osborne John (James) 1929– . English dramatist. He was one of the first Angry Young Men (anti- establishment writers of the 1950s) of British theatre with his debut play, *Look Back in Anger* 1956. Other plays include *The Entertainer* 1957, *Luther* 1960, and *Watch It Come Down* 1976.

Pinero Arthur Wing 1855–1934. English dramatist. A leading exponent of the 'well-made' play, he enjoyed great contemporary success with his farces *The Magistrate* 1885, *Dandy Dick* 1886, and *The Cabinet Minister* 1890. A departure to more substantial social drama came with *The Second Mrs Tanqueray* 1893, and the comedies *Trelawny of the 'Wells'* 1898 and *The Gay Lord Quex* 1899.

Pinter Harold 1930– . English dramatist and director. Many of his plays are ambiguous comedies on the theme of the breakdown of communication, broadly in the tradition of the Theatre of the Absurd. They include *The Birthday Party* 1958; *The Caretaker* 1960; *The Homecoming* 1965; and a series of one-act plays, *The Lover* 1963, *Silence* and *Landscape* 1969, and *No Man's Land* 1975. His plays entered the political arena with *Mountain Language* 1988.

Pirandello Luigi 1867–1936. Italian dramatist and novelist. His plays revolve around the themes of the futility of human endeavour and the impossibility of defining reality, and include *Sei personaggi in cerca d'autore/Six Characters in Search of an Author* 1921 and *Enrico Quarto/Henry IV* 1922. Nobel Prize for Literature 1934.

Racine Jean 1639–99. French dramatist and exponent of the classical tragedy in French drama. His subjects came from Greek mythology and he observed the rules of classical Greek drama. Most of his tragedies have women in the title role—for example, *Andromaque* 1667, *Iphigénie* 1674, and *Phèdre* 1677. After the contemporary failure of *Phèdre*, he gave up writing for the secular stage, but was persuaded by Madame de Maintenon, the second wife of Louis XIV, to write two religious dramas, *Esther* 1689 and *Athalie* 1691, which achieved posthumous success.

Reinhardt Max. Stage name of Max Goldmann 1873–1943. Austrian actor, director, and manager whose Expressionist style was predominant in German theatre and film during the 1920s and 1930s. He excelled in lavish spectacles—for example, *Oedipus Rex* in Munich

1910 and *The Miracle* at Olympia, London, 1911, which are remembered for his control of huge crowds on stage, and use of new lighting techniques and stage devices. Reinhardt also directed small-scale intimate dramas in the smaller Berlin theatres and founded the Salzburg Festival in 1917.

Sartre Jean-Paul 1905–80. French writer and philosopher. A founder of existentialism, he expressed its tenets in his plays, which include *Les Mouches/The Flies* 1943, a retelling of the Orestes myth, and *Huis-clos/In Camera* 1944, in which three characters are confined in a hell of their own making. In 1951 his most ambitious, but less theatrically successful, play *Le Diable et le Bon Dieu* was written, followed by *Nekrassov* 1955 and *Les Séquestrés d'Altona/The Condemned of Altona* 1959. He refused the Nobel Prize for Literature in 1964.

Schiller Johann Christoph Friedrich von 1759–1805. German dramatist, poet, and historian. He was a leading exponent of the *Sturm und Drang* ('storm and stress') movement. His first play *Die Räuber/The Robbers* 1782 was an immediate success, particularly with the young. This was followed by *Kabale und Liebe/Love and Intrigue* 1784 and a romantic historical tragedy, *Don Carlos* 1789. His later works include the historical trilogy *Wallenstein* 1798–9, and the classical dramas *Maria Stuart* 1800, *Die Jungfrau von Orleans/The Maid of Orleans* 1801, and *Wilhelm Tell* 1804.

Shakespeare William 1564–1616. English playwright and poet. Established in London by 1589 as an actor and a playwright, he was England's unrivalled dramatist until his death, and is considered the greatest English dramatist. His plays, written in blank verse, can be broadly divided into *lyric plays*, including *Romeo and Juliet* and *A Midsummer Night's Dream*; *comedies*, including *The Comedy of Errors*, *As You Like It*, *Much Ado About Nothing*, and *Measure For Measure*; *historical plays*, such as *Henry VI* (in three parts), *Richard III*, and *Henry IV* (in two parts), which often showed cynical political wisdom; and *tragedies*, such as *Hamlet*, *Macbeth*, and *King Lear*.

For the first 200 years after his death, Shakespeare's plays were frequently performed in cut or revised form (Nahun Tate's *King Lear* was given a happy ending), and it was not until the 19th century, with the critical assessments of Coleridge and Hazlitt, that the original texts were restored. Since then the plays have been consistently performed throughout the world, and have exerted an immeasurable influence on the history of the theatre.

Shaw George Bernard 1856–1950. Irish dramatist and critic. A prolific writer, he allied himself with a new and essentially political and polemical movement in the theatre, aiming in his work to engage the audience's social conscience and intellect as well as its emotions. His plays include *Mrs Warren's Profession* (1893, but banned until 1902 because it dealt with prostitution), *Arms and the Man* 1894, *Candida* 1895, the epic *Man and Superman* 1905, *Major Barbara* 1905, *Pygmalion* 1913 (adapted as the musical *My Fair Lady*), *Heartbreak House* 1920, and *St Joan* 1923. Nobel Prize for Literature 1925.

Shepard Sam 1943– . US dramatist and actor. His work combines colloquial American dialogue with striking visual imagery, and includes *The Tooth of Crime* 1972 and *Buried Child* 1978, for which he won the Pulitzer Prize. *Seduced* 1979 is based on the life of the recluse Howard Hughes. He has acted in a number of films, including *The Right Stuff* 1983, *Fool for Love* 1986, based on his play of the same name, and *Steel Magnolias* 1989.

Sheridan Richard Brinsley 1751–1816. Irish dramatist and theatre manager. His plays were masterpieces of the 'comedy of manners'—a more refined version of the earlier and coarser Restoration dramas, and include *The Rivals* 1775, celebrated for the character of Mrs Malaprop; *The School for Scandal* 1777; and *The Critic* 1779. Sheridan was manager of the Drury Lane Theatre from 1776, and became a member of parliament 1780.

Simon (Marvin) Neil 1927– . US playwright. His stage plays include the wryly comic *Barefoot in the Park* 1963, *The Odd Couple* 1965, and *The Sunshine Boys* 1972, and the more serious, autobiographical trilogy *Brighton Beach Memoirs* 1983, *Biloxi Blues* 1985, and *Broadway Bound* 1986. He has also written screenplays and co-written musicals.

Sophocles 496–406. Greek dramatist who, with Aeschylus and Euripides, is one of the three great tragedians. He modified the form of tragedy by introducing a third actor, developing stage scenery, and reducing the chorus to a lyrical device emphasising changes of mood rather than directly affecting the action. Sophocles wrote over 100 plays, of which seven tragedies and a large fragment of a satyr play (a tragedy treated in a grotesquely comic fashion) survive. These include *Ajax* about 450, *Antigone* about 441, *Oedipus Rex* about 425, *Electra* about 409, and *Oedipus at Colonus* about 406.

Stanislavsky Konstantin Sergeivich 1863–1938. Russian actor, director, and teacher of acting. He was a cofounder of the Moscow Art Theatre 1898 and achieved his greatest success as a director with his productions of Chekhov and Gorky. He rejected the declamatory style of acting in favour of a more realistic approach concentrating on the psychological development of character. He described his techniques in *My Life in Art* 1924, *An Actor Prepares* 1926, and other works, which had great influence on acting in Europe and the USA.

Stoppard Tom 1937– . Czechoslovak-born British playwright, whose works use wit and wordplay to explore logical and philosophical ideas. He wrote *Rosencrantz and Guildenstern are Dead* 1967 (the film of which he directed 1989). This was followed by comedies including *The Real Inspector Hound* 1968, *Jumpers* 1972, *Travesties* 1974, *Dirty Linen* 1976, *The Real Thing* 1982, and *Hapgood* 1988.

Strindberg August 1849–1912. Swedish dramatist and novelist. His plays, influential in the development of dramatic technique, are in a variety of styles including historical plays, symbolic dramas (the two-part *Dödsdansen/The Dance of Death* 1901), and 'chamber plays', such as *Spoksonaten/The Ghost [Spook] Sonata* 1907. *Fadern/ The Father* 1887 and *Fröken Julie/Miss Julie* 1888 are both powerful studies of human frailty and hostility between the sexes.

Synge J(ohn) M(illington) 1871–1909. Irish playwright, a leading figure in the Irish dramatic revival of the early 20th century. His six plays show a poetic ear for the speech patterns of the Aran Islands and West Ireland. They include *In the Shadow of the Glen* 1903, *Riders to the Sea* 1904, and *The Playboy of the Western World* 1907, which caused riots at the Abbey Theatre, Dublin, when first performed.

Vega, Lope Felix de (Carpio) 1562–1635. Spanish dramatist and poet, one of the founders of modern Spanish drama. He wrote over 1,500 plays (of which 426 are still in existence), mostly tragicomedies. He set out his views on drama in *Arte nuevo de hacer comedias/The New Art of Writing Plays* 1609, in which he adopts a practical approach while reaffirming the classical form. *Fuenteovejuna/The Sheep Wall* 1614 has been acclaimed in this century as the first proletarian drama.

Warner Deborah 1959– . English theatre director who founded the Kick Theatre company 1980. Discarding period costume and furnished sets, she adopted an uncluttered approach to the classics, including productions of many Shakespeare plays and Sophocles' *Electra*.

Webster John c 1580–1634. English dramatist who ranks after Shakespeare as the greatest tragedian of his time and is the Jacobean whose works are most frequently revived today. His two great plays *The White Devil* about 1612 and *The Duchess of Malfi* 1613/14 are dark, violent tragedies obsessed with death and decay, and infused with poetic brilliance.

Wilde Oscar (Fingal O'Flahertie Wills) 1854–1900. Irish writer. In the theatre he is best known for his elegant, stylish comedies with witty dialogue, such as *Lady Windermere's Fan* 1892, *A Woman of No Importance* 1893, *An Ideal Husband* 1895, and his most consistently successful play, *The Importance of Being Earnest* 1895. The drama *Salome* 1893, based on the biblical character, was written in French; considered scandalous by the British censor, it was first performed in Paris 1896 with the actress Sarah Bernhardt in the title role.

Williams Tennessee. Pen name of Thomas Lanier Williams 1911–1983. US playwright, an exponent of psychological realism with a marked interest in the visual elements of the theatre and a mastery of language. His plays, usually set in the Deep South against a background of decadence and degradation, include *The Glass Menagerie* 1945, *A Streetcar Named Desire* 1947, and *Cat on a Hot Tin Roof* 1955.

Actors

Who do you think are the better actors and actresses—people who appear:

Mainly in the theatre	48
Mainly in cinema films	20
Mainly on television	18
Don't know	15

SCIENCE AND TECHNOLOGY

TERMS AND TECHNIQUES

absolute dating methods that determine age in calendar years by reference to a fixed time scale. Also called chronometric dating, it usually incorporates a measure of uncertainty, expressed as a standard deviation.

accelerator mass spectrometry (AMS) a new radiocarbon dating method that determines the actual number of carbon-14 atoms in a sample rather than the small numbers of carbon-14 atoms that decay radioactively during the measurement time of the conventional method. This method requires only a tiny sample, and its measurement time is only about one hour (as opposed to days for radiocarbon dating), but it is expensive.

aerial photography (or aerial archaeology) technique for taking photographs from a high level, particularly useful in distinguishing surface features (such as crop marks, soil marks, shadow marks) not clearly visible from ground level and which indicate the presence of ancient features; for example, crops will show differences in growth and colour if they are growing over a buried wall foundation or other stone feature.

aerial reconnaissance techniques used in the recording and interpretation of archaeological sites from the air, and also useful in discovering new sites. *Thermal prospection* (also called thermography) is an expensive remote-sensing method that uses heat sensors in aircraft which scan the varying temperatures of remains below ground. Images produced from LANDSAT satellites have been used to discover ancient sites and landscapes (in particular Mayan sites in Mesoamerica); SLAR (sideways looking aerial radar) from NASA aircraft has also been used to reveal ancient sites and field systems.

anthropology the study of humanity's physical characteristics and culture, generally divided into the three subdisciplines of physical (biological) anthropology, social (cultural) anthropology, and archaeology.

archaeology the study of the human past through the systematic recovery and analysis of material remains. Its aims are to recover, describe and classify this material, to describe the form and behaviour of past societies, and to understand the reasons for this behaviour. A truly interdisciplinary subject, it has borrowed many of its major theoretical and methodological concepts and approaches from history and anthropology.

methods Principal activities include preliminary field (or site) surveys, excavation (where necessary), and the classification, dating, and interpretation of finds. Related disciplines that have been useful in archaeological reconstruction include stratigraphy (the study of geological strata), dendrochronology (the establishment of chronological sequences through the study of tree rings), palaeobotany (the study of ancient pollens, seeds, and grains), epigraphy (the study of inscriptions), and numismatics (the study of coins). Since 1958 radiocarbon dating has been used and refined to establish the age of archaeological strata and associated materials.

archaeomagnetic dating dating technique based on the palaeomagnetism of archaeological materials such as baked clay structures (hearths, kilns, ovens). When originally heated, their magnetic particles realigned with the Earth's magnetic field at the time, and since that field changes over time, local and regional chronologies of field-direction can be built up and independently dated. In England for example such curves have been established for the last 2000 years, allowing for any sample to be dated within that span to within approximately 50 years.

archaeozoology (or zooarchaeology) a branch of archaeology involving the analysis of animal remains for information on physiology and ecology; for the interpretation of these remains in association with artifacts and people; and for data on subsistence, dietary and butchering patterns, animal domestication, and palaeoenvironment.

artifact any movable object that has been used, modified, or manufactured by humans, such as a tool, weapon or vessel.

assemblage a collection of artifacts occurring together at a particular time and place that can be considered a single analytic unit. Frequently repeated assemblages that represent a broad range of human activity are termed an archaeological culture.

atomic absorption spectrometry a technique used to determine quantitatively the chemical composition of artifactual metals, minerals, and rocks, in order to identify raw material sources, to relate artifacts of the same material, or to trace trade routes. A sample of the material is atomized in a flame, and its light intensity measured. The method is slow and destructive.

attribute a characteristic element of a particular archaeological culture or group; or a specific element of an individual artifact, such as the rim of a pot or the base of a projectile point, or a type of decoration, raw material, or colour.

auger a tool used to collect sediment and soil samples below ground without hand excavation, or to determine the depth and type of archaeological deposits. The auger may be hand- or machine-powered.

bosing a subsurface detection technique for locating buried pits or ditches, carried out by striking the surface of the ground with a heavy wooden mallet; a duller sound is produced over any disturbance.

Bronze Age stage of prehistory and early history when bronze became the first metal worked extensively and used for tools and weapons. The second 'age' in the three-age system, it

ARCHAEOLOGY: CHRONOLOGY

14th–16th centuries	The Renaissance revived interest in classical Greek and Roman art and architecture, including ruins and buried art and artefacts.
1748	The buried Roman city of Pompeii was discovered under ash from Vesuvius.
1784	Thomas Jefferson dug an Indian burial mound on the Rivanna River in Virginia and wrote a report on his finds.
1790	John Frere identified Old Stone Age (Palaeolithic) tools together with large extinct animals.
1822	Champollion deciphered Egyptian hieroglyphics.
1836	C J Thomsen devised the Stone, Bronze, and Iron Age classification.
1840s	A H Layard excavated the Assyrian capital of Nineveh.
1868	Great Zimbabwe ruins in E Africa first seen by Europeans.
1871	Heinrich Schliemann began excavations at Troy.
1879	Ice Age paintings were first discovered at Altamira, Spain.
1880s	A H Pitt-Rivers set new standards in meticulous excavation, recording, and typological studies, based on the principles of stratigraphy.
1891	W M F Petrie began excavating Akhetaton in Egypt.
1899–1935	A J Evans excavated Minoan Knossos in Crete.
1900–44	Max Uhle began the systematic study of the civilizations of Peru.
1911	The Inca city of Machu Picchu discovered by Hiram Bingham in the Andes.
1911–12	Piltdown skull 'discovered'; proved a fake 1949.
1914–18	Osbert Crawford developed the technique of aerial survey of sites.
1922	Tutankhamen's tomb in Egypt opened by Howard Carter.
1935	Dendrochronology (dating events in the distant past by counting tree rings) developed by Andrew E Douglass; useful where preserved timbers are present.
1939	Anglo-Saxon ship-burial treasure found at Sutton Hoo, England.
1940	Lascaux, the most spectacular decorated cave of the Ice Age, discovered by four boys in the Dordogne, France.
1947	The first of the Dead Sea Scrolls discovered.
1948	*Proconsul* prehistoric ape discovered by Mary Leakey in Kenya; several early hominid fossils found by Louis Leakey in Olduvai Gorge 1950s–1970s.
1953	Michael Ventris deciphered Minoan Linear B.
1960s	Radiocarbon and thermoluminescence measurement developed as aids for dating remains.
1961	Swedish warship *Wasa* raised at Stockholm.
1963	W B Emery pioneered rescue archaeology at Abu Simbel before the site was flooded by the Aswan Dam.
1974	Tomb of Shi Huangdi discovered in China.
1975	Hominid nicknamed 'Lucy', *c.* 3 million years old, discovered at Hadar, Ethiopia.
1976	Footprints of hominids, *c.* 3.8 million years old, found in hardened mud at Laetoli, Tanzania.
1978	Tomb attributed to Philip II of Macedon (Alexander the Great's father) discovered in Greece.
1979	The Aztec capital Tenochtitlán excavated beneath a zone of Mexico City.
1982	The English king Henry VIII's warship *Mary Rose* of 1545 was raised and studied with new techniques in underwater archaeology.
1985	The tomb of Maya, Tutankhamen's treasurer, discovered at Saqqara, Egypt.
1988	Turin Shroud established as of medieval date by radiocarbon dating.
1989	Remains of Globe and Rose Theatres discovered in London, where many of Shakespeare's plays were originally performed.
1991	Body of man from 5300 years ago, with clothing, bow, arrows, a copper axe and other implements found preserved in Italian Alps.

developed out of the Stone Age, preceded the Iron Age, and may be dated 5000–1200 BC in the Middle East and about 2200–500 BC in Europe. Mining and metalworking were the first specialized industries, and the invention of the wheel during this time revolutionized transport. Agricultural productivity (which began during the Neolithic period, about 10,000 BC), and hence the size of the population that could be supported, was transformed by the ox-drawn plough. Recent discoveries in Thailand suggest that the Far East, rather than the Middle East, was the cradle of the Bronze Age.

cognitive archaeology the study of past ways of thought from material remains, and of the meanings evoked by the symbolic nature of material culture.

computerized axial tomography (CAT) a technique for looking inside bodies or mummies without disturbing them. X-ray scans made at intervals produce a series of cross-sectional 'slices' that the computer can reformat to create images from any angle.

context an artifact's context may refer to its matrix (the sediment or material surrounding it), its provenance (its 3-dimensional position within that matrix), and its association with other artifacts in the matrix.

contract archaeology archaeological survey and/ or excavation, today increasingly required by state legislation, most often in advance of highway construction or urban development.

core solid cylinder of sediment or soil collected with a coring device and used to evaluate the geological context and stratigraphy of archaeological material or to obtain palaeobotanical samples; a stone blank from which flakes or blades are removed.

cross-dating method of demonstrating contemporaneity of two cultural groups by establishing links between them, for example the presence of objects of both groups in one another's archaeological contexts.

cultural anthropology (social anthropology) a subdiscipline of anthropology that analyzes human culture and society, the non-biological and behavioural aspects of humanity. Two principal branches are ethnography (the study at first hand of living cultures) and ethnology (the comparison of cultures using ethnographic evidence).

cultural resource management (CRM) the legally mandated protection of archaeological sites located on public lands in the USA that are threatened by destruction through development.

dendrochronology dating technique that uses tree-ring sequences to date timbers and other logs from archaeological structures and sites. This technique is based on the principle that every year trees add a ring of growth, and by counting these rings their age can be determined. An unbroken series of rings can be built up and extended back for centuries by 'overlapping' identical sequences preserved on modern and ancient timbers; subsequently, any piece of wood found in the area can have its rings checked against the master sequence and its precise age established. 'Floating' chronologies, which do not extend to the present day, have been built up in many regions worldwide and allow for relative dating between structures and sites.

In North America, sequences of tree rings extending back over 8,000 years have been obtained by using cores from the bristle-cone pine (*Pinus aristata*), which can live for over 4,000 years. Such sequences have proved very useful for calibrating, or correcting, radiocarbon dates, which were found to have serious discrepancies due to a differences in the atmosphere's carbon-14 content over time.

diffusion the spread of ideas, objects or cultural traits from one culture or society to another, rather than their independent invention; for example a diffusionist school of thought held that Egypt was the source of metallurgy and megalithic building, whereas it is now accepted that these traits arose independently in different areas.

dowsing unconventional and controversial method for locating subsurface features by holding out a twig, rod, or pendulum and waiting for it to move. Although used at times in archaeology, it is not taken seriously by most archaeologists.

electrolysis a cleaning process in archaeological conservation, especially of material from underwater archaeology, involving immersing the object in a chemical solution, and passing a weak current between it and a surrounding metal grill. Corrosive salts move slowly from the object (cathode) to the grill (anode), leaving the artifact clean.

electron spin resonance (ESR) is a non-destructive dating method applicable to teeth, bone, heat-treated flint, ceramics, sediments and stalagmitic concretions.

It enables electrons, displaced by natural radiation and then trapped in the structure, to be measured; their number indicate the age of the specimen.

environmental archaeology a subfield of archaeology aimed at identifying processes, factors and conditions of past biological and physical environmental systems and how they relate to cultural systems. It is an eminently interdisciplinary field, where archaeologists and natural scientists combine to reconstruct the human uses of plants and animals and how societies adapted to changing environmental conditions.

eolith naturally shaped or fractured stone found in Lower Pleistocene deposits and once believed by some archaeologists to be the oldest known artifact type, dating to the pre-Palaeolithic era. They are now recognized as not humanly made.

ethnoarchaeology the study of human behaviour, and of the material culture of living societies, in order to see how materials enter the archaeological record, and hence to provide hypotheses explaining the production, use, and disposal patterns of ancient material culture.

ethnography the description and analysis of individual contemporary cultures, using anthropological techniques like participant observation (where the anthropologist lives in the society being studied) and a reliance on informants. Ethnography has provided many data of use to the archaeologist as analogies.

ethnology the use of ethnographic data in a comparative analysis to understand how cultures work and why they change, with a view to deriving general principles about human society.

excavation the systematic recovery of archaeological data through the exposure of buried sites and artifacts. Excavation is destructive, and is therefore accompanied by a comprehensive recording of all material found and its three-dimensional locations (its context). As much material and information as possible must be recovered from any 'dig'. A full record of all the techniques employed in the excavation itself must also be made, so that future archaeologists will be able to evaluate the results of the work accurately.

CHRONOLOGICAL CHART SHOWING MAJOR CULTURAL DEVELOPMENTS WORLDWIDE

Years AD/BC	North Europe	Mediterranean	Near East	Egypt and Africa	
1,500				Great Zimbabwe	
1,000	Medieval states	BYZANTINE EMPIRE			
500			ISLAM		
AD	ROMAN EMPIRE	ROMAN EMPIRE		Towns (*Africa*) AXUM	
BC					
500	IRON AGE	CLASSICAL GREECE	PERSIA BABYLON	LATE PERIOD	
1,000			ASSYRIA		
1,500		Iron	HITITES	NEW KINGDOM	
		MYCENAE		MIDDLE KINGDOM	
2,000	BRONZE AGE (*Stonehenge*)	MINOAN	Iron	OLD KINGDOM (*Pyramids*)	
2,500					
			SUMER		
3,000				EARLY DYNASTIC	
3,500			Writing Cities Wheeled vehicles	Towns (*Egypt*)	
4,000					
4,500	Megaliths	Copper (*Balkans*)			
5,000	Farming, pottery				
5,500			Irrigation		
6,000					
6,500		Farming, pottery	Copper	Cattle (*North Africa*)	
7,000			Pottery		
7,500			Wheat, rye etc	Pottery (*Sudan*)	
8,000					
8,500					
9,000			Sheep		
9,500					
10,000					

Information supplied by Paul Bahn

Besides being destructive, excavation is also costly. For both these reasons, it should be used only as a last resort. It can be partial, in which only a sample of the site is investigated, or total. Samples are chosen either by informed guesswork, in which case excavators investigate those areas they feel will be most productive, or statistically, in which case the sample is drawn using various statistical techniques, so as to ensure that it is representative. An important goal of excavation is a full understanding of a site's stratigraphy, that is the vertical layering of a site. These layers or levels can be defined naturally (e.g. soil changes), culturally (e.g.

different occupation levels), or arbitrarily (e.g. 10 cm/4 in levels). Excavation can also be done horizontally, to uncover larger areas of a particular layer to reveal the spatial relationships between artifacts and features in that layer. Known as open-area excavation, this is used especially where single-period deposits lie close to the surface and the time dimension is represented by lateral movement rather than by the placing of one building on top of the preceding one.

Most excavators employ a flexible combination of vertical and horizontal digging to adapt to the nature of their site and the questions they are seeking to answer.

India	East Asia and Pacific	North America	Meso-America	South America	Years AD/BC
				INCA	1,500
		Cahokia	AZTEC		1,000
	New Zealand settled	Chaco	"TOLTEC"	CHIMU	
	States (Japan)	HOPEWELL			500
			MAYA		
	Great Wall	PUEBLOS			AD
MAURYAN	(China)		TEOTIHUACAN	MOCHE	
	Cast iron				BC
Iron	(China)				500
	Lapita	Maize		CHAVIN	1,000
	(Polynesia)	(Southwest)	OLMEC		
	SHANG (China)				1,500
					2,000
INDUS	Walled villages				2,500
	(China)			Temple-mounds	3,000
				Maize, llama	3,500
				cotton	
					4,000
					4,500
					5,000
	Rice-millet		Maize		5,500
	(China)			Manioc	
				Pottery	6,000
			Beans, squash,	(Amazonia)	
			peppers	Beans, squash	6,500
Farming	Gardens			peppers	7,000
	(New Guinea)				7,500
					8,000
					8,500
					9,000
					9,500
	Pottery (Japan)				10,000

experimental archaeology the controlled replication of ancient technologies and behaviour in order to provide hypotheses that can be tested by actual archaeological data. Experiments can range in size from the reproduction of ancient tools, to the construction of whole villages and ancient subsistence practice.

feature a non-portable element of a site, such as a hearth, wall, post-hole, or activity area. Some are constructed (eg houses, storerooms, burial features) while others simply form over time, such as heaps of shells, or quarry areas.

field survey the examination of the surface of the earth for evidence of archaeological remains, without recourse to excavation. Surveys can be carried out unsystematically, where **field walking** takes place over areas suspected of having archaeological material, and the location of any finds or surface features encountered is plotted; or systematically, where the area is divided into a grid and a sample of its sectors are walked, making the survey more representative of the whole and hence more accurate.

fission-track dating dating method based on the natural and spontaneous nuclear fission of uranium-238 and its physical product, linear atomic displacements (tracks) created along the trajectory of released energized fission fragments. Knowing the rate of fission (a constant), the uranium content of the material and the number of fission tracks by counting, the age of the material can be determined. The method is most widely used to date volcanic deposits adjacent to archaeological material.

geomagnetic reversal a periodic reversal in the Earth's magnetic field (where magnetic north becomes south, and vice versa), occurring most recently *c.* 700,000 years ago. A sequence of such reversals stretching back millions of years has been built up with the aid of potassium-argon dating. Finding part of the sequence in the rocks of early hominid sites in Africa provides a useful method of checking other dating methods.

grid system an excavation technique that divides a site into squares to facilitate the recording of excavated objects and features. The practice includes both the vertical and horizontal dimensions by retaining intact baulks (standing sections) of earth between the excavated squares of the grid so that different layers can be traced and correlated across the site of the vertical profiles.

hoard a deliberately buried group of valuables or prized possessions, often in times of conflict or war, which were never reclaimed. Coins, objects in precious metals, and scrap metal are the most common objects found in hoards. In July 1991 the largest hoard found in Britain was discovered, consisting of 7,000 15th-century coins; it was declared treasure trove.

Iron Age the developmental stage of human technology when weapons and tools were made from iron. Iron was produced in Thailand by about 1600 BC but was considered inferior in strength to bronze until about 1000 when metallurgical techniques improved and the alloy steel was produced by adding carbon during the smelting process. In Europe it begins around 1100 BC, and early Iron Age cultures are represented by the Villanovans in Italy and Hallstatt and La Tène in central and western Europe; it is also the time when Celtic art flourished. The end of the period overlaps with the expansion of imperial Rome around the 1st Century BC, but beyond the borders of the Empire it is generally taken to end much later, around the 4th–6th centuries AD.

isotopic analysis the analysis of ratios of the principal isotopes preserved in human bone in order to reconstruct ancient diet, based on the principle that different food categories (e.g. marine resources) leave specific chemical signatures in the body.

landscape archaeology the study of human occupation and activities on landscapes, in particular the patterning of settlements and sites within that broad perspective through time.

magnetometer device for measuring the intensity of the earth's magnetic field; distortions in this field occur when archaeological structures such as kilns and hearths are present, or pits and ditches. The technique allows for such features to be located without disturbing the ground, and for excavation to be focussed on the likeliest area.

material culture the physical, humanly-made re-

Europe's Oldest Boats?

Archaeologists in Paris have established that the site of the city was occupied in the Neolithic period and have discovered France's earliest bow as well as three oak boats, the oldest ever found in Europe.

Excavations began in January at Bercy, in eastern Paris, as archaeologists led by Philippe Marquis monitored development work on the future 'Centre International du Vin et de l'Alimentation', where the bulldozers have permitted them for the first time to reach a depth of 15 m/50 ft, 5 m/16 ft below the level of the Seine. Because this level is so damp, it has preserved hundreds of objects. The finds included the bones of wild cattle, boars, red deer, wolves, beavers, otters, freshwater turtles, carp, and pike; pottery; and axes of flint and polished stone which reveal the date (4500 BC) of Paris's first sedentary settlement.

The most important finds are an almost complete bow 1.5 m/5 ft long, and three oak canoes dating to 4300–3700 BC. The canoes measure 3.45 m/11 ft 4 in, 4.15 m/13 ft 7 in and 5.35 m/17 ft 7 in; the biggest, which was found upside down, is virtually intact: a cast was made of it before removal. The boats' presence proves that the Seine used to pass to the east of Bercy, and mooring posts have also been found along the ancient water course.

The archaeologists have explored 500 sq m/600 sq yd, and have until the end of 1992 to work at the site. Meanwhile, two of the boats are being kept in vats in a warehouse, while the least well preserved is still at the site. They will eventually be sent to Denmark for treatment, and will then be displayed in a new museum at Bercy.

---

mains of past societies (tools, buildings, etc.) which constitute the major source of evidence for archaeology.

Mesolithic the Middle Stone Age developmental stage of human technology and of prehistory, following the Palaeolithic and preceeding the Neolithic. While the environment changed with the withdrawal of the Pleistocene ice sheets around 10,000 years ago, the old Palaeolithic hunting and gathering way of life continued during the Mesolithic; changes in the tool assemblages however reflect adaptations to environmental changes, with the flint industries of this period characterized by microliths (very small flint tools) in great number. With the introduction of farming and stock-rearing the Mesolithic gave way to the Neolithic (occurring in Britain around 4000 BC).

metal detector electronic device for detecting metal on or beneath the surface of the ground. It is used to survey areas for buried metallic objects, occasionally by archaeologists. However, their indiscriminate use by 'treasure hunters' led to their banning on recognized archaeological

MOLECULAR ARCHAEOLOGY

Over the last decade biochemists have introduced techniques that allow tiny traces of DNA to be amplified into quantities that can be studied by geneticists. The genes of people who lived 50,000 years ago can be studied and compared with the genes of people alive today.

The most important technique is cloning, where the DNA traces are introduced to bacteria, which reproduce them along with their own DNA. In 1985, Svante Paabo of the University of Munich cloned DNA from an Egyptian mummy that lived over 4,000 years ago. In 1988 he went on to amplify mitochondrial DNA from a brain thought to be 7,000 years old, which had been found preserved in Florida. In 1989 researchers at Oxford University amplified DNA from human bone.

It is not an easy task to obtain ancient DNA. First researches were made with soft tissues that had dried, such as those from Egyptian mummies. Other obvious sources, such as bodies preserved in peat bogs, were less useful, because the tannic acid that preserved the bodies also destroyed the DNA.

However, in Windover, Florida, unusual circumstances have combined to offer scientists an opportunity to study the DNA of bog people—a limestone spring continually dribbles into a peat bog that contains many well-preserved bodies. The calcium bicarbonate in the spring water buffers the acidity of the peat and prevents the tannic acid from destroying the DNA.

The Windover bodies have yielded considerable information, in particular concerning the immune systems of the local population 8,000 years ago. Scientists working with the bodies are hopeful that they will be able to tell which diseases the population was immune to. They have also found that the DNA from different bodies is very similar, suggesting that the population was isolated and inbred.

DNA is also well preserved by freeze-drying. This is not a particularly common way for bodies to be preserved, but one specimen emerged in 1991, high up in the Alps near the border between Austria and Italy. Nicknamed the Iceman, the body is thought to be 5,000 years old, a healthy man who died of exposure when caught in a storm on a high Alpine pass. Scientists are hoping to clone and study DNA not only from the Iceman, but also from parasitic organisms to which he was playing host.

Other sources of DNA are bones themselves. Unfortunately, extracting DNA from them results in destruction of the bone—although there are a number of Neanderthal skeletons that could give fascinating information, scientists are as yet unwilling to sacrifice priceless specimens. Molecular archaeology will need to become more established, or to develop new techniques, for this source to be exploited.

Bone has been shown to give DNA samples in at least one case. This is a 50,000-year-old vertebra from a skeleton found in Iraq. The specimen was so fragmentary as to be worthless for conventional archaeologists, so it was sent for DNA recovery to Los Alamos National Laboratory in the USA. DNA that corresponds to primate DNA has been found, but there is no doubt that it has been damaged by age.

It is not only DNA that can be usefully studied by molecular archaeologists. At the Smithsonian Institute in Washington DC, techniques have been developed for studying the antibodies that have soaked into the bones of individuals suffering from disease. So far, immuno-globulins from two skeletal populations have been identified. The scientists hope that the technique will enable them to trace the effects of disease on human populations. A comparative study of infections in Europe and America might resolve the contention that syphilis was brought to Europe by Columbus's returning crew.

Molecular archaeology is in its infancy. As it proves its worth, curators of ancient specimens are more likely to sacrifice at least a part of their collection for the knowledge that it will yield. The growth of biochemical knowledge of our ancestors is then likely to be exponential.

---

sites in some countries; in Britain the law forbids the use of metal detectors on 'scheduled' (that is nationally important) sites.

metallographic examination a method of analyzing the manufacturing techniques of metal artifacts. A cross-sectional slice of an artifact is polished, etched to highlight internal structures, and examined under a metallurgical microscope. The reflected light of the microscope enhances uneven surfaces revealing grain size, shape and boundaries, inclusions, fabric, defects, and other detail.

microwear analysis (or *usewear analysis*) the examination of the surface and working edge of an artifact for signs of use (such as damage or residue), often by means of a high-powered microscope. The technique is principally used in the study of stone tools, which suffer diagnostic damage or polishing when used to cut, saw, or pierce other materials.

Neolithic last period of the Stone Age, characterized by settled communities based on agriculture and the domestication of animals, and identified by sophisticated, finely honed stone tools, and ceramic wares. The earliest neolithic communities appeared about 9000 BC in southwest Asia, followed by Egypt, India, and China. In Europe farming began in about 6500 BC in the Balkans and Aegean, spreading north and east. Sometimes called the Neolithic Revolution, the period marks the most important single development of humanity as it brought with it sedentarism, which in turn encouraged population growth and greater specialization.

New Archaeology a development in the 1960s

WORLD'S OLDEST WOODEN CONSTRUCTION?

Archaeologists have discovered what they think is the world's oldest surviving wooden structure in northwest Germany. It is a well dating to 5,300 BC. It is so well preserved that they can tell how it was built and even what tools were used.

The team, from the Landschaftsverband Rheinland, led by Jurgen Weiner, have been excavating since mid-1989 in a gravel pit at Kuckhoven near Erkelenz, south of Monchengladbach. A settlement of the Linearbandkeramik (LBK) culture, dating to the early Neolithic period, is under threat and will be destroyed by gravel extraction in a few years.

Most LBK settlements were villages of farmers and shepherds. The archaeologists have uncovered postholes which show that the people lived in long timber houses. Sites of the period are normally on good loess soils near streams or rivers. The Kuckhoven site was a puzzle since it lay on an expanse of loess which was 3 km/1.8 mi from the nearest watercourse. The solution to this puzzle proved to be the presence of a great well.

Excavation revealed the first fragments of wood in late 1990. Further digging in summer 1991 located a shaft at a depth of 7 m/23 ft below the present ground surface. The shaft had vertical walls of 5–6 m/16–20 ft, and abundant wooden fragments in its centre. A test pit revealed a further 7.6 m/25 ft of shaft below and two rectangular wooden well-frames in the middle. The outer frame is 3 m/10 ft square. The inner frame is newer. It is 1.6 m/5.2 ft square and placed in the northwest corner of the larger square. It was probably built after the older one was damaged. Fragments of wickerwork have been found, and this material may have been used to line the upper part of the shaft.

The 200 oak planks discovered so far are up to 15 cm/6 in thick and 50 cm/20 in wide. After the trees were felled, their trunks—up to a metre in diameter—must have been split with the stone axes of the period. The stone used for axe heads in this area came from what is now Belgium. There are clear marks of these stone tools on the heavy planks; other tools, probably chisels made of cattle bones, were used to cut rectangular mortises in them. In this way, the beams could be joined into the 3 m box-frame, the slots being caulked with moss. Archaeologists have also recovered the remains of several tools from the well, including two composite mattocks with wooden blades and hafts. These tools may have been used to dig the well or to fill it. They are the only such tools ever recovered from an LBK settlement. We can expect more finds when the shaft is completely emptied, since wells which fell into disuse—perhaps after they dried up—were often used as rubbish tips.

Initial results from radiocarbon dating put the well at 5300–4900 BC. These results have been confirmed and made more precise by analysis of the tree-rings on the planks. We can now say that the oak trees were felled in 5303 BC, probably in the autumn or winter. The well was built in the following spring or summer, its shaft more than 15 m/50 ft deep. The lowest 8 m/26 ft are beautifully preserved.

Why is the Kuckhoven find so important? There are several reasons. First, it is the oldest surviving wooden construction in the world. Before it was discovered no one knew that Neolithic people had mastered the particular carpentry technique employed at the site. Second, its timbers are making a crucial contribution to tree-ring data for this period in Europe. The remarkable conditions of preservation of the well are caused by a combination of s il chemistry and the great dampness around the structure. They have ensured that a Rhineland museum will eventually be able to display a unique and perfectly conserved Neolithic well-shaft.

aimed at making archaeology more scientific, now more often referred to as Processual Archaeology. It proposed that archaeology should openly state its assumptions and use specific scientific procedures. Some adherents of New Archaeology believed that laws of human behaviour were obtainable by using the correct methodologies.

palaeobotany (archaeobotany) the recovery and identification of plant remains from archaeological contexts, and their use in the reconstruction of past environments.

palaeontology the study of the fossil remains of ancient life forms and their environment and evolution; human palaeontology is the study of the origins of the human species.

Palaeolithic earliest stage of human technology and development of the Stone Age, beginning with the emergence of hominids and the production of the earliest stone tools (approximately 3 million years ago), and lasting till the retreat of the ice sheets about 10,000 years ago. Its subdivisions are the Lower Palaeolithic, in which the earliest hominids appear (*Australopithecus* and *Homo erectus*); the Middle Palaeolithic, the age of the Neanderthals; and the Upper Palaeolithic, marked by the appearance of *Homo sapiens* and the remarkable cave art of western Europe (for example the caves at Lascaux). The final stage also saw the colonization of the New World and Australia.

phosphate analysis a technique of taking soil samples at regular intervals from the surface of a site and its surroundings to identify, through chemical analysis of phosphorus concentrations in the soil, human settlements and activity and burial areas within sites. Excrement and bone are relatively high in phosphorus content, so human activity and remains tend to produce comparatively large concentrations of phosphates.

physical anthropology (biological anthropology) a subdiscipline of anthropology that studies human biological or physical characteristics and how they evolved.

pollen analysis (palynology) the study of fossil and living pollen and spores, utilized in palaeoenvironmental and palaeoclimatic reconstruction, in identifying natural and humanly induced vegetation changes, and in developing relative chronologies.

Since different genera (and sometimes species) of pollen have distinct characteristics of size, shape, and markings on the coat, the study of these pollen grains can reveal information on the dominant flora, and thus the climate, of a particular period. Pollen grains are extremely resistant and therefore well-preserved in rocks and particularly abundant in peat.

potassium-argon dating an isotopic dating method based on the radioactive decay of potassium-40 to the stable isotope argon-40. The method is used primarily to date volcanic layers in stratigraphic sequences with archaeological deposits, and the palaeomagnetic reversal timescale. Ages are based on the known half-life of 40K, and the ratio of 40K/40Ar. The method is routinely applied from about 100,000 to 30 million years ago.

prehistory the period of human history for which there is no contemporary documentary evidence; it constitutes the longest segment of the human past, and is the major object of study of archaeology. Prehistory and history can overlap in time—for example, prehistoric Iron Age cultures existed at the same time as the historic Roman culture; and in our own age, 'prehistoric' societies have existed contemporaneously with modern ones, for example the Kung Bushmen or the Australian aborigines.

protohistory period following prehistory but prior to the appearance of history as documented in written records.

radiocarbon dating a radiometric dating technique used for determining the age of carbon-bearing materials including wood and plant remains, bone, peat, and shell. It is based on the radioactive decay of the carbon-14 isotope in the sample to nitrogen, with the release of (beta) particles that is initiated when an organism dies and ceases to exchange carbon-14 with the atmosphere. After death the carbon-14 content is a function of time and is determined by counting (beta) particles with either a proportional gas or a liquid scintillation counter for a period of time.

The method yields reliable ages back to c. 30,000 years, but its results require correction since the atmospheric production rate of carbon-14 has not been constant through time. Radiocarbon dates from tree rings showed that material before 1000 BC had been exposed to greater concentrations of carbon-14. Now radiocarbon dates are calibrated against calendar dates obtained from tree rings, or, for earlier periods, against uranium/thorium dates obtained from coral. A new advance, AMS (accelerator mass spectrometry) requires only tiny samples of the material being dated, and counts the atoms of carbon-14 directly, disregarding their decay.

relative dating dating methods that measure differences in age utilizing an ordinal scale, for example, they include sequencing of events or objects relative to one another but without linkage to ages in calendar years.

remote sensing general term for reconnaissance and surface survey techniques that provide information without disturbing subsurface archaeological deposits.

rescue archaeology (or *salvage archaeology*) the branch of archaeology that deals with the impact of contemporary construction and other developments on archaeological sites, and the various laws enacted to mitigate the threat. It involves the location and recording (usually by rapid excavation) of archaeological sites in advance of their destruction.

resistivity survey a geophysical survey method used to locate buried features and structures with a resistivity meter. An electrical current is passed through the soil between electrodes and the resistance (normally a consequence of moisture content) is recorded. In this way buried features can be detected through their differential retention of groundwater (so, for example, a stone feature will show greater resistance than the soil around it, and a damp pit will show less).

seriation a relative dating technique that organizes artifacts temporally, according to their relative popularity. Evolutionary seriation is based on changes that represent essentially technological improvements, while stylistic seriation is based on gradual changes in the frequencies of stylistic attributes, so that the greater the similarity in style, the closer in age artifacts are to each other.

site any location where there is evidence for past human behaviour. A site can be as small as an isolated find, which is either a single artifact or a small number of artifacts, or as large as an ancient city. Sites are classified according to function: major types include domestic/habitation sites, kill sites, processing/butchering sites.

site catchment analysis (SCA) the definition of the site catchment, the total area from which the site's contents have been derived (i.e. the full inventory of its artifactual and non-artifactual remains, and their sources), and an assessment of the catchment's economic potential.

site exploitation territory (SET) the territory surrounding a site that was habitually exploited by the site's inhabitants. Territories are normally seen as having a radius of one hour walking distance for farmers, and a two-hour distance for hunter-gatherers.

sondage a deep test-pit, employed to investigate a site's stratigraphy prior to carrying out larger-scale excavation.

AMAZON FINDS

Recent research on the lower Amazon, Brazil, has unearthed the oldest pottery in the western hemisphere. It suggests that the tropical lowlands, not the Andes, were the cradle of civilization in South America.

There has been little professional archaeological work in Amazonia. Before antibiotics and immunization, the area could be lethal. Scholars who worked there often died young of tropical diseases, and their discoveries remained unpublished or ignored in foreign-language journals. In the 20th century, most archaeological research in South America has been directed elsewhere.

Experts used to claim that the tropical rainforest would have prevented prehistoric human occupation in the lowlands. They assumed that the Andes were the centre of cultural development, and that intruders from there brought horticulture to the lowlands. These intruders displaced the hunter-gatherers who could not develop early agriculture, ceramics, or complex societies because of the poverty of tropical resources.

This view ignored environmental and archaeological evidence to the contrary. The rainforests of Amazonia may be short on resources, but this vast region also has large areas of alluvial soils. They are as fertile as the flood plains of the Nile, Ganges, and other great rivers. They have a riverine seasonal forest and savanna rich in fish, game, and plants.

Between 1830 and 1945 researchers had already discovered that the region had deep, stratified middens, earthworks, elaborate pottery, and other artefacts. Researchers in the 19th century assigned some middens to the early Holocene. More recently, they generally assumed that this material was only 1,400 years old. Only a few pioneers such as American archaeologist Donald Lathrap continued to argue for Amazonia's chronological priority and cultural complexity.

In 1987, archaeologists carried out new excavations at the prehistoric shell-midden of Taperinha, near Santarem in Brazil. This mound is over 6 m/20 ft tall and covers several hectares. It lies on the edge of an ancient terrace of the lower Amazon. The excavations, under the direction of Anna Roosevelt, exposed 48 strata of freshwater mussel-shells, charcoal, animal bones, 383 fragile potsherds, and a few human bones. Radiocarbon dates were obtained from four samples of charcoal, five of shell, and two of elemental carbon and humic-fulvic acids from the base of a pot. The results spanned the period from 8,050 to 6,950 years ago. A thermoluminescence date from a fragment of the same pottery gave a result of $7,110 \pm 1,422$ years ago.

The Taperinha pottery is grit-tempered and brown-red. Some of it is decorated with painted patterns or an incised rim. The tests show that it is at least 1,000 years older than the previous earliest ceramics of South America, from Colombia in the fourth millennium BC. It is 3,000 years older than the first pottery in the Andes or Mesoamerica.

The upper part of the region's shell-mounds contains numerous grinding stones. These may reflect the beginnings of root horticulture. From about 4,000 years ago there were ceramic-stage villages with manioc horticulture, two millennia before the Central Andes had reached that stage.

Roosevelt argues that the broad Amazon floodplain may have been one of the most densely inhabited zones in the prehistoric New World. Ancient middens are almost continuous along the banks of the lower Amazon, often several metres deep. Some areas of the floodplain are densely covered with earthworks over hundreds of square kilometres. By about 2,000 years ago there were populous agricultural chiefdoms, here and in the upper Amazon, with settlements of urban scale and complexity.

Roosevelt's investigations on the immense Marajo Island at the Amazon's mouth have revealed a complex society of the 5th to the 14th centuries AD. It features monumental earthen mounds, cemeteries of elaborate funerary urns, and a rich material culture with complex, varied art styles. There are numerous large 'Marajoara' sites. Some comprise 20 to 40 individual mounds over areas of several square kilometres. There are no obvious images of chiefs, but this was probably a ranked or stratified society. It was not based on intensive agriculture but on a mixed diet, mainly seeds and fish. Analysis of human remains suggests that the population lived better than many modern Amazonians.

The 17th-century Europeans who came to this region found populous chieftaincies supported by agriculture, foraging, trade, and tribute. Unfortunately they fought and defeated them to make way for their vast ranches. None of the indigenous people still existed by 1850 when scholarly research was beginning. Only archaeology can resurrect this neglected culture which may hold the key to the origins of many of South America's cultural achievements.

This ceramic object is a pubic cover once worn by the Marajo peoples of Amazonia.

ROMAN LEAD

Here is an unusual example of putting archaeology to practical use. Physicists are using Roman lead recovered from a 2,000-year-old shipwreck to help them detect very low levels of radioactivity.

The wreck lies off the coast of Sardinia. It is that of a freighter (*onerarius magnus*); its keel, reinforced with huge iron nails almost a metre long, seems purpose-built for carrying heavy cargoes of metal. About 1,500 lead ingots, each weighing roughly 35 kg/80 lb, lie scattered across the sandy seabed. Their shape and weight suggest that they were made in the early 1st century BC, probably from lead mined and smelted in Sardinia or southern Spain. Trace-element analysis should establish the precise source.

Archaeologist Donatella Salvi is cooperating with two physicists, Gianni Fiorentini and Ettore Fiorini. They hope to use some of the lead for the heavy shielding that they need for their work. In their laboratory, which lies beneath the mountain of Gran Sasso in the Apennines, they are trying to detect exotic particles of matter such as neutrinos, muons, and magnetic monopoles. The number of these particles passing through the mountain is so low that the physicists need to eliminate stray signals from natural radioactivity.

Modern lead is unsuitable for effective shielding, since it has radioactivity of its own in an isotope called lead-210. Low-activity lead is too expensive to produce in the necessary quantities. The Roman lead has had over 2,000 years in which to lose almost all its lead-210, which has a half-life of only 22 years. It has been protected from cosmic radiation and nuclear fallout by 35 m/120 ft of seawater. Measurements show that its radioactivity is extremely low.

---

spectrographic analysis technique used to analyze the component elements in a compound, based on the principle that light given off upon volatization breaks up into a distinctive pattern when split into a spectrum by a prism. By analyzing the pattern of lines in the spectrum the composition of elements present in a compound can be determined. The technique has been especially useful in metal analysis, but is also applied to pottery, obsidian, and glass.

step-trenching excavation technique used on very deep sites such as Near Eastern 'tells' (mounds) where a large area opened at the top gradually narrows as the dig descends in a series of large steps.

Stone Age the developmental stage of humans in prehistory before the use of metals, when tools and weapons were made of stone (especially flint), wood, bone, and antler. The Stone Age is subdivided into the Old or Palaeolithic, the Middle or Mesolithic, and the New or Neolithic. The people of the Old Stone Age were hunters, whereas the Neolithic people took the first steps in agriculture, the domestication of animals, weaving, and pottery.

stratigraphy the study of the formation, composition, sequence, and correlation of stratified sediment, soils and rocks. Stratigraphy is the principal means by which the context of archaeological deposits is evaluated, chronologies are constructed, and events are sequenced. It is invaluable for interpreting the sequence of deposition of the site and thereby the relative ages of artifacts, features and other phenomena in the site.

thermoluminescence (TL) is used to date fired archaeological material such as pottery and burned flint tools. When the material was originally fired, any electrons trapped in it by radiation escaped, emitting light known as thermoluminescence, and thereby setting the TL clock to zero. By measuring the amount of TL emitted when the material is reheated, and knowing its radioactive content, one can calculate the lapse of time since the original firing.

thin-section analysis technique using a sample chip—ground down to a paper thin sheet and mounted on a glass slide—that is utilized in petrological analysis of the mineralogical composition of ceramics, stone artifacts and soils.

Three Age System scheme first formulated by Christian Thomsen (1788–1865) between 1816–19 to divide prehistory into a Stone Age, Bronze Age, and Iron Age. Subsequently, the Stone Age was subdivided into the Old and the New (the Palaeolithic and Neolithic); the Middle (Mesolithic) Stone Age was added later, as well as the Copper Age (inserted between the New Stone Age and Bronze Age). While providing a valuable and valid classification system for prehistoric material, it did not provide dates but only a sequence of developmental stages, which, furthermore, were not necessarily followed in that order by different societies.

trace element analysis the study (e.g. by neutron activation analysis or X-ray fluorescence) of elements that occur naturally in minor amounts in minerals in soil and sediment. Trace elements can be identified by various analyses and may serve as 'fingerprints' for some artifact raw material sources.

typology the systematic organization of artifacts into types on the basis of their shared attributes. The two objectives are classification, i.e. grouping objects according to their shape, leading to a type series; and, through the comparison of different types, to discover how these types relate to eachother. The latter process can lead to seriation, which demonstrates the *development* of a type of artifact (the development may be related to function, technological advance, fashion, etc.). Such information requires an independent dating source for at least several examples in the series in order to establish the rate of change.

underwater reconnaissance geophysical methods

BITUMEN AND BEESWAX—A RECIPE FOR THE DEAD

French scientists have finally ended the debate about the way the ancient Egyptians mummified the dead. They have proved that the Egyptians used bitumen, far earlier than people thought, and have pinpointed the most likely sources of the material.

The word 'mummy' comes from the Persian *mumia* meaning bitumen or pitch. The 'mummy mountain' in Persia was famous for the black, bituminous substance that oozed from it and was said to have medicinal properties. The blackened appearance of many preserved bodies from ancient Egypt led early scholars to assume that the corpses had been soaked in bitumen. Hence the word *mumia* was applied to them, and it was presumed that, like the Persian substance, they could be used effectively in medicines.

More recently, Egyptologists have assumed that the corpses had been coated with resins that eventually turned black, and that the Persians had later confused this blackness with bitumen. The few papyri concerning the rituals of Egyptian mum-mification do not mention bitumen as an ingredient. Diodorus of Sicily (a contemporary of Caesar) does note that bitumen was ex-ported from the Dead Sea to Egypt for mum-mification.

In the late 1980s, two French geo-chemists, Jacques Connan and Daniel Dessort, analysed parts of an Egyptian mummy in Lyon's Musée Guimet. They discovered definite traces of bitumen, whose character-istics pointed to the Dead Sea as its source. Together with similar results by German and Israeli scientists this showed the use of bitumen in mummies dating from Ptolemaic and Roman times—about 400 BC to AD 300. Connan and Dessort have now identified

bitumen in another dozen mummies dating from the reign of Rameses II (*c.* 1200 BC) to the Roman period, thus pushing the practice far back in time. They have used petroleum geochemistry techniques to identify steranes and terpanes—geochemical fossils—in hydrocarbon fractions of the balms. These prove that bitumen was an important ingredient in the embalming process. Other substances detected include conifer resin and beeswax.

The geochemists have pinpointed two principal sources. The first, already noted in their earlier study, is the Dead Sea, where asphalts occur in floating blocks. The second is the region of Hit-Abu Jir in Iraq, where asphalt used to be exported to Babylon for use as mortar in brick walls.

The quantity of steranes and terpanes in the natural asphalts and the balms suggests that the embalmers used between 3% and 81% of bitumen in their mixture, but mostly from 10% to 30%. This underlines the fact that the 'recipes' used in mummification varied: beeswax is also sometimes abundant and sometimes totally absent.

Why was bitumen so important to the Egyptians, and why did they import it from so far away? The answer may be simply its supposed medicinal, antiseptic, and preserv-ative properties. But the use of bitumen on corpses may also have been linked to a belief in rebirth, which was symbolized by the colour black in ancient Egypt.

In any case, the puzzle of Egypt's 'black mummies' seems to have been solved, and Connan and Dessort are now turning their attention to the question of whether bitumen was also used on the very earliest mummies, those dating from 2600 BC to 1300 BC.

---

of underwater survey including the proton magnetometer, towed behind a survey vessel to detect iron and steel objects that distort the earth's magnetic field; side-scan sonar, that transmits sound waves in a fan-shaped beam to produce a graphic image of subsurface features on the sea-bed; and a sub-bottom profiler that emits sound pulses that bounce back from fea-tures and objects buried under the sea-floor.

X-ray diffraction analysis a physical technique used to identify the mineralogy of material such as ceramics, stone, sediments and weathering products on metals. The sample is ground to powder, and exposed to X-rays

at various angles; the diffraction patterns pro-duced are compared with reference standards for identification.

X-ray fluorescence spectrometry (XRF) a physi-cal technique used to determine the major and trace elements in the chemical composition of materials such as ceramics, obsidian and glass that may help in identifying the material source. The sample is bombarded with X-rays, and the wavelengths of the released energy, or fluorescent X-rays, are detected and measured. Different elements have unique wavelengths, while their concentrations can be estimated from the intensity of the released X-rays.

SPACE EXPLORATION

Ames Research Center NASA installation at Mountain View, California, for research into aeronautics and life sciences. Ames has managed the Pioneer series of planetary probes and is involved in the search for extraterrestrial life.

Apollo project US space project to land a person on the Moon, achieved 20 July 1969, when Neil Armstrong was the first to set foot there. He was accompanied on the Moon's surface by Col Edwin E Aldrin Jr; Michael Collins remained in the orbiting command module.

Apollo-Soyuz test project joint US-Soviet space mission in which an Apollo and a Soyuz craft docked while in orbit around the Earth on 17 July 1975. The craft remained attached for two days and crew members were able to move from one craft to the other through an airlock attached to the nose of the Apollo. The mission was designed to test rescue procedures as well as having political significance.

Ariane series of launch vehicles built by the European Space Agency (first flight 1979). The launch site is at Kourou in French Guiana. Ariane is a three-stage rocket using liquid fuels. Small solid-fuel and liquid-fuel boosters can be attached to its first stage to increase carrying power.

Ariel series of six UK satellites launched by the US 1962–79, the most significant of which was Ariel 5, 1974, which made a pioneering survey of the sky at X-ray wavelengths.

astronaut person making flights into space; the term *cosmonaut* is used for any astronaut from the former Soviet Union.

astronautics the science of space travel.

astronomy the science of the celestial bodies: the Sun, the Moon, and the planets; the stars and galaxies; and all other objects in the universe. It is concerned with their positions, motions, distances, and physical conditions, and with their origins and evolution. Astronomy thus divides into fields such as astrophysics, celestial mechanics, and cosmology.

Baikonur main launch site for spacecraft located at Tyuratam, Kazakhstan.

Cape Canaveral promontory on the Atlantic coast of Florida, USA, 367 km/228 mi N of Miami, used as a rocket launch site by NASA.

Cassini a joint space probe of NASA and the European Space Agency to the planet Saturn. Cassini is scheduled to be launched in Nov 1996 and will go into orbit around Saturn in Sept 2004, dropping off a sub-probe, Huygens, to land on Saturn's largest moon, Titan.

communications satellite a relay station in space for sending telephone, television, telex, and other messages around the world. Messages are sent to and from the satellites via ground stations. Most communications satellites are in geostationary orbit, appearing to hang fixed over one point on the Earth's surface.

Cosmos name used from the 1960s for nearly all Soviet artificial satellites. Over 2,100 Cosmos satellites had been launched by Jan 1991.

Delta rocket a US rocket used to launch many scientific and communications satellites since 1960, based on the Thor ballistic missile. Several increasingly powerful versions were produced as satellites became larger and heavier. Solid-fuel boosters were attached to the first stage to increase lifting power.

Edwards Air Force Base military USAF centre in California, situated on a dry lake bed, often used as a landing site by the Space Shuttle.

Energia the most powerful Soviet space rocket, first launched 15 May 1987. Used to launch the Soviet Space Shuttle, the Energia booster has the capacity, with the use of strap-on boosters, of launching payloads of up to 190 tonnes/195 tons into Earth orbit.

European Space Agency (ESA) an organization of European countries (Austria, Belgium, Denmark, France, Germany, Ireland, Italy, the Netherlands, Norway, Spain, Sweden, Switzerland, and the UK) that engages in space research and technology. It was founded 1975, with headquarters in Paris.

Explorer a series of US scientific satellites. *Explorer 1*, launched Jan 1958, was the first US satellite in orbit and discovered the Van Allen radiation belts around the Earth.

Galileo spacecraft launched from the space shuttle *Atlantis* Oct 1989, on a six-year journey to Jupiter. It flew past Venus (Feb 1990) and the Earth (Dec 1990), and is scheduled to pass the Earth again Dec 1992, using the gravitational fields of these planets to accelerate it towards its final destination.

Gemini project US space programme (1965–66) in which astronauts practised rendezvous and docking of spacecraft, and working outside their spacecraft, in preparation for the Apollo Moon landings.

geostationary orbit the circular path 35,900 km/ 22,300 mi above the Earth's equator on which a satellite takes 24 hours, moving from west to east, to complete an orbit, thus appearing to hang stationary over one place on the Earth's surface. Geostationary orbits are particularly used for communications satellites and weather satellites. They were first thought of by the author Arthur C Clarke. A *geosynchronous orbit* lies at the same distance from Earth but is inclined to the equator.

Giotto space probe built by the European Space Agency to study Halley's comet. Launched by an Ariane rocket in July 1985, *Giotto* passed within 600 km/375 mi of the comet's nucleus on 13 March 1986. On 2 July 1990 it flew 23,000 km/14,000 mi from Earth, which diverted its path to encounter another comet, Grigg-Skjellerup, on 10 July 1992.

Goddard Space Flight Center NASA installation at Greenbelt, Maryland, responsible for the operation of NASA's unmanned scientific satellites, including the Hubble Space Telescope. It is also home of the National Space Science Data centre, a repository of data collected by

---

ASTRONOMY: CHRONOLOGY

2300 BC	Chinese astronomers made their earliest observations.
2000	Babylonian priests made their first observational records.
1900	Stonehenge was constructed: first phase.
365	The Chinese observed the satellites of Jupiter with the naked eye.
3rd cent. BC	Aristarchus argued that the Sun is the centre of the solar system.
2nd cent. AD	Ptolemy's complicated Earth-centred system was promulgated, which dominated the astronomy of the Middle Ages.
1543	Copernicus revived the ideas of Aristarchus in *De Revolutionibus*.
1608	Lippershey invented the telescope, which was first used by Galileo 1609.
1609	Kepler's first two laws of planetary motion published (the third appeared 1619).
1632	The world's first official observatory was established in Leiden, the Netherlands.
1633	Galileo's theories were condemned by the Inquisition.
1675	The Royal Greenwich Observatory was founded in England.
1687	Newton's *Principia* was published, including his 'law of universal gravitation'.
1718	Halley predicted the return of the comet named after him, observed 1758.
1781	Herschel discovered Uranus and recognized stellar systems beyond our Galaxy.
1796	Laplace elaborated his theory of the origin of the solar system.
1801	Piazzi discovered the first asteroid, Ceres.
1814	Fraunhofer first studied absorption lines in the solar spectrum.
1846	Neptune was identified by Galle, following predictions by Adams and Leverrier.
1887	The earliest photographic star charts were produced.
1889	E E Barnard took the first photographs of the Milky Way.
1908	Fragment of comet fell at Tunguska, Siberia.
1920	Eddington began the study of interstellar matter.
1923	Hubble proved that the galaxies are systems independent of the Milky Way, and by 1930 had confirmed the concept of an expanding universe.
1930	The planet Pluto was discovered by Clyde Tombaugh at the Lowell Observatory, Arizona, USA.
1931	Jansky founded radioastronomy.
1945	Radar contact with the Moon was established by Z Bay of Hungary and the US Army Signal Corps Laboratory.
1948	The 5-m Hale reflector telescope was installed at Mount Palomar, California, USA.
1955	The Jodrell Bank telescope dish in England was completed.
1957	The first Sputnik satellite (USSR) opened the age of space observation.
1962	The first X-ray source was discovered in Scorpius.
1963	The first quasar was discovered.
1967	The first pulsar was discovered by Jocelyn Bell and Antony Hewish.
1969	The first crewed Moon landing was made by US astronauts.
1976	A 6-m reflector telescope was installed at Mount Semirodniki (USSR).
1977	Uranus was discovered to have rings.
1977	The spacecraft *Voyager 1* and *2* were launched, passing Jupiter and Saturn 1979–81.
1978	The spacecraft *Pioneer Venus 1* and *2* reached Venus.
1978	A satellite of Pluto, Charon, was discovered by James Christy of the US Naval Observatory.
1986	Halley's comet returned. *Voyager 2* flew by Uranus.
1987	Bright supernova visible to the naked eye for the first time since 1604.
1989	*Voyager 2* flew by Neptune.
1991	The space probe *Galileo* flew past the asteroid Gaspra.
1992	COBE satellite detects ripples from the Big Bang that mark the first stage in the formation of galaxies.

satellites.

Hipparcos acronym for the **high precision parallax collecting satellite** launched by the European Space Agency in Aug 1989. Named after the Greek astronomer Hipparchus, it is the world's first astrometry satellite, designed to provide precise positions and apparent motions of stars. The accuracy of these measurements from space is far greater than from ground-based telescopes.

Hubble Space Telescope (HST) telescope placed into orbit around the Earth, at an altitude of 610 km/380 mi, by the Space Shuttle *Dis-* covery in April 1990. It has a main mirror 2.4 m/94 in wide, which suffers from spherical aberration and so cannot be focused properly. Yet, because it is above the atmosphere, the HST outperforms ground-based telescopes. Computer techniques are being used to improve the images from the telescope until the arrival of a maintenance mission to install corrective optics.

Intelsat International Telecommunications Satellite Organization, established 1964 to operate a worldwide system of communications satellites. More than 100 countries are members of

Intelsat, with headquarters in Washington DC. Intelsat satellites are stationed in geostationary orbit (maintaining their positions relative to the Earth) over the Atlantic, Pacific, and Indian Oceans. The first Intelsat satellite was *Early Bird*, launched 1965.

IRAS the Infrared Astronomy Satellite, a joint US/UK/Dutch satellite, launched 1983, surveyed the sky at infrared wavelengths, studying areas of star formation, distant galaxies, possible embryo planetary systems around other stars, and discovering five new comets in our own solar system.

Jet Propulsion Laboratory NASA installation at Pasadena, California, operated by the California Institute of Technology. It is the command centre for NASA's deep space probes such as the Voyager, Magellan, and Galileo missions, with which it communicates via the Deep Space Network of radio telescopes at Goldstone, California; Madrid, Spain; and Canberra, Australia.

Johnson Space Center NASA installation at Houston, Texas, home of mission control for manned space missions. It is the main centre for the selection and training of astronauts.

Kennedy Space Center the NASA launch site on Merritt Island, near Cape Canaveral, Florida, used for Apollo and space-shuttle launches.

Kourou second-largest town of French Guiana, NW of Cayenne, site of the Guiana Space Centre of the European Space Agency. Situated near the equator, it is an ideal site for launches of satellites into geostationary orbit.

Landsat a series of satellites used for monitoring Earth resources. The first was launched 1972.

Magellan a NASA space probe to Venus, launched in May 1989, went into orbit around Venus in Aug 1990 to make a detailed map of the planet by radar. It revealed volcanoes, meteorite craters, and fold mountains on the planet's surface.

Mariner spacecraft series of US space probes that explored the planets Mercury, Venus, and Mars 1962–75.

Marshall Space Flight Center NASA installation at Huntsville, Alabama, where the Saturn series of rockets and the Space Shuttle engines were developed. It also manages various payloads for the Space Shuttle, including the Spacelab space station.

Mir Soviet space station, the core of which was launched 20 Feb 1986. *Mir* is intended to be a permanently occupied space station.

Moon probe crewless spacecraft used to investigate the Moon. Early probes flew past the Moon or crash-landed on it, but later ones achieved soft landings or went into orbit. Soviet probes included the Luna series. US probes (Ranger, Surveyor, Lunar Orbiter) prepared the way for the Apollo crewed flights.

NASA National Aeronautics and Space Administration, the US government agency, founded 1958, for spaceflight and aeronautical research. Its headquarters are in Washington DC and its main installation is at the Kennedy Space Center.

Pioneer probes a series of US solar-system space probes 1958–78. The probes *Pioneer 4–9* went into solar orbit to monitor the Sun's activity during the 1960s and early 1970s. *Pioneer 5*, launched 1960, was the first of a series to study the solar wind between the planets. *Pioneer 10*, launched Mar 1972, was the first probe to reach Jupiter (Dec 1973) and to leave the solar system 1983. *Pioneer 11*, launched April 1973, passed Jupiter Dec 1974, and was the first probe to reach Saturn (Sept 1979), before also leaving the solar system. *Pioneer 10* and *11* carry plaques containing messages from Earth in case they are found by other civilizations among the stars. Pioneer Venus probes were launched May and Aug 1978. One orbited Venus, and the other dropped three probes onto the surface. In early 1990 *Pioneer 10* was 7.1 billion km from the Sun.

Plesetsk rocket-launching site 170 km/105 mi S of Archangel, Russia. From here the former USSR launched artificial satellites from 1966, mostly military.

Proton rocket Soviet space rocket introduced 1965, used to launch heavy satellites, space probes, and the *Salyut* and *Mir* space stations.

Redstone rocket short-range US military missile, modified for use as a space launcher. Redstone rockets launched the first two Mercury flights. A modified Redstone, *Juno 1*, launched the first US satellite, *Explorer 1*, in 1958.

rocket projectile driven by the reaction of gases produced by a fast-burning fuel. Unlike jet engines, which are also reaction engines, modern rockets carry their own oxygen supply to burn their fuel and are totally independent of any surrounding atmosphere. As rockets are the only form of propulsion available that can function in a vacuum, they are essential to exploration in outer space. Multistage rockets have to be used, consisting of a number of rockets joined together.

ROSAT joint US/German/UK satellite launched 1990 to study cosmic sources of X-rays and extremely short ultraviolet wavelengths, named after Wilhelm Röntgen, the discoverer of X-rays.

Salyut series of seven space stations launched by the USSR 1971–82. *Salyut* was cylindrical in shape, 15 m/50 ft long, and weighed 19 tonnes. It housed two or three cosmonauts at a time, for missions lasting up to eight months.

satellite any small body that orbits a larger one, either natural or artificial. Natural satellites that orbit planets are called moons. The first *artificial satellite*, Sputnik 1, was launched into orbit around the Earth by the USSR 1957. Artificial satellites are used for scientific purposes, communications, weather forecasting, and military applications. The largest artificial satellites can be seen by the naked eye.

Saturn rocket family of large US rockets, developed by Wernher von Braun for the Apollo project. The two-stage Saturn IB was used for launching Apollo spacecraft into orbit around the Earth. The three-stage Saturn V sent Apollo spacecraft to the Moon, and launched the

COSMOLOGY: HAVE WE SEEN THE CREATION?

Lumpiness is the overriding characteristic of the universe. Most of its visible material is collected into stars, separated by several light years. The stars in turn are collected in vast aggregations called galaxies, millions of light years apart. On the grandest scale, even the galaxies are clustered.

In April 1992, US astronomers announced that they had detected the first steps in the formation of the overall structure of the universe, from the results of a satellite called COBE, the Cosmic Background Explorer. It was hailed variously as the discovery of the century and, more realistically, the discovery of the decade. But it also pointed out the unsettling fact that the visible stars and galaxies account for only a small fraction of all the matter in the universe.

'We have found the primordial, the oldest things you can imagine coming from the universe,' said an ecstatic Dr George Smoot of the University of California, Berkeley, leader of the team that made the discovery. 'This begins the golden age of cosmology. It is going to change our view of the universe and our place within it.' Dr Michael Turner of the University of Chicago said: 'These astronomers have found the Holy Grail of cosmology.'

All modern cosmology starts from the basic fact, discovered in 1929 by Edwin Hubble at Mount Wilson Observatory in California, that the universe is expanding like a balloon. The inevitable conclusion, arrived at by imagining the expansion run in reverse, is that the universe must once have been compressed into a super-dense blob that exploded for some reason. That explosion is known as the Big Bang and, from the current rate of expansion of the universe, it is estimated to have occurred about 15 billion years ago. Direct evidence for the Big Bang turned up in 1965 when two workers at the Bell Telephone Laboratories in New Jersey, Arno Penzias and Robert Wilson, detected a faint hiss from the universe at short radio wavelengths. This is known as the cosmic background radiation, and is interpreted as being the heat from the Big Bang explosion that has been cooled by the subsequent expansion of the universe. Penzias and Wilson won a Nobel prize for this discovery.

But there was a problem. The background radiation was too smooth to account for the lumpiness of the currently observed universe. Slight differences in temperature would be expected from denser areas of gas where the galaxies formed but, try as they might, astronomers could not find them. The Big Bang theory looked as though it might be in trouble.

COBE, launched by the US space agency NASA in Nov 1989, has changed all that. It has measured the temperature of the background radiation with new precision, 2.735°C above absolute zero. And, as Dr Smoot announced at the American Physical Society meeting in Washington DC on 23 April 1992, it has detected the sought-after temperature variations, which appear like ripples on the background radiation. They amount to a mere 30 millionths of a degree, and it is a tribute to the precision of COBE that they could be detected at all.

The findings are in line with the predictions made by a modern version of the Big Bang, called the inflationary theory. According to this, the universe expanded very rapidly during the first fraction of a second of its existence, before settling down to the more leisurely rate of expansion observed today.

There is a catch, though. The density fluctuations detected by COBE would not, on their own, be enough to explain the formation of the galaxies. There must also be vast amounts of unseen dark matter in the universe to supply additional gravitational attraction.

'We need such invisible matter to explain how galaxies formed in the early universe and gathered themselves together into huge clusters. Ordinary matter would be attracted into regions of concentrated dark matter, and the universe as we know it today could develop, eventually leading to the formation of galaxies, stars, and planets,' said Dr Edward Wright of the University of California, Los Angeles.

If the astronomers are right, over 90% of the universe consists of unseen matter. At present, no one knows what this dark matter is, or how to detect it. The most popular view is that it consists of unknown atomic particles which have been given fanciful names such as axions, gravitinos, and photinos.

Other possibilities are immense black holes, or countless numbers of small, faint stars. Astronomers are hoping to get more clues to the nature of the dark matter from COBE.

Skylab space station. The liftoff thrust of a Saturn V was 3,500 tonnes. After Apollo and Skylab, the Saturn rockets were retired in favour of the Space Shuttle.

Skylab US space station, launched 14 May 1973, made from the adapted upper stage of a Saturn V rocket. At 75 tonnes, it was the heaviest object ever put into space, and was 25.6 m/84 ft long. Skylab contained a workshop for carrying out experiments in weightlessness, an observatory for monitoring the Sun, and cameras for photographing the Earth's surface.

Soyuz continuing series of Soviet spacecraft, capable of carrying up to three cosmonauts.

Soyuz spacecraft consist of three parts: a rear section containing engines; the central crew compartment; and a forward compartment that gives additional room for working and living space. They are now used for ferrying crews up to space stations, though they were originally used for independent space flight.

Spacelab a small space station built by the European Space Agency, carried in the cargo bay of the Space Shuttle, in which it remains throughout each flight, returning to Earth with the Shuttle. Spacelab consists of a pressurized module in which astronauts can work, and a series of **pallets**, open to the vacuum of

CAN ASTRONOMERS SAVE THE WORLD?

Sixty-five million years ago, it is thought that a rock from space several kilometres wide crashed into the Earth, spraying so much dust into the atmosphere that it temporarily changed the climate, wiping out the dinosaurs and numerous other species alive at the time. Were such an event to happen today, it would be humans, alongside other animal species, that would become extinct.

The threat is real, say astronomers, for another collision could happen at any time. In 1991 a rock the size of a house whistled past the Earth at half the distance of the Moon—a hair's breadth in interplanetary terms and the nearest miss yet recorded. The Spacewatch telescope at the University of Arizona, set up to look for such near-Earth asteroids, is finding them at the rate of one or two a month. In all, there could be thousands of them up to a few kilometres in diameter,

packing the destructive power of a million Hiroshima bombs. Statistically, there is more chance of being killed by an asteroid than dying in an air crash, said a NASA panel that reported on the asteroid hazard in 1992.

Not surprisingly, the NASA report calls for more funding to build a network of new telescopes, dedicated to providing an early warning of hazardous asteroids. The NASA scientists think it would take 25 years to identify most of the dangerous asteroids that might be on a collision course with Earth.

Having detected a killer asteroid, they would have to decide what to do with it. One possibility considered by the NASA scientists is to use rockets to nudge it into another orbit clear of the Earth. Blowing it up would not be such a good idea, since that would create a shower of smaller objects that might be just as deadly.

space, on which equipment is mounted.

space probe any instrumented object sent beyond Earth to collect data from other parts of the solar system and from deep space. The first probe was the Soviet *Lunik 1*, which flew past the Moon 1959. The first successful planetary probe was the US *Mariner 2*, which flew past Venus 1962, using transfer orbit. The first space probe to leave the solar system was *Pioneer 10* 1983. Space probes include *Giotto*, the Moon probes, and the Mariner, Pioneer, Viking, and Voyager series. Japan launched its first space probe in Feb 1990.

space shuttle reusable crewed spacecraft. The first was launched 12 April 1981 by the USA. It was developed by NASA to reduce the cost of using space for commercial, scientific, and military purposes. After leaving its payload in space, the space-shuttle orbiter can be flown back to Earth to land on a runway, and is then available for reuse.

space sickness or **space adaptation syndrome** a feeling of nausea, sometimes accompanied by vomiting, experienced by about 40% of all astronauts during their first few days in space. It is akin to travel sickness, and is thought to be caused by confusion of the body's balancing mechanism, located in the inner ear, by weightlessness. The sensation passes after a few days as the body adapts.

space station any large structure designed for human occupation in space for extended periods of time. Space stations are used for carrying out astronomical observations and surveys of Earth, as well as for biological studies and the processing of materials in weightlessness. The first space station was *Salyut 1*, and the USA has launched *Skylab*. NASA plans to build a larger space station, to be called *Freedom*, in orbit during the 1990s, in cooperation with other countries, including the European Space Agency, which is building a module called *Columbus*, and Japan, also building a module.

space suit a protective suit worn by astronauts and cosmonauts in space. It provides an insulated, air-conditioned cocoon in which people can live and work for hours at a time while outside the spacecraft. Inside the suit is a cooling garment that keeps the body at a comfortable temperature even during vigorous work. The suit provides air to breathe, and removes exhaled carbon dioxide and moisture. The suit's outer layers insulate the occupant from the extremes of hot and cold in space (−150°C/−240°F in the shade to +180°C/350°F in sunlight), and from the impact of small meteorites. Some space suits have a jet-propelled backpack, which the wearer can use to move about.

Sputnik a series of ten Soviet Earth-orbiting satellites. *Sputnik 1* was the first artificial satellite, launched 4 Oct 1957. It weighed 84 kg/185 lb, with a 58 cm/23 in diameter, and carried only a simple radio transmitter which allowed scientists to track it as it orbited Earth. It burned up in the atmosphere 92 days later. Sputniks were superseded in the early 1960s by the Cosmos series.

Telstar US communications satellite, launched 10 July 1962, which relayed the first live television transmissions between the USA and Europe. *Telstar* orbited the Earth in 158 minutes, and so had to be tracked by ground stations, unlike the geostationary satellites of today.

Titan rocket family of US space rockets, developed from the Titan intercontinental missile. Two-stage Titan rockets launched the Gemini crewed missions. More powerful Titans, with additional stages and strap-on boosters, were used to launch spy satellites and space probes, including Viking and Voyager.

Tyuratam site of the Baikonur Cosmodrome, Kazakhstan.

Ulysses joint NASA/ESA probe to study the Sun's poles, launched 1990 by the Space Shuttle *Discovery*. In Feb 1992 Jupiter's gravity swung it

SPACE DIARY—MAIN LAUNCHES MAY 1991–MAY 1992

Launch date	Flight	Remarks
1991		
5 June	STS 40	Space Shuttle *Columbia* carried Life Sciences Laboratory. *Crew*: Bryan O'Connor, Sidney Gutierrez, James Bagian, Tamara Jernigan, Rhea Seddon, Drew Gaffney, Millie Hughes-Fulford. Landed Edwards Air Force Base 14 June
2 August	STS 43	Space Shuttle *Atlantis* launched TDRS-E communications satellite. *Crew*: John Blaha, Michael Baker, Shannon Lucid, David Low, James Adamson. Landed Kennedy Space Center 11 August
13 September	Soyuz TM-13	Space Shuttle *Discovery* launched Upper Atmosphere Research Satellite to monitor ozone levels. *Crew:* John Creighton, Kenneth Reightler, James Buchli, Mark Brown, Sam Gemar. Landed Edwards Air Force Base 18 September
2 October	Soyuz TM-13	Franz Viehböck of Austria launched with Aleksander Volkov and Toktar Aubakirov to *Mir* space station. Franz Viehböck returned in *Soyuz TM-12* on 10 October with Anatoli Artsebarsky and Aubakirov. Volkov remained aboard with Sergei Krikalev
24 November	STS 44	Space Shuttle *Atlantis* launched Defense Support Program early warning satellite. *Crew*: Fred Gregory, Tom Henricks, James Voss, Story Musgrave, Mario Runco, Tom Hennen. Landed Edwards Air Force Base 1 December
1992		
22 January	STS 42	Space Shuttle *Discovery* carried International Microgravity Laboratory 1. *Crew*: Ronald Grabe, Stephen Oswald, Norman Thagard, William Readdy, David Hilmers, Roberta Bondar (Canada), Ulf Merbold (ESA). Landed Edwards Air Force Base 30 January
17 March	Soyuz TM-14	Klaus-Dietrich Flade of Germany launched with Aleksandr Viktorenko and Aleksandr Kaleri to Mir space station. Flade landed March 25 in *Soyuz TM-13* with Aleksandr Volkov and Sergei Krikalev
24 March	STS 45	Space Shuttle *Atlantis* carried Atmospheric Laboratory. *Crew*: Charles Bolden, Brian Duffy, Kathryn Sullivan, David Leestma, Michael Foale, Dirk Frimout (Belgium), Byron Lichtenberg. Landed Kennedy Space Center 2 April
7 May	STS 49	Maiden flight of Space Shuttle *Endeavor*. Rescue of Intelsat VI satellite and practice of space station assembly techniques. *Crew*: Daniel Brandenstein, Kevin Chilton, Bruce Melnick, Pierre Thuot, Richard Hieb, Kathryn Thornton, Thomas Akers. Landed Edwards Air Force Base May 16. Brandenstein now has the record flight time aboard the Space Shuttle: 789 hours on four flights

onto a path that loops it first under the Sun's south pole and then over the north pole to study the Sun and solar wind at latitudes not observable from the Earth.

Vanguard an early series of US Earth-orbiting satellites and their associated rocket launcher. *Vanguard 1* was the second US satellite, launched 17 March 1958 by the three-stage Vanguard rocket. Tracking of its orbit revealed that Earth is slightly pear-shaped. The series ended Sept 1959 with *Vanguard 3*.

Viking probes two US space probes to Mars, each one consisting of an orbiter and a lander. They were launched 20 Aug and 9 Sept 1975. They transmitted colour pictures, and analysed the soil. No definite signs of life were found.

Voskhod Soviet spacecraft used in the mid-1960s; it was modified from the single-seat Vostok, and was the first spacecraft capable of carrying two or three cosmonauts. During *Voskhod 2*'s flight 1965, Alexei Leonov made the first space walk.

Vostok the first Soviet spacecraft, used 1961–63. Vostok was a metal sphere 2.3 m/7.5 ft in diameter, capable of carrying one cosmonaut. It made flights lasting up to five days. *Vostok 1* carried the first person into space, Yuri Gagarin.

Voyager probes two US space probes, originally Mariners. *Voyager 1*, launched 5 Sept 1977, passed Jupiter March 1979, and reached Saturn Nov 1980. *Voyager 2* was launched earlier, 20 Aug 1977, on a slower trajectory that took it past Jupiter July 1979, Saturn Aug 1981, Uranus Jan 1986, and Neptune Aug 1989. Like the Pioneer probes, the Voyagers are on their way out of the solar system. Their tasks now include helping scientists to locate the position of the heliopause, the boundary at which the influence of the Sun gives way to the forces exerted by other stars. Both *Voyagers* carry specially coded long-playing records called 'Sounds of Earth' for the enlightenment of any other civilizations that might

SHUTTLE ASTRONAUTS GRAB GLORY

The US space agency NASA had billed STS-49, the 47th space-shuttle mission, as the most dramatic for years, but even they could not have foreseen just how extraordinary it would become.

It was the first flight of *Endeavor*, a new shuttle built at a cost of $2 billion to replace *Challenger*, which had exploded in Jan 1986, killing its crew. The main aim of STS-49 was to salvage a satellite called *Intelsat VI*, stranded in the wrong orbit for two years because of a launch-rocket failure. A subsidiary goal was to give the crew experience of working in space. In the event, they got more experience than they expected.

The flight began straightforwardly, with a launch on 7 May and a rendezvous three days later with *Intelsat*. Astronaut Pierre Thuot was manoeuvred on the end of the shuttle's robot arm towards the satellite. Thuot was supposed to attach a bar to the underside of *Intelsat* so it could be pulled into the cargo bay, where he and Rick Hieb would attach a new rocket motor to it. But the capture bar would not clamp on properly. They tried again the next day, still without success.

After discussions with ground controllers, it was decided to try a new approach—the first ever three-person space walk. A trio of astronauts would try to grab *Intelsat* by hand. In one of the trickiest shuttle manoeuvres yet attempted, Commander Dan Brandenstein nudged *Endeavor* to within arm's length of the slowly spinning satellite, with Thuot on the end of the robot arm, Hieb standing on the edge of the cargo bay, and Thomas Akers in the cargo bay. With the satellite surrounded, the astronauts were able to hold it firmly while they attached the capture bar. The rest of the rescue plan went smoothly. After a record-breaking space walk lasting 8 hours 29 minutes, longer even than the Apollo walks on the Moon, the three exhausted men returned to *Endeavor*. *Intelsat* was then released from the cargo bay and its newly attached rocket was fired to put it into the correct orbit, from where it would relay telephone calls and pictures of the Barcelona Olympic Games across the Atlantic. The satellite's owners, a consortium of more than 120 nations, had paid NASA $93 million for the rescue.

Because of the delays, controllers extended the mission for an extra day to complete one more space walk, this time involving Kathryn Thornton, only the third woman to walk in space. She and Akers practised techniques for building the *Freedom* space station. The walk lasted 7 hours 45 minutes, the second longest in history. NASA administrator Daniel Goldin commented that the risky mission had 'brought the magic back into the space programme'.

---

find them.

weightlessness condition in which there is no gravitational force acting on a body, either because gravitational force is cancelled out by equal and opposite acceleration, or because the body is so far outside a planet's gravitational field that no force is exerted upon it.

THE SOLAR SYSTEM

Apollo asteroid member of a group of asteroids whose orbits cross that of the Earth. They are named after the first of their kind, Apollo, discovered 1932 and then lost until 1973. Apollo asteroids are so small and faint that they are difficult to see except when close to Earth (Apollo is about 2 km/1.2 mi across).

asteroid or *minor planet* any of many thousands of small bodies, composed of rock and iron, that orbit the Sun. Most lie in a belt between the orbits of Mars and Jupiter, and are thought to be fragments left over from the formation of the solar system. About 100,000 may exist, but their total mass is only a few hundredths the mass of the Moon.

aurora coloured light in the night sky near the Earth's magnetic poles, called *aurora borealis*, 'northern lights', in the northern hemisphere and *aurora australis* in the southern hemisphere. An aurora is usually in the form of a luminous arch followed by folded bands and rays, usually green but often showing shades of blue and red, and sometimes yellow or white. Auroras are caused at heights of over 100 km/60 mi by a fast stream of charged particles from solar flares and low-density 'holes' in the Sun's corona. These are guided by the Earth's magnetic field towards the north and south magnetic poles, where they enter the upper atmosphere and bombard the gases in the atmosphere, causing them to emit visible light.

Baily's beads bright spots of sunlight seen around the edge of the Moon for a few seconds immediately before and after a total eclipse of the Sun, caused by sunlight shining between mountains at the Moon's edge. Sometimes one bead is much brighter than the others, producing the so-called *diamond ring* effect. The effect was described 1836 by the English astronomer Francis Baily (1774-1844).

Callisto second largest moon of Jupiter, 4,800 km/3,000 mi in diameter, orbiting every 16.7 days at a distance of 1.9 million km/1.2 million mi from the planet. Its surface is covered with large craters.

Ceres the largest asteroid, 940 km/584 mi in diameter, and the first to be discovered (by Giuseppe Piazzi 1801). Ceres is a rock that orbits the Sun every 4.6 years at an average distance of 414 million km/257 million mi. Its mass is about one-seventieth (0.014) of that of the Moon.

Chiron unusual solar-system object orbiting between Saturn and Uranus, discovered 1977 by US astronomer Charles T Kowal (1940–). Initially classified as an asteroid, it is now believed to be a giant cometary nucleus about 200 km/120 mi across, composed of ice with a dark crust of carbon dust.

chromosphere a layer of mostly hydrogen gas about 10,000 km/6,000 mi deep above the visible surface of the Sun (the photosphere). It appears pinkish-red during eclipses of the Sun.

comet small, icy body orbiting the Sun, usually on a highly elliptical path. A comet consists of a central nucleus a few kilometres across, often likened to a dirty snowball because it consists mostly of ice mixed with dust. As the comet approaches the Sun the nucleus heats up, releasing gas and dust which form a tenuous coma, up to 100,000 km/60,000 mi wide, around the nucleus. Gas and dust stream away from the coma to form one or more tails, which may extend for millions of kilometres.

corona a faint halo of hot (about 2,000,000°C/3,600,000°F) and tenuous gas around the Sun, which boils from the surface. It is visible at solar eclipses or through a **coronagraph**, an instrument that blocks light from the Sun's brilliant disc. Gas flows away from the corona to form the solar wind.

crater a hollow in the ground caused by the impact of a meteorite, asteroid or comet. The Moon and inner planets, as well as many of the moons of the outer planets, are heavily cratered by impacts. Over 100 features on Earth up to 140 km/87 mi in diameter are believed to be the results of meteorite impact, although some are so eroded that they no longer look like craters. The most famous meteorite crater on Earth is the Barringer crater in Arizona, 1.2 km/0.75 mi in diameter, formed in prehistoric times by an iron meteorite weighing perhaps 100,000 tons.

crescent the curved shape of the Moon when it appears less than half-illuminated.

Deimos one of the two moons of Mars. It is irregularly shaped, 15 × 12 × 11 km/9 × 7.5 × 7 mi orbits at a height of 24,000 km/15,000 mi every 1.26 days, and is not as heavily cratered as the other moon, Phobos. Deimos was discovered 1877 by US astronomer Asaph Hall (1829–1907), and is thought to be an asteroid captured by Mars' gravity.

Earth the third planet from the Sun. It is almost spherical, flattened slightly at the poles, and is composed of three concentric layers: the core, the mantle, and the crust. 70% of the surface (including the north and south polar icecaps) is covered with water. The Earth is surrounded by a life-supporting atmosphere and is the only planet on which life is known to exist.
mean distance from the Sun 149,500,000 km/92,860,000 mi
equatorial diameter 12,756 km/7,923 mi
circumference 40,070 km/24,900 mi
rotation period 23 hr 56 min 4.1 sec
year (complete orbit, or sidereal period) 365 days 5 hr 48 min 46 sec. Earth's average speed around the Sun is 30 kps/18.5 mps; the plane of its orbit is inclined to its equatorial plane at an angle of 23.5°, the reason for the changing seasons
atmosphere nitrogen 78.09%; oxygen 20.95%; argon 0.93%; carbon dioxide 0.03%; and less than 0.0001% neon, helium, krypton, hydrogen, xenon, ozone, radon
surface land surface 150,000,000 sq km/57,500,000 sq mi (greatest height above sea level 8,872 m/29,118 ft Mount Everest); water surface 361,000,000 sq km/139,400,000 sq mi (greatest depth 11,034 m/36,201 ft Mariana Trench in the Pacific). The interior is thought to be an inner core about 2,600 km/1,600 mi in diameter, of solid iron and nickel; an outer core about 2,250 km/1,400 mi thick, of molten iron and nickel; and a mantle of mostly solid rock about 2,900 km/1,800 mi thick, separated by the Mohorovičić discontinuity from the Earth's crust. The crust and the topmost layer of the mantle form about 12 major moving plates, some of which carry the continents. The plates are in constant, slow motion, called tectonic drift
satellite the Moon
age 4.6 billion years. The Earth was formed with the rest of the Solar System by consolidation of interstellar dust. Life began about 3.5 billion years ago.

eclipse the passage of an astronomical body through the shadow of another. The term is usually used for solar and lunar eclipses, which may be either partial or total, but also, for example, for eclipses by Jupiter of its satellites. An eclipse of a star by a body in the solar system is called an occultation.

Encke's comet the comet with the shortest known orbital period, 3.3 years. It is named after German mathematician and astronomer Johann Franz Encke (1791–1865) who in 1819 calculated the orbit from earlier sightings.

Eros an asteroid, discovered 1898, that can pass 22 million km/14 million mi from the Earth, as in 1975. Eros was the first asteroid to be discovered that has an orbit coming within that of Mars. It is elongated, measures about 36 × 12 km/22 × 7 mi, rotates around its shortest axis every 5.3 hours, and orbits the Sun every 1.8 years.

Europa the fourth largest moon of the planet Jupiter, diameter 3,140 km/1,950 mi, orbiting 671,000 km/417,000 mi from the planet every 3.55 days. It is covered by ice and crisscrossed by thousands of thin cracks, each some 50,000 km/30,000 mi long.

flare, solar a brilliant eruption on the Sun above a sunspot, thought to be caused by release of magnetic energy. Flares reach maximum brightness within a few minutes, then fade away over about an hour. They eject a burst of atomic particles into space at up to 1,000 kps/600 mps. When these particles reach Earth they can cause radio blackouts, disruptions of the Earth's magnetic field, and auroras.

Ganymede the largest moon of the planet Jupiter, and the largest moon in the solar system, 5,260 km/3,270 mi in diameter (larger than

ECLIPSES 1993

Date	Type of eclipse	Time of maximum eclipse (UT)	Main area of visibility
21 May	Sun partial	14h 20m	Northern North America, Greenland, Northern Europe
4 June	Moon total	13h 00m	Pacific Ocean, Australasia
13 November	Sun partial	21h 46m	Antarctica
29 November	Moon total	06h 26m	North and South America, Europe, west Africa

the planet Mercury). It orbits Jupiter every 7.2 days at a distance of 1.1 million km/ 700,000 mi. Its surface is a mixture of cratered and grooved terrain.

Halley's comet a comet that orbits the Sun about every 76 years, named after Edmond Halley, who calculated its orbit. It is the brightest and most conspicuous of the periodic comets. Recorded sightings go back over 2,000 years. It travels around the Sun in the opposite direction to the planets. Its orbit is inclined at almost 20° to the main plane of the solar system and ranges between the orbits of Venus and Neptune. It will next reappear 2061.

heliosphere region of space through which the solar wind flows outwards from the Sun. The *heliopause* is the boundary of this region, believed to lie about 100 astronomical units from the Sun, where the flow of the solar wind merges with the interstellar gas.

Icarus an Apollo asteroid 1.5 km/1 mi in diameter, discovered 1949. It orbits the Sun every 409 days at a distance of 28 million–186 million km/28 million–300 million mi (0.19–2.0 astronomical units). It was the first asteroid known to approach the Sun closer than does the planet Mercury. In 1968 it passed 6 million km/4 million mi from the Earth.

inferior planet a planet (Mercury or Venus) whose orbit lies within that of the Earth, best observed when at its greatest elongation from the Sun, either at eastern elongation in the evening (setting after the Sun) or at western elongation in the morning (rising before the Sun).

interplanetary matter gas and dust thinly spread through the solar system. The gas flows outwards from the Sun as the solar wind. Fine dust lies in the plane of the solar system, scattering sunlight to cause the zodiacal light. Swarms of dust shed by comets enter the Earth's atmosphere to cause meteor showers.

Io the third largest moon of the planet Jupiter, 3,630 km/2,260 mi in diameter, orbiting in 1.77 days at a distance of 422,000 km/ 262,000 mi. It is the most volcanically active body in the solar system, covered by hundreds of vents that erupt not lava but sulphur, giving Io an orange-coloured surface.

Jupiter the fifth planet from the Sun, and the largest in the solar system (equatorial diameter 142,800 km/88,700 mi), with a mass more than twice that of all the other planets combined, 318 times that of the Earth's. It takes 11.86 years to orbit the Sun, at an average distance of 778 million km/484 million mi, and has at least 16 moons. It is largely composed of hydrogen and helium, liquefied by pressure in its interior, and probably with a rocky core larger than the Earth. Its main feature is the Great Red Spot, a cloud of rising gases, revolving anticlockwise, 14,000 km/8,500 mi wide and some 30,000 km/20,000 mi long.

Lagrangian points the five locations in space where the centrifugal and gravitational forces of two bodies neutralize each other; a third, less massive body located at any one of these points will be held in equilibrium with respect to the other two. Three of the points, L1–L3, lie on a line joining the two large bodies. The other two points, L4 and L5, which are the most stable, lie on either side of this line. Their existence was predicted 1772 by Joseph Louis Lagrange.

magnetosphere the volume of space, surrounding a planet, controlled by the planet's magnetic field, and acting as a magnetic 'shell'. The Earth's extends 64,000 km/40,000 mi towards the Sun, but many times this distance on the side away from the Sun.

mare (plural *maria*) dark lowland plain on the Moon. The name comes from Latin 'sea', because these areas were once wrongly thought to be water.

Mars the fourth planet from the Sun, average distance 227.9 million km/141.6 million mi. It revolves around the Sun in 687 Earth days, and has a rotation period of 24 hr 37 min. It is much smaller than Venus or Earth, with diameter 6,780 km/4,210 mi, and mass 0.11 that of Earth. Mars is slightly pear-shaped, with a low, level northern hemisphere, which is comparatively uncratered and geologically 'young', and a heavily cratered 'ancient' southern hemisphere.

Mercury the closest planet to the Sun, at an average distance of 58 million km/36 million mi. Its diameter is 4,880 km/3,030 mi, its mass 0.056 that of Earth. Mercury orbits the Sun every 88 days, and spins on its axis every 59 days. On its sunward side the surface temperature reaches over 400°C/752°F, but on the 'night' side it falls to −170°C/−274°F. Mercury has an atmosphere with minute traces of argon and helium. In 1974 the US space probe *Mariner 10* discovered that its surface is cratered by meteorite impacts. Mercury has no moons.

meteor a flash of light in the sky, popularly known as a *shooting* or *falling star*, caused by a particle of dust, a *meteoroid*, entering the atmosphere at speeds up to 70 kps/45 mps and burning up by friction at a height of around 100 km/60 mi. On any clear night, several *sporadic* meteors can be seen each hour.

meteorite a piece of rock or metal from space that reaches the surface of the Earth, Moon, or other body. Most meteorites are thought to be fragments from asteroids, although some may be pieces from the heads of comets. Most are stony, although some are made of iron and a few have a mixed rock-iron composition. Meteorites provide evidence for the nature of the solar system and may be similar to the Earth's core and mantle, neither of which can be observed directly.

moon any natural satellite that orbits a planet. Mercury and Venus are the only planets in the solar system that do not have moons.

Moon the natural satellite of Earth, 3,476 km/ 2,160 mi in diameter, with a mass 0.012 (approximately one-eightieth) that of Earth. Its surface gravity is only 0.16 (one-sixth) that of Earth. Its average distance from Earth is 384,404 km/238,857 mi, and it orbits in a west-to-east direction every 27.32 days (the *sidereal month*). It spins on its axis with one side permanently turned towards Earth. The Moon has no atmosphere or water. Much of our information about the Moon is derived from photographs and measurements taken by US and Soviet Moon probes; from geological samples brought back by US Apollo astronauts and by Soviet Luna probes; and from experiments set up by the US astronauts 1969–72.

Neptune the eighth planet in average distance from the Sun. Neptune orbits the Sun every 164.8 years at an average distance of 4.497 billion km/2.794 billion mi. It is a giant gas (hydrogen, helium, methane) planet, with a diameter of 48,600 km/30,200 mi and a mass 17.2 times that of Earth. Its rotation period is 16 hours 7 minutes. The methane in its atmosphere absorbs red light and gives the planet a blue colouring. It is believed to have a central rocky core covered by a layer of ice. Neptune has eight known moons.

occultation the temporary obscuring of a star by a body in the solar system. Occultations are used to provide information about changes in an orbit, and the structure of objects in space, such as radio sources.

Oort cloud spherical cloud of comets beyond Pluto, extending out to about 100,000 astronomical units (1.5 light years) from the Sun. The gravitational effect of passing stars and the rest of our Galaxy disturbs comets from the cloud so that they fall in towards the Sun on highly elongated orbits, becoming visible from Earth. As many as 10 trillion comets may reside in the Oort cloud, named after Jan Oort who postulated it in 1950.

Phobos one of the two moons of Mars, discovered 1877 by the US astronomer Asaph Hall (1829–1907). It is an irregularly shaped lump of rock, cratered by meteorite impacts. Phobos is 27 × 22 × 19 km/17 × 13 × 12 mi across, and orbits Mars every 0.32 days at a distance of 9,400 km/5,840 mi from the planet's centre. It is thought to be an asteroid captured by Mars' gravity.

photosphere the visible surface of the Sun, which emits light and heat. About 300 km/200 mi deep, it consists of incandescent gas at a temperature of 5,800K (5,530°C/9,980°F).

planet a large celestial body in orbit around a star, composed of rock, metal, or gas. There are nine planets in the solar system: Mercury, Venus, Earth, Mars, Jupiter, Saturn, Uranus, Neptune, and Pluto.

Pluto the smallest and, usually, outermost planet of the solar system. The existence of Pluto was predicted by calculation by Percival Lowell and the planet was located by Clyde Tombaugh 1930. It orbits the Sun every 248.5 years at an average distance of 5.9 billion km/3.6 billion mi. Its highly elliptical orbit occasionally takes it within the orbit of Neptune, such as 1979–99. Pluto has a diameter of about 2,300 km/1,400 mi, and a mass about 0.002 that of Earth. It is of low density, composed of rock and ice, with frozen methane on its surface and a thin atmosphere.

prominence bright cloud of gas projecting from the Sun into space 100,000 km/60,000 mi or more. *Quiescent prominences* last for months, and are held in place by magnetic fields in the Sun's corona. *Surge prominences* shoot gas into space at speeds of 1,000 kps/600 mps. *Loop prominences* are gases falling back to the Sun's surface after a solar flare.

satellite any small body that orbits a larger one, either natural or artificial. Natural satellites that orbit planets are called moons. The first

LARGEST PLANETARY SATELLITES

planet	satellite	diameter in km	mean distance from centre of primary in km	orbital period in days	reciprocal mass (planet = 1)
Jupiter	Ganymede	5,262	1,070,000	7.16	12,800
Saturn	Titan	5,150	1,221,800	15.95	4,200
Jupiter	Callisto	4,800	1,883,000	16.69	17,700
Jupiter	Io	3,630	421,600	1.77	21,400
Earth	Moon	3,476	384,400	27.32	81.3
Jupiter	Europa	3,138	670,900	3.55	39,700
Neptune	Triton	2,700	354,300	5.88	770

artificial satellite, *Sputnik 1*, was launched into orbit around the Earth by the USSR 1957. Artificial satellites are used for scientific purposes, communications, weather forecasting, and military applications. The largest artificial satellites can be seen by the naked eye.

Saturn the second largest planet in the solar system, sixth from the Sun, and encircled by bright and easily visible equatorial rings. Viewed through a telescope it is ochre. Saturn orbits the Sun every 29.46 years at an average distance of 1,427,000,000 km/ 886,700,000 mi. Its equatorial diameter is 120,000 km/75,000 mi, but its polar diameter is 12,000 km/7,450 mi smaller, a result of its fast rotation and low density, the lowest of any planet. Saturn spins on its axis every 10 hours 14 minutes at its equator, slowing to 10 hours 40 minutes at high latitudes. Its mass is 95 times that of Earth, and its magnetic field 1,000 times stronger. Saturn is believed to have a small core of rock and iron, encased in ice and topped by a deep layer of liquid hydrogen. There are over 20 known moons, its largest being Titan. The rings visible from Earth begin about 14,000 km/9,000 mi from the planet's cloudtops and extend out to about 76,000 km/47,000 mi. Made of small chunks of ice and rock (averaging 1 m/3 ft across), they are 275,000 km/170,000 mi rim to rim, but only 100 m/300 ft thick. The Voyager probes showed that the rings actually consist of thousands of closely spaced ringlets, looking like the grooves in a gramophone record.

solar system the Sun and all the bodies orbiting it: the nine planets (Mercury, Venus, Earth, Mars, Jupiter, Saturn, Uranus, Neptune, and Pluto), their moons, the asteroids, and the comets. It is thought to have formed from a cloud of gas and dust in space about 4.6 billion years ago. The Sun contains 99% of the mass of the solar system. The edge of the solar system is not clearly defined, marked only by the limit of the Sun's gravitational influence, which extends about 1.5 light years, almost halfway to the nearest star, Alpha Centauri, 4.3 light years away.

solar wind a stream of atomic particles, mostly protons and electrons, from the Sun's corona, flowing outwards at speeds of between 300 kps/ 200 mps and 1,000 kps/600 mps.

spicules, solar short-lived jets of hot gas in the upper chromosphere of the Sun. Spiky in appearance, they move at high velocities along lines of magnetic force to which they owe their shapes, and last for a few minutes each. Spicules appear to disperse material into the corona.

Sun the star at the centre of the solar system. Its diameter is 1,392,000 km/ 865,000 mi; its temperature at the surface is about 5,800K (5,530°C/9,980°F), and at the centre 15,000,000K (15,000,000°C/ 27,000,000°F). It is composed of about 70% hydrogen and 30% helium, with other elements making up less than 1%. The Sun's energy is generated by nuclear fusion reactions that turn hydrogen into helium at its centre. It is about 4.7 billion years old, with a predicted lifetime of 10 billion years.

sunspot a dark patch on the surface of the Sun, actually an area of cooler gas, thought to be caused by strong magnetic fields that block the outward flow of heat to the Sun's surface. Sunspots consist of a dark central **umbra**, about 4,000K (3,700°C/6,700°F), and a lighter surrounding **penumbra**, about 5,500K (5,200°C/9,400°F). They last from several days to over a month, ranging in size from 2,000 km/1,250 mi to groups stretching for over 100,000 km/62,000 mi. The number of sunspots visible at a given time varies from none to over 100 in a cycle averaging 11 years.

superior planet planet that is farther away from the Sun than the Earth: that is, Mars, Jupiter, Saturn, Uranus, Neptune, and Pluto.

tektite small, rounded glassy stone, found in certain regions of the Earth, such as Australasia. They are probably the scattered drops of molten rock thrown out by the impact of a large meteorite.

Titan largest moon of the planet Saturn, with a diameter of 5,150 km/3,200 mi and a mean distance from Saturn of 1,222,000 km/ 759,000 mi. It was discovered 1655 by Christiaan Huygens, and is the second largest moon in the solar system (Ganymede, of Jupiter, is larger).

Uranus the seventh planet from the Sun, discovered by William Herschel 1781. It is twice as far out as the sixth planet, Saturn. Uranus has a diameter of 50,800 km/31,600 mi and a mass 14.5 times that of Earth. It orbits the Sun in 84 years at an average distance of 2,870 million km/1,783 million mi. The spin axis of Uranus is tilted at 98°, so that one pole points towards the Sun, giving extreme seasons. It has 15 moons, and in 1977 was discovered to have thin rings around its equator.

Venus the second planet from the Sun. It orbits the Sun every 225 days at an average distance of 108.2 million km/67.2 million mi and can approach the Earth to within 38 million km/ 24 million mi, closer than any other planet. Its diameter is 12,100 km/7,500 mi and its mass is 0.82 that of Earth. Venus rotates on its axis more slowly than any other planet, once every 243 days and from east to west, the opposite direction to the other planets (except Uranus). Venus is shrouded by clouds of sulphuric acid droplets that sweep across the planet from east to west every four days. The atmosphere is almost entirely carbon dioxide, which traps the Sun's heat by the greenhouse effect and raises the planet's surface temperature to 480°C/900°F, with an atmospheric pressure 90 times that at Earth's surface.

zodiacal light a cone-shaped light sometimes seen extending from the Sun along the ecliptic, visible after sunset or before sunrise. It is due to thinly spread dust particles in the central plane of the solar system. It is very faint, and requires a dark, clear sky to be seen.

TECHNICAL TERMS

aberration of starlight the apparent displacement of a star from its true position, due to the combined effects of the speed of light and the speed of the Earth in orbit around the Sun (about 30 kps/18.5 mps).

albedo the fraction of the incoming light reflected by a body such as a planet. A body with a high albedo, near 1, is very bright, while a body with a low albedo, near 0, is dark. The Moon has an average albedo of 0.12, Venus 0.65, Earth 0.37.

aphelion the point at which an object, travelling in an elliptical orbit around the Sun, is at its furthest from the Sun.

apogee the point at which an object, travelling in an elliptical orbit around the Earth, is at its furthest from the Earth.

arc minute, arc second units for measuring small angles, used in geometry, surveying, map-making, and astronomy. An arc minute is one-sixtieth of a degree, and an arc second one-sixtieth of an arc minute.

astrometry the measurement of the precise positions of stars, planets, and other bodies in space.

astronomical unit unit (symbol AU) equal to the mean distance of the Earth from the Sun: 149,597,870 km/92,955,800 mi. It is used to describe planetary distances. Light travels this distance in approximately 8.3 minutes.

calendar the division of the year into months, weeks, and days and the method of ordering the years. From year one, an assumed date of the birth of Jesus, dates are calculated backwards (BC 'before Christ', or BCE 'before common era') and forwards (AD, Latin, *anno domini* 'in the year of the Lord' or CE 'common era'). The *lunar month* (period between one new moon and the next) naturally averages 29.5 days, but the Western calendar uses for convenience a *calendar month* with a complete number of days, 30 or 31 (Feb has 28). For adjustments, since there are slightly fewer than six extra hours a year left over, they are added to Feb as a 29th day every fourth year (*leap year*), century years being excepted unless they are divisible by 400. For example 1896 was a leap year; 1900 was not.

celestial mechanics the branch of astronomy that deals with the calculation of the orbits of celestial bodies, their gravitational attractions (such as those that produce Earth's tides), and also the orbits of artificial satellites and space probes. It is based on the laws of motion and gravity laid down by Newton.

celestial sphere imaginary sphere surrounding the Earth, on which the celestial bodies seem to lie. The positions of bodies such as stars, planets and galaxies are specified by their coordinates on the celestial sphere. The equivalents of latitude and longitude on the celestial sphere are called declination and right ascension (which is measured in hours from 0 to 24). The *celestial poles* lie directly above the Earth's poles, and the *celestial equator* lies over the Earth's equator. The celestial sphere appears to rotate once around the Earth each day, actually a result of the rotation of the Earth on its axis.

conjunction the alignment of two celestial bodies as seen from Earth. A superior planet (or other object) is in conjunction when it lies behind the Sun. An inferior planet (or other object) comes to *inferior conjunction* when it passes between the Earth and the Sun; it is at *superior conjunction* when it passes behind the Sun. *Planetary conjunction* takes place when a planet is closely aligned with another celestial object, such as the Moon, a star, or another planet.

cosmology the study of the structure of the universe. Modern cosmology began in the 1920s with the discovery that the universe is expanding, which suggested that it began in an explosion, the Big Bang. An alternative view, the steady-state theory, claimed that the universe has no origin, but is expanding because new matter is being continually created.

day the time taken for the Earth to rotate once on its axis. The *solar day* is the time that the Earth takes to rotate relative to the Sun. It is divided into 24 hours, and is the basis of our civil day. The *sidereal day* is the time that the Earth takes to rotate once relative to the stars. It is 3 minutes 56 seconds shorter than the solar day, because the Sun's position against the background of stars as seen from Earth changes as the Earth orbits it.

declination the coordinate on the celestial sphere (imaginary sphere surrounding the Earth) that corresponds to latitude on the Earth's surface. Declination runs from 0° at the celestial equator to 90° at the north and south celestial poles.

ecliptic the path, against the background of stars, that the Sun appears to follow each year as the Earth orbits the Sun. It can be thought of as the plane of the Earth's orbit projected on to the celestial sphere (imaginary sphere around the Earth).

elongation the angular distance between the Sun and a planet or other solar-system object. This angle is 0° at conjunction, 90° at quadrature, and 180° at opposition.

equinox the points in spring and autumn at which the Sun's path, the ecliptic, crosses the celestial equator, so that the day and night are of approximately equal length. The *vernal equinox* occurs about 21 March and the *autumnal equinox*, 23 Sept.

escape velocity minimum velocity with which an object must be projected for it to escape from the gravitational pull of a planetary body. In the case of the Earth, the escape velocity 11.2 kps/6.9 mps; the Moon 2.4 kps/1.5 mps; Mars 5 kps/3.1 mps; and Jupiter 59.6 kps/37 mps.

exobiology the study of life forms that may possibly exist elsewhere in the universe, and of the effects of extraterrestrial environments on Earth organisms.

geostationary orbit the circular path 35,900 km/22,300 mi above the Earth's equator on which a satellite takes 24 hours, moving from west to east, to complete an orbit, thus appearing to hang stationary over one place on the Earth's surface. Geostationary orbits are particularly used for communications satellites and weather satellites. They were first thought of by the author Arthur C Clarke. A *geosynchronous orbit* lies at the same distance from Earth but is inclined to the equator.

gravitational lens the bending of light by a gravitational field, predicted by Einstein's general theory of relativity. The effect was first detected in 1917 when the light from stars was found to be bent as it passed the totally eclipsed Sun. More remarkable is the splitting of light from distant quasars into two or more images by intervening galaxies. In 1979 the first double image of a quasar produced by gravitational lensing was discovered and a quadruple image of another quasar was later found.

gravity the force of attraction that arises between objects by virtue of their masses. On Earth, gravity is the force of attraction between any object in the Earth's gravitational field and the Earth itself.

Greenwich Mean Time (GMT) local time on the zero line of longitude (the *Greenwich meridian*), which passes through the Old Royal Observatory at Greenwich, London. It was replaced 1972 by coordinated universal time (UTC).

Hertzsprung-Russell diagram a graph on which the surface temperatures of stars are plotted against their luminosities. Most stars, including the Sun, fall into a narrow band called the *main sequence*. When a star grows old it moves from the main sequence to the upper right part of the graph, into the area of the giants and supergiants. At the end of its life, as the star shrinks to become a white dwarf, it moves again, to the bottom left area. It is named after the Dane Ejnar Hertzsprung and the American Henry Norris Russell, who independently devised it in the years 1911–13.

Hubble's constant a measure of the rate at which the universe is expanding, named after Edwin Hubble. Observations suggest that galaxies are moving apart at a rate of 50–100 kps/30–60 mps for every million parsecs of distance. This means that the universe, which began at one point according to the Big Bang theory, is between 10 billion and 20 billion years old.

Hubble's law the law that relates a galaxy's distance from us to its speed of recession as the universe expands, announced in 1929 by Edwin Hubble. He found that galaxies are moving apart at speeds that increase in direct proportion to their distance apart. The rate of expansion is known as Hubble's constant.

inclination the angle between the ecliptic and the plane of the orbit of a planet, asteroid, or comet. In the case of satellites orbiting a planet, it is the angle between the plane of

orbit of the satellite and the equator of the planet.

light year the distance travelled by a beam of light in a vacuum in one year, approximately 9.46 trillion (million million) km/5.88 trillion miles.

magnitude measure of the brightness of a star or other celestial object. The larger the number denoting the magnitude, the fainter the object. Zero or first magnitude indicates some of the brightest stars. Still brighter are those of negative magnitude, such as Sirius, whose magnitude is –1.46. *Apparent magnitude* is the brightness of an object as seen from Earth, *absolute magnitude* the brightness at a standard distance of 10 parsecs (32.6 light years).

month unit of time based on the motion of the Moon around the Earth. The time from one new or full Moon to the next (the *synodic* or *lunar month*) is 29.53 days. The time for the Moon to complete one orbit around the Earth relative to the stars (the *sidereal month*) is 27.32 days. The *solar month* equals 30.44 days, and is exactly one-twelfth of the solar or tropical year, the time taken for the Earth to orbit the Sun. The *calendar month* is a human invention, devised to fit the calendar year.

nadir the point on the celestial sphere vertically below the observer and hence diametrically opposite the *zenith*.

nutation a slight 'nodding' of the Earth in space, caused by the varying gravitational pulls of the Sun and Moon. Nutation changes the angle of the Earth's axial tilt (average 23.5°) by about 9 seconds of arc to either side of its mean position, a complete cycle taking just over 18.5 years.

opposition the moment at which a body in the solar system lies opposite the Sun in the sky as seen from the Earth and crosses the meridian at about midnight.

orbit the path of one body in space around another, such as the orbit of Earth around the Sun, or the Moon around Earth. When the two bodies are similar in mass, as in a double star, both bodies move around their common centre of mass. The movement of objects in orbit follows Kepler's laws, which apply to artificial satellites as well as to natural bodies.

parallax the change in the apparent position of an object against its background when viewed from two different positions. Nearby stars show a shift owing to parallax when viewed from different positions on the Earth's orbit around the Sun. A star's parallax is used to deduce its distance.

parsec a unit (symbol pc) used for distances to stars and galaxies. One parsec is equal to 3.2616 light years, 2.063×10^5 astronomical units, and 3.086×10^{13} km.

perigee the point at which an object, travelling in an elliptical orbit around the Earth, is at its closest to the Earth.

perihelion the point at which an object, travelling in an elliptical orbit around the Sun, is at its closest to the Sun.

phase the apparent shape of the Moon or a planet

when all or part of its illuminated hemisphere is facing Earth. The Moon undergoes a full cycle of phases from new (when between Earth and the Sun) through first quarter (when at 90° eastern elongation from the Sun), full (when opposite the Sun), and last quarter (when at 90° western elongation from the Sun). The inferior planets can also undergo a full cycle of phases, as can an asteroid passing inside the Earth's orbit.

precession a slow wobble of the Earth on its axis, like that of a spinning top. The gravitational pulls of the Sun and Moon on the Earth's equatorial bulge cause the Earth's axis to trace out a circle on the sky every 25,800 years. The position of the celestial poles is constantly changing owing to precession, as are the positions of the equinoxes (the points at which the celestial equator intersects the Sun's path around the sky). The *precession of the equinoxes* means that there is a gradual westward drift in the ecliptic—the path that the Sun appears to follow—and in the coordinates of objects on the celestial sphere; this is why the dates of the astrological signs of the zodiac no longer correspond to the times of year when the Sun actually passes through the constellations. For example, the Sun passes through Leo from mid-Aug to mid-Sept, but the astrological dates for Leo are between about 23 July and 22 Aug.

proper motion the gradual change in the position of a star that results from its motion in orbit around our Galaxy, the Milky Way. Proper motions are slight and undetectable to the naked eye, but can be accurately measured on telescopic photographs taken many years apart. Barnard's Star is the star with the largest proper motion, 10.3 arc seconds per year.

red shift the lengthening of the wavelengths of light from an object as a result of the object's motion away from us. It is an example of the Doppler effect. The red shift in light from galaxies is evidence that the universe is expanding.

right ascension the coordinate on the celestial sphere that corresponds to longitude on the surface of the Earth. It is measured in hours, minutes, and seconds eastwards from the point where the Sun's path, the ecliptic, intersects the celestial equator; this point is called the *vernal equinox.*

sidereal period the orbital period of a planet around the Sun, or a moon around a planet, with reference to a background star. The sidereal period of a planet is in effect its 'year'. A synodic period is a full circle as seen from Earth.

singularity the point at the centre of a black hole at which it is predicted that the infinite gravitational forces will compress the infalling mass of the collapsing star to infinite density. It is a point in space-time at which the known laws of physics break down. Also, it is thought, in the Big Bang theory of the origin of the universe, to be the point from which the expansion of the universe began.

solstice either of the points at which the Sun is farthest north or south of the celestial equator each year. The *summer solstice*, when the Sun is farthest north, occurs around 21 June; the *winter solstice* around 22 Dec.

speckle interferometry technique whereby large telescopes can achieve high resolution of astronomical objects despite the adverse effects of the atmosphere through which light from the object under study must pass. It involves the taking of large numbers of images, each under high magnification and with short exposure times. The pictures are then combined to form the final picture. The technique was introduced by the French astronomer Antoine Labeyrie 1970.

synodic period the time taken for a planet or moon to return to the same position in its orbit as seen from the Earth; that is, from one opposition to the next. It differs from the sidereal period because the Earth is moving in orbit around the Sun.

transfer orbit elliptical path followed by a spacecraft moving from one orbit to another, designed to save fuel although at the expense of a longer journey time.

transit the passage of a smaller object across the visible disc of a larger one. Transits of the inferior planets occur when they pass directly between the Earth and Sun, and are seen as tiny dark spots against the Sun's disc.

universal time (UT) another name for Greenwich Mean Time. It is based on the rotation of the Earth, which is not quite constant. Since 1972, UT has been replaced by *coordinated universal time* (UTC), which is based on uniform atomic time.

year a unit of time measurement, based on the orbital period of the Earth around the Sun.

zenith the uppermost point of the celestial horizon, immediately above the observer; the nadir is below, diametrically opposite.

zodiac the zone of the heavens containing the paths of the Sun, Moon, and planets. When this was devised by the ancient Greeks, only five planets were known, making the zodiac about 16° wide. The stars in it are grouped into 12 signs (constellations), each 30° in extent: Aries, Taurus, Gemini, Cancer, Leo, Virgo, Libra, Scorpius, Sagittarius, Capricornus, Aquarius, and Pisces. Because of the precession of the equinoxes, the current constellations do not cover the same areas of sky as the zodiacal signs of the same name.

STARS, GALAXIES, AND THE UNIVERSE

Algol or *Beta Persei* an eclipsing binary, a pair of rotating stars in the constellation Perseus, one of which eclipses the other every 69 hours, causing its brightness to drop by two thirds.

Alpha Centauri or *Rigil Kent* the brightest star

THE DAY OF TWO DAWNS

A total eclipse of the Sun is one of the most awesome sights in nature. Astronomers travel the world to see the precious few minutes of totality during which the Sun's bright disc is obscured so that its faint outer layers spring into view. On 11 July 1991, their task was made easier when the path of a total eclipse crossed Hawaii, site of one of the world's largest collections of telescopes.

Not only professional astronomers, but also tens of thousands of tourists, came to see what was billed as the Day of Two Dawns. As eclipse fever gripped the island, would-be eclipse watchers sported eclipse T-shirts, drank from eclipse coffee mugs, ate eclipse pastries, and even received eclipse haircuts.

Shortly after sunrise on 11 July, the Moon began to take its first bite out of the solar disc. For the next hour the eclipse progressed and the sky darkened until, at 7.30 a.m., the Moon completely blotted out the Sun, casting a deep twilight over the landscape. But many spectators were disappointed, for unexpected cloud obscured much of the event. Even for those lucky scientists in the observatory on the peak of Mauna Kea, volcanic dust from the eruption of Mount Pinatubo in the Philippines added a high-altitude haze.

Where it was clear, observers thrilled to the delicate detail in the Sun's pearly halo of gas called the corona, and watched two clouds of pink hydrogen gas that thrust outwards into space from the Sun's rim. After just over four minutes the Sun emerged from behind the Moon so that Hawaii experienced its second dawn of the day. The eclipse shadow raced away over the Pacific to Mexico, where more people saw totality than at any other eclipse in history. As seen from Mexico, totality lasted 6.9 minutes, longer than any eclipse until the year 2132.

The next total eclipse of the Sun to be visible from the British Isles will be on the morning of 11 August 1999 when the Moon's shadow will cross Cornwall, bringing two minutes of darkness. The rest of the British Isles will see a large partial eclipse.

---

in the constellation Centaurus and the third brightest star in the sky. It is actually a tr ple star (see binary star); the two brighter stars orbit each other every 80 years, and the third, Proxima Centauri is the closest star to the Sun, 4.2 light years away, 0.1 light years closer than the other two.

Andromeda galaxy galaxy 2.2 million light years away from Earth in the constellation Andromeda, and the most distant object visible to the naked eye. It is the largest member of the Local Group of galaxies. Like the Milky Way, it is a spiral orbited by several companion galaxies but contains about twice as many stars. It is about 200,000 light years across.

Barnard's star second closest star to the Sun, six light years away in the constellation Ophiuchus. It is a faint red dwarf of 10th magnitude, visible only through a telescope. It is named after the US astronomer Edward E Barnard (1857–1923), who discovered in 1916 that it has the fastest proper motion of any star, crossing 1 degree of sky every 350 years.

Big Bang the hypothetical 'explosive' event that marked the origin of the universe as we know it. At the time of the Big Bang, the entire universe was squeezed into a hot, superdense state. The Big Bang explosion threw this compacted material outwards, producing the expanding universe. The cause of the Big Bang is unknown; observations of the current rate of expansion of the universe suggest that it took place about 15 billion years ago.

binary star a pair of stars moving in orbit around their common centre of mass. Observations show that most stars are binary, or even multiple – for example, the nearest star system to the Sun, Alpha Centauri.

black hole object in space whose gravity is so great that nothing can escape from it, not even light. Thought to form when massive stars shrink at the ends of their lives, a black hole sucks in more matter, including other stars, from the space around it. Matter that falls into a black hole is squeezed to infinite density at the centre of the hole. Black holes can be detected because gas falling towards them becomes so hot that it emits X-rays.

brown dwarf hypothetical object less massive than a star, but heavier than a planet. Brown dwarfs would not have enough mass to ignite nuclear reactions at their centres, but would shine by heat released during their contraction from a gas cloud. Because of the difficulty of detection, no brown dwarfs have been spotted with certainty, but some astronomers believe that vast numbers of them may exist throughout the Galaxy.

Cepheid variable yellow supergiant star that varies regularly in brightness every few days or weeks as a result of pulsations. The time that a Cepheid variable takes to pulsate is directly related to its average brightness; the longer the pulsation period, the brighter the star.

constellation one of the 88 areas into which the sky is divided for the purposes of identifying celestial objects. The first constellations were simple, arbitrary patterns of stars in which early civilizations visualized gods, sacred beasts, and mythical heroes. The current list of 88 constellations was adopted by the International Astronomical Union, astronomy's governing body, in 1930; it is derived from a list of 48 known to the ancient Greeks.

cosmic background radiation the electromagnetic radiation, also known as the 3° radiation, left over from the original formation of the universe in the Big Bang around 15 billion years ago. It corresponds to an overall background temperature of 3K

(−270°C/−454°F), or 3°C/37°F above absolute zero.

Crab nebula cloud of gas 6,000 light years from Earth, in the constellation Taurus. It is the remains of a star that exploded as a supernova (observed as a brilliant point of light on Earth 1054). At its centre is a pulsar that flashes 30 times a second. The name comes from its crablike shape.

double star two stars that appear close together. Most double stars attract each other due to gravity, and orbit each other, forming a genuine binary star, but other double stars are at different distances from Earth, and lie in the same line of sight only by chance. Through a telescope both types of double star will look the same.

eclipsing binary a binary (double) star in which the two stars periodically pass in front of each other as seen from Earth.

galaxy a congregation of millions or billions of stars, held together by gravity. *Spiral galaxies*, such as the Milky Way, are flattened in shape, with a central bulge of old stars surrounded by a disc of younger stars, arranged in spiral arms like a Catherine wheel. *Barred spirals* are spiral galaxies that have a straight bar of stars across their centre, from the ends of which the spiral arms emerge. The arms of spiral galaxies contain gas and dust from which new stars are still forming. *Elliptical galaxies* contain old stars and very little gas. They include the most massive galaxies known, containing a trillion stars. At least some elliptical galaxies are thought to be formed by mergers between spiral galaxies. There are also irregular galaxies. Most galaxies occur in clusters, containing anything from a few to thousands of members.

globular cluster spherical or near-spherical star cluster from approximately 10,000 to millions of stars. More than a hundred globular clusters are distributed in a spherical halo around our Galaxy. They consist of old stars, formed early in our Galaxy's history. Globular clusters are also found around other galaxies.

interstellar molecules over 50 different types of molecules existing in gas clouds in our Galaxy. Most have been detected by their radio emissions, but some have been found by the absorption lines they produce in the spectra of starlight. The most complex molecules, many of them based on carbon, are found in the dense clouds where stars are forming. They may be significant for the origin of life elsewhere in space.

Local Group a cluster of about 30 galaxies that includes our own, the Milky Way. Like other groups of galaxies, the Local Group is held together by the gravitational attraction among its members, and does not expand with the expanding universe. Its two largest galaxies are the Milky Way and the Andromeda galaxy; most of the others are small and faint.

Magellanic Clouds in astronomy, the two galaxies nearest to our own Galaxy. They are irregularly shaped, and appear as detached parts of the Milky Way, in the southern constellations Dorado and Tucana.

Milky Way faint band of light crossing the night sky, consisting of stars in the plane of our Galaxy. The name Milky Way is often used for the Galaxy itself. It is a spiral galaxy, about 100,000 light years in diameter, containing at least 100 billion stars. The Sun is in one of its spiral arms, about 25,000 light years from the centre.

Mira or **Omicron Ceti** the brightest long-period pulsating variable star, located in the constellation Cetus. Mira was the first star discovered to vary periodically in brightness.

nebula a cloud of gas and dust in space. Nebulae are the birthplaces of stars. An *emission nebula*, such as the Orion nebula, glows brightly because its gas is energized by stars that have formed within it. In a *reflection nebula*, starlight reflects off grains of dust in the nebula, such as surrounds the stars of the Pleiades cluster. A *dark nebula* is a dense cloud, composed of molecular hydrogen, which partially or completely absorbs light behind it. Examples include the Coalsack nebula in Crux and the Horsehead nebula in Orion. Some nebulae are produced by gas thrown off from dying stars.

neutron star a very small, 'superdense' star composed mostly of neutrons. They are thought to form when massive stars explode as supernovae, during which the protons and electrons of the star's atoms merge, due to intense gravitational collapse, to make neutrons. A neutron star may have the mass of up to three Suns, compressed into a globe only 20 km/12 mi in diameter. If its mass is any greater, its gravity will be so strong that it will shrink even further to become a black hole. Being so small, neutron stars can spin very quickly. The rapidly 'flashing' radio stars called pulsars are believed to be neutron stars. The 'flashing' is caused by a rotating beam of radio energy similar in behaviour to a lighthouse beam of light.

nova (plural *novae*) a faint star that suddenly erupts in brightness by 10,000 times or more. Novae are believed to occur in close double star systems, where gas from one star flows to a companion white dwarf. The gas ignites, and is thrown off in an explosion at speeds of 1,500 kps/930 mps or more. Unlike a supernova, the star is not completely disrupted by the outburst.

Olbers' paradox a question put forward 1826 by Heinrich Olbers, who asked: If the universe is infinite in extent and filled with stars, why is the sky dark at night? The answer is that the stars do not live infinitely long, so there is not enough starlight to fill the universe. A wrong answer, frequently given, is that the expansion of the universe weakens the starlight.

Orion nebula a luminous cloud of gas and dust 1,500 light years away, in the constellation Orion, from which stars are forming. It is about 15 light years in diameter, and contains enough gas to make a cluster of thousands of stars. At the nebula's centre is a group of hot young stars, called the *Trapezium*, which make the surrounding gas glow. The nebula is visible to the naked eye as a misty patch below the belt of Orion.

oscillating universe a theory that states that the gravitational attraction of the mass within the universe will eventually slow down and stop the expansion of the universe. The outward motions of the galaxies will then be reversed, eventually resulting in a 'Big Crunch' where all the matter in the universe would be contracted into a small volume of high density. This could undergo a further Big Bang, thereby creating another expansion phase. The theory suggests that the universe would alternately expand and collapse through alternate Big Bangs and Big Crunches.

planetary nebula a shell of gas thrown off by a star at the end of its life. Planetary nebulae have nothing to do with planets. They were named by William Herschel, who thought their rounded shape resembled the disc of a planet. After a star such as the Sun has expanded to become a red giant, its outer layers are ejected into space to form a planetary nebula, leaving the core as a white dwarf at the centre.

Polaris or *Pole Star* or *North Star* the bright star closest to the north celestial pole, and the brightest star in the constellation Ursa Minor. Its position is indicated by the 'pointers' in Ursa Major. Polaris is a yellow supergiant about 500 light years away.

Proxima Centauri the closest star to the Sun, 4.2 light years away. It is a faint red dwarf, visible only with a telescope, and is a member of the Alpha Centauri triple-star system.

pulsar celestial source that emits pulses of energy at regular intervals, ranging from a few seconds to a few thousandths of a second. They were discovered 1967, and are thought to be rapidly rotating neutron stars, which flash at radio and other wavelengths as they spin. Over 400 radio pulsars are known in our Galaxy, although a million or so may exist.

quasar (from *quasi*-stellar object or QSO) any of a class of celestial objects far beyond our Galaxy, discovered 1963–65. Quasars appear starlike, but each emits more energy than 100 giant galaxies. They are thought to be young, distant galaxies with brilliant centres. Their brilliance is caused by stars and gas falling towards an immense black hole at their nucleus. The light from quasars shows a large red shift, unlike starlight, indicating that they are far off in the universe, the furthest lying over 10 billion light years away. Some quasars emit radio waves, which is how they were first identified in 1963, but most are radio-quiet. About 3,000 are now known to exist.

radio galaxy galaxy that is a strong source of electromagnetic waves of radio wavelengths. All galaxies, including our own, emit some radio waves, but radio galaxies are up to a million times more powerful.

red dwarf any star that is cool, faint, and small (about one-tenth the mass and diameter of the Sun). They burn slowly, and have estimated lifetimes of 100 billion years. Red dwarfs may be the most abundant type of star, but are difficult to see because they are so faint. Two of the closest stars to the Sun, Proxima Centauri and Barnard's Star, are red dwarfs.

red giant any large bright star with a cool surface. It is thought to represent a late stage in the evolution of a star like the Sun, as it runs out of hydrogen fuel at its centre. Red giants have diameters between 10 and 100 times that of the Sun. They are very bright because they are so large, although their surface temperature is lower than that of the Sun, about 2,000–3,000K (1,700°C/3,000°F–2,700°C/5,000°F).

Seyfert galaxy a type of galaxy whose small, bright centre is caused by hot gas moving at high speed around a massive central object, possibly a black hole. Almost all Seyferts are spiral galaxies. They seem to be closely related to quasars, but are about 100 times fainter. They are named after their discoverer Carl Seyfert (1911–60).

star luminous globe of gas, producing its own heat and light by nuclear reactions. Stars are born from nebulae, and consist mostly of hydrogen and helium gases. Surface temperatures range from 2,000°C/3,600°F to above 30,000°C/54,000°F, and the corresponding colours range from red to blue-white. The brightest stars have masses 100 times that of the Sun, and emit as much light as millions of suns; they live for less than a million years before exploding as supernovae. The faintest stars are the red dwarfs, less than one-thousandth the brightness of the Sun.

star cluster group of related stars, usually held together by gravity. Members of a star cluster are thought to form together from one large cloud of gas in space. *Open clusters* such as the Pleiades contain from a dozen to many hundreds of young stars, loosely scattered over several light years. *Globular clusters* are larger and much more densely packed, containing perhaps 100,000 old stars.

steady-state theory theory that the universe appears the same wherever (and whenever) viewed. This seems to be refuted by the existence of cosmic background radiation, however.

supernova the explosive death of a star, which temporarily attains a brightness of 100 million Suns or more, so that it can shine as brilliantly as a small galaxy for a few days or weeks.

universe all of space and its contents, the study of which is called cosmology. The universe is thought to be between 10 billion and 20 billion years old, and is mostly empty space, dotted with galaxies for as far as telescopes can see. The most distant detected galaxies and quasars lie 10 billion light years or more from Earth, and are moving farther apart as the universe expands. Several theories attempt to explain how the universe came into being and evolved, for example, the Big Bang theory of an expanding universe originating in a single

ASTRONOMERS ROYAL

John Flamsteed	1675–1719
Edmond Halley	1720–1742
James Bradley	1742–1762
Nathaniel Bliss	1762–1764
Nevil Maskelyne	1765–1811
John Pond	1811–1835
George Airy	1835–1881
William Christie	1881–1910
Frank Dyson	1910–1933
Harold Spencer Jones	1933–1955
Richard Woolley	1956–1971
Martin Ryle	1972–1982
F Graham Smith	1982–1990
Arnold Wolfendale	1991–

explosive event, and the contradictory steady-state theory.

variable star a star whose brightness changes, either regularly or irregularly, over a period ranging from a few hours to months or even years. The Cepheid variables regularly expand and contract in size every few days or weeks.

white dwarf a small, hot star, the last stage in the life of a star such as the Sun. White dwarfs have a mass similar to that of the Sun, but only 1% of the Sun's diameter, similar in size to the Earth. Most have surface temperatures of 8,000°C/14,400°F or more, hotter than the Sun. Yet, being so small, their overall luminosities may be less than 1% of that of the Sun.

TELESCOPES AND OBSERVATORIES

Algonquin Radio Observatory site in Ontario, Canada, of the 46 m/150 ft radio telescope of the National Research Council of Canada, opened 1966.

Arecibo site in Puerto Rico of the world's largest single-dish radio telescope, 305 m/1,000 ft in diameter. It is built in a natural hollow, and uses the rotation of the Earth to scan the sky. It has been used both for radar work on the planets and for conventional radio astronomy, and is operated by Cornell University, USA.

astrolabe ancient navigational instrument, forerunner of the sextant. Astrolabes usually consisted of a flat disc with a sighting rod that could be pivoted to point at the Sun or bright stars. From the altitude of the Sun or star above the horizon, the local time could be estimated.

astrophotography the use of photography in astronomical research. The first successful photograph of a celestial object was the daguerreotype plate of the Moon taken by John W Draper (1811–1882) of the USA in March 1840. The first photograph of a star, Vega, was taken by US astronomer William C Bond (1789–1859) in 1850.

Australia Telescope an array of radio telescopes at three locations in Australia, operated by the Commonwealth Scientific and Industrial Research Organization (CSIRO). Six 22-m/72-ft dishes in a line 6 km/10 mi long at Culgoora, New South Wales, form the so-called Compact Array which can be used in combination with another 22–m dish at Siding Spring, NSW, and the 64-m/210-ft radio telescope at Parkes, NSW.

charge-coupled device (CCD) device for forming images electronically, using a layer of silicon that releases electrons when struck by incoming light. The electrons are stored in pixels and read off into a computer at the end of the exposure. CCDs have now almost entirely replaced photographic film for applications such as astrophotography where extreme sensitivity to light is paramount.

David Dunlap Observatory Canadian observatory at Richmond Hill, Ontario, operated by the University of Toronto, with a 1.88-m/74-in reflector, the largest optical telescope in Canada, opened 1935.

Dominion Astrophysical Observatory Canadian observatory near Victoria, British Columbia, the site of a 1.85-m/73-in reflector opened 1918, operated by the National Research Council of Canada. The associated Dominion Radio Astrophysical Observatory at Penticton, BC, operates a 26-m/84-ft radio dish and an aperture synthesis radio telescope.

Effelsberg site near Bonn, Germany, of the world's largest fully steerable radio telescope, the 100-m/328-ft radio dish of the Max Planck Institute for Radio Astronomy, opened 1971.

European Southern Observatory observatory operated jointly by Belgium, Denmark, France, Germany, Italy, the Netherlands, Sweden and Switzerland with headquarters near Munich. Its telescopes, located at La Silla, Chile, include a 3.6-m/142-in reflector opened 1976 and the 3.58-m/141-in New Technology Telescope opened 1990. By 1988 work began on the Very Large Telescope, consisting of four 8-m/315-in reflectors mounted independently but capable of working in combination.

Jodrell Bank site in Cheshire, England, of the Nuffield Radio Astronomy Laboratories of the University of Manchester. Its largest instrument is the 76 m/250 ft radio dish (the Lovell Telescope), completed 1957 and modified 1970. A 38 m × 25 m/125 ft × 82 ft elliptical radio dish was introduced 1964, capable of working at shorter wavelengths. These radio telescopes are used in conjunction with six smaller dishes up to 230 km/143 mi apart in an array called MERLIN (multi-element radio-linked interferometer network) to produce detailed maps of radio sources.

Keck Telescope the world's largest optical telescope, with a mirror 10 m/33 ft in diameter, consisting of 36 hexagonal sections. It is situated on Mauna Kea, Hawaii, and was scheduled to open spring 1992. An identical telescope is under construction next to it, due for completion 1996. Both telescopes are jointly owned by the California Institute of Technology and the University of California.

NEW PLANETS . . . NO PLANETS?

Astronomers at Jodrell Bank, Cheshire, created a sensation in July 1991 when they announced that they had detected a planet orbiting a pulsar (a celestial body that emits regular energy pulses). But in Jan 1992 they admitted they had made a mistake, and that the planet does not exist.

The initial 'discovery' came when they found that radio flashes from the pulsar were varying regularly every six months.

A planet orbiting the pulsar every six months would cause such an effect, but so would the movement of the Earth around the Sun. The astronomers thought they had taken the Earth's movement into account, which left the 'planet' as the only answer. But they had got the position of the pulsar slightly wrong. When they reanalysed their data using the correct position for the pulsar, the effect vanished.

Despite this retraction, two US astronomers have announced evidence for two planets around another pulsar. They say they are sure they have not made the same mistake as the Jodrell Bank team. Other astronomers are checking the claim.

Kitt Peak National Observatory observatory in the Quinlan Mountains near Tucson, Arizona, operated by AURA (Association of Universities for Research into Astronomy). Its main telescopes are the 4-m/158-in Mayall reflector, opened 1973, and the McMath Solar Telescope, opened 1962, the world's largest of its type. Among numerous other telescopes on the site is a 2.3-m/90-in reflector owned by the Steward Observatory of the University of Arizona.

Las Campanas Observatory site in Chile of the 2.5-m/100-in Du Pont telescope of the Carnegie Institution of Washington, opened 1977.

Lick Observatory observatory of the University of California and Mount Hamilton, California. Its main instruments are the 3.04-m/120-in Shane reflector, opened 1959, and a 91-cm/36-in refractor, opened 1988, the second-largest refractor in the world.

Lowell Observatory founded by Percival Lowell at Flagstaff, Arizona, with a 61-cm/24-in refractor opened in 1896. The observatory now operates other telescopes at a nearby site on Anderson Mesa including the 1.83-m/72-in Perkins reflector of Ohio State and Ohio Wesleyan Universities.

Mauna Kea astronomical observatory in Hawaii, USA, built on a dormant volcano at 4,200 m/13,784 ft above sea level. Because of its elevation high above clouds, atmospheric moisture, and artificial lighting, Mauna Kea is ideal for infrared astronomy. The first telescope on the site was installed 1970.

McDonald Observatory the observatory of the University of Texas on Mount Locke, Texas, site of a 2.72-m/107-in reflector opened 1969 and a 2.08-m/82-in reflector opened 1939.

Mills Cross a type of radio telescope consisting of two rows of aerials at right angles to each other, invented 1953 by the Australian radio astronomer Bernard Mills (1920–   ). The cross-shape produces a narrow beam useful for pinpointing the positions of radio sources.

Mount Wilson site near Los Angeles of the 2.5-m/100-in Hooker telescope opened 1917 with which Edwin Hubble discovered the expansion of the Universe, closed in 1985 when the Carnegie Institution withdrew its support. Two solar telescopes in towers 18.3 m/60 ft and 45.7 m/150 ft tall, and a 1.5-m/60-in reflector opened 1908, still operate there.

Mullard Radio Astronomy Observatory the radio observatory of the University of Cambridge, England. Its main instrument is the Ryle Telescope, eight dishes 12.8 m/42 ft wide in a line of 5 km/3 mi long, opened 1972.

Multiple Mirror Telescope unique telescope on Mount Hopkins, Arizona, opened 1979, consisting of six 1.83-m/72-in mirrors mounted in a hexagon, the light-collecting area of which equals that of a single mirror 4.5 m/176 in diameter. It is planned to replace the six mirrors with a single mirror 6.5 m/256 in wide.

observatory a site or facility for observation of natural phenomena. The modern observatory dates from the invention of the telescope. Most early observatories were near towns, but with the advent of big telescopes, clear skies with little background light, and hence high, remote sites, became essential. The most powerful optical telescopes covering the sky are at Mauna Kea; Mount Palomar; Kitt Peak, Arizona; La Palma, Canary Islands; Cerro Tololo and La Silla, Chile; Siding Spring, Australia; and Mount Semirodniki, the Caucasus. Radio astronomy observatories include Jodrell Bank; the Mullard, Cambridge, England; Arecibo; Effelsberg, Germany; and Parkes. Observatories are also carried on aircraft or sent into orbit as satellites, in space stations, and on the Space Shuttle. The Hubble Space Telescope was launched into orbit in April 1990. The Very Large Telescope is under construction by the European Southern Observatory (ESO) in the mountains of N Chile and is expected to be in operation by 1997.

Palomar, Mount the location, since 1948, of an observatory, 80 km/50 mi NE of San Diego, California, USA. It has a 5 m/200 in diameter reflector called the Hale.

Parkes the site in New South Wales of the Australian National Radio Astronomy Observatory, featuring a radio telescope of 64 m/210 ft aperture, run by the Commonwealth Scientific and Industrial Research Organization.

planetarium complex optical projection device by means of which the motions of stars and planets are reproduced on a domed ceiling representing the sky.

radio telescope instrument for detecting radio waves from the universe. Radio telescopes usually consist of a metal bowl that collects and focuses radio waves the way a concave mirror collects and focuses light waves. Other radio telescopes are shaped like long troughs, and some consist of simple rod-shaped aerials. Radio telescopes are much larger than optical telescopes, because the wavelengths they are detecting are much longer than the wavelength of light. A large dish such as that at Jodrell Bank, England, can see the radio sky less clearly than a small optical telescope sees the visible sky. The largest single dish is 305 m/1,000 ft across, at Arecibo, Puerto Rico.

Royal Greenwich Observatory the national astronomical observatory of the UK, founded 1675 at Greenwich, SE London, England, to provide navigational information for sailors. After World War II it was moved to Herstmonceux Castle, Sussex; in 1990 it was transferred to Cambridge. It also operates telescopes on La Palma in the Canary Islands, including the 4.2-m/165-in William Herschel Telescope, commissioned 1987.

Siding Spring Mountain peak 400 km/250 mi NW of Sydney, site of the UK Schmidt Telescope, opened 1973, and the 3.9-m/154-in **Anglo-Australian Telescope**, opened 1975, which was the first big telescope to be fully computer-controlled. It is one of the most powerful telescopes in the southern hemisphere.

South African Astronomical Observatory national observatory of South Africa at Sutherland, founded in 1973 after the merger of the Royal Observatory, Cape Town, and the Republic Observatory, Johannesburg, and operated by the Council for Scientific and Industrial Research of South Africa. Its main telescope is a 1.88-m/74-in reflector formerly at the Radcliffe Observatory, Pretoria.

sundial instrument measuring time by means of a shadow cast by the Sun. Almost completely superseded by the proliferation of clocks, it survives ornamentally in gardens. The dial is marked with the hours at graduated distances, and a style or gnomon (parallel to Earth's axis and pointing to the north) casts the shadow.

telescope device for collecting and focusing light and other forms of electromagnetic radiation. A telescope produces a magnified image, which makes the object seem nearer, and it shows objects fainter than can be seen by the eye alone. A telescope with a large aperture, or opening, can distinguish finer detail and fainter objects than one with a small aperture. The **refracting telescope** uses lenses, and the **reflecting telescope** uses mirrors. A third type, the **catadioptric telescope**, with a combination of lenses and mirrors, is used increasingly.

US Naval Observatory US government observatory in Washington, DC, which provides the nation's time service and publishes almanacs for navigators, surveyors, and astronomers. It contains a 66-cm/26-in refracting telescope opened 1873. A 1.55-m/61-in reflector for measuring positions of celestial objects was opened 1964 at Flagstaff, Arizona.

Very Large Array (VLA) the largest and most complex single-site radio telescope in the world. It is located on the Plains of San Augustine, 80 km/50 mi west of Socorro, New Mexico. It consists of 27 dish antennae, each 25 m/82 ft in diameter, arranged along three equally spaced arms forming a Y-shaped array. Two of the arms are 21 km/13 mi long, and the third, to the north, is 19 km/11.8 mi long. The dishes are mounted on railway tracks enabling the configuration and size of the array to be altered as required.

Yerkes Observatory astronomical centre in Wisconsin, USA, founded by George Hale in 1897. It houses the world's largest refracting optical telescope, with a lens of diameter 102 cm/40 in.

Zelenchukskaya site of the world's largest single-mirror optical telescope, with a mirror 6 m/236 in diameter, in the Caucasus Mountains of Russia. At the same site is the RATAN 600 radio telescope, consisting of radio reflectors in a circle 600 m/2,000 ft diameter.

CLASSIFICATION

analytical chemistry branch of chemistry that deals with the determination of the chemical composition of substances. *Qualitative analysis* determines the identities of the substances in a given sample; *quantitative analysis* determines how much of a particular substance is present.

biochemistry science concerned with the chemistry of living organisms: the structure and reactions of proteins (such as enzymes), nucleic acids, carbohydrates, and lipids.

inorganic chemistry the branch of chemistry dealing with the chemical properties of the elements and their compounds, excluding the more complex covalent compounds of carbon, which are considered in organic chemistry.

organic chemistry branch of chemistry that deals with carbon compounds. Organic compounds form the chemical basis of life and are more abundant than inorganic compounds. The basis of organic chemistry is the ability of carbon to form long chains of atoms, branching chains, rings, and other complex structures. In a typical organic compound, each carbon atom forms bonds covalently with each of its neighbouring carbon atoms in a chain or ring, and additionally with other atoms, commonly hydrogen, oxygen, nitrogen, or sulphur. Compounds containing only carbon and hydrogen are known as *hydrocarbons*.

physical chemistry branch of chemistry concerned with examining the relationships between the chemical compositions of substances and the physical properties that they display. Most chemical reactions exhibit some physical phenomenon (change of state, temperature, pressure, or volume, or the use or production of electricity), and the measurement and study of such phenomena has led to many chemical theories and laws.

INORGANIC CHEMISTRY

ammonia NH_3 colourless pungent-smelling gas, lighter than air and very soluble in water. It is made on an industrial scale by the Haber process, and used mainly to produce nitrogenous fertilizers, some explosives, and nitric acid.

carbon nonmetallic element, symbol C, atomic number 6, relative atomic mass 12.011. It is one of the most widely distributed elements, both inorganically and organically, and occurs in combination with other elements in all plants and animals.

The atoms of carbon can link with one another in rings or chains, giving rise to innumerable complex compounds. It occurs in nature (1) in the pure state in the crystalline forms of graphite and diamond; (2) as

calcium carbonate ($CaCO_3$) in carbonaceous rocks such as chalk and limestone; (3) as carbon dioxide (CO_2) in the atmosphere; and (4) as hydrocarbons in the fossil fuels petroleum, coal, and natural gas. Noncrystalline forms of pure carbon include charcoal and coal. When added to steel, carbon forms a wide range of alloys. In its elemental form, it is widely used as a moderator in nuclear reactors; as colloidal graphite it is a good lubricant, which, when deposited on a surface in a vacuum, obviates photoelectric and secondary emission of electrons. The radioactive isotope C-14 (half-life 5,730 years) is widely used in archaeological dating and as a tracer in biological research.

gold heavy, precious, yellow, metallic element; symbol Au, atomic number 79, relative atomic mass 197.0. It is unaffected by temperature changes and is highly resistant to acids. For manufacture, gold is alloyed with another strengthening metal, its purity being measured in carats on a scale of 24. In 1990 the three leading gold-producing countries were: South Africa, 605.4 tonnes; USA, 295 tonnes; and USSR, 260 tonnes. Like silver, gold is used in printed circuits and for electrical contacts because of its excellent electrical conductivity.

halogen any of a group of five nonmetallic elements with similar chemical bonding properties: fluorine, chlorine, bromine, iodine, and astatine. They form a linked group in the periodic table of the elements, descending from fluorine, the most reactive, to astatine, the least reactive. They combine directly with most metals to form salts, such as common salt (NaCl). Each halogen has seven electrons in its valence shell, which accounts for the chemical similarities displayed by the group.

hydrochloric acid HCl solution of hydrogen chloride (a colourless, acidic gas) in water. The concentrated acid is about 35% hydrogen chloride and is corrosive. The acid is a typical strong, monobasic acid forming only one series of salts, the chlorides. It has many industrial uses, including recovery of zinc from galvanized scrap iron and the production of chlorine. It is also produced in the stomachs of animals for the purposes of digestion.

hydrogen colourless, odourless, gaseous, nonmetallic element, symbol H, atomic number 1, relative atomic mass 1.00797. It is the lightest of all the elements and occurs on Earth chiefly in combination with oxygen as water. Hydrogen is the most abundant element in the universe, where it accounts for 93% of the total number of atoms and 76% of the total mass. It is a component of most stars, including the Sun, whose heat and light are produced through the nuclear-fusion process that converts hydrogen into helium. When subjected to a pressure 500,000 times greater than that of the Earth's atmosphere, hydrogen becomes a solid with metallic properties. Its industrial uses include the hardening of oils and fats by hydrogenation.

metal any of a class of chemical elements with certain chemical characteristics and physical

BIOCHEMISTRY: CHRONOLOGY

c.1830	Johannes Müller discovered proteins.
1833	Anselme Payen and J F Persoz first isolated an enzyme.
1862	Haemoglobin was first crystallized.
1869	The genetic material DNA (deoxyribonucleic acid) was discovered by Friedrich Mieschler.
1899	Emil Fischer postulated the 'lock-and-key' hypothesis to explain the specificity of enzyme action.
1913	Leonor Michaelis and M L Menten developed a mathematical equation describing the rate of enzyme-catalyzed reactions.
1915	The hormone thyroxine was first isolated from thyroid-gland tissue.
1920	The chromosome theory of heredity was postulated by Thomas Hunt Morgan; growth hormone was discovered by Herbert McLean Evans and J A Long.
1921	Insulin was first isolated from the pancreas by Frederick Grant Banting and Charles Best.
1926	Insulin was obtained in pure crystalline form.
1927	Thyroxine was first synthesized.
1928	Alexander Fleming discovered penicillin.
1931	Paul Karrer deduced the structure of retinol (vitamin A); vitamin D compounds were obtained in crystalline form by Adolf Windaus and Askew, independently of each other.
1932	Charles Glen King isolated ascorbic acid (vitamin C).
1933	Tadeusz Reichstein synthesized ascorbic acid.
1935	Richard Kuhn and Karrer established the structure of riboflavin (vitamin B_2).
1936	Robert Williams established the structure of thiamine (vitamin B_1); biotin was isolated by Kogl and Tonnis.
1937	Niacin was isolated and identified by Conrad Arnold Elvehjem.
1938	Pyridoxine (vitamin B_6) was isolated in pure crystalline form.
1939	The structure of pyridoxine was determined by Kuhn.
1940	Hans Krebs proposed the citric acid (Krebs) cycle; Hickman isolated retinol in pure crystalline form; Williams established the structure of pantothenic acid; biotin was identified by Albert Szent-Györgyi, Vincent Du Vigneaud, and co-workers.
1941	Penicillin was isolated and characterized by Howard Florey and Ernst Chain.
1943	The role of DNA in genetic inheritance was first demonstrated by Oswald Avery, Colin MacLeod, and Maclyn McCarty.
1950	The basic components of DNA were established by Erwin Chargaff; the alpha-helix structure of proteins was established by Linus Pauling and R B Corey.
1953	James Watson and Francis Crick determined the molecular structure of DNA.
1956	Mahlon Hoagland and Paul Zamecnick discovered transfer RNA (ribonucleic acid); mechanisms for the biosynthesis of RNA and DNA were discovered by Arthur Kornberg and Severo Ochoa.
1957	Interferon was discovered by Alick Isaacs and Jean Lindemann.
1958	The structure of RNA was determined.
1960	Messenger RNA was discovered by Sydney Brenner and François Jacob.
1961	Marshall Warren Nirenberg and Ochoa determined the chemical nature of the genetic code.
1965	Insulin was first synthesized.
1966	The immobilization of enzymes was achieved by Chibata.
1968	Brain hormones were discovered by Roger Guillemin and Andrew Victor Schally.
1975	J Hughes and Hans Walter Kosterlitz discovered encephalins.
1976	Guillemin discovered endorphins.
1977	Baxter isolated the genetic code for human growth hormone.
1978	Human insulin was first produced by genetic engineering.
1979	The biosynthetic production of human growth hormone was announced by Howard Goodman and J Baxter of the University of California, and by D V Goeddel and Seeburg of Genentech.
1982	Louis Chedid and Michael Sela developed the first synthesized vaccine.
1984	Alec Jeffreys developed genetic fingerprinting at the University of Leicester.
1983	The first commercially available product of genetic engineering (Humulin) was launched.
1985	Alec Jeffreys devised genetic fingerprinting.
1990	Jean-Marie Lehn, Ulrich Koert, and Margaret M Harding at Louis Pasteur University, France reported the synthesis of a new class of compounds, called nucleohelicates, that mimic the double helical structure of DNA, turned inside out.

properties; they are good conductors of heat and electricity; opaque but reflect light well; malleable, which enables them to be cold-worked and rolled into sheets; and ductile, which permits them to be drawn into thin wires. Metallic elements comprise about 75% of the 109 elements shown in the periodic table of the elements. They form alloys with each other, bases with the hydroxyl radical (OH), and replace the hydrogen in an acid to form a salt. The majority are found in nature in the combined form only, as compounds or mineral ores; about 16 of them also occur in the elemental form, as native metals. Their chemical properties are largely determined by the extent to which their atoms can lose one or more electrons to form positive ions.

nitric acid HNO_3 fuming acid obtained by the oxidation of ammonia or the action of sulphuric acid on potassium nitrate. It is a highly corrosive acid, dissolving most metals, and a strong oxidizing agent. It is used in the making of nitrates, explosives, plastics, and dyes.

nitrogen colourless, odourless, tasteless, gaseous, nonmetallic element, symbol N, atomic number 7, relative atomic mass 14.0067. It forms almost 80% of the Earth's atmosphere by volume and is a constituent of all plant and animal tissues (in proteins and nucleic acids). Nitrogen is obtained for industrial use by the liquefaction and fractional distillation of air. It is used in the Haber process to make ammonia, NH_3, and to provide an inert atmosphere for certain chemical reactions. Its compounds are used in the manufacture of foods, drugs, fertilizers, dyes, and explosives.

nonmetal one of a set of elements (around 20 in total) with certain physical and chemical properties opposite to those of metals. Nonmetals accept electrons, and are sometimes called electronegative elements.

oxygen colourless, odourless, tasteless, nonmetallic, gaseous element, symbol O, atomic number 8, relative atomic mass 15.9994. It is the most abundant element in the Earth's crust (almost 50% by mass), forms about 21% by volume of the atmosphere, and is present in combined form in water, carbon dioxide, silicon dioxide (quartz), iron ore, calcium carbonate (limestone), and many other substances. Life on Earth evolved using oxygen, which is a by-product of photosynthesis and the basis for respiration in plants and animals. Oxygen is essential for combustion (burning), and is used with ethyne (acetylene) in high-temperature oxyacetylene welding and cutting torches. Ozone is an allotrope of oxygen.

phosphate salt or ester of phosphoric acid. Phosphates are used as fertilizers, and are required for the development of healthy root systems. They are involved in many biochemical processes, often as part of complex molecules, such as adenosine triphosphate (ATP).

plutonium silvery-white, radioactive, metallic element, symbol Pu, atomic number 94, relative atomic mass 239.13. It occurs in nature in minute quantities, but is produced in quantity only synthetically. Plutonium is one of the three elements capable of nuclear fission (the others are thorium and uranium), and is used as a fuel in fast-breeder reactors and in making nuclear weapons. It has a long half-life (24,000 years) during which time it remains highly toxic, and poses considerable disposal problems.

silicon brittle, nonmetallic element, symbol Si, atomic number 14, relative atomic mass 28.086. It is the second most abundant element (after oxygen) in the Earth's crust and occurs in amorphous and crystalline forms. In nature it is found only in combination with other elements, chiefly with oxygen in silica (silicon dioxide, SiO_2) and the silicates. These form the mineral quartz, which makes up most sands and gravels. Silicon is used in alloys and to make transistors and semiconductors.

silver white, lustrous, extremely malleable and ductile, metallic element, symbol Ag, atomic number 47, relative atomic mass 107.868. It occurs in nature in ores and as a free metal; the chief ores are sulphides, from which the metal is extracted by smelting with lead. It is one of the best metallic conductors of both heat and electricity; its most useful compounds are the chloride and bromide, which darken on exposure to light and are the basis of photographic emulsions.

sulphur brittle, pale-yellow, nonmetallic element, symbol S, atomic number 16, relative atomic mass 32.064. It occurs in three forms: two crystalline (called rhombic and monoclinic, following the arrangements of the atoms within the crystals) and one amorphous. It burns in air with a blue flame and a stifling odour. Sulphur is widely used in the manufacture of sulphuric acid (used to treat phosphate rock to make fertilizers) and in making paper, matches, gunpowder and fireworks, in vulcanizing rubber, and in medicines and insecticides.

sulphuric acid H_2SO_4 a dense, viscous, colourless liquid that is extremely corrosive. It gives out heat when added to water and can cause severe burns. Sulphuric acid is used extensively in the chemical industry, in the refining of petrol, and in the manufacture of fertilizers, detergents, explosives, and dyes. It forms the acid component of car batteries.

transuranic element or **transuranium element** chemical element with an atomic number of 93 or more—that is, with a greater number of protons in the nucleus than has uranium. All transuranic elements are radioactive. Neptunium and plutonium are found in small quantities in nature; the others are synthesized in nuclear reactions.

uranium hard, silvery-white, radioactive, metallic element, symbol U, atomic number 92, relative atomic mass 238.029. It is the most abundant radioactive element in the Earth's crust, its decay giving rise to essentially all the radioactive elements in nature; its final decay product is the stable element lead. Uranium is one of the three elements capable of nuclear fission; the isotope uranium-235 is used as a fuel in nuclear reactors and in making nuclear weapons.

water H_2O liquid without colour, taste, or odour, an oxide of hydrogen. It is the most abundant substance on Earth, and is essential to all forms of life. Water begins to freeze solid at 0°C/32°F, and to boil at 100°C/212°F. When liquid, it is virtually incompressible; frozen, it expands by 1/11 of its volume. It acts as an efficient solvent, particularly when hot.

ORGANIC CHEMISTRY

alcohol any member of a group of organic chemical compounds characterized by the presence of one or more aliphatic OH (hydroxyl) groups in the molecule, and which form esters with acids. The main uses of alcohols are as solvents for gums, resins, lacquers, and varnishes; in the making of dyes; for essential oils in perfumery; and for medical substances in pharmacy. Alcohol (ethanol) is produced naturally in the fermentation process and is consumed as part of alcoholic beverages.

aldehyde any of a group of organic chemical compounds prepared by oxidation of primary alcohols, so that the OH (hydroxyl) group loses its hydrogen to give an oxygen joined by a double bond to a carbon atom (the aldehyde group, with the formula CHO).

aliphatic compound organic chemical compound are also aliphatic, as in the alicyclic compound cyclohexane (C_6H_{12}) or the heterocyclic piperidine ($C_5H_{11}N$). Compare aromatic compound.

alkane member of a group of hydrocarbons having the general formula C_nH_{2n+2}, commonly known as *paraffins*. Lighter alkanes, such as methane, ethane, propane, and butane, are colourless gases; heavier ones are liquids or solids. In nature they are found in natural gas and petroleum. As alkanes contain only single covalent bonds, they are said to be saturated.

alkene member of a group of hydrocarbons having the general formula C_nH_{2n}, formerly known as olefins. Lighter alkenes, such as ethene and propene, are gases, obtained from the cracking of oil fractions. Alkenes are unsaturated compounds, characterized by one or more double bonds between adjacent carbon atoms. They react by addition, and many useful compounds, such as poly(ethene), are made from them.

alkyne member of a group of hydrocarbons with the general formula C_nH_{2n-2}, formerly known as the acetylenes. They are unsaturated compounds, characterized by one or more triple bonds between adjacent carbon atoms. Lighter alkynes, such as ethyne, are gases; heavier ones are liquids or solids.

amino acid water-soluble organic molecule, mainly composed of carbon, oxygen, hydrogen, and nitrogen, containing both a basic in which the bonding electrons are localized within the vicinity of the bonded atoms. Its carbon atoms are joined in straight chains, as in hexane (C_6H_{14}), or in branched chains, as in 2-methylpentane ($CH_3CH(CH_3)CH_2CH_2CH_3$). Cyclic compounds that do not have delocalized electrons

CRYSTAL GAZING

The image you see on a laptop-computer screen or on the face of a digital watch is brought about by a liquid-crystal display (LCD). Such a device consists of a layer of liquid crystal sandwiched between two filters that polarize light in different directions. It works because the rod-shaped liquid-crystal molecules can alter the way polarized light passes through them, and because they are sensitive to an electric field. When an electric field is applied to a particular region of the LCD, the liquid-crystal molecules in that region line up in an orderly way and allow light polarized by the first filter to pass through them. This light cannot pass through the second filter and so the display appears black in that region. Switch off the field and the crystals become disorderly and interfere with the polarized light from the first filter. Because this light is now unpolarized, it can pass through the second filter and so the display appears transparent.

A good example of modern technology, you might think. But, in fact, liquid crystals are widespread in biological systems. The membrane of every living cell behaves like a liquid crystal, and the fatty substance myelin

that sheathes the nerve cells also has liquid-crystal properties. Myelin was first observed by German pathologist Rudolf Virchow in 1853. Two years later, it was found to affect polarized light just as many crystals did. Five years later, Otto Lehman made the first synthetic liquid crystal, cholesteryl benzoate. He observed that his new substance had apparently two melting points, and that between these temperatures it was neither a liquid nor a crystal. Many scientists are now of the opinion that liquid crystals are the fourth state of matter—the simple schoolbook definition of the three states of matter as solid, liquid, and gas, is no longer sufficient.

New understanding of liquid crystals is aiding biological research and leading to the development of plastic materials with astonishing mechanical and electrical properties. The Du Pont Corporation manufactures Kevlar, a fibre stronger than steel, from liquid-crystal plastics based on aromatic polyamides. At the General Electric Company, researchers have developed liquid-crystal materials ideal for making erasable compact discs. A similar technology produces plastic materials that can encode holograms.

amine group (NH_2) and an acidic carboxyl (COOH) group. When two or more amino acids are joined together, they are known as peptides; proteins are made up of interacting polypeptides (peptide chains consisting of more than three amino acids) and are folded or twisted in characteristic shapes.

aromatic compound organic chemical compound in which some of the bonding electrons are delocalized (shared amongst several atoms within the molecule and not localized in the vicinity of the atoms involved in bonding). The commonest aromatic compounds have ring structures, the atoms comprising the ring being either all carbon or containing one or more different atoms (usually nitrogen, sulphur, or oxygen). Typical examples are benzene (C_6H_6) and pyridine (C_6H_5N).

ester organic compound formed by the reaction between an alcohol and an acid, with the elimination of water. Unlike salts, esters are covalent compounds.

ethanoic acid common name *acetic acid* CH_3CO_2H one of the simplest fatty acids (a series of organic acids). In the pure state it is a colourless liquid with an unpleasant pungent odour; it solidifies to an icelike mass of crystals at 16.7°C/62.4°F, and hence is often called glacial ethanoic acid. Vinegar contains 5% or more ethanoic acid, produced by fermentation.

ether any of a series of organic chemical compounds having an oxygen atom linking the carbon atoms of two hydrocarbon radical goups (general formula R-O-R); also the common name for ethoxyethane $C_2H_5OC_2H_5$ (also called diethyl ether). Ethoxyethane is a colourless, volatile, inflammable liquid, slightly soluble in water, miscible with ethanol. It is prepared by treatment of ethanol with excess concentrated sulphuric acid at 140°C/284°F. It is used as an anaesthetic by vapour inhalation and as an external cleansing agent before surgical operations. It is also used as a solvent, and in the extraction of oils, fats, waxes, resins, and alkaloids.

fatty acid or *carboxylic acid* organic compound consisting of a hydrocarbon chain, up to 24 carbon atoms long, with a carboxyl group (–COOH) at one end.

functional group a small number of atoms in an arrangement that determines the chemical properties of the group and of the molecule to which it is attached (for example, the carboxyl group COOH, or the amine group NH_2). Organic compounds can be considered as structural skeletons, with a high carbon content, with functional groups attached.

homologous series a series of organic chemicals with similar chemical properties whose members differ by a constant relative molecular mass.

hydrocarbon any of a class of chemical compounds containing only hydrogen and carbon (for example, the alkanes and alkenes). Hydrocarbons are obtained industrially principally from petroleum and coal tar.

isomer chemical compound having the same molecular composition and mass as another, but with different physical or chemical properties owing to the different structural arrangement of its constituent atoms. For example, the organic compounds butane ($CH_3(CH_2)CH_3$) and methyl propane ($CH_3CH(CH_3)CH_3$) are isomers, each possessing four carbon atoms and ten hydrogen atoms but differing in the way that these are arranged with respect to each other.

ketone member of the group of organic compounds containing the carbonyl group (C=O) bonded to two atoms of carbon (instead of one carbon and one hydrogen as in aldehydes). Ketones are liquids or low-melting-point solids, slightly soluble in water.

lipid any of a large number of esters of fatty acids, commonly formed by the reaction of a fatty acid with glycerol. They are soluble in alcohol but not in water. Lipids are the chief constituents of plant and animal waxes, fats, and oils.

phenol member of a group of aromatic chemical compounds with weakly acidic properties, which are characterized by a hydroxyl (OH) group attached directly to an aromatic ring. The simplest of the phenols, derived from benzene, is also known as phenol and has the formula C_6H_5OH. It is sometimes called *carbolic acid* and can be extracted from coal tar. Pure phenol consists of colourless, needle-shaped crystals, which take up moisture from the atmosphere. It has a strong and characteristic smell and was once used as an antiseptic. It is, however, toxic by absorption through the skin.

polyester synthetic resin formed by the condensation of polyhydric alcohols (alcohols containing more than one hydroxyl group) with dibasic acids (acids containing two replaceable hydrogen atoms). Polyesters are thermosetting plastics, used in making synthetic fibres, such as Dacron and Terylene, and constructional plastics. With glass fibre added as reinforcement, polyesters are used in car bodies and boat hulls.

polymer compound made up of a large, long-chain or branching matrix composed of many repeated simple units (*monomers*). There are many polymers, both natural (cellulose, chitin, lignin) and synthetic (polyethylene and nylon, types of plastic). Synthetic polymers belong to two groups: thermosoftening and thermosetting.

polyunsaturate type of fat or oil containing a high proportion of triglyceride molecules whose fatty-acid chains contain several double bonds. By contrast, the fatty-acid chains of the triglycerides in saturated fats (such as lard) contain only single bonds. Polyunsaturated fats are generally considered healthier for human nutrition than are saturated fats, and are widely used in margarines and cooking oils.

saturated compound organic compound, such as

TRANSURANIC ELEMENTS

atomic number	name	symbol	year of discovery	source of first preparation identified	isotope	half life of first isotope identified
actinide series						
93	neptunium	Np	1940	irradiation of uranium-238 with neutrons	Np-239	2.35 days
94	plutonium	Pu	1941	Bombardment of uranium-238 with deuterons	Pu-238	86.4 years
95	americium	Am	1944	irradiation of plutonium-239 with neutrons	Am-241	458 years
96	curium	Cm	1944	bombardment of plutonium-239 with helium nuclei	Cm-242	162.5 days
97	berkelium	Bk	1949	bombardment of americium-241 with helium nuclei	Bk-243	4.5 hours
98	californium	Cf	1950	bombardment of curium-242 with helium nuclei	Cf-245	44 minutes
99	einsteinium	Es	1952	irradiation of uranium-238 with neutrons in first thermonuclear explosion	Es-253	20 days
100	fermium	Fm	1953	irradiation of uranium-238 with neutrons in first thermonuclear explosion	Fm-235	16 hours
101	mendelevium	Md	1955	bombardment of einsteinium-253 with helium nuclei	Md-256	1.5 hours
102	nobelium	No	1958	bombardment of curium-246 with carbon nuclei	No-255	3 seconds
103	lawrencium	Lr	1961	bombardment of californium-252 with boron nuclei	Lr-257	8 seconds
super-heavy elements						
104	unnilquadium* (also called rutherfordium or kurchatovium)	Unq	1964/ 1969	bombardment of californium-249 with carbon-12 nuclei	U4-257	4 seconds
105	unnilpentium* (also called hahnium or nielsbohrium)	Unp	1967/ 1970	bombardment of californium-249 with nitrogen-15 nuclei	U5-260	1.6 seconds
106	unnilhexium*	Unh	1974	bombardment of californium-249 with oxygen-18 nuclei	U6-263	0.9 seconds
107	unnilseptium*	Uns	1976	bombardment of bismuth-209 with nuclei of chromium-54	U7	2 milliseconds
108	unniloctium*	Uno	1984	bombardment of lead-208	U8-265	a few milliseconds
109	unnilennium*	Une	1982	bombardment of bismuth-209	U9	5 milliseconds

* Names for elements 104–109 are as proposed by the International Union for Pure and Applied Chemistry.

propane, that contains only single covalent bonds. Saturated organic compounds can only undergo further reaction by substitution reactions, as in the production of chloropropane from propane.

unsaturated compound chemical compound in which two adjacent atoms are bonded by a double or triple covalent bond.

STRUCTURE

atom the smallest unit of matter that can take part in a chemical reaction, and which cannot be broken down chemically into anything simpler. An atom is made up of protons and neutrons in a central nucleus surrounded by electrons. The atoms of the various elements differ in atomic number, relative atomic mass, and chemical behaviour. There are 109 different types of atom, corresponding with the 109 known elements as listed in the periodic table of the elements.

atomic number or *proton number* the number (symbol Z) of protons in the nucleus of an atom. It is equal to the positive charge on the nucleus. In a neutral atom, it is also equal to the number of electrons surrounding the nucleus. The 109 elements are arranged in the periodic table of the elements according to their atomic number.

bond the result of the forces of attraction that hold together atoms of an element or elements to form a molecule. The principal types

DISCOVERY OF THE ELEMENTS

Date	Element (symbol)	Discoverer
prehistoric knowledge	antimony (Sb)	
	arsenic (As)	
	bismuth (Bi)	
	carbon (C)	
	copper (Cu)	
	gold (Au)	
	iron (Fe)	
	lead (Pb)	
	mercury (Hg)	
	silver (Ag)	
	sulphur (S)	
	tin (Sn)	
	zinc (Zn)	
1557	platinum (Pt)	Julius Scaliger
1669	phosphorus (P)	Hennig Brand
1735	cobalt (Co)	Georg Brandt
1751	nickel (Ni)	Axel Cronstedt
1755	magnesium (Mg)	Joseph Black (isolated by Humphry Davy 1808)
1766	hydrogen (H)	Henry Cavendish
1771	fluorine (F)	Karl Scheele (isolated by Henri Moissan 1886)
1772	nitrogen (N)	Daniel Rutherford
1774	chlorine (Cl)	Scheele
	manganese (Mn)	Johann Gottlieb Gahn
	oxygen (O)	Joseph Priestley and Karl Scheele, independently of each other
1778	molybdenum (Mo)	detected by Karl Scheele (isolated by Peter Jacob Hjelm 1782)
1782	tellurium (Te)	Franz Müller
1783	tungsten (W)	Juan José Elhuyar and Fausto Elhuyar
1789	uranium (U)	Martin Klaproth (isolated by Eugène Péligot 1841)
	zirconium (Zr)	Klaproth
1790	titanium (Ti)	William Gregor
1794	yttrium (Y)	Johan Gadolin
1797	chromium (Cr)	Louis-Nicolas Vauquelin
1798	beryllium (Be)	Vauquelin (isolated by Friedrich Wöhler and Antoine-Alexandre-Brutus Bussy 1828)
1801	vanadium (V)	Andrés del Rio (disputed), or Nils Sefström 1830
	niobium (Nb)	Charles Hatchett
1802	tantalum (Ta)	Anders Ekeberg
1803	cerium (Ce)	Jöns Berzelius and Wilhelm Hisinger, and independently by Klaproth
	iridium (Ir)	Smithson Tennant
	osmium (Os)	Tennant
	palladium (Pd)	William Wollaston
	rhodium (Rh)	Wollaston
1807	potassium (K)	Humphry Davy
	sodium (Na)	Davy
1808	barium (Ba)	Davy
	boron (B)	Davy, and independently by Joseph Gay-Lussac and Louis-Jacques Thénard
	calcium (Ca)	Davy
	strontium (Sr)	Davy
1811	iodine (I)	Bernard Courtois
1817	cadmium (Cd)	Friedrich Strohmeyer
	lithium (Li)	Johan Arfwedson
	selenium (Se)	Jöns Berzelius
1823	silicon (Si)	Berzelius
1824	aluminium (Al)	Hans Oersted (also attributed to Friedrich Wöhler 1827)
1826	bromine (Br)	Antoine-Jérôme Balard
1827	ruthenium (Ru)	G W Osann (isolated by Karl Klaus 1844)
1828	thorium (Th)	Berzelius
1839	lanthanum (La)	Carl Mosander
1842	erbium (Er)	Mosander
1843	terbium (Tb)	Mosander
1860	caesium (Cs)	Robert Bunsen and Gustav Kirchoff
1861	rubidium (Rb)	Bunsen and Kirchoff
	thallium (Tl)	William Crookes (isolated by Crookes and Lamy, independently of each other 1862)
1863	indium (In)	Ferdinand Reich and Hieronymus Richter
1868	helium (He)	Pierre Janssen
1875	gallium (Ga)	Paul Lecoq de Boisbaudran
1876	scandium (Sc)	Lars Nilson
1878	ytterbium (Yb)	Jean Charles de Marignac
1879	holmium (Ho)	Per Cleve
	samarium (Sm)	Lecoq de Boisbaudran
	thulium (Tm)	Cleve
1885	neodymium (Nd)	Carl von Welsbach
	praseodymium (Pr)	von Welsbach
1886	dysprosium (Dy)	Lecoq de Boisbaudran
	gadolinium (Gd)	Lecoq de Boisbaudran
	germanium (Ge)	Clemens Winkler
1894	argon (Ar)	John Rayleigh and William Ramsay
1898	krypton (Kr)	Ramsay and Morris Travers
	neon (Ne)	Ramsay and Travers
	polonium (Po)	Marie and Pierre Curie
	radium (Ra)	Marie Curie
	xenon (Xe)	Ramsay and Travers
1899	actinium (Ac)	André Debierne
1900	radon (Rn)	Friedrich Dorn
1901	europium (Eu)	Eugène Demarçay
1907	lutetium (Lu)	Georges Urbain and von Welsbach, independently of each other
1913	protactinium (Pa)	Kasimir Fajans and O Göhring
	hafnium (Hf)	Dirk Coster and Georg von Hevesy
1925	rhenium (Re)	Walter Noddack, Ida Tacke, and Otto Berg
1937	technetium (Tc)	Carlo Perrier and Emilio Segrè
1939	francium (Fr)	Marguérite Perey

DISCOVERY OF THE ELEMENTS Cont.

1940	astatine (At)	Dale R Corson, K R MacKenzie, and Segrè
	neptunium (Np)	Edwin M McMillan and Philip Abelson
	plutonium (Pu)	Glenn T Seaborg, McMillan, Joseph W Kennedy, and Arthur C Wahl
1944	americium (Am)	Seaborg, Ralph A James, Leon O Morgan, and Albert Ghiorso
	curium (Cm)	Seaborg, James, and Ghiorso
1945	promethium (Pm)	J A Marinsky, Lawrence E Glendenin, and Charles D Coryell
1949	berkelium (Bk)	Seaborg, Stanley G Thompson, and Ghiorso
1950	californium (Cf)	Seaborg, Thompson, Kenneth Street Jr, and Ghiorso
1952	einsteinium (Es)	Ghiorso and co-workers
	fermium (Fm)	Ghiorso and co-workers
1955	mendelevium (Md)	Ghiorso, Bernard G Harvey, Gregory R Choppin, Thompson, and Seaborg
1958	nobelium (No)	Ghiorso, Torbjørn Sikkeland, J R Walton, and Seaborg
1961	lawrencium (Lr)	Ghiorso, Sikkeland, Almon E Larsh, and Robert M Latimer
1964	unnilquadium (Unq)	claimed by Soviet scientist Georgii Flerov and co-workers (disputed by US workers)
1967	unnilpentium (Unp)	claimed by Flerov and co-workers (disputed by US workers)
1969	unnilquadium (Unq)	claimed by US scientist Albert Ghiorso and co-workers (disputed by Soviet workers)
1970	unnilpentium (Unp)	claimed by Ghiorso and co-workers (disputed by Soviet workers)
1974	unnilhexium (Unh)	claimed by Flerov and co-workers, and, independently, by Ghiorso and co-workers
1976	unnilseptium (Uns)	Flerov and Yuri Oganessian (confirmed by German scientist Peter Armbruster and co-workers)
1982	unnilennium (Une)	Armbruster and co-workers
1984	unniloctium (Uno)	Armbruster and co-workers

of bonding are ionic, covalent, metallic, and intermolecular (such as hydrogen bonding).

compound chemical substance made up of two or more elements bonded together, so that they cannot be separated by physical means. Compounds are held together by ionic or covalent bonds.

covalent bond chemical bond in which the two combining atoms share a pair of electrons. It is often represented by a single line drawn between the two atoms. Covalently bonded substances include hydrogen (H_2), water (H_2O), and most organic substances.

electron stable, negatively charged elementary particle, a constituent of all atoms and the basic particle of electricity. A beam of electrons will undergo diffraction (scattering), and produce interference patterns, in the same way as electromagnetic waves such as light; hence they may also be regarded as waves.

electronegativity the power of an atom in a molecule to attract electrons. Nonmetals such as fluorine and chlorine have the highest values of electronegativity; metals have low values.

element substance that cannot be split chemically into simpler substances. The atoms of a particular element all have the same number of protons in their nuclei (the same atomic number). Of the 109 known elements, 95 occur in nature (those with atomic numbers 1–95). Those from 96 to 109 do not occur in nature and are produced synthetically in particle accelerators. Eighty-one of the elements are stable; all the others, which include atomic numbers 43, 61, and from 84 up, are radioactive. The relationship between elements is displayed in the periodic table.

formula a representation of a molecule, radical, or ion, in which the component chemical elements are represented by their symbols. An *empirical formula* indicates the simplest ratio of the elements in a compound, without indicating how many of them there are or how they are combined. A *molecular formula* gives the number of each type of element present in one molecule. A *structural formula* shows the relative positions of the atoms and the bonds between them. For example, for ethanoic acid, the empirical formula is CH_2O, the molecular formula is $C_2H_4O_2$, and the structural formula is CH_3COOH.

ion an atom, or group of atoms, which is either positively charged (*cation*) or negatively charged (*anion*), as a result of the loss or gain of electrons during chemical reactions or exposure to certain forms of radiation.

ionic bond or *electrovalent bond* bond produced when atoms of one element donate electrons to another element that accepts the electrons, forming positively and negatively charged ions respectively. The electrostatic attraction between the oppositely charged ions constitutes the bond.

isotope one of two or more atoms that have the same atomic number (same number of protons), but which contain a different number

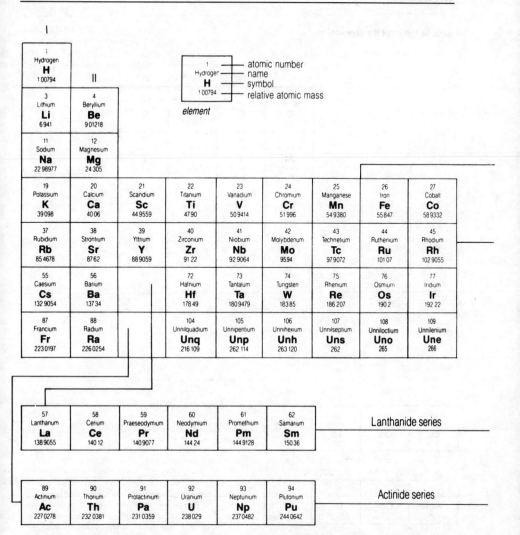

| 1 |
| Hydrogen |
| **H** |
| 1 00794 |

atomic number
name
symbol
relative atomic mass

element

of neutrons, thus differing in their atomic masses.

They may be stable or radioactive, naturally occurring or synthesized. The term was coined by English chemist Frederick Soddy, pioneer researcher in atomic disintegration.

lone pair a pair of electrons in the outermost shell of an atom that are not used in bonding. In certain circumstances, they will allow the atom to bond with atoms, ions, or molecules (such as boron trifluoride, BF_3) that are deficient in electrons, forming coordinate covalent (dative) bonds in which they provide both of the bonding electrons.

molecule the smallest unit of an element or compound that can exist and still retain the characteristics of the element or compound. A molecule of an element consists of one or more like atoms; a molecule of a compound consists of two or more different atoms bonded together. They vary in size and complexity from the hydrogen molecule (H_2) to the large macromolecules of proteins. They are held together by ionic bonds, in which the atoms gain or lose electrons to form ions, or covalent bonds, where electrons from each atom are shared in a new molecular orbital.

neutron one of the three chief subatomic particles (the others being the proton and the electron). Neutrons have about the same mass as protons but no electric charge, and occur in the nuclei of all atoms except hydrogen. They contribute to the mass of atoms but do not affect their chemistry, which depends on the proton or electron numbers. For instance, isotopes of a single element (with different masses) differ only in the number of neutrons in their nuclei and have identical chemical properties.

periodic table of the elements in chemistry, a table setting out the classification of the elements following the statement by Russian chemist Dmitri Mendeleyev 1869 that 'the properties of elements are in periodic depend-

periodic table   of the elements   0

					0
					2 Helium **He** 4.00260

III	IV	V	VI	VII	
5 Boron **B** 10.81	6 Carbon **C** 12.011	7 Nitrogen **N** 14.0067	8 Oxygen **O** 15.9994	9 Fluorine **F** 18.99840	10 Neon **Ne** 20.179
13 Aluminium **Al** 26.98154	14 Silicon **Si** 28.086	15 Phosphorus **P** 30.97376P	16 Sulphur **S** 32.06	17 Chlorine **Cl** 35.453	18 Argon **Ar** 39.948

28 Nickel **Ni** 58.70	29 Copper **Cu** 63.546	30 Zinc **Zn** 65.38	31 Gallium **Ga** 69.72	32 Germanium **Ge** 72.59	33 Arsenic **As** 74.9216	34 Selenium **Se** 78.96	35 Bromine **Br** 79.904	36 Krypton **Kr** 83.80
46 Palladium **Pd** 106.4	47 Silver **Ag** 107.868	48 Cadmium **Cd** 112.40	49 Indium **In** 114.82	50 Tin **Sn** 118.69	51 Antimony **Sb** 121.75	52 Tellurium **Te** 127.75	53 Iodine **I** 126.9045	54 Xenon **Xe** 131.30
78 Platinum **Pt** 195.09	79 Gold **Au** 196.9665	80 Mercury **Hg** 200.59	81 Thallium **Tl** 204.37	82 Lead **Pb** 207.37	83 Bismuth **Bi** 207.2	84 Polonium **Po** 210	85 Astatine **At** 211	86 Radon **Rn** 222.0176

63 Europium **Eu** 151.96	64 Gadolinium **Gd** 157.25	65 Terbium **Tb** 158.9254	66 Dysprosium **Dy** 162.50	67 Holmium **Ho** 164.9304	68 Erbium **Er** 167.26	69 Thulium **Tm** 168.9342	70 Ytterbium **Yb** 173.04	71 Lutetium **Lu** 174.97
95 Americium **Am** 243.0614	96 Curium **Cm** 247.0703	97 Berkelium **Bk** 247.0703	98 Californium **Cf** 251.0786	99 Einsteinium **Es** 252.0828	100 Fermium **Fm** 257.0951	101 Mendelevium **Md** 258.0986	102 Nobelium **No** 259.1009	103 Lawrencium **Lr** 260.1054

ence upon their atomic weight'. (Today elements are classified by their atomic number rather than by their relative atomic mass.) The properties of the elements are a direct consequence of the electronic (and nuclear) structure of their atoms. Striking similarities exist between the chemical properties of the elements in each of the table's vertical columns (called *groups*), which are numbered I–VII and then 0 (from left to right) to reflect the number of electrons in the outermost unfilled shell and hence the maximum valency. A gradation of properties may be traced along the horizontal rows (called *periods*). Metallic character increases across a period from right to left, and down a group. A large block of elements, between groups II and III, contains the transition elements, characterized by displaying more than one valency state.

proton (Greek 'first') positively charged subatomic particle, a fundamental constituent of any atomic nucleus. Its lifespan is effectively infinite.

relative atomic mass the mass of an atom. It depends on the number of protons and neutrons in the atom, the electrons having negligible mass. It is calculated relative to one-twelfth the mass of an atom of carbon-12. If more than one isotope of the element is present, the relative atomic mass is calculated by taking an average that takes account of the relative proportions of each isotope, resulting in values that are not whole numbers. The term *atomic weight*, although commonly used, is strictly speaking incorrect.

valency the measure of an element's ability to combine with other elements, expressed as the number of atoms of hydrogen (or any other standard univalent element) capable of uniting with (or replacing) its atoms. The number of electrons in the outermost shell of the atom dictates the combining ability of an element.

Isomer

butane CH₃(CH₂)₂CH₃

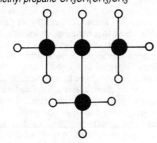

methyl propane CH₃CH(CH₃)CH₃

○ hydrogen atom

● carbon atom

— covalent bond

REACTIVITY

acid compound that, in solution in an ionizing solvent (usually water), gives rise to hydrogen ions (H^+ or protons). In modern chemistry, acids are defined as substances that are proton donors and accept electrons from a base to form ionic bonds. Acids react with bases to form salts, and they act as solvents. Strong acids are corrosive; dilute acids have a sour or sharp taste, although in some organic acids this may be partially masked by other flavour characteristics. Acids are classified as monobasic, dibasic, tribasic, and so forth, according to the number of hydrogen atoms, replaceable by bases, in a molecule.

activation energy the energy required in order to start a chemical reaction. Some elements and compounds will react together merely by bringing them into contact (spontaneous reaction). For others it is necessary to supply energy in order to start the reaction, even if there is ultimately a net output of energy. This initial energy is the activation energy.

alkali chemical compound classed as a base that is soluble in water. Alkalis neutralize acids and are soapy to the touch. The hydroxides of metals are alkalis; those of sodium (sodium hydroxide, NaOH) and of potassium (potassium hydroxide, KOH) being chemically powerful.

base a substance that accepts protons, such as the hydroxide ion (OH^- and ammonia (NH_3). Bases react with acids to give a salt. Those that

dissolve in water are called alkalis.

catalyst substance that alters the rate of a chemical or biochemical reaction without itself undergoing any permanent change. In practice, most catalysts are used to speed up reactions, particularly in industrial processes. They work by introducing an entirely different reaction mechanism that lowers the activation energy. Enzymes are natural biological catalysts.

chain reaction a mechanism that produces a succession of reactions, usually involving free radicals, where the products of one stage are the reactants of the next. A chain reaction is characterized by the continual generation of reactive substances.

chemical equation method of indicating the reactants and products of a chemical reaction by using chemical symbols and formulae. A chemical equation gives two basic pieces of information: (1) the reactants (on the left-hand side) and products (right-hand side); and (2) the reacting proportions (stoichiometry)—that is, how many units of each reactant and product are involved. The equation must balance; that is, the total number of atoms of a particular element on the left-hand side must be the same as the number of atoms of that element on the right-hand side.

chemical equilibrium condition in which the products of a reversible chemical reaction are formed at the same rate at which they decompose back into the reactants, so that the concentration of each reactant and product remains constant.

decomposition the process whereby a chemical compound is reduced to its component substances.

dissociation the process whereby a single compound splits into two or more smaller products, which may be capable of recombining to form the reactant.

enthalpy of reaction or *heat of reaction* the energy released or absorbed during a chemical reaction. When heat is given out and the temperature rises, the reaction is called an exothermic reaction. When the temperature falls and heat is absorbed, the reaction is called an endothermic reaction.

free radical an atom or molecule that has an unpaired electron and is therefore highly reactive. Most free radicals are very short-lived. If free radicals are produced in living organisms they can be very damaging.

ion exchange process whereby an ion in one compound is replaced by a different ion, of the same charge, from another compound. It is the basis of a type of chromatography in which the components of a mixture of ions in solution are separated according to the ease with which they will replace the ions on the polymer matrix through which they flow. Ion-exchange resins are used to soften water by exchanging the dissolved ions responsible for the water's hardness with others that do not have this effect.

neutralization a process occurring when the excess acid (or excess base) in a substance is reacted with added base (or added acid) so that the resulting substance is neither acidic nor basic.

oxidation the loss of electrons, gain of oxygen, or loss of hydrogen by an atom, ion, or molecule during a chemical reaction.

rate of reaction the speed at which a chemical reaction proceeds. It is usually expressed in terms of the concentration (usually in moles per litre) of a reactant consumed, or product formed, in unit time; so the units would be moles per litre per second (mol l^{-1} s^{-1}). The rate of a reaction may be affected by the concentration of the reactants, the temperature of the reactants, and the presence of a catalyst. If the reaction is entirely in the gas state, pressure affects the rate, and, for solids, the particle size.

reaction the coming together of two or more atoms, ions or molecules with the result that a chemical change takes place. The nature of the reaction is portrayed by a chemical equation.

reactivity series chemical series produced by arranging the metals in order of their ease of reaction with reagents such as oxygen, water, and acids. This arrangement aids the understanding of the properties of metals, helps to explain differences between them, and enables predictions to be made about a metal's behaviour, based on a knowledge of its position or properties.

redox reaction chemical change where one reactant is reduced and the other reactant oxidized. The reaction can only occur if both reactants are present and each changes simultaneously. For example, hydrogen reduces copper(II) oxide to copper while it is itself oxidized to water. The corrosion of iron and the reactions taking place in electric and electolytic cells are just a few instances of redox reactions.

reduction the gain of electrons, loss of oxygen, or gain of hydrogen by an atom, ion, or molecule during a chemical reaction.

salt any compound formed from an acid and a base through the replacement of all or part of the hydrogen in the acid by a metal or electropositive radical. *Common salt* is sodium chloride.

strength of acids and bases the ability of acids and bases to dissociate in solution with water, and hence to produce a low or high pH respectively.

PROPERTIES

boiling point for any given liquid, the temperature at which any further application of heat will convert the liquid to vapour. The temperature remains at this point until all the liquid has vapourized. It is invariable under similar conditions of pressure—for example, the boiling point of water under standard atmospheric pressure is 100°C/212°F. The lower the pressure, the lower the boiling point and vice versa.

buffer mixture of chemical compounds chosen to maintain a steady pH.

colloid substance composed of extremely small particles of one material (the dispersed phase) evenly and stably distributed in another material (the continuous phase). The size of the dispersed particles (1–1,000 nanometres/0.000039–0.039 in across) is less than that of particles in suspension but greater than that of molecules in true solution. Colloids involving gases include *aerosols* (dispersions of liquid or solid particles in a gas, as in fog or smoke) and *foams* (dispersions of gases in liquids). Those involving liquids include *emulsions* (in which both the dispersed and the continuous phases are liquids) and *sols* (solid particles dispersed in a liquid). Sols in which both phases contribute to a molecular three-dimensional network have a jellylike form and are known as *gels*; gelatine, starch 'solution', and silica gel are common examples.

diffusion the spontaneous and random movement of molecules or particles in a fluid (gas or liquid) from a region in which they are at a high concentration to a region in which they are at a low concentration, until a uniform concentration is achieved throughout. No mechanical mixing or stirring is involved. For instance, if a drop of ink is added to water, its molecules will diffuse until their colour becomes evenly distributed throughout.

dipole the uneven distribution of magnetic or electrical characteristics within a molecule or substance so that it behaves as though it possesses two equal but opposite poles or charges, a finite distance apart. The uneven distribution of electrons within a molecule composed of atoms of different electronegativities may result in an apparent concentration of electrons towards one end of the molecule and a deficiency towards the other, so that it forms a dipole consisting of apparently separated positive and negative charges. A bar magnet behaves as though its magnetism were concentrated in separate north and south magnetic poles because of the uneven distribution of its magnetic field.

emulsion colloid consisting of a stable dispersion of a liquid in another liquid—for example, oil and water in some cosmetic lotions.

freezing point for any given liquid, the temperature at which any further removal of heat will convert the liquid into the solid state. The temperature remains at this point until all the liquid has solidified. It is invariable under similar conditions of pressure—for example, the freezing point of water under standard atmospheric pressure is 0°C/32°F.

immiscible term describing liquids that will not mix with each other, such as oil and water. When two immiscible liquids are shaken together, a turbid mixture is produced. This normally forms separate layers on being left to stand.

mixture a substance containing two or more compounds that still retain their separate physical and chemical properties. There is no chemical bonding between them and they can be separated from each other by physical means (compare compound).

pH scale for measuring acidity or alkalinity. A pH of 7.0 indicates neutrality, below 7 is acid, while above 7 is alkaline.

precipitation the formation of a suspension of solid, insoluble particles in a liquid as a result of a reaction within the liquid between two or more soluble substances. If the particles settle, they form a *precipitate*; if the particles are very small and remain in suspension, they form a *colloidal precipitate*.

radioactivity spontaneous alteration of the nuclei of radioactive atoms, accompanied by the emission of radiation. It is the property exhibited by the radioactive isotopes of stable elements and all isotopes of radioactive elements.

solute substance that is dissolved in another substance.

solution two or more substances mixed to form a single, homogenous phase. One of the substances (usually the one present in greatest quantity) is the *solvent* and the others (*solutes*) are said to be dissolved in it. A solution is said to be saturated when no more solutes will dissolve in it.

solvent substance, usually a liquid, that will dissolve another substance. Although the commonest solvent is water, in popular use the term refers to low-boiling-point organic liquids, which are harmful if used in a confined space. They can give rise to respiratory problems, liver damage, and neurological complaints.

sublimation the conversion of a solid to vapour without passing through the liquid phase.

CHEMICALS WE USE

acesulfame-K non-carbohydrate sweetener that is up to 300 times as sweet as sugar. It is used in soft drinks, desserts, and puddings.

additive chemical added to a substance for technological advantage. Examples are the anti-knock agents used in petroleum fuels and the fungicides added to wallpaper pastes. In food technology, an additive is any natural or artificial chemical that is added to a processed food in order to prolong its shelf life, alter its colour or flavour, or improve its nutritional value.

Many chemical food additives are used and they are subject to regulation, since individuals may be affected by constant exposure even to traces of certain additives and may suffer side effects ranging from headaches and hyperactivity to cancer. Within the EC, approved additives are given an official E number.

aspartame non-carbohydrate sweetener used in foods under the tradename Nutrasweet. It is about 200 times as sweet as sugar and, unlike saccharine, has no aftertaste.

caramel complex mixture of substances produced by heating sugars, without charring, until they turn brown. Caramel is used as colouring and flavouring in foods. Its production in the manufacture of sugar confection gives rise to a toffee-like sweet of the same name.

carbohydrate chemical compound composed of carbon, hydrogen, and oxygen, with the basic formula $C_m(H_2O)_n$, and related compounds with the same basic structure but modified functional groups. The simplest carbohydrates are sugars (*monosaccharides*, such as glucose and fructose, and *disaccharides*, such as sucrose), which are soluble compounds, some with a sweet taste. When these basic sugar units are joined together in long chains or branching structures they form *polysaccharides*, such as starch and glycogen, which often serve as food stores in living organisms.

cyclamate derivative of cyclohexysulphamic acid, formerly used as an artificial sweetener.

dough mixture consisting primarily of flour, water, and yeast, which is used in the manufacture of bread. The preparation of dough involves thorough kneading and standing in a warm place to 'prove' (increase in volume) so that the enzymes in the dough can break down the starch from the flour into smaller sugar molecules, which are then fermented by the yeast. This releases carbon dioxide, which causes the dough to rise.

drug any of a range of chemicals voluntarily or involuntarily introduced into the bodies of humans and animals in order to enhance or suppress a biological function. Most drugs in use are medicines (pharmaceuticals), used to prevent or treat diseases, or to relieve their symptoms; they include antibiotics, cytotoxic drugs, immunosuppressives, sedatives, and pain-relievers (analgesics).

fat naturally occurring, soft, greasy substance that forms a rich source and store of energy in animals and plants. It consists chiefly of triglycerides (lipids containing three fatty acid molecules linked to a molecule of glycerol) and phospholipids, but also contains fat-soluble vitamins, minerals, and other substances in small amounts. Animal fat contains cholesterol, which is believed to be a major contributor to heart disease in humans.

fructose $C_6H_{12}O_6$ a sugar that occurs naturally in honey, the nectar of flowers, and many sweet fruits; it is commercially prepared from glucose. Fructose is a monosaccharide, whereas the more familar cane or beet sugar is a disaccharide, made up of two monosaccharide units: fructose and glucose. It is sweeter than cane sugar.

glucose or *grape-sugar* $C_6H_{12}O_6$ monosaccharide sugar present in the blood, and found also in honey and fruit juices. It is a source of energy for the body, being produced from other sugars and starches to form the 'energy currency' of many biochemical reactions also involving ATP.

lactic acid or *2-hydroxypropanoic acid* CH_3-

BUCKYBALLS: A NEW FORM OF CARBON

Chemists regard a diamond as just another form of carbon, an element familiar to everyone as soot, which is practically pure carbon. Equally everyday is the graphite in a 'lead' pencil, another form of carbon. The chemical difference between graphite and diamond is that the carbon atoms in each substance are arranged differently. The carbon atoms of graphite are arranged in flat, hexagonal patterns, rather like the cells of a honeycomb. Because graphite molecules are flat, they slide over one another easily. In contrast, the carbon atoms in a diamond are interlinked three-dimensionally, giving the substance its extraordinary hardness. And there until recently the matter rested: carbon was an element that came in two forms—diamond and graphite. Now chemists are excited about a third form of carbon, in which the atoms are linked together in a molecule that looks very like a soccer ball. The new form of carbon is a cagelike molecule consisting of 60 carbon atoms that make a perfect sphere. It has been named 'buckminsterfullerene' in honour of the US architect Buckminster Fuller's work, which included spherical domes.

The story of the discovery of these exotic new molecules involves soot, outer space, and lasers. It starts when two scientists, Donald Huffman from the University of Arizona, Tucson, and Wolfgang Kratschmer, were working at the Max Planck Institute for Nuclear Physics in Heidelberg, Germany. They were heating graphite rods under special conditions and examining the soot made in the process: they speculated that a similar process might take place in outer space, contributing to clouds of interstellar dust.

Meanwhile the team of Harold Kroto and David Walton at the University of Sussex had been on the trail of interstellar molecules made up of long chains of carbon atoms that might have originated in the atmosphere that surrounds red giant stars. Enlisting the help of researchers at Rice University in Houston, Texas, who were using a giant laser to blast atoms from the surface of different target substances, Kroto and his team soon found the long-chained carbon molecules. But they were struck by a surprising discovery of a very stable molecule that contained exactly 60 carbon atoms.

Now Richard Smalley of the Rice team set out to make a model of the new molecule, using scissors, sticky tape, and paper. He soon found that a hexagonal arrangement of carbon atoms was impossible, but that a perfect sphere could be formed from 20 hexagons and 12 pentagons. Such a sphere has 60 vertices. Chemists attribute the stability of the new form of carbon to this closed cage structure.

However, chemists like to prove the structures of the molecules they make: the evidence so far was merely speculative.

Ordinary soot absorbs ultraviolet light in a characteristic way, and the new molecule also showed a characteristic ultraviolet fingerprint. The problem was to make enough of the new carbon so that exact measurements could be made. If it could be crystallized, then an X-ray analysis would enable the precise distances between the carbon atoms to be determined. The Heidelberg team forged ahead, and produced milligrams of red-brown crystals by evaporating a solution of their product in benzene. The X-ray results confirmed that the molecules were indeed spherical, and that the paper model of 20 hexagons and 12 pentagons was correct.

This result was clinched when Kroto and his colleagues, using nuclear magnetic resonance spectroscopy, not only confirmed the new 60-atom structure but also provided evidence for a family of fullerenes, as the new forms of carbon are now called. Structures containing 28, 32, 50, 60, and 70 carbon atoms are known. Chemists affectionately term such molecules 'buckyballs'.

In many ways, these new discoveries in carbon chemistry are as important as the key discovery more than a century ago of the structure of benzene. When in 1865 German chemist Friederich Kekulé proposed a ring structure for this important organic molecule, the whole field of aromatic chemistry opened up, leading to dyestuffs in the first instance, and millions of new substances since. The fullerene family holds similar promise.

Chemists at Exxon's laboratories in New Jersey have already played a part in the fullerene story, and are interested in the lubricating properties of the new materials. Sumio Iijima, a Japanese scientist, has synthesized tubelike structures based on the fullerene idea, which are naturally called 'buckytubes'.

Other teams have now done work that suggests that such molecules may have interesting electrical properties: they may have semiconducting abilities. Cagelike molecules can contain other atoms, such as metals: a group of researchers from the University of California at Los Angeles have produced a 'doped' fullerene that behaves as a superconductor. No evidence has been found that buckminsterfullerene exists in space, but some is almost certainly produced every time you light a candle.

CHOHCOOH organic acid, a colourless, almost odourless liquid, produced by certain bacteria during fermentation and by active muscle cells when they are exercised hard and are experiencing oxygen debt. It occurs in yoghurt, buttermilk, sour cream, poor wine, and certain plant extracts, and is used in food preservation and in the preparation of pharmaceuticals.

monosodium glutamate (MSG) $NaC_5H_8NO_4$ a white, crystalline powder, the sodium salt of glutamic acid (an amino acid). It is used to enhance the flavour of many packaged and 'fast foods', and in Chinese cooking. Ill ef-

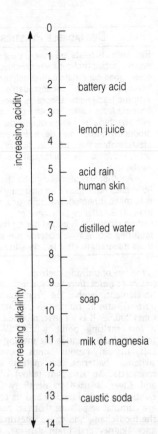

Ph

0	
1	
2	battery acid
3	
	lemon juice
4	
5	acid rain
	human skin
6	
7	distilled water
8	
9	
	soap
10	
11	milk of magnesia
12	
13	caustic soda
14	

increasing acidity

increasing alkalinity

fects, such as dizziness and heart palpitations, may arise from its overconsumption, and some people are very sensitive to it, even in small amounts. MSG is prepared commercially from vegetable protein, such as sugar beet pulp.

oil inflammable substance, usually insoluble in water, and chiefly composed of carbon and hydrogen. Oils may be solids (fats and waxes) or liquids. The three main types are: *essential oils*, obtained from plants; *fixed oils*, obtained from animals and plants; and *mineral oils*, obtained chiefly from the refining of petroleum. Eight of the 14 top-earning companies in the USA in 1990 (led by Exxon with $7 billion in sales) are in the global petroleum industry.

plaster of Paris form of calcium sulphate, obtained from gypsum; it is mixed with water for making casts and moulds.

protein complex, biologically important substance composed of amino acids joined by peptide bonds. Other types of bond, such as sulphur–sulphur bonds, hydrogen bonds, and cation bridges between acid sites, are responsible for creating the protein's characteristic three-dimensional structure, which may be fibrous, globular, or pleated.

saccharin or *ortho-sulpho benzimide* $C_7H_5NO_3S$

sweet, white, crystalline solid derived from coal tar and substituted for sugar. Since 1977 it has been regarded as potentially carcinogenic. Its use is not universally permitted and it has been largely replaced by other sweetening agents.

salt, common or *sodium chloride* NaCl white crystalline solid, found dissolved in sea water and as rock salt (halite) in large deposits and salt domes. Common salt is used extensively in the food industry as a preservative and for flavouring, and in the chemical industry in the making of chlorine and sodium. While common salt is an essential part of our diet, some medical experts believe that excess salt can lead to high blood pressure and increased risk of heart attacks.

sodium bicarbonate or *bicarbonate of soda* (technical name *sodium hydrogencarbonate*) $NaHCO_3$ white crystalline solid that neutralizes acids and is used in medicine to treat acid indigestion. It is also used in baking powders—it releases carbon dioxide in the presence of water and heat, which makes the dough or cakemix rise.

starch widely distributed, high-molecular-mass carbohydrate, produced by plants as a food store; main dietary sources are cereals, legumes, and tubers, including potatoes. It consists of varying proportions of two glucose polymers (polysaccharides): straight-chain (amylose) and branched (amylopectin) molecules.

steroid any of a group of cyclic, unsaturated alcohols (lipids without fatty acid components), which, like sterols, have a complex molecular structure consisting of four carbon rings. Steroids include the sex hormones, such as testosterone, the corticosteroid hormones produced by the adrenal gland, bile acids, and cholesterol. The term is commonly used to refer to anabolic steroids, a class of hormones used in medicine and, usually illicitly, in sport to stimulate tissue growth.

sucrose or *cane sugar* or *beet sugar* $C_{12}H_{22}O_{10}$ a sugar found in the pith of sugar cane and in sugar beets. It is popularly known as sugar. Sucrose is a disaccharide sugar, each of its molecules being made up of two simple sugar (monosaccharide) units: glucose and fructose.

sulphur dioxide SO_2 pungent gas produced by burning sulphur in air or oxygen. It is widely used for disinfecting food vessels and equipment, and as a preservative in some food products. It occurs in industrial flue gases and is a major cause of acid rain.

thaumatin naturally occurring, non-carbohydrate sweetener derived from the bacterium *Thaumatococcus danielli*. Its sweetness is not sensed as quickly as that of other sweeteners, and it is not as widely used in the food industry.

urea waste product formed in the liver when nitrogen compounds are broken down, and excreted in urine. When purified, it is a white, crystalline solid. In industry it is used to make plastics, pharmaceuticals, and fertilizers.

HARMFUL CHEMICALS

arsenic brittle, greyish-white, weakly metallic element, symbol As, atomic number 33, relative atomic mass 74.92. It occurs in many ores and occasionally in its elemental state, and is widely distributed, being present in minute quantities in the soil, the sea, and the human body. In larger quantities, it is poisonous, accumulating in the body and causing vomiting, diarrhoea, tingling and possibly numbness in the limbs, and collapse.

carbon monoxide CO colourless, odourless gas formed when carbon is oxidized in a limited supply of air. It is a poisonous constituent of car exhaust fumes, forming a stable compound with haemoglobin in the blood, thus preventing the haemoglobin from transporting oxygen to the body tissues.

DDT abbreviation for *dichloro-diphenyl-trichloroethane* $(ClC_6H_4)_2CHCCl_3$ insecticide discovered in 1939 by Swiss chemist Paul Müller. It is useful in the control of insects that spread malaria, but resistant strains develop. DDT is highly toxic and persists in the environment and in living tissue. Its use is now banned in most countries.

dioxin any of a family of over 200 organic chemicals, all of which are heterocyclic hydrocarbons. The term is commonly applied, however, to only one member of the family, 2,3,7,8-tetrachlorodibenzodioxin (2,3,7,8- TCDD), a highly toxic chemical that occurred as an impurity in a defoliant (Agent Orange) used in the Vietnam War, and in the weedkiller 2,4,5-T. It has been associated with a disfiguring skin complaint (chloracne), birth defects, miscarriages, and cancer.

halon organic chemical compound containing one or two carbon atoms, together with bromine and other halogens. The most commonly used are halon 1211 (bromochlorodifluoromethane) and halon 1301 (bromotrifluoromethane). The halons are gases and are widely used in fire extinguishers. As destroyers of the ozone layer, they are up to ten times more effective than chlorofluorocarbons (CFCs), to which they are chemically related.

lead heavy, soft, malleable, grey, metallic element, symbol Pb (from Latin *plumbum*), atomic number 82, relative atomic mass 207.19. It is used in making batteries, glass, ceramics, and alloys such as pewter and solder. Lead is a cumulative poison, causing abdominal pain, anaemia, and nerve or brain damage. The addition of lead tetraethyl, $Pb(C_2H_5)_4$, to leaded petrol to improve the performance of car engines has resulted in atmospheric pollution by lead compounds, which can lead to impaired learning ability in children exposed to this pollution over long periods of time. This has prompted a shift

DEGRADABLE PLASTICS

Research chemists are now finding ways to make plastics that rot away quickly. ICI has a very good candidate called polyhydroxybutyrate, or PHB. This biodegradable plastic, with the trade name Biopol, is made by bacteria from sugar, and when it is finished with, bacteria in the soil rapidly digest it, producing carbon dioxide. In this way, the plastic enters the carbon cycle and is naturally recycled like ordinary animal and plant waste.

Another way of making sure that plastic litter does not become an unsightly menace is to make it photodegradable, or sensitive to light. By altering polythene chemically—carbon monoxide is added during the manufacturing process—a material is made that loses its strength after two days in sunlight.

to the use of unleaded petrol.

mercury or *quicksilver* heavy, silver-grey, metallic element, symbol Hg (from Latin *hydrargyrum*), atomic number 80, relative atomic mass 200.59. It is a dense, mobile liquid with a low melting point (−38.87°C/−37.96°F). Industrial uses include the making of chemicals, mercury-vapour lamps, power-control switches, batteries, barometers, and thermometers. An amalgam (alloy) of mercury and silver is used in dentistry for filling cavities in teeth. Mercury and its compounds are cumulative poisons that can contaminate the food chain, and cause intestinal disturbance, kidney and brain damage, and birth defects in humans. Eating fish and shellfish caught from seas in which mercury wastes have been dumped is the major cause of poisoning.

nicotine $C_{10}H_{14}N_2$ an alkaloid (nitrogenous compound) obtained from the dried leaves of the tobacco plant *Nicotiana tabacum* and used as an insecticide. It is the component of cigarette smoke that causes physical addiction. A colourless oil, soluble in water, it turns brown on exposure to the air.

ozone O_3 highly reactive pale-blue gas with a penetrating odour. Ozone is an allotrope of oxygen, made up of three atoms of oxygen. It is formed when the molecule of the stable form of oxygen (O_2) is split by ultraviolet radiation or electrical discharge. It forms a layer in the upper atmosphere, which protects life on Earth from ultraviolet rays, a cause of skin cancer. At lower atmospheric levels it is an air pollutant and contributes to the greenhouse effect.

radon colourless, odourless, gaseous, radioactive, nonmetallic element, symbol Rn, atomic number 86, relative atomic mass 222. It is formed by the radioactive decay of radium in rocks and soil. In certain areas, such as Devon, Cornwall, and SE Scotland, the gas forms a natural hazard, seeping upwards into houses and increasing the probability of the inhabitants contracting lung cancer.

NOBEL PRIZE FOR CHEMISTRY

prizewinners

1952	Archer Martin (UK) and Richard Synge (UK): invention of partition chromatography
1953	Hermann Staudinger (Germany): discoveries in macromolecular chemistry
1954	Linus Pauling (USA): nature of chemical bonds, especially in complex substances
1955	Vincent Du Vigneaud (USA): investigations into biochemically important sulphur compounds, and the first synthesis of a polypeptide hormone
1956	Cyril Hinshelwood (UK) and Nikoly Semenov (USSR): mechanism of chemical reactions
1957	Alexander Todd (UK): nucleotides and nucleotide coenzymes
1958	Frederick Sanger (UK): structure of proteins, especially insulin
1959	Jaroslav Heyrovský (Czechoslovakia): polarographic methods of chemical analysis
1960	Willard Libby (USA): radiocarbon dating in archaeology, geology, and geography
1961	Melvin Calvin (USA): assimilation of carbon dioxide by plants
1962	Max Perutz (UK) and John Kendrew (UK): structures of globular proteins
1963	Karl Ziegler (Germany) and Giulio Natta (Italy): chemistry and technology of high polymers
1964	Dorothy Crowfoot Hodgkin (UK): crystallographic determination of the structures of biochemical compounds, notably penicillin and cyanocobalamin (vitamin B_{12})
1965	Robert Woodward (USA): organic synthesis
1966	Robert Mulliken (USA): molecular orbital theory of chemical bonds and structures
1967	Manfred Eigen (Germany), Ronald Norrish (UK), and George Porter (UK): investigation of rapid chemical reactions by means of very short pulses of energy
1968	Lars Onsager (USA): discovery of reciprocal relations, fundamental for the thermodynamics of irreversible processes
1969	Derek Barton (UK) and Odd Hassel (Norway): concept and applications of conformation
1970	Luis Federico Leloir (Argentina): discovery of sugar nucleotides and their role in carbohydrate biosynthesis
1971	Gerhard Herzberg (Germany): electronic structure and geometry of molecules, particularly free radicals
1972	Christian B Anfinsen (USA), Stanford Moore (USA), and William H Stein (USA): amino-acid structure and biological activity of the enzyme ribonuclease
1973	Ernst Fischer (Germany) and Geoffrey Wilkinson (UK): chemistry of organometallic sandwich compounds
1974	Paul J Flory (USA): physical chemistry of macromolecules
1975	John Cornforth (Australia): stereochemistry of enzyme- catalysed reactions. Vladimir Prelog (Yugoslavia): stereochemistry of organic molecules and their reactions
1976	William N Lipscomb (USA): structure and chemical bonding of boranes (compounds of boron and hydrogen)
1977	Ilya Prigogine (USSR): themodynamics of irreversible and dissipative processes
1978	Peter Mitchell (UK): biological energy transfer and chemiosmotic theory
1979	Herbert C Brown (USA) and Georg Wittig (Germany): use of boron and phosphorus compounds, respectively, in organic syntheses
1980	Paul Berg (USA): biochemistry of nucleic acids, especialy recombinant-DNA. Walter Gilbert (USA) and Frederick Sanger (UK): base sequences in nucleic acids
1981	Kenichi Fukui (Japan) and Roald Hoffmann (USA): theories concerning chemical reactions
1982	Aaron Klug (UK): crystallographic electron microscopy: structure of biologically important nucleic-acid–protein complexes
1983	Henry Taube (USA): electron-transfer reactions in inorganic chemical reactions
1984	Bruce Merrifield (USA): chemical syntheses on a solid matrix
1985	Herbert A Hauptman (USA) and Jerome Karle (USA): methods of determining crystal structures
1986	Dudley R Herschbach (USA), Yuan T Lee (USA), and John C Polanyi (Canada): dynamics of chemical elementary processes
1987	Donald J Cram (USA), Jean-Marie Lehn (France), and Charles J Pedersen (USA): molecules with highly selective structure-specific interactions
1988	Johann Deisenhofer (Germany), Robert Huber (Germany), and Hartmut Michel (Germany): three-dimensional structure of the reaction centre of photosynthesis
1989	Sydney Altman (USA) and Thomas Cech (USA): discovery of catalytic function of RNA
1990	Elias James Corey (USA): new methods of synthesizing chemical compounds
1991	Richard Ernst (USA): perfecting sharp imaging in NMR spectroscopy, now widely used in medical scanning.

ARTEFACTS AND PROCESSES

adhesive substance that sticks two surfaces together. Natural adhesives (glues) include gelatin in its crude industrial form (made from bones, hide fragments, and fish offal) and vegetable gums. Synthetic adhesives include thermoplastic and thermosetting resins, which are often stronger than the substances they join; mixtures of epoxy resin and hardener that set by chemical reaction; and elastomeric (stretching) adhesives for flexible joints. Superglues are fast-setting adhesives used in very small quantities.

alloy metal blended with some other metallic or nonmetallic substance to give it special qualities, such as resistance to corrosion, greater hardness, or tensile strength. Useful alloys include bronze, brass, cupronickel, duralumin, German silver, gunmetal, pewter, solder, steel, and stainless steel. The most recent alloys include the superplastics: alloys that can stretch 100% at specific temperatures, permitting, for example, their injection into moulds as easily as plastic.

anode the positive electrode of an electrolytic cell, towards which negative particles (anions), usually in solution, are attracted.

battery any energy-storage device allowing release of electricity on demand. It is made up of one or more electrical cells.

brewing the making of beer, ale, or other alcoholic beverage from malt and barley by steeping (mashing), boiling, and fermenting. Mashing the barley releases its sugars. Yeast is then added, which contains the enzymes needed to convert the sugars into ethanol (alcohol) and carbon dioxide. Hops are added to give a bitter taste.

cathode the negative electrode of an electrolytic cell, towards which positive particles (cations), usually in solution, are attracted.

chromatography technique used for separating the components of a mixture. This is brought about by means of two immiscible substances, one of which (the *mobile phase*) transports the sample mixture through the other (the stationary phase). The mobile phase may be a gas or a liquid; the stationary phase may be a liquid or a solid, and may be in a column, on paper, or in a thin layer on a glass or plastic support. The components of the mixture are adsorbed or impeded by the stationary phase to different extents and therefore become separated.

cracking reaction where a large alkane molecule is broken down by heat into a smaller alkane and a small alkene molecule. The reaction is carried out at a high temperature (600°C or higher) and often in the presence of a catalyst. It is the main method of preparation of alkenes and is also used to manufacture petrol from the higher-boiling-point fractions obtained from the fractional distillation (fractionation) of crude oil.

detergent surface-active cleansing agent. The common detergents are made from hydrocarbons and sulphuric acid, and their long-chain molecules have a type of structure similar to that of soap molecules: a salt group at one end attached to a long hydrocarbon 'tail'. They have the advantage over soap in that they do not produce scum by forming insoluble salts with the calcium and magnesium ions present in hard water.

distillation technique used to purify liquids or to separate mixtures of liquids possessing different boiling points.

electrophoresis powerful technique used to separate and identify chemical compounds in a mixture. By applying an electric field to a mixture of chemicals in solution, they are made to migrate at different speeds within a plastic gel or piece of filter paper. Genetic fingerprinting depends on this technique.

fermentation the breakdown of sugars by bacteria and yeasts using a method of respiration without oxygen (anaerobic). Fermentation processes have long been utilized in baking bread, making beer and wine, and producing cheese, yoghurt, soy sauce, and many other foodstuffs.

indicator chemical compound that changes its structure and colour in response to its environment. The commonest chemical indicators detect changes in pH (for example, litmus), or in the oxidation state of a system (redox indicators).

litmus dye obtained from various lichens and used in chemistry as an indicator to test the acidic or alkaline nature of aqueous solutions; it turns red in the presence of acid, and blue in the presence of alkali.

soap a mixture of the sodium salts of various fatty acids: palmitic, stearic, and oleic acid. It is made by the action of sodium hydroxide (caustic soda) or potassium hydroxide (caustic potash) on fats of animal or vegetable origin. Soap makes grease and dirt disperse in water in a similar manner to a detergent.

universal indicator a mixture of pH indicators, used to gauge the acidity or alkalinity of a solution. Each component changes colour at a different pH value, and so the indicator is capable of displaying a range of colours, according to the pH of the test solution, from red (at pH1) to purple (at pH13).

Industrial Chemical Processes

---

c.1100	Alcohol was first distilled.
1746	John Roebuck invented the lead-chamber process for the manufacture of sulphuric acid.
1790	Nicolas Leblanc developed a process for making sodium carbonate from sodium chloride (common salt).
1827	John Walker invented phosphorus matches.
1831	Peregrine Phillips developed the contact process for the production of sulphuric acid; it was first used on an industrial scale 1875.
1834	Justus von Liebig developed melamine.
1835	Tetrachloroethene (vinyl chloride) was first prepared.
1850	Ammonia was first produced from coal gas.
1855	A technique was patented for the production of cellulose nitrate (nitrocellulose) fibres, the first artificial fibres.
1856	Henry Bessemer developed the Bessemer converter for the production of steel.
1857	William Henry Perkin set up the first synthetic-dye factory.
1861	Ernest Solvay patented a method for the production of sodium carbonate from sodium chloride and ammonia; the first production plant was established 1863.
1862	Alexander Parkes produced the first known synthetic plastic (Parkesine, or xylonite) from cellulose nitrate, vegetable oils, and camphor; it was the forerunner of celluloid.
1864	William Siemens and Pierre Emile Martin developed the Siemens–Martin process (open-hearth method) for the production of steel.
1868	Henry Deacon invented the Deacon process for the production of chlorine by the catalytic oxidation of hydrogen chloride.
1869	Celluloid was first produced from cellulose nitrate and camphor.
1880	The first laboratory preparation of polyacrylic substances.
1886	Charles M Hall and Paul-Louis-Toussaint Héroult developed, independently of each other, a method for producing aluminium by the electrolysis of aluminium oxide.
1891	Rayon was invented. Herman Frasch patented the Frasch process for the recovery of sulphur from underground deposits. Lindemann produced the first epoxy resins.
1894	Carl Kellner and Hamilton Castner developed, independently of each other, a method for the production of sodium hydroxide by the electrolysis of brine.
1895	The Thermit reaction for the reduction of metallic oxides to their molten metals was developed by Johann Goldschmidt.
1902	Friedrich Wilhelm Ostwald patented a process for the production of nitric acid by the catalytic oxidation of ammonia.
1908	Fritz Haber invented the Haber process for the production of ammonia from nitrogen and hydrogen. Heike Kamerlingh-Onnes prepared liquid helium.
1909	The first totally synthetic plastic (Bakelite) was produced by Leo Baekeland.
1912	I Ostromislensky patented the use of plasticizers in the manufacture of plastic, rendering the product (PVC) mouldable.
1913	The thermal cracking of petroleum was established.
1919	Elwood Haynes patented non-rusting stainless steel.
1927	The commercial production of polyacrylic polymers began.
1930	Freons were first prepared and used in refrigeration plants. William Chalmers produced the polymer of methyl methacrylate (later marketed as Perspex).
1933	E W Fawcett and R O Gibson first produced polyethylene.
1935	The catalytic cracking of petroleum was introduced. Triacetate film (used as base for photographic film) was developed.
1937	Wallace Carothers invented nylon; polyurethanes were first produced.
1938	Roy Plunkett first produced polytetrafluoroethene (PTFE, marketed as Teflon).
1943	The industrial production of silicones was initiated.
1941	J R Whinfield invented Terylene.
1955	Artificial diamonds were first produced.
1959	The Du Pont company developed Lycra.
1963	Leslie Phillips and co-workers at the Royal Aircraft Establishment, Farnborough invented carbon fibre.
1980	Japanese company Nippon Oil patented the use of methyl-tert-butyl ether (MTBE) as a lead-free antiknock additive to petrol.
1984	About 2,500 people died in Bhopal, central India when poisonous methyl isocyanate gas escaped from a chemical plant owned by US company Union Carbide.
1990	ICI began production of the hydrofluorocarbon Klea 134a, a substitute for CFCs in refrigerators and air-conditioning systems.

HOW COMPUTERS WORK

Despite their impressive capabilities, computers are really only able to perform the simplest of tasks: adding or multiplying two numbers together; determining whether one number is higher than another; and so on. It is their ability to perform these tasks extremely quickly and in a predefined sequence that gives them their apparent power.

At the heart of the computer is a *CPU* (central processing unit). The CPU is built around an **arithmetic and logic unit** (ALU) which performs all the basic computations. It includes a set of registers that provide limited storage for immediate data and results. The whole thing is coordinated by an internal *clock*.

The CPU is supported by **memory**. This is used to store large amounts of data, as well as programs (instructions). There are two main types of memory. **Internal memory** is readily available to the CPU. It can be accessed very quickly, but its contents are lost when the power is removed. **External memory** is used for longer-term storage. It is usually in the form of a physical device such as a tape or disc. These generally provide a higher capacity than internal memory, but are considerably slower. The CPU cannot access external memory directly, so data has to be transferred to internal memory before it can be used.

The CPU communicates with external devices by means of a **bus**. This carries data between the various types of memory, and also to and from the **ports**, to which peripherals such as keyboards, screens, and printers are attached.

Programming

Computers have no intelligence of their own. They work by carrying out the detailed instructions provided by a programmer. The programmer's job is to break down the required task into a series of simple steps.

Programs are written in a **programming language**, designed for the convenience of the programmer. They are then translated into **machine code**, which the computer can execute. The translation is itself done by the computer, using a special program called a **compiler** (which performs the translation before the program is run) or an **interpreter** (which translates each part of the program as it is being executed).

Types of computer

There are four main classes of computer, corresponding roughly to memory capacity and processing speed. **Microcomputers** (also called **personal computers** or **PCs**) are the smallest and least expensive. They are widely used in the home, in schools, and in businesses of all sizes. **Minicomputers** are generally larger, and are found in universities and larger companies. They often support up to a hundred simultaneous users. **Mainframes** support many hundreds of simultaneous users and have very large storage capacities. They are found in large organizations such as banks and government departments. **Supercomputers** are the most powerful of all. There are few of them in the world, and they are used for specialized scientific tasks such as nuclear research and weather forecasting.

Computers are also classified by **generation**. The first generation of computers was developed in the 1940s and 1950s, and made from valves and wire circuits. Second-generation computers, emerging in the early 1960s, incorporated transistors and printed circuits. The third generation, from the late 1960s to the present, used integrated circuits. Fourth-generation computers are the most commonly used today, and are based on microprocessors and large-scale integrations. Finally, a fifth generation is emerging, using very large-scale integration (VLSI) and parallel processors.

COMPUTER HARDWARE

disc the commonest type of external storage, used for storing large volumes of data. A magnetic disc is rotated at high speed in a disc-drive unit as a read/write (playback or record) head passes over its surfaces to 'read' the magnetic variations that encode the data. **Floppy discs** are the least expensive type. They typically hold between 360 kilobytes and 1.4 megabytes, and are small and light enough to be sent through the post. **Hard discs** are much faster and have higher capacities, sometimes hundreds of megabytes. They are permanently housed in a sealed case. Recently, optical **compact discs** have emerged as an alternative to magnetic discs. They use a laser beam to read data encoded as tiny pits on the disc's surface. They have enormous capacities (sometimes over a billion bytes) but cannot always be written directly by the computer.

graphics tablet or **bit pad** input device in which

THE COMPUTER GIANTS

World rank			
'90	'89	Company	Revenue (US$m)
1	1	IBM	67,090.0
2	2	Digital	13,072.3
3	4	Fujitsu	12,361,5
4	3	NEC	12,350.3
5	6	Hitachi	9,590.9
6	5	Unisys	9,302.0
7	7	Hewlett-Packard	9,300.0
8	N/A	Siemens/Nixdorf	7,735.1
9	10	Olivetti	6,414.5
10	8	Groupe Bull	6,349.6
11	11	Apple	5,740.0
12	12	NCR	5,617.0
13	13	Toshiba	4,764.5
14	14	Canon	4,669.2
15	15	Matsushita	3,731.0

Source: Datamation

NOT JUST DIRE STRAITS: THE CD SHOWS ITS VERSATILITY

The compact disc (CD) is one of the most successful 'formats' ever invented. The 5-inch silver disc in its clear jewel case looks attractive, is easy to store and handle, performs well, seems not to deteriorate, and very rarely goes wrong. It thus commands a premium price over compact audio cassettes and VHS video cassettes, which are less attractive, more awkward to assemble and, because of their thin tape and complex plastic parts, prone to fail. Now the CD format is being extended into other areas. As well as hi-fi sound, CDs can also be used for computer programs, text, graphics, speech, animation, photographic images, and even full-screen, full-motion video (FMV for short) with a quality that compares with VHS.

CDs are already an important form of computer storage with products on CD-ROM (read-only memory). One CD can hold about 550 megabytes of data or about 90 million words of text. This is easily enough to hold a very large encyclopedia, a year's issues of a newspaper, several years' issues of most journals, or hundreds of novels. CD-ROMs are already available with all UK addresses and postcodes, all UK telephone numbers, and the full Oxford English Dictionary. Obviously the cost of pressing a CD—now less than 50 p—is far less than the cost of producing the paper equivalents. And the CD is more powerful, since you can search in seconds for, say, every York Road in the country.

But a CD is not limited to holding numbers or text. The electronic edition of *The Hutchinson Encyclopedia* is a good example of a so-called 'multimedia' disc. With a PC that runs Windows, you have access not only to 1.8 million words of text but also to over 2,000 pictures, tables, maps, and accompanying sound sequences. If, for instance, you were to look up the entry for Martin Luther King, you would be able to read his biography, browse through pictures of his life and times, then listen to his famous 'I have a dream' speech as delivered almost thirty years ago.

Volume production has brought down the prices of drives and discs, and standards have been established for IBM PC-compatible computers by the Multimedia PC Council, so this kind of thing is becoming popular. Of course it is still not a mass market, but there are other plans to promote the use of CDs in the home. The most important are CD-i and Photo CD.

CD-i (for Compact Disc Interactive) is a new format launched in the UK in May 1992 with the backing of Philips, Sony, Matsushita, and other consumer electronics firms. CD-i extends the CD-ROM format by providing for interleaved sound and graphics, and later it will be expanded to include FMV.

CD-i is best thought of as 'interactive television': the sound and graphics are better than TV quality. But instead of just 'playing back' a CD-i disc, you can interact with it. For example, Time-Life's 35 mm Photography disc provides 25 'workshops' where you learn the basics by controlling a simulated camera. CD-i games, like the Palm Springs Open golf game, can be based on video footage rather than computer graphics.

Photo CD, a CD-i-compatible format developed by Kodak and Philips, puts 35 mm snapshots onto CDs as a sort of high-quality 'digital negative'. Not only can you display your snaps on TV, you can zoom in on selected parts, crop, recolour, and otherwise manipulate them.

CD-i and Photo CD players look like an ordinary CD players, and also play CD-DA (standard Digital Audio) discs. The fact that the CD-i or Photo CD player includes a powerful microcomputer with a real-time operating system—something like an Apple Macintosh or Commodore Amiga—is nowhere mentioned in the promotional literature. But computer and video games suppliers can achieve similar effects by adding CD drives to their machines, rather than by adding computers to their players. Early examples of this approach include Fujitsu's FM-Towns computer, NEC's PC Engine games console, and Commodore's Amiga-based CDTV system. With Nintendo and Sega entering this market for Christmas 1992, the technology will be widely adopted.

For gamers, CDs have huge benefits in removing the space restrictions that limit the use of high-quality sound and graphics. Instead of being limited to one or two megabytes of code, authors will be able to use about five hundred. Piracy will be less of a problem too, and users won't have to worry about fragile floppy discs being damaged or corrupted.

Ten years ago, when the compact disc was launched, it seemed expensive and of limited appeal. The new CD-i format might seem that way too, today, but in the next decade it promises to become even more ubiquitous. Indeed, Motorola is already planning to put all the CD-i electronics on a single microchip, making the additional cost marginal. CD-i machines will then completely replace CD players for all but a few audiophiles.

A Kodak Photo CD can store in digital format up to a hundred colour photographs, each of which may be displayed on the screen of a Photo CD player, and manipulated electronically to zoom in on selected parts.

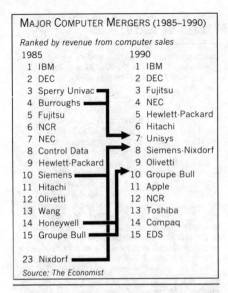

MAJOR COMPUTER MERGERS (1985–1990)

Ranked by revenue from computer sales

1985		1990	
1	IBM	1	IBM
2	DEC	2	DEC
3	Sperry Univac	3	Fujitsu
4	Burroughs	4	NEC
5	Fujitsu	5	Hewlett-Packard
6	NCR	6	Hitachi
7	NEC	7	Unisys
8	Control Data	8	Siemens-Nixdorf
9	Hewlett-Packard	9	Olivetti
10	Siemens	10	Groupe Bull
11	Hitachi	11	Apple
12	Olivetti	12	NCR
13	Wang	13	Toshiba
14	Honeywell	14	Compaq
15	Groupe Bull	15	EDS
23	Nixdorf		

Source: The Economist

a stylus or cursor is moved by hand over a flat surface. The computer can keep track of the position of the stylus, so enabling the operator to input drawings or diagrams.

joystick an input device that signals to a computer the direction and extent of displacement of a hand-held lever. It is similar to the joystick used to control the flight of an aircraft.

keyboard the commonest input device, used by the operator to input data and instructions into the computer. It resembles a typewriter keyboard but with additional keys. Most keyboards have a separate numeric keypad (like a calculator) as well as special keys for controlling the cursor and performing predefined functions (such as calling up a help screen).

light pen an input device resembling an ordinary pen, used to indicate locations on a computer screen. With certain computer-aided design (CAD) programs, the light pen can be used to instruct the computer to change the shape, size, position, and colours of sections of a screen image.

memory the part of the system used to store data and programs. *RAM* (random-access memory) is the type most commonly used for internal memory. It is made of a collection of integrated circuits (chips). It can be both read from and written to by the computer, but its contents are lost when the power is removed. By contrast, *ROM* (read-only memory) cannot be altered by the computer, and its contents are retained when the machine is switched off. It is used to hold data and programs that will rarely or never need altering, such as the computer's operating system. External memory devices include discs and magnetic tape.

modem (*mo*dulator-*dem*odulator) device that enables computers to send and receive data over a telephone line. It converts digital signals to analogue and back again.

mouse input device used to control a pointer on the screen. Moving the mouse across a desktop causes corresponding movement of the pointer. In this way, the operator can manipulate objects on the screen and make menu selections.

plotter output device for drawing pictures, diagrams, and plans. Flatbed plotters move a pen across the paper while roller plotters roll the paper past the pen as it moves from side to side.

printer device for producing printed copies of text and graphics. Types include *dot matrix*, which uses patterns of dots to create characters and images, the quality of which varies with the number of 'pins' in the print head (9-pin is low quality, 24-pin is much higher); *laser*, which produces very high-quality text and graphics but is more expensive to operate; and *ink-jet*, which produces a quality approaching that of the laser printer.

screen or *monitor* output device on which the computer displays information for the benefit of the operator. The commonest type is the *cathode-ray tube* (CRT), which is similar to a television screen. Portable computers often use *liquid crystal display* (LCD) screens. These are harder to read than CRTs, but require less power, making them suitable for battery operation.

touch screen an input device allowing the user to communicate with the computer by touching a display screen with a finger. In this way, the user can point to a required menu option or item of data. Touch screens are used less widely than other pointing devices such as the joystick or mouse.

VDU (visual display unit) single device incorporating a keyboard and screen. They are frequently used with mainframes and minicomputers, but less so with personal computers.

USES OF COMPUTERS

artificial intelligence (AI) the creation of computer programs that can perform actions comparable with those of an intelligent human. Current AI research covers areas such as planning (for robot behaviour), language understanding, pattern recognition, and knowledge representation.

CAD (computer-aided design) the use of computers for creating and editing design drawings. CAD is widely used in architecture, electronics, and engineering; for example, in the motor industry, where it is used to assist in designing cars.

CAL (computer-assisted learning) the use of computers in education and training, where the computer displays instructional material to a student and asks questions about the information given. The student's answers determine the sequence of the lessons.

CAM (computer-aided manufacturing) the use of computers to control production processes—in

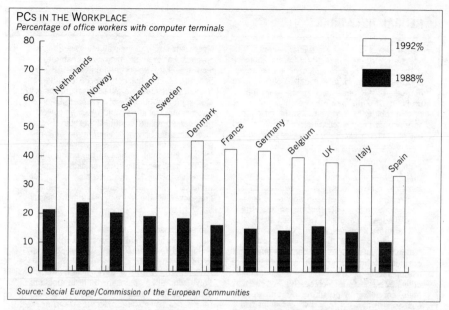

PCs IN THE WORKPLACE
Percentage of office workers with computer terminals

□ 1992%
■ 1988%

Source: Social Europe/Commission of the European Communities

particular, machine tools and robots.

computer game or ***video game*** a computer-controlled game in which the computer (usually) opposes the human player. Computer games typically employ fast, animated graphics and synthesized sound.

computer graphics the use of computers to display and manipulate information in pictorial form. The output may be as simple as a pie chart, or as complex as an animated sequence in a science-fiction film, or a seemingly three-dimensional engineering blueprint. Input may be achieved by drawing with a mouse or stylus on a graphics tablet, or by drawing directly on to the screen with a light pen. Computer graphics are increasingly used in computer-aided design (CAD), and to generate models and simulations in engineering, meteorology, medicine and surgery, and other fields of science.

databases and record-keeping systems many computer applications involve some form of structured data storage, or database. For example, an accounting system might be built around a database containing details of customers and suppliers. In larger computers, the database is organized in such a way that it is available to any program that needs it, without the programs needing to be aware of how the data are actually stored. The term database is also sometimes used for simple record-keeping systems, such as mailing lists, in which there are facilities for searching, sorting, and producing reports.

desktop publishing (DTP) small-scale typesetting and page make-up. DTP programs can produce originals, containing text and graphics, with text set in different typefaces and sizes. The pages can be previewed on the screen before final printing on a laser printer.

electronic mail or ***E-mail*** system in which people use computers to send messages to each other. Messages are stored in 'mailboxes' in a computer until the recipient is ready to read them. There are several large public systems, such as British Telecom's Dialcom, which have many thousands of subscribers.

expert system program for giving advice, such as diagnosing an illness or interpreting the law, based on knowledge derived from a human expert.

point-of-sale system system that records purchases in shops, typically operating through computerized cash registers. Point-of-sale systems are often used for the automatic updating of stock figures, and for transferring money from the shopper's bank account to the shop's.

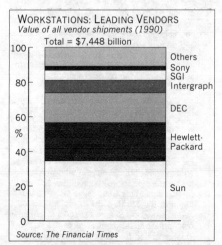

WORKSTATIONS: LEADING VENDORS
Value of all vendor shipments (1990)

Total = $7,448 billion

Others
Sony
SGI
Intergraph

DEC

Hewlett-Packard

Sun

Source: The Financial Times

NEURAL NETWORKS

Neural networks–strictly *artificial* neural networks—represent a radically different approach to computing. They are called *neural* networks because they are loosely modelled on the networks of neurons—nerve cells—that make up brains. Neural networks are characterized by their ability to *learn*, and can be described as *trainable pattern recognizers*. The study and use of neural networks is sometimes called *neurocomputing*.

Brain power

Brains perform remarkable computational feats: recognizing music from just a few seconds of a recording, or faces seen only once before—accomplishments that defeat even the most modern computers. Yet brains stumble with arithmetic and make errors with simple logic. The reason for these anomalies might be found in the differences between brain and computer architecture—their internal structure and operating mechanisms. Conventional computers possess distinct processing and memory units, controlled by programs, but animal nervous systems and neural networks are instead made up of highly interconnected webs of simple processing units. They have no specific memory locations, information instead being stored as patterns of interconnections between the processing units. Neural networks are not programmed, but are trained by example. They can, therefore, learn things that cannot easily be stated in programs, making them attractive in a wide range of application areas. Although neural networks are a form of parallel processing, the essence of the approach can be simulated on ordinary computers. Indeed, many packages are now available to enable personal computers to function as neurocomputers. Dedicated neural computing hardware, however, runs far faster.

Neurocomputing can be considered a branch of artificial intelligence. Artificial intelligence has two principal motivations: technology and psychology. The first concerns the use of computers to mimic biological intelligence and perform technologically useful tasks. The second is about understanding human perception and understanding. Neural networks have had dramatic effects on both—indeed, a distinct approach to psychology called *connectionism*, or *parallel distributed processing*, has grown up around them.

High hopes and disappointments

Although neurocomputing might seem a recent development, in fact research started at around the same time as the early work on digital computers. In the 1940s McCulloch and Pitts devised simple electrical networks, crudely modelling neural circuits, which could perform simple logical computations. More sophisticated networks, called *perceptrons*, followed in the 1950s—the ancestors of modern neural networks. Simple networks of amplifiers, perceptrons could learn to recognize patterns. This generated tremendous excitement, but significant limits to their abilities were discovered. For example, they were unable to learn the exclusive-OR relation (a logical relationship, 'A *or* B but *not* A and B together'). Marvin Minsky and Seymour Papert of the Massachusetts Institute of Technology proved that certain problems could never be solved by the perceptrons. They published their results in an important book—*Perceptrons*—and research into neural networks effectively ceased for over a decade. At around the end of the 1970s, however, theoretical breakthroughs made it possible for more complex neural networks to be developed, which overcame these problems, and the flurry of excitement began again.

The way ahead

Neural networks are of interest to computer technologists because they have the potential to offer solutions to a range of problems that have proved difficult to solve using conventional computing approaches. These problems include pattern recognition, machine learning, time series forecasting, machine vision, and robot control. Underpinning all this is their ability to *learn*. In a famous example, a neural network was trained to recognize speech—with eerily realistic results. The network, called NET-talk, was developed by T J Sejnowski and C R Rosenberg at Johns Hopkins University in the USA. It was linked to a computer that could produce synthetic speech, so its progress could be heard. After producing formless noise for a few hours, it started babbling like a baby. Overnight training improved its performance still further so that it could read text with 95% accuracy. No conventionally programmed computer could do this.

Although humans often have to be taught, a great deal of important learning takes place unsupervised. We are not *taught* to speak our first language, we acquire it from experience. Neural networks cannot learn entire languages, but an important area of neurocomputing research is concerned with *unsupervised learning*. One of the most important approaches, discovered by David Willshaw of Edinburgh University, enables the neural network automatically to find patterns in batches of data. This has been applied by Finnish researcher Teuvo Kohonen to producing a phonetic typewriter, which converts speech to text.

Some people think that traditional approaches to artificial intelligence, such as expert systems, have been superseded by neurocomputing. This is wrong. Neural networks are less suitable for some problems than expert systems, and vice versa. There are other concerns about neural systems, such as the time required to train the network, and the difficulties of having a network explain the decision it has reached. The future of artificial intelligence rests with combined techniques, producing *hybrid systems* that exploit techniques best suited to the task in hand.

simulation the representation of real-life situations in a computer program. For example, the program might simulate traffic flow to assist planners to decide the effect of changes to road layouts.

speech recognition techniques whereby a computer can understand ordinary speech. Spoken words are divided into 'frames', each lasting about one-thirtieth of a second, which are converted to a wave form. These are then compared with a series of stored frames to determine the most likely word. Research into speech recognition started in 1938, but the technology became sufficiently developed for commercial applications only in the late 1980s.

spreadsheet program that mimics a sheet of ruled paper, divided into columns and rows. The user enters values in the sheet, then instructs the program to perform some operation on them, such as totalling a column or finding the average of a series of numbers. Highly complex numerical analyses can be built up from these simple steps. Spreadsheets are widely used for bookkeeping, forecasting, financial control, analysing results of experiments, and so on.

virtual reality advanced form of computer simulation, in which a participant has the illusion of being part of an artificial environment. The participant views the environment through two tiny 3-D television screens built into a visor. Sensors detect movements of the head or body, causing the apparent viewing position to change. Gloves (datagloves) fitted with sensors may be worn, which allow the participant seemingly to pick up and move objects in the environment. The technology is still under development but is expected to have widespread applications; for example, in military and surgical training, architecture, and home entertainment.

word processing the use of a program that allows the operator to type text into the computer memory, and then to retrieve it, alter it, and manipulate it in various ways before finally printing it on paper. Word processing is often used to speed up the typing of successive drafts of a long document and for creating large numbers of personalized letters. Many word processors include facilities for checking spellings, looking up synonyms, and adding graphics to the text.

workstation high-performance desktop computer with strong graphics capabilities, traditionally used for engineering (CAD and CAM), scientific research, and desktop publishing. Frequently based on fast RISC (reduced instruction-set computer) chips, workstations generally offer more processing power than microcomputers (although the distinction between workstations and the more powerful microcomputer models is becoming increasingly blurred). Most workstations use Unix as their operating system, and have good networking facilites.

TERMS

ASCII (acronym from American standard code for information interchange) a coding system in which numbers (between 0 and 127) are assigned to letters, digits, and punctuation symbols. For example, 45 represents a hyphen and 65 a capital A. The first 32 codes are used for control functions, such as carriage return and backspace. Strictly speaking, ASCII is a seven-bit code, but an eighth bit (binary digit) is often used to provide parity or to allow for extra characters. The system is widely used for the storage of text and for the transmission of data between computers. Although computers work in binary code, ASCII numbers are usually quoted as decimal or hexadecimal numbers.

binary number system or **binary number code** system of numbers to base two, using combinations of the digits 1 and 0. Binary numbers play a key role in digital computers, in which they form the basis of the internal coding of information, the values of bits (short for 'binary digits') being represented as on/off (1 and 0) states of switches and high/low voltages in circuits.

bit the smallest unit of information; a binary digit or place in a binary number. A byte contains 8 bits.

boot or **bootstrap** the process of starting up the computer. Most computers have a small, built-in program whose only job is to load a slightly larger program, usually from a disc, which in turn loads the main operating system.

buffer part of the memory used to hold data while it is waiting to be used. For example, a program might store data in a printer buffer until the printer is ready to print it.

byte a basic unit of storage of information. A byte contains 8 bits and can hold either a single character (letter, digit, or punctuation symbol) or a number between 0 and 255. Not all computers use bytes, although the unit is widely used in microcomputers.

chip alternative term for **integrated circuit**, a complete electronic circuit on a slice of silicon (or other semiconductor) crystal only a few millimetres square.

client-server architecture a system in which the mechanics of storing data are separated from the programs that use the data. For example, the 'server' might be a central database, typically located on a large computer that is reserved for this purpose. The 'client' would be an ordinary program that requests data from the server as needed.

data facts, figures, and symbols stored in computers. The term is often used to mean raw, unprocessed facts, as distinct from information, to which a meaning or interpretation has been applied.

data compression techniques for reducing the amount of storage needed for a given amount of data. They include word tokenization (in which frequently used words are stored as shorter codes), variable bit lengths (in which common characters are represented by fewer bits than less common ones), and run-length encoding (in which a repeated value is stored once along with a count).

DOS (acronym from *d*isc *o*perating *s*ystem) an operating system specifically designed for use with disc storage; also used as an alternative name for a particular operating system, Microsoft MS-DOS.

function a small part of a program that supplies a specific value; for example, the square root of a specified number, or the current date. Most programming languages incorporate a number of built-in functions; some allow programmers to write their own. A function may have one or more arguments (the values on which the function operates). A *function key* on a keyboard is one which, when pressed, performs a designated task, such as ending a program.

fuzzy logic form of knowledge representation suitable for notions, such as 'hot' or 'loud', that cannot be defined precisely but which depend on their context. The central idea of fuzzy logic is *probability of set membership*. For instance, referring to someone 5 ft 9 in tall, the statement 'this person is tall' (this person is a member of the set of tall people) might be about 70% true if that person is a man, and about 85% true if that person is a woman. Fuzzy logic enables computerized devices to reason more like humans, responding effectively to complex messages from their control panels and sensors. For example, a vacuum cleaner launched in 1992 by Japanese manufacturer Matsushita uses fuzzy logic to adjust its sucking power in response to messages from its sensors about the type of dirt on the floor, its distribution, and its depth.

gigabyte a unit of memory equal to 1,024 megabytes. It is also used, less precisely, to mean 1,000 million bytes.

hacking unauthorized access to a computer, either for fun or for malicious or fraudulent purposes. Hackers generally use microcomputers and telephone lines to obtain access.

hardware the mechanical, electrical, and electronic components of a computer system, as opposed to the various programs, which constitute software.

hexadecimal number system number system to the base 16. In hex (as it is commonly known) the decimal numbers 0–15 are represented by the characters 0, 1, 2, 3, 4, 5, 6, 7, 8, 9, A, B, C, D, E, F. Hexadecimal numbers are easy to convert to the computer's internal binary code and are more compact than binary numbers.

hypertext system for viewing information (both text and pictures) on a computer's screen in such a way that related items of information can easily be reached. For example, the program might display a map of a country; if the user points (with a mouse) to a particular city, the program displays information about that city.

image compression one of a number of methods used to reduce the amount of information required to represent an image, so that it takes up less computer memory and can be transmitted more rapidly and economically via telecommunications systems. It plays a major role in fax transmission and in videophone and multimedia systems.

integrated circuit or *chip* a miniaturized electronic circuit produced on a single crystal, or chip, of a semiconducting material such as silicon. It may contain more than a million transistors, resistors, and capacitors and yet measure only 5 mm/0.2 in square and 1 mm/0.04 in thick. The IC is encapsulated within a plastic or ceramic case, and linked via gold wires to metal pins with which it is connected to a printed circuit board and the other components that make up electronic devices such as computers and calculators.

interface the point of contact between two programs or pieces of equipment. The term is most often used for the physical connection between the computer and a peripheral device. For example, a printer interface is the cabling and circuitry used to transfer data from the computer to the printer and to compensate for differences in speed and coding systems.

kilobyte (KB) a unit of memory equal to 1,024 bytes.

laptop computer portable microcomputer, small enough to be used on the operator's lap. It consists of a single unit, incorporating a keyboard, floppy disc or hard disc drives, and a screen. The screen often forms a lid that folds back in use. It uses a liquid crystal or gas plasma display, rather than the bulkier and heavier cathode ray tubes found in most VDUs. A typical laptop computer measures about 360 mm × 380 mm × 100 mm, and weighs 3–7 kg.

macro in programming, a new command created by combining a number of existing ones. For example, if the language has separate commands for obtaining data from the keyboard and for displaying data on the screen, the programmer might create a macro that performs both these tasks in one command. A *macro key* is a key on the keyboard that combines the effects of several individual key presses.

megabyte a unit of memory equal to 1,024 kilobytes. It is also used, less precisely, to mean 1 million bytes.

microprocessor a computer's central processing unit (CPU) contained on a single integrated circuit. The appearance of the first microprocessors in 1971 heralded the introduction of the microcomputer. The microprocessor has led to a dramatic fall in the size and cost of computers and to the introduction of dedicated computers in washing machines, cars, and so on.

MS-DOS (abbreviation of *Microsoft Disc Operating System*) operating system produced by the Microsoft Corporation, widely used on microcomputers with 16-bit microprocessors. A version called PC-DOS is sold by IBM specifically for its range of personal computers. MS-DOS and PC-DOS are usually referred to

COMPUTING: CHRONOLOGY

1614	Scottish mathematician John Napier invented logarithms.
1623	Wilhelm Schickard (1592–1635) invented the mechanical calculating machine.
1672–74	Gottfried Wilhelm Leibniz built his first calculator, the Stepped Reckoner.
1801	Joseph-Marie Jacquard developed an automatic loom controlled by punched cards.
1820	First mass-produced calculator, the Arithmometer, invented by Charles Thomas de Colmar (1785–1870).
1822	Charles Babbage developed the difference engine, a device for calculating the values of logarithms and trigometric functions.
1830s	Babbage created the first design for the analytical engine, a calculating machine capable of being driven by an external program.
1890	Herman Hollerith developed the punched-card ruler for the USA census.
1936	Alan Turing published the mathematical theory of computing.
1938	Konrad Zuse constructed the first binary calculator, using Boolean algebra.
1939	J V Atanasoff of Iowa State University became the first to use electronic means for mechanizing arithmetical operations.
1943	The Colossus electronic code-breaker was developed by Alan Turing and his team at Bletchley Park, England; the first electronic program-controlled calculator, the Harvard University Mark I (or Automatic Sequence-Controlled Calculator), was completed.
1945	ENIAC (electronic numerator, integrator, analyser and computer), the first general purpose, fully electronic digital computer, was completed at the University of Pennsylvania, USA.
1948	The first stored-program computer, the Manchester University (England) Mark I, was developed.
1951	Ferranti Mark I, the first commercially produced computer, was launched; Whirlwind, the first real-time computer, was built for the USA air-defence system; transistors began to be developed.
1953	Magnetic-core memory was developed.
1958	The first integrated circuit was produced.
1963	PDP-8, the first minicomputer, was built by Digital Equipment (DEC); the first electronic calculator was developed by the Bell Punch Company.
1964	IBM System/360, the first compatible family of computers, was launched.
1965	The first supercomputer, the Control Data CD6600, was developed.
1971	The first microprocessor, the Intel 4004, was introduced.
1974	CLIP-4, the first computer with a parallel architecture, was developed.
1975	The first personal computer, Altair 8800, was produced.
1981	The Xerox Star system, the first WIMP (windows, icons, menus and pointing devices) system, was developed. IBM launched its Personal Computer (PC).
1985	The Inmos T414 Transputer, the first 'off-the-shelf' RISC microprocessor for building parallel computers, was launched.
1988	The first optical microchip, which uses light instead of electricity, was developed.
1989	Wafer-scale silicon memory chips, able to store 200 million characters, were launched.
1990	Microsoft releases Windows 3, a windowing environment for PCs.
1991	IBM developed the world's fastest high-capacity memory chip, SRAM (static random access memory), able to send or receive 8 billion bits of information per second.

as DOS. MS-DOS first appeared in the early 1980s, and was based on an earlier system for computers with 8-bit microprocessors, CP/M.

multitasking or **multiprogramming** a system in which one processor appears to run several different programs (or different parts of the same program) at the same time. All the programs are held in memory together and each is allowed to run for a certain period, for example while other programs are waiting for a peripheral device to work or for input from an operator. The ability to multitask depends on the operating system rather than the type of computer.

neural network artificial network of processors that attempts to mimic the structure of neurons in the human brain. Neural networks may be electronic, optical, or simulated by computer software. The chief characteristic of neural networks is their ability to learn large amounts of imprecise data and decide whether they match a pattern or not. Networks of this type may be used in developing robot vision, matching fingerprints, and analysing fluctuations in stock-market prices. However, it is thought unlikely by scientists that such networks will ever be able accurately to imitate the human brain, which is very much more complicated; it contains around 10 billion neurons, whereas current artificial networks contain only a hundred or so.

operating system (OS) a program that controls the basic operation of a computer. A typical OS controls the peripheral devices, organ-

THE MULTIMEDIA EXPERIENCE

Star Wars film director George Lucas said that 'sound is 50% of the movie-going experience.' Adding sound can transform computer programs, and multimedia promises even more —animation, sound, photographs, and video, in addition to traditional text and graphics. *Multimedia Beethoven*, for example, allows the user to hear Beethoven's music and follow the score while exploring his life and times. Multimedia applications include interactive training, presentation graphics, point-of-sale merchandising systems, information services—and, of course, entertainment.

Apart from making rudimentary sounds, standard PCs only display visual information, so adaptations are required to enable sound and video to be handled. In addition, most multimedia systems include CD-ROM drives (which are the same as audio compact discs, simply used to store a different kind of data), since huge amounts of data are involved in most multimedia applications, and CD-ROMs are suitable for both storage and distribution of such quantities of information.

High-quality multimedia presentations are difficult to produce, since few people are accustomed to manipulating so many different media within a single program.

Early efforts will probably suffer from 'over-production' difficulties similar to those first encountered by amateur desk-top publishing users: the multimedia equivalent of too many different fonts. The emergence of improved authoring tools may help users to avoid these problems, and still develop multimedia presentations relatively easily.

Standards for multimedia systems are beginning to emerge. A number of companies, including AT&T, Microsoft, Tandy, and many others have formed the Multimedia PC Marketing Council. They plan to use the trademark MPC to indicate compatibility with the MPC specification originally announced in 1990. Apple and NeXT machines also represent viable multimedia platforms, though neither has the same installed user base as the PC.

As the computer price–performance ratio continues to improve, the cost of the hardware required to run multimedia applications will become generally affordable. Multimedia remains in its infancy, but as it matures, we can expect to see increasing numbers of applications designed with multimedia in mind.

---

izes the filing system, provides a means of communicating with the operator, and runs other programs.

pixel (contraction of 'picture element') a single dot on a computer screen. All screen images are made up of a collection of pixels, with each pixel being either off (dark) or on (illuminated, possibly in colour). The number of pixels available determines the screen's resolution. Typical resolutions of microcomputer screens vary from 320×200 pixels to 640×480 pixels, but screens with over 1,000 pixels are now quite common for graphic (pictorial) displays.

procedure a small part of a computer program, which performs a specific task, such as clearing the screen or sorting a file. In some program-

ming languages there is an overlap between procedures, functions, and subroutines. Careful use of procedures is an element of structured programming. A **procedural language**, such as BASIC, is one in which the programmer describes a task in terms of how it is to be done, as opposed to a **declarative language**, such as PROLOG, in which it is described in terms of the required result.

RISC (acronym from *r*educed *i*nstruction-*s*et *c*omputer) a processor on a single integrated circuit, or chip, that is faster and more powerful than others in common use today. By reducing the range of operations the processor can carry out, the chips are able to optimize those operations to execute more quickly.

PORTABLE COMPUTERS: THE WORLD MARKET

Forecast of unit shipments in '000s

	1991	1992	1993	1994
United States	1,313	1,687	2,022	2,284
Western Europe	973	1,309	1,620	1,883
Japan	1,054	1,458	2,018	2,726
Rest of the world	522	711	912	1,136
WORLD TOTAL	3,862	5,165	6,572	8,029

Percentage growth rate for the figures above

United States	27	28	20	13
Western Europe	49	35	24	16
Japan	41	38	38	35
Rest of the world	55	36	28	25
WORLD TOTAL	39	34	27	22

Source: The Financial Times

PROGRAMMING LANGUAGES: A SELECTION

language	main uses	description
assembler languages	jobs needing detailed control of the hardware, fast execution, and small program sizes	fast and efficient but require considerable effort and skill
BASIC (*b*eginner's *a*ll-purpose *s*ymbolic *i*nstruction *c*ode)	in education and the home, and among nonprofessional programmers, such as engineers	easy to learn; early versions (derived from FORTRAN) lacked the features of other languages
C	systems programming; general programming	fast and efficient; widely used as a general-purpose language; especially popular among professional programmers
COBOL (*c*ommon *b*usiness-*o*riented *l*anguage)	business programming	strongly oriented towards data processing work; easy to learn but very verbose; widely used on mainframes
FORTRAN (*fo*rmula *tran*slation)	scientific and computational work	based on mathematical formulae; popular among engineers, scientists, and mathematicians
LISP (*lis*t *p*rocessing)	artificial intelligence	symbolic language with a reputation for being hard to learn; popular in the academic and research communities
Modula-2	systems and real-time programming; general programming	highly structured; intended to replace Pascal for 'real-world' applications
PASCAL	general-purpose language	highly structured; widely used for teaching programming in universities
PROLOG (*pro*gramming in *log*ic	artificial intelligence	symbolic-logic programming system, originally intended for theorem solving but now used more generally in artificial intelligence

Computers based on RISC chips became commercially available in the late 1980s, but are less widespread than traditional processors.

software a collection of programs and procedures for making a computer perform a specific task, as opposed to the machine and circuitry itself, known as hardware. Software is created by programmers and either distributed on a suitable medium, such as the floppy disc, or built into the computer in the form of firmware. Examples of software include operating systems, compilers, and application programs, such as payrolls. No computer can function without some form of software.

Unix operating system designed for minicomputers but becoming increasingly popular on large microcomputers, workstations, and supercomputers. It was developed by Bell Laboratories in the late 1960s, and is closely related to the programming language C. Its wide range of functions and flexibility have made it widely used by universities and in commercial software.

virtual memory a technique whereby a portion of external memory is used as an extension of internal memory. The contents of an area of RAM are stored on, say, a hard disc while they are not needed, and brought back into main memory when required. The process, known as paging or segmentation, is hidden from the programmer, to whom the computer's internal memory appears larger than it really is.

virus piece of software that can be transferred from one computer to another and can replicate itself over and over again without the user being aware of its presence. Some viruses are relatively harmless, but others can damage or destroy data. They are written by anonymous programmers, often maliciously, and are usually spread by 'infected' floppy discs. Antivirus software can be used to detect and destroy well-known viruses, but new viruses continually appear and these may bypass existing antivirus programs.

word a unit of storage. The size of a word varies from one computer to another. In a popular microcomputer, it is 16 bits or 2 bytes; on many mainframes it is 32 bits.

WYSIWYG (pronounced 'whizzywig'; acronym from *w*hat *y*ou *s*ee *i*s *w*hat *y*ou *g*et) a program that attempts to display on the screen a faithful representation of the final printed output. For example, a WYSIWYG word processor would show actual line widths, page breaks, and the sizes and styles of type.

THE INTERIOR OF THE EARTH

asthenosphere a division of the Earth's structure lying beneath the lithosphere, at a depth of approximately 70 km/45 mi to 260 km/160 mi. It is thought to be the soft, partially molten layer of the mantle on which the rigid plates of the Earth's surface move to produce the motions of plate tectonics.

bed a single sedimentary rock unit with a distinct set of physical characteristics or contained fossils, readily distinguishable from those of beds above and below. Well-defined partings called *bedding planes* separate successive beds or strata.

continent any one of the large land masses of Earth, as distinct from ocean. They are Asia, Africa, North America, South America, Europe, Australia, and Antarctica. Continents are constantly moving and evolving a process known as Plate Tectonics. A continent does not end at the coastline; its boundary is the edge of the shallow continental shelf (part of the continental crust, made of sial), which may extend several hundred miles or kilometres out to sea.

core the innermost part of the structure of Earth. It is divided into an inner core, the upper boundary of which is 1,700 km/1,060 mi from the centre, and an outer core, 1,820 km/1,130 mi thick. Both parts are thought to consist of iron-nickel alloy, with the inner core being solid and the outer core being liquid. The temperature may be 3,000°C/5,400°F.

craton or *shield* the core of a continent, a vast tract of highly deformed metamorphic rock around which the continent has been built. Intense mountain-building periods shook these shield areas in Precambrian times before stable conditions set in.

crust the outermost part of the structure of Earth, consisting of two distinct parts, the oceanic crust and the continental crust. The *oceanic* crust is on average about 10 km/6.2 mi thick and consists mostly of basaltic types of rock. By contrast, the *continental* crust is primarily granitic in composition and more complex in its structure. Because of the movements of plate tectonics, the oceanic crust is in no place older than about 200 million years. However, parts of the continental crust are over three billion years old.

diagenesis or *lithification* the physical and chemical changes by which a sediment becomes a sedimentary rock. The main processes involved include compaction of the grains, and the cementing of the grains together by the growth of new minerals deposited by percolating groundwater.

earthquake shaking or convulsion of the Earth's surface, the scientific study of which is called seismology. Earthquakes result from a build-up of stresses within rocks until strained to fracturing point. Most occur along faults (fractures or breaks) in the Earth's crust. Plate tectonic movements generate the major proportion of all earthquakes; as two plates move past each other, they can become jammed and deformed, and earthquakes occur when they spring free. Most earthquakes happen under the sea. Their force is measured on the Richter scale.

epicentre the point on the Earth's surface immediately above the seismic focus of an earthquake. Most damage usually takes place at an earthquake's epicentre. The term sometimes refers to a point directly above or below a nuclear explosion ('at ground zero').

fault a fracture in the Earth's crust along which the two sides have moved as a result of differing strains in the adjacent rock bodies. Displacement of rock masses horizontally or vertically along a fault may be microscopic, or it may be massive, causing major earthquakes.

fold a bend in rock beds. If the bend is arched up in the middle it is called an *anticline*; if it sags downwards in the middle it is called a *syncline*. The line along which a bed of rock folds is called its axis. The axial plane is the plane joining the axes of successive beds.

geochemistry the science of chemistry as it applies to geology. It deals with the relative and absolute abundances of the chemical elements and their isotopes in the Earth, and also with the chemical changes that accompany geologic processes.

geophysics branch of geology using physics to study the Earth's surface, interior, and atmosphere. Studies also include winds, weather, tides, earthquakes, volcanoes, and their effects.

geothermal energy energy produced by the use of natural steam, subterranean hot water, and hot dry rock for heating and electricity generation. Hot water is pumped to the surface and converted to steam or run through a heat exchanger; or dry steam is directed through turbines to produce electricity.

geyser a natural spring that intermittently dis-

continent

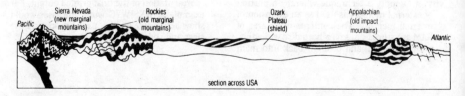

section across USA

THE RISE AND FALL OF SOUTH AMERICAN CIVILIZATIONS

The year 1992 sees the 500th anniversary of the landing of Christopher Columbus in the Americas. This event is seen as the beginning of the final destruction of the complex and sophisticated civilizations that existed on those continents. Yet the influx of foreigners was not the only problem to beset these ancient peoples, particularly in the region of the Andes. Many of their problems were due to the geology of the land that they occupied.

The Andes are one of the most active mountain-building areas on Earth. The whole scheme of plate tectonics describes the surface of the Earth as being composed of individual plates, each growing from one edge at an ocean ridge, moving slowly across the Earth's surface, and being destroyed at the other edge, by being dragged down or 'subducted' beneath the next plate. The action of subduction generates mountain ranges as the edges of the plates are crumpled, and volcanoes as the subducting plate is melted and the molten material is injected upwards through the mountains above. Earthquakes accompany the movement, and the pulling down of the subducting plate produces an ocean trench, just offshore of the mountain range. All these conditions are seen along the west coast of South America. The Nazca Plate of the eastern Pacific ocean floor is being subducted beneath the western edge of the South American continent. The Peru–Chile Trench lies just offshore. The Andes mountains run the length of the continent, and are continually rising. The whole system is riddled with volcanoes, the region of Bolivia and Peru having the greatest density of volcanoes in the world. Peru alone has 22 that are currently active.

Since the earliest days of civilization these regions have been occupied. And it is hardly surprising that natural disaster has followed natural disaster, leading to a very complex history of a succession of cultures and settlements. About 900 BC there were many thriving settlements along the Peruvian coast. Their economy was based on fishing. The prolific fishing grounds just offshore were fed by algae that thrived on nutrient-rich water welling up from the deeps of the Peru–Chile Trench. These settlements were suddenly destroyed at about that time. Archaeological evidence (damaged buildings and silt deposits on top of cobblestones) indicates that they were engulfed by a tsunami—what journalists call a 'tidal wave'. The movements of the plates in this area produce frequent earthquakes. When the earthquakes occur at sea the resulting disturbance can send giant sea waves far inland. The direct result of this disaster was the establishment of an important religious centre, Chavin de Huantar, 3,000 m/9,900 ft above sea level in the Andes. This was the first of the great mountain civilizations and existed for 500 years.

One of the largest of the Andean civilizations was the Chimu of the Moche river valley in Peru, which existed for 500 years and died out just before the European invasions. It was an agriculturally based society, farming the fertile but arid coastal plain. Complex irrigation systems based on long canals spread the water from the Moche river. However, the continuing plate-tectonic movement meant that the land was rising and tilting continuously, as the Andes were continuing to grow. Periodically the canals would dry up because the slope altered, and a new irrigation system had to be installed. A side-effect of this was that irrigation technology and engineering were pushed to new frontiers. Also, the armies of labourers brought in from neighbouring conquered areas had to be found other work once each irrigation system was completed, and their energies were diverted into building the great cities for their conquerors. Eventually the change in the topography meant that the river had cut so deeply into its bed as the surrounding land rose that there was no practical remedy to the failure of the irrigation systems. The civilization perished.

Even now this area is subjected to disasters. Some 20,000 died in 1970 when a landslide, triggered by an earthquake, destroyed the Peruvian town of Yungay. Thousands more died in a mudslide that engulfed the Colombian town of Armero in 1985. The fishing grounds off the coast are still there, but are becoming increasingly subject to the El Niño effect, in which a change of the wind pattern alters the current system and the nutritious water fails to rise from the bottom of the Peru–Chile Trench. As a result the fish stocks collapse, and with them the economy of the local fishing communities.

Buildings in Armero, Colombia, partially collapsed after the eruption of Nevado El Ruiz.

Major 20th-Century Earthquakes

date	place	magnitude (Richter scale)	number of deaths
1906	San Francisco, USA	8.3	3,000
1908	Messina, Italy	7.5	83,000
1915	Avezzano, Italy	7.5	29,980
1920	Gansu, China	8.6	100,000
1923	Tokyo, Japan	8.3	99,330
1927	Nan-Shan, China	8.3	200,000
1932	Gansu, China	7.6	70,000
1935	Quetta, India	7.5	30,000
1939	Erzincan, Turkey	7.9	30,000
1939	Chillán, Chile	8.3	28,000
1948	USSR	7.3	110,000
1970	N Peru	7.7	66,794
1976	Tangshan, China	8.2	242,000
1978	NE Iran	7.7	25,000
1980	El Asnam, Algeria	7.3	20,000
1985	Mexico City, Mexico	8.1	5,000
1988	Armenia, USSR	6.9	25,000
1990	NW Iran	7.7	50,000

charges an explosive column of steam and hot water into the air.

intrusion mass of igneous rock that has formed by 'injection' of molten rock, or magma, into existing cracks beneath the surface of the Earth, as distinct from a volcanic rock mass which has erupted from the surface. Intrusion features include vertical cylindrical structures such as stocks and necks, sheet structures such as dykes that cut across the strata and sills that push between them, and laccoliths, which are blisters that push up the overlying rock.

lava molten material that erupts from a volcano and cools to form extrusive igneous rock. A lava high in silica is viscous and sticky and does not flow far, wheras low-silica lava can flow for long distances.

lithosphere the topmost layer of the Earth's structure, forming the jigsaw of plates that take part in the movements of plate tectonics. The lithosphere comprises the crust and a portion of the upper mantle. It is regarded as being rigid and moves about on the semi-molten asthenosphere. The lithosphere is about 75 km/47 mi thick.

magma molten material beneath the Earth's surface from which igneous rocks are formed. Lava is magma that has reached the surface, losing some of its components on the way.

mantle the intermediate zone of the Earth between the crust and the core. It is thought to consist of silicate minerals such as olivine and spinel.

Mercalli scale a scale used to measure the intensity of an earthquake. It differs from the Richter scale, which measures *magnitude*. It is named after the Italian seismologist Giuseppe Mercalli (1850–1914).

metamorphism geological term referring to the changes in rocks of the Earth's crust caused by increasing pressure and temperature. The resulting rocks are metamorphic rocks. All metamorphic changes take place in solid rocks. If the rocks melt and then harden, they become igneous rocks.

Mohorovičić discontinuity also *Moho* or *M-discontinuity* boundary that separates the Earth's crust and mantle, marked by a rapid increase in the speed of earthquake waves. It follows the variations in the thickness of the crust and is found approximately 32 km/20 mi below the continents and about 10 km/6 mi below the oceans. It is named after the Yugoslav geophysicist Andrija Mohorovičić (1857–1936) who suspected its presence after analysing seismic waves from the Kulpa Valley earthquake 1909.

petrology branch of geology that deals with the study of rocks, their mineral compositions, and their origins.

Richter scale a scale based on measurement of seismic waves, used to determine the magnitude of an earthquake at the epicentre. The magnitude of an earthquake differs from the intensity, measured by the Mercalli scale, which is subjective and varies from place to place for the same earthquake.

sial in geochemistry and geophysics, term denoting the substance of the Earth's continental crust, as distinct from the sima of the ocean crust. The name is derived from *si*lica and *al*umina, its two main chemical constituents.

sima in geochemistry and geophysics, term denoting the substance of the Earth's oceanic crust, as distinct from the sial of the continental crust. The name is derived from *si*lica and *ma*gnesia, its two main chemical constituents.

volcano vent in the Earth's crust from which molten rock, lava, ashes, and gases are ejected. Usually it is cone-shaped with a pitlike opening at the top called the crater. Some volcanoes, for example Stromboli and Vesuvius in Italy, eject the material with explosive violence; others, for example on Hawaii, are quiet and the lava simply rises into the crater and flows over the rim.

THE SURFACE OF THE EARTH

abyssal zone dark ocean area 2,000–6,000 m/6,500–19,500 ft deep; temperature 4°C/39°F. Three-quarters of the area of the deep ocean floor lies in the abyssal zone. It is too far from the surface for photosynthesis to take place. Some fish and crustaceans living there are blind or have their own light sources. The region above is the bathyal zone; the region below, the hadyal zone.

alluvial deposit a layer of broken rocky matter, or sediment, formed from material that has been carried in suspension by a river or stream and dropped as the velocity of the current changes. River plains and deltas are made entirely of alluvial deposits, but smaller pockets can be found in the beds of upland torrents.

Antarctic Circle an imaginary line that encircles the South Pole at latitude 66° 32| S. The line encompasses the continent of Antarctica and

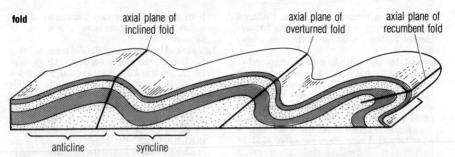

fold — axial plane of inclined fold — axial plane of overturned fold — axial plane of recumbent fold

anticline — syncline

the Antarctic Ocean.

anticline a fold in the rocks of the Earth's crust in which the layers or beds bulge upwards to form an arch (seldom preserved intact).

aquifer any rock formation containing water that can be extracted by a well. The rock of an aquifer must be porous and permeable (full of interconnected holes) so that it can absorb water.

archipelago a group of islands, or an area of sea containing a group of islands. The islands of an archipelago are usually volcanic in origin, and they sometimes represent the tops of peaks in areas around continental margins flooded by the sea.

Arctic Circle an imaginary line that encircles the North Pole at latitude 66° 32ǀ N. Within this line there is at least one day in the summer during which the sun never sets, and at least one day in the winter during which the sun never rises.

artesian well a well in which water rises from its aquifer under natural pressure. Such a well may be drilled into an aquifer that is confined by impermeable beds both above and below. If the water table (the top of the region of water saturation) in that aquifer is above the level of the well head, hydrostatic pressure will force the water to the surface.

badlands a barren landscape cut by erosion into a maze of ravines, pinnacles, gullies and sharp-edged ridges. South Dakota and Nebraska, USA, are examples.

caldera a very large basin-shaped crater. Calderas are found at the tops of volcanoes, where the original peak has collapsed into an empty chamber beneath. The basin, many times larger than the original volcanic vent, may be flooded, producing a crater lake, or the flat floor may contain a number of small volcanic cones, produced by volcanic activity after the collapse.

crater a bowl-shaped topographic feature, usually round and with steep sides. Craters are formed by explosive events such as the eruption of a volcano or by the impact of a meteorite. A caldera is a much larger feature.

delta a roughly fanlike tract of land at a river's mouth, formed by deposited silt or sediment. Familiar examples of large deltas are those of the Mississippi, Ganges and Brahmaputra, Rhône, Po, Danube, and Nile; the shape of the Nile delta is like the Greek letter Δ, and thus gave rise to the name.

desert area without sufficient rainfall and, consequently, vegetation to support human life. Scientifically, this term includes the ice areas of the polar regions. Almost 33% of Earth's land surface is desert, and this proportion is increasing.

dune a mound or ridge of wind-drifted sand. Loose sand is blown and bounced along by the wind, up the windward side of a dune. The sand particles then fall to rest on the lee side, while more are blown up from the windward side. In this way a dune moves gradually downwind.

equator the *terrestrial equator* is the great circle whose plane is perpendicular to the Earth's axis (the line joining the poles). Its length is 40,092 km/24,901.8 mi, divided into 360 degrees of longitude. The *celestial equator* is the circle in which the plane of the Earth's equator intersects the celestial sphere.

erosion the processes whereby the rocks and soil of the Earth's surface are loosened, worn away, and transported (weathering does not involve transportation). There are two types, chemical and physical. *Chemical erosion* involves the alteration of the mineral component of the rock, by means of rainwater or the substances dissolved in it, and its subsequent movement. *Physical erosion* involves the breakdown and transportation of exposed rocks by physical forces. In practice the two work together.

fjord or *fiord* narrow sea inlet enclosed by high cliffs. Fjords are found in Norway and elsewhere. *Fiordland* is the deeply indented SW coast of South Island, New Zealand; one of the most beautiful inlets is Milford Sound.

flood plain the area bordering a stream or river over which water spreads in time of flood. When stream discharge exceeds channel capacity, water rises over the channel banks and floods the adjacent low-lying lands. A river flood plain can be regarded as part of its natural domain, statistically certain to be claimed by the river at repeated intervals. By plotting floods that have occurred and extrapolating from that data we can speak of ten-year floods, 100-year floods, 500-year floods, and so forth, based on the statistical probability of flooding across certain parts of the flood plain.

glacier a body of ice, originating in mountains in snowfields above the snowline, which traverses land surfaces (glacier flow). It moves slowly down a valley or depression, and is constantly replenished from its source. The scenery produced by the erosive action of glaciers is characteristic and includes U-shaped valleys, corries, arêtes, and various features formed by the deposition of moraine (rocky debris).

ground water the water formed underground in porous rock strata and soils and issuing as springs and streams. The ground-water table (or water table) is the boundary between two zones of rock or soil. Below the water table the pores are completely filled with water (called the saturated zone); above the water table is an unsaturated zone. Sandy or other kinds of beds that are filled with ground water are called aquifers. Most ground water near the surface moves slowly through the ground while the water table stays in the same place. The depth of the water table reflects the balance between the rate of infiltration, called recharge, and the rate of discharge at springs or rivers or pumped water wells. The force of gravity makes underground water run 'downhill' underground just as it does above the surface. The greater the slope and the permeability, the greater the speed. Velocities vary from 100 cm/40 in per day to 0.5 cm/0.2 in.

International Date Line (IDL) a modification of the 180th meridian that marks the difference in time between E and W. The date is put forward a day when crossing the line going W, and back a day when going E. The IDL was chosen at the International Meridian Conference in 1884.

island an area of land surrounded entirely by water. Australia is classed as a continent rather than an island, because of its size.

landslide a sudden downward movement of a mass of soil or rocks from a cliff or steep slope. Landslides happen when a slope becomes unstable, usually because the base has been undercut or certain boundaries of materials within the mass have become wet and slippery.

latitude and longitude angular distances defining position on the globe. *Latitude* (abbreviation lat.) is the angular distance of any point from the equator, measured N or S along the Earth's curved surface, equalling the angle between the respective horizontal planes. It is measured in degrees, minutes, and seconds, each minute equalling one nautical mile (1.85 km/1.15 mi) in length. *Longitude* (abbreviation long.) is the angle between the terrestrial meridian through a place, and a standard meridian now taken at Greenwich, England. At the equator one degree of longitude measures approximately 113 km/70 mi.

meander a loop-shaped curve in a river flowing across flat country. As a river flows, any curve in its course is accentuated by the current. The current is fastest on the outside of the curve where it cuts into the bank; on the curve's inside the current is slow and deposits any transported material. In this way the river changes its course across the floodplain.

meridian half a great circle drawn on the Earth's surface passing through both poles and thus through all places with the same longitude. Terrestrial longitudes are usually measured from the Greenwich Meridian.

moraine rocky debris or till carried along and deposited by a glacier. Material eroded from the side of a glaciated valley and carried along the glacier's edge is called lateral moraine; that worn from the valley floor and carried along the base of the glacier is called ground moraine. Rubble dropped at the foot of a melting glacier is called terminal moraine.

peat fibrous organic substance found in bogs and

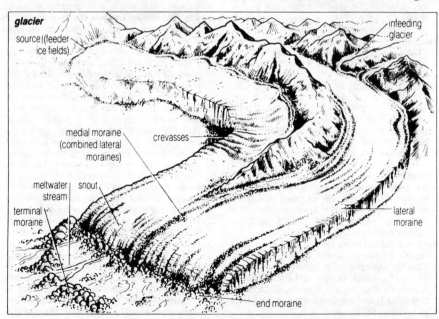

glacier

source (feeder ice fields)

infeeding glacier

medial moraine (combined lateral moraines)

crevasses

meltwater stream

snout

terminal moraine

lateral moraine

end moraine

latitude and magnitude

Point X lies on longitude 60°W

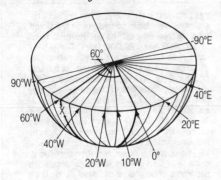

Point X lies on latitude 20°S

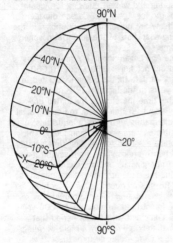

Together longitude 60°W latitude 20°S places point X on a precise position on the globe.

formed by the incomplete decomposition of plants such as sphagnum moss. The USSR, Canada, Finland, Ireland, and other places have large deposits, which have been dried and used as fuel from ancient times. Peat can also be used as a soil additive.

permafrost condition in which a deep layer of soil does not thaw out during the summer but remains at below 0°C/32°F for at least two years, despite thawing of the soil above. It is claimed that 26% of the world's land surface is permafrost.

plain or *grassland* land, usually flat, upon which grass predominates. The plains cover large areas of the Earth's surface, especially between the deserts of the tropics and the rainforests of the equator, and have rain in one season only. In such regions the climate belts move north and south during the year, bringing rainforest

conditions at one time and desert conditions at another. Examples include the North European Plain, the High Plains of the USA and Canada, and the Russian Plain, also known as the steppe.

plateau elevated area of fairly flat land, or a mountainous region in which the peaks are at the same height. An *intermontane plateau* is one surrounded by mountains. A *piedmont plateau* is one that lies between the mountains and low-lying land. A *continental plateau* rises abruptly from low-lying lands or the sea.

polder area of flat reclaimed land that used to be covered by a river, lake, or the sea. Polders have been artificially drained and protected from flooding by building dykes. They are common in the Netherlands, where the total land area has been increased by nearly one-fifth since AD 1200.

poles geographic north and south points of the axis about which the Earth rotates. The magnetic poles are the points towards which a freely suspended magnetic needle will point; however, they vary continually.

In 1985 the magnetic north pole was some 350 km/218 mi NW of Resolute Bay, Northwest Territories, Canada. It moves northwards about 10 km/6 mi each year, although it can vary in a day about 80 km/50 mi from its average position. It is relocated every decade in order to update navigational charts. Migrating birds are believed to orientate themselves partly using the Earth's magnetic field.

rift valley valley formed by the subsidence of a block of the Earth's crust between two or more parallel faults. Rift valleys are steep-sided and form where the crust is being pulled apart, as at ocean ridges, or in the Great Rift Valley of E Africa.

sand loose grains of rock, sized 0.02–2.00 mm/ 0.0008–0.0800 in in diameter, consisting chiefly of quartz, but owing their varying colour to mixtures of other minerals. It is used in cement-making, as an abrasive, in glass-making, and for other purposes.

scarp and dip the two slopes formed when a sedimentary bed outcrops as a landscape feature. The scarp is the slope that cuts across the bedding plane; the dip is the opposite slope which follows the bedding plane. The scarp is usually steep, while the dip is a gentle slope.

sediment any loose material that has 'settled' – deposited from suspension in water, ice, or air, generally as the water current or wind speed decreases. Typical sediments are, in order of increasing coarseness, clay, mud, silt, sand, gravel, pebbles, cobbles, and boulders.

soil loose covering of broken rocky material and decaying organic matter overlying the bedrock of the Earth's surface. Various types of soil develop under different conditions: deep soils form in warm wet climates and in valleys; shallow soils form in cool dry areas and on slopes. *Pedology*, the study of soil, is significant because of the relative importance of different soil types to agriculture.

stalactite and stalagmite cave structures formed

FOSSILIZED ATMOSPHERE

Many present-day environmental fears arise from changes in the composition of the atmosphere. CFCs from aerosols and refrigerators drift to the stratosphere where they break down the ozone layer. Sulphur dioxide from factory chimneys forms sulphuric acid in the atmosphere which falls as acid rain. The build up of carbon dioxide, water vapour, and other gases keeps in the Earth's surface heat, producing the so-called greenhouse effect. Soot particles from blazing oil wells at the site of the Gulf War caused a lowering of temperatures downwind. It is therefore important to chart the natural changes in the atmospheric gases so that we know what effect such changes have had in the past.

A current experiment that is shedding light on the subject is GRIP—the Greenland Icecore Project. The ice of the Greenland icecap is formed from snow which has been compacted by more snow falling upon it. The ice formed each year contains the atmospheric impurities that were trapped in the snow during that year and can be analysed. The dates of each layer can be accurately counted, rather like the rings of a tree. In the summer the acidity of the atmosphere increases and this increases the electrical conductivity of the snow. The variations in the conductivity in the ice core give the number of years represented. Big increases in acidity, and hence conductivity, are produced by sulphur dioxide from volcanic eruptions, and such increases can be compared with eruptions from known dates and provide a check on the dating. Teams from Denmark, Switzerland, France, Germany, Iceland, the UK, Belgium and Italy, coordinated by the European Science Foundation, began in 1988 to drill into the thickest portion of the Greenland icecap and collect continuous samples. The samples are in the form of cylindrical cores of ice, each about 2.5 m/8 ft long, which are brought to the surface and analysed on site before they become contaminated. The on-site laboratory is located in a trench in the ice at the well-head, manned by between 30 and 50 people during the summer season.

The ice is moving outwards under pressure at the edges of the icecap, but the GRIP drilling site is almost central and the ice has been quite stationary. Other drilling programmes have been carried out in the Greenland ice, reaching depths equivalent to dates of 100,000 and 120,000 years. The GRIP team hope to reach ice that is between 300,000 and 500,000 years old, at a depth of 3 km/2 mi , during the summer of 1992.

Relative proportions of oxygen-18 and oxygen-16 in the ice give a clue to the atmospheric temperatures of the time—an increase in oxygen-18 showing warmer conditions. High concentrations of chlorine in the ice show that the water that formed it came from the sea. Large proportions of sodium show that the ice came from land-derived water. Air circulation patterns can be determined from such studies. Dust particles are highly concentrated in the ice that formed during the last glacial phase of the Ice Age—because the sea levels were lower and more land was exposed to strong winds. At this time most dust was deposited during spring and winter, allowing for accurate dating of the Ice Age years. Carbon dioxide and methane are present in tiny bubbles in the ice, giving snapshots of the actual atmosphere of the time.

The Ice Age began about 1.7 million years ago, and did not finish until about 10,000 years ago—a date that is being readjusted to 11,500 years in the light of GRIP research. During this time the climate fluctuated dramatically about 20 times, with the cold glacial periods alternating with mild 'interglacials', in which climates were warmer than today. The GRIP borehole should for the first time sample ice, and hence atmosphere, from several glacials and interglacials and allow climatologists to examine the circumstances of the climate's change. Results produced so far show high concentrations of ammonium, produced by extensive forest fires, from about 12,000 years ago. This coincided with a cool period that was immediately followed by a rapid warming. Perhaps the carbon dioxide from these fires generated a greenhouse effect.

The GRIP programme is producing an extremely detailed and accurate plot of how the Earth's climate has changed since the Ice Age. The understanding of these natural variations is essential if we are to understand the artificial climatic variations that are currently being produced by the impact of civilization.

by the deposition of calcite dissolved in ground water. *Stalactites* grow downwards from the roofs or walls and can be icicle-shaped, straw-shaped, curtain-shaped, or formed as terraces. *Stalagmites* grow upwards from the cave floor and can be conical, fir-cone-shaped, or resemble a stack of saucers. Growing stalactites and stalagmites may meet to form a continuous column from floor to ceiling.

syncline geological term for a fold in the rocks of the Earth's crust in which the layers or beds dip inwards, thus forming a trough-like structure with a sag in the middle. The opposite structure, with the beds arching upwards, is an anticline.

topography the surface shape and aspect of the land, and its study. Topography deals with relief and contours, the distribution of mountains and valleys, the patterns of rivers, and all other features, natural and artificial, that produce the landscape.

tropics the area between the tropics of Cancer and Capricorn, defined by the parallels of latitude approximately 23°30| N and S of the equator. They are the limits of the area of Earth's surface in which the Sun can be directly overhead.

water table level of ground below which the rocks

LARGEST DESERTS

Name/Location	Area* sq km	sq m
Sahara, N Africa	8,600,000	3,320,000
Arabian, SW Asia	2,330,000	900,000
Gobi, Mongolia and NE China	1,166,000	450,000
Patagonian, Argentina	673,000	260,000
Great Victoria, SW Australia	647,000	250,000
Great Basin, SW USA	492,000	190,000
Chihuahuan, Mexico	450,000	175,000
Great Sandy, NW Australia	400,000	150,000
Sonoran, SW USA	310,000	120,000
Kyzyl Kum, Kazakhstan-Uzbekistan	300,000	115,000
Takla Makan, N China	270,000	105,000
Kalahari, SW Africa	260,000	100,000

*Desert areas are very approximate, because clear physical boundaries may not occur

are saturated with water. Thus above the water table water will drain downwards, and where the water table cuts the surface of the ground, a spring results. The water table usually follows surface contours, and it varies with rainfall. In many irrigated areas the water table is lowering because of the extracted water. That below N China, for example, is sinking at a rate of 1 m/3 ft a year.

weathering process by which exposed rocks are broken down by the action of rain, frost, wind, and other elements of the weather. Two types of weathering are recognized: physical and chemical. They usually occur together.

ATMOSPHERE AND OCEAN

barometer instrument that measures atmospheric pressure as an indication of weather. Most often used are the *mercury barometer* and the *aneroid barometer*.

bathyal zone the upper part of the ocean, which lies on the Continental shelf at a depth of between 200 m/656 ft and 2,000 m/6,561 ft.

beach strip of land bordering the sea, normally consisting of boulders and pebbles on exposed coasts or sand on sheltered coasts. It is usually defined by the high- and low-water marks.

Beaufort scale system of recording wind velocity, devised in 1806 by Francis Beaufort. It is a numerical scale ranging from 0 to 17, calm being indicated by 0 and a hurricane by 12; 13–17 indicate degrees of hurricane force.

climate weather conditions at a particular place over a period of time. Climate encompasses all the meteorological elements and the factors that influence them. The primary factors that determine the variations of climate over the surface of the Earth are: (a) the effect of latitude and the tilt of the Earth's axis to the plane of the orbit about the Sun (66.5°); (b) the large-scale movements of different wind belts over the Earth's surface; (c) the temperature difference between land and sea; (d) contours of the ground; and (e) location of the area in relation to ocean currents. Catastrophic variations to climate may be caused by the impact of another planetary body, or by clouds resulting from volcanic activity. The most important local or global meteorological changes brought about by human activity are those linked with ozone depleters and the greenhouse effect.

cloud water vapour condensed into minute water particles that float in masses in the atmosphere. Clouds, like fogs or mists, which occur at lower levels, are formed by the cooling of air charged with water vapour, which generally condenses around tiny dust particles.

Coriolis effect a result of the deflective force of the Earth's west to east rotation. Winds, ocean currents, and aircraft are deflected to the right of their direction of travel in the Northern hemisphere and to the left in the Southern hemisphere.

current the flow of a body of water or air moving in a definite direction. There are three basic types of oceanic currents: *drift currents* are broad and slow-moving; *stream currents* are narrow and swift-moving; and *upwelling currents* bring cold, nutrient-rich water from the ocean bottom.

doldrums area of low atmospheric pressure along the equator, largely applied to oceans at the convergence of the NE and SE trade winds. To some extent the area affected moves N and S with seasonal changes.

drought period of prolonged dry weather. The area of the world subject to serious droughts, such as the Sahara, is increasing because of destruction of forests, overgrazing, and poor agricultural practices.

estuary river mouth widening into the sea, where fresh water mixes with salt water and tidal effects are felt.

exosphere the uppermost layer of the atmosphere. It is an ill-defined zone above the thermosphere, beginning at about 700 km/435 mi and fading off into the vacuum of space. The gases are extremely thin, with hydrogen as the main constituent.

fog cloud that collects at the surface of the Earth, composed of water vapour that has condensed

WEATHERING

physical weathering

temperature changes	weakening rocks by expansion and contraction
frost	wedging rocks apart by the expansion of water on freezing
rain	making loose slopes unstable
wind	wearing away rocks by sandblasting, and moving sand dunes along
unloading	the loosening of rock layers by release of pressure after the erosion and removal of those layers above

chemical weathering

carbonation	the breakdown of calcite by reaction with carbonic acid in rainwater
hydrolysis	the breakdown of feldspar into china clay by reaction with carbonic acid in rainwater
oxidation	the breakdown of iron-rich minerals due to rusting
hydration	the expansion of certain minerals due to the uptake of water

gravity

soil creep	the slow downslope movement of surface material
landslide	the rapid downward movement of solid material
avalanche	scouring by ice, snow, and accumulated debris

rivers

abrasion	wearing away stream beds and banks by trundling boulders along
corrasion	the wear on the boulders themselves as they are carried along

glaciers

deepening	of valleys by the weight of ice
scouring	of rock surfaces by embedded rocky debris

sea

hydraulic effect	expansion of air pockets in rocks and cliffs by constant hammering by waves
abrasion	see *Rivers* above
corrosion	see *Rivers* above

on particles of dust in the atmosphere. Cloud and fog are both caused by the air temperature falling below dew point. The thickness of fog depends on the number of water particles it contains. Usually, fog is formed by the meeting of two currents of air, one cooler than the other, or by warm air flowing over a cold surface. Sea fogs commonly occur where warm and cold currents meet and the air above them mixes.

front the interface between two air masses of dif-
rift valley

ferent temperature or humidity. A **cold front** marks the line of advance of a cold air mass from below, as it displaces a warm air mass; a **warm front** marks the advance of a warm air mass pushing a cold one forward.

frost condition of the weather when the air temperature is below freezing, 0°C/32°F. Water in the atmosphere is deposited as ice crystals on the ground or exposed objects. As cold air is heavier than warm, ground frost is more common than hoar frost, which is formed by

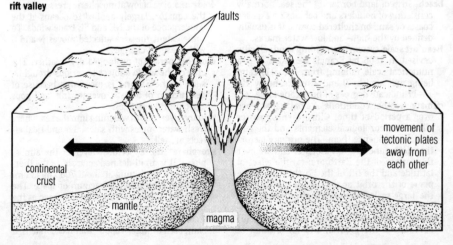

Cloud

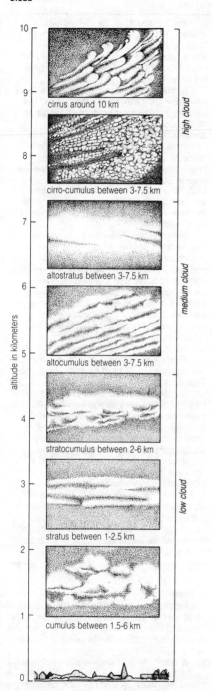

THE WORST POLLUTERS

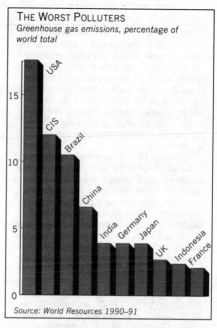

Greenhouse gas emissions, percentage of world total

Source: World Resources 1990–91

the Earth and re-emitted from the surface, is prevented from escaping by various gases in the air. The result is a rise in the Earth's temperature; in a garden greenhouse, the glass walls have the same effect. The main greenhouse gases are carbon dioxide, methane, and chlorofluorocarbons. Fossil-fuel consumption and forest fires are the main causes of carbon dioxide buildup; methane is a byproduct of agriculture (rice, cattle, sheep). Water vapour is another greenhouse gas. The United Nations Environment Programme estimates an increase in average world temperatures of 1.5°C/2.7°F with a consequent rise of 20 cm/7.7 in in sea level by 2025.

gyre the circular surface rotation of ocean water in each major sea (a type of current). Gyres are large and permanent, and occupy the N and S halves of the three major oceans. Their movements are dictated by the prevailing winds and the Coriolis effect. Gyres move clockwise in the northern hemisphere and anticlockwise in the southern hemisphere.

hail precipitation in the form of pellets of ice (hailstones). It is caused by the circulation of moisture in strong convection currents, usually within cumulonimbus clouds.

hurricane revolving storm in tropical regions, called **typhoon** in the N Pacific. It originates between 5° and 20° N or S of the equator, when the surface temperature of the ocean is above 27°C/80°F. A central calm area, called the eye, is surrounded by inwardly spiralling winds (anticlockwise in the N hemisphere) of up to 320 kph/200 mph. A hurricane is accompanied by lightning and torrential rain, and can cause extensive damage. In meteorology, a hurricane is a wind of force 12 or more on

the condensation of water particles in the same way that dew collects.

greenhouse effect in the Earth's atmosphere, the trapping of solar radiation, which, absorbed by

EL NIÑO, 1991–92

El Niño is the name that climatologists give to a change in the currents and winds of the eastern Pacific Ocean. The effect results in the warming of the surface waters of the area with subsequent damage to local fisheries. It usually happens about Christmas-time—hence the name, which means 'the Child'—and appears at irregular intervals of a few years. Attempts are now being made to analyse past patterns so that the event can be predicted.

In early 1991 climatologists at the National Weather Service's Climate Analysis Centre in Camp Springs, Maryland, at the Lamont–Doherty Geological Observatory in Palisades, New York, and at the Scripps Institution of Oceanography in La Jolla, California, independently predicted that there would be a small El Niño event beginning in summer 1991. The event did take place, with a number of alarming effects.

The northeasterly trade winds that bring moisture to Australia failed, giving rise to the worst drought on that continent for 200 years. Eucalyptus trees, normally well adapted to dry conditions, have been drying out and dying, with some forests in Queensland recording a death rate of 50%. The level of the Darling and other rivers is so low that sunlight reaching the bed has given rise to a bloom of cyanobacteria, poisoning the water. Fertilizer runoff adds to this problem. The consequence is that many of Australia's unique animals, such as koalas and platypuses, are dying in large numbers.

Further north there has been a change in the regular pattern of typhoons or hurricanes. A permanent high-pressure area over the western Pacific tends to deflect the typhoons from Japan, but in September and October 1991 this high-pressure area collapsed. El Niño, which causes a warming of the east Pacific, also causes a cooling of the west Pacific, and in this instance prevented the formation of the high-pressure area. Japan was subjected to severe typhoons in September and October, producing rainfall that was about 3.6 times the average.

Further south, in the Philippines, typhoon Thelma killed 6,000 in November. Most deaths were the result of mudslides. Illegal logging operations in the hills had left large areas of bare soil that washed away in the torrential rains.

In the eastern Pacific the El Niño effects have been felt further north than usual. The warming of the waters produced heavy rains in British Columbia and southern Alaska in January 1992. In February the storms hit California, dropping 30 cm/12 in of rain in four days and causing extensive flooding. These conditions are only expected in the area once in 50 years or so. The unpredictability of El Niño and its effects is shown by the fact that rains failed to materialize along the Peruvian coast as they usually do during an El Niño event.

With all these side-effects, as well as the inevitable failure of the fish harvests, it is important that the effects should be accurately predicted in the future so that adequate preparations can be made. The recent history of the climates of the Pacific Ocean is being studied to try to detect the patterns. A new tool in this study is the single-celled alga *Emiliana huxleyi*. This blooms in the summer and dies back in the winter, giving rise to bottom sediments that are alternately rich and poor in their remains. The layering can be used for accurate dating. Scientists at Stanford University in California and the University of Bristol have found that this alga synthesizes an organic molecule called an alkenone, and that the chemical bonding in this molecule depends on the temperature of the surrounding water. By studying the layering of the sediment, and the structure of the alkenone molecules, it has been possible to produce a very accurate profile of the changing sea temperatures of the eastern Pacific between 1915 and 1988. Up to now these studies have been carried out using the different isotopes of carbon and oxygen in carbonates formed at different times, but the alkenone molecules are much more stable.

---

the Beaufort scale.

The most intense hurricane recorded in the Caribbean/Atlantic sector was Hurricane Gilbert in 1988, with sustained winds of 280 kph/175 mph and gusts of over 320 kph/200 mph.

In Oct 1987 and Jan 1990, allegedly hurricane-force winds were experienced in S England. Although not technically hurricanes, they were the strongest winds there for three centuries.

isobar a line drawn on maps and weather charts linking all places with the same atmospheric pressure (usually measured in millibars).

When used in weather forecasting, the distance between individual isobars is an indica-

tion of the barometric gradient.

jet stream a narrow band of very fast wind (velocities of over 150 kph/95 mph) found at altitudes of 10–16 km/6–10 mi in the upper troposphere or lower stratosphere. Jet streams usually occur about the latitudes of the Westerlies (35°–60°).

lagoon coastal body of shallow salt water, usually with limited access to the sea. The term is normally used to describe the shallow sea area cut off by a coral reef or barrier islands.

magnetic storm a sudden disturbance affecting the Earth's magnetic field, causing anomalies in radio transmissions and magnetic compasses. It is probably caused by sunspot activity.

Mediterranean climate climate characterized by hot dry summers and warm wet winters. Mediterranean zones are situated in either hemisphere on the western side of continents, between latitudes of 30° and 60°.

mesosphere layer in the Earth's atmosphere above the stratosphere and below the thermosphere. It lies between about 50 km/31 mi and 80 km/50 mi above the ground.

meteorology the scientific observation and study of the atmosphere, so that weather can be accurately forecasted. Data from meteorological stations and weather satellites is collated by computer at central agencies such as the Meteorological Office in Bracknell, near London, and a forecast and weather maps based on current readings are issued at regular intervals.

monsoon a wind system that dominates the climate of a wide region, with seasonal reversals of direction; in particular, the wind in S Asia that blows towards the sea in winter and towards the land in summer, bringing heavy rain. The monsoon may cause destructive flooding all over India and SE Asia from April to Sept. Thousands of people are rendered homeless each year. The Guinea monsoon is a southwesterly wind that blows in W Africa from April to Sept, throughout the rainy season.

ocean ridge topographical feature of the seabed indicating the presence of a constructive plate margin produced by the rise of magma to the surface. It can rise thousands of metres above the surrounding abyssal plain.

ocean trench topographical feature of the seabed indicating the presence of a destructive plate margin (produced by the movements of plate tectonics). The subduction or dragging downward of one plate of the lithosphere beneath

CONTINENTS ON THE MOVE

The former existence of Pangaea has been accepted for a long time. Between about 250 and 100 million years ago—for most of the time that the dinosaurs were alive—all the continents of the Earth were fused into one vast landmass that scientists call Pangaea. Since then this supercontinent has split up and the individual pieces have been moving apart, in the process popularly known as 'continental drift'. The rate of movement is slow, only a few centimetres per year, but the Atlantic Ocean is now 30 m/100 ft wider than it was when Christopher Columbus crossed it 500 years ago.

Before the time of Pangaea there was a completely different set of continents, and it was these continental masses that drifted together to form the supercontinent 250 million years ago. Recent research shows that there was another supercontinent in the far distant past, and probably others before that. Other research suggests that there were continents on the Earth as early as 100 million years after the Earth formed, and that 40% of today's continental material was in existence by 3,800 million years ago. It seems that since then all the continental material has been coming together in supercontinents and drifting apart quite regularly, in cycles of about 400 million years or so.

another means that the ocean floor is pulled down.

ooze sediment of fine texture consisting mainly of organic matter found on the ocean floor at depths greater than 2,000 m/6,600 ft. Several kinds of ooze exist, each named after its constituents.

rain (technically termed *precipitation*) separate

HIGHEST MOUNTAINS

Name	* m	* ft	Location
Everest	8,850	29,030	China-Nepal
K2	8,610	28,250	Kashmir-Jammu
Kangchenjunga	8,590	28,170	India-Nepal
Lhotse	8,500	27,890	China-Nepal
Kangchenjunga S Peak	8,470	27,800	India-Nepal
Makalu I	8,470	27,800	China-Nepal
Kangchenjunga W Peak	8,420	27,620	India-Nepal
Llotse E Peak	8,380	27,500	China-Nepal
Dhaulagiri	8,170	26,810	Nepal
Cho Oyu	8,150	26,750	China-Nepal
Manaslu	8,130	26,660	Nepal
Nanga Parbat	8,130	26,660	Kashmir-Jammu
Annapurna I	8,080	26,500	Nepal
Gasherbrum I	8,070	26,470	Kashmir-Jammu
Broad-highest	8,050	26,400	Kashmir-Jammu
Gasherbrum II	8,030	26,360	Kashmir-Jammu
Gosainthan	8,010	26,290	China
Broad-middle	8,000	26,250	Kashmir-Jammu

* Heights are given to the nearest 10 m/ft.

Some Environmental Monitoring Programmes Using Satellite Remote Sensing

Programme	Agency	Status	Objectives
POES: Polar-orbiting Operational Environment Satellites	NOAA	Operational since 1970	Weather observations
METEOSAT: Meteorology Satellite	ESA	Operational since 1977	Weather observations
LANDSAT: Land Remote Sensing Satellite	EOSAT	Operational since 1972	Vegetation, crop and land-use inventory
LAGEOS-1: Laser Geodynamics Satellite-1	NASA	Operational since 1976	Geodynamics, gravity field
SPOT-1: Système Probatoire d'Observation de la Terre-1	France	Operational since 1986	Land use, earth resources
IRS: Indian Remote Sensing Satellite (e.g. Rohini-2)	India	Operational since 1981	Earth resources
MOS-1: Marine Observation Satellite-1	NASDA (Japan)	Operational since 1987	State of sea surface and atmosphere
LAGEOS-2: Laser Geodynamics Satellite-2	NASA-PSN (Italy)	Operational since 1988	Geodynamics, gravity field
ERS-1: Earth Remote Sensing Satellite-1	ESA	Launch 1990	Imaging of oceans, ice fields, land areas
N-ROSS: Navy Remote Sensing System	US Navy	Launch 1991	Ocean topography, surface winds, ice extent
JERS-1: Japan Earth Remote Sensing Satellite-1	NASDA (Japan)	Launch 1991	Earth resources
TOPEX/POSEIDON: Ocean Topography Experiment	NASA-CNES (France)	Start 1987, Launch 1991	Ocean surface topography
RADARSAT: Canadian Radar Satellite	Canada	Start 1986, Launch 1991	Studies of Arctic ice, ocean studies, earth resources
GRM: Geopotential Research Mission	NASA	Start 1989, Launch 1992	Measure global geoid and magnetic field
EOS: Earth Observing System/ Polar-Orbiting Platforms	NASA	Start 1989, Launch 1994	Long-term global earth observations
European Polar Orbiting Platform (Columbus)	ESA	Planned	Long term comprehensive research, operational and commercial earth observations
Rainfall mission	NASA	Start 1991, Launch 1994	Tropical precipitation measurements
REPRESENTATIVE SPACE SHUTTLE INSTRUMENTS			
ATMOS: Atmospheric Trace Molecules Observed by Spectroscopy	NASA	Current	Atmospheric chemical composition
ACR: Active Cavity Radiometer	NASA	Current	Solar energy output
SUSIM: Solar Ultraviolet Spectral Irradiance Monitor	NASA	Current	Ultraviolet solar observations
MAPS: Measurement of Air Pollution from Shuttle	NASA	Current/in development	Tropospheric carbon monoxide
INDIVIDUAL INSTRUMENTS FOR LONG-TERM GLOBAL OBSERVATIONS			
Total Ozone Monitor	NASA	Planned	Monitor global ozone
Laser Ranger:	NASA	Planned	Continental motions
Scanning Radar Altimeter	NASA	Planned	Continental topography

CNES Centre National d'Études Spatiales (France); EOSAT The EOSAT Company; ESA European Space Agency; NASDA Japan Space Agency; NOAA National Oceanic and Atmospheric Administration (USA); NSF National Science Foundation (USA); PSN Piano Spaziale Nazionale (Italian National Space Plan); USGS United States Geological Survey
Source: UNEP Environmental Data Report 89/90

GEOLOGICAL TIME CHART

eon	era	period	epoch	millions of years ago	life forms
Phanerozoic	Cenozoic	Quaternary	Holocene	0.01	
			Pleistocene	1.64	humans appear
		Tertiary	Pliocene	5.2	
			Miocene	23.5	
			Oligocene	35.5	
			Eocene	56.6	
			Palaeocene	65	mammals flourish
	Mesozoic	Cretaceous		146	heyday of dinosaurs
		Jurassic		208	first birds
		Triassic		245	first mammals and dinosaurs
	Palaeozoic	Permian		290	reptiles expand
		Carboniferous		363	first reptiles
		Devonian		409	first amphibians
		Silurian		439	first land plants
		Ordovician		510	first fish
		Cambrian		570	first fossils
Proterozoic	Precambrian			2500	earliest living things
Archaean				4600	

drops of water that fall to the Earth's surface from clouds. The drops are formed by the accumulation of droplets that condense from water vapour in the air.

tornado extremely violent revolving storm with swirling, funnel-shaped clouds, caused by a rising column of warm air propelled by strong wind. A tornado can rise to a great height, but with a diameter of only a few hundred metres or less. Tornadoes move with wind speeds of 160–480 kph/100–300 mph, destroying everything in their path. They are common in the central USA and Australia.

trade wind prevailing wind that blows towards the equator from the northeast and southeast. Trade winds are caused by hot air rising at the equator and the consequent movement of air from north and south to take its place. The winds are deflected towards the west because of the Earth's west-to-east rotation. The unpredictable calms known as the doldrums lie at their convergence.

troposphere lower part of the Earth's atmosphere extending about 10.5 km/6.5 mi from the Earth's surface, in which temperature decreases with height to about −60°C/−76°F except in local layers of temperature inversion. The **tropopause** is the upper boundary of the troposphere above which the temperature increases slowly with height.

tsunami (Japanese 'harbour wave') giant wave generated by an undersea earthquake or other disturbance. In the open ocean it may take the form of several successive waves, travelling at tens of kilometres per hour but with an amplitude (height) of approximately a metre. In the coastal shallows, tsunamis slow down and build up, producing towering waves that can sweep inland and cause great loss of life and property.

wind lateral movement of the Earth's atmosphere from high- to low-pressure areas. Although modified by features such as land and water, there is a basic worldwide system of trade winds, Westerlies, monsoons, and others.

SCOTTISH TSUNAMI

Evidence suggests that a tsunami or tidal wave hit northeast Scotland about 7,000 years ago. Recent excavations in Inverness have revealed a level of Mesolithic (Middle Stone Age) occupation, dating from 7,235 to 7,080 years ago. Covering it is coarse white marine sand. In appearance, altitude and thickness this sand is very like a sand layer often found in coastal sediments in eastern Scotland. The layer can be dated at around 7,000 years ago, and seems to suggest a very short-lived event. It is usually 5–15 cm/2–6 in thick, and lies 8–9 m above sea level. Scholars now believe that a series of tsunamis deposited the sand.

These waves would have been triggered by a massive submarine landslide on the continental slope off the southwestern coast of Norway. This would have involved the movement of up to 1,700 cu km/400 cu mi over an area a quarter the size of Scotland. It is hard to estimate the size and speed of the waves that would have struck the Scottish coast. Based on the sand layer's altitude compared to present-day mudflats, the biggest waves were probably at least 8 m/26 ft high. The tsunami probably lasted only a few hours.

A few other Mesolithic sites in the region also lie under sand layers, which in the past were interpreted simply as exceptional tides. It now looks as though the sand is a valuable marker of a dramatic event in British prehistory.

THE DEVELOPING EARTH

Archaean or *Archaeozoic* the earliest eon of geological time; the first part of the Precambrian era, from the formation of Earth up to about 2,500 million years ago. It is a time when no life existed, and with every new discovery of ancient life its upper boundary is being pushed further back.

Cambrian period of geological time 570–510 million years ago; the first period of the Palaeozoic era. All invertebrate animal life appeared, and marine algae was widespread. The earliest fossils with hard shells, such as trilobites, date from this period.

Carboniferous period of geological time 363–290 million years ago, the fifth period of the Palaeozoic era. In the USA it is regarded as two periods: the Mississippian (lower) and the Pennsylvanian (upper). Typical of the lower-Carboniferous rocks are shallow-water limestones, while upper-Carboniferous rocks have delta deposits with coal (hence the name). Amphibians were abundant, and reptiles evolved.

continental drift theory proposed by the German meteorologist Alfred Wegener in 1915 that, about 200 million years ago, Earth consisted of a single large continent (Pangaea) that subsequently broke apart to form the continents known today. Such vast continental movements could not be satisfactorily explained until the study of plate tectonics in the 1960s.

Cretaceous period of geological time 146-65 million years ago. It is the last period of the Mesozoic era, during which angiosperm (seed-bearing) plants evolved, and dinosaurs and other reptiles reached a peak before almost complete extinction at the end of the period. Chalk is a typical rock type of the second half of the period.

dating the science of determining the age of geological structures, rocks, and fossils, and placing them in the context of geological time.

Devonian period of geological time 409-363 million years ago, the fourth period of the Palaeozoic era. Many desert sandstones from North America and Europe date from this time. The first land plants flourished in the Devonian period, corals were abundant in the seas, amphibians evolved from air-breathing fish, and

MAJOR ICE AGES

name	date (years ago)
Pleistocene	1.7 million–10,000
Permo-Carboniferous	330–250 million
Ordovician	440–430 million
Verangian	615–570 million
Sturtian	820–770 million
Gnejso	940–880 million
Huronian	2,700–1,800 million

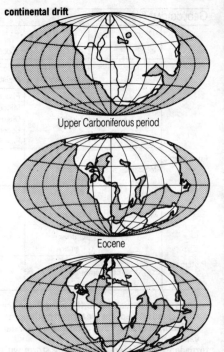

continental drift

Upper Carboniferous period

Eocene

Lower Quaternary

insects developed on land.

epoch a subdivision of a geologic period in the geologic time scale. Epochs are sometimes given their own names (such as the Paleocene, Eocene, Oligocene, Miocene, and Pliocene epochs comprising the Tertiary period), or they are referred to as the late, early, or middle portions of a given period (as the Late Cretaceous or the Middle Triassic epoch).

era any of the major divisions of geologic time, each including several periods, but smaller than an eon. The currently recognized eras all fall within the Phanerozoic eon—or the vast span of time, starting about 590 million years ago, when fossils are found to become abundant. The eras in ascending order are the Palaeozoic, Mesozoic, and Cenozoic. We are living in the Recent epoch of the Quaternary period of the Cenozoic era.

geological time time scale embracing the history of the Earth from its physical origin to the present day. Geological time is divided into eras (Precambrian, Palaeozoic, Mesozoic, Cenozoic), which in turn are divided into periods, epochs, ages, and finally chrons.

Gondwanaland or *Gondwana* land mass, including the continents of South America, Africa, Australia, and Antarctica, that formed the southern half of Pangaea, the 'supercontinent' or world continent that existed between 250 and 200 million years ago. The northern half was Laurasia. The baobab tree of Africa and Australia is a relic of Gondwanaland.

Holocene epoch of geological time that began

10,000 years ago, the second epoch of the Quaternary period. The glaciers retreated, the climate became warmer, and humans developed significantly.

Iapetus Ocean or *Proto-Atlantic* sea that existed in early Palaeozoic times between the continent that was to become Europe and that which was to become North America. The continents moved together in the late Palaeozoic, obliterating the ocean. When they moved apart once more, they formed the Atlantic.

ice age any period of glaciation occurring in the Earth's history, but particularly that in the Pleistocene epoch, immediately preceding historic times. On the North American continent, glaciers reached as far south as the Great Lakes, and an ice sheet spread over N Europe, leaving its remains as far south as Switzerland. There were several glacial advances separated by interglacial stages during which the ice melted and temperatures were higher than today.

K-T boundary geologists' shorthand for the boundary between the rocks of the Cretaceous and the Tertiary periods. It marks the extinction of the dinosaurs and in many places reveals a layer of iridium, possibly deposited by a meteorite that may have caused the extinction by its impact.

Laurasia former land mass or supercontinent, formed by the fusion of North America, Greenland, Europe, and Asia. It made up the northern half of Pangaea, the 'world continent' that is thought to have existed between 250 and 200 million years ago. The southern half was Gondwanaland.

mass extinction an event that produced the extinction of many species at about the same time. One notable example is the boundary between the Cretaceous and Tertiary periods (known as the K-T boundary) that saw the extinction of the dinosaurs and other big reptiles, and many of the marine invertebrates as well. Mass extinctions have taken place several times during Earth's history. The Age of Man may eventually be regarded as another.

Mesozoic era of geological time 245-65 million years ago, consisting of the Triassic, Jurassic, and Cretaceous periods. At the beginning of the era, the continents were joined together as Pangaea; dinosaurs and other giant reptiles dominated the sea and air; and ferns, horsetails, and cycads thrived in a warm climate worldwide. By the end of the Mesozoic era, the continents had begun to assume their present positions, flowering plants were dominant and many of the large reptiles and marine fauna were becoming extinct.

Ordovician period of geological time 510-439 million years ago; the second period of the Palaeozoic era. Animal life was confined to the sea: reef-building algae and the first jawless fish are characteristic.

palaeomagnetism the science of the reconstruction of the Earth's ancient magnetic field and the former positions of the continents from the evidence of *remanent magnetization* in ancient rocks; that is, traces left by the Earth's magnetic field in igneous rocks before they cool. Palaeomagnetism shows that the Earth's magnetic field has reversed itself—the magnetic north pole becoming the magnetic south pole, and vice versa—at approximate half-million-year intervals, with shorter reversal periods in between the major spans.

palaeontology the study of ancient life that encompasses the structure of ancient organisms and their environment, evolution, and ecology, as revealed by their fossils.

Palaeozoic era of geological time 570-245 million years ago. It comprises the Cambrian, Ordovician, Silurian, Devonian, Carboniferous, and Permian periods. The Cambrian, Ordovician, and Silurian constitute the Lower Palaeozoic; the Devonian, Carboniferous, and Permian make up the Upper Palaeozoic. The era includes the evolution of hard-shelled multicellular life forms in the sea; the invasion of land by plants and animals; and the evolution of fish, amphibians, and early reptiles. The earliest identifiable fossils date from this era. The climate was mostly warm with short ice ages. The continents were very different from the present ones but, towards the end of the era, all were joined together as a single world continent called Pangaea.

Pangaea or *Pangea* world continent, named by Alfred Wegener, that existed between 250 and 200 million years ago, made up of all the continental masses. It may be regarded as a combination of Laurasia in the north and Gondwanaland in the south, the rest of Earth being covered by the Panthalassa ocean.

Panthalassa ocean that covered the surface of the Earth not occupied by the world continent Pangaea between 250 and 200 million years ago.

Permian period of geological time 290-245 million years ago, the last period of the Palaeozoic era. Its end was marked by a significant change in marine life, including the extinction of many corals and trilobites. Deserts were widespread, and terrestrial amphibians and mammal-like reptiles flourished. Cone-bearing plants (gymnosperms) came to prominence.

Phanerozoic eon in Earth history, consisting of the most recent 570 million years. It comprises the Palaeozoic, Mesozoic, and Cenozoic eras. The vast majority of fossils come from this eon, owing to the evolution of hard shells and internal skeletons. The name means 'interval of well-displayed life'.

plate tectonics concept that attributes continental drift and seafloor spreading to the continual formation and destruction of the outermost layer of the Earth. This layer is seen as consisting of major and minor plates, curved to the planet's spherical shape and with a jigsaw fit to one another. Convection currents within the Earth's mantle produce upwellings of new material along joint lines at the surface, forming ridges (for example the Mid-Atlantic Ridge). The new material extends the plates, and these move away from the ridges. Where

OIL: ARE WE LOOKING IN THE RIGHT PLACE?

Petroleum is perhaps the most important mineral resource in the world. Whole economies grow and collapse over variations in its price. 1991 saw a war—the Gulf War—waged over it. Yet it is not an inexhaustible resource. The world's known supply may run out some time next century.

As a result there is a constant search for new deposits. An understanding of how oil is formed and how it is emplaced is essential in the hunt. Crude oil—petroleum—is formed from the organic remains of living creatures. Animals and plants are buried in the sediments of the sea bed. If they are buried quickly their organic substances may not oxidize and decay away. When this sediment is compressed into sedimentary rock, the organic chemicals—the hydrocarbons—may form droplets of petroleum, which can float upwards through the water contained in the rocks above. If they meet a layer that is impervious to the flow, the droplets gradually build up until the pores of the rocks are filled with oil, resulting in a reservoir. Hence the oil geologist looks for the source rocks (rocks that are likely to have produced oil) and then the reservoir rocks (rocks that have concentrated it and now contain it). Source rocks and reservoir rocks are both sedimentary, having formed from layers of sand, silt, and mud, and so oil geologists tend to be specialists in sedimentary rocks.

However, back in the early 1980s, a single dissenting voice expressed a differing view. It was the voice of Dr Thomas Gold of Cornell University, Ithaca, New York. His theory was that hydrocarbons formed deep below the Earth's crust. The original matter of the solar system was rich in carbon—as can be seen today in carbonaceous meteorites and the black colour of the nucleus of Halley's Comet. This carbon was incorporated into the Earth's mantle as the planet solidified. For as long as the Earth has existed the carbon has been seeping out, oxidizing on the way up to form the gas carbon dioxide—an abundant product of volcanic eruptions. It is theoretically possible that the great pressures inside the Earth can turn the carbon into methane and the other chemicals that constitute petroleum. Should these chemicals migrate towards the surface without oxidizing—and Gold's theory is that cracks in solid igneous rocks like granite would provide suitable pathways—then they may accumulate in sedimentary traps close to the surface as deposits of petroleum. The places to look for source rocks would then be in areas of very old broken igneous rocks close to sedimentary basins in which oil is known to have accumulated.

Gold's theories were dismissed out of hand by the petroleum industry but he did manage to obtain backing for an exploratory borehole from the Swedish State Power Board and the American Gas Research Institute. The site chosen was a geological structure called the Siljan Ring in central Sweden. It is an ancient meteorite crater punched into the Precambrian granitic rock that forms the core of the European continent. The site would provide the cracked igneous rock required by the theory, and was in the same general region as the North Sea oilfields. Drilling began in July 1986 and the whole project was all but dismissed and forgotten by the rest of the scientific world.

On 7 October 1991, when the eyes of the world were on the devastation of the Gulf War, and the oil industry was desperately trying to extinguish the blazing oil installations and cap the wrecked wells to prevent millions of gallons of oil from pouring into the desert and the sea, an announcement was made from the Siljan Ring project. Oil had been struck at a depth of 2.8 km/1.7 mi. The full extent has yet to be determined, but the immediate implication is that the standard theory of petroleum formation, on which the entire oil industry is based, needs to be closely examined.

---

two plates collide, one overrides the other and the lower is absorbed back into the mantle. These 'subduction zones' occur in the ocean trenches.

Precambrian the time from the formation of Earth (4.6 billion years ago) up to 570 million years ago. Its boundary with the succeeding Cambrian period marks the time when animals first developed hard outer parts (exoskeletons) and so left abundant fossil remains. It comprises about 85% of geological time and is divided into two eons: the Archaean and the Proterozoic.

Proterozoic eon of geological time, 2.5 billion to 570 million years ago, the second division of the Precambrian era. It is defined as the time of simple life, since many rocks dating from this eon show traces of biological activity, and some contain the fossils of bacteria and algae.

Quaternary period of geological time that began 1.64 million years ago and is still in process. It is divided into the Pleistocene and Holocene epochs.

seafloor spreading growth of the ocean crust outwards (sideways) from mid-ocean ridges. The concept of seafloor spreading has been combined with that of continental drift and incorporated into plate tectonics.

stratigraphy branch of geology that deals with the sequence of formation of sedimentary rock layers and the conditions under which they were formed. Its basis was developed by William Smith (1769–1839), a British canal engineer.

stromatolite mound produced in shallow water by mats of algae that trap mud particles. Another mat grows on the trapped mud layer and this traps another layer of mud and so on. The stromatolite grows to heights of a metre or so. They are uncommon today but their fossils are among the earliest evidence for living things—over 2,000 million years old.

tectonics the study of the movements of rocks on the Earth's surface. On a small scale tectonics involves the formation of folds and faults, but on a large scale plate tectonics deals with the movement of the Earth's surface as a whole.

Tertiary period of geological time 65–1.64 million years ago, divided into five epochs: Palaeocene, Eocene, Oligocene, Miocene, and Pliocene. During the Tertiary, mammals took over all the ecological niches left vacant by the extinction of the dinosaurs, and became the prevalent land mammals. The continents took on their present positions, and climatic and vegetation zones as we know them became established. Within the geological time column the Tertiary follows the Cretaceous period and is succeeded by the Quarternary period.

Triassic period of geological time 245-208 million years ago, the first period of the Mesozoic era. The continents were fused together to form the world continent Pangaea. Triassic sediments contain remains of early dinosaurs and other reptiles now extinct. By late Triassic times, the first mammals had evolved.

TERMS

The chief direct sources of energy are oil, coal, wood, and natural gas, and indirectly, electricity produced by the use of such fuels or derived from water power or nuclear fission. Increasing costs and the prospect of exhaustion of coal, oil and gas resources, led in the 1980s to consideration of alternative sources. These included solar power, which provides completely 'clean' energy; wind and wave power; tidal power, which like geothermal power, is geographically limited in application; utilization of organic waste, such as chicken manure; photosynthetic power, produced by the use of simple, fast-reproducing plants as fuel; and nuclear power, by fusion rather than fission.

biofuel any solid, liquid, or gaseous fuel produced from organic (once living) matter, either directly from plants or indirectly from industrial, commercial, domestic, or agricultural wastes. There are three main avenues for the development of biofuels: combustion of dry organic wastes (such as refuse, industrial and agricultural wastes, straw, wood, and peat); digestion of wet wastes in the absence of oxygen (anaerobic digestion) to produce biogas (containing up to 60% methane), or fermentation of sugar cane or corn to produce alcohol; and energy forestry (producing fast-growing wood for fuel).

electricity generation and supply electricity is the most useful and most convenient form of energy there is. It can readily be converted into heat and light, and used to power machines. Because electricity flows readily through wires, it can be made, or generated, in one place and distributed to anywhere it is needed. Electricity is generated at power stations, where a suitable energy source is made to drive turbines that spin the electricity generators. The generators produce alternating current (AC), and the producing units are generally called turboalternators. The main energy sources for electricity generation are coal, oil, water power (hydroelectricity), natural gas, and nuclear power, with limited contributions from wind power, tidal power, and geothermal power. Nuclear fuel provides the cheapest form of electricity generation in Britain, but environmental considerations may limit its future development.

Electricity is generated at power stations at a voltage of about 25,000 volts, which is not a suitable voltage for long-distance transmission. For minimal power loss transmission must take place at very high voltage—up to 400,000 volts or more. The generated voltage is therefore increased, or stepped-up, by a transformer. The resulting high voltage electricity is then fed into the main arteries of the grid system. This is an interconnected network of power stations and distribution centres covering a large area, sometimes (as in the UK) countrywide, even (as in Europe) from country to country. After transmission to a local substation, the line voltage is reduced by a step-down transformer and distributed by consumers.

fossil fuel fuel, such as coal, oil, or natural gas, formed from the fossilized remains of plants that lived hundreds of millions of years ago. Fossil fuels are a nonrenewable resource and will eventually run out. Extraction of coal causes considerable environmental pollution, and burning coal contributes to problems of acid rain and the greenhouse effect.

geothermal energy either subterranean hot water pumped to the surface and converted to steam or run through a heat exchanger, or dry steam from an underground source, directed through turbines to produce electricity. The 'hot dry rock' system pumps cold water into fractured rocks deep underground and then extracts the heated water.

heat pump machine, run by electricity, that cools the interior of a building by removing heat from the interior air and pumping it out or, conversely, heats the inside by extracting energy from the exterior atmosphere, or from a hot-water source, and pumping it in. A heat pump may transfer more than twice as much energy, in the form of heat, as is needed to run it.

heat storage means of storing heat for later release. It is usually achieved by using materials that undergo phase changes at ordinary temperatures—for example, sodium pyrophosphate, which freezes at 7°C. This salt is used to store off-peak heat in the home, being liquefied by cheap heat during the night, and then freezing, if the temperature falls below 7°C, to give off heat during the day. Other developments include the use of plastic crystals that change their structure, rather than melt, when heated. These can be incorporated in clothing or curtains.

hydroelectric power electricity generated by water power. In a typical hydroelectric-power (HEP) scheme water stored in a reservoir, often created by damming a river, is piped into water turbines, coupled to electricity generators. In pumped-storage plants water flowing through the turbines is recycled. A tidal-power station is a HEP plant that exploits the rise and fall of the tides. Today about one-fifth of the world's electricity comes from hydroelectric power. Such plants have a prodigious generating capacity. The Grand Coulee plant in Washington State, USA, has a power output of some 10,000 megawatts. The Itaipu power station on the Parana

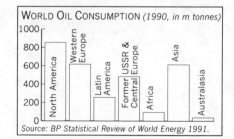

World Oil Consumption (1990, in m tonnes)

Source: BP Statistical Review of World Energy 1991.

FUSION POWER COMES A LITTLE CLOSER

Harnessing the source of the Sun's power—nuclear power—is one of the dreams of the modern age. Its proponents promise almost limitless fuel, not radioactive waste, and inherent safety. But until recently, fusion power has seemed more of a mirage than a realistic hope. The first commercial reactors are not expected to be operating before 2040. Difficult scientific and technical questions remain to be answered before a clear-cut development path can be laid out. An important step along the road to fusion power was taken on 9 November 1991. In an experiment that lasted two seconds, a 1.7 megawatt (MW) pulse of power was produced by the Joint European Torus (JET) at Culham, Oxfordshire, England. This was the first time a substantial amount of fusion power had been produced in a controlled experiment, as opposed to a bomb.

The £75 million-a-year JET project began in 1978. One of the first problems to be solved was how to control enormously hot hydrogen plasma—a form of matter seen in normal circumstances on Earth only in the centre of a lightning bolt, or in a neon advertising sign. The solution is to contain the plasma in a magnetic 'bottle' which holds the plasma away from the walls of the reactor. A great deal of research was needed to establish the correct shape of magnetic bottle necessary to hold the plasma stable. The US physicist Edward Teller, pioneer of the hydrogen bomb, said that trying to confine a plasma with lines of magnetic force was like trying to confine a jelly with rubber bands. The successful design, called a tokamak, was developed in the USSR in the early 1950s and adopted by the JET team in 1973. The plasma is contained in a doughnut-shaped vacuum vessel called a torus. Inside the torus, the plasma can be heated to a temperature 20 times hotter than that of the centre of the Sun at a density sufficient to start a fusion reaction. At these temperatures and densities, hydrogen atoms break apart and then re-form to make helium and a neutron, and, in the process, release energy.

The early exploratory experiments at Culham have been done with a plasma of deuterium, a form of hydrogen, to avoid any significant radioactive contamination of the machine. However, this is rather like trying to start a fire with damp straw. In future self-sustaining reactors, the plasma will be a mixture of deuterium and tritium, a radioactive type of hydrogen. The recent experiment was a test of the use of tritium. It was the first time tritium had been used. The plasma was a 11/89 tritium–deuterium mixture, and behaved exactly

as predicted. Scientists are confident that a 50/50 deuterium–tritium plasma will produce almost enough energy for breakeven, but this is not due for testing before 1994. An unresolved problem is that impurities from the wall of the containment enter the plasma as the temperature increases, reducing performance. The next step, therefore, is to install a magnetic diverter to strip impurities out of the plasma.

The success of the JET experiment strengthens the belief that fusion power is a practical possibility and has stimulated work in other countries. In the USA, the Tokamak Fusion Test Reactor is due to begin tritium–deuterium experiments in the summer of 1993. Researchers hope these experiments will approach breakeven. Also, the USA, the Commonwealth of Independent States, Japan, and the European Community have agreed to design jointly the next generation of fusion reactors, called the International Thermonuclear Experimental Reactor, or ITER. This reactor will be the largest tokamak ever built, about 25 m/80 ft high. The plasma chamber will measure 4.3m by 8.4 m/14 ft by 27 ft. ITER will generate more than 1,000 times MW of power. The scientific and engineering knowledge gained from ITER should enable a fusion reactor power station to be built.

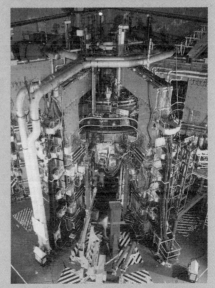

The exterior of the Joint European Torus (JET). Inside, it gets hotter than the Sun.

river (Brazil/Paraguay) has a potential capacity of 12,000 megawatts.

natural gas mixture of flammable gases found in the Earth's crust (often in association with petroleum), now one of the world's three main fossil fuels (with coal and oil). Natural gas is a mixture of hydrocarbons, chiefly methane, with ethane, butane, and propane.

nuclear energy energy from the inner core or nucleus of atoms, as opposed to energy released in chemical processes such as burning.

nuclear fission as in an atom bomb, is achieved by allowing a neutron to strike the nucleus of an atom of uranium-235, which then splits apart to release perhaps two to three other

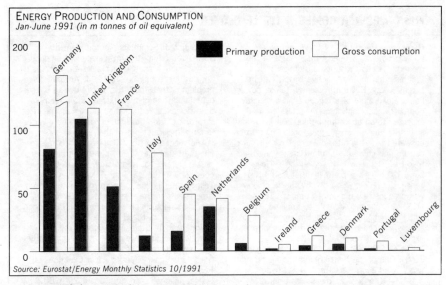

ENERGY PRODUCTION AND CONSUMPTION
Jan-June 1991 (in m tonnes of oil equivalent)

■ Primary production □ Gross consumption

Source: Eurostat/Energy Monthly Statistics 10/1991

neutrons. If the material is pure uranium-235, a chain reaction is set up when these neutrons in turn strike other nuclei. This happens with great rapidity, resulting in the tremendous burst of energy associated with the atom bomb. However, the process can be controlled by absorbing excess neutrons in 'control rods' (which may be made of steel alloyed with boron), and slowing down the speed of those neutrons allowed to act. This is what happens inside a nuclear power plant.

nuclear fusion is the release of thermonuclear energy by the combination of hydrogen nuclei to form helium nuclei. It is the process that takes place in a hydrogen bomb and, as a continuing reaction, in the Sun and other stars. Attempts to harness it for commercial power production have so far not succeeded.

reactors there are various types of (fission) reactor in use. In a gas-cooled reactor, a circulating gas under pressure (such as carbon dioxide) removes heat from the core of the reactor, which usually contains natural uranium and has neutron-absorbing control rods made of boron. The Calder Hall reactor is of this type. An advanced gas-cooled reactor (AGR) generally has enriched uranium oxide as its fuel. A water-cooled reactor, such as the steam-generating heavy-water reactor at Winfrith, Dorset, has water circulating through the hot core. The water is converted to steam, which drives turbo-alternators for generating electricity. In a pressurized water reactor (PWR) the coolant consists of a sealed system of pressurized heavy water (deuterium oxide), which heats ordinary water to form steam in heat exchangers. The spent fuel from either type of reactor contains some plutonium, which can be extracted and used as fuel for the so-called fast breeder reactor (such as the one at Dounreay, Scotland). This produces more plutonium than it consumes (hence its name)

by converting uranium placed as a blanket round the main core. The usual coolant is liquid sodium, a substance that is difficult to handle. A major danger with any type of reactor is the possibility of meltdown, which can result in the release of radioactive material. Problems can also arise over the processing of nuclear fuel and disposal of nuclear waste.

nuclear accidents the most serious have been:
April 1986 at Chernobyl (USSR): a leak from a non-pressurized boiling-water reactor, one of the largest in the Soviet Union, caused by overheating. The resulting clouds of radioactive isotopes were traced as far away as Sweden. Vast tracts of land and hundreds of people were contaminated.
1979 at Three Mile Island, Harrisburg, USA: a pressurized water reactor leaked radioactive matter as a result of a combination of mechanical and electrical failure, as well as operator error.
1957 at Windscale (now Sellafield), England: fire destroyed the core of a reactor, releasing large quantities of radioactive fumes into the atmosphere.

nuclear waste is produced in three forms:
gas usually in small enough quantity to be released into the atmosphere;
solid irradiated fuel-element cans and other equipment. When of low activity, this is packaged for sea disposal (for example, at a site 450 km/300 mi off Land's End), but this is controversial. High-activity waste may be combustible (plutonium being recovered from the incinerator), or may be buried, the latter being another source of controversy;
liquid high-activity liquid wastes pose the greatest problems of all. Storage has been proposed in salt mines, granite formations, or 'clay basins'; or on or under the seabed. However, no container can be guaranteed (as international

RUSSIAN NUCLEAR POWER STATIONS: SAFETY UNDER SCRUTINY

Russian officials played down the seriousness of a leak of radioactive iodine from a Chernobyl-type nuclear reactor near St Petersburg on 24 March 1992. Minatom, Russia's atomic energy ministry, said 'Releases of inert gases and iodine to the environment don't exceed the requirements of sanitary rules and regulation'. Nevertheless, the incident sparked fears of another Chernobyl-type disaster, and there is a growing consensus that Russia's nuclear technology is out of date and dangerous.

The incident took place at Sosnovy Bor, 100 km/60 mi west of St Petersburg on the Gulf of Finland. Sosnovy Bor is the home of four 16-year-old RMBK reactors. In these reactors, the fuel channels form a honeycomb structure within the graphite core through which cooing water flows; damage to the core in one of the reactors caused the accident. After Chernobyl, all RMBK reactors were fitted with extra safety systems. At Sosnovy Bor, the emergency control systems appeared to work correctly, shutting down the reactor immediately. Nevertheless, a week later Alexi Yablokov, a government ecology adviser, criticized the traditional Russian love of secrecy, and said that the accident had released 109 times more radiation than had been officially acknowledged. In April, a group of Western nuclear experts visited the Sosnovy Bor site and were disturbed by the high levels of radiation in the plant and the old-fashioned control technology. This prompted the authorities in Ukraine to shut down the remaining reactors at Chernobyl for maintenance and safety checks. In October 1991 a faulty electrical device had caused a 3-hour fire in the turbine hall serving one of the reactors

at Chernobyl—more trouble for the blighted installation.

Two reactors were recently shut down in the central Siberian city of Krasnoyarsk. The reactors were said to be a danger to civilian health and the environment. The old-fashioned reactors were cooled by water taken from and pumped back into the Yenisey River. The river, already heavily polluted by industry, flows for 2,011 km/1,250 mi through Siberia. Pollution has already made water from 75% of Russia's rivers, lakes and reservoirs unfit to drink. Understandably, the local population at Krasnoyarsk feared that plutonium, a dangerous poison from the reactors, would find its way to the river. The reactor which was allowed to continue operating at Krasnoyarsk is underground and uses modern, 'closed cycle' technology which cannot cause pollution.

The emerging pattern is one of old-fashioned and unsafe technology. Unfortunately, the solution to the problem is far from easy. The country relies on nuclear power. Its 45 nuclear plants produce well over 200 billion units of electricity each year. St Petersburg is the country's biggest consumer of nuclear power with four 1,000 MW units producing 23 billion units. Other large nuclear power complexes are situated at Kursk (23 billion units), Smolensk (19 billion units), Balakovo (12 billion units), Kalinin (12 billion units), and Kola (12 billion units). The smallest population of nuclear consumers live in the northern Siberian mining town of Bilibino. Their four 12 MW stations help keep the Siberian winters at bay. What will keep them warm if Russia's nuclear power is judged unsafe?

ACCIDENTS AND STOPPAGES AT NUCLEAR REACTORS IN THE FORMER USSR

Jan 1991—March 1992

	reactors	stoppages	accidents
Pressurised-water reactors			
Balakovsk (Russia)	3	50	
Zaporozhe (Ukraine)	5	47	
Tver (Russia)	2	16	
Kola Peninsula (Russia)	4	22	
Novovoronezh (Russia	3	15	
Rovno (Ukraine)	3	29	
Khmelnitsky (Ukraine)	1	6	
Southern Ukraine	3	15	
Boiling-water (RBMK) reactors			
Ignalina (Lithuania)	2	7	1
Kursk (Russia)	4	11	
St Petersburg (Russia)	4	11	1
Chernobyl (Ukraine)	3	10	2
Others			
Beloyarsk (Russia)	1	5	
Bilibino (Russia)	4	10	1
Total	45	270	5

Source: The Economist

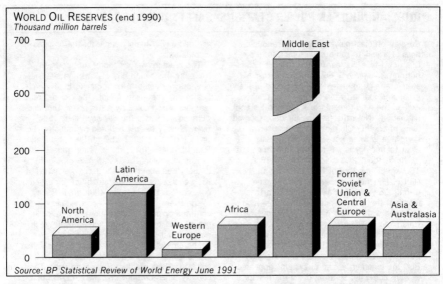

WORLD OIL RESERVES (end 1990)
Thousand million barrels

Source: BP Statistical Review of World Energy June 1991

authorities require) against decay, volcanic action, and so on, for 100,000 years. The most promising of the proposed methods involves the vitrification of liquid waste into solid glass cylinders, which might then be placed in titanium-cobalt alloy containers and deposited on other planets. If these containers were stored beneath the sea they would start to corrode after 1,000 years, and would dissolve within the following 1,000 years.

petroleum or *crude oil* natural mineral oil, a thick greenish-brown flammable liquid found underground in permeable rocks, and consisting of hydrocarbons mixed with oxygen, sulphur, nitrogen, and other elements in varying proportions. The products derived from petroleum include the fossil fuels oil and petrol (gasoline). Eight of the 14 top-earning companies in the USA in 1990 (led by Exxon with $7 billion in sales) are in the global petroleum industry.

Petroleum is thought to be derived from ancient organic material that has been converted by, first, bacterial action, then heat and pressure. The exploitation of oilfields began with the first commercial well in Pennsylvania 1859. The USA led in production until the 1960s, when the Middle East outproduced other areas, their immense reserves leading to a worldwide dependence on cheap oil for transport and industry. In 1961 the Organization of the Petroleum Exporting Countries (OPEC) was established to avoid exploitation of member countries; after OPEC's price rises in 1973, the International Energy Agency (IEA) was established 1974 to protect the interests of oil-consuming countries. New technologies were introduced to pump oil from offshore and from the Arctic (the Alaska pipeline) in an effort to avoid a monopoly by OPEC.

The burning of petroleum fuel is one cause of air pollution. The transport of oil can lead to

major catastrophes—for example, the *Torrey Canyon* tanker lost off SW England 1967, which led to an agreement by the international oil companies 1968 to pay compensation for massive shore pollution. The 1989 oil spill in Alaska from the *Exxon Valdez* damaged the area's fragile environment, despite clean-up efforts.

renewable resource natural resource that is replaced by natural processes in a reasonable amount of time. Soil, water, forests, plants, and animals are all renewable resources as long as they are properly conserved. Solar, wind, wave, and geothermal energies are based on renewable resources.

solar energy energy derived from the Sun's radiation. A solar furnace, such as that built in 1970 at Odeillo in the French Pyrenees, has thousands of mirrors to focus the Sun's rays; it produces uncontaminated, intensive heat for industrial and scientific or experimental purposes. Other solar heaters produce less energy and may have industrial or domestic uses. They usually consist of a black (heat-absorbing) panel containing pipes through which air or water is circulated, either by thermal convection or by a pump. Solar energy may also be harnessed indirectly using solar cells, made up of panels of semiconductor material (usually silicon) that generate electricity when illuminated by sunlight. Because of their high cost and low-power output, solar cells have found few applications outside space probes and artificial satellites.

tidal power station hydroelectric power plant that uses the 'head' of water created by the rise and fall of the ocean tides to spin the water turbines. An example is at St Malo, France.

turbine an engine in which steam, water or gas is made to spin a rotating shaft. Turbines are among the most powerful machines. Steam turbines are used to drive ships' propellers

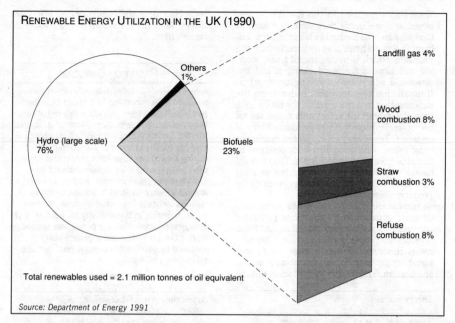

RENEWABLE ENERGY UTILIZATION IN THE UK (1990)

Others
1%

Hydro (large scale)
76%

Biofuels
23%

Landfill gas 4%

Wood
combustion 8%

Straw
combustion 3%

Refuse
combustion 8%

Total renewables used = 2.1 million tonnes of oil equivalent

Source: Department of Energy 1991

and the generators in power stations; water turbines spin the generators in hydroelectric power plants; and gas turbines, in the guise of jet engines, power most aircraft, and drive machines in industry. The high-temperature, high-pressure steam for steam turbines is raised in boilers heated by furnaces burning coal, oil or gas, or by nuclear energy. A steam turbine consists of a shaft, or rotor, which rotates inside a fixed casing (stator). The rotor carries 'wheels' consisting of blades, or vanes. The stator has vanes set between the vanes of the rotor, which direct the steam through the rotor vanes at the optimum angle.

water mill machine that harnesses the energy in flowing water to produce mechanical power, typically for milling (grinding) grain. Water from a stream is directed against the paddles of a water wheel to make it turn. Simple gearing transfers this motion to the millstones. The modern equivalent of the water wheel is the water turbine, used in hydroelectric power plants.

wave power power obtained by harnessing the energy of water waves. Various schemes have been advanced since 1973, when oil prices rose dramatically and an energy shortage threatened. In 1974 English engineer Stephen Salter developed the duck—a floating boom whose segments nod up and down with the waves. The nodding motion can be used to drive pumps and spin generators. Another device, developed in Japan, uses an oscillating water column to harness wave power.

windmill a mill with sails or vanes that, by the action of wind upon them, drive machinery for grinding corn, pumping water, and so on.

NUCLEAR POWER: CHRONOLOGY

1896	French physicist Henri Becquerel discovered radioactivity.
1905	German physicist Albert Einstein demonstrated that mass can be converted into energy.
1911	New Zealander Ernest Rutherford proposed the nuclear model of the atom.
1919	Rutherford split the atom, by bombarding a nitrogen nucleus with alpha particles.
1939	Otto Hahn, Fritz Strassman, and Lise Meitner announced the discovery of nuclear fission.
1942	Enrico Fermi built the first nuclear reactor in Chicago.
1951	First nuclear electricity generated by the Experimental Breeder Reactor at Idaho, USA.
1954	The first reactor for generating electricity built in the Soviet Union.
1956	The first large-scale nuclear power station opened at Calder Hall, England.
1957	The first pressurized water reactor built in Shippingport, Pennsylvania, USA.
1959	The first fast breeder reactor built at Dounreay, Scotland.
1991	First production of significant amount of fusion power (1.7 MW) by JET reactor at Culham, Oxfordshire, England.

Windmills were used in the East in ancient times, and in Europe they were first used in Germany and the Netherlands in the 12th century. The main types of early windmill are the *post mill*, which is turned round a post when the direction of the wind changes, and the *tower mill*, which has a revolving turret on top. It usually has a device (fantail) that keeps the sails pointing into the wind. In the USA a light type of windmill with steel sails supported on a long steel girder shaft was introduced for use on farms. The energy crisis has led to modern experiments with wind turbines, designed to use wind power on a major scale. They usually have a propeller-type rotor mounted on a tall shell tower. The turbine drives a generator for producing electricity.

wind turbine windmill of advanced aerodynamic design connected to an electricity generator and used in wind-power installations. Wind turbines can be either large propeller-type rotors mounted on a tall tower, or flexible metal strips fixed to a vertical axle at top and bottom. The world's largest wind turbine is on Hawaii, in the Pacific Ocean. It has two blades 50 m/164 ft long on top of a tower 20 storeys high.

RADIATION DANGERS

A recent United Nations agency report has revealed an astonishing fact about coal-fired power stations: they give out more radiation than nuclear power stations. The International Atomic Energy Agency compared six energy sources for the amount of radiation given off during operation. Coal-fired power stations top the list, producing 4 man-sieverts of radiation per gigawatt-year. Radiation units are notoriously difficult to visualize; man-sieverts indicate the radiation dose received by each worker in the industry for each unit of energy produced. Nuclear power was second with 2.5 man-sievert per gigawatt-year, followed by geothermal energy, peat burning, oil plants, and natural gas.

Energy sources

How serious, if at all, are the health and environmental hazards posed by power stations running on coal or nuclear energy?

Very serious	42
Moderately serious	38
Not very serious	9
Not at all serious	3
Don't know	7

Which of the following types of 'renewable' energy do you think the UK ought to develop?

Wind	53
Wave	36
Something else	2
None of these	11

Do you think that the Government should or should not do more to increase the proportions of electricity coming from 'renewable' sources in the UK?

Should	87
Should not	3
Don't know	10

And would you prefer to see a greater proportion of your power coming from these 'renewable' sources, even if some are slightly more expensive than traditional fuel sources?

Would prefer	77
Would not prefer	9
Don't know	14

THE NATURAL WORLD

biodiversity shortened form of *biological diversity*, a measure of variation amongst living things, in terms of different species, genetic differences within species, and different ecosystems. Research suggests that biodiversity is far greater than previously realized, especially amongst smaller organisms. Up to 80% of the earth's species have yet to be identified and described. Maintenance of the Earth's biodiversity is important for ecological stability, and as a resource for research into agriculture, medicine, etc. Habitat destruction, pollution, and other environmentally damaging factors have led to the most massive and most rapid loss of biodiversity in the history of the planet; in recognition of this, an international convention for the preservation of biodiversity was adopted at the Earth Summit in Rio de Janeiro in June 1992; it was signed by over 100 countries, including the UK but not the USA.

carbon cycle the sequence by which carbon circulates and is recycled through the natural world. The carbon element from carbon dioxide, released into the atmosphere by living things as a result of respiration, is taken up by plants during photosynthesis and converted into carbohydrates; the oxygen component is released back into the atmosphere. The simplest link in the carbon cycle, however, occurs when an animal eats a plant and carbon is transferred from, say, a leaf cell to the animal body. Today, the carbon cycle is in danger of being disrupted by the increased consumption and burning of fossil fuels, and the burning of large tracts of tropical forests, as a result of which levels of carbon dioxide are building up in the atmosphere and probably contributing to the greenhouse effect.

climate weather conditions at a particular place over a period of time. Climate encompasses all the meteorological elements and the factors that influence them. The primary factors that determine the variations of climate over the surface of the Earth are: (a) the effect of latitude and the tilt of the Earth's axis to the plane of the orbit about the Sun (66.5°); (b) the large-scale movements of different wind belts over the Earth's surface; (c) the temperature difference between land and sea; (d) contours of the ground; and (e) location of the area in relation to ocean currents. Catastrophic variations to climate may be caused by the impact of another planetary body, or by clouds resulting from volcanic activity.

The most important local or global meteorological changes brought about by human activity are those linked with ozone depleters and the greenhouse effect.

deforestation the destruction of forest for timber, fuelwood, charcoal burning, and clearing for agriculture and extractive industries such as mining, without planting new trees to replace those lost (reafforestation) or working on a cycle that allows the natural forest to regenerate. Deforestation causes fertile soil to be blown away or washed into rivers, leading to soil erosion, drought, flooding, and loss of wildlife.

Deforestation is taking place in both tropical rainforests and temperate forests.

desertification the creation of deserts by changes in climate, or by human-aided processes such as overgrazing, destruction of forest belts, and exhaustion of the soil by too intensive cultivation without restoration of fertility; all usually prompted by the pressures of expanding populations. The process can be reversed by special planting (marram grass, trees) and by the use of water-absorbent plastic grains (a polymer absorbent of 40 times its own weight of water), which, added to the sand, enable crops to be grown. About 135 million people are directly affected by desertification, mainly in Africa, the Indian subcontinent, and South America.

firewood the principal fuel for some 2.5 billion people, mainly in the Third World. In principle a renewable energy source, firewood is being cut far faster than the trees can regenerate in many areas of Africa and Asia, leading to deforestation. (In Mali, for example, wood provides 97% of total energy consumption, and deforestation is running at an estimated 9,000 hectares a year.) The heat efficiency of firewood can be increased by use of stoves, but many people cannot afford to buy these.

fossil fuel fuel, such as coal, oil, and natural gas, formed from the fossilized remains of plants that lived hundreds of millions of years ago. Fossil fuels are a nonrenewable resource and will eventually run out. Extraction of fossil fuels causes considerable environmental pollution, and burning coal contributes to acid rain and the greenhouse effect.

habitat the localized environment in which an organism lives, and which provides for all (or almost all) of its needs. The diversity of habitats found within the Earth's ecosystem is enormous, and they are changing all the time. Some can be considered inorganic or physical, for example the Arctic ice cap. Others are more complex, for instance a woodland floor or a forest. Some habitats are so precise that they are called *microhabitats*, such as the area under a stone where a particular type of insect lives. Most habitats provide a home for many species.

hedge or *hedgerow* row of closely planted shrubs or low trees, generally acting as a land division and windbreak. Hedges also serve as a source of food and as a refuge for wildlife, and provide a habitat not unlike the understorey of a natural forest.

mangrove any of several shrubs and trees, especially of the mangrove family Rhizophoraceae, found in the muddy swamps of tropical coasts and estuaries. By sending down aerial roots from their branches, they rapidly form close-growing mangrove thickets. Their timber is impervious to water and resists marine worms.

national park land set aside and conserved for public enjoyment. The first was Yellowstone National Park, USA, established 1872. National parks include not only the most scenic places, but also places distinguished for their historic, prehistoric, or scientific interest, or for their superior recreational assets. They range from areas the size of small countries to pockets of just a few hectares.

There are ten national parks in England and Wales; they are run by National Park Authorities and are financed by national government (75%) and local government (25%).

nature reserve area set aside to protect a habitat and the wildlife that lives within it, with only restricted admission for the public. A nature reserve often provides a sanctuary for rare species. The world's largest is Etosha Reserve, Namibia, with an area of 99,520 sq km/ 38,415 sq mi.

niche in ecology, the 'place' occupied by a species in its habitat, including all chemical, physical, and biological components, such as what it eats, the time of day at which the species feeds, temperature, moisture, the parts of the habitat that it uses (for example, trees or open grassland), the way it reproduces, and how it behaves. It is believed that no two species can occupy exactly the same niche, because they would be in direct competition for the same resources at every stage of their life cycle.

nonrenewable resource natural resource, such as coal or oil, that takes thousands or millions of years to form naturally and can therefore not be replaced once it is consumed. The main energy sources used by humans are nonrenewable resources.

oceanography the study of the oceans, their origin, composition, structure, history, and wildlife (seabirds, fish, plankton, and other organisms). It involves the study of water movements—currents, waves, and tides—and the chemical and physical properties of the seawater. It deals with the origin and topography of the ocean floor—ocean trenches and ridges formed by plate tectonics, and continental shelves from the submerged portions of the continents. Much oceanography uses computer simulations to plot the possible movements of the waters, and many studies are carried out by remote sensing.

The World Ocean Circulation Experiment, begun 1990 and set to last seven years, involves researchers from 44 countries examining the physics of the ocean and its role in the climate of the Earth. It is based at Southampton University, England.

overfishing fishing at rates that exceed the sustained-yield cropping of fish species, resulting in a net population decline. For example, in the North Atlantic, herring has been fished to the verge of extinction and the cod and haddock populations are severely depleted. In the Third World, use of huge factory ships, often by Western fisheries, has depleted stocks for locals who cannot otherwise obtain protein.

rainforest dense forest found on or near the equa-tor where the climate is hot and wet (tropical rainforest) or in warm, damp temperate areas. Over half the tropical rainforests are in Central and South America, the rest in SE Asia and Africa. Although covering approximately 8% of the Earth's land surface, they make up about 50% of all growing wood on the planet, and harbour at least 40% of the Earth's species (plants and animals). Rainforests are being destroyed at an increasing rate as their valuable timber is harvested and land cleared for agriculture, causing deforestation, soil erosion, and flooding. By 1990 50% of the world's rainforest had been removed. If clearance continues at the present rate, all of the world's primary (undisturbed) rainforest will disappear or be damaged within the next 30 years.

Rainforests can be divided into several kinds: tropical, montane, upper montane or cloud, mangrove, subtropical, and temperate. They are characterized by a great diversity of species, usually of tall broad-leaved evergreen trees, with many climbing vines and ferns, some of which are main sources of raw materials for medicines. Rainforests are some of the most complex and diverse ecosystems on the planet and help to regulate global weather patterns. When deforestation occurs, the microclimate of the mature forest disappears; soil erosion and flooding become major problems since the forest protects the shallow tropical soil.

Deforestation may lead to global warming of the atmosphere, and contribute to the greenhouse effect. It also causes the salt level in the ground to rise to the surface, making the land unsuitable for farming or ranching.

renewable resource a natural resource that is replaced by natural processes in a reasonable amount of time. Soil, water, forests, plants, and animals are all renewable resources as long as they are properly conserved. Solar, wind, wave, and geothermal energies are based on renewable resources.

PROTECTION OF NATURAL AREAS

Selected OECD countries (1990)

	No. of sites	Total size (km²)	% of territory
Canada (incl. Alaska)	523	701,255	7.0
USA	961	982,974	10.5
Japan	65	24,024	6.4
Australia	728	456,544	5.9
Austria	129	15,939	19.0
France	80	47,787	2.3
W Germany	54	29,559	11.9
Ireland	6	268	0.4
Italy	108	13,006	4.3
Netherlands	68	3,550	8.7
Spain	161	35,111	7.0
Sweden	99	17,584	3.9
Switzerland	15	1,112	2.7
UK	138	46,392	18.9
World	6,940	6,514,676	4.9

Source: OECD Environmental Data 1991

TROPICAL MARINE AREAS UNDER THREAT

Mangroves

Niger River delta, Nigeria	Exploited for timber, fuel, fodder and urban expansion.
Kenya and Tanzania	Cleared for fuelwood, building materials and tourist resorts.
Indus River mouth, Pakistan	Over-exploitation for fuel, fodder and building material.
Sundarbans, India and Bangladesh	Over-exploitation for fuel, fodder, timber and fishponds.
Malaysia and Gulf of Thailand	Destruction for fish and shellfish ponds and agricultural land.
Philippines	Destruction for timber, tannin, fuelwood and fish and shellfish ponds.
Indonesia	Massive destruction for logging and woodchip industries, fish and shellfish ponds and for building materials and fuelwood.
Queensland, Australia	Town and tourist development.
US south coast, Texas to Florida	Over-development of coastline for urban expansion, resorts, housing estates. Also used as rubbish dumps.
Panama	Cleared for fish and shrimp ponds.
Ecuador	Cleared for fish and shrimp ponds.
Caribbean	All mangrove stands disturbed. Main threats: tourism and coastal land development.

Seagrasses

East Africa	Under threat from heavy sedimentation of shallow coastal waters caused by erosion of agricultural lands.
Southeast Asia	Under threat from loss of mangroves, coastal development, urban expansion and bucket dredging for tin.
Caribbean and Gulf of Mexico	Under threat from dredge and fill operations, loss of mangroves, coastal development for tourism, oil production.

Coral reefs

East Africa	Coral mining for building materials, blast fishing, tourist trade and sedimentation.
The Gulf	Oil and industrial pollution, sedimentation.
Thailand and Malaysia	Tourist resorts, bucket dredging for tin, over-fishing.
Philippines	Blast fishing, coral mining, collection for tourist trade and use of poisons.
Southern Japan – Ryukyu Archipelago	Destroyed by coastal development and sedimentation.
Indonesia	Destroyed by blast fishing, coral mining, tourist trade and coastal development.
South Pacific	Tourism, sedimentation from coastal development.
Wider Caribbean	Collection for tourist trade, coastal development, mangrove destruction/sedimentation and damage by boat anchors.

Source: World Wildlife Fund

slash and burn simple agricultural method whereby natural vegetation is cut and burned, and the clearing then farmed for a few years until the soil loses its fertility, whereupon farmers move on and leave the area to regrow. Although this is possible with a small, widely dispersed population, it becomes unsustainable with more people and is now a cause of deforestation.

soil erosion the wearing away and redistribution of the Earth's soil layer. It is caused by the action of water, wind, and ice, and also by improper methods of agriculture. If unchecked, soil erosion results in the formation of deserts. It has been estimated that 20% of the world's cultivated topsoil was lost between 1950 and 1990.

If the rate of erosion exceeds the rate of soil formation (from rock), then the land will decline and eventually become infertile. The removal of forests or other vegetation often leads to serious soil erosion, because plant roots bind soil, and without them the soil is free to wash or blow away, as in the American dust bowl. The effect is worse on hillsides, and there has been devastating loss of soil where forests have been cleared from mountainsides, as in Madagscar. Improved agricultural practices are needed to combat soil erosion. Wind-breaks, such as hedges or strips planted with coarse grass, are valuable. Organic farming can reduce soil erosion by as much as 75%.

sustained-yield cropping the removal of surplus individuals from a population of organisms so that the population maintains a constant size. This usually requires selective removal of animals of all ages and both sexes to ensure a balanced population structure. Taking too many individuals can result in a population decline, as in overfishing.

water Water covers 70% of the Earth's surface; less than 0.01% is fresh water. It occurs as standing (oceans, lakes) and running (rivers, streams) water, and in the form of rain and vapour, and supports all forms of life on Earth.

Water supply in sparsely populated regions usually comes from underground water rising to the surface in natural springs, supplemented by pumps and wells. Urban sources are deep artesian wells, rivers, and reservoirs, usually formed from enlarged lakes or dammed and flooded valleys, from which water is conveyed by pipes, conduits, and aqueducts to filter beds. As water seeps through layers of shingle, gravel, and sand, harmful organisms are removed and the water is then distributed by pumping or gravitation through mains and pipes. Often other substances are added

THE EARTH SUMMIT: PROGRESS AND SETBACKS

In June 1992 over a hundred of the world's heads of state met in Rio de Janeiro, Brazil, to take part in the United Nations Conference on Environment and Development (UNCED). The meeting, popularly known as the Earth Summit, was unique in a number of ways. It was the largest gathering of world leaders in history. It was by far the largest conference ever to be held about the environment. And it succeeded in agreeing upon two globally important treaties, with countries signing up faster then ever before.

Yet for an event that might almost be compared with the formation of the United Nations in terms of global significance, the meeting gave the distinct impression of being something of a damp squib. Economic interests watered down many of the finer ideals on which the conference had been set up. Although there were many fine words, there was little money to back them up. The rift between North and South was, if anything, widened rather than healed by the discussions in Rio. The Earth Summit was a UN-sponsored meeting to discuss issues relating to environment and development, and the links between the two. It began with very high ideals, some of which had been whittled away in the two-year build-up process. This had included a number of preparatory conferences (precons) in different parts of the world. By the time the conference was actually launched, much had already been argued about, and won or lost, during the precon process.

In the event, two significant treaties were signed at Rio, although not by everybody. A treaty on climate change was agreed, calling on countries to commit themselves to stabilize emissions of greenhouse gases by the year 2000, and asking signatories to act before the convention becomes effective. A second treaty, on biodiversity, was originally drafted to ensure that signatories took steps to preserve plant and animal life, but eventually also included rights to exploit life in their territories as well. Unfortunately, both of the treaties were significantly weakened by the time they reached Rio, mainly because of opposition from the rich countries and especially the USA. The greenhouse treaty was originally supposed to be binding, but was weakened through softer wording, less commitment, and a reduction in the support provided by the rich countries to the poor to help in meeting the targets. The biodiversity treaty, which the USA refused to sign owing to fears of losing rights to exploit other country's biological resources in biotechnology, had some high-sounding ideals but little money. Again, the rich nations opposed moves to include provision for substantial financial support for the poorer countries in conservation of biodiversity.

A gain for the environmental lobby was the agreement reached on Agenda 21, an ambitious 500-page plan to protect the environment, with 115 specific clean-up programmes. This caused a furore in discussion because of the enormous costs it was calculated as requiring, some $625 billion a year, most of which was to have come from the South. In practice, and in line with much of the rest of UNCED, far less money was available and the Agenda, although agreed, is non-binding.

The largest single failure of the conference was the failure to agree on any binding treaty on forests. Instead, a non-binding statement of principles to conserve forests was agreed, which few people expect to make much difference to practical forest-management policies. Here, the main opposition came from the South, and was spearheaded by Malaysia which already has a massive logging programme and plans to continue the exploitation. Malaysia's threat to pull out of UNCED unless the treaty was dropped had a large influence over its abandonment. Here, ironically, the USA was a prime supporter, but there was failure even to agree the need for a convention in the future.

So, was the Earth Summit a success or failure? It was a failure in that it did not produce the major shift towards greater protection for the environment that was originally hoped. Yet it did result in an unprecedented statement of concern by most of the world's leaders, and it did result in two major treaties being signed. As one environmental lobbyist said, if you read the small print on what was agreed there are a lot of hooks to hang countries on if they don't meet up to the requirements. The UNCED meeting was not the solution to the world's problems that some people were looking for, but it was a step in the right direction.

Brazilian Indian Chief Kanhok Caiapo with Maurice Strong, Earth Summit general secretary, during the opening ceremony of the International Indigenous People's Conference in Rio de Janeiro.

to the water, such as chlorine and fluorine; aluminium sulphate is the most widely used chemical in water treatment. In towns, besides industrial demands, domestic and municipal (road washing, sewage) needs account for about 1354l/30 gal per head each day. In coastal desert areas, such as the Arabian peninsula, desalination plants remove salt from sea water. The Earth's waters, both fresh and saline, have been polluted by industrial and domestic chemicals, many of which are toxic and others radioactive.

The British water industry was privatized 1989, and in 1991 the UK was taken to court for failing to meet EC drinking-water standards on nitrate and pesticide levels.

wetlands areas where land and freshwater meet, including marshes, fens, wet meadows, ponds, lakes, and both lowland and upland bogs. They constitute vital habitats for many unique life forms, particularly plants and birds.

Loss of wetlands is now a worldwide environmental problem, as a result of drainage for agriculture, plantation forestry, and urban expansion. There have been a number of attempts to protect wetlands through international treaties—such as the Ramsar Convention which protects over 460 important waterfowl sites around the world—but drainage schemes continue in many countries. Creation of new wetland areas is taking place on some nature reserves.

wilderness area of uncultivated and uninhabited land, which is usually located some distance from towns and cities. In the USA wilderness areas are specially designated by Congress and protected by federal agencies.

wildlife trade international trade in live plants and animals, and in wildlife products such as skins, horns, shells, and feathers. The trade has made some species virtually extinct, and whole ecosystems (for example, coral reefs) are threatened. Wildlife trade is to some extent regulated by CITES.

Species almost eradicated by trade in their products include many of the largest whales, crocodiles, marine turtles, and some wild cats. Until recently, some 2 million snake skins were exported from India every year. Populations of black rhino and African elephant have collapsed because of hunting for their tusks (ivory), and poaching remains a problem in cases where trade is prohibited.

ENVIRONMENTAL POLLUTANTS

acid rain acidic rainfall, thought to be caused principally by the release into the atmosphere of sulphur dioxide (SO_2) and oxides of nitrogen. Sulphur dioxide is formed from the burning of fossil fuels such as coal that contain high quantities of sulphur, and nitrogen oxides

WETLANDS OF INTERNATIONAL IMPORTANCE

Selected countries (1990)

	No. of sites	Total area km²
Canada	30	129,373
USA	8	11,158
Japan	3	99
Australia	39	44,779
New Zealand	5	381
Austria	5	1,024
Belgium	6	96
Denmark	27	7,342
Finland	11	1,013
France	1	850
West Germany	21	3,253
Greece	11	1,074
Iceland	2	575
Ireland	21	124
Italy	45	545
Netherlands	17	3,064
Norway	14	163
Portugal	2	306
Spain	17	1,287
Sweden	30	3,912
Switzerland	2	18
UK	44	1,733
Yugoslavia	2	181

Note: Wetlands designated by the contracting parties of the Convention on Wetlands of International Importance, especially as a waterfowl habitat.
Source: IUCN

are contributed from fossil fuels, industrial activities, and car exhaust fumes.

Acid rain is linked with damage to and death of forests and lake organisms in Scandinavia, Europe, and eastern North America. It also results in damage to buildings and statues. US and European power stations burning fossil fuel release some 8 grams of sulphur dioxides and 3 grams of nitrogen oxides per kilowatt-hour. According to DOE figures emissions of sulphur dioxide from power stations would have to be decreased by 81% in order to arrest such damage.

aerosol particles of liquid or solid suspended in a gas. Fog is a common natural example. Aerosol cans, which contain pressurized gas mixed with a propellant, are used to spray liquid in the form of tiny drops of such products as scents and cleaners. Most aerosols used chlorofluorocarbons (CFCs) as propellants until these were found to cause destruction of the ozone layer in the stratosphere.

The international community has agreed to phase out the use of CFCs, but most so-called 'ozone-friendly' aerosols also use ozone-depleting chemicals, although they are not as destructive as CFCs. Some of the products sprayed, such as pesticides, can be directly toxic to humans.

air pollution contamination of the atmosphere caused by the discharge, accidental or deliberate, of a wide range of toxic substances. Often the amount of the released substance is relatively high in a certain locality, so the harmful effects are more noticeable. The cost of preventing any discharge of pollutants into the air is prohibitive, so attempts are more usually made to reduce gradually the amount of discharge and to disperse this as quickly as possible by using a very tall chimney, or by intermittent release.

carbon dioxide CO_2 colourless gas, slightly soluble in water and denser than air, produced by living things during the processes of respiration and the decay of organic matter; its increasing density is contributing to global warming (see greenhouse effect in this section).

Britain has 1% of the world's population, yet it produces 3% of CO_2 emissions; the USA has 5% of the world's population and produces 25% of CO_2 emissions.

chlorofluorocarbon (CFC) synthetic chemical, which is odourless, nontoxic, nonflammable, and chemically inert. CFCs are used as propellants in aerosol cans, refrigerants in refrigerators and air conditioners, and in the manufacture of foam boxes for take-away food cartons. They are partly responsible for the destruction of the ozone layer. In June 1990 representatives of 93 nations, including the UK and the USA, agreed to phase out production of CFCs and various other ozone-depleting chemicals by the end of the century, and subsequent negotiations have increased controls even further.

When CFCs are released into the atmosphere, they drift up slowly into the stratosphere, where, under the influence of ultraviolet radiation from the Sun, they break down into chlorine atoms which destroy the ozone layer and allow harmful radiation from the Sun to reach the Earth's surface. CFCs can remain in the atmosphere for more than 100 years.

dioxin any of a family of over 200 organic chemicals, of which 2,3,7,8-tetrachlorodibenzodioxin (2,3,7,8-TCDD) is the most widespread. A highly toxic chemical, it has been associated with a disfiguring skin complaint (chloracne), birth defects, miscarriages, and cancer.

Disasters involving accidental release of large amounts of dioxin into the environment have occurred at Seveso in Italy and Times Beach in Missouri, USA. Small amounts of dioxins are released by the burning of a wide range of chlorinated materials (treated wood, exhaust fumes from fuels treated with chlorinated additives, and plastics). The discovery of dioxin contamination in food and mothers' breast milk has led the EC to decrease significantly dioxin emissions from incinerators.

UK government figures released 1989 showed dioxin levels 100 times higher than guidelines it has set for environmental dioxin in breast milk, suggesting dioxin contamination is more widespread than previously thought.

eutrophication the excessive enrichment of rivers, lakes, and shallow sea areas, primarily by nitrate fertilizers, washed from the soil by rain, and by phosphates from fertilizers and detergents in municipal sewage. These encourage the growth of algae and bacteria which use up the oxygen in the water, thereby making it uninhabitable for fishes and other animal life.

global warming projected imminent climate change attributed to the greenhouse effect.

greenhouse effect in the Earth's atmosphere, the trapping of solar radiation, which, absorbed by the Earth and re-emitted from the surface, is prevented from escaping by various gases in the air. The result is a rise in the Earth's temperature; in a garden greenhouse, the glass walls have the same effect. The main greenhouse gases are carbon dioxide, methane, and chlorofluorocarbons. Fossil-fuel consumption and forest fires are the main causes of carbon dioxide buildup; methane is a byproduct of agriculture (rice, cattle, sheep). Water vapour is another greenhouse gas. United Nations Environment Programme estimates an increase in average world temperatures of 1.5°C/2.7°F with a consequent rise of 20 cm/7.7 in in sea level by 2025.

The concentration of carbon dioxide in the atmosphere is estimated to have risen by 25% since the Industrial Revolution, and 10% since 1950; the rate of increase is now 0.5% a year. Chlorofluorocarbon levels are rising by 5% a year, and nitrous oxide levels by 0.4% a year, resulting in a global warming effect of 0.5% since 1900, and a rise of about 0.1°C a year in the temperature of the world's oceans during the 1980s. Arctic ice was 6–7 m/20–23 ft thick in 1976 and had reduced to 4–5 m/13–17 ft by 1987.

Low-lying areas and entire countries are threatened by flooding, and crops will be affected by the change in climate.

Dubbed the 'greenhouse effect' by Swedish scientist Svante Arrhenius, it was first predicted in 1827 by French mathematician Joseph Fourier (1768–1830).

A computer model from the British Meteorological Office predicts a warming of 2.7°C for a doubling of carbon dioxide.

leaching process by which substances are washed out of the soil. Fertilizers leached out of the soil find their way into rivers and cause water pollution. In tropical areas, leaching of the soil after deforestation removes scarce nutrients and leads to a dramatic loss of soil fertility.

mercury heavy, silver-grey, metallic element, symbol Hg. Mercury is a cumulative poison that can contaminate the food chain, and cause intestinal disturbance, kidney and brain damage, and birth defects in humans. The discharge into the sea of organic mercury compounds such as dimethylmercury is the major cause of mercury poisoning in the latter half of the twentieth century. Between 1953 and 1975, 684 people in the Japanese fishing village of Minamata were poisoned (115 fatally) by organic mercury wastes that had been dumped into the bay and had accumulated in the bodies of fish and shellfish.

nitrate any salt of nitric acid, containing the

NO_3^- ion. Nitrates in the soil, whether naturally occurring or from inorganic or organic fertilizers, can be used by plants to make proteins and nucleic acids. Being soluble in water, nitrates are leached out by rain into streams and reservoirs. High levels are now found in drinking water in arable areas. These may be harmful to newborn babies, and it is possible that they contribute to stomach cancer, although the evidence for this is unproven. The UK current standard is 100 milligrams per litre, double the EC limits to be implemented by 1993.

oil spill oil released by damage to or discharge from a tanker or oil installation. An oil spill kills all shore life, clogging up the feathers of birds and suffocating other creatures. At sea toxic chemicals leach into the water below, poisoning sea life. Mixed with dust, the oil forms globules that sink to the seabed, poisoning sea life there as well.

In March 1989 the *Exxon Valdez* spilled oil in Alaska's Prince William Sound, covering 12,400 sq km/4,800 sq mi and killing at least 34,000 sea birds, 10,000 sea otters, and up to 16 whales. The world's largest oil spill was in the Gulf in Jan 1991, the result of deliberate action on the part of the Iraquis during the Gulf War.

ozone O_3 highly reactive pale-blue gas with a penetrating odour. It forms a layer in the upper atmosphere, which protects life on Earth from ultraviolet rays, a cause of skin cancer. At lower atmospheric levels it is an air pollutant and contributes to the greenhouse effect. At ground level, ozone can cause asthma attacks, stunted growth in plants, and corrosion of certain materials. It is produced by the action of sunlight on car exhaust fumes, and is a major air pollutant in hot summers.

A continent-sized hole has formed over Antarctica as a result of damage to the ozone layer caused in part by chlorofluorocarbons (CFCs). In 1989 ozone depletion was 50% over the Antarctic compared with 3% over the Arctic. However, ozone depletion over the polar regions is the most dramatic manifestation of a general global effect. At ground level, ozone is so dangerous that the US Environment Protection Agency recommends people should not be

exposed for more than one hour a day to ozone levels of 120 parts per billion (ppb), while the World Health Organization recommends a lower 76–100 ppb. It is known that even at levels of 60 ppb ozone causes respiratory problems, and may cause the yields of some crops to fall. In the USA, the annual economic loss due to ozone has been estimated at $5.4 billion.

ozone depleter any chemical that destroys the ozone in the stratosphere. Most ozone depleters are chemically stable compounds containing chlorine or bromine, which remain unchanged for long enough to drift up to the upper atmosphere. The best known are chlorofluorocarbons (CFCs), but many other ozone depleters are known, including halons, used in some fire extinguishers; methyl chloroform and carbon tetrachloride, both solvents; some CFC substitutes; and the pesticide methyl bromide.

packaging material, usually of metal, paper, or plastic, used to protect products, make them easier to display, and as a form of advertising. Packaging is in part responsible for the magnitude of the waste problem globally, and environmentalists have targeted packaging materials as being wasteful of energy and resources.

pesticide any chemical used in farming, gardening, and indoors to combat pests. Pesticides are of three main types: *insecticides* (to kill insects), *fungicides* (to kill fungal diseases), and *herbicides* (to kill plants, mainly those considered weeds). The safest pesticides are those made from plants, such as the insecticides pyrethrum and derris. Pesticides cause a number of pollution problems through spray drift on to surrounding areas, direct contamination of users or the public, and as residues on food. The aid organization Oxfam estimates that pesticides cause about 10,000 deaths worldwide every year.

More potent are synthetic products, such as chlorinated hydrocarbons. These products, including DDT and dieldrin, are highly toxic to wildlife and human beings, so their use is now restricted by law in some areas and is declining. Safer pesticides such as malathion are based on organic phosphorus compounds, but they still

Major Oil Spills From Tankers

Over 30,000 tonnes, worldwide (1983–1991)

Year	Name of ship/flag	Country affected	Quantity spilled (tonnes)
1983	Castello de Belver/Spain	S. Africa	255,525
1984	Assimi/n.a.	Oman	51,431
	Pericles/n.a.	Qatar	46,631
1985	Neptunia/Liberia	Iran	60,000
	Nova/Liberia	Iran	71,120
1988	Athenian Venture/Cyprus	Canada	30,000
	Odyssey/Liberia	Canada	140,000
1989	Exxon Valdez/USA	USA (Alaska)	35,000
	Kharg 5/n.a.	Morocco	70,000
1991	Le Haven/Cyprus	Italy	n.a.

Source: OECD Environmental Data 1991

SIGNS OF HOPE, SIGNS OF STRESS

One of the main factors contributing to the collapse of Soviet-style communism in E Europe was growing public discontent about the state of the environment. The Polish Ecology Club was the first legally independent organization to be established in Poland after the rise of Solidarity. Environmental issues were rallying calls to the former opposition in Czechoslovakia and Hungary, and Hungarian opposition to a dam on the Danube drew international attention. Yet now that the countries of central and E Europe are opening up for the first time in decades, the overall state of the environment is by no means clear, as was once assumed by people in the west.

The best-known environmental problems in the central European countries are connected with various forms of pollution. Inefficient industrial processes, lax environmental standards, and the intrinsically higher pollution levels from the sulphur-rich lignite coal found in some of the former communist countries have combined to cause extremely high air-pollution levels in places. For example, in the mid-1980s Poland had annual emissions of sulphur and nitrogen oxides almost identical to those coming from the UK but with a population not much more than half the size of Britain's, meaning that there was roughly twice as much acidic pollution per person. East Germany emitted more air pollution than West Germany, despite having not much more than a quarter

Emissions from the brown coal power station Bloxberg blacken the sky above the river Lausitz in former East Germany.

of the population. Yet Britain and Germany had at that time some of the highest air-pollution emissions of W European countries.

The extent of environmental damage in the east includes results for the east include severely damaged forests, crumbling historical buildings, as in the heavily polluted Polish city of Kraków, and evidence that human cancer levels have increased in areas of high pollution. Children are kept home from school on 'bad days' in the most polluted areas of Czechoslovakia.

There are other serious pollution problems. Freshwater pollution is reaching crisis levels in some areas. The Volga-Caspian basin, source of most of the world's caviar, contains 700 times the legal levels of petroleum products and 113 times the permitted levels of surface pollution from synthetic products. This has led to fears of 'ecological disaster', according to Professor Vladimir Lukyanenko, a top Russian biologist. Large areas of the Siberian taiga are said to be polluted by oil from spillage during drilling. Children in the Bulgarian town of Kuklen have such high levels of lead in their blood that they would be sent for detoxification in the USA. Infant mortality rates in Czechoslovakia are 60% higher than in the west.

Yet in other ways ecological conditions in E Europe are superior to those found in the west. The largest remaining areas of natural or ancient forest in Europe are found in the east, where they serve as a vital reservoir of biodiversity. There are large populations of rare animals, such as bear and wolf.

Unfortunately, these irreplaceable forests are now being slated for logging, often by western companies moving into rich new markets in the east. Russia has some 40% of the world's temperate timber, mainly in Siberia, where plans to log huge areas of this are rapidly gaining pace. Latvia is already developing forestry in areas that would be classed as internationally important nature reserves in most other European countries.

The west is playing a role in the increasing damage from agrochemical pollution as well. Although some parts of E Europe have long been run with extremely intensive agricultural systems, other areas are effectively still practising peasant farming.

These places have a chance to develop organic and low-input farming systems with produce that would find a ready market in the west. However, western aid funding and the agrochemical companies are pushing the development of the type of intensive agriculture that is gradually being abandoned, or at least severely modified, in the rest of Europe.

E Europe is an ecological disaster area in some respects. However, in other ways it has the potential to provide a reservoir of biodiversity that has long been destroyed in most W European countries. It is important that the 'help' coming from the west does not destroy the good in the process of trying to correct things that are wrong.

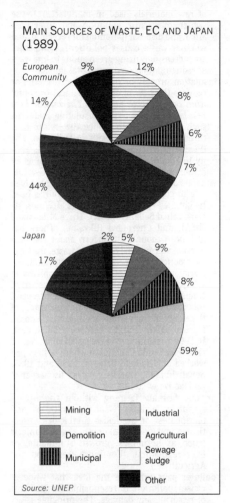

MAIN SOURCES OF WASTE, EC AND JAPAN (1989)

European Community

9% · 12% · 8% · 6% · 7% · 44% · 14%

Japan

2% · 5% · 9% · 8% · 59% · 17%

Mining — Industrial

Demolition — Agricultural

Municipal — Sewage sludge

Other

Source: UNEP

present hazards to health.

Pesticides were used to deforest SE Asia during the Vietnam War, causing death and destruction to the area's ecology and lasting health and agricultural problems.

In 1985, 400 different chemicals were approved in the UK for use as pesticides.

pollution the harmful effect on the environment of by-products of human activity, principally industrial and agricultural processes—for example noise, smoke, car emissions, chemical effluents in seas and rivers, pesticides, sewage, and household waste. Pollution contributes to the greenhouse effect.

Pollution control involves higher production costs for the industries concerned, but failure to implement adequate controls will result in further irreversible environmental damage and an increase in the incidence of diseases such as cancer.

In the UK 1987 air pollution caused by carbon monoxide emission from road transport was measured at 5.26 million tonnes. In Feb 1990 the UK had failed to apply 21 European Community Laws on air and water pollution and faced prosecution before the European Court of Justice on 31 of the 160 EC directives in force.

The existence of 1,300 toxic waste tips in the UK in 1990 posed a considerable threat of increased water pollution.

slurry form of manure composed mainly of liquids. Slurry is collected and stored on many farms, especially when large numbers of animals are kept in factory units. When slurry tanks are accidentally or deliberately breached, large amounts can spill into rivers, killing fish and causing eutrophication. Slurry pollution has increased dramatically in the UK in recent years.

Waldsterben (German 'forest death') tree dieback (disease where first the young shoots die, then the larger branches) related to air pollution, common throughout the industrialized world. It appears to be caused by a mixture of pollutants, and the precise chemical mix varies between locations, but it includes acid rain, ozone, sulphur dioxide, and nitrogen oxides.

Waldsterben was first noticed in the Black Forest of Germany during the late 1970s, and is spreading to many Third World countries, such as China. Despite initial hopes that Britain's trees had not been damaged, research has now shown them to be among the most badly affected in Europe.

waste materials that are no longer needed and are discarded. Examples are household waste, industrial waste (which often contains toxic chemicals), medical waste (which may contain organisms that cause disease), and nuclear waste (which is radioactive). By recycling, some waste materials can be reclaimed for further use.

There has been a tendency to increase the amount of waste generated per person in industrialized countries, particularly through the growth in disposable consumer products, creating a 'throwaway society'. In the USA, 40 tonnes of solid waste is generated annually per person. In Britain, the average person throws away about ten times their own body weight in household refuse each year.

water pollution any addition to fresh or sea water that disrupts biological processes or causes a health hazard. Common pollutants include nitrate, pesticides, and sewage, though a huge range of industrial contaminants also enter water—legally, accidentally, and through illegal dumping.

weedkiller or *herbicide* chemical that kills some or all plants. Selective herbicides are effective with cereal crops because they kill all broad-leaved plants without affecting grasslike leaves. Those that kill all plants include sodium chlorate and paraquat. The widespread use of weedkillers in agriculture has led to a dramatic increase in crop yield but also to pollution of soil and water supplies and killing birds and small animals, as well as creating a health hazard for humans.

ENVIRONMENTAL ISSUES

biodegradable capable of being broken down by living organisms, principally bacteria and fungi. Biodegradable substances, such as food and sewage, can therefore be rendered harmless by natural processes. The process of decay leads to compaction and liquefaction, and to the release of nutrients that are then recycled by the ecosystem. Nonbiodegradable substances, such as glass, heavy metals, and most types of plastic, present major problems of disposal.

catalytic converter device for reducing toxic emissions from the internal-combustion engine. It converts harmful exhaust products to relatively harmless ones by passing exhaust gases over a mixture of catalysts. *Oxidation catalysts* convert hydrocarbons into carbon dioxide and water; *three-way catalysts* convert oxides of nitrogen back into nitrogen. Catalytic converters are standard in the USA, where a 90% reduction in pollution from cars was achieved without loss of engine performance or fuel economy.

compost organic material decomposed by bacteria under controlled conditions to make a nutrient-rich natural fertilizer for use in gardening or farming. A well-made compost heap reaches a high temperature during the composting process, killing most weed seeds that might be present.

ecology the study of the relationship among organisms and the environments in which they live, including all living and nonliving components. The term was coined by the biologist Ernst Haeckel 1866.

Ecology may be concerned with individual organisms (for example, behavioural ecology, feeding strategies), with populations (for example, population dynamics), or with entire communities (for example, competition between species for access to resources in an ecosystem, or predator–prey relationships). A knowledge of ecology is essential in addressing many environmental problems, such as the consequences of pollution.

energy conservation methods of reducing energy use through insulation, increasing energy efficiency, and changes in patterns of use. Profligate energy use by industrialized countries contributes greatly to air pollution and the greenhouse effect when it draws on nonrenewable energy sources.

The average annual decrease in energy consumption in relation to gross national product 1973–87 was 1.2% in France, 2% in the UK, 2.1% in the USA, and 2.8% in Japan.

green audit inspection of a company's accounts to assess the total environmental impact of its activities or of a particular product or process.

For example, a green audit of a manufactured product looks at the impact of production (including energy use and the extraction of raw materials used in manufacture), use (which may cause pollution and other hazards), and disposal (potential for recycling, and whether waste causes pollution). Companies are increasingly using green audits to find ways of reducing their environmental impact.

insulation process or material that prevents or reduces the flow of electricity, heat or sound from one place to another. *Thermal* or *heat insulation* makes use of insulating materials such as fibreglass to reduce the loss of heat through the roof and walls of buildings. The U-value of a material is a measure of its ability to conduct heat—a material chosen as an insulator should therefore have a low U-value.

nuclear safety the use of nuclear energy has given rise to concern over safety. Anxiety has been heightened by accidents such as at Windscale (now called Sellafield) (UK), Three Mile Island (USA), and Chernobyl (Ukraine). There has also been mounting concern about the production and disposal of nuclear waste, the toxic by-products of the nuclear energy industry. Burial on land or at sea raises problems of safety, environmental pollution, and security. Nuclear waste may have an active life of several thousand years and there are no guarantees of the safety of the various methods of disposal. Nuclear safety is still a controversial subject. In 1990 a scientific study revealed an increased risk of leukemia in children whose fathers had worked at Sellafield between 1950 and 1985. Sellafield is the world's greatest discharger of radioactive waste.

organic farming farming without the use of synthetic fertilizers (such as nitrates and phosphates) or pesticides (herbicides, insecticides ,and fungicides) or other agrochemicals (such as hormones, growth stimulants, or fruit regulators). (For more, see Food and Agriculture.)

polluter pays principle the idea that whoever causes pollution is responsible for the cost of repairing any damage. The principle is accepted in British law but has in practice often been ignored; for example, farmers causing the death of fish through slurry pollution have not been fined the full costs of restocking the river.

recycling processing of industrial and household waste (such as paper, glass, and some metals and plastics) so that it can be reused, thus saving expenditure on scarce raw materials, slowing down the depletion of nonrenewable resources, and helping to reduce pollution.

Producing steel from scrap reduces energy

SOURCES OF MARINE POLLUTION

Source	All potential pollutants (%)
Land-based discharges	44.0
Atmospheric inputs	33.0
Marine transport	12.0
Dumping	10.0
Oil exploration/production	1.0

Source: The Times Guide to the Environment 1990

BIOSPHERE II: UNDER THREAT?

In May 1991, the largest ecological test project ever—a 'planet in a bottle'—got underway in the Arizona desert. Under a glass dome, a number of different habitats were recreated (tropical rainforest, salt marsh, desert, coral reef, and savanna, as well as a section for intensive agriculture), and representatives of nearly 4,000 species, including eight humans, were sealed in the biosphere for two years. The aim of the experiment was to see how effectively the recycling of air, water, and waste could work in an enclosed environment, and whether a stable ecosystem could be created (ultimately BSII is a prototype space colony). BSII is in fact not the second in a series: Earth itself is regarded as Biosphere I.

The cost of setting up and maintaining the project was estimated at $100 million, some of which will be covered by paying visitors, who can view the inhabitants through the geodesic glass dome.

The intention was for the biospherians to be entirely self-sufficient, except for electricity (provided by a 3.7-megawatt power station on the outside), and a computer link with the outside world. But the experiment's validity came into question in Nov 1991, when it was reported that BSII contained a device for cleansing air of carbon dioxide. A project spokeswoman conceded that the machine, installed shortly before the facility was occupied, was not 'natural', but was considered a minor aid in stabilizing the atmosphere during initial fluctuations in carbon dioxide. In Dec about 600,000 cubic feet of air, or 10% of the air in the glass and steel structure, was pumped in. Despite denials from the project's top systems engineer, the move was suspected to be a means of dealing with a rising carbon dioxide level and could be viewed as one which invalidates the test project.

---

consumption by 65%, air pollution by 85%, water pollution by 76%, and eliminates mining wastes. Making recycled paper cuts energy use by 25%–60%, air pollution by 74%, and water pollution by 35%. Recycling aluminium cuts energy use by 95%; recycling glass, by 33%.

reuse multiple use of a product (often forms of packaging), by returning it to the manufacturer or processor each time. Many such returnable items are sold with a deposit which is reimbursed if the item is returned. Reuse is usually more energy- and resource-efficient than recycling unless there are large transport or cleaning costs.

sewage disposal the disposal of human excreta and other waterborne waste products from houses, streets, and factories. Conveyed through sewers to sewage works, sewage has to undergo a series of treatments to be acceptable for discharge into rivers or

the sea, according to various local laws and ordinances.

In the industrialized countries of the West, most industries are responsible for disposing of their own wastes. Government agencies establish industrial waste-disposal standards. In most countries, sewage systems for residential areas are the responsibility of local authorities. The solid waste (sludge) may be spread over fields as a fertilizer or, in a few countries, dumped at sea.

Raw sewage, or sewage that has not been treated properly, is one serious source of water pollution and a cause of eutrophication. A significant proportion of bathing beaches in densely populated regions have unacceptably high bacterial content, largely as a result of untreated sewage being discharged into rivers and the sea.

The use of raw sewage as a fertilizer (long practised in China) has the drawback that disease-causing microorganisms can survive in the soil and be transferred to people or animals by consumption of subsequent crops. Sewage sludge is safer, but may contain dangerous levels of heavy metals and other industrial contaminants.

waste disposal methods used for getting rid of waste material. Methods of waste disposal vary according to the materials in the waste and include incineration, burial at designated sites, and dumping at sea. Organic waste can be treated and reused as fertilizer (see sewage disposal). Nuclear and toxic waste is usually buried or dumped at sea, which, while addressing the short-term disposal problem, creates a potential toxic 'time bomb' with long-term consequences for marine life.

Waste disposal is an ever-increasing problem. Environmental groups, such as Greenpeace and Friends of the Earth, are campaigning for more recycling, a change in life style so that less waste (from consumer packaging to nuclear materials) is produced, and for safer methods of disposal.

The industrial waste dumped every year by the UK in the North Sea includes 550,000 tonnes/541,310 tons of fly ash from coal-fired power stations. The British government agreed in 1989 to stop North Sea dumping from 1993, but dumping in the heavily polluted Irish Sea will continue. Industrial pollution is responsible for serious ecological damage, including an epidemic that killed hundreds of seals in 1989.

In 1987, Britain dumped more than 4,700 tonnes/4,626 tons of sewage sludge into the North Sea, and 4,200 tonnes/4,134 tons into the Irish Sea and other coastal areas. Also dumped in British coastal waters, other than the Irish Sea, were 6,462 tonnes/6,360 tons of zinc, 2,887 tonnes/2,841 tons of lead, 1,306 tonnes/1,285 tons of chromium, and 8 tonnes/7.8 tons of arsenic. Dumped into the Irish Sea were 916 tonnes/902 tons of zinc, 297 tonnes/298 tons of lead, 200 tonnes/197 tons of chromium, and 1 tonne/0.98 tons of arsenic.

TEN WAYS TO REDUCE DAMAGE TO THE ENVIRONMENT

1. Minimize use of your car, and travel by bike, bus or train instead.
2. Avoid aerosols where possible, and if you do use them, only choose those clearly marked 'ozone friendly'.
3. Do not buy tropical hardwood products, unless they are certified as coming from sustainably managed forests by an independent body.
4. Select the most energy-efficient electrical appliances you can find.
5. Save energy by draught-stripping and insulating your home.
6. Recycle waste paper, bottles, and aluminium cans, and compost all vegetable and garden waste.
7. Choose recycled paper products wherever possible.
8. Save water by having a shower instead of a bath, installing a dual flush toilet, and using a water butt for the garden.
9. Always buy organically grown food where it is available.
10. Avoid overconsumption.

WORKING TOWARDS A BETTER ENVIRONMENT

CITES abbreviation for *Convention on International Trade in Endangered Species*, an international convention founded in 1973 (under the auspices of the International Union for the Conservation of Nature) to regulate the trade in endangered species of animals and plants; it is signed by 81 countries. When voluntary codes such as CITES fail to stem the trade in particular species, national and international bans sometimes come into effect (for example those operated by the European Community on most whale products).

Council for the Protection of Rural England countryside conservation group with a brief that extends from planning controls to energy policy. A central organization campaigns on national issues and 42 local groups lobby on regional matters. The *Campaign for the Protection of Rural Wales* is the Welsh equivalent.

Countryside Council for Wales Welsh nature conservation body formed 1991 by the fusion of the Welsh office of the former Nature Conservancy Council and the Welsh Countryside Commission. It is government-funded and administers conservation and land-use policies within Wales.

Earth Summit official name of the United Nations Conference on Environment and Development that took place in Rio de Janeiro, Brazil in June 1992. (See feature in this section).

English Nature English nature conservation body formed 1991 after the break up of the national Nature Conservancy Council into separate bodies for England, Scotland, and Wales. It is government-funded and responsible for designating and managing national nature reserves and other conservation areas, advising government ministers on policies, providing advice and information, and commissioning or undertaking relevant scientific research.

Environmentally Sensitive Area (ESA) scheme introduced by the UK Ministry of Agriculture 1984, as a result of EC legislation, to protect some of the most beautiful areas of the British countryside from the loss and damage caused by agricultural change. The first areas to be designated ESAs are in the Pennine Dales, the North Peak District, the Norfolk Broads, the Breckland, the Suffolk River Valleys, the Test Valley, the South Downs, the Somerset Levels and Moors, West Penwith, Cornwall, the Shropshire Borders, the Cambrian Mountains, and the Lleyn Peninsula.

In these ESAs farmers are encouraged to use traditional methods to preserve the value of the land as a wildlife habitat. A farmer who joins the scheme agrees to manage the land in this way for at least five years. In return for this agreement, the Ministry of Agriculture pays the farmer a sum that reflects the financial losses incurred as a result of reconciling conservation with commercial farming.

Environmentally Sensitive Areas now amount to some 110,495 hectares, or 1% of England's farmland.

Environmental Protection Agency US agency set up 1970 to control water and air quality, industrial and commercial wastes, pesticides, noise, and radiation. In its own words, it aims to protect 'the country from being degraded, and its health threatened, by a multitude of human activities initiated without regard to long-ranging effects upon the life-supporting properties, the economic uses, and the recreational value of air, land, and water'.

Friends of the Earth (FoE or FOE) environmental pressure group, established in the UK 1971, that aims to protect the environment and to promote rational and sustainable use of the Earth's resources. It campaigns on issues such as acid rain; air, sea, river, and land pollution; recycling; disposal of toxic wastes; nuclear power and renewable energy; the destruction of rainforests; pesticides; and agriculture. FoE has branches in 30 countries.

Gaia hypothesis theory that the Earth's living and nonliving systems form an inseparable whole that is regulated and kept adapted for life by living organisms themselves. The planet therefore functions as a single organism, or a giant cell. Since life and environment are so closely linked, there is a need for humans to understand and maintain the physical environment and living things around them. The Gaia hypothesis was elaborated by James Lovelock in the 1970s.

Green Party political party aiming to 'preserve the planet and its people', based on the premise that incessant economic growth is unsustainable. The leaderless party structure reflects a general commitment to decentralization. Green parties

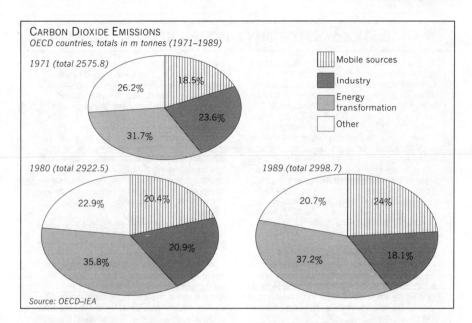

CARBON DIOXIDE EMISSIONS
OECD countries, totals in m tonnes (1971–1989)

1971 (total 2575.8)
26.2%
18.5%
23.6%
31.7%

Mobile sources
Industry
Energy transformation
Other

1980 (total 2922.5)
22.9%
20.4%
20.9%
35.8%

1989 (total 2998.7)
20.7%
24%
18.1%
37.2%

Source: OECD–IEA

sprang up in W Europe in the 1970s and in E Europe from 1988. Parties in different countries are linked to one another but unaffiliated to any pressure group. They had a number of parliamentary seats in 1989: Austria 8, Belgium 11, Finland 4, Italy 20, Luxembourg 2, Republic of Ireland 1, Sweden 20, Switzerland 9, West Germany 42; and 24 members of the European Parliament (Belgium 3, France 9, Italy 3, Portugal 1, West Germany 8).

Greenpeace international environmental pressure group, founded 1971, with a policy of nonviolent direct action backed by scientific research. During a protest against French atmospheric nuclear testing in the S Pacific 1985, its ship *Rainbow Warrior* was sunk by French intelligence agents, killing a crew member.

Henry Doubleday Research Association gardening group founded by Lawrence Hills to investigate organic growing techniques. It runs the *National Centre for Organic Gardening*, a 22-acre demonstration site, at Ryton on Dunsmore near Coventry, England. The association is named after the man who first imported Russian comfrey, a popular green manuring crop.

International Union for the Conservation of Nature (IUCN) an organization established by the United Nations to promote the conservation of wildlife and habitats as part of the national policies of member states. It has formulated guidelines and established research programmes (such as the International Biological Programme, IBP), and set up advisory bodies (such as Survival Services Commission, SSC). In 1980 it launched the *World Conservation Strategy* to highlight particular problems, designating a small number of areas as *World Heritage Sites* to ensure their survival

as unspoilt habitats (for example, Yosemite National Park in the USA, and the Simen Mountains in Ethiopia). This was followed in 1991 by the publication *Caring for the Earth*.

Montréal Protocol international agreement, signed 1987, to reduce production of ozone-depleting chemicals (see ozone depleters in Enviromental Pollutants section) by 35% by 1999 and thus protect the ozone layer. The protocol (under the Vienna Convention for the Protection of the Ozone Layer) was scheduled for review in 1992. The green movement criticized the agreement as inadequate, arguing that an 85% reduction in ozone depleters would be necessary just to stabilize the ozone layer at 1987 levels.

National Rivers Authority UK environmental agency launched Sept 1989. It is responsible for managing water resources, investigating pollution controls, and taking over flood controls and land drainage from the former ten regional water authorities of England and Wales.

National Trust British trust founded 1895 for the preservation of land and buildings of historic interest or beauty, incorporated by Act of Parliament 1907. It is the largest private landowner in Britain. The National Trust for Scotland was established 1931.

Natural Environment Research Council (NERC) UK organization established by royal charter 1965 to undertake and support research in the earth sciences, to give advice both on exploiting natural resources and on protecting the environment, and to support education and training of scientists in these fields of study. Research areas include geothermal energy, industrial pollution, waste disposal, satellite surveying, acid rain, biotechnology, atmospheric circulation, and climate. Research is carried out principally within the UK but also in

IS AIR TRAVEL ENVIRONMENTALLY UNACCEPTABLE?

Air travel is one of the world's fastest-growing energy users, and it is also potentially one of our most environmentally damaging activities. Although the environmental impact of aircraft is generally equated with the problems of noise and perhaps with fuel consumption, it now seems likely that the most significant impact is the effect that airliners and military aircraft have on the ozone layer, and on global warming.

The ozone layer is a thin but vital gaseous layer in the upper atmosphere (stratosphere), which helps prevent harmful solar radiation from reaching the Earth. It is currently thinning in places, owing to the effects of several chemically stable pollutants that reach the stratosphere and destroy ozone molecules. Global warming is a complex series of known and suspected climatic effects that are occurring because a greater amount of solar heat is being trapped inside the Earth's atmosphere as a result of increased levels of pollutants, including carbon dioxide, methane, and nitrogen oxides. These problems are still by no means fully understood.

Flying is now seen as virtually indispensable for many people in the wealthy countries of the North, and for the rich minority in the South. In 1989, scheduled services carried more than one billion passengers worldwide, with about a quarter of the flights being international. Over the past five years, passenger numbers have increased by 5% a year on average, with a proportionately greater increase in international flights. The main reasons for air travel differ between countries, but holidays and pleasure trips make up an increasing proportion of journeys in the richest countries. In the UK, for example, only about 20% of 1989 flights were for business, with the remainder being divided between package holidays (38%), other holidays, visiting relatives, and so on. Flying is the standard way of getting around countries where internal distances are especially large, such as the USA, Australia, and the European Community. The International Civil Aviation Authority expects this rate of increase to continue for some time, which means that the demand for air transport would approximately double by 2005.

In general, pollution emissions from aircraft form a relatively small proportion of total global pollution levels.

However, the pollutants are released at very high altitudes, and thus injected directly into the stratosphere, where they may do more harm. Pollutants persist longer at high altitudes than they do near the ground, and some important atmospheric chemical reactions, such as ozone formation, occur in the stratosphere.

The impact that aircraft could have on ozone is complex, and varies with a number of factors, including altitude. At medium altitudes (the troposphere), the nitrogen oxide (NOx) emissions from aircraft could help *produce* ozone, which, at that height above the planet's surface, has a significant global-warming potential.

However, in the stratosphere NOx could have the opposite effect—*destroying* ozone. In addition, high-level clouds could be formed in part by water emissions from aircraft.

Both these factors would help increase the net influx of radiation and thus in turn increase global warming. Stratospheric ozone loss has a number of other detrimental effects, including causing skin cancer and eye cataracts.

Despite the potential seriousness of the problem, there has been comparatively little detailed research on the impact of aircraft on global warming. The various different effects make firm predictions even more difficult than is usually the case in atmospheric chemistry. A report published by the World Wide Fund for Nature (WWF) in 1991 suggested that the contribution made by aircraft to global warming could be anything between 2% and 43% of the total. This means that the global-warming potential of aircraft may be anything from small but significant to so large that up to a quarter of our efforts at reducing global warming should be directed at aircraft.

That said, it is difficult to see what can be done to reduce the impact in the short term except to persuade people to cut down on air travel. The development of high-speed trains and other improved forms of land transport, as well as the increasing sophistication of communication networks, could help reduce business travel in the future. But with the bulk of travel being for pleasure in many countries, pleas for a reduction in flying are likely to meet with entrenched opposition. Future research will show how important air transport really is in terms of global warming. If the pessimistic figures are correct, a major rethink of air-transport costs and availability seems inevitable.

interest by one of the regional bodies of the UK government's Nature Conservancy Council. Numbers fluctuate, but there were over 5,000 SSSIs in 1991, covering about 6% of Britain. Although SSSIs enjoy some legal protection, this does not in practice always prevent damage or destruction; during 1989, for example, 44 SSSIs were so badly damaged that they were no longer worth protecting.

Soil Association the foremost UK organization promoting organic agriculture as a healthier alternative for consumers and producers. Established in 1946, its objectives are to research, develop, and promote sustainable relationships between the soil, plants, animals, people, and the biosphere, with the goal of producing healthier food and improving the environment. It also sets the Standards for Organic Agriculture; administers and monitors the Symbol Scheme (the Symbol is a quality mark for organically grown food); researches and publishes findings on organic issues; lobbies the government for changes in agriculture; and promotes educational programmes for the general public on organic farming.

World Wide Fund for Nature (WWF, formerly the *World Wildlife Fund*) international organization established 1961 to raise funds for conservation by public appeal. Its headquarters are in Gland, Switzerland. Projects include conservation of particular species, for example, the tiger and giant panda, and of special areas.

Suppose your family's regular washing powder cost £3 per packet but there is concern about its effect on the environment. How much would you be prepared to pay for an environmentally-friendly powder?

£3.10	16
£3.50	27
£4.00	21
Nothing extra	35

Coal and gas power stations contribute to the greenhouse effect, and atmospheric pollution would be reduced if we used less electricity generated by this method. Would you be willing to:

Pay more for cleaner ways to generate electricity	50
Endure daily rationing to reduce pollution	17
Could not face cuts at all	23
Don't know	12

Science has brought us vast benefits, ranging from longer life to global communications to labour-saving devices. But would you give all this up to be in a truly natural world that is free from man-made radiation and pollution?

Yes, definitely	21
Yes, probably	20
Not sure	23
No, probably not	21
No, definitely not	14
Don't know	0

Roads and the environment

In building roads it sometimes happens that roads have to be built through or across sites of natural beauty or historical interest. Some people say the roads could be rerouted, or built through tunnels, but usually at extra cost and time. What do you think is more important: to protect the sites, to pay more for the roads, or to let the roads be built through the areas as originally planned?

Protect sites	75
Go through as planned	12
Don't know/other reply	13

FOOD AND DRINK

beer alcoholic drink made from fermented malt (germinating barley or other grain) and water, flavoured with hops. It contains between 1% and 6% alcohol. The medieval distinction between beer (containing hops) and *ale* (without hops) has now fallen into disuse and beer has come to be used strictly as a generic term including ale, stout, and lager. *Stout* is a sweet, dark beer, fermented at the top of the brewing vessel and strongly flavoured with roasted grain; *lager* is a light beer, bottom fermented and matured over a longer period.

biscuit a small, flat, brittle cake of baked dough. The basic components of biscuit dough are weak flour and fat. Other ingredients such as eggs, sugar, nuts, chocolate, dried fruit, and spices may be added to vary the flavour and texture. Originally made from slices of unleavened bread baked until hard and dry, biscuits could be stored for several years, and were a useful, though dull, source of carbohydrate on long sea voyages and military campaigns. The first biscuit factory opened in Carlisle, northern England, in 1815. The UK is Europe's largest producer and consumer of factory-made biscuits.

bread food baked from a dough of flour, liquid (water or milk) and salt. Many other ingredients may be added to vary the flavour or texture. The dough may be leavened (raised, usually by the action of yeast) or unleavened. Bread has been a staple of human diet in many civilizations as long as agriculture has been practised. Potato, banana, and cassava bread are among some local varieties, but most breads are made from cereals such as wheat, barley, rye, and oats, which form elastic proteins called glutens when mixed with water. Traditionally bread has been made from whole grains, which were ground into a rough meal. White bread was developed by the end of the 19th century by roller-milling, which removed the wheat germ and produced a fine flour to satisfy fashionable consumer demand. In modern manufacturing processes, fermentation is speeded up using ascorbic acid (vitamin C) and potassium bromide, with fast-acting flour improvers. Today, some of the nutrients removed in the processing of bread are synthetically replaced.

bulghur wheat or *bulgar* or *burghul* cracked wholewheat, made by cooking the grains, then drying and cracking them. It is widely eaten in the Middle East. Coarser bulghur may be cooked in the same way as rice; more finely ground bulghur is mixed with minced meat to make a paste that may be eaten as a dip with salad, or shaped and stuffed before being grilled or fried.

butter solid yellowish fat made by churning cream. It is usually salted. In the UK, butter typically consists of about 82% fat,

0.4% protein, and up to 16% water; it contains 1,300 micrograms of vitamin A per 100 g/3.5 oz in summer, and 500 micrograms per 100 g/3.5 oz in winter.

cake a baked food item made from a mixture of weak flour, sugar, eggs, and fat (usually butter or margarine). Other ingredients such as nuts, chocolate, and fresh or dried fruits can be added, and pastry is sometimes used as a base. Cakes may be eaten to celebrate occasions such as birthdays or weddings, and a specific type of cake is often associated with a particular event—for example, heavy fruit cakes covered with marzipan and icing that are traditionally eaten at Christmas. Easter cakes include the fruited simnel cake and the pyramid-shaped Russian *pashka*, made from sweetened curd cheese and filled with dried fruit and nuts. The UK is Europe's biggest producer of factory-made cakes.

cereal, breakfast food prepared from the seeds of cereal crops. Breakfast cereals fall into two groups: those that require cooking (oats, cooked in milk to make porridge); and ready-to-eat cereals. The second group accounts for the major share of the market; it includes refined and sweetened varieties as well as whole cereals such as muesli. Whole cereals are more nutritious and provide more fibre than the refined cereals, which often have vitamins and flavourings added to replace those lost in the refining process.

cheese food made from the curds (solids) of soured milk from cows, sheep, or goats, separated from the whey (liquid), then salted, put into moulds, and pressed into firm blocks. Cheese is ripened with bacteria or surface fungi, and kept for a time to mature before being eaten.

Soft cheeses may be ripe or unripe, and include the low-fat cottage cheese, fromage frais, and quark, and the high-fat soft cheeses such as Bel Paese, Camembert, and Neufchâtel.

Semi-hard cheeses are ripened by bacteria (Munster) or by bacteria and surface fungi (Port-Salut, St Paulin, and Gouda); they may also have penicillin moulds injected into them (Roquefort, Gorgonzola, Blue Stilton, and Wensleydale).

Hard cheeses are ripened by bacteria, for example Cheddar, Cheshire, and Caciocavallo; some have large holes in them (Emmental and Gruyère).

Very hard cheeses, such as Parmesan and Spalen, are made with skimmed milk.

Processed cheese is made with dried skimmed milk powder and additives.

Whey cheese is made by heat coagulation of the proteins from whey; examples are Mysost and Primost.

In France (from 1980) cheese has the same *appellation contrôlée* status as wine if it is made only in a special defined area—for example, Cantal and Roquefort are *appellation contrôlée* cheeses, but not Camembert and Brie, which are made in more than one region.

COMPOSITION OF CHEESES

cheese	fat (%)	protein (%)	calcium (mg/100g)	salt (mg/100g)	(Kcal/100g)
Cheddar	32.2	25	750	700	398
Roquefort	31.5	21.5	315	–	368
Camembert	minimum 26.0	17.5	105	–	299
Emmental	28.0	27.5	925	710	370
processed	28.0	25	850	1,150	360
cottage	0.3	17	90	290	86

cider a fermented drink made from the juice of the apple; in the USA the term cider usually refers to unfermented (non-alcoholic) apple juice. Cider has been made for more than 2,000 years, and for many centuries has been a popular drink in France and England, which are now its main centres of production.

A similar drink, *perry*, is made from the fermented juice of sour pears. It is produced commercially in France, Germany, and SW England.

cocoa and chocolate food products made from the cacao (or cocoa) bean, fruit of a tropical tree *Theobroma cacao*, native to Central America but now cultivated mainly in W Africa. Chocolate as a drink was introduced to Europe from the New World by the Spanish in the 16th century; solid chocolate was first produced in the late 18th century.

Preparation takes place in the importing country and consists chiefly of roasting, winnowing and grinding the nib (the edible portion of the bean) to form a thick paste consisting of cocoa solids and fat (cocoa butter). If *cocoa* for drinking is required, a proportion of the cocoa butter is removed by hydraulic pressure and the remaining cocoa is reduced by further grinding and sieving to a fine powder. *Plain chocolate* is made by removing some of the cocoa butter and adding a little sugar. It is dark, with a slightly bitter flavour. *Milk chocolate* is sweeter and made by adding condensed or powdered milk and a larger amount of sugar. In the UK cheaper vegetable fats are widely substituted for milk and chocolate need contain only 20% cocoa solids. *White chocolate* contains cocoa butter but no cocoa solids, and is flavoured with sugar and vanilla.

coffee beverage made by infusing the roasted and ground beanlike seeds of evergreen shrubs of the genus *Coffea*. It contains a stimulant, caffeine. Coffee drinking began in Arab regions in the 14th century but did not become common in Europe until 300 years later, when the first coffee houses were opened in Vienna, and soon after in Paris and London. The world's largest producers of coffee are Brazil, Colombia, and the Ivory Coast; others include Indonesia (Java), Ethiopia, India, Hawaii, and Jamaica.

The flavour of coffee beans depends on the variety grown, the location of the plantation, and the manner in which the beans were processed—for example, *Arabica* beans, grown at high altitudes, are considered finer than the cheaper *Robusta* and *Liberian* varieties.

Manufacturers, therefore, blend beans from a number of sources in order to achieve a consistent product.

cream the part of milk that has the highest fat content; it can be separated by centrifugation or gravity (if milk is left to stand, the upper layer will be cream, the lower layer skimmed milk). If cream is to be whipped successfully, it must contain at least 30% fat. In the UK, *single cream* has a fat content of 18%; the thicker *double cream* has a fat content of 48%. *Clotted cream* is made by scalding double cream and skimming off the yellow crust produced. It should contain 55% fat and 4% protein.

egg the shell-covered egg of a domestic chicken, duck, or goose, or of a game bird such as quail. It is a highly nutritious food: the albumin, or egg white, of a chicken's egg is 10% protein; the yolk is 33% fat and 15% protein, and contains vitamins A, B, and D. The yolk also contains cholesterol, a fatty substance associated with heart disease in humans.

Eggs have many uses in cooking. They can be used for thickening sauces, binding and coating crumbly foods, and for raising batters and cakes; whisked egg white gives a foamy texture to soufflés and desserts; and yolk acts as an emulsifier, keeping oil in suspension in mixtures such as mayonnaise.

fish the flesh or roe (eggs) of freshwater or saltwater fish. The nutritional composition of fish is similar to that of meat, although the fat content is generally lower and most of the fat takes the form of polyunsaturated oil. Oily fish have a fat content of 8–20%, and include salmon, mackerel, and herring. White fish such as cod, haddock, and whiting contain only 0.4–4% fat. Fish are good sources of vitamin B and iodine, and extracts from the livers of fatty fish are used commercially as sources of vitamins A and D.

flour foodstuff made by grinding starchy vegetable materials, usually cereal grains, into a fine powder. Flour may also be made from root vegetables such as potato and cassava, and from pulses such as soya beans and chick peas. The most commonly used cereal flour is *wheat flour*. It may contain varying proportions of bran (husk) and wheatgerm (embryo), ranging from 100% wholemeal flour to refined white flour, which has less than 75% of the whole grain. *Granary flour* contains malted flakes of wheat. The properties of flour depend on the strain of wheat used. Bread requires strong ('hard') flour with a high gluten content (gluten is a protein that enables the dough to stretch during rising).

Trends in Food Consumption (UK, 1986–1990)

kg per capita per year	1986	1987	1988	1989	1990
Liquid wholemilk (litres)	87.02	82.66	77.05	70.25	62.62
Skimmed milk (litres)	20.76	23.12	27.33	32.43	36.92
Cream	0.74	0.89	0.74	0.96	0.59
Yoghurt	4.14	4.21	4.58	4.80	5.02
Cheese, natural	5.75	5.61	5.66	5.54	5.45
Eggs (number)	156	150	139	119	114
Beef & veal	9.70	9.98	9.37	8.89	7.72
Mutton & lamb	4.44	3.91	4.10	4.41	4.30
Pork	5.36	4.67	4.86	4.64	4.38
Bacon & ham, uncooked	5.44	5.11	5.13	4.93	4.45
Broiler chicken, uncooked	7.11	7.47	7.50	7.24	7.56
Poultry uncooked incl. frozen	10.19	11.32	11.09	10.77	3.39
White fish	1.53	1.37	1.44	1.38	2.27
Frozen convenience fish products	1.52	1.42	1.06	1.50	1.44
Butter	3.34	3.16	2.94	2.59	2.37
Margarine	6.04	5.86	5.59	5.12	4.70
Sugar	11.86	11.03	10.23	9.52	8.90
Potatoes	57.15	54.29	53.71	52.46	51.85
Cabbages, fresh	5.35	5.08	4.79	4.61	4.35
Brussel sprouts, fresh	2.06	1.75	1.75	1.51	1.46
Canned veg. excl. pulses, potatoes, tomatoes	1.80	1.73	1.70	1.56	1.56
Frozen chips/potato products	3.53	3.87	3.97	4.15	3.80
Oranges, fresh	4.56	3.98	4.61	4.41	4.16
Grapes	0.93	1.00	1.26	1.19	1.22
Bananas, fresh	4.51	4.73	5.28	5.90	6.47
Canned peaches, pears, pineapples	1.74	1.67	1.63	1.64	1.43
White bread	24.38	23.61	22.93	22.60	21.76
Brown bread	5.57	5.40	5.75	5.39	5.09
Wholewheat & wholemeal bread	7.95	6.98	6.39	6.06	5.63
Flour	6.10	5.80	5.29	4.83	4.70
Rice	1.30	1.71	1.33	1.57	1.49
Tea	2.57	2.52	2.43	2.37	2.24
Coffee, bean & ground	0.24	0.21	0.23	0.21	0.21
Coffee, instant	0.81	0.77	0.77	0.74	0.71
Mineral water (litres)	0.77	1.11	1.34	2.74	2.89
Ice-cream, mousse (litres)	4.55	4.64	4.69	4.86	4.88
Salt	1.00	0.84	0.74	0.64	0.62

Source: Lifestyle Pocket Book 1992/NTC

Durum flour also has a high gluten content, and is used for pasta. Cakes and biscuits are made from weak ('soft') flour containing less gluten. Much of the flour available now is bleached to whiten it; bleaching also destroys some of its vitamin content, so synthetic vitamins are added to replace them.

fruit in botany, the ripened ovary of a flower, including the seeds that it encloses; in popular terms, a fruit is any sweet, fleshy plant item, such as an orange, strawberry, or rhubarb stalk. The latter definition excludes many true botanical fruits such as tomatoes, cucumbers, and wheat grains. When eaten, fruits provide energy, fibre, vitamins, minerals, and enzymes, but little protein.

Broadly, fruits are divided into three agricultural categories on the basis of the climate in which they grow. **Temperate fruits** require a cold season for satisfactory growth. In order of abundance, these include, apples, pears, plums, peaches, apricots, cherries, and soft fruits, such as raspberries and strawberries. **Subtropical fruits** require warm conditions but can survive light frosts; they include oranges and other citrus fruits, dates, pomegranates, and avocados. **Tropical fruits** cannot tolerate temperatures that drop close to freezing point; they include bananas, mangoes, pineapples, papayas, and litchis. Technical advances in storage and transport have made tropical fruits available to consumers in temperate areas, and fresh temperate fruits available all year in major markets.

fruit juice juice extracted from fruits, either by pressing (citrus fruits), or by spinning at high speeds in a centrifuge (other fruits). Although fruit juice provides no fibre, its nutritional value is close to that of the whole fruit. The most widely used juices are orange, apple, grapefruit, pineapple, and tomato. Most fruit juices are transported in concentrated form, and are diluted and pasteurized before being packaged. Concentrated juices may be used as sweeteners in cooking.

herb any plant with a distinctive smell or taste, used in flavouring food, in medicine, or in perfumery. Most herbs are temperate plants; they include bay, thyme, borage, mint, chives, and tarragon. Their leaves and stems release aromatic oils on being crushed, chopped, or heated, and may be used fresh, dried, or freeze-dried.

honey sweet syrup produced by honey bees from the nectar of flowers. It is stored in honey-combs and made in excess of their needs as food for the winter. Honey comprises various sugars, mainly fructose and glucose, with enzymes, colouring matter, acids, and pollen grains. It has antibacterial properties and was widely used in ancient Egypt, Greece, and Rome as a wound salve.

ice cream rich, creamy, frozen confectionery, made commercially from the early 20th century from various milk products, sugar, and fruit and nut flavourings, usually with additives to improve keeping qualities and ease of serving. In the UK, the sale is permitted of ice cream made with 'non-milk' animal or vegetable fat. Water ices and sorbets are frozen fruit juices and do not contain milk or cream. Sherbet is a frozen dessert of watered fruit juice, egg white, and sugar, like an ice, but with gelatin and milk added.

lard the melted and clarified edible fat of pigs. It can be heated to very high temperatures without burning.

liqueur alcoholic liquor made by infusing flavouring substances (fruits, herbs, spices) in alcohol. For example, crème de cassis is an infusion of blackcurrants in rum, and maraschino is an infusion of cherries in brandy. Specific recipes are closely guarded commercial secrets. Originally liqueurs were used as medicines and are still thought of as aids to digestion.

margarine butter substitute made from animal fats and/or vegetable oils. The French chemist Hippolyte Mège-Mouries invented margarine in 1889. Today, margarines are usually made with vegetable oils, such as soy, corn (maize), or sunflower oil, giving a product low in saturated fats, and fortified with vitamins A and D.

meat flesh of animals taken as food; in Western countries, it is chiefly provided by the muscle tissue of domesticated cattle (beef and veal), sheep (lamb and mutton), pigs (pork), and poultry. Beef, lamb, and mutton are termed **red meats**; poultry, pork, and veal are termed **white meats**. Meat has a high protein content and is a good source of B-vitamins and iron; its fat tends to have a high proportion of saturated fatty acids. Major exporters include Argentina, Australia, New Zealand, Canada, the USA, and Denmark (chiefly bacon). The practice of cooking meat is at least 600,000 years old. More than 40% of the world's grain is now fed to animals intended for meat consumption. **Game** is meat obtained from wild animals and birds, such as deer, hare, grouse, pheasant, and wild duck. It has a stronger flavour than that of farm-reared animals, and is thought to be less easy to digest. Before being cooked, therefore, it is stored suspended ('hung') in a cool place to make it more tender. At one time, game was hung until it was almost rotten ('high'), but it is now stored for a shorter period (2–8 days). **Offal** comprises the edible internal organs of an animal, and also its head, feet, tail, tongue, and bone marrow. It is generally cheaper than other meats.

Meat substitutes include textured vegetable protein (TVP), usually made from soya beans, and Quorn (developed by Rank Hovis McDougall), which is made from mycoprotein, a tiny relative of mushrooms that grows prolifically in culture. Both are rich in protein and low in fat.

milk the secretion of the mammary glands of female mammals, with which they suckle their young (during lactation). Over 85% is water, the remainder comprising protein, fat, lactose (a sugar), calcium, phosphorus, iron, and vitamins. The milk of cows, goats, and sheep is often consumed by humans, but only Western societies drink milk after infancy; for people in most of the world, milk causes flatulence and diarrhoea. Milk composition varies among species; human milk contains less protein and more lactose than that of cows. **Skimmed milk** is what remains when the cream has been separated from milk. It is readily dried. **Semi-skimmed milk** is milk from which just over half of the cream has been removed. **Evaporated milk** is milk reduced by heat until it reaches about half its volume. **Condensed milk** is concentrated to about a third of its original volume with added sugar.

Composition Of Milks

source	protein (g/100ml)	fat (g/100 ml)	carbohydrate (g/100ml)	energy (Kcal/100 ml)
cow	3.5	3.5	5.0	65
buffalo	4.3	7.5	4.5	105
camel	3.7	4.2	4.0	70
ewe	6.5	7.0	5.0	110
goat	3.7	5.0	4.5	75
mare	1.3	1.2	5.5	30
reindeer	10.5	22.5	2.5	250
human	1.1	6.2	7.5	70

mineral water water with mineral constituents gathered from the rocks with which it comes in contact, and bottled at source. Some mineral waters are naturally sparkling; others are artificially carbonated with carbon dioxide under pressure. Fears about the quality of tap water in many areas of the UK contributed to the greatly increased sales of mineral water from the 1980s.

The most widely sold mineral water in the UK is Perrier, from the French village of Vergèze in W Provence. It is naturally carbonated, but the gas is removed at source and then used to recarbonate the water during bottling. In 1990 minute traces of benzene, a cancer-causing chemical, were found in samples of Perrier, and 160 million bottles were recalled. Production was resumed once charcoal filters at the bottling plant had been replaced.

mushroom the fruiting body of certain fungi, consisting of an upright stem and a spore-producing cap with radiating gills on the undersurface. Many species are inedible or even poisonous. Cultivated edible mushrooms are usually species of the genus *Agaricus*. Edible wild, or field, mushrooms include the cep *Boletus edulis*, the chanterelle *Cantharellus cibarius*, and the horn of plenty *Cratellus cornicupoides*, all woodland species; and the horse mushroom *Agaricus arvensis* and shaggy ink cap *Coprinus comatus*, found in grassland. The most prized mushrooms are truffles (various species of *Tuber*), which fruit underground, and morels (species of *Morchella*).

mustard a strong-tasting condiment made from the whole, crushed, or ground seeds of the black, brown, or white mustard plants. Its main use is as an accompaniment for meat, though it can also be used in sauces and dressings, and with fish. English mustard is made from finely ground black and white mustard seed mixed with turmeric. French Dijon mustard contains black and brown mustard seed, verjuice (the juice of unripe grapes), oil, and white wine. Other varieties are made with vinegar, and may be flavoured with herbs or garlic.

nut in botany, a dry, single-seeded fruit; commonly, an edible seed or fruit with a woody shell, such as a coconut, almond, walnut, peanut (groundnut), Brazil nut, or hazel nut. The edible parts of most nuts provide a concentrated, nutritious food, containing vitamins, minerals, and enzymes, about 50% fat, and 10–20% protein, although a few, such as chestnuts, are high in carbohydrates and have only a moderate protein content of 5%. Nuts also provide edible oils.

oil, cooking a fat that is liquid at room temperature, extracted from the seeds or fruits of certain plants and used for frying, salad dressings, and sauces and condiments such as mayonnaise and mustard. Plants used for cooking oil include sunflower, olive, maize (corn), soya, peanut, and rape. Vegetable oil is a blend of more than one type of oil. Most oils are hot pressed and refined, a process that leaves them without smell or flavour. Cold-pressed, unrefined oils keep their flavour. Oils are generally low in cholesterol and contain a high proportion of polyunsaturated or monounsaturated fatty acids, although all except soya and corn oil become saturated when heated.

pasta food made from a dough of durum-wheat flour or semolina, water, and, sometimes, egg, and cooked in boiling water. It is usually served with a sauce. Pasta is creamy-yellow in colour, but may be coloured green with spinach, or red with tomato. It is available either fresh or dried, and comes in a wide variety of shapes: in narrow strands (spaghetti, vermicelli), flat or in ribbons (lasagne, tagliatelle, fettucine), shell-shaped (conchiglie, lumache), butterfly-shaped (farfalle), tubular (cannelloni, macaroni, penne), and twisted (fusilli). Some varieties are sold ready stuffed with a meat, cheese, herb, or vegetable filling (ravioli, agnolotti, tortellini).

pastry a baked dough made from flour, fat, water, and salt. It makes a useful base or container for soft, moist fillings, and is widely used for tarts, pies, quiches, and pasties. Richer pastries may include eggs, yeast, or sugar. Types include: short pastry, flaked pastries, suet crust, filo, choux. **Puff pastry** is made with a higher proportion of fat. Its preparation involves repeated folding, which, with the fat, makes it flaky.

pepper hot, aromatic spice derived from the berry of the climbing plant *Piper nigrum*, native to the E Indies. The dried berries (corns) may be crushed or ground to release their flavour, or may be used whole. Green peppercorns are berries that have been harvested while unripe, and dried or canned; black peppercorns are unripe berries that have been left to darken and shrivel in the Sun; and white peppercorns are dried ripe berries that have had their outer husks removed. Black peppercorns are hotter but less aromatic than white peppercorns. The mild pink peppercorns that became fashionable in the 1980s are the fruits of a different plant, a member of the poison ivy family.

potato the tuberous root of the perennial plant *Solanum tuberosum*, native to the Andes of South America. One of the most versatile of foods, the potato is cultivated in many varieties, particularly in temperate regions. It is a good source of carbohydate, fibre, and vitamin C, and also contains some protein, phosphates, and iron. The unrelated *sweet potato*, native to tropical America, has a sweet, orange or yellow flesh, and is rich in vitamin A.

Potato varieties can be grouped according to when their tubers mature: *new* or *early potatoes* are gathered in the spring and summer, are generally small and waxy, and are suitable for boiling in their skins and canning; the larger *maincrop potatoes* are lifted in the autumn, are more floury in texture,

Average Daily Energy Requirements (Kcal/day)

	Light activity	Moderate activity	Heavy activity
Men	2,015	2,314	2,730
Women	2,496	2,624	2,912

and are suitable for mashing and baking, and for commercial processing into products such as frozen chips, crisps and snacks, and potato flour.

pulse dried seed, such as a pea, bean, or lentil, gathered from the pod of a leguminous plant. Pulses provide a concentrated source of vegetable protein, and make a vital contribution to the diet in countries where meat is scarce, and among vegetarians.

Soya beans are the major temperate protein crop in the West; most are used for oil production or for animal feed. In Asia, most are processed into soya milk and tofu (beancurd). *Miso* is soya beans fermented with cereal grains, water, and salt, used in soups and sauces; soya sauce is beans fermented with salt; *tamari* is similar to soya sauce but stronger, having been matured for up to two years. *Peanuts* (groundnuts), which are not true nuts but pulses grown in underground pods, dominate pulse production in the tropical world. They yield a valuable oil and form the basis for numerous processed foods, such as peanut butter. Canned *baked beans* are usually a variety of haricot bean.

rice grain of *Oryza sativa*, the principal cereal of the wet regions of the tropics, but grown also in the Po valley of Italy, and in the USA in Louisiana, the Carolinas, and California. Boiled or ground into flour, it forms the staple food of one-third of the world population. It is rich in carbohydrate and contains 8–9% protein. Brown rice (rice that has not been husked) has valuable B-vitamins that are lost in husking, or polishing. Most of the rice eaten in the world is, however, sold in polished form.

salt, common or *sodium chloride* NaCl white crystalline solid, found dissolved in sea water and as rock salt (halite) in large deposits and salt domes. It is used extensively in the food industry as a preservative and for flavouring. While common salt is an essential part of our diet, some medical experts believe that excess salt can lead to high blood pressure and increased risk of heart attacks.

sauce a liquid used in cooking or served with food to add to its flavour. Sauces may be thick or thin, hot or cold, sweet or savoury. There are sauces suitable for serving with almost any dish, ranging from the simplest vinaigrette, a cold mixture of oil, vinegar, and seasonings, to cooked sauces containing cream, wine, egg yolks, or herbs.

shellfish common name for any aquatic invertebrate with a shell, including both molluscs and crustaceans. Many species are eaten, including oyster, scallop, crab, lobster, shrimp, mussel, and clam. Shellfish are high in protein and minerals. They do not keep well, and should only be used if known to be fresh. They become tough if overcooked; some are eaten raw.

soft drink a non-alcoholic drink, usually sweetened. Soft drinks may be carbonated (made fizzy by the introduction of carbon dioxide under pressure), as in lemonade, ginger ale, and tonic water. Many fruit-flavoured drinks contain no fruit, consisting only of water, sugar or artificial sweetener, and synthetic flavourings. In the UK, undiluted fruit squash must contain stipulated amounts of fruit or of fruit juice. In 1990, the British public drank 4.1 billion litres of soft drinks, at a cost of £5 billion. Coca-Cola and Schweppes is the largest soft-drink company in the UK, with 40% of the market.

spice any aromatic vegetable substance used as a condiment and for flavouring food. Spices are mostly obtained from tropical plants, and include pepper, nutmeg, ginger, and cinnamon. They have little food value but increase the appetite and may facilitate digestion.

spirit strong alcoholic liquor, distilled from the fruit, seeds, roots, or stems of certain plants. Fruit-based spirits include Calvados (apples), and brandy (grapes); grain-based spirits include whisky (malted barley, with other grains sometimes added), gin (barley, maize, or rye), sake (rice); others include rum (sugar cane), and tequila (agave). Spirits are usually matured for several years before use; they may be drunk on their own, diluted, or iced. Sake, from Japan, is heated before serving.

stock liquid used as a base for soups, stews, or sauces. *White stock* is made from poultry or veal, and vegetables boiled together in water. *Brown stock* is made from red meat or bones, and vegetables, browned in fat before being boiled in water.

sugar a sweet, soluble crystalline carbohydrate, such as sucrose, glucose, fructose, maltose, and lactose. It is easily digested and forms a major source of energy. The term is popularly used to refer only to sucrose, the type most commonly used in cooking and in the food industry as a sweetener and (in high concentrations) preservative. A high consumption of sucrose is associated with tooth decay and

Relative Sweetness Of Artificial Sweeteners

Artificial sweetener	Relative sweetness (sucrose = 1.0)
thaumatin	3,000
saccharin	300
aspartame	200
acesulfame-K	150
cyclamate	30

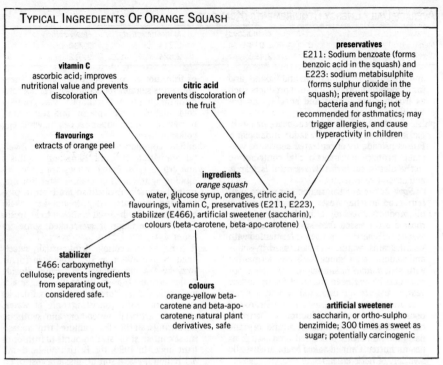

TYPICAL INGREDIENTS OF ORANGE SQUASH

vitamin C
ascorbic acid; improves nutritional value and prevents discoloration

citric acid
prevents discoloration of the fruit

preservatives
E211: Sodium benzoate (forms benzoic acid in the squash) and E223: sodium metabisulphite (forms sulphur dioxide in the squash); prevent spoilage by bacteria and fungi; not recommended for asthmatics; may trigger allergies, and cause hyperactivity in children

flavourings
extracts of orange peel

ingredients
orange squash
water, glucose syrup, oranges, citric acid, flavourings, vitamin C, preservatives (E211, E223), stabilizer (E466), artificial sweetener (saccharin), colours (beta-carotene, beta-apo-carotene)

stabilizer
E466: carboxymethyl cellulose; prevents ingredients from separating out, considered safe.

colours
orange-yellow beta-carotene and beta-apo-carotene; natural plant derivatives, safe

artificial sweetener
saccharin, or ortho-sulpho benzimide; 300 times as sweet as sugar; potentially carcinogenic

obesity. In the UK, sucrose may not be used in baby foods.

The main sources of sucrose are tropical sugar cane *Saccharum officinarum*, which accounts for about two-thirds of production, and temperate sugar beet *Beta vulgaris*. Minor quantities are produced from the sap of maple trees, and from sorghum and date palms. Raw sugar crystals obtained by heating the juice of sugar canes are processed to form brown sugars, such as Muscovado and Demerara, or refined and sifted to produce white sugars, such as granulated, caster, and icing. The syrup that is drained away from the raw sugar is *molasses*; it may be processed to form golden syrup or treacle, or fermented to produce rum. Molasses obtained from sugar beet juice is too bitter for human consumption.

sweetener, artificial or *noncaloric sweetener* a chemical that adds sweetness to food without providing energy; for example, saccharin and aspartame (Nutrasweet). Artificial sweeteners are used in the food industry and by dieters and diabetics. Thaumatin, aspartame, and acesulfame-K are banned in foods intended for babies and young children. Cyclamate is banned completely in the UK and USA; acesulfame-K is banned in the USA.

sweets confectionery made mainly from sucrose sugar. Other ingredients include glucose, milk, nuts, fat (animal and vegetable), and fruit. Boiled-sugar sweets contain sugar, glucose, colour, and flavouring, and are boiled, cooled, and shaped. *Chewing gum* consists of synthetic or vegetable gum with colour, flavouring, and sometimes sweetener added. *Toffee* and *caramel* are made from sugar, glucose, animal fat, milk, and cream or vegetable fat, heated and shaped. The USA is the biggest producer of sweets, though the UK has the highest consumption, with millions of pounds spent each year on advertising.

tea beverage made by infusing the dried leaves of the evergreen shrub *Camellia sinensis*. Known in China as early as 2737 BC, tea was first brought to Europe AD 1610 and rapidly became a fashionable drink. In 1823 it was found growing wild in N India, and plantations were later established in Assam and Sri Lanka; producers today include Africa, South America, Georgia, Azerbaijan, Indonesia, and Iran.

The young leaves and shoots of the tea plant are picked every five years. After 24 hours spread on shelves in withering lofts, they are broken up by rolling machines to release the essential oils, and then left to ferment. This process is halted by passing the leaves through ovens where moisture is removed and the blackish-brown **black tea** emerges ready for sifting into various grades. *Green tea* is steamed and quickly dried before fermentation, remaining partly green in colour.

vegetable any food plant, especially leafy plants (cabbage and lettuce), roots and tubers (carrots, parsnips, and potatoes), pulses (peas, lentils, and beans), and even flowers (cauliflower, broccoli, and artichoke). Tomatoes, peppers, aubergines, and cucumbers are generally regarded as vegetables but are technically fruits. Green leafy vegetables and potatoes are good sources of vitamin C, though much is lost in cooking, and pulses are a main source of protein. Cooking softens vegetables by dissolving pectins and hemicellulose and gelatinizing starch.

vinegar acidic liquid produced by the souring of alcoholic liquids, such as wine, beer, or cider, and used to flavour food and as a preservative in pickling. The souring yeasts and bacteria oxidize the alcohol to ethanoic (acetic) acid. *Malt vinegar* is brown and made from malted cereals; *white vinegar* is distilled from it. *Balsamic vinegar* is wine vinegar aged in wooden barrels. Other sources of vinegar include sherry and fermented fruits and honey.

wine alcoholic beverage, usually made from fermented grape pulp, although wines have also traditionally been made from many other fruits such as damsons and elderberries. *Red wine* is the product of the grape with the skin; *white wine* of the inner pulp of the grape. The sugar content is converted to alcohol (ethanol) by the yeast *Saccharomyces ellipsoideus*, which lives on the skin of the grape. Most wines have an alcohol content of 10–12%. For *dry wine* the fermentation is allowed to go on longer than for *sweet* or *medium* wine. Champagne (sparkling wine from the Champagne region of France) and other, similar, *méthode champenoise* wines are bottled while still fermenting, but other sparkling wines are artificially carbonated. The largest wine-producing countries are Italy, France, Russia, Georgia, Moldova, Armenia, and Spain; others include almost all European countries, Australia, South Africa, the USA, and Chile.

A *vintage wine* is produced during a good year (as regards quality of wine, produced by favourable weather conditions) in recognized vineyards of a particular area; France has a guarantee of origin (*appellation controlée*), as do Italy (*Denominazione di Origine Controllata*), Spain (*Denominacíon Controllata*), and Germany (a series of graded qualities running from *Qualitätswein* to *Beerenauslese*).

wine, fortified wine that has extra alcohol added to raise its alcohol content to about 20%. Fortified wines keep well because the alcohol kills the microorganisms that spoil natural wines. Port, which originates from Oporto in Portugal, is made by adding brandy to wine before fermentation is complete; sherry, originally made in Jerez in Spain, is a dry wine fortified after fermentation and later blended with sugar for sweet sherry; vermouth is flavoured with bitter herbs. Marsala, from Sicily, is fortified after fermentation and then heated gradually.

yoghurt or *yogurt* or *yoghourt* semi-solid, curdlike dairy product made from milk fermented with bacteria. It is drunk plain throughout the Asian and Mediterranean regions, but honey, sugar, and fruit are usually added in Europe and the USA, and the product made solid and creamy, to be eaten by spoon. Heat-treated, homogenized milk is inoculated with a culture of *Streptococcus lactis* and *Lactobacillus bulgaricus* in equal amounts, which change the lactose in the milk to lactic acid. Acetaldehyde gives yoghurt its characteristic flavour. Commercially, fruit, flavourings, and colouring and thickening agents are added to the fermented yoghurt.

FOOD TECHNOLOGY

food technology the commercial processing of foodstuffs in order to render them more palatable or digestible, or to preserve them from spoilage. Food spoils because of the action of enzymes within the food that change its chemical composition, or because of the growth of bacteria, moulds, yeasts, and other microorganisms. Fatty or oily foods also suffer oxidation of the fats, giving them an unpleasant rancid flavour. Traditional forms of processing include boiling, frying, flour-milling, bread-making, yoghurt- and cheese-making, brewing, and various methods of *food preservation*, such as salting, smoking, pickling, drying, bottling, and preserving in sugar. Modern food technology still employs traditional methods, but also uses many novel processes and additives, which allow a wider range of foodstuffs to be preserved.

additive any natural or artificial chemical added to prolong the shelf life of processed foods, alter the colour or flavour of food, or improve its nutritional value. Many additives are used and they are subject to regulation, since individuals may be affected by constant exposure even to traces of certain chemicals, and may suffer side effects ranging from headaches and hyperactivity to cancer. Additives approved for use throughout the European Community are given an official E number.

flavours are used to alter or intensify a food's taste. They may be natural or artificial, and include artificial sweeteners.

enhancers heighten the flavour or smell of foods without imparting their own taste—for example, monosodium glutamate (MSG).

colourings enhance the visual appeal of foods.

nutrients enhance food value or replace nutrients lost in processing.

preservatives slow down the rate of spoilage by controlling the growth of bacteria and fungi.

antioxidants prevent fatty foods from going rancid by inhibiting their natural oxidation.

emulsifiers and *stabilizers* modify the texture and consistency of food, and prevent the ingredients of a mixture from separating out.

leavening agents are substances other than yeast that lighten the texture of baked products—for example, sodium bicarbonate.

E Numbers: A Selection of Food Additives

number	name	typical use
	COLOURS	
E102	tartrazine	soft drinks
E104	quinoline yellow	
E110	sunset yellow	biscuits
E120	cochineal	alcoholic drinks
E122	carmoisine	jams and preserves
E123	amaranth	
E124	ponceau 4R	dessert mixes
E127	erythrosine	glacé cherries
E131	patent blue V	
E132	indigo carmine	
E142	green S	pastilles
E150	caramel	beers, soft drinks, sauces, gravy browning
E151	black PN	
E160 (b)	annatto; bixin; norbixin	crisps
E180	pigment rubine (lithol rubine BK)	
	ANTIOXIDANTS	
E310	propyl gallate	vegetable oils; chewing gum
E311	octyl gallate	
E312	dodecyl gallate	
E320	butylated hydroxynisole (BHA)	beef stock cubes; cheese spread
E321	butylated hydroxytoluene (BHT)	chewing gum
	EMULSIFIERS AND STABILIZERS	
E407	carageenan	quick-setting jelly mixes; milk shakes
E413	tragacanth	salad dressings; processed cheese
	PRESERVATIVES	
E210	benzoic acid	
E211	sodium benzoate	beer, jam, salad cream, soft drinks, fruit pulp
E212	potassium benzoate	fruit-based pie fillings, marinated herring and mackerel
E213	calcium benzoate	
E214	ethyl para-hydroxy-benzoate	
E215	sodium ethyl para-hydroxy-benzoate	
E216	propyl para-hydroxy-benzoate	
E217	sodium propyl para-hydroxy-benzoate	
E218	methyl para-hydroxy-benzoate	
E220	sulphur dioxide	
E221	sodium sulphate	dried fruit, dehydrated vegetables, fruit juices and syrups,
E222	sodium bisulphite	sausages, fruit-based dairy desserts, cider, beer,
E223	sodium metabisulphite	and wine; also used to prevent browning of peeled
E224	potassium metabisulphite	potatoes and to condition biscuit doughs
E226	calcium sulphite	
E227	calcium bisulphite	
E249	potassium nitrite	
E250	sodium nitrite	bacon, ham, cured meats, corned beef and
E251	sodium nitrate	some cheeses
E252	potassium nitrate	
	OTHERS	
E450 (a)	disodium dihydrogen diphosphate	buffers, sequestrants, emulsifying salts,
	trisodium diphosphate	stabilizers, texturizers
	tetrasodium diphosphate	raising agents,
	tetrapotassium diphosphate	used in whipping cream, fish and meat
E450 (b)	pentasodium triphosphate	products, bread, processed cheese,
	pentapotassium triphosphate	canned vegetables

acidulants sharpen the taste of foods but may also perform a buffering function in the control of acidity.

bleaching agents whiten flours.

anticaking agents prevent powdered products from coagulating into solid lumps.

humectants control the humidity of foods by absorbing and retaining moisture.

clarifying agents are used in fruit juices, vinegars, and other fermented liquids. Gelatin is the most common.

firming agents restore the texture of vegetables that may be damaged during processing.

foam regulators may be used in beer to provide a controlled 'head' on top of the poured product.

canning preservation of food in hermetically sealed steel, aluminium, or plastic containers (cans) by the application of heat. The high temperature destroys microorganisms and enzymes, and the can's seal prevents recontamination. Beverages may also be canned to preserve the carbon dioxide that makes drinks fizzy.

curing method of preserving meat by soaking it in salt (sodium chloride) solution, with saltpetre (sodium nitrate) added to give the meat its pink colour and characteristic taste. The nitrates in cured meats are converted to nitrites and nitrosamines by bacteria, and these are potentially carcinogenic to humans.

deep freezing method of preserving food by lowering its temperature to $-18°C/0°F$ or below. It stops almost all spoilage processes, although there may be some residual enzyme activity in uncooked vegetables, which is why these are blanched (dipped in hot water to destroy the enzymes) before freezing. Microorganisms cannot grow or divide while frozen, but most remain alive and can resume activity once defrosted. Commercial techniques freeze foods rapidly in order to prevent the growth

GATT AND THE URUGUAY ROUND

In Sept 1986 an attempt to secure a package of multilateral agreements on reducing trade barriers, in pursuance of the basic objectives of the General Agreement on Tariffs and Trade (GATT), was launched at Punta del Este, Uruguay. Because of the location of its inception it became known as the Uruguay Round. The original intention was that negotiations would run for four years, with agreement to be reached by 31 Dec 1990. This target date was passed without a successful conclusion and a new set of time objectives were set but by 1992 the Round was still deadlocked.

The Uruguay Round was intended to continue the freeing of international trade embodied in the rules of the GATT, which include: non-discrimination (a country is not permitted to set different tariffs on the same goods for different countries); reciprocity (tariff reductions should be balanced country by country); and the impartial settlement of trade disputes through the GATT machinery.

The main obstacle in the path of progress in settling the Uruguay Round has been a disagreement between the USA and the European Community over agricultural exports and farm subsidies. The EC wanted to introduce direct income support payments for farmers, to compensate partly for cuts in price support subsidies. The USA wanted these support payments to be treated like other farm supports and reduced according to the framework agreed within the Uruguay Round. The USA also wanted the volume of EC agricultural exports to be reduced, and argued for a greater reduction in price subsidies than the EC was willing to make. In its turn, the EC proposed that the volume of US cereal substitutes to the Community should be reduced.

The political will to secure an agreement has, at times, been sadly lacking. In the USA, presidential election year is always seen as a difficult time for taking hard, possibly unpopular, decisions, while in Europe the tail-end of the Commission presidency tends to create a similar tardiness.

In March 1992 a spokesman for President Bush was speaking about 'the possible collapse' of the Uruguay Round and at about the same time it was reported that the US administration was considering an exemption from the GATT rules for four key sector areas: sea transport, air transport, financial services, and telecommunications. EC officials argued that such a move would undermine attempts to reach an overall GATT agreement and even the GATT secretariat, unusually, criticized the USA, saying that its emphasis on regional and bilateral agreements would erode the whole basis of GATT principles.

A meeting at the end of April 1992 between President Bush and EC Commission president, Jacques Delors, resulted in a communiqué expressing hope and commitment but no concrete progress. However, agreement in Brussels a month later to accept a major reform of the Common Agricultural Policy (CAP) offered more hope. Although EC commissioners and ministers have always insisted that CAP reform is quite separate from the Uruguay Round, it is undoubtedly true that European agreement to reduce agricultural export subsidies would go a long way towards satisfying US demands for what it sees as 'fairer' competition, and so possibly unblock the log jam which US–EC disagreement has created.

In December 1992 the GATT secretary-general, Arthur Dunkel, put forward proposals which he hoped would satisfy governments on both sides of the Atlantic: first, a cut in domestic farm subsidies by 20% by 1999; second, a reduction in the volume and value of subsidized exports; and third, the conversion of quotas and other non-tariff restrictions on farm trade into tariffs, which would then be gradually reduced. The CAP reforms would go some significant way to meeting Mr Dunkel's propositions.

The prospects of the Uruguay Round being successfully concluded during 1992 are therefore probably the brightest they have ever been, despite the political uncertainties in Washington and Brussels. One thing seems certain: if they fail it is inconceivable that they would be prolonged yet again. Most informed observers see 1992 as a make or break year.

---

of large ice crystals, which would damage the food tissue on thawing.

dehydration preservation of food by reducing its moisture content by 80% or more. It inhibits the activity of moulds and bacteria, and reduces the mass and volume of foods, thereby lowering distribution costs. Products such as dried milk and instant coffee are made by spraying the liquid into a rising column of dry, heated air.

freeze-drying method of preserving food by freezing it and then placing it in a vacuum chamber so that the ice is forced out as water vapour. Many of the substances that give products such as coffee their typical flavour are volatile, and would be lost in a normal drying process because they would evaporate along with the water. In the freeze-drying process these volatile compounds do not pass into the ice that is to be sublimed, and are therefore largely retained.

hydrogenation method by which liquid oils are transformed into solid products, such as margarine. Vegetable oils contain double carbon-to-carbon bonds and are therefore examples of unsaturated compounds. When hydrogen is added to these double bonds, the oils become saturated and more solid in consistency.

irradiation method of preserving food by subjecting it to low-level gamma radiation in order to kill microorganisms. Although the process is now legal in several countries, uncertainty remains about possible long-term effects on consumers of irradiated food. The process does not make the food radioactive, but some vitamins, such as vitamin C, are destroyed and many molecular changes take place including the initiation of free radicals, which may be further changed into a range of unknown and unstable chemicals. Irradiation also eradicates the smell, taste, and poor appearance of bad or ageing food products.

pasteurization treatment of food to reduce the number of microorganisms it contains and so protect consumers from disease. Harmful bacteria are killed and the development of others is delayed. For milk, the method involves heating it to 72°C/161°F for 15 seconds followed by rapid cooling to 10°C/50°F or lower. However, the process also kills beneficial bacteria and reduces the nutritive property of milk.

pickling method of preserving food by soaking it in acetic acid (found in vinegar), which stops the growth of moulds. In sauerkraut, lactic acid, produced by bacteria, has the same effect.

puffing method of processing cereal grains. The grains are first subjected to high pressures, and then suddenly ejected into a normal atmospheric pressure, causing each grain to expand sharply. This type of process is used to make puffed wheat cereals and puffed rice cakes.

refrigeration method of preserving food by lowering its temperature to below 5°C/41°F (or below 3°C/37°F for cooked foods). It slows the processes of spoilage, but is less effective for foods with a high water content. Although a convenient form of preservation, this process cannot kill microorganisms, nor stop their growth completely, and a failure to realize its limitations causes many cases of food poisoning. Refrigerator temperatures should be checked as the efficiency of the machinery can decline with age.

smoking method of preserving fresh oily meats (such as pork and goose) or fish (such as herring and salmon). Before being smoked, the food is first salted or soaked in brine, then hung to dry. Meat is hot-smoked over a fast-burning wood fire, which is covered with sawdust, producing thick smoke and partly cooking the meat. Fish may be hot-smoked or cold-smoked over a slow-burning wood fire, which does not cook it. Modern refrigeration techniques mean that food does not need to be smoked to help it keep, so factory-smoked foods tend to be smoked just enough to give them a smoky flavour, with colours added to give them the appearance of traditionally smoked food.

ultra-heat treatment (UHT) preservation of milk by raising its temperature to 132°C/269°F or more. It uses higher temperatures than pasteurization, and kills all bacteria present, giving the milk a long shelf life but altering the flavour.

AGRICULTURE

agriculture the cultivation of land and the raising of animals in order to provide food for human nourishment, fodder for animals, or commodities such as wool and cotton. The units for managing agricultural production vary from small holdings and individually owned farms, to corporate-run farms and collective farms run by entire communities.

The first agricultural communities appeared about 9000 BC in southwest Asia, followed by Egypt, India, and China; in Europe farming began around 6500 BC in the Balkans and Aegean, and then spread north and east. Previously, food had been obtained only by hunting and by gathering wild vegetation. The selective breeding of reliable and productive animals and crop plants, and the improvement of soil by ploughing, irrigation, crop rotation, and the use of organic fertilizers such as manure and ashes meant that communities could become more stable, giving rise to fixed villages and towns and to complicated social systems. Reorganization of farming along more scientific and productive lines took place in Europe in the 18th century in response to dramatic population growth. Mechanization made considerable progress in Europe and the USA during the 19th century. After World War II, there was a dramatic increase in the use of agricultural chemicals: herbicides (weed-killers), insecticides, fungicides, and inorganic fertilizers. In the 1960s high-yielding species were developed for the *green revolution* of the Third World, and the industrialized countries began intensive farming of cattle, poultry, and pigs. In the 1980s, hybridization of species by genetic engineering, and pest control by the use of chemicals such as pheromones (scents emitted by animals) were developed. However, there was also a reaction against some forms of intensive agriculture because of the pollution and habitat destruction caused. One result of this was a growth of alternative methods, including organic farming.

agricultural revolution the sweeping changes that took place in British agriculture over the period 1750–1850 in response to the increased demand for food from a rapidly expanding population. Changes during the latter half of the 18th century include the enclosure of open fields, the introduction of four-year crop rotation, together with new fodder crops such as turnip, and the development of improved breeds of livestock.

agrochemical artificially produced chemical used in modern, intensive agricultural systems. Agrochemicals include inorganic nitrate and phosphate fertilizers, pesticides, some animal-feed additives, and drugs. Many are responsible for pollution and almost all are avoided by organic farmers.

agronomy the study of crops and soils, a branch of agricultural science. Agronomy includes such topics as selective breeding (of plants and animals), irrigation, pest control, and soil analysis and modification.

artificial insemination (AI) mating achieved by mechanically injecting previously collected semen into the uterus without genital contact. It is commonly used with cattle because it allows farmers to select the type and quality of bull required for a herd, and to control the timing and organization of a breeding programme. The practice of artificially inseminating pigs has also become widespread in recent years.

bovine spongiform encephalopathy (BSE) or *mad-cow disease* disease of cattle, allied to scrapie, that renders the brain spongy and may drive an animal mad. It has been identified only in the UK, where more than 14,000 cases had been confirmed between the first diagnosis Nov 1986 and June 1990. The source of the disease has been traced to manufactured protein feed incorporating the rendered brains of scrapie-infected sheep. BSE is very similar to, and may be related to, Creutzfeld–Jakob disease and kuru, which affect humans.

cash crop crop grown solely for sale rather than for the farmer's own use—for example, coffee, cotton, or sugar beet. Many Third World countries grow cash crops to meet their debt repayments rather than grow food for their people. The price for these crops depends on financial interests, such as those of the multinational companies and the International Monetary Fund.

cattle large, ruminant, even-toed, hoofed mammals of the genus *Bos*, family Bovidae. Fermentation in the four-chambered stomach allows cattle to make good use of the grass that normally forms the greater part of their diet. They are bred to achieve maximum yields of meat (beef cattle) or milk (dairy cattle). The old established beef breeds are mostly British in origin—for example, the Hereford, the Aberdeen Angus, the Devon, and the Beef Shorthorn. In recent years, more interest has been shown in other European breeds, their tendency to have less fat being more suited to modern tastes. Examples include the Charolais and the Limousin from central France, and the Simmental, originally from Switzerland. For dairying purposes, a breed raised in many countries is variously known as the Friesian, Holstein, or Black and White. It can give enormous milk yields, up to 13,000 l/3,450 gal in a single lactation, and will produce calves ideally suited for intensive beef production. Other dairying types include the Jersey and Guernsey, whose milk has a high butterfat content, and the Ayrshire, a smaller breed capable of staying outside all year.

cereal grass grown for its edible, nutrient-rich, starchy seeds. The term refers primarily to wheat, oats, rye, barley, and triticale (a cross between wheat and rye), but may also refer to maize (corn), millet, sorghum, and rice. Cereals contain about 75% complex carbohydrates

and 10% protein, plus fats and roughage. They store easily. In 1990, world production exceeded 2 billion tonnes. If all the world's cereal crop were consumed as wholegrain products directly by humans, everyone would obtain adequate protein and carbohydrate; however, a large proportion of cereal production in affluent nations is used as animal feed to boost the production of meat, dairy products, and eggs.

collective farm (Russian *kolkhoz*) farm in which a group of farmers pool their land, domestic animals, and agricultural implements, retaining as private property enough only for the members' own requirements. The profits of the farm are divided among its members. Collective farming is practised in parts of the former USSR, China, and Israel.

combine harvester or *combine* machine used for harvesting cereals and other crops, so called because it combines the actions of reaping (cutting the crop) and threshing (beating the ears so that the grain separates).

Common Agricultural Policy (CAP) system that allows the member countries of the European Community (EC) jointly to organize and control agricultural production within their boundaries. The objectives of the CAP were outlined in the Treaty of Rome: to increase agricultural productivity, to provide a fair standard of living for farmers and their employees, to stabilize markets, and to assure the availability of supply at a price that was reasonable to the consumer. The CAP is increasingly criticized for its role in creating overproduction, and consequent environmental damage, and for the high price of food subsidies.

crop rotation the system of regularly changing the crops grown on a piece of land. The crops are grown in a particular order in order to utilize and add to the nutrients in the soil and

MORE FOOD, BUT NOT WHERE IT MATTERS

Record harvests in 1990 boosted world food output by 4%, with production of all foods exceeding 2 billion tonnes. World cereal production rose by almost 5%, to 1,784 million tonnes, and for global cereal stocks increased for the first time in four years. Bumper harvests were recorded in North America, Mexico, China, India, Bangladesh, and what was then the USSR. Wheat production grew by an unprecedented 11%, with increases in most of the countries listed above and also in Turkey and Iran. Overall gains were also recorded for rice in Asia, and for global production of milk (after several years of stagnation), roots and tubers, pulses, and meat. Some gains were due to increased acreage of farmland, while others, such as that of pulses in Asia, relied on productivity growth on existing land.

Unfortunately, this optimistic global average masks regional problems in the very places where it matters most. Increases were concentrated in the industrialized world, where food shortages do not exist to any appreciable extent, and output was not so high in those areas of the world already threatened by food scarcity. For example, although overall Third World cereal output increased moderately, this varied markedly by region, with Asian output up by 10% while production actually fell by 11% in Latin America and by 7.5% in Africa. Production of cassava and yams in Africa, the staple foods over large areas, remained stagnant, lagging behind population growth. Cereals and roots are vital basic foods in most Third World countries, and even quite small reductions in availability can tip a country or region into serious food shortages.

Indeed, food production is failing to match population growth in most of the Third World countries studied by the Food and Agricultural Organization (FAO). An FAO analysis of food output in 72 poor countries between 1985 and 1989 found that in 49 countries (68%), food production per head of population fell significantly. Problems were greatest in Africa, where 80% of the countries studied were failing to increase food production at a pace that matched population growth, but other areas were also affected.

Although the relationship between population growth and food supply is complex, it does not appear that overall resource constraints are the only, or even the biggest, problem at present. In several of the most populous developing countries—India, China, Indonesia, Brazil, and Colombia—food production exceeded population growth during the period 1985–89. And population density remains far higher in many of the rich countries, including the UK, than in most developing countries. Other factors, such as the impact of droughts and desertification, political instability, lack of finance, international debt, poor infrastructure and transport networks, and environmental degradation, are also important.

For the poorest people, and especially those with no access to land, subtle distinctions in the statistics of food production per head of population literally mean the difference between life and death. Famines continue to break out sporadically in some areas, including the devastated environment of the Horn of Africa. Although a change of government in Ethiopia has recently reduced political conflict and brought about peace in Eritrea and Tigré, the economy and social structure of the country lie in ruins. Elsewhere in the region, political stability has deteriorated. Civil wars in Somalia and Sudan, threats of increased unrest in Kenya, and local conflicts in several other countries are combining with the factors described above to threaten famine on a scale not experienced for 50 years.

While famines make news, the much more common problems of chronic malnourishment continue to affect most Third World countries. This increases risk of disease, reduces productivity, and shortens lifespan, quite apart from the everyday suffering it causes.

At the same time, virtually all world agricultural systems face uncertainty about their future. Global climate change, for example, could have very serious implications for world agricultural productivity. A 1990 report of the Intergovernmental Panel on Climate Change concluded that the areas likely to suffer most in any predicted climate fluctuations would be the very ones where food is already in short supply. This is far from the only problem facing agriculture. Desertification and rapid soil erosion currently threaten the majority of the world's agricultural areas. Significant crop losses through atmospheric pollution have already occurred in many countries. Other forms of pollution and environmental degradation take their toll. The increase in global food production is welcome, but there is still comparatively little grounds for optimism about the future food security of large parts of the world.

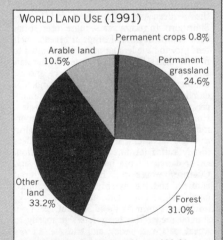

WORLD LAND USE (1991)

Permanent crops 0.8%
Arable land 10.5%
Permanent grassland 24.6%
Other land 33.2%
Forest 31.0%

Sources: Philips Geographical Digest 1992–3/ Heinemann–Philips Atlases

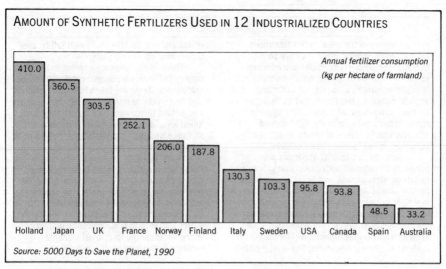

AMOUNT OF SYNTHETIC FERTILIZERS USED IN 12 INDUSTRIALIZED COUNTRIES

Annual fertilizer consumption
(kg per hectare of farmland)

410.0 — Holland
360.5 — Japan
303.5 — UK
252.1 — France
206.0 — Norway
187.8 — Finland
130.3 — Italy
103.3 — Sweden
95.8 — USA
93.8 — Canada
48.5 — Spain
33.2 — Australia

Source: 5000 Days to Save the Planet, 1990

to prevent the build-up of insect and fungal pests. Including a legume crop (member of the pea family, such as clover or alfalfa) in the rotation helps build up nitrate in the soil because the roots contain bacteria capable of fixing nitrogen from the air. In the 18th century a four-year rotation was widely adopted, in which an autumn-sown cereal such as wheat, was followed by a root crop, a spring cereal such as barley, and a legume crop.

dairying the business of producing and handling milk and milk products, such as cream, butter, and cheese. It is now usual for dairy farms to concentrate on the production of milk and for factories to take over the handling, processing, and distribution of milk as well as the manufacture of dairy products. In the UK, the Milk Marketing Board (1933), to which all producers must sell their milk, forms a connecting link between small farms and factories.

deer farming method of producing venison through the controlled breeding and rearing of deer on farms rather than hunting them in the wild. British deer-farming enterprises have been growing in number during the 1980s as more farmers seek to diversify into new sources of income. The meat is sold largely to the restaurant trade, and there is a market for the antlers and skin.

factory farming the intensive rearing of poultry or other animals for food, usually on high-protein foodstuffs and in confined quarters. Chickens for eggs and meat, and calves for veal are commonly farmed in this way. Some countries restrict the use of antibiotics and growth hormones as aids to factory farming, because they can persist in the flesh of the animals after they are slaughtered. The European Commission banned steroid hormones for beef cattle at the end of 1985. Many people object to factory farming for moral as well as health reasons.

fallow term describing land that is ploughed and tilled but left unsown for a season to allow it to regain its fertility.

fertilizer substance containing some or all of a range of about 20 chemical elements necessary for healthy plant growth, used to compensate the deficiencies of poor or depleted soil. Fertilizers may be *organic*—for example farmyard manure, composts, bonemeal, blood, and fishmeal; or *inorganic*, in the form of compounds, mainly of nitrogen, potassium, and phosphorus, which have been used on a very much increased scale since 1945.

fibre crop plant that is grown for the fibres that can be extracted from its tissues. Temperate areas produce flax and hemp; tropical and subtropical areas produce cotton, jute, and sisal. Cotton dominates fibre-crop production.

field enclosed area of land used for farming. Twentieth-century developments in agricultural science and technology have encouraged farmers to amalgamate and enlarge their fields, often to as much as 40 hectares/100 acres.

fish farming or *aquaculture* raising fish and shellfish (molluscs and crustaceans) under controlled conditions in tanks and ponds, sometimes in offshore pens. It has been practised for centuries in the Far East, where Japan alone produces some 100,000 tonnes of fish a year. In the 1980s one-tenth of the world's consumption of fish was farmed, notably carp, catfish, trout, salmon, turbot, eel, mussels, clams, oysters, and shrimp.

foot-and-mouth disease contagious eruptive viral disease of cloven-hoofed mammals (such as cattle and sheep), characterized by blisters in the mouth and around the hooves. In cattle it causes deterioration of milk yield and abortions. In the UK, affected herds are destroyed; inoculation is practised in Europe, and in the USA, a vaccine was developed in the 1980s.

forage crop plant that is grown to feed livestock, for example, grass, clover, and kale (a form of cabbage). Forage crops cover a greater area of the world than food crops, and grass, which dominates this group, is the world's most

---

Humane Slaughter?

Many people are troubled by the treatment farm animals receive when they are sent to slaughter. There is considerable concern about the standards and upkeep of abbatoirs (slaughterhouses), and interest in finding ways to minimize the stress and suffering of animals when they are killed. New hygiene rules introduced within the EC focused attention on the issue of safety when many abbatoirs failed to meet basic criteria.

In the UK, up to 300 abbatoirs are currently threatened with closure on grounds of safety, after almost half failed inspections by Ministry of Agriculture vets in 1989. This is viewed with mixed emotions by animal welfare groups. While they welcome tightening standards, they are concerned that fewer abbatoirs mean that animals will be transported over longer distances; the total number

of abbatoirs in Britain could well fall by over three-quarters in just a decade.

There is also growing interest in the concept of humane slaughter, whereby elaborate precautions are taken to reduce pain and fear in the animals. This includes use of equipment to stun animals before they are killed and, in some cases, mobile abbatoirs so that animals do not have to be moved from familiar surroundings.

A particular problem with respect to humane slaughter is posed by the requirements of Jewish and Muslim ritual slaughter in which cattle, sheep, goats, and poultry are killed by slitting their throats while still conscious. Proponents claim that animals suffer less with this method than with conventional stunning, but ritual slaughter remains a sharp focus of controversy.

---

abundant crop, though much of it is still in an unimproved state.

game farming protected rearing of gamebirds such as pheasants, partridges, and grouse for subsequent shooting. Game farms provide plenty of woodland and brush, which the birds require for cover, and may also plant special crops for them to feed on.

green revolution a popular term for the changes in agricultural methods that have taken place in developing countries since the 1960s and 1970s. The intent is to provide more and better food for their populations, albeit with a heavy reliance on chemicals and machinery. The green revolution was abandoned by some countries in the 1980s. Much of the food produced is exported as cash crops, so that local diet does not always improve.

harrow implement used to break up the furrows left by the plough and reduce the soil to a fine consistency, or tilth, and to cover the seeds after sowing. The traditional harrow consists of spikes set in a frame; modern harrows use sets of discs.

hay preserved grass or clover used as a winter feed for livestock. The grass is cut and allowed to dry in the field before being baled and removed for storage in a barn. The optimum period for cutting is when the grass has just come into flower and contains most feed value. One hectare of grass can produce up to 7.5 tonnes/7.3 tons of hay.

herbicide or **weedkiller** chemical used to kill plants or check their growth. Herbicides may be nonselective, killing all plants, or selective, killing only broad-leaved weeds and leaving narrow-leaved cereals unharmed. Nonselective herbicides include sodium chlorate and paraquat. Widespread use of weedkillers has led to a dramatic increase in crop yield but also to pollution of soil and water and to a decline in wildflowers.

horticulture the growing of flowers, fruit, and

vegetables. The growth of industrial towns in the 19th century led to the development of commercial horticulture in the form of nurseries and market gardens, pioneering methods such as glasshouses, artificial heat, herbicides (weedkillers), and pesticides, inorganic fertilizers, and machinery. In the UK, over half a million acres are devoted to commercial horticulture, and vegetables account for almost three-quarters of the produce.

insecticide any chemical pesticide used to kill insects. Among the most effective insecticides are synthetic chlorinated organic chemicals such as DDT (dichloro-diphenyl-trichloroethane) and dieldrin. However, these have proved persistent in the environment and are also poisonous to animal life, including humans, and are consequently banned in many countries. Other synthetic insecticides include organic phosphorus compounds such as malathion. Insecticides prepared from plants, such as derris and pyrethrum, are safer to use but need to be applied frequently and carefully.

irrigation artificial water supply for dry agricultural areas by means of dams and channels. An example is the channelling of the annual Nile flood in Egypt, which has been done from earliest times to its present control by the Aswan High Dam. Drawbacks to irrigation are that it tends to concentrate salts, ultimately causing infertility, and rich river silt is retained at dams, to the impoverishment of the land and fisheries below them.

legume plant of the family Leguminosae, which has a pod containing dry seeds. The family includes peas, beans, lentils, clover, and alfalfa (lucerne). Legumes are widely grown because of their specialized roots, which have nodules containing bacteria capable of fixing nitrogen from the air and increasing the nitrate content of the soil. The edible seeds of legumes are called *pulses*; they provide a concentrated source of vegetable protein, and make a vital contribution to human diets in poor countries where meat is scarce, and among vegetarians. Soya beans are the major temperate pulse crop in the West; most are used for oil production or for animal feed; some are processed into 'meat substitutes'. In Asia, most are processed into soya milk and beancurd. Peanuts dominate pulse production in the tropical world and are generally consumed as human food.

ley area of temporary grassland, sown for grazing or to produce hay or silage for a period of one to ten years before being ploughed and cropped. Short-term leys are often incorporated in systems of crop rotation.

milking machine machine that uses suction to milk cows. The first milking machine was invented in the USA by L O Colvin in 1860. Later it was improved so that the suction was regularly released by a pulsating device, since it was found that continuous suction is harmful to cows.

oil crop plant grown for the oil that can be pressed from its seeds or fruit. Cool temperate areas grow rapeseed and linseed; warm temperate regions produce sunflowers, olives, and soya beans; tropical regions produce groundnuts (peanuts), palm oil, and coconuts. Some of the major vegetable oils, such as soya bean oil, peanut oil, and cottonseed oil, are derived from crops grown primarily for other purposes. Most vegetable oils are used as both edible oils and as ingredients of other products such as soaps, varnishes, printing inks, and paints.

organic farming farming without the use of synthetic fertilizers (such as nitrates and phosphates) or pesticides (herbicides, insecticides, and fungicides) or other agrochemicals (such as hormones, growth stimulants, or fruit regulators). In place of synthetic fertilizers, compost, manure, seaweed, or other substances derived from living things are used (hence the name 'organic'); growing a nitrogen-fixing legume such as clover, then ploughing it back into the soil, also fertilizes the ground. Crop rotation is a central element. Organic farming methods produce food without pesticide residues and reduce pollution. They are more labour intensive, and therefore more expensive, but use less fossil fuel. Soil structure is improved by organic methods, and recent studies show that a conventional farm can lose four times as much soil as an organic farm through erosion.

pesticide any chemical used to combat pests. Pesticides are of three main types: *insecticides* (to kill insects), *fungicides* (to kill fungi), and *herbicides* (to kill plants, mainly those considered weeds). Such chemicals cause a number of pollution problems through spray drift on to surrounding areas, direct contamination of users or the public, and as residues on food. The aid organization Oxfam estimates that the indiscriminate use of pesticides causes about 10,000 deaths worldwide every year.

pig even-toed hoofed mammal of the family Suidae. Pigs are omnivorous, and have simple, non-ruminating stomachs and thick hides.

Over 400 varieties have been bred over the centuries, many of which have all but disappeared in more recent times with the development of intensive rearing systems. The Berkshire, Chester White, Poland, China, Saddleback, Yorkshire, Duroc, Tamworth, and Razorback are the main surviving breeds. Indoor rearing methods favour the large white breeds, such as the Chester White and the originally Swedish Landrace, over coloured varieties, which tend to be hardier and can survive better outdoors. Since 1960, hybrid pigs, produced by crossing two or more breeds, have become popular for their heavy lean carcasses.

plough implement used for tilling the soil. The plough dates from about 3500 BC, when oxen were used to pull a simple wooden blade, or ard. The present tractor-drawn plough consists of many 'bottoms', each comprising a curved ploughshare and angled mouldboard, and designed so that it slices into the ground and turns the soil over.

poultry domestic birds such as chickens, turkeys, ducks, and geese. Good egg-laying breeds of chicken are Leghorns, Minorcas, and Anconas; varieties most suitable for eating are Dorkings, Australorps, Brahmas, and Cornish; those useful for both purposes are Orpingtons, Rhode Island Reds, Wyandottes, Plymouth Rocks, and Jersey White Giants. Most farm poultry are hybrids, selectively crossbred for certain characteristics, including feathers and down. Since World War II, the development of battery-produced eggs and the intensive breeding of broiler fowls and turkeys has doubled egg yields and increased the availability of poultry meat. However, this form of factory farming has also aroused public concern about the conditions in which the birds are kept, and has led to a growing interest in deep-litter and free-range systems. In 1988-89 the UK egg industry suffered a major blow when it was discovered that salmonella was present in large quantities of eggs. Chickens were slaughtered and farmers lost large amounts of money. Eggs were declared safe only if heated to a high enough temperature to kill the bacteria.

root crop ambiguous term for several different types of crop, which may or may not be cultivated for their true roots; in agriculture, it usually refers to turnips, swedes, and beets, whereas in trade statistics it refers to the tubers of potatoes, sweet potatoes, cassava, and yams. Roots have a high carbohydrate content, but their protein content rarely exceeds 2%. Consequently, communities relying almost exclusively upon roots may suffer from protein deficiency. Potatoes, cassava, and yams are second in importance only to cereals as human food. Food production for a given area from roots is greater than from cereals.

scrapie fatal disease of sheep and goats that attacks the central nervous system, causing deterioration of the brain cells. It is believed to be caused by a submicroscopic organism known as a prion and may be related to bovine spongiform encephalopathy, the disease

GENETIC ENGINEERING: CURSE OR CURE FOR AGRICULTURE?

Over the next decade, the use of genetic engineering may initiate the greatest changes in agriculture since the large-scale introduction of artificial pesticides and fertilizers. Normally sober scientists have been making predictions usually associated with pulp science fiction: strains of wheat capturing their own nutrients from the air; cube-shaped tomatoes for easy packing; crops that fight off pests without pesticides; cattle producing three times the current levels of milk; entirely new farm animals purpose-created for maximum productivity ...

But does genetic engineering really offer such massive advantages? At present, there are sharp divisions of opinion between those who see biotechnology as an important step forward for farmers and growers, and those who see it as a largely irrelevant development which will bring with it a whole new set of health and environmental problems.

The word 'biotechnology' covers many different techniques. In its simplest form, biotechnology includes traditional crop breeding, which has been practised at least since the Sumerians developed settled agriculture in the Middle East 6,000 years ago. Modern developments in biotechnology have taken two main forms:

(1) the use of *tissue culture* of plants and *embryo transfer* in animals to speed up conventional breeding techniques, allowing the creation of large numbers of individuals from a single plant and a rapid increase in rates of selective breeding, production of virus-free plants, export of livestock in embryo form, and so on;

(2) the *transfer of genetic material* between cells of different individuals, or different species, usually by means of an infecting virus or plasmid, thus directly and permanently changing the nature of the organism.

Transfer of genetic material is fundamentally different from streamlined breeding techniques. In the latter case, the fundamentals of crop breeding still apply, with approximately the same constraints on which species can interbreed. In genetic transfer, genes and gene sequences can in theory be taken from any species and be placed in another to gain a specific result.

So far, despite the existence of 500 companies and 150 research organizations, there is no commercially available product made by gene transfer. It is now tacitly admitted that making usable products by genetic manipulation has proved harder than was first hoped. There is also a growing concern about the

health and safety aspects of releasing genetically manipulated organisms, which may have undetermined hazards for humans or the environment. Nonetheless, there are many products under development, aimed specifically at farmers and growers. These include crops resistant to specific diseases and viral attack; crops resistant to herbicides, so that these can be sprayed at higher concentrations for weed control; plants capable of capturing their own supplies of nitrogen from the air by means of genetically modified bacteria (something that occurs naturally in members of the pea and bean family); genetically manipulated animal feed to boost productivity; and artificial hormones to increase meat, milk, or wool production.

Supporters of biotechnology argue that genetic engineering offers the chance to break away from the current heavy reliance on polluting agrochemicals, and to make food production more efficient in an increasingly hungry world. However, there are questions hanging over the safety of several of these techniques. Using genetic manipulation to boost resistance to herbicides would *increase* the use of agrochemicals if it was widely adopted. Stimulating plants' innate abilities to fight off pests usually involves raising the concentration of 'natural pesticides' in the plant; in cases of severe pest attack, these toxic chemicals can rise to 300 times the background level and pose similar problems to those from pesticide residues in food. Changes to animals' hormone levels have seldom been achieved in the past without causing either suffering for the animals or attendant problems for people eating the products. Plans to introduce bovine somatotropin (BST) into the UK as a means of boosting milk production met with entrenched opposition from both farmers and consumers. We don't know the side effects of any new organism or characteristic and, once in use, the genetically manipulated organisms may well be impossible to recall.

Also, benefits may not be evenly distributed. The likelihood that companies will patent life forms for the first time inevitably means that an increasing cost will accrue for using the products of biotechnology. As in the case of the 'green revolution' of the 1960s, when improved strains of cereals were introduced into the Third World, it is likely to be the rich that benefit most, leaving the poorer farmers even worse off than before. Whatever the final outcome, the debate over the pros and cons of biotechnology is sure to escalate over the next few years.

of cattle known as 'mad-cow disease'.

scythe harvesting tool with long wooden handle and sharp, curving blade. It was in common use in the Middle East and Europe from the dawn of agriculture until the early 20th century, by which time it had generally been replaced by machinery.

seed drill machine for sowing cereals and other seeds, developed by Jethro Tull in England

1701. The seed is stored in a hopper and delivered by tubes into furrows in the ground. The furrows are made by a set of blades, or coulters, attached to the front of the drill. A harrow drawn behind the drill covers up the seeds.

sheep ruminant, even-toed, hoofed mammal of the genus *Ovis*, family Bovidae. Various breeds of sheep are reared worldwide for meat, wool, milk, and cheese, and for rotation on arable land to maintain its fertility. Over 50 breeds were developed in the UK, but only a small proportion are still in full commercial use. They are grouped into three principal categories. The hardy *upland* breeds, such as the Scottish Blackface and Welsh Mountain, are able to survive in a bleak, rugged environment. The *shortwool* varieties, such as the Down breeds of Hampshire and Suffolk, are well adapted to thrive on the lush grassland of lowland areas. *Longwool* breeds, such as the Leicesters and Border Leicesters, were originally bred for their coarse, heavy fleeces, but are now crossed with hill-sheep flocks to produce fat lambs.

silage green fodder preserved through controlled fermentation in an airtight tower (silo) or pit. The term also refers to stacked crops that may be preserved indefinitely.

subsistence farming farming in which the produce is enough to feed only the farmer and family and there is no surplus to sell.

tenant farming system whereby farmers rent their holdings from a landowner in return for the use of agricultural land.

threshing process of separating cereal grains from the plant. Traditionally, the work was carried out by hand in winter months using the flail, a jointed beating stick. Today, threshing is done automatically inside the combine harvester at the time of cutting.

topsoil the upper, cultivated layer of soil, which may vary in depth from 8–45 cm/3–18 in. It contains organic matter, the decayed remains of vegetation, which plants need for active growth, along with a variety of soil organisms, including earthworms.

tractor a powerful motor vehicle, commonly having large rear wheels or caterpillar tracks, used for pulling farm machinery and loads. It is usually powered by a diesel engine and has a power-takeoff mechanism for driving machinery, and a hydraulic lift for raising and lowering implements.

There is concern over the side-effects of some preservatives in food, but if they were banned many foods would quickly turn bad and stomach upsets could become more likely. Which of the following is most important to you?

Additive-free food	15
Food with a long shelf-life but with additives	5
Lower-priced food	9
Fresh produce	68
None of these	2

Which of these foods have you/would you dare eat?

Jellied eels	21
Frogs legs	34
Snails	28
Caviar	40
Oysters	35
Raw fish	25
Tripe	19
Haggis	42
Sweetbreads	24
None of these	27

EVOLUTIONARY BIOLOGY

adaptation any change in the structure or function of an organism that allows it to survive and reproduce more effectively in its environment. In evolution, adaptation is thought to occur as a result of random variation in the genetic make-up of organisms (produced by mutation and recombination) coupled with natural selection.

artificial selection selective breeding of individuals that exhibit the particular characteristics that a plant or animal breeder wishes to develop. In plants, desirable features might include resistance to disease, high yield (in crop plants), or attractive appearance. In animal breeding, selection has led to the development of particular breeds of cattle for improved meat or milk production.

cladistics a method of biological classification (taxonomy) that uses a formal step-by-step procedure for objectively assessing the extent to which organisms share particular characters, and for assigning them to taxonomic groups. These taxonomic groups (species, genus, family) are termed *clades*.

competition the interaction between two or more organisms, or groups of organisms (for example, species), that use a common resource which is in short supply. Competition invariably results in a reduction in the numbers of one or both competitors, and in evolution contributes both to the decline of certain species and to the evolution of adaptations.

convergent evolution the independent evolution of similar structures in species (or other taxonomic groups) that are not closely related, as a result of living in a similar way. Thus, birds and bats have wings, not because they are descended from a common winged ancestor, but because their respective ancestors independently evolved flight.

evolution slow process of change from one form to another, as in the evolution of the universe from its formation in the Big Bang to its present state, or in the evolution of life on Earth.

extinction the complete disappearance of a species. In the past, extinctions are believed to have occurred because species were unable to adapt quickly enough to a naturally changing environment. Today, most extinctions are due to human activity. Some species, such as the dodo of Mauritius, the moas of New Zealand, and the passenger pigeon of North America, were exterminated by hunting. Others become extinct when their habitat is destroyed. (See feature in *Natural History*.)

human species, origins of evolution of humans from ancestral primates. The African apes (gorilla and chimpanzee) are shown by anatomical and molecular comparisons to be the closest living relatives of humans. Molecular studies put the date of the split between the human and African ape lines at 5–10 million years ago. There are no ape or **hominid** (of the human group) fossils from this period; the oldest known hominids, found in Ethiopia and Tanzania, date from 3.5 million years ago. These creatures are known as *Australopithecus afarensis*, and they walked upright. They were either direct ancestors or an offshoot of the line that led to modern humans. They might have been the ancestors of *Homo habilis* (considered by some to be a species of *Australopithecus*), who appeared about a million years later, had slightly larger bodies and brains, and were probably the first to use stone tools. *Australopithecus robustus* and *A. gracilis* also lived in Africa at the same time, but these are not generally considered to be our ancestors.

Lamarckism theory of evolution advocated during the early 19th century by French naturalist Jean Baptiste de Lamarck (1744–1829). It differed from the Darwinian theory of evolution in that it was based on the idea that acquired characteristics were inherited: he argued that particular use of an organ or limb strengthens it, and that this development may be 'preserved by reproduction'. For example, he suggested that giraffes have long necks because they are continually stretching them to reach high leaves; according to the theory, giraffes that have lengthened their necks by stretching will pass this characteristic on to their offspring.

mutation a change in the genes produced by a change in the DNA that makes up the hereditary material of all living organisms. Mutations, the raw material of evolution, result from mistakes during replication (copying) of DNA molecules. Only a few improve the organism's performance and are therefore favoured by natural selection. Mutation rates are increased by certain chemicals and by radiation.

natural selection the process whereby gene frequencies in a population change through certain individuals producing more descendants than others because they are better able to survive and reproduce in their environment. The accumulated effect of natural selection is to produce adaptations such as the insulating coat of a polar bear or the spadelike forelimbs of a mole. The process is slow, relying firstly on random variation in the genes of an organism being produced by mutation and the genetic recombination of sexual reproduction. It was recognized by Charles Darwin and Alfred Russel Wallace as the main process driving evolution.

neo-Darwinism the modern theory of evolution, built up since the 1930s by integrating Darwin's theory of evolution through natural selection with the theory of genetic inheritance founded on the work of Mendel.

phylogeny the historical sequence of changes that occurs in a given species during the course of its evolution. It was once erroneously associated with ontogeny (the process of development of a living organism).

punctuated equilibrium model evolutionary theory developed by Niles Eldridge and

MOLECULE WATCHING—THE DANCE OF DNA

One of the most exciting biological break-throughs of recent times has been the development of techniques for watching the behaviour of individual molecules. New techniques enable scientists to see large molecules, and to follow their movements and interactions with other molecules. The first application of these ideas has been in the study of DNA and proteins inside the cell, but they are also beginning to be used in the study of polymers in materials science.

Optical microscopes cannot resolve something as small as a molecule—the wavelength of visible light is larger than most molecules, so no matter how powerful the lens system, molecules cannot be seen. However, by combining the molecule to be studied with a fluorescent dye, a complex that glows can be formed. Light shining on the complex makes it fluoresce, and the glowing molecule can be tracked as it moves against a dark background.

The actual structure of the complex still cannot be resolved. However, the technique is exciting in the study of movements of molecules, such as DNA. Several groups in the USA have now witnessed the movement of individual DNA molecules, bending and stretching in solution or twirling and dancing through gels. Once the problem of the precise amount of dye to use had been overcome—too little gives too faint an image, whereas too much causes the whole subject to glow—groups could explore many aspects of DNA movement, and could easily record the movements on video.

One of the first problems the technique has helped with is in the understanding of electrophoretic gels. Such gels are widely used in the separation of DNA fragments. An electric current draws the fragments along the gel, with shorter pieces moving further than longer pieces. The fluorescent-dye technique has enabled researchers to understand why this happens.

As a DNA fragment moves through the gel, it encounters pores. The electric current attracts the charged fragments to move through these pores, but the shape of the fragment slows it down.

The molecule bunches and stretches like an earthworm, and sometimes the rear of the molecule swings and is attracted through a different pore. All these movements have been observed using the dye technique, and this has led to the realization that the longer the fragment, the more difficulty it has with moving and passing through pores. Thus the longer fragments move more slowly across the gel.

A similar observation has been made in two-dimensional electrophoresis. In this technique, once electrophoresis has started, a new electric field is applied across the gel, normally at right angles to the first. Now the molecules have to turn a corner to follow the field. With large fragments, several parts of the molecule are attracted by the field, and so the molecule begins to kink. Eventually, one part of the molecule is more attracted than the rest, so this

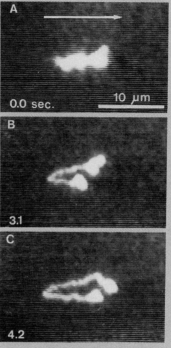

DNA molecule moving through a gel under the influence of an electric field and observed using a fluorescence microscope.

part leads towards the attracting electricity. Once again, this process serves to slow down large fragments, and so separate them from smaller ones.

A variation in the technique has been to combine DNA fragments with other chemicals as well as dyes. For example, by joining one end of the fragment to a cover slip and the other to a magnetic bead, the strength of the DNA can be measured. DNA is a helical structure, like a spring, and its elasticity and breaking point can be measured just as in a wire spring. Instead of putting extra weight on the wire spring, the magnetic field is increased, and the length of the molecule measured on the video screen. The ratio between the force of the field and the length of the DNA corresponds to the stiffness of the molecule. The stiffness can be altered by changing the conditions—for example, lowering the salt concentration increases the stiffness.

The exciting prospect for the future is that individual molecules can be altered and manoeuvred while they are being observed on television. The possibility then is that DNA pieces could be precisely assembled, almost on factory assembly lines.

Custom-built DNA could be produced, ready for whatever biological task had been assigned to it.

BIOLOGY: CHRONOLOGY

c 500 BC	First studies of the structure and behaviour of animals, by the Greek Alcmaeon of Creton.
c 450	Hippocrates of Cos undertook the first detailed studies of human anatomy.
c 350	Aristotle laid down the basic philosophy of the biological sciences and outlined a theory of evolution.
c 300	Theophrastus carried out the first detailed studies of plants.
c AD 175	Galen established the basic principles of anatomy and physiology.
c 1500	Leonardo da Vinci studied human anatomy to improve his drawing ability and produced detailed anatomical drawings.
1628	William Harvey described the circulation of the blood and the function of the heart as a pump.
1677	Anthony van Leeuwenhoek greatly improved the microscope and used it to describe spermatozoa as well as many microorganisms.
1736	Carolus (Carl) Linnaeus published his systematic classification of plants, so establishing taxonomy.
1768–79	James Cook's voyages of discovery in the Pacific revealed an undreamed-of diversity of living species, prompting the development of theories to explain their origin.
1796	Edward Jenner established the practice of vaccination against smallpox, laying the foundations for theories of antibodies and immune reactions.
1809	Jean-Baptiste Lamarck advocated a theory of evolution through inheritance of acquired characters.
1839	Theodor Schwann proposed that all living matter is made up of cells.
1857	Louis Pasteur established that microorganisms are responsible for fermentation, creating the discipline of microbiology.
1859	Charles Darwin published *On the Origin of Species*, expounding his theory of the evolution of species by natural selection.
1866	Gregor Mendel pioneered the study of inheritance with his experiments on peas, but achieved little recognition.
1900	Mendel's work was rediscovered and the science of genetics founded.
1935	Konrad Lorenz published the first of many major studies of animal behaviour, which founded the discipline of ethology.
1953	James Watson and Francis Crick described the molecular structure of the genetic material, DNA.
1964	William Hamilton recognized the importance of inclusive fitness, so paving the way for the development of sociobiology.
1975	Discovery of endogenous opiates (the brain's own painkillers) opened up a new phase in the study of brain chemistry.
1976	Har Gobind Khorana and his colleagues constructed the first artificial gene to function naturally when inserted into a bacterial cell, a major step in genetic engineering.
1982	Establishment of gene databases at Heidelberg, Germany for the European Molecular Biology Laboratory, and at Los Alamos, USA for the US National Laboratories.
1985	Isolation of the first human cancer gene, retinoblastoma, by researchers at the Massachusetts Eye and Ear Infirmary and the Whitehead Institute, Massachusetts.
1988	Human Genome Organization (HUGO) established in Washington, DC, with the aim of mapping the complete sequence of DNA.

Stephen Jay Gould in 1972 to explain discontinuities in the fossil record. It claims that periods of rapid change alternate with periods of relative stability (stasis), and that the appearance of new lineages is a separate process from the gradual evolution of adaptive changes within a species.

saltation (Latin *saltare* 'to leap') the idea that an abrupt genetic change can occur in an individual, which then gives rise to a new species. The idea has now been largely discredited, although the appearance of polyploid individuals (possessing three or more sets of chromosomes) can be considered an example.

species a distinguishable group of organisms that resemble each other or consist of a few distinctive types (as in polymorphism), and that can all interbreed to produce fertile offspring. Species are the lowest level in the system of biological classification.

variation difference between individuals of the same species, found in any sexually reproducing population. Variations may be almost unnoticeable in some cases, obvious in others, and can concern many aspects of the organism. Typically, variation in size, behaviour, biochemistry, or colouring may be found. The cause of the variation can be genetic (that is, inherited), environmental, or more usually a combination of the two. The origins of variation can be traced to the recombination of the genetic material during the formation of the gametes, and, more rarely, to mutation.

REPRODUCTION

Reproduction is the process by which a living organism produces other organisms similar to itself. Reproduction may be sexual or asexual.

sexual reproduction requires the union, or fertilization, of gametes (specialized reproductive cells, such as eggs and sperm). These are usually produced by two different individuals, although self-fertilization occurs in a few hermaphrodites such as tapeworms. Most organisms other than bacteria and cyanobacteria show some sort of sexual process. Except in some lower organisms, the gametes are of two distinct types called eggs and sperm. The organisms producing the eggs are called females, and those producing the sperm, males. The fusion of a male and female gamete produces a *zygote*, from which a new individual develops.

Asexual reproduction does not involve the manufacture and fusion of sex cells, nor the necessity for two parents. The process carries a clear advantage in that there is no need to search for a mate nor to develop complex pollinating mechanisms; every asexual organism can reproduce on its own. Asexual reproduction can therefore lead to a rapid population build-up.

In evolutionary terms, the disadvantage of asexual reproduction arises from the fact that only identical individuals, or clones, are produced—there is no variation. In the field of horticulture, where standardized production is needed, this is useful, but in the wild, an asexual population that cannot adapt to a changing environment is at risk of extinction.

binary fission a type of asexual reproduction, whereby a single-celled organism divides into two smaller 'daughter' cells. It can also occur in a few simple multicellular organisms, such as sea anemones, producing two smaller sea anemones of equal size.

budding a type of asexual reproduction in which an outgrowth develops from a cell to form a new individual. Most yeasts reproduce in this way. In a suitable environment, yeasts grow rapidly, forming long chains of cells as the buds themselves produce further buds before being separated from the parent. Simple invertebrates, such as hydra, can also reproduce by budding.

In horticulture, the term is used for a technique of plant propagation whereby a bud (or scion) and a sliver of bark from one plant are transferred to an incision made in the bark of another plant (the stock). This method of grafting is often used for roses.

parthenogenesis the development of an ovum (egg) without any genetic contribution from a male. Parthenogenesis is the normal means of reproduction in a few plants (for example,

MAJOR DATABASES STORING INFORMATION ON THE GENOME

Location	Sponsor	Work
Los Alamos National Laboratory New Mexico, USA	Dept of Energy and the National Institutes of Health, Washington DC	Gen Bank (contains the DNA sequences that make up human genes)
European Molecular Biology Laboratory, Heidelberg, Germany	15 European states and the EC	Nucleotide Sequence Data Library (contains the DNA sequences that make up human genes)
National Institute of Genetics, Mishima, Japan	Science and Technology Agency, Tokyo	DNA Database of Japan
Laboratory of Molecular Biology, Cambridge, UK	Medical Research Council, London	Nematode worm
Johns Hopkins University, Baltimore, Maryland, USA	Howard Hughes Medical Institute, Bethesda	Genome Database
Johns Hopkins University, Baltimore, Maryland, USA	National Institutes of Health	OMIM, the Online Mendelian Inheritance in Man
Brookhaven National Laboratory, Upton, New York, USA	Dept of Energy	Protein DataBank (contains 3-D coordinates associated with each protein)
Georgetown University, Washington DC	National Institutes of Health	Protein Identification Resource (contains sequences of the amino acids that make up proteins)
Jackson Laboratory, Bar Harbor, Maine, USA	National Institutes of Health	Homology Database and Project (contains genetic data on humans, mice and 23 other species)

Source: The New Scientist 1990

pregnancy

not to scale

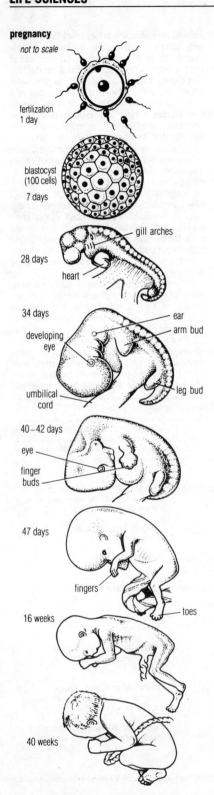

fertilization
1 day

blastocyst
(100 cells)
7 days

gill arches

28 days

heart

34 days

ear

developing
eye

arm bud

umbilical
cord

leg bud

40–42 days

eye

finger
buds

47 days

fingers

toes

16 weeks

40 weeks

dandelions) and animals (for example, certain fish). Some sexually reproducing species, such as aphids, show parthenogenesis at some stage in their life cycle.

In most cases, there is no fertilization at all, but in a few the stimulus of being fertilized by a sperm is needed to initiate development, although the male's chromosomes are not absorbed into the nucleus of the ovum. Parthenogenesis can be artificially induced in many animals (such as rabbits) by cooling, pricking, or applying acid to an egg.

THE LIFE CYCLE

The life cycle is the sequence of developmental stages through which members of a given species pass. Most vertebrates have a simple life cycle consisting of fertilization of sex cells or gametes, a period of development as an embryo, a period of juvenile growth after hatching or birth, an adulthood including sexual reproduction, and finally death. Invertebrate life cycles are generally more complex and may involve major reconstitution of the individual's appearance (metamorphosis) and completely different styles of life. Thus dragonflies live an aquatic life as larvae and an aerial life during the adult phase. In many invertebrates and protozoa there is a sequence of stages in the life cycle, and in parasites different stages often occur in different host organisms. Plants have a special type of life cycle with two distinct phases, known as alternation of generations.

birth is the act of producing live young from within the body of female animals. Both viviparous and ovoviviparous animals give birth to young. In viviparous animals, embryos obtain nourishment from the mother via a placenta or other means. In ovoviviparous animals, fertilized eggs develop and hatch in the oviduct of the mother and gain little or no nourishment from maternal tissues.

ageing is the period of deterioration of the physical condition of a living organism that leads to death; in biological terms, the entire life process. Three current theories attempt to account for ageing. The first suggests that the process is genetically determined, to remove individuals that can no longer reproduce. The second suggests that it is due to the accumulation of mistakes during the replication of DNA at cell division. The third suggests that it is actively induced by pieces of DNA that move between cells, or by cancer-causing viruses; these may become abundant in old cells and induce them to produce unwanted proteins or interfere with the control functions of their DNA.

death is the cessation of all life functions, so that the molecules and structures associated with living things become disorganized and indistinguishable from similar molecules found in non-living things. Large molecules such as proteins break down into simpler, soluble components. Eventually the organism partly dissolves into the soil or evaporates into the air, leaving behind skeletal material. Living organisms expend large amounts of energy preventing their complex molecules from breaking up; cellular repair and replacement are vital processes in multicellular organisms. At death this energy is no longer available, and the processes of disorganization become inevitable.

Biologists have a problem in explaining the phenomenon of death. If proteins, other complex molecules, and whole cells can be repaired or replaced, why cannot a multicellular organism be immortal? The most favoured explanation is an evolutionary one. Organisms must die in order to make way for new ones, which, by virtue of sexual reproduction, may vary slightly in relation to the previous generation. Most environments change constantly, if slowly; without this variation organisms would be unable to adapt to the changes.

In human beings, death used to be pronounced when a person's breathing and heartbeat stopped. The advent of mechanical aids has made this point sometimes difficult to determine, and in controversial cases a person is now pronounced dead when the brain ceases to control the vital functions.

alternation of generations the typical life cycle of terrestrial plants and some seaweeds, in which there are two distinct forms occurring alternately: *diploid* (having two sets of chromosomes) and *haploid* (one set of chromosomes). The diploid generation produces haploid spores by meiosis, and is called the sporophyte, while the haploid generation produces gametes (sex cells), and is called the gametophyte. The gametes fuse to form a diploid zygote which develops into a new sporophyte; thus the sporophyte and gametophyte alternate.

allele (or allelomorph) one of a pair of genes that occupy the same relative position (locus) on homologous chromosomes, and are responsible for the occurrence of contrasting characteristics—for example, blue and brown eyes in humans are determined by different alleles of the gene for eye colour. Organisms with two sets of chromosomes (diploid) will have two copies of each gene. If the two alleles are identical the individual is said to be homozygous at that locus; if different, heterozygous.

chromosome structure in a cell nucleus that carries the genes. Each chromosome consists of one very long strand of DNA, coiled and folded to produce a compact chromosome. The point on a chromosome where a particular gene occurs is known as its locus. Most higher organisms have two copies of each chromosome (they are diploid) but some have only one (they are haploid).

diploid having two sets of chromosomes in each cell. In sexually reproducing species, one set is derived from each parent, the gametes, or sex cells, of each parent being haploid (having only one set of chromosomes) due to meiosis (reduction cell division).

embryo early development stage of an animal or a plant following fertilization of an ovum (egg cell), or activation of an ovum by parthenogenesis.

In animals the embryo exists either within an egg (where it is nourished by food contained in the yolk), or in mammals, in the uterus of the mother. In mammals (except marsupials) the embryo is fed through the placenta. In humans the term embryo describes the fertilized egg during its first seven weeks of existence; from the eighth week onwards it is referred to as a fetus. The plant embryo is found within the seed in higher plants. It sometimes consists of only a few cells, but usually includes a root; a shoot (or primary bud); and one or two cotyledons, which nourish the growing seedling.

fertilization in sexual reproduction, the union of two gametes (sex cells, often called egg and sperm) to produce a zygote, which combines the genetic material contributed by each parent. In self-fertilization the male and female gametes come from the same plant; in cross-fertilization they come from different plants. Self-fertilization rarely occurs in animals; usually even hermaphrodite animals cross-fertilize each other.

gamete cell that functions in sexual reproduction by merging with another gamete to form a zygote. Examples of gametes include sperm and egg cells. In most organisms, the gametes are haploid (they contain half the number of chromosomes of the parent), owing to reduction division or meiosis.

gene unit of inherited material, encoded by a strand of DNA, and transcribed by RNA. In higher organisms, genes are located on the chromosomes. The term 'gene', coined in 1909 by the Danish geneticist Wilhelm Johannsen (1857–1927), refers to the inherited factor that consistently affects a particular character in an individual—for example the gene for eye colour. Also termed a Mendelian gene, after Gregor Mendel, it occurs at a particular point or locus on a particular chromosome and may have several variants or alleles, each specifying a particular form of that character—for example the alleles for blue or brown eyes. Some alleles show dominance. These mask the effect of other alleles known as recessive.

genome the full complement of genes carried by a single (haploid) set of chromosomes in the nucleus of any cell, organism, or species.

genotype the particular set of alleles possessed by a given organism. The term is often used in conjunction with the phenotype (physical appearance) of the organism.

haploid having a single set of chromosomes in each cell. Most higher organisms are diploid—that is, they have two sets—but some plants, such as mosses, liverworts, and many seaweeds are haploid. Male honey bees are haploid because they develop from eggs that have not been fertilized.

hermaphrodite an organism that has both male

and female sex organs. Hermaphroditism is the norm in species such as earthworms and snails, and is common in flowering plants. Cross-fertilization is the rule among hermaphrodites, with the parents functioning as male and female simultaneously, or as one or the other sex at different stages in their development.

heterozygous in a living organism, having two different alleles for any one trait. In homozygous organisms, by contrast, both chromosomes carry the same allele. In an outbreeding population (one that produces offspring outside a particular family/tribe/group) an individual organism will generally be heterozygous for some genes but homozygous for others.

homozygous in a living organism, having two identical alleles for a given trait. Individuals homozygous for a trait always breed true, that is they produce offspring that resemble them in appearance when bred with a genetically similar individual; inbred varieties or species are homozygous for almost all traits.

karyotype the set of chromosomes characteristic of a given species. It is described as the number, shape, and size of the chromosomes in a single cell of an organism. In humans for example, the karyotype consists of 46 chromosomes, in mice 40, crayfish 200, and in fruit flies 8.

The diagrammatic representation of a complete chromosome set is called a *karyogram*.

larva the stage between hatching and adulthood in those species in which the young have a different appearance and way of life from the adults. Examples include tadpoles (frogs) and caterpillars (butterflies and moths). Larvae are typical of the invertebrates, and some (for example, shrimps) have two or more distinct larval stages. Among vertebrates, it is only the amphibians and some fishes that have a larval stage. The process whereby the larva changes into another stage, such as a pupa (chrysalis) or adult, is known as metamorphosis.

meiosis a process of cell division in which the number of chromosomes in the cell is halved. It only occurs in eukaryotic cells, and is part of a life cycle that involves sexual reproduction because it allows the genes of two parents to be combined without the total number of chromosomes increasing.

metamorphosis period during the life cycle of many invertebrates, most amphibians, and some fish, during which the individual's body changes from one form to another through a major reconstitution of its tissues. For example, adult frogs are produced by metamorphosis from tadpoles, and butterflies are produced from caterpillars following metamorphosis within a pupa.

ovum (plural *ova*) the female gamete (sex cell) before fertilization. In animals it is called an egg, and is produced in the ovaries. In plants, where it is also known as an egg cell or oosphere, the ovum is produced in an ovule. The ovum is nonmotile. It must be fertilized by a male gamete before it can develop further, except in

cases of parthenogenesis.

phenotype the physical traits, collectively, displayed by an organism. It is determined both by its genetic constitution (genotype) and the environment.

The phenotype is not a direct reflection of the genotype—for example, two plants may have the same genotype for height, but if one receives less sunlight it will become paler and taller than the other. The phenotype can also differ (in organisms with the same genotype) because some alleles are masked by the presence of other, dominant alleles, in a phenomenon known as penetrance, or the extent to which a gene exhibits its effect. Such variations in the effects of a gene are thought to be influenced by the effect of other genes present and by the environment.

pollen the grains of seed plants that contain the male gametes. In angiosperms pollen is produced within anthers; in most gymnosperms it is produced in male cones. A pollen grain is typically yellow and, when mature, has a hard outer wall. Pollen of insect-pollinated plants is often sticky and spiny and larger than the smooth, light grains produced by wind-pollinated species. The study of pollen grains is known as palynology, and the study of fossil grains (well-preserved in many kinds of rock and especially numerous in peat) can reveal the dominant flora—and hence the climate—in past geological eras.

pregnancy in humans, the period during which an embryo grows within the womb. It begins at conception and ends at birth, and the normal length is 40 weeks. Menstruation usually stops on conception. About one in five pregnancies fails, but most of these failures occur very early on, so the woman may notice only that her period is late. After the second month, the breasts become tense and tender, and the areas round the nipples become darker. Enlargement of the uterus can be felt at about the end of the third month, and thereafter the abdomen enlarges progressively. Pregnancy in animals is called gestation.

pupa the nonfeeding, largely immobile stage of some insect life cycles, in which larval tissues are broken down, and adult tissues and structures are formed. In many insects, it is *exarate*, with the appendages (legs, antennae, wings) visible outside the pupal case; in butterflies and moths, the pupa is called a chrysalis, and is *obtect*, with the appendages developing inside the case.

replication production of two identical molecules of DNA from the parent molecule; it occurs during cell division (mitosis and meiosis). The two new single strands that are formed (from the splitting of the double-stranded parent molecule) each control the synthesis of a new strand complementary to itself.

sperm or *spermatozoon* the male gamete of animals. Each sperm cell has a head capsule containing a nucleus, a middle portion containing mitochondria (which provide energy), and a long tail (flagellum).

zygote ovum (egg) after fertilization but before it undergoes cleavage to begin embryonic development.

THE MAINTENANCE OF LIFE

aerobic using molecular oxygen (usually dissolved in water) for the efficient release of energy. Almost all living organisms are aerobic. They use oxygen to convert glucose to carbon dioxide and water, thereby releasing energy. Most aerobic organisms die in the absence of oxygen, but certain organisms and cells, such as muscle cells, can function for short periods anaerobically (without oxygen).

anaerobic not requiring oxygen for the release of energy food. Anaerobic organisms include many bacteria, yeasts, and internal parasites. *Obligate anaerobes* such as archaebacteria cannot function in the presence of oxygen; but *facultative anaerobes*, like the fermenting yeasts and some bacteria, can function with or without oxygen. Anaerobic organisms release 19 times less of the available energy from their food than do aerobic organisms.

autotroph any living organism that synthesizes organic substances from inorganic molecules by using light or chemical energy. Autotrophs are the *primary producers* in all food chains since the materials they synthesize and store are the energy sources of all other organisms. All green plants and many planktonic organisms are autotrophs, using sunlight to convert carbon dioxide and water into sugars by photosynthesis.

basal metabolic rate (BMR) the amount of energy needed by an animal just to stay alive. It is measured when the animal is awake but resting, and includes the energy required to keep the heart beating, sustain breathing, repair tissues, and keep the brain and nerves functioning. Measuring the animal's consumption of oxygen gives an accurate value for BMR, because oxygen is needed to release energy from food.

BMR varies from one species to another, and from males to females. In humans, it is highest in children and declines with age. Disease, including mental illness, can make it rise or fall. Hormones from the thyroid gland control the BMR.

biosynthesis the synthesis of organic chemicals from simple inorganic ones by living cells—for example, the conversion of carbon dioxide and water to glucose by plants during photosynthesis. Other biosynthetic reactions produce cell constituents including proteins and fats.

carnivore animal that eats other animals. Although it is sometimes confined to animals that eat the flesh of vertebrate prey, the term is often used more broadly to include any animal that eats other animals, even microscopic ones. Carrion-eaters may or may not be included.

chemosynthesis method of making protoplasm (contents of a cell) using the energy from chemical reactions, in contrast to the use of light energy employed for the same purpose in photosynthesis. The process is used by certain bacteria, which can synthesize organic compounds from carbon dioxide and water using the energy from special methods of respiration.

decomposer any organism that breaks down dead matter. Decomposers play a vital role in the ecosystem by freeing important chemical substances, such as nitrogen compounds, locked up in dead organisms or excrement. They feed on some of the released organic matter, but leave the rest to filter back into the soil or pass in gas form into the atmosphere. The principal decomposers are bacteria and fungi, but earthworms and many other invertebrates are often included in this group. The nitrogen cycle relies on the actions of decomposers.

food chain or *food web* in ecology, the sequence of organisms through which energy and other nutrients are successively transferred. Since many organisms feed at several different levels (for example, omnivores feed on both fruit and meat), the relationships often form a complex web rather than a simple chain.

The sequence of the food chain comprises the autotrophs, or producers, which are principally plants and photosynthetic microorganisms, and a series of heterotrophs, or consumers, which are the herbivores that feed on the producers; the carnivores that feed on the herbivores; and the decomposers that break down the dead bodies and waste products of all four groups (including their own), ready for recycling.

gas exchange the exchange of gases between living organisms and the atmosphere, principally oxygen and carbon dioxide.

herbivore an animal that feeds on green plants or their products, including seeds, fruit, and nectar. The most numerous type of herbivore is thought to be the zooplankton, tiny invertebrates in the surface waters of the oceans that feed on small photosynthetic algae. Herbivores are more numerous than other animals because their food is the most abundant. They form a link in the food chain between plants and carnivores.

heterotroph any living organism that obtains its energy from organic substances produced by other organisms. All animals and fungi are heterotrophs, and they include herbivores, carnivores, and saprotrophs (those that feed on dead animal and plant material).

nitrogen cycle the process of nitrogen passing through the ecosystem. Nitrogen, in the form of inorganic compounds (such as nitrates) in the soil, is absorbed by plants and turned into organic compounds (such as proteins) in plant tissue. A proportion of this nitrogen is eaten by herbivores, with some of this in turn being passed on to the carnivores, which feed on the herbivores. The nitrogen is ultimately returned to the soil as excrement, and when organisms die and decompose.

omnivore animal that feeds on both plant and animal material. Omnivores have digestive adaptations intermediate between those of herbivores and carnivores, with relatively unspecialized digestive systems and gut microorganisms that can digest a variety of foodstuffs.

photosynthesis the process by which green plants, photosynthetic bacteria, and cyanobacteria use light energy from the Sun to produce food molecules (carbohydrates) from carbon dioxide and water. There are two stages. During the *light reaction* sunlight is used to split water (H_2O) into oxygen (O_2), protons (hydrogen ions, H^+), and electrons, and oxygen is given off as a by-product. In the second-stage *dark reaction*, where sunlight is not required, the protons and electrons are used to convert carbon dioxide (CO_2) into carbohydrates (CH_2O). Photosynthesis depends on the ability of chlorophyll to capture the energy of sunlight and to use it to split water molecules.

Photosynthesis by cyanobacteria was responsible for the appearance of oxygen in the Earth's atmosphere 2 billion years ago, and photosynthesis by plants maintains the oxygen level today.

respiration biochemical process whereby food molecules are progressively broken down (oxidized) to release energy in the form of ATP. In most organisms this requires oxygen, but in some bacteria the oxidant is the nitrate or sulphate ion instead. In all higher organisms, respiration occurs in the mitochondria. Respiration is also used to mean breathing, although this is more accurately described as a form of gas exchange.

THE MACROSCOPIC WORLD

ANIMAL

(or *metazoan*) member of the kingdom Animalia, one of the major categories of living things, the science of which is *zoology*. Animals are all heterotrophs (they obtain their energy from organic substances produced by other organisms); they have eukaryotic cells (the genetic material is contained within a distinct nucleus) bounded by a thin cell membrane rather than the thick cell wall of plants. In the past, it was common to include the single-celled protozoa with the animals, but these are now classified as protists, together with single-celled plants. Thus all animals are multicellular. Most are capable of moving around for at least part of their life cycle.

Types
invertebrate
animal without a backbone. The invertebrates comprise over 95% of the million or so existing animal species and include the sponges, coelenterates, flatworms, nematodes, annelid worms, arthropods, molluscs, echinoderms, and primitive aquatic chordates such as sea squirts and lancelets.

annelid any segmented worm of the phylum Annelida. Annelids include earthworms, leeches, and marine worms such as lugworms. They have a distinct head and soft body, which is divided into a number of similar segments shut off from one another internally by mem-

nitrogen cycle

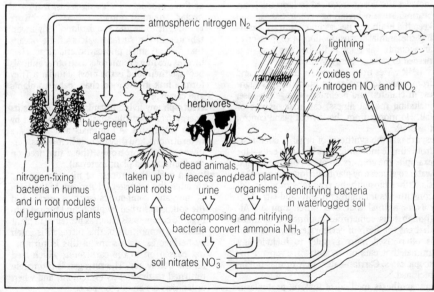

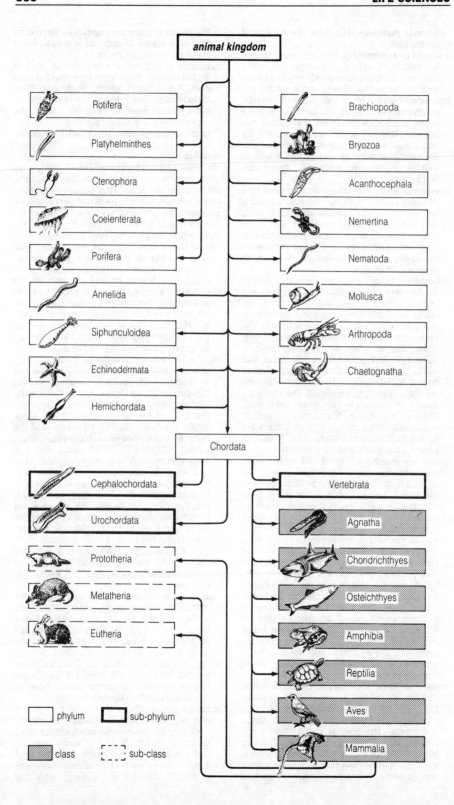

branous partitions, but there are no jointed appendages.

arachnid or *arachnoid* type of arthropod, including spiders, scorpions, and mites. They differ from insects in possessing only two main body regions, the cephalophorax and the abdomen.

arthropod member of the phylum Arthropoda; an invertebrate animal with jointed legs and a segmented body with a horny or chitinous casing (exoskeleton), which is shed periodically and replaced as the animal grows. Included are arachnids such as spiders and mites, as well as crustaceans, millipedes, centipedes, and insects.

crustacean one of the class of arthropods that includes crabs, lobsters, shrimps, woodlice, and barnacles. The external skeleton is made of protein and chitin hardened with lime. Each segment bears a pair of appendages that may be modified as sensory feelers (antennae), as mouthparts, or as swimming, walking, or grasping structures.

echinoderm marine invertebrate of the phylum Echinodermata ('spiny-skinned'), with a basic body structure divided into five sectors. Included are starfishes (or sea stars), brittlestars, sea-lilies, sea-urchins, and sea-cucumbers. The skeleton is external, made of a series of limy plates, and echinoderms generally move by using tube-feet, small water-filled sacs that can be protruded or pulled back to the body.

flatworm invertebrate of the phylum Platyhelminthes. Some are free-living, but many are parasitic (for example, tapeworms and flukes). The body is simple and bilaterally symmetrical, with one opening to the intestine. Many are hermaphroditic (with both male and female sex organs), and practise self-fertilization.

insect any member of the class Insecta among the arthropods or jointed-legged animals. An insect's body is divided into head, thorax, and abdomen. The head bears a pair of feelers or antennae, and attached to the thorax are three pairs of legs and usually two pairs of wings. The scientific study of insects is termed entomology. More than one million species are known, and several thousand new ones are discovered every year. Insects vary in size from 0.02 cm/0.007 in to 35 cm/13.5 in in length.

jellyfish marine invertebrate of the phylum Cnidaria (coelenterates) with an umbrella-shaped body composed of a semi-transparent gelatinous substance, with a fringe of stinging tentacles. Most adult jellyfishes move freely, but during parts of their life cycle many are polyp-like and attached. They feed on small animals that are paralyzed by stinging cells in the jellyfishes' tentacles.

mollusc any invertebrate of the phylum Mollusca. The majority of molluscs are marine animals, but some inhabit fresh water, and a few are terrestrial. They include bivalves, snails, slugs, and squids. The body is soft, limbless, and cold-blooded. There is no internal skeleton, but most species have a hard shell covering the body. Molluscs vary in diet, the carnivorous species feeding chiefly upon other members of

the phylum. Some are vegetarian. Reproduction is by means of eggs and is sexual; many species are hermaphrodite.

nematode unsegmented worm of the phylum Aschelminthes. Nematodes are pointed at both ends, with a tough, smooth outer skin. They include many free-living soil and water forms, but a large number are parasites, such as the roundworms and pinworms that live in humans, or the eelworms that attack plant roots.

vertebrate
any animal with a backbone. The 41,000 species of vertebrates include mammals, birds, reptiles, amphibians, and fishes. They include most of the larger animals, but in terms of numbers of species are only a tiny proportion of the world's animals. The zoological taxonomic group Vertebrata is a subgroup of the phylum Chordata.

amphibian member of the vertebrate class Amphibia (Greek 'double life'), which generally spend their larval (tadpole) stage in fresh water, transferring to land at maturity and generally returning to water to breed. Like fish and reptiles, they continue to grow throughout life, and cannot maintain a temperature greatly differing from that of their environment. The class includes caecilians, worm-like in appearance; salamanders, frogs, and toads.

bird backboned animal of the class Aves, the biggest group of land vertebrates, characterized by warm blood, feathers, wings, breathing through lungs, and egg-laying by the female. Birds are bipedal, with the front limb modified to form a wing and retaining only three digits. The heart has four chambers, and the body is maintained at a high temperature (about 41°C/106°F). Most birds fly, but some groups (such as ostriches) are flightless, and others include flightless members. Many communicate by sounds, or by visual displays, in connection with which many species are brightly coloured, usually the males. Birds have highly developed patterns of instinctive behaviour. Hearing and eyesight are well developed, but the sense of smell is usually poor. Typically the eggs are brooded in a nest and, on hatching, the young receive a period of parental care. There are nearly 8,500 species of birds.

fish aquatic vertebrate that uses gills for obtaining oxygen from water. There are three main groups, not closely related: the bony fishes or Osteichthyes (these include goldfish, cod, tuna, and constitute the majority of living fishes, about 20,000 species); the cartilaginous fishes or Chondrichthyes (sharks, rays, of which there are fewer than 600 known species); and the jawless fishes or Agnatha (hagfishes, lampreys).

mammal any vertebrate that suckles its young and has hair. Mammals maintain a constant body temperature in varied surroundings. Most mammals give birth to live young, but the platypus and echidna lay eggs. There are over 4,000 species, adapted to almost every way of life. The smallest shrew weighs only 2 g/

skeleton

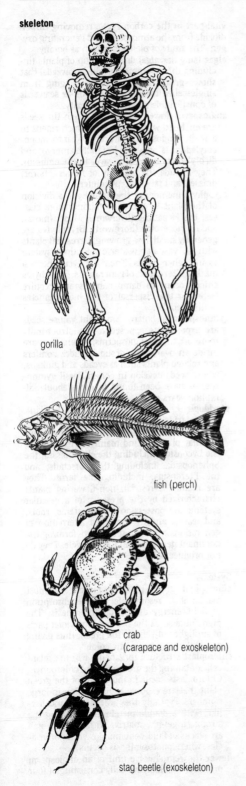

gorilla

fish (perch)

crab
(carapace and exoskeleton)

stag beetle (exoskeleton)

0.07 oz, the largest whale up to 150 tonnes.

reptile class (Reptilia) of vertebrates. Unlike amphibians, reptiles have hard- shelled, yolk-filled eggs that are laid on land and from which fully formed young are born. Some snakes and lizards retain their eggs and give birth to live young. Reptiles are cold-blooded, produced from eggs, and the skin is usually covered with scales. The metabolism is slow, and in some cases (some large snakes) intervals between meals may be months. Reptiles date back over 300 million years. They include snakes, lizards, crocodiles, turtles, tortoises, and the tuatara.

Systems

alimentary canal in animals, the tube through which food passes; it extends from the mouth to the anus. It is a complex organ, adapted for digestion. In human adults, it is about 9 m/ 30 ft long, consisting of the mouth cavity, pharynx, oesophagus, stomach, and the small and large intestines.

bone the hard connective tissue comprising the skeleton of most vertebrate animals. It consists of a network of collagen fibres impregnated with inorganic salts, especially calcium phospate. Enclosed within this solid matrix are bone cells, blood vessels, and nerves. In strength, the toughest bone is comparable with reinforced concrete. There are two types of bone: those that develop by replacing cartilage and those that form directly from connective tissue. The latter are usually platelike in shape, and form in the skin of the developing embryo. Humans have about 206 distinct bones in the skeleton. The interior of long bones consists of a spongy matrix filled with a soft marrow that produces blood cells.

brain in higher animals, a mass of interconnected nerve cells, forming the anterior part of the central nervous system, whose activities it coordinates and controls. In vertebrates, the brain is contained by the skull. An enlarged portion of the upper spinal cord, the *medulla oblongata*, contains centres for the control of respiration, heartbeat rate and strength, and blood pressure. Overlying this is the *cerebellum*, which is concerned with coordinating complex muscular processes such as maintaining posture and moving limbs. The cerebral hemispheres (*cerebrum*) are paired outgrowths of the front end of the forebrain, in early vertebrates mainly concerned with the senses, but in higher vertebrates greatly developed and involved in the integration of all sensory input and motor output, and in intelligent behaviour. In the brain, nerve impulses are passed across synapses by neurotransmitters, in the same way as in other parts of the nervous system.

In mammals the cerebrum is the largest part of the brain, carrying the *cerebral cortex*. As cerebral complexity grows, the surface of the brain becomes convoluted into deep folds. In higher mammals, there are large unassigned areas of the brain that seem to be connected with intelligence, personality, and higher mental faculties. Language is controlled in two special regions usually in the left side of the brain: *Broca's area* governs the ability to talk, and *Wernicke's area* is responsible for the comprehension of spoken and written words.

In 1990, scientists at Johns Hopkins University, Baltimore, succeeded in culturing human brain cells.

circulatory system the system of vessels in an animal's body that transports essential substances (blood or other circulatory fluid) to and from the different parts of the body. Except for simple animals such as sponges and coelenterates (jellyfishes, sea anemones, corals), all animals have a circulatory system.

muscle contractile animal tissue that produces locomotion and maintains the movement of body substances. Muscle is made of long cells that can contract to between one-half and one-third of their relaxed length. *Striped* muscles are activated by motor nerves under voluntary control; their ends are usually attached via tendons to bones. *Involuntary* or *smooth* muscles are controlled by motor nerves of the autonomic nervous system, and located in the gut, blood vessels, iris, and various ducts. *Cardiac* muscle occurs only in the heart, and is also controlled by the autonomic nervous system.

nervous system the system of interconnected nerve cells of most invertebrates and all vertebrates. It is composed of the central and autonomic nervous systems. It may be as simple as the nerve net of coelenterates (for example, jellyfishes) or as complex as the mammalian nervous system, with a central nervous system comprising brain and spinal cord, and a peripheral nervous system connecting up with sensory organs, muscles, and glands.

skeleton the rigid or semirigid framework that supports an animal's body, protects its internal organs, and provides anchorage points for its muscles. The skeleton may be composed of bone and cartilage (vertebrates), chitin (arthropods), calcium carbonate (molluscs and other invertebrates, or silica (many protists).

It may be internal, forming an *endoskeleton*, or external, forming an *exoskeleton*. Another type of skeleton, found in invertebrates such as earthworms, is the *hydrostatic skeleton*. This gains partial rigidity from fluid enclosed within a body cavity. Because the fluid cannot be compressed, contraction of one part of the body results in extension of another part, giving peristaltic motion.

PLANT

an organism that carries out photosynthesis, has cellulose cell walls and complex eukaryotic cells, and is immobile. A few parasitic plants have lost the ability to photosynthesize but are still considered to be plants.

Plants are autotrophs, that is, they make carbohydrates from water and carbon dioxide, and are the primary producers in all food chains, so that all animal life is dependent on them. They play a

vital part in the carbon cycle, removing carbon dioxide from the atmosphere and generating oxygen. The study of plants is known as botany.

algae (singular **alga**) diverse group of plants (including those commonly called seaweeds) that shows great variety of form, ranging from single-celled forms to multicellular seaweeds of considerable size and complexity.

angiosperm flowering plant in which the seeds are enclosed within an ovary, which ripens to a fruit. Angiosperms are divided into monocotyledons (single seed leaf in the embryo) and dicotyledons (two seed leaves in the embryo). They include the majority of flowers, herbs, grasses, and trees except conifers.

bryophyte member of the Bryophyta, a division of the plant kingdom containing three classes, the Hepaticae (liverwort), Musci (moss), and Anthocerotae (hornwort). Bryophytes are generally small, low-growing, terrestrial plants with no vascular (water-conducting) system as in higher plants. Their life cycle shows a marked alternation of generations. Bryophytes chiefly occur in damp habitats and require water for the dispersal of the male gametes (antherozoids).

gymnosperm in botany, any plant whose seeds are exposed, as opposed to the structurally more advanced angiosperms, where they are inside an ovary. The group includes conifers and related plants such as cycads and ginkgos, whose seeds develop in cones. Fossil gymnosperms have been found in rocks about 350 million years old.

pteridophyte simple type of vascular plant. The pteridophytes comprise four classes: the Psilosida, including the most primitive vascular plants, found mainly in the tropics; the Lycopsida, including the club mosses; the Sphenopsida, including the horsetails; and the Pteropsida, including the ferns. They are mainly terrestrial, non-flowering plants characterized by the presence of a vascular system; the possession of true stems, roots, and leaves; and by a marked alternation of generations, with the sporophyte forming the dominant generation in the life cycle. They do not produce seeds.

Systems

chlorophyll green pigment present in most plants; it is responsible for the absorption of light energy during photosynthesis. The pigment absorbs the red and blue-violet parts of sunlight but reflects the green, thus giving plants their characteristic colour.

chloroplast structure (organelle) within a plant cell containing the green pigment chlorophyll. Chloroplasts occur in most cells of the green plant that are exposed to light, often in large numbers. Typically, they are flattened and disc-like, with a double membrane enclosing the stroma, a gel-like matrix. Within the stroma are stacks of fluid-containing cavities, or vesicles, where photosynthesis occurs.

flower the reproductive unit of an angiosperm or flowering plant, typically consisting of four whorls of modified leaves: sepals, petals, stamens, and carpels. These are borne on a central axis or receptacle. The many variations in size, colour, number and arrangement of parts are closely related to the method of pollination. Flowers adapted for wind pollination typically have reduced or absent petals and sepals and long, feathery stigmas that hang outside the flower to trap airborne pollen. In contrast, the petals of insect-pollinated flowers are usually conspicuous and brightly coloured.

In size, flowers range from the tiny blooms of duckweeds scarcely visible with the naked eye to the gigantic flowers of the Malaysian *Rafflesia*, which can reach over 1 m/3 ft across.

leaf lateral outgrowth on the stem of a plant, and in most species the primary organ of photosynthesis. The chief leaf types are cotyledons (seed leaves), scale leaves (on underground stems), foliage leaves, and bracts (in the axil of which a flower is produced).

Structurally the leaf is made up of mesophyll cells surrounded by the epidermis and usually, in addition, a waxy layer, termed the cuticle, which prevents excessive evaporation of water from the leaf tissues by transpiration. The epidermis is interrupted by small pores, or stomata through which gas exchange occurs.

root the part of a plant that is usually underground, and whose primary functions are anchorage and the absorption of water and dissolved mineral salts. Roots usually grow downwards and towards water (that is, they are positively geotropic and hydrotropic; see tropism). Plants, such as epiphytic orchids that grow above ground, produce aerial roots that absorb moisture from the atmosphere. Others, such as ivy, have climbing roots arising from the stems that serve to attach the plant to trees and walls.

THE MICROSCOPIC WORLD

archaebacteria three groups of bacteria whose DNA differs significantly from that of other bacteria (called the 'eubacteria'). All are strict anaerobes, that is, they are killed by oxygen. This is thought to be a primitive condition and to indicate that the archaebacteria are related to the earliest life forms, which appeared about 4 billion years ago, when there was little oxygen in the Earth's atmosphere.

bacillus member of a group of rodlike bacteria that occur everywhere in the soil and air. Some are responsible for diseases such as anthrax or for causing food spoilage.

bacteria (singular *bacterium*) microscopic unicellular organisms with prokaryotic cells (lacking true nuclei and other specialized cell structures), divided into groups on the basis of such characteristics as the rigidity and shape of the cell wall, type of colony, and type and products of metabolism. The large majority of bacteria are *eubacteria*, which have a rigid cell wall.

They usually reproduce by binary fission, and since this may occur approximately every

---

BIGGEST ORGANISM FOUND

The largest living organism has been found in northern Michigan, USA. Surprisingly, it is neither a mammal nor a tree, but a fungus. The fungus *Armillaria bulbosa* covers over 15 ha/37 acres and is estimated to weigh 100,000 kg/220,500 lb.

The fungus infects tree roots, and the main part of it is made up of millions of fine underground tubes known as hyphae. The recently discovered specimen is completely below the surface, which is why something of this size has not been previously observed. The scientists who discovered it think it may have been in existence for 1500 years.

---

20 minutes, a single bacterium is potentially capable of producing 16 million copies of itself in a day.

blue-green algae single-celled, primitive organisms that resemble bacteria in their internal cell organization, sometimes joined together in colonies or filaments. Blue-green algae are among the oldest known living organisms; remains have been found in rocks up to 3.5 billion years old. They are widely distributed in aquatic habitats, on the damp surfaces of rocks and trees, and in the soil.

Blue-green algae and bacteria are prokaryotic organisms. Some can fix nitrogen and thus are necessary to the nitrogen cycle, while others follow a symbiotic existence—for example, living in association with fungi to form lichens.

cell a self-contained portion of living matter bordered by a membrane, the smallest unit capable of an independent existence. All living organisms consist of one or more cells, with the exception of viruses. Bacteria, protozoa and many other microorganisms consist of single cells, whereas a human is made up of billions of cells. Essential features of a cell are the membrane, which encloses it and restricts the flow of substances in and out; the jellylike material within, often known as protoplasm, the ribosomes, which carry out protein synthesis, and the DNA, which forms the hereditary material.

coccus (plural *cocci*) member of a group of globular bacteria, some of which are harmful to humans. The cocci contain the subgroups *streptococci*, where the bacteria associate in straight chains, and *staphylococci*, where the bacteria associate in branched chains.

cytoplasm the part of the cell outside the nucleus. Strictly speaking, this includes all the organelles (mitochondria, chloroplasts, and so on), but often cytoplasm refers to the jellylike matter in which the organelles are embedded (correctly termed the cytosol). In many cells, the cytoplasm is made up of two parts: the *ectoplasm* (or plasmagel), a dense gelatinous outer layer concerned with cell movement, and the *endoplasm* (or plasmasol), a more fluid inner part where most of the organelles are found.

eukaryote an organism whose cells have a distinct nucleus which carries the genetic material on

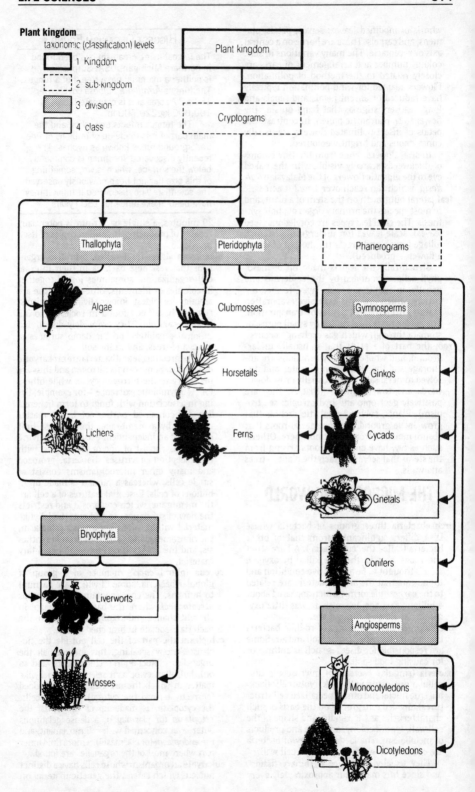

Plant kingdom

taxonomic (classification) levels

- 1 Kingdom
- 2 sub-kingdom
- 3 division
- 4 class

Plant kingdom

Cryptograms

Thallophyta

Pteridophyta

Phanerograms

Algae

Clubmosses

Gymnosperms

Horsetails

Ginkos

Lichens

Ferns

Cycads

Bryophyta

Gnetals

Conifers

Liverworts

Angiosperms

Mosses

Monocotyledons

Dicotyledons

chromosomes. All organisms, except bacteria and blue-green algae, which belong to the prokaryote grouping, are eukaryotes.

methanogenic bacteria one of a group of primitive bacteria (archaebacteria). They give off methane gas as a by-product of their metabolism, and are common in sewage treatment plants and hot springs, where the temperature is high and oxygen is absent.

microorganism or **microbe** living organism invisible to the naked eye but visible under a microscope. Microorganisms include viruses and single-celled organisms such as bacteria, protozoa, yeasts, and some algae. The term has no taxonomic significance in biology. The study of microorganisms is known as microbiology.

nucleus the central, membrane-enclosed part of a eukaryotic cell, containing the genetic material, DNA.

prokaryote an organism whose cells lack organelles (specialized segregated structures such as nuclei, mitochondria, and chloroplasts). Prokaryote DNA is not arranged in chromosomes but forms a coiled structure called a **nucleoid**. The prokaryotes comprise only the **bacteria** and **blue-green algae**; all other organisms are eukaryotes.

protist a single-celled organism which has a eukaryotic cell, but which is not a member of the plant, fungal, or animal kingdoms. The main protists are protozoa.

protozoa group of single-celled organisms without rigid cell walls. Some, such as amoeba, ingest other cells, but most are saprotrophs or parasites. The group is polyphyletic (containing organisms which have different evolutionary origins).

virus infectious particle consisting of a core of nucleic acid (DNA or RNA) enclosed in a protein shell. Viruses are acellular and able to function and reproduce only if they can invade a living cell to use the cell's system to replicate themselves. In the process they may disrupt or alter the host cell's own DNA. The healthy human body reacts by producing an antiviral protein, interferon, which prevents the infection spreading to adjacent cells.

Among diseases caused by viruses are canine distemper, chickenpox, common cold, herpes, influenza, rabies, smallpox, yellow fever, AIDS, and many plant diseases.

THE NEW SYNTHESIS

amino acid water-soluble organic molecule, mainly composed of carbon, oxygen, hydrogen, and nitrogen, containing both a basic amine group (NH_2) and an acidic carboxyl (COOH) group. When two or more amino acids are joined together, they are known as peptides; proteins are made up of interacting polypeptides (peptide chains consisting of more than three amino acids) and are folded or twisted in characteristic shapes.

Many different proteins are found in the cells of living organisms, but they are all made up of the same 20 amino acids, joined together in varying combinations, (although other types of amino acid do occur infrequently in nature). Eight of these, the **essential amino acids**, cannot be synthesized by humans and must be obtained from the diet. Children need a further two amino acids that are not essential for adults. Other animals also need some preformed amino acids in their diet, but green plants can manufacture all the amino acids they need from simpler molecules, relying on energy from the sun and minerals (including nitrates) from the soil.

amylase one of a group of enzymes that breaks down starches into their component molecules (sugars) for use in the body. It occurs widely in both plants and animals. In humans, it is found in saliva and in pancreatic juices.

basepair the linkage of two base (purine or pyrimidine) molecules in DNA. They are found in nucleotides, and form the basis of the genetic code.

One base lies on one strand of the DNA double helix, and one on the other, so that the base pairs link the two strands like the rungs of a ladder. In DNA, there are four bases: adenine and guanine (purines) and cytosine and thymine (pyrimidines). Adenine always pairs with thymine, and cytosine with guanine.

codon a triplet of bases in a molecule of DNA or RNA that directs the placement of a particular amino acid during the process of protein synthesis. There are 64 codons in the genetic code.

cytochrome protein responsible for part of the process of respiration by which food molecules are broken down in aerobic organisms. Cytochromes are part of the electron transport chain, which uses energized electrons to reduce molecular oxygen (O_2) to oxygen ions (O^{2-}). These combine with hydrogen ions (H^+) to form water (H_2O), the end product of aerobic respiration. As electrons are passed from one cytochrome to another energy is released and used to make ATP.

DNA **deoxyribonucleic acid** complex two stranded molecule that contains, in chemically coded form, all the information needed to build, control, and maintain a living organism. DNA is a ladderlike double-stranded nucleic acid that forms the basis of genetic inheritance in all organisms, except for a few viruses that have only RNA. In eukaryotic organisms, it is organized into chromosomes and contained in the cell nucleus.

enzyme biological catalyst produced in cells, and capable of speeding up the chemical reactions necessary for life. Enzymes are not themselves destroyed by this process. They are large, complex proteins, and are highly specific, each chemical reaction requiring its own particular enzyme. Digestive enzymes include amylases (which digest starch), lipases (which digest fats), and proteases (which digest protein).

ELECTRONIC LIFE

One of the problems with studying life sciences is that changes in ecosystems and the evolution of life forms takes place over long periods of time. Scientists have attempted to simulate life processes in computers, so that such changes can be studied with artificial life. Now researchers at the University of Delaware have made significant advances with such computer-generated organisms.

Tierra: a new form of life ...

Under the direction of Thomas Ray, an electronic world, known as Tierra, has been created. Life, death, competition, and reproduction are all modelled in computer terms, and the electronic organisms can be viewed as coloured patterns on a computer screen. A simple program, written to replicate itself, will rapidly fill the screen with progeny. More complex programming sets free numerous organisms to reproduce and compete with each other for limited resources.

Tierra uses a concept known as a virtual computer—a software program that models a computer inside the real computer. This is a safety device to prevent any of the electronic organisms getting out of control and behaving like computer viruses. An interesting feature of the virtual computer is a block of memory termed the 'soup'. This is analogous to the 'primordial soup'—the mixture of organic molecules in which life is thought to have evolved. The electronic organisms use this memory to grow and to change.

Changes, or mutations, to the electronic organisms are what makes Tierra such a fascinating environment. Changes come about in two ways—either by random flips in the memory soup (the memory changes from 0 to 1 or vice versa) or by inaccurate copying of the organisms' template during replication, which happens about once in every 2,000 instructions copied. Provided that important instructions are unaltered, the mutant organism can still function. Just as in the evolution of life, the occasional mutation is actually of benefit to the organism, and it can compete with greater success against other Tierran life.

... and death

There is also a monitoring program, known as the reaper. This program comes into operation when over three-quarters of the memory soup is occupied (that is, at high population levels). Its function is to simulate death, and it removes both the oldest creatures and those least efficient at replicating.

Tierra was first run in 1990 with a single ancestor organism some 80 instructions long. Almost immediately a creature evolved that was only 22 instructions long and could reproduce six times as rapidly as the ancestor. Large creatures—one of 23,000 instructions—also arose, but died out because they could not compete with the smaller, faster-reproducing organisms.

Parasites emerged—programs that could not reproduce themselves, but could use the instructions of other organisms to do so. These programs were at an advantage because they were smaller and reproduced more quickly. However, a 79-instruction creature evolved, which was similar to the ancestor but immune to parasites. This creature dominated Tierra until a new parasite evolved which could evade the dominant creature's defences.

A model for evolution and ecology

Fascinating though the Tierran system is, what use is it to life science in general? Thomas Ray suggests that it will be important to two groups in particular. Ecologists and evolutionary biologists will find the interaction of creatures and the emerging population patterns of significance.

For ecologists, one most important question is the extent to which competition structures community. Tierra has shown both competitive exclusion, with weaker organisms driven to extinction, and coexistence, where different organisms have developed stable communities, despite shortages of resources.

Another ecological concept that can be tested is the 'keystone predator' effect, where the addition of a new predator stimulates diversity in a system. This theory is particularly difficult to test in the real world because of the environmental damage that could be caused by such an addition. There are no such constraints in Tierra.

Evolutionary biologists are also interested in the system because it demonstrates population cycling—hosts and parasites followed each other in peaks and declines. Despite the example of the snowshoe hare and the Canadian lynx, such cycles are difficult to observe in the real world.

Tierran evolution is also marked by punctuated equilibrium, where a period of stability is followed by rapid evolutionary change. The punctuated-equilibrium model has been controversial among biologists, but its demonstration in the Tierran system gives it extra credibility.

Tierra is already a powerful modelling and teaching tool. With its unpredictable and mutating organisms, it will also figure strongly in the debate about what life actually is.

Other enzymes play a part in the conversion of food energy into ATP; the manufacture of all the molecular components of the body; the replication of DNA when a cell divides; the production of hormones; and the control of movement of substances into and out of cells.

Enzymes have many medical and industrial uses, from washing powders to drug production, and as research tools in molecular biology. They can be extracted from bacteria and moulds, and genetic engineering now makes it possible to tailor the enzyme for a specific purpose, and greatly increase the rate of production.

genetic code the way in which instructions for building proteins, the basic structural molecules of living matter, are 'written' in the genetic material DNA. This relationship between the sequence of bases (the subunits in a DNA molecule) and the sequence of amino acids (the subunits of a protein molecule) is the basis of heredity. The code employs codons of three bases each; it is the same in almost all organisms, except for a few minor differences recently discovered in some protozoa.

mitochondria (singular *mitochondrion*) membrane-enclosed organelles within eukaryotic cells, containing enzymes responsible for energy production during aerobic respiration. These rodlike or spherical bodies are thought to be derived from free-living bacteria that, at a very early stage in the history of life, invaded larger cells and took up a symbiotic way of life inside. Each still contains its own small loop of DNA, and new mitochondria arise by division of existing ones.

molecular biology the study of the molecular basis of life, including the biochemistry of molecules such as DNA, RNA, and proteins, and the molecular structure and function of the various parts of living cells.

nucleotide organic compound consisting of a purine (adenine or guanine) or a pyrimidine (thymine, uracil, or cytosine) base linked to a sugar (deoxyribose or ribose) and a phosphate group. DNA and RNA are made up of long chains of nucleotides.

operon group of genes that are found next to each other on a chromosome, and are turned on and off as an integrated unit. They usually produce enzymes that control different steps in the same biochemical pathway. Operons were discovered 1961 (by the French biochemists F Jacob and J Monod) in bacteria; they are less common in higher organisms where the control of metabolism is a more complex process.

peptide a molecule comprising two or more amino acid molecules (not necessarily different) joined by *peptide bonds*, whereby the acid group of one acid is linked to the amino group of the other (–CO.NH). The number of amino acid molecules in the peptide is indicated by referring to it as a di-, tri-, or polypeptide (two, three, or many amino acids).

protein complex, biologically important substance composed of amino acids joined by peptide bonds. Other types of bond, such as sulphur–sulphur bonds, hydrogen bonds, and cation bridges between acid sites, are responsible for creating the protein's characteristic three-dimensional structure, which may be fibrous, globular, or pleated.

Proteins are essential to all living organisms. As *enzymes* they regulate all aspects of metabolism. Structural proteins such as *keratin* and *collagen* make up the skin, claws, bones, tendons, and ligaments; *muscle* proteins produce movement; *haemoglobin* transports oxygen; and *membrane* proteins regulate the movement of substances into and out of cells.

ribosome the protein-making machinery of the cell. Ribosomes are located on the endoplasmic reticulum (ER) of eukaryotic cells, and are made of proteins and a special type of RNA, ribosomal RNA. They receive messenger RNA (copied from the DNA) and amino acids, and 'translate' the messenger RNA by using its chemically coded instructions to link amino acids in a specific order, to make a strand of a particular protein.

RNA *ribonucleic acid* nucleic acid involved in the process of translating DNA, the genetic material into proteins. It is usually single-stranded, unlike the double-stranded DNA, and consists of a large number of nucleotides strung together, each of which comprises the sugar ribose, a phosphate group, and one of four bases (uracil, cytosine, adenine, or guanine). RNA is copied from DNA by the formation of base pairs, with uracil taking the place of thymine. Although RNA is normally associated only with the process of protein synthesis, it makes up the hereditary material itself in some viruses, such as retroviruses.

translation in living cells, the process by which proteins are synthesized. During translation, the information coded as a sequence of nucelotides in messenger RNA is transformed into a sequence of amino acids in a peptide chain. The process involves the 'translation' of the genetic code. See also transcription.

NEW TECHNIQUES

abzyme an artificially created antibody that can be used like an enzyme to accelerate reactions.

autoradiography technique for following the movement of molecules within an organism, especially a plant, by labelling with a radioactive isotope that can be traced on photographs. It is used to study photosynthesis, where the pathway of radioactive carbon dioxide can be traced as it moves through the various chemical stages.

bacteriophage virus that attacks bacteria. Such viruses are now of use in genetic engineering.

biosensor device based on microelectronic circuits that can directly measure medically significant variables for the purpose of diagnosis or monitoring treatment. One such device measures the blood sugar level of diabetics using a single drop of blood, and shows the result on a liquid crystal display within a few minutes.

biotechnology the industrial use of living organisms to manufacture food, drugs, or other products. The brewing and baking industries have long relied on the yeast microorganism for fermentation purposes, while the dairy industry employs a range of bacteria and fungi to convert milk into cheeses and yoghurts. Recent advances include genetic engineering, in which single-celled organisms with modified

DNA
how a cell divides

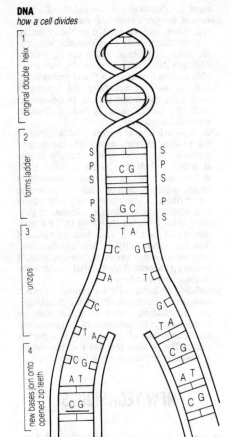

1 original double helix

2 forms ladder

3 unzips

4 new bases join onto opened zip teeth

5 two new identical double strands

S P S C G P S
S P G C S
S T A P
C G
A T
C G
T A
C G
A T
C G

C G
A T
C G

Key

S sugars	G guanine
P phosphates	A adenine
C cytosine	T thymine

DNA are used to produce insulin and other drugs. Enzymes, whether extracted from cells or produced artificially, are central to most biotechnological applications.

cosmid fragment of DNA from the human genome inserted into a bacterial cell. The bacterium replicates the fragment along with its own DNA. In this way the fragments are copied for a gene library. Cosmids are characteristically 40,000 base pairs in length. The most commonly used bacterium is *Escherichia coli*. A yeast artificial chromosome works in the same way.

electron microscope instrument that produces a magnified image by using a beam of electrons

instead of light rays, as in an optical microscope. An *electron lens* is an arrangement of electromagnetic coils that control and focus the beam. Electrons are not visible to the eye, so instead of an eyepiece there is a fluorescent screen or a photographic plate on which the electrons form an image. The wavelength of the electron beam is much shorter than that of light, so much greater magnification and resolution (ability to distinguish detail) can be achieved.

A *high-resolution electron microscope* (HREM) can produce a magnification of 7 million times ($\times$ 7,000,000). The development of the electron microscope has made possible the observation of very minute organisms, viruses, and even large molecules. A *transmission electron microscope* passes the electron beam through a very thin slice of a specimen. A *scanning electron microscope* looks at the exterior of a specimen.

electroporation a technique of introducing foreign DNA into pollen with a strong burst of electricity, used in creating genetically-engineered plants.

fluorescence microscopy technique for examining samples under a microscope without slicing them into thin sections. Instead, fluorescent dyes are introduced into the tissue and used as a light source for imaging purposes.

gene bank collection of seeds or other forms of genetic material, such as tubers, spores, bacterial or yeast cultures, live animals and plants, frozen sperm and eggs, or frozen embryos. These are stored for possible future use in agriculture, plant and animal breeding, or in medicine, genetic engineering, or the restocking of wild habitats where species have become extinct. Gene banks will be increasingly used as the rate of extinction increases, depleting the Earth's genetic variety (biodiversity).

gene therapy proposed medical technique for curing or alleviating inherited diseases or defects. Although not yet a practical possibility for most defects, some of the basic techniques are available as a result of intensive research in genetic engineering.

genetic engineering the deliberate manipulation of genetic material by biochemical techniques. It is often achieved by the introduction of new DNA, usually by means of a virus or plasmid. This can be for pure research or to breed functionally specific plants, animals or bacteria. These organisms with a foreign gene added are said to be transgenic.

In genetic engineering, the splicing and reconciliation of genes is used to increase knowledge of cell function and reproduction, but it can also achieve practical ends. For example, plants grown for food could be given the ability to fix nitrogen, found in some bacteria, and so reduce the need for expensive fertilizers, or simple bacteria may be modified to produce rare drugs. Developments in genetic engineering have led to the production of human insulin, human growth hormone and a number of other bone-marrow stimulating hormones.

ULTRASAURUS—THE WORLD'S BIGGEST DINOSAUR

Some 30 km/18 m west of Denver, in the foothills of the Rocky Mountains, lies the small town of Morrison. Its main claim to fame is a huge natural amphitheatre which hosts rock concerts and operas. The amphitheatre is known as Red Rocks Stadium and, indeed, all the rocks around Morrison are a striking red. The town gives its name to the Morrison formation, a stratum of rocks laid down in Jurassic times. The formation meets the surface both east and west of the high Rocky Mountains, and both areas have proved rich in dinosaur fossils. In particular, the Uncompahgre region of western Colorado has yielded enormous numbers of dinosaur remains. And some of those remains have been huge ...

Biggest of all has been the Ultrasaurus. Two specimens of *Ultrasaurus macintoshi* have been found that indicate that this dinosaur was 30 m/98 ft long and weighed a gigantic 100 tonnes—possibly as much as 130 tonnes. The weight is close to the theoretical limit for a land vertebrate: mathematical calculations suggest that a terrestrial creature weighing 140 tonnes would need legs so large that they would be almost impossible to move.

It seems obvious to suggest that such a monster is a rarity, yet Ultrasaurus must have been reasonably successful. Other Ultrasaur bones have been found elsewhere in the Morrison formation, and remains of the closely related *Ultrasaurus tabriensis* have recently been discovered in Cretaceous rocks in South Korea. The presence of Ultrasaur remains in both Jurassic and Cretaceous rocks also suggests that the creature inhabited the Earth for quite a time.

Americans have been quick to celebrate the discovery of this enormous creature. A life-size model has been erected in Paradise Park, Honolulu, Hawaii, and a smaller (but still 7 m/23 ft high) model has been put up in New York's Central Park, where 1,000 local children have been involved in painting it.

Other enormous dinosaurs have also been found in the Morrison formation. From the same region of the Uncompahgre, *Supersaurus viviane* may not have had the same bulk as Ultrasaurus, but probably stood considerably taller. Its height is estimated to have been 16 m/52 ft, and its length to be in the same 30 m/98 ft region. Some way further to the south, in Albuquerque, New Mexico, the rocks have yielded the remains of Seismosaurus. An estimated weight of 50 tonnes is again less than that of Ultrasaurus, but this dinosaur was over 36 m/118 ft long. Its hefty size gave it its name—Seismosaurus translates as 'earthquake lizard'.

Seismosaurus may be the longest dinosaur of which remains have been found, but there are signs that others may have been longer still. In Morocco, recently discovered footprints and tracks appear to have been made by a dinosaur a massive 48 m/157 ft long. Two of these would occupy the length of a football pitch.

However, as yet no bones of such creatures have been found. Other important dinosaur finds have been made recently in Argentina. The oldest known dinosaur, Herrerasaurus, has been excavated from rock formations in the foothills of the Andes.

This dinosaur, named after an early dinosaur hunter, José Herrera, who discovered parts of the skeleton, is estimated to be 230 million years old. At only 2.5 m/8.2 ft long and with an estimated weight of 100 kg/220 lbs, this is tiny compared to Ultrasaurus, but the find may be of considerable significance. Herrerasaurus has a jaw with dual hinging, a feature that was thought not to have evolved until some 50 million years later.

Recent years have seen an explosion of dinosaur finds, as likely formations are recognized and better techniques of excavation are exploited. Further finds may fill in gaps in the dinosaur story, or make us more aware of how little we know about them.

New strains of animals have also been produced; a new strain of mouse was patented in the USA 1989 (the application was rejected in the European patent office). A vaccine against a sheep parasite (a larval tapeworm) has been developed by genetic engineering; most existing vaccines protect against bacteria and viruses.

There is a risk that when transplanting genes between different types of bacteria (*Escherichia coli*, which lives in the human intestine, is often used) new and harmful strains might be produced. For this reason strict safety precautions are observed, and the altered bacteria are disabled in some way so they are unable to exist outside the laboratory.

molecular clock the use of rates of mutation in genetic material to calculate the length of time elapsed since two related species diverged from each other during evolution. The method can be based on comparisons of the DNA or of widely occurring proteins, such as haemoglobin.

Since mutations are thought to occur at a constant rate, the length of time that must have elapsed in order to produce the difference between two species can be estimated. This information can be compared with the evidence obtained from palaeontology to reconstruct evolutionary events.(See feature in this section.)

protein engineering the creation of synthetic proteins designed to carry out specific tasks. For example, an enzyme may be designed to remove grease from soiled clothes and remain stable at the high temperatures in a washing machine.

restriction enzyme enzyme that breaks a chain of DNA into two pieces at a specific point. The point along the DNA chain at which the enzyme can work is restricted to places where

EXTRA LETTER FOR GENETIC CODE

The genetic code consists of four bases: adenine, guanine, cytosine, and uracil. Arranged in combinations of three, these bases instruct cells to arrange 20 amino acids into sequences of proteins. Scientists in Switzerland and California have now found a way of introducing an extra base into the sequence, and using this extra base to incorporate a new amino acid into proteins.

The new base is *iso-cytosine*. The researchers incorporated this base into a length of RNA as an artificial triplet (*iso*-C)AG (iso-cytosine, adenine, and guanine). They also produced the complementary triplet, which was incorporated into a molecule of transfer RNA. The new transfer RNA then slotted iodotyrosine, an artificially produced amino acid, into a polypeptide chain.

The achievement opens the possibility of producing completely artificial proteins, designed for individual tasks. However, if this is to work economically the extended code must also be introduced into DNA (only RNA has been attempted so far), and organisms found that will copy the code without error.

---

a specific sequence of base pairs occurs.

Different restriction enzymes will break a DNA chain at different points. The overlap between the fragments is used in determining the sequence of base pairs in the DNA chain.

sequencing determining the sequence of chemical subunits within a large molecule. Techniques for sequencing amino acids in proteins were established in the 1950s, insulin being the first for which the sequence was completed. Major efforts are now being made to determine the sequence of base pairs within DNA.

transgenic organism plant, animal, bacterium, or other living organism which has had a foreign gene added to it by means of genetic engineering.(See feature in this section.)

yeast artificial chromosome (YAC) fragment of DNA from the human genome inserted into a yeast cell. The yeast replicates the fragment along with its own DNA. In this way the fragments are copied to be preserved in a gene library. YACs are characteristically between 250,000 and 1 million base pairs in length. A cosmid works in the same way.

The new science of genetic engineering raises moral questions as important as those that were raised by the creation of the atom bomb. For example, scientists will soon be able to treat many major inherited diseases. But the same discoveries could also mean that employers could reject those more susceptible to disease. Where does the responsibility lie in tackling moral and ethical issues such as these?

Politics/government	46
Referendum	26
Scientists	26
The church	10
Legal profession	1
Academics in universities	11
None of these	13

Surrogacy

Do you tend to approve or disapprove of a woman (known as the surrogate mother) carrying a child for another woman who is unable to bear children?

Approve	43
Disapprove	39
Don't know	18

A woman in America is carrying twins for her daughter who is unable to bear children. Eggs from her daughter were fertilized with sperm from her son-in-law and implanted in her. What about this particular case, where the mother will be bearing her daughter's children? Do you think this is a good idea or a bad idea?

Good idea	39
Bad idea	47
Don't know	15

Sex of child

Imagine it were possible to choose the sex of a child before birth. Do you think parents should be able to have this choice or should they leave it to chance?

Choice	21
Left to chance	74
Don't know	5

TERMS

abacus method of calculating with a handful of stones on 'a flat surface' (Latin *abacus*), familiar to the Greeks and Romans, and used by earlier peoples, possibly even in ancient Babylon; it still survives in the more sophisticated bead-frame form of the Russian *schoty* and the Japanese *soroban*. The abacus has principles in common with the electronic calculator.

abscissa in coordinate geometry, the horizontal or *x* coordinate, that is, the distance of a point from the vertical or *y*-axis. For example, a point with the coordinates (3,4) has an abscissa of 3.

algebra system of arithmetic applying to any set of non-numerical symbols, and the axioms and rules by which they are combined or operated upon. It is used in many branches of mathematics, such as matrix algebra and Boolean algebra, the method of algebraic reasoning devised in the 19th century by English mathematician George Boole and used in working out the logic for computers.

alternate angle in geometry, one of a pair of angles that lie on opposite sides of a transversal (a line cutting two other lines). If the two other lines are parallel, the alternate angles are equal.

altitude in geometry, the perpendicular distance from a vertex (corner) of a triangle to the base (the side opposite the vertex). In ordinary terms, the altitude is the height of the triangle.

angle in geometry, an amount of rotation. Angles are measured in degrees or radians. An angle of 90° (90 degrees) is a right angle. Angles of less than 90° are called **acute angles**; angles of more than 90° but less than 180° are **obtuse angles**. A **reflex angle** is an angle of more than 180° but less than 360°. **Complementary angles** are two angles that add up to 90°; **supplementary angles** are two angles that add up to 180°.

apex the highest point, or vertex, of a solid or plane (two-dimensional) figure, with respect to a particular base plane or line.

Arabic numerals or **Hindu–Arabic numerals** the symbols 0, 1, 2, 3, 4, 5, 6, 7, 8, 9, early forms of which were in use among the Arabs before being adapted by the peoples of Europe during the Middle Ages in place of Roman numerals. They appear to have originated in India, and reached Europe by way of Spain.

arc in geometry, a section of a curve. A circle has two types of arc. An arc that is less than a semicircle is called a **minor arc**; an arc that is greater than a semicircle is a **major arc**.

area a measure of surface, measured in square units (such as m² or km²).

arithmetic branch of mathematics that concerns all questions involving numbers, as in counting, measuring, or weighing. Simple arithmetic already existed in prehistoric times. The fundamental operations are addition and subtraction, and multiplication and division. Fractions, percentages, and ratios are developed from these operations.

Modular arithmetic deals with events recurring in regular cycles, and is used in describing the functioning of petrol engines, electrical generators, and so on. For example in the modulo-twelve system, the answer to a question as to what time it will be in five hours if it is now ten o'clock, can be expressed $10 \pm 5 \pm 3$.

associative operation an operation that is independent of the grouping of the numbers, terms, or symbols concerned. For example, multiplication is associative, as $4 \times (3 \times 2) = (4 \times 3) \times 2 = 24$; however, division is not, as $12 \div (4 \div 2) = 6$, but $(12 \div 4) \div 2 = 1.5$. Compare commutative operation and distributive operation.

base the number of different single-digit symbols used in a particular number system. Thus our usual (decimal) counting system of numbers (with symbols 0, 1, 2, 3, 4, 5, 6, 7, 8, 9) has the base 10. In the binary number system, which has only the symbols 1 and 0, the base is 2.

bearing angle that a fixed, distant point makes with true or magnetic north at the point of observation, or the angle of the path of a moving object with respect to the north lines. Bearings are measured in degrees and given as three-digit numbers increasing clockwise. For instance, NW would be denoted as 045M or 045T, depending on whether the reference line were magnetic (M) or true (T) north.

binomial in algebra, an expression consisting of two terms, such as $a + b, a - b$. The *binomial theorem*, discovered by English mathematician and physicist Isaac Newton (1642–1727) and first published in 1676, is a formula calculating any power of a binomial quantity.

calculus branch of mathematics that permits the manipulation of continuously varying quantities, used in practical problems involving such matters as changing speeds, problems

AREAS OF COMMON TWO-DIMENSIONAL SHAPES

rectangle	*lb*
length *l*, breadth *b*,	
square	*l*²
side *l*	
triangle	1/2*lh*
side *l*, perpendicular height *h*	
parallelogram	*lh*
side *l*, perpendicular height *h*	
circle	π*r*²
radius *r*	

SURFACE AREAS OF COMMON THREE-DIMENSIONAL SHAPES

sphere	4π*r*²
radius *r*	
cylinder (closed)	2π*r*(*h* + *r*)
height *h*, radius of cross section *r*	
cube	6*l*²
side *l*	

Circle

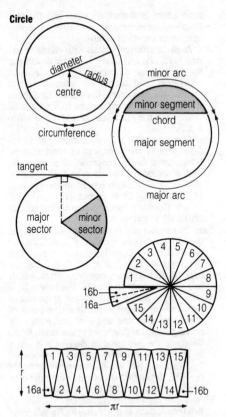

resulting divisions of its area are termed major and minor **sectors**. The area of a circle (πr^2) can be shown by dividing a circle into very thin sectors and reassembling them to make an approximate rectangle.

circumference in geometry, the curved line that encloses a plane, or two-dimensional, figure—for example, a circle or an ellipse. Its length varies according to the nature of the curve.

coefficient the number part in front of an algebraic term, signifying multiplication. For example, in the expression $4x^2 + 2xy - x$, the coefficient of x^2 is 4 (because $4x^2$ means $4 \times x^2$), that of xy is 2 and that of x is -1 (because $-1 \times x = -x$). In some algebraic expressions, coefficients are represented by letters called constants, that stand for numbers - for example, in the equation $ax^2 + bx + c = 0$, a, b and c are constants.

commutative operation an operation that is independent of the order of the numbers or symbols concerned. For example, addition is commutative: the result of adding $4 + 2$ is the same as that of adding $2 + 4$; subtraction is not: $4 - 2 = 2$, but $2 - 4 = -2$. Compare associative operation and distributive operation.

complement in set theory, all the members of a universal set that are not members of a particular set. A set and its complement add up to the whole. For example, if the universal set is the set of all positive whole numbers and the set S is the set of all even numbers, then the complement of S (denoted $S]$) is the set of all odd numbers.

concave (of a surface) curving inwards, or away from the eye. For example, a bowl appears concave when viewed from above. In geometry, a concave polygon is one that has an interior angle greater than 180°. Compare convex.

concentric (of two or more circles) having the same centre but different radii.

cone in geometry, a solid figure having a plane (two-dimensional) curve as its base and tapering to a point (the vertex). The line joining the vertex to the centre of the base is called the axis of the cone. A circular cone has a circle as its base; a cone that has its axis at right angles to the base is called a right cone. A circular cone of perpendicular height h and base of radius r has a volume V equal to $1/3 \, \pi r^2 h$. The distance from the edge of the base of a cone to the vertex is called the slant height. In a right circular cone of slant height l, the curved surface area is $\pi r l$, and the area of the base is πr^2. Therefore, the total surface area $A = \pi r l + \pi r^2 = \pi r(l + r)$.

congruent (of two or more plane or solid figures) having the same shape and size. With plane congruent figures, one figure will fit on top of the other exactly, though this may first require rotation and/or reflection (making a mirror image) of one of the figures.

conic section in geometry, curve obtained when a cone is intersected by a plane (two-dimensional surface). If the intersecting plane cuts both extensions of the cone it yields a hyperbola; if it

of flight, varying stresses in the framework of a bridge, and alternating current theory. **Integral calculus** deals with the method of summation, or adding together the effects of continuously varying quantities. **Differential calculus** deals in a similar way with rates of change. Many of its applications arose from the study of the gradients of the tangents to curves.

cardinal number one of a series of numbers 0, 1, 2, 3, 4 ... Cardinal numbers relate to quantity, whereas ordinal numbers (first, second, third, fourth ...) relate to order.

chord a straight line joining any two points on a curve. The chord that passes through the centre of a circle (its longest chord) is the diameter. The longest and shortest chords of an ellipse (a regular oval) are called the major and minor axes.

circle a path followed by a point that moves so as to keep a constant distance, the **radius**, from a fixed point, the **centre**. The longest distance in a straight line from one side of a circle to the other is called the **diameter**. It is twice the radius. The ratio of the distance all the way round the circle—the **circumference**—to the diameter is an irrational number called **pi** (π), roughly equal to 3.14159. A circle of diameter d and radius r has a circumference C equal to πd, or $2\pi r$, and an area A equal to πr^2. If a circle is divided up by two radii, then the

THE MATHEMATICS OF CHAOS

Why are tides predictable years ahead, whereas weather forecasts often go wrong within a few days?

Both tides and weather are governed by natural laws. Tides are caused by the gravitational attraction of the Sun and Moon; the weather by the motion of the atmosphere under the influence of heat from the Sun. The law of gravitation is not noticeably simpler than the laws of fluid dynamics; yet for weather the resulting behaviour seems to be far more complicated.

The reason for this is *chaos*, which lies at the heart of one of the most exciting and most rapidly expanding areas of mathematical research, the theory of nonlinear dynamic systems.

It has been known for a long time that dynamic systems—systems that change with time according to fixed laws—can exhibit regular patterns, such as repetitive cycles. Thanks to new mathematical techniques, emphasizing shape rather than number, and to fast and sophisticated computer graphics, we now know that dynamic systems can also behave randomly. The difference lies not in the complexity of the formulae that define their mathematics, but in the geometrical features of the dynamics. This is a remarkable discovery: random behaviour in a system whose mathematical description contains no hint whatsoever of randomness.

Simple geometric structure produces simple dynamics. For example, if the geometry shrinks everything towards a fixed point, then the motion tends towards a steady state. But if the dynamics keep stretching things apart and then folding them together again, the motion tends to be chaotic—like food being mixed in a bowl. The motion of the Sun and Moon, on the kind of timescale that matters when we want to predict the tides, is a series of regular cycles, so prediction is easy. The changing patterns of the weather involve a great deal of stretching and folding, so here chaos reigns.

The geometry of chaos can be explored using theoretical mathematical techniques such as topology—'rubber-sheet geometry'—but the most vivid pictures are obtained using computer graphics. The geometric structures of chaos are *fractals*: they have detailed form on all scales of magnification. Order and chaos, traditionally seen as opposites, are now viewed as two aspects of the same basic process, the evolution of a system in time. Indeed, there are now examples where both order and chaos occur naturally within a single geometrical form.

Does chaos make randomness predictable? Sometimes. If what looks like random behaviour is actually governed by a dynamic system, then short-term prediction becomes possible. Long-term prediction is not as easy, however. In chaotic systems any initial error of measurement, however small, will grow rapidly and eventually ruin the prediction. This is known as the butterfly effect : if a butterfly flaps its wings, a month later the air disturbance created may cause a hurricane.

Chaos can be applied to many areas of science, such as chemistry, engineering, computer sicence, biology, electronics, and astronomy. For example, although the short-term motions of the Sun and Moon are not chaotic, the long-term motion of the Solar System *is* chaotic. It is impossible to predict on which side of the Sun Pluto will lie in 200 million years' time. Saturn's satellite *Hyperion* tumbles chaotically. Chaos caused by Jupiter's gravitational field can fling asteroids out of orbit, towards the Earth. Disease epidemics, locust plagues, and irregular heartbeats are more down-to-earth examples of chaos, on a more human timescale.

Chaos places limits on science: it implies that even when we know the equations that govern a system's behaviour, we may not in practice be able to make effective predictions. On the other hand, it opens up new avenues for discovery, because it implies that apparently random phenomena may have simple, non-random explanations. So chaos is changing the way scientists think about what they do: the relation between determinism and chance, the role of experiment, the computability of the world, the prospects for prediction, and the interaction between mathematics, science, and nature. Chaos cuts right across traditional subject boundaries, and distinctions between pure and applied mathematicians, between mathematicians and physicists, between physicists and biologists, become meaningless when compared to the unity revealed by their joint efforts.

is parallel to the side of the cone it produces a parabola. Other intersecting planes produce a circle or an ellipse. Conic sections were first discovered by the ancient Greeks.

constant a fixed quantity or one that does not change its value in relation to variables. For example, in the algebraic expression $y^2 = x$ m2 3, the number 3 is a constant; so too are a and b in the general equation $ax \pm b = 0$.

converse the reversed order of a conditional statement; the converse of the statement 'if a..., then b...' is 'if b..., then a...'. The converse does not always hold true; for example, the converse of 'if $x = 3$, then $x^2 = 9$' is 'if $x^2 = 9$, then $x = 3$', which is not true, as x could also be –3.

convex curving outwards, or towards the eye. For example, the outer surface of a ball appears convex. In geometry, the term is used to describe any polygon possessing no interior angle greater than 180°. Compare concave.

coordinate geometry or *analytical geometry* a system of geometry in which points, lines, shapes, and surfaces are represented by algebraic expressions. In plane (two-dimensional) coordinate geometry, the plane is usually defined by two axes at right angles to each other, the horizontal x-axis (abscissa) and the vertical y-axis (ordinate), crossing at 0, the origin. A

Mathematical Symbols

$a{\rightarrow}b$	a implies b	$a{\div}b{=}c$	$a{\div}b$, read as 'a divided by b', denotes
x	unknown	$a/b{=}c$	division. a is the dividend, b is the divisor,
∞	infinity		c is the quotient.
$a{\sim}b$	numerical difference between a and b		In the fraction a/b, a is the numerator
$a{\approx}b$	a approximately equal to b		b the denominator
$a{=}b$	a equal to b	$a{:}b$	ratio of a to b
$a{\equiv}b$	a identical with b (for formulae only)	$a^b{=}c$	a^b, read as 'a to the power b', a is the base,
$a{>}b$	a greater than b		b the exponent, or index
$a{<}b$	a smaller than b	$^b\!\sqrt{a}{=}c$	$^b\sqrt{a}$, is the bth root of a, b being known
$a{\neq}b$	a not equal to b		as the root exponent. In the special case
$b{<}a{<}c$	a greater than b and smaller than c, that		of $^2\sqrt{a}{=}c$, c is known as the square
	is, a lies between the values b and c but		root of a, and the root exponent is
	cannot equal either		usually omitted, that is, $^2\sqrt{a}=\sqrt{a}$
$a{\geqslant}b$	a equal to or greater than b, that is,	$n!$	factorial of the positive integer n, denotes
	a at least as great as b		$n{\times}(n{-}1){\times}(n{-}2){\times}(n{-}3)\ldots3{\times}2{\times}1$
$a{\leqslant}b$	a equal to or less than b, that is, a at	$\int$	indefinite integral
	most as great as b	$\int_a^b f(x)dx$	definite integral, or integral between $x{=}a$
$b{\leqslant}a{\leqslant}c$	a lies between the values b and c and		and $x{=}b$
	could take the values b and c	e	exponential constant and the base of
$\lvert a\rvert$	absolute value of a: this is always positive,		natural (Napierian) logarithms
	for example $\lvert{-}5\rvert{=}5$		$=2.7182818284\ldots$
$+$	addition sign, positive	π	ratio of the circumference of a circle to its
$-$	subtraction sign, negative		diameter $=3.1415925535\ldots$
$\times$ or .	multiplication sign, times	$p{\in}S$	p is a member of the set S
$\div$	division sign, divided by	$p{\notin}S$	p is not a member of S
$a{+}b{=}c$	$a{+}b$, read as 'a plus b', denotes the	$S{\subset}T$	S is a subset of T, all members of S are also
	addition of a and b. The result of the		members of the larger set T
	addition, c, is also known as the sum.	$T{\not\subset}S$	T is not a subset of S, not all members of
$a{-}b{=}c$	$a{-}b$, read as 'a minus b', denotes		T are members of S
	subtraction of b from a	$S{\cap}T$	intersection of sets S and T, denotes all
	$a{-}b$, or c is the difference. Subtraction is		elements that are members of both S and T
	the opposite of addition.	$S{\cup}T$	union of sets S and T, denotes all elements
$a{\times}b{=}c$	$a{\times}b$, read as 'a multiplied by b', denotes		that are members of either S or T
$ab{=}c$	multiplication of a by b; c is the product,	S'	complement of set S, denotes all elements
$a.b{=}c$	a and b are factors of c		that are not members of S
		$\mathbb{U}$, $\mathscr{E}$	universal set, the union of any set and its complement
		$\{\,\}$, $\emptyset$	empty set, set that has no members

point on the plane can be represented by a pair of Cartesian coordinates, which define its position in terms of its distance along the x-axis and along the y-axis from O. These distances are respectively the x and y coordinates of the point.

Lines are represented as equations; for example, $y = 2x + 1$ gives a straight line, and $y = 3x^2 + 2x$ gives a parabola (a curve). Different lines and curves can be drawn by plotting the coordinates of points that satisfy their equations and joining up the points. One of the advantages of coordinate geometry is that geometrical solutions can be obtained without drawing but by manipulating algebraic expressions. For example, the coordinates of the point of intersection of two straight lines can be determined by finding the unique values of x and y that satisfy both of the equations for the lines, that is, by solving them as a pair of simultaneous equations. The curves studied in simple coordinate geometry are the conic sections (circle, ellipse, parabola, and hyperbola) each of which has its own characteristic equation.

cosine in trigonometry, a function of an angle in a right-angled triangle found by dividing the length of the side adjacent to the angle by the length of the hypotenuse (the longest side).

cube in geometry, a solid figure whose faces are all squares. It has six equal-area faces and 12 equal-length edges. If the length of one edge is l, the volume of the cube V is equal to l^3 and its surface area A equals $6l^2$.

cuboid in geometry, a solid figure whose faces are all rectangles. A brick is a cuboid.

curve in geometry, the locus of a point moving according to specified conditions. The best-known of all curves is the circle, which is the locus of all points equidistant from a given

cycloid

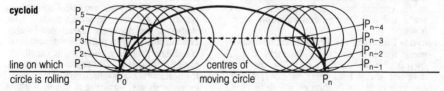

line on which circle is rolling • centres of moving circle

point (the centre). Other common geometrical curves are the ellipse, parabola, and hyperbola, which are also produced when a cone is cut by a plane (two-dimensional surface) at different angles. Many curves have been invented for the solution of special problems in geometry and mechanics—for example, the cissoid and the cycloid.

cybernetics (Greek *kubernan*, 'to steer') science concerned with how systems organize, regulate, and reproduce themselves, and also how they evolve and learn. In the laboratory inanimate objects are created that behave like living systems. Uses range from the creation of electronic artificial limbs to the running of the fully automated factory where decision-making machines operate at up to managerial level. Cybernetics was founded and named in 1947 by US mathematician Norbert Wiener.

cycloid in geometry, a curve resembling a series of arches traced out by a point on the circumference of a circle that rolls along a straight line. It has such applications as studying the motion of wheeled vehicles along roads and tracks.

cylinder in geometry, a tubular solid figure with a circular cross-section, ordinarily understood to be a right cylinder (that is, having its curved surface at right angles to the base). The volume V of a cylinder of radius r and height h is given by $V = \pi r^2 h$. Its total surface area A has the formula $A = 2\pi r\,(h + r)$ where $2\pi rh$ is the curved surface area, and $2\pi r^2$ is the area of both ends.

decimal fraction fraction expressed by the use of the decimal point, that is, a fraction in which the denominator is any higher power of 10. Thus 3/10, 51/100, 23/1,000 are decimal fractions and are normally expressed as 0.3, 0.51, 0.023. The use of decimals greatly simplifies addition and multiplication of fractions, though not all fractions can be expressed exactly as decimal fractions. The regular use of the decimal point appears to have been introduced about 1585, but the occasional use of decimal fractions can be traced back as far as the 12th century.

degree (symbol °) a unit of measurement of an angle. One complete revolution, or circle, is divided into 360°; a degree is subdivided into 60 minutes (symbol '). A quarter-turn, or right angle is 90°; a half-turn, or the angle on a straight line, is 180°.

denominator the number or symbol that appears below the line in a vulgar fraction. For example, the denominator of 3/4 is 4. The denominator represents the fraction's divisor, or the number of equal parts into which the whole may be considered to have been divided. Compare numerator.

differentiation a procedure for finding the rate of change of one variable quantity relative to another. Together, differentiation and integration of functions make up calculus.

distributive operation an operation, such as multiplication, that bears a relationship to another operation, such as addition, such that

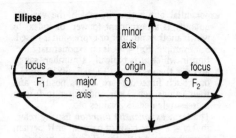

Ellipse

$a \times (b + c) = (a \times b) + (a \times c)$. For example, $3 \times (2 + 4) = (3 \times 2) + (3 \times 4) = 18$. Multiplication may be said to be distributive over addition. Addition is not, however, distributive over multiplication because $3 + (2 \times 4) \neq (3 + 2) \times (3 + 4)$. Compare associative operation and commutative operation.

ellipse in geometry, a curve joining all points (loci) around two fixed points (foci) so that the sum of the distances from those points is always constant. The diameter passing through the foci is the major axis, and the diameter bisecting this at right angles is the minor axis. An ellipse is one of a series of curves known as conic sections; a slice across a cone that is not made parallel to, or does not pass through, the base will produce an ellipse.

epicycloid in geometry, a curve resembling a series of arches traced out by a point on the circumference of a circle that rolls around another circle of a different diameter. If the two circles have the same diameter, the curve is a *cardioid*. Greek mathematicians thought that planets moved in small circles (epicycles) while completing a large circle (the deferent) round the Earth.

equation expression that represents the equality of two expressions involving constants and/or variables, and thus usually includes an equals sign (=). For example, the equation $A = \pi r^2$ equates the area A of a circle of radius r to the product πr^2. The algebraic equation $y = mx + c$ is the general one in coordinate geometry for a straight line.

If a mathematical equation is true for all variables in a given domain, it is sometimes called an identity and denoted by $\equiv$.

equilateral having all sides of equal length. For example, a square and a rhombus are both equilateral four-sided figures. An equilateral triangle, to which the term is most often applied, has all three sides equal and all three angles equal (at 60°).

exponent or *power* or *index* a number that indicates the number of times a term is multiplied by itself. It is written a superior small numeral. For example, in x^2 the exponent is 2 and signifies $x \times x$; in 4^5 the exponent is 5 and signifies $4 \times 4 \times 4 \times 4 \times 4$. Exponents obey certain rules. Terms that contain them are multiplied by adding the exponents - for example, $x^2 \times x^5 = x^7$; and divided by subtracting the exponents - for example, $y^5 \div y^3 = y^2$. Any number with an exponent of 0 is equal to 1, for example, $x^0 = 1$ and $99^0 = 1$.

exponential a function in which the variable quantity is an exponent (power, or index) to which another number or expression is raised. For example, $f(x) = a^x$ is an exponential function in which a is typically a number, say 5, and x is the exponent (0.1, 0.5, m210, and so on). Such functions are always positive and their values get closer and closer to 0 with increasingly negative values of x.

The term *exponential function* usually refers to $f(x) = e^x$, the basis of natural, or Naperian, logarithms and definitive of many natural phenomena of growth and decay (such as the radioactive decay of various isotopes). In this expression e is an irrational number equal to 2.71828... *Exponential growth* is a form of increase in numbers in which the rate of growth is slow at first but then rises sharply. It applies, for example, to uncontrolled population growth.

factor a number that divides into another number exactly. For example, the factors of 64 are 1, 2, 4, 8, 16, 32, and 64. In algebra, certain kinds of polynomials (expressions consisting of several or many terms) can be factorized. For example, the factors of $x^2 + 3x + 2$ are $x + 1$ and $x + 2$, since $x^2 + 3x + 2 = (x + 1)(x + 2)$.

factorial of a positive number, the product of all the whole numbers (integers) inclusive between 1 and the number itself. A factorial is indicated by the symbol !. For example, 6! $= 1 \times 2 \times 3 \times 4 \times 5 \times 6 = 720$. Zero factorial, 0!, is defined as 1.

fractal (Latin *fractus*, 'broken') an irregular shape or surface produced by a procedure of repeated subdivision. Generated on a computer screen, fractals are used in creating models for geographical or biological processes (for example, the creation of a coastline by erosion or accretion, or the growth of plants). They are also used for computer art.

fraction a number that indicates one or more equal parts of a whole. The usual way of denoting this is to place below a horizontal line the number of equal parts into which the unit is divided (denominator), and above the line the number of these parts comprising the fraction (numerator); thus 2/3 or 3/4. Such fractions are called *vulgar* or *simple fractions*. The denominator can never be zero.

A *proper fraction* is one in which the numerator is less than the denominator. An *improper fraction* is one in which the numerator is larger than the denominator—for example, 3/2. An improper fraction can therefore be expressed as a mixed number, for example, 11/2. A *decimal fraction* has as its denominator a power of 10 (10, 100, 1,000, and so on), but this is omitted and is expressed instead by the position of the numerator after a dot or point (the decimal point)—for example, 0.4 is 4/10, 0.04 is 4/100, and 0.004 is 4/1,000.

function a procedure that defines a relationship between quantities, usually variables. For example, in the algebraic expression $y = 4x^3 \pm 2$, the variable y is a function of the variable x,

generally written as $f(x)$. Functions are commonly used in applied mathematics, physics, and science generally—for example, the formula $t = 2\pi(l/g)^{1/2}$ shows that, for a simple pendulum, the time of swing t is a function of its length l and of no other variable quantity (π and g, the acceleration due to gravity, are constants).

geometry branch of mathematics concerned with the properties of space, usually in terms of plane (two-dimensional) and solid (three-dimensional) figures. It probably originated in Egypt, in land measurements necessitated by the periodic inundations of the River Nile, and was soon extended into surveying and navigation. Early geometers were Thales, Pythagoras, and Euclid. Analytical methods were introduced and developed by Descartes in the 17th century. The subject is usually divided into *pure geometry*, which embraces roughly the plane and solid geometry dealt with in Euclid's *Elements*, and *analytical* or *coordinate geometry*, in which problems are solved using algebraic methods. A third, quite distinct, type includes the *non-Euclidean geometries*, which proved significant in the development of the theory of relativity and in the formulation of atomic theory.

group a finite or infinite set of elements that can be combined by an operation; formally, a group must satisfy certain conditions. For example, the set of all integers (positive or negative whole numbers) forms a group with regard to addition because: (1) addition is associative, that is, the sum of two or more integers is the same regardless of the order in which the integers are added; (2) adding two integers gives another integer; (3) the set includes an identity element 0, which has no effect on any integer to which it is added (for example, 0 + 3 = 3); and (4) each integer has an inverse (for instance, 7 has the inverse –7), such that the sum of an integer and its inverse is 0. *Group theory* is the study of the properties of groups.

helix in geometry, a three-dimensional curve resembling a screw thread. It is generated by a line that encircles a cylinder or cone at a constant angle. Formally, a group must satisfy certain conditons G that can be combined by an operation *, provided the following four conditions are satisfied (a, b, and c are all elements, or members, of G): (1) the set is closed under *, that is, if $a * b = p$, then p must be a member of G; (2) G contains an identity element I such that $a * I = I * a = a$; (3) each element a has an inverse a^{-1} such that $a * a^{-1} = 1$; (4) the operation is associative, that is, $(a * b) * c = a * (b * c)$. *Group theory* is the study of the properties of groups.

hyperbola in geometry, a curve formed by cutting a right circular cone with a plane (two-dimensional surface) so that the angle between the plane and the base is greater than the angle between the base and the side of the cone. It is a member of the family of curves known as conic sections.

hypotenuse the longest side of a right-angled triangle, that is, the side opposite the right angle.

infinity quantity that is larger than any fixed assignable quantity; symbol ∞. By convention, the result of dividing any number by zero is regarded as infinity.

integer a positive or negative whole number—for example, 3 and 0. Fractions, such as $\frac{1}{2}$ and 0.35, are known as nonintegral numbers.

integration a method in calculus of evaluating definite or indefinite integrals. An example of a definite integral can be thought of as finding the area under a curve (as represented by an algebraic expression or function) between particular values of the function's variable. In practice, integral calculus provides scientists with a powerful tool for doing calculations that involve a continually varying quantity (such as determing the position at any given instant of a space rocket that is accelerating away from Earth). Its basic principles were discovered in the late 1660s independently by the German philosopher Gottfried Leibniz and the British scientist Isaac Newton.

interest in finance, a sum of money paid to an investor in return for the loan, usually expressed as percentage per annum. *Simple interest* is interest calculated as a straight percentage of the amount invested. In *compound interest*, the interest earned over a period of time (for example, per annum) is added to the investment, so that at the end of the next period interest is paid on that total.

A sum of £100 invested at 10% per annum simple interest for five years earns £10 a year, giving a total of £50 interest (and at the end of the period the investor receives a total of £150). The same sum of £100 invested for five years at 10% compound interest earns a total of £61.05 interest (with £161.05 returned at the end of the period). Generally, for a sum S invested at $x\%$ simple interest for y years, the total amount returned is $S + xyS/100$. If it is invested at $x\%$ compound interest for y years, the total amount returned is $S\,[(100 + x)/100]^y$.

linear equation an equation involving two variables (x, y), of the general form $y = mx + c$, where m and c are constants. In coordinate geometry, such an equation plotted using Cartesian coordinates gives a straight-line graph of slope m; c is the value of y where the line crosses the y-axis. Linear equations can be used to describe the behaviour of buildings, bridges, and other static structures.

locus (Latin 'place') in geometry, the path traced by a moving point. For example, the locus of a point that moves so that it is always at the same distance from another fixed point is a circle; the locus of a point that is always at the same distance from two fixed points is a straight line that perpendicularly bisects the line joining them.

logarithm or **log** the exponent of a number to a specified base. If $b^a = x$, then a is the logarithm of x to the base b. Before the advent of cheap electronic calculators, the multiplication and division of large numbers could be simplified by substituting respectively the addition and subtraction of those numbers' logarithms. Tables of logarithms and antilogarithms are available (usually to the base 10) that show conversions of numbers to logarithms, and vice versa.

For any two numbers x and y (where $x = b^a$ and $y = b^c$), $x \times y = b^a + b^c = b^{a+c}$. Therefore, the product of x and y can be found by adding their logarithms (a and b), and looking up this figure in antilogarithm tables. For example, to multiply 6,560 × 980, one would look up the logarithms of these numbers (3.8169 and 2.9912), add them together (6.8081), then look up the antilogarithm of this to get the answer (6,428,000). Natural, or Naperian, logarithms are to the base e, an irrational number equal to approximately 2.7183. Log tables (to the base e) were first published 1614 by Scottish mathematician John Napier; base-10 logs were introduced from 1624 by Henry Briggs of England and Adriaen Vlacq of the Netherlands.

magic square a square array of different numbers in which the rows, columns, and diagonals add up to the same total. A simple example employing the numbers 1 to 9, with a total of 15, is:

```
6  7  2
1  5  9
8  3  4
```

matrix a square $(n \times n)$ or rectangular $(m \times n)$ array of elements (numbers or algebraic variables). They are a means of condensing information about mathematical systems and can be used for, among other things, solving simultaneous linear equations and transformations.

maximum and minimum points at which the slope of a curve representing a function in coordinate geometry changes from positive to negative (maximum), or from negative to positive (minimum). A tangent to a curve at a maximum or minimum has zero gradient (is horizontal). Maxima and minima can be found by differentiating the function for the curve and setting the differential to zero (the value of the slope at the turning point). For example, differentiating the function for the parabola $y = 2x^2 - 8x$ gives $dy/dx = 4x - 8$. Setting this equal to zero gives $x = 2$, so that $y = -8$ (found by substituting $x = 2$ into the parabola equation). Thus the function has a minimum at the point (2, -8).

mean a measure of the average of a number of terms or quantities. The simple *arithmetic mean* is the average value of the quantities, that is, the sum of the quantities divided by their number. The *weighted mean* takes into account the frequency of the terms that are summed; it is calculated by multiplying each term by the number of times it occurs, summing the results and dividing this total by the total number of occurrences. The *geometric mean* is the corresponding root of the product of the quantities.

modulus the positive value of a real number, irrespective of its sign, indicated by a pair of vertical lines. Thus $|3|$ is 3; and $|-5|$ is 5.

number a symbol used in counting or measuring. In mathematics, there are various kinds of numbers. The everyday number system is the decimal ('proceeding by tens') system, using the base 10. *Real numbers* include all rational numbers (integers, or whole numbers, and fractions) and irrational numbers (those not expressible as fractions). *Complex numbers* are of the form $a + ib$, where a and b are real numbers and i is the square root of -1 (an imaginary number). The complex numbers include real numbers (when b is zero).

The numerals, 0, 1, 2, 3, 4, 5, 6, 7, 8, 9, give a counting system which, to the base ten, continues 10, 11, 12, 13, and so on. These are positive whole numbers, with fractions represented as 1/4, 1/2, 3/4 and so on, or as decimal fractions (0.25, 0.5, 0.75 and so on). They are also rational numbers. Irrational numbers cannot be represented as fractions and require symbols, such as $\sqrt{2}$, π, and e: they can be expressed numerically only as the (inexact) approximations 1.414, 3.142 and 2.728 (to three places of decimals) respectively.

numerator the number or symbol that appears above the line in a vulgar fraction. For example, the numerator of 5/6 is 5. The numerator represents the fraction's dividend and indicates how many of the equal parts indicated by the denominator (number or symbol below the line) comprise the fraction.

ordinal number one of the series first, second, third, fourth,.... . Ordinal numbers relate to order, whereas cardinal numbers (1, 2, 3, 4,...) relate to quantity, or count.

ordinate in coordinate geometry, the vertical or y coordinate, that is, the distance of a point from the horizontal or x-axis. For example, a point with the coordinates (3,4) has an ordinate of 4.

origin in coordinate geometry, the point at which the horizontal x-axis and vertical y-axis cross, and therefore the point at which both x and y equal 0.

parabola in geometry, a curve formed by cutting a right circular cone with a plane (two-dimensional figure) parallel to the sloping side of the cone; it is one of the family of curves known as conic sections. A parabola can also be defined as a path traced out by a point that moves in such a way that it is always the same distance from a fixed point (focus) and a fixed straight line (directrix). The corresponding solid figure, the *paraboloid*, is formed by rotating a parabola about its axis. The parabola is a common shape for headlamp reflectors, dish-shaped microwave and radar aerials, and for radiotelescopes. A source of radiation placed at the focus of a paraboloidal reflector is propagated as a parallel beam.

parallel lines and parallel planes straight lines or planes (two-dimensional surfaces) that always remain the same perpendicular distance from one another no matter how far they

Polygon

	number of sides	sum of interior angles (degrees)
triangle	3	180
quadrilateral	4	360
pentagon	5	540
hexagon	6	720
heptagon	7	900
octagon	8	1,080
decagon	10	1,440
duodecagon	12	1,800
icosagon	20	3,240

are extended. This is a principle of Euclidean geometry. Some non-Euclidean geometries, such as elliptical and hyperbolic geometry, however, reject Euclid's parallel axiom.

parallelogram in geometry, a quadrilateral (four-sided plane figure) with opposite pairs of sides equal in length and parallel, and opposite angles equal. When all four sides are equal in length, the parallelogram is known as a rhombus; when the internal angles are right angles, it is a rectangle or square. The diagonals of a parallelogram bisect each other. Its area is the product of the length of one side and the perpendicular distance between this side and the side parallel to it.

percentage a way of representing a number as a fraction of 100. Thus 45 per cent (or 45%) equals 45/100, and 45% of 20 is $45/100 \times 20 = 9$. In general, if a quantity x changes to y, the percentage change is $100(x - y)/x$. Thus, if the number of people in a room changes from 40 to 50, the percentage increase is $(100 \times 10)/40 = 25\%$. To express a fraction as a percentage, its denominator must first be converted to 100, for example, $1/8 = 12.5/100 = 12.5\%$. The use of percentages often makes it easier to compare fractions that do not have a common denominator.

perimeter the line enclosing a plane (two-dimensional) figure, or the distance measured around the figure's boundary. For example, the perimeter of a square is its four sides (or four times the length of one side); the perimeter of a circle is its circumference.

permutation a specified arrangement of a group of objects. In general, the number of permutations of a items taken b at a time is given by $a!/(a\ m2\ b)!$, where the symbol ! stands for factorial (the product of all the integers (whole numbers) up to and including the number). For example, the number of permutations of four letters taken from any group of six different letters is $6!/2! = (1 \times 2 \times 3 \times 4 \times 5 \times 6)/(1 \times 2) = 360$. The theoretical number of four-letter 'words' that can be made from an alphabet of 26 letters is $26!/22! = 358,800$.

perpendicular or *normal* term describing a line that is oriented at right angles (90°) to another line or to a plane (two-dimensional) surface. A vertical line is perpendicular to a horizontal line.

polygon in geometry, a plane (two-dimensional) figure with three or more straight-line sides. Common polygons have their own names, which define the number of sides (for example, triangle, quadrilateral, pentagon). These are all convex polygons, having no interior angle greater than 180°. In general, the more sides a polygon has, the larger the sum of its internal angles and, in the case of a convex polygon, the more closely it approximates a circle.

polyhedron in geometry, a solid figure with four or more plane, or two-dimensional, faces. Common polyhedra have their own names (for example, pyramid, tetrahedron, cube, cuboid, prism). The more faces there are on a polyhedron, the more closely it approximates a sphere. There are only five types of regular polyhedra (with all faces the same size and shape), as was deduced by early Greek mathematicians; they are the tetrahedron (four equilateral triangular faces), cube (six square faces), octahedron (eight equilateral triangles), dodecahedron (12 regular pentagons) and icosahedron (20 equilateral triangles).

prime number a number that can be divided only by 1 or itself, that is, having no other factors. There is an infinite number of primes, the first ten of which are 2, 3, 5, 7, 11, 13, 17, 19, 23, and 29 (by definition, the number 1 is excluded from the set of prime numbers). The number 2 is the only even prime because all other even numbers have 2 as a factor.

In 1989 researchers at Amdahl Corporation, Sunnyvale, California, calculated the largest known prime number. It has 65,087 digits, and is more than a trillion trillion trillion times as large as the previous record holder. It took over a year of computation to locate the number and prove it was a prime.

prism in geometry, a solid figure whose cross-section is constant in planes drawn perpendicular to its axis. A cylinder is a prism of circular cross-section.

probability the likelihood or chance that something will happen, often expressed as 'odds' or as a fraction. In general, the probability that n particular events will happen out of a total of m possible events is n/m. A certainty has a probability of 1; an impossibility has a probability of 0.

In tossing an unbiased coin the chance that it will land heads is the same as the chance that it will land tails, that is, 1 to 1 or 'even'; mathematically this probability is expressed as 1/2 or 0.5. The odds against any chosen number coming up on the roll of an unbiased dice are 5 to 1; the probability is 1/6 or 0.1666... If two dice are rolled there are $6 \times 6 = 36$ different possible combinations. A double (two numbers the same) occurs in six of these combinations; thus the probability is 6/36 or 0.1666...

Probability theory was first developed by French mathematicians Blaise Pascal and Pierre de Fermat, initially in response to a request to calculate the odds of being dealt various hands at cards. Today probability plays a major part in the mathematics of atomic theory and finds application in insurance and statistical studies.

progression sequence of numbers each formed by a specific relationship to its predecessor: an *arithmetical progression* has numbers that increase or decrease by a common sum or difference (for example, 2, 4, 6, 8, 10); a *geometric progression* has numbers each bearing a fixed ratio to its predecessor (for example, 3, 6, 12, 24, 48), and a *harmonic progression* is a sequence with numbers whose reciprocals are in arithmetic progression (for example, 1, 1/2, 1/3, 1/4, 1/5).

proportional related by a constant ratio. Two variable quantities x and y are proportional if, for all values of x, $y = ax$, where a is a constant. This means that if x increases, y increases in a linear fashion. A graph of x against y would be a straight line passing through the origin (the point $x = 0$, $y = 0$). y is *inversely proportional* to x if the graph of y against $1/x$ is a straight line through the origin. The corresponding equation is $y = a/x$. Many laws of science relate quantities that are proportional.

pyramid in geometry, a solid figure with triangular side-faces meeting at a common vertex (point) and with a polygon as its base. The volume of a pyramid, no matter how many faces it has, is equal to the area of the base multiplied by one-third of the perpendicular height. A pyramid with a triangular base is called a tetrahedron; the Egyptian pyramids have square bases.

Pythagoras' theorem in geometry, theorem stating that in a right-angled triangle, the area of the square on the hypotenuse (the longest side) is equal to the sum of the areas of the squares drawn on the other two sides. If the hypotenuse is h units long and the lengths of the other sides are a and b, then $h^2 = a^2 + b^2$. The theorem provides a way of calculating the length of any side of a right-angled triangle if the lengths of the other two sides are known.

quadratic equation an equation containing as its highest exponent, or power, the square of a single unknown variable, such as x, for example, $3x^2 + 2x + 2 = 0$. The general formula of such equations is $ax^2 + bx + c = 0$, in which a, b, and c are real numbers, and only the coefficient a cannot equal 0. In coordinate geometry, a quadratic equation represents a parabola.

Depending on the value of $b^2 - 4ac$ (the *discriminant*), the roots, or solutions, of a quadratic equation are either two real roots or two complex roots (when $b^2 - 4ac < 0$, two different real roots; when $b^2 - 4ac = 0$, two equal real roots; and when $b^2 - 4ac > 0$, two different complex roots). Some quadratic equations can be solved by factorization, or the the values of x may be found by using the formula $x = [-b \pm \sqrt{(b^2 - 4ac)}]/2a$.

radian in geometry, an alternative unit to the degree for measuring angles. It is the angle at the centre of a circle when the centre is joined to the two ends of an arc (part of the circumference) equal in length to the radius of the circle. There are 2π (approximately 6.284) radians in a full circle (360°); 1 radian is approximately 57°, and 1° is $\pi/180$ or approximately 0.0175 radians. Radians are commonly used to specify angles in polar coordinates.

ratio measure of the relative size of two quantities or of two measurements (in similar units), expressed as a proportion. For example, the ratio of vowels to consonants in the alphabet is 5:21; the ratio of 500 m to 2 km is 500:2,000, or 1:4.

reciprocal of a quantity, that quantity divided into 1. Thus the reciprocal of 2 is 1/2 (= 0.5); of 150 is 1/150 (= 0.00666666...); of x^2 is $1/x^2$ or x^{-2}.

rectangle a quadrilateral (four-sided figure) with opposite sides equal and parallel, and with each interior angle a right angle (90°). The diagonals of a rectangle bisect each other. Its area A is the product of its length l and breadth b; that is, $A = l \times b$. A rectangle is a special case of a parallelogram. A rectangle with all four sides equal is a square.

rhombus a diamond-shaped plane figure, a parallelogram with four equal sides (opposite sides are equal in length and parallel) and no internal angle that is a right angle (otherwise it is a square). Its diagonals bisect each other at right angles. The area of a rhombus is equal to the length of a side multiplied by its height (the perpendicular distance between opposite sides).

right-angled triangle a triangle in which one of the angles is a right angle (90°). It is the basic form of triangle for defining trigonometrical ratios (for example, sine, cosine and tangent) and for which Pythagoras' theorem holds true. The longest side of a right-angled triangle is called the *hypotenuse*. Its area is equal to half the product of the other two sides. A triangle constructed on the diameter of a circle with its opposite vertex (corner) on the circumference is a right-angled triangle, a fundamental theorem in geometry first credited to the Greek mathematician Thales about 580 BC.

Roman numerals an old number system using different symbols from today's Arabic numerals (the ordinary numbers 1, 2, 3, 4, 5, and so on). The seven key symbols in Roman numerals as represented today (originally they were a little different) are I (= 1), V (= 5), X (= 10), L (= 50), C (= 100), D (= 500), and M (= 1,000). There is no zero. The first fifteen Roman numerals are I, II, III, IV (or IIII), V, VI, VII, VIII, IX, X, XI, XII, XIII, XIV, and XV; the multiples of 10 from 20 to 90 are XX, XXX, XL, L, LX, LXX, LXXX, and XC; and the year 1992 becomes MCMXCII. Although addition and subtraction are fairly straightforward using Roman numerals, the

topology

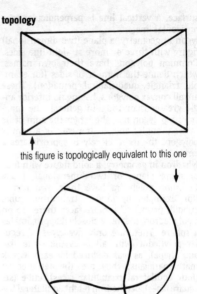

this figure is topologically equivalent to this one

absence of a zero makes other arithmetic operations (such as multiplication) clumsy and difficult.

scalar quantity any quantity that has magnitude but no direction, as distinct from a vector quantity, which has direction as well as magnitude. Speed, mass, and volume are scalar quantities.

set any collection of defined things (elements), provided the elements are distinct and that there is a rule to decide whether an element is a member of the set. It is usually denoted by a capital letter and indicated by curly brackets { }. For example, L = {letters of the alphabet} represents the set that consists of all the letters of the alphabet. The symbol ϵ stands for 'is a member of'; thus p ϵ L means that p belongs to the set consisting of all letters, and 4 $\notin$ L means that 4 does not belong to the set consisting of all letters.

A *finite set* has a limited number of members, such as {letters of the alphabet}; an *infinite set* has an unlimited number of members, such as {all whole numbers}; an *empty* or *null set* has no members, such as the number of people who have swum across the Atlantic Ocean, written as { } or ∅. Sets with some members in common are *intersecting sets*; for example, if R = {red playing cards} and F = {face cards}, then R and F share the members that are red face cards. Sets with no members in common are *disjoint sets*, such as {minerals} and {vegetables}. Sets contained within others are *subsets*; for example, {vowels} is a subset of {letters of the alphabet}. The set that contains all the elements of all the sets under consideration is known as the *universal set*; the *complement* of a set consists of all elements within the universal set that

Triangle

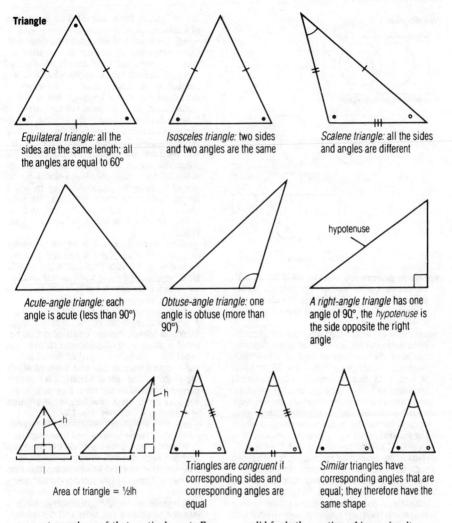

Equilateral triangle: all the sides are the same length; all the angles are equal to 60°

Isosceles triangle: two sides and two angles are the same

Scalene triangle: all the sides and angles are different

Acute-angle triangle: each angle is acute (less than 90°)

Obtuse-angle triangle: one angle is obtuse (more than 90°)

A right-angle triangle has one angle of 90°, the *hypotenuse* is the side opposite the right angle

Area of triangle = ½lh

Triangles are *congruent* if corresponding sides and corresponding angles are equal

Similar triangles have corresponding angles that are equal; they therefore have the same shape

are not members of that particular set. For example, if the universal set is the set of all positive whole numbers and the designated set S is the set of all even numbers, then the complement of S (denoted S') is the set of all odd numbers. Sets and their interrelationships are often illustrated by a **Venn diagram**.

significant figures the figures in a number that, by virtue of their place value, express the magnitude of that number to a specified degree of accuracy. The final significant figure is rounded up if the following digit is, greater than five. For example, 5,463,254 to three significant figures is 5,460,000; 3.462891 to four significant figures is 3.463.

simultaneous equations two or more algebraic equations that contain two or more unknown quantities that may have a unique solution. For example, in the case of two linear equations with two unknown variables, such as (i) $x + 3y = 6$ and (ii) $3y - 2x = 4$, the solution will be those unique values of x and y that are valid for both equations. Linear simultaneous equations can be solved by using algebraic manipulation to eliminate one of the variables, coordinate geometry, or matrices.

sine in trigonometry, a function of an angle in a right-angled triangle found by dividing the length of the side opposite to the angle by the length of the hypotenuse (the longest side). Various properties in physics vary sinsoidally, that is, they can be represented diagramatically by a sine wave (a graph obtained by plotting values of angles against the values of their sines). Examples include simple harmonic motion, such as the way alternating current (AC) electricity varies with time.

speed the rate at which an object moves. Speed in kilometres per hour is calculated by dividing the distance travelled in kilometres by the time taken in hours. Speed is a scalar quantity, as the direction of motion is not taken into consideration. This makes it different from velocity, which is a vector quantity.

Ven diagram

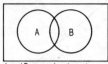

A and B are overlapping sets

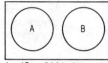

A and B are disjoint sets

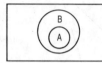

A is the subset of B

sphere in geometry, a circular solid figure with all points on its surface the same distance from the centre. For a sphere of radius r, the volume $V = 4/3\pi(12)r^3$, and the surface area $A = 4\pi r^2$.

square root a number that when squared (multiplied by itself) equals another given number. For example, the square root of 25 (written $\sqrt{25}$) is ± 5, because $+5 \times +5 = 25$, and $(-5) \times (-5) = 25$. As an exponent, a square root is represented by 1/2; for example, $16^{1/2} = \pm 4$. Negative numbers (less than 0) do not have square roots that are real numbers. Their roots are represented by complex numbers, in which the square root of -1 is given the symbol i (that is, $i^2 = -1$). Thus the square root of -4 is $\pm 2i$.

statistics the branch of mathematics concerned with the collection and interpretation of data. For meaningful interpretation, there should be a large amount of data to analyse. For example, faced with the task of determining the mean (average) age of the children in a school, an exact mean could be obtained by averaging the ages of every pupil in the school. A statistically acceptable answer might be obtained by calculating the average based on the ages of a representative sample, consisting say of a random tenth of the pupils from each class.

tangent in trigonometry, a function of an angle in a right-angled triangle, defined as the ratio of the length of the side opposite the angle (not the right angle) to the length of the side adjacent to it; a way of expressing the gradient of a line. In geometry, a tangent is a straight line that touches a curve and has the same slope as the curve at the point of contact. At a maximum or minimum, the tangent to a curve has zero gradient.

tetrahedron in geometry, a solid figure (polyhedron) with four triangular faces; that is, a pyramid on a triangular base. A regular tetrahedron has equilateral triangles as its faces; it can be constructed by joining four points that

are equidistant from each other on the surface of a sphere.

topology the branch of geometry that deals with those properties of a figure that remain unchanged even when the figure is transformed (bent, stretched)—for example, when a square painted on a rubber sheet is deformed by distorting the sheet. Topology has scientific applications, as in the study of turbulence in flowing fluids. The map of the London Underground system is an example of the topological representation of a network; connectivity (the way the lines join together) is preserved, but shape and size are not. The topological theory, proposed 1880, that only four colours are required in order to produce a map in which no two adjoining countries have the same colour, inspired extensive research, and was proved 1972 by Kenneth Appel and Wolfgang Haken.

trapezium (North American **trapezoid**) in geometry, a four-sided plane figure quadrilateral with two of its sides parallel. If the parallel sides have lengths a and b and the perpendicular distance between them is h (the height of the trapezium), its area $A = 1/2h(a + b)$.

triangle in geometry, a three-sided plane figure. A **scalene triangle** has no two sides equal; an **isosceles triangle** has two equal sides (and two equal angles); an **equilateral triangle** has three equal sides (and three equal angles of 60°). A right-angled triangle has one angle of 90°. If the length of one side of a triangle is l and the perpendicular distance from that side to the opposite corner is h (the height, or altitude, of the triangle), its area $A = 1/2l \times h$.

trigonometry branch of mathematics that solves problems relating to plane and spherical triangles. Its principles are based on the fixed proportions of angles and sides in a right-angled triangle, the simplest of which are the sine, cosine, and tangent (so-called trigonometrical ratios).

It is possible, using trigonometry, to calculate the lengths of the sides and the sizes of the angles of a right-angled triangle as long as one angle (other than the right-angle) and one side are known. Trigonometry is of practical importance in navigation and surveying, and simple harmonic motion in physics.

variable a changing quantity (one that can take various values), as opposed to a constant. For example, in the algebraic expression $y = 4x^3 + 2$, the variables are x and y, whereas 4 and 2 are constants.

vector quantity a physical quantity such as velocity or acceleration that has both magnitude and direction, as distinct from a scalar quantity (such as speed, density, or mass), which has magnitude but no direction. A vector is often represented geometrically by an arrow on a line of length equal to its magnitude and in technical writing it is denoted by **bold type**. Vectors can be added graphically by constructing a parallelogram of vectors.

velocity the speed of an object in a given direction. Velocity is a vector quantity, since its direction is as important as its magnitude (or speed).

Venn diagram a diagram representing a set or sets and the logical relationships between them. Sets are drawn as circles. An area of overlap between two circles (sets) contains elements that are common to both sets, and thus represents a third set. Circles that do not overlap represent sets with no elements in common (disjoint sets). The method is named after English logician John Venn (1834–1923).

vertex a corner of a plane (two-dimensional) or solid shape. In a polygon, it is the point of intersection of two sides; in a polyhedron it is the point where two edges meet. For example, a square has four vertices; a cube has eight.

volume the space occupied by a three-dimensional solid object.

VOLUMES OF COMMON THREE-DIMENSIONAL SHAPES

cuboid	lbh
length l, breadth b, height h	
cube	l^3
side l	
cylinder	$\pi r^2 h$
height h, radius of cross section r	
cone	$1/3\pi r^2 h$
height h, radius of base r	
sphere	$4/3\pi r^3$
radius r	

THE GREAT MATHEMATICIANS

Archimedes c. 287–212 BC. Greek mathematician who made discoveries in geometry, hydrostatics, and mechanics. He used geometrical techniques to measure the areas and volumes of curved figures, such as the sphere, determined an approximate value for π, and devised a system of notation for very large numbers. He also formulated a law of fluid displacement (Archimedes' principle), and is credited with the invention of the Archimedes screw, a cylindrical device for raising water.

Bernoulli Swiss family that produced many capable mathematicians in the 17th, 18th, and 19th centuries, in particular the brothers *Jakob* (1654–1705) and *Johann* (1667–1748), who were pioneers of Leibniz's calculus. Jakob used calculus to study the forms of many curves arising in practical situations, and studied probability; *Bernoulli numbers*, a complex series of fractions used in higher mathematics, are named after him. Johann discovered exponential calculus and contributed to many areas of applied mathematics, including the problem of a particle moving in a gravitational field. His son *Daniel* (1700–1782) investigated calculus and probability, and made discoveries in hydrodynamics.

Boole George 1814–1864. English mathematician whose work *The Mathematical Analysis of Logic* 1847 established the basis of modern mathematical logic, and whose *Boolean algebra* can be used in designing computers.

Cantor Georg 1845–1918. German mathematician who followed his work on number theory and trigonometry by considering the foundations of mathematics. He defined real numbers and produced a treatment of irrational numbers using a series of transfinite numbers. Cantor's set theory has been used in the development of topology and real function theory.

Cauchy Augustin Louis 1789–1857. French mathematician, celebrated for his rigorous methods of analysis. His prolific output included work on complex functions, determinants, and probability, and on the convergence of infinite series. In calculus, he refined the concepts of the definite integral.

Descartes René 1596–1650. French mathematician and philosopher. He believed that commonly accepted knowledge was doubtful because of the subjective nature of the senses, and attempted to rebuild human knowledge using as his foundation 'cogito ergo sum' ('I think, therefore I am'). He aimed to express the physical sciences in mathematical terms, and founded coordinate geometry as a way of defining and manipulating geometrical shapes by means of algebraic expressions. Cartesian coordinates, the means by which points are represented in this system, were named after him.

Eratosthenes c. 276–c. 194 BC. Greek geographer and mathematician whose map of the ancient world was the first to contain lines of latitude and longitude. He calculated the Earth's circumference with an error of about 10%. His mathematical achievements include a method for duplicating the cube, and for finding prime numbers (*Eratosthenes' sieve*).

Euclid c. 330–c. 260 BC. Greek mathematician from Alexandria who wrote the *Stoicheia/Elements* in 13 books, of which nine deal with plane and solid geometry, and four with arithmetic. His great achievement lay in the systematic arrangement of previous discoveries, based on axioms, definitions, and theorems.

Euler Leonhard 1707–1783. Swiss mathematician. He developed the theory of differential equations and the calculus of variations, and worked in astronomy and optics. He was a pupil of Johann Bernoulli.

Fermat Pierre de 1601–1665. French mathematician who with Blaise Pascal founded the theory of probability and the modern theory of numbers, and who made contributions to coordinate geometry. *Fermat's last theorem* states that equations of the form $x^n + y^n = z^n$, where x, y, z, and n are all integers, have no solutions if $n < 2$. There is no general proof of this, so it remains a conjecture rather than a theorem.

Fibonacci Leonardo (also known as Leonardo of Pisa) c. 1170–c. 1250. Italian mathematician. In 1202 he published *Liber abaci/Book of the*

Abacus (based in part on his knowledge of the work of the Persian mathematician al-Khwārizmī), which was instrumental in the introduction of Hindu–Arabic numerals into Europe. It also described special sequences of numbers, now called **Fibonacci numbers**, in which each number is the sum of its two predecessors (for example, 1, 1, 2, 3, 5, 8, 13...). From 1960, interest developed in these sequences' unusual characteristics and their possible applications in botany, psychology, and astronomy. For example, the number of petals and sepals on flowers, the spirals in a spider's web, and the distances between the planets and the Sun, all fit such sequences.

Galois Evariste 1811–1832. French mathematician who originated the theory of groups. His attempts to gain recognition for his work were largely thwarted by the French mathematical establishment, critical of his lack of formal qualifications. Galois was killed in a duel before he was 21. The night before, he had hurriedly written out his unpublished discoveries on group theory, the importance of which would come to be appreciated more and more as the 19th century progressed.

Gauss Karl Friedrich 1777–1855. German mathematician. He found four different proofs of the fundamental theorem of algebra, which states that every equation has at least one root, and developed a form of non-Euclidean geometry. Gauss also worked on the mathematical development of electric and magnetic theory.

Gödel Kurt 1906–1978. Austrian-born US mathematician and philospher who proved that a mathematical system always contains statements that can be neither proved nor disproved within the system; in other words, as a science, mathematics can never be totally consistent and totally complete. He was a friend of Einstein and worked on relativity, constructing a mathematical model of the Universe that made travel back through time theoretically possible.

Hilbert David 1862–1943. German mathematician who attempted to put mathematics on a logical foundation through defining it in terms of a number of basic principles, which Kurt Gödel later showed to be impossible; none the less, his attempt greatly influenced 20th-century mathematics. Hilbert proposed a set of 23 unsolved problems in 1900 for future mathematicians to solve, a programme that has inspired mathematical research ever since.

Khwārizmī, al- Muhammad ibn-Mūsāc 780–c.850. Persian mathematician who wrote a book on algebra, from part of whose title (*al-jabr*, 'transposition') comes the word 'algebra'. His work helped to introduce to the West the Hindu–Arabic decimal number system, including the symbol for zero. The word 'algorithm' (the process of steps used to solve mathematical problems) is a corruption of his name.

Lagrange Joseph Louis 1736–1813. French mathematician who presided over the commission that introduced the metric system in 1793.

His *Mécanique analytique* 1788 applied mathematical analysis, using principles established by Newton to such problems as the movements of planets when affected by each other's gravitational force.

Leibniz Gottfried Wilhelm 1646–1716. German mathematician and philosopher. Independently of, but concurrently with, the British scientist Isaac Newton he developed calculus. In his metaphysical works, such as *The Monadology* 1714, he argued that everything consisted of innumerable units, **monads**, whose individual properties determined each thing's past, present, and future.

Lobachevsky Nikolai Ivanovich 1792–1856. Russian mathematician who founded non-Euclidean geometry concurrently with, but independently of, Karl Gauss and the Hungarian János Bulyai (1802–1860). Lobachevsky published the first account of the subject in 1829, but his work went unrecognized until Georg Riemann's system was published.

Lorenz Ludwig Valentine 1829–1891. Danish mathematician and physicist who developed mathematical formulae to describe various phenomena, such as the relationship between refraction of light and the density of a pure transparent substance, and the relationship between a metal's electrical and thermal conductivity and temperature.

Mandelbrot Benoit B 1924– . Polish-born US scientist who coined the term **fractal geometry** to describe 'self-similar' shape, a motif that repeats indefinitely, each time smaller.

Markov Andrei 1856–1922. Russian mathematician who formulated the **Markov chain**, a concept that holds that a chain of events is governed only by established probability and is uninfluenced by the past history of earlier links in the chain.

Möbius August Ferdinand 1790–1868. German mathematician, considered one of the founders of topology. He discovered the **Möbius strip**, a structure made by giving a half twist to a flat strip of paper and joining the ends together. It has certain remarkable properties, arising from the fact that it has only one edge and one side. If cut down the centre of the strip, instead of two new strips of paper, only one long strip is produced.

Napier John 1550–1617. Scottish mathematician who invented logarithms in 1614, and 'Napier's Bones', an early mechanical calculating device for multiplication and division.

Newton Isaac 1642–1727. English physicist and mathematician who laid the foundations of physics as a modern discipline. He discovered the law of gravity, showed that white light is composed of many colours, and developed the three standard laws of motion still in use today. In mathematics, Newton discovered differential and integral calculus (although it was Gottfried Leibniz's notation that was finally adopted), and the binomial theorem. Most of the last 30 years of his life were taken up by studies and experiments in alchemy.

Pascal Blaise 1623–1662. French mathematician

Pascal triangle

```
                  1
               1     1
            1     2     1
         1     3     3     1
      1     4     6     4     1
   1     5    10    10     5     1
1     6    15    20    15     6     1
1  7   21    35    35    21     7     1
```

---

physicist who worked on conic sections and (with Pierre de Fermat) probability theory. *Pascal's triangle* is an array of numbers with 1 at the apex and in which each number is the sum of the pair of numbers above it. Plotted at equal distances along a horizontal axis, the numbers in the rows give the binomial probability distribution with equal probability of success and failure, such as when tossing coins.

Poincaré Jules Henri 1854–1912. French mathematician who developed the theory of differential equations and was a pioneer in relativity theory. He suggested that Isaac Newton's laws for the behaviour of the universe could be the exception rather than the rule. However, the calculation was so complex and time-consuming that he never managed to realise its full implication. He also published the first paper devoted entirely to topology.

Pythagoras c. 580–c. 500 BC. Greek mathematician and philosopher who formulated Pythagoras' theorem. Much of his work concerned numbers, to which he assigned mystical properties. For example, he classified numbers into triangular ones (1, 3, 6, 10,...) which can be represented as a triangular array, and square ones (1, 4, 9, 16,...) which form squares. He also observed that any two adjacent triangular numbers add to a square number (for example, $1 + 3 = 4$, $3 = 6 = 9$, $6 + 10 = 16$, and so on).

Riemann Georg Friedrich Bernhard 1826–1866. German mathematician whose system of non-Euclidean geometry, thought at the time to be a mere mathematical curiosity, was used by Einstein to develop his general theory of relativity.

Rubik Erno 1944– . Hungarian architect who invented the *Rubik Cube* 1974, a plastic multi-coloured puzzle that can be manipulated and rearranged in only one correct way and in around 43 trillion wrong ones. Intended to help his students understand three-dimensional design, it became a fad that swept the world.

Thales c. 624–c. 547 BC. Greek philosopher and scientist. He advanced geometry as an abstract study, predicted an eclipse of the Sun 585 BC, and as a philosophical materialist, theorized that water was the first principle of all things, that the Earth floated on water, and so proposed an explanation for earthquakes.

Turing Alan Mathison 1912–1954. British mathematician and logician. In 1936 he described a 'universal computing machine' that could theoretically be programmed to solve any problem capable of solution by a specially designed machine. This concept, now called the *Turing machine*, foreshadowed the digital computer.

Von Neumann John 1903–1957. Hungarian-born US mathematician and scientist. He invented his celebrated 'rings of operators' (called Von Neumann algebras) in the late 1930s, and also contributed to set theory, games theory, cybernetics (with his theory of self-reproducing automata, called *Von Neumann machines*), and the development of the atomic and hydrogen bombs.

Wiener Norbert 1894–1964. US mathematician, credited with the establishment of the science of cybernetics in his book *Cybernetics* 1948. He laid the foundation of the study of stochastic processes (those dependent on random events), including Brownian movement (evidence of constant random motion of molecules).

SOME ENDANGERED SPECIES

aye-aye

The enormous size of Africa, the existence of extensive wildlife parks, and the sheer scale of wilderness areas have given many people the impression that efforts to protect African wildlife have been paying off. Unfortunately, failures have continued to outstrip the few successes. Deforestation throughout the continent, the advancing desert, conversion of the savannah into farmland, illegal poaching, and the impact of overfishing are all having catastrophic effects on many wild species. Some areas, such as the huge island of Madagascar, are already at crisis point. In this section we focus on just some of the animals and plants threatened with serious declines and extinctions in the world's largest continent.

MAMMALS

African elephant the world's largest land animal *Loxodonta africana*, ruthlessly hunted by poachers throughout E Africa for the ivory from its tusks. Numbers collapsed during the 1980s owing to overhunting, and elephant populations in several countries are threatened with extinction. A ban on trading ivory introduced 1990 resulted in an apparent drop in poaching but it is too early to be certain what long-term effects this will have. (See feature in this section.)

African palm squirrel a smallish rodent *Epixerus ebii* living in dense tropical rainforest in western Africa and little known, having seldom been seen alive. The species has probably always been quite scarce, but is now threatened by rainforest destruction over a large part of its range.

aye-aye nocturnal primate *Daubentonia madagascariensis* that lives in trees and feeds on fruit and insect larvae, extracting the latter from rotten wood with an elongated middle finger. One of at least 25 endemic primate species threatened by catastrophic deforestation in Madagascar, it is confined to a few scattered individuals in coastal districts, although a breeding colony has been established

on an offshore island from animals raised in zoos.

Barbary macaque or *Barbary ape* an Old World primate *Macaca sylvanus* living mainly in the Mahgreb countries of northern Africa, and especially in the forests of the Atlas mountains. A tame population exists on Gibraltar. The macaque is threatened by illegal logging, which is devastating some of the ancient forests in the area. Although it is breeding well in captivity, forest loss may confound attempts to reintroduce this species into the wild.

black rhinoceros formerly the most numerous African rhinoceros *Diuceros bicornis*. It numbered almost 70,000 at the beginning of the 1970s but had been reduced to just 3,000 twenty years later and is in extreme danger of extinction. It is slaughtered by poachers for its horns, which some cultures believe have aphrodisiac properties. Some game wardens now saw off horns to reduce the reason for killing. The rhino is also threatened by loss of habitat and its own low reproduction rate which makes recovery of numbers difficult.

black wildebeest or *white-tailed gnu* once found over much of southern Africa, *Connochaetes gnou* was reduced to the point of extinction by the hunting and agricultural practices of early European settlers. Numbers fell to 1,700 by 1965. A coordinated breeding programme has raised populations to 3,000 again, and selected reintroductions are being attempted, but the animal remains in a precarious position.

bushman's rabbit or *riverine rabbit* a wild rodent *Bunolagus monticularis* found in dense riverine bush in South Africa. It lives in small populations, and individuals are only seen very occasionally; it is now at extreme risk of extinction owing to loss of habitat to agriculture. Very little is known about its life or habits.

Cape mountain zebra a zebra subspecies confined to South Africa. *Equus zebra zebra* almost became extinct in the 1940s and still only has a population of 450, despite attempts at conservation. The main population is in Mountain Zebra Park in the east of the country, although some zebras have now been moved to other parks in an attempt to build up other viable breeding herds.

cheetah a large wild cat *Acinonyx jubatus*. It is the world's fastest mammal, and can reach speeds

African elephant

IVORY TRADE—WILL THE BAN HOLD?

A disastrous crash in the population of the African elephant during the 1980s reduced overall populations by more than half and has prompted serious fears for the future of the species in the wild. Numbers throughout the continent fell from 1.3 million in 1979 to an estimated 625,000 just ten years later. In Zaire, less than a quarter of the population remained alive at the end of the decade and in Tanzania more than two thirds of the native elephants disappeared over the same period.

Although habitat destruction is affecting elephant populations in some areas, the predominant reason for the decline is a huge and often illegal trade in ivory. Prices for ivory are now so high that poachers are often prepared to face the risk of death to obtain tusks, and fierce gun battles between hunters and game wardens have become common in some areas. Poachers have killed around 22,000 elephants annually in Tanzania since 1981 and similar drastic declines have occurred over much of the animal's range. Ivory is particularly prized for carving and in addition to other destinations considerable amounts of African elephant ivory is imported into India to make up the shortfall in ivory from the largely domesticated Indian elephants.

International concern about the effects of the slaughter resulted in a number of country-wide bans at the end of the 1980s. The UK banned import of raw and worked ivory in 1989, and this move was soon followed by similar bans in the rest of the European Community and the USA. Dubai, a major trading centre for ivory, also announced a ban. Japan, the destination for almost a quarter of the world's ivory, gave a commitment that it would import ivory only from those African countries authorized to trade by the Convention on International Trade in Endangered Species. CITES is an international treaty which controls trade in wild plant and animal products through agreements between signatories, and has a number of categories for free, controlled and prohibited trade depending on the degree to which the species is endangered. In 1991, following intense pressure from conservationists, CITES voted to move the African elephant on to Appendix I of the treaty, thus effectively prohibiting any international trade in ivory.

The CITES move was extremely controversial. Conservation organizations such as the World Wide Fund for Nature (WWF) had lobbied for the ban as the only effective way of removing the incentive for continued poaching. However, five southern African countries—including Zimbabwe and Botswana—claimed to be managing flourishing elephant herds which were funded and conserved partly because of the profits made from ivory produced by a regular cull, or from big-game hunting managed in the same way. Zimbabwe has found that money from big-game hunting expeditions killing 100–200 elephants a year outweighs profits from poaching. There is some justification for the claim that this helps to protect elephants, and several countries managed to build up their elephant numbers in reverse of the overall decline during the 1980s. The trading countries argued that without an international market the incentive to manage their elephant stocks would disappear and it would be difficult to justify setting aside good land for elephants.

Unfortunately, the presence of any ivory in the international trade makes it far easier for poachers to launder their proceeds. Import and export controls cannot detect even quite large discrepancies in amounts traded from particular countries and there are sufficient dishonest traders to keep poached ivory flooding on to the market.

Whatever the misgivings, preliminary research suggested that the CITES ban had resulted in a rapid reduction of poaching, and it was cautiously applauded by conservation groups. However, in 1992 a fresh and determined attempt was made to overturn the ban within CITES.

Poaching has diminished following a total ban on international trade in ivory.

VIVISECTION: EXPERIMENTS AND PROCEDURES ON LIVING ANIMALS IN THE UK

Categories	1989	1990
Total numbers of procedures on animals (incl experiments)	3,315,125	3,207,094
Number of procedures without anaesthetic	2,094,866	2,205,360
Total number of animals used*	X	3,100,553
Fundamental research	702,715	625,240
Applied research	2,612,410	2,414,008
Selection of medical, dental & vet products	1,158,561	1,079,235
Animals used in toxicity testing of medical products	289,716	291,032
Animals used in toxicity testing of non-medical products	254,482	266,843
Animals used in education & training	12,099	10,382
Procedures on cats	4,762	4,392
in respiratory & cardiovascular research	1,839	1,803
in nervous system & behavioural research	998	869
Procedures on primates	5,280	5,284
in toxicity tests of medical & vet products	1,949	2,123
in toxicity tests of non-medical products	226	28
in nervous & behavioural research	1,154	909
Procedures on dogs	12,625	11,433
in respiratory & cardiovascular research	3,800	3,697
in toxicity tests of medical & vet products	4,563	3,327
in digestive research	2,080	1,333
Procedures on mice	1,744,880	1,636,332
Alcohol research	1,114	1,429
Toxicity tests of cosmetics & toiletries	12,090	4,365
Toxicity tests of food additives	5,710	10,822
Toxicity tests of tobacco & its substitutes	387	659
Toxicity tests of household products	4,017	1,486
Deliberately causing animals to have cancer	73,531	59,616
Test for cancer-causing chemicals	47,285	37,478
Procedures deliberately causing psychological stress	8,325	11,093
Application of substances to the eye	107,015	115,991
of which, Draize tests on rabbits	4,273	4,008
Injection of germs into brain or spinal cord	55,150	64,586
LD50 and LC50 toxicity tests**	73,130	98,631
Procedures required by legislation, British & overseas	670,000	686,733
No. of project licence holders (in charge of research projects)	4,205	4,500
No. of visits to laboratories by inspectors	2,775	2,829
Reported infringements of the law or of licence conditions	14	X
No. reported to the Director of Public Prosecutions	0	X
No. of licences revoked	1	2+?

* Details re number of animals used available for first time in 1990
** 1989 and 1990 figures are not directly comparable. 1990 figures include all quantitative short-term tests which have death as end point.
Source: Statistics of Scientific Procedures on Living Animals Great Britain/HMSO

of 110 kph/70 mph for short bursts when running down prey. Cheetahs roam wild over much of Africa and parts of Asia and the Middle East, but face threats both from ranchers who shoot them as vermin and from general habitat destruction that is reducing the prey on which they feed, especially gazelles.

Heaviside's dolphin or *benguela dolphin* a coastal species *Cephalorhynchus heavisidii* confined to the coastal waters of Namibia. It is one of the least-known dolphins, and seldom studied by biologists when alive; there are only a handful of recordings in existence. It is thought that about a hundred a year are killed in purse seine nets from fishing boats, which could have a serious impact on such an apparently rare species.

hunting dog or *painted dog* a wild dog *Lycaon pictus* which once roamed over virtually the whole of sub-Saharan Africa. A pack might have a range of almost 4,000 km/2,500 mi, hunting game such as zebra and antelope. Individuals can run at 50 kph/30 mph for up to 5 km/3 mi, with short bursts of even higher speeds. The species is now reduced to a fraction of its original population, and the maximum pack size found today is usually about 20, whereas in the past several hundred might have hunted together. Habitat destruction and the decline of large game herds have played a part in its decline, but the hunting dog has also suffered badly from the effects of distemper which was introduced into east Africa early in the 20th century.

Juntink's duiker a small and shy antelope *Cephalophus jentinki* that plunges into bushes when startled. It is acutely threatened by deforestation in its remaining habitat in west Africa

The Importing of Live Animals

Customs & Excise seizures of live animals and prosecutions under UK conservation controls

1989	Animals seized	1990
239	reptiles, amphibians	1,567
47	birds	744 + 12 eggs (export)
3	mammals	8

Prosecutions:

1989	1990
Number of offenders 5	Number of offenders 5
Total fines £2,100 plus 1 sentence of 6 months suspended for 2 years. Costs awarded £1,550.	Total fines £1,000 plus 3 prison sentences totalling 63 months.

Source: Wildlife Trade Monitoring Unit/CITES

where it is also hunted. One captive breeding colony exists in Texas and there are hopes of establishing others as the immediate future for this species in the wild appears to be bleak.

lemur prosimian primate of the family *Lemuridae*, inhabiting Madagascar and the Comoro Islands. There are about 16 species, ranging from mouse-sized to dog-sized animals; they are arboreal, and some species are nocturnal. They feed on fruit, insects, and small animals. Many are threatened with extinction owing to loss of their forest habitat and, in some cases, from hunting.

mountain gorilla highly endangered ape subspecies *Gorilla gorilla beringei* found in bamboo and rainforest on the Rwanda, Zaïre, and Uganda borders in central Africa, with a total population of under 400. It is threatened by deforestation and illegal hunting for skins and the zoo trade.

rhim or **sand gazelle** a smallish gazelle *Gazella leptocerus* that has already disappeared over most of its former range of north Africa. Populations are fragmented and often isolated. It is one of several highly threatened gazelle species in northern Africa and the Sahara.

sacred baboon or **hamadryas** a medium-sized ba-

sacred baboon

boon *Papio hamadryas* that was once sacred in Egypt but has since become extinct there owing to competition for land. It occurs in troops of up to 500. It is still found in Ethiopia on dry savannah where there are rocky cliffs and hillsides, but is threatened by habitat changes and perhaps also hunting.

scimitar oryx a medium-sized oryx *Oryx dammah*. It has startling, swept-back horns which have made it a prime target for hunters. It was once found over virtually the whole of the Sahel. Numbers started to decline sharply in the 1950s and the animals were reduced to scattered groups by the 1970s, then reached the edge of extinction by the 1980s. The initial cause of decline was the destruction of grasslands, but savage hunting annihilated the remainder. There are captive breeding herds and plans to reintroduce the species in Tunisia.

triple nose-leaf bat one of many threatened bats in Africa, *Triaenops persicus* is found scattered along much of the coastal regions of east Africa and faces threats from disturbance of the caves in which it breeds. Tourism development, resulting in disturbance to coral caves which the bats inhabit, is a particular problem.

white-collared mangabey lives in troops of about 20 in forest areas of midwest Africa. *Cerocebus torquatus* is threatened mainly by forest destruction but is also hunted for food in some places and in Sierra Leone it is killed as a pest because troops sometimes raid crops.

lemur

FRESH THREATS TO TIGERS

The tiger has always held a special place in the hearts of the conservation movement. The largest and most famous of the wild cats, the tiger once roamed over vast areas of Asia, living mainly in the dense tropical rainforests. Although declining for many centuries as a result of human pressure, the tiger was probably first seriously threatened by the hunting parties organized by the British Raj in India, which increased the scale of a kill long practised by the maharajahs and other local rulers. After a disastrous population decline, tigers were afforded some protection in many areas, but soon faced further and even more serious threats from the large-scale destruction of their habitat by deforestation, and a relentless onslaught from hunters and poachers.

Before World War II, there were eight known subspecies of tiger. Of these, three are almost certainly extinct and a fourth, the Amoy tigers south of the Chang Jiang in China, are reduced to about 50 individuals, which face almost certain extinction through illegal hunting. A tiny remnant population of Siberian tigers are also highly threatened in China, although 400 or so are well protected across the border in Russia. Although government sources claim that there are 2,000 Indochinese tigers in Thailand, Myanmar, and Malaysia, wildlife experts dispute the figures, and these tigers are also highly at risk from poaching. The Sumatran tiger is relatively well protected in some reserves in Indonesia and the massive Bengal tiger of India and Nepal has now regained a total population believed to be around 5,000 following a determined conservation programme.

The tiger was one of the first animals in the Third World to be the subject of serious conservation policies. In India, for example, Indira Gandhi, as prime minister, launched Operation Tiger, which established a network of more than 20 tiger reserves throughout the country. In these areas, predominantly made up of natural forest, wildlife reigns supreme. Human visitors are only allowed into select areas, accompanied by professional guides, leaving most of the habitat entirely to nature. Tiger numbers in India thus stabilized and started to rise.

However, threats to tigers are increasing once again. The pressures that cause deforestation—including population growth, concentration of agricultural land into fewer hands, and the need for foreign capital—are not removed simply by creating a reserve. In some areas, forest reserves are under pressure from encroachment by people desperate for land or fuel.

The reserves are mostly at maximum population capacity for tigers so that there is no further room for expansion. And conserving dangerous and potentially deadly animals does not meet with universal approval from the people living in close proximity to reserves. Democratic pressure to reduce tiger numbers may well be coming in the near future.

Unfortunately, tigers are threatened by more than encroachment. Long desired by people in the West as stuffed trophies, they still have a very high market value in Chinese-speaking regions for some of their products. Wine that includes tiger bones is believed to be a tonic and dried tiger penises are valued as aphrodisiacs. (Rhinoceros horn is similarly believed to have aphrodisiac properties, which also vastly increases the number killed by poachers.) TRAFFIC, an organization that monitors the wildlife trade, estimates that bones from almost 150 tigers were imported into Korea between 1985 and 1990. In March 1992, two ethnic Chinese were arrested in France in possession of 24 tiger penises. These bizarre beliefs are seriously threatening the future of several unique tiger populations.

Stopping the trade in tiger products will not prove easy. In 1992, China applied to the Convention on International Trade in Endangered Species (CITES) for a waiver on the total ban on trade in tiger products to allow trade in those from a tiger farm in the northeast of the country. Although they withdrew the request after stiff opposition from conservationists, it is widely believed that they will keep trying. Policing the illegal trade will become even more difficult if indeterminate amounts of 'farmed tiger' products start entering the international market. Despite continued and dedicated efforts by many wildlife experts and conservationists, the future of the tiger is still far from assured.

Farm animal? Despite a CITES ban, China has been pressing for legal trade in 'farmed' tiger products.

Animals Protected in UK Under the Wildlife and Countryside Act 1981

common name	species	scientific name
adder [1]		Vipera berus
anemone [4]	Ivell's sea	Edwardsia ivelli
	starlet sea	Nematostella vectensis
apus [4]		Triops cancriformis
bat	all species	–
beetle	rainbow leaf	Chrysolina cerealis
	violet click [4]	Limoniscus violaceus
burbot		Lota lota
butterfly	heath fritillary	Mellicta athalia or Melitaea athalia
	large blue	Maculinea arion
	swallowtail	Papilio machaon
cat [4]	wild	Felis silvestris
cicada [4]	New Forest	Cicadetta montana
crayfish [4] [2]	white-clawed	Austropotamobius pallipes
cricket	field	Gryllus campestris
	mole	Gryllotalpa gryllotalpa
dolphin [4]		Cetacea species
dormouse [4]		Muscardinus avellanarius
dragonfly	Norfolk aeshna	Aeshna isosceles
frog [1]	common	Rana temporaria
grasshopper	wart-biter	Decticus verrucivorus
leech [4]	medicinal	Hirudo medicinalis
lizard	sand	Lacerta agilis
	viviparous [3]	Lacerta vivipara
marten [4]	pine	Martes martes
moth	barberry carpet	Pareulype berberata
	black-veined	Siona lineata or Idaea lineata
	Essex emerald	Thetidia smaragdaria
	New Forest burnet	Zygaena viciae
	reddish buff	Acosmetica caliginosa
	viper's bugloss [4]	Hadena irregularis
newt	great crested (warty)	Triturus cristatus
	palmate [1]	Triturus helveticus
	smooth [1]	Triturus vulgaris
otter	common	Lutra lutra
porpoise [4]		Cetacea species
sandworm [4]	lagoon	Armandia cirrhosa
sea mat [4]	trembling	Victorella pavida
shrimp [4]	fairy	Chirocephalus diaphanus
	lagoon sand	Gammarus insensibilis
slowworm [3]		Anguis fragilis
snail	glutinous	Myxas glutinosa
	sandbowl	Catinella avenaria
snake	grass [3]	Natrix natrix
	smooth	Coronella austriaca
spider	great raft	Dolomedes plantarius
	ladybird	Eresus niger
squirrel	red	Sciurus vulgaris
toad	common [1]	Bufo bufo
	natterjack	Bufo calamita
turtle [4]	leatherback	Dermochelyidae
	marine (all species)	Chelonidae
vendace [4]		Coregonus albula
walrus [4]		Odobenus rosmarus
whale [4]		Cetacea species
whitefish [4]		Coregonus lavaretus

It is normally an offence to kill, injure, take, possess, or sell any of the above-mentioned animals (whether live or dead) and to disturb its place of shelter and protection or to destroy that place.
[1] species for which the offence relates to sale only [2] species for/which the offence relates to taking and sale only
[3] species for which the offence relates to killing, injuring, and sale [4] species added to the list in 1986
Sources: *Protecting Britain's Wildlife: A Brief Guide* (DOE), and *IUCN, Red List of Threatened Animals 1988*

BIRDS

Bannerman's turaco a parrot-like bird *Tauraco bannermani* apparently confined to the mountain forests of Cameroon and endangered by the rapid deforestation of Mount Oku to establish farms. One of several species threatened by the probability of further losses to the already fragmented and shrunken forest resources of west Africa.

Madagascar teal or *Bernier's* teal a small duck *Anas bernieri* apparently confined to a few small lakes and marshy areas in western Madagascar and now severely threatened with extinction. It is thought that there are at most a few hundred teal left alive and the opening of an airstrip nearby greatly increases the risk of sport shooting.

Sokoke scops owl a small African owl *Otus ieneae* thought to be entirely confined to the threatened Arabuko Sokoke Forest in Kenya. Only discovered in 1965, the owl is typical of many of the continent's little-known species, confined to a few limited and specialized habitats and thus extremely vulnerable to change. There are currently efforts to establish a national park in the forest.

REPTILES AND AMPHIBIANS

geometric tortoise a tiny South African tortoise *Psammobates geometricus* which only grows to 10–12 cm/4–5 in in length and is acutely threatened by habitat loss, which has shrunk to just 4% of the reptile's original range. Remaining areas are mainly fragmented and suffering from the invasion of alien plant species that the tortoise is unable to eat.

Nile crocodile a large crocodile *Crocodylus niloticus* which once spread over most of Africa and into the Middle East but is now increasingly threatened. Although habitat destruction has damaged some populations the main menace has come from hunting. In what is now Tanzania, for example, 12,509

RAW FURSKINS BROUGHT TO THE UK

not incl. tanned, dressed furs*

Import (numbers unless stated)

1989		1990
2,967,180	Mink	1,482,769
83,302	Rabbit, hare	88,216
569,664	Lamb**	11,022
12,010	Beaver	15,305
353,107	Muskrat	133,323
383,117	Fox	124,611
1,193	Seal	6,400
2,601	Sea otter, Nutria***	51,229
100	Marmots	2,100
4,500	Wild feline	–
37,107kg	Others	49,152kg

* Approx 100,000 in 1990 **Astrakan, Persian etc
***S. American coypu

Source: Wildlife Trade Monitoring Unit/CITES

skins were exported in 1950. Although now protected in many areas, it still suffers from poaching and remaining populations are increasingly fragmented.

PLANTS

marsh rose a shrub 1–4 m/3–13 ft high *Orothamnus zeyheri*. It grows in South Africa and is under threat, partly because of picking for its beautiful flowerheads. Further threats come from fungi, probably introduced by footwear or equipment, and by changes in management practice that have prevented periodic fires which are necessary for seed germination. Ironically, populations have reached such critically low levels that uncontrolled fires could wipe out remaining adults. Although protected, it remains highl threatened.

palm *Willmania carinensis* a small palm tree

FASHION VICTIMS

A selection of CITES statistics on imports of animal skins (1989)

African elephant-skin pieces		(min.)	2,822 m²
Alligator watchstraps			10,200
Caiman crocodilus crocodilus skins			4,002
Caiman crocodilus crocodilus watchstraps			32,131*
Tupinambis teguixin (lizard) skins			27,040
Varanus niloticus (Nile monitor) skins			25,397
ditto	watchstraps		9,558
Varanus salvator (lizard) skins			218,135
ditto	skin pieces		10,000
ditto	watchstraps		53,185
Python reticulatus skins			85,827
Pytas mucosus (Indian rat snake) handbags			11,787
ditto	pairs of shoes		43,237
ditto	skins		320,397

* Items from other crocodile species also imported
Source: Wildlife Trade Monitoring Unit/CITES

ANIMAL RIGHTS AND WRONGS

At first sight, the animal-rights movement has never had it so good. New legislation is being introduced into many countries aimed specifically at improving animal welfare: in Britain cramped farrowing crates for pigs will be illegal from 1998; Switzerland has banned battery hen farming; the European Community is struggling with the ethics of livestock transportation; and Thailand is under international pressure to halt its trade in live birds. Vegetarians and vegans (people who eat no animal products at all) are on the increase. A growing proportion of meat eaters will buy products only from free-range animals. There are many popular campaigns to protect animals, such as those against tuna fishing nets that endanger dolphins.

However, some rights of animals are also under attack. In Britain, illegal dog fighting and badger baiting have increased recently, despite efforts by the League Against Cruel Sports, whose activists often have to live in hiding from the 'sportsmen' they confront. New developments in genetic engineering threaten greater suffering for farm livestock. Animals are increasingly transported long distances, and may suffer as a result. There is certainly no smooth transition towards increased animal rights.

A glance at the history of animal welfare shows that this should come as no surprise; although concern goes back a long way, campaigners have always faced strong opposition. The Parsee faith of E India, probably the world's oldest religion, teaches a philosophy of total nonviolence to animals such that extreme adherents even wear gauze over their mouths to prevent themselves from accidentally swallowing flies. Yet animal rights in India are not noticeably better than in surrounding countries.

Animal-welfare campaigners have long been accused of diverting attention from more pressing problems. Yet, the issues of animal and human rights have usually progressed side by side. The Royal Society for the Prevention of Cruelty to Animals was started in 1824 by William Wilberforce and Sir Thomas Fowell Buxton, who were also leading abolitionists of the slave trade. The Franciscan order pioneered animal-rights issues in the Christian tradition and also preached against the wealth and corruption of the established church. Mahatma Gandhi worked against imperialism and the Indian caste system, and refused to eat meat on moral grounds.

The contemporary animal-rights movement has two new components. A detailed philosophical framework has been established, and in addition some campaigners have also become more extreme, even considering direct attacks on humans justifiable. In 1976, Peter Singer, an Australian philosopher, published *Animal Liberation*, in which he argued that treating animals in ways that would be considered unacceptable to humans was morally indefensible. He coined the word 'speciesism'

Ninety six per cent of the UK's 38 million egg-laying hens are kept in battery cages. Confined for their entire lives in these crowded cages, they have no room to move, stretch their wings, or perch.

to describe prejudice against animals and compared this to racism or sexism.

Singer succeeded in switching the whole emphasis of the debate from one in which animal welfare was seen as a nonessential indulgence of a civilized society to one in which animal-rights campaigners argued that animals should be put on equal terms with humans.

For a minority of extreme and usually anonymous activists, *Animal Liberation* has become a tract for revolutionary action. Members of several shadowy animal-rights groups have carried out firebomb attacks on laboratories where animal experiments take place, threatened individuals, set booby traps, and mounted graffiti campaigns and property attacks against fur traders and others. The more traditional groups have been outraged by such tactics and argue against anything but a nonviolent strategy.

Many individuals, both inside and outside the animal-rights movement, are currently confused and uncertain about how to proceed. Polls show that most people think that keeping chickens in battery cages is wrong, but most also continue to buy battery eggs. People campaign against fur coats but wear leather jackets. Others balk at animal experiments but use cosmetics tested on laboratory animals. The rights of animals continue to be abused in some areas while a steady increase in legislation protecting them continues in most countries.

In 1780, the Utilitarian Jeremy Bentham wrote of animals: 'The question is not, can they reason? Nor, can they talk? But, *can they suffer?*' In the late 20th century, most people accept that animals can indeed suffer, and a growing number are prepared to make changes in their lives to reduce this suffering.

confined to Djibouti, Somalia, and South Yemen, growing along river valleys. Although cultivated, it is now extremely rare and endangered in the wild. The main threats come from grazing by cattle and sheep, and from felling for building timber; the palm is one of the few trees producing straight and durable timber in the area.

spiral aloe or *kharetsa* a perennial succulent *Aloe polyphylla* confined to mountains in Lesotho. An attractive species valued by the horticultural trade, this succulent has been endangered by uprooting for sale to collectors. It is now legally protected and is known from about 50 localities, but remains vulnerable.

yeheb nut a small tree *Cordeauxia adulis* found in Ethiopia and Somalia and formerly much valued as a food source for its nuts. Although cultivated as a food crop in Kenya and Sudan, it is now critically endangered in the wild and has at most three known sites remaining. Overgrazing by cattle and goats has prevented regeneration, and nuts are taken for consumption thus preventing reseeding. Although reintroduction would theoretically be possible from cultivated trees, the continuing grazing pressure would make establishment unlikely without proper management.

Are you in favour of:

	Yes	No	Don't know
Keeping animals in zoos	18	73	9
Keeping a dog	65	23	11
Keeping a cat	63	27	10

TERMS

absolute zero the lowest temperature theoretically possible, zero kelvin, equivalent to $-273.16°C/-459.67°F$, at which molecules are motionless. Although the third law of thermodynamics indicates the impossibility of reaching absolute zero exactly, a temperature within 3×10^{-8} kelvin of it was produced in 1984 by Finnish scientists. Near absolute zero, the physical properties of some materials change substantially; for example, some metals lose their electrical resistance and become superconductive. See cryogenics.

acoustics in general, the experimental and theoretical science of sound and its transmission; in particular, that branch of the science that has to do with the phenomena of sound in a particular space such as a room or theatre.

analogue signal in electronics, current or voltage that conveys or stores information, and varies continuously in the same way as the information it represents. Analogue signals are prone to interference and distortion.

centre of mass or *centre of gravity* the point in or near an object from which its total weight appears to originate and can be assumed to act. A symmetrical homogeneous object such as a sphere or cube has its centre of mass at its physical centre; a hollow shape (such as a cup) may have its centre of mass in space inside the hollow.

chain reaction in nuclear physics, a fission reaction that is maintained because neutrons released by the splitting of some atomic nuclei themselves go on to split others, releasing even more neutrons. Such a reaction can be controlled (as in a nuclear reactor) by using moderators to absorb excess neutrons. Uncontrolled, a chain reaction produces a nuclear explosion (as in an atom bomb).

critical mass in nuclear physics, the minimum mass of fissile material that can undergo a continuous chain reaction. Below this mass, too many neutrons escape from the surface for a chain reaction to carry on; above the critical mass, the reaction may accelerate into a nuclear explosion.

cryogenics science of very low temperatures (approaching absolute zero), including the production of very low temperatures and the exploitation of special properties associated with them, such as the disappearance of electrical resistance (superconductivity).

diffraction the spreading of a wave motion (such as light or sound) as it passes an obstacle and expands into a region not exposed directly to incoming waves behind the obstacle. This accounts for interference phenomena observed at the edges of opaque objects, or discontinuities between different media in the path of a wave train. The phenomena give rise to slight spreading of light into coloured bands at the shadow of a straight edge.

digital in electronics and computing, a term meaning 'coded as numbers'. A digital system uses two-state, either on/off or high/low voltage pulses, to encode, receive, and transmit information. A *digital display* shows discrete values as numbers (as opposed to an analogue signal, such as the continuous sweep of a pointer on a dial). *Digital electronics* is the technology that underlies digital techniques. Low-power, miniature, integrated circuits (chips) provide the means for the coding, storage, transmission, processing, and reconstruction of information of all kinds.

dynamics in mechanics, the mathematical and physical study of the behaviour of bodies under the action of forces that produce changes of motion in them.

efficiency in a machine, the useful work output (work done by the machine) divided by the work input (work put into the machine), usually expressed as a percentage. Because of losses caused by friction, efficiency is always less than 100%, although it can approach this for electrical machines with no moving parts (such as a transformer).

elasticity the ability of a solid to recover its shape once deforming forces (stresses modifying its dimensions or shape) are removed. An

FUNDAMENTAL CONSTANTS

Constant	Symbol	Value in SI Units
acceleration of free fall	g	9.80665 m s^{-2}
Avogadro's constant	N_A	6.02252×10^{23} mol^{-1}
Boltzmann's constant	$k = R/N_A$	1.380622×10^{-23} J K^{-1}
electronic charge	e	1.602192×10^{-19} C
electronic rest mass	m_e	9.109558×10^{-31} kg
Faraday's constant	F	9.648670×10^4 C mol^{-1}
gas constant	R	8.31434 J K^{-1} mol^{-1}
gravitational constant	G	6.664×10^{-11} N m^2 kg^{-2}
Loschmidt's number	N_L	2.68719×10^{25} m^{-3}
neutron rest mass	m_n	1.67492×10^{-27} kg
Planck's constant	h	6.626196×10^{-34} J s
proton rest mass	m_p	1.672614×10^{-27} kg
speed of light	c	2.99792458×10^8 m s^{-1}
standard atmospheric pressure	P	1.01325×10^5 Pa
Stefan–Boltzmann constant	σ	5.6697×10^{-8} W m^{-2} K^{-4}

elastic material obeys Hooke's law: that is, its deformation is proportional to the applied stress up to a certain point, called the *elastic limit*, beyond which additional stress will deform it permanently. Elastic materials include metals and rubber; however, all materials have some degree of elasticity.

electric current the flow of electrically charged particles through a conducting circuit due to the presence of a potential difference. The current at any point in a circuit is the amount of charge flowing per second; it is measured in amperes. Current carries electrical energy from a power supply, such as a battery of electrical cells, to the components of the circuit where it is converted into other forms of energy, such as heat, light, or motion. It may be either direct (DC) or alternating (AC).

electricity all phenomena caused by electric charge, whether static or in motion. Electric charge is caused by an excess or deficit of electrons in the charged substance, and an electric current by the movement of electrons around a circuit. Substances may be electrical conductors, such as metals, which allow the passage of electricity through them, or insulators, such as rubber, which are extremely poor conductors. Substances with relatively poor conductivities that can be improved by the addition of heat or light are known as semiconductors.

electric potential the relative electrical state of an object. A charged conductor, for example, has a higher potential than the earth, whose potential is taken by convention to be zero. An electric cell (battery) has a potential in relation to emf (electromotive force), which can make current flow in an external circuit. The difference in potential between two points—the *potential difference*—is expressed in volts; that is, a 12V battery has a potential difference of 12 volts between its negative and positive terminals.

electrodynamics the branch of physics dealing with electric currents and associated magnetic forces. Quantum electrodynamics (QED) studies the interaction between charged particles and their emission and absorption of electromagnetic radiation. This field combines quantum theory and relativity theory, making accurate predictions about subatomic processes involving charged particles such as electrons and protons.

electromagnetic waves oscillating electric and magnetic fields travelling together through space at a speed of nearly 300,000 km/186,000 mi per second. The (limitless) range of possible wavelengths or frequencies of electromagnetic waves, which can be thought of as making up the *electromagnetic spectrum*, includes radio waves, infrared radiation, visible light, ultraviolet radiation, X-rays, and gamma rays.

energy the capacity for doing work. Potential energy (PE) is energy deriving from position; thus a stretched spring has elastic PE, and an object raised to a height above the Earth's surface, or the water in an elevated reservoir, has gravitational PE. A lump of coal and a tank of petrol, together with the oxygen needed for their combustion, have chemical energy. Other sorts of energy include electrical and nuclear energy, and light and sound. Moving bodies possess kinetic energy (KE). Energy can be converted from one form to another, but the total quantity stays the same (in accordance with the conservation of energy principle that governs many natural phenomena). For example, as an apple falls, it loses gravitational PE but gains KE.

engine a device for converting stored energy into useful work or movement. Most engines use a fuel as their energy store. The fuel is burnt to produce heat energy—hence the name 'heat engine'—which is then converted into movement. Heat engines can be classified according to the fuel they use (petrol engine or diesel engine), or according to whether the fuel is burnt inside (internal combustion engine) or outside (steam engine) the engine, or according to whether they produce a reciprocating or rotary motion (turbine or Wankel engine).

entropy in thermodynamics, a parameter representing the state of disorder of a system at the atomic, ionic, or molecular level; the greater the disorder, the higher the entropy. Thus the fast-moving disordered molecules of water vapour have higher entropy than those of more ordered liquid water, which in turn have more entropy than the molecules in solid crystalline ice.

equilibrium an unchanging condition in which the forces acting on a particle or system of particles (body) cancel each other, or in which energy is distributed among the particles of a system in the most probable way; or the state in which a body is at rest or moving at constant velocity. A body is in *thermal equilibrium* if no heat enters or leaves it, so that all its parts are at the same temperature as its surroundings.

field the region of space by which an object exerts a force on another separate object because of certain properties they both possess. For example, there is a force of attraction between any two objects that have mass, where one is in the gravitational field of the other. Other fields of force include electric fields (caused by electric charges) and magnetic fields (caused by magnetic poles), either of which can involve attractive or repulsive forces.

force any influence that tends to change the state of rest or the uniform motion in a straight line of a body. The action of an unbalanced or resultant force results in the acceleration of a body in the direction of action of the force or it may, if the body is unable to move freely, result in its deformation. Force is a vector quantity, possessing both magnitude and direction; its unit is the newton.

forces, fundamental the four fundamental interactions believed to be at work in

THE ROAD AHEAD FOR PARTICLE PHYSICS

British physicists have recently proposed a strategy for future research in particle physics. In a report, *Particle Physics 2000*, the UK Science and Engineering Research Council (SERC) sets out the areas of the subject considered most promising for future research.

The past decade has seen the development of the Standard Model of the elementary particles and the forces acting on them. The model supposes that matter comprises two distinct families of elementary particles, quarks and leptons. Normal matter is built from two types of quark, *u* and *d*, which form protons and neutrons. Two types of lepton, the electron and the electron neutrino, are also found in the everyday world. This pattern of pairs of elementary particles is repeated in two heavier 'generations' of particles, each with two quarks and two leptons, which are revealed in accelerator experiments.

However, although the Standard Model is astonishingly successful, it cannot be the whole story. In its current form, it contains many constants, such as the mass of particles, which are not predicted but are measured in experiments and inserted into theory 'by hand'. The SERC report identifies three crucial unresolved problems. First, what determines the masses of the elementary particles? This is arguably the central question in particle physics today. Peter Higgs of Edinburgh University has proposed that particles acquire mass through interactions with a new particle, the Higgs boson, but there is no experimental evidence for this mechanism. To investigate the origin of mass, SERC supports the proposed Large Hadron Collider, a particle accelerator planned for construction at CERN, the European particle physics laboratory near Geneva, by 1999. The new machine would be powerful enough to reveal the Higgs boson if it exists.

Second, why are there three generations of quarks and leptons? The existence of three generations is known to explain another of nature's puzzling features, CP violation—the inherent lack of symmetry in the weak nuclear force. Understanding the mechanism and size of this asymmetry is a subtle and challenging problem. It will lead towards the explanation of another mystery – why does matter dominate over antimatter in the Universe? The problem will be tackled by experiments on the HERA accelerator at DESY, the German national particle physics laboratory in Hamburg. The machine will collide electrons with protons. It will work as a powerful electron microscope, yielding a high-resolution picture of the protons and the quarks within them. The experiments will probe for evidence of structure in quarks and leptons, which would indicate that these particles are themselves built from more fundamental particles—a possible explanation for the three generations.

The third crucial question concerns the nature of the 'dark matter' forming more than 90% of the mass of the Universe. This material produces no radiation and can only be detected through its gravitational attraction. Its existence almost certainly indicates physics beyond the Standard Model, possibly the existence of new particles. Extremely sensitive detectors are needed to find it. To have escaped detection so far, dark matter must have very little interaction with ordinary matter. The best hope is to look for the very low-energy recoil produced when nuclei collide with particles of dark matter. The challenge is to devise techniques that can detect this energy, which will cause rises in temperature as small as one millionth of a degree. Prototype detectors have been developed at the Rutherford Appleton Laboratory, near Oxford, and set up in a salt and potash mine at Boulby, Cleveland.

Theorists have already shown that two of the four fundamental forces of nature—electromagnetism and the weak force—are aspects of a single force, the electroweak force. This suggests that the strong nuclear and electroweak forces can in turn be brought together in a 'grand unified theory'. The past ten years have seen several attempts to include gravity with the other forces in a consistent framework.. The most exciting work is on the superstring theory, which replaces point particles with the oscillations of one-dimensional 'strings'. As yet there is no hint of experimental support but the new accelerators might turn these promising ideas into fact.

A general trend in particle theory is the increasing use of high-speed computers to calculate the interactions between particles. This trend will continue, with machines capable of performing 1,000 billion arithmetical operations per second being available by 1994. Towards the end of the decade machines 100 times faster are likely. The techniques developed will find application in other theoretical studies, for example in theoretical chemistry and fluid dynamics.

---

the physical universe. There are two long-range forces: *gravity*, which keeps the planets in orbit around the Sun, and acts between all particles that have mass; and the *electromagnetic force*, which stops solids from falling apart, and acts between all particles with electric charge. There are two very short-range forces: the *weak force*, responsible for the reactions that fuel the Sun and for the emission of beta particles from certain nuclei; and the **strong force**, which binds together the protons and neutrons in the nuclei of atoms.

frequency the number of periodic oscillations, vibrations, or waves occurring per unit of time. The unit of frequency is the hertz (Hz), one hertz being equivalent to one cycle per second. Human beings can hear sounds from objects vibrating in the range 20—15,000 Hz.

electromagnetic waves

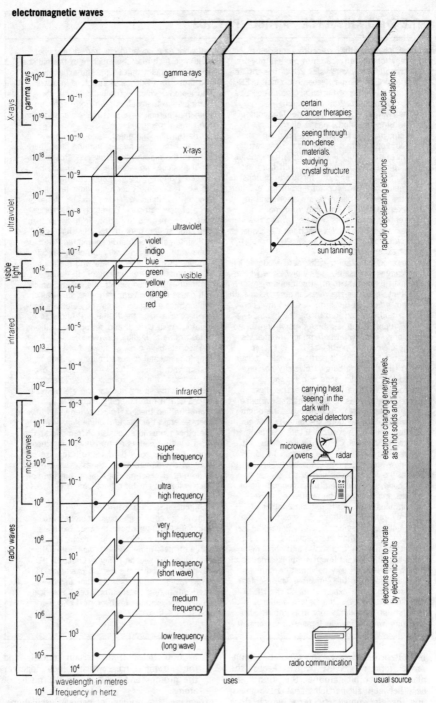

Ultrasonic frequencies well above 15,000 Hz can be detected by mammals such as bats.

friction the force that opposes the relative motion of two bodies in contact. The *coefficient of friction* is the ratio of the force required to achieve this relative motion to the force pressing the two bodies together.

fundamental constant a physical quantity that is constant in all circumstances throughout the whole universe. Examples are the electric charge of an electron, the speed of light, Planck's constant, and the gravitational constant.

grand unified theory (GUT) a sought-for theory that would combine the theory of the strong nuclear force (called quantum chromodynamics) with the theory of the weak and electromagnetic forces. The search for the grand unified theory is part of a larger programme seeking a unified field theory, which would combine all the forces of nature (including gravity) within one framework.

gravity the force of attraction that arises between objects by virtue of their masses. On Earth, gravity is the force of attraction between any object in the Earth's gravitational field and the Earth itself.

half-life the time taken for the strength of a radioactive source to decay to half its original value. It may vary from millionths of a second to billions of years. Radioactive substances decay exponentially; thus the time taken for the first 50% of the isotope to decay will be the same as the time taken by the next 25%, and by the 12.5% after that, and so on. For example, carbon-14 takes about 5,730 years for half the material to decay; another 5,730 for half of the remaining half to decay; then 5,730 years for half of that remaining half to decay, and so on. Plutonium-239, one of the most toxic of all radioactive substances, has a half-life of about 24,000 years. In theory, the decay process is never complete and there is always some residual radioactivity.

heat form of internal energy possessed by a substance by virtue of the kinetic energy in the motion of its molecules or atoms. Heat energy is transferred by conduction, convection, and radiation. It always flows from a region of higher temperature (heat intensity) to one of lower temperature. Its effect on a substance may be simply to raise its temperature, or to cause it to expand, melt (if a solid), vaporize (if a liquid), or increase its pressure (if a confined gas).

hydrodynamics the science of nonviscous fluids (such as water, alcohol, and ether) in motion.

hydrostatics the branch of statics dealing with the mechanical problems of fluids in equilibrium—that is, in a static condition. Practical applications include shipbuilding and dam design.

inertia the tendency of an object to remain in a state of rest or uniform motion until an external force is applied, as stated by Isaac Newton's first law of motion (see Newton's laws of motion).

interference the phenomenon of two or more wave motions interacting and combining to produce a resultant wave of larger or smaller amplitude (depending on whether the combining waves are in or out of phase with each other). Interference of white light (multiwavelength) results in spectral coloured fringes, for example, the iridescent colours of oil films seen on water or soap bubbles. Interference of sound waves of similar frequency produces the phenomenon of beats, often used by musicians when tuning an instrument. With monochromatic light (of a single wavelength), interference produces patterns of light and dark bands. This is the basis of holography, for example. Interferometry can also be applied to radio waves, and is a powerful tool in modern astronomy.

kinetic theory theory describing the physical properties of matter in terms of the behaviour—principally movement—of its component atoms or molecules. The temperature of a substance is dependent on the velocity of movement of its constituent particles, increased temperature being accompanied by increased movement. A gas consists of rapidly moving atoms or molecules and, according to kinetic theory, it is their continual impact on the walls of the containing vessel that accounts for the pressure of the gas. The slowing of molecular motion as temperature falls, according to kinetic theory, accounts for the physical properties of liquids and solids, culminating in the concept of no molecular motion at absolute zero (0 K/–273°C). By making various assumptions about the nature of gas molecules, it is possible to derive from the kinetic theory the various gas laws (such as Avogadro's law, Boyle's law, and Charles's law).

laser (acronym for *light amplification by stimulated emission of radiation*) a device for producing a narrow beam of light, capable of travelling over vast distances without dispersion, and of being focused to give enormous power densities (10^8 watts per cm^2 for high-energy lasers). It operates on a principle similar to that of the maser (a high-frequency microwave amplifier or oscillator). The uses of lasers include communications (a laser beam can carry much more information than can radio waves), cutting, drilling, welding, satellite tracking, medical and biological research, and surgery.

lens in optics, a piece of a transparent material, such as glass, with two polished surfaces—one concave or convex, and the other plane, concave, or convex—that modifies rays of light. A convex lens brings rays of light together; a concave lens makes the rays diverge. Lenses are essential to spectacles, microscopes, telescopes, cameras, and almost all optical instruments.

lever a simple machine consisting of a rigid rod pivoted at a fixed point called the fulcrum, used for shifting or raising a heavy load or applying force in a similar way. Levers are classified into orders according to where the effort is applied, and the load-moving force developed, in relation to the position of the fulcrum. A *first-order* lever has the load and the effort on opposite sides of the fulcrum—for example, a see-saw or pair of scissors. A *second-order* lever has the load and the effort on the same side of the fulcrum, with the load nearer the fulcrum—for example, nutcrackers or a

FOCUSED ATOMS

According to quantum theory, every particle is also a wave. George Thomson and Clinton Davisson shared the 1937 Nobel Prize in Physics for demonstrating that electrons are waves—as well as particles, of course. This discovery led on to the electron microscope, which uses electron waves instead of light waves as in an ordinary microscope. Because electron waves have shorter wavelengths than light waves, finer details can be revealed by the electron microscope. However, to produce the very small wavelengths that are needed, it is necessary to use high-energy electrons. This can often damage the object being examined, so scientists have looked at the possibility of using atoms instead of electrons. Because atoms are more massive than electrons, short wavelengths can be achieved at lower energies, thus reducing the chance of damage.

German and US experiments have recently shown that it is possible to focus a beam of helium atoms. This is done by using a device called a Fresnel plate, consisting of alternate bands of transmitting and absorbing material which get thinner towards the edges of the plate. Helium atoms emerging from a thin split and passing through the Fresnel plate are focused, just as sunlight passing through a magnifying glass is focused to a small point. When the technology of atomic focusing is developed, atomic microscopes capable of discerning details as small as a billionth of a metre across should be possible, using low-energy beams.

---

wheelbarrow. A *third-order* lever has the effort nearer the fulcrum than the load with both on the same side of it—for example, a pair of tweezers or tongs.

light   electromagnetic waves in the visible range, having a wavelength, from about 400 nanometers in the extreme violet to about 770 nanometers in the extreme red. Light is considered to exhibit particle and wave properties, and the fundamental particle, or quantum, of light is called the photon. The speed of light (and of all electromagnetic radiation) in a vacuum is approximately 300,000 km/186,000 mi per second, and is a universal constant denoted by c.

luminescence   emission of light from a body when its atoms are excited by means other than raising its temperature. Short-lived luminescence is called fluorescence; longer-lived luminescence is called phosporescence.

magnetism   branch of physics dealing with the properties of magnets and magnetic fields. Magnetic fields are produced by moving charged particles: in electromagnets, electrons flow through a coil of wire connected to a battery; in magnets, spinning electrons within the atoms generate the field.

mass   the quantity of matter in a body as measured by its inertia. Mass determines the acceleration produced in a body by a given force acting on it, the acceleration being inversely proportional to the mass of the body. The mass also determines the force exerted on a body by gravity on Earth, although this attraction varies slightly from place to place. In the SI system, the base unit of mass is the kilogram.

mechanics   branch of physics dealing with the motions of bodies and the forces causing these motions, and also with the forces acting on bodies in equilibrium. It is usually divided into dynamics and statics.

mirror   any polished surface that reflects light; often made from 'silvered' glass (in practice, a mercury alloy coating of glass). A plane (flat) mirror produces a same-size, erect 'virtual' image located behind the mirror at the same distance from it as the object is in front of it. A spherical concave mirror produces a reduced, inverted real image in front or an enlarged, erect virtual image behind it (as with a shaving mirror), depending on how close the object is to the mirror. A spherical convex mirror produces a reduced, erect virtual image behind it (as with a car's rear-view mirror).

Newton's laws of motion   three laws that form the basis of Newtonian mechanics. (1) Unless acted upon by an external resultant, or unbalanced, force, an object at rest stays at rest, and a moving object continues moving at the same speed in the same straight line. Put more simply, the law says that, if left alone, stationary objects will not move and moving objects will keep on moving at a constant speed in a straight line. (2) A resultant or unbalanced force applied to an object produces a rate of change of momentum that is directly proportional to the force and is in the direction of the force. (3) When an object A applies a force to an object B, B applies an equal and opposite force to A; that is, to every action there is an equal and opposite reaction.

nuclear fission   process whereby an atomic nucleus breaks up into two or more major fragments with the emission of two or three neutrons. It is accompanied by the release of energy in the form of gamma radiation and the kinetic energy of the emitted particles.

nuclear fusion   process whereby two atomic nuclei are fused, with the release of a large amount of energy. Very high temperatures and pressures are thought to be required in order for the process to happen. Under these conditions the atoms involved are stripped of all their electrons so that the remaining particles, which together make up plasma, can come close together at very high speeds and overcome the mutual repulsion of the positive charges on the atomic nuclei. At very close range another nuclear force will come into play, fusing the particles together to form a larger nucleus. As fusion is accompanied by the release of large amounts of energy, the process might one day be harnessed to form the basis of commercial energy production. Methods of achieving controlled fusion are

PHYSICS: CHRONOLOGY

c. 400 BC	The first 'atomic' theory was put forward by Democritus.
c. 250	Archimedes' principle of buoyancy was established.
c. 1610	The principle of falling bodies descending to earth at the same speed was established by Italian astronomer Galileo.
1642	The principles of hydraulics were put forward by French mathematician, physicist, and philosopher Blaise Pascal.
1662	Boyle's law concerning gas was established by Irish physicist Robert Boyle.
c. 1665	English physicist Isaac Newton put forward the law of gravity, stating that the Earth exerts a constant force on falling bodies.
1690	The wave theory of light was propounded by Dutch physicist Christiaan Huygens.
1704	The corpuscular theory of light was put forward by Isaac Newton.
1764	Specific and latent heats were described by Scottish chemist Joseph Black.
1771	The link between nerve action and electricity was discovered by Italian anatomist and physiologist Luigi Galvani.
c. 1787	Charles's law relating the pressure, volume, and temperature of a gas was established by French physicist and physical chemist Jacques Alexandre César Charles.
1798	The link between heat and friction was discovered by Anglo-American physicist Benjamin Thomson Rumford.
1800	Italian physicist Alessandro Volta invented the electric cell.
1801	Interference of light was discovered by British physicist Thomas Young.
1808	The 'modern' atomic theory was propounded by British physicist and chemist John Dalton.
1811	Avogadro's hypothesis relating volumes and numbers of molecules of gases was proposed by Italian physicist and chemist Amedeo Avogadro.
1815	Refraction of light was explained by French physicist Augustin Fresnel.
1819	The discovery of electromagnetism was made by Danish physicist Hans Oersted.
1821	The dynamo principle was described by British physicist and chemist Michael Faraday; the thermocouple was discovered by German physicist Thomas Seebeck.
1822	The laws of electrodynamics were established by French physicist and mathematician André Ampère.
1824	Thermodynamics as a branch of physics was proposed by French physicist Sadi Carnot.
1827	Ohm's law of electrical resistance was established by German physicist Georg Ohm; Brownian motion resulting from molecular vibrations was observed by British botanist Robert Brown.
1829	The law of gaseous diffusion established by Scottish chemist Thomas Graham.
1831	Electromagnetic induction was discovered by Faraday.
1834	Faraday discovered self-induction.
1842	The principle of conservation of energy was observed by German physician and physicist Julius von Mayer.
1849	A measurement of speed of light was put forward by French physicist Armand Fizeau (1819–1896).
1851	The rotation of the Earth was demonstrated by French physicist Jean Foucault.
1859	Spectrographic analysis was made by German chemist Robert Bunsen and German physicist Gustav Kirchhoff.
1873	Light was conceived as electromagnetic radiation by Scottish physicist James Maxwell.
1877	A theory of sound as vibrations in an elastic medium was propounded by British physicist John Rayleigh.
1887	The existence of radio waves was predicted by German physicist Heinrich Hertz.
1895	X-rays were discovered by German physicist Wilhelm Röntgen.
1896	The discovery of radioactivity was made by French physicist Antoine Becquerel.
1897	The electron was discovered by Joseph John Thomson.
1899	New Zealand physicist Ernest Rutherford discovered alpha and beta rays.
1900	Quantum theory was propounded by German physicist Max Planck; the discovery of gamma rays was made by French physicist Paul-Ulrich Villard (1860–1934).
1904	The theory of radioactivity was put forward by Rutherford and British chemist Frederick Soddy.
1905	German–Swiss physicist Albert Einstein propounded his special theory of relativity.
1911	The discovery of the atomic nucleus was made by Rutherford.
1913	The Geiger counter was invented by German physicist Hans Geiger and Walther Müller; the orbiting electron atomic theory was propounded by Danish physicist Niels Bohr.

PHYSICS: CHRONOLOGY (CONT.)

1916	Einstein put forward his general theory of relativity; mass spectrography was discovered by British physicist William Aston.
1927	The uncertainty principle of atomic physics was established by German physicist Werner Heisenberg.
1928	Wave mechanics was introduced by Austrian physicist Erwin Schrödinger.
1931	The cyclotron was developed by US physicist Ernest Lawrence.
1932	The discovery of the neutron was made by James Chadwick.
1933	The positron, the antiparticle of the electron, was discovered by US physicist Carl David Anderson.
1934	Artificial radioactivity was developed by Frédéric and Irène Joliot-Curie.
1939	The discovery of nuclear fission was made by German chemists Otto Hahn and Fritz Strassman (1902–).
1942	The first controlled nuclear chain reaction was achieved by US physicist Enrico Fermi.
1956	The neutrino, an elementary particle, was discovered experimentally by US physicists Fred Reines and Clyde Cowan.
1963	US scientist Theodore Maiman developed the first laser.
1964	US physicist Murray Gell-Mann predicted the existence of the quark.
1983	Evidence of W and Z particles confirmed at CERN, validating the link between the weak and electromagnetic forces.
1986	First high-temperature superconductor discovered, able to conduct electricity without resistance at a temperature of 35K.
1989	CERN's Large Electron–Positron Collider (LEP), a particle accelerator with a circumference of 27 km/16.8 mi, came into operation.
1991	LEP experiments demonstrated the existence of three generations of elementary particles.

therefore the subject of research around the world.

optics the branch of physics that deals with the study of light and vision—for example, shadows and mirror images, lenses, microscopes, telescopes, and cameras. For all practical purposes light rays travel in straight lines, although Einstein demonstrated that they may be 'bent' by a gravitational field. On striking a surface they are reflected or refracted with some absorption of energy, and the study of this is known as geometrical optics.

power the rate of doing work or consuming energy. Its SI unit is the watt (joule per second).

pressure measure of the force acting normally (at right angles) to a body per unit surface area. Its SI unit is the pascal (newton per square metre).In a fluid (liquid or gas), pressure increases with depth. At the edge of Earth's atmosphere, pressure is zero, whereas at ground level it is about 100 kPa.

quantum theory the theory that energy does not have a continuous range of values, but is, instead, absorbed or radiated discontinuously, in multiples of definite, indivisible units called quanta. Just as earlier theory showed how light, generally seen as a wave motion, could also in some ways be seen as composed of discrete particles (photons), quantum mechanics shows how atomic particles such as electrons may also be seen as having wavelike properties. Quantum

HIGH-TEMPERATURE SUPERCONDUCTORS MAKE PROGRESS

Chemists from the universities of Birmingham and Cambridge, England, have produced a ceramic oxide superconductor that loses electrical resistance at −145ºC, the highest temperature at which complete loss of resistance—superconductivity—has been observed. The new material is a compound of thallium, barium, calcium, copper and oxygen, with an approximate formula $Tl_2Ba_2Ca_2Cu_3O_x$. The material is made in a complex but basically 'low-tech' process. The first step is to grind together a mixture of thallium oxide, barium peroxide, calcium oxide and copper oxide and compress the mixture into a pellet. Next, the pellet is wrapped in gold foil and heated at 910ºC in oxygen for 3 hours. Then the pellet is heated at 750ºC for 10 days. The last step is to reheat the pellet in oxygen at low pressure.

Researchers in Japan and the USA have recently succeeded in making transistors, used in electronics, using high-temperature superconducting ceramics rather than semiconductors. The new devices show electrical resistance 100 times lower than that of semiconductor transistors. The speed of the superconducting transistors is 10 times higher, too. However, there are problems involved in using the new devices. They have to be cooled to −245ºC, and their low resistance would be a problem in some applications. They are unlikely to replace conventional transistors in computer chips.

mechanics is the basis of particle physics, modern theoretical chemistry, and the solid-state physics that describes the behaviour of the silicon chips used in computers.

radiation emission of radiant energy as particles or waves—for example, heat, light, alpha particles, and beta particles.

radioactivity spontaneous alteration of the nuclei of radioactive atoms, accompanied by the emission of radiation. It is the property exhibited by the radioactive isotopes of stable elements and all isotopes of radioactive elements.

radioisotope contraction of *radioactive isotope* a naturally occurring or synthetic radioactive form of an element. Most radioisotopes are made by bombarding a stable element with neutrons in the core of a nuclear reactor. The radiations given off by radioisotopes are easy to detect (hence their use as tracers), can in some instances penetrate substantial thicknesses of materials, and have profound effects on living matter. Although dangerous, radioisotopes are used in the fields of medicine, industry, agriculture, and research.

reflection the throwing back or deflection of waves, such as light or sound waves, when they hit a surface. The *law of reflection* states that the angle of incidence (the angle between the ray and a perpendicular line drawn to the surface) is equal to the angle of reflection (the angle between the reflected ray and a perpendicular to the surface).

refraction the bending of a wave of light, heat, or sound when it passes from one medium to another. Refraction occurs because waves travel at different velocities in diferent media.

relativity the theory of the relative rather than absolute character of motion and mass and the interdependence of matter, time, and space, as developed by Albert Einstein in two phases:

special theory (1905) Starting with the premises that (1) the laws of nature are the same for all observers in unaccelerated motion, and (2) the speed of light is independent of the motion of its source, Einstein postulated that the time interval between two events was longer for an observer in whose frame of reference the events occur in different places than for the observer for whom they occur at the same place.

general theory of relativity (1915) The geometrical properties of space-time were to be conceived as modified locally by the presence of a body with mass. A planet's orbit around the Sun (as observed in three-dimensional space) arises from its natural trajectory in modified space-time; there is no need to invoke, as Isaac Newton did, a force of gravity coming from the Sun and acting on the planet. Einstein's theory predicted slight differences in the orbits of the planets from Newton's theory, which were observable in the case of Mercury. The new theory also said light rays should bend when they pass by a massive object, owing to the object's effect on local space-time. The predicted bending of starlight was observed during the eclipse of the Sun 1919, when light from distant stars passing close to the Sun was not masked by sunlight.

resistance that property of a substance that restricts the flow of electricity through it, associated with the conversion of electrical energy to heat; also the magnitude of this property. Resistance depends on many factors, such as the nature of the material, its temperature, dimensions, and thermal properties; degree of impurity; the nature and state of illumination of the surface; and the frequency and magnitude of the current. The unit of resistance is the ohm.

resonance rapid and uncontrolled increase in the size of a vibration when the vibrating object is subject to a force varying at its natural frequency. In a trombone, for example, the length of the air column in the instrument is adjusted until it resonates with the note being sounded. Resonance effects are also produced by many electrical circuits. Tuning a radio, for example, is done by adjusting the natural frequency of the receiver circuit until it coincides with the frequency of the radio waves falling on the aerial.

semiconductor crystalline material with an electrical conductivity between that of metals (good) and insulators (poor).

SI units (French *Système International d'Unités*) standard system of scientific units used by scientists worldwide. Originally proposed in 1960, it replaces the m.k.s., c.g.s., and f.p.s. systems. It is based on seven basic units: the metre (m) for length, kilogram (kg) for weight, second (s) for time, ampere (A) for electrical current, kelvin (K) for temperature, mole (mol) for amount of substance, and candela (cd) for luminosity.

sound physiological sensation received by the ear, originating in a vibration (pressure variation in the air) that communicates itself to the air, and travels in every direction, spreading out as an expanding sphere. All sound waves in air travel with a speed dependent on the temperature; under ordinary conditions, this is about 330 m/1,070 ft per second. The pitch of the sound depends on the number of vibrations imposed on the air per second, but the speed is unaffected. The loudness of a sound is dependent primarily on the amplitude of the vibration of the air.

spectroscopy the study of spectra associated with atoms or molecules in solid, liquid, or gaseous phase. Spectroscopy can be used to identify unknown compounds and is an invaluable tool in science, medicine, and industry (for example, in checking the purity of drugs).

spectrum (plural *spectra*) an arrangement of frequencies or wavelengths when electromagnetic radiations are separated into their constituent parts. Visible light is part of the electromagnetic spectrum and most sources emit waves over a range of wavelengths that can be broken up or 'dispersed'; white light can be separated into red, orange, yellow, green, blue, indigo, and violet. The visible spectrum was first studied by Newton, who showed in

SI Prefixes

Multiple	Prefix	Symbol	Example	
1,000,000,000,000 (10^{12})	tera	T	TV	(teravolt)
1,000,000,000 (10^9)	giga	G	GW	(gigawatt)
1,000,000 (10^6)	mega	M	MHz	(megahertz)
1,000 (10^3)	kilo	K	Kg	(kilogram)
1/10 (10^{-1})	deci	d	dC	(decicoulomb)
1/100 (10^{-2})	centi	c	cm	(centimetre)
1/1,000 (10^{-3})	milli	m	mA	(milliampere)
1/1,000,000 (10^{-6})	micro	μ	μF	(microfarad)
1/1,000,000,000 (10^{-9})	nano	n	nm	(nanometre)
1/1,000,000,000,000 (10^{-12})	pico	p	ps	(picosecond)

1672 how white light could be broken up into different colours.

states of matter the forms (solid, liquid, or gas) in which material can exist. Whether a material is solid, liquid, or gas depends on its temperature and the pressure on it. The transition between states takes place at definite temperatures, called melting point and boiling point.

statics branch of mechanics concerned with the behaviour of bodies at rest and forces in equilibrium, and distinguished from dynamics.

stress and strain measures of the deforming force applied to a body (stress) and of the resulting change in its shape (strain). For a perfectly elastic material, stress is proportional to strain (*Hooke's law*).

surface tension the property that causes the surface of a liquid to behave as if it were covered with a weak elastic skin; this is why a needle can float on water. It is caused by the exposed surface's tendency to contract to the smallest possible area because of unequal cohesive forces between molecules at the surface. Allied phenomena include the formation of droplets, the concave profile of a meniscus, and the capillary action by which water soaks into a sponge.

temperature the state of hotness or coldness of a body, and the condition that determines whether or not it will transfer heat to, or receive heat from, another body according to the laws of thermodynamics. It is measured in degrees Celsius (before 1948 called centigrade), kelvin, or Fahrenheit.

tension reaction force set up in a body that is subjected to stress. In a stretched string or wire it exerts a pull that is equal in magnitude but opposite in direction to the stress being applied at its ends. Tension originates in the net attractive intermolecular force created when a stress causes the mean distance separating a material's molecules to become greater than the equilibrium distance. It is measured in newtons.

thermodynamics branch of physics dealing with the transformation of heat into and from other forms of energy. It is the basis of the study of the efficient working of engines, such as the steam and internal combustion engines. The three laws of thermodynamics are (1) energy can be neither created nor destroyed, heat and mechanical work being mutually convertible; (2) it is impossible for an unaided self-acting machine to convey heat from one body to another at a higher temperature; and (3) it is impossible by any procedure, no matter how idealized, to reduce any system to the absolute zero of temperature (0K–273°C) in a finite number of operations. Put into mathematical form, these laws have widespread applications in physics and chemistry.

ultrasound pressure waves similar in nature to sound waves but occurring at frequencies above 20,000 Hz (cycles per second), the approximate upper limit of human hearing (15–16 Hz is the lower limit). Ultrasonics is concerned with the study and practical application of these phenomena.

viscosity the resistance of a fluid to flow, caused by its internal friction, which makes it resist flowing past a solid surface or other layers of

SI Units

Quantity	SI unit	Symbol
absorbed radiation dose	gray	Gy
amount of substance	mole*	mol
electric capacitance	farad	F
electric charge	coulomb	C
electric conductance	siemens	S
electric current	ampere*	A
energy or work	joule	J
force	newton	N
frequency	hertz	Hz
illuminance	lux	lx
inductance	henry	H
length	metre*	m
luminous flux	lumen	lm
luminous intensity	candela*	cd
magnetic flux	weber	Wb
magnetic flux density	tesla	T
mass	kilogram*	kg
plane angle	radian	rad
potential difference	volt	V
power	watt	W
pressure	pascal	Pa
radiation dose equivalent	sievert	Sv
radiation exposure	roentgen	r
radioactivity	becquerel	Bq
resistance	ohm	Ω
solid angle	steradian	sr
sound intensity	decibel	dB
temperature	°Celsius	°C
temperature, thermodynamic	kelvin*	K
time	second*	s
*SI base unit		

the fluid. It applies to the motion of an object moving through a fluid as well as the motion of a fluid passing by an object.

wave a disturbance travelling through a medium (or space).

There are two types: in a **longitudinal wave** (such as a sound wave) the disturbance is parallel to the wave's direction of travel; in a **transverse wave** (such as an electromagnetic wave) it is perpendicular. The medium (for example the Earth, for seismic waves) is not permanently displaced by the passage of a wave.

weight the force exerted on an object by gravity. The weight of an object depends on its mass—the amount of material in it—and the strength of the Earth's gravitational pull, which decreases with height. Consequently, an object weighs less at the top of a mountain than at sea level. On the Moon, an object weighs only one-sixth of its weight on Earth, because the pull of the Moon's gravity is one-sixth that of the Earth.

work a measure of the result of transferring energy from one system to another to cause an object to move. Work should not be confused with energy (the capacity to do work, which is also measured in joules) or with power (the rate of doing work, measured in joules per second).

PARTICLE PHYSICS

The study of the properties of the particles that make up all atoms, and of their interactions. More than 300 subatomic particles have now been identified by physicists, categorized into several classes according to their mass, electric charge, spin, magnetic moment, and interaction. Subatomic particles include the **elementary particles** (quarks, leptons, and gauge bosons), which are indivisible and so can be considered the fundamental units of matter; and the **hadrons** (baryons, such as protons and neutrons, and mesons), which are composite particles made up of two or three quarks. Some subatomic particles have been shown to change from one form to another.

antimatter a form of matter in which most of the attributes (such as electrical charge, magnetic moment, and spin) of elementary particles are reversed. Such particles (called antiparticles) can be created in particle accelerators, such as those at CERN in Geneva and at Fermilab in the USA.

baryon a heavy subatomic particle made up of three indivisible elementary particles called quarks. The baryons form a subclass of the hadrons, and comprise the nucleons (protons and neutrons) and hyperons.

boson a subatomic particle whose spin can only take values that are whole numbers or zero. Bosons may be classified as gauge bosons (carriers of the four fundamental forces) or

mesons. All subatomic particles are either bosons or fermions.

electron an elementary particle of negative charge, which cannot be subdivided; it is a constituent of all atoms, and a member of the class of particles known as leptons. The electrons in each atom surround the nucleus in shells, the number being equal to the atom's atomic number (the number of protons in the nucleus). This electron structure is responsible for the chemical properties of the atom (see atomic structure).

fermion a subatomic particle whose spin can only take values that are half-integers, such as $\frac{1}{2}$ or $1\frac{1}{2}$. Fermions may be classified as leptons, such as the electron, and baryons, such as the proton and neutron. All subatomic particles are either fermions or bosons.

gauge boson or **field particle** any of the elementary particles that carry the four fundamental forces. Gauge bosons include the photon, the graviton, the gluons, and the weakons.

gluon a gauge boson that carries the strong force responsible for binding quarks together to form the strongly interacting subatomic particles known as hadrons. There are eight kinds of gluon.

graviton a gauge boson that is the postulated carrier of the gravitational force.

hadron a strongly interacting subatomic particle made up of indivisible elementary particles called quarks. The hadrons are grouped into the baryons (protons, neutrons, and hyperons) and the mesons (particles with masses between those of electrons and protons). Since the 1960s, particle physicists' main interest has been the elucidation of hadron structure.

lepton a light elementary particle that does not interact strongly with other particles or nuclei. The leptons include six particles: the electron, muon, and tau, and their neutrinos, the electron neutrino, muon neutrino, and tau neutrino, plus their six antiparticles.

meson a subatomic particle made up of two indivisible elementary particles called quarks. The mesons have masses intermediate between those of the leptons (such as the electron) and those of the baryons (such as the proton and neutron). They are found in cosmic radiation, and are emitted by nuclei under bombardment by very high-energy particles. The mesons form a subclass of the hadrons and include the kaons, pions, psi, and upsilon.

neutrino any of three uncharged elementary particles (and their antiparticles) of the lepton class, having a mass too close to zero to be measured. The most familiar type, the electron neutrino, is emitted in the beta decay of a nucleus. The other two are the muon neutrino and the tau neutrino.

neutron one of the three main subatomic particles, the others being the proton and the electron. It belongs to the baryon group of the hadrons. Neutrons have about the same mass as protons but no electric charge, and occur in the nuclei of all atoms except hydrogen. They contribute to the mass of atoms but do not af-

LASERS AND CHIPS

Imagine lasers so small that a million could be packed into an area of 0.5 sq cm/0.04 sq in. This would have been a flight of fancy a few years ago, but no longer. Laser science has made great strides recently, largely by adopting the technology used to make complex integrated circuits or chips.

The most familiar laser is perhaps the helium-neon gas laser, the type used at supermarket check-outs to read bar codes. However, semiconductor lasers are much more widespread. They are used in compact disc players, CD-ROMs or optical discs, fibre optic communications networks, and laser printers. Over 25 million semiconductor lasers were sold last year.

Simple semiconductor lasers are made from two layers of semiconductor material, gallium arsenide, formed into a small cube or chip. The layers are 'doped' with different kinds of impurities. In one layer, the impurities add extra electrons; in the other layer, they create electron vacancies or 'holes'. Applying a voltage across the junction between the layers causes electrons and holes to move towards the junction where they combine, releasing heat and light. If the edges of the chip are made to reflect some of the light back into the junction, the emission of more light is stimulated—this is the laser action which amplifies the intensity of the light. Eventually the light is intense enough to escape from one end of the chip, producing a narrow beam of laser light.

The key to improving semiconductor lasers is to confine the light to a small region around the junction; this produces more light and less heat. The development of molecular beam epitaxy, a technique which deposits atoms layer by layer, made possible the production of extremely thin layers to act as the laser, sandwiched between thicker barrier layers. The resulting devices, called quantum well lasers, are more efficient and are already used in some commercial semiconductor lasers. Although the output of a quantum well laser is small, it is possible to pack an array of these lasers on to a chip. Although each laser emits only a small amount of light, the total output is sufficient for some applications.

The next step forward was the strained layer laser. These depend upon the fact that it is possible to vary the composition of the barrier layers either side of the thin laser layer. In the past few years this technique has been used to make lasers which produce light of various colours. The technique was used in the most dramatic breakthrough in semiconductor technology in 1991—the first semiconductor laser emitting green light, with a wavelength of 525 nm, at room temperature. The shortest wavelengths previously reported were around 600 nm, a red-orange colour. Commercial lasers emit red or near infrared light with wavelength of 635 nm or more.

Another recent innovation has been to produce semiconductor lasers that shine their light upwards from the chip surface rather than from the chip edge. This can be done by incorporating sloping reflective mirrors into the chip, or by etching small grooves into the sides of the chip to diffract light sideways. A more sophisticated approach is to place reflective surfaces above and below the junction layer so that the laser beam is generated perpendicular to the junction layer. Such devices are called vertical-cavity lasers. The reflective layers can be made circular and packed closely together in an array on the chip. This is how the million lasers, roughly one-tenth the thickness of a human hair, were packed on to a single chip.

In some laser arrays, each laser can be turned off and on independently. This can be done up to 5 billion times a second in a two-by-eight array, to produce 800 billion pulses of light a second. Other arrays can combine the output of many laser elements to produce a single beam of higher power. It is possible for each laser element on a chip to produce a different wavelength of light because the distance between the reflective layers determines the wavelength of light produced.

Researchers have barely begun to explore the possibilities of these devices. One obvious application is in fibre optic communications; each laser element could be used to transmit a message using a different wavelength. The chips could be used in extremely fast, high-quality laser printers and in optical computers which process information coded as pulses of light instead of electric currents.

Laser on a penny: cleaved coupled-cavity (C^3) laser seen through a scanning electron microscope.

PRINCIPAL SUBATOMIC PARTICLES

	Group	Particle	Symbol	Charge	Mass (MeV)	Spin	Lifetime (sec)
elementary particle	quark	up	u	2/3	336	½	?
		down	d	−1/3	336	½	?
		(top)	t	(2/3)	(<600,000)	(½)	?
		bottom	b	−1/3	4,700	½	?
		strange	s	−1/3	540	½	?
		charm	c	2/3	1,500	½	?
	lepton	electron	e^-	−1	0·511	½	stable
		electron neutrino	ν_e	0	(0)	½	stable
		muon	μ^-	−1	105·66	½	$2·2 \times 10^{-6}$
		muon neutrino	ν_μ	0	(0)	½	stable
		tau	τ^-	−1	1,784	½	$3·4 \times 10^{-13}$
		tau neutrino	ν_τ	0	(0)	½	?
	gauge boson	photon	γ	0	0	1	stable
		graviton	g	0	(0)	2	stable
		gluon	g	0	0	1	?
		weakon	$W^\pm$	±1	81,000	1	?
			Z	0	94,000	1	?
hadron	meson	pion	π^+	1	139·57	0	$2·6 \times 10^{-8}$
			π^0	0	134·96	0	$8·3 \times 10^{-17}$
		kaon	K^+	1	493·67	0	$1·2 \times 10^{-8}$
			K_s^0	0	497·67	0	$8·9 \times 10^{-11}$
			K_L^0	0	497·67	0	$5·18 \times 10^{-8}$
		psi	Ψ	0	3,100	1	$6·3 \times 10^{-2}$
		upsilon	Υ	0	9,460	1	$\sim 1 \times 10^{-20}$
	baryon	nucleon					
		proton	p	1	938·28	½	stable
		nucleon	n	0	939·57	½	920
		hyperon					
		lambda	Λ	0	1,115·6	½	$2·63 \times 10^{-10}$
		sigma	Σ^+	1	1,189·4	½	$8·0 \times 10^{-11}$
			Σ^-	−1	1,197·3	½	$1·5 \times 10^{-10}$
			Σ^0	0	1,192·5	½	$5·8 \times 10^{-20}$
		xi	Ξ^-	−1	1,321·3	½	$1·64 \times 10^{-10}$
			Ξ^0	0	1,314·9	½	$2·9 \times 10^{-10}$
		omega	Ω	−1	1,672·4	3/2	$8·2 \times 10^{-11}$

? indicates that the particle's lifetime has yet to be determined
( ) indicates that the property has been deduced but not confirmed
MeV = million electron volts

fect their chemistry. For instance, the isotopes of a single element differ only in the number of neutrons in their nuclei but have identical chemical properties. Outside a nucleus, a free neutron is radioactive, decaying with a half-life of 11.6 minutes into a proton, an electron, and an antineutrino.

nucleus the positively charged central part of an atom, which is only one-ten-thousandth the diameter of the atom but constitutes almost all its mass. Except for hydrogen nuclei, which have only protons, nuclei are primarily composed of both protons and neutrons. Surrounding the nuclei are electrons, which contain a negative charge equal to the protons, thus giving the atom a neutral charge.

photon the elementary particle or quantum of energy in which light or other forms of electromagnetic radiation is emitted. It has both particle and wave properties; it has no charge, is considered massless, but possesses momentum and energy. It is one of the gauge bosons and is the carrier of the electromagnetic

force, one of the fundamental forces of nature.

proton (Greek 'first') a positively charged subatomic particle, a constituent of the nucleus of all atoms. It belongs to the baryon subclass of the hadrons. A proton is extremely long-lived, with a lifespan of at least 10^{32} years. It carries a unit positive charge equal to the negative charge of an electron. Its mass is almost 1,836 times that of an electron, or 1.67×10^{-24} g. The number of protons in the atom of an element is equal to the atomic number of that element.

quantum chromodynamics (QCD) a theory describing the interactions of quarks, the elementary particles that make up hadrons (such as protons and neutrons). In quantum chromodynamics, quarks are considered to interact by exchanging gauge bosons called gluons, which carry the strong nuclear force, and whose role is to 'glue' quarks together. The mathematics involved in the theory is complex, and although a number of successful predictions have been made, as yet the theory does not compare in accuracy with quantum electrodynamics, upon which it is modelled.

quantum electrodynamics (QED) a theory describing the interaction of charged subatomic particles within electric and magnetic fields. It combines quantum theory and relativity, and considers charged particles to interact by the exchange of photons. QED is remarkable for the accuracy of its predictions—for example, it has been used to calculate the value of some physical quantities to an accuracy of ten decimal places, a feat equivalent to calculating the distance between New York and Los Angeles to within the thickness of a hair. The theory was developed by US physicists Richard Feynman and Julian Schwinger, and by Japanese physicist Sin-Itiro Tomonaga.

quark an elementary particle that is the fundamental constituent of all hadrons (baryons, such as neutrons and protons, and mesons). There are six types, or 'flavours': up, down, top, bottom, strange, and charm, each of which has three varieties, or 'colours': red, yellow, and blue (visual colour is not meant, although the analogy is useful in many ways). To each quark there is an antiparticle, called an antiquark.

spin the intrinsic angular momentum of a subatomic particle, nucleus, atom, or molecule, which continues to exist even when the particle comes to rest. A particle in a specific energy state has a particular spin, just as it has a particular electric charge and mass. According to quantum theory, this is restricted to discrete and indivisible values, specified by a spin quantum number. Because of its spin, a charged particle acts as a small magnet and is affected by magnetic fields.

standard model the modern theory of elementary particles and their interactions. According to the standard model, subatomic particles are classified as leptons (light particles, such as electrons), hadrons (particles, such as neutrons and protons, that are formed from quarks), and gauge bosons. Leptons and hadrons interact by exchanging gauge bosons, each of which is responsible for a different fundamental force: photons mediate the electromagnetic force, which affects all charged particles; gluons mediate the strong nuclear force, which affects quarks; gravitons mediate the gravitational force; and the weakons mediate the weak nuclear force.

superstring theory a mathematical theory developed in the 1980s to explain the properties of elementary particles and the forces between them (in particular, gravity and the nuclear forces) in a way that combines relativity and quantum theory. In string theory, the fundamental objects in the universe are not pointlike particles but extremely small stringlike objects. These objects exist in a universe of ten dimensions, although, for reasons not yet understood, only three space dimensions and one dimension of time are discernable. There are many unresolved difficulties with superstring theory, but some physicists think it may be the ultimate 'theory of everything'

that explains all aspects of the universe within one framework.

supersymmetry a theory that relates the two classes of elementary particle, the fermions and the bosons. According to supersymmetry, each fermion particle has a boson partner particle, and vice versa. It has not been possible to marry up all the known fermions with the known bosons, and so the theory postulates the existence of other, as-yet undiscovered fermions, such as the photinos (partners of the photons), gluinos (partners of the gluons), and gravitinos (partners of the gravitons). Using these ideas, it has become possible to develop a theory of gravity—called supergravity—that extends Einstein's work and considers the gravitational, nuclear, and elecromagnetic forces to be manifestations of an underlying superforce. Supersymmetry has been incorporated into the superstring theory, and appears to be a crucial ingredient in the 'theory of everything' sought by scientists.

uncertainty principle or *indeterminacy principle* the principle that it is meaningless to speak of a particle's position, momentum, or other parameters, except as results of measurements; measuring, however, involves an interaction (such as a photon of light bouncing off the particle under scrutiny), which must disturb the particle, though the disturbance is noticeable only at an atomic scale. The principle implies that one cannot, even in theory, predict the moment-to-moment behaviour of such a system.

weakon a gauge boson that carries the weak force, one of the fundamental forces of nature. There are three types of weakon, the positive and negative W particles and the neutral Z particle.

THE GREAT PHYSICISTS

Ampère André Marie 1775–1836. French physicist and mathematician who made many discoveries in electromagnetism and electrodymanics. He followed up the work of Hans Oersted on the interaction between magnets and electric currents, developing a rule for determining the direction of the magnetic field associated with an electric current. The ammeter and ampere are named after him.

Bohr Niels Henrik David 1885–1962. Danish physicist. After work with Ernest Rutherford at Manchester, he became professor at Copenhagen in 1916, and founded there the Institute of Theoretical Physics of which he became director in 1920. He was awarded the Nobel Prize for Physics 1922. Bohr fled from the Nazis in World War II and took part in work on the atomic bomb in the USA. In 1952, he helped to set up CERN, the European nuclear research organization, in Geneva.

Boyle Robert 1627–1691. Irish physicist and chemist, who published the seminal *The*

Skeptical Chymist 1661. He was the first chemist to collect a sample of gas, formulated ***Boyle's law*** on the compressibility of a gas in 1662, and was one of the founders of the Royal Society.

Broglie, de Louis, 7th Duc de Broglie 1892--1987. French theoretical physicist. He established that all subatomic particles can be described either by particle equations or by wave equations, thus laying the foundations of wave mechanics. He was awarded the 1929 Nobel Prize for Physics.

Carnot (Nicolas Leonard) Sadi 1796–1832. French scientist and military engineer who founded the science of thermodynamics; his pioneering work was *Réflexions sur la puissance motrice du feu/On the Motive Power of Fire*, which considered the changes that would take place in an idealized, frictionless steam engine.

Cavendish Henry 1731–1810. British physicist. He discovered hydrogen (which he called 'inflammable air') 1766, and determined the compositions of water and of nitric acid.

Chadwick James 1891–1974. British physicist. In 1932 he discovered the particle in the nucleus of an atom that became known as the neutron because it has no electric charge. He was awarded a Nobel prize 1935.

Curie Marie (born Sklodovska) 1867–1934. Polish scientist who investigated radioactivity with her French husband Pierre (1859–1906). In 1898 she reported the possible existence of a new, powerfully radioactive element in pitchblende ores. Her husband abandoned his own researches to assist her, and in the same year they announced the existence of polonium and radium. They isolated the pure elements in 1902. Both scientists refused to take out a patent on their discoveries and were awarded, with Becquerel, the Nobel Prize for Physics 1903. Marie Curie was awarded the Nobel Prize for Chemistry 1911.

Dirac Paul Adrien Maurice 1902–1984. British physicist who worked out a version of quantum mechanics consistent with special relativity. The existence of the positron (positive electron) was one of its predictions. He shared a Nobel Prize for Physics 1933.

Einstein Albert 1879–1955. German-born US physicist who formulated the theories of relativity, and worked on radiation physics and thermodynamics. In 1905 he published the special theory of relativity, and in 1915 issued his general theory of relativity. His latest conception of the basic laws governing the universe was outlined in his unified field theory, made public 1953.

Faraday Michael 1791–1867. English chemist and physicist. In 1821 he began experimenting with electromagnetism, and ten years later discovered the induction of electric currents and made the first dynamo. He subsequently found that a magnetic field will rotate the plane of polarization of light. Faraday also investigated electrolysis.

Fermi Enrico 1901–1954. Italian-born US physicist, who proved the existence of new radioactive elements produced by bombardment with neutrons, and discovered nuclear reactions produced by low-energy neutrons. His theoretical work included study of the weak nuclear force, one of the fundamental forces of nature, and (with Paul Dirac) of the quantum statistics of fermion particles. He was awarded a Nobel prize 1938.

Feynman Richard Phillips 1918–1988. US physicist whose work provided the foundations for quantum electrodynamics. For his work on the theory of radiation he was awarded a share of the Nobel Prize for Physics 1965. As a member of the committee investigating the *Challenger* space-shuttle disaster 1986, he demonstrated the lethal faults in the rubber seals on the shuttle's booster rocket. Towards the end of his life he became widely known for his revealing autobiography *Surely you're Joking Mr Feynman!*.

Foucault Jean Bernard Léon 1819–1868. French physicist who used a pendulum to demonstrate the rotation of the Earth on its axis, and invented the gyroscope.

Gabor Dennis 1900–1979. Hungarian-born British physicist. In 1947 he invented the holographic method of three-dimensional photography and in 1958 invented a type of colour-television tube of greatly reduced depth. He was awarded a Nobel prize 1971.

Galileo properly Galileo Galilei 1564–1642. Italian mathematician, astronomer, and physicist. He developed the astronomical telescope and was the first to see sunspots, the four main satellites of Jupiter, mountains and craters on the Moon, and the appearance of Venus going through 'phases', thus proving it was orbiting the Sun. In mechanics, Galileo discovered that freely falling bodies, heavy or light, had the same, constant acceleration (although the story of his dropping cannonballs from the Leaning Tower of Pisa is questionable) and that a body moving on a perfectly smooth horizontal surface would neither speed up nor slow down.

Gell-Mann Murray 1929– . US physicist. In 1964 he formulated the theory of the quark as one of the fundamental constituents of matter. He was awarded a Nobel prize 1969.

Glashow Sheldon Lee 1932– . US particle physicist. He proposed the existence of a fourth 'charmed' quark 1964, and argued that quarks must have properties analogous with colour. Glashow went on to consider ways in which the weak and the electromagnetic forces (two of the fundamental forces of nature) could be unified as a single force now called the electroweak force. He shared the Nobel Prize for Physics 1979 with Abdus Salam and Steven Weinberg.

Hawking Stephen William 1942– . English physicist. He discovered that the strong gravitational field around a black hole can radiate particles of matter. Commenting on Einstein's remark, 'God does not play dice with the universe,' Hawking said: 'God not only plays dice, he throws them where they can't be seen.' Confined to a wheelchair because of a muscular disease, he performs complex mathematical calculations entirely in his head. His books include *A Brief History of Time* 1988.

Heisenberg Werner Carl 1901–1976. German physicist who developed quantum theory and formulated the uncertainty principle, which concerns matter, radiation, and their reactions, and places absolute limits on the achievable accuracy of measurement. He was awarded a Nobel prize 1932.

Hertz Heinrich 1857–1894. German physicist who studied electromagnetic waves, showing that their behaviour resembles that of light and heat waves.

Hooke Robert 1635–1703. English scientist and inventor. *Hooke's law* states that the deformation of a body is proportional to the magnitude of the deforming force, provided that the body's elastic limit is not exceeded. Hooke's inventions included a telegraph system, the spirit-level, marine barometer, and sea gauge. He coined the term 'cell' in biology.

Josephson Brian 1940– . British physicist, a leading authority on superconductivity. In 1973 he shared a Nobel prize for his theoretical predictions of the properties of a supercurrent through a tunnel barrier (the Josephson junction).

Joule James Prescott 1818–1889. British physicist whose work on the relations between electrical, mechanical, and chemical effects led to the discovery of the first law of thermodynamics.

Kelvin William Thomson, 1st Baron Kelvin 1824–1907. Irish physicist who introduced the *kelvin scale*, the absolute scale of temperature. His work on the conservation of energy 1851 led to the second law of thermodynamics.

Lawrence Ernest O(rlando) 1901–1958. US physicist. His invention of the cyclotron pioneered the production of artificial radioisotopes. He was awarded a Nobel prize in 1939.

Maxwell James Clerk 1831–1879. Scottish physicist. His major achievement was in the understanding of electromagnetic waves: *Maxwell's equations* bring together electricity, magnetism, and light in one set of relations. He contributed to every branch of physical science—gases, optics, and colour sensation. His theoretical work in magnetism prepared the way for wireless telegraphy and telephony.

Michelson Albert Abraham 1852–1931. German-born US physicist. In conjunction with Edward Morley, he performed in 1887 the *Michelson–Morley experiment* to detect the motion of the Earth through the postulated ether (a medium believed to be necessary for the propagation of light). The failure of the experiment indicated the nonexistence of the ether, and led Einstein to his theory of relativity. Michelson was the first American to be awarded a Nobel prize 1907.

Newton Isaac 1642–1727. English physicist and mathematician who laid the foundations of physics as a modern discipline. He discov-

ered the law of gravity, showed that white light is composed of many colours, and developed the three standard laws of motion still in use today. His *Philosophiae naturalis principia mathematica* (usually referred to as *Principia*) was published in three volumes 1686–87, with the aid of the astronomer and physicist Edmund Halley.

Ohm Georg Simon 1787–1854. German physicist who studied electricity and discovered the fundamental law that bears his name. The SI unit of electrical resistance is named after him, and the unit of conductance (the reverse of resistance) was formerly called the mho, which is Ohm spelt backwards.

Pauli Wolfgang 1900–1958. Austrian physicist who originated the *exclusion principle*: in a given system no two fermions (electrons, protons, neutrons, or other elementary particles of half-integral spin) can be characterized by the same set of quantum numbers. He also predicted the existence of neutrinos. He won a Nobel prize 1945 for his work on atomic structure.

Planck Max 1858–1947. German physicist who framed the quantum theory 1900. His research into the manner in which heated bodies radiate energy led him to report that energy is emitted only in indivisible amounts, called quanta, the magnitudes of which are proportional to the frequency of the radiation. His discovery ran counter to classical physics and is held to have marked the commencement of the modern science. Planck was awarded the Nobel Prize for Physics 1918.

Powell Cecil Frank 1903–1969. English physicist, awarded a Nobel prize 1950 for his use of photographic emulsion as a method of tracking charged nuclear particles.

Rutherford Ernest 1871–1937. New Zealand physicist, a pioneer of modern atomic science. His main research was in the field of radioactivity, and he discovered alpha, beta, and gamma rays. He named the nucleus, and was the first to recognize the ionizing nature of the atom. Nobel prize 1908

Salam Abdus 1926– . Pakistani physicist. In 1967 he proposed a theory linking the electromagnetic and weak forces, also arrived at independently by Steven Weinberg. In 1979 he was the first person from his country to receive a Nobel prize, which he shared with Weinberg and Sheldon Glashow.

Schrödinger Erwin 1887–1961. Austrian physicist who advanced the study of wave mechanics (see quantum theory). Born in Vienna, he became senior professor at the Dublin Institute for Advanced Studies 1940. He shared (with Paul Dirac) a Nobel prize 1933.

Shockley William 1910–1989. US physicist and amateur geneticist who worked with John Bardeen and Walter Brattain on the invention of the transistor. They were jointly awarded a Nobel prize 1956. During the 1970s Shockley was criticized for his claim that blacks were genetically inferior to whites in terms of intelligence.

Nobel Prize For Physics

prizewinners

1964 Charles Townes (USA), Nikolai Basov (USSR), and Aleksandr Prokhorov (USSR): quantum electronics leading to construction of oscillators and amplifiers based on maser-laser principle

1965 Sin-Itiro Tomonaga (Japan), Julian Schwinger (USA), and Richard Feynman (USA): quantum electrodynamics

1966 Alfred Kastler (France): development of optical pumping, whereby atoms are raised to higher energy levels by illumination

1967 Hans Bethe (USA): theory of nuclear reactions, and discoveries concerning production of energy in stars

1968 Luis Alvarez (USA): elementary-particle physics, and discovery of resonance states, using hydrogen bubble chamber and data analysis

1969 Murray Gell-Mann (USA): classification of elementary particles, and study of their interactions

1970 Hannes Alfvén (Sweden): magnetohydrodynamics and its applications in plasma physics. Louis Néel (France): antiferromagnetism and ferromagnetism in solid-state physics

1971 Dennis Gabor (UK): invention and development of holography

1972 John Bardeen (USA), Leon Cooper (USA), and John Robert Schrieffer (USA): theory of superconductivity

1973 Leo Eskai (Japan) and Ivar Giaver (USA): tunnelling phenomena in semiconductors and superconductors. Brian Josephson (UK): theoretical predictions of the properties of a supercurrent through a tunnel barrier

1974 Martin Ryle (UK) and Antony Hewish (UK): development of radioastronomy, particularly aperture-synthesis technique, and the discovery of pulsars

1975 Aage Bohr (Denmark), Ben Mottelson (Denmark), and James Rainwater (USA): discovery of connection between collective motion and particle motion in atomic nuclei, and development of theory of nuclear structure

1976 Burton Richter (USA) and Samuel Ting (USA): discovery of the psi meson

1977 Philip Anderson (USA), Nevill Mott (UK), and John Van Vleck (USA): electronic structure of magnetic and disordered systems

1978 Pyotr Kapitza (USSR): low-temperature physics. Arno Penzias (Germany), and Robert Wilson (USA): discovery of cosmic background radiation

1979 Sheldon Glashow (USA), Abdus Salam (Pakistan), and Steven Weinberg (USA): unified theory of weak and electromagnetic fundamental forces, and prediction of the existence of the weak neutral current

1980 James W Cronin (USA) and Val Fitch (USA): violations of fundamental symmetry principles in the decay of neutral kaon mesons

1981 Nicolaas Bloemergen (USA) and Arthur Schawlow (USA): development of laser spectroscopy. Kai Siegbahn (Sweden): high-resolution electron spectroscopy

1982 Kenneth Wilson (1936– , USA): theory for critical phenomena in connection with phase transitions

1983 Subrahmanyan Chandrasekhar (USA): theoretical studies of physical processes in connection with structure and evolution of stars. William Fowler (USA): nuclear reactions involved in the formation of chemical elements in the universe

1984 Carlo Rubbia (Italy) and Simon van der Meer (Netherlands): contributions to the discovery of the W and Z particles (weakons)

1985 Klaus von Klitzing (Germany): discovery of the quantized Hall effect

1986 Erns Ruska (Germany): electron optics, and design of the first electron microscope. Gerd Binnig (Germany) and Heinrich Rohrer (Switzerland): design of scanning tunnelling microscope

1987 Georg Bednorz (Germany) and Alex Müller (Switzerland): superconductivity in ceramic materials

1988 Leon M Lederman (USA), Melvin Schwartz (USA), and Jack Steinberger (Germany): neutrino-beam method, and demonstration of the structure of leptons through discovery of muon neutrino

1989 Norman Ramsey (USA): measurement techniques leading to discovery of caesium atomic clock. Hans Dehmelt (USA) and Wolfgang Paul (Germany): ion-trap method for isolating single atoms

1990 Jerome Friedman (USA), Henry Kendall (USA), and Richard Taylor (Canada): experiments demonstrating that protons and neutrons are made up of quarks

1991 Pierre-Gilles de Gennes (France): work on disordered systems including polymers and liquid crystals; development of mathematical methods for studying the behaviour of molecules in a liquid on the verge of solidifying.

THE QUANTUM TURNSTILE

Every physics undergraduate struggles with the mathematics of the 'quantum box'—a very small box containing a single particle. The box is a simple system in which the effects of quantum theory are important. At very low temperatures, quantum theory predicts that the particle can have only certain fixed energies—these are the energy levels characteristic of quantum systems. If the particle does not have the energy corresponding to the lowest empty energy level, it cannot enter the box. Recently, physicists have discovered how to make such boxes, and have studied the way electrons jump in and out of them.

Scientists at the AT&T Bell Laboratories in New Jersey have constructed quantum boxes from a sandwich of semiconductor material. The outer layers of the sandwich are made of an electrically insulating material. The thin inner layer is made of gallium arsenide doped with impurities to improve its electrical conductivity. A ring-shaped electrode is fixed on top of the sandwich, and a conducting layer is placed underneath. When a negative voltage is applied to the circular electrode, electrons in the sandwich are repelled towards the centre of the ring, effectively confining them in a microscopic box just 1 micrometre wide.

The device acts as an electrical capacitor which stores electrical charge, and precise measurements of the capacitance reveals the passage of electrons into and out of the box. Initially, to empty the box, the negative voltage on the ring electrode is raised. The voltage is then slowly lowered until, at a certain threshold voltage, the capacitance suddenly changes, as a single electron enters the box. The capacitance then stays steady until a second electron jumps into the box, taking up the second energy level.

A related series of experiments at the Delft University of Technology in the Netherlands has electrons jumping in one side of the quantum box and out of the other. The Dutch experiment has a rectangular upper electrode and thus produces a rectangular-shaped quantum box. Negative voltages are applied to contacts at the ends of the rectangle. If the voltage at one end is gradually lowered, an electron will eventually enter the box at that end. If the voltage is then raised, the electron is trapped. The negative voltage at the other end can then be lowered to let the electron escape from the end opposite to the one that it entered. The box has become a quantum turnstile, shuffling individual electrons in one end and out the other. This technique may turn out to be a practical means of regulating electrical current very precisely; an exact number of electrons can be allowed to flow. If a rapidly alternating voltage is applied to the end contacts, the in-and-out movement of electrons can be speeded up, because the sequence of voltage changes needed is produced automatically. An alternating voltage with frequency of 10 MHz shunts 10 million electrons a second (a million millionth of an ampere) through the box. If the current can be increased a thousand times, a new, accurate standard for measuring electrical currents might be possible.

Thomson J(oseph) J(ohn) 1856–1940. English physicist who discovered the electron. He was responsible for organizing the Cavendish atomic research laboratory at Cambridge University. His work inaugurated the electrical theory of the atom, and his elucidation of positive rays and their application to an analysis of neon led to Frederick Aston's discovery of isotopes. He was awarded a Nobel prize 1906.

Volta Alessandro 1745–1827. Italian physicist who invented the first electric cell (the voltaic pile), the electrophorus (an early electrostatic generator), and an electroscope.

Watt James 1736–1819. Scottish engineer who developed the steam engine. He made Newcomen's steam engine vastly more efficient by cooling the used steam in a condenser separate from the main cylinder.

Weinberg Steven 1933– . US physicist, who in 1967 demonstrated, together with Abdus Salam, that the weak force and the electromagnetic force (two of the fundamental forces) are variations of a single underlying force, now called the electroweak force. Weinberg and Salam shared a Nobel prize with Sheldon Glashow in 1979.

CONSTRUCTION

bridge a construction that provides a continuous path or road over water, valleys, ravines, or above other roads. Bridges may be classified into four main groups:

arch bridges, for example, Sydney Harbour bridge (steel arch) with a span of 503 m/ 1,650 ft;

beam or **girder bridges**, as at Rio-Niteroi (1974), Guanabara Bay, Brazil, the world's longest continuous box-and-plate girder bridge: centre span 300 m/984 ft; length 13.9 km/8 mi 3,363 ft;

cantilever bridges, for example, the Forth rail bridge, which is 1,658 m/5,440 ft long and has two main spans, each consisting of two cantilevers, one from each tower;

suspension bridges, such as the Humber bridge, the world's longest-span suspension bridge with a centre span of 1,410 m/4,626 ft.

Steel is pre-eminent in the construction of long-span bridges because of its high strength-to-weight ratio, but in other circumstances reinforced concrete has the advantage of lower maintenance costs.

canal a man-made waterway constructed for drainage, irrigation, or navigation.

irrigation canals carry water for irrigation from rivers, reservoirs, or wells, and are carefully designed to maintain an even flow of water over the whole length. Irrigation canals fed from the Nile have maintained life in Egypt since the earliest times; the Murray Basin project of Victoria, Australia, and the Imperial and Central Valley project of California, USA, are examples of 19th- and 20th-century irrigation-canal development.

navigation and ship canals constructed at one level between locks, canals frequently link with other forms of waterway—natural rivers, modified river channels, and sea links—to

bridge
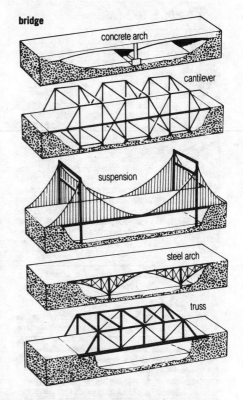

form a waterway system. The world's two major international ship canals are the Suez Canal and the Panama Canal which provide invaluable short cuts for shipping respectively between Europe and the East and between the east and west coasts of the Americas. The first major British canal was the Bridgewater Canal from Worsley to Manchester 1761–76; the engineer was Brindley and the canal was constructed for the 3rd Duke of Bridgewater

THE WORLD'S MOST REMARKABLE BRIDGES

Angostura	*Cuidad Bolivar, Venezuela*
	Suspension-type bridge; span 712 m/2,336 ft; total length 1,678 m/5,507 ft
Bendorf Bridge	*Coblenz, Germany*
	3-span cement girder bridge; main span 208 m/682 ft ; total length 1030 m/3,378 ft
Bosphorus Bridge	*Istanbul, Turkey* (linking Europe to Asia)
	Suspension bridge; total length 1,074 m/3,524 ft
Gladesville Bridge	*Sydney, Australia*
	Concrete arch bridge; 305 m/1,000 ft span – world's longest concrete arch
Humber Bridge	*Kingston upon Hull, England*
	Suspension bridge; total span 1410 m/4,626 ft – world's longest suspension span
Lake Pontchartrain Causeway	*New Orleans, USA*
	Multiple span; 38,421 m/126,055 ft – the world's longest multiple span
Oosterscheldebrug	*Flushing/Rotterdam, Netherlands*
	Traffic causeway over Zeeland sea arm; total length 19 km 3.125 mi
Rio-Niteroi	*Guanabara Bay, Brazil*
	Continuous box and plate girder bridge; 14 km/8.7 mi length – the world's longest box girder bridge
Tagus River Bridge	*Lisbon, Portugal*
	Main span 1013 m/3,323 ft
Zoo Bridge	*Cologne, Germany*
	Steel box girder bridge; main span 259 m/850 ft

A BRIDGE TOO FAR?

London has a new bridge across the Thames. The Dartford bridge, 30 km/19 mi downstream from central London, is the longest cable-stayed bridge in Europe, with a main span of 450 m/1,476 ft. It was also one of the swiftest construction jobs ever for a large bridge—barely six years from conception to opening. The Dartford bridge represents a design that has been eagerly adopted by bridge designers and builders worldwide as a cost-effective way of building long-span bridges. The race is on to build bigger and better cable-stayed bridges. Leading the field, at the moment, is the 465 m/1,526 ft Annacis bridge near Vancouver. The second Hooghly River bridge at Calcutta, begun in 1974 and nearing completion, has a main span of 457 m/1,499 ft. The Rama IX bridge across Bangkok's Chao Phraya River, opened in late 1987, has a main span of 450 m/1,476 ft. Another giant, when completed, is the 490 m/1,607 ft span of the Ikuchi bridge between the Japanese islands of Honshu and Shikoku. Norway is planning to finish a 530 m/1,739 ft Skarnsundet bridge across a fjord northeast of Trondheim at around the same time. By mid-1994, the French plan to complete a cable-stayed bridge of 856 m/2,808 ft spanning the mouth of the Seine at Honfleur. By the end of the century, the Japanese expect to have completed a cable-stayed bridge of 890 m/2,919 ft between Honshu and Shikoku. But are designers pressing the new cable-stayed technology too far, beyond its safe limits, without adequate testing or accumulated experience?

Large bridges have traditionally been suspension bridges. Both forms of bridge rely on cables to support their weight. The suspension bridge uses cables draped between towers at each end, from which the bridge is suspended by vertical steel ropes. The longest suspension bridge is the ten-year-old bridge over the Humber River in northeast England. Its main span is 1,410 m/4,626 ft. Cable-stayed bridges rely on diagonal cables connected directly between the bridge deck and the supporting towers at each end. Generally, the spans of cable-stayed bridges have been less than 350 m/1,150 ft, so the new bridges represent a quantum leap in size.

Bridge designers remember the last time their discipline took a quantum leap forward. In the 1930s, maximum bridge lengths doubled. Then, in November 1940, the collapse of the 860-m/2,821-ft bridge over the Tacoma Narrows, Washington State, revealed the fragility of that advance. Even now engineers do not know for certain what caused the Tacoma bridge collapse, but a likely culprit was the bridge deck's flexibility. The wind could twist the deck which presented a large flat side surface to the wind.

The Annacis bridge is just 250 km/155 mi north of the Tacoma Narrows and its builders studied the Tacoma collapse before finalizing their design. The bridge deck was made thinner, and the edges were streamlined to reduce interaction with side winds. Also, the deck was a concrete and steel composite, with concrete slabs on top of a structural steel framework. Composite decks are common on bridges supported by columns, but had not previously been widely used on suspension bridges.

Attention was paid to the composition and arrangement of the cables, too, since these affect the bridge's stiffness. The simplest cable arrangement is to attach the cables along the centre-line of the bridge and to uprights in the same vertical plane at each end of the bridge. However, a more rigid structure results if the cables are attached to the sides of the bridge and to two uprights at each end of the bridge. The cables themselves are made by winding together many thin steel wires, each a few millimetres across, to produce a final cable around 160 mm/6.3 in in diameter. Experience on the Annacis bridge encouraged designers to press ahead with more ambitious projects with apparent confidence. But the giant bridges being planned are large steps into the unknown.

The Dartford bridge in east London is the longest cable-stayed bridge in Europe.

THE WORLD'S HIGHEST DAMS

Name	Country	Height above lowest formation
Rogun*	Tajikistan	335 m/1,099 ft
Nurek	Tajikistan	300 m/984 ft
Grand Dixence	Switzerland	285 m/935 ft
Inguri	Georgia	272 m/892 ft
Boruca*	Costa Rica	267 m/875 ft
Chicoasen	Mexico	261 m/856 ft
Tehri*	India	261 m/856 ft
Kambaratinsk*	Kyrgyzstan	255 m/836 ft
Kishau*	India	253 m/830 ft
Sayano-Shushensk*	Russia	245 m/804 ft
Guavio	Colombia	243 m/797 ft
Mica	Canada	242 m/794 ft
Ertan*	China	240 m/787 ft
Mauvoisin	Switzerland	237 m/778 ft
Chivor	Colombia	237 m/778 ft
Kishau*	India	236 m/774 ft
El Cajon	Honduras	234 m/768 ft
Chirkey	Russia	233 m/765 ft

* under construction

to carry coal from his collieries to Manchester. Brindley overcame great difficulties in the route. Today many of Britain's canals form part of an interconnecting system of waterways some 4,000 km/2,500 mi long. Although most have fallen out of commercial use, many have been restored for recreation and the use of pleasure craft.

dam a structure built to hold back water in order to prevent flooding, provide water for irrigation and storage, or generate hydroelectric power. The world's largest dam is the Pati dam on the Paraná river, Argentina, which has a volume of 238 million cu m/933 million cu ft. Like all the biggest dams it is an **earth-and-rock-fill dam**, also called an **embankment dam**. Such dams are generally built on broad valley sites. Deep, narrow gorges, however, dictate a concrete dam, the enormous strength of reinforced concrete being able to withstand the enormous water pressures involved. Many concrete dams are triangular in cross-section, with their vertical face pointing upstream. Their sheer weight holds them in position, and they are called **gravity dams**. Some concrete dams, however, are more slight and are built in the shape of an arch, with the curve facing

upstream. The **arch dam** derives its strength from its shape, just as an arch bridge does. A valuable development in arid regions, as in parts of Brazil, is the **underground dam**, where water is stored among sand and stones on a solid rock base, with a wall to ground level, so avoiding rapid evaporation.

skyscraper a building so tall that it appears to 'scrape the sky', developed in New York, USA, where land prices were high and the geology adapted to such methods of construction. Skyscrapers are now found in cities throughout the world. The world's tallest free-standing structure is the CN (Canadian National) Tower, Toronto, 555 m/1,821 ft. The tallest building in the UK is the office tower of the Canary Wharf development in London Docklands, 259 m/850 ft.

In Manhattan, New York, are the Empire State Building (1931), 102 storeys and 381 m/1,250 ft high, and the twin towers of the World Trade Center, 415 m/1,361 ft, but these were surpassed 1973 by the Sears Tower, 443 m/1,454 ft, in Chicago. Chicago was the home of the first skyscraper, the Home Insurance Building (1885), which was built ten storeys high with an iron and steel frame. Most skyscrapers are constructed around a rigid loadbearing steel frame; the walls simply hang from the frame (curtain walling), and can therefore be made from relatively flimsy materials such as glass and aluminium. Another type of construction, central-core construction, has the lifts and staircases enclosed to form the skyscraper's core. Unit-slab construction involves building each storey on top of the last.

tunnel tunnelling is an increasingly important branch of civil engineering in mining, transport, and other areas. In the 19th century there were two major advances: the use of compressed air within the tunnel to balance the external pressure of water and of the tunnel shield to support the rockface and assist excavation. In recent years there have been notable developments in tunnel linings, such as concrete segments and steel liner plates, and in the use of rotary diggers and cutters, and of explosives. Famous tunnels include the world's longest road tunnel, the St Gotthard (1980), Switzerland, 16.3 km/10.1 mi long; the world's longest rail tunnel, the Seikan (1975), under Tsugaru Strait linking Honshu and Hokkaido, Japan, 53.85 km/33.5 mi long; the Orange-Fish River tunnel (1975), South

THE CHANNEL TUNNEL: RECENT DEVELOPMENTS

1984	Construction of a tunnel agreed in principle at an Anglo-French summit.
1986	Anglo-French treaty signed; design submitted by a consortium called the Channel Tunnel Group accepted.
1987	Legislation completed; Anglo-French treaty ratified.
1987 (Nov)	Construction began in earnest.
1990 (Dec)	First breakthrough of service tunnel.
1991 (May)	Breakthrough of first rail tunnel.
1991 (June)	Completion of second rail tunnel.
1993 (Sept)	Tunnel scheduled to be operational.

THE PLASTIC HOUSE

Finland's largest petrochemical group, Neste Chemicals, has recently produced a house that is three-quarters plastic. Conventional houses might be around 5% plastic, the plastics being used for pipes and waste traps, or as imitation wooden beams. In 1989 the US chemicals giant GE Plastics built a house in Pittsfield, Massachusetts, which contained 30% plastic. The GE house, however, looked no different from conventional homes; the plastic roof panels were dressed up to resemble traditional American wooden shingles. The Finnish house, called the Nestehaus, wears its plastic proudly. Plastics are clearly visible in the structural columns, roof, and staircases.

Although more expensive than traditional homes, the plastic house should be cheaper to run; a two-year cost assessment programme is under way. The main advantages are freedom from corrosion, light weight, and good insulation. The designers believe that a house could be built almost entirely of plastics. Nonplastics would only have to be used for some structural members, where strength is needed. And, of course, no true Finn would consider a plastic sauna—only wood would do there!

The structure of the house is based on round load-bearing columns of fibreglass-reinforced plastic pipes. Steel reinforcing bars are inserted and concrete, impregnated with polypropylene fibres, is poured in. The high strength-to-weight ratio allows the columns to have a diameter of only 128 mm/ 5 in, although they have to be used in groups of two or three. If conventional reinforced concrete columns and beams were used they would need to be about 300 mm/12 in across. The supporting cross-beams are made from rectangular-shaped pipes of the same reinforced plastic filled with the same concrete mixture. The curtain walls are made from fibreglass-reinforced plastic into which triple glazing or insulating panels are inserted. Nonloadbearing insulating wall panels consist of blocks of expanded polystyrene 300 mm/12 in thick with a thin plastic skin. These are four times better insulators than the same thickness of brick or concrete block. They keep the house warm enough for shirt sleeves even in the cold of a Finnish winter.

The floors consist of polystyrene blocks reinforced with steel, and covered with concrete. The foundations are moulded polystyrene blocks that insulate as well as support. Concrete and reinforcing bars fill the voids between the polystyrene blocks. Inside the house, a spiral staircase made entirely of plastics dominates. The floor is covered with PVC; recycled granulated plastics are used in the bathroom. Kitchen work surfaces are marble-effect polyester and cabinets are lined with plastics. Drainage pipes are the standard PVC while hot-water pipes are polyethylene. Built primarily to test the limits of plastics technology, the Nestehaus has shown that plastics could be used far more widely in buildings. Shall we see the day when the notoriously conservative British housebuyer swaps bricks and mortar for polystyrene?

WORLD'S LONGEST RAILWAY TUNNELS

Tunnel	Date	Km/Mi
Seikan	1985	54/33.5
Dai-shimizu	1979	23/14
Simplon No. 1 and 2	1906, 1922	19/12
Kanmon	1975	19/12
Apennine	1934	18/11
Rokko	1972	16/10
Mt MacDonald	1989	15/9.1
Gotthard	1882	14/9
Lotschberg	1913	14/9
Hokuriku	1962	14/9
Mont Canis (Frejus)	1871	13/8
Shin-Shimizu	1961	13/8
Aki	1975	13/8
Cascade	1929	13/8
Flathead	1970	13/8
Keijo	1970	11/7
Lierasen	1973	11/7
Santa Lucia	1977	10/6
Arlberg	1884	10/6
Moffat	1928	10/6
Shimizu	1931	10/6

Source: The World Almanac and Book of Facts 1991, 1990 Pharos Books

Africa 82 km/50 mi long, constructed for irrigation; and the Chesapeake Bay Bridge tunnel (1963), USA, 28 km/17.5 mi long.

A tunnel beneath the English Channel was planned as a military measure by Napoleon in 1802. Excavations were made from both shores in the late 1870s and early 1880s, but work was halted by Parliament for security reasons. In 1986 a scheme for a Channel Tunnel (or Chunnel), in the form of twin rail tunnels, was approved by the French and British governments. Excavation began November 1987 and should be completed 1993.

TELECOMMUNICATIONS AND VIDEO TECHNOLOGY

Telecommunications are communications over a distance. For centuries bonfires have been used as a method of conveying a simple message, such as 'The Armada is coming' (1588). The first mechanical telecommunications systems were the **semaphore** and **heliograph** (which used flashes of sunlight). But the forerunner of the mod-

telecommunications

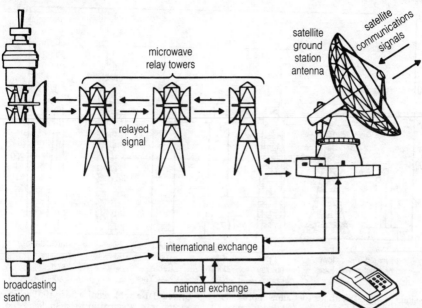

ern telecommunications age was the *electric telegraph*. The earliest practicable instrument was invented by William Cooke and Charles Wheatstone in the UK in 1837, and used by railway companies, the first public line being laid between Paddington and Slough in 1843. In the USA Morse invented a signalling code, Morse code, which is still used, and a recording telegraph, first used commercially between England and France in 1851. As a result of Heinrich Hertz's discoveries using electromagnetic waves, Guglielmo Marconi pioneered a *wireless telegraph*, ancestor of the radio. He established wireless communication between England and France 1899 and across the Atlantic 1901. The modern telegraph uses teleprinters to send coded messages along telecommunications lines. They are keyboard-operated machines that transmit a five-unit baudot code. The receiving teleprinter automatically prints the received message.

Long-distance voice communication was pioneered in 1876 by Alexander Graham Bell, when he invented the *telephone* as a result of Michael Faraday's discovery of electromagnetism. Today it is possible to communicate with most countries by telephone cable, several thousand simultaneous conversations being carried. However, the chief method of relaying long-distance calls on land is *microwave radio transmission*. The drawback to this is that the transmissions follow a straight line from tower to tower, so that over the sea the system becomes impracticable.

A solution was put forward in 1945 by Arthur C Clarke in *Wireless World*, when he proposed a system of *communications satellites* in an orbit 35,900 km/27,300 mi above the equator, where they would circle the Earth in exactly 24 hours, and thus appear fixed in the sky.

Such a system is now in operation internationally, operated by Intelsat. The satellites are called geostationary satellites, or synchronous satellites (syncoms). The first to be successfully launched, by Delta rocket from Cape Canaveral, was *Syncom 2* in July 1963. Numbers of such satellites are now in use, concentrated over heavy traffic areas such as the Atlantic, Indian, and Pacific Oceans. Telegraphy, telephony, and television transmissions are carried simultaneously by high-frequency radio waves. They are beamed to the satellites from large dish antennae or Earth stations, which connect with international networks. The number of stations continues to increase. In the UK Goonhilly and Madley are the main Earth stations.

In 1980 the Post Office opened its first System X (all electronic, digital) telephone exchange in London, a method already adopted in the USA. Other recent advances include the use of fibre-optic cables consisting of fine glass fibres for telephone lines instead of the usual copper cables. The telecommunications signals are transmitted along the fibres on pulses of laser light. Procedures, technical standards, frequencies, and so on, in telecommunications are controlled by the International Telecommunications Union (ITU).

cellphone or *cellular radio* mobile radio telephone, one of a network connected to the telephone system by a computer-controlled communication system. Service areas are divided into small 'cells', about 5 km/3 mi across, each with a separate low-power transmitter.

The cellular system allows the use of the same set of frequencies with the minimum risk of interference. Nevertheless, in crowded city areas, cells can become overloaded. This has led to a move away from analogue transmis-

skyscraper

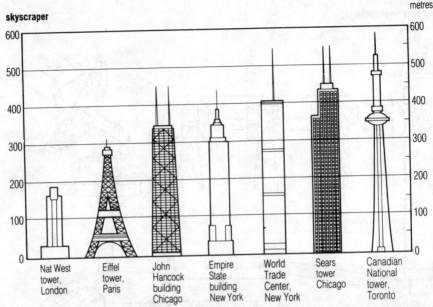

sions to digital methods that allow more calls to be made within a limited frequency range.

fax common name for *facsimile transmission* or *telefax*: the transmission of images over a telecommunications link, usually the telephone network. When placed in a fax machine, the original image is scanned by a transmitting device and converted into coded signals, which travel via the telephone lines to the receiving fax machine, where an image is created that is a copy of the original. Photographs as well as printed text and drawings may be sent.

radio the transmission and reception of radio waves. The theory of electromagnetic waves was first developed by James Clerk Maxwell 1864, given practical confirmation in the laboratory 1888 by Heinrich Hertz, and put to practical use by Marconi, who in 1901 achieved reception of a signal in Newfoundland transmitted from Poldhu in Cornwall.

radio transmission a microphone converts sound waves (pressure variations in the air) into an audiofrequency electrical signal. An oscillator produces a carrier wave of high frequency; different stations are allocated different transmitting carrier frequencies. A modulator superimposes the audiofrequency signal on the carrier. There are two main ways of doing this: amplitude modulation (AM), used for long- and medium-wave broadcasts, in which the strength of the carrier is made to fluctuate in time with the audio signal; and frequency modulation (FM), as used for VHF broadcasts, in which the frequency of the carrier is made

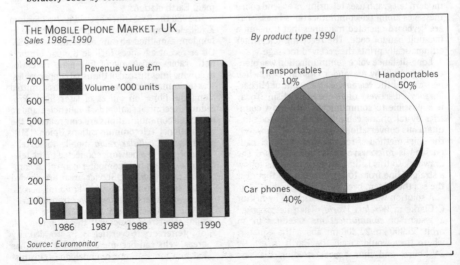

THE MOBILE PHONE MARKET, UK
Sales 1986–1990

By product type 1990

Source: Euromonitor

ELECTROPOLYMERS LEAVE THE LABORATORY

Polymers that conduct electricity—called electropolymers—are set to revolutionize material technology. New electrically conducting polymers can now be produced and, just as important, be fabricated for use in many varied applications: aircraft de-icing heaters, cable shielding, gas sensors, lightweight electrodes in batteries, solar cells, and anti-static clothing, for example. Some pilot commercial production plants have been set up, and these products are now beginning to reach the marketplace.

Early conducting polymers were essentially insulators, embedded with a network of conducting particles which overlapped, allowing the flow of electricity. The new electropolymers, however, are intrinsically conducting, allowing the free movement of charge carriers—electrons or holes—along their molecular backbones. To conduct electricity in this way, a polymer must have a special structure. The chain of atoms which form its backbone must be joined together with double or triple bonds. Electrons can flow freely through chains of such bonds. A polymer, such as polythene, that only has single bonds cannot conduct electricity.

One electropolymer, called poly(sulphur nitride) was discovered in 1910. This material has a metallic lustre, becomes superconducting at very low temperatures, and is a true metal, despite containing no metal atoms. Crystals of poly(sulphur nitride) have a conductivity of up to 1,000 siemens per centimetre (S/cm). This is about one-tenth the conductivity of the metal mercury, and 1% of the conductivity of metals like silver and copper. The problem with poly(sulphur nitride) is that it tarnishes in air, just like better-known metals, and is difficult to fabricate.

A number of other electropolymers are now known, although much attention has centred on polyacetylene because of its high electrical conductivity and potential electronics applications. Other promising materials are polypyrrole (a substance chemically related to ammonia), polyaniline, and a group of substances halfway between ordinary covalent organic compounds and ionic salts, known as conducting adducts.

Finding ways to turn these raw materials into useful products has not been easy. Many of these substances are unstable. All decompose or become non-conducting when melted, making them unsuitable for injection moulding. However, varying the chemical composition of the polymers without interfering with the conducting backbone of atoms has produced useful materials. Polypyrrole, for example, deteriorates rapidly in air but replacing chloride ions in its structure produces a material that can be washed in water, is stable in air, and loses only 10% of its conductivity in a year.

The first product is a black sheet with a conductivity of 10 S/cm. This is intended for use as cable screening, where it has advantages over aluminium-coated polyester or copper braiding: it does not fray, has no holes in it, and is more flexible. Another product is a light-brown powder, intended for use in floor tiles and table tops which are sufficiently conducting to eliminate static electricity. Paints containing the new materials are being developed. These could be used in gas sensors because gas molecules absorbed by a painted surface change the conductivity of the paint, producing an electrical signal. Ammonia, nitrogen dioxide, sulphur dioxide and other acid or alkaline gases have been shown to produce the necessary effect. Conductive paints could also protect enclosures against radio-frequency noise. Explosives could be made safer by using electropolymers as antistatic binders for the explosive; accidental discharge of static electricity, with disastrous consequences, would be reduced.

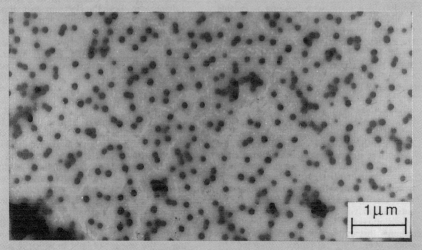

A diluted dispersion of colloidal polypyrrole paint particles, seen in a transmission electron micrograph.

TELECOMMUNICATIONS: CHRONOLOGY

1794	Claude Chappe in France built a long-distance signalling system using semaphore.
1839	Charles Wheatstone and William Cooke devised an electric telegraph in England.
1843	Samuel Morse transmitted the first message along a telegraph line in the USA, using his Morse code of signals—short (dots) and long (dashes).
1858	The first transatlantic telegraph cable was laid.
1876	American Alexander Graham Bell invented the telephone.
1877	Thomas Edison invented the carbon transmitter for the telephone.
1894	Guglielmo Marconi pioneered wireless telegraphy in Italy, later moving to England.
1900	Reginald Fessenden in the USA first broadcast voice by radio.
1901	Marconi transmitted the first radio signals across the Atlantic.
1904	John Ambrose Fleming invented the thermionic valve.
1920	Stations in Detroit and Pittsburgh began regular radio broadcasts.
1922	The BBC began its first radio transmissions, for the London station 2LO.
1932	The Post Office introduced the Telex in the UK.
1956	The first transatlantic telephone cable was laid.
1962	Telstar pioneers transatlantic satellite communications, transmitting live TV pictures.
1966	Charles Kao in England advanced the idea of using optical fibres for telecommunications transmissions.
1969	Live TV pictures were sent from astronauts on the Moon back to Earth.
1975	The Post Office announced Prestel, the world's first viewdata system, using the telephone lines to link a computer data bank with the TV screen.
1977	The first optical fibre cable was installed in California.
1984	First commercial cellphone service started in Chicago, USA.
1988	Integrated Services Digital Network (ISDN), an international system for sending signals in digital format along optical fibres and coaxial cable, launched in Japan.
1989	The first transoceanic optical-fibre cable, capable of carrying 40,000 simultaneous telephone conversations was laid between Europe and the USA.
1991	ISDN introduced in the UK.
1992	Videophones, made possible by advances in image compression and the development of ISDN, introduced in the UK.

to fluctuate. The transmitting aerial emits the modulated electromagnetic waves, which travel outwards from it.

radio reception a receiving aerial produces minute voltages in response to the waves sent out by a transmitter. A tuned circuit selects a particular voltage frequency, usually by means of a variable capacitor connected across a coil of wire. (The effect is similar to altering the tension in a piano wire, making it capable of vibrating at a different frequency.) A demodulator disentangles the audio signal from the carrier, which is now discarded, having served its purpose. An amplifier boosts the audio signal for feeding to the loudspeaker, which produces sound waves.

superheterodyne receiver the most widely used type of radio receiver, in which the incoming signal is mixed with a signal of fixed frequency generated within the receiver circuits. The resulting signal, called the intermediate-frequency (i.f.) signal, has a frequency between that of the incoming signal and the internal signal. The intermediate frequency is near the optimum frequency of the amplifier to which the i.f. signal is passed. This arrangement ensures greater gain and selectivity. The superheterodyne system is also used in basic television receivers.

telephone instrument for communicating by voice over long distances, invented by Alexander Graham Bell 1876. The transmitter (mouthpiece) consists of a carbon microphone, with a diaphragm that vibrates when a person speaks into it. The diaphragm vibrations compress grains of carbon to a greater or lesser extent, altering their resistance to an electric current passing through them. This sets up variable electrical signals, which travel along the telephone lines to the receiver of the person being called. There they cause the magnetism of an electromagnet to vary, making a diaphragm above the electromagnet vibrate and give out sound waves, which mirror those that entered the mouthpiece originally.

The standard instrument has a handset, which houses the transmitter (mouthpiece), and receiver (earpiece), resting on a base, which has a dial or push-button mechanism for dialling a telephone number. Some telephones combine a push-button mechanism and mouthpiece and earpiece in one unit. A cordless telephone is of this kind, connected to a base unit not by wires but by radio. It can be used at distances up to about 100 m/330 ft from the base unit. In 1988 Japan and in 1990 Britain introduced an integrated services digital network, providing fast transfer of computerized information.

television the reproduction at a distance by radio waves of visual images.

history in 1873 it was realized that since the electrical properties of selenium vary according to the amount of light to which it is exposed, light could be converted into electrical impulses, making it possible to transmit such

TELEVISION CHRONOLOGY

1878	William Crookes in England invented the Crookes tube, which produced cathode rays.
1884	Paul Nipkow in Germany built a mechanical scanning device, the Nipkow disc, a rotating disc with a spiral pattern of holes in it.
1897	Karl Ferdinand Braun, also in Germany, modified the Crookes tube to produce the ancestor of the modern TV receiver picture tube.
1906	Boris Rosing in Russia began experimenting with the Nipkow disc and cathode-ray tube, eventually succeeding in transmitting some crude TV pictures.
1923	Vladimir Zworykin in the USA invented the first electronic camera tube.
1926	John Logie Baird demonstrated a workable TV system, using mechanical scanning by Nipkow disc.
1928	Baird demonstrated colour TV.
1929	The BBC began experimental broadcasting of TV programmes, using Baird's system.
1936	The BBC began regular broadcasting using Baird's system from Alexandra Palace, London.
1940	Experimental colour TV transmission began in the USA, using the modern system of colour reproduction.
1953	Successful colour TV transmissions began in the USA.
1956	The first videotape recorder was produced in California, USA by the Ampex Corporation.
1962	TV signals were transmitted across the Atlantic via the *Telstar* satellite.
1970	The first videodisc system was announced by Decca in the UK and by AEG–Telefunken in Germany, but it was not perfected until the 1980s, when laser scanning was used for playback.
1975	Sony introduced their videocassette tape-recorder system, Betamax, for domestic viewers, six years after their professional U-Matic system; the British Post Office (now British Telecom) announced their Prestel viewdata system.
1973	The BBC and Independent Television introduced the world's first teletext systems, Ceefax and Oracle, respectively.
1979	Matsushita in Japan developed a pocket-sized flat-screen TV set, using a liquid-crystal display (LCD).
1986	Data broadcasting using digital techniques was developed; an enhancement of teletext was produced.
1989	The Japanese began broadcasting high-definition television; satellite television was introduced in the UK.
1990	Independent Television introduced a digital stereo sound system (NICAM); MAC, a European system allowing greater picture definition, more data, and sound tracks, was introduced.
1992	All-digital high-definition television demonstrated in the USA.

impulses over a distance and then reconvert them into light. The chief difficulty was seen to be the 'splitting of the picture' so that the infinite variety of light and shade values might be transmitted and reproduced. In 1908 Alan Archibald Campbell Swinton pointed out that cathode-ray tubes would best effect transmission and reception. Mechanical devices were used at the first practical demonstration of actual television, given by John Logie Baird in London on 27 Jan 1926, and cathode-ray tubes were used experimentally by the BBC from 1934. The world's first public television service was started from the BBC station at the Alexandra Palace, in N London, on 2 Nov 1936.

technology for transmission, a television camera converts the pattern of light it receives into a pattern of electrical charges. This is scanned line-by-line by a beam of electrons from an electron gun, resulting in variable electrical signals that represent the visual picture. These vision signals are combined with a radio carrier wave and broadcast. The TV aerial picks up the wave and feeds it to the receiver (TV set). This separates out the vision signals, which pass to the picture tube (a cathode-ray tube). The broad end of the tube, upon which the scene is to appear, has its inside surface coated with a fluorescent material. The vision signals control the strength of a beam of electrons from an electron gun, aimed at the screen and making it glow more or less brightly. At the same time the beam is made to scan across the screen line-by-line, mirroring the action of the gun in the TV camera. The result is a re-creation spot-by-spot, line-by-line of the pattern of light that entered the camera. 25 pictures are built up each second with interlaced scanning (30 in USA), with a total of 625 lines (in Europe, but 525 lines in the USA and Japan).

colour television Baird gave a demonstration of colour television in London in 1928, but it was not until Dec 1953 that the first successful system was adopted for broadcasting, in the USA. This is called the NTSC system, since it was developed by the National Television System Committee, and variations of it have been developed in Europe—for example, the SECAM (sequential and memory) system in France and the PAL (phase alternation by line) in West Germany. All three differ only in the way colour signals are prepared for transmission. When there was no agreement on a universal European system 1964, in 1967 the UK, West Germany, the Netherlands, and Switzerland adopted PAL while France and the USSR adopted SECAM. In 1989 the European Community agreed to harmonize TV channels from 1991, allowing any station to show programmes anywhere in the EC.

The method of colour reproduction in television is related to that used in colour photography and printing. It uses the principle that any colours can be made by mixing the primary colours red, green, and blue in appropriate proportions. In colour television the receiver reproduces only three basic colours: red, green and blue. The effect of yellow, for example, is reproduced by combining equal amounts of red and green light, while white is formed by a mixture of all three basic colours. Signals indicate the amounts of red, green, and blue light to be generated at the receiver.

To transmit each of these three signals in the same way as the single-brightness signal in monochrome (black-and-white) television would need three times the normal bandwidth, and reduce the number of possible stations and programmes to one-third of that possible with monochrome television. The three signals are therefore coded into one complex signal, which is transmitted as a more-or-less normal black-and-white signal, and produces a satisfactory—or compatible—picture on ordinary black-and-white receivers. A fraction of each primary red, green, and blue signal is added together to produce the normal brightness, or luminance, signal. The minimum of extra colouring information is then sent by a special subcarrier signal, which is superimposed on the brightness signal. This extra colouring information corresponds to the hue and saturation of the transmitted colour, but without any of the fine detail of the picture. The impression of sharpness is conveyed only by the brightness signal, the colouring being added as a broad colour wash. The various colour systems differ only in the way in which the colouring information is sent on the subcarrier signal.

The colour receiver has to amplify the complex signal and decode it back to the basic red, green and blue signals; these primary signals are then applied to a colour cathode-ray tube. The colour display tube is the heart of any colour receiver. Many designs of colour picture tube have been invented; the most successful of these is known as the 'shadow mask tube'. It operates on similar electronic principles to the black-and-white television picture tube, but the screen is composed of a fine mosaic of over one million dots arranged in an orderly fashion. One-third of the dots glow red when bom-

barded by electrons, one-third glow green, and one-third blue. There are three sources of electrons, respectively modulated by the red, green, and blue signals. The tube is so arranged that the shadow mask allows only the red signals to hit red dots, the green signals to hit green dots, and the blue signals to hit blue dots. The glowing dots are so small that from a normal viewing distance the colours merge into one another and a picture with a full range of colours is seen.

high-definition television (HDTV) system offering a significantly greater number of scanning lines, and therefore a clearer picture, than the 625 lines (Europe) or 525 lines (USA and Japan) of established television systems. In 1989 the Japanese broadcasting station NHK and a consortium of manufacturers launched the Hi-Vision system, based on analogue technology, with 1125 lines and a wide-screen format. A European system, HD-MAC, which is partly digital, partly analogue, is under development. A fully digital system has been demonstrated in the USA.

TV channels in addition to transmissions received by all viewers, the 1970s and 1980s saw the growth of pay-television cable networks, which are received only by special subscribers, and of devices, such as those used in the Qube system (USA), which allow the viewers' opinions to be transmitted instantaneously to the studio via a response button, so that, for example, a home viewing audience can vote in a talent competition. The number of programme channels continues to increase, following the introduction of satellite television (in the UK, Sky Television 1989 and British Satellite Broadcasting 1990, which merged to form British Sky Broadcasting 1990).

Further use of the television set has been brought about by videotext and the use of video recorders to tape programmes for playback later or to play prerecorded videocassettes, and by their use as computer screens and for security systems. Extended-definition television gives a clear enlargement from a microscopic camera and was first used in 1989 in neurosurgery to enable medical students to watch brain operations.

video camera or **camcorder** portable television camera that takes moving pictures electronically on magnetic tape. It produces an electrical output signal corresponding to rapid line-by-line scanning of the field of view. The output is recorded on videotape and is played back on a television screen via a video tape recorder (VTR).

video disc disc with pictures (and sounds) recorded on it, played back by laser. It works in the same way as a compact disc. The video disc (originated by Baird 1928; commercially available from 1978) is chiefly used to provide commercial films for private viewing. Most systems use a 30 cm/12 in rotating vinyl disc coated with a reflective material. Laser scanning recovers picture and sound signals from the surface where they are recorded as a spiral of microscopic pits.

video tape recorder (VTR) device for recording visuals and sound on cassettes or spools of magnetic tape. The first commercial VTR was launched 1956 for the television broadcasting industry, but from the late 1970s cheaper models developed for home use—to record broadcast programmes for future viewing and to view rented or purchased video cassettes of commercial films. ,

Video recording works in the same way as audio tape recording: the picture information is stored as a line of varying magnetism, or track, on a plastic tape covered with magnetic material. The main difficulty—the huge amount of information needed to reproduce a picture—is overcome by arranging the video track diagonally across the tape. During recording, the tape is wrapped around a drum in a spiral fashion. The recording head rotates inside the drum. The combination of the forward motion of the tape and the rotation of the head produces a diagonal track. The audio signal accompanying the video signal is recorded as a separate track along the edge of the tape.

Two VTR systems were introduced by Japanese firms in the 1970s. The Sony Betamax was considered technically superior, but Matsushita's VHS (Video Home Service) had larger marketing resources behind it and after some years became the sole system on the market. Super-VHS is an improved version of the VHS system, launched 1989, with higher picture definition and colour quality.

videotext system in which information (text) is displayed on a television (video) screen. There are two basic systems, known as teletext and viewdata. In the teletext system information is broadcast with the ordinary television signals, whereas in viewdata information is relayed to the screen from a central data bank via the telephone network. Both systems require the use of a television receiver with special decoder.

ELECTRONICS

electronics the branch of science that deals with the emission of electrons from conductors and semiconductors, with the subsequent manipulation of these electrons, and with the construction of electronic devices. The first electronic device was the thermionic valve, or vacuum tube, in which electrons moved in a vacuum, and led to such inventions as radio, television, radar, and the digital computer. Replacement of valves with the comparatively tiny and reliable transistor in 1948 revolutionized electronic development. Modern electronic devices are based on minute integrated circuits (silicon chips), wafer-thin crystal slices holding tens of thousands of electronic components.

By using solid-state devices such as integrated circuits, extremely complex electronic circuits can be constructed, leading to the development of digital watches, pocket calculators, powerful microcomputers, and word processors.

electron stable, negatively charged elementary particle, a constituent of all atoms and the basic particle of electricity. A beam of electrons will undergo diffraction (scattering), and produce interference patterns, in the same way as electromagnetic waves such as light; hence they may also be regarded as waves.

integrated circuit popularly called *silicon chip* complete miniaturized electronic circuit produced on a single crystal, or chip, of a semiconducting material such as silicon. It may contain many thousands of transistors, resistors, and capacitors, and yet measure only 5 mm/0.2 in square and 1 mm/0.04 in thick.

The integrated circuit is encapsulated within a plastic or ceramic case, and linked via gold wires to metal pins with which it is connected to a printed circuit board and the other components that make up electronic devices such as computers and calculators. The discovery in

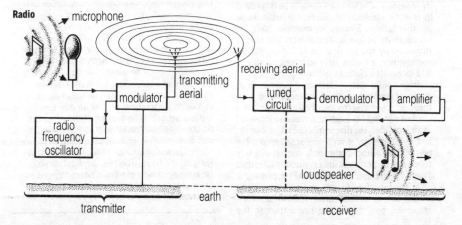

Radio
microphone
transmitting aerial
receiving aerial
modulator
tuned circuit
demodulator
amplifier
radio frequency oscillator
loudspeaker
earth
transmitter
receiver

ELECTRONICS: CHRONOLOGY

1897	Discovery of the electron by English physicist John Joseph Thomson.
1904	Diode valve, which allows flow of electricity in one direction only, invented by English physicist Ambrose Fleming.
1906	Triode electron valve, the first device to control an electric current, invented by US physicist Lee De Forest.
1947	John Bardeen, William Shockley, and Walter Brattain invented the junction germanium transistor at the Bell Laboratories, New Jersey, USA.
1952	British physicist G W A Dunner proposed the integrated circuit.
1953	Jay Forrester of the Massachusetts Institute of Technology, USA, built a magnetic memory smaller than existing vacuum-tube memories.
1954	Silicon transistor perfected by Gordon Teal of Texas Instruments, USA.
1958	The first integrated circuit, containing five components, built by US electrical physicist Jack Kilby.
1961	Steven Hofstein designed the field-effect transistor used in modern integrated circuits.
1971	The first microprocessor, the Intel 4004, designed by Ted Hoff in the USA; it contained 2,250 components and could add two four-bit numbers in 11-millionths of a second.
1974	The Intel 8080 microprocessor introduced; it contained 4,500 components and could add two eight-bit numbers in 2.5-millionths of a second.
1981	The Hewlett-Packard Superchip introduced; it contained 450,000 components and could multiply two 32-bit numbers in 1.8-millionths of a second.
1985	The Inmos T414 Transputer introduced, the first microprocessor designed for use in parallel computers.
1988	The first optical microchip, which uses light instead of electricity, was developed.
1989	Wafer-scale silicon memory chips introduced: the size of a beer mat, they are able to store 200 million characters.
1990	Memory chips capable of holding 4 million bits of information began to be mass-produced in Japan. The chips can store the equivalent of 520,000 characters, or the contents of a 16-page newspaper. Each chip contains 9 million components packed on a piece of silicon less than 15 mm long by 5 mm wide.

the early 1970s of the means to produce integrated circuits began the so-called computer revolution.

microprocessor a computer's central processing unit, contained on a single integrated circuit. The appearance of the first microprocessors 1971 heralded the introduction of the microcomputer. The microprocessor has led to a dramatic fall in the size and cost of computers and to the introduction of dedicated computers in washing machines, cars, and so on.

semiconductor crystalline material with an electrical conductivity between that of metals (good) and insulators (poor). The conductivity of semiconductors can usually be improved by minute additions of different substances or by other factors. Silicon, for example, has poor conductivity at low temperatures, but this is improved by the application of light, heat, or voltage; hence its use in transistors, rectifiers, and integrated circuits (silicon chips).

transistor solid-state electronic component made of semiconducting material and with three or more electrodes, that can regulate a current passing through it. A transistor can act as an amplifier, oscillator, photocell, or switch, and usually operates on a very small amount of power. Transistors commonly consist of a tiny sandwich of germanium or silicon, alternate layers having different electrical properties.

A crystal of pure germanium or silicon would act as an insulator (nonconductor). However, by introducing impurities in the form of atoms of other materials (for example, boron, arsenic, or indium) in minute amounts, the germanium and silicon layers may be made either *n-type*, having an excess of electrons, or *p-type*, having a deficiency of electrons. This enables electrons

---

THE SILICON CILIATE

Ciliates are micro-organisms that move themselves by rippling the hairs on their bodies in wavelike undulations. Scientists in Japan have been able to imitate nature by building tiny plastic hairs on a silicon chip. Using the standard production techniques for silicon chips, the scientists have produced arrays of tiny hairs, each about half a millimetre long, on a base of silicon. Each hair is made of two different types of plastic, with a thin metal wire sandwiched between. The hairs normally stand upright but, when a current flows in the wire, the hairs curl and lie flat. The hairs can be made to stand up and lie down ten times a second. The heating of the wires can be computer-controlled so that the hairs can curl and uncurl in unison, producing wave-like ripples powerful enough to move light objects lying on the hairs. The best application so far envisaged is to use the devices to position computer chips precisely, so that automatic tests can be done.

FIBRE OPTICS SET PULSES RACING

Recently British Telecom demonstrated a system capable of broadcasting 384 video channels to nearly 40 million potential viewers within an area 50 km/31 m in diameter. The system, called a broadcast network, uses optical fibres to transmit signals from a central station. This is just one of the developments possible using the latest optical-fibre technology. It should eventually be possible to integrate telephone, computer, and television into a total system giving businesses access to vast databases, enabling researchers to utilize supercomputers located thousands of kilometres away, and allowing home viewers to choose programmes from large video libraries without leaving their armchairs.

Light-wave technology has progressed rapidly, with five generations, or major stages of advance, since 1975. The first generation could carry far more information than earlier telephony systems using copper wires. These systems and the ones that followed consisted of a few basic components: encoders and decoders, a transmitter, a receiver, optical fibres, and repeaters. The encoder first converted a message into an electrical signal. The transmitter, which converted the signal into light, was a light-emitting diode that produced infrared radiation. The fibres were made of high-purity silica glass, so clear that you could see through a sheet 35 km/22 mi thick. Despite the purity of the glass, the light signal weakened as it propagated. This necessitated the use of amplifiers or repeaters along the line. Finally, the receiver converted the light into an electrical signal and the decoder reconstructed the message from the electrical signal.

The second generation allowed much more information to be transmitted along a line by reducing the size of the fibres, which greatly reduced the dispersion of the light signal, and by using wavelengths which were attenuated less by silica. The third generation developed around the laser diode chip, which could produce high-speed pulses of laser light at the wavelength at which silica glass is most transparent. The fourth generation consisted of systems relying on changes to the light's frequency rather than its intensity to carry information. By the end of the 1980s, it was apparent that these systems could only be improved by the development of better amplifiers.

The breakthrough was the development of the erbium-doped fibre amplifier. The main components are a laser diode and a length of optical fibre doped with small amounts of erbium. The laser powers the amplifier by providing infrared radiation which is absorbed by the erbium atoms in the fibre. When a light signal is sent down the fibre, these atoms release their extra energy, amplifying the signal. Research at Southampton University, England, and the AT&T Bell Laboratory in New Jersey demonstrated the practicality of the new amplifiers in the late 1980s. In early 1989, the Nippon Telegraph and Telephone (NTT) Research Laboratories near Tokyo produced a prototype communications link using erbium-doped fibre amplifiers interspersed between lengths of ordinary fibre. The system carried over 2 billion bits of information per second over a distance of 2 km/1.25 mi, a performance comparable with earlier fibre-optic systems.

The Japanese success started a race to extend the capabilities of the new technology. In the middle of 1989, both NTT and the Bell laboratories reported transmission rates of about 10 billion bits per second over distances of 150 km/94 mi. By the end of 1989, the world record was a transmission of 1.2 billion bits per second over the incredible distance of 904 km/562 mi. Then in early 1990, NTT sent 2.5 billion bits of information per second through 2,223 km/1,381 mi of fibre using erbium amplifiers, each 16 m/52 ft long, separated by 80 km/50 mi of standard optical fibre. Experimental systems at AT&T have since achieved even higher transmission rates: 2.4 billion bits per second over lines of 21,000 km/13,000 mi and 5 billion bits over 9,000 km/5,600 mi. AT&T plan to lay such cables across the Pacific Ocean, each cable carrying 500,000 simultaneous telephone calls.

The latest work promises to increase the transmission rate even further using pulses of light, called solitons, with special properties. Solitons are extremely short pulses—lasting about 10 trillionths of a second—which propagate along optical fibres without distortion. Each pulse or soliton can represent a bit of information, and transmission rates of at least 5 billion bits per second over distances of 10,000 km/6,200 mi should be possible. Furthermore, several soliton signals can be transmitted at once. This approach could bring the total transmission rate up to 50 billion bits per second. No other technology can compete with these rates.

to flow from one layer to another in one direction only. Transistors have had a great impact on the electronics industry, and are now made in thousands of millions each year. They perform many of the same functions as the thermionic valve, but have the advantages of greater reliability, long life, compactness, and instantaneous action, no warming-up period being necessary. They are widely used in most electronic equipment, including portable radios and televisions, computers, satellites, and space research, and are the basis of the integrated circuit (silicon chip). They were invented at Bell Telephone Laboratories in the USA in 1948 by John Bardeen and Walter Brittain, developing the work of William Shockley.

Transputer electronic device that increases the

computing power of a computer, launched 1985 by UK company Inmos. In the circuits of a standard computer the processing of data takes place in sequence. In a Transputer's circuits processing takes place in parallel, greatly reducing computing time for programs written specifically for the Transputer.

valve or ***electron tube*** a glass tube containing gas at low pressure, which is used to control the flow of electricity in a circuit. Three or more metal electrodes are inset into the tube By varying the voltage on one of them, called the grid electrode, the current through the valve can be controlled, and the valve can act as an amplifier. They have been replaced for most applications by transistors. However, they are still used in high-power transmitters and amplifiers, and in some hi-fi systems.

Science and technology influence most areas of life today. How well equipped do you feel you are to make sense of latest developments in, say, electronics and biotechnology?

Very well	7
Well	26
Neither	28
Badly	26
Very badly	29
Very badly	9
Don't know	4

Which, if any, of these branches of science and technology do you feel will most improve the quality of life for people in the long term?

Medical research	43
Environmental research	20
Alternative forms of energy	16
Agriculture/food research	11
Computers/information technology	4
Nuclear energy	1
Robotics/automation	1
Space exploration	1
None of these	4

We rely on modern technology every day of the week. Which of the following is the most important to you?

Telephones	27
Motor vehicles	20
Central heating	10
Televisions	10
Painkillers	9
Contraceptives	6
Cash cards	6
Frozen food	4
Answering machines	1
None of them/don't know	6

THE WORLD

LEADERS OF THE
MODERN WORLD

Adenauer Konrad 1876–1967. German Christian Democrat politician, chancellor of West Germany 1949–63. With the French president de Gaulle he achieved the postwar reconciliation of France and Germany and strongly supported all measures designed to strengthen the Western bloc in Europe.

Allende Gossens Salvador 1908–1973. Chilean Marxist politician, president from 1970 until his death during a military coup in 1973.

Amin Dada Idi 1926– Ugandan politician, president 1971–79. He led the coup that deposed Milton Obote 1971, expelled the Asian community 1972, and exercised a reign of terror over his people. He fled to Libya when insurgent Ugandan and Tanzanian troops invaded the country 1979.

Aquino (Maria) Corazón (born Cojuangco) 1933– . President of the Philippines 1986, when she was instrumental in the nonviolent overthrow of President Ferdinand Marcos. She sought to rule in a conciliatory manner, but encountered opposition from left (communist guerrillas) and right (army coup attempts), and her land reforms have been seen as inadequate. She did not contest the presidency in 1992 and was succeeded by her endorsed candidate, Fidel Ramos.

Arafat Yassir 1929– . Palestinian nationalist politician, cofounder of al-Fatah 1956 and president of the Palestine Liberation Organization (PLO) from 1969. In the 1970s his activities in pursuit of an independent homeland for Palestinians made him a prominent figure in world politics, but in the 1980s the growth of factions within the PLO effectively reduced his power. He was forced to evacuate Lebanon 1983, but remained leader of most of the PLO and in 1990 persuaded it to recognize formally the state of Israel. He supported Saddam Hussein's invasion of Kuwait 1990.

Attlee Clement (Richard), 1st Earl 1883–1967. British Labour politician. In the coalition government during World War II he was Lord Privy Seal 1940–42, dominions secretary 1942–43, and Lord President of the Council 1943–45, as well as deputy prime minister from 1942. As prime minister 1945–51 he introduced a sweeping programme of nationalization and a whole new system of social services.

Babangida Ibrahim 1941– . Nigerian politician and soldier, president from 1985. He became head of the Nigerian army in 1983 and in 1985 led a coup against President Buhari, assuming the presidency himself. Responding to calls for a return to civilian rule, in Jan 1992 he announced dates for assembly and presidential elections in Nov and Dec 1992.

Balfour Arthur James, 1st Earl of Balfour 1848–1930. British Conservative politician, prime minister 1902–05 and foreign secretary 1916–19, when he issued the Balfour Declaration 1917 and was involved in peace negotiations after World War I, signing the Treaty of Versailles.

Banda Hastings Kamuzu 1902– . Malawi politican, president from 1966. He led his country's independence movement and was prime minister of Nyasaland (the former name of Malawi) from 1963. He became Malawi's first president in 1966 and in 1971 was named president for life; his rule has been authoritarian. Despite civil unrest during 1992, he has resisted calls for free, multiparty elections.

Bandaranaike Sirimavo (born Ratwatte) 1916– . Sri Lankan politician, who succeeded her husband Solomon Bandaranaike to become the world's first female prime minister 1960–65 and 1970–77, but was expelled from parliament 1980 for abuse of her powers while in office. She was largely responsible for the new constitution 1972.

Bandaranaike Solomon West Ridgeway Dias 1899–1959. Sri Lankan nationalist politician. In 1951 he founded the Sri Lanka Freedom party and in 1956 became prime minister, pledged to a socialist programme and a neutral foreign policy. He failed to satisfy extremists and was assassinated by a Buddhist monk.

Begin Menachem 1913–1992. Israeli politician, born in Poland. He was a leader of the extremist Irgun Zvai Leumi organization in Palestine from 1942; was prime minister of Israel 1977–83, as head of the right-wing Likud party; and in 1978 shared a Nobel Peace Prize with President Sadat of Egypt for work on the Camp David Agreements for a Middle East peace settlement. (See *Obituaries* for more.)

Ben Bella Ahmed 1916– . Algerian leader of the National Liberation Front (FLN) from 1952; prime minister of independent Algeria 1962–65, when he was overthrown by Boumédienne and detained until 1980. He founded a new party, Mouvement pour la Démocratie en Algérie, in 1985. In 1990 he returned to Algeria.

Beneš Eduard 1884–1948. Czechoslovak politician. He worked with Thomas Masaryk towards Czechoslavak nationalism from 1918 and was foreign minister and representative at the League of Nations. He was president of the republic from 1935 until forced to resign by the Germans; he headed a government in exile in London during World War II. He returned home as president 1945 but resigned again after the Communist coup 1948.

Ben-Gurion David. Adopted name of David Gruen 1886–1973. Israeli statesman and socialist politician, one of the founders of the state of Israel, the country's first prime minister 1948–53, and again 1955–63.

Bérégovoy Pierre 1925– . French socialist politician and prime minister from 1992. A longstanding Mitterand ally and a former wartime resistance fighter, he was a successful finance minister before replacing Edith Cresson as prime minister April 1992.

Bevan Aneurin 1897–1960. British Labour politician. Son of a Welsh miner, and himself a miner at 13, he became member of Parliament for Ebbw Vale 1929–60. As minister of health 1945–51, he inaugurated the National Health Service (NHS); he was minister of labour Jan–April 1951, when he resigned (with Harold Wilson) on the introduction of NHS charges and led a Bevanite faction against the government. In 1956 he became chief labour spokesman on foreign affairs, and deputy leader of the Labour party 1959. He was a good speaker.

Bevin Ernest 1881–1951. British Labour politician. Chief creator of the Transport and General Workers' Union, he was its general secretary from 1921 to 1940, when he entered the war cabinet as minister of labour and National Service. He organized the 'Bevin boys', chosen by ballot to work in the coal mines as war service, and was foreign secretary in the Labour government 1945–51.

Bhutto Benazir 1953– . Pakistani politician, leader of the Pakistan People's Party (PPP) from 1984 (in exile until 1986), and prime minister of Pakistan 1988–90, when the opposition manoeuvred her from office and charged her with corruption. She was the first female leader of a Muslim state.

Bhutto Zulfikar Ali 1928–1979. Pakistani politician, president 1971–73; prime minister from 1973 until the 1977 military coup led by General Zia ul Haq. In 1978 he was sentenced to death for conspiring to murder a political opponent and was hanged the following year.

Bildt Carl 1949– . Swedish conservative politician, leader of the Moderate Party, and prime minister from 1991. He took office at the head of what he called a 'bourgeois coalition', pledging to break the pattern of economic stagnation, to undertake a major policy of deregulation, and to negotiate membership in the European Community.

Bokassa Jean-Bédel 1921– . President and later self-proclaimed emperor of the Central African Republic 1966–79. Commander in chief from 1963, in Dec 1965 he led the military coup that gave him the presidency. On 4 Dec 1976 he proclaimed the Central African Empire and one year later crowned himself as emperor for life. His regime was characterized by arbitrary state violence and cruelty. Overthrown in 1979, Bokassa was in exile until 1986. Upon his return he was sentenced to death, but this was commuted to life imprisonment 1988.

Bolger Jim (James) Brendan 1935– . New Zealand politician and prime minister. A successful sheep and cattle farmer, Bolger was elected as a member of Parliament 1972. He held a variety of cabinet posts under Robert Muldoon's leadership 1977–84, and was an effective, if uncharismatic leader of the opposition from March 1986, leading the National Party to electoral victory Oct 1990.

As prime minister he enjoyed a brief honeymoon period but his failure to honour election pledges, leading to cuts in welfare provision, resulted in a sharp fall in his and his party's popularity.

Botha P(ieter) W(illem) 1916– . South African politician. Prime minister from 1978, he initiated a modification of apartheid, which later slowed in the face of Afrikaner (Boer) opposition. In 1984 he became the first executive state president. In 1989 he unwillingly resigned both party leadership and presidency after suffering a stroke, and was succeeded by F W de Klerk.

Boumédienne Houari. Adopted name of Mohammed Boukharouba 1925–1978. Algerian politician who brought the nationalist leader Ben Bella to power by a revolt 1962, and superseded him as president in 1965 by a further coup.

Boutros Ghali Boutros 1923– . Egyptian diplomat and politician, deputy prime minister 1991–92, United Nations secretary general from 1992. He worked towards peace in the Middle East in the foreign ministry posts he held 1977–91, and established his reputation as a key negotiator in the 1978 Camp David talks between Egypt and Israel.

Brandt Willy. Adopted name of Karl Herbert Frahm 1913– . West German socialist politician, federal chancellor (premier) 1969–74. He played a key role in the remoulding of the Social Democratic Party (SPD) as a moderate socialist force (leader 1964–87). As mayor of West Berlin 1957–66, Brandt became internationally known during the Berlin Wall crisis 1961. He received the Nobel Peace Prize 1971.

Brezhnev Leonid Ilyich 1906–1982. Soviet leader. A protégé of Stalin and Khrushchev, he came to power (after he and Kosygin forced Khrushchev to resign) as general secretary of the Soviet Communist Party (CPSU) 1964–82 and was president 1977–82. Domestically he was conservative; abroad the USSR was established as a military and political superpower during the Brezhnev era, extending its influence in Africa and Asia.

Brundtland Gro Harlem 1939– . Norwegian Labour politician. Environment minister 1974–76, she briefly took over as prime minister 1981, and was elected prime minister in 1986 and again in 1990. She chaired the World Commission on Environment and Development which produced the *Brundtland Report* 1987.

Bush George 1924– . 41st president of the USA from 1989, a Republican. He was director of the Central Intelligence Agency (CIA) 1976–81 and US vice president 1981–89. He faced economic recession in the USA and was the driving force behind international opposition to Iraq's invasion of Kuwait 1990. Evidence came to light in 1987 linking him with the Irangate scandal. His responses as president to the Soviet leader Gorbachev's diplomatic initiatives were initially criticized as inadequate, but sending US troops to depose his former ally, General Noriega of Panama, proved a popular move at home. Success in the 1991 Gulf War against Iraq temporarily raised his standing; but his failure to tackle domestic problems lowered his popularity ratings in the run-up to the 1992 presidential election.

Buthelezi Chief Gatsha 1928– . Zulu leader and politician, chief minister of KwaZulu, a black 'homeland' in the Republic of South Africa from 1970. He is founder and president of Inkatha 1975, a paramilitary organization for attaining a nonracial democratic political system. As constitutional talks between the government and representatives of the black community proceeded, he was strongly criticized by ANC leaders for his alleged complicity in the killing of ANC supporters by members of Inkatha and the security services.

Callaghan (Leonard) James, Baron Callaghan 1912– . British Labour politician. As chancellor of the Exchequer 1964–67, he introduced corporation and capital-gains taxes, and resigned following devaluation. He was home secretary 1967–70 and prime minister 1976–79 in a period of increasing economic stress.

Carlsson Ingvar (Gösta) 1934– . Swedish socialist politician, leader of the Social Democratic Party, deputy prime minister 1982–86 and prime minister 1986–91. His party was defeated in the Sept 1991 general elections; he was succeeded by Moderate Party leader Carl Bildt.

Carter Jimmy (James Earl) 1924– . the 39th president of the USA 1977–81, a Democrat. In 1976 he narrowly wrested the presidency from Gerald Ford. Features of his presidency were the return of the Panama Canal Zone to Panama, the Camp David Agreements for peace in the Middle East, and the Iranian seizure of US embassy hostages. He was defeated by Ronald Reagan 1980.

Castro (Ruz) Fidel 1927– . Cuban Communist politician, prime minister 1959–76 and president from 1976. He led two unsuccessful coups against the right-wing Batista regime and led the revolution that overthrew the dictator 1959. From 1979 he was also president of the nonaligned movement, although promoting the line of the USSR, which subsidized his regime. The demise of the Soviet Union left him as one of the last few remaining communist leaders in the world.

Cavaco Silva Anibal 1939– . Portuguese politician, finance minister 1980–81, and prime minister and Social Democratic Party (PSD) leader from 1985. Under his leadership Portugal joined the European Community 1985 and the Western European Union 1988. He was re-elected in the 1991 elections.

Ceaușescu Nicolae 1918–1989. Romanian politician, leader of the Romanian Communist Party (RCP), in power 1965–89. He pursued a policy line independent of and critical of the USSR. He appointed family members, including his wife *Elena Ceaușescu*, to senior state and party posts, and governed in an increasingly repressive manner, zealously implementing schemes that impoverished the nation. The Ceaușescus were overthrown in a bloody revolutionary coup Dec 1989 and executed.

Chamberlain (Arthur) Neville 1869–1940. British Conservative politician, son of Joseph Chamberlain. He was prime minister 1937–40; his policy of appeasement towards the fascist dictators Mussolini and Hitler (with whom he concluded the Munich Agreement 1938) failed to prevent the outbreak of World War II. He resigned 1940 following the defeat of the British forces in Norway.

Chiang Kai-shek Pinyin *Jiang Jie Shi* 1887–1975. Chinese Nationalist Guomindang (Kuomintang) general and politician, president of China 1928–31 and 1943–49, and of Taiwan from 1949, where he set up a US-supported right-wing government on his expulsion from the mainland by the Communist forces. He was a commander in the civil war that lasted from the end of imperial rule 1911 to the Second Sino-Japanese War and beyond, having split with the Communist leader Mao Zedong 1927.

Chirac Jacques 1932– . French conservative politician, prime minister 1974–76 and 1986–88. He established the neo-Gaullist Rassemblement pour la République (RPR) 1976, and became mayor of Paris 1977.

Chissano Joaquim 1939– . Mozambique nationalist politician, president from 1986; foreign minister 1975–86.

Churchill Winston (Leonard Spencer) 1874–1965. British Conservative politician. In Parliament from 1900, as a Liberal until 1923, he held a number of ministerial offices, including First Lord of the Admiralty 1911–15 and chancellor of the Exchequer 1924–29. Absent from the cabinet in the 1930s, he returned Sept 1939 to lead a coalition government 1940–45, negotiating with Allied leaders in World War II; he was again prime minister 1951–55. Nobel Prize for Literature 1953.

Collor de Mello Fernando 1949– . Brazilian politician and president from 1990. He was little known in national politics until the presidential campaign of 1989, which he conducted on a platform of abolishing government corruption and entrenched privileges. After two years in office he was criticized for past wrongdoings but denied the allegations and resisted calls for his resignation.

Craxi Bettino 1934– . Italian socialist politician, leader of the Italian Socialist Party (PSI) from 1976, prime minister 1983–87.

Cresson Edith 1934– . French politician and founder member of the Socialist Party, prime minister 1991–92. Cresson held successive ministerial portfolios in François Mitterrand's government 1981–86 and 1988–90. Her government was troubled by a struggling economy, a series of strikes, and unrest in many of the country's poor suburban areas, which eventually forced her resignation; she was replaced as prime minister April 1992 by Pierre Bérégovoy.

Dalai Lama 14th incarnation 1935– . Spiritual and temporal head of the Tibetan state until 1959, when he went into exile in protest against Chinese annexation and oppression. He settled at Dharmsala in the Punjab, India, and his people continue to demand his return. He was awarded the Nobel Peace Prize 1989 in recognition of his commitment to the nonviolent liberation of his homeland.

Tibetan Buddhists believe that each Dalai Lama is a reincarnation of his predecessor and also of Avalokiteśvara.

de Gaulle Charles André Joseph Marie 1890–1970. French general and first president of the Fifth Republic 1959–69. He organized the Free French troops fighting the Nazis 1940–44, was head of the provisional French government 1944–46, and leader of his own Gaullist party. In 1958 the national assembly asked him to form a government during France's economic recovery and to solve the crisis in Algeria. He became president at the end of 1958, having changed the constitution to provide for a presidential system, and served until 1969.

de Klerk F(rederik) W(illem) 1936– . South African National Party politician, president from 1989. Trained as a lawyer, he entered the South African parliament in 1972. He served in the cabinets of B J Vorster and P W Botha 1978–89, and in Feb and Aug 1989 successively replaced Botha as National Party leader and state president. Projecting himself as a pragmatic conservative who sought gradual reform of the apartheid system, he won the Sept 1989 elections for his party, but with a reduced majority. In Feb 1990 he ended the ban on the African National Congress opposition movement and released its effective leader, Nelson Mandela, and in 1991 promised the end of all apartheid legislation. During the prolonged constitutional talks his relations with the black community and the ANC leadership fluctuated greatly, with allegations of duplicity and procrastination levelled against him.

Delors Jacques 1925– . French socialist politician, finance minister 1981–84. As president of the European Commission from 1984 he has overseen significant budgetary reform and the move towards a free European Community market in 1993, with increased powers residing in Brussels. The refusal of the Danish people to ratify the Maastricht treaty in June 1992 came as a shock, but he accepted the opportunity of extending his term of office for another two years.

Deng Xiaoping or *Teng Hsiao-ping* 1904– . Chinese political leader. A member of the Chinese Communist Party (CCP) from the 1920s, he took part in the Long March 1934–36. He was in the Politburo from 1955 until ousted in the Cultural Revolution 1966–69. Reinstated in the 1970s, he gradually took power and introduced a radical economic modernization programme. He retired from the Politburo in 1987 and from his last official position (as chair of State Military Commission) Mar 1990, but remained influential behind the scenes.

Diouf Abdou 1935– . Senegalese politician, president from 1980. He became prime minister 1970 under President Leopold Senghor and, on his retirement, succeeded him, being re-elected in 1983 and 1988.

Douglas-Home Alec, Baron Home of the Hirsel 1903– . British Conservative politician. He was foreign secretary 1960-63, and succeeded Harold Macmillan as prime minister 1963. He renounced his peerage (as 14th Earl of Home) to fight (and lose) the general election 1963, and resigned as party leader 1965. He was again foreign secretary 1970-74, when he received a life peerage. His brother is the playwright William Douglas Home.

Dubček Alexander 1921– . Czechoslovak politician, chair of the federal assembly from 1989. He was a member of the resistance movement during World War II, and became first secretary of the Communist Party 1967–69. He launched a liberalization campaign (called the Prague Spring) that was opposed by the USSR and led to the Soviet invasion of Czechoslovakia in 1968. He was arrested by Soviet troops and expelled from the party 1970.

In 1989 he gave speeches at pro-democracy rallies, and in Dec, after the fall of the hardline regime, he was elected speaker of the National Assembly in Prague.

Duvalier François 1907–1971. Right-wing president of Haiti 1957–71. Known as *Papa Doc*, he ruled as a dictator, organizing the Tontons Macoutes ('bogeymen') as a private security force to intimidate and assassinate opponents of his regime. He rigged the 1961 elections in order to have his term of office extended until 1967, and in 1964 declared himself president for life. He was excommunicated by the Vatican for harassing the church, and was succeeded on his death by his son Jean-Claude Duvalier.

Duvalier Jean-Claude 1951– . Right-wing president of Haiti 1971–86. Known as *Baby Doc*, he succeeded his father François Duvalier, becoming, at the age of 19, the youngest president in the world. He continued to receive support from the USA but was pressured into moderating some elements of his father's regime, yet still tolerated no opposition. In 1986, with Haiti's economy stagnating and with increasing civil disorder, Duvalier fled to France, taking much of the Haitian treasury with him.

Eden Anthony, 1st Earl of Avon 1897–1977. British Conservative politician, foreign secretary 1935–38, 1940–45, and 1951–55; prime minister 1955–57, when he resigned after the failure of the Anglo-French military intervention in the Suez Crisis.

Eisenhower Dwight David ('Ike') 1890–1969. the 34th president of the USA 1953–60, a Republican. A general in World War II, he commanded the Allied forces in Italy 1943, then the Allied invasion of Europe, and from Oct 1944 all the Allied armies in the West. As president he promoted business interests at home and conducted the Cold War abroad. His vice president was Richard Nixon.

Ershad Hussain Mohammad 1930– . Military ruler of Bangladesh 1982–90. He became chief of staff of the Bangladeshi army 1979 and assumed power in a military coup 1982. As president from 1983, Ershad introduced a successful rural-oriented economic programme. He was re-elected 1986 and lifted martial law, but faced continuing political opposition, which forced him to resign in Dec 1990. In Jan 1991 he was formally charged with corruption in connection with alleged misappropriation of arms contract funds, and placed on trial.

Farouk 1920–1965. King of Egypt 1936–52. He succeeded his father Fuad I. In 1952 a coup headed by General Muhammed Neguib and Colonel Gamal Nasser compelled him to abdicate, and his son Fuad II was temporarily proclaimed in his place.

Franco Francisco (Paulino Hermenegildo Teódulo Bahamonde) 1892–1975. Spanish dictator from 1939. As a general, he led the insurgent Nationalists to victory in the Spanish Civil War 1936–39, supported by Fascist Italy and Nazi Germany, and established a dictatorship. In 1942 Franco reinstated the Cortes (Spanish parliament), which in 1947 passed an act by which he became head of state for life.

Gandhi Indira (born Nehru) 1917–1984. Indian politician. Prime minister of India 1966–77 and 1980–84, and leader of the Congress Party 1966–77 and subsequently of the Congress (I) party. She was assassinated 1984 by members of her Sikh bodyguard, resentful of her use of troops to clear malcontents from the Sikh temple at Amritsar.

Gandhi Mohandas Karamchand, called *Mahatma* ('Great Soul') 1869–1948. Indian Nationalist leader. A pacifist, he led the struggle for Indian independence from the UK by advocating nonviolent noncooperation (*satyagraha*, defence of and by truth) from 1915. He was imprisoned several times by the British authorities and was influential in the Nationalist Congress Party and in the independence negotiations 1947. He was assassinated by a Hindu nationalist in the violence that followed the partition of British India into India and Pakistan.

Gandhi Rajiv 1944–1991. Indian politician, prime minister from 1984, following his mother Indira Gandhi's assassination, to Nov 1989. As prime minister, he faced growing discontent with his party's elitism and lack of concern for social issues. He was assassinated by a bomb at an election rally, for which the Tamil Tigers were responsible.

García Perez Alan 1949– . Peruvian politician, leader of the moderate, left-wing APRA party; president 1985–90.

Geingob Hage Gottfried 1941– . Namibian politician and prime minister. He played a major role in the South West Africa's People's Organization (SWAPO), acting as a petitioner to the United Nations 1964–71, to obtain international recognition for SWAPO. He was appointed founding director of the United Nations Institute for Namibia in Lusaka, 1975. Geingob became first prime minister of an independent Namibia March 1990.

Giscard d'Estaing Valéry 1926– . French conservative politician, president 1974–81. He was finance minister to de Gaulle 1962–66 and Pompidou 1969–74. As leader of the Union pour la Démocratie Française, which he formed in 1978, Giscard sought to project himself as leader of a 'new centre'. In recent years he has become more active and influential in the European Parliament.

Goh Chok Tong 1941– . Singapore politician, prime minister from 1990. A trained economist, Goh became a member of Parliament for the ruling People's Action Party 1976. Rising steadily through the party ranks, he was appointed deputy prime minister 1985, and subsequently chosen by the cabinet as Lee Kuan Yew's successor.

González Márquez Felipe 1942– . Spanish socialist politician, leader of the Socialist Workers' Party (PSOE), prime minister from 1982.

Gorbachev Mikhail Sergeyevich 1931– . Soviet president, in power from 1985 to 1991. As general secretary of the Communist Party (CPSU) from 1985, and president of the Supreme Soviet from 1988, he introduced liberal reforms at home and an opening up to the west (*perestroika* and *glasnost*), and attempted to halt the arms race abroad. He became head of state 1989 and in March 1990 he was formally elected to a five-year term as executive president with greater powers. At home, his plans for economic reform at home failed to avert a food crisis in the winter of 1990–91 and his desire to preserve a single, centrally controlled USSR met with resistance from Soviet republics seeking greater autonomy. He was awarded the Nobel Peace Prize 1990, but his international reputation suffered in the light of the harsh repression of nationalist demonstrations in the Baltic states early in 1991. An attempted coup by communist hardliners 19–21 Aug weakened his authority and strengthened that of the Russian president, Boris Yeltsin. On 23 Aug Gorbachev resigned as general secretary of the Communist Party, and on 25 Dec as president of the Soviet Union.

Havel Vaclav 1936– . Czech playwright and a leader of Civic Forum movement. As a playwright in Prague, his works, which criticised the Communist regime, were banned throughout Eastern Europe from 1968 and he was subsequently imprisoned or placed under house arrest. In 1988 he founded a monthly dissident publication, the *People's Newspaper*.

In 1989, he became a presidential candidate after the resignation of the communist Gustav Husak. Following the overthrow of the communist regime, he was elected state president by the federal assembly Dec 1989. In 1992 he failed to win re-election as president, but remained head of state pending a formal split of Czechoslovakia.

Hawke Bob (Robert) 1929– . Australian Labor politician, on the right wing of the party. He was president of the Australian Council of Trade Unions 1970–80 and prime minister 1983–91. He was deposed as prime minister in Dec 1991 by his parliamentary colleagues and replaced by Paul Keating.

Heath Edward (Richard George) 1916– . British Conservative politician, party leader 1965–75. As prime minister 1970–74 he took the UK into the European Community but was brought down by economic and industrial relations crises at home. In 1990 he undertook a mission to Iraq in an attempt to secure the release of British hostages. Declining a peerage to which, as a former prime minister, he would have been entitled, he remained in the House of Commons and in 1992 was awarded the Order of the Garter.

Hitler Adolf 1889–1945. German Nazi dictator, born in Austria. Führer (leader) of the Nazi party from 1921, author of *Mein Kampf/My Struggle* 1925–27. As chancellor of Germany from 1933 and head of state from 1934, he created a dictatorship by playing party and state institutions against each other, creating new offices and appointments, and continually creating new offices and appointments. After Hitler became chancellor, the Nazis built approximately 5,000 concentration camps to imprison ideological and political opponents and those considered 'misfits' of the Aryan state; over 6 million people, mostly Jews, died in the camps.

His position was not seriously challenged until the 'Bomb Plot' 20 July 1944 to assassinate him. In foreign affairs, he reoccupied the Rhineland and formed an alliance with the fascist dictator Mussolini 1936, annexed Austria 1938, and occupied the Sudetenland under the Munich Agreement. The rest of Czechoslovakia was annexed March 1939. The Hitler–Stalin pact was followed in Sept by the invasion of Poland, bringing Britain and France into the war. He committed suicide as Berlin fell to the Allies at the end of World War II.

Ho Chi Minh adopted name of Nguyen That Tan 1890–1969. North Vietnamese Communist politician, premier and president 1954–69. Having trained in Moscow shortly after the Russian Revolution, he headed the communist Vietminh from 1941 and fought against the French during the Indochina War 1946–54, becoming president and prime minister of the republic at the armistice. Aided by the Communist bloc, he did much to develop industrial potential. He relinquished the premiership 1955, but continued as president. In the years before his death, Ho successfully led his country's fight against US-aided South Vietnam in the Vietnam War 1954–75.

Honecker Erich 1912– . German communist politician, in power 1973–89, elected chair of the council of state (head of state) 1976.

He governed in an outwardly austere and efficient manner and, while favouring East–West détente, was a loyal ally of the USSR. In Oct 1989, following a wave of pro-democracy demonstrations, he was replaced as leader of the Socialist Unity Party (SED) and head of state by Egon Krenz, and in Dec expelled from the Communist Party.

Hoxha Enver 1908–1985. Albanian Communist politician, the country's leader from 1954. He founded the Albanian Communist Party 1941, and headed the liberation movement 1939–44. He was prime minister 1944–54, combining with foreign affairs 1946–53, and from 1954 was first secretary of the Albanian Party of Labour. In policy he was a Stalinist and independent of both Chinese and Soviet communism.

Hun Sen 1950– . Cambodian political leader, prime minister from 1985. Originally a member of the Khmer Rouge army, he defected in 1977 to join Vietnam-based anti-Khmer Cambodian forces.

Hussein Saddam 1937– . Iraqi left-wing politician, in power from 1968, president from 1979. Ruthless in the pursuit of his objectives, he fought a bitter war against Iran 1980–88 and dealt harshly with Kurdish rebels seeking a degree of independence, using chemical weapons against civilian populations. In 1990 he ordered the invasion and annexation of Kuwait, provoking an international crisis and a United Nations embargo, followed by military reprisal. Iraq's defeat in the Gulf War by a UN coalition undermined his position as the country's leader; when the Kurds rebelled again, following the end of the Gulf War, he sent the remainder of his army to crush them, bringing international charges of genocide against him and causing hundreds of thousands of Kurds to flee their homes in northern Iraq.

Iliescu Ion 1930– . Romanian president. Iliescu was elected a member of the Romanian Communist Party (PCR) central committee 1968, becoming its propaganda secretary 1971. Conflict over the launching of a 'cultural revolution', and the growth of Nicolae Ceaușescu's personality cult led to Iliescu's removal from national politics: he was sent to Timișoara as chief of party propaganda. At the outbreak of the 'Christmas revolution' 1989, Iliescu was one of the first leaders to emerge, heading the National Salvation Front (NSF), and becoming president of the Provisional Council of National Unity Feb 1990. He won an overwhelming victory in the presidential elections in May, despite earlier controversy over his hard line.

Jaruzelski Wojciech 1923– . Polish general, communist leader from 1981, president from 1985. He imposed martial law for the first year of his rule, suppressed the opposition, and banned trade-union activity, but later released many political prisoners. In 1989, elections in favour of the free trade union Solidarity forced Jaruzelski to speed up democratic reforms, overseeing a transition to a new form of 'socialist pluralist' democracy, stepping down as president 1990.

Jayawardene Junius Richard 1906– . Sri Lankan politician. Leader of the United Nationalist Party from 1973, he became prime minister 1977 and the country's first president 1978–88.

Jiang Zemin 1926– . Chinese political leader. The son-in-law of Li Xiannian, he joined the Chinese Communist Party's politburo in 1987 after serving in the Moscow embassy and as mayor of Shanghai. He succeeded Zhao Ziyang as party leader after the Tiananmen Square massacre of 1989. A cautious proponent of economic reform coupled with unswerving adherence to the party's 'political line', he subsequently replaced Deng Xiaoping as head of the influential central military commission.

Jinnah Muhammad Ali 1876–1948. Indian politician, Pakistan's first governor general from 1947. He was president of the Muslim League from 1934, and by 1940 was advocating the need for a separate state of Pakistan; at the 1946 conferences in London he insisted on the partition of British India into Hindu and Muslim states.

Johnson Lyndon Baines 1908–1973. the 36th president of the USA 1963–69, a Democrat. He was born in Stonewall, Texas, elected to Congress 1937–49 and the Senate 1949–60. His persuasive powers and hard work on domestic issues led J F Kennedy to ask him to be his vice presidential running mate 1960; Johnson brought critical Southern support which won a narrow victory. He assumed the presidency upon the assassination of J F Kennedy.

Kádár János 1912–1989. Hungarian Communist leader, in power 1956–88, after suppressing the national uprising. As Hungarian Socialist Workers' Party (HSWP) leader and prime minister 1956–58 and 1961–65, Kádár introduced a series of market-socialist economic reforms, while retaining cordial political relations with the USSR.

Kaifu Toshiki 1932– . Japanese conservative politician, prime minister 1989–91. A protégé of former premier Takeo Miki, he was selected as a compromise choice as Liberal Democratic Party (LDP) president and prime minister in Aug 1989, following the resignation of Sosuke Uno. Having lost the support of important factional leaders in the LDP, Kaifu declined to seek re-election as party leader in Oct 1991. Kiichi Miyazawa was elected party leader, and took office as Kaifu's successor Nov 1991.

Kaunda Kenneth (David) 1924– . Zambian politician. Imprisoned in 1958–60 as founder of the Zambia African National Congress, he became in 1964 first prime minister of Northern Rhodesia, then first president of Zambia. In 1973 he introduced one-party rule. He supported the nationalist movement in Southern Rhodesia, now Zimbabwe, and survived a coup attempt 1980 thought to have been promoted by South Africa. He was elected chair of the Organization of African Unity 1987. In 1990 his popularity fell and he was faced with wide anti-government demonstrations, leading to the acceptance of a multiparty political system. Kaunda was defeated in elections held Oct 1991 by union leader Frederick Chiluba.

Keating Paul 1954– . Australian politician, Labor Party (ALP) leader and prime minister from 1991. He was treasurer and deputy leader of the ALP 1983–91, and also held several posts in Labor's shadow ministry 1976–83. As finance minister 1983–91 under Bob Hawke, Keating was unpopular with the public for his harsh economic policies. He successfully challenged Hawke for the ALP party leadership Dec 1991.

Kennedy John F(itzgerald) 1917–1963. 35th president of the USA 1961–63, a Democrat. Kennedy was the first Roman Catholic and the youngest person to be elected president. In foreign policy he carried through the unsuccessful Bay of Pigs invasion of Cuba, and in 1963 secured the withdrawal of Soviet missiles from the island. His programme for reforms at home, called the *New Frontier*, was posthumously executed by Lyndon Johnson. Kennedy was assassinated while on a state visit to Dallas, Texas, on 22 Nov 1963 by Lee Harvey Oswald (1939–1963), who was in turn shot dead by Jack Ruby.

Kenyatta Jomo. Assumed name of Kamau Ngengi c. 1894–1978. Kenyan nationalist politician, prime minister from 1963, as well as first president of Kenya from 1964 until his death. He led the Kenya African Union from 1947 (*KANU* from 1963) and was active in liberating Kenya from British rule.

Khaddhafi or *Gaddafi* or *Qaddafi*, Moamer al 1942– . Libyan revolutionary leader. Overthrowing King Idris 1969, he became virtual president of a republic, although he nominally gave up all except an ideological role 1974. He favours territorial expansion in N Africa reaching as far as Zaire, has supported rebels in Chad, and proposed mergers with a number of countries. His theories, based on those of the Chinese communist leader Mao Zedong, are contained in a *Green Book*. After the Gulf War, he made major efforts to improve relations with the West.

Khomeini Ayatollah Ruhollah 1900–1989. Iranian Shi'ite Muslim leader, born in Khomein, central Iran. Exiled for opposition to the Shah from 1964, he returned when the Shah left the country 1979, and established a fundamentalist Islamic republic. His rule was marked by a protracted war with Iraq, and suppression of opposition within Iran, executing thousands of opponents.

Khrushchev Nikita Sergeyevich 1894–1971. Soviet politician, secretary general of the Communist Party 1953–64, premier 1958–64. He emerged as leader from the power struggle following Stalin's death and was the first official to denounce Stalin, in 1956. His destalinization programme gave rise to revolts in Poland and Hungary 1956. Because of problems with the economy and foreign affairs (a breach with China 1960; conflict with the USA in the Cuban missile crisis 1962), he was ousted by Leonid Breszhnev and Alexei Kosygin.

Kim Il Sung 1912– . North Korean Communist politician and marshal. He became prime minister 1948 and president 1972, retaining the presidency of the Communist Workers' party. He likes to be known as the 'Great Leader' and has campaigned constantly for the reunification of Korea. His son *Kim Jong Il* (1942–), known as the 'Dear Leader', has been named as his successor.

King Martin Luther Jr 1929–1968. US civil-rights campaigner, black leader, and Baptist minister. He first came to national attention as leader of the Montgomery, Alabama bus boycott 1955, and was one of the organizers of the massive (200,000 people) march on Washington DC 1963 to demand racial equality. An advocate of nonviolence, he was awarded the Nobel Peace Prize 1964. He was assassinated in Memphis, Tennessee by James Earl Ray. King's birthday (15 Jan) is observed on the third Monday in Jan as a public holiday in the USA.

Kohl Helmut 1930– . German conservative politician, leader of the Christian Democratic Union (CDU) from 1976, West German chancellor 1982–90 and chancellor of the newly united Germany from 1990. His miscalculation of the true costs of reunification and their subsequent effects on the German economy led to a dramatic fall in his popular esteem.

Kravchuk Leonid 1934– . Ukrainian politician, president from 1991. Formerly a member of the Ukrainian Communist Party (UCP), he became its ideology chief in the 1980s. After the suspension of the UCP Aug 1991, Kravchuk became an advocate of independence and market-centred economic reform, and was popularly elected president Dec 1991, at the same time as a referendum voted overwhelmingly in favour of independence from the USSR.

Landsbergis Vyutautus 1932– . Lithuanian politician and president from 1990. He became active in nationalist politics in the 1980s, founding and eventually chairing the anticommunist Sajudis independence movement 1988. When Sajudis swept to victory in the republic's elections March 1990, Landsbergis chaired the Supreme Council of Lithuania, becoming, in effect, president. He immediately drafted the republic's declaration of independence from the USSR which, after initial Soviet resistance, was recognized Sept 1991. He is also a musicologist, specializing in 19th-and 20th-century Lithuanian music, and taught at the Vilnius Conservatoire before coming to power.

Lange David (Russell) 1942– . New Zealand Labour Party prime minister 1983–89. Lange, a barrister, was elected to the House of Representatives in 1977. Labour had a decisive win in the 1984 general election on a non-nuclear military policy, which Lange immediately put into effect, despite criticism from the USA. He introduced a free-market economic policy and

was re-elected 1987. He resigned Aug 1989 over a disagreement with his finance minister.

Lee Kuan Yew 1923– . Singapore politician, prime minister 1959–90. Lee founded the anticommunist Socialist People's Action Party 1954 and entered the Singapore legislative assembly 1955. He was elected the country's first prime minister 1959, and took Singapore out of the Malaysian federation 1965. He remained in power until his resignation in 1990. He was succeeded by Goh Chok Tong.

Lenin Vladimir Ilyich. Adopted name of Vladimir Ilyich Ulyanov 1870–1924. Russian revolutionary, first leader of the USSR, and communist theoretician. Active in the 1905 Revolution, Lenin had to leave Russia when it failed, settling in Switzerland 1914. He returned to Russia after the February revolution of 1917. He led the Bolshevik revolution in Nov 1917 and became leader of a Soviet government, concluded peace with Germany, and organized a successful resistance to White Russian (pro-tsarist) uprisings and foreign intervention 1918–20. His modification of traditional Marxist doctrine to fit conditions prevailing in Russia became known as *Marxism-Leninism*, the basis of communist ideology.

Li Peng 1928– . Chinese communist politician, a member of the Politburo from 1985, and head of government from 1987. During the pro-democracy demonstrations 1989 he supported the massacre of students by Chinese troops and the subsequent executions of others. He favours maintaining firm central and party control over the economy, and seeks improved relations with the USSR.

Lloyd George David 1863–1945. Welsh Liberal politician, prime minister 1916–22. A pioneer of social reform, as chancellor of the Exchequer 1908–15 he introduced old-age pensions 1908 and health and unemployment insurance 1911. High unemployment, intervention in the Russian Civil War, and use of the military police force the Black and Tans in Ireland eroded his support as prime minister, and creation of the Irish Free State 1921 and his pro-Greek policy against the Turks caused the collapse of his coalition government.

Lumumba Patrice 1926–1961. Congolese politician, prime minister of Zaïre 1960. Imprisoned by the Belgians, but released in time to attend the conference giving the Congo independence 1960, he led the National Congolese Movement to victory in the subsequent general election. He was deposed in a coup d'état, and murdered some months later.

MacDonald (James) Ramsay 1866–1937. British politician, first Labour prime minister Jan–Oct 1924 and 1929–31. He joined the Independent Labour Party 1894, and became first secretary of the new Labour Party 1900. In Parliament he led the party 1906–14 and 1922–31 and was prime minister of the first two Labour governments. Failing to deal with worsening economic conditions, he left the party to form a coalition government 1931, which was increasingly dominated by Conservatives, until he was replaced by Stanley Baldwin 1935.

Machel Samora 1933–1986. Mozambique nationalist leader, president 1975–86. Machel was active in the liberation front Frelimo from its conception 1962, fighting for independence from Portugal. He became Frelimo leader 1966, and Mozambique's first president from independence 1975 until his death in a plane crash near the South African border.

Macmillan (Maurice) Harold, 1st Earl of Stockton 1894–1986. British prime minister 1957–63. Conservative MP for Stockton 1924–29 and 1931–45; and for Bromley 1945–64. As minister of housing 1951–54 he achieved the construction of 300,000 new houses a year. He became foreign secretary 1955 and was chancellor of the Exchequer from 1955 to 1957. He became prime minister on the resignation of Anthony Eden after the Suez crisis. Macmillan led the Conservative Party to victory in the 1959 elections on the slogan 'You've never had it so good' (the phrase was borrowed from a US election campaign). Internationally, his realization of the 'wind of change' in Africa advanced the independence of former colonies. In 1963 he attempted to negotiate British entry to the European Economic Community, but was blocked by the French president de Gaulle. Much of his career as prime minister was spent trying to maintain a UK nuclear weapon, and he was responsible for the purchase of US Polaris missiles 1962. Macmillan's nickname Supermac was coined by the cartoonist Vicky. Created 1st Earl of Stockton 1984.

Major John 1943– . British Conservative politician, foreign secretary 1989, chancellor of the Exchequer 1989–90, and elected prime minister in the Conservative Party leadership election in Nov 1990. He retained his position by winning a narrow victory in the 1992 general election.

Makarios III 1913–1977. Cypriot politician, Greek Orthodox archbishop 1950–77. A leader of the Resistance organization EOKA, he was exiled by the British to the Seychelles 1956–57 for supporting armed action to achieve union with Greece (*enosis*). He was president of the republic of Cyprus 1960–77 (briefly deposed by a Greek military coup July–Dec 1974).

Mandela Nelson (Rolihlahla) 1918– . South African politician and lawyer. As organizer of the banned African National Congress (ANC), he was acquitted of treason 1961, but was given a life sentence 1964 on charges of sabotage and plotting to overthrow the government. In prison he became a symbol of unity for the worldwide anti-apartheid movement. In Feb 1990 he was released, the ban on the ANC having been lifted. As ANC president he established an international reputation, and domestically he has led the constitutional talks with the South African government.

Manley Michael 1924– . Jamaican politician, prime minister 1972–80 and 1989–92, in his last term adopting more moderate socialist policies. He resigned the premiership because of ill health March 1992 and was succeeded by P J Patterson. Manley left parliament April 1992. His father, Norman Manley (1893–1969), was founder of the People's National Party and prime minister 1959–62.

Mao Zedong or **Mao Tse-tung** 1893–1976. Chinese political leader and Marxist theoretician. A founder of the Chinese Communist Party (CCP) 1921, Mao soon emerged as its leader. He organized the Long March 1934–36 and the war of liberation 1937–49, following which he established a People's Republic and Communist rule in China; he headed the CCP and government until his death. His influence diminished with the failure of his 1958–60 Great Leap Forward, but he emerged dominant again during the 1966–69 Cultural Revolution. Mao adapted communism to Chinese conditions, as set out in the *Little Red Book*.

Marcos Ferdinand 1917–1989. Filipino right-wing politician, president from 1965 to 1986, when he was forced into exile in Hawaii. He was backed by the USA when in power, but in 1988 US authorities indicted him and his wife *Imelda Marcos* (1931–) for racketeering, embezzlement, and defrauding US banks; she was acquitted after his death. She returned to the Philippines, unsuccessfully contesting the 1992 presidential election.

Masire Quett Ketumile Joni 1925– . President of Botswana from 1980. In 1962, with Seretse Khama, he founded the Botswana Democratic Party (BDP) and in 1965 was made deputy prime minister. After independence, in 1966, he became vice president and, on Khama's death in 1980, president, continuing a policy of nonalignment.

Mazowiecki Tadeusz 1927– . Polish politician, founder member of Solidarity, and Poland's first postwar noncommunist prime minister 1989–1990. Forced to introduce unpopular economic reforms, he was knocked out in the first round of the Nov 1990 presidential elections, resigning in favour of his former colleague, Lech Walesa.

Mazzini Giuseppe 1805–1872. Italian nationalist. He was a member of the revolutionary society, the Carbonari, and founded in exile the nationalist movement Giovane Italia (Young Italy) 1832. Returning to Italy on the outbreak of the 1848 revolution, he headed a republican government established in Rome, but was forced into exile again on its overthrow 1849. He acted as a focus for the movement for Italian unity.

Meir Golda 1898–1978. Israeli Labour (*Mapai*) politician. Born in Russia, she emigrated to the USA 1906, and in 1921 went to Palestine. She was foreign minister 1956–66 and prime minister 1969–74. Criticism of the Israelis' lack of preparation for the 1973 Arab-Israeli War led to election losses for Labour and, unable to form a government, she resigned.

Menem Carlos Saul 1935– . Argentine politician, president from 1989; leader of the Peronist (Justice Party) movement. As president, he improved relations with the UK, and eventually engineered a successful revival of his country's economy.

Milosevic Slobodan 1941– . Serbian communist politician. A leading figure in the Yugoslavian Communist Party (LCY) in the republic of Serbia, he became Serbian party chief and president in 1986 and campaigned to reintegrate Kosovo and Vojvodina provinces into 'greater Serbia'. Milosevic was re-elected president in multiparty elections held Dec 1990. His actions contributed to the eventual breakup of Yugoslavia, and his persecution of non-Serbs earned him international criticism and eventually opposition from his own people.

Mitterrand François 1916– . French socialist politician, president from 1981. He held ministerial posts in 11 governments 1947–1958. He founded the French Socialist Party (PS) 1971. In 1985 he introduced proportional representation, allegedly to weaken the growing opposition from left and right. He enjoyed years of unrivalled popularity, but dissatisfaction with his social and economic policies in 1992 resulted in a sharp fall in his public esteem.

Miyazawa Kiichi 1920– . Japanese right-wing politician, prime minister from Nov 1991. After holding a number of key government posts, he became leader of the ruling Liberal Democratic Party and subsequently prime minister.

Mobutu Sese-Seko-Kuku-Ngbeandu-Wa-Za-Banga 1930– . Zairean president from 1965. He assumed the presidency by coup, and created a unitary state under his centralized government. He abolished secret voting in elections 1976 in favour of a system of acclamation at mass rallies. His personal wealth is estimated at $3–4 billion, and more money is spent on the presidency than on the entire social-services budget. The harshness of some of his policies and charges of corruption have attracted widespread international criticism.

Moi Daniel arap 1924– . Kenyan politician, president from 1978. Originally a teacher, he became minister of home affairs in 1964, vice president in 1967, and succeeded Jomo Kenyatta as president. From 1988 his rule became increasingly authoritarian and in 1991, in the face of widespread criticism, he promised an eventual introduction of multiparty politics.

Mubarak Hosni 1928– . Egyptian politician, president from 1981. He commanded the air force 1972–75 (and was responsible for the initial victories in the Egyptian campaign of 1973 against Israel), when he became an active vice president to Anwar Sadat, and succeeded him on his assassination. He has continued to pursue Sadat's moderate policies, and has significantly increased the freedom of the press and of political association, while trying to repress the growing Islamic fundamentalist movement. He gave his full support to the United Nations during the Gulf War.

Mugabe Robert (Gabriel) 1925– . Zimbabwean politician, prime minister from 1980 and president from 1987. He was in detention in Rhodesia for nationalist activities 1964–74, then carried on guerrilla warfare from Mozambique. As leader of ZANU he was in an uneasy alliance with Joshua Nkomo of ZAPU (Zimbabwe African People's Union) from 1976. The two parties merged 1987. Economic problems, including the failure to anticipate and respond to the 1991–92 drought in southern Africa, adversely affected his popularity.

Muldoon Robert David 1921– . New Zealand National Party politician, prime minister 1975–84. He resigned from parliament Nov 1991, because of his dissatisfaction with the policies of the National Party government of Jim Bolger.

Mulroney Brian 1939– . Canadian politician. A former business executive, he replaced Joe Clark as Progressive Conservative party leader 1983, and achieved a landslide in the 1984 election to become prime minister. He won the 1988 election on a platform of free trade with the USA, but with a reduced majority.

Mussolini Benito 1883–1945. Italian dictator from 1925 to 1943. As founder of the Fascist Movement 1919 and prime minister from 1922, he became known as *Il Duce* ('the leader'). He invaded Ethiopia 1935–36, intervened in the Spanish Civil War 1936–39 in support of Franco, and conquered Albania 1939. In June 1940 Italy entered World War II supporting Hitler. Forced by military and domestic setbacks to resign 1943, Mussolini established a breakaway government in N Italy 1944–45, but was killed trying to flee the country.

Najibullah Ahmadzai 1947– . Afghan communist politician, a member of the Politburo from 1981, and leader of the ruling People's Democratic Party of Afghanistan (PDPA) from 1986, later state president. His attempts to broaden the support of the PDPA regime had little success, but his government survived the withdrawal of Soviet troops Feb 1989, eventually falling April 1992.

Nakasone Yasuhiro 1917– . Japanese conservative politician, leader of the Liberal Democratic Party (LDP) and prime minister 1982–87. He stepped up military spending and increased Japanese participation in international affairs, with closer ties to the USA. He was forced to resign his party post May 1989 as a result of having profited from insider trading in the Recruit scandal. He was the leader until 1990 of a right-wing faction of the LDP.

Nasser Gamal Abdel 1918–1970. Egyptian politician, prime minister 1954–56 and from 1956 president of Egypt (the United Arab Republic 1958–71). In 1952 he was the driving power behind the Neguib coup, which ended the monarchy. His nationalization of the Suez Canal 1956 led to an Anglo-French invasion and the Suez Crisis, and his ambitions for an Egyptian-led union of Arab states led to disquiet in the Middle East (and in the West). Nasser was also an early and influential leader of the non-aligned movement.

Nazarbayev Nursultan 1940– . Kazakhstan politician, president from 1990. In the Soviet period he was prime minister of the republic 1984–89, and leader 1989–91 of the Kazakh Communist Party, which established itself as the independent Socialist Party of Kazakhstan (SPK) Sept 1991. He was elected president of the new Republic of Kazakhstan by over 98% of the electorate. He advocates free-market policies, yet enjoys the support of the environmentalist lobby. He joined the Kazakh Communist Party at 22 and left it after the failed Soviet coup 1991.

Nehru Jawaharlal 1889–1964. Indian nationalist politician, prime minister from 1947. Before the partition (the division of British India into India and Pakistan) he led the socialist wing of the Nationalist Congress Party, and was second in influence only to Mohandas Gandhi. He was imprisoned nine times by the British 1921–45 for political activities. As prime minister from the creation of the dominion (later republic) of India Aug 1947, he originated the idea of nonalignment (neutrality towards major powers). His daughter was Prime Minister Indira Gandhi.

Nixon Richard (Milhous) 1913– . 37th president of the USA 1969–74, a Republican. He attracted attention as a member of the Un-American Activities Committee 1948, and was vice president to Eisenhower 1953–61. As president he was responsible for US withdrawal from Vietnam, and forged new links with China, but at home his culpability in the cover-up of the Watergate scandal and the existence of a 'slush fund' for political machinations during his re-election campaign 1972 led to his resignation 1974 after being threatened with impeachment.

Nkomo Joshua 1917– . Zimbabwean politician, president of ZAPU (Zimbabwe African People's Union) from 1961 and a leader of the black nationalist movement against the white Rhodesian regime. He was a member of Robert Mugabe's cabinet in 1980–82 and from 1987.

Nkrumah Kwame 1909–1972. Ghanaian nationalist politician, prime minister of the Gold Coast (Ghana's former name) 1952–57 and of newly independent Ghana 1957– 60. He became Ghana's first president 1960 but was overthrown in a coup 1966. His policy of 'African socialism' led to links with the Communist bloc.

Noriega Manuel Antonio Morena 1940– . Panamanian soldier and politician, effective ruler of Panama from 1982 until arrested by the USA 1989 and detained for trial on drug-trafficking charges. He was eventually convicted April 1992, receiving a life sentence.

Nujoma Sam 1929– . Namibian left-wing politician, president from 1990, founder and leader of SWAPO (the South-West Africa People's Organization) from 1959. He was exiled in 1960 and controlled guerrillas from Angolan bases until the first free elections were held 1989, taking office early the following year.

Nyerere Julius (Kambarage) 1922– . Tanzanian socialist politician, president 1964–85. Originally a teacher, he devoted himself from 1954 to the formation of the Tanganyika African National Union and subsequent campaigning for independence. He became chief minister 1960, was prime minister of Tanganyika 1961–62, president of the newly formed Tanganyika Republic 1962–64, and first president of Tanzania 1964–85.

Obote (Apollo) Milton 1924– . Ugandan politician who led the independence movement from 1961. He became prime minister 1962 and was president 1966–71 and 1980–85, being overthrown by first Idi Amin and then Lt-Gen Tito Okello.

Ortega (Saavedra) Daniel 1945– . Nicaraguan socialist politician, head of state 1981–90. He was a member of the Sandinista Liberation Front (FSLN), which overthrew the regime of Anastasio Somoza 1979. US-sponsored Contra guerrillas opposed his government from 1982.

Ozal Turgut 1927– . Turkish Islamic right-wing politician, prime minister 1983–89, president from 1989.

Palme (Sven) Olof 1927–1986. Swedish social-democratic politician, prime minister 1969–76 and 1982–86. He entered government 1963, holding several posts before becoming leader of the Social Democratic Labour Party (SAP) 1969. He was assassinated Feb 1986.

Papandreou Andreas 1919– . Greek socialist politician, founder of the Pan-Hellenic Socialist Movement (PASOK), and prime minister 1981–89, when he became implicated in the alleged embezzlement and diversion of funds to the Greek government of $200 million from the Bank of Crete, headed by George Koskotas, and lost the election.

Pérez de Cuéllar Javier 1920– . Peruvian diplomat, secretary-general of the United Nations 1982–1991. A delegate to the first UN General Assembly 1946–47, he subsequently held several ambassadorial posts. He raised the standing of the UN by his successful diplomacy in ending the Iran-Iraq war in 1988 and securing the independence of Namibia 1989. Under his leadership the UN responded decisively to Iraq's invasion of Kuwait 1990. He was replaced 1 Jan 1992 by Boutros Boutros Ghali of Egypt.

Perón Juan (Domingo) 1895–1974. Argentine politician, dictator 1946–55 and from 1973 until his death. He took part in the military coup 1943, and his popularity with the *descamisados* ('shirtless ones') led to his election as president 1946. He instituted social reforms, but encountered economic difficulties. After the death of his second wife Eva Perón he lost popularity, and was deposed in a military coup 1955. He returned from exile to the presidency 1973, but died in office 1974,

PRIME MINISTERS OF BRITAIN

Sir Robert Walpole	(Whig)	1721	Lord J Russell	(Liberal)	1865
Earl of Wilmington	(Whig)	1742	Earl of Derby	(Conservative)	1866
Henry Pelham	(Whig)	1743	Benjamin Disraeli	(Conservative)	1868
Duke of Newcastle	(Whig)	1754	W E Gladstone	(Liberal)	1886
Duke of Devonshire	(Whig)	1756	Benjamin Disraeli	(Conservative)	1874
Duke of Newcastle	(Whig)	1757	W E Gladstone	(Liberal)	1880
Earl of Bute	(Tory)	1762	Marquess of Salisbury	(Conservative)	1885
George Grenville	(Whig)	1763	W E Gladstone	(Liberal)	1886
Marquess of Rockingham	(Whig)	1765	Marquess of Salisbury	(Conservative)	1886
Duke of Grafton	(Whig)	1766	W E Gladstone	(Liberal)	1892
Lord North	(Tory)	1770	Earl of Roseberry	(Liberal)	1894
Marquess of Rockingham	(Whig)	1782	Marquess of Salisbury	(Conservative)	1895
Earl of Shelbourne	(Whig)	1782	Sir H Campbell-Bannerman	(Liberal)	1905
Duke of Portland	(Coalition)	1783	H H Asquith	(Liberal)	1908
William Pitt	(Tory)	1783	H H Asquith	(Coalition)	1915
Henry Addington	(Tory)	1801	D Lloyd George	(Coalition)	1916
William Pitt	(Tory)	1804	A Bonar Law	(Conservative)	1922
Lord Grenville	(Whig)	1806	Stanley Baldwin	(Conservative)	1923
Duke of Portland	(Tory)	1807	Ramsay MacDonald	(Labour)	1924
Spencer Percival	(Tory)	1809	Stanley Baldwin	(Conservative)	1924
Earl of Liverpool	(Tory)	1812	Ramsay MacDonald	(Labour)	1929
George Canning	(Tory)	1827	Ramsay MacDonald	(National)	1931
Viscount Goderich	(Tory)	1827	Stanley Baldwin	(National)	1935
Duke of Wellington	(Tory)	1828	N Chamberlain	(National)	1937
Earl Grey	(Whig)	1830	Sir Winston Churchill	(Coalition)	1940
Viscount Melbourne	(Whig)	1834	Clement Attlee	(Labour)	1945
Sir Robert Peel	(Conservative)	1834	Sir Winston Churchill	(Conservative)	1951
Viscount Melbourne	(Whig)	1835	Sir Anthony Eden	(Conservative)	1955
Sir Robert Peel	(Conservative)	1841	Harold Macmillan	(Conservative)	1957
Lord J Russell	(Liberal)	1846	Sir Alec Douglas-Home	(Conservative)	1963
Earl of Derby	(Conservative)	1852	Harold Wilson	(Labour)	1964
Lord Aberdeen	(Peelite)	1852	Edward Heath	(Conservative)	1970
Viscount Palmerston	(Liberal)	1855	Harold Wilson	(Labour)	1974
Earl of Derby	(Conservative)	1858	James Callaghan	(Labour)	1976
Viscount Palmerston	(Liberal)	1859	Margaret Thatcher	(Conservative)	1979
			John Major	(Conservative)	1990

and was was succeeded by his third wife Isabel Perón.

Pinochet (Ugarte) Augusto 1915– . Military ruler of Chile from 1973, when a coup backed by the US Central Intelligence Agency ousted and killed President Salvador Allende. Pinochet took over the presidency and governed ruthlessly, crushing all opposition. He was voted out of power when general elections were held in Dec 1989 but remains head of the armed forces until 1997. In 1990 his attempt to reassert political influence was firmly censured by President Patricio Aylwin.

Pol Pot (also known as *Saloth Sar, Tol Saut,* and *Pol Porth*) 1925– . Cambodian politician and Communist Party leader; a member of the anti-French resistance under Ho Chi Minh in the 1940s. As leader of the Khmer Rouge, he overthrew the government 1975 and proclaimed Democratic Kampuchea with himself as premier. His policies were to evacuate cities and put people to work in the countryside. The Khmer Rouge also carried out a systematic large-scale extermination of the Western-influenced educated and middle classes (3–4 million) before the regime was overthrown by a Vietnamese invasion 1979. Pol Pot continued to help lead the Khmer Rouge until their withdrawal in 1989; in

that year too he resigned from his last position within the Khmer Rouge. Despite the reinstatement of legitimate government in Kampuchea, he continued to exercise a clandestine influence on the country's affairs.

Primo de Rivera Miguel 1870–1930. Spanish soldier and politician, dictator from 1923 as well as premier from 1925. He was captain-general of Catalonia when he led a coup against the ineffective monarchy and became virtual dictator of Spain with the support of Alfonso XIII. He resigned 1930.

Rabin Yitzhak 1922– . Israeli Labour politician, prime minister 1974–77, 1992– . Rabin was minister for defence under the conservative Likud coalition government 1984-90. His policy of favouring Palestinian self-government in the occupied territories contributed to the success of the centre-left party in the 1992 elections. Shortly after taking office he visited Egypt's President Hosni Mubarak July 1992 as the first step in negotiating an Arab–Israeli peace accord.

Rafsanjani Hojatoleslam Ali Akbar Hashemi 1934– . Iranian politician and cleric, president from 1989. After training as a mullah (Islamic teacher) under Ayatollah Khomeini in Qom, he acquired considerable wealth through his construction business but kept in touch with his exiled mentor. When the Ayatollah returned after the revolution of 1979–80, Rafsanjani became the speaker of the Iranian parliament and, after Khomeini's death, state president and effective political leader.

Ramos Fidel (Eddie) 1928– . Philippine politician, president from 1992. He was Corazón Aquino's staunchest ally as defence secretary when numerous coup attempts were made against her. He was her chosen successor when he won the presidency May 1992.

Ramphal Shridath Surendranath ('Sonny') 1928– . Guyanese politician. He was minister of foreign affairs and justice 1972–75 and secretary-general of the British Commonwealth 1975–90.

Rao P V Narasimha 1921– . Indian politician and prime minister from 1991. He served in the cabinets of both Indira and Rajiv Gandhi. When he was elected Congress (I) president, in succession to Rajiv Gandhi, in May 1991, he was seen only as an interim leader, but following the June 1991 general election he became prime minister at the head of a minority Congress (I) government.

Reagan Ronald (Wilson) 1911– . 40th president of the USA 1981–89, a Republican. He was governor of California 1966–74, and a former Hollywood actor. Reagan was a hawkish and popular president. He adopted an aggressive policy in Central America, attempting to overthrow the government of Nicaragua, and invading Grenada 1983. In 1987, Irangate was investigated by the Tower Commission; Reagan admitted that USA–Iran negotiations had become an 'arms for hostages deal', but denied knowledge of resultant funds being illegally sent to the Contras in Nicaragua. He increased military spending (sending the national budget deficit to record levels), cut social programmes, introduced deregulation of domestic markets, and cut taxes. His Strategic Defense Initiative ('Star Wars'), announced 1983, proved controversial owing to its enormous cost and unfeasibility. He was succeeded by George Bush.

Reynolds Albert 1933– . Irish politician, prime minister from 1992. He joined Fianna Fáil 1977 and held various ministerial posts, including minister for industry and commerce 1987–88 and minister of finance 1989–92. Reynolds was a successful businessman before entering politics. He became prime minister after Charles Haughey was forced to resign 1992.

Robinson Mary 1944– . Irish Labour politician, president from 1990. She became a professor of law at 25 and has campaigned for women's rights in Ireland.

Rocard Michel 1930– . French socialist politician, prime minister 1988–91. A former radical, he joined the Socialist Party (PS) 1973, emerging as leader of its moderate social-democratic wing. He held ministerial office under François Mitterrand 1981–85.

Roh Tae-woo 1932– . South Korean right-wing politician and general. He held ministerial office from 1981 under President Chun, and became chair of the ruling Democratic Justice Party 1985. He was elected president 1987, amid allegations of fraud and despite being connected with the massacre of about 2,000 anti-government demonstrators 1980.

Roosevelt Franklin Delano 1882–1945. 32nd president of the USA 1933–45, a Democrat. He served as governor of New York 1929–33. Becoming president amid the Depression, he launched the *New Deal* economic and social reform programme, which made him popular with the people. After the outbreak of World War II he introduced Lend-Lease for the supply of war materials and services to the Allies and drew up the Atlantic Charter of solidarity. Once the USA had entered the war 1941 he spent much time in meetings with Allied leaders (including the Québec, Tehran, and Yalta conferences).

Sadat Anwar 1918–1981. Egyptian politician. Succeeding Nasser as president 1970, he restored morale by his handling of the Egyptian campaign in the 1973 war against Israel. In 1974 his plan for economic, social, and political reform to transform Egypt was unanimously adopted in a referendum. In 1977 he visited Israel to reconcile the two countries, and shared the Nobel Peace Prize with Israeli prime minister Menachem Begin 1978. He was assassinated by Islamic fundamentalists.

Salazar Antonio de Oliveira 1889–1970. Portuguese prime minister 1932–68 who exercised a virtual dictatorship. A corporative constitution on the Italian model was introduced 1933, and until 1945 Salazar's National Union, founded 1930, remained the only legal party. Salazar was also foreign minister 1936–47 and during World War II he maintained Portuguese neutrality. But he fought long colonial wars in Africa (Angola and Mozambique) that impeded his country's economic development.

Sarney (Costa) José 1930– . Brazilian politician, member of the Democratic Movement (PMDB), president 1985–90.

Schmidt Helmut 1918– . German socialist politician, member of the Social Democratic Party (SPD), chancellor of West Germany 1974–83. As chancellor, Schmidt introduced social reforms and continued Brandt's policy of Ostpolitik. With the French president Giscard d'Estaing, he instigated annual world and European economic summits. He was a firm supporter of NATO and of the deployment of US nuclear missiles in West Germany during the early 1980s.

Shamir Yitzhak 1915– . Israeli right-wing politician, born in Poland; prime minister 1983–84 and 1986–92; leader of the Likud (Consolidation Party). He was foreign minister under Menachem Begin 1980–83, and again foreign minister in the Peres unity government 1984–86.

Shuskevich Stanislav 1934– . Byelorussian politician, president of Belarus from 1991. An eminent scientist and supporter of democratic

PRESIDENTS OF THE UNITED STATES OF AMERICA

name	party	took office
1. George Washington	(Federalist)	1789
2. John Adams	(Federalist)	1797
3. Thomas Jefferson	(Democratic Republican)	1801
4. James Madison	(Democratic Republican)	1809
5. James Monroe	(Democratic Republican)	1817
6. John Quincy Adams	(Democratic Republican)	1825
7. Andrew Jackson	(Democrat)	1829
8. Martin Van Buren	(Democrat)	1837
9. William Henry Harrison	(Whig)	1841
10. John Tyler	(Whig)	1841
11. James Knox Polk	(Democrat)	1845
12. Zachary Taylor	(Whig)	1849
13. Millard Fillmore	(Whig)	1850
14. Franklin Pierce	(Democrat)	1853
15. James Buchanan	(Democrat)	1857
16. Abraham Lincoln	(Republican)	1861
17. Andrew Johnson	(Democrat)	1865
18. Ulysses Simpson Grant	(Republican)	1869
19. Rutherford Birchard Hayes	(Republican)	1877
20. James Abram Garfield	(Republican)	1881
21. Chester Alan Arthur	(Republican)	1881
22. Grover Cleveland	(Democrat)	1885
23. Benjamin Harrison	(Republican)	1889
24. Grover Cleveland	(Republican)	1893
25. William McKinley	(Republican)	1897
26. Theodore Roosevelt	(Republican)	1901
27. William Howard Taft	(Republican)	1909
28. Woodrow Wilson	(Democrat)	1913
29. Warren Gamaliel Harding	(Republican)	1921
30. Calvin Coolidge	(Republican)	1923
31. Herbert C Hoover	(Republican)	1929
32. Franklin Delano Roosevelt	(Democrat)	1933
33. Harry S Truman	(Democrat)	1945
34. Dwight D Eisenhower	(Republican)	1953
35. John F Kennedy	(Democrat)	1961
36. Lyndon B Johnson	(Democrat)	1963
37. Richard M Nixon	(Republican)	1969
38. Gerald R Ford	(Republican)	1974
39. James Earl Carter	(Democrat)	1977
40. Ronald Reagan	(Republican)	1981
41. George Bush	(Republican)	1989

change, he was in the forefront of the movement that established the Commonwealth of Independent States (CIS) as the successor to the Soviet Union.

Sihanouk Prince Norodom 1922– . Cambodian politician and head of state from 1991. Elected king of Cambodia in 1941, he abdicated in 1955 to become an elected politician, leading the Popular Socialist Community. In 1960 he was elected head of state but deposed by a military coup in 1970. Fleeing to Beijing, he formed a joint resistance front with Pol Pot, overthrowing the military government in 1975 and returning as head of state. In 1976 he was ousted by the communist Khmer Rouge and formed a government-in-exile in North Korea while a civil war raged in Cambodia. A peace agreement was eventually signed in Paris Oct 1991, and he returned from exile Nov 1991 under the auspices of a UN-brokered peace settlement to head a new coalition comprising all Cambodia's warring factions, including the Khmer Rouge. On his return, Sihanouk called for an international trial of the leaders of the Khmer Rouge on charges of genocide.

Smith Ian Douglas 1919– . Rhodesian politician. He was a founder of the Rhodesian Front 1962 and prime minister 1964–79. In 1965 he made a unilateral declaration of Rhodesia's independence and, despite United Nations sanctions, maintained his regime with tenacity. In 1979 he was succeeded as prime minister by Bishop Abel Muzorewa, when the country was renamed Zimbabwe. He was suspended from the Zimbabwe parliament in April 1987 and resigned in May as head of the white opposition party.

Soares Mario 1924– . Portuguese socialist politician, president from 1986. Exiled in 1970, he returned to Portugal in 1974, and, as leader of the Portuguese Socialist Party, was prime minister 1976–78. He resigned as party leader in 1980, but in 1986 he was elected Portugal's first socialist president.

Stalin Joseph. Adopted name (Russian 'steel') of Joseph Vissarionovich Djugashvili 1879–1953. Soviet politician. A member of the October Revolution Committee 1917, Stalin became general secretary of the Communist Party 1922. After Lenin's death 1924, Stalin sought to create 'socialism in one country' and clashed with Trotsky, who denied the possibility of socialism inside Russia until revolution had occurred in W Europe. Stalin won this ideological struggle by 1927, and a series of five-year plans was launched to collectivize industry and agriculture from 1928. All opposition was eliminated in the Great Purge 1936–38. During World War II, Stalin intervened in the military direction of the campaigns against Nazi Germany. His role was denounced after his death by Khrushchev and other members of the Soviet regime.

Stroessner Alfredo 1912– . Military leader and president of Paraguay 1954–89. As head of the armed forces from 1951, he seized power in a coup in 1954 sponsored by the right-wing ruling Colorado Party. Accused by his opponents of harsh repression, his regime spent heavily on the military to preserve his authority. He was overthrown by a military coup and gained asylum in Brazil.

Suharto Raden 1921– . Indonesian politician and general. He ousted Sukarno to become president in 1967. He ended confrontation with Malaysia, invaded East Timor in 1975, and reached a cooperation agreement with Papua New Guinea 1979. His authoritarian rule met domestic opposition from the left, but it brought considerable economic success. He was re-elected in 1973, 1978, 1983, and 1988.

Sukarno Achmed 1901–1970. Indonesian nationalist, president 1945–67. During World War II he cooperated in the local administration set up by the Japanese, replacing Dutch rule. After the war he became the first president of the new Indonesian republic, becoming president-for-life in 1966; he was ousted by Suharto.

Tambo Oliver 1917– . South African nationalist politician, in exile 1960–90, president of the African National Congress (ANC) 1977–91.

Thatcher Margaret Hilda (Baroness Thatcher of Kesteven) (born Roberts) 1925– . British Conservative politician, prime minister 1979–1990. She was education minister 1970–74 and Conservative Party leader 1975–90. In 1982 she sent British troops to recapture the Falkland Islands from Argentina. She confronted trade-union power during the miners' strike 1984–85, sold off majority stakes in many public utilities to the private sector, and reduced the influence of local government through such measures as the abolition of metropolitan councils, the control of expenditure through 'rate-capping', and the introduction of the community charge or poll tax from 1989. In 1990 splits in the cabinet over the issues of Europe and consensus government forced her resignation. An astute Parliamentary tactician, she tolerated little disagreement, either from the opposition or from within her own party. She was created a life peer 1992.

Tito adopted name of Josip Broz 1892–1980. Yugoslav soldier and communist politician, in power from 1945. In World War II he organized the National Liberation Army to carry on guerrilla warfare against the German invasion 1941, and was created marshal 1943. As prime minister 1946–53 and president from 1953, he followed a foreign policy of 'positive neutralism'.

Trotsky Leon. Adopted name of Lev Davidovitch Bronstein 1879–1940. Russian revolutionary. He joined the Bolshevik party and took a leading part in the seizure of power 1917 and raising the Red Army that fought the Civil War 1918–20. In the struggle for power that followed Lenin's death 1924, Stalin defeated Trotsky, and this and other differences with the Communist Party led to his exile 1929. He settled in Mexico, where he was assassinated with an ice pick at Stalin's instigation. Trotsky believed in world revolution and in permanent revolution, and was an uncompromising, if liberal, idealist.

Trudeau Pierre (Elliott) 1919– . Canadian Liberal politician. He was prime minister 1968–79 and won again by a landslide Feb 1980. In 1980 his work helped to defeat the Québec independence movement in a referendum. He repatriated the constitution from Britain 1982, but by 1984 had so lost support that he resigned.

Truman Harry S 1884–1972. 33rd president of the USA 1945–53, a Democrat. In Jan 1945 he became vice president to F D Roosevelt, and president when Roosevelt died in Apr that year. He used the atom bomb against

Japan, launched the Marshall Plan to restore W Europe's economy, and nurtured the European Community and NATO (including the rearmament of West Germany).

Tutu Desmond (Mpilo) 1931– . South African priest, Anglican archbishop of Cape Town and general secretary of the South African Council of Churches 1979–84. One of the leading figures in the struggle against apartheid in the Republic of South Africa, he received the 1984 Nobel Peace Prize.

Ulbricht Walter 1893–1973. East German communist politician, in power 1960–71. He lived in exile in the USSR during Hitler's rule 1933–45. A Stalinist, he became first secretary of the Socialist Unity Party in East Germany 1950 and (as chair of the Council of State from 1960) was instrumental in the building of the Berlin Wall 1961. He established East Germany's economy and recognition outside the Eastern European bloc.

U Thant 1909–1974. Burmese diplomat, secretary general of the United Nations 1962–71. He helped to resolve the US-Soviet crisis over the Soviet installation of missiles in Cuba, and he made the controversial decision to withdraw the UN peacekeeping force from the Egypt–Israel border 1967.

Vassilou Georgios Vassos 1931– . Cypriot politician, president from 1988. A self-made millionaire, he entered politics as an independent and in 1988 won the presidency, with Communist Party support. He has since, with United Nations help, tried unsuccessfully to heal the rift between the Greek and Turkish communities.

Vranitzky Franz 1937– . Austrian politician, federal chancellor since 1986. A successful banker, he joined the moderate, left-of-centre Social Democratic Party (SPÖ) and became finance minister in 1984. He succeeded Fred Sinowatz as federal chancellor in 1986, heading an SPÖ–ÖVP (Austrian People's Party) coalition.

Waldheim Kurt 1918– . Austrian politician and diplomat, president 1986–92. He was secretary general of the United Nations 1972–81, having been Austria's representative there 1964–68 and 1970–71. He was elected president of Austria despite revelations that during World War II he had been an intelligence officer in an army unit responsible for transporting Jews to death camps.

Walesa Lech 1943– . Polish trade-union leader and president of Poland from 1990, founder of Solidarity (Solidarność) in 1980, an organization, independent of the Communist Party, which forced substantial political and economic concessions from the Polish government 1980–81 until being outlawed. During his presidency, his public standing diminished and economic problems increased. Nobel Peace Prize 1983.

Weizmann Chaim 1874–1952. Zionist leader, the first president of Israel (1948–52), and chemist. Born in Russia, he became a naturalized British subject, and as director of the Admiralty laboratories 1916–19 discovered a process for manufacturing acetone, a solvent. He conducted the negotiations leading up to the Balfour Declaration, by which Britain declared its support for an independent Jewish state. He became head of the Hebrew University in Jerusalem, then in 1948 became the first president of the new republic of Israel.

Wilson (Thomas) Woodrow 1856–1924. 28th president of the US 1913–21, a Democrat. He kept the US out of World War I until 1917 and in Jan 1918 issued his Fourteen Points as a basis for a just peace settlement. At the peace conference in Paris he secured the inclusion of the League of Nations covenant in individual peace treaties, but these were not ratified by Congress, so the US did not join the League. He was awarded the Nobel Peace Prize 1919.

Wilson (James) Harold, Baron Wilson of Rievaulx 1916– . British Labour politician, party leader from 1963, prime minister 1964–70 and 1974–76. His premiership was dominated by the issue of UK admission to membership of the European Community, the social contract (unofficial agreement with the trade unions), and economic difficulties.

Yeltsin Boris Nikolayevich 1931– . Russian reform politician, president of the Russian Republic from 1990, as well as prime minister from Nov 1990. He was Moscow Communist Party chief 1985–87, when he was dismissed after criticizing the slow pace of political and economic reform. He was re-elected in March 1989 with a 89% share of the vote, defeating an 'official Communist Party' candidate, and was elected to the Supreme Soviet in May 1989. He supported the Baltic states in their calls for greater independence and demanded increas-

ingly more radical economic reform. In April 1991 the Russian Republic congress voted him emergency powers. Yeltsin's strong reformist stance was strengthened by his leading a successful opposition to the attempted right-wing coup 19–21 Aug 1991; after the coup he emerged as the most influential politician within the Commonwealth of Independent States which succeeded the Soviet Union.

Zhao Ziyang 1918– . Chinese politician, prime minister from 1980, and secretary of the Chinese Communist Party (CCP) 1987–89. His reforms included self-management and incentives for workers and factories. He lost his secretaryship and other posts after the Tiananmen Square massacre in Beijing June 1989.

Zhelev 1935– . Bulgarian politician and president since 1990. A former professor of philosophy, he was expelled from the Bulgarian Communist Party because of his criticisms of Lenin; in 1989 he became head of the opposition movement in Bulgaria, the Democratic Forces coalition. He was nominated, unopposed, for the presidency in 1990 after the demise of the 'reform communist' regime, and was directly elected to the post 1992. He is a proponent of market-centred economic reform.

Zia ul-Haq Mohammad 1924–1988. Pakistani general, in power from 1977 until his death, probably an assassination, in an aircraft explosion. He became army chief of staff 1976, led the military coup against Zulfiqar Ali Bhutto 1977, and became president 1978. Zia introduced a fundamentalist Islamic regime and restricted political activity.

THE ANCIENT WORLD

Africa

14 million BC Africa, which is considered the 'cradle-continent', probably produced the first human-like creatures

3–5 million direct line of descent of modern humans established from E Africa

c. 60000 American Indians entered N America from Asia

15000 agriculture first practised in Egypt

10000–2000 the originally fertile Sahara became a barrier desert between northern and southern Africa

9000 Marmes man, earliest human remains found in N America

5450–2500 era of Saharan rock and cave paintings, as in the Tassili

c. 3000 first dynasties of Mesopotamia: King Gilgamesh; Bronze Age civilizations: Minoan, Mycenaean

2800–2205 Sage kings in China, earliest Chinese dynasty; civilization spread to all of China

2500–1500 Indus valley civilization

1950 first Babylonian Empire established

625 birth of Buddha

550 birth of Confucius

246 Shi Huangdi, Emperor of China, succeeded to the throne of Qin. He had reunited the country as an empire by 221, and built the Great Wall of China

Egypt

5000 BC Egyptian culture already well established in the Nile Valley

3200 Menes united Lower Egypt (the Delta) with his own kingdom of Upper Egypt to form the Egyptian state

2800 Imhotep built step pyramid at Sakkara

c. 2600 Old Kingdom reached the height of its power and the kings of the 4th Dynasty built the pyramids at Gîza

c. 2200–1800 Middle Kingdom, under which the unity lost towards the end of the Old Kingdom was restored

1730 invading Asiatic Hyksos established their kingdom in the Delta

c. 1580 New Kingdom established by the 18th Dynasty, following the eviction of the Hyksos, with its capital at Thebes; high point of Egyptian civilization

c. 1321 19th Dynasty

1191 Ramses III defeated the Indo-European 'Sea Peoples', but after him there was decline and eventual anarchy

8th–7th centuries brief interlude of rule by kings from Nubia

666 the Assyrians under Ashurbanipal occupied Thebes

525 after a brief resurgence of independence, Egypt became a Persian province following conquest by Cambyses

332 conquest by Alexander; on the division of his empire, Egypt went to Ptolemy, whose descend-

ants ruled until Cleopatra's death in 30 BC

30 conquest by the Roman Emperor Augustus: Egypt a province of the Roman and Byzantine empires

641 AD conquest by the Arabs, so that the Christianity of later Roman rule was replaced by Islam

Greece

c. 1600–1200 BC Mycenean civilization

c. 1180 Siege of Troy

c. 1100 Dorian invasion, and the rise of the Greek city states, of which the greatest were Athens and Sparta

750–550 trading colonies founded round the Mediterranean, Black Sea, and elsewhere

5th century Persian Empire sought to establish its rule over the Greeks

490 Persians defeated at Marathon

480 The Spartans defended Thermopylae to the death against a fresh invasion by Xerxes, but the Persians were defeated at sea (Salamis 480) and on land (Plataea 479)

461–429 Pericles attempted to convert the alliance against the Persians into the basis of a Greek empire

431–404 Peloponnesian War prompted by Sparta's suspicion of Pericles's ambitions, with the resultant destruction of the political power of Athens

378–371 Sparta, successor to Athens in the leadership, overthrown by Thebes

358–336 Philip II of Macedon seized his opportunity to establish supremacy over Greece

334–331 Philip's son Alexander the Great defeated the decadent Persian Empire, and went on to found his own

3rd century BC Greek cities formed the Achaean and Aetolian Leagues to try and maintain their independence against Macedon, Egypt, and Rome

146 BC Greece annexed by Rome

330 AD capital of Roman Empire transferred to Constantinople

529 closure of the University of Athens by Justinian ended Greek cultural dominance

Persia

550 BC Cyrus II became king of the Medes and Persians, founding the Persian Empire, which at its height was to include Babylonia, Assyria, Asia Minor, Egypt, Thrace, and Macedonia

521 Darius I became king of Persia

499 revolt of the Ionian Greeks against Persian rule

490 Darius I defeated by the Greeks at Marathon

480 Xerxes I victorious at Thermopylae, which Leonidas, king of Sparta, and 1,000 men defended to the death against the Persians; Athens captured but Greek navy victorious at Salamis

479 Greeks under Spartan general Pausanias victorious at Plataea, driving the Persians from the country

334–326 conquest by Alexander the Great

Rome

753 BC traditional date for the foundation of Rome

510 the Etruscan dynasty of the Tarquins was expelled, and a republic was established, governed by two consuls, elected annually by the popular assembly, and a council of elders or senate. The concentration of power in the hands of the aristocracy aroused the opposition of the plebeian masses

390 Rome sacked by Gauls

367 the plebeians secured the right to elect tribunes, the codification of the laws, and the right to marry patricians; it was enacted that one consul must be a plebeian

338 the cities of Latium formed into a league under Roman control

343–290 the Etruscans to the north were subdued during the 5th and 4th centuries, and the Samnites to the southeast

280–272 the Greek cities of the south were conquered

264–241 first Punic War, ending in a Roman victory and the annexation of Sicily

238 Sardinia seized from Carthage and became a Roman province

226–222 Roman conquest of Cisalpine Gaul (Lombardy); conflict with Carthage, which was attempting to conquer Sicily

218 Hannibal invaded Italy and won a brilliant series of victories

202 victory over Hannibal at Zama, followed by surrender of Carthage and relinquishing of its Spanish colonies

148 three wars with Macedon were followed by its conversion into a province

146 after a revolt Greece became in effect a Roman province. In the same year Carthage was annexed. On the death of the king of Pergamum, Rome succeeded to his kingdom in Asia Minor

133 Tiberius Gracchus put forward proposals for agrarian reforms and was murdered by the senatorial party

123 Tiberius's policy was taken up by his brother Gaius Gracchus, who was likewise murdered

109–106 the leadership of the democrats passed to Marius

91–88 Social War: a revolt of the Italian cities compelled Rome to grant citizenship to all Italians

87–84 while Sulla was repelling an invasion of Greece by Mithridates, Marius seized power

82 on his return Sulla established a dictatorship and ruled by terror

70 Sulla's changes were reversed by Pompey and Crassus

66–62 defeat of Mithridates and annexation of Syria and the rest of Asia Minor

60 Pompey formed an alliance with the democratic leaders Crassus and Julius Caesar

51 Gaul conquered by Caesar as far as the Rhine

49 Caesar's return to Italy (crossing the Rubicon) led to civil war between Caesar and Pompey

48 defeat of Pompey at Pharsalus

44 Caesar's dictatorship ended by his assassination

32 the Empire divided between Caesar's nephew Octavian in the west, and Antony in the east; war between them

31 defeat of Antony at Actium

30 with the deaths of Antony and Cleopatra Egypt was annexed

27 Octavian took the name Augustus; he was by now absolute ruler, although in title only *Princeps* (first citizen)

43 AD Augustus made the Rhine and the Danube the frontiers of the Empire; Claudius added Britain

96–180 under the Flavian emperors Nerva, Trajan, Hadrian, Antoninus Pius, and Marcus Aurelius the Empire enjoyed a golden age

115 Trajan conquered Macedonia; peak of Roman territorial expansion

180 death of Marcus Aurelius. A century of war and disorder followed, during which a succession of generals were placed on the throne by their armies

284–305 Diocletian reorganized the Empire as a centralized autocracy

324–37 Constantine I realized the political value of Christianity and became a convert

330 Constantine removed the capital to Constantinople, and the Empire was divided

410 the Goths overran Greece and Italy, sacked Rome, and finally settled in Spain. The Vandals conquered Italy

451–2 the Huns raided Gaul and Italy

476 the last Western emperor was deposed

MEDIEVAL AND EARLY MODERN

300–1500 AD period of the great medieval states in Africa: Ghana, Mali, Songhai, Benin, Ife

320–550 Gupta dynasty in India

4th century Christianity became the established religion of the Roman Empire

4th–6th centuries Western Europe overrun by Anglo-Saxons, Franks, Goths, and Lombards

570 birth of Muhammad

7th–8th centuries Islamic expansion began in N, E, and Central Africa. Christendom threatened by Moorish invasions

800 Charlemagne given title of Emperor by the Pope

c. 1000 Leif Ericsson traditionally reached N America

1073 Gregory VII began 200 years of conflict between the Empire and the Papacy

1096–1291 the Crusades were undertaken to recover the Holy Land from the Muslims

1192 first Muslim kingdom of India established

12th century setting up of German, Flemish, and Italian city states in Europe, which in the 14th and 15th centuries fostered the Renaissance

12th–14th centuries height of Moundbuilder and Pueblo cultures in N America

12th–15th centuries era of Arab travellers in Africa, such as Ibn Batuta, and of trade (for example Kilwa)

1280 Kublai Khan became emperor of China

1395 Tamerlane defeated the Golden Horde, the invading Mongol-Tartar army which had terror-

ized Europe from 1237
1398 Tamerlane captured Delhi
1453 Constantinople captured by the Turks
1488 Diaz rounded the Cape of Good Hope
1492, 12 Oct Columbus first sighted land in the Caribbean
16th century arrival of Europeans in S America, with the Spanish (Pizarro) and Portuguese conquest. American Indians were either killed, assimilated, or, where unsuitable as slave labour, replaced by imported slaves from Africa
1526 Babur established the Mogul Empire in India
1565 first Spanish settlements in N America
16th–17th centuries Europe dominated by rivalry of France and the Hapsburgs, the Protestant Reformation, and the Catholic Counter-Reformation
1607 first permanent English settlement in N America at Jamestown, Virginia
17th century beginnings of the British East India Company in India. Era of absolute monarchies in Europe (notably Louis XIV)
18th century War of Austrian Succession and Seven Years' War ended in loss of French colonial empire to Britain and the emergence of Prussia as a leading European power. Height of the Atlantic and Indian Ocean slave trade
1789–95 French Revolution and the overthrow of Louis XVI

REVOLUTIONS

REVOLUTION
The word can be used to describe any rapid, far-reaching or violent change in the political, social or economic structure of society. It has usually been applied to different forms of political change; the American Revolution (War of Independence) where colonists broke free from their colonial ties and established a sovereign, independent state; the French Revolution where an absolute monarchy was overthrown by opposition from inside the country and a popular rising; and the Russian Revolution where a repressive monarchy was overthrown by those seeking to institute widespread social and economic changes in line with a socialist model. While political revolutions are often associated with violence, there are other types of change which often have just as much impact on society. Most notable is the Industrial Revolution, a process which has imposed massive changes on economies and societies since the mid-18th century. In the 1980s, a 'silicon' revolution was underway, involving the increasing use of computers to undertake tasks formerly done 'by hand'.
American Revolution the revolt 1775–83 of the British North American colonies that resulted in the establishment of the United States of America. It was caused by colonial resentment at the contemporary attitude that commercial or industrial interests of any colony should be subordinate to those of the mother country;

and by the unwillingness of the colonists to pay for a standing army. It was also fuelled by the colonists anti-monarchist sentiment and a desire to participate in the policies affecting them.
1773 a government tax on tea which led citizens disguised as N American Indians to board the ships carrying the tea and throw it into the harbour (the **Boston Tea Party**)
1774–75 the **First Continental Congress** held in Philadelphia to call for civil disobedience in reply to British measures
1775 19 April hostilities began at Lexington and Concord, Massachusetts, the first shots being fired when British troops, sent to seize illegal military stores, were attacked by the local militia. The first battles was **Bunker Hill** Massachusetts, 17 June 1775, in which the colonists were defeated; George Washington was appointed colonial commander soon afterwards
1776 the **Second Continental Congress** on 4 July issued the **Declaration of Independence**.
27 Aug at **Long Island** Washington was defeated, forced to evacuate New York and retire to Pennsylvania, but re-crossed the Delaware to win successes at **Trenton** (26 Dec) and **Princeton** (3 Jan 1777)
1777 a British plan, for Sir William Howe (advancing from New York) and General Burgoyne (from Canada) to link up, miscarried. Burgoyne surrendered at **Saratoga** (17 Oct) but Howe invaded Pennsylvania, defeating Washington at **Brandywine** (11 Sept) and **Germantown** (4 Oct), and occupying Philadelphia; Washington wintered at Valley Forge 1777–78
1778 France and Spain entered the war on the American side
1780 12 May capture of **Charleston**, the most notable of a series of British victories in the American south, but they alienated support by attempting to enforce conscription
1781 19 Oct Cornwallis, besieged in **Yorktown** by Washington and the French fleet, surrendered
1782 peace negotiations opened
1783 3 Sept **Treaty of Paris** American independence recognized.
Industrial Revolution the sudden acceleration of technical development which occurred in Europe from the late 18th century, and which transferred the balance of political power from the landowner to the industrial capitalist, and created an organized industrial working class. The great achievement of the first phase (to 1830) was the invention of the steam engine in Britain, originally developed for draining mines, but rapidly put to use in factories and in the railways. In the second phase, from 1830 to the early 20th century, the Industrial Revolution enlarged its scope from Europe to the world, with some initial exploitation of 'colonial' possessions by European powers as a preliminary to their independent development, and the internal combustion engine and electricity were developed. Then in 1911

Rutherford split the atom at Manchester and the prospect of nuclear power opened, and electronic devices were developed which made possible automation, with the eventual prospect of even managerial decision-making being in the hands of 'machines'.

French Revolution the forcible abolition of the *Ancien Régime* 'old order of things' (feudalism and absolute monarchy) 1789–99.

1789 5 May the States General (an assembly of the three 'estates', nobles, clergy, and commons) met at Versailles, bent on establishing a new constitution; 17 June National Assembly formed by the Third Estate (commons); 14 Jul Bastille was taken by the mob when Louis XVI attempted repressive moves

1791 20 June flight of the royal family to Varennes; 14 Sept Louis, brought back as a prisoner, accepted the new constitution

1792 20 April war declared on Austria, which threatened to suppress the revolution; 10 Aug royal palace stormed by the French mob; 21 Sept First Republic proclaimed

1793 21 Jan Louis XVI executed; 2 June overthrow of the moderate Girondins by the Jacobins; rule of the dictatorial Committee of Public Safety; 5 Sept the mass executions of the Terror began

1794 27 July (9 Thermidor under the Revolutionary calendar) fall of Robespierre and end of the Terror; the Directory (a body of five directors) established to hold a middle course between Royalism and Jacobinism. It ruled until Napoleon seized power in 1799.

Bastille a fortress prison in Paris, stormed by the mob at the beginning of the revolution on 14 July 1789, when it was found to contain only seven prisoners. The governor and most of the garrison were killed and the building razed.

Commune of Paris first body which took this name between 1789–1794 and acted as the municipal government of Paris from the storming of the Bastille to the fall of Robespierre.

Jacobins extremist republican club founded at Versailles in 1789, which later used a former Jacobin (Dominican) friary as its headquarters in Paris. It was led by Robespierre and closed after his execution in 1794.

Girondins right wing republicans of the French Revolution whose leaders came from the Gironde departement of France.

Robespierre Maximilien. French politician, 'the Sea Green Incorruptible'. As Jacobin leader in the National Convention, he supported the execution of Louis XVI and the overthrow of the Girondins, and as dominant member of the Committee of Public Safety instituted the Reign of Terror in 1793. His extremist zeal made him enemies on both left and right, resulting in his overthrow and death by guillotining in July 1794.

Danton Georges Jacques. French lawyer and leading revolutionary. Influential in the early years of the revolution in Paris, he was instrumental in organizing the rising of 10 Aug 1792 which overthrew the monarchy. He also helped to instigate the revolutionary tribunal

and the Committee of Public Safety in 1793. He led the Committee until July 1793 but was then superseded by Robespierre. An attempt to reassert his power failed and he was guillotined in 1794.

Marat Jean Paul 1743–93. French revolutionary leader and journalist. He was the idol of the Paris revolutionary crowds, and was elected in 1792 to the National Convention, where he carried on a long struggle with the Girondins, ending in their overthrow in May 1793. In Jul he was murdered by Charlotte Corday.

Revolutions of 1848 a series of revolts in various parts of Europe against monarchial rule. While some of the revolutionaries had republican ideas, many more were motivated by economic grievances. The revolution began in France and then spread to Italy, the Austrian Empire, and to Germany where the short-lived Frankfurt Parliament put forward ideas about German political unity. None of the revolutions enjoyed any lasting success, and most were violently suppressed within a few months.

Indian Mutiny (1857–58) the revolt of the Bengal Army against the British in India. The movement was confined to the North, from Bengal to the Punjab, and Central India. Most support came from the army and recently dethroned princes, but in some areas it developed into a peasant rising or general revolt. Outstanding episodes were the seizure of Delhi by the rebels, and its seige and recapture by the British, and the defence of Lucknow by a British garrison. The mutiny led to the end of rule by the East Indian Co. and its replacement by direct Crown administration.

Paris Commune the second body to bear this name. A provisional government of Socialist and left-wing Republicans, elected in March 1871 after an attempt by the right-wing National Assembly at Versailles to disarm the Paris National Guard, it held power until May, when the Versailles troops captured Paris and massacred at least 20,000 people. It is famous as the first socialist government in history.

Chinese Revolution a series of major political upheavals which began in 1911 with a nationalist revolt which overthrew the Chiing imperial dynasty in 1912. Led by Sun Yat-Sen (1923–5) and then by Chiang Kai-Shek (1925–49), the nationalists came under increasing pressure from the growing communist movement. The 6,000 mile 'Long March' of the Chinese communists (1934–5) to escape from the nationalist forces saw Mao Tse-Tung emerge as leader. After World War II, the conflict expanded into open civil war (1946–9) with the nationalists finally being defeated at Nanking. This effectively established communist rule in China under the leadership of Mao.

Sun Yat-Sen or *Sun Zhong Shan* 1867–1925. Chinese revolutionary, founder of the Guomindang, and moving spirit behind the revolution of 1911 which overthrew the Manchu dynasty. He was briefly president 1912, but the reactionaries gained the ascendant, and he broke away to try to establish an independent republic in S China based on Canton. He lacked organizational ability, but his three 'people's principles' of nationalism, democracy, and social reform were influential.

Chiang Kai-Shek Chinese statesman (Pinyin: *Jiang Jie Shi*). He took part in the Revolution of 1911, and after the death of Sun Yat-sen was made Commander-in-Chief of the Guomindang armies in S China in 1925. The initial collaboration with the communists, broken in 1927, was resumed following the Xi An incident, and he nominally headed the struggle against the Japanese invaders, receiving the Japanese surrender in 1945. Civil War then resumed between communists and nationalists, and ended in the defeat of Chiang in 1949, and the limitation of his rule to Taiwan.

Mao Zedong or **Mao Tse-Tung** 1893–1976. Chinese statesman, the 'Great Helmsman'. Born in Hunan, he became the leader of the communists in 1927. After the rupture with the nationalists, led by Chiang Kai-shek, Mao Zedong and his troops undertook the 'Long March' of 10,000 km/6000 mi 1934–5 from SE to NW China, the prelude to his ascent to power. Again in nominal alliance with Chiang against the Japanese 1937–45, he subsequently defeated him, and proclaimed the People's Republic of China in 1949. As Chairman of the Communist Party, he provided the pattern for the development of the country through the Great Leap Forward of 1959, and the Cultural Revolution of 1966 based on his thoughts contained in the *Little Red Book*. His reputation plunged after his death, but was later somewhat restored.

Russian Revolution the name given to the two revolutions of March and Nov 1917 which began with the overthrow of the Romanov Imperial dynasty and ended with the the establishment of a state run by Lenin and the Bolsheviks. The revolution of March 1917 arose in part from the repressive nature of Tsarist government but primarily as a result of the mismanagement of the war after 1914. Riots in St Petersburg led to the abdication of Tsar Nicholas II and the formation of a provisional government under Kerensky. The provisional government ruled until Oct 1917 but found its power increasingly undermined by the soldiers' and workers' soviets in Petrograd (St Petersburg) and Moscow. During this period, the Bolsheviks under Lenin's guidance, had concentrated on gaining control of the soviets and advocating an end to the war and land reform. Under the slogan 'All power to the Soviets', they staged a coup on the night of 6–7 Nov which overthrew the government. The second All-Russian Congress of Soviets, which met the following day, proclaimed itself the new government of Russia. The Bolshevik seizure of power led to peace with Germany through the Treaty of Brest-Litovsk, but also to civil war as anti-Bolshevik elements within the army attempted to seize power. The war lasted until 1920, when the Red Army, organized by Trotsky, finally overcame 'white' opposition.

Lenin Vladimir Ilich Ulyanov 1870–1924. Born 22 April 1870 at Simbinsk (Ulyanovsk), Vladimir Ilich Ulyanov was converted to Marxism in 1889 and exiled to Siberia in 1895 as a result of subversive activity. After 1900, he spent most of his time in Western Europe, emerging as the leader of the more radical Bolshevik section of Russian Social Democracy. Returning to Russia in April 1917 with German help, Lenin assumed control of the Bolshevik movement and was instrumental in organizing the coup of 6–7 Nov. From then until his death in 1924, he effectively controlled Russia, establishing Bolshevik rule and the beginnings of communism. In addition he consolidated his position as a great Marxist theoretician, modifying traditional Marxist doctrine to fit the objective conditions prevailing in Russia, a doctrine known as Marxism-Leninism which became the basis of communist ideology.

Trotsky Leon 1879–1940. Born 7 Nov 1879 at Yanovka. Communist theorist, agitator, and collaborator with Lenin after the two met in exile in London in 1902. Trotsky was a leading member of the Bolshevik movement in 1917 and helped organize the overthrow of the Provisional Government. He was instrumental in building up the Red Army to the point where it could win the Civil War and acted as Commissioner for Foreign Affairs until 1924. He was ousted during the power struggle which followed Lenin's death, but he remained active in opposing Stalin's rule until he was assassinated in Aug 1940.

Cuban Revolution 1959 name given to the overthrow of the Batista regime in Jan 1959 by Fidel Castro and the 26 July Movement. Having led abortive coups in 1953 and 1956, Castro succeeded in overthrowing Batista with a force of only 5,000 men. Politically non-aligned, Castro was increasingly forced to seek Eastern Bloc help for government as a result of US opposition—which culminated in the abortive 'Bay of Pigs' invasion of 1961 sponsored by the CIA. The missile crisis of 1962 highlighted Russian involvement in Cuba. Between 1959 and 1974, Cuba, led by Castro, his brother Raúl, and initially Che Guevara, adopted economic and social policies based on the principles of Marxism-Leninism and relied almost exclusively on communist help. After 1974, in an attempt to stabilize the economy, Castro reintroduced incentives into society with the maxim that each 'should receive according to his work' rather than according to his need.

Castro Ruz Fidel 1927– . Cuban Prime Minister. Of wealthy parentage Castro was educated at Jesuit schools and, after studying law at the University of Havana, he gained a reputation through his work for poor clients. He strongly opposed the Batista dictatorship, and with his brother Raúl took part in an unsuccessful attack on the Army barracks at Santiago de Cuba in 1953. After spending some time in exile in the USA and Mexico, Castro attempted a secret landing in Cuba in 1956

Chinese Dynasties

c. 2200–c. 1500 BC	The *Xia dynasty*, a bronze age early civilization, with further agricultural developments, including irrigation, and the first known use of writing in this area.
c. 1500–c. 1066 BC	The *Shang dynasty* is the first of which we have documentary evidence. Writing became well-developed; bronze vases survive in ceremonial burials. The first Chinese calendar was made.
c. 1066–221 BC	During the *Zhou dynasty*, the feudal structure of society broke down in a period of political upheaval, though iron, money, and written laws were all in use, and philosophy flourished. The dynasty ended in the 'Warring States' period (403–221 BC), with the country divided into small kingdoms.
221–206 BC	The *Qin* dynasty corresponds to the reign of Shih Huang Ti, who curbed the feudal nobility and introduced orderly bureaucratic government; he had roads and canals built and began the Great Wall of China to keep out invaders from the north.
206 BC–AD 220	The *Han dynasty* was a long period of peace, during which territory was incorporated, the keeping of historical records was systematized, and an extensive civil service set up. Art and literature flourished, and Buddhism was introduced. The first census was taken in AD 2, registering a population of 57 million. Chinese caravans traded with the Parthians.
220–581	The area was divided under *Three Kingdoms*: the Wei, Shu, and Wu. Confucianism was superseded by Buddhism and Taoism; glass was introduced from the West. Following prolonged fighting, the Wei became the most powerful kingdom, eventually founding the *Jin dynasty* (265–304), which expanded to take over from the barbarian invaders who ruled much of China at that time, but from 305 to 580 lost the territory they had gained to the Tatar invaders from the north.
581–618	Reunification came with the *Sui dynasty* when the government was reinstated, the barbarian invasions stopped, and the Great Wall refortified.
618–907	During the *Tang dynasty* the system of government became more highly developed and centralized, and the empire covered most of SE and much of central Asia. Sculpture, painting, and poetry flourished again, and trade relations were established with the Islamic world and the Byzantine Empire.
907–960	The period known as the *Five Dynasties and Ten Kingdoms* held war, economic depression, and loss of territory in N China, central Asia, and Korea, but printing was developed, including the first use of paper money, and porcelain traded to Islamic lands.
960–1279	The *Sung dynasty* was a period of calm and creativity. Central government was restored, and movable type was invented. At the end of the dynasty, the northern and western frontiers were neglected, and Mongol invasions took place. Marco Polo visited the court of the Great Khan in 1275.
1279–1368	The *Yuan dynasty* saw the beginning of Mongol rule in China, with Kublai Khan on the throne in Beijing 1293; there were widespread revolts. Marco Polo served the Kublai Khan.
1368–1644	The Mongols were expelled by the first of the native Chinese *Ming dynasty*, who expanded the empire. Chinese ships sailed to the Sunda Islands 1403, Ceylon 1408, and the Red Sea 1430. Mongolia was captured by the second Ming emperor. Architecture developed and Beijing flourished as the new capital. Portuguese explorers reached Macao 1516 and Canton 1517; other Europeans followed. Chinese porcelain arrived in Europe 1580. The Jesuits reached Beijing 1600.
1644–1912	The last of the dynasties was the *Manchu* or *Ching*, who were non-Chinese nomads from Manchuria. Initially trade and culture flourished, but during the 19th century it seemed that China would be partitioned among the US and European imperialist nations, since all trade was conducted through treaty ports in their control. The *Boxer Rebellion* 1900 against Western influence was suppressed by European troops.
1911–12	Revolution broke out, and the infant emperor Henry P'u-i was deposed.

in which all but 11 of his supporters were killed. He eventually gathered an army of over 5,000 which overthrew Batista in 1959 and he became Prime Minister a few months later. He became president in 1976, and in 1979 also president of the Non-Aligned Movement. His brother Raúl was appointed Minister of Armed Forces in 1959.

Guevara Ernesto 'Che' 1928–67. Revolutionary. Born in Argentina, he was trained as a doctor, but in 1953 left the country because of his opposition to Peron. In effecting the Cuban revolution of 1959, he was second only to Castro and his brother, but in 1965 moved on to fight against white mercenaries in the Congo, and then to Bolivia, where he was killed in an unsuccessful attempt to lead a peasant rising. His revolutionary technique using minimum resources has been influential, but his orthodox Marxism has been obscured by romanticizing disciples.

Chilean Revolution 1970–73. Name given to the period between 1970 and 1973 and the Presidency of Salvador Allende, the world's first democratically elected Marxist head of state. Allende was brought to power in 1970 as the head of the Popular Unity alliance of socialists, communists, and radicals, a victory which owed more to the disunity of the Christian Democrat opposition than a major shift in voter preferences. Allende was committed to extensive social and economic reforms to be carried out within the existing political structure—the so-called 'peaceful road to socialism'. Nationalization of key industries and increased contacts with Eastern Bloc countries strained Chile's traditional economic relations with the USA and the West. His failure to stabilize the economy created widespread opposition; Allende was unable to fulfil the expectations of his supporters or quell the fears of his opponents about the pace of change. This led to increasing political polarization which culminated in a military coup in Sept 1973. The Allende regime was overthrown and replaced by a four-man junta led by General Pinochet.

Allende Gossens Salvador 1908– . Born in Valparaiso, Chile, Allende became a Marxist activist in the 1930s and rose to prominence as a left-wing presidential candidate in 1952, 1958, and 1964. In each election he had the support of the socialist and communist movements but was defeated by the Christian Democrats and Nationalists. Elected in 1970 as the candidate of the Popular Front alliance, Allende never succeeded in keeping the electoral alliance together in government. His failure to solve the country's economic problems or to deal with political subversion allowed the army to stage the 1973 coup which brought about Allende's death, and those of many of his supporters.

Nicaraguan Revolution the revolt led by the FSLN (Sandinist National Liberation Front, named after Augusto Cesar Sandino, killed by the National Guard in 1934) against the dictatorship established by the father of the president Anastasio 'Tacho' Somoza. The dictatorship of the Somoza family had been underwritten by US support but this was of little help in 1978–9 when the Sandinistas mounted a full scale challenge to the regime and the hated National Guard. Somoza was forced into exile and assassinated in Paraguay in 1980. Since the revolution, the Sandinistas have taken political control of the country, introducing socialist policies and receiving help from Eastern Bloc countries and US aid dried up. The Sandinista government has had to contend with severe economic problems and also the activities of a counter-revolutionary movement, the Contras, operating in the north of the country with US monetary and technical support.

Iranian Revolution the revolution in Iran 1979 which deposed the shah 15 Jan and led to the popular return of Ayatollah Khomeini 1 Feb. Opposition to the shah's one-party regime (introduced 1975) became so great that he was forced to quit the country, leaving the way open for Khomeini's return. Khomeini, exiled for 25 years, had led an effective campaign from France. He appointed Mehdi Bazargan as prime minister 1979–80; real power however, remained with Khomeini's Islamic Revolutionary Council. Revolutionary forces took control of the country, and Khomeini announced the establishment of the Islamic Republic, in which a return was made to the strict observance of Muslim principles and tradition. The harshness of the Islamic codes caused increasing opposition to Khomeini's regime, which led to a power struggle after his death 1989. The more moderate Hoshemi Rafsanjani became president.

Revolutions of 1989 a series of revolutions in various countries of Eastern Europe against communist rule. By 1990 most had moved from monist to pluralist political systems.

Mikhail Gorbachev's official encouragement of *perestroika* (radical restructuring), and *glasnost* (greater political openness), largely for economic reasons, unleashed a wave of simmering discontent: both within the USSR (notably in the Baltic states of Estonia, Latvia, and Lithuania, and in Byelorussia, the Ukraine, and Moldova) and in several East European countries. Until the late 1980s, any potentially damaging discontent, however widespread, had been kept in check by the use of, or threat of military force controlled from Moscow—as in the termination of the Prague Spring experiment 1968 in Czechoslovakia.

Bulgaria, Czechoslovakia, East Germany, Hungary, Poland, Romania, Albania, and Yugoslavia were not as 'reluctantly content' with their lot as had been supposed, though they still subscribed to a form of one-party communism. Though many of the countries achieved bloodless coups (Bulgaria, Czechoslovakia, and Hungary), some were more dramatic: Romania's 'Christmas Revolution' 1989, in which Nicolae Ceauşescu was shot, was short and bloody. East Germany's revolution witnessed the symbolic dismantling of the Berlin Wall Nov 1989, with formal unification of East and West Germany Oct 1990. In Yugoslavia, the multi-party systems established in Slovenia and Croatia led to several republics calling for secession, and fighting between Serbs and Croats in Croatia 1991.

HOLY ROMAN EMPERORS

Carolingian Kings and Emperors

Charlemagne, Charles the Great   800–14

Louis I, the Pious	814–40
Lothair I	840–55
Louis II	855–75
Charles II, the Bald	875–77
Charles III, the Fat	881–87
Guido of Spoleto	891–94
Lambert of Spoleto (co-emperor)	892–98
Arnulf (rival)	896–901
Louis III of Provence	901–05
Berengar	905–24
Conrad I of Franconia (rival)	911–18

Saxon Kings and Emperors

Henry I, the Fowler	918–36
Otto I, the Great	936–73
Otto II	973–83
Otto III	938–1002
Henry II, the Saint	1002–24

Franconian (Salian) Emperors

Conrad II	1024–39
Henry III, the Black	1039–56
Henry IV	1056–1106
Rudolf of Swabia (rival)	1077–80
Hermann of Luxembourg (rival)	1081–93
Conrad of Franconia (rival)	1093–1101
Henry V	1106–25
Lothair II	1126–37

Hohenstaufen Kings and Emperors

Conrad III	1138–52
Frederick Barbarossa	1152–90
Henry VI	1190–97
Otto IV	1198–1215
Philip of Swabia (rival)	1198–1208
Frederick II	1215–50
Henry Raspe of Thuringia (rival)	1246–67
William of Holland (rival)	1247–56
Conrad IV	1250–54
The Great Interregnum	1254–73

Rulers from Various Noble Families

Richard of Cornwall (rival)	1257–72
Alfonso X of Castile (rival)	1257–73
Rudolf I, Habsburg	1273–91
Adolf I of Nassau	1292–98
Albert I, Habsburg	1298–1303
Henry VII, Luxembourg	1308–13
Louis IV of Bavaria	1314–47
Frederick of Habsburg (co-regent)	1314–25
Charles IV, Luxembourg	1347–78
Wenceslas of Bohemia	1378–1400
Frederick III of Brunswick	1400
Rupert of the Palatinate	1400–10
Sigismund, Luxembourg	1411–37

Habsburg Emperors

Albert II	1438–39
Frederick III	1440–93
Maximilian I	1493–1519
Charles V	1519–56
Ferdinand I	1556–64

Maximilian II	1564–76
Rudolf II	1576–1612
Matthais	1612–19
Ferdinand II	1619–37
Ferdinand III	1637–57
Leopold I	1658–1705
Joseph I	1705–11
Charles VI	1711–40
Charles VII of Bavaria	1742–45

Habsburg-Lorraine Emperors

Francis I of Lorraine	1745–65
Joseph II	1765–90
Leopold II	1790–92
Francis II	1792–1806

ENGLISH SOVEREIGNS FROM 900

Name	Date of accession	Relationship
West Saxon Kings		
Edward the Elder	901	son of Alfred the Great
Athelstan	925	son of Edward I
Edmund	940	half-brother of Athelstan
Edred	946	brother of Edmund
Edwy	955	son of Edmund
Edgar	959	brother of Edwy
Edward the Martyr	975	son of Edgar
Ethelred II	978	son of Edgar
Edmund Ironside	1016	son of Ethelred
Danish Kings		
Canute	1016	son of Sweyn
Hardicanute	1040	son of Canute
Harold I	1035	son of Canute
West Saxon Kings (restored)		
Edward the Confessor	1042	son of Ethelred II
Harold II	1066	son of Godwin
Norman Kings		
William I	1066	
William II	1087	son of William I
Henry I	1100	son of William I
Stephen	1135	grandson of William II
House of Plantagenet		
Henry II	1154	son of Matilda (daughter of Henry I)
Richard I	1189	son of Henry II
John	1199	son of Henry II
Henry III	1216	son of John
Edward I	1272	son of Henry III
Edward II	1307	son of Edward I
Edward III	1327	son of Edward II
Richard II	1377	son of the Black Prince

(son of Edward III)

House of Lancaster

Henry IV	1399	son of John of Gaunt
Henry V	1413	son of Henry IV
Henry VI	1422	son of Henry V

House of York

Edward IV	1461	son of Richard, Duke of York
Edward V	1483	son of Edward IV
Richard III	1483	brother of Edward IV

House of Tudor

Henry VII	1485	son of Edmund Tudor, Earl of Richmond
Henry VIII	1509	son of Henry VII
Edward VI	1547	son of Henry VIII
Mary I	1553	daughter of Henry VIII
Elizabeth I	1558	daughter of Henry VIII

House of Stuart

James I	1603	great-grandson of Margaret (daughter of Henry VII)
Charles I	1625	son of James I

The Commonwealth

House of Stuart (restored)

Charles II	1660	son of Charles I
James II	1685	son of Charles I
William III and Mary	1689	son of Mary (daughter of Charles I)/ daughter of James II
Anne	1702	daughter of James II

House of Hanover

George I	1714	son of Sophia (granddaughter of James I)
George II	1727	son of George I
George III	1760	son of Frederick (son of George II)
George IV	1820	son of George III
William IV	1830	son of George III
Victoria	1837	daughter of Edward (son of George III)

House of Saxe-Coburg

Edward VII	1901	son of Victoria

House of Windsor

George V	1910	son of Edward VII
Edward VIII	1936	son of George V
George VI	1936	son of George V
Elizabeth II	1952	daughter of George VI

KINGS OF FRANCE

Valois Kings of France

Philip VI	1328–50
John	1350–64
Charles V	1364–80
Charles VI	1380–1422
Charles VII	1422–61
Louis XI	1461–83
Charles VIII	1483–98
Louis XII	1498–1515
Francis I	1515–47
Henry II	1547–59
Francis II	1559–60
Charles IX	1560–74
Henry III	1574–89

Bourbon Kings of France

Henry IV	1589–1610
Louis XIII	1610–43
Louis XIV	1643–1715
Louis XV	1715–74
Louis XVI	1774–93

KINGS OF ITALY

Vittorio Emanuele II	1861–78
Umberto I	1878–1900
Vittorio Emanuele III	1900–46
Umberto II	1946 (abdicated)

HABSBURGS

Emperors of Austria

Franz I and II	1804–35
Ferdinand I	1835–48

Emperors of Austria-Hungary

Franz Josef	1848–1916
Karl	1916–18 (abdicated)

RUSSIAN RULERS
1547–1917

House of Rurik

Ivan 'the Terrible'	1547–84
Theodore I	1548–98
Irina	1598

House of Gudonov

Boris Gudonov	1598–1605
Theodore II	1605

Usurpers

Dimitri III	1605–06
Basil IV	1606–10
Interregnum	1610–13

House of Romanov

Michael Romanov	1613–45
Alexis	1645–76
Theodore III	1676–82
Peter I and Ivan V (brothers)	1682–96
Peter I 'Peter the Great' (Tsar)	1689–1721
Peter I (Emperor)	1721–25
Catherine I	1725–27
Peter II	1727–30
Anna Ivanovna	1730–40
Ivan VI	1740–41
Elizabeth	1741–62
Peter III	1762
Catherine II 'Catherine the Great'	1762–96
Paul I	1796–1801
Alexander I	1801–25
Nicholas I	1825–55
Alexander II	1855–81
Alexander III	1881–94
Nicholas II	1894–1917

From Colonialism to Independence: The Break-up of the Empires

Belgium

current name	colonial names and history	colonized	independent
Zaïre	Belgian Congo	1885	1960

France

current name	colonial names and history	colonized	independent
Cambodia	Kampuchea 1970–89	1863	1953
Laos	French Indochina (protectorate)	1893	1954
Vietnam	Tonkin, Annam, Cochin-China to 1954	1858	1954
	North and South Vietnam 1954–76		
Burkina Faso	Upper Volta to 1984	1896	1960
Central African Republic	Ubangi-Shari	19th century	1960
Chad	French Equatorial Africa	19th century	1960
Côte d'Ivoire	Ivory Coast to 1986	1883	1960
Madagascar		1896	1960
Mali	French Sudan	19th century	1960
Niger		1912	1960
Algeria	colonized in 19th century; incorporated into France 1881	c. 1840	1962

The Netherlands

current name	colonial names and history	colonized	independent
Indonesia	Netherlands Indies	17th century	1949
Suriname	British colony 1650–67	1667	1975

Portugal

current name	colonial names and history	colonized	independent
Brazil		1532	1822
Uruguay	province of Brazil	1533	1828
Mozambique		1505	1975
Angola		1491	1975

Spain

current name	colonial names and history	colonized	independent
Paraguay	viceroyalty of Buenos Aires	1537	1811
Argentina	viceroyalty of Buenos Aires	16th century	1816
Chile		1541	1818
Costa Rica		1563	1821
Mexico	viceroyalty of New Spain	16th century	1821
Peru		1541	1824
Bolivia		16th century	1825
Ecuador	Greater Colombia 1822–30	16th century	1830
Venezuela	captaincy-general of Caracas to 1822	16th century	1830
	Greater Colombia	1822–30	
Honduras	federation of Central America 1821–38	1523	1838
El Salvador	federation of Central America 1821–39	16th century	1839
Guatemala	federation of Central America 1821–39	16th century	1839
Dominican Republic	Hispaniola to 1821	16th century	1844
	ruled by Haiti to 1844		
Cuba		1512	1898
Colombia	viceroyalty of New Granada to 1819	16th century	1903
	Greater Colombia to 1830		
Panama	part of Colombia to 1903	16th century	1903
Philippines	Spain 1565–1898, US 1898–1946	1565	1946

United Kingdom

current name	colonial names and history	colonized	independent
India	British E India Co. 18th century–1858	18th century	1947
Pakistan	British E India Co. 18th century–1858	18th century	1947
Sri Lanka	Portuguese, Dutch 1602–1796; Ceylon 1802–1972	16th century	1948
Ghana	Gold Coast	1618	1957

FROM COLONIALISM TO INDEPENDENCE: THE BREAK-UP OF THE EMPIRES (Cont.)

current name	colonial names and history	colonized	independent
Nigeria		1861	1960
Cyprus	Turkish to 1878, then British rule	1878	1960
Sierra Leone	British protectorate	1788	1961
Tanzania	German E Africa to 1921; British mandate from League of Nations/UN as Tanganyika	19th century	1961
Jamaica	Spanish to 1655	17th century	1962
Trinidad & Tobago	Spanish 1532–1797; British 1797–1962	1532	1962
Uganda	British protectorate	1894	1962
Kenya	British colony from 1920	1895	1963
Malaysia	British interests from 1786; Federation of Malaya 1957–63	1874	1963
Malawi	British protectorate of Nyasaland 1907–53; Federation of Rhodesia & Nyasaland 1953–64	1891	1964
Malta	French 1798–1814	1798	1964
Zambia	N Rhodesia – British protectorate; Federation of Rhodesia & Nyasaland 1953–64	1924	1964
The Gambia		1888	1965
Singapore	Federation of Malaya 1963–65	1858	1965
Guyana	Dutch to 1796; British Guiana 1796–1966	1620	1966
Botswana	Bechuanaland – British protectorate	1885	1966
Lesotho	Basutoland	1868	1966
Mauritius		1814	1968
Bangladesh	British E India Co. 18th cent–1858; British India 1858–1947; E Pakistan 1947–71	18th century	1971
Zimbabwe	S Rhodesia from 1923; UDI under Ian Smith 1965–79	1895	1980

CONTINENTS

Africa second largest of the continents, three times the area of Europe

area 30,097,000 sq km/11,620,451 sq mi

largest cities (population over 1 million) Cairo, Algiers, Lagos, Kinshasa, Abidjan, Cape Town, Nairobi, Casablanca, El Gîza, Addis Ababa, Luanda, Dar-es Salaam, Ibadan, Douala, Mogadishu

physical dominated by a uniform central plateau comprising a southern tableland with a mean altitude of 1,070 m/3,000 ft that falls northwards to a lower elevated plain with a mean altitude of 400 m/1,300 ft. Although there are no great alpine regions or extensive coastal plains, Africa has a mean altitude of 610 m/2,000 ft, two times greater than Europe. The highest points are Mount Kilimanjaro 5,900 m/19,364 ft, and Mount Kenya 5,200 m/17,058 ft; the lowest point is Lac Assal in Djibouti 144 m/471 ft below sea level. Compared with other continents, Africa has few broad estuaries or inlets and therefore has proportionately the shortest coastline (24,000 km/15,000 mi). The geographical extremities of the continental mainland are Cape Hafun in the E, Cape Almadies in the W, Ras Ben Sekka in the N, and Cape Agulhas in the S. The Sahel is a narrow belt of savanna and scrub forest which covers 700 million hectares of west and central Africa; 75% of the continent lies within the tropics

features Great Rift Valley, containing most of the great lakes of E Africa (except Lake Victoria); Atlas Mountains in NW; Drakensberg mountain range in SE; Sahara Desert (world's largest desert) in N; Namib, Kalahari, and Great Karoo deserts in S; Nile, Zaïre, Niger, Zambezi, Limpopo, Volta, and Orange rivers

products has 30% of the world's minerals including diamonds (51%) and gold (47%); produces 11% of the world's crude petroleum, 58% of the world's cocoa (Ivory Coast, Ghana, Cameroon, Nigeria), 23% of the world's coffee (Uganda, Ivory Coast, Zaïre, Ethiopia, Cameroon, Kenya), 20% of the world's groundnuts (Senegal, Nigeria, Sudan, Zaïre), and 21% of the world's hardwood timber (Nigeria, Zaïre, Tanzania, Kenya)

population (1988) 610 million; more than double the 1960 population of 278 million, and rising to an estimated 900 million by 2000; annual growth rate 3% (10 times greater than Europe); 27% of the world's undernourished people live in sub-Saharan Africa where an estimated 25 million are facing famine

language over 1,000 languages spoken in Africa; Niger-Kordofanian languages including Mandinke, Kwa, Lingala, Bemba, and Bantu (Zulu, Swahili, Kikuyu), spoken over half of Africa from Mauritania in the W to South Africa; Nilo-Saharan languages, including Dinka, Shilluk, Nuer, and Masai, spoken in Central Africa from the bend of the Niger river to the foothills of Ethiopia; Afro-Asiatic (Hamito-Semitic) languages, including Arabic, Berber, Ethiopian, and Amharic, N of Equator; Khoisan languages with 'click' consonants spoken in SW by Bushmen, Hottentots, and Nama people of Namibia

religion Islam in the N and on the E coast as far S as N Mozambique; animism below the Sahara, which survives alongside Christianity (both Catholic and Protestant) in many central and S areas.

Antarctica an ice-covered continent surrounding the South Pole

area 13,900,000 sq km/5,400,000 sq mi (the size of Europe and the USA combined)

physical formed of two blocks of rock with an area of about 8 million sq km/3 million sq mi, Antarctica is covered by a cap of ice that flows slowly towards its 22,400 km/14,000 mi coastline, reaching the sea in high ice cliffs. The most southerly shores are near the 78th parallel in the Ross and Weddell Seas. E Antarctica is a massive block of ancient rocks that surface in the Transantarctic Mountains of Victoria Land. Separated by a deep channel, W Antarctica is characterized by the mountainous regions of Graham Land, the Antarctic Peninsula, Palmer Land and Ellsworth Land; the highest peak is Vinson Massif (5,139 m/16,866 ft). Little more than 1% of the land is ice-free. With an estimated volume of 24 million cu m/283 million cu ft, the ice-cap has a mean thickness of 1,880 m/6,170 ft and in places reaches depths of 5,000 m/16,000 ft or more. Each annual layer of snow preserves a record of global conditions, and where no melting at the surface of the bedrock has occurred the ice can be a million years old. Occupying 10% of the world's surface, the continent contains 90% of the world's ice and 70% of its fresh water. Winds are strong and temperatures are cold, particularly in the interior where temperatures can drop to −70°C/−100°F and below. Precipitation is largely in the form of snow or hoar-frost rather than rain which rarely exceeds 50 mm/2 in in a year (less than the Sahara Desert). The Antarctic ecosystem is characterized by large numbers of relatively few species of higher plants and animals, and a short food chain from tiny marine plants to whales, seals, penguins, and other sea birds. Only two species of vascular plant are known, but there are about 60 species of moss, 100 species of lichen, and 400 species of algae. The crabeater seal is the most numerous wild large mammal in the world

features Mount Erebus on Ross Island is the world's southernmost active volcano; the Ross Ice Shelf is formed by several glaciers coalescing in the Ross Sea

products cod, Antarctic icefish, and krill are fished in Antarctic waters. Whaling, which began in the early 20th century ceased during the 1960s as a result of over-whaling. Petroleum, coal, and minerals such as palladium and platinum exist, but their exploitation is prevented

---

ANTARCTIC EXPLORATION

1773–77	English explorer James Cook first sailed in Antarctic seas, but exploration was difficult before the development of iron ships able to withstand ice pressure.
1819–21	Antarctica circumnavigated by Russian explorer Fabian Bellingshausen.
1823	British navigator James Weddell sailed into the sea named after him.
1841–42	Scottish explorer James Ross sighted the Great Ice Barrier named after him.
1895	Norwegian explorer Carsten Borchgrevink was one of the first landing party on the continent.
1898	Borchgrevink's British expedition first wintered in Antarctica.
1901–04	English explorer Robert Scott first penetrated the interior of the continent.
1907–08	English explorer Ernest Shackleton came within 182 km/113 mi of the Pole.
1911	Norwegian explorer Roald Amundsen reached the Pole, 14 Dec, overland with dogs.
1912	Scott reached the Pole, 18 Jan, initially aided by ponies.
1928–29	US naval officer Richard Byrd made the first flight to the Pole.
1935	US explorer Lincoln Ellsworth first flew across Antarctica.
1946–48	US explorer Finn Ronne's expedition proved the Antarctic to be one continent.
1957–58	English explorer Vivian Fuchs made the first overland crossing.
1959	Soviet expedition from the West Ice Shelf to the Pole.
1959	International Antarctic Treaty suspended all territorial claims, reserving an area south of 60° S latitude for peaceful purposes.
1961–62	Bentley Trench discovered, which suggested that there may be an Atlantic-Pacific link beneath the Continent.
1966–67	Specially protected areas established internationally for animals and plants.
1979	Fossils of ape-like humanoids resembling E Africa's Proconsul found 500 km/300 mi from the Pole.
1980	International Convention on the exploitation of resources—oil, gas, fish, and krill.
1982	First circumnavigation of Earth (2 Sept 1979–29 Aug 1982) via the Poles by English explorers Ranulph Fiennes and Charles Burton.
1990	Longest unmechanized crossing (6,100 km/3,182 mi) completed by a 6-person international team, using only skis and dogs.
1991	Antarctic Treaty imposing a 50-year ban on mining activity secured.

---

by a 50-year ban on commercial mining agreed by 39 nations in 1991

population no permanent residents; settlement limited to scientific research stations with maximum population of 2,000 to 3,000 during the summer months. Sectors of Antarctica are claimed by Argentina, Australia, Chile, France, the UK, Norway, and New Zealand

history following multi-national scientific co-operation in Antarctica during the International Geophysical Year of 1957–58, 12 countries signed an Antarctic Treaty with a view to promoting scientific research and keeping Antarctica free from conflict. After it came into effect 1961, a further 27 countries acceded to the treaty. In response to overfishing in Antarctic waters, the Conservation of Antarctic Marine Living Resources was agreed 1980. In 1988 the Convention on the Regulation of Antarctic Mineral Resource Activities gave any signatory the right to veto mining activity on environmental grounds. While this provided a means of regulation, environmental pressure groups felt it would not prevent commercial exploitation. In 1991 an agreement was signed extending the Antarctic Treaty and imposing a 50-year ban on mining activity.

Arctic, the that part of the northern hemisphere surrounding the North Pole; arbitrarily defined as the region lying N of the Arctic Circle (66° 32'N) or N of the tree line. There is no Arctic continent—the greater part of the region comprises the Arctic Ocean which is the world's smallest ocean. Arctic climate, fauna, and flora extend over the islands and northern edges of continental land masses that surround the Arctic Ocean (Svalbard, Iceland, Greenland, Siberia, Scandinavia, Alaska, and Canada)

area 36,000,000 sq km/14,000,000 sq mi

physical pack-ice floating on the Arctic Ocean occupies almost the entire region between the North Pole and the coasts of North America and Eurasia, covering an area that ranges in diameter from 3,000 km/1,900 mi to 4,000 km/2,500 mi. The pack-ice reaches a maximum extent in Feb when its outer limit (influenced by the cold Labrador Current and the warm Gulf Stream) varies from 50°N along the coast of Labrador to 75°N in the Barents Sea N of Scandinavia. In spring the pack-ice begins to break up into ice floes which are carried by the S-flowing Greenland Current to the Atlantic Ocean. Arctic ice is at its minimum area in August. The greatest concentration of icebergs in Arctic regions is found in Baffin Bay. They are derived from the glaciers of W Greenland, then carried along Baffin Bay and down into the N Atlantic where they melt off Labrador and Newfoundland. The Bering Straits are icebound for more than six months each year, but the Barents Sea between Scandinavia and Svalbard is free of ice and is

ARCTIC EXPLORATION

60,000–35,000 BC	Ancestors of the Inuit and American Indians began migration from Siberia to North America by the 'lost' landbridge of Beringia.
320 BC	Pytheas, Greek sailor contemporary with Alexander the Great, possibly reached Iceland.
9th–10th centuries AD	Vikings colonized Iceland and Greenland, which then had a much warmer climate.
c. 1000	Norwegian sailor Leif Ericsson reached Baffin Island (NE of Canada) and Labrador.
1497	Genoese pilot Giovanni Caboto first sought the Northwest Passage as a trade route around North America for Henry VII of England.
1553	English navigator Richard Chancellor tried to find the Northeast Passage around Siberia and first established direct English trade with Russia.
1576	English sailor Martin Frobisher reached Frobisher Bay, but found only 'fools' gold' (iron pyrites) for Elizabeth I of England.
1594–97	Dutch navigator Willem Barents made three expeditions in search of the Northeast Passage.
1607	English navigator Henry Hudson failed to cross the Arctic Ocean, but his reports of whales started the northern whaling industry.
1670	Hudson's Bay Company started the fur trade in Canada.
1728	Danish navigator Vitus Bering passed Bering Strait.
1829–33	Scottish explorer John Ross discovered the North Magnetic Pole.
1845	Mysterious disappearance of English explorer John Franklin's expedition to the Northwest Passage stimulated further exploration.
1878–79	Swedish navigator Nils Nordensköld was the first European to discover the Northeast Passage.
1893–96	Norwegian explorer Fridtjof Nansen's ship *Fram* drifted across the Arctic, locked in the ice, proving that no Arctic continent existed.
1903–06	Norwegian explorer Roald Amundsen sailed through the Northwest Passage.
1909	US explorer Robert Peary, Matt Henson, and four Inuit reached the North Pole on 2 April.
1926	US explorer Richard Byrd and Floyd Bennett flew to the Pole on 9 May.
1926	Italian aviator Umberto Nobile and Amundsen crossed the Pole (Spitzbergen–Alaska) in the airship *Norge* on 12 May.
1954	First regular commercial flights over the short-cut polar route by Scandinavian Airlines.
1958	The US submarine *Nautilus* crossed the Pole beneath the ice.
1960	From this date a Soviet nuclear-powered icebreaker has kept open a 4,000 km/2,500 mi Asia-Europe passage along the north coast of Siberia 150 days a year.
1969	First surface crossing, by dog sled, of the Arctic Ocean (Alaska–Spitzbergen) by Wally Herbert, British Transarctic Expedition, Feb–May.
1977	The Soviet icebreaker *Arktika* made the first surface voyage to the Pole.
1982	First circumnavigation of the Earth (2 Sept 1979–29 Aug 1982) via the Poles by Ranulph Fiennes and Charles Burton.
1988	Canadian and Soviet skiers attempted the first overland crossing from the USSR to Canada via the Pole.

navigable throughout the year. Arctic coastlines, which have emerged from the sea since the last Ice Age, are characterized by deposits of gravel and disintegrated rock

climate permanent ice sheets and year-round snow cover are found in regions where average monthly temperatures remain below 0°C/32°F, but on land areas where one or more summer months have average temperatures between freezing point and 10°C/50°F, a stunted, treeless tundra vegetation is found. Mean annual temperatures range from –23°C at the North Pole to –12°C on the coast of Alaska. In winter the sun disappears below the horizon for a time, but the cold is less severe than in parts of inland Siberia or Antarctica. During the short summer season there is a maximum of 24 hours of daylight at the summer solstice on the Arctic Circle and six months constant light at the North Pole. Countries with Arctic coastlines established the International Arctic Sciences Committee in 1987 to study ozone depletion and climatic change

flora and fauna the plants of the relatively infertile Arctic tundra (lichens, mosses, grasses, cushion plants, and low shrubs) spring to life during the short summer season and remain dormant for the remaining ten months of the year. There are no annual plants, only perennials. Animal species include reindeer, caribou, musk ox, fox, hare, lemming, wolf, polar bear, seal, and walrus. There are few birds except in summer when insects, especially mosquitoes, are plentiful

natural resources the Arctic is rich in coal (Svalbard, Russia), oil and natural gas (Alaska, Canadian Arctic, Russia), and mineral resources including gold, silver, copper, uranium, lead, zinc, nickel, and bauxite. Because of climatic conditions, the Arctic is not suited to navigation and the exploitation of these resources

population there are about one million aboriginal people including the Aleuts of Alaska, North American Indians, the Lapps of Scandinavia and Russia, the Yakuts, Samoyeds, Komi, Chukchi, Tungus, and Dolgany of Russia, and the Inuit of Siberian Russia, the Canadian Arctic, and Greenland.

Asia largest of the continents, occupying one third of the total land surface of the world

area 44,000,000 sq km/17,000,000 sq mi

largest cities (population over 5 million) Tokyo, Shanghai, Osaka, Beijing, Seoul, Calcutta, Bombay, Jakarta, Bangkok, Tehran, Hong Kong, Delhi, Tianjin, Karachi

physical lying in the eastern hemisphere, Asia extends from the Arctic Circle to just over 10° S of the Equator. The Asia mainland, which forms the greater part of the Eurasian continent, lies entirely in the northern hemisphere and stretches from Cape Chelyubinsk at its N extremity to Cape Piai at the S tip of the Malay Peninsula. From Dezhneva Cape in the E, the mainland extends W over more than 165° longitude to Cape Baba in Turkey. Containing the world's highest mountains and largest inland seas, Asia can be divided into five physical units:
1) at the heart of the continent, a central triangle of plateaux at varying altitudes (Tibetan Plateau, Tarim Basin, Gobi Desert), surrounded by huge mountain chains which spread in all directions (Himalayas, Karakoram, Hindu Kush, Pamirs, Kunlun, Tien Shan, Altai);
2) the western plateaux and ranges (Elburz, Zagros, Taurus, Great Caucasus mountains) of Afghanistan, Iran, N Iraq, Armenia, and Turkey;
3) the lowlands of Turkestan and Siberia which stretch N of the central mountains to the Arctic Ocean and include large areas in which the subsoil is permanently frozen;
4) the fertile and densely populated E lowlands and river plains of Korea, China, and Indochina, and the islands of the East Indies and Japan;
5) the southern plateaux of Arabia, and the Deccan, with the fertile alluvial plains of the Euphrates, Tigris, Indus, Ganges, Brahmaputra, and Irrawaddy rivers.

In Asiatic Russia are the largest areas of coniferous forest (taiga) in the world. The climate shows great extremes and contrasts, the heart of the continent becoming bitterly cold in winter and extremely hot in summer. When the heated air over land rises, moisture-laden air from the surrounding seas flows in, bringing heavy monsoon rain to all SE Asia, China, and Japan between May and Oct

features Mount Everest at 8,872 m/29,118 ft, is the world's highest mountain; Dead Sea –394 m/–1,293 ft is the world's lowest point below sea level; rivers (over 3,200 km/ 2,000 mi) include Chiang Jiang (Yangtze), Huang He (Yellow River), Ob-Irtysh, Amur, Lena, Mekong, Yeni sei; lakes (over 18,000 sq km/7,000 sq mi) include Caspian Sea (the largest inland sea in the world), Aral Sea, Baikal (largest freshwater lake in Eurasia), Balkhash; deserts include the Gobi, Takla Makan, Syrian Desert, Arabian Desert, Negev

products 62% of the population are employed in agriculture; Asia produces 46% of the world's cereal crops (91% of the world's rice); other crops include mangoes (India), groundnuts (India, China), 84% of the world's copra (Philippines, Indonesia), 93% of the world's rubber (Indonesia, Malaysia, Thailand), tobacco (China), flax (China, Russia), 95% of the world's jute (India, Bangladesh, China), cotton (China, India, Pakistan), silk (China, India), fish (Japan, China, Korea, Thailand); China produces 55% of the world's tungsten; 45% of the world's tin is produced by Malaysia, China, and Indonesia; Saudi Arabia is the world's largest producer of oil

population (1988) 3 billion; the world's largest, though not the fastest growing population, amounting to more than half the total number of people in the world; between 1950 and 1990 the death rate and infant mortality rate were reduced by more than 60%; annual growth rate 1.7%; projected to increase to 3.55 billion by 2000

language predominantly tonal languages (Chinese, Japanese) in the E, Indo-Iranian languages (Hindi, Urdu, Persian) in S Asia, Altaic languages (Mongolian, Turkish) in W and Central Asia, Semitic languages (Arabic, Hebrew) in the SW

religion the major religions of the world had their origins in Asia—Judaism and Christianity in the Middle East, Islam in Arabia, Buddhism, Hinduism, and Sikhism in India, Confucianism in China, and Shinto in Japan.

Europe second smallest continent, occupying 8% of the Earth's surface

area 10,400,000 sq km/4,000,000 sq mi

largest cities (population over 1.5 million) Athens, Barcelona, Berlin, Birmingham, Bucharest, Budapest, Hamburg, Istanbul, Kharkov, Kiev, Lisbon, London, Madrid, Manchester, Milan, Moscow, Paris, Rome, St Petersburg, Vienna, Warsaw

physical conventionally occupying that part of Eurasia to the west of the Ural Mountains, north of the Caucasus Mountains, and north of the Sea of Marmara; Europe lies entirely in the northern hemisphere between 36° N and the Arctic Ocean. About two-thirds of the continent is a great plain which covers the whole of European Russia and spreads westward through Poland to the Low Countries and the Bay of Biscay. To the north lie the Scandinavian highlands rising to 2,470 m/8,110 ft at Glittertind in the Jotenheim Range of Norway. To the south, a series of mountain ranges stretch from east to west (Caucasus, Balkans, Carpathians, Apennines, Alps, Pyrenees, and Sierra Nevada). The most westerly point of the mainland is Cape Roca in Portugal; the most southerly location is Tarifa Point in Spain; the most northerly point on the mainland is Nordkynn in Norway. A line from the Baltic to the Black Sea divides Europe between an eastern continental region and a western region characterized by a series of peninsulas that include Scandinavia (Norway, Sweden, and Finland), Jutland (Denmark and Germany), Iberia (Spain and Portugal), and Italy and the Balkans (Greece, Albania, Croatia, Slovenia, Bosnia-Herzegovina, Yugoslavia, Bulgaria, and European Turkey). Because of the large number of bays, inlets, and peninsulas, the coastline is longer in proportion to its size than that of any other continent. The largest islands adjacent to continental Europe are the British Isles, Novaya Zemlya, Sicily, Sardinia, Crete, Corsica, Gotland (in the Baltic Sea) and the Balearic Islands; more distant islands include Iceland, Svalbard, Franz Josef Land, Madeira, the Azores, and the Canary Islands. The greater part of Europe falls within the northern temperate zone which is modified by the Gulf Stream in the northwest; Central Europe has warm summers and cold winters; the Mediterranean coast has comparatively mild winters and hot summers

features Mount Elbruz 5,642 m/18,517 ft in the Caucasus mountains is the highest peak in Europe; Mont Blanc 4,807 m/15,772 ft is the highest peak in the Alps; lakes (over 5,100 sq km/2,000 sq mi) include Ladoga, Onega, Vänern; rivers (over 800 km/500 mi) include the Volga, Danube, Dnieper, Ural, Don, Pechora, Dneister, Rhine, Loire, Tagus, Ebro, Oder, Prut, Rhône

products nearly 50% of the world's cars are produced in Europe (Germany, France, Italy, Spain, Russia, Georgia, Ukraine, Latvia, Belarus, UK); Europe produces 43% of the world's barley (Germany, Spain, France, UK), 41% of its rye (Poland, Germany), 31% of its oats (Poland, Germany, Sweden, France), and 24% of its wheat (France, Germany, UK, Romania); Italy, Spain, and Greece produce more than 70% of the world's olive oil

population (1985) 496 million (excluding Turkey and the ex-Soviet republics); annual growth rate 0.3%, projected population of 512 million by 2000

language mostly Indo-European, with a few exceptions, including Finno-Ugrian (Finnish and Hungarian), Basque and Altaic (Turkish); apart from a fringe of Celtic, the NW is Germanic; Letto-Lithuanian languages separate the Germanic from the Slavonic tongues of E Europe; Romance languages spread E-W from Romania through Italy and France to Spain and Portugal

religion Christianity (Protestant, Roman Catholic, Eastern Orthodox), Muslim (Turkey, Albania, Bosnia-Herzegovina, Yugoslavia, Bulgaria), Judaism.

North America third largest of the continents (including Greenland and Central America), and more than twice the size of Europe

area 24,000,000 sq km/9,400,000 sq mi

largest cities (population over 1 million) Mexico City, New York, Chicago, Toronto, Los Angeles, Montreal, Guadalajara, Monterrey, Philadelphia, Houston, Guatemala City, Vancouver, Detroit, San Diego, Dallas

physical occupying the N part of the landmass of the western hemisphere between the Arctic Ocean and the tropical SE tip of the isthmus that joins Central America to South America; the northernmost point on the mainland is the tip of Boothia Peninsula in the Canadian Arctic; the northernmost point on adjacent islands is Cape Morris Jesup on Greenland; the most westerly point on the mainland is Cape Prince of Wales, Alaska; the most westerly point on adjacent islands is Attu Island in the Aleutians; the most easterly point on the mainland lies on the SE coast of Labrador; the highest point is Mount McKinley, Alaska 6,194 m/20,320 ft; the lowest point is Badwater in Death Valley –86 m/–282 ft. In Canada and the USA, the Great Plains of the interior separate mountain belts to the E (Appalachians, Laurentian Highlands) and W (Rocky Mountains, Coast Mountains, Cascade Range, Sierra Nevada). The W range extends S into Mexico as the Sierra Madre. The Mississippi river system drains from the central Great Plains into the Gulf of Mexico; low coastal plains on the Atlantic coast are indented by the Gulf of St Lawrence, Bay of Fundy, Delaware Bay, Chesapeake Bay; the St Lawrence and Great Lakes form a rough crescent (with Lake Winnipeg, Lake Athabasca, the Great Bear, and the Great Slave lakes) around the exposed rock of the great Canadian/Laurentian shield, into which Hudson Bay breaks from the north; Greenland (the largest island in the world next to Australia) is a high, ice-covered plateau with a deeply indented coastline of fjords

features Lake Superior (the largest body of freshwater in the world); Grand Canyon on the Colorado river; Redwood National Park, California has some of the world's tallest trees; San Andreas Fault, California; deserts: Death Valley, Mojave, Sonoran; rivers (over 1,600 km/1,000 mi) include Mississippi, Missouri, Mackenzie, Rio Grande, Yukon, Arkansas, Colorado, Saskatchewan-Bow, Columbia, Red, Peace, Snake

products with abundant resources and an ever-expanding home market, the USA's fast-growing industrial and technological strength has made it less dependent on exports and a dominant economic power throughout the continent. Canada is the world's leading producer of nickel, zinc, uranium, potash, and linseed, and the world's second largest producer of asbestos, silver, titanium, gypsum, sulphur, and molybdenum; Mexico is the world's leading producer of silver and the fourth largest oil producer; the USA is the world's leading producer of salt and the second largest producer of oil and cotton; nearly 30% of the world's beef and veal is produced in North America *population* (1988) 417 million, rising to an estimated 450 million by 2000; annual growth rate from 1980 to 1985: Canada 1.08%, USA 0.88%, Mexico 2.59%, Honduras 3.39%; the native American Indian, Inuit, and Aleut peoples are now a minority within a population predominantly of European immigrant origin. Many Africans were brought in as part of the slave trade

language English predominates in Canada, USA, and Belize; Spanish is the chief language of the countries of Latin America and a sizeable minority in the USA; French is spoken by about 25% of the population of Canada, and by people of the French *département* of St Pierre and Miquelon; indigenous non-European minorities, including the Inuit of Arctic Canada, the Aleuts of Alaska, North American Indians, and the Maya of Central America, have their own languages and dialects

religion Christian and Jewish religions predominate; 97% of Latin Americans, 47% of Canadians, and 21% of those living in the USA are Roman Catholic

Oceania a general term for the islands of the central and S Pacific, including Australia, New Zealand, and the E half of New Guinea; although situated in the world's largest ocean, Oceania is the smallest continent in the world in terms of land surface

area 8,500,000 sq km/3,300,000 sq mi (land area)

largest cities (population over 500,000) Sydney, Melbourne, Brisbane, Perth, Adelaide, Auckland

physical stretching from the Tropic of Cancer in the N to the S tip of New Zealand, Oceania can be broadly divided into groups of volcanic and coral islands on the basis of the ethnic origins of their inhabitants: Micronesia (Guam, Kiribati, Mariana, Marshall, Caroline Islands), Melanesia (Papua New Guinea, Vanuatu, New Caledonia, Fiji, Solomon Islands), and Polynesia (Tonga, Samoa, Line Islands, Tuvalu, French Polynesia, Pitcairn); Australia (the largest island in the world) occupies more than 90% of the land surface; the highest point is Mount Wilhelm, Papua New Guinea 4,509 m/ 14,793 ft; the lowest point is Lake Eyre, South Australia –16 m/–52 ft; the longest river is the Murray in SE Australia 2,590 km/1,609 mi

features the Challenger Deep in the Mariana Trench –11,034 m/–36,201 ft is the greatest known depth of sea in the world; Ayers Rock in Northern Territory, Australia is the world's largest monolith; the Great Barrier Reef is the longest coral reef in the world; Mount Kosciusko 2,229 m/7,316 ft in New South Wales, is the highest peak in Australia; Mount Cook 3,764 m/21,353 ft is the highest peak in New Zealand

products with a small home market, Oceania has a manufacturing sector dedicated to servicing domestic requirements and a large export-oriented sector, 70% of which is based on exports of primary agricultural or mineral products. Australia is a major producer of bauxite, nickel, silver, cobalt, gold, iron ore, diamonds, lead, and uranium; New Caledonia is a source of cobalt, chromite, and nickel; Papua and New Guinea produce gold and copper.

Agricultural products include coconuts, copra, palm oil, coffee, cocoa, phosphates (Nauru), rubber (Papua New Guinea), 40% of the world's wool (Australia, New Zealand); New Zealand and Australia are, respectively, the world's second and third largest producers of mutton and lamb; fishing and tourism are also major industries

population 26 million, rising to 30 million by 2000; annual growth rate from 1980 to 1985 1.5%; Australia accounts for 65% of the population; 1% of Australia's population is Aboriginal and 9% of the people of New Zealand are Maori

language English, French (French Polynesia, New Caledonia, Wallis and Fatuna, Vanuatu); a wide range of indigenous Aboriginal, Maori, Melanesian, Micronesian, and Polynesian languages and dialects (over 700 in Papua New Guinea) are spoken

religion predominantly Christian; 30% of the people of Tonga adhere to the Free Wesleyan Church; 70% of the people of Tokelau adhere to the Congregational Church; French overseas territories are largely Roman Catholic.

South America fourth largest of the continents, nearly twice as large as Europe, occupying 13% of the world's land surface

area 17,864,000 sq km/6,900,000 sq mi

largest cities (population over 2 million) Buenos Aires, São Paulo, Rio de Janeiro, Bogotá, Santiago, Lima, Caracas, Janeiro, Belo Horizonte

physical occupying the S part of the landmass of the western hemisphere, the South American continent stretches from Point Gallinas on the Caribbean coast of Colombia to Cape Horn at the southern tip of Horn Island which lies adjacent to Tierra del Fuego; the most southerly point on the mainland is Cape Froward on the Brunswick peninsula, S Chile; at its maximum width (5,120 km/3,200 mi) the continent stretches from Point Pariñas, Peru in the extreme W to Point Coqueiros, just N of Recife, Brazil, in the E; five-sixths of the continent lies in the southern hemisphere and two-thirds within the tropics. South America can be divided into the following physical regions: 1) the Andes mountain system which begins as three separate ranges in the N and stretches the whole length of the W coast approximately 7,200 km/4,500 mi; the highest peak is Aconcagua 6,960 m/22,834 ft; the width of the Andes ranges from 40 km/25 mi in Chile to 640 km/400 mi in Bolivia; a narrow coastal belt lies between the Andes and the Pacific Ocean;
2) the uplifted remains of the old continental mass, with interior plains at an elevation of 610–1,520 m/2,000–5,000 ft, are found in the E and NE, in the Brazilian Highlands (half the area of Brazil) and Guiana Highlands;

3) the plain of the Orinoco river is an alluvial tropical lowland lying between the Venezuelan Andes and the Guiana Highlands;

4) the tropical Amazon Plain stretches over 3,200 km/2,000 mi from the E foothills of the Andes to the Atlantic ocean, separating the Brazilian and Guiana highlands; once an inland sea, the Amazon basin was filled with sediment and then uplifted;

5) the Pampa-Chaco plain of Argentina, Paraguay, and Bolivia occupies a former bay of the Atlantic that has been filled with sediment brought down from the surrounding highlands;

6) the Patagonian Plateau in the S consists of a series of terraces that rise from the Atlantic Ocean to the foothills of the Andes; glaciation, wind, and rain have dissected these terraces and created rugged land forms

features Lake Titicaca (world's highest navigable lake); La Paz (highest capital city in the world); Atacama Desert; Inca ruins at Machu Picchu; rivers include the Amazon (world's largest and second longest), Parana, Madeira, São Francisco, Purus, Paraguay, Orinoco, Araguaia, Negro, Uruguay

products produces 44% of the world's coffee (Brazil, Colombia), 22% of its cocoa (Brazil), 35% of its citrus fruit, meat (Argentina, Brazil), soybeans (Argentina, Brazil), cotton (Brazil), linseed (Argentina); Argentina is the world's second largest producer of sunflower seed; Brazil is the world's largest producer of bananas, its second largest producer of tin, and its third largest producer of manganese, tobacco, and mangoes; Peru is the world's second largest producer of silver; Chile is the world's largest producer of copper

population (1988) 285 million, rising to 550 million by 2000; annual growth rate from 1980 to 1985 2.3%

language Spanish, Portuguese (chief language in Brazil), Dutch (Surinam), French (French Guiana), Amerindian languages; Hindi, Javanese, and Chinese spoken by descendants of Asian immigrants to Surinam and Guyana; a variety of Creole dialects spoken by those of African descent

religion 90–95% Roman Catholic; local animist beliefs among Amerindians; Hindu and Muslim religions predominate among the descendants of Asian immigrants in Surinam and Guyana.

Emigration

If you were free to do so, would you like to go and settle in another country? If Yes; which country would you settle in if you were to emigrate from Britain?

Australia	15
Canada	7
New Zealand	5
USA	5
Europe	4
Other	7
Don't know	3
No, would not	54
'Speaking a foreign language'	
In	76
Out	17
Don't know	7

COUNTRIES

Afghanistan (Republic of)
(Jamhuria Afghanistan)

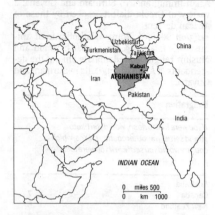

area 652,090 sq km/251,707 sq mi
capital Kabul
towns Kandahar, Herat, Mazar-i-Sharif
physical mountainous in centre and NE, plains in N and SW
environment an estimated 95% of the urban population is without access to sanitation services
features Hindu Kush mountain range (Khyber and Salang passes, Wakhan salient and Panjshir Valley), Amu Darya (Oxus) River, Helmand River, Lake Saberi
interim head of state Burhanuddin Rabbani from 1992
head of government Ustad Sabour Fareed from 1992
political system transitional
political parties Homeland Party (Hezb-i-Watan, formerly People's Democratic Party of Afghanistan (PDPA)) Marxist-Leninist; Hezb-i-Islami and Jamiat-i-Islami, Islamic fundamentalist mujaheddin; National Liberation Front, moderate mujaheddin
exports dried fruit, natural gas, fresh fruit, carpets; small amounts of rare minerals, karakul lamb skins, and Afghan coats
currency afgháni
population (1989) 15,590,000 (more than 5 million became refugees after 1979); growth rate 0.6% p.a.
life expectancy (1986) men 43, women 41
languages Pushtu, Dari (Persian)
religion Muslim (80% Sunni, 20% Shi'ite)
literacy men 39%, women 8% (1985 est)
GNP $3.3 bn (1985); $275 per head
GDP $1,858 million; $111 per head

chronology
1747 Afghanistan became an independent emirate.
1839–42 and 1878–80 Afghan Wars instigated by Britain to counter the threat to British India from expanding Russian influence in Afghanistan.
1919 Afghanistan recovered full independence following Third Afghan War.
1953 Lt-Gen Daud Khan became prime minister and introduced reform programme.
1963 Daud Khan forced to resign and constitutional monarchy established.
1973 Monarchy overthrown in coup by Daud Khan.
1978 Daud Khan ousted by Taraki and the PDPA.
1979 Taraki replaced by Hafizullah Amin; Soviet Union

entered country to prop up government; they installed Babrak Karmal in power. Amin executed.
1986 Replacement of Karmal as leader by Dr Najibullah Ahmadzai. Partial Soviet troop withdrawal.
1988 New non-Marxist constitution adopted.
1989 Complete withdrawal of Soviet troops; state of emergency imposed in response to intensification of civil war.
1990 PDPA renamed the Homeland Party; President Najibullah elected its president.
1991 UN peace plan accepted by President Najibullah but rejected by the mujaheddin. US and Soviet military aid withdrawn.
1992 Mujaheddin began talks with Russians and Kabul government. Pakistan withdrew military aid to the mujaheddin and declared support for UN peace plan. Najibullah regime overthrown by mujaheddin alliance. June: Burhannudin Rabbani named head of state for four-month interim period. July :Ustad Abdul Sabour Fareed, a fundamentalist, became prime minister. New administration ruled to abolish all laws contrary to Shari'a (Islamic law).

Albania (Republic of)
(Republika e Shqipërisë)

area 28,748 sq km/11,097 sq mi
capital Tiranë
towns Shkodër, Elbasan, Vlorë, chief port Durrës
physical mainly mountainous, with rivers flowing E–W, and a narrow coastal plain
features Dinaric Alps, with wild boar and wolves
head of state Sali Berisha from 1992
head of government Alexander Meksi from 1992
political system emergent democracy
political parties Socialist Party of Albania (SPA, formerly Party of Labour of Albania (PLA)), Marxist-Leninist; Democratic Party (DP); Amonia (Greek minority party)
exports crude oil, bitumen, chrome, iron ore, nickel, coal, copper wire, tobacco, fruit, vegetables
currency lek
population (1990 est) 3,270,000; growth rate 1.9% p.a.
life expectancy men 69, women 73
languages Albanian, Greek
religion Muslim 70%, although all religion banned 1967–90
literacy 75% (1986)
GNP $2.8 bn (1986 est); $900 per head
GDP $1,313 million; $543 per head

chronology
c. 1468 Albania made part of the Ottoman Empire.

1912 Independence achieved from Turkey.
1925 Republic proclaimed.
1928–39 Monarchy of King Zog.
1939–44 Under Italian and then German rule.
1946 Communist republic proclaimed under the leadership of Enver Hoxha.
1949 Admitted into Comecon.
1961 Break with Khrushchev's USSR.
1967 Albania declared itself the 'first atheist state in the world'.
1978 Break with 'revisionist' China.
1985 Death of Hoxha.
1987 Normal diplomatic relations restored with Canada, Greece, and West Germany.
1988 Attendance of conference of Balkan states for the first time since the 1930s.
1990 One-party system abandoned; first opposition party formed.
1991 April: PLA won first multiparty elections; Ramiz Alia re-elected president; country renamed Republic of Albania. June: prime minister Nano resigned, replaced by Ylli Bufi who formed new interim caretaker government. Dec: Bufi resigned; DP withdrew from coalition; Vilson Ahmeti formed new government.
1992 Former communist officials arrested on corruption charges. Sali Berisha elected president; Alexander Meksi chosen to succeed Ahmeti.

Algeria (Democratic and Popular Republic of)
(al-Jumhuriya al-Jazairiya ad-Dimuqratiya ash-Shabiya)

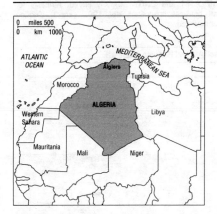

area 2,381,741 sq km/919,352 sq mi
capital al-Jazair (Algiers)
towns Qacentina/Constantine; ports are Ouahran/Oran, Annaba/Bône
physical coastal plains backed by mountains in N; Sahara desert in S
features Atlas mountains, Barbary Coast, Chott Melrhir depression, Hoggar mountains
head of state Ali Kafi from 1992
head of government to be decided
political system semi-military rule
political parties National Liberation Front (FLN), nationalist socialist; Islamic Salvation Front (FIS), Islamic fundamentalist
exports oil, natural gas, iron, wine, olive oil
currency dinar
population (1990 est) 25,715,000 (83% Arab, 17% Berber); growth rate 3.0% p.a.
life expectancy men 59, women 62
languages Arabic (official); Berber, French
religion Sunni Muslim (state religion)
literacy men 63%, women 37% (1985 est)
GDP $64.6 bn; $2,796 per head

chronology
1954 War for independence from France led by the FLN.
1962 Independence achieved from France, Republic declared. Ben Bella elected prime minister.
1963 Ben Bella elected Algeria's first president.
1965 Ben Bella deposed by military, led by Colonel Houari Boumédienne.
1976 New constitution approved.
1978 Death of Boumédienne.
1979 Benjedid Chadli elected president. Ben Bella released from house arrest. FLN adopted new party structure.
1981 Algeria helped secure release of US prisoners in Iran.
1983 Chadli re-elected.
1988 Riots in protest at government policies; 170 killed. Reform programme introduced. Diplomatic relations with Egypt restored.
1989 Constitutional changes proposed, leading to limited political pluralism.
1990 Fundamentalist Islamic Salvation Front (FIS) won Algerian municipal and provincial elections.
1991 President Benjedid Chadli promised multiparty elections. Dec: Islamic Salvation Front (FIS) won first round of elections.
1992 Jan: Chadli resigned; military took control of government; second round of elections cancelled; Mohamed Boudiaf became president. March: FIS ordered to disband. June: Boudiaf assassinated, Ali Kafi chosen as new head of state. Sid Ahmed Ghozali resigned as prime minister.

Andorra (Principality of)
(Principat d'Andorra)

area 468 sq km/181 sq mi
capital Andorra-la-Vella
towns Les Escaldes
physical mountainous, with narrow valleys
features the E Pyrenees, Valira River
heads of state Joan Marti i Alanis (bishop of Urgel, Spain) and François Mitterrand (president of France)
head of government Oscar Riba Reig from 1989
political system semi-feudal co-principality
political party Democratic Party of Andorra
exports main industries tourism and tobacco
currency French franc and Spanish peseta
population (1990) 51,000 (30% Andorrans, 61% Spanish, 6% French)
languages Catalan (official); Spanish, French
religion Roman Catholic
literacy 100% (1987)
GDP $300 million (1985)

chronology
1278 Treaty signed making Spanish bishop and French count joint rulers of Andorra (through marriage the king of France later inherited the count's right).
1970 Extension of franchise to third-generation women and second-generation men.
1976 First political organization (Democratic Party of Andorra) formed.
1977 Franchise extended to first-generation Andorrans.
1981 First prime minister appointed by General Council.
1982 With the appointment of an Executive Council, executive and legislative powers were separated.
1991 Representatives of the ruling co-princes set timetable for writing the state's first constitution.

Angola (People's Republic of)
(República Popular de Angola)

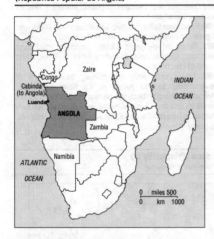

area 1,246,700 sq km/481,226 sq mi
capital and chief port Luanda
towns Lobito and Benguela, also ports; Huambo, Lubango
physical narrow coastal plain rises to vast interior plateau with rainforest in NW; desert in S
features Cuanza, Cuito, Cubango, and Cunene rivers; Cabinda enclave
head of state and government José Eduardo dos Santos from 1979
political system socialist republic
political parties People's Movement for the Liberation of Angola–Workers' Party (MPLA–PT), Marxist-Leninist; National Union for the Total Independence of Angola (UNITA)
exports oil, coffee, diamonds, palm oil, sisal, iron ore, fish
currency kwanza
population (1989 est) 9,733,000 (largest ethnic group Ovimbundu); growth rate 2.5% p.a.
life expectancy men 40, women 44
languages Portuguese (official); Bantu dialects
religion Roman Catholic 68%, Protestant 20%, animist 12%
literacy 20%
GDP $2.7 bn; $432 per head

chronology
1951 Angola became an overseas territory of Portugal.
1956 First independence movement formed, the People's Movement for the Liberation of Angola (MPLA).
1961 Unsuccessful independence rebellion.
1962 Second nationalist movement formed, the National Front for the Liberation of Angola (FNLA).
1966 Third nationalist movement formed, the National

Union for the Total Independence of Angola (UNITA).
1975 Independence achieved from Portugal. Transitional government of independence formed from representatives of MPLA, FNLA, UNITA, and Portuguese government. MPLA proclaimed People's Republic of Angola under the presidency of Dr Agostinho Neto. FNLA and UNITA proclaimed People's Democratic Republic of Angola.
1976 MPLA gained control of most of the country. South African troops withdrawn, but Cuban units remained.
1977 MPLA restructured to become the People's Movement for the Liberation of Angola–Workers' Party (MPLA–PT).
1979 Death of Neto, succeeded by José Eduardo dos Santos.
1980 Constitution amended to provide for an elected people's assembly. UNITA guerrillas, aided by South Africa, continued raids against the Luanda government and bases of the South West Africa People's Organization (SWAPO) in Angola.
1984 The Lusaka Agreement.
1985 South African forces officially withdrawn.
1986 Further South African raids into Angola. UNITA continuing to receive South African support.
1988 Peace treaty, providing for the withdrawal of all foreign troops, signed with South Africa and Cuba.
1989 Cease-fire agreed with UNITA broke down and guerrilla activity restarted.
1990 Peace offer by rebels. Return to multiparty politics promised.
1991 Peace agreement signed, civil war between MPLA–PT and UNITA officially ended. Amnesty for all political prisoners. Sept 1992 general election announced.

Antigua and Barbuda (State of)

area Antigua 280 sq km/108 sq mi, Barbuda 161 sq km/62 sq mi, plus Redonda 1 sq km/0.4 sq mi
capital and chief port St John's
towns Codrington (on Barbuda)
physical low-lying tropical islands of limestone and coral with some higher volcanic outcrops; no rivers and low rainfall result in frequent droughts and deforestation
features Antigua is the largest of the Leeward Islands; Redonda is an uninhabited island of volcanic rock rising to 305 m/1,000 ft
head of state Elizabeth II from 1981 represented by governor general
head of government Vere C Bird from 1981
political system liberal democracy
political parties Antigua Labour Party (ALP), moderate, left-of-centre; Progressive Labour Movement (PLM), left-of-centre

exports sea-island cotton, rum, lobsters
currency Eastern Caribbean dollar
population (1989) 83,500; growth rate 1.3% p.a.
life expectancy 70 years
language English
media no daily newspaper; weekly papers all owned by political parties
religion Christian (mostly Anglican)
literacy 90% (1985)
GDP $173 million (1985); $2,200 per head

chronology
1493 Antigua visited by Christopher Columbus.
1632 Antigua colonized by English settlers.
1667 Treaty of Breda formally ceded Antigua to Britain.
1871–1956 Antigua and Barbuda administered as part of the Leeward Islands federation.
1967 Antigua and Barbuda became an associated state within the Commonwealth, with full internal independence.
1971 PLM won the general election by defeating the ALP.
1976 PLM called for early independence, but ALP urged caution. ALP won the general election.
1981 Independence from Britain achieved.
1983 Assisted US invasion of Grenada.
1984 ALP won a decisive victory in the general election.
1985 ALP re-elected.
1989 Another sweeping general election victory for the ALP.

Argentina (Republic of)
(República Argentina)

area 2,780,092 sq km/1,073,116 sq mi
capital Buenos Aires (to move to Viedma)
towns Rosario, Córdoba, Tucumán, Mendoza, Santa Fe; ports are La Plata and Bahía Blanca
physical mountains in W, forest and savanna in N, pampas (treeless plains) in E central area, Patagonian plateau in S; rivers Colorado, Salado, Paraná, Uruguay, Río de la Plata estuary
territories part of Tierra del Fuego; disputed claims to S Atlantic islands and part of Antarctica
environment an estimated 20,000 sq km/7,700 sq mi of land has been swamped with salt water
features Andes mountains, with Aconcagua the highest peak in the W hemisphere; Iguaçú Falls
head of state and government Carlos Menem from 1989
political system emergent democratic federal republic

political parties Radical Civic Union Party (UCR), moderate centrist; Justicialist Party, right-wing Peronist
exports livestock products, cereals, wool, tannin, peanuts, linseed oil, minerals (coal, copper, molybdenum, gold, silver, lead, zinc, barium, uranium); the country has huge resources of oil, natural gas, hydroelectric power
currency austral
population (1990 est) 32,686,000 (mainly of Spanish or Italian origin, only about 30,000 American Indians surviving); growth rate 1.5% p.a.
life expectancy men 66, women 73
languages Spanish (official); English, Italian, German, French
religion Roman Catholic (state-supported)
literacy men 96%, women 95% (1985 est)
GDP $70.1 bn (1990); $2,162 per head

chronology
1816 Independence achieved from Spain, followed by civil wars.
1946 Juan Perón elected president, supported by his wife 'Evita'.
1952 'Evita' Perón died.
1955 Perón overthrown and civilian administration restored.
1966 Coup brought back military rule.
1973 A Peronist party won the presidential and congressional elections. Perón returned from exile in Spain as president, with his third wife, Isabel, as vice president.
1974 Perón died, succeeded by Isabel.
1976 Coup resulted in rule by a military junta led by Lt-Gen Jorge Videla. Congress dissolved, and hundreds of people, including Isabel Perón, detained.
1976–83 Ferocious campaign against left-wing elements, the 'dirty war'.
1978 Videla retired. Succeeded by General Roberto Viola, who promised a return to democracy.
1981 Viola died suddenly. Replaced by General Leopoldo Galtieri.
1982 With a deteriorating economy, Galtieri sought popular support by ordering an invasion of the British-held Falkland Islands. After losing the short war, Galtieri was removed and replaced by General Reynaldo Bignone.
1983 Amnesty law passed and 1853 democratic constitution revived. General elections won by Dr Raúl Alfonsín and his party. Armed forces under scrutiny.
1984 National Commission on the Disappearance of Persons (CONADEP) reported on over 8,000 people who had disappeared during the 'dirty war' of 1976–83.
1985 A deteriorating economy forced Alfonsín to seek help from the IMF and introduce an austerity programme.
1986 Unsuccessful attempt on Alfonsín's life.
1988 Unsuccessful army coup attempt.
1989 Carlos Menem, of the Justicialist Party, elected president. Alfonsín handed over power before required date of Dec 1989. Thirty-day state of emergency declared, after rioting following price measures and dramatic inflation (120% in June, with an annual rate of approximately 12,000%).
1990 Full diplomatic relations with the UK restored. Menem elected Justicialist Party leader. Revolt by army officers thwarted. Inflation over the year to Nov 1990 at 1,838%.

Armenia (Republic of)

area 29,800 sq km/11,500 sq mi
capital Yerevan
towns Kumayri (formerly Leninakan)
physical mainly mountainous (including Mount Ararat), wooded
features State Academia Theatre of Opera and Ballet; Yerevan Film Studio

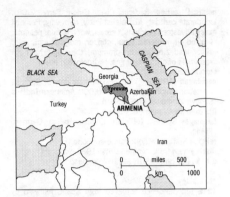

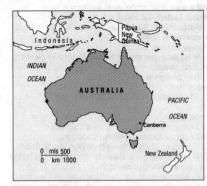

head of state Levon Ter-Petrossian from 1990
head of government Gagik Arutyunyan
political system emergent democracy
products copper, molybdenum, cereals, cotton, silk
population (1991) 3,580,000 (90% Armenian, 5% Azerbaijani, 2% Russian, 2% Kurd)
language Armenian
religion traditionally Armenian Christian

chronology
1918 Became an independent republic.
1920 Occupied by the Red Army.
1936 Became a constituent republic of the USSR.
1988 Feb: demonstrations in Yerevan called for transfer of Nagorno-Karabakh from Azerbaijan to Armenian control. Dec: earthquake claimed around 25,000 lives and caused extensive damage.
1989 Jan-Nov: strife-torn Nagorno-Karabakh placed under 'temporary' direct rule from Moscow. Pro-autonomy Armenian National Movement founded. Nov: civil war erupted with Azerbaijan over Nagorno-Karabakh.
1990 March: Armenia boycotted USSR constitutional referendum. Aug: nationalists secured control of Estonian supreme soviet; former dissident Levon Ter-Petrossian indirectly elected president; independence declared. Nakhichevan affected by Nagorno-Karabakh dispute.
1991 March: overwhelming support for independence in referendum. Dec: Armenia joined new Commonwealth of Independent States (CIS); Nagorno-Karabakh declared its independence; Armenia granted diplomatic recognition by USA.
1992 Jan: admitted into CSCE. Conflicts over Nagorno-Karabakh and Nakhichevan continued.

Australia (Commonwealth of)

---

area 7,682,300 sq km/2,966,136 sq mi
capital Canberra
towns Adelaide, Alice Springs, Brisbane, Darwin, Melbourne, Perth, Sydney, Hobart, Geelong, Newcastle, Townsville, Wollongong
physical the world's smallest, flattest, and driest continent (40% lies in the tropics, one-third is desert, and one-third is marginal grazing); Great Sandy Desert; Gibson Desert; Great Victoria Desert; Simpson Desert; the Great Barrier Reef (largest coral reef in the world, stretching 2,000 km/1,250 mi off E coast of Queensland); Great Dividing Range and Australian Alps in the E (Mt Kosciusko, 2,229 m/7,136 ft, Australia's highest peak). The fertile SE region is watered by the Darling, Lachlan, Murrumbridgee, and Murray rivers; rivers in the interior are seasonal. Lake Eyre basin and Nullarbor Plain in the S

territories Norfolk Island, Christmas Island, Cocos (Keeling) Islands, Ashmore and Cartier Islands, Coral Sea Islands, Heard Island and McDonald Islands, Australian Antarctic Territory
environment an estimated 75% of Australia's northern tropical rainforest has been cleared for agriculture or urban development since Europeans first settled there in the early 19th century
features Ayers Rock; Arnhem Land; Gulf of Carpentaria; Cape York Peninsula; Great Australian Bight; unique animal species include the kangaroo, koala, platypus, wombat, Tasmanian devil, and spiny anteater; of 800 species of bird, the budgerigar, cassowary, emu, kookaburra, lyre bird, and black swan are also unique as a result of Australia's long isolation from other continents
head of state Elizabeth II from 1952 represented by governor general
head of government Paul Keating from 1991
political system federal constitutional monarchy
political parties Australian Labor Party (ALP), moderate left-of-centre; Liberal Party of Australia, moderate, liberal, free-enterprise; National Party of Australia (formerly Country Party), centrist non-metropolitan
exports world's largest exporter of sheep, wool, diamonds, alumina, coal, lead and refined zinc ores, and mineral sands; other exports include cereals, beef, veal, mutton, lamb, sugar, nickel (world's second largest producer), iron ore; principal trade partners are Japan, the USA, and EC member states
currency Australian dollar
population (1990 est) 16,650,000; growth rate 1.5% p.a.
life expectancy men 75, women 80
languages English, Aboriginal languages
religion Anglican 26%, other Protestant 17%, Roman Catholic 26%
literacy 98.5.% (1988)
GDP $220.96 bn (1988); $14,458 per head

chronology
1901 Creation of Commonwealth of Australia.
1911 Site acquired for capital at Canberra.
1927 Seat of government moved to Canberra.
1942 Statute of Westminster Adoption Act gave Australia autonomy from UK in internal and external affairs.
1944 Liberal Party founded by Robert Menzies.
1951 Australia joined New Zealand and the USA as a signatory to the ANZUS Pacific security treaty.
1966 Menzies resigned after being Liberal prime minister for 17 years, and was succeeded by Harold Holt.
1967 A referendum was passed giving Aborigines full citizenship rights.
1968 John Gorton became prime minister after Holt's death.
1971 Gorton succeeded by William McMahon, heading a Liberal–Country Party coalition.

1972 Gough Whitlam became prime minister, leading a Labor government.

1975 Senate blocked the government's financial legislation; Whitlam dismissed by the governor general, who invited Malcolm Fraser to form a Liberal–Country Party caretaker government. The action of the governor general, John Kerr, was widely criticized.

1977 Kerr resigned.

1978 Northern Territory attained self-government.

1983 Australian Labor Party, returned to power under Bob Hawke, convened meeting of employers and unions to seek consensus on economic policy to deal with growing unemployment.

1986 Australia Act passed by UK government, eliminating last vestiges of British legal authority in Australia.

1988 Labor foreign minister Bill Hayden appointed governor general designate. Free-trade agreement with New Zealand signed.

1990 Hawke won record fourth election victory, defeating Liberal Party by small majority.

1991 Hawke defeated in challenge for Labor Party leadership by Paul Keating who consequently became prime minister.

Austria (Republic of)
(Republik Österreich)

area 83,8500 sq km/32,374 sq mi

capital Vienna

towns Graz, Linz, Salzburg, Innsbruck

physical landlocked mountainous state, with Alps in W and S and low relief in E where most of the population is concentrated

environment Hainburg, the largest primeval rainforest left in Europe, under threat from a dam project (suspended 1990)

features Austrian Alps (including Grossglockner and Brenner and Semmering passes); Lechtaler and Allgauer Alps N of river Inn; Carnic Alps on Italian border; river Danube

head of state Thomas Klestil from 1992

head of government Franz Vranitzky from 1986

political system democratic federal republic

political parties Socialist Party of Austria (SPÖ), democratic socialist; Austrian People's Party (ÖVP), progressive centrist; Freedom Party of Austria (FPÖ), moderate left-of-centre; United Green Party of Austria (VGÖ), conservative ecological; Green Alternative Party (ALV), radical ecological

exports lumber, textiles, clothing, iron and steel, paper, machinery and transport equipment, foodstuffs

currency schilling

population (1990 est) 7,595,000; growth rate 0.1% p.a.

life expectancy men 70, women 77

language German

religion Roman Catholic 85%, Protestant 6%

literacy 98% (1983)

GDP $183.3 bn (1987); $11,337 per head

chronology

1867 Emperor Franz Josef established dual monarchy of Austria–Hungary.

1914 Archduke Franz Ferdinand assassinated by a Serbian nationalist; Austria–Hungary invaded Serbia, precipitating World War I.

1918 Habsburg empire ended, republic proclaimed.

1938 Austria incorporated into German Third Reich by Hitler (the *Anschluss*).

1945 Under Allied occupation, 1920 constitution reinstated and coalition government formed by the SPÖ and the ÖVP.

1955 Allied occupation ended, and the independence of Austria formally recognized.

1966 ÖVP in power with Josef Klaus as chancellor.

1970 SPÖ formed a minority government, with Dr Bruno Kreisky as chancellor.

1983 Kreisky resigned, was replaced by Dr Fred Sinowatz, leading a coalition.

1986 Dr Kurt Waldheim elected president. Sinowatz resigned, succeeded by Franz Vranitzky. No party won an overall majority; Vranitzky formed a coalition of the SPÖ and the ÖVP, with ÖVP leader, Dr Alois Mock, as vice chancellor.

1989 Austria sought European Community membership.

1990 Vranitzky re-elected.

1991 Bid for EC membership endorsed by the Community.

1992 Thomas Klestil elected president.

Azerbaijan (Republic of)

area 86,600 sq km/33,400 sq mi

capital Baku

towns Gyandzha (formerly Kirovabad), Sumgait

physical Caspian Sea; the country ranges from semidesert to the Caucasus mountains

head of state and government Abulfaz Elchibey from 1992

political system emergent democracy

political parties Republican Democratic Party, ex-communist dominated; Popular Front, democratic nationalist; Islamic Party, fundamentalist

products oil, iron, copper, fruit, vines, cotton, silk, carpets

population (1990) 7,145,600 (83% Azeri, 6% Russian, 6% Armenian)

language Turkic

religion traditionally Shi'ite Muslim

chronology
1917-1918 A member of the anti-Bolshevik Transcaucasian Federation.
1918 Became an independent republic.
1920 Occupied by the Red Army.
1922-36 Formed part of the Transcaucasian Federal Republic with Georgia and Armenia.
1936 Became a constituent republic of the USSR.
1988 Riots followed Nagorno-Karabakh's request for transfer to Armenia.
1989 Jan-Nov: strife-torn Nagorno-Karabakh placed under 'temporary' direct rule from Moscow. Azerbaijan Popular Front established. Nov: civil war erupted with Armenia over Nagorno-Karabakh.
1990 Jan: Soviet troops despatched to Baku to restore order; state of emergency declared in Baku. Aug: Communists won parliamentary elections. Nakhichevan affected by Nagorno-Karabakh dispute.
1991 Aug: Azerbaijan leadership supported attempted anti-Gorbachev coup in Moscow; independence declared; state of emergency lifted. Sept: former communist Ayaz Mutalibov elected president. Dec: joined new Commonwealth of Independent States (CIS); Nagorno-Karabakh declared independence; independence of Azerbaijan acknowledged by USA but diplomatic recognition withheld.
1992 Jan: admitted into CSCE; signed cooperation agreement with Turkey. March: Mutalibov resigned following Azeri defeats in Nagorno-Karabakh, replaced by Yakub Mamedov. May: Mutalibov briefly restored to power, but ousted; replaced as interim president by his deputy leader, Isa Gambarov. June: Albufaz Elchibey, leader of the Popular Front, elected president.

Bahamas (Commonwealth of the)

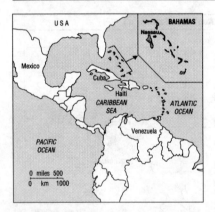

area 13,864 sq km/5,352 sq mi
capital Nassau on New Providence
towns Alice Town, Andros Town, Hope Town, Spanish Wells, Freeport, Moss Town, George Town
physical comprises 700 tropical coral islands and about 1,000 cays
features desert islands: only 30 are inhabited; Blue Holes of Andros, the world's longest and deepest submarine caves; the Exumas are a narrow spine of 365 islands
principal islands Andros, Grand Bahama, Great Abaco, Eleuthera, New Providence, Berry Islands, Biminis, Great Inagua, Acklins, Exumas, Mayaguana, Crooked Island, Long Island, Cat Island, Rum Cay, Watling (San Salvador) Island
head of state Elizabeth II from 1973 represented by governor general
head of government Lynden Oscar Pindling from 1967
political system constitutional monarchy

political parties Progressive Liberal Party (PLP), centrist; Free National Movement (FNM), centre-left
exports cement, pharmaceuticals, petroleum products, crawfish, salt, aragonite, rum, pulpwood; over half the islands' employment comes from tourism
currency Bahamian dollar
population (1990 est) 251,000; growth rate 1.8% p.a.
languages English and some Creole
media three independent daily newspapers
religion 29% Baptist, 23% Anglican, 22% Roman Catholic
literacy 95% (1986)
GDP $2.7 bn (1987); $11,261 per head

chronology
1964 Independence achieved from Britain.
1967 First national assembly elections.
1972 Constitutional conference to discuss full independence.
1973 Full independence achieved.
1983 Allegations of drug trafficking by government ministers.
1984 Deputy prime minister and two cabinet ministers resigned. Pindling denied any personal involvement and was endorsed as party leader.
1987 Pindling re-elected despite claims of frauds.

Bahrain (State of)
(Dawlat al Bahrayn)

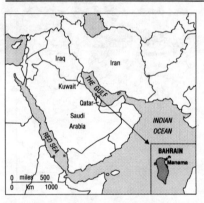

area 688 sq km/266 sq mi
capital Manama on the largest island (also called Bahrain)
towns Muharraq, Jidd Hafs, Isa Town; oil port Mina Sulman
physical 35 islands, composed largely of sand-covered limestone; generally poor and infertile soil; flat and hot
environment a wildlife park features the oryx on Bahrain; most of the south of the island is preserved for the ruling family's falconry
features causeway linking Bahrain to mainland Saudi Arabia; Sitra island is a communications centre for the lower Persian Gulf and has a satellite-tracking station
head of state and government Sheik Isa bin Sulman al-Khalifa (1933–) from 1961
political system absolute emirate
political parties none
exports oil, natural gas, aluminium, fish
currency Bahrain dinar
population (1990 est) 512,000 (two-thirds are nationals); growth rate 4.4% p.a.
life expectancy men 67, women 71
languages Arabic (official); Farsi, English, Urdu
religion 85% Muslim (Shi'ite 60%, Sunni 40%)
literacy men 79%, women 64% (1985 est)
GDP $3.5 bn (1987); $7,772 per head

chronology
1861 Became British protectorate.
1968 Britain announced its intention to withdraw its forces. Bahrain formed, with Qatar and the Trucial States, the Federation of Arab Emirates.
1971 Qatar and the Trucial States withdrew from the federation and Bahrain became an independent state.
1973 New constitution adopted, with an elected national assembly.
1975 Prime minister resigned and national assembly dissolved. Emir and his family assumed virtually absolute power.
1986 Gulf University established in Bahrain. A causeway was opened linking the island with Saudi Arabia.
1988 Bahrain recognized Afghan rebel government.
1991 Bahrain joined UN coalition that ousted Iraq from its occupation of Kuwait.

Bangladesh (People's Republic of)
(Gana Prajatantri Bangladesh)
(formerly *East Pakistan*)

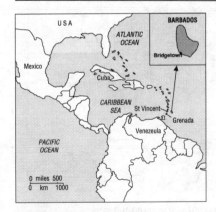

area 144,000 sq km/55,585 sq mi
capital Dhaka (formerly Dacca)
towns ports Chittagong, Khulna
physical flat delta of rivers Ganges (Padma) and Brahmaputra (Jamuna), the largest estuarine delta in the world; annual rainfall of 2,540 mm/100 in; some 75% of the land is less than 3 m/10 ft above sea level and vulnerable to flooding and cyclones; hilly in extreme SE and NE
environment deforestation on the slopes of the Himalayas increases the threat of flooding in the coastal lowlands of Bangladesh which are also subject to devastating monsoon storms. The building of India's Farakka Barrage has reduced the flow of the Ganges in Bangladesh and permitted salt water to intrude further inland. Increased salinity has destroyed fisheries, contaminated drinking water, and damaged forests
features tribal cultures with a population of just over 1 million occupy the tropical Chittagong Hill Tracts, Mymensingh and Sylhet districts
head of state Abdur Rahman Biswas from 1991
head of government Begum Khaleda Zia from 1991
political system emergent democratic republic
political parties Bangladesh Nationalist Party (BNP), Islamic right-of-centre; Awami League, secular, moderate socialist; Jatiya Dal (National Party), Islamic nationalist
exports jute, tea, garments, fish products
currency taka
population (1991 est) 107,992,100; growth rate 2.17% p.a.

life expectancy men 50, women 52
language Bangla (Bengali)
religion Sunni Muslim 85%, Hindu 14%
literacy men 43%, women 22% (1985 est)
GDP $17.6 bn (1987); $172 per head

chronology
1947 Formed into eastern province of Pakistan on partition of British India.
1970 Half a million killed in flood.
1971 Bangladesh emerged as independent nation, under leadership of Sheik Mujibur Rahman, after civil war.
1975 Mujibur Rahman assassinated. Martial law imposed.
1976–77 Maj-Gen Zia ur-Rahman assumed power.
1978–79 Elections held and civilian rule restored.
1981 Assassination of Maj-Gen Zia.
1982 Lt-Gen Ershad assumed power in army coup. Martial law reimposed.
1986 Elections held but disputed. Martial law ended.
1987 State of emergency declared in response to opposition demonstrations.
1988 Assembly elections boycotted by main opposition parties. State of emergency lifted. Islam made state religion. Monsoon floods left 30 million homeless and thousands dead.
1989 Power devolved to Chittagong Hill Tracts to end 14-year conflict between local people and army-protected settlers.
1990 Following mass antigovernment protests, President Ershad resigned; Shahabuddin Ahmad became interim president.
1991 Feb: elections resulted in coalition government with BNP dominant. April: cyclone disaster killed around 139,000 and left up to 10 million homeless. Sept: parliamentary government restored; by-elections gave BNP an absolute majority; Abdur Rahman Biswas elected president.

Barbados

area 430 sq km/166 sq mi
capital Bridgetown
towns Speightstown, Holetown, Oistins
physical most easterly island of the West Indies; surrounded by coral reefs; subject to hurricanes June–Nov
features highest point Mount Hillaby 340 m/1,115 ft
head of state Elizabeth II from 1966 represented by governor general Hugh Springer from 1984
head of government prime minister Erskine Lloyd Sandiford from 1987
political system constitutional monarchy
political parties Barbados Labour Party (BLP), moderate

left-of-centre; Democratic Labour Party (DLP), moderate left-of-centre; National Democratic Party (NDP), centre
exports sugar, rum, electronic components, clothing, cement
currency Barbados dollar
population (1990 est) 260,000; growth rate 0.5% p.a.
life expectancy men 70, women 75
languages English and Bajan (Barbadian English dialect)
media two independent daily newspapers
religion 70% Anglican, 9% Methodist, 4% Roman Catholic
literacy 99% (1984)
GDP $1.4 bn (1987); $5,449 per head

chronology
1627 Became British colony; developed as a sugar plantation economy, initially on basis of slavery (slaves freed 1834).
1951 Universal adult suffrage introduced. BLP won general election.
1954 Ministerial government established.
1961 Independence achieved from Britain. DLP, led by Errol Barrow, in power.
1966 Barbados achieved full independence within Commonwealth. Barrow became the new nation's first prime minister.
1972 Diplomatic relations with Cuba established.
1976 BLP, led by Tom Adams, returned to power.
1983 Barbados supported US invasion of Grenada.
1985 Adams died suddenly; Bernard St John became prime minister.
1986 DLP, led by Barrow, returned to power.
1987 Barrow died, succeeded by Erskine Lloyd Sandiford.
1989 New NDP opposition formed.
1991 DLP, under Erskine Sandiford, won general election.

Belarus (Republic of)

area 207,600 sq km/80,100 sq mi
capital Mensk (Minsk)
towns Gomel, Vitebsk, Mogilev, Bobruisk, Grodno, Brest
physical more than 25% forested; rivers W Dvina, Dnieper and its tributaries, including the Pripet and Beresina; the Pripet Marshes in the E; mild and damp climate
features Belovezhskaya Pushcha (scenic forest reserve)
head of state Stanislav Shushkevich from 1991
head of government Vyacheslav Kebich from 1990
political system emergent democracy
products peat, agricultural machinery, fertilizers, glass, textiles, leather, salt, electrical goods, meat, dairy produce
currency rouble and dukat

population (1990) 10,200,000 (77% Byelorussian 'Eastern Slavs', 13% Russian, 4% Polish, 1% Jewish)
language Byelorussian, Russian
religion Roman Catholic, Russian Orthodox, with Baptist and Muslim minorities

chronology
1918-19 Briefly independent from Russia.
1937-41 More than 100,000 people were shot in mass executions ordered by Stalin.
1941-44 Occupied by Nazi Germany.
1945 Became a founding member of the United Nations.
1986 April: large areas contaminated by fallout from Chernobyl disaster.
1989 Byelorussian Popular Front established as well as a more extreme nationalist organization, the Tolaka group.
1990 Sept: Byelorussian established as state language and republican sovereignty declared.
1991 April: Mensk hit by nationalist-backed general strike, calling for disbandment of Communist Party workplace cells. Aug: declared independence from Soviet Union in wake of failed anti-Gorbachev coup; suspended Communist Party. Sept: changed name to Republic of Belarus; Shushkevich elected president. Dec: Commonwealth of Independent States (CIS) formed in Mensk; diplomatic recognition accorded by USA.
1992 Jan: admitted into CSCE.

Belgium (Kingdom of)
(French *Royaume de Belgique*, Flemish *Koninkrijk België*)

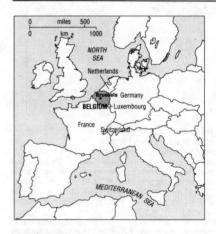

area 30,510 sq km/11,784 sq mi
capital Brussels
towns Ghent, Liège, Charleroi, Bruges, Mons, Namur, Leuven; ports are Antwerp, Ostend, Zeebrugge
physical fertile coastal plain in NW, central rolling hills rise eastwards, hills and forest in SE
environment a 1989 government report judged the drinking water in Flanders to be 'seriously substandard' and more than half the rivers and canals in that region to be in a 'very bad' condition
features Ardennes Forest; rivers Scheldt and Meuse
head of state King Baudouin from 1951
head of government Jean-Luc Dehaene from 1992
political system liberal democracy
political parties Flemish Christian Social Party (CVP), centre-left; French Social Christian Party (PSC), centre-left; Flemish Socialist Party (SP), left-of-centre; French Socialist Party (PS), left-of-centre; Flemish Liberal Party (PVV), moderate centrist; French Liberal Reform Party (PRL), moderate centrist; Flemish People's Party (VU),

federalist; Flemish Green Party (Agalev); French Green
Party (Ecolo)
exports iron, steel, textiles, manufactured goods,
petrochemicals, plastics, vehicles, diamonds
currency Belgian franc
population (1990 est) 9,895,000 (comprising Flemings
and Walloons); growth rate 0.1% p.a.
life expectancy men 72, women 78
languages in the N (Flanders) Flemish (a Dutch dialect,
known as *Vlaams*) 55%; in the S (Wallonia) Walloon (a
French dialect) 32%; bilingual 11%; German (E border)
0.6%; all are official
religion Roman Catholic 75%
literacy 98% (1984)
GDP $111 bn (1986); $9,230 per head

chronology
1830 Belgium became an independent kingdom.
1914 Invaded by Germany.
1940 Again invaded by Germany.
1948 Belgium became founding member of Benelux
Customs Union.
1949 Belgium became founding member of Council of
Europe and NATO.
1951 Leopold III abdicated in favour of his son Baudouin.
1952 Belgium became founding member of European
Coal and Steel Community (ECSC).
1957 Belgium became founding member of the European
Economic Community (EEC).
1971 Steps towards regional autonomy taken.
1972 German-speaking members included in the cabinet
for the first time.
1973 Linguistic parity achieved in government
appointments.
1974 Separate regional councils and ministerial
committees established.
1978 Wilfried Martens succeeded Leo Tindemans as
prime minister.
1980 Open violence over language divisions. Regional
assemblies for Flanders and Wallonia and a three-
member executive for Brussels created.
1981 Short-lived coalition led by Mark Eyskens was
followed by the return of Martens.
1987 Martens head of caretaker government after breakup of coalition.
1988 Following a general election, Martens formed a new
CVP–PS–SP–PSC–VU coalition.
1992 Martens-led coalition collapsed; Jean-Luc Dehaene
formed a new CVP-led coalition.

Belize
(formerly *British Honduras*)

area 22,963 sq km/8,864 sq mi
capital Belmopan
towns ports Belize City, Dangriga and Punta Gorda; Orange
Walk, Corozal
physical tropical swampy coastal plain, Maya Mountains
in S, over 90% under forest
environment in 1986 the world's first jaguar reserve was
created in the Cockscomb Mountains
features world's second longest barrier reef; Maya ruins
head of state Elizabeth II from 1981 represented by
governor general
head of government George Price from 1989
political system constitutional monarchy
political parties People's United Party (PUP), left-of-
centre; United Democratic Party (UDP), moderate
conservative
exports sugar, citrus fruits, rice, fish products, bananas
currency Belize dollar (3.25 = £1 July 1991)
population (1990 est) 180,400 (including Mayan
minority in the interior); growth rate 2.5% p.a.
life expectancy (1988) 60 years

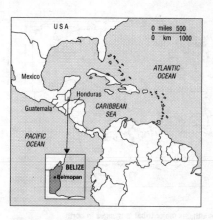

languages English (official); Spanish (widely spoken),
native Creole dialects
media no daily newspaper; several independent weekly
tabloids
religion Roman Catholic 60%, Protestant 35%
literacy 93% (1988)
GDP $247 million (1988); $1,220 per head

chronology
1862 Belize became a British colony.
1954 Constitution adopted, providing for limited internal
self-government. General election won by George Price.
1964 Self-government achieved from the UK (universal
adult suffrage introduced).
1965 Two-chamber national assembly introduced, with
Price as prime minister.
1970 Capital moved from Belize City to Belmopan.
1973 British Honduras became Belize.
1975 British troops sent to defend the disputed frontier
with Guatemala.
1977 Negotiations undertaken with Guatemala but no
agreement reached.
1980 United Nations called for full independence.
1981 Full independence achieved. Price became prime
minister.
1984 Price defeated in general election. Manuel
Esquivel formed the government. The UK reaffirmed
its undertaking to defend the frontier.
1989 Price and the PUP won the general election.
1991 Diplomatic relations with Guatemala established.

Benin (People's Republic of)
(*République Populaire du Bénin*)

area 112,622 sq km/43,472 sq mi
capital Porto Novo (official), Cotonou (de facto)
towns Abomey, Natitingou, Parakou; chief port Cotonou
physical flat to undulating terrain; hot and humid in S;
semiarid in N
features coastal lagoons with fishing villages on stilts;
Niger River in NE
head of state and government Nicéphore Soglo from
1991
political system socialist pluralist republic
political parties Party of the People's Revolution of Benin
(PRPB); other parties from 1990
exports cocoa, peanuts, cotton, palm oil, petroleum,
cement, sea products
currency CFA franc
population (1990 est) 4,840,000; growth rate 3% p.a.
life expectancy men 42, women 46
languages French (official); Fon 47% and Yoruba 9% in

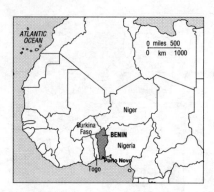

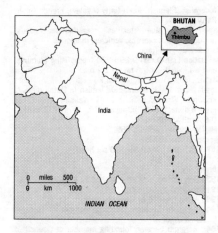

south; six major tribal languages in north
religion animist 65%, Christian 17%, Muslim 13%
literacy men 37%, women 16% (1985 est)
GDP $1.6 bn (1987); $365 per head

chronology
1851 Under French control.
1958 Became self-governing dominion within the French Community.
1960 Independence achieved from France.
1960–72 Acute political instability, with switches from civilian to military rule.
1972 Military regime established by General Mathieu Kerekou.
1974 Kerekou announced that the country would follow a path of 'scientific socialism'.
1975 Name of country changed from Dahomey to Benin.
1977 Return to civilian rule under a new constitution.
1980 Kerekou formally elected president by the national revolutionary assembly.
1989 Marxist-Leninism dropped as official ideology. Strikes and protests against Kerekou's rule mounted; demonstrations banned and army deployed against protesters.
1990 Referendum support for multiparty politics.
1991 Multiparty elections held. Kerekou defeated in presidential elections by Nicéphore Soglo.

religion 75% Lamaistic Buddhist (state religion), 25% Hindu
literacy 5%
GDP $250 million (1987); $170 per head

chronology
1865 Trade treaty with Britain signed.
1907 First hereditary monarch installed.
1910 Anglo-Bhutanese Treaty signed.
1949 Indo-Bhutan Treaty of Friendship signed.
1952 King Jigme Dorji Wangchuk installed.
1953 National assembly established.
1959 4,000 Tibetan refugees given asylum.
1968 King established first cabinet.
1972 King died and was succeeded by his son Jigme Singye Wangchuk.
1979 Tibetan refugees told to take Bhutanese citizenship or leave; most stayed.
1983 Bhutan became a founding member of the South Asian Regional Association for Cooperation organization (SAARC).
1988 King imposes 'code of conduct' suppressing Nepalese customs.
1990 Hundreds of people allegedly killed during demonstrations.

Bhutan (Kingdom of)
(Druk-yul)

area 46,500 sq km/17,954 sq mi
capital Thimbu (Thimphu)
towns Paro, Punakha, Mongar
physical occupies S slopes of the Himalayas; cut by valleys formed by tributaries of the Brahmaputra; thick forests in S
features Gangkar Punsum (7,529 m/24,700 ft) is one of the world's highest unclimbed peaks
head of state and government Jigme Singye Wangchuk from 1972
political system hereditary monarchy
political parties none officially; illegal Bhutan People's Party (BPP)
exports timber, talc, fruit and vegetables, cement, distilled spirits, calcium carbide
currency ngultrum; also Indian currency
population (1990 est) 1,566,000; growth rate 2% p.a. (75% Ngalops and Sharchops, 25% Nepalese)
life expectancy men 44, women 43
languages Dzongkha (official, a Tibetan dialect), Sharchop, Bumthap, Nepali, and English

Bolivia (Republic of)
(República de Bolivia)

area 1,098,581 sq km/424,052 sq mi
capital La Paz (seat of government), Sucre (legal capital and seat of judiciary)
towns Santa Cruz, Cochabamba, Oruro, Potosí
physical high plateau (Altiplano) between mountain ridges (cordilleras); forest and lowlands (llano) in the E
features Andes, lakes Titicaca (the world's highest navigable lake, 3,800 m/12,500 ft) and Poopó; La Paz is world's highest capital city (3,600 m/11,800 ft)
head of state and government Jaime Paz Zamora from 1989
political system emergent democratic republic
political parties National Revolutionary Movement (MNR), centre-right; Nationalist Democratic Action Party (ADN), extreme right-wing; Movement of the Revolutionary Left (MIR), left-of-centre
exports tin, antimony (second largest world producer), other nonferrous metals, oil, gas (piped to Argentina), agricultural products, coffee, sugar, cotton
currency boliviano
population (1990 est) 6,730,000; (Quechua 25%,

Bosnia-Herzegovina (Republic of)

Aymara 17%, mestizo (mixed) 30%, European 14%);
growth rate 2.7% p.a.
life expectancy men 51, women 54
languages Spanish, Aymara, Quechua (all official)
religion Roman Catholic 95% (state-recognized)
literacy men 84%, women 65% (1985 est)
GDP $4.2 bn (1987); $617 per head

chronology
1825 Liberated from Spanish rule by Simón Bolívar; independence achieved (formerly known as Upper Peru).
1952 Dr Víctor Paz Estenssoro elected president.
1956 Dr Hernán Siles Zuazo became president.
1960 Estenssoro returned to power.
1964 Army coup led by vice president.
1966 General René Barrientos became president.
1967 Uprising, led by 'Che' Guevara, put down with
US help.
1969 Barrientos killed in plane crash, replaced by Vice
President Siles Salinas. Army coup deposed him.
1970 Army coup put General Juan Torres González in
power.
1971 Torres replaced by Col Hugo Banzer Suárez.
1973 Banzer promised a return to democratic
government.
1974 Attempted coup prompted Banzer to postpone
elections and ban political and trade union activity.
1978 Elections declared invalid after allegations of fraud.
1980 More inconclusive elections followed by another
coup, led by General Luis García. Allegations of
corruption and drug trafficking led to cancellation of
US and EC aid.
1981 García forced to resign. Replaced by General Celso
Torrelio Villa.
1982 Torrelio resigned. Replaced by military junta led by
General Guido Vildoso. Because of worsening economy,
Vildoso asked congress to install a civilian administration.
Dr Siles Zuazo chosen as president.
1983 Economic aid from USA and Europe resumed.
1984 New coalition government formed by Siles.
Abduction of president by right-wing officers. The
president undertook a five-day hunger strike as an
example to the nation.
1985 President Siles resigned. Election result inconclusive; Dr Paz Estenssoro, at the age of 77, chosen by
congress as president.
1989 Jaime Paz Zamora (MIR) elected president in power-
sharing arrangement with Hugo Banzer Suárez, pledged
to maintain fiscal and monetary discipline and preserve
free-market policies.

area 51,129 sq km/19,745 sq mi
capital Sarajevo
towns Banja Luka, Mostar, Prijedor, Tuzla, Zenica
physical barren, mountainous country
features part of the Dinaric Alps, limestone gorges
population (1990) 4,300,000 including 44% Muslims,
33% Serbs, 17% Croats; a complete patchwork of ethi-
cally mixed communities
head of state Alija Izetbegović from 1990
head of government to be decided
political system emergent democracy
political parties Party of Democratic Action (SDA),
Muslim-orientated; Serbian Democratic Party (SDS);
Christian Democratic Union (HDS); League of
Communists
products citrus fruits and vegetables; iron, steel, and
leather goods; textiles
language Serbian variant of Serbo-Croat
religion Sunni Muslim, Serbian Orthodox, Roman Catholic

chronology
1918 Incorporated in the future Yugoslavia.
1941 Occupied by the Nazis.
1945 Became republic within Yugoslav Socialist
Federation.
1980 Upsurge in Islamic nationalism.
1990 Ethnic violence erupted between Muslims and Serbs
Nov-Dec: communists defeated in multi-party elections;
coalition formed by Serb, Muslim, and Croat parties.
1991 May: Serbia-Croatia conflict spread disorder into
Bosnia-Herzegovina. Aug: Serbia revealed plans to annex
the SE part of the republic. Oct: 'sovereignty' declared.
Nov: plebiscite by Serbs favoured remaining within
Yugoslavia; Serbs and Croats established autonomous
communities.
1992 Feb-March: Muslims and Croats voted overwhelmingly in favour of independence; referendum
boycotted by Serbs. April: USA and EC recognized
Bosnian independence. Ethnic hostilities escalated, with
Serb forces occupying E and Croat forces much of W; state
of emergency declared; all-out civil war ensued.
June: Canadian/French UN forces drafted into Sarajevo
in attempt to relieve three-month siege of city by Serbs.

Botswana (Republic of)

area 582,000 sq km/225,000 sq mi
capital Gaborone
towns Mahalpye, Serowe, Tutume, Francistown

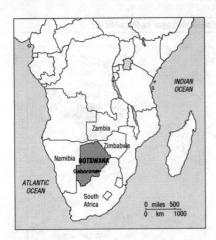

physical desert in SW, plains in E, fertile lands and swamp in N

environment the Okavango Swamp is threatened by plans to develop the area for mining and agriculture

features Kalahari Desert in SW; Okavango Swamp in N, remarkable for its wildlife; Makgadikgadi salt pans in E; diamonds mined at Orapa and Jwaneng in partnership with De Beers of South Africa

head of state and government Quett Ketamile Joni Masire from 1980

political system democratic republic

political parties Botswana Democratic Party (BDP), moderate centrist; Botswana National Front (BNF), moderate left-of-centre

exports diamonds (third largest producer in world), copper, nickel, meat products, textiles

currency pula

population (1990 est) 1,218,000 (80% Bamangwato, 20% Bangwaketse); growth rate 3.5% p.a.

life expectancy (1988) 59 years

languages English (official), Setswana (national)

religion Christian 50%, animist 50%

literacy (1988) 84%

GDP $2.0 bn (1988); $1,611 per head

chronology

1885 Became a British protectorate.

1960 New constitution created a legislative council.

1963 End of rule by High Commission.

1965 Capital transferred from Mafeking to Gaborone. Internal self-government granted. Sir Seretse Khama elected head of government.

1966 Independence achieved from Britain. New constitution came into effect; name changed from Bechuanaland to Botswana; Seretse Khama elected president.

1980 Seretse Khama died; succeeded by Vice President Quett Masire.

1984 Masire re-elected.

1985 South African raid on Gaborone.

1987 Joint permanent commission with Mozambique established, to improve relations.

1989 The BDP and Masire re-elected.

Brazil (Federative Republic of)
(República Federativa do Brasil)

area 8,511,965 sq km/3,285,618 sq mi

capital Brasília

towns São Paulo, Belo Horizonte, Curitiba, Manaus, Fortaleza; ports are Rio de Janeiro, Belém, Recife, Pôrto Alegre, Salvador

physical the densely forested Amazon basin covers the northern half of the country with a network of rivers; the south is fertile; enormous energy resources, both hydroelectric (Itaipú dam on the Paraná, and Tucuruí on the Tocantins) and nuclear (uranium ores)

environment Brazil has one-third of the world's tropical rainforest. It contains 55,000 species of flowering plants (the greatest variety in the world) and 20% of all the bird species of the world. During the 1980s at least 7% of the Amazon rainforest was destroyed by settlers who cleared the land for cultivation and grazing

features Mount Roraima, Xingu National Park; Amazon delta; Rio harbour

head of state and government Fernando Afonso Collor de Mello from 1989

political system emergent democratic federal republic

political parties Social Democratic Party (PDS), moderate left-of-centre; Brazilian Democratic Movement Party (PMDB), centre-left; Liberal Front Party (PFL), moderate left-of-centre; Workers' Party (PT), left-of-centre; National Reconstruction Party (PRN), centre-right

exports coffee, sugar, soya beans, cotton, textiles, timber, motor vehicles, iron, chrome, manganese, tungsten and other ores, as well as quartz crystals, industrial diamonds, gemstones; the world's sixth largest arms exporter

currency cruzado (introduced 1986; value = 100 cruzeiros, the former unit); inflation 1990 was 1,795%

population (1990 est) 153,770,000 (including 200,000 Indians, survivors of 5 million, especially in Rondônia and Mato Grosso, mostly living on reservations); growth rate 2.2% p.a.

life expectancy men 61, women 66

languages Portuguese (official); 120 Indian languages

religion Roman Catholic 89%; Indian faiths

literacy men 79%, women 76% (1985 est)

GDP $352 bn (1988); $2,434 per head

chronology

1822 Independence achieved from Portugal; ruled by Dom Pedro, son of the refugee King John VI of Portugal.

1889 Monarchy abolished and republic established.

1891 Constitution for a federal state adopted.

1930 Dr Getúlio Vargas became president.

1945 Vargas deposed by the military.

1946 New constitution adopted.

1951 Vargas returned to office.

1954 Vargas committed suicide.

1956 Juscelino Kubitschek became president.

1960 Capital moved to Brasília.

1961 João Goulart became president.

1964 Bloodless coup made General Castelo Branco president; he assumed dictatorial powers, abolishing free political parties.
1967 New constitution adopted. Branco succeeded by Marshal da Costa e Silva.
1969 Da Costa e Silva resigned and a military junta took over.
1974 General Ernesto Geisel became president.
1978 General Baptista de Figueiredo became president.
1979 Political parties legalized again.
1984 Mass calls for a return to fully democratic government.
1985 Tancredo Neves became first civilian president in 21 years. Neves died and was succeeded by the vice president, José Sarney.
1988 New constitution approved, transferring power from the president to the congress. Measures announced to halt large-scale burning of Amazonian rainforest for cattle grazing.
1989 Forest Protection Service and Ministry for Land Reform abolished. International concern over how much of the Amazon has been burned. Fernando Collor (PRN) elected president Dec, pledging free-market economic policies.
1990 Government won the general election offset by mass abstentions.
1992 Calls for Collor's resignation followed accusations of corruption.

Brunei (The Islamic Sultanate of)
(Negara Brunei Darussalam)

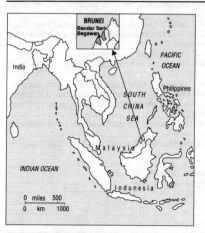

area 5,765 sq km/2,225 sq mi
capital Bandar Seri Begawan
towns Tutong, Seria, Kuala Belait
physical flat coastal plain with hilly lowland in W and mountains in E; 75% of the area is forested; the Limbang valley splits Brunei in two, and its cession to Sarawak 1890 is disputed by Brunei
features Temburong, Tutong, and Belait rivers; Mount Pagon (1,850 m/6,070 ft)
head of state and of government HM Muda Hassanal Bolkiah Mu'izzaddin Waddaulah, Sultan of Brunei, from 1968
political system absolute monarchy
political parties Brunei National United Party (BNUP)
exports liquefied natural gas (world's largest producer) and oil, both expected to be exhausted by the year 2000
currency Brunei dollar
population (1990 est) 372,000 (65% Malay, 20% Chinese—few Chinese granted citizenship); growth rate 12% p.a.

life expectancy 74 years
languages Malay (official), Chinese (Hokkien), English
religion 60% Muslim (official)
literacy 95%
GDP $3.4 bn (1985); $20,000 per head

chronology
1888 Brunei became a British protectorate.
1941–45 Occupied by Japan.
1959 Written constitution made Britain responsible for defence and external affairs.
1962 Sultan began rule by decree.
1963 Proposal to join Malaysia abandoned.
1967 Sultan abdicated in favour of his son, Hassanal Bolkiah..
1971 Brunei given internal self-government.
1975 UN resolution called for independence for Brunei.
1984 Independence achieved from Britain, with Britain maintaining a small force to protect the oil and gas fields.
1985 A 'loyal and reliable' political party, the Brunei National Democratic Party (BNDP), legalized.
1986 Death of former sultan, Sir Omar. Formation of multiethnic BNUP.
1988 BNDP banned.

Bulgaria (Republic of)
(Republika Bulgaria)

area 110,912 sq km/42,812 sq mi
capital Sofia
towns Plovdiv, Ruse; Black Sea ports Burgas and Varna
physical lowland plains in N and SE separated by mountains that cover three-quarters of the country
environment pollution has virtually eliminated all species of fish once caught in the Black Sea. Vehicle exhaust emissions in Sofia have led to dust concentrations more than twice the medically accepted level
features key position on land route from Europe to Asia; Black Sea coast; Balkan and Rhodope mountains; Danube River in N
head of state Zhelyu Zhelev from 1990
head of government Filip Dimitrov from 1991
political system emergent democratic republic
political parties Union of Democratic Forces (UDF), right-of-centre; Bulgarian Socialist Party (BSP), the former communist party (BCP); the Movement for Rights and Freedoms (MRF), represents the Turkish-speaking minority in Bulgaria
exports textiles, leather, chemicals, nonferrous metals, timber, machinery, tobacco, cigarettes (world's largest exporter)

currency lev
population (1990 est) 8,978,000 (including 900,000–
1,500,000 ethnic Turks, concentrated in S and NE);
growth rate 0.1% p.a.
life expectancy men 69, women 74
languages Bulgarian, Turkish
religion Eastern Orthodox Christian 90%, Sunni Muslim
10%
literacy 98%
GDP $25.4 bn (1987); $2,836 per head

chronology
1908 Bulgaria became a kingdom independent of Turkish
rule.
1944 Soviet invasion of German-occupied Bulgaria.
1946 Monarchy abolished and communist-dominated
people's republic proclaimed.
1947 Soviet-style constitution adopted.
1949 Death of Georgi Dimitrov, the communist
government leader.
1954 Election of Todor Zhivkov as Communist Party
general secretary; made nation a loyal satellite of USSR.
1971 Constitution modified; Zhivkov elected president.
1985–89 Large administrative and personnel changes
made haphazardly under Soviet stimulus.
1987 New electoral law introduced multicandidate
elections.
1989 Programme of 'Bulgarianization' resulted in mass
exodus of Turks to Turkey. Nov: Zhivkov ousted by Petar
Mladenov. Dec: opposition parties allowed to form.
1990 April: BCP renamed Bulgarian Socialist Party
(BSP). Aug: Dr Zheylyu Zhelev elected president.
Nov: government headed by Andrei Lukanov resigned,
replaced Dec by coalition led by Dimitur Popov.
1991 July: new constitution adopted. Oct: Union of
Democratic Forces (UDF) beat BSP in general election by
narrow margin; formation of first noncommunist, UDF-
minority government under Filip Dimitrov.
1992 Zhelev became Bulgaria's first directly elected
president. Relations with West greatly improved.

Burkina Faso (The People's Democratic Republic of)
(formerly *Upper Volta*)

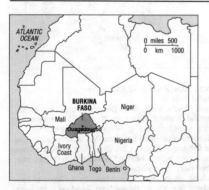

area 274,122 sq km/105,811 sq mi
capital Ouagadougou
towns Bobo-Dioulasso, Koudougou
physical landlocked plateau with hills in W and SE;
headwaters of the river Volta; semiarid in N, forest and
farmland in S
environment tropical savanna exposed to overgrazing and
deforestation
features linked by rail to Abidjan in Ivory Coast, Burkina
Faso's only outlet to the sea
head of state and government Blaise Compaoré from
1987

political system emergent democratic republic
political parties Organization for Popular Democracy–
Workers' Movement (ODP–MT), nationalist left-wing;
FP–Popular Front, left-of-centre, umbrella grouping
exports cotton, groundnuts, livestock, hides, skins,
sesame, cereals
currency CFA franc
population (1990 est) 8,941,000; growth rate 2.4% p.a.
life expectancy men 44, women 47
languages French (official); about 50 native Sudanic
languages spoken by 90% of population
religion animist 53%, Sunni Muslim 36%, Roman
Catholic 11%
literacy men 21%, women 6% (1985 est)
GDP $1.6 bn (1987); $188 per head

chronology
1958 Became a self-governing republic within the French
Community.
1960 Independence achieved from France, with Maurice
Yaméogo as the first president.
1966 Military coup led by Col Lamizana. Constitution
suspended, political activities banned, and a supreme
council of the armed forces established.
1969 Ban on political activities lifted.
1970 Referendum approved a new constitution leading to
a return to civilian rule.
1974 After experimenting with a mixture of military and
civilian rule, Lamizana reassumed full power.
1977 Ban on political activities removed. Referendum
approved a new constitution based on civilian rule.
1978 Lamizana elected president.
1980 Lamizana overthrown in bloodless coup led by Col
Zerbo.
1982 Zerbo ousted in a coup by junior officers. Major
Ouédraogo became president and Thomas Sankara prime
minister.
1983 Sankara seized complete power.
1984 Upper Volta renamed Burkina Faso, 'land of upright
men'.
1987 Sankara killed in coup led by Blaise Compaoré.
1989 New government party ODP–MT formed by merger
of other pro-government parties. Coup against Compaoré
foiled.
1991 New constitution approved. Compaoré re-elected
president.
1992 Multiparty elections won by FP–Popular Front.

Burundi (Republic of)
(*Republika y'Uburundi*)

area 27,834 sq km/10,744 sq mi
capital Bujumbura
towns Gitega, Bururi, Ngozi, Muyinga
physical landlocked grassy highland straddling watershed
of Nile and Congo

features Lake Tanganyika, Great Rift Valley
head of state and government Pierre Buyoya from 1987
political system one-party military republic
political party Union for National Progress (UPRONA), nationalist socialist
exports coffee, cotton, tea, nickel, hides, livestock, cigarettes, beer, soft drinks; there are 500 million tonnes of peat reserves in the basin of the Akanyaru River
currency Burundi franc
population (1990 est) 5,647,000 (of whom 15% are the Nilotic Tutsi, still holding most of the land and political power, 1% are Pygmy Twa, and the remainder Bantu Hutu); growth rate 2.8% p.a.
life expectancy men 45, women 48
languages Kirundi (a Bantu language) and French (both official), Kiswahili
religion Roman Catholic 62%, Protestant 5%, Muslim 1%, animist 32%
literacy men 43%, women 26% (1985)
GDP $1.1 bn (1987); $230 per head
chronology
1962 Separated from Ruanda-Urundi, as Burundi, and given independence as a monarchy under King Mwambutsa IV.
1966 King deposed by his son Charles, who became Ntare V; he was in turn deposed by his prime minister, Capt Michel Micombero, who declared Burundi a republic.
1972 Ntare V killed, allegedly by the Hutu ethnic group. Massacres of 150,000 Hutus by the rival Tutsi ethnic group, of which Micombero was a member.
1973 Micombero made president and prime minister.
1974 UPRONA declared the only legal political party, with the president as its secretary general.
1976 Army coup deposed Micombero. Col Jean-Baptiste Bagaza appointed president by the Supreme Revolutionary Council.
1981 New constitution adopted, providing for a national assembly.
1984 Bagaza elected president as sole candidate.
1987 Bagaza deposed in coup Sept. Major Pierre Buyoya headed new Military Council for National Redemption.
1988 Some 24,000 majority Hutus killed by Tutsis. First Hutu prime minister appointed.
1992 New constitution approved.

Cambodia (State of)
(formerly *Khmer Republic 1970–76, Democratic Kampuchea 1976–79, People's Republic of Kampuchea 1979–89*)

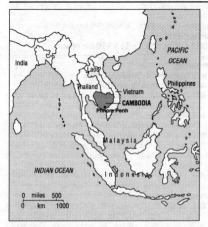

area 181,035 sq km/69,880 sq mi
capital Phnom Penh
towns Battambang, the seaport Kompong Som

physical mostly flat forested plains with mountains in SW and N; Mekong River runs N–S
features ruins of ancient capital Angkor; Lake Tonle Sap
head of state Prince Norodom Sihanouk from 1991
head of government Hun Sen from 1985
political system transitional
political parties Cambodian People's Party (CPP), reform socialist (formerly the communist Kampuchean People's Revolutionary Party (KPRP)); Party of Democratic Kampuchea (Khmer Rouge), ultranationalist communist; Khmer People's National Liberation Front (KPNLF), anticommunist
exports rubber, rice, pepper, wood, cattle
currency Cambodian riel
population (1990 est) 6,993,000; growth rate 2.2% p.a.
life expectancy men 42, women 45
languages Khmer (official), French
religion Theravāda Buddhist 95%
literacy men 78%, women 39% (1980 est)
GDP $592 mn (1987); $83 per head

chronology
1863–1941 French protectorate.
1941–45 Occupied by Japan.
1946 Recaptured by France.
1953 Independence achieved from France.
1970 Prince Sihanouk overthrown by US-backed Lon Nol.
1975 Lon Nol overthrown by Khmer Rouge.
1978–79 Vietnamese invasion and installation of Heng Samrin government.
1982 The three main anti-Vietnamese resistance groups formed an alliance under Prince Sihanouk.
1987 Partial withdrawal of Vietnamese troops.
1988 Vietnamese troop withdrawal continued.
1989 Sept: completion of Vietnam withdrawal. Nov: UN peace proposal rejected by Phnom Penh government.
1991 Oct: Peace agreement signed in Paris, providing for a UN Transitional Authority in Cambodia (UNTAC) to administer country in transition period in conjunction with all-party Supreme National Council; communism abandoned. Nov: Sihanouk returned as head of state.
1992 Political prisoners released; freedom of speech and party formation restored.

Cameroon (Republic of)
(République du Cameroun)

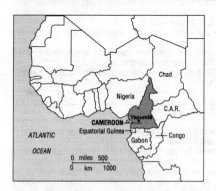

area 475,440 sq km/183,638 sq mi
capital Yaoundé
towns chief port Douala; Nkongsamba, Garoua
physical desert in far north in the Lake Chad basin, mountains in W, dry savanna plateau in the intermediate area, and dense tropical rainforest in the south
environment the Korup National Park preserves 1,300 sq km/500 sq mi of Africa's fast-disappearing

tropical rainforest. Scientists have identified nearly 100 potentially useful chemical substances produced naturally by the plants of this forest

features Mount Cameroon 4,070 m/13,358 ft, an active volcano on the coast, W of the Adamawa Mountains

head of state and of government Paul Biya from 1982

political system emergent democratic republic

political parties Democratic Assembly of the Cameroon People (RDPC), nationalist left-of-centre; Social Democratic Front (SDF), centre-left; Social Movement for New Democracy (MSND), left-of-centre; Union of the Peoples of Cameroon (UPC), left-of-centre

exports cocoa, coffee, bananas, cotton, timber, rubber, groundnuts, gold, aluminium, crude oil

currency CFA franc

population (1990 est) 11,109,000; growth rate 2.7% p.a.

life expectancy men 49, women 53

languages French and English in pidgin variations (official); there has been some discontent with the emphasis on French—there are 163 indigenous peoples with their own African languages

media heavy government censorship

religion Roman Catholic 35%, animist 25%, Muslim 22%, Protestant 18%

literacy men 68%, women 45% (1985 est)

GDP $12.7 bn (1987); $1,170 per head

chronology

1884 Treaty signed establishing German rule.

1916 Captured by Allied forces in World War I.

1922 Divided between Britain and France.

1946 French Cameroon and British Cameroons made UN trust territories.

1960 French Cameroon became the independent Republic of Cameroon. Ahmadou Ahidjo elected president.

1961 Northern part of British Cameroon merged with Nigeria and southern part joined the Republic of Cameroon to become the Federal Republic of Cameroon.

1966 One-party regime introduced.

1972 New constitution made Cameroon a unitary state, the United Republic of Cameroon.

1973 New national assembly elected.

1982 Ahidjo resigned and was succeeded by Paul Biya.

1983 Biya began to remove his predecessor's supporters; accused by Ahidjo of trying to create a police state. Ahidjo went into exile in France.

1984 Biya re-elected; defeated a plot to overthrow him. Country's name changed to Republic of Cameroon.

1988 Biya re-elected.

1990 Widespread public disorder. Biya granted amnesty to political prisoners.

1991 Biya promised multiparty elections for 1992. Constitutional changes made.

1992 Ruling RDPC won in first multiparty elections for 28 years.

Canada (Dominion of)

area 9,970,610 sq km/3,849,674 sq mi

capital Ottawa

towns Toronto, Montréal, Vancouver, Edmonton, Calgary, Winnipeg, Québec, Hamilton, Saskatoon, Halifax

physical mountains in W, with low-lying plains in interior and rolling hills in E. Climate varies from temperate in S to arctic in N

environment sugar maples are dying in E Canada as a result of increasing soil acidification; nine rivers in Nova Scotia are now too acid to support salmon or trout reproduction

features St Lawrence Seaway, Mackenzie River; Great Lakes; Arctic Archipelago; Rocky Mountains; Great Plains or Prairies; Canadian Shield; Niagara Falls; the world's second largest country

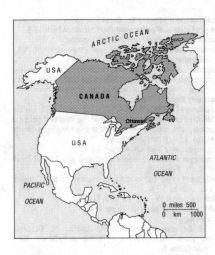

head of state Elizabeth II from 1952 represented by governor general

head of government Brian Mulroney from 1984

political system federal constitutional monarchy

political parties Progressive Conservative Party, free-enterprise, right-of-centre; Liberal Party, nationalist, centrist; New Democratic Party (NDP), moderate, left-of-centre

exports wheat, timber, pulp, newsprint, fish (salmon), furs (ranched fox and mink exceed the value of wild furs), oil, natural gas, aluminium, asbestos (world's second largest producer), coal, copper, iron, zinc, nickel (world's largest producer), uranium (world's largest producer), motor vehicles and parts, industrial and agricultural machinery, fertilizers, chemicals

currency Canadian dollar

population (1990 est) 26,527,000—including 300,000 North American Indians, of whom 75% live on over 2,000 reservations in Ontario and the four western provinces; some 300,000 Métis (people of mixed race) and 19,000 Inuit (or Eskimo, of whom 75% live in the Northwest Territories). Over half Canada's population lives in Ontario and Québec. Growth rate 1.1% p.a.

life expectancy men 72, women 79

languages English, French (both official) (about 70% speak English, 20% French, and the rest are bilingual); there are also North American Indian languages and the Inuit Inuktitut

religion Roman Catholic 46%, Protestant 35%

literacy 99%

GDP $412 bn (1987); $15,910 per head

chronology

1867 Dominion of Canada founded.

1949 Newfoundland joined Canada.

1957 Progressive Conservatives returned to power after 22 years in opposition.

1961 NDP formed.

1963 Liberals elected under Lester Pearson.

1968 Pearson succeeded by Pierre Trudeau.

1979 Joe Clark, leader of the Progressive Conservatives, formed a minority government; defeated on budget proposals.

1980 Liberals under Trudeau returned with a large majority. Québec referendum rejected demand for independence.

1982 Canada Act removed Britain's last legal control over Canadian affairs; 'patriation' of Canada's constitution.

1983 Clark replaced as leader of the Progressive Conservatives by Brian Mulroney.

1984 Trudeau retired and was succeeded as Liberal leader and prime minister by John Turner. Progressive

Conservatives won the federal election with a large majority, and Mulroney became prime minister.
1988 Conservatives re-elected with reduced majority on platform of free trade with the USA.
1989 Free-trade agreement signed. Turner resigned as Liberal Party leader, and Ed Broadbent as NDP leader.
1990 Collapse of Meech Lake accord. Canada joined the coalition opposing Iraq's invasion of Kuwait.
1991 Mulroney presented a package of constitutional reforms to parliament.
1992 Gradual withdrawal of Canadian forces in Europe announced.

Cape Verde (Republic of)
(República de Cabo Verde)

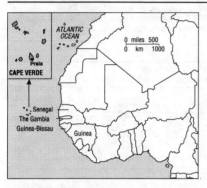

area 4,033 sq km/1,557 sq mi
capital Praia
towns Mindelo, Sal-Rei, Porto Novo
physical archipelago of ten volcanic islands 565 km/350 mi W of Senegal; the windward (Barlavento) group includes Santo Antão, São Vicente, Santa Luzia, São Nicolau, Sal, and Boa Vista; the leeward (Sotovento) group comprises Maio, São Tiago, Fogo, and Brava; all but Santa Luzia are inhabited
features strategic importance guaranteed by its domination of western shipping lanes; Sal, Boa Vista, and Maio lack water supplies but have fine beaches
head of state Mascarenhas Monteiro from 1991
head of government Carlos Viega from 1991
political system socialist pluralist state
political parties African Party for the Independence of Cape Verde (PAICV), African nationalist; Movement for Democracy (MPD)
exports bananas, salt, fish
currency Cape Verde escudo
population (1990 est) 375,000 (including 100,000 Angolan refugees); growth rate 1.9% p.a.
life expectancy men 57, women 61
language Creole dialect of Portuguese
religion Roman Catholic 80%
literacy men 61%, women 39% (1985)
GDP $158 million (1987); $454 per head

chronology
15th century First settled by Portuguese.
1951–74 Ruled as an overseas territory by Portugal.
1974 Moved towards independence through a transitional Portuguese–Cape Verde government.
1975 Independence achieved from Portugal. National people's assembly elected. Aristides Pereira became the first president.
1980 Constitution adopted providing for eventual union with Guinea-Bissau.
1981 Union with Guinea-Bissau abandoned and the

constitution amended; became one-party state.
1991 First multiparty elections held. New party, MPD, won majority in assembly. Pereira replaced by Mascarenhas Monteiro.

Central African Republic
(République Centrafricaine)

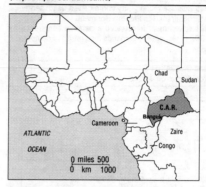

area 622,436 sq km/240,260 sq mi
capital Bangui
towns Berbérati, Bouar, Bossangoa
physical landlocked flat plateau, with rivers flowing N and S, and hills in NE and SW. Dry in N, rainforest in SW
environment an estimated 87% of the urban population is without access to safe drinking water
features Kotto and Mbali river falls; the Oubangui River rises 6 m/20 ft at Bangui during the wet season (June–Nov)
head of state and government André Kolingba from 1981
political system one-party military republic
political parties Central African Democratic Assembly (RDC), nationalist; all political activity has been banned since the 1981 coup, but the main opposition groups, although passive, still exist. They are the Patriotic Front Ubangi Workers' Party (FPO-PT), the Central African Movement for National Liberation (MCLN), and the Movement for the Liberation of the Central African People (MPLC)
exports diamonds, uranium, coffee, cotton, timber, tobacco
currency CFA franc
population (1990 est) 2,879,000 (more than 80 ethnic groups); growth rate 2.3% p.a.
life expectancy men 41, women 45
languages Sangho (national), French (official), Arabic, Hunsa, and Swahili
religion 25% Protestant; 25% Roman Catholic; 10% Muslim; 10% animist
literacy men 53%, women 29% (1985 est)
GDP $1 bn (1987); $374 per head

chronology
1960 Central African Republic achieved independence from France; David Dacko elected president.
1962 The republic made a one-party state.
1965 Dacko ousted in military coup led by Col Bokassa.
1966 Constitution rescinded and national assembly dissolved.
1972 Bokassa declared himself president for life.
1977 Bokassa made himself emperor of the Central African Empire.
1979 Bokassa deposed by Dacko following violent repressive measures by the self-styled emperor, who went into exile.
1981 Dacko deposed in a bloodless coup, led by General André Kolingba, and an all-military government established.

1983 Clandestine opposition movement formed.
1984 Amnesty for all political party leaders announced. President Mitterrand of France paid a state visit.
1985 New constitution promised, with some civilians in the government.
1986 Bokassa returned from France, expecting to return to power; he was imprisoned and his trial started. General Kolingba re-elected.
1988 Bokassa found guilty and received death sentence, later commuted to life imprisonment.
1991 Government announced a national conference for 1992 in response to demands for a return to democracy.

Chad (Republic of)
(République du Tchad)

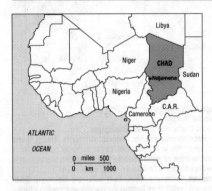

area 1,284,000 sq km/495,624 sq mi
capital Ndjamena (formerly Fort Lamy)
towns Sarh, Moundou, Abéché
physical landlocked state with mountains and part of Sahara Desert in N; moist savanna in S; rivers in S flow NW to Lake Chad
head of state and government Idriss Deby from 1990
political system emergent democratic republic
political parties National Union for Independence and Revolution (UNIR), nationalist; Alliance for Democracy and Progress (RDP), centre-left; Union for Democracy and Progress (UPDT), centre-left
exports cotton, meat, livestock, hides, skins
currency CFA franc
population (1990 est) 5,064,000; growth rate 2.3% p.a. Nomadic tribes move N–S seasonally in search of water
life expectancy men 42, women 45
languages French, Arabic (both official), over 100 African languages spoken
religion Muslim 44% (N), Christian 33%, animist 23% (S)
literacy men 40%, women 11% (1985 est)
GDP $980 million (1986); $186 per head

chronology
1960 Independence achieved from France, with François Tombalbaye as president.
1963 Violent opposition in the Muslim north, led by the Chadian National Liberation Front (Frolinat), backed by Libya.
1968 Revolt quelled with France's help.
1975 Tombalbaye killed in military coup led by Félix Malloum. Frolinat continued its resistance.
1978 Malloum tried to find a political solution by bringing the former Frolinat leader Hissène Habré into his government but they were unable to work together.
1979 Malloum forced to leave the country; an interim government was set up under General Goukouni. Habré continued his opposition with his Army of the North (FAN).

1981 Habré now in control of half the country. Goukouni fled and set up a 'government in exile'.
1983 Habré's regime recognized by the Organization for African Unity (OAU), but in the north Goukouni's supporters, with Libya's help, fought on. Eventually a cease-fire was agreed, with latitude 16°N dividing the country.
1984 Libya and France agreed to a withdrawal of forces.
1985 Fighting between Libyan-backed and French-backed forces intensified.
1987 Chad, France, and Libya agreed on cease-fire proposed by OAU.
1988 Full diplomatic relations with Libya restored.
1989 Libyan troop movements reported on border; Habré re-elected, amended constitution.
1990 President Habré ousted in coup led by Idriss Deby. New constitution adopted.
1991 Several anti-government coups foiled.
1992 Anti-government coup foiled. Two new opposition parties approved.

Chile (Republic of)
(República de Chile)

area 756,950 sq km/292,257 sq mi
capital Santiago
towns Concepción, Viña del Mar, Temuco; ports Valparaíso, Antofagasta, Arica, Iquique, Punta Arenas
physical Andes mountains along E border, Atacama Desert in N, fertile central valley, grazing land and forest in S
territories Easter Island, Juan Fernández Islands, part of Tierra del Fuego, claim to part of Antarctica
features Atacama Desert is one of the driest regions in the world
head of state and government Patricio Aylwin from 1990
political system emergent democratic republic
political parties Christian Democratic Party (PDC), moderate centrist; National Renewal Party (RN), right-wing
exports copper (world's leading producer), iron, molybdenum (world's second largest producer), nitrate, pulp and paper, steel products, fishmeal, fruit
currency peso
population (1990 est) 13,000,000 (the majority are of European origin or are mestizos, of mixed American Indian and Spanish descent); growth rate 1.6% p.a.
life expectancy men 64, women 73
language Spanish
religion Roman Catholic 89%

literacy 94% (1988)
GDP $18.9 bn (1987); $6,512 per head

chronology
1818 Achieved independence from Spain.
1964 PDC formed government under Eduardo Frei.
1970 Dr Salvador Allende became the first democratically elected Marxist president; he embarked on an extensive programme of nationalization and social reform.
1973 Government overthrown by the CIA-backed military, led by General Augusto Pinochet. Allende killed. Policy of repression began during which all opposition was put down and political activity banned.
1983 Growing opposition to the regime from all sides, with outbreaks of violence.
1988 Referendum on whether Pinochet should serve a further term resulted in a clear 'No' vote.
1989 President Pinochet agreed to constitutional changes to allow pluralist politics. Patricio Aylwin (PDC) elected president; Pinochet remained as army commander in chief.
1990 Salvador Allende officially restored to favour. Aylwin reached accord on end to military junta government. Pinochet censured by president.

China (People's Republic of)
(Zhonghua Renmin Gonghe Guo)

area 9,596,960 sq km/3,599,975 sq mi
capital Beijing (Peking)
towns Chongqing (Chungking), Shenyang (Mukden), Wuhan, Nanjing (Nanking), Harbin; ports Tianjin (Tientsin), Shanghai, Qingdao (Tsingtao), Lüda (Lü-ta), Guangzhou (Canton)
physical two-thirds of China is mountains or desert (N and W); the low-lying E is irrigated by rivers Huang He (Yellow River), Chang Jiang (Yangtze-Kiang), Xi Jiang (Si Kiang)
features Great Wall of China; Gezhouba Dam; Ming Tombs; Terracotta Warriors (Xi'ain); Gobi Desert; world's most populous country
head of state Yang Shangkun from 1988
head of government Li Peng from 1987
political system communist republic
political party Chinese Communist Party (CCP), Marxist-Leninist-Maoist
exports tea, livestock and animal products, silk, cotton, oil, minerals (China is the world's largest producer of tungsten and antimony), chemicals, light industrial goods
currency yuan
population (1990 est) 1,130,065,000 (the majority are Han or ethnic Chinese; the 67 million of other ethnic

groups, including Tibetan, Uigur, and Zhuang, live in border areas). The number of people of Chinese origin outside China, Taiwan, and Hong Kong is estimated at 15–24 million. Growth rate 1.2% p.a.
life expectancy men 67, women 69
language Chinese, including Mandarin (official), Cantonese, and other dialects
religion officially atheist, but traditionally Taoist, Confucianist, and Buddhist; Muslim 13 million; Catholic 3–6 million (divided between the 'patriotic' church established 1958 and the 'loyal' church subject to Rome); Protestant 3 million
literacy men 82%, women 66% (1985 est)
GDP $293.4 bn (1987); $274 per head

chronology
1949 People's Republic of China proclaimed by Mao Zedong.
1954 Soviet-style constitution adopted.
1956–57 Hundred Flowers Movement encouraged criticism of the government.
1958–60 Great Leap Forward commune experiment to achieve 'true communism'.
1960 Withdrawal of Soviet technical advisers.
1962 Sino-Indian border war.
1962–65 Economic recovery programme under Liu Shaoqi; Maoist 'socialist education movement' rectification campaign.
1966–69 Great Proletarian Cultural Revolution; Liu Shaoqi overthrown.
1969 Ussuri River border clashes with USSR.
1970–76 Reconstruction under Mao and Zhou Enlai.
1971 Entry into United Nations.
1972 US president Nixon visited Beijing.
1975 New state constitution. Unveiling of Zhou's 'Four Modernizations' programme.
1976 Deaths of Zhou Enlai and Mao Zedong; appointment of Hua Guofeng as prime minister and Communist Party chair. Vice Premier Deng Xiaoping in hiding. Gang of Four arrested.
1977 Rehabilitation of Deng Xiaoping.
1979 Economic reforms introduced. Diplomatic relations opened with USA. Punitive invasion of Vietnam.
1980 Zhao Ziyang appointed prime minister.
1981 Hu Yaobang succeeded Hua Guofeng as party chair. Imprisonment of Gang of Four.
1982 New state constitution adopted.
1984 'Enterprise management' reforms for industrial sector.
1986 Student prodemocracy demonstrations.
1987 Hu was replaced as party leader by Zhao, with Li Peng as prime minister. Deng left Politburo but remained influential.
1988 Yang Shangkun became state president. Economic reforms encountered increasing problems; inflation rocketed.
1989 Over 2,000 killed in prodemocracy student demonstrations in Tiananmen Square; international sanctions imposed.
1991 March: EC and Japanese sanctions lifted. May: normal relations with USSR resumed. Sept: UK prime minister John Major visited Beijing. Nov: relations with Vietnam normalized.
1992 China promised to sign 1968 Nuclear Non-Proliferation Treaty. Full diplomatic relations with Israel established.

Colombia (Republic of)
(República de Colombia)

area 1,141,748 sq km/440,715 sq mi
capital Bogotá
towns Medellín, Cali, Bucaramanga; ports Barranquilla, Cartagena, Buenaventura
physical the Andes mountains run N–S; flat coastland

in W and plains (llanos) in E; Magdalena River runs N to Caribbean Sea; includes islands of Providencia, San Andrés, and Mapelo

features Zipaquira salt mine and underground cathedral; Lake Guatavita, source of the legend of 'El Dorado'

head of state and government Cesar Gaviria Trujillo from 1990

political system emergent democratic republic

political parties Liberal Party (PL), centrist; April 19 Movement (M-19); National Salvation Movement; Conservative Party, right-of-centre

exports emeralds (world's largest producer), coffee (world's second largest producer), cocaine (country's largest export), bananas, cotton, meat, sugar, oil, skins, hides, tobacco

currency peso

population (1990 est) 32,598,800 (mestizo 68%, white 20%, Amerindian 1%); growth rate 2.2% p.a.

life expectancy men 61, women 66; Indians 34

language Spanish

religion Roman Catholic 95%

literacy men 89%, women 87% (1987); Indians 40%

GDP $31.9 bn (1987); $1,074 per head

chronology

1886 Full independence achieved from Spain. Conservatives in power.

1930 Liberals in power.

1946 Conservatives in power.

1948 Left-wing mayor of Bogotá assassinated; widespread outcry.

1949 Start of civil war, 'La Violencia', during which over 250,000 people died.

1957 Hoping to halt the violence, Conservatives and Liberals agreed to form a National Front, sharing the presidency.

1970 National Popular Alliance (ANAPO) formed as a left-wing opposition to the National Front.

1974 National Front accord temporarily ended.

1975 Civil unrest because of disillusionment with the government.

1978 Liberals, under Julio Turbay, revived the accord and began an intensive fight against drug dealers.

1982 Liberals maintained their control of congress but lost the presidency. The Conservative president, Belisario Betancur, granted guerrillas an amnesty and freed political prisoners.

1984 Minister of justice assassinated by drug dealers; campaign against them stepped up.

1986 Virgilio Barco Vargas, Liberal, elected president by record margin.

1989 Drug cartel assassinated leading presidential candidate; Vargas declared antidrug war; bombing campaign by drug lords killed hundreds; police killed

José Rodríguez Gacha, one of the most wanted cartel leaders.

1990 Cesar Gaviria Trujillo elected president. Liberals maintained control of congress.

1991 New constitution prohibited extradition of Colombians wanted for trial in other countries; several leading drug traffickers arrested. Oct: Liberal Party won general election.

Comoros (Federal Islamic Republic of)
(Jumhuriyat al-Qumur al-Itthādīyah al-Islāmiyah)

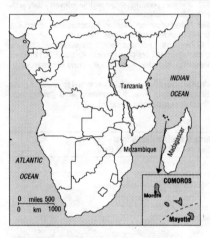

area 1,862 sq km/719 sq mi

capital Moroni

towns Mutsamudu, Domoni, Fomboni

physical comprises the volcanic islands of Njazídja, Nzwani, and Mwali (formerly Grande Comore, Anjouan, Moheli); at N end of Mozambique Channel

features active volcano on Njazídja; poor tropical soil

head of state and government Said Mohammad Djohar (interim administration)

political system authoritarian nationalism

political parties Comoran Union for Progress (Udzima), nationalist Islamic; National Union for Congolese Democracy (UNDC), left-of-centre; Popular Democratic Movement (MDP), centrist

exports copra, vanilla, cocoa, sisal, coffee, cloves, essential oils

currency CFA franc

population (1990 est) 459,000; growth rate 3.1% p.a.

life expectancy men 48, women 52

languages Arabic (official), Comorian (Swahili and Arabic dialect), Makua, French

religion Muslim (official) 86%, Roman Catholic 14%

literacy 15%

GDP $198 million (1987); $468 per head

chronology

1975 Independence achieved from France, but Mayotte remained part of France. Ahmed Abdallah elected president. The Comoros joined the United Nations.

1976 Abdallah overthrown by Ali Soilih.

1978 Soilih killed by mercenaries working for Abdallah. Islamic republic proclaimed and Abdallah elected president.

1979 The Comoros became a one-party state; powers of the federal government increased.

1985 Constitution amended to make Abdallah head of government as well as head of state.

1989 Abdallah killed by French mercenaries who took control of government; under French and South African

pressure, mercenaries left Comoros, turning authority over to French administration and interim president Said Mohammad Djohar.
1990 Antigovernment coup foiled.

Congo (Republic of)
(République du Congo)

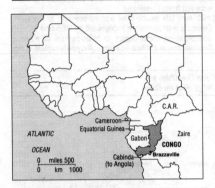

area 342,000 sq km/132,012 sq mi
capital Brazzaville
towns chief port Pointe-Noire; N'Kayi, Loubomo
physical narrow coastal plain rises to central plateau then falls into northern basin. Zaïre (Congo) River on the border with Zaire; half the country is rainforest
environment an estimated 93% of the rural population is without access to safe drinking water
features 70% of the population lives in Brazzaville, Pointe-Noire, or in towns along the railway linking these two places
head of state and government Denis Sassou-Nguessou from 1979
political system emergent democracy
political parties Congolese Labour Party (PCT), (Marxist-Leninist ideology abandoned 1990) left-wing; Union for Congolese Democracy (UDC), left-of-centre; National Union for Democracy and Progress (UNDP), left-of-centre
exports timber, petroleum, cocoa, sugar
currency CFA franc
population (1990 est) 2,305,000 (chiefly Bantu); growth rate 2.6% p.a.
life expectancy men 45, women 48
languages French (official); many African languages
religion animist 50%, Christian 48%, Muslim 2%
literacy men 79%, women 55% (1985 est)
GDP $2.1 bn (1983); $500 per head

chronology
1910 Became part of French Equatorial Africa.
1960 Achieved independence from France, with Abbé Youlou as the first president.
1963 Youlou forced to resign. New constitution approved, with Alphonse Massamba-Débat as president.
1964 The Congo became a one-party state.
1968 Military coup, led by Capt Marien Ngouabi, ousted Massamba-Débat.
1970 A Marxist state, the People's Republic of the Congo, was announced, with the PCT as the only legal party.
1977 Ngouabi assassinated. Col Yhombi-Opango became president.
1979 Yhombi-Opango handed over the presidency to the PCT, who chose Col Denis Sassou-Nguessou as his successor.
1984 Sassou-Nguessou elected for another five-year term.

1990 The PCT abandoned Marxist-Leninism and promised multiparty politics.
1991 1979 constitution suspended pending the introduction of multiparty democracy. Possible postponement of multiparty elections announced. Country renamed the Republic of Congo.
1992 New constitution approved.

Costa Rica (Republic of)
(République de Costa Rica)

area 51,000 sq km/19,735 sq mi
capital San José
towns ports Limón, Puntarenas
physical high central plateau and tropical coasts; Costa Rica was once entirely forested, containing an estimated 5% of the Earth's flora and fauna. By 1983 only 17% of the forest remained; half of the arable land had been cleared for cattle ranching, which led to landlessness, unemployment (except for 2,000 politically powerful families), and soil erosion; the massive environmental destruction also caused incalculable loss to the gene pool
environment one of the leading centres of conservation in Latin America, with more than 10% of the country protected by national parks, and tree replanting proceeding at a rate of 150 sq km/60 sq mi per year
features Poas Volcano; Guayabo pre-Colombian ceremonial site
head of state and government Rafael Calderón from 1990
political system liberal democracy
political parties National Liberation Party (PLN), left-of-centre; Christian Socialist Unity Party (PUSC), centrist coalition; ten minor parties
exports coffee, bananas, cocoa, sugar, beef
currency colón
population (1990 est) 3,032,000 (including 1,200 Guaymi Indians); growth rate 2.6% p.a.
life expectancy men 71, women 76
language Spanish (official)
religion Roman Catholic 95%
literacy men 94%, women 93% (1985 est)
GDP $4.3 bn (1986); $1,550 per head

chronology
1821 Independence achieved from Spain.
1949 New constitution adopted. National army abolished. José Figueres, cofounder of the PLN, elected president; he embarked on ambitious socialist programme.
1958-73 Mainly conservative administrations.
1974 PLN regained the presidency and returned to socialist policies.
1978 Rodrigo Carazo, conservative, elected president.

Sharp deterioration in the state of the economy.
1982 Luis Alberto Monge of the PLN elected president. Harsh austerity programme introduced to rebuild the economy. Pressure from the USA to abandon neutral stance and condemn Sandinista regime in Nicaragua.
1983 Policy of neutrality reaffirmed.
1985 Following border clashes with Sandinista forces, a US-trained antiguerrilla guard formed.
1986 Oscar Arias Sánchez won the presidency on a neutralist platform.
1987 Oscar Arias Sánchez won Nobel Peace Prize for devising a Central American peace plan.
1990 Rafael Calderón (PUSC) elected president.

Croatia (Republic of)

area 56,538 sq km/21,824 sq mi
capital Zagreb
towns chief port: Rijeka (Fiume); other ports: Zadar, Sibenik, Split, Dubrovnik
physical Adriatic coastline with large islands; very mountainous, with part of the Karst region and the Julian and Styrian Alps; some marshland
features popular sea resorts along the extensive Adriatic coastline
head of state Franjo Tudjman from 1990
head of government Franjo Greguric from 1991
political system emergent democracy
political parties Christian Democratic Union (HDZ), right-wing, nationalist; Coalition of National Agreement, centrist; Communist Party, reform-communist
products cereals, potatoes, tobacco, fruit, livestock, metal goods, textiles
currency Croatian dinar
population (1990) 4,760,000 including 75% Croats, 12% Serbs, and 1% Slovenes
language Croatian variant of Serbo-Croatian
religion Roman Catholic (Croats); Orthodox Christian (Serbs)
GNP $7.9 bn (1990); $1,660 per head

chronology
1918 Became part of the kingdom which united the Serbs, Croats, and Slovenes.
1929 The kingdom of Croatia, Serbia, and Slovenia became Yugoslavia. Croatia continued its campaign for autonomy.
1941 Became a Nazi puppet state following German invasion.
1945 Became constituent republic of Yugoslavia.
1970s Separatist demands resurfaced. Crackdown against anti-Serb separatist agitators.

1989 Formation of opposition parties permitted.
1990 April-May: Communists defeated by Tudjman-led Croatian Democratic Union (HDZ) in first free election since 1938. Sept: 'sovereignty' declared. Dec: new constitution adopted.
1991 Feb: assembly called for Croatia's secession. March: Serb-dominated Krajina announced secession from Croatia. June: Croatia declared independence; military conflict with Serbia; internal civil war ensued. July onwards: civil war intensified. Oct: Croatia formally seceded from Yugoslavia.
1992 Jan: UN peace plan accord reached at Sarajevo; Croatia's independence recognized by USA and EC. UN peacemaking force began to take control of Krajina; Croatian forces continued to shell Krajina's capital, Knin.

Cuba (Republic of)
(República de Cuba)

area 110,860 sq km/42,820 sq mi
capital Havana
towns Santiago de Cuba, Camagüey
physical comprises Cuba, the largest and westernmost of the West Indies, and smaller islands including Isle of Youth; low hills; Sierra Maestra mountains in SE
features 3,380 km/2,100 mi of coastline, with deep bays, sandy beaches, coral islands and reefs; more than 1,600 islands surround the Cuban mainland
head of state and government Fidel Castro Ruz from 1959
political system communist republic
political party Communist Party of Cuba (PCC), Marxist-Leninist
exports sugar, tobacco, coffee, nickel, fish
currency Cuban peso
population (1990 est) 10,582,000; 37% are white of Spanish descent, 51% mulatto, and 11% are of African origin; growth rate 0.6% p.a.
life expectancy men 72, women 75
language Spanish
religion Roman Catholic 85%; also Episcopalians and Methodists
literacy men 96%, women 95% (1988)
disposable national income $15.8 bn (1983); $1,590 per head

chronology
1492 Christopher Columbus landed in Cuba and claimed it for Spain.
1898 USA defeated Spain in Spanish-American War; Spain gave up all claims to Cuba.
1901 Cuba achieved independence; Tomás Estrada Palma became first president of the Republic of Cuba.
1933 Fulgencia Batista seized power.

1944 Batista retired.
1952 Batista seized power again to begin an oppressive regime.
1953 Fidel Castro led an unsuccessful coup against Batista.
1956 Second unsuccessful coup by Castro.
1959 Batista overthrown by Castro. Constitution of 1940 replaced by a 'Fundamental Law', making Castro prime minister, his brother Raúl Castro his deputy, and Che Guevara his number three.
1960 All US businesses in Cuba appropriated without compensation; USA broke off diplomatic relations.
1961 USA sponsored an unsuccessful invasion at the Bay of Pigs. Castro announced that Cuba had become a communist state, with a Marxist-Leninist programme of economic development.
1962 Cuba expelled from the Organization of American States (OAS). Soviet nuclear missiles installed but subsequently removed from Cuba at US insistence.
1965 Cuba's sole political party renamed Cuban Communist Party (PCC). With Soviet help, Cuba began to make considerable economic and social progress.
1972 Cuba became a full member of the Moscow-based Council for Mutual Economic Assistance (CMEA).
1976 New socialist constitution approved; Castro elected president.
1976-81 Castro became involved in extensive international commitments, sending troops as Soviet surrogates, particularly to Africa.
1982 Cuba joined other Latin American countries in giving moral support to Argentina in its dispute with Britain over the Falklands.
1984 Castro tried to improve US-Cuban relations by discussing exchange of US prisoners in Cuba for Cuban 'undesirables' in the USA.
1988 Peace accord with South Africa signed, agreeing to withdrawal of Cuban troops from Angola.
1989 Reduction in Cuba's overseas military activities. Castro reaffirmed communist orthodoxy.
1991 Soviet troops withdrawn.
1992 Castro reaffirmed his faith in communism.

Cyprus (Greek Republic of Cyprus)
(Kypriakí Dimokratía) in the south, and *Turkish Republic of Northern Cyprus (Kíbris Cumhuriyeti)* in the north

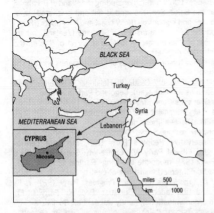

area 9,251 sq km/3,571 sq mi, 37% in Turkish hands
capital Nicosia (divided between Greeks and Turks)
towns ports Limassol, Larnaca, Paphos (Greek); Morphou, and ports Kyrenia and Famagusta (Turkish)
physical central plain between two E–W mountain ranges
features archaeological and historic sites; Mount Olympus 1,953 m/6,406 ft (highest peak); beaches

heads of state and government Georgios Vassiliou (Greek) from 1988, Rauf Denktaş (Turkish) from 1976
political system democratic divided republic
political parties Democratic Front (DIKO), centre-left; Progressive Party of the Working People (AKEL), socialist; Democratic Rally (DISY), centrist; Socialist Party (EDEK), socialist; *Turkish zone:* National Unity Party (NUP), Communal Liberation Party (CLP), Republican Turkish Party (RTP), New British Party (NBP)
exports citrus, grapes, raisins, Cyprus sherry, potatoes, clothing, footwear
currency Cyprus pound and Turkish lira
population (1990 est) 708,000 (Greek Cypriot 78%, Turkish Cypriot 18%); growth rate 1.2% p.a.
life expectancy men 72, women 76
languages Greek and Turkish (official), English
religion Greek Orthodox 78%, Sunni Muslim 18%
literacy 99% (1984)
GDP $3.7 bn (1987); $5,497 per head

chronology
1878 Came under British administration.
1955 Guerrilla campaign began against the British for enosis (union with Greece), led by Archbishop Makarios and General Grivas.
1956 Makarios and enosis leaders deported.
1959 Compromise agreed and Makarios returned to be elected president of an independent Greek-Turkish Cyprus.
1960 Independence achieved from Britain, with Britain retaining its military bases.
1963 Turks set up their own government in northern Cyprus. Fighting broke out between the two communities.
1964 UN peacekeeping force installed.
1971 Grivas returned to start a guerrilla war against the Makarios government.
1974 Grivas died. Military coup deposed Makarios, who fled to Britain. Nicos Sampson appointed president. Turkish army sent to northern Cyprus to confirm Turkish Cypriots' control; military regime in southern Cyprus collapsed; Makarios returned. Northern Cyprus declared itself the Turkish Federated State of Cyprus (TFSC), with Rauf Denktaş as president.
1977 Makarios died; succeeded by Spyros Kyprianou.
1983 An independent Turkish Republic of Northern Cyprus (TRNC) proclaimed but recognized only by Turkey.
1984 UN peace proposals rejected.
1985 Summit meeting between Kyprianou and Denktaş failed to reach agreement.
1988 Georgios Vassiliou elected president. Talks with Denktaş began, under UN auspices.
1989 Vassiliou and Denktaş agreed to draft an agreement for the future reunification of the island, but peace talks were abandoned Sept.
1991 Turkish offer of peace talks rejected by Cyprus and Greece.

Czechoslovakia (Czech and Slovak Federative Republic)
(Česká a Slovenská federativní)

area 127,903 sq km/49,371 sq mi
capital Prague
towns Bratislava, Brno, Ostrava
physical Carpathian Mountains, rivers Morava, Labe (Elbe), Vltava (Moldau); hills and plateau; Danube plain in S
environment Czechoslovakia is the most polluted country in E Europe. Pollution is worst in N Bohemia which produces 70% of the country's coal and 45% of its coal-generated electricity. Up to 20 times the permissible level of sulphur dioxide is released over Prague where

75% of the drinking water fails to meet the country's health standards

features divided by valley of the Morava into the densely populated Czech area with good communications in W, and the sparsely populated, mainly agricultural Slovak area in E; summer and winter resort areas in Western Carpathian, Bohemian, and Sudetes mountain ranges

head of state to be decided

head of government Václav Klaus from 1992

political system emergent democratic republic

political parties Civic Democratic Party (CDP), right-of-centre, Czech-based (formerly part of Civic Forum); Civic Movement (CM), left-of-centre, Czech-based (formerly part of Civic Forum); Civic Democratic Union-Public Against Violence (PAV), Slovakia-based; Movement for Democratic Slovakia (MFDS), Slovak-nationalist; Communist Party of Czechoslovakia (CCP), Marxist-Leninist; Christian Democratic Movement (CDM), centrist

exports machinery, vehicles, timber, ceramics, glass, textiles, lignite, magnesite, mercury

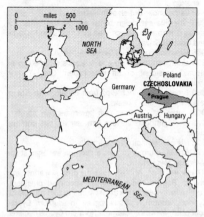

currency koruna

population (1990 est) 15,695,000 (63% Czech, 31% Slovak, with Hungarian, Polish, German, Russian, and other minorities); growth rate 0.4% p.a.

life expectancy men 68, women 75

languages Czech and Slovak (official)

religion Roman Catholic 75%, Protestant 15%

literacy 99% (1981)

GDP $148.5 bn (1987); $3,127 per head

chronology

1918 Independence achieved from Austro-Hungarian Empire; Czechs and Slovaks formed Czechoslovakia as independent nation.

1938 Infamous Munich Agreement gave Sudetenland to Nazi Germany, as 'appeasement', but six months later Hitler occupied entire nation. Beneš headed government in exile until 1945.

1945 Liberation of Czechoslovakia from Nazis by USSR and USA.

1948 Communists assumed power in coup and new constitution framed.

1968 'Prague Spring' experiment with liberalization ended by Soviet invasion and occupation.

1969 Czechoslovakia became a federal state; Husák elected Communist Party leader.

1977 Emergence and suppression of Charter 77 human-rights movement.

1985-86 Criticism of Husák rule by new Soviet leadership.

1987 Husák resigned as communist leader, remaining president; replaced by Miloš Jakeš.

1988 Personnel overhaul of party and state bodies, including replacement of Prime Minister Štrougal by the technocrat Adamec.

1989 Communist regime overthrown in Nov-Dec bloodless 'gentle revolution'. Communist monopoly of power ended, with new 'Grand Coalition' government formed. Václav Havel appointed state president.

1990 22,000 prisoners released. Havel announced agreement with USSR for complete withdrawal of Soviet troops. Devolution of more powers to federal republics.

1991 Bill of rights passed. Steps taken towards privatization. Splits appeared in reform coalitions, with the emergence of new parties. Last Soviet troops withdrawn. Increasing Czech and Slovak separatism.

1992 Václav Klaus, leader of the CDP, became prime minister. Klaus and Vladimir Meciar, leader of the MFDS, sought solution to separatist issue; formal split into Czech and Slovak republics agreed for end Sept, with interim caretaker government, following Slovak gains in assembly elections. Havel resigned.

Denmark (Kingdom of)
(Kongeriget Danmark)

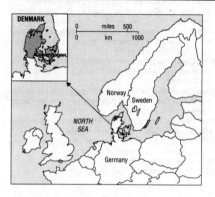

area 43,075 sq km/16,627 sq mi

capital Copenhagen

towns Aarhus, Odense, Aalborg, Esbjerg, all ports

physical comprises the Jutland peninsula and about 500 islands (100 inhabited) including the island of Bornholm in the Baltic Sea; the land is flat and cultivated; sand dunes and lagoons on the W coast and long inlets (fjords) on the E; the main island is Sjælland (Zealand), where most of Copenhagen is located (the rest of it is on the island of Amager)

territories the dependencies of Faeroe Islands and Greenland

features Kronborg Castle in Helsingør (Elsinore); Tivoli Gardens (Copenhagen); Legoland Park in Sillund

head of state Queen Margrethe II from 1972

head of government Poul Schlüter from 1982

political system liberal democracy

political parties Social Democrats (SD), left-of-centre; Conservative People's Party (KF), moderate centre-right; Liberal Party (V), centre-left; Socialist People's Party (SF), moderate left-wing; Radical Liberals (RV), radical internationalist left-of-centre; Centre Democrats (CD), moderate centrist; Progress Party (FP), radical antibureaucratic; Christian People's Party (KrF), interdenominational, family values; Left Socialists

exports bacon, dairy produce, eggs, fish, mink pelts, car and aircraft parts, electrical equipment, textiles, chemicals

currency kroner (11.34 = £1 July 1991)

population (1990 est) 5,134,000; growth rate 0% p.a.

life expectancy men 72, women 78

languages Danish (official); there is a German-speaking minority

religion Lutheran 97%
literacy 99% (1983)
GDP $85.5 bn (1987); $16,673 per head

chronology
1940-45 Occupied by Germany.
1945 Iceland's independence recognized.
1947 Frederik IX succeeded Christian X.
1948 Home rule granted for Faeroe Islands.
1949 Became a founding member of NATO.
1960 Joined European Free Trade Association (EFTA).
1972 Margrethe II became Denmark's first queen in nearly 600 years.
1973 Left EFTA and joined European Economic Community (EEC).
1979 Home rule granted for Greenland.
1985 Strong non-nuclear movement in evidence.
1990 General election; another coalition government formed.
1992 Rejection of Maastricht Treaty in national referendum.

Djibouti (Republic of)
(Jumhouriyya Djibouti)

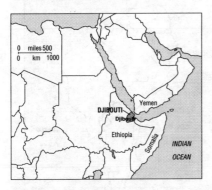

area 23,200 sq km/8,955 sq mi
capital (and chief port) Djibouti
towns Tadjoura, Obock, Dikhil
physical mountains divide an inland plateau from a coastal plain; hot and arid
features terminus of railway link with Ethiopia; Lac Assal salt lake is the second lowest point on Earth (−144 m/−471 ft)
head of state and government Hassan Gouled Aptidon from 1977
political system authoritarian nationalism
political party People's Progress Assembly (RPP), nationalist
exports acts mainly as a transit port for Ethiopia
currency Djibouti franc (285.00 = £1 July 1991)
population (1990 est) 337,000 (Issa 47%, Afar 37%, European 8%, Arab 6%); growth rate 3.4% p.a.
life expectancy 50
languages French (official), Somali, Afar, Arabic
religion Sunni Muslim
literacy 20% (1988)
GDP $378 million (1987); $1,016 per head

chronology
1884 Annexed by France as part of French Somaliland.
1967 French Somaliland became the French Territory of the Afars and the Issas.
1977 Independence achieved from France; Hassan Gouled elected president.
1979 All political parties combined to form the People's Progress Assembly (RPP).

1981 New constitution made RPP the only legal party. Gouled re-elected. Treaties of friendship signed with Ethiopia, Somalia, Kenya, and Sudan.
1984 Policy of neutrality reaffirmed.
1987 Gouled re-elected for a final term.

Dominica (Commonwealth of)

area 751 sq km/290 sq mi
capital Roseau, with a deepwater port
towns Portsmouth, Marigot
physical second largest of the Windward Islands, mountainous central ridge with tropical rainforest
features of great beauty, it has mountains of volcanic origin rising to 1,620 m/5,317 ft; Boiling Lake (an effect produced by escaping subterranean gas)
head of state Clarence Seignoret from 1983
head of government Eugenia Charles from 1980
political system liberal democracy
political parties Dominica Freedom Party (DFP), centrist; Labour Party of Dominica (LPD), left-of-centre coalition
exports bananas, coconuts, citrus, lime, bay oil
currency E Caribbean dollar (4.38 = £1 July 1991), pound sterling, French franc
population (1990 est) 94,200 (mainly black African in origin, but with a small Carib reserve of some 500); growth rate 1.3% p.a.
life expectancy men 57, women 59
language English (official), but the Dominican *patois* still reflects earlier periods of French rule
media one independent weekly newspaper
religion Roman Catholic 80%
literacy 80%
GDP $91 million (1985); $1,090 per head

chronology
1763 Became British possession.
1978 Independence achieved from Britain. Patrick John, leader of Dominica Labour Party (DLP), elected prime minister.
1980 Dominica Freedom Party (DFP), led by Eugenia Charles, won convincing victory in general election.
1981 Patrick John implicated in plot to overthrow government.
1982 John tried and acquitted.
1985 John retried and found guilty. Regrouping of left-of-centre parties resulted in new Labour Party of Dominica (LPD). DFP, led by Eugenia Charles, re-elected.
1990 Charles elected to a third term.
1991 Integration into Windward Islands confederation proposed.

Dominican Republic
(República Dominicana)

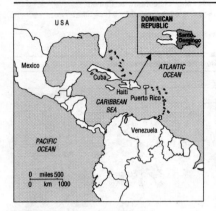

area 48,442 sq km/18,700 sq mi
capital Santo Domingo
towns Santiago de los Caballeros, San Pedro de Macoris
physical comprises eastern two-thirds of island of Hispaniola; central mountain range with fertile valleys
features Pico Duarte 3,174 m/10,417 ft, highest point in Caribbean islands; Santo Domingo is the oldest European city in the western hemisphere
head of state and government Joaquín Ricardo Balaguer from 1986
political system democratic republic
political parties Dominican Revolutionary Party (PRD), moderate left-of-centre; Christian Social Reform Party (PRSC), independent socialist; Dominican Liberation Party (PLD), nationalist
exports sugar, gold, silver, tobacco, coffee, nickel
currency peso (20.75 = £1 July 1991)
population (1989 est) 7,307,000; growth rate 2.3% p.a.
life expectancy men 61, women 65
language Spanish (official)
religion Roman Catholic 95%
literacy men 78%, women 77% (1985 est)
GDP $4.9 bn (1987); $731 per head

chronology
1492 Visited by Christopher Columbus.
1844 Dominican Republic established.
1930 Military coup established dictatorship of Rafael Trujillo.
1961 Trujillo assassinated.
1962 First democratic elections resulted in Juan Bosch, founder of the PRD, becoming president.
1963 Bosch overthrown in military coup.
1965 US Marines intervene to restore order and protect foreign nationals.
1966 New constitution adopted. Joaquín Balaguer, leader of PRSC, became president.
1978 PRD returned to power, with Silvestre Antonio Guzmán as president.
1982 PRD re-elected, with Jorge Blanco as president.
1985 Blanco forced by International Monetary Fund to adopt austerity measures to save the economy.
1986 PRSC returned to power, with Balaguer re-elected president.
1990 Balaguer re-elected.

Ecuador (Republic of)
(República del Ecuador)

area 270,670 sq km/104,479 sq mi
capital Quito

towns Cuenca; chief port Guayaquil
physical coastal plain rises sharply to Andes Mountains which are divided into a series of cultivated valleys; flat, low-lying rainforest in the E
environment about 25,000 species became extinct 1965-90 as a result of environmental destruction
features Ecuador is crossed by the equator, from which it derives its name; Galápagos Islands; Cotopaxi is world's highest active volcano; rich wildlife in rainforest of Amazon basin
head of state and government Rodrigo Borja Cevallos from 1988
political system emergent democracy
political parties Progressive Democratic Front coalition, left-of-centre (composed of six individual parties); Concentration of Popular Forces (CFP), right-of-centre; Social Christian Party (PSC), right-wing; Conservative Party (PC), right-wing; others
exports bananas, cocoa, coffee, sugar, rice, fruit, balsa wood, fish, petroleum
currency sucre (1,657.66 = £1 July 1991, official rate)
population (1989 est) 10,490,000; (mestizo 55%, Indian 25%, European 10%, black African 10%); growth rate 2.9% p.a.

life expectancy men 62, women 66
languages Spanish (official), Quechua, Jivaro, and other Indian languages
religion Roman Catholic 95%
literacy men 85%, women 80% (1985 est)
GDP $10.6 bn (1987); $1,069 per head

chronology
1830 Independence achieved from Spain.
1925-48 Great political instability; no president completed his term of office.
1948-55 Liberals in power.
1956 First conservative president in 60 years.
1960 Liberals returned, with José Velasco as president.
1961 Velasco deposed and replaced by the vice president.
1962 Military junta installed.
1968 Velasco returned as president.
1972 A coup put the military back in power.
1978 New democratic constitution adopted.
1979 Liberals in power but opposed by right- and left-wing parties.
1982 Deteriorating economy provoked strikes, demonstrations, and a state of emergency.
1983 Austerity measures introduced.
1984-85 No party with a clear majority in the national

congress; Febres Cordero narrowly won the presidency for the Conservatives.
1988 Rodrigo Borja elected president for moderate left-wing coalition.
1989 Guerrilla left-wing group, *Alfaro Vive, Carajo* ('Alfaro lives, Dammit'), numbering about 1,000, laid down arms after nine years.

Egypt (Arab Republic of)
(Jumhuriyat Misr al-Arabiya)

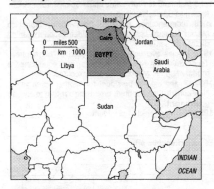

area 1,001,450 sq km/386,990 sq mi
capital Cairo
towns Gîza; ports Alexandria, Port Said, Suez, Damietta
physical mostly desert; hills in E; fertile land along Nile valley and delta; cultivated and settled area is about 35,500 sq km/13,700 sq mi
environment the building of the Aswan Dam (opened 1970) on the Nile has caused widespread salinization and an increase in waterborne diseases in villages close to Lake Nasser. A dramatic fall in the annual load of silt deposited downstream has reduced the fertility of cropland and has led to coastal erosion and the consequent loss of sardine shoals
features Aswan High Dam and Lake Nasser; Sinai; remains of ancient Egypt (pyramids, Sphinx, Luxor, Karnak, Abu Simbel, El Faiyum)
head of state and government Hosni Mubarak from 1981
political system democratic republic
political parties National Democratic Party (NDP), moderate left-of-centre; Socialist Labour Party, right-of-centre; Socialist Liberal Party, free-enterprise; New Wafd Party, nationalist
exports cotton and textiles, petroleum, fruit and vegetables
currency Egyptian pound (5.40 = £1 July 1991)
population (1989 est) 54,779,000; growth rate 2.4% p.a.
life expectancy men 57, women 60
language Arabic (official); ancient Egyptian survives to some extent in Coptic
media there is no legal censorship, but the largest publishing houses, newspapers, and magazines are owned and controlled by the state, as is all television. Questioning of prevalent values, ideas, and social practices is discouraged
religion Sunni Muslim 95%, Coptic Christian 5%
literacy men 59%, women 30% (1985 est)
GDP $34.5 bn (1987); $679 per head

chronology
1914 Egypt became a British protectorate.
1936 Independence achieved from Britain. King Fuad succeeded by his son Farouk.
1946 Withdrawal of British troops except from Suez Canal Zone.
1952 Farouk overthrown by army in bloodless coup.

1953 Egypt declared a republic, with General Neguib as president.
1956 Neguib replaced by Col Gamal Nasser. Nasser announced nationalization of Suez Canal; Egypt attacked by Britain, France, and Israel. Cease-fire agreed because of US intervention.
1958 Short-lived merger of Egypt and Syria as United Arab Republic (UAR). Subsequent attempts to federate Egypt, Syria, and Iraq failed.
1967 Six Day War with Israel ended in Egypt's defeat and Israeli occupation of Sinai and Gaza Strip.
1970 Nasser died suddenly, succeeded by Anwar Sadat.
1973 Attempt to regain territory lost to Israel led to fighting; cease-fire arranged by US secretary of state Henry Kissinger.
1977 Sadat's visit to Israel to address the Israeli parliament was criticized by Egypt's Arab neighbours.
1978-79 Camp David talks in the USA resulted in a treaty between Egypt and Israel. Egypt expelled from the Arab League.
1981 Sadat assassinated, succeeded by Hosni Mubarak.
1983 Improved relations between Egypt and the Arab world; only Libya and Syria maintained a trade boycott.
1984 Mubarak's party victorious in the people's assembly elections.
1987 Mubarak re-elected. Egypt readmitted to Arab League.
1988 Full diplomatic relations with Algeria restored.
1989 Improved relations with Libya; diplomatic relations with Syria restored. Mubarak proposed a peace plan.
1990 Gains for independents in general election.
1991 Participation in Gulf War on US-led side. Major force in convening Middle East peace conference in Spain.

El Salvador (Republic of)
(República de El Salvador)

area 21,393 sq km/8,258 sq mi
capital San Salvador
towns Santa Ana, San Miguel
physical narrow coastal plain, rising to mountains in N with central plateau
features smallest and most densely populated Central American country; Mayan archaeological remains
head of state and government Alfredo Cristiani from 1989
political system emergent democracy
political parties Christian Democrats (PDC), anti-imperialist; National Republican Alliance (ARENA), right-wing; National Conciliation Party (PCN), right-wing; Farabundo Marti Liberation Front (FMLN), left-wing
exports coffee, cotton, sugar
currency colón (13.02 = £1 July 1991)
population (1989 est) 5,900,000 (mainly of mixed Spanish and Indian ancestry; 10% Indian); growth rate 2.9% p.a.

life expectancy men 63, women 66
languages Spanish, Nahuatl
religion Roman Catholic 97%
literacy men 75%, women 69% (1985 est)
GDP $4.7 bn (1987); $790 per head

chronology
1821 Independence achieved from Spain.
1931 Peasant unrest followed by a military coup.
1961 Following a coup, PCN established and in power.
1969 'Soccer' war with Honduras.
1972 Allegations of human-rights violations and growth of left-wing guerrilla activities. General Carlos Romero elected president.
1979 A coup replaced Romero with a military-civilian junta.
1980 Archbishop Oscar Romero assassinated; country on verge of civil war. José Duarte became first civilian president since 1931.
1981 Mexico and France recognized the guerrillas as a legitimate political force but the USA actively assisted the government in its battle against them.
1982 Assembly elections boycotted by left-wing parties and held amid considerable violence.
1986 Duarte sought a negotiated settlement with the guerrillas.
1988 Duarte resigned.
1989 Alfredo Cristiani (ARENA) elected president in rigged elections; rebel attacks intensified.
1991 UN-sponsored peace accord signed by representatives of the government and the socialist guerrilla groups, the FMLN.
1992 Peace accord validated; FMLN became political party.

Equatorial Guinea (Republic of)
(República de Guinea Ecuatorial)

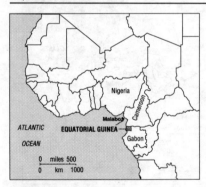

area 28,051 sq km/10,828 sq mi
capital Malabo (Bioko)
towns Bata, Mbini (Río Muni)
physical comprises mainland Río Muni, plus the small islands of Corisco, Elobey Grande and Elobey Chico, and Bioko (formerly Fernando Po) together with Annobón (formerly Pagalu)
features volcanic mountains on Bioko
head of state and government Teodoro Obiang Nguema Mbasogo from 1979
political system one-party military republic
political party Democratic Party of Equatorial Guinea (PDGE), militarily controlled
exports cocoa, coffee, timber
currency ekuele; CFA franc (498.25 = £1 July 1991)
population (1988 est) 336,000 (plus 110,000 estimated to live in exile abroad); growth rate 2.2% p.a.
life expectancy men 44, women 48

language Spanish (official); pidgin English is widely spoken, and on Annobón (whose people were formerly slaves of the Portuguese) a Portuguese dialect; Fang and other African dialects spoken on Río Muni
religion nominally Christian, mainly Catholic, but in 1978 Roman Catholicism was banned
literacy 55% (1984)
GDP $90 million (1987); $220 per head

chronology
1778 Fernando Po (Bioko Island) ceded to Spain.
1885 Mainland territory came under Spanish rule; colony known as Spanish Guinea.
1968 Independence achieved from Spain. Francisco Macias Nguema became first president, soon assuming dictatorial powers.
1979 Macias overthrown and replaced by his nephew, Teodoro Obiang Nguema Mbasogo, who established a military regime. Macias tried and executed.
1982 Obiang elected president for another seven years. New constitution adopted, promising a return to civilian government.
1989 Obiang re-elected president.

Estonia (Republic of)

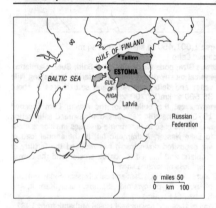

area 45,000 sq km/17,000 sq mi
capital Tallinn
towns Tartu, Narva, Kohtla-Järve, Pärnu
physical lakes and marshes in a partly forested plain; 774 km/481 mi of coastline; mild climate
features Lake Peipus and Narva River forming boundary with Russian Federation; Baltic islands, the largest of which is Saaremaa Island
head of state Arnold Rüütel from 1988
head of government Tiit Vahl from 1992
political system emergent democracy
political parties Estonian Popular Front (Rahvarinne), nationalist; Association for a Free Estonia, nationalist; International Movement, ethnic Russian; Estonian Green Party, environmentalist
products oil and gas (from shale), wood products, flax, dairy and pig products
currency kroon
population (1989) 1,573,000 (Estonian 62%, Russian 30%, Ukrainian 3%, Byelorussian 2%)
language Estonian, allied to Finnish
religion traditionally Lutheran

chronology
1918 Estonia declared its independence. March: Soviet forces, who had tried to regain control from occupying German forces during World War I, were overthrown by German troops. Nov: Soviet troops took control after German withdrawal.

1919 Soviet rule overthrown with help of British navy; Estonia declared a democratic republic.
1934 Fascist coup replaced government.
1940 Estonia incorporated into USSR.
1941-44 German occupation during World War II.
1944 USSR regained control.
1980 Beginnings of nationalist dissent.
1988 Adopted own constitution, with power of veto on all centralized Soviet legislation. Estonian Popular Front (Rahvarinne) established to campaign for democracy. Estonia's supreme soviet (state assembly) voted to declare the republic 'sovereign' and autonomous in all matters except military and foreign affairs; rejected by USSR as unconstitutional.
1989 Estonian replaced Russian as main language.
1990 Feb: Communist Party monopoly of power abolished; multiparty system established. March: pro-independence candidates secured majority after republic elections; coalition government formed with Popular Front leader, Edgar Savisaar, as prime minister; Arnold Rüütel became president. May: pre-war constitution partially restored.
1991 March: independence plebiscite overwhelmingly approved. Aug: full independence declared after abortive anti-Gorbachev coup; Communist Party outlawed. Sept: independence recognized by Soviet government and Western nations; admitted into UN and CSCE.
1992 Jan: Savisaar resigned due to his government's inability to alleviate food and energy shortages; new government formed by Tiit Vahl.

Ethiopia (People's Democratic Republic of)

(Hebretesebawit Ityopia, formerly also known as Abyssinia)

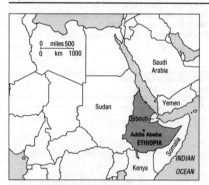

area 1,221,900 sq km/471,653 sq mi
capital Addis Ababa
towns Asmara (capital of Eritrea), Dire Dawa; ports Massawa, Assab
physical a high plateau with central mountain range divided by Rift Valley; plains in E; source of Blue Nile River
environment more than 90% of the forests of the Ethiopian highlands have been destroyed since 1900
features Danakil and Ogaden deserts; ancient remains (at Aksum, Gondar, Lalibela, amongst others); only African country to retain its independence during the colonial period
head of state and government Meles Zenawi from 1991
political system transition to democratic socialist republic
political parties Ethiopian People's Revolutionary Democratic Front (EPRDF), nationalist, left-of-centre; Tigré People's Liberation Front (TPLF); Eritrean People's Liberation Front (EPLF); Ethiopian People's Democratic Movement (EPDM); Oromo People's Democratic Organization (OPDO)

exports coffee, pulses, oilseeds, hides, skins
currency birr (3.34 = £1 July 1991)
population (1989 est) 47,709,000 (Oromo 40%, Amhara 25%, Tigré 12%, Sidamo 9%); growth rate 2.5% p.a.
life expectancy 38
languages Amharic (official), Tigrinya, Orominga, Arabic
religion Sunni Muslim 45%, Christian (Ethiopian Orthodox Church, which has had its own patriarch since 1976) 40%
literacy 35% (1988)
GDP $4.8 bn (1987); $104 per head

chronology
1889 Abyssinia reunited by Menelik II.
1930 Haile Selassie became emperor.
1962 Eritrea annexed by Haile Selassie; resistance movement began.
1974 Haile Selassie deposed and replaced by a military government led by General Teferi Benti. Ethiopia declared a socialist state.
1977 Teferi Benti killed and replaced by Col Mengistu Haile Mariam.
1977-79 'Red Terror' period in which Mengistu's regime killed thousands of innocent people.
1981-85 Ethiopia spent at least $2 billion on arms.
1984 WPE declared the only legal political party.
1985 Worst famine in more than a decade; Western aid sent and forcible internal resettlement programmes undertaken.
1987 New constitution adopted, Mengistu Mariam elected president. New famine; food aid hindered by guerrillas.
1988 Mengistu agreed to adjust his economic policies in order to secure IMF assistance. Influx of refugees from Sudan.
1989 Coup attempt against Mengistu foiled. Peace talks with Eritrean rebels mediated by former US president Carter reported some progress.
1990 Rebels captured port of Massawa. Mengistu announced new reforms.
1991 Mengistu overthrown; transitional government set up by EPRDF. EPLF secured Eritrea; Eritrea's right to secede recognized. Meles Zenawi elected Ethiopia's new head of state and government. Isaias Afwerki became secretary general of provisional government in Eritrea.

Fiji (Republic of)

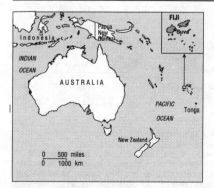

area 18,333 sq km/7,078 sq mi
capital Suva
towns ports Lautoka and Levuka
physical comprises 844 Melanesian and Polynesian islands and islets (about 110 inhabited), the largest being Viti Levu (10,429 sq km/4,028 sq mi) and Vanua Levu (5,550 sq km/2,146 sq mi); mountainous, volcanic, with tropical rainforest and grasslands

features almost all islands surrounded by coral reefs; high volcanic peaks; crossroads of air and sea services between N America and Australia
head of state Ratu Sir Penaia Ganilau from 1987
head of government Ratu Sir Kamisese Mara from 1970
political system democratic republic
political parties Alliance Party (AP), moderate centrist Fijian; National Federation Party (NFP), moderate left-of-centre Indian; Fijian Labour Party (FLP), left-of-centre Indian; United Front, Fijian
exports sugar, coconut oil, ginger, timber, canned fish, gold; tourism is important
currency Fiji dollar (2.45 = £1 July 1991)
population (1989 est) 758,000 (46% Fijian, holding 80% of the land communally, and 49% Indian, introduced in the 19th century to work the sugar crop); growth rate 2.1% p.a.
life expectancy men 67, women 71
languages English (official), Fijian, Hindi
religion Hindu 50%, Methodist 44%
literacy men 88%, women 77% (1980 est)
GDP $1.2 bn (1987); $1,604 per head

chronology
1874 Fiji became a British crown colony.
1970 Independence achieved from Britain; Ratu Sir Kamisese Mara elected as first prime minister.
1987 April: general election brought to power an Indian-dominated coalition led by Dr Timoci Bavadra. May: military coup by Col Sitiveni Rabuka removed new government at gunpoint; Governor General Ratu Sir Penaia Ganilau regained control within weeks. Sept: second military coup by Rabuka proclaimed Fiji a republic and suspended the constitution. Oct: Fiji ceased to be a member of the Commonwealth. Dec: civilian government restored with Rabuka retaining control of security as minister for home affairs.
1989 New constitution proposed.

left-of-centre; National Coalition Party (KOK), moderate right-of-centre; Centre Party (KP), centrist, rural-orientated; Finnish People's Democratic League (SKDL), left-wing; Swedish People's Party (SFP), independent Swedish-orientated; Finnish Rural Party (SMP), farmers and small businesses; Democratic Alternative, left-wing; Green Party
exports metal, chemical and engineering products (ice-breakers and oil rigs), paper, sawn wood, clothing, fine ceramics, glass, furniture
currency markka (6.96 = £1 July 1991)
population (1989 est) 4,990,000; growth rate 0.5% p.a.
life expectancy men 70, women 78
languages Finnish 93%, Swedish 6% (both official), small Saami and Russian-speaking minorities
religion Lutheran 97%, Eastern Orthodox 1.2%
literacy 99%
GDP $77.9 bn (1987); $15,795 per head

chronology
1809 Finland annexed by Russia.
1917 Independence declared from Russia.
1920 Soviet regime acknowledged independence.
1939 Defeated by USSR in 'Winter War'.
1941 Allowed Germany to station troops in Finland to attack USSR; USSR bombed Finland.
1944 Concluded separate armistice with USSR.
1948 Finno-Soviet Pact of Friendship, Cooperation, and Mutual Assistance signed.
1955 Finland joined the UN and the Nordic Council.
1956 Urho Kekkonen elected president; re-elected 1962, 1968, 1978.
1973 Trade treaty with EEC signed.
1977 Trade agreement with USSR signed.
1982 Koivisto elected president; re-elected 1988.
1989 Finland joined Council of Europe.
1991 Big swing to the centre in general election. New coalition government formed.
1992 Formal application for EC membership.

Finland (Republic of)
(Suomen Tasavalta)

area 338,145 sq km/130,608 sq mi
capital Helsinki
towns Tampere, Rovaniemi, Lahti; ports Turku, Oulu
physical most of the country is forest, with low hills and about 60,000 lakes; one-third is within the Arctic Circle; archipelago in S; includes Åland Islands
features Helsinki is the most northerly national capital on the European continent; at the 70th parallel there is constant daylight for 73 days in summer and 51 days of uninterrupted night in winter
head of state Mauno Koivisto from 1982
head of government Esko Ahoi from 1991
political system democratic republic
political parties Social Democratic Party (SDP), moderate

France (French Republic)
(République Française)

area (including Corsica) 543,965 sq km/209,970 sq mi
capital Paris
towns Lyons, Lille, Bordeaux, Toulouse, Nantes, Strasbourg; ports Marseille, Nice, Le Havre
physical rivers Seine, Loire, Garonne, Rhône, Rhine; mountain ranges Alps, Massif Central, Pyrenees, Jura, Vosges, Cévennes; the island of Corsica
territories Guadeloupe, French Guiana, Martinique, Réunion, St Pierre and Miquelon, Southern and Antarctic

Territories, New Caledonia, French Polynesia, Wallis and Futuna

features Ardennes forest, Auvergne mountain region, Riviera, Mont Blanc (4,810 m/15,781 ft), caves of Dordogne with relics of early humans; largest W European nation

head of state François Mitterrand from 1981

head of government Pierre Bérégovoy from 1992

political system liberal democracy

political parties Socialist Party (PS), left-of-centre; Rally for the Republic (RPR), neo-Gaullist conservative; Union for French Democracy (UDF), centre-right; Republican Party (RP), centre-right; French Communist Party (PCF), Marxist-Leninist; National Front, far-right; Greens, environmentalist

exports fruit (especially apples), wine, cheese, wheat, automobiles, aircraft, iron and steel, petroleum products, chemicals, jewellery, silk, lace; tourism is very important

currency franc (9.96 = £1 July 1991)

population (1990 est) 56,184,000 (including 4,500,000 immigrants, chiefly from Portugal, Algeria, Morocco, and Tunisia); growth rate 0.3% p.a.

life expectancy men 71, women 79

language French (regional dialects include Basque, Breton, Catalan, Provençal)

religion Roman Catholic 90%, Protestant 2%, Muslim 1%

literacy 99% (1984)

GNP $568 bn (1983); $7,179 per head

chronology

1944–46 De Gaulle provisional government; start of Fourth Republic.

1954 Indochina achieved independence.

1956 Morocco and Tunisia achieved independence.

1957 Entry into EEC.

1958 Recall of de Gaulle following Algerian crisis; start of Fifth Republic.

1959 De Gaulle became president.

1962 Algeria achieved independence.

1966 France withdrew from military wing of NATO.

1968 'May events' crisis.

1969 De Gaulle resigned following referendum defeat; Pompidou became president.

1974 Giscard d'Estaing elected president.

1981 Mitterrand elected Fifth Republic's first socialist president.

1986 'Cohabitation' experiment, with the conservative Jacques Chirac as prime minister.

1988 Mitterrand re-elected. Moderate socialist Michel Rocard became prime minister. Matignon Accord on future of New Caledonia approved by referendum.

1989 Greens gained 11% of vote in elections to European Parliament.

1991 French forces were part of the US-led coalition in the Gulf War. Edith Cresson became France's first woman prime minister. Mitterrand's popularity rating fell rapidly.

1992 March: Socialist Party humiliated in regional and local elections; Greens and National Front polled strongly. April: Cresson replaced by Pierre Bérégovoy.

Gabon (Gabonese Republic)
(République Gabonaise)

area 267,667 sq km/103,319 sq mi

capital Libreville

towns Port-Gentil and Owendo (ports); Masuku (Franceville)

physical virtually the whole country is tropical rainforest; narrow coastal plain rising to hilly interior with savanna in E and S; Ogooué River flows N–W

features Schweitzer hospital at Lambaréné; Trans-Gabonais railway

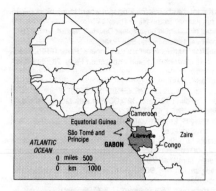

head of state and government Omar Bongo from 1967

political system authoritarian nationalism

political parties Gabonese Democratic Party (PDG), nationalist; Morena Movement of National Recovery, left-of-centre

exports petroleum, manganese, uranium, timber

currency CFA franc (498.25 = £1 July 1991)

population (1988) 1,226,000 including 40 Bantu groups; growth rate 1.6% p.a.

life expectancy men 47, women 51

languages French (official), Bantu

religion 96% Christian (Roman Catholic 65%), small Muslim minority (1%), animist 3%

literacy men 70%, women 53% (1985 est)

GDP $3.5 bn (1987); $3,308 per head

chronology

1889 Gabon became part of the French Congo.

1960 Independence from France achieved; Léon M'ba became the first president.

1964 Attempted coup by rival party foiled with French help. M'ba died; he was succeeded by his protégé, Albert-Bernard Bongo.

1968 One-party state established.

1973 Bongo re-elected; converted to Islam, he changed his first name to Omar.

1986 Bongo re-elected.

1989 Coup attempt against Bongo defeated.

1990 Widespread fraud alleged in first multiparty elections since 1964.

Gambia (Republic of The)

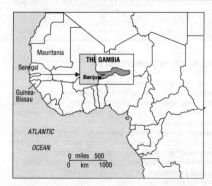

area 10,402 sq km/4,018 sq mi

capital Banjul

towns Serekunda, Bakau, Georgetown

physical banks of the river Gambia flanked by low hills

features smallest state in black Africa; stone circles;

Karantaba obelisk marking spot where Mungo Park began his journey to the Niger River 1796

head of state and government Dawda Jawara from 1970

political system liberal democracy

political parties Progressive People's Party (PPP), moderate centrist; National Convention Party (NCP), left-of-centre

exports groundnuts, palm oil, fish

currency dalasi (14.26 = £1 July 1991)

population (1990 est) 820,000; growth rate 1.9% p.a.

life expectancy 42 (1988 est)

languages English (official), Mandinka, Fula and other native tongues

media no daily newspaper; two official weeklies sell about 2,000 copies combined and none of the other independents more than 700

religion Muslim 90%, with animist and Christian minorities

literacy men 36%, women 15% (1985 est)

GDP $189 million (1987); $236 per head

chronology

1843 The Gambia became a crown colony.

1965 Independence achieved from Britain as a constitutional monarchy within the Commonwealth, with Dawda K Jawara as prime minister.

1970 Declared itself a republic, with Jawara as president.

1972 Jawara re-elected.

1981 Attempted coup foiled with the help of Senegal.

1982 Formed with Senegal the Confederation of Senegambia; Jawara re-elected.

1987 Jawara re-elected.

1989 Confederation of Senegambia dissolved.

Georgia (Republic of)

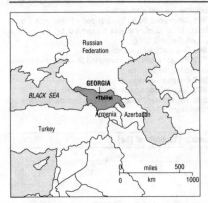

area 69,700 sq km/26,911 sq mi

capital Tbilisi

towns Kutaisi, Rustavi, Batumi, Sukhumi

physical largely mountainous with a variety of landscape from the subtropical Black Sea shores to the ice and snow of the crest line of the Caucasus; chief rivers are Kura and Rioni

features holiday resorts and spas on the Black Sea; good climate; two autonomous republics, Abkhazia and Adzharia; one autonmous region, S Ossetia

interim head of state Eduard Shevardnadze from 1992

head of government Tengiz Sigua from 1992

political system transitional

political parties over 100 including: Georgian Popular Front, moderate nationalist; National Democratic Party of Georgia, radical nationalist; the National Independence Party; the Monarchist Party, pro-monarchist

products tea, citrus and orchard fruits, tung oil, tobacco, vines, silk, hydroelectricity

population (1990) 5,500,000 (70% Georgian, 8% Armenian, 8% Russian, 6% Azeri, 3% Ossetian, 2% Abkhazian)

language Georgian

religion Georgian Church, independent of the Russian Orthodox Church since 1917

chronology

1918-21 Independent republic.

1921 Uprising quelled by Red Army and Soviet republic established.

1922-36 Linked with Armenia and Azerbaijan as the Transcaucasian Republic.

1936 Became separate republic within USSR.

1981-88 Increasing demands for autonomy, spearheaded from 1988 by the Georgian Popular Front.

1989 March-April: Abkhazians demanded secession from Georgia, provoking inter-ethnic clashes. April: Georgian Communist Party (GCP) leadership purged. July: state of emergency imposed in Abkhazia; inter-ethnic clashes in S Ossetia. Nov: economic and political sovereignty declared.

1990 March: Georgian Communist Party's monopoly of power ended. Oct: S Ossetia declared independence, but not recognized; nationalist coalition triumphed in supreme soviet elections. Nov: former anti-Communist dissident Zviad Gamsakhurdia indirectly elected president. Dec: GCP seceded from Communist Party of USSR and called for Georgian independence; state of emergency imposed in Tskhnivali and Dzhava in S Ossetia.

1991 Jan: national guard established. Feb: Georgia boycotted USSR referendum. March: independence plebiscite approved. April: declared independence from USSR. May: Gamsakhurdia popularly elected president. Aug: Communist Party outlawed and all relations with USSR severed in wake of failed anti-Gorbachev coup. Sept: anti-Gamsakhurdia demonstrations and takeover of TV station; state of emergency declared. Dec: USA acknowledged Georgian independence but withheld diplomatic recognition. Georgia failed to new join Commonwealth of Independent States (CIS).

1992 Jan: Gamsakhurdia fled to Armenia; Sigua appointed prime minister by ruling military council; admitted into CSCE. March: Eduard Shevardnadze appointed interim president by new state council (provisional parliament). July: admitted into UN.

Germany (Federal Republic of)
(Bundesrepublik Deutschland)

area 357,041 sq km/137,853 sq mi

capital Berlin

towns Cologne, Munich, Essen, Frankfurt-am-Main, Dortmund, Stuttgart, Düsseldorf, Leipzig, Dresden, Chemnitz, Magdeburg; ports Hamburg, Kiel, Cuxhaven, Bremerhaven, Rostock
physical flat in N, mountainous in S with Alps; rivers Rhine, Weser, Elbe flow N, Danube flows SE, Oder, Neisse flow N along Polish frontier; many lakes, including Müritz
environment acid rain causing *Waldsterben* (tree death) affects more than half the country's forests; industrial E Germany has the highest per-capita sulphur dioxide emissions in the world
features Black Forest, Harz Mountains, Erzgebirge (Ore Mountains), Bavarian Alps, Fichtelgebirge, Thüringer Forest
head of state Richard von Weizsäcker from 1984
head of government Helmut Kohl from 1982
political system liberal democratic federal republic
political parties Christian Democratic Union (CDU), right-of-centre; Christian Social Union (CSU), right-of-centre; Social Democratic Party, left-of-centre; Free Democratic Party (FDP), liberal; Greens, environmentalist; Republicans, far-right; Party of Democratic Socialism (PDS), reform-communist (formerly Socialist Unity Party: SED)
exports machine tools (world's leading exporter), cars, commercial vehicles, electronics, industrial goods, textiles, chemicals, iron, steel, wine, lignite (world's largest producer), uranium, coal, fertilizers, plastics
currency Deutschmark (2.94 = £1 July 1991)
population (1990) 78,420,000 (including nearly 5,000,000 'guest workers', *Gastarbeiter*, of whom 1,600,000 are Turks; the rest are Yugoslavs, Italians, Greeks, Spanish, and Portuguese); growth rate −0.7% p.a.
life expectancy men 68, women 74
languages German, Sorbian
religion Protestant 42%, Roman Catholic 35%
literacy 99% (1985)
GNP $1,250 bn (1989); $16,200 per head

chronology
1945 Germany surrendered; country divided into four occupation zones (US, French, British, Soviet).
1948 Blockade of West Berlin.
1949 Establishment of Federal Republic under the 'Basic Law' Constitution with Adenauer as chancellor; establishment of the German Democratic Republic as an independent state.
1953 Uprising in East Berlin suppressed by Soviet troops.
1954 Grant of full sovereignty to both West Germany and East Germany.
1957 West Germany was a founder-member of the EEC; recovery of Saarland.
1961 Construction of Berlin Wall.
1963 Retirement of Chancellor Adenauer.
1964 Treaty of Friendship and Mutual Assistance signed between East Germany and USSR.
1969 Willy Brandt became chancellor of West Germany.
1971 Erich Honecker elected Socialist Unity Party (SED) leader in East Germany.
1972 Basic Treaty between West Germany and East Germany; treaty ratified 1973, normalizing relations between the two.
1974 Resignation of Brandt; Helmut Schmidt became chancellor.
1975 East German friendship treaty with USSR renewed for 25 years.
1982 Helmut Kohl became West German chancellor.
1987 Official visit of Honecker to the Federal Republic.
1988 Death of West German Bavarian CSU leader Franz-Josef Strauss.
1989 West Germany: rising support for far right in local and European elections, declining support for Kohl. East Germany: mass exodus to West Germany began. Honecker replaced by Egon Krenz. National borders opened in Nov, including Berlin Wall. Reformist Hans

Modrow appointed prime minister. Krenz replaced.
1990 March: East German multiparty elections won by a coalition led by the right-wing CDU. 3 Oct: official reunification of East and West Germany. 2 Dec: first all-German elections since 1932, resulting in a victory for Kohl.
1991 Kohl's popularity declined after tax increase. The CDU lost its Bundesrat majority to the SPD. Racism continued with violent attacks on foreigners.
1992 Prolonged public sector strike for higher wages.

Ghana (Republic of)

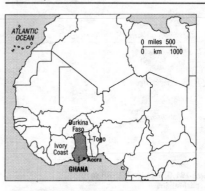

area 238,305 sq km/91,986 sq mi
capital Accra
towns Kumasi, and ports Sekondi-Takoradi, Tema
physical mostly tropical lowland plains; bisected by river Volta
environment forested areas have shrunk from 8.2 million sq km/3.17 million sq mi at the beginning of the 20th century to 1.9 million sq km/730,000 sq mi by 1990
features world's largest artificial lake, Lake Volta; relics of traditional kingdom of Ashanti: 32,000 chiefs and kings
head of state and government Jerry Rawlings from 1981
political system military republic
exports cocoa, coffee, timber, gold, diamonds, manganese, bauxite
currency cedi (593.10 = £1 July 1991)
population (1990 est) 15,310,000; growth rate 3.2% p.a.
life expectancy men 50, women 54
languages English (official) and African languages
media all media are government-controlled and the two daily newspapers are government-owned
religion animist 38%, Muslim 30%, Christian 24%
literacy men 64%, women 43% (1985 est)
GNP $3.9 bn (1983); $420 per head

chronology
1957 Independence achieved from Britain, within the Commonwealth, with Kwame Nkrumah as president.
1960 Ghana became a republic.
1964 Ghana became a one-party state.
1966 Nkrumah deposed and replaced by General Joseph Ankrah.
1969 Ankrah replaced by General Akwasi Afrifa, who initiated a return to civilian government.
1970 Edward Akufo-Addo elected president.
1972 Another coup placed Col Acheampong at the head of a military government.
1978 Acheampong deposed in a bloodless coup led by Frederick Akuffo; another coup put Flight-Lt Jerry Rawlings in power.
1979 Return to civilian rule under Hilla Limann.
1981 Rawlings seized power again, citing the incompetence of previous governments. All political parties banned.

1989 Coup attempt against Rawlings foiled.
1992 New multi-party constitution approved. Partial lifting of ban on political parties.

Greece (Hellenic Republic)
(Elliniki Dimokratia)

area 131,957 sq km/50,935 sq mi
capital Athens
towns Larisa; ports Piraeus, Thessaloníki, Patras, Iráklion
physical mountainous; a large number of islands, notably Crete, Corfu, and Rhodes
environment acid rain and other airborne pollutants are destroying the classical buildings and ancient monuments of Athens
features Corinth canal; Mount Olympus; the Acropolis; many classical archaeological sites; the Aegean and Ionian Islands
head of state Christos Sartzetakis from 1985
head of government Xenophon Zolotas from 1989
political system democratic republic
political parties Panhellenic Socialist Movement (PASOK), democratic socialist; New Democracy Party (ND), centre-right; Democratic Renewal (DR); Communist Party; Greek Left Party
exports tobacco, fruit, vegetables, olives, olive oil, textiles, aluminium, iron and steel
currency drachma (321.37 = £1 July 1991)
population (1990 est) 10,066,000; growth rate 0.3% p.a.
life expectancy men 72, women 76
language Greek
religion Greek Orthodox 97%
literacy men 96%, women 89% (1985)
GDP $40.9 bn (1987); $4,093 per head

chronology
1829 Independence achieved from Turkish rule.
1912-13 Balkan Wars; Greece gained much land.
1941-44 German occupation of Greece.
1946 Civil war between royalists and communists; communists defeated.
1949 Monarchy re-established with Paul as king.
1964 King Paul succeeded by his son Constantine.
1967 Army coup removed the king; Col George Papadopoulos became prime minister. Martial law imposed, all political activity banned.
1973 Republic proclaimed, with Papadopoulos as president.
1974 Former premier Constantine Karamanlis recalled from exile to lead government. Martial law and ban on political parties lifted; restoration of the monarchy rejected by a referendum.

1975 New constitution adopted, making Greece a democratic republic.
1980 Karamanlis resigned as prime minister and was elected president.
1981 Greece became full member of EEC. Andreas Papandreou elected Greece's first socialist prime minister.
1983 Five-year defence and economic cooperation agreement signed with USA; ten-year economic cooperation agreement signed with USSR.
1985 Papandreou re-elected.
1988 Relations with Turkey improved. Major cabinet reshuffle after mounting criticism of Papandreou.
1989 Papandreou defeated. Tzannis Tzannetakis became prime minister; his all-party government collapsed. Xenophon Zolotas formed new unity government. Papandreou charged with corruption.
1990 Siting of US bases agreed.
1992 Papandreou acquitted. His call for a general election rejected by government.

Grenada

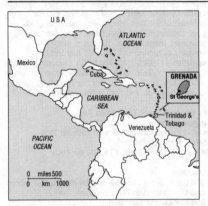

area (including the Grenadines, notably Carriacou) 340 sq km/131 sq mi
capital St George's
towns Grenville, Hillsborough (Carriacou)
physical southernmost of the Windward Islands; mountainous
features Grand-Anse beach; Annandale Falls; the Great Pool volcanic crater
head of state Elizabeth II from 1974 represented by governor general
head of government Ben Jones from 1989
political system emergent democracy
political parties New National Party (NNP), centrist; Grenada United Labour Party (GULP), nationalist left-of-centre
exports cocoa, nutmeg, bananas, mace
currency Eastern Caribbean dollar (4.39 = £1 July 1991)
population (1990 est) 84,000, 84% of black African descent; growth rate −0.2% p.a.
life expectancy 69
language English (official); some French patois spoken
media two independent weekly newspapers
religion Roman Catholic 60%
literacy 85% (1985)
GDP $139 million (1987); $1,391 per head

chronology
1974 Independence achieved from Britain; Eric Gairy elected prime minister.
1979 Gairy removed in bloodless coup led by Maurice Bishop; constitution suspended and a People's Revolutionary Government established.

1982 Relations with the USA and Britain deteriorated as ties with Cuba and the USSR strengthened.

1983 After Bishop's attempt to improve relations with the USA, he was overthrown by left-wing opponents. A coup established the Revolutionary Military Council (RMC), and Bishop and three colleagues were executed. The USA invaded Grenada, accompanied by troops from other E Caribbean countries; RMC overthrown, 1974 constitution reinstated.

1984 The newly formed NNP won 14 of the 15 seats in the house of representatives and its leader, Herbert Blaize, became prime minister.

1989 Herbert Blaize lost leadership of NNP, remaining as head of government; he died and was succeeded by Ben Jones.

1991 Integration into Windward Islands confederation proposed.

Guatemala (Republic of)
(República de Guatemala)

area 108,889 sq km/42,031 sq mi

capital Guatemala City

towns Quezaltenango, Puerto Barrios (naval base)

physical mountainous; narrow coastal plains; limestone tropical plateau in N; frequent earthquakes

environment between 1960 and 1980 nearly 57% of the country's forest was cleared for farming

features Mayan archaeological remains, including site at Tikal

head of state and government Jorge Serrano Elías from 1991

political system democratic republic

political parties Guatemalan Christian Democratic Party (PDCG), Christian centre-left; Centre Party (UCN), centrist; National Democratic Cooperation Party (PDCN), centre-right; Revolutionary Party (PR), radical; Movement of National Liberation (MLN), extreme right-wing; Democratic Institutional Party (PID), moderate conservative; Solidarity Action Movement (MAS), right-wing

exports coffee, bananas, cotton, sugar, beef

currency quetzal (7.93 = £1 July 1991)

population (1990 est) 9,340,000 (Mayaquiche Indians 54%, mestizos (mixed race) 42%); growth rate 2.8% p.a. (87% of under-fives suffer from malnutrition)

life expectancy men 57, women 61

languages Spanish (official); 40% speak 18 Indian languages

religion Roman Catholic 80%, Protestant 20%

literacy men 63%, women 47% (1985 est)

GDP $7 bn (1987); $834 per head

chronology
1839 Independence achieved from Spain.

1954 Col Carlos Castillo became president in US-backed coup, halting land reform.

1963 Military coup made Col Enrique Peralta president.

1966 Cesar Méndez elected president.

1970 Carlos Araña elected president.

1974 General Kjell Laugerud became president. Widespread political violence precipitated by the discovery of falsified election returns in March.

1978 General Fernando Romeo became president.

1981 Growth of antigovernment guerrilla movement.

1982 General Angel Anibal became president. Army coup installed General Ríos Montt as head of junta and then as president; political violence continued.

1983 Montt removed in coup led by General Mejía Victores, who declared amnesty for the guerrillas.

1985 New constitution adopted; PDCG won congressional elections; Vinicio Cerezo elected president.

1989 Coup attempt against Cerezo foiled. Over 100,000 people killed, and 40,000 reported missing since 1980.

1991 Jorge Serrano Elías of the Solidarity Action Movement elected president. Diplomatic relations with Belize established.

Guinea (Republic of)
(République de Guinée)

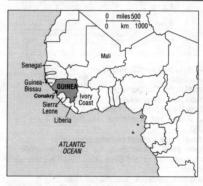

area 245,857 sq km/94,901 sq mi

capital Conakry

towns Labé, Nzérékoré, Kankan

physical flat coastal plain with mountainous interior; sources of rivers Niger, Gambia, and Senegal; forest in SE

environment large amounts of toxic waste from industrialized countries have been dumped in Guinea

features Fouta Djallon, area of sandstone plateaux, cut by deep valleys

head of state and government Lansana Conté from 1984

political system military republic

political parties none since 1984

exports coffee, rice, palm kernels, alumina, bauxite, diamonds

currency syli or franc (1,007.50 free rate, 487.50 public transaction rate = £1 July 1991)

population (1990 est) 7,269,000 (chief peoples are Fulani, Malinke, Susu); growth rate 2.3% p.a.

life expectancy men 39, women 42

languages French (official), African languages

media state-owned, but some criticism of the government tolerated; no daily newspaper

religion Muslim 85%, Christian 10%, local 5%

literacy men 40%, women 17% (1985 est)

GNP $1.9 bn (1987); $369 per head

chronology
1958 Full independence achieved from France; Sékou Touré elected president.

1977 Strong opposition to Touré's rigid Marxist policies forced him to accept return to mixed economy.

1980 Touré returned unopposed for fourth seven-year term.
1984 Touré died. Bloodless coup established a military committee for national recovery, led by Col Lansana Conté.
1985 Attempted coup against Conté while he was out of the country was foiled by loyal troops.
1991 Antigovernment general strike in May called by National Confederation of Guinea Workers (CNTG).

Guinea-Bissau (Republic of)
(República da Guiné-Bissau)

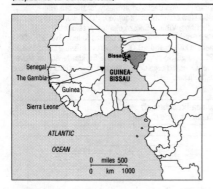

area 36,125 sq km/13,944 sq mi
capital Bissau
towns Mansôa, São Domingos
physical flat coastal plain rising to savanna in E
features the archipelago of Bijagós
head of state and government João Bernardo Vieira from 1980
political system socialist pluralist republic
political party African Party for the Independence of Portuguese Guinea and Cape Verde (PAIGC), nationalist socialist
exports rice, coconuts, peanuts, fish, timber
currency peso (1,056.25 = £1 July 1991)
population (1989 est) 929,000; growth rate 2.4% p.a.
life expectancy 42; 1990 infant mortality rate was 14.8%
languages Portuguese (official), Crioulo (Cape Verdean dialect of Portuguese), African languages
religion animism 54%, Muslim 38%, Christian 8%
literacy men 46%, women 17% (1985 est)
GDP $135 million (1987); $146 per head

chronology
1956 PAIGC formed to secure independence from Portugal.
1973 Two-thirds of the country declared independent, with Luiz Cabral as president of a state council.
1974 Independence achieved from Portugal.
1980 Cape Verde decided not to join a unified state. Cabral deposed, and João Vieira became chair of a council of revolution.
1981 PAIGC confirmed as the only legal party, with Vieira as its secretary general.
1982 Normal relations with Cape Verde restored.
1984 New constitution adopted, making Vieira head of government as well as head of state.
1989 Vieira re-elected.
1991 Other parties legalized. Multiparty elections promised.

Guyana (Cooperative Republic of)

area 214,969 sq km/82,978 sq mi
capital and port Georgetown

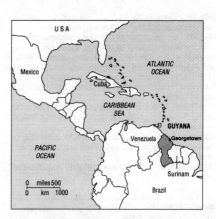

towns New Amsterdam, Mabaruma
physical coastal plain rises into rolling highlands with savanna in S; mostly tropical rainforest
features Mount Roraima; Kaietur National Park, including Kaietur Fall on the Potaro (tributary of Essequibo) 250 m/821 ft
head of state and government Desmond Hoyte from 1985
political system democratic republic
political parties People's National Congress (PNC), Afro-Guyanan nationalist socialist; People's Progressive Party (PPP), Indian Marxist-Leninist
exports sugar, rice, rum, timber, diamonds, bauxite, shrimps, molasses
currency Guyanese dollar (206.37 = £1 July 1991)
population (1989 est) 846,000 (51% descendants of workers introduced from India to work the sugar plantations after the abolition of slavery, 30% black, 5% Amerindian); growth rate 2% p.a.
life expectancy men 66, women 71
languages English (official), Hindi, Amerindian
media one government-owned daily newspaper; one independent paper published three times a week, on which the government puts pressure by withholding foreign exchange for newsprint; one weekly independent in the same position. There is also legislation that restricts exchange of information between public officials, government, and the press
religion Christian 57%, Hindu 33%, Sunni Muslim 9%
literacy men 97%, women 95% (1985 est)
GNP $359 million (1987); $445 per head

chronology
1831 Became British colony under name of British Guiana.
1953 Assembly elections won by left-wing PPP; Britain suspended constitution and installed interim administration, fearing communist takeover.
1961 Internal self-government granted.
1966 Independence achieved from Britain.
1970 Guyana became a republic within the Commonwealth.
1980 Forbes Burnham became first executive president under new constitution.
1985 Burnham died; succeeded by Desmond Hoyte.

Haiti (Republic of)
(République d'Haïti)

area 27,750 sq km/10,712 sq mi
capital Port-au-Prince
towns Cap-Haïtien, Gonaïves, Les Cayes
physical mainly mountainous and tropical; occupies W third of Hispaniola Island in Caribbean Sea; seriously

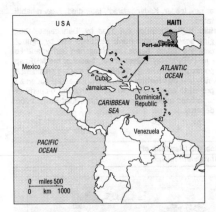

deforested
features oldest black republic in the world; only French-speaking republic in the Americas; island of La Tortuga off N coast was formerly a pirate lair
interim head of state Joseph Nerette from 1991
head of government Marc Bazin from 1991
political system transitional
political party National Progressive Party (PNP), right-wing military
exports coffee, sugar, sisal, cotton, cocoa, bauxite
currency gourde (8.12 = £1 July 1991)
population (1990 est) 6,409,000; growth rate 1.7% p.a.; one of highest population densities in the world; about 1.5 million Haitians live outside Haiti (in USA and Canada); about 400,000 live in virtual slavery in the Dominican Republic, where they went or were sent to cut sugar cane
life expectancy men 51, women 54
languages French (official, spoken by literate 10% minority), Creole (spoken by 90% black majority)
religion Christianity 95% of which 80% is Roman Catholic, voodoo 4%
literacy men 40%, women 35% (1985 est)
GDP $2.2 bn (1987); $414 per head

chronology
1804 Independence achieved from France.
1915 Haiti invaded by USA; remained under US control until 1934.
1957 Dr François Duvalier (Papa Doc) elected president.
1964 Duvalier pronounced himself president for life.
1971 Constitution amended to allow president to nominate his successor. Duvalier died, succeeded by his son, Jean-Claude (Baby Doc); thousands murdered during Duvalier era.
1986 Duvalier deposed; replaced by Lt-Gen Henri Namphy as head of a governing council.
1988 Feb: Leslie Manigat became president. Namphy staged a military coup in June, but another coup in Sept led by Brig-Gen Prosper Avril replaced him with a civilian government under military control.
1989 Coup attempt against Avril foiled; US aid resumed.
1990 Opposition elements expelled; Ertha Pascal-Trouillot acting president.
1991 Jean-Bertrand Aristide elected president but later overthrown in military coup led by Brig-Gen Raoul Cedras. Efforts to reinstate Aristide failed. Joseph Nerette became interim head of state; Marc Bazin appointed premier.

Honduras (Republic of)
(República de Honduras)

area 112,100 sq km/43,282 sq mi
capital Tegucigalpa

towns San Pedro Sula; ports La Ceiba, Puerto Cortés
physical narrow tropical coastal plain with mountainous interior, Bay Islands
features archaeological sites; Mayan ruins at Copán
head of state and government Rafael Leonardo Callejas from 1990
political system democratic republic
political parties Liberal Party of Honduras (PLH), centre-left; National Party (PN), right-wing
exports coffee, bananas, meat, sugar, timber (including mahogany, rosewood)
currency lempira (9.16 = £1 July 1991)
population (1989 est) 5,106,000 (90% mestizo (mixed), 10% Indians and Europeans); growth rate 3.1% p.a.

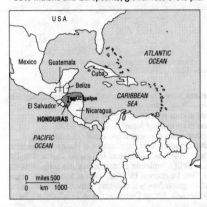

life expectancy men 58, women 62
languages Spanish (official), English, Indian languages
religion Roman Catholic 97%
literacy men 61%, women 58% (1985 est)
GDP $3.5 bn (1987); $758 per head

chronology
1838 Independence achieved from Spain.
1980 After more than a century of mostly military rule, a civilian government was elected, with Dr Roberto Suazo as president; the commander in chief of the army, General Gustavo Alvarez, retained considerable power.
1983 Close involvement with the USA in providing naval and air bases and allowing Nicaraguan counter-revolutionaries ('Contras') to operate from Honduras.
1984 Alvarez ousted in coup led by junior officers, resulting in policy review towards USA and Nicaragua.
1985 José Azcona elected president after electoral law changed, making Suazo ineligible for presidency.
1989 Government and opposition declared support for Central American peace plan to demobilize Nicaraguan Contras based in Honduras; Contras and their dependents in Honduras in 1989 thought to number about 55,000.
1990 Rafael Callejas (PN) elected president.

Hungary (Republic of)
(Magyar Köztársaság)

area 93,032 sq km/35,910 sq mi
capital Budapest
towns Miskolc, Debrecen, Szeged, Pécs
physical Great Hungarian Plain covers E half of country; Bakony Forest, Lake Balaton, and Transdanubian Highlands in the W; rivers Danube, Tisza, and Raba
environment an estimated 35-40% of the population live in areas with officially 'inadmissible' air and water pollution. In Budapest lead levels have reached 30 times the maximum international standards

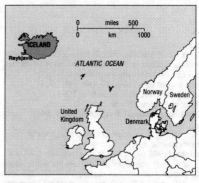

as new leader. Kádár 'retired', later died; Nagy rehabilitated.

1990 HSP reputation damaged by 'Danubegate' bugging scandal. March-April: elections won by right-of-centre coalition, headed by Hungarian Democratic Forum (MDF). May: József Antall, leader of the MDF, appointed premier. Aug: Arpád Göncz elected president.

1991 Jan: devaluation of currency. June: legislation approved to compensate owners of land and property expropriated under Communist regime. Last Soviet troops departed.

Iceland (Republic of)
(Lýdveldid Ísland)

---

features more than 500 thermal springs; Hortobágy National Park; Tokay wine area
head of state Arpád Göncz from 1990
head of government József Antall from 1990
political system emergent democratic republic
political parties over 50, including Hungarian Socialist Party (HSP), left-of-centre; Hungarian Democratic Forum (MDF), umbrella prodemocracy grouping; Alliance of Free Democrats (SzDSz), radical free-market opposition group heading coalition with Alliance of Young Democrats, Social Democrats, and Smallholders Party, right-wing
exports machinery, vehicles, iron and steel, chemicals, fruit and vegetables
currency forint (126.15 = £1 July 1991)
population (1990 est) 10,546,000 (Magyar 92%, Romany 3%, German 2.5%; Hungarian minority in Romania has caused some friction between the two countries); growth rate 0.2% p.a.
life expectancy men 67, women 74
language Hungarian (or Magyar), one of the few languages of Europe with non-Indo-European origins; it is grouped with Finnish, Estonian, and others in the Finno-Ugric family
religion Roman Catholic 67%, other Christian denominations 25%
literacy men 99.3%, women 98.5% (1980)
GDP $26.1 bn (1987); $2,455 per head

chronology
1918 Independence achieved from Austro-Hungarian empire.
1919 A communist state formed for 133 days.
1920-44 Regency formed under Admiral Horthy, who joined Hitler's attack on the USSR.
1945 Liberated by USSR.
1946 Republic proclaimed; Stalinist regime imposed.
1949 Soviet-style constitution adopted.
1956 Hungarian national uprising; workers' demonstrations in Budapest; democratization reforms by Imre Nagy overturned by Soviet tanks, Kádár installed as party leader.
1968 Economic decentralization reforms.
1983 Competition introduced into elections.
1987 VAT and income tax introduced.
1988 Kádár replaced by Károly Grosz. First free trade union recognized; rival political parties legalized.
1989 May: border with Austria opened. July: new four-man collective leadership of HSWP. Oct: new 'transitional constitution' adopted, founded on multiparty democracy and new presidentialist executive. HSWP changed name to Hungarian Socialist Party, with Nyers

area 103,000 sq km/39,758 sq mi
capital Reykjavík
towns Akureyri, Akranes
physical warmed by the Gulf Stream; glaciers and lava fields cover 75% of the country; active volcanoes (Hekla was once thought the gateway to Hell), geysers, hot springs, and new islands created offshore (Surtsey in 1963); subterranean hot water heats 85% of Iceland's homes
features Thingvellir, where the oldest parliament in the world first met AD 930; shallow lake Mývatn (38 sq km/15 sq mi) in N
head of state Vigdís Finnbogadóttir from 1980
head of government Davíd Oddsson from 1991
political system democratic republic
political parties Independence Party (IP), right-of-centre; Progressive Party (PP), radical socialist; People's Alliance (PA), socialist; Social Democratic Party (SDP), moderate, left-of-centre; Citizens' Party, centrist; Women's Alliance, women and family orientated
exports cod and other fish products, aluminium, diatomite
currency krona (102.25 = £1 July 1991)
population (1990 est) 251,000; growth rate 0.8% p.a.
life expectancy men 74, women 80
language Icelandic, the most archaic Scandinavian language, in which some of the finest sagas were written
religion Evangelical Lutheran 95%
literacy 99.9% (1984)
GDP $3.9 bn (1986); $16,200 per head

chronology
1944 Independence achieved from Denmark.
1949 Joined NATO and Council of Europe.
1953 Joined Nordic Council.
1976 'Cod War' with UK.
1979 Iceland announced 200-mile exclusive fishing zone.
1983 Steingrímur Hermannsson appointed to lead a coalition government.
1985 Iceland declared itself a nuclear-free zone.

1987 New coalition government formed by Thorsteinn Pálsson after general election.
1988 Vigdís Finnbogadóttir re-elected president for a third term; Hermannsson led new coalition.
1991 Davíd Oddsson led new IP–SDP (Independence Party and Social Democratic Party) centre-right coalition, becoming prime minister in the general election.

India (Republic of)
(Hindi *Bharat*)

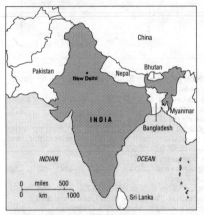

area 3,166,829 sq km/1,222,396 sq mi
capital New Delhi
towns Bangalore, Hyderabad, Ahmedabad, Kanpur, Pune, Nagpur; ports Calcutta, Bombay, Madras
physical Himalaya mountains on N border; plains around rivers Ganges, Indus, Brahmaputra; Deccan peninsula S of the Narmada River forms plateau between Western and Eastern Ghats mountain ranges; desert in W; Andaman and Nicobar Islands, Lakshadweep (Laccadive Islands)
environment the controversial Narmada Valley Project is the world's largest combined hydroelectric-irrigation scheme. In addition to displacing a million people, the damming of the holy Narmada River will submerge large areas of forest and farmland and create problems of waterlogging and salinization
features Taj Mahal monument; Golden Temple, Amritsar; archaeological sites and cave paintings (Ajanta); world's second most populous country
head of state Shankar Dyal Sharma from 1992
head of government P V Narasimha Rao from 1991
political system liberal democratic federal republic
political parties All India Congress Committee (I), or Congress (I), cross-caste and cross-religion left-of-centre; National Front (including Janata Dal), left-of-centre; Bharatiya Janata Party (BJP), conservative Hindu-chauvinist; Communist Party of India (CPI), pro-Moscow Marxist-Leninist; Communist Party of India–Marxist (CPI–M), West Bengal-based moderate socialist
exports tea (world's largest producer), coffee, fish, iron and steel, leather, textiles, clothing, polished diamonds
currency rupee (34.09 = £1 July 1991)
population (1991 est) 844,000,000 (920 women to every 1,000 men); growth rate 2.0% p.a.
life expectancy men 56, women 55
languages Hindi (widely spoken in N India), English, and 14 other official languages: Assamese, Bengali, Gujarati, Kannada, Kashmiri, Malayalam, Marathi, Oriya, Punjabi, Sanskrit, Sindhi, Tamil, Telugu, Urdu
media free press; government-owned broadcasting
religion Hindu 80%, Sunni Muslim 10%, Christian 2.5%, Sikh 2%

literacy men 57%, women 29% (1985 est)
GDP $220.8 bn (1987); $283 per head

chronology
1947 Independence achieved from Britain.
1950 Federal republic proclaimed.
1962 Border skirmishes with China.
1964 Death of Prime Minister Nehru. Border war with Pakistan over Kashmir.
1966 Indira Gandhi became prime minister.
1971 War with Pakistan leading to creation of Bangladesh.
1975-77 State of emergency proclaimed.
1977-79 Janata Party government in power.
1980 Indira Gandhi returned in landslide victory.
1984 Indira Gandhi assassinated; Rajiv Gandhi elected with record majority.
1987 Signing of 'Tamil' Colombo peace accord with Sri Lanka; Indian Peacekeeping Force (IPKF) sent there. Public revelation of Bofors scandal.
1988 New opposition party, Janata Dal, established by former finance minister V P Singh. Voting age lowered from 21 to 18.
1989 Congress (I) lost majority in general election, after Gandhi associates implicated in financial misconduct; Janata Dal minority government formed, with V P Singh prime minister.
1990 Central rule imposed in Jammu and Kashmir. V P Singh resigned; new minority Janata Dal government formed by Chandra Shekhar. Interethnic and religious violence in Punjab and elsewhere.
1991 Central rule imposed in Tamil Nadu. Shekhar resigned; elections called for May. May: Rajiv Gandhi assassinated. June: elections resumed, resulting in a Congress (I) minority government led by P V Narasimha Rao. Separatist violence continued.
1992 Congress (I) won control of state assembly and a majority in parliament in Punjab state elections. Split in Janata Dal opposition resulted in creation of National Front coalition party (including rump of Janata Dal party). July: Shankar Dyal Sharma elected president.

Indonesia (Republic of)
(*Republik Indonesia*)

area 1,919,443 sq km/740,905 sq mi
capital Jakarta
towns Bandung; ports Surabaya, Semarang, Tandjung-priok
physical comprises 13,677 tropical islands, of the Greater Sunda group (including Java and Madura, part of Borneo (Kalimantan), Sumatra, Sulawesi and Belitung), and the Lesser Sundas/Nusa Tenggara (including Bali, Lombok, Sumbawa, Sumba, Flores, and Timor), as well as Malaku/Moluccas and part of New Guinea (Irian Jaya)

environment a comparison of primary forest and 30-year-old secondary forest has shown that logging in Kalimantan has led to a 20% decline in tree species
head of state and government T N J Suharto from 1967
political system authoritarian nationalist republic
political parties Golkar, military-bureaucrat-farmers ruling party; United Development Party (PPP), moderate Islamic; Indonesian Democratic Party (PDI), nationalist Christian
exports coffee, rubber, timber, palm oil, coconuts, tin, tea, tobacco, oil, liquid natural gas
currency rupiah (3,175.66 = £1 July 1991)
population (1989 est) 187,726,000 (including 300 ethnic groups); growth rate 2% p.a.; Indonesia has the world's largest Muslim population; Java is one of the world's most densely populated areas
life expectancy men 52, women 55
language Indonesian (official), closely allied to Malay; Javanese is the most widely spoken local dialect
religion Muslim 88%, Christian 10%, Buddhist and Hindu 2%
literacy men 83%, women 65% (1985 est)
GDP $69.7 bn (1987); $409 per head

chronology
17th century Dutch colonial rule established.
1942 Occupied by Japan; nationalist government established.
1945 Japanese surrender; nationalists declared independence under Sukarno.
1949 Formal transfer of Dutch sovereignty.
1950 Unitary constitution established.
1963 Western New Guinea (Irian Jaya) ceded by the Netherlands.
1965-66 Attempted communist coup; General Suharto imposed emergency administration, carried out massacre of hundreds of thousands.
1967 Sukarno replaced as president by Suharto.
1975 Terrorists seeking independence for S Moluccas seized train and Indonesian consulate in the Netherlands, held Western hostages.
1976 Forced annexation of former Portuguese colony of East Timor.
1986 Institution of 'transmigration programme' to settle large numbers of Javanese on sparsely populated outer islands, particularly Irian Jaya.
1988 Partial easing of travel restrictions to East Timor. Suharto re-elected for fifth term.
1989 Foreign debt reaches $50 billion; Western creditors offer aid on condition that concessions are made to foreign companies and that austerity measures are introduced.
1991 Democracy forums launched to promote political dialogue. Massacre in East Timor severely damaged Indonesia's international reputation.

Iran (Islamic Republic of)
(Jomhori-e-Islami-e-Irân; until 1935 Persia)

area 1,648,000 sq km/636,128 sq mi
capital Tehran
towns Isfahan, Mashhad, Tabriz, Shiraz, Ahvaz; chief port Abadan
physical plateau surrounded by mountains, including Elburz and Zagros; Lake Rezayeh; Dasht-Ekavir Desert; occupies islands of Abu Musa, Greater Tunb and Lesser Tunb in the Gulf
features ruins of Persepolis; Mount Demavend 5,670 m/18,603 ft
Leader of the Islamic Revolution Seyed Ali Khamenei from 1989
head of government Ali Akbar Hoshemi Rafsanjani from 1989
political system authoritarian Islamic republic

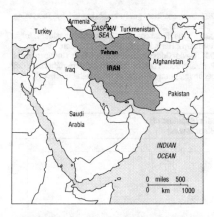

political party Islamic Republican Party (IRP), fundamentalist Islamic
exports carpets, cotton textiles, metalwork, leather goods, oil, petrochemicals, fruit
currency rial (112.50 = £1 July 1991)
population (1989 est) 51,005,000 (including minorities in Azerbaijan, Baluchistan, Khuzestan/Arabistan, and Kurdistan); growth rate 3.2% p.a.
life expectancy men 57, women 57
languages Farsi (official), Kurdish, Turkish, Arabic, English, French
religion Shi'ite Muslim (official) 92%, Sunni Muslim 5%, Zoroastrian 2%, Jewish, Baha'i, and Christian 1%
literacy men 62%, women 39% (1985 est)
GDP $86.4 bn (1987); $1,756 per head

chronology
1946 British, US, and Soviet forces left Iran.
1951 Oilfields nationalized by Prime Minister Muhammad Mossadeq.
1953 Mossadeq deposed and the US-backed shah took full control of the government.
1975 The shah introduced single-party system.
1978 Opposition to the shah organized from France by Ayatollah Khomeini.
1979 Shah left the country; Khomeini returned to create Islamic state. Revolutionaries seized US hostages at embassy in Tehran; US economic boycott.
1980 Start of Iran–Iraq War.
1981 US hostages released.
1984 Egyptian peace proposals rejected.
1985 Fighting intensified in Iran–Iraq War; UN secretary general's peace moves unsuccessful.
1988 Cease-fire; talks with Iraq began.
1989 Khomeini called for the death of British writer Salman Rushdie. June: Khomeini died; Ali Khamenei elected interim Leader of the Revolution; speaker of Iranian parliament Hoshemi Rafsanjani elected president. Secret oil deal with Israel revealed.
1990 Generous peace terms with Iraq accepted. Normal relations with UK restored.
1991 Imprisoned British businessman, Roger Cooper, released. Nearly one million Kurds arrived in Iran from Iraq, fleeing persecution by Saddam Hussein after the Gulf War.
1992 Pro-Rafsanjani moderates won assembly elections.

Iraq (Republic of)
(al Jumhouriya al 'Iraqia)

area 434,924 sq km/167,881 sq mi
capital Baghdad
towns Mosul and port of Basra

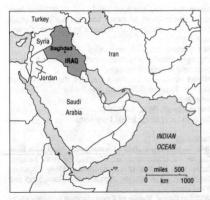

physical mountains in N, desert in W; wide valley of rivers Tigris and Euphrates NW–SE

environment a chemical weapons plant covering an area of 65 sq km/25 sq mi, and situated 80 km/50 mi NW of Baghdad, has been described by the UN as the largest toxic waste dump in the world

features reed architecture of the marsh Arabs; ancient sites of Eridu, Babylon, Nineveh, Ur, Ctesiphon

head of state and government Saddam Hussein al-Tikriti from 1979

political system one-party socialist republic

political party Arab Ba'ath Socialist Party, nationalist socialist

exports oil (prior to UN sanctions), wool, dates (80% of world supply)

currency Iraqi dinar (0.59 = £1 July 1991)

population (1989 est) 17,610,000 (Arabs 77%, Kurds 19%, Turks 2%); growth rate 3.6% p.a.

life expectancy men 62, women 63

languages Arabic (official); Kurdish, Assyrian, Armenian

religion Shi'ite Muslim 60%, Sunni Muslim 37%, Christian 3%

literacy men 68%, women 32% (1980 est)

GDP $42.3 bn (1987); $3,000 per head

chronology

1920 Iraq became a British League of Nations protectorate.

1921 Hashemite dynasty established, with Faisal I installed by Britain as king.

1932 Independence achieved from British protectorate status.

1958 Monarchy overthrown; Iraq became a republic.

1963 Joint Ba'athist-military coup headed by Col Salem Aref.

1968 Military coup put Maj-Gen al-Bakr in power.

1979 Al-Bakr replaced by Saddam Hussein.

1980 War between Iraq and Iran broke out.

1985 Fighting intensified.

1988 Cease-fire; talks began with Iran. Iraq used chemical weapons against Kurdish rebels seeking greater autonomy.

1989 Unsuccessful coup against President Hussein; Iraq launched ballistic missile in successful test.

1990 Peace treaty favouring Iran agreed. Aug: Iraq invaded and annexed Kuwait, precipitating another Gulf crisis. US forces massed in Saudi Arabia at request of King Fahd. UN resolutions ordered Iraqi withdrawal from Kuwait and imposed total trade ban on Iraq; UN resolution sanctioning force approved. All foreign hostages released.

1991 16 Jan: US-led forces began aerial assault on Iraq; Iraq's infrastructure destroyed by bombing. 23–28 Feb: land-sea-air offensive to free Kuwait successful. Uprisings of Kurds and Shi'ites brutally suppressed by surviving Iraqi troops. Talks between Kurdish leaders

and Saddam Hussein about Kurdish autonomy. Allied troops withdrew after establishing 'safe havens' for Kurds in the north. A rapid reaction force left near the Turkish border. Allies threatened to bomb strategic targets in Iraq if full information about nuclear facilities denied to United Nations.

Ireland (Republic of)
(Irish *Eire*)

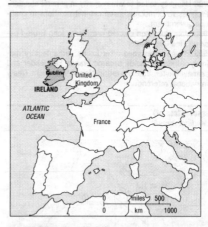

area 70,282 sq km/27,146 sq mi

capital Dublin

towns ports Cork, Dun Laoghaire, Limerick, Waterford

physical central plateau surrounded by hills; rivers Shannon, Liffey, Boyne

features Bog of Allen, source of domestic and national power; Macgillicuddy's Reeks, Wicklow Mountains; Lough Corrib, lakes of Killarney; Galway Bay and Aran Islands

head of state Mary Robinson from 1990

head of government Albert Reynolds from 1992

political system democratic republic

political parties Fianna Fáil (Soldiers of Destiny), moderate centre-right; Fine Gael (Irish Tribe), moderate centre-left; Labour Party, moderate left-of-centre; Progressive Democrats, radical free-enterprise

exports livestock, dairy products, Irish whiskey, microelectronic components and assemblies, mining and engineering products, chemicals, clothing; tourism is important

currency punt (1.10 = £1 July 1991)

population (1989 est) 3,734,000; growth rate 0.1% p.a.

life expectancy men 70, women 76

languages Irish Gaelic and English (both official)

religion Roman Catholic 94%

literacy 99% (1984)

GDP $21.9 (1987); $6,184 per head

chronology

1916 Easter Rising: nationalists against British rule seized the Dublin general post office and proclaimed a republic; the revolt was suppressed by the British army and most of the leaders were executed.

1918-21 Guerrilla warfare against British army led to split in rebel forces.

1921 Anglo-Irish Treaty resulted in creation of the Irish Free State (Southern Ireland).

1937 Independence achieved from Britain.

1949 Eire left the Commonwealth and became the Republic of Ireland.

1973 Fianna Fáil defeated after 40 years in office; Liam Cosgrave formed a coalition government.

1977 Fianna Fáil returned to power, with Jack Lynch as prime minister.
1979 Lynch resigned, succeeded by Charles Haughey.
1981 Garret FitzGerald formed a coalition.
1983 New Ireland Forum formed, but rejected by the British government.
1985 Anglo-Irish Agreement signed.
1986 Protests by Ulster Unionists against the agreement.
1987 General election won by Charles Haughey.
1988 Relations with UK at low ebb because of disagreement over extradition decisions.
1989 Haughey failed to win majority in general election. Progressive Democrats given cabinet positions in coalition government.
1990 Mary Robinson elected president; John Bruton became Fine Gael leader.
1992 Haughey resigned after losing parliamentary majority. Albert Reynolds became Fianna Fáil leader and prime minister. Vote pro ratification of Maastricht Treaty in national referendum.

Israel (State of)
(Medinat Israel)

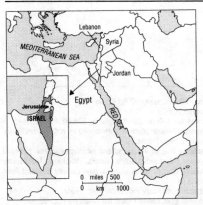

area 20,800 sq km/8,029 sq mi (as at 1949 armistice)
capital Jerusalem (not recognized by the United Nations)
towns ports Tel Aviv/Jaffa, Haifa, Acre, Eilat; Bat-Yam, Holon, Ramat Gan, Petach Tikva, Beersheba
physical coastal plain of Sharon between Haifa and Tel Aviv noted since ancient times for fertility; central mountains of Galilee, Samariq, and Judea; Dead Sea, Lake Tiberias, and river Jordan Rift Valley along the E are below sea level; Negev Desert in the S; Israel occupies Golan Heights, West Bank, and Gaza
features historic sites: Jerusalem, Bethlehem, Nazareth, Masada, Megiddo, Jericho; caves of the Dead Sea scrolls
head of state Chaim Herzog from 1983
head of government Yitzhak Rabin from 1992
political system democratic republic
political parties Israel Labour Party, moderate left-of-centre; Consolidation Party (Likud), right-of-centre
exports citrus and other fruit, avocados, chinese leaves, fertilizers, diamonds, plastics, petrochemicals, textiles, electronics (military, medical, scientific, industrial), electro-optics, precision instruments, aircraft and missiles
currency shekel (4.01 = £1 July 1991)
population (1989 est) 4,477,000 (including 750,000 Arab Israeli citizens and over 1 million Arabs in the occupied territories); under the Law of Return 1950, 'every Jew shall be entitled to come to Israel as an immigrant'; those from the East and E Europe are Ashkenazim, and from Mediterranean Europe (Spain, Portugal, Italy, France, Greece) and Arab N Africa are Sephardim (over 50% of the population is now of Sephardic descent). Be-

tween Jan 1990 and April 1991, 250,000 Soviet Jews emigrated to Israel. An Israeli-born Jew is a Sabra; about 500,000 Israeli Jews are resident in the USA. Growth rate 1.8% p.a.
life expectancy men 73, women 76
languages Hebrew and Arabic (official); Yiddish, European and W Asian languages
religion Israel is a secular state, but the predominant faith is Judaism 83%; also Sunni Muslim, Christian, and Druse
literacy Jewish 88%, Arab 70%
GDP $35 bn (1987); $8,011 per head

chronology
1948 Independent State of Israel proclaimed with Ben-Gurion as prime minister; attacked by Arab nations, Israel won the War of Independence. Many displaced Arabs settled in refugee camps in the Gaza Strip and West Bank.
1952 Col Gamal Nasser of Egypt stepped up blockade of Israeli ports and support of Arab guerrillas in Gaza.
1956 Israel invaded Gaza and Sinai.
1959 Egypt renewed blockade of Israeli trade through Suez Canal.
1963 Ben-Gurion resigned, succeeded by Levi Eshkol.
1964 Palestine Liberation Organization (PLO) founded with the aim of overthrowing the state of Israel.
1967 Israel victorious in the Six Day War. Gaza, West Bank, E Jerusalem, Sinai, and Golan Heights captured.
1968 Israel Labour Party formed, led by Golda Meir.
1969 Golda Meir became prime minister.
1973-74 Yom Kippur War: Israel attacked by Egypt and Syria. Golda Meir succeeded by Itzhak Rabin.
1975 Suez Canal reopened.
1977 Menachem Begin elected prime minister. Egyptian president addressed the Knesset.
1978 Camp David talks.
1979 Egyptian-Israeli agreement signed. Israel agreed to withdraw from Sinai.
1980 Jerusalem declared capital of Israel.
1981 Golan Heights formally annexed.
1982 Israel pursued PLO fighters into Lebanon.
1983 Agreement reached for withdrawal from Lebanon.
1985 Israeli prime minister Shimon Peres had secret talks with King Hussein of Jordan.
1986 Itzhak Shamir took over from Peres under power-sharing agreement.
1988 Criticism of Israel's handling of Palestinian uprising in occupied territories; PLO acknowledged Israel's right to exist.
1989 New Likud—Labour coalition government formed under Shamir. Limited progress achieved on proposals for negotiations leading to elections in occupied territories.
1990 Coalition collapsed due to differences over peace process; international condemnation of Temple Mount killings. New Shamir right-wing coalition formed.
1991 Shamir gave cautious response to Middle East peace proposals. Some Palestinian prisoners released. Peace talks began in Barcelona.
1992 Israelis and Palestinians held first direct negotiations. Shamir lost majority in Knesset when fundamentalists withdrew from coalition. Labour Party, led by Yitzhak Rabin, won in June elections; coalition government formed under Rabin.

Italy (Republic of)
(Repubblica Italiana)

---

area 301,300 sq km/116,332 sq mi
capital Rome
towns Milan, Turin; ports Naples, Genoa, Palermo, Bari, Catania, Trieste
physical mountainous (Maritime Alps, Dolomites, Apennines) with narrow coastal lowlands; rivers

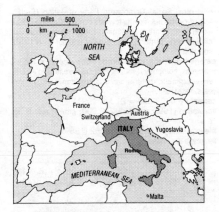

Po, Adige, Arno, Tiber, Rubicon; islands of Sicily, Sardinia, Elba, Capri, Ischia, Lipari, Pantelleria; lakes Como, Maggiore, Garda
environment Milan has the highest recorded level of sulphur dioxide pollution of any city in the world. The Po River, with pollution ten times higher than officially recommended levels, is estimated to discharge 234 tonnes of arsenic into the sea each year
features continental Europe's only active volcanoes: Vesuvius, Etna, Stromboli; historic towns include Venice, Florence, Siena, Rome; Greek, Roman, Etruscan archaeological sites
political parties Christian Democratic Party (DC), Christian, centrist; Democratic Party of the Left (PDS), pro-European socialist; Italian Socialist Party (PSI), moderate socialist; Italian Social Movement—National Right (MSI—DN), neofascist; Italian Republican Party (PRI), social democratic, left-of-centre; Italian Social Democratic Party (PSDI), moderate left-of-centre; Liberals (PLI), right-of-centre
exports wine (world's largest producer), fruit, vegetables, textiles (Europe's largest silk producer), clothing, leather goods, motor vehicles, electrical goods, chemicals, marble (Carrara), sulphur, mercury, iron, steel
head of state Oscar Luigi Scalfaro from 1992
head of government Giulio Amato from 1992
political system democratic republic
currency lira (2,187.00 = £1 July 1991)
population (1990 est) 57,657,000; growth rate 0.1% p.a.
life expectancy men 73, women 80 (1989)
language Italian; German, French, Slovene, and Albanian minorities
religion Roman Catholic 100% (state religion)
literacy 97% (1989)
GDP $748 bn; $13,052 per head (1988)

chronology
1946 Monarchy replaced by a republic.
1948 New constitution adopted.
1954 Trieste returned to Italy.
1976 Communists proposed establishment of broad-based, left–right government, the 'historic compromise'; rejected by Christian Democrats.
1978 Christian Democrat Aldo Moro, architect of the historic compromise, kidnapped and murdered by Red Brigade guerrillas.
1983 Bettino Craxi, a Socialist, became leader of broad coalition government.
1987 Craxi resigned; succeeding coalition fell within months.
1988 Christian Democrats' leader Ciriaco de Mita established a five-party coalition including the Socialists.
1989 De Mita resigned after disagreements within his coalition government; succeeded by Giulio Andreotti. De

Mita lost leadership of Christian Democrats; Communists formed 'shadow government'.
1991 Referendum approved electoral reform.
1992 Ruling coalition lost its majority in general election. President Cossiga resigned, replaced by Oscar Luigi Scalfaro. Attempts made to construct new coalition, with Giulio Andreotti (DC) as interim prime minister. June: Giuliano Amato, deputy leader of PDS, accepted premiership; new government formed.

Ivory Coast (Republic of)
(République de la Côte d'Ivoire)

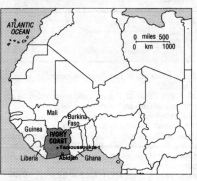

area 322,463 sq km/124,471 sq mi
capital Yamoussoukro
towns Bouaké, Daloa, Man; ports Abidjan, San-Pédro
physical tropical rainforest (diminishing as exploited) in S; savanna and low mountains in N
environment an estimated 85% of the country's forest has been destroyed by humans
features Vridi canal, Kossou dam, Monts du Toura
head of state and government Félix Houphouët-Boigny from 1960
political system emergent democratic republic
political party Democratic Party of the Ivory Coast (PDCI), nationalist, free-enterprise
exports coffee, cocoa, timber, petroleum products
currency franc CFA (498.25 = £1 July 1991)
population (1990 est) 12,070,000; growth rate 3.3% p.a.
life expectancy men 52, women 55 (1989)
languages French (official), over 60 native dialects
media the government has full control of the media
religion animist 65%, Muslim 24%, Christian 11%
literacy 35% (1988)
GDP $7.6 bn (1987); $687 per head

chronology
1904 Became part of French West Africa.
1958 Achieved internal self-government.
1960 Independence achieved from France, with Félix Houphouët-Boigny as president of a one-party state.
1985 Houphouët-Boigny re-elected, unopposed.
1986 Name changed officially from Ivory Coast to Côte d'Ivoire.
1990 Houphouët-Boigny and PDCI re-elected.
1991 Anti-government demonstrations.

Jamaica

area 10,957 sq km/4,230 sq mi
capital Kingston
towns Montego Bay, Spanish Town, St Andrew
physical mountainous tropical island
features Blue Mountains (so called because of the haze over them) renowned for their coffee; partly undersea

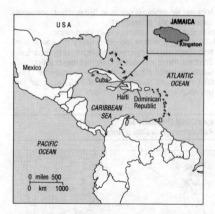

of-centre; Social Democratic Party of Japan (SDJP), left-of-centre but moving towards centre; Komeito (Clean Government Party), Buddhist-centrist; Democratic Socialist Party, centrist; Japanese Communist Party (JCP), socialist
exports televisions, cassette and video recorders, radios, cameras, computers, robots, other electronic and electrical equipment, motor vehicles, ships, iron, steel, chemicals, textiles
currency yen (223.50 = £1 July 1991)
population (1990 est) 123,778,000; growth rate 0.5% p.a.
life expectancy men 76, women 82 (1989)
language Japanese

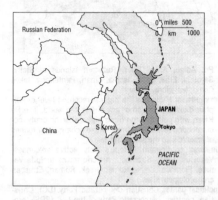

ruins of pirate city of Port Royal, destroyed by an earthquake 1692
head of state Elizabeth II from 1962 represented by governor general (Howard Cooke from 1991)
head of government P J Patterson from 1992
political system constitutional monarchy
political parties Jamaica Labour Party (JLP), moderate, centrist; People's National Party (PNP), left-of-centre
exports sugar, bananas, bauxite, rum, cocoa, coconuts, liqueurs, cigars, citrus
currency Jamaican dollar (J$16.16 = £1 July 1991)
population (1990 est) 2,513,000 (African 76%, mixed 15%, Chinese, Caucasian, East Indian); growth rate 2.2% p.a.
life expectancy men 75, women 78 (1989)
languages English, Jamaican creole
media one daily newspaper 1834–1988 (except 1973–82), privately owned; sensational evening and weekly papers
religion Protestant 70%, Rastafarian
literacy 82% (1988)
GDP $2.9 bn; $1,187 per head (1989)

chronology
1494 Columbus reached Jamaica.
1509-1655 Occupied by Spanish.
1655 Captured by British.
1944 Internal self-government introduced.
1962 Independence achieved from Britain, with Alexander Bustamante of the JLP as prime minister.
1967 JLP re-elected under Hugh Shearer.
1972 Michael Manley of the PNP became prime minister.
1980 JLP elected, with Edward Seaga as prime minister.
1983 JLP re-elected, winning all 60 seats.
1988 Island badly damaged by Hurricane Gilbert.
1989 PNP won a decisive victory with Michael Manley returning as prime minister.
1992 Manley resigned, succeeded by P J Patterson.

Japan *(Nippon)*

area 377,535 sq km/145,822 sq mi
capital Tokyo
towns Fukuoka, Kitakyushu, Kyoto, Sapporo; ports Osaka, Nagoya, Yokohama, Kobe, Kawasaki
physical mountainous, volcanic; comprises over 1,000 islands, the largest of which are Hokkaido, Honshu, Kyushu, and Shikoku
features Mount Fuji, Mount Aso (volcanic)
head of state (figurehead) Emperor Akihito from 1989
head of government Kiichi Miyazawa from 1991
political system liberal democracy
political parties Liberal Democratic Party (LDP), right-

religion Shinto, Buddhist (often combined), Christian; 30% claim a personal religious faith
literacy 99% (1989)
GDP $2.4 trillion; $19,464 per head (1989)

chronology
1867 End of shogun rule; executive power passed to emperor. Start of modernization of Japan.
1894-95 War with China; Formosa (Taiwan) and S Manchuria gained.
1902 Formed alliance with Britain.
1904-05 War with Russia; Russia ceded southern half of Sakhalin.
1910 Japan annexed Korea.
1914 Joined Allies in World War I.
1918 Received German Pacific islands as mandates.
1931-32 War with China; renewed 1937.
1941 Japan attacked US fleet at Pearl Harbor 7 Dec.
1945 World War II ended with Japanese surrender. Allied control commission took power. Formosa and Manchuria returned to China.
1946 Framing of 'peace constitution'. Emperor Hirohito became figurehead ruler.
1952 Full sovereignty regained.
1958 Joined United Nations.
1968 Bonin and Volcano Islands regained.
1972 Ryukyu Islands regained.
1974 Prime Minister Tanaka resigned over Lockheed bribes scandal.
1982 Yasuhiro Nakasone elected prime minister.
1987 Noboru Takeshita chosen to succeed Nakasone.
1988 Recruit scandal cast shadow over government and opposition parties.
1989 Emperor Hirohito died; succeeded by his son Akihito. Many cabinet ministers implicated in Recruit scandal and Takeshita resigned; succeeded by Sosuke Uno. Aug: Uno resigned after sex scandal; succeeded by Toshiki Kaifu.
1990 Feb: new house of councillors' elections won by LDP. Public-works budget increased by 50% to encourage imports.

1991 Japan contributed billions of dollars to the Gulf War and its aftermath. Kaifu succeeded by Kiichi Miyazawa.
1992 Over 100 politicians implicated in new financial scandal.

Jordan (Hashemite Kingdom of)
(Al Mamlaka al Urduniya al Hashemiyah)

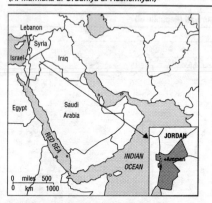

area 89,206 sq km/34,434 sq mi (West Bank 5,879 sq km/2,269 sq mi)
capital Amman
towns Zarqa, Irbid, Aqaba (the only port)
physical desert plateau in E; rift valley separates E and W banks of the river Jordan
features lowest point on Earth below sea level in the Dead Sea (−396 m/−1,299 ft); archaeological sites at Jerash and Petra
head of state King Hussein ibn Talai from 1952
head of government Mudar Badran from 1989
political system constitutional monarchy
political parties none (banned 1976; ban lifted 1991)
exports potash, phosphates, citrus, vegetables
currency Jordanian dinar (JD1.09 = £1 July 1991)
population (1990 est) 3,065,000 (including Palestinian refugees); West Bank (1988) 866,000; growth rate 3.6% p.a.
life expectancy men 67, women 71
languages Arabic (official), English
religion Sunni Muslim 92%, Christian 8%
literacy 71% (1988)
GDP $4.3 bn (1987); $1,127 per head (1988)

chronology
1946 Independence achieved from Britain as Transjordan.
1949 New state of Jordan declared.
1950 Jordan annexed West Bank.
1953 Hussein ibn Talai officially became king of Jordan.
1958 Jordan and Iraq formed Arab Federation that ended when the Iraqi monarchy was deposed.
1967 Israel captured and occupied West Bank. Martial law imposed.
1976 Lower house dissolved, elections postponed until further notice.
1982 Hussein tried to mediate in Arab-Israeli conflict.
1984 Women voted for the first time.
1985 Hussein and Yassir Arafat put forward framework for Middle East peace settlement. Secret meeting between Hussein and Israeli prime minister.
1988 Hussein announced decision to cease administering the West Bank as part of Jordan, passing responsibility to Palestine Liberation Organization, and the suspension of parliament.
1989 Prime Minister Zaid al-Rifai resigned; Hussein promised new parliamentary elections followed criticism of economic policies. Riots over price increases

up to 50% following fall in oil revenues. 80-member parliament elected and Mudar Badran appointed prime minister. First parliamentary elections for 22 years; Muslim Brotherhood won 25 of 80 seats but exiled from government; martial law provisions lifted.
1990 Hussein unsuccessfully tried to mediate after Iraq's invasion of Kuwait. Massive refugee problems as thousands fled to Jordan from Kuwait and Iraq.
1991 Ban on political parties removed. 24 years of martial law ended.

Kazakhstan (Republic of)

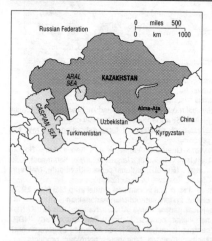

area 2,717,300 sq km/1,049,150 sq mi
capital Alma-Ata
towns Karaganda, Semipalatinsk, Petropavlovsk
physical Caspian and Aral seas, Lake Balkhash; Steppe region
features Baikonur Cosmodrome (space launch site at Tyuratam, near Baikonur)
head of state Nursultan Nazarbayev from 1990
head of government Sergey Tereshchenko
political system emergent democracy
products grain, copper, lead, zinc, manganese, coal, oil
population (1990) 16,700,000 (40% Kazakh, 38% Russian, 6% Germans, 5% Ukrainians)
language Russian; Kazakh, related to Turkish
religion Sunni Islam

chronology
1920 Autonomous republic in USSR.
1936 Joined the USSR and became a full union republic.
1950s Site of Nikita Khrushchev's ambitious 'virgin lands' agricultural extension programme.
1960s A large influx of Russian settlers turned the Kazakhs into a minority in their own republic.
1986 Riots in Alma-Alta after Gorbachev ousted local communist leader.
1989 June: Nazarbayev became leader of the Kazakh Communist Party (KCP) and instituted economic and cultural reform programmes.
1990 Feb: Nazarbayev became head of state.
1991 March: Kazakh voters supported continued union with USSR. Aug: attempted anti-Gorbachev Moscow coup condemned by Nazarbayev; Communist Party abolished and replaced by independent Socialist Party of Kazakhstan (SPK). Dec: joined new Commonwealth of Independent States (CIS); recognition of independence accorded by USA.
1992 Jan: admitted into CSCE.

Kenya (Republic of)
(Jamhuri ya Kenya)

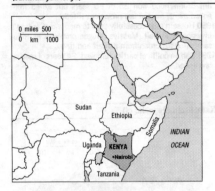

area 582,600 sq km/224,884 sq mi
capital Nairobi
towns Kisumu, port Mombasa
physical mountains and highlands in W and centre; coastal plain in S; arid interior and tropical coast
environment the elephant faces extinction as a result of poaching
features Great Rift Valley, Mount Kenya, Lake Nakuru (salt lake with world's largest colony of flamingos), Lake Turkana (Rudolf), national parks with wildlife, Malindini Marine Reserve, Olduvai Gorge
head of state and government Daniel arap Moi from 1978
political system authoritarian nationalism
political parties Kenya African National Union (KANU), nationalist, centrist; National Democratic Party (NDP), centrist (launched 1991, not accepted by government)
exports coffee, tea, pineapples, petroleum products
currency Kenya shilling (46.57 = £1 July 1991)
population (1990 est) 25,393,000 (Kikuyu 21%, Luo 13%, Luhya 14%, Kelenjin 11%; Asian, Arab, European); growth rate 4.2% p.a.
life expectancy men 59, women 63 (1989)
languages Kiswahili (official), English; there are many local dialects
religion Protestant 38%, Roman Catholic 28%, indigenous beliefs 26%, Muslim 6%
literacy 50% (1988)
GDP $6.9 bn (1987); $302 per head (1988)

chronology
1895 British East African protectorate established.
1920 Kenya became a British colony.
1944 African participation in politics began.
1950 Mau Mau campaign began.
1953 Nationalist leader Jomo Kenyatta imprisoned by British authorities.
1956 Mau Mau campaign defeated, Kenyatta released.
1963 Achieved internal self-government, with Kenyatta as prime minister.
1964 Independence achieved from Britain as a republic within the Commonwealth, with Kenyatta as president.
1978 Death of Kenyatta. Succeeded by Daniel arap Moi.
1982 Attempted coup against Moi foiled.
1983 Moi re-elected.
1984 Over 2,000 people massacred by government forces at Wajir.
1985-86 Thousands of forest villagers evicted and their homes destroyed to make way for cash crops.
1988 Moi re-elected. 150,000 evicted from state-owned forests.
1989 Moi announced release of all known political prisoners. Confiscated ivory burned in attempt to stop elephant poaching.

1990 Despite antigovernment riots, Moi refused multiparty politics.
1991 Increasing demands for political reform; Moi announced that multiparty politics would be established.
1992 Proposals for constitutional reforms announced.

Kiribati (Republic of)

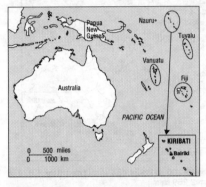

area 717 sq km/277 sq mi
capital and port Bairiki (on Tarawa Atoll)
physical comprises 33 Pacific coral islands: the Kiribati (Gilbert), Rawaki (Phoenix), and Line Islands, Banaba (Ocean Island), and Kiritimati (Christmas Island)
environment the islands are threatened by the possibility of a rise in sea level caused by global warming. A rise of 30 cm by the year 2040 will make existing fresh water brackish and undrinkable
features island groups crossed by equator and International Date Line
head of state and government Teatao Teannaki from 1991
political system liberal democracy
political parties National Progressive Party, governing faction; opposition parties: Christian Democratic Party and the Kiribati United Party
exports copra, fish
currency Australian dollar ($A2.11 = £1 July 1991)
population (1990 est) 65,600 (Micronesian); growth rate 1.7% p.a.
languages English (official), Gilbertese
religion Roman Catholic 48%, Protestant 45%
literacy 90% (1985)
GDP $26 million (1987); $430 per head (1988)

chronology
1892 Gilbert and Ellice Islands proclaimed a British protectorate.
1937 Phoenix Islands added to colony.
1950s UK tested nuclear weapons on Kiritimati (formerly Christmas Island).
1962 USA tested nuclear weapons on Kiritimati.
1975 Ellice Islands separated to become Tuvalu.
1977 Gilbert Islands granted internal self-government.
1979 Independence achieved from Britain, within the Commonwealth, as the Republic of Kiribati, with Ieremia Tabai as president.
1982 and 1983 Tabai re-elected.
1985 Fishing agreement with Soviet state-owned company negotiated, prompting formation of Kiribati's first political party, the opposition Christian Democrats.
1987 Tabai re-elected.
1991 Tabai re-elected but not allowed under constitution to serve further term; Teatao Teannaki elected as president.

Korea, North (Democratic People's Republic of)
(Chosun Minchu-chui Inmin Konghwa-guk)

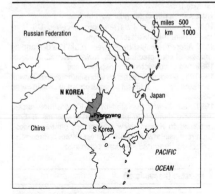

area 120,538 sq km/46,528 sq mi
capital Pyongyang
towns Chongjin, Nampo, Wonsan
physical wide coastal plain in W rising to mountains cut by deep valleys in interior
environment the building of a hydroelectric dam at Kumgangsan on a tributary of the Han River has been opposed by South Korea as a potential flooding threat to central Korea
features separated from South Korea by a military demarcation line; the richer of the two Koreas in mineral resources (copper, iron ore, graphite, tungsten, zinc, lead, magnesite, gold, phosphor, phosphates)
head of state Kim Il Sung from 1972 (also head of Korean Workers' Party)
head of government Yon Hyong Muk from 1988
political system communism
political parties Korean Workers' Party (KWP), Marxist-Leninist-Kim Il Sungist (leads Democratic Front for the Reunification of the Fatherland, including North Korean Democratic Party and Religious Chungwoo Party)
exports coal, iron, copper, textiles, chemicals
currency won (1.58 = £1 July 1991)
population (1990 est) 23,059,000; growth rate 2.5% p.a.
life expectancy men 67, women 73 (1989)
language Korean
religion traditionally Buddhist, Confucian, but religious activity now curtailed by the state
literacy 99% (1989)
GNP $20 bn; $3,450 per head (1988)

chronology
1910 Korea formally annexed by Japan.
1945 Russian and US troops entered Korea, forced surrender of Japanese, and divided the country in two. Soviet troops occupied North Korea.
1948 Democratic People's Republic of Korea declared.
1950 North Korea invaded South Korea to unite the nation, beginning the Korean War.
1953 Armistice agreed to end Korean War.
1961 Friendship and mutual assistance treaty signed with China.
1972 New constitution, with executive president, adopted. Talks took place with South Korea about possible reunification.
1980 Reunification talks broke down.
1983 Four South Korean cabinet ministers assassinated in Rangoon, Burma (Myanmar), by North Korean army officers.
1985 Increased relations with the USSR.
1989 Increasing evidence shown of nuclear-weapons development.

1990 Diplomatic contacts with South Korea and Japan suggested the beginning of a thaw in North Korea's relations with the rest of the world.
1991 Became a member of the United Nations. Signed non-aggression agreement with South Korea, signalling a move towards a formal peace treaty, and nuclear weapons pact.
1992 Signed Nuclear Safeguard Agreement, allowing international inspection of its nuclear facilities.

Korea, South (Republic of)
(Daehan Minguk)

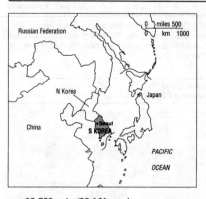

area 98,799 sq km/38,161 sq mi
capital Seoul
towns Taegu, ports Pusan, Inchon
physical southern end of a mountainous peninsula separating the Sea of Japan from the Yellow Sea
features Chomsongdae (world's earliest observatory); giant Popchusa Buddha; granite peaks of Soraksan National Park
head of state Roh Tae Woo from 1988
head of government Chung Won Shik from 1991
political system emergent democracy
political parties Democratic Liberal Party (DLP), right-of-centre; Democratic Party, left-of-centre; Unification National Party, right-of-centre
exports steel, ships, chemicals, electronics, textiles and clothing, plywood, fish
currency won (1,172.52 = £1 July 1991)
population (1990 est) 43,919,000; growth rate 1.4% p.a.
life expectancy men 66, women 73 (1989)
language Korean
media freedom of the press achieved 1987; large numbers of newspapers with large circulations. It is still prohibited to say anything favourable about North Korea
religion traditionally Buddhist, Confucian, and Chondokyo; Christian 28%
literacy 92% (1989)
GNP $171bn (1988); $2,180 per head (1986)

chronology
1910 Korea formally annexed by Japan.
1945 Russian and US troops entered Korea, forced surrender of Japanese, and divided the country in two. US military government took control of South Korea.
1948 Republic proclaimed.
1950-53 War with North Korea.
1960 President Syngman Rhee resigned amid unrest.
1961 Military coup by General Park Chung-Hee. Industrial growth programme.
1979 Assassination of President Park.
1980 Military takeover by General Chun Doo Hwan.
1987 Adoption of more democratic constitution following student unrest. Roh Tae Woo elected president.

1988 Former president Chun, accused of corruption, publicly apologized and agreed to hand over his financial assets to the state. Seoul hosted Summer Olympic Games.

1989 Roh reshuffled cabinet, threatened crackdown on protesters.

1990 Two minor opposition parties united with Democratic Justice Party to form ruling Democratic Liberal Party.

Diplomatic relations established with the USSR.

1991 Violent mass demonstrations against the government. New opposition grouping, the Democratic Party, formed. Prime Minister Ro Jai Bong replaced by Chung Won Shik. Non-aggression and nuclear pacts signed with North Korea.

1992 DLP lost absolute majority in March general election; substantial gains made by Democratic Party and newly formed Unification National Party (UNP), led by Chung Ju Wong.

Kuwait (State of)
(Dowlat al Kuwait)

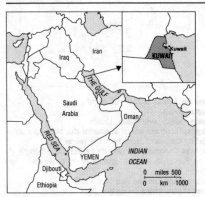

area 17,819 sq km/6,878 sq mi
capital Kuwait (also chief port)
towns Jahra, Ahmadi, Fahaheel
physical hot desert; islands of Failaka, Bubiyan, and Warba at NE corner of Arabian Peninsula
environment during the Gulf War 1990-91, 650 oil wells were set alight and about 300,000 tonnes of oil were released into the waters of the Gulf leading to pollution haze, photochemical smog, acid rain, soil contamination, and water pollution
features there are no rivers and rain is light; the world's largest desalination plants, built in the 1950s
head of state and government Jabir al-Ahmad al-Jabir al-Sabah from 1977
political system absolute monarchy
political parties none
exports oil
currency Kuwaiti dinar (KD0.48 = £1 July 1991)
population (1990 est) 2,080,000 (Kuwaitis 40%, Palestinians 30%); growth rate 5.5% p.a.
life expectancy men 72, women 76 (1989)
languages Arabic 78%, Kurdish 10%, Farsi 4%
religion Sunni Muslim 45%, Shi'ite minority 30%
literacy 71% (1988)
GNP $19.1 bn; $10,410 per head (1988)

chronology
1914 Britain recognized Kuwait as an independent sovereign state.
1961 Full independence achieved from Britain, with Sheik Abdullah al-Salem al-Sabah as emir.
1965 Sheik Abdullah died; succeeded by his brother, Sheik Sabah.

1977 Sheik Sabah died; succeeded by Crown Prince Jabir.
1983 Shi'ite guerrillas bombed targets in Kuwait; 17 arrested.
1984 Shi'ite terrorists convicted.
1987 Kuwaiti oil tankers reflagged, received US Navy protection; missile attacks by Iran.
1988 Aircraft hijacked by pro-Iranian Shi'ites demanding release of convicted terrorists; Kuwait refused.
1989 Two of convicted terrotists released.
1990 Prodemocracy demonstrations suppressed. Kuwait annexed by Iraq. Emir set up government in exile in Saudi Arabia.
1991 Feb: Kuwait liberated by US-led coalition forces; extensive damage to property and environment. Emir returned to Kuwait. New government omitted opposition representatives. Trials of alleged Iraqi collaborators criticized. Promised elections postponed.

Kyrgyzstan (Republic of)

area 198,500 sq km/76,641 sq mi
capital Bishkek (formerly Frunze)
towns Osh, Przhevalsk, Kyzyl-Kiya, Tormak
physical mountainous, an extension of the Tian Shan range
head of state Askar Akayev from 1990
head of government Tursunbek Chyngyshev
political system emergent democracy
political party Democratic Kyrgyzstan, nationalist reformist; Asaba (Banner) Party and Free Kyrgyzstan Party, both opposition groupings
products cereals, sugar, cotton, coal, oil, sheep, yaks, horses
population (1990) 4,400,000 (52% Kyrgyz, 22% Russian, 13% Uzbek, 3% Ukrainian, 2% German)
language Kyrgyz, a Turkic language
religion Sunni Islam

chronology
1917-1924 Part of an independent Turkestan republic.
1924 Became autonomous republic within USSR.
1936 Became full union republic within USSR.
1990 June: ethnic clashes resulted in state of emergency being imposed in Bishkek. Nov: Askar Akayev chosen as state president.
1991 March: Kyrgyz voters endorsed maintenance of Union in USSR referendum. Aug: President Akayev condemned anti-Gorbachev attempted coup in Moscow; Kyrgyz Communist Party, which supported the coup, suspended. Oct: Akayev directly elected president. Dec: joined new Commonwealth of Independent States (CIS) and independence recognized by USA.
1992 Jan: admitted into CSCE.

Laos (Lao People's Democratic Republic)
(Saathiaranagroat Prachhathippatay Prachhachhon Lao)

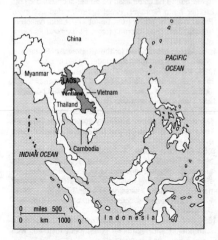

area 236,790 sq km/91,400 sq mi
capital Vientiane
towns Luang Prabang (the former royal capital), Pakse, Savannakhet
physical landlocked state with high mountains in E; Mekong River in W; jungle covers nearly 60% of land
features Plain of Jars, where prehistoric people carved stone jars large enough to hold a person
head of state Kaysone Phomvihane from 1991
head of government General Khamtay Siphandon from 1991
political system communism, one-party state
political party Lao People's Revolutionary Party (only legal party)
exports hydroelectric power from the Mekong is exported to Thailand, timber, teak, coffee, electricity
currency new kip (K.1,137.50 = £1 July 1991)
population (1990 est) 4,024,000 (Lao 48%, Thai 14%, Khmer 25%, Chinese 13%); growth rate 2.2% p.a.
life expectancy men 48, women 51 (1989)
languages Lao (official), French
religion Theravāda Buddhist 85%, animist beliefs among mountain dwellers
literacy 45% (1991)
GNP $500 million (1987); $180 per head (1988)

chronology
1893-1945 Laos was a French protectorate.
1945 Temporarily occupied by Japan.
1946 Retaken by France.
1950 Granted semi-autonomy in French Union.
1954 Independence achieved from France.
1960 Right-wing government seized power.
1962 Coalition government established; civil war continued.
1973 Vientiane cease-fire agreement.
1975 Communist-dominated republic proclaimed with Prince Souphanouvong as head of state.
1986 Phoumi Vongvichit became acting president.
1988 Plans announced to withdraw 40% of Vietnamese forces stationed in the country.
1989 First assembly elections since communist takeover.
1990 Draft constitution published.
1991 Constitution approved. Kaysone Phomvihane elected president. General Khamtay Siphandon named as new premier.

Latvia (Republic of)

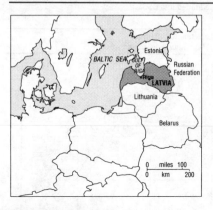

area 63,700 sq km/24,595 sq mi
capital Riga
towns Daugavpils, Liepāja, Jurmala, Jelgava, Ventspils
physical wooded lowland (highest point 312 m/1,024 ft), marshes, lakes; 472 km/293 mi of coastline; mild climate
features Western Dvina River; Riga is largest port on the Baltic after Leningrad
head of state Anatolijs Gorbunov from 1988
head of government Ivars Godmanis from 1990
political system emergent democratic republic
political parties Latvian Popular Front, nationalist; Latvian Social-Democratic Workers' Party
products electronic and communications equipment, electric railway carriages, motorcycles, consumer durables, timber, paper and woollen goods, meat and dairy products
currency Latvian rouble
population (1990) 2,700,000 (52% Latvian, 34% Russian, 5% Byelorussian, 3% Ukrainian)
language Latvian
religion mostly Lutheran Protestant, with a Roman Catholic minority

chronology
1917 Soviets and Germans contested for control of Latvia.
1918 Feb: Soviet forces overthrown by Germany. Nov: Latvia declared independence. Dec: Soviet rule restored after German withdrawal.
1919 Soviet rule overthrown by British naval and German forces May–Dec; democracy established.
1934 Coup replaced established government.
1939 German–Soviet secret agreement placed Latvia under Russian influence.
1940 Incorporated into USSR as constituent republic.
1941-44 Occupied by Germany.
1944 USSR regained control.
1980 Nationalist dissent began to grow.
1988 Latvian Popular Front established to campaign for independence. Prewar flag readopted; official status given to Latvian language.
1989 Popular Front swept local elections.
1990 Jan: Communist Party's monopoly of power abolished. March-April: Popular Front secured majority in elections. April: Latvian Communist Party split into pro-independence and pro-Moscow wings. May: unilateral declaration of independence from USSR, subject to transitional period for negotiation.
1991 Jan: Soviet troops briefly seized key installations in Riga. March: overwhelming vote for independence in referendum. Aug: full independence declared at time of anti-Gorbachev coup; Communist Party outlawed. Sept:

independence recognized by Soviet government and Western nations; United Nations membership granted; admitted into CSCE.

Lebanon (Republic of)
(al-Jumhouria al-Lubnaniya)

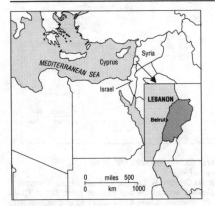

area 10,452 sq km/4,034 sq mi
capital and port Beirut
towns ports Tripoli, Tyre, Sidon
physical narrow coastal plain; Bekka valley N–S between Lebanon and Anti-Lebanon mountain ranges
features Mount Hermon; Chouf Mountains; archaeological sites at Baalbeck, Byblos, Tyre; until the civil war, the financial centre of the Middle East
head of state Elias Hrawi from 1989
head of government Rashid al-Solh from 1992
political system emergent democratic republic
political parties Phalangist Party, Christian, radical, right-wing; Progressive Socialist Party (PSP), Druse, moderate, socialist; National Liberal Party (NLP), Maronite, centre-left; Parliamentary Democratic Front, Sunni Muslim, centrist; Lebanese Communist Party (PCL), nationalist, communist
exports citrus and other fruit, vegetables; industrial products to Arab neighbours
currency Lebanese pound (Leb.1469.00 = £1 July 1991)
population (1990 est) 3,340,000 (Lebanese 82%, Palestinian 9%, Armenian 5%); growth rate –0.1% p.a.
life expectancy men 65, women 70 (1989)
languages Arabic, French (both official), Armenian, English
religion Muslim 57% (Shi'ite 33%, Sunni 24%), Christian (Maronite and Orthodox) 40%, Druse 3%
literacy 75% (1989)
GNP $1.8 bn; $690 per head (1986)

chronology
1920–41 Administered under French mandate.
1944 Independence achieved.
1948–49 Lebanon joined first Arab war against Israel. Palestinian refugees settled in the south.
1964 Palestine Liberation Organization (PLO) founded in Beirut.
1967 More Palestinian refugees settled in Lebanon.
1971 PLO expelled from Jordan; established headquarters in Lebanon.
1975 Outbreak of civil war between Christians and Muslims.
1976 Cease-fire agreed; Syrian-dominated Arab deterrent force formed to keep the peace but considered by Christians as an occupying force.
1978 Israel invaded S Lebanon in search of PLO fighters. International peacekeeping force established. Fighting broke out again.

1979 Part of S Lebanon declared an 'independent free Lebanon'.
1982 Bachir Gemayel became president but was assassinated before he could assume office; succeeded by his brother Amin Gemayel. Israel again invaded Lebanon. Palestinians withdrew from Beirut under supervision of international peacekeeping force. PLO moved its headquarters to Tunis.
1983 Agreement reached for the withdrawal of Syrian and Israeli troops but abrogated under Syrian pressure.
1984 Most of international peacekeeping force withdrawn. Muslim militia took control of W Beirut.
1985 Lebanon in chaos; many foreigners taken hostage.
1987 Syrian troops sent into Beirut.
1988 Agreement on a Christian successor to Gemayel failed; he established a military government; Selim al-Hoss set up rival government; threat of partition hung over the country.
1989 Christian leader, General Michel Aoun declared 'war of liberation' against Syrian occupation; Saudis and Arab League sponsored talks resulted in new constitution recognizing Muslim majority; Rene1 Muhawad named president, assassinated after 17 days in office; Elias Hrawi named successor; Aoun occupied presidential palace, rejected constitution.
1990 Irish hostage Brian Keenan released. General Aoun surrendered and legitimate government restored, with Umar Karami as prime minister.
1991 Government extended control to the whole country. Treaty of cooperation with Syria signed. Western hostages Terry Anderson, Joseph Cicippio, Thomas Sutherland, and Terry Waite released. General Aoun pardoned.
1992 Karami resigned as prime minister; succeeded by Rashid al-Solh. Remaining Western hostages released.

Lesotho (Kingdom of)

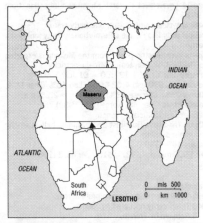

area 30,355 sq km/11,717 sq mi
capital Maseru
towns Teyateyaneng, Mafeteng, Roma, Quthing
physical mountainous with plateaus, forming part of South Africa's chief watershed
features Lesotho is an enclave within South Africa
political system military-controlled monarchy
head of state King Letsie III from 1990
head of government Elias Tutsoane Ramaema from 1991
political parties Basotho National Party (BNP), traditionalist, nationalist; Basutoland Congress Party (BCP); Basotho Democratic Alliance (BDA)
exports wool, mohair, diamonds, cattle, wheat, vegetables
currency maluti (4.68 = £1 July 1991)
population (1990 est) 1,757,000; growth rate 2.7% p.a.

life expectancy men 59, women 62 (1989)
languages Sesotho, English (official), Zulu, Xhosa
religion Protestant 42%, Roman Catholic 38%
literacy 59% (1988)
GNP $408 million; $410 per head (1988)

chronology
1868 Basutoland became a British protectorate.
1966 Independence achieved from Britain, within the Commonwealth, as the Kingdom of Lesotho, with Moshoeshoe II as king and Chief Leabua Jonathan as prime minister.
1970 State of emergency declared and constitution suspended.
1973 Progovernment interim assembly established; BNP won majority of seats.
1975 Members of the ruling party attacked by guerrillas backed by South Africa.
1985 Elections cancelled because no candidates opposed BNP.
1986 South Africa imposed border blockade, forcing deportation of 60 African National Congress members. General Lekhanya ousted Chief Jonathan in coup. National assembly abolished. Highlands Water Project agreement signed with South Africa.
1990 Moshoeshoe II dethroned by military council; replaced by his son Mohato as King Letsie III.
1991 Lekhanya ousted in military coup led by Col Elias Tutsoane Ramaema. Political parties permitted to operate.

Liberia (Republic of)

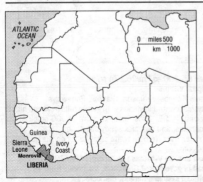

area 111,370 sq km/42,989 sq mi
capital and port Monrovia
towns ports Buchanan, Greenville
physical forested highlands; swampy tropical coast where six rivers enter the sea
features nominally the world's largest merchant navy as minimal registration controls make Liberia's a flag of convenience; the world's largest rubber plantations
head of state and government Amos Sawyer from 1990
political parties National Democratic Party of Liberia (NDLP), nationalist; Liberian Action Party; Liberian Unity Party; United People's Party; Unity Party
political system emergent democratic republic
exports iron ore, rubber (Africa's largest producer), timber, diamonds, coffee, cocoa, palm oil
currency Liberian dollar (1.61 = £1 July 1991)
population (1990 est) 2,644,000 (95% indigenous); growth rate 3% p.a.
life expectancy men 53, women 56 (1989)
languages English (official), over 20 Niger-Congo languages
media two daily newspapers, one published under government auspices, the other independent and with the largest circulation (10,000 copies)

religion animist 65%, Muslim 20%, Christian 15%
literacy men 47%, women 23% (1985 est)
GNP $973 million; $410 per head (1987)

chronology
1847 Founded as an independent republic.
1944 William Tubman elected president.
1971 Tubman died; succeeded by William Tolbert.
1980 Tolbert assassinated in coup led by Samuel Doe, who suspended the constitution and ruled through a People's Redemption Council.
1984 New constitution approved. National Democratic Party of Liberia (NDPL) founded by Doe.
1985 NDPL won decisive victory in general election. Unsuccessful coup against Doe.
1990 Rebels under former government minister Charles Taylor controlled nearly entire country by July. Doe killed during a bloody civil war between rival rebel factions. Amos Sawyer became interim head of government.
1991 Amos Sawyer re-elected president. Rebel leader Charles Taylor agreed to work together with Sawyer. Peace agreement failed but later revived; peacekeeping force drafted into republic.

Libya (Great Socialist People's Libyan Arab Jamahiriya)
(al-Jamahiriya al-Arabiya al-Libya al-Shabiya al-Ishtirakiya al-Uzma)

area 1,759,540 sq km/679,182 sq mi
capital Tripoli
towns ports Benghazi, Misurata, Tobruk
physical flat to undulating plains with plateaux and depressions stretch S from the Mediterranean coast to an extremely dry desert interior
environment plan to pump water from below the Sahara to the coast risks rapid exhaustion of nonrenewable supply (Great Manmade River Project)
features Gulf of Sirte; rock paintings of about 3000 BC in the Fezzan; Roman city sites include Leptis Magna, Sabratha
political system one-party socialist state
head of state and government Moamer al-Khaddhafi from 1969
political party Arab Socialist Union (ASU), radical, left-wing
exports oil, natural gas
currency Libyan dinar (LD0.48 = £1 July 1991)
population (1990 est) 4,280,000 (including 500,000 foreign workers); growth rate 3.1% p.a.
life expectancy men 64, women 69 (1989)
language Arabic
religion Sunni Muslim 97%
literacy 60% (1989)
GNP $20 bn; $5,410 per head (1988)

chronology
1911 Conquered by Italy.
1934 Colony named Libya.
1942 Divided into three provinces: Fezzan (under French control); Cyrenaica, Tripolitania (under British control).
1951 Achieved independence as the United Kingdom of Libya, under King Idris.
1969 King deposed in a coup led by Col Moamer al-Khaddhafi. Revolution Command Council set up and the Arab Socialist Union (ASU) proclaimed the only legal party.
1972 Proposed federation of Libya, Syria, and Egypt abandoned.
1980 Proposed merger with Syria abandoned. Libyan troops began fighting in Chad.
1981 Proposed merger with Chad abandoned.
1986 US bombing of Khaddhafi's headquarters, following allegations of his complicity in terrorist activities.
1988 Diplomatic relations with Chad restored.
1989 USA accused Libya of building a chemical-weapons factory and shot down two Libyan planes; reconciliation with Egypt.
1992 Khaddhafi under international pressure to send suspected Lockerbie bombers for trial outside Libya.

Liechtenstein (Principality of)
(Fürstentum Liechtenstein)

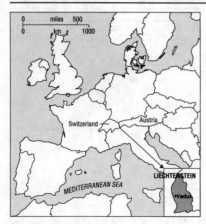

area 160 sq km/62 sq mi
capital Vaduz
towns Balzers, Schaan, Ruggell
physical landlocked alpine; includes part of Rhine Valley in W
features no airport or railway station; easy tax laws make it an international haven for foreign companies and banks (some 50,000 companies are registered)
head of state Prince Hans Adam II from 1989
head of government Hans Brunhart from 1978
political system constitutional monarchy
political parties Fatherland Union (VU); Progressive Citizens' Party (FBP)
exports microchips, dental products, small machinery, processed foods, postage stamps
currency Swiss franc (2.52 = £1 July 1991)
population (1990 est) 30,000 (33% foreign); growth rate 1.4% p.a.
life expectancy men 78, women 83 (1989)
language German (official); an Alemannic dialect is also spoken
religion Roman Catholic 87%, Protestant 8%
literacy 100% (1989)
GNP $450 million (1986)
GDP $1 bn (1987); $32,000 per head

chronology
1342 Became a sovereign state.
1434 Present boundaries established.
1719 Former counties of Schellenberg and Vaduz constituted as the Principality of Liechtenstein.
1921 Adopted Swiss currency.
1923 United with Switzerland in a customs union.
1938 Prince Franz Josef II came to power.
1984 Prince Franz Joseph II handed over power to Crown Prince Hans Adam. Vote extended to women in national elections.
1989 Prince Franz Joseph II died; Hans Adam II succeeded him. Liechtenstein sought admission to United Nations.
1990 Became a member of the United Nations.
1991 Became seventh member of European Free Trade Association (EFTA).

Lithuania (Republic of)

area 65,200 sq km/25,174 sq mi
capital Vilnius
towns Kaunas, Klaipeda, Siauliai, Panevezys
physical central lowlands with gentle hills in W and higher terrain in SE; 25% forested; some 3,000 small lakes, marshes, and complex sandy coastline
features river Nemen; white sand dunes on Kursiu Marios lagoon
head of state Vytautas Landsbergis from 1990
head of government Gediminas Vagnorius from 1991
political system emergent democracy
political parties Lithuanian Restructuring Movement (Sajudis), nationalist; Democratic Party, centrist; Humanism and Progress Party, reformist; Social Democratic Party, left-of-centre; Green Party, ecological; Christian Democratic Party, right-of-centre; Democratic Labour Party, 'reform communist'
products heavy engineering, electrical goods, shipbuilding, cement, food processing, bacon, dairy products, cereals, potatoes
currency Lithuanian rouble (no commercial exchange rate)
population (1990) 3,700,000 (Lithuanian 80%, Russian 9%, Polish 7%, Byelorussian 2%)
language Lithuanian
religion predominantly Roman Catholic

chronology
1918 Independence declared following withdrawal of German occupying troops at end of World War I; USSR attempted to regain power.
1919 Soviet forces overthrown by Germans, Poles, and nationalist Lithuanians; democratic republic established.
1920-39 Province and city of Vilnius occupied by Poles.
1926 Coup overthrew established government; Antanas Smetona became president.

1939 Secret German–Soviet agreement brought most of Lithuania under Soviet influence.
1940 Incorporated into USSR as constituent republic.
1941 Lithuania revolted against USSR and established own government. During World War II Germany again occupied the country.
1944 USSR resumed rule.
1944-52 Lithuanian guerrillas fought USSR.
1972 Demonstrations against Soviet government.
1980 Growth in nationalist dissent, influenced by Polish example.
1988 Popular front formed, the Lithuanian Restructuring Movement (Sajudis) to campaign for increased autonomy.
1989 Lithuanian declared the state language; flag of independent interwar republic readopted. Communist Party split into pro-Moscow and nationalist wings. Communist local monopoly of power ablished.
1990 Feb: nationalist Sajudis won elections. March: Vytautas Landsbergis became president; unilateral declaration of independence resulted in temporary Soviet blockade.
1991 Jan: Prime Minister Kazimiera Prunskiene resigned; replaced by Albertas Shiminas. Soviet paratroopers briefly occupied political and communications buildings in Vilnius. Sept: independence recognized by Soviet government and Western nations; Gediminas Vagnorius elected prime minister; Communist Party outlawed; admitted into UN and CSCE.

Luxembourg (Grand Duchy of)
(Grand-Duché de Luxembourg)

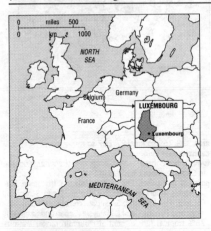

area 2,586 sq km/998 sq mi
capital Luxembourg
towns Esch-sur-Alzette, Dudelange
physical on the river Moselle; part of the Ardennes (Oesling) forest in N
features seat of the European Court of Justice, Secretariat of the European Parliament, international banking centre; economically linked with Belgium
head of state Grand Duke Jean from 1964
head of government Jacques Santer from 1984
political system liberal democracy
political parties Christian Social Party (PCS), moderate, left-of-centre; Luxembourg Socialist Workers' Party (POSL), moderate, socialist; Democratic Party (PD), centre-left; Communist Party of Luxembourg, pro-European left-wing
exports pharmaceuticals, synthetic textiles, steel
currency Luxembourg franc (60.30 = £1 July 1991)
population (1990 est) 369,000; growth rate 0% p.a.
life expectancy men 71, women 78 (1989)

languages French (official), local Letzeburgesch, German
religion Roman Catholic 97%
literacy 100% (1989)
GNP $4.9 bn; $13,380 per head (1988)

chronology
1354 Became a duchy.
1482 Under Habsburg control.
1797 Ceded, with Belgium, to France.
1815 Treaty of Vienna created Luxembourg a grand duchy, ruled by the king of the Netherlands.
1830 With Belgium, revolted against Dutch rule.
1890 Link with Netherlands ended with accession of Grand Duke Adolphe of Nassau-Weilburg.
1948 With Belgium and the Netherlands, formed the Benelux customs union.
1960 Benelux became fully effective economic union.
1961 Prince Jean became acting head of state on behalf of his mother, Grand Duchess Charlotte.
1964 Grand Duchess Charlotte abdicated; Prince Jean became grand duke.
1974 Dominance of Christian Social Party challenged by Socialists.
1979 Christian Social Party regained pre-eminence.

Madagascar (Democratic Republic of)
(Repoblika Demokratika n'i Madagaskar)

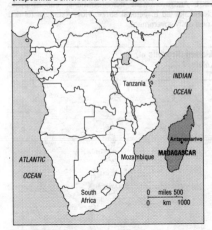

area 587,041 sq km/226,598 sq mi
capital Antananarivo
towns chief port Toamasina, Antseranana, Fianarantsoa, Toliary
physical temperate central highlands; humid valleys and tropical coastal plains; arid in S
environment according to 1990 UN figures, 93% of the forest area has been destroyed and about 100,000 species have been made extinct
features one of the last places to be inhabited, it evolved in isolation with unique animals (such as the lemur, now under threat from deforestation)
head of state Didier Ratsiraka from 1975
head of government Guy Razanamasy from 1991
political system emergent democratic republic
political parties National Front for the Defence of the Malagasy Socialist Revolution (FNDR); AKFM-Congress and AKFM-Renewal, both left-of-centre; Social Democratic Party (PSD), centre-left
exports coffee, cloves, vanilla, sugar, chromite, shrimps
currency Malagasy franc (2,968.50 = £1 July 1991)
population (1990 est) 11,802,000, mostly of Malayo-Indonesian origin; growth rate 3.2% p.a.
life expectancy men 50, women 53 (1989)
languages Malagasy (official), French, English

religion animist 50%, Christian 40%, Muslim 10%
literacy 53% (1988)
GNP $2.1 bn (1987); $280 per head (1988)

chronology
1885 Became a French protectorate.
1896 Became a French colony.
1960 Independence achieved from France, with Philibert Tsiranana as president.
1972 Army took control of the government.
1975 Martial law imposed under a national military directorate. New Marxist constitution proclaimed the Democratic Republic of Madagascar, with Didier Ratsiraka as president.
1976 Front-Line Revolutionary Organization (AREMA) formed.
1977 National Front for the Defence of the Malagasy Socialist Revolution (FNDR) became the sole legal political organization.
1980 Ratsiraka abandoned Marxist experiment.
1983 Ratsiraka re-elected, despite strong opposition from radical socialist National Movement for the Independence of Madagascar (MONIMA) under Monja Jaona.
1989 Ratsiraka re-elected for third term after restricting opposition parties.
1990 Political opposition legalized; 36 new parties created.
1991 Antigovernment demonstrations; opposition to Ratsiraka led to general strike. Nov: Ratsiraka formed new unity government.

Malawi (Republic of)
(Malaŵi)

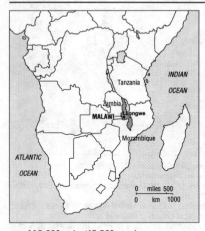

area 118,000 sq km/45,560 sq mi
capital Lilongwe
towns Blantyre (largest city and commercial centre), Mzuzu, Zomba
physical landlocked narrow plateau with rolling plains; mountainous W of Lake Malawi
features one-third is water, including lakes Malawi, Chilara, and Malombe; Great Rift Valley; Nyika, Kasungu, and Lengare national parks; Mulanje Massif; Shire River
head of state and government Hastings Kamuzu Banda from 1966 for life
political system one-party republic
political party Malawi Congress Party (MCP), multiracial, right-wing
exports tea, tobacco, cotton, peanuts, sugar
currency kwacha (K.4.75 = £1 July 1991)
population (1990 est) 9,080,000 (nearly 1 million refugees from Mozambique); growth rate 3.3% p.a.

life expectancy men 46, women 50 (1989)
languages English, Chichewa (both official)
religion Christian 75%, Muslim 20%
literacy 25% (1989)
GNP $1.2 bn (1987); $160 per head (1988)

chronology
1891 Became the British protectorate Nyasaland.
1964 Independence achieved from Britain, within the Commonwealth, as Malawi.
1966 Became a one-party republic, with Hastings Banda as president.
1971 Banda was made president for life.
1977 Banda started a programme of moderate liberalization, releasing some political detainees and allowing greater freedom of the press.
1986-89 Influx of nearly 1 million refugees from Mozambique.
1992 Country-wide industrial riots caused many fatalities. Calls for multiparty politics.

Malaysia

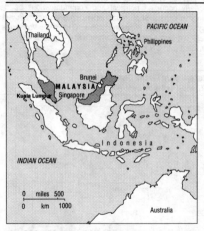

area 329,759 sq km/127,287 sq mi
capital Kuala Lumpur
towns Johor Baharu, Ipoh, Georgetown (Penang), Kuching in Sarawak, Kota Kinabalu in Sabah
physical comprises Peninsular Malaysia (the nine Malay states—Johore, Kedah, Kelantan, Negri Sembilan, Pahang, Perak, Perlis, Selangor, Trengganu—plus Malacca and Penang); and E Malaysia (Sabah and Sarawak); 75% tropical jungle; central mountain range; swamps in E
features Mount Kinabalu (highest peak in SE Asia); Niah caves (Sarawak)
head of state Rajah Azlan Muhibuddin Shah (sultan of Perak) from 1989
head of government Mahathir bin Mohamad from 1981
political system liberal democracy
political parties New United Malays' National Organization (UMNO Baru), Malay-orientated nationalist; Malaysian Chinese Association (MCA), Chinese-orientated conservative; Gerakan Party, Chinese-orientated left-of-centre; Malaysian Indian Congress (MIC), Indian-orientated; Democratic Action Party (DAP), left-of-centre multiracial, but Chinese dominated; Pan- Malayan Islamic Party (PAS), Islamic; Spirit of 1946 (Semangat '46), moderate, multiracial
exports pineapples, palm oil, rubber, timber, petroleum (Sarawak), bauxite
currency ringgit (4.52 = £1 July 1991)
population (1990 est) 17,053,000 (Malaysian 47%,

Chinese 32%, Indian 8%, others 13%); growth rate 2% p.a.
life expectancy men 65, women 70 (1989)
languages Malay (official), English, Chinese, Indian, and local languages
religion Muslim (official), Buddhist, Hindu, local beliefs
literacy 80% (1989)
GNP $34.3 bn; $1,870 per head (1988)

chronology
1786 Britain established control.
1826 Became a British colony.
1963 Federation of Malaysia formed, including Malaya, Singapore, Sabah (N Borneo), and Sarawak (NW Borneo).
1965 Secession of Singapore from federation.
1969 Anti-Chinese riots in Kuala Lumpur.
1971 Launch of *bumiputra* ethnic-Malaya-oriented 'new economic policy'.
1981 Election of Dr Mahathir bin Mohamad as prime minister.
1982 Mahathir bin Mohamad re-elected.
1986 Mahathir bin Mohamad re-elected.
1987 Arrest of over 100 opposition activists, including DAP leader, as Malay-Chinese relations deteriorated.
1988 Split in ruling UMNO party over Mahathir's leadership style; new UMNO formed.
1989 Semangat '46 set up by former members of UMNO including ex-premier Tunku Abdul Rahman.
1990 Mahathir bin Mohamad re-elected.
1991 New economic growth programme launched.

Maldives (Republic of)
(Divehi Jumhuriya)

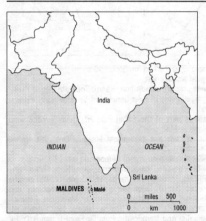

area 298 sq km/115 sq mi
capital Malé
towns Seenu
physical comprises 1,196 coral islands, grouped into 12 clusters of atolls, largely flat, none bigger than 13 sq km/5 sq mi, average elevation 1.8 m/6 ft; 203 are inhabited
environment the threat of rising sea level has been heightened by the frequency of flooding in recent years
features tourism developed since 1972
head of state and government Maumoon Abdul Gayoom from 1978
political system authoritarian nationalism
political parties none; candidates elected on the basis of personal influence and clan loyalties
exports coconuts, copra, bonito (fish related to tuna), garments
currency Rufiya (16.20 = £1 July 1991)

population (1990 est) 219,000; growth rate 3.7% p.a.
life expectancy men 60, women 63 (1989)
languages Divehi (Sinhalese dialect), English
religion Sunni Muslim
literacy 36% (1989)
GNP $69 million (1987); $410 per head (1988)

chronology
1887 Became a British protectorate.
1953 Long a sultanate, the Maldive Islands became a republic within the Commonwealth.
1954 Sultan restored.
1965 Achieved full independence outside the Commonwealth.
1968 Sultan deposed; republic reinstated with Ibrahim Nasir as president.
1978 Nasir retired; replaced by Maumoon Abdul Gayoom.
1982 Rejoined the Commonwealth.
1983 Gayoom re-elected.
1985 Became a founder member of South Asian Association for Regional Cooperation (SAARC).
1988 Gayoom re-elected. Coup attempt by mercenaries thought to have the backing of former president Nasir was foiled by Indian paratroops.

Mali (Republic of)
(République du Mali)

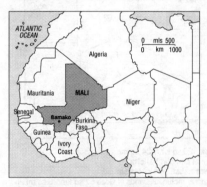

area 1,240,142 sq km/478,695 sq mi
capital Bamako
towns Mopti, Kayes, Ségou, Timbuktu
physical landlocked state with river Niger and savanna in S; part of the Sahara in N; hills in NE; Senegal River and its branches irrigate the SW
environment a rising population coupled with recent droughts has affected marginal agriculture. Once in surplus, Mali has had to import grain every year since 1965
features ancient town of Timbuktu; railway to Dakar is the only outlet to the sea
head of state and government Alpha Oumar Konare from 1992
political system emergent democratic republic
political parties Alliance for Democracy in Mali (ADEMA), centrist; National Committee for Democratic Initiative (CNID), centre-left; Sudanese Union–African Democratic Rally (US–RDA), Sudanese nationalist
exports cotton, peanuts, livestock, fish
currency franc CFA (498.25 = £1 July 1991)
population (1990 est) 9,182,000; growth rate 2.9% p.a.
life expectancy men 44, women 47 (1989)
languages French (official), Bambara
religion Sunni Muslim 90%, animist 9%, Christian 1%
literacy 10% (1989)
GNP $1.6 bn (1987); $230 per head (1988)

chronology
1895 Came under French rule.
1959 With Senegal, formed the Federation of Mali.
1960 Became the independent Republic of Mali, with Modibo Keita as president.
1968 Keita replaced in an army coup by Moussa Traoré.
1974 New constitution made Mali a one-party state.
1976 New national party, the Malian People's Democratic Union, announced.
1983 Agreement between Mali and Guinea for eventual political and economic integration signed.
1985 Conflict with Burkina Faso lasted five days; mediated by International Court of Justice.
1991 Demonstrations against one-party rule. Moussa Traoré ousted in a coup led by Lt-Col Amadou Toumani Toure. New constitution agreed, subject to referendum.
1992 Referendum endorsed new democratic constitution. Alliance for Democracy in Mali (ADEMA) won multiparty elections; Alpha Oumar Konare elected president.

1962 Nationalists elected, with Borg Olivier as prime minister.
1964 Independence achieved from Britain, within the Commonwealth. Ten-year defence and economic aid treaty with UK signed.
1971 Mintoff re-elected. 1964 treaty declared invalid and negotiations began for leasing the NATO base in Malta.
1972 Seven-year NATO agreement signed.
1974 Became a republic.
1979 British military base closed.
1984 Mintoff retired and was replaced by Mifsud Bonnici as prime minister and MLP leader.
1987 Edward Fenech Adami (Nationalist) elected prime minister.
1989 Vincent Tabone elected president. USA–USSR summit held offshore.
1990 Formal application made for EC membership.
1992 Nationalist Party re-elected in general election.

Malta (Republic of)
(Repubblika Ta'Malta)

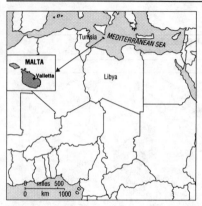

area 320 sq km/124 sq mi
capital and port Valletta
towns Rabat; port of Marsaxlokk
physical includes islands of Gozo 67 sq km/26 sq mi and Comino 2.5 sq km/1 sq mi
features occupies strategic location in central Mediterranean; large commercial dock facilities
head of state Vincent Tabone from 1989
head of government Edward Fenech Adami from 1987
political system liberal democracy
political parties Malta Labour Party (MLP), moderate, left-of-centre; Nationalist Party, Christian, centrist, pro-European
exports vegetables, knitwear, handmade lace, plastics, electronic equipment
currency Maltese lira (Lm 0.55 = £1 July 1991)
population (1990 est) 373,000; growth rate 0.7% p.a.
life expectancy men 72, women 77 (1987)
languages Maltese, English
religion Roman Catholic 98%
literacy 90% (1988)
GNP $1.6 bn; $4,750 per head (1988)
chronology
1814 Annexed to Britain by the Treaty of Paris.
1947 Achieved self-government.
1955 Dom Mintoff of the Malta Labour Party (MLP) became prime minister.
1956 Referendum approved MLP's proposal for integration with the UK. Proposal opposed by the Nationalist Party.
1958 MLP rejected the British integration proposal.

Mauritania (Islamic Republic of)
(République Islamique de Mauritanie)

area 1,030,700 sq km/397,850 sq mi
capital Nouakchott
towns port of Nouadhibou, Kaédi, Zouérate
physical valley of river Senegal in S; remainder arid and flat
features part of the Sahara Desert; dusty sirocco wind blows in March
head of state and government Maaouia Ould Sid Ahmed Taya from 1984
political system emergent democratic republic
political parties Democratic and Social Republican Party (PRDS), centre-left, militarist; Union of Democratic Forces (UFD), centre-left; Rally for Democracy and National Unity (RDUN), centrist; Mauritian Renewal Party (PMR), centrist; Umma, Islamic fundamentalist; Socialist and Democratic Popular Front Union (UDSP), left-of-centre
exports iron ore, fish, gypsum
currency ouguiya (134.97 = £1 March 1990)
population (1990 est) 2,038,000 (30% Arab-Berber, 30% black Africans, 30% Haratine—descendants of black slaves, who remained slaves until 1980); growth rate 3% p.a.
life expectancy men 43, women 48 (1989)
languages French (official), Hasaniya Arabic, black African languages
religion Sunni Muslim 99%
literacy 17% (1987)
GNP $843 million; $480 per head (1988)

chronology
1903 Became a French protectorate.
1960 Independence achieved from France, with Moktar Ould Daddah as president.

1975 Western Sahara ceded by Spain. Mauritania occupied the southern area and Morocco the north. Polisario Front formed in Sahara to resist the occupation by Mauritania and Morocco.
1978 Daddah deposed in bloodless coup; replaced by Mohamed Khouna Ould Haidalla. Peace agreed with Polisario Front.
1981 Diplomatic relations with Morocco broken.
1984 Haidalla overthrown by Maaouia Ould Sid Ahmed Taya. Polisario regime formally recognized.
1985 Relations with Morocco restored.
1989 Violent clashes between Mauritanians and Senegalese. Arab-dominated government expelled thousands of Africans into N Senegal; governments had earlier agreed to repatriate each other's citizens (about 250,000).
1991 Amnesty for political prisoners. Multiparty elections promised. Calls for resignation of President Taya.
1992 First multiparty elections won by ruling PRDS. Diplomacy with Senegal resumed.

Mauritius (Republic of)

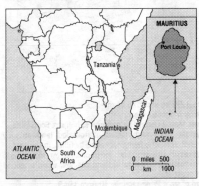

area 1,865 sq km/720 sq mi; the island of Rodrigues is part of Mauritius; there are several small island dependencies
capital Port Louis
towns Beau Bassin-Rose Hill, Curepipe, Quatre Bornes
physical mountainous, volcanic island surrounded by coral reefs
features unusual wildlife includes flying fox and ostrich; it was the home of the dodo (extinct from about 1680)
interim head of state Veerasamy Ringadoo from 1992
head of government Aneerood Jugnauth from 1982
political system liberal democratic republic
political parties Mauritius Socialist Movement (MSM), moderate socialist-republican; Mauritius Labour Party (MLP), centrist, Hindu-orientated; Mauritius Social Democratic Party (PMSD), conservative, Francophile; Mauritius Militant Movement (MMM), Marxist-republican; Rodriguais People's Organization (OPR), left-of-centre
exports sugar, knitted goods, tea
currency Mauritius rupee (27.05 = £1 July 1991)
population (1990 est) 1,141,900, 68% of Indian origin; growth rate 1.5% p.a.
life expectancy men 64, women 71 (1989)
languages English (official), French, creole, Indian languages
religion Hindu 51%, Christian 30%, Muslim 17%
literacy 94% (1989)
GNP $1.4 bn (1987); $1,810 per head (1988)

chronology
1814 Annexed to Britain by the Treaty of Paris.
1968 Independence achieved from Britain within the Commonwealth, with Seewoosagur Ramgoolam as prime minister.
1982 Aneerood Jugnauth became prime minister.
1983 Jugnauth formed a new party, the Mauritius Socialist Movement. Ramgoolam appointed governor general. Jugnauth formed a new coalition government.
1985 Ramgoolam died, succeeded by Veersamy Ringadoo.
1987 Jugnauth's coalition re-elected.
1990 Attempt to create a republic failed.
1991 Jugnauth's ruling MSM–MMM–OPR coalition won general election; pledge to secure republican status by 1992.
1992 Mauritius became a republic whilst remaining a member of the Commonwealth. Ringadoo became interim president.

Mexico (United States of)
(Estados Unidos Mexicanos)

area 1,958,201 sq km/756,198 sq mi
capital Mexico City
towns Guadalajara, Monterrey; port Veracruz
physical partly arid central highlands; Sierra Madre mountain ranges E and W; tropical coastal plains
environment during the 1980s, smog levels in Mexico City exceeded World Health Organization standards on more than 300 days of the year. Air is polluted by 130,000 factories and 2.5 million vehicles
features Rio Grande; 3,218 km/2,000 mi frontier with USA; resorts Acapulco, Cancun, Mexicali, Tijuana; Baja California, Yucatan peninsula; volcanoes, including Popocatepetl; pre-Columbian archaeological sites
head of state and government Carlos Salinas de Gortari from 1988
political system federal democratic republic
political parties Institutional Revolutionary Party (PRI), moderate, left-wing; National Action Party (PAN), moderate Christian socialist
exports silver, gold, lead, uranium, oil, natural gas, handicrafts, fish, shellfish, fruits and vegetables, cotton, machinery
currency peso (free rate 4,900.00 = £1 July 1991)
population (1990 est) 88,335,000 (60% mixed descent, 30% Indian, 10% Spanish descent); 50% under 20 years of age; growth rate 2.6% p.a.
life expectancy men 67, women 73
languages Spanish (official) 92%, Nahuatl, Maya, Mixtec
religion Roman Catholic 97%
literacy men 92%, women 88% (1989)
GNP $126 bn (1987); $2,082 per head

chronology
1821 Independence achieved from Spain.
1846-48 Mexico at war with USA; loss of territory.

1848 Maya Indian revolt suppressed.
1864-67 Maximilian of Austria was emperor of Mexico.
1917 New constitution introduced, designed to establish permanent democracy.
1983-84 Financial crisis.
1985 Institutional Revolutionary Party (PRI) returned to power. Earthquake in Mexico City.
1986 IMF loan agreement signed to keep the country solvent until at least 1988.
1988 PRI candidate Carlos Salinas Gotari elected president. Debt reduction accords negotiated with USA.
1991 PRI won general election. President Salinas promised constitutional reforms.

Moldova (Republic of)

area 33,700 sq km/13,012 sq mi
capital Chisinau (Kishinev)
towns Tiraspol, Beltsy, Bendery
physical hilly land lying largely between the rivers Prut and Dnestr; northern Moldova comprises the level plain of the Beltsy Steppe and uplands; the climate is warm and moderately continental
features Black Earth region
head of state Mircea Snegur from 1989
head of government Valeriu Muravski
political system emergent democracy
political parties Moldavian Popular Front (MPF), Romanian nationalist; Gagauz-Khalky People's Movement (GKPM), Gagauz separatist
products wine, tobacco, canned goods
population (1990) 4,400,000 (Moldavian 64%, Ukrainian 14%, Russian 13%, Gagauzi 4%, Bulgarian 2%)
language Moldavian, allied to Romanian
religion Russian Orthodox

chronology
1940 Bessarabia in the E became part of the Soviet Union whereas the W part remained in Romania.
1941 Bessarabia taken over by Romania-Germany.
1944 Red army reconquered Bessarabia.
1946-47 Widespread famine.
1988 A popular front, the Democratic Movement for Perestroika, campaigned for accelerated political reform.
1989 Jan-Feb: nationalist demonstrations in Chisinau. May: Moldavian Popular Front established. July: Snegur became head of state. Aug: Moldavian language granted official status triggering clashes between ethnic Russians and Moldavians. Nov: Gagauz-Khalky People's Movement formed to campaign for Gagauz autonomy.
1990 Feb: Popular Front polled strongly in supreme soviet elections. June: economic and political sovereignty declared; renamed Republic of Moldova. Oct: Gagauz held unauthorized elections to independent parliament; state of emergency declared after inter-ethnic clashes.

1991 March: Moldova boycotted the USSR's constitutional referendum. Aug: independence declared after abortive anti-Gorbachev coup; Communist Party outlawed. Sept: Dnestr region declared independence from Moldova. Dec: Moldova joined new Commonwealth of Independent States (CIS); independence acknowledged by USA but diplomatic recognition withheld.
1992 Jan: admitted into CSCE. State of emergency imposed as civil war with secessionist Trans-Dnestr region escalated.

Monaco (Principality of)

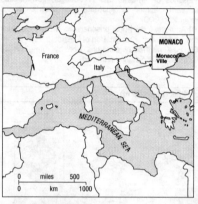

area 1.95 sq km/0.75 sq mi
capital Monaco-Ville
towns Monte Carlo, La Condamine; heliport Fontvieille
physical steep and rugged; surrounded landwards by French territory; being expanded by filling in the sea
features aquarium and oceanographic centre; Monte Carlo film festival, motor races, and casinos; world's second smallest state
head of state Prince Rainier III from 1949
head of government Jean Ausseil from 1986
political system constitutional monarchy under French protectorate
political parties National and Democratic Union (UND); Democratic Union Movement; Monaco Action; Monégasque Socialist Party
exports some light industry; economy dependent on tourism and gambling
currency French franc (9.96 = £1 July 1991)
population (1989) 29,000; growth rate –0.5% p.a.
languages French (official), English, Italian
religion Roman Catholic 95%
literacy 99% (1985)

chronology
1861 Became an independent state under French protection.
1918 France given a veto over succession to the throne.
1949 Prince Rainier III ascended the throne.
1956 Prince Rainier married US actress Grace Kelly.
1958 Birth of male heir, Prince Albert.
1959 Constitution of 1911 suspended.
1962 New constitution adopted.

Mongolia (State of)
(Outer Mongolia until *1924; People's Republic of Mongolia* until *1991)*

area 1,565,000 sq km/604,480 sq mi
capital Ulaanbaatar
towns Darhan, Choybalsan
physical high plateau with desert and steppe (grasslands)

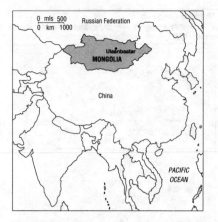

features Altai Mountains in SW; salt lakes; part of Gobi Desert in SE
head of state Punsalmaagiyn Ochirbat from 1990
head of government Dashiyn Byambasuren from 1990
political system emergent democracy
political parties Mongolian People's Revolutionary Party (MPRP), reform-communist; Mongolian Democratic Party (MDP), main opposition party; Mongolian Democratic Union
exports meat and hides, minerals, wool, livestock, grain, cement, timber
currency tugrik (5.45 = £1 July 1991)
population (1990 est) 2,185,000; growth rate 2.8% p.a.
life expectancy men 63, women 67 (1989)
languages Khalkha Mongolian (official), Chinese, Russian and Turkic languages
religion officially none (Tibetan Buddhist Lamaism suppressed 1930s)
literacy 89% (1985)
GNP $3.6 bn; $1,820 per head (1986)

chronology
1911 Outer Mongolia gained autonomy from China.
1915 Chinese sovereignty reasserted.
1921 Chinese rule overthrown with Soviet help.
1924 People's Republic proclaimed.
1946 China recognized Mongolia's independence.
1966 20-year friendship, cooperation, and mutual-assistance pact signed with USSR. Relations with China deteriorated.
1984 Yumjaagiyn Tsedenbal, effective leader, deposed and replaced by Jambyn Batmonh.
1987 Soviet troops reduced; Mongolia's external contacts broadened.
1989 Further Soviet troop reductions.
1990 Democratization campaign launched by Mongolian Democratic Union. Ochirbat's Mongolian People's Revolutionary Party elected in free multiparty elections. Mongolian script readopted.
1991 Massive privatization programme launched as part of move towards a market economy. The word 'Republic' dropped from country's name.
1992 New constitution introduced. Worsening economic situation. Prime minister's resignation refused.

Morocco (Kingdom of)
(al-Mamlaka al-Maghrebia)

---

area 458,730 sq km/177,070 sq mi (excluding Western Sahara)
capital Rabat
towns Marrakesh, Fez, Meknès; ports Casablanca, Tangier, Agadir
physical mountain ranges NE–SW; fertile coastal plains in W
features Atlas Mountains; the towns Ceuta (from 1580) and Melilla (from 1492) are held by Spain; tunnel crossing the Strait of Gibraltar to Spain proposed 1985
head of state Hassan II from 1961
head of government Azzedine Laraki from 1985
political system constitutional monarchy
political parties Constitutional Union (UC), right-wing; National Rally of Independents (RNI), royalist; Popular Movement (MP), moderate socialist; Istiqlal, nationalist, right-of-centre; Socialist Union of Popular Forces (USFP), progressive socialist; National Democratic Party (PND), moderate, nationalist
exports dates, figs, cork, wood pulp, canned fish, phosphates
currency dirham (DH) (14.76 = £1 July 1991)
population (1990 est) 26,249,000; growth rate 2.5% p.a.

life expectancy men 62, women 65 (1989)
languages Arabic (official) 75%, Berber 25%, French, Spanish
religion Sunni Muslim 99%
literacy men 45%, women 22% (1985 est)
GNP $18.7 bn; $750 per head (1988)

chronology
1912 Morocco divided into French and Spanish protectorates.
1956 Independence achieved as the Sultanate of Morocco.
1957 Sultan restyled king of Morocco.
1961 Hassan II came to the throne.
1969 Former Spanish province of Ifni returned to Morocco.
1972 Major revision of the constitution.
1975 Western Sahara ceded by Spain to Morocco and Mauritania.
1976 Guerrilla war in Western Sahara with the Polisario Front. Sahrawi Arab Democratic Republic (SADR) established in Algiers. Diplomatic relations between Morocco and Algeria broken.
1979 Mauritania signed a peace treaty with Polisario.
1983 Peace formula for Western Sahara proposed by the Organization of African Unity (OAU); Morocco agreed but refused to deal directly with Polisario.
1984 Hassan signed an agreement for cooperation and mutual defence with Libya.
1987 Cease-fire agreed with Polisario, but fighting continued.
1988 Diplomatic relations with Algeria restored.
1989 Diplomatic relations with Syria restored.

Mozambique (People's Republic of)
(*República Popular de Moçambique*)

area 799,380 sq km/308,561 sq mi
capital and chief port Maputo
towns Beira, Nampula
physical mostly flat tropical lowland; mountains in W
features rivers Zambezi, Limpopo; 'Beira Corridor' rail, road, and pipeline link with Zimbabwe
head of state and government Joaquim Alberto Chissano from 1986
political system emergent democratic republic
political party National Front for the Liberation of Mozambique (Frelimo), Marxist-Leninist; Renamo or Mozambique National Resistance (MNR), former rebel movement
exports prawns, cashews, sugar, cotton, tea, petroleum products, copra
currency metical (replaced escudo 1980) (2,462.87 ∞ £1 July 1991)
population (1990 est) 14,718,000 (mainly indigenous Bantu peoples; Portuguese 50,000); growth rate 2.8% p.a.; nearly 1 million refugees in Malawi
life expectancy men 45, women 48 (1989)
languages Portuguese (official), 16 African languages
religion animist 60%, Roman Catholic 18%, Muslim 16%
literacy men 55%, women 22% (1985 est)
GDP $4.7 bn; $319 per head (1987)

chronology
1505 Mozambique became a Portuguese colony.
1962 Frelimo (liberation front) established.
1975 Independence achieved from Portugal as a socialist republic, with Samora Machel as president and Frelimo as the sole legal party.
1977 Renamo resistance group formed.
1983 Re-establishment of good relations with Western powers.
1984 Nkomati accord of nonagression signed with South Africa.
1986 Machel killed in air crash; succeeded by Joaquim Chissano.
1988 Tanzania announced withdrawal of its troops. South Africa provided training for Mozambican forces.
1989 Frelimo offered to abandon Marxist-Leninism; Chissano re-elected. Renamo continued attacks on government facilities and civilians.
1990 One-party rule officially ended. Partial cease-fire agreed.
1991 Peace talks resumed in Rome, delaying democratic process. Attempted antigovernment coup thwarted.

Myanmar (Union of)
(*Thammada Myanmar Naingngandaw*) (formerly *Burma* until 1989)

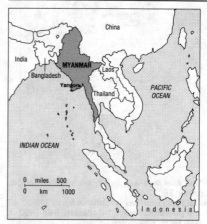

area 676,577 sq km/261,228 sq mi
capital and chief port Yangon (formerly Rangoon)
towns Mandalay, Moulmein, Pegu
physical over half is rainforest; rivers Irrawaddy and Chindwin in central lowlands ringed by mountains in N, W, and E
environment landslides and flooding during the rainy season (June–Sept) are becoming more frequent as a result of deforestation
features ruined cities of Pagan and Mingun
head of state and government Than Shwe from 1992
political system military republic
political parties National Unity Party (NUP), military-socialist ruling party; National League for Democracy (NLD), pluralist opposition grouping
exports rice, rubber, jute, teak, jade, rubies, sapphires
currency kyat (K 10.79 = £1 July 1991)
population (1990 est) 41,279,000; growth rate 1.9% p.a. (includes Shan, Karen, Raljome, Chinese, and Indian minorities)
life expectancy men 53, women 56 (1989)
language Burmese
religion Hinayana Buddhist 85%, animist, Christian
literacy 66% (1989)
GNP $9.3 bn (1988); $210 per head (1989)

chronology
1886 United as province of British India.
1937 Became crown colony in the British Commonwealth.
1942-45 Occupied by Japan.
1948 Independence achieved from Britain. Left the Commonwealth.
1962 General Ne Win assumed power in army coup.
1973-74 Adopted presidential-style 'civilian' constitution.
1975 Opposition National Democratic Front formed.
1986 Several thousand supporters of opposition leader Suu Kyi arrested.
1988 Government resigned after violent demonstrations. General Saw Maung seized power in military coup Sept; over 1,000 killed.
1989 Martial law declared; thousands arrested including advocates of democracy and human rights. Country renamed Myanmar and capital Yangon.
1990 Breakaway opposition group formed 'parallel government' on rebel-held territory.
1991 Martial law and human-rights abuses continued. Military offensives continued. Opposition leader, Aung San Suu Kyi, received Nobel Peace Prize.

1992 Jan-April: Pogrom against Muslim community in Arakan province, W Myanmar, carried out with army backing. April: Saw Maung replaced by Than Shwe. Several political prisoners liberated.

Namibia (Republic of)
(formerly *South West Africa*)

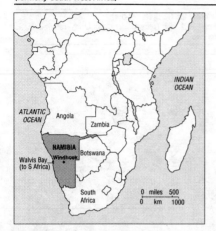

area 824,300 sq km/318,262 sq mi
capital Windhoek
towns Swakopmund, Rehoboth, Rundu
physical mainly desert
features Namib and Kalahari deserts; Orange River; Caprivi Strip links Namibia to Zambezi River; includes the enclave of Walvis Bay (area 1,120 sq km/432 sq mi)
head of state and government Sam Nujoma from 1990
political system democratic republic
political parties South-West Africa People's Organization (SWAPO), socialist Ovambo-orientated; Democratic Turnhalle Alliance (DTA), moderate, multiracial coalition; United Democratic Front (UDF), disaffected ex-SWAPO members; National Christian Action (ACN), white conservative
exports diamonds, uranium, copper, lead, zinc
currency South African rand (R 4.68 = £1 July 1991)
population (1990 est) 1,372,000 (85% black African, 6% European)
life expectancy blacks 40, whites 69
languages Afrikaans (spoken by 60% of white population), German, English (all official), several indigenous languages
religion 51% Lutheran, 19% Roman Catholic, 6% Dutch Reformed Church, 6% Anglican
literacy whites 100%, nonwhites 16%
GNP $1.6 bn; $1,300 per head (1988)

chronology
1884 German and British colonies established.
1915 German colony seized by South Africa.
1920 Administered by South Africa, under League of Nations mandate, as British South Africa.
1946 Full incorporation in South Africa refused by United Nations (UN).
1958 South-West Africa People's Organization (SWAPO) set up to seek racial equality and full independence.
1966 South Africa's apartheid laws extended to the country.
1968 Redesignated Namibia by UN.
1978 UN Security Council Resolution 435 for the granting of full sovereignty accepted by South Africa and then rescinded.
1988 Peace talks between South Africa, Angola, and Cuba led to agreement on full independence for Namibia.

1989 Unexpected incursion by SWAPO guerrillas from Angola into Namibia threatened agreed independence. Transitional constitution created by elected representatives; SWAPO dominant party.
1990 Liberal multiparty 'independence' constitution adopted; independence achieved. Sam Nujoma elected president.
1991 Joint administration of Walvis Bay agreed with South Africa.

Nauru (Republic of)
(*Naoero*)

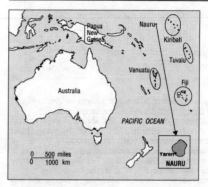

area 21 sq km/8 sq mi
capital (seat of government) Yaren District
physical tropical island country in SW Pacific; plateau encircled by coral cliffs and sandy beaches
features lies just S of equator; one of three phosphate rock islands in the Pacific
head of state and government Bernard Dowiyogo from 1989
political system liberal democracy
political party Democratic Party of Nauru (DPN), opposition to government
exports phosphates
currency Australian dollar ($A2.11 = £1 July 1991)
population (1990 est) 8,100 (mainly Polynesian; Chinese 8%, European 8%); growth rate 1.7% p.a.
languages Nauruan (official), English
religion Protestant 66%, Roman Catholic 33%
literacy 99% (1988)
GNP $160 million (1986); $9,091 per head (1985)

chronology
1888 Annexed by Germany.
1920 Administered by Australia, New Zealand, and UK until independence, except 1942-45, when it was occupied by Japan.
1968 Independence achieved from Australia, New Zealand, and UK with 'special member' Commonwealth status. Hammer DeRoburt elected president.
1976 Bernard Dowiyogo elected president.
1978 DeRoburt re-elected.
1986 DeRoburt briefly replaced as president by Kennan Adeang.
1987 DeRoburt re-elected; Adeang established the Democratic Party of Nauru.
1989 DeRoburt replaced by Kensas Aroi, who was later succeeded by Bernard Dowiyogo.

Nepal (Kingdom of)
(*Nepal Adhirajya*)

area 147,181 sq km/56,850 sq mi
capital Katmandu
towns Pátan, Moráng, Bhádgáon

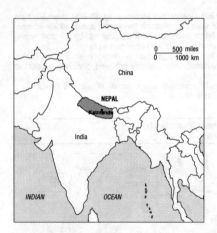

physical descends from the Himalayan mountain range in N through foothills to the river Ganges plain in S

environment described as the world's highest rubbish dump, Nepal attracts 270,000 tourists, trekkers, and mountaineers each year. An estimated 1,100 lbs of rubbish is left by each expedition trekking or climbing in the Himalayas. Since 1952 the foothills of the Himalayas have been stripped of 40% of their forest cover

features Mount Everest, Mount Kangchenjunga; the only Hindu kingdom in the world; Lumbini, birthplace of the Buddha

head of state King Birendra Bir Bikram Shah Dev from 1972

head of government Girija Prasad Koirala from 1991

political system constitutional monarchy

political parties Nepali Congress Party (NCP), left-of-centre; United Nepal Communist Party (UNCP), Marxist-Leninist-Maoist; United Liberation Torchbearers; Democratic Front, radical republican

exports jute, rice, timber, oilseed

currency Nepalese rupee (54.29 = £1 July 1991)

population (1990 est) 19,158,000 (mainly known by name of predominant clan, the Gurkhas; the Sherpas are a Buddhist minority of NE Nepal); growth rate 2.3% p.a.

life expectancy men 50, women 49 (1989)

language Nepali (official); 20 dialects spoken

religion Hindu 90%; Buddhist, Muslim, Christian

literacy men 39%, women 12% (1985 est)

GNP $3.1 bn (1988); $160 per head (1986)

chronology

1768 Nepal emerged as unified kingdom.

1815-16 Anglo-Nepali 'Gurkha War'; Nepal became a British-dependent buffer state.

1846-1951 Ruled by the Rana family.

1923 Independence achieved from Britain.

1951 Monarchy restored.

1959 Constitution created elected legislature.

1960-61 Parliament dissolved by king; political parties banned.

1980 Constitutional referendum held following popular agitation.

1981 Direct elections held to national assembly.

1983 Overthrow of monarch-supported prime minister.

1986 New assembly elections returned a majority opposed to panchayat system of partyless government.

1988 Strict curbs placed on opposition activity; over 100 supporters of banned opposition party arrested; censorship imposed.

1989 Border blockade imposed by India in treaty dispute.

1990 Panchayat system collapsed after mass pro-democracy demonstrations; new constitution introduced; elections set for May 1991.

1991 Nepali Congress Party, led by Girija Prasad Koirala, won the general election.

1992 Communist-led demonstrations in Katmandu and Patan demanded government's resignation at time of economic austerity.

Netherlands (Kingdom of the)

(Koninkrijk der Nederlanden), popularly referred to as Holland

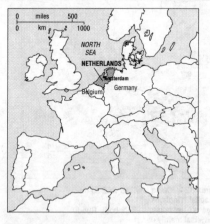

area 41,863 sq km/16,169 sq mi

capital Amsterdam

towns The Hague (seat of government), Utrecht, Eindhoven, Maastricht; chief port Rotterdam

physical flat coastal lowland; rivers Rhine, Scheldt, Maas; Frisian Islands

territories Aruba, Netherlands Antilles (Caribbean)

environment the country lies at the mouths of three of Europe's most polluted rivers, the Maas, Rhine, and Scheldt. Dutch farmers contribute to this pollution by using the world's highest quantities of nitrogen-based fertilizer per hectare/acre per year

features polders (reclaimed land) make up over 40% of the land area; dyke (Afsluitdijk) 32 km/20 mi long 1932 has turned the former Zuider Zee inlet into the freshwater IJsselmeer; Delta Project series of dams 1986 forms sea defence in Zeeland delta of the Maas, Scheldt, and Rhine

head of state Queen Beatrix Wilhelmina Armgard from 1980

head of government Ruud Lubbers from 1989

political system constitutional monarchy

political parties Christian Democratic Appeal (CDA), Christian, right-of-centre; Labour Party (PvdA), moderate, left-of-centre; People's Party for Freedom and Democracy (VVD), free enterprise, centrist

exports dairy products, flower bulbs, vegetables, petrochemicals, electronics

currency guilder (3.31 = £1 July 1991)

population (1990 est) 14,864,000 (including 300,000 of Dutch-Indonesian origin absorbed 1949-64 from former colonial possessions); growth rate 0.4% p.a.

life expectancy men 74, women 81 (1989)

language Dutch

religion Roman Catholic 40%, Protestant 31%

literacy 99% (1989)

GNP $223 bn (1988); $13,065 per head (1987)

chronology

1940-45 Occupied by Germany during World War II.

1947 Joined Benelux customs union.

1948 Queen Juliana succeeded Queen Wilhelmina to the throne.
1949 Became a founding member of North Atlantic Treaty Organization (NATO).
1953 Dykes breached by storm; nearly 2,000 people and tens of thousands of cattle died in flood.
1958 Joined European Economic Community.
1980 Queen Juliana abdicated in favour of her daughter Beatrix.
1981 Opposition to Cruise missiles averted their being sited on Dutch soil.
1989 Prime Minister Lubbers resigned; new Lubbers-led coalition elected.
1991 Netherlands Communist Party wound up.

New Zealand (Dominion of)

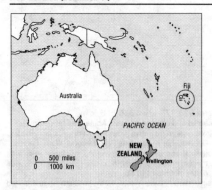

area 268,680 sq km/103,777 sq mi
capital and port Wellington
towns Hamilton, Palmerston North, Christchurch, Dunedin; port Auckland
physical comprises North Island, South Island, Stewart Island, Chatham Islands, and minor islands; mainly mountainous
overseas territories Tokelau (three atolls transferred 1926 from former Gilbert and Ellice Islands colony); Niue Island (one of the Cook Islands, separately administered from 1903: chief town Alafi); Cook Islands are internally self-governing but share common citizenship with New Zealand; Ross Dependency in Antarctica
features Ruapehu on North Island, 2,797 m/9,180 ft, highest of three active volcanoes; geysers and hot springs of the Rotorua district; Lake Taupo (616 sq km/238 sq mi), source of Waikato River; Kaingaroa state forest. On South Island are the Southern Alps and Canterbury Plains
head of state Elizabeth II from 1952 represented by governor general (Catherine Tizard from 1990)
head of government Jim Bolger from 1990
political system constitutional monarchy
political parties Labour Party, moderate, left-of-centre; New Zealand National Party, free enterprise, centre-right; Alliance Party, left-of-centre, ecologists
exports lamb, beef, wool, leather, dairy products, processed foods, kiwi fruit; seeds and breeding stock; timber, paper, pulp, light aircraft
currency New Zealand dollar ($NZ2.90 = £1 July 1991)
population (1990 est) 3,397,000 (European (mostly British) 87%; Polynesian (mostly Maori) 12%); growth rate 0.9% p.a.
life expectancy men 72, women 78 (1989)
languages English (official), Maori
religion Protestant 50%, Roman Catholic 15%
literacy 99% (1989)
GNP $37 bn; $11,040 per head (1988)

chronology
1840 New Zealand became a British colony.
1907 Created a dominion of the British Empire.
1931 Granted independence from Britain.
1947 Independence within the Commonwealth confirmed by the New Zealand parliament.
1972 National Party government replaced by Labour Party, with Norman Kirk as prime minister.
1974 Kirk died; replaced by Wallace Rowling.
1975 National Party returned, with Robert Muldoon as prime minister.
1984 Labour Party returned under David Lange.
1985 Non-nuclear military policy created disagreements with France and the USA.
1987 National Party declared support for the Labour government's non-nuclear policy. Lange re-elected. New Zealand officially classified as a 'friendly' rather than 'allied' country by the USA because of its non-nuclear military policy.
1988 Free-trade agreement with Australia signed.
1989 Lange resigned over economic differences with finance minister (he cited health reasons); replaced by Geoffrey Palmer.
1990 Palmer replaced by Mike Moore. Labour Party defeated by National Party in general election; Jim Bolger became prime minister.
1991 Formation of amalgamated Alliance Party set to challenge two-party system.

Nicaragua (Republic of)
(República de Nicaragua)

area 127,849 sq km/49,363 sq mi
capital Managua
towns León, Granada; chief ports Corinto, Puerto Cabezas, El Bluff
physical narrow Pacific coastal plain separated from broad Atlantic coastal plain by volcanic mountains and lakes Managua and Nicaragua
features largest state of Central America and most thinly populated; Mosquito Coast, Fonseca Bay, Corn Islands
head of state and government Violeta Barrios de Chamorro from 1990
political system emergent democracy
political parties Sandinista National Liberation Front (FSLN), Marxist-Leninist; Democratic Conservative Party (PCD), centrist; National Opposition Union (UNO), loose, US-backed coalition
exports coffee, cotton, sugar, bananas, meat
currency cordoba (C$8.12 = £1 July 1991)
population (1990) 3,606,000 (70% mestizo, 15% Spanish descent, 10% Indian or black); growth rate 3.3% p.a.
life expectancy men 61, women 63 (1989)
languages Spanish (official), Indian, English

religion Roman Catholic 95%
literacy 66% (1986)
GNP $2.1 bn; $610 per head (1988)

chronology
1838 Independence achieved from Spain.
1926-1933 Occupied by US marines.
1936 General Anastasio Somoza elected president; start of near-dictatorial rule by Somoza family.
1962 Sandinista National Liberation Front (FSLN) formed to fight Somoza regime.
1979 Somoza government ousted by FSLN.
1982 Subversive activity against the government promoted by the USA. State of emergency declared.
1984 The USA mined Nicaraguan harbours.
1985 Denunciation of Sandinista government by US president Reagan. FSLN won assembly elections.
1987 Central American peace agreement cosigned by Nicaraguan leaders.
1988 Peace agreement failed. Nicaragua held talks with Contra rebel leaders. Hurricane left 180,000 people homeless.
1989 Demobilization of rebels and release of former Somozan supporters; cease-fire ended.
1990 FSLN defeated by UNO, a US-backed coalition; Violeta Barrios de Chamorro elected president. Antigovernment riots.

Niger (Republic of)
(République du Niger)

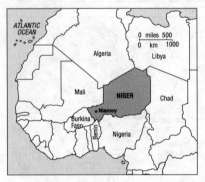

area 1,186,408 sq km/457,953 sq mi
capital Niamey
towns Zinder, Maradi, Tahoua
physical desert plains between hills in N and savanna in S; river Niger in SW, Lake Chad in SE
features part of the Sahara Desert and subject to Sahel droughts
head of state Ali Saibu from 1987
head of government to be elected
political system military republic
political parties banned from 1974
exports peanuts, livestock, gum arabic, uranium
currency franc CFA (498.25 = £1 July 1991)
population (1990 est) 7,691,000; growth rate 2.8% p.a.
life expectancy men 48, women 50 (1989)
languages French (official), Hausa, Djerma, and other minority languages
religion Sunni Muslim 85%, animist 15%
literacy men 19%, women 9% (1985 est)
GNP $2.2 bn; $310 per head (1987)

chronology
1960 Achieved full independence from France; Hamani Diori elected president.
1974 Diori ousted in army coup led by Seyni Kountché.
1977 Cooperation agreement signed with France.

1987 Kountché died; replaced by Col Ali Saibu.
1989 Ali Saibu elected president without opposition.
1990 Multiparty politics promised.
1991 Saibu stripped of executive powers; transitional government formed, headed by André Salifou with Amadou Cheiffou as prime minister.
1992 Transitional government collapsed.

Nigeria (Federal Republic of)

area 923,773 sq km/356,576 sq mi
capital and chief port Lagos; Abuja (capital-designate)
towns administrative headquarters Abuja; Ibadan, Ogbomosho, Kano; ports Port Harcourt, Warri, Calabar
physical arid savanna in N; tropical rainforest in S, with mangrove swamps along the coast; river Niger forms wide delta; mountains in SE
environment toxic waste from northern industrialized countries has been dumped in Nigeria
features harmattan (dry wind from the Sahara); rich artistic heritage, for example, Benin bronzes
head of state and government Ibrahim Babangida from 1985
political system emergent democratic republic
political parties Social Democratic Party (SDP), left-of-centre; National Republican Convention (NRC), right-of-centre
exports petroleum (largest oil resources in Africa), cocoa, peanuts, palm oil (Africa's largest producer), cotton, rubber, tin
currency naira (16.98 = £1 July 1991)
population (1991) 88,514,500 (Yoruba in W, Ibo in E, and Hausa-Fulani in N); growth rate 3.3% p.a.
life expectancy men 47, women 49 (1989)
languages English (official), Hausa, Ibo, Yoruba
media all radio and television stations and almost 50% of all publishing owned by the federal government or the Nigerian states
religion Sunni Muslim (50%) in N, Christian (40%) in S, local beliefs (10%)
literacy men 54%, women 31% (1985 est)
GNP $78 bn (1987); $790 per head (1984)

chronology
1914 N Nigeria and S Nigeria united to become Britain's largest African colony.
1954 Nigeria became a federation.
1960 Independence achieved from Britain within the Commonwealth.
1963 Became a republic, with Nnamdi Azikiwe as president.
1966 Military coup, followed by a counter-coup led by General Yakubu Gowon. Slaughter of many members of the Ibo tribe in north.
1967 Conflict over oil revenues led to declaration of an independent Ibo state of Biafra and outbreak of civil war.
1970 Surrender of Biafra and end of civil war.

1975 Gowon ousted in military coup; second coup put General Olusegun Obasanjo in power.
1979 Shehu Shagari became civilian president.
1983 Shagari's government overthrown in coup by Maj-Gen Muhammadu Buhari.
1985 Buhari replaced in a bloodless coup led by Maj-General Ibrahim Babangida.
1989 Two new political parties approved. Babangida promised a return to pluralist politics; date set for 1992.
1991 Nine new states created. Babangida confirmed his commitment to democratic rule for 1992.
1992 Multiparty elections won by Babangida's Social Democratic Party.

Sweden.
1905 Links with Sweden ended; full independence achieved.
1940-45 Occupied by Germany.
1949 Joined North Atlantic Treaty Organization (NATO).
1952 Joined Nordic Council.
1957 King Haakon VII succeeded by his son Olaf V.
1960 Joined European Free Trade Association (EFTA).
1972 Accepted into membership of European Economic Community; application withdrawn after a referendum.
1988 Gro Harlem Brundtland awarded Third World Prize.
1989 Jan P Syse became prime minister.
1990 Brundtland returned to power.
1991 King Olaf V died; succeeded by his son Harald V.

Norway (Kingdom of)
(Kongeriket Norge)

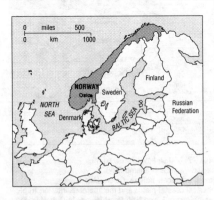

area 387,000 sq km/149,421 sq mi (includes Svalbard and Jan Mayen)
capital Oslo
towns Bergen, Trondheim, Stavanger
physical mountainous with fertile valleys and deeply indented coast; forests cover 25%; extends N of Arctic Circle
territories dependencies in the Arctic (Svalbard and Jan Mayen) and in Antarctica (Bouvet and Peter I Island, and Queen Maud Land)
environment an estimated 80% of the lakes and streams in the southern half of the country have been severely acidified by acid rain
features fjords, including Hardanger and Sogne, longest 185 km/115 mi, deepest 1,245 m/4,086 ft; glaciers in north; midnight sun and northern lights
head of state Harald V from 1991
head of government Gro Harlem Brundtland from 1990
political system constitutional monarchy
political parties Norwegian Labour Party (DNA), moderate, left-of-centre; Conservative Party, progressive, right-of-centre; Christian People's Party (KrF), Christian, centre-left; Centre Party (SP), left-of-centre, rural-oriented
exports petrochemicals from North Sea oil and gas, paper, wood pulp, furniture, iron ore and other minerals, high-tech goods, sports goods, fish
currency krone (11.43 = £1 July 1991)
population (1990 est) 4,214,000; growth rate 0.3% p.a.
life expectancy men 73, women 80 (1989)
languages Norwegian (official); there are Saami (Lapp) and Finnish-speaking minorities
religion Evangelical Lutheran (endowed by state) 94%
literacy 100% (1989)
GNP $89 bn (1988); $13,790 per head (1984)

chronology
1814 Became independent from Denmark; ceded to

Oman (Sultanate of)
(Saltanat 'Uman)

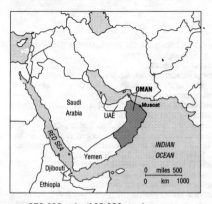

area 272,000 sq km/105,000 sq mi
capital Muscat
towns Salalah, Nizwa
physical mountains to N and S of a high arid plateau; fertile coastal strip
features Jebel Akhdar highlands; Kuria Muria islands; Masirah Island is used in aerial reconnaissance of the Arabian Sea and Indian Ocean; exclave on Musandam Peninsula controlling Strait of Hormuz
head of state and government Qaboos bin Said from 1970
political system absolute monarchy
political parties none
exports oil, dates, silverware, copper
currency rial Omani (0.62 = £1 July 1991)
population (1990 est) 1,305,000; growth rate 3.0% p.a.
life expectancy men 55, women 58 (1989)
languages Arabic (official), English, Urdu, other Indian dialects
religion Ibadhi Muslim 75%, Sunni Muslim, Shi'ite Muslim, Hindu
literacy 20% (1989)
GNP $7.5 bn (1987); $5,070 per head (1988)

chronology
1951 The Sultanate of Muscat and Oman achieved full independence from Britain. Treaty of Friendship with Britain signed.
1970 After 38 years' rule, Sultan Said bin Taimur replaced in coup by his son Qaboos bin Said. Name changed to Sultanate of Oman.
1975 Left-wing rebels in south defeated.
1982 Memorandum of Understanding with UK signed, providing for regular consultation on international issues.
1985 Diplomatic ties established with USSR.

Pakistan (Islamic Republic of)

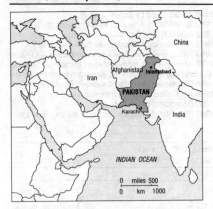

area 796,100 sq km/307,295 sq mi; one-third of Kashmir under Pakistani control
capital Islamabad
towns Karachi, Lahore, Rawalpindi, Peshawar
physical fertile Indus plain in E; Baluchistan plateau in W, mountains in N and NW
environment about 68% of irrigated land is waterlogged or suffering from salinization
features the 'five rivers' (Indus, Jhelum, Chenab, Ravi, and Sutlej) feed the world's largest irrigation system; Tarbela (world's largest earthfill dam); K2 mountain; Khyber Pass; sites of the Indus Valley civilization
head of state Ghulam Ishaq Khan from 1988
head of government Nawaz Sharif from 1990
political system emergent democracy
political parties Pakistan People's Party (PPP), moderate, Islamic, socialist; Islamic Democratic Alliance (IDA), including the Pakistan Muslim League (PML), Islamic conservative; Mohajir National Movement (MQM), Sind-based *mohajir* (Muslims previously living in India) settlers
exports cotton textiles, rice, leather, carpets
currency Pakistan rupee (39.00 = £1 July 1991)
population (1990 est) 113,163,000 (66% Punjabi, 13% Sindhi); growth rate 3.1% p.a.
life expectancy men 54, women 55 (1989)
languages Urdu and English (official); Punjabi, Sindhi, Pashto, Baluchi, other local dialects
religion Sunni Muslim 75%, Shi'ite Muslim 20%, Hindu 4%
literacy men 40%, women 19% (1985 est)
GDP $39 bn (1988); $360 per head (1984)

chronology
1947 Independence achieved from Britain, Pakistan formed following partition of British India.
1956 Proclaimed a republic.
1958 Military rule imposed by General Ayub Khan.
1969 Power transferred to General Yahya Khan.
1971 Secession of East Pakistan (Bangladesh). After civil war, power transferred to Zulfiqar Ali Bhutto.
1977 Bhutto overthrown in military coup by General Zia ul-Haq; martial law imposed.
1979 Bhutto executed.
1981 Opposition Movement for the Restoration of Democracy formed. Islamization process pushed forward.
1985 Nonparty elections held, amended constitution adopted, martial law and ban on political parties lifted.
1986 Agitation for free elections launched by Benazir Bhutto.
1988 Zia introduced Islamic legal code, the *Shari'a*. He was killed in a military plane crash in Aug. Benazir Bhutto elected prime minister in Nov.

1989 Pakistan rejoined the Commonwealth.
1990 Army mobilized in support of Muslim separatists in Indian Kashmir. Bhutto dismissed. Islamic Democratic Alliance (IDA), led by Nawaz Sharif, won Oct general election.
1991 *Sharia* (Islamic legal code) bill enacted; privatization and economic deregulation programme launched.

Panama (Republic of)
(República de Panamá)

area 77,100 sq km/29,768 sq mi
capital Panamá (Panama City)
towns Cristóbal, Balboa, Colón, David
physical coastal plains and mountainous interior; tropical rainforest in E and NW; Pearl Islands in Gulf of Panama
features Panama Canal; Barro Colorado Island in Gatún Lake (reservoir supplying the canal), a tropical forest reserve since 1923; Smithsonian Tropical Research Institute
head of state and government Guillermo Endara from 1989
political system emergent democratic republic
political parties Democratic Revolutionary Party (PRD), right-wing; Labour Party (PALA), right-of-centre; Panamanian Republican Party (PPR), right-wing; Nationalist Liberal Republican Movement (MOLIRENA), left-of-centre; Authentic Panamanian Party (PPA), centrist; Christian Democratic Party (PDC), centre-left
exports bananas, petroleum products, copper, shrimps, sugar
currency balboa (1.61 = £1 July 1991)
population (1990 est) 2,423,000 (70% mestizo (mixed race), 14% W Indian, 10% European descent, 6% Indian (Cuna, Choco, Guayami)); growth rate 2.2% p.a.
life expectancy men 71, women 75 (1989)
languages Spanish (official), English
religion Roman Catholic 93%, Protestant 6%
literacy 87% (1989)
GNP $4.2 bn (1988); $1,970 per head (1984)

chronology
1821 Achieved independence from Spain; joined Gran Colombia.
1903 Full independence achieved on separation from Colombia.
1974 Agreement to negotiate full transfer of the Panama Canal from the USA to Panama.
1977 USA–Panama treaties transferred the canal to Panama, effective 1999, with the USA guaranteeing its protection and an annual payment.
1984 Nicolás Ardito Barletta elected president.
1985 Barletta resigned; replaced by Eric Arturo del Valle.

1987 General Noriega resisted calls for his removal, despite suspension of US military and economic aid.

1988 Del Valle replaced by Manuel Solis Palma. Noriega, charged with drug smuggling by the USA, declared a state of emergency.

1989 Opposition won election; Noriega declared results invalid; Francisco Rodríguez sworn in as president; coup attempt against Noriega failed; Noriega declared head of government by assembly; 'state of war' with the USA announced; US invasion deposed Noriega; Guillermo Endara installed as president; Noriega sought asylum in Vatican embassy; later surrendered and taken to US for trial.

1991 Attempted anti-government coup foiled. Army abolished.

1992 Noriega found guilty of drugs offences.

Papua New Guinea

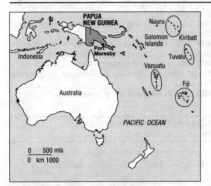

area 462,840 sq km/178,656 sq mi

capital Port Moresby (on E New Guinea)

towns Lae, Rabaul, Madang

physical mountainous; includes tropical islands of New Ireland, New Britain, and Bougainville; Admiralty Islands, D'Entrecasteaux Islands, and Louisiade Archipelago

features one of world's largest swamps on SW coast; world's largest butterfly, orchids; Sepik River

head of state Elizabeth II, represented by governor general

head of government Paias Wingti from 1992

political system liberal democracy

political parties Papua New Guinea Party (Pangu Pati: PP), urban-and coastal-oriented nationalist; People's Democratic Movement (PDM), 1985 breakaway from the PP; National Party (NP), highlands-based; Melanesian Alliance (MA), Bougainville-based autonomy; People's Progress Party (PPP), conservative

exports copra, coconut oil, palm oil, tea, copper, gold, coffee

currency kina (1.56 = £1 July 1991)

population (1989 est) 3,613,000 (Papuans, Melanesians, Negritos, various minorities); growth rate 2.6% p.a.

life expectancy men 53, women 54 (1987)

languages English (official); pidgin English, 715 local languages

religion Protestant 63%, Roman Catholic 31%, local faiths

literacy men 55%, women 36% (1985 est)

GNP $2.5 bn; $730 per head (1987)

chronology

1883 Annexed by Queensland; became the Australian Territory of Papua.

1884 NE New Guinea annexed by Germany; SE claimed by Britain.

1914 NE New Guinea occupied by Australia.

1921–42 Held as a League of Nations mandate.

1942–45 Occupied by Japan.

1975 Independence achieved from Australia, within the Commonwealth, with Michael Somare as prime minister.

1980 Julius Chan became prime minister.

1982 Somare returned to power.

1985 Somare challenged by deputy prime minister, Paias Wingti, who later formed a five-party coalition government.

1988 Wingti defeated on no-confidence vote and replaced by Rabbie Namaliu, who established a six-party coalition government.

1989 State of emergency imposed on Bougainville in response to separatist violence.

1991 Peace accord signed with Bougainville secessionists. Economic boom as gold production doubled. Wiwa Korowi elected as new governor general. Deputy prime minister, Ted Diro, resigned having been found guilty of corruption.

1992 Wingti re-elected as premier in July elections.

Paraguay (Republic of)
(República del Paraguay)

area 406,752 sq km/157,006 sq mi

capital Asunción

towns Puerto Presidente Stroessner, Pedro Juan Caballero; port Concepción

physical low marshy plain and marshlands; divided by Paraguay River; Paraná River forms SE boundary

features Itaipú dam on border with Brazil; Gran Chaco plain with huge swamps

head of state and government General Andrés Rodríguez from 1989

political system emergent democracy

political parties National Republican Association (Colorado Party), right-of-centre; Liberal Party (PL), right-of-centre; Radical Liberal Party (PLR), centrist

exports cotton, soya beans, timber, vegetable oil, maté

currency guaraní (2,145.28 = £1 July 1991)

population (1990 est) 4,660,000 (95% mixed Guarani Indian--Spanish descent); growth rate 3.0% p.a.

life expectancy men 67, women 72 (1989)

languages Spanish 6% (official), Guarani 90%

religion Roman Catholic 97%

literacy men 91%, women 85% (1985 est)

GNP $7.4 bn; $1,000 per head (1987)

chronology

1811 Independence achieved from Spain.

1865–70 War with Argentina, Brazil, and Uruguay; much territory lost.
1932–35 Territory won from Bolivia during the Chaco War.
1940–48 Presidency of General Higinio Morínigo.
1948–54 Political instability; six different presidents.
1954 General Alfredo Stroessner seized power.
1989 Stroessner ousted in coup led by General Andrés Rodríguez. Rodríguez elected president; Colorado Party won the congressional elections.
1991 Colorado Party successful in assembly elections.

Peru (Republic of)
(República del Perú)

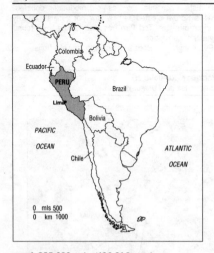

area 1,285,200 sq km/496,216 sq mi
capital Lima, including port of Callao
towns Arequipa, Iquitos, Chiclayo, Trujillo
physical Andes mountains NW–SE cover 27% of Peru, separating Amazon river-basin jungle in NE from coastal plain in W; desert along coast N–S
environment an estimated 3,000 out of the 8,000 sq km/3,100 sq mi of coastal lands under irrigation are either waterlogged or suffering from saline water. Only half the population have access to clean drinking water
features Lake Titicaca; Atacama Desert; Nazca lines, monuments of Machu Picchu, Chan Chan, Charín de Huantar
head of state and government Alberto Fujimori from 1990
political system democratic republic
political parties American Popular Revolutionary Alliance (APRA), moderate, left-wing; United Left (IU), left-wing; Change 90, centrist
exports coca, coffee, alpaca, llama and vicuña wool, fish meal, lead (largest producer in South America), copper, iron, oil
currency new sol (1.38 = £1 July 1991)
population (1990 est) 21,904,000 (46% Indian, mainly Quechua and Aymara; 43% mixed Spanish–Indian descent); growth rate 2.6% p.a.
life expectancy men 61, women 66
languages Spanish 68%, Quechua 27% (both official), Aymara 3%
religion Roman Catholic 90%
literacy men 91%, women 78% (1985 est)
GNP $19.6 bn (1988); $940 per head (1984)

chronology
1824 Independence achieved from Spain.
1849–74 Some 80,000–100,000 Chinese labourers ar-

rived in Peru to fill menial jobs such as collecting guano.
1902 Boundary dispute with Bolivia settled.
1927 Boundary dispute with Colombia settled.
1942 Boundary dispute with Ecuador settled.
1948 Army coup, led by General Manuel Odría, installed a military government.
1963 Return to civilian rule, with Fernando Belaúnde Terry as president.
1968 Return of military government in a bloodless coup by General Juan Velasco Alvarado.
1975 Velasco replaced, in a bloodless coup, by General Morales Bermúdez.
1980 Return to civilian rule, with Fernando Belaúnde as president.
1981 Boundary dispute with Ecuador renewed.
1985 Belaúnde succeeded by Social Democrat Alan García Pérez.
1987 President García delayed the nationalization of Peru's banks after a vigorous campaign against the proposal.
1988 García pressured to seek help from the International Monetary Fund.
1989 Mario Vargas Llosa entered presidential race; his Democratic Front won municipal elections Nov.
1990 Alberto Fujimori defeated Vargas Llosa in presidential elections. Assassination attempt on president failed.
1992 Fujimori sided with army to avert coup.

Philippines (Republic of the)
(Republika ng Pilipinas)

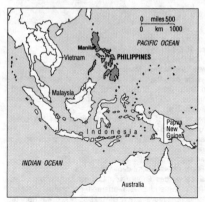

area 300,000 sq km/115,800 sq mi
capital Manila (on Luzon)
towns Quezon City (Luzon), Zamboanga (Mindanao); ports Cebu, Davao (on Mindanao), and Iloilo
physical comprises over 7,000 islands; volcanic mountain ranges traverse main chain N–S; 50% still forested. The largest islands are Luzon 108,172 sq km/41,754 sq mi and Mindanao 94,227 sq km/36,372 sq mi; others include Samar, Negros, Palawan, Panay, Mindoro, Leyte, Cebu, and the Sulu group
environment cleared for timber, tannin, and the creation of fish ponds, the mangrove forest was reduced from an area of 5,000 sq km/1,930 sq mi to 380 sq km/146 sq mi between 1920 and 1988
features Luzon, site of Clark Field, US air base used as a logistical base in Vietnam War; Subic Bay, US naval base; Pinatubo volcano (1,759 m/5,770 ft); Mindanao has active volcano Apo (2,954 m/9,690 ft) and mountainous rainforest
head of state and government Fidel Ramos from 1992
political system emergent democracy
political parties People's Power, including the PDP--

Laban Party and the Liberal Party, centrist pro-Aquino; Nationalist Party, Union for National Action (UNA), and Grand Alliance for Democracy (GAD), conservative opposition groupings; Mindanao Alliance, island-based decentralist body

exports sugar, copra (world's largest producer) and coconut oil, timber, copper concentrates, electronics, clothing
currency peso (43.00 = £1 July 1991)
population (1990 est) 66,647,000 (93% Malaysian); growth rate 2.4% p.a.
life expectancy men 63, women 69 (1989)
languages Tagalog (Filipino, official); English and Spanish
religion Roman Catholic 84%, Protestant 9%, Muslim 5%
literacy 88% (1989)
GNP $38.2 bn; $667 per head (1988)

chronology
1542 Named the Philippines (Filipinas) by Spanish explorers.
1565 Conquered by Spain.
1898 Ceded to the USA after Spanish–American War.
1935 Granted internal self-government.
1942–45 Occupied by Japan.
1946 Independence achieved from USA.
1965 Ferdinand Marcos elected president.
1983 Opposition leader Benigno Aquino murdered by military guard.
1986 Marcos overthrown by Corazon Aquino's People's Power movement.
1987 'Freedom constitution' adopted, giving Aquino mandate to rule until June 1992. People's Power won majority in congressional elections. Attempted right-wing coup suppressed. Communist guerrillas active. Government in rightward swing.
1988 Land Reform Act gave favourable compensation to large estate-holders.
1989 Referendum on southern autonomy failed; Marcos died in exile; Aquino refused his burial in Philippines. Sixth coup attempt suppressed with US aid; Aquino declared state of emergency.
1990 Seventh coup attempt survived by President Aquino.
1991 June: eruption of Mount Pinatubo, hundreds killed. USA agreed to give up Clark Field airbase but keep Subic Bay naval base for ten more years. Sept: Philippines Senate voted to urge withdrawal of all US forces. US renewal of Subic Bay lease rejected. Nov: Imelda Marcos returned.
1992 Fidel Ramos elected to replace Aquino.

Poland (Republic of)
(Polska Rzeczpospolita)

area 127,886 sq km/49,325 sq mi
capital Warsaw
towns Lódź, Kraków, Wroclaw, Poznań, Katowice, Bydgoszcz, Lublin; ports Gdańsk, Szczecin, Gdynia
physical part of the great plain of Europe; Vistula, Oder, and Neisse rivers; Sudeten, Tatra, and Carpathian mountains on S frontier
environment atmospheric pollution derived from coal (producing 90% of the country's electricity), toxic waste from industry, and lack of sewage treatment have resulted in the designation of 27 ecologically endangered areas. Half the country's lakes have been seriously contaminated and three-quarters of its drinking water does not meet official health standards
features last wild European bison (only in protected herds)
head of state Lech Walesa from 1990
head of government Hanna Suchocka from 1992
political system emergent democratic republic

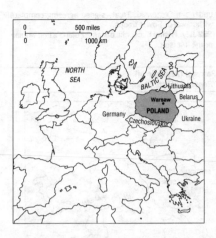

political parties Democratic Union, centrist, ex-Solidarity; Democratic Left Alliance, ex-communist; Centre Alliance, right-of-centre, Walesa-linked; Social Democratic Party of the Polish Republic, 1990 successor to Polish United Workers' Party (PUWP), social democratic; Union of Social Democrats, radical breakaway from PUWP formed 1990; Solidarność (Solidarity) Parliamentary Club (OKP), anticommunist coalition
exports coal, softwood timber, chemicals, machinery, ships, vehicles, meat, copper (Europe's largest producer)
currency zloty (18,684.00 = £1 July 1991)
population (1990 est) 38,363,000; growth rate 0.6% p.a.
life expectancy men 66, women 74 (1989)
languages Polish (official), German
religion Roman Catholic 95%
literacy 98% (1989)
GNP $276 bn (1988); $2,000 per head (1986)

chronology
1918 Poland revived as independent republic.
1939 German invasion and occupation.
1944 Germans driven out by Soviet forces.
1945 Polish boundaries redrawn at Potsdam Conference.
1947 Communist people's republic proclaimed.
1956 Poznań riots. Gomulka installed as Polish United Workers' Party (PUWP) leader.
1970 Gomulka replaced by Gierek after Gdańsk riots.
1980 Solidarity emerged as a free trade union following Gdańsk disturbances.
1981 Martial law imposed by General Jaruzelski.
1983 Martial law ended.
1984 Amnesty for political prisoners.
1985 Zbigniew Messner became prime minister.
1987 Referendum on economic reform rejected.
1988 Solidarity-led strikes and demonstrations called off after pay increases. Messner resigned; replaced by the reformist Mieczyslaw F Rakowski.
1989 Solidarity relegalized. April: new 'socialist pluralist' constitution formed. June: widespread success for Solidarity in assembly elections, the first open elections in 40 years. July: Jaruzelski elected president. Sept: 'Grand coalition', first non-Communist government since World War II formed; economic restructuring undertaken on free-market lines; W Europe and US create $1 bn aid package.
1990 Jan: PUWP dissolved; replaced by Social Democratic Party and breakaway Union of Social Democrats. Lech Walesa elected president; Dec: prime minister Mazowiecki resigned.
1991 Oct: Multiparty general election produced inconclusive result. Five-party centre-right coalition formed

under Jan Olszewski. Treaty signed agreeing complete withdrawal of Soviet troops.
1992 July: Hanna Suchocka became Poland's first woman prime minister.

Portugal (Republic of)
(República Portuguesa)

area 92,000 sq km/35,521 sq mi (including the Azores and Madeira)
capital Lisbon
towns Coimbra, ports Porto, Setúbal
physical mountainous in N, plains in S
features rivers Minho, Douro, Tagus (Tejo), Guadiana; Serra da Estrêla mountains
head of state Mario Alberto Nobre Lopes Soares from 1986
head of government Aníbal Cavaco Silva from 1985
political system democratic republic
political parties Social Democratic Party (PSD), moderate, left-of-centre; Socialist Party (PS), progressive socialist; Democratic Renewal Party (PRD), centre-left; Democratic Social Centre Party (CDS), moderate, left-of-centre
exports wine, olive oil, resin, cork, sardines, textiles, clothing, pottery, pulpwood
currency escudo (254.10 = £1 July 1991)
population (1990 est) 10,528,000; growth rate 0.5% p.a.
life expectancy men 71, women 78 (1989)
language Portuguese
religion Roman Catholic 97%
literacy men 89%, women 80% (1985)
GNP $33.5 bn (1987); $2,970 per head (1986)

chronology
1928–68 Military dictatorship under António de Oliveira Salazar.
1968 Salazar succeeded by Marcello Caetano.
1974 Caetano removed in military coup led by General Antonio Ribeiro de Spínola. Spínola replaced by General Francisco da Costa Gomes.
1975 African colonies became independent.
1976 New constitution, providing for return to civilian rule, adopted. Minority government appointed, led by Socialist Party leader Mario Soares.
1978 Soares resigned.
1980 Francisco Balsemão formed centre-party coalition after two years of political instability.
1982 Draft of new constitution approved, reducing powers of presidency.
1983 Centre-left coalition government formed.
1985 Aníbal Cavaco Silva became prime minister.
1986 Mario Soares elected first civilian president in 60 years. Portugal joined European Community.

1988 Portugal joined Western European Union.
1989 Constitution amended to allow major state enterprises to be denationalized.
1991 Mario Soares re-elected president; Social Democrats (PSD) majority slightly reduced in assembly elections.

Qatar (State of)
(Dawlat Qatar)

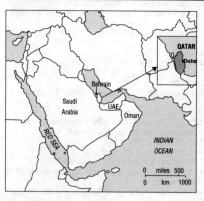

area 11,400 sq km/4,402 sq mi
capital and chief port Doha
town Dukhan, centre of oil production
physical mostly flat desert with salt flats in S
features negligible rain and surface water; only 3% is fertile, but irrigation allows self-sufficiency in fruit and vegetables; extensive oil discoveries since World War II
head of state and government Sheik Khalifa bin Hamad al-Thani from 1972
political system absolute monarchy
political parties none
exports oil, natural gas, petrochemicals, fertilizers, iron, steel
currency riyal (5.89 = £1 July 1991)
population (1990 est) 498,000 (half in Doha; Arab 40%, Indian 18%, Pakistani 18%); growth rate 3.7% p.a.
life expectancy men 68, women 72 (1989)
languages Arabic (official), English
religion Sunni Muslim 95%
literacy 60% (1987)
GNP $5.9 bn (1983); $35,000 per head

chronology
1916 Qatar became a British protectorate.
1970 Constitution adopted, confirming the emirate as an absolute monarchy.
1971 Independence achieved from Britain.
1972 Emir Sheik Ahmad replaced in bloodless coup by his cousin, Crown Prince Sheik Khalifa.

Romania

area 237,500 sq km/91,699 sq mi
capital Bucharest
towns Braşov, Timişoara, Cluj–Napoca, Iaşi; ports Galaţi, Constanta, Brăila
physical mountains surrounding a plateau, with river plains S and E
environment although sulphur dioxide deposits are low, only 20% of the country's rivers can provide drinkable water
features Carpathian Mountains, Transylvanian Alps; river Danube; Black Sea coast; mineral springs

Sept: prime minister Petre Roman resigned following riots, succeeded by Theodor Stolojan heading a new cross-party coalition government. Dec: new constitution endorsed by referendum.

head of state Ion Iliescu from 1989
head of government Theodor Stolojan from 1991
political system emergent democratic republic
political parties National Salvation Front (NSF), reform socialist; Civic Alliance (CA), right-of-centre; Convention for Democracy, umbrella organization for right-of-centre National Liberal Party (NLP) and ethnic-Hungarian Union of Democratic Magyars (UDM)
exports petroleum products and oilfield equipment, electrical goods, cars, cereals
currency leu (101.48 = £1 July 1991)
population (1990 est) 23,269,000 (Romanians 89%, Hungarians 7.9%, Germans 1.6%); growth rate 0.5% p.a.
life expectancy men 67, women 73 (1989)
languages Romanian (official), Hungarian, German
media television is state-run; there are an estimated 900 newspapers and magazines, but only the progovernment papers have adequate distribution and printing facilities
religion Romanian Orthodox 80%, Roman Catholic 6%
literacy 98% (1988)
GNP $151 bn (1988); $6,400 per head

chronology
1944 Pro-Nazi Antonescu government overthrown.
1945 Communist-dominated government appointed.
1947 Boundaries redrawn. King Michael abdicated and People's Republic proclaimed.
1949 New Soviet-style constitution adopted. Joined Comecon.
1952 Second new Soviet-style constitution.
1955 Romania joined Warsaw Pact.
1958 Soviet occupation forces removed.
1965 New constitution adopted.
1974 Ceauşescu created president.
1985–86 Winters of austerity and power cuts.
1987 Workers demonstrated against austerity programme.
1988–89 Relations with Hungary deteriorated over 'systematization programme'.
1989 Announcement that all foreign debt paid off. Razing of villages and building of monuments to Ceauşescu; Communist orthodoxy reaffirmed; demonstrations violently suppressed; massacre in Timisoara; army joined uprising; heavy fighting; bloody overthrow of Ceauşescu regime in 'Christmas Revolution'; Ceauşescu and wife tried and executed; estimated 10,000 dead in civil warfare; power assumed by new military-dissident-reform communist National Salvation Front, headed by Ion Iliescu.
1990 Securitate replaced by new Romanian Intelligence Service (RIS); religious practices resumed; mounting strikes and protests against effects of market economy.
1991 April: treaty on co-operation and good neighbourliness signed with USSR. Aug: privatization law passed.

Russian Federation

area 17,075,500 sq km/6,591,100 sq mi
capital Moscow
towns St Petersburg (Leningrad), Nizhni-Novgorod (Gorky), Rostov-on-Don, Samara (Kuibyshev), Tver (Kalinin), Volgograd, Vyatka (Kirov), Ekaterinburg (Sverdlovsk)
physical fertile Black Earth district; extensive forests; the Ural Mountains with large mineral resources
features the heavily industrialized area around Moscow; Siberia; includes 16 autonomous republics (capitals in brackets): Bashkir (Ufa); Buryat (Ulan-Ude); Checheno-Ingush (Grozny); Chuvash (Cheboksary); Dagestan (Makhachkala); Kabardino-Balkar (Nalchik); Kalmyk (Elista); Karelia (Petrozavodsk); Komi (Syktyvkar); Mari (Yoshkar-Ola); Mordovia (Saransk); Vladikavkaz (formerly Ordzhonikidze); Tatarstan (Kazan); Tuva (Kizyl); Udmurt (Izhevsk); Yakut (Yakutsk)
head of state and government Boris Yeltsin from 1990/91
political system emergent democracy
political parties Democratic Russia, liberal-radical, pro-Yeltsin; Congress of Civil and Patriotic Groups (CCDG), right-wing; Civic Union, right-of-centre; Nashi (Ours), far-right, Russian imperialist coalition; Communist (Bolshevik) Party, Stalinist-communist
products iron ore, coal, oil, gold, platinum, and other minerals, agricultural produce
currency rouble
population (1990) 148,000,000 (82% Russian, Tatar 4%, Ukrainian 3%, Chuvash 1%)
language Great Russian
religion traditionally Russian Orthodox

chronology
1945 Became a founding member of United Nations.
1988 Aug: Democratic Union formed in Moscow as political party opposed to totalitarianism. Oct: Russian language demonstrations in Leningrad and Tsarist flag raised.
1989 March: Boris Yeltsin elected to USSR Congress of People's Deputies. Sept: conservative-nationalist Russian United Workers' Front established in Sverdlovsk.
1990 May: anticommunist May Day protests in Red Square, Moscow; Yeltsin narrowly elected RSFSR president by Russian parliament. June: economic and political sovereignty declared; Ivan Silaev became Russian prime minister. July: Yeltsin resigned his party membership. Aug: Tatarstan declared sovereignty. Dec: rationing introduced in some cities; private land ownership allowed.
1991 March: Yeltsin secured the support of Congress of Peoples' Deputies for direct election of an executive president. June: Yeltsin elected president under a liberal-

radical banner. July: Yeltsin issued a sweeping decree to remove Communist Party cells from workplaces; sovereignty of the Baltic republics recognized by the republic. Aug: Yeltsin stood out against abortive anti-Gorbachev coup, emerging as key power-broker within Soviet Union; national guard established and pre-revolutionary flag restored. Sept: Silaev resigned as Russian premier. Nov: Yeltsin also named as prime minister; CPSU and Russian Communist Party banned; Yeltsin's goverment gained control of Russia's economic assets and armed forces. Oct: Checheno-Ingush declared its independence. Dec: Yeltsin negotiated formation of new confederal Commonwealth of Independent States (CIS); Russian independence recognized by USA and EC.
1992 Jan: admitted into CSCE; assumed former USSR's permanent seat on UN Security Council; prices freed; Yeltsin proposed further major reductions in strategic nuclear weapons. Feb: Yeltsin-Bush summit meeting; Yeltsin administration rocked by neo-communist demonstrations in Moscow and criticism of vice president Rutskoi as living standards plummet. March: 18 out of 20 republics signed treaty agreeing to remain within loose Russian Federation; Tatarstan and Checheno-Ingush refused to sign.

Rwanda (Republic of)
(Republika y'u Rwanda)

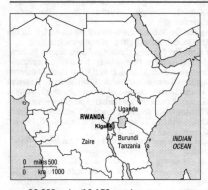

area 26,338 sq km/10,173 sq mi
capital Kigali
towns Butare, Ruhengeri
physical high savanna and hills, with volcanic mountains in NW
features part of lake Kivu; highest peak Mount Karisimbi 4,507 m/14,792 ft; Kagera River (whose headwaters are the source of the Nile) and National Park
head of state and government Maj-Gen Juvenal Habyarimana from 1973
political system one-party military republic
political party National Revolutionary Movement for Development (MRND), nationalistic, socialist
exports coffee, tea, pyrethrum
currency franc (213.03 = £1 July 1991)
population (1990 est) 7,603,000 (Hutu 90%, Tutsi 9%, Twa 1%); growth rate 3.3% p.a.
life expectancy men 49, women 53 (1989)
languages Kinyarwanda, French (official); Kiswahili
religion Roman Catholic 54%, animist 23%, Protestant 12%; Muslim 9%
literacy men 50% (1989)
GNP $2.3 bn (1987); $323 per head (1986)

chronology
1916 Belgian troops occupied Rwanda; League of Nations mandated Rwanda and Burundi to Belgium as Territory of Ruanda-Urundi.
1959 Interethnic warfare between Hutu and Tutsi.

1962 Independence from Belgium achieved, with Grégoire Kayibanda as president.
1972 Renewal of interethnic fighting.
1973 Kayibanda ousted in a military coup led by Maj-Gen Juvenal Habyarimana.
1978 New constitution approved; Rwanda remained a military-controlled state.
1980 Civilian rule adopted.
1988 Refugees from Burundi massacres streamed into Rwanda.
1990 Rwandan Patriotic Army attacked government. Constitutional reforms promised.

St Christopher (St Kitts)—Nevis (Federation of)

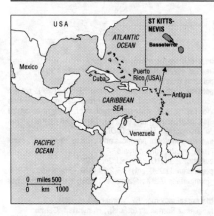

area 269 sq km/104 sq mi (St Christopher 176 sq km/68 sq mi, Nevis 93 sq mi/36 sq mi)
capital Basseterre (on St Christopher)
towns Charlestown (largest on Nevis)
physical both islands are volcanic
features fertile plains on coast; black beaches
head of state Elizabeth II from 1983 represented by governor general
head of government Kennedy Simmonds from 1980
political system federal constitutional monarchy
political parties People's Action Movement (PAM), centre-right; Nevis Reformation Party (NRP), Nevis-separatist; Labour Party, moderate, left-of-centre
exports sugar, molasses, electronics, clothing
currency E Caribbean dollar (EC$4.39 = £1 July 1991)
population (1990 est) 45,800; growth rate 0.2% p.a.
life expectancy men 69/women 72
language English
media no daily newspaper; two weekly papers, published by the governing and opposition party respectively — both receive advertising support from the government
religion Anglican 36%, Methodist 32%, other protestant 8%, Roman Catholic 10% (1985 est)
literacy 90% (1987)
GNP $40 million (1983); $870 per head

chronology
1871-1956 Part of the Leeward Islands Federation.
1958-62 Part of the Federation of the West Indies.
1967 St Christopher, Nevis, and Anguilla achieved internal self-government, within the British Commonwealth, with Robert Bradshaw, Labour Party leader, as prime minister.
1971 Anguilla returned to being a British dependency.
1978 Bradshaw died; succeeded by Paul Southwell.
1979 Southwell died; succeeded by Lee L Moore.
1980 Coalition government led by Kennedy Simmonds.
1983 Full independence achieved within the Commonwealth.

1984 Coalition government re-elected.
1989 Prime Minister Simmonds won a third successive term.

St Lucia

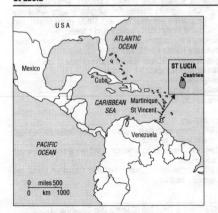

area 617 sq km/238 sq mi
capital Castries
towns Vieux-Fort, Soufrière
physical mountainous island with fertile valleys; mainly tropical forest
features volcanic peaks; Gros and Petit Pitons
head of state Elizabeth II from 1979 represented by governor general
head of government John Compton from 1982
political system constitutional monarchy
political parties United Workers' Party (UWP), moderate, left-of-centre; St Lucia Labour Party (SLP), moderate, left-of-centre; Progressive Labour Party (PLP), moderate, left-of-centre
exports coconut oil, bananas, cocoa, copra
currency E Caribbean dollar (EC$4.39 = £1 July 1991)
population (1990 est) 153,000; growth rate 2.8% p.a.
life expectancy men 68, women 73 (1989)
languages English, French patois
media two independent biweekly newspapers
religion Roman Catholic 90%
literacy 78% (1989)
GNP $166 million; $1,370 per head (1987)

chronology
1814 Became a British crown colony following Treaty of Paris.
1967 Acquired internal self-government as a West Indies associated state.
1979 Independence achieved from Britain within the Commonwealth, with John Compton, leader of the United Workers' Party (UWP), as prime minister. Allan Louisy, leader of the St Lucia Labour Party (SLP), replaced Compton as prime minister.
1981 Louisy resigned; replaced by Winston Cenac.
1982 Compton returned to power at the head of a UWP government.
1987 Compton re-elected with reduced majority.
1991 Integration with Windward Islands proposed.
1992 UWP won general election.

St Vincent and the Grenadines

area 388 sq km/150 sq mi, including islets of the Northern Grenadines 43 sq km/17 sq mi
capital Kingstown
towns Georgetown, Chateaubelair

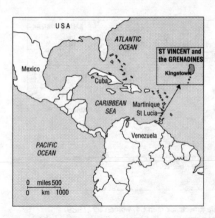

physical volcanic mountains, thickly forested
features Mustique, one of the Grenadines, a holiday resort; Soufrière volcano
head of state Elizabeth II from 1979 represented by governor general
head of government James Mitchell from 1984
political system constitutional monarchy
political parties New Democratic Party (NDP), moderate, left-of-centre; St Vincent Labour Party (SVLP), moderate, left-of-centre
exports bananas, taros, sweet potatoes, arrowroot, copra
currency E Caribbean dollar (EC$4.39 = £1 July 1991)
population (1990 est) 106,000; growth rate -4% p.a.
life expectancy men 69, women 74 (1989)
languages English, French patois
media government-owned radio station; two privately-owned weekly newspapers, subject to government pressure
religion 47% Anglican, 28% Methodist, 13% Roman Catholic
literacy 85% (1989)
GNP $188 million; $1,070 per head (1987)

chronology
1783 Became a British crown colony.
1958-62 Part of the West Indies Federation.
1969 Achieved internal self-government.
1979 Achieved full independence from Britain within the Commonwealth, with Milton Cato as prime minister.
1984 James Mitchell replaced Cato as prime minister.
1989 Mitchell decisively re-elected.
1991 Integration with Windward Islands proposed.

Samoa, Western (Independent State of)
(Samoa i Sisifo)

area 2,830 sq km/1,093 sq mi
capital Apia (on Upolu island)
physical comprises South Pacific islands of Savai'i and Upolu, with two smaller tropical islands and islets; mountain ranges on main islands
features lava flows on Savai'i
head of state King Malietoa Tanumafili II from 1962
head of government Tofilau Eti Alesana from 1988
political system liberal democracy
political parties Human Rights Protection Party (HRPP), led by Tofilau Eti Alesana; the Va'ai Kolone Group (VKG); Christian Democratic Party (CDP), led by Tupua Tamasese Efi. All 'parties' are personality-based groupings
exports coconut oil, copra, cocoa, fruit juice, cigarettes, timber
currency talà (3.84 = £1 July 1991)
population (1989) 169,000; growth rate 1.1% p.a.

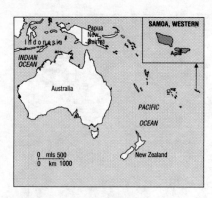

life expectancy men 64, women 69 (1989)
languages English, Samoan (official)
religion Protestant 70%, Roman Catholic 20%
literacy 90% (1989)
GNP $110 million (1987); $520 per head

chronology
1899-1914 German protectorate.
1920-61 Administered by New Zealand.
1959 Local government elected.
1961 Referendum favoured independence.
1962 Independence achieved within the Commonwealth, with Fiame Mata Afa Mulinu'u as prime minister.
1975 Mata Afa died.
1976 Tupuola Taisi Efi became first nonroyal prime minister.
1982 Va'ai Kolone became prime minister; replaced by Tupuola Efi. Assembly failed to approve budget; Tupuola Efi resigned; replaced by Tofilau Eti Alesana.
1985 Tofilau Eti resigned; head of state invited Va'ai Kolone to lead the government.
1988 Elections produced a hung parliament, with first Tupuola Efi as prime minister and then Tofilau Eti Alesana.
1990 Universal adult suffrage introduced.
1991 Tofilau Eti Alesana re-elected. Fiame Naome became first woman in cabinet.

San Marino (Republic of)
(Repubblica di San Marino)

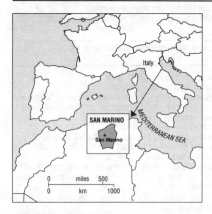

area 61 sq km/24 sq mi
capital San Marino
towns Serravalle (industrial centre)
physical on the slope of Mount Titano

features surrounded by Italian territory; one of the world's smallest states
head of state and government two captains regent, elected for a six-month period
political system direct democracy
political parties San Marino Christian Democrat Party (PDCS), right-of-centre; Democratic Progressive Party (PDP), left-of-centre; Socialist Unity Party (PSU) and Socialist Party (PSS), both left-of-centre
exports wine, ceramics, paint, chemicals, building stone
currency Italian lira (2,187.00 = £1 July 1991)
population (1990 est) 23,000; growth rate 0.1% p.a.
life expectancy men 70, women 77
language Italian
religion Roman Catholic 95%
literacy 97% (1987)

chronology
1862 Treaty with Italy signed; independence recognized under Italy's protection.
1947-86 Governed by a series of left-wing and centre-left coalitions.
1986 Formation of Communist and Christian Democrat 'grand coalition'.

São Tomé e Príncipe (Democratic Republic of)

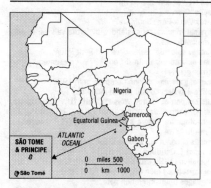

area 1,000 sq km/386 sq mi
capital São Tomé
towns Santo Antonio, Santa Cruz
physical comprises two main islands and several smaller ones, all volcanic; thickly forested and fertile
head of state and government Miguel Trovoada from 1991
political system emergent democratic republic
political parties Movement for the Liberation of São Tomé e Príncipe (MLSTP), nationalist socialist; Democratic Convergence Party—Reflection Group (PCD—GR), centre-left
exports cocoa, copra, coffee, palm oil and kernels
currency dobra (303.87 = £1 July 1991)
population (1990 est) 125,000; growth rate 2.5% p.a.
life expectancy men 62, women 62
languages Portuguese (official), Fang (Bantu)
religion Roman Catholic 80%, animist
literacy men 73%, women 42% (1981)
GNP $32 million (1987); $384 per head (1986)

chronology
1471 Discovered by Portuguese.
1522-1973 A province of Portugal.
1973 Achieved internal self-government.
1975 Independence achieved from Portugal, with Manuel Pinto da Costa as president.
1984 Formally declared a nonaligned state.
1987 Constitution amended.
1988 Unsuccessful coup attempt against da Costa.

1990 New constitution approved.
1991 First multiparty elections held; Miguel Trovoada replaced Pinto da Costa.

Saudi Arabia (Kingdom of)
(al-Mamlaka al-'Arabiya as-Sa'udiya)

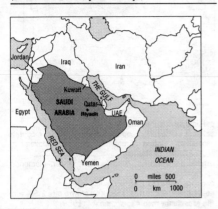

area 2,200,518 sq km/849,400 sq mi
capital Riyadh
towns Mecca, Medina, Taif; ports Jidda, Dammam
physical desert, sloping to the Persian Gulf from a height of 2,750 m/9,000 ft in the W
environment oil pollution caused by the Gulf War 1990-91 has affected 460 km/285 mi of the Saudi coastline, threatening desalination plants and damaging the wildlife of saltmarshes, mangrove forest, and mudflats
features Nafud Desert in N and the Rub'al Khali (Empty Quarter) in S, area 650,000 sq km/250,000 sq mi; with a ban on women drivers, there are an estimated 300,000 chauffeurs
head of state and government King Fahd Ibn Abdul Aziz from 1982
political system absolute monarchy
political parties none
exports oil, petroleum products
currency rial (6.07 = £1 July 1991)
population (1990 est) 16,758,000 (16% nomadic); growth rate 3.1% p.a.
life expectancy men 64, women 67 (1989)
language Arabic
religion Sunni Muslim; there is a Shi'ite minority
literacy men 34%, women 12% (1980 est)
GNP $70 bn (1988); $6,170 per head (1988)

chronology
1926-32 Territories united and kingdom established.
1953 King Ibn Saud died and was succeeded by his eldest son, Saud.
1964 King Saud forced to abdicate; succeeded by his brother, Faisal.
1975 King Faisal assassinated; succeeded by his half-brother, Khalid.
1982 King Khalid died; succeeded by his brother, Crown Prince Fahd.
1987 Rioting by Iranian pilgrims caused 400 deaths in Mecca; diplomatic relations with Iran severed.
1990 Iraqi troops invaded and annexed Kuwait and massed on Saudi Arabian border. King Fahd called for help from US and UK forces.
1991 King Fahd provided military and financial assistance in Gulf War. Calls from religious leaders for 'consultative assembly' to assist in government of kingdom. Saudi Arabia attended Middle East peace conference.
1992 Formation of a 'consultative council' seen as possible move towards representative government.

Senegal (Republic of)
(République du Sénégal)

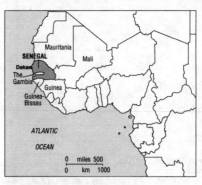

area 196,200 sq km/75,753 sq mi
capital and chief port Dakar
towns Thiès, Kaolack
physical plains rising to hills in SE; swamp and tropical forest in SW
features river Senegal; the Gambia forms an enclave within Senegal
head of state and government Abdou Diouf from 1981
political system emergent socialist democratic republic
political parties Senegalese Socialist Party (PS), democratic socialist; Senegalese Democratic Party (PDS), left-of-centre
exports peanuts, cotton, fish, phosphates
currency franc CFA (498.25 = £1 July 1991)
population (1990 est) 7,740,000; growth rate 3.1% p.a.
life expectancy men 51, women 54 (1989)
languages French (official); African dialects are spoken
religion Muslim 80%, Roman Catholic 10%, animist
literacy men 37%, women 19% (1985 est)
GNP $2 bn (1987); $380 per head (1984)

chronology
1659 Became a French colony.
1854-65 Interior occupied by French.
1902 Became a territory of French West Africa.
1959 Formed the Federation of Mali with French Sudan.
1960 Independence achieved from France, but withdrew from the federation. Léopold Sédar Senghor, leader of the Senegalese Progressive Union (UPS), became president.
1966 UPS declared the only legal party.
1974 Pluralist system re-established.
1976 UPS reconstituted as Senegalese Socialist Party (PS). Prime Minister Abdou Diouf nominated as Senghor's successor.
1980 Senghor resigned; succeeded by Diouf. Troops sent to defend Gambia.
1981 Military help again sent to Gambia.
1982 Confederation of Senegambia came into effect.
1983 Diouf re-elected. Post of prime minister abolished.
1988 Diouf decisively re-elected.
1989 Violent clashes between Senegalese and Mauritanians in Dakar and Nouakchott killed more than 450 people; over 50,000 people repatriated from both countries. Senegambia federation abandoned.
1991 Constitutional changes outlined.
1992 Diplomatic links with Mauritania re-established.

Seychelles (Republic of)

area 453 sq km/175 sq mi
capital Victoria (on Mahé island)

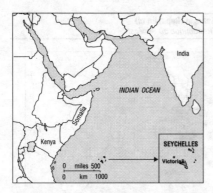

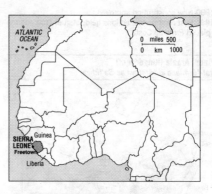

towns Cascade, Port Glaud, Misere

physical comprises two distinct island groups, one concentrated, the other widely scattered, totalling over 100 islands and islets

features Aldabra atoll, containing world's largest tropical lagoon; the unique 'double coconut' (*coco de mer*); tourism is important

head of state and government France-Albert René from 1977

political system one-party socialist republic

political party Seychelles People's Progressive Front (SPPF), nationalistic socialist

exports copra, cinnamon

currency Seychelles rupee (8.80 = £1 July 1991)

population (1990) 71,000; growth rate 2.2% p.a.

life expectancy 66 years (1988)

languages creole (Asian, African, European mixture) 95%, English, French (all official)

religion Roman Catholic 90%

literacy 80% (1989)

GNP $175 million; $2,600 per head (1987)

chronology

1744 Became a French colony.

1794 Captured by British.

1814 Ceded by France to Britain; incorporated as a dependency of Mauritius.

1903 Became a separate British colony.

1975 Internal self-government agreed.

1976 Independence achieved from Britain as a republic within the Commonwealth, with James Mancham as president.

1977 Albert René ousted Mancham in an armed coup and took over presidency.

1979 New constitution adopted; Seychelles People's Progressive Front (SPPF) sole legal party.

1981 Attempted coup by South African mercenaries thwarted.

1984 René re-elected.

1987 Coup attempt foiled.

1989 René re-elected.

1991 Multiparty politics promised.

1992 Mancham returned from exile.

Sierra Leone (Republic of)

area 71,740 sq km/27,710 sq mi

capital Freetown

towns Koidu, Bo, Kenema, Makeni

physical mountains in E; hills and forest; coastal mangrove swamps

features hot and humid climate (3,500 mm/138 in rainfall p.a.)

head of state and government military council headed by Capt Valentine Strasser from 1992

political system transitional

political parties All People's Congress (APC), moderate socialist; United Front of Political Movements (UNIFORM), centre-left

exports palm kernels, cocoa, coffee, ginger, diamonds, bauxite, rutile

currency leone (371.45 = £1 July 1991)

population (1990 est) 4,168,000; growth rate 2.5% p.a.

life expectancy men 41, women 47 (1989)

languages English (official), local languages

media no daily newspapers; 13 weekly papers, of which 11 are independent but only one achieves sales of over 5,000 copies

religion animist 52%, Muslim 39%, Protestant 6%, Roman Catholic 2% (1980 est)

literacy men 38%, women 21% (1985 est)

GNP $965 million (1987); $320 per head (1984)

chronology

1808 Became a British colony.

1896 Hinterland declared a British protectorate.

1961 Independence achieved from Britain within the Commonwealth, with Milton Margai, leader of Sierra Leone People's Party (SLPP), as prime minister.

1964 Milton succeeded by his half-brother, Albert Margai.

1967 Election results disputed by army, who set up a National Reformation Council and forced the governor general to leave.

1968 Army revolt made Siaka Stevens, leader of the All People's Congress (APC), prime minister.

1971 New constitution adopted, making Sierra Leone a republic, with Stevens as president.

1978 APC declared only legal party. Stevens sworn in for another seven-year term.

1985 Stevens retired; succeeded by Maj-Gen Joseph Momoh.

1989 Attempted coup against President Momoh foiled.

1991 Referendum endorsed multiparty politics.

1992 Military take-over; President Momoh fled. National Provisional Ruling Council (NPRC) established under Capt Valentine Strasser.

Singapore (Republic of)

area 622 sq km/240 sq mi

capital Singapore City

towns Jurong, Changi

physical comprises Singapore Island, low and flat, and 57 small islands

features Singapore Island is joined to the mainland by causeway across Strait of Johore; temperature range 21–34° = 69–93°F

head of state Wee Kim Wee from 1985

head of government Goh Chok Tong from 1990

political system liberal democracy with strict limits on dissent

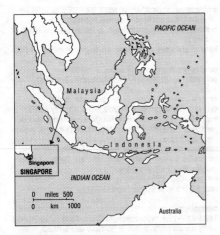

political parties People's Action Party (PAP), conservative; Workers' Party (WP), socialist; Singapore Democratic Party (SDP), liberal pluralist
exports electronics, petroleum products, rubber, machinery, vehicles
currency Singapore dollar (S$2.86 = £1 July 1991)
population (1990 est) 2,703,000 (Chinese 75%, Malay 14%, Tamil 7%); growth rate 1.2% p.a.
life expectancy men 71, women 77 (1989)
languages Malay (national tongue), Chinese, Tamil, English (all official)
religion Buddhist, Taoist, Muslim, Hindu, Christian
literacy men 93%, women 79% (1985 est)
GDP $19.9 bn (1987); $7,616 per head

chronology
1819 Singapore leased to British East India Company.
1858 Placed under crown rule.
1942 Invaded and occupied by Japan.
1945 Japanese removed by British forces.
1959 Independence achieved from Britain; Lee Kuan Yew became prime minister.
1963 Joined new Federation of Malaysia.
1965 Left federation to become an independent republic.
1984 Opposition made advances in parliamentary elections.
1986 Opposition leader convicted of perjury and prohibited from standing for election.
1988 Ruling conservative party elected to all but one of available assembly seats; increasingly authoritarian rule.
1990 Lee Kuan Yew resigned as prime minister; replaced by Goh Chok Tong.
1991 People's Action Party (PAP) and Goh Chok Tong re-elected.

Slovenia (Republic of)

area 20,251 sq km/7,817 sq mi
capital Ljubljana
towns Maribor, Kranj, Celji; chief port: Koper
physical mountainous; rivers: Sava, Drava
head of state Milan Kucan from 1990
head of government Janez Drnovsek from 1992
political system emergent democracy
political parties Democratic Opposition of Slovenia (DEMOS), six-party, right-of-centre coalition; Party of Democratic Reform, reform-communist
products grain, sugarbeet, livestock, timber, cotton and woollen textiles, steel, vehicles
currency tolar

population (1990) 2,000,000 (91% Slovene, 3% Croat, 2% Serb)
language Slovene, resembling Serbo-Croatian, written in Roman characters
religion Roman Catholic

chronology
1918 United with Serbia and Croatia.
1929 The kingdom of Serbs, Croats, and Slovenes took the name of Yugoslavia.
1945 Became a constituent republic of Yugoslav Socialist Federal Republic.
mid-1980s The Slovenian Communist Party liberalized itself and agreed to free elections. The Yugoslav counter-intelligence (KOV) began repression.
1989 Jan: Social Democratic Alliance of Slovenia launched as first political organization independent of Communist Party. Sept: constitution changed to allow secession from federation.
1990 Feb: Slovene League of Communists, renamed as the Party of Democratic Reform, severed its links with the Yugoslav League of Communists. April: nationalist DEMOS coalition secured victory in first multiparty parliamentary elections; Milan Kucan became president. July: sovereignty declared. Dec: independence overwhelmingly approved in referendum.
1991 June: independence declared; 100 killed after federal army intervened; cease-fire brokered by EC. July: cease-fire agreed between federal troops and nationalists. Oct: withdrawal of Yugoslav National Army (JNA) completed.
1992 USA and EC recognized Slovenia's independence; admitted into CSCE.

Solomon Islands

area 27,600 sq km/10,656 sq mi
capital Honiara (on Guadalcanal)
towns Gizo, Yandina
physical comprises all but the northernmost islands (which belong to Papua New Guinea) of a Melanesian archipelago stretching nearly 1,500 km/900 mi. The largest is Guadalcanal (area 6,500 sq km/2,510 sq mi); others are Malaita, San Cristobal, New Georgia, Santa Isabel, Choiseul; mainly mountainous and forested
features rivers ideal for hydroelectric power
head of state Elizabeth II represented by governor general
head of government Solomon Mamaloni from 1989
political system constitutional monarchy
political parties People's Alliance Party (PAP), centre-left; Solomon Islands United Party (SIUPA), right-of-centre
exports fish products, palm oil, copra, cocoa, timber
currency Solomon Island dollar (SI$4.44 = £1 July 1991)

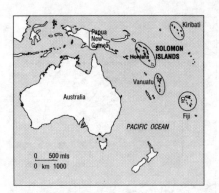

population (1990 est) 314,000 (Melanesian 95%, Polynesian 4%); growth rate 3.9% p.a.
life expectancy men 66, women 71
language English (official); there are some 120 Melanesian dialects
religion Anglican 34%, Roman Catholic 19%, South Sea Evangelical 17%
literacy 60% (1989)
GNP $141 million; $420 per head (1987)

chronology
1893 Solomon Islands placed under British protection.
1978 Independence achieved from Britain within the Commonwealth, with Peter Kenilorea as prime minister.
1981 Solomon Mamaloni replaced Kenilorea as prime minister.
1984 Kenilorea returned to power, heading a coalition government.
1986 Kenilorea resigned after allegations of corruption; replaced by his deputy, Ezekiel Alebua.
1988 Kenilorea elected deputy prime minister. Joined Vanuatu and Papua New Guinea to form the Spearhead Group, aiming to preserve Melanesian cultural traditions and secure independence for the French territory of New Caledonia.
1989 Solomon Mamaloni (People's Action Party) elected prime minister; formed PAP-dominated coalition.
1990 Mamaloni resigned as PAP party leader, but continued as head of national unity government.

Somalia (Somali Democratic Republic)
(Jamhuriyadda Dimugradiga Somaliya)

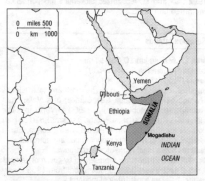

area 637,700 sq km/246,220 sq mi
capital Mogadishu
towns Hargeisa, Kismayu, port Berbera
physical mainly flat, with hills in N

environment destruction of trees for fuel and by grazing livestock has led to an increase in desert area
features occupies a strategic location on the Horn of Africa
head of state and government Ali Mahdi Mohammed from 1991
political system one-party socialist republic
political party Somali Revolutionary Socialist Party (SRSP), nationalist, socialist
exports livestock, skins, hides, bananas, fruit
currency Somali shilling (4,257.50 = £1 July 1991)
population (1990 est) 8,415,000 (including 350,000 refugees from Ethiopia and 50,000 in Djibouti); growth rate 3.1% p.a.
life expectancy men 53, women 53 (1989)
languages Somali, Arabic (both official), Italian, English
religion Sunni Muslim 99%
literacy 40% (1986)
GNP $1.5 bn; $290 per head (1987)

chronology
1884-87 British protectorate of Somaliland established.
1889 Italian protectorate of Somalia established.
1960 Independence achieved from Italy and Britain.
1963 Border dispute with Kenya; diplomatic relations with the UK broken.
1968 Diplomatic relations with the UK restored.
1969 Army coup led by Maj-Gen Mohamed Siad Barre; constitution suspended, Supreme Revolutionary Council set up; name changed to Somali Democratic Republic.
1978 Defeated in eight-month war with Ethiopia. Armed insurrection began in north.
1979 New constitution for socialist one-party state adopted.
1982 Antigovernment Somali National Movement formed. Oppressive countermeasures by government.
1987 Barre re-elected president.
1989 Dissatisfaction with government and increased guerrilla activity in north.
1990 Civil war intensified. Constitutional reforms promised.
1991 Mogadishu captured by rebels; Barre fled; Ali Mahdi Mohammed named president; free elections promised. Secession of NE Somalia, as the Somaliland Republic, announced. Cease-fire signed, but later collapsed. Thousands of casualties as a result of heavy fighting in capital.
1992 Relief efforts to ward off impending famine severely hindered by unstable political situation.

South Africa (Republic of)
(Republiek van Suid-Afrika)

area 1,223,181 sq km/472,148 sq mi (includes Walvis Bay and independent black homelands)
capital and port Cape Town (legislative), Pretoria (administrative), Bloemfontein (judicial)
towns Johannesburg; ports Durban, Port Elizabeth, East London
physical southern end of large plateau, fringed by mountains and lowland coastal margin
territories Marion Island and Prince Edward Island in the Antarctic
features Drakensberg Mountains, Table Mountain; Limpopo and Orange rivers; the Veld and the Karoo; part of Kalahari Desert; Kruger National Park
head of state and government F W de Klerk from 1989
political system racist, nationalist republic, restricted democracy
political parties White: National Party (NP), right-of-centre, racist; Conservative Party of South Africa (CPSA), extreme right, racist; Democratic Party (DP), left-of-centre, multiracial. Coloureds: Labour Party of South Africa, left-of-centre; People's Congress Party,

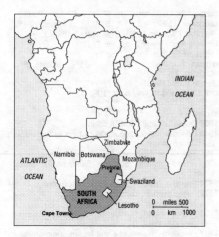

right-of-centre. Indian: National People's Party, right-of-centre; Solidarity Party, left-of-centre

exports maize, sugar, fruit, wool, gold (world's largest producer), platinum, diamonds, uranium, iron and steel, copper; mining and minerals are largest export industry, followed by arms manufacturing

currency rand (R4.68, commercial rate = £1 July 1991)

population (1990 est) 39,550,000 (73% black: Zulu, Xhosa, Sotho, Tswana; 18% white: 3% mixed, 3% Asian); growth rate 2.5% p.a.

life expectancy whites 71, Asians 67, blacks 58

languages Afrikaans and English (both official), Bantu

religion Dutch Reformed Church 40%, Anglican 11%, Roman Catholic 8%, other Christian 25%, Hindu, Muslim

literacy whites 99%, Asians 69%, blacks 50% (1989)

GNP $81 bn; $1,890 per head (1987)

chronology

1910 Union of South Africa formed from two British colonies and two Boer republics.

1912 African National Congress (ANC) formed.

1948 Apartheid system of racial discrimination initiated by Daniel Malan, leader of National Party (NP).

1955 Freedom Charter adopted by ANC.

1958 Malan succeeded as prime minister by Hendrik Verwoerd.

1960 ANC banned.

1961 South Africa withdrew from Commonwealth and became a republic.

1962 ANC leader Nelson Mandela jailed.

1964 Mandela, Walter Sisulu, Govan Mbeki, and five other ANC leaders sentenced to life imprisonment.

1966 Verwoerd assassinated; succeeded by B J Vorster.

1976 Soweto uprising.

1977 Death in custody of Pan African Congress activist Steve Biko.

1978 Vorster resigned and was replaced by Pieter W Botha.

1984 New constitution adopted, giving segregated representation to Coloureds and Asians and making Botha president. Nonaggression pact with Mozambique signed but not observed.

1985 Growth of violence in black townships.

1986 Commonwealth agreed on limited sanctions. US Congress voted to impose sanctions. Some major multinational companies closed down their South African operations.

1987 Government formally acknowledged the presence of its military forces in Angola.

1988 Botha announced 'limited constitutional reforms'. South Africa agreed to withdraw from Angola and recognize Namibia's independence as part of regional peace accord.

1989 Botha gave up NP leadership and state presidency. F W de Klerk became president. ANC activists released; beaches and public facilities desegregated. Elections held in Namibia to create independence government.

1990 ANC ban lifted; Nelson Mandela released from prison. NP membership opened to all races. Oliver Tambo returned. Daily average of 35 murders and homicides recorded.

1991 Mandela and Zulu leader Buthelezi urged end to fighting between ANC and Inkatha. Mandela elected ANC president. Revelations of government support for Inkatha threatened ANC cooperation. De Klerk announced repeal of remaining apartheid laws. South Africa readmitted to international sport. USA lifted sanctions. PAC and Buthelezi withdrew from negotiations over new constitution.

1992 Constitution leading to all-races majority rule approved by whites-only referendum. Boipatong killings, allegedly by Inkatha supporters with police backing, threatened constitutional talks.

Spain
(España)

area 504,750 sq km/194,960 sq mi

capital Madrid

towns Zaragoza, Seville, Murcia, Córdoba; ports Barcelona, Valencia, Cartagena, Málaga, Cádiz, Vigo, Santander, Bilbao

physical central plateau with mountain ranges; lowlands in S

territories Balearic and Canary Islands; in N Africa: Ceuta, Melilla, Alhucemas, Chafarinas Is, Peñón de Vélez

features rivers Ebro, Douro, Tagus, Guadiana, Guadalquivir; Iberian Plateau (Meseta); Pyrenees, Cantabrian Mountains, Andalusian Mountains, Sierra Nevada

head of state King Juan Carlos I from 1975

head of government Felipe González Márquez from 1982

political system constitutional monarchy

political parties Socialist Workers' Party (PSOE), democratic socialist; Popular Alliance (AP), centre-right; Christian Democrats (DC), centrist; Liberal Party (PL), left-of-centre

exports citrus fruits, grapes, pomegranates, vegetables, wine, sherry, olive oil, canned fruit and fish, iron ore, cork, vehicles, textiles, petroleum products, leather goods, ceramics

currency peseta (184.10 = £1 July 1991)

population (1990 est) 39,623,000; growth rate 0.2% p.a.

life expectancy men 74, women 80 (1989)

languages Spanish (Castilian, official), Basque, Catalan, Galician, Valencian, Majorcan
religion Roman Catholic 99%
literacy 97% (1989)
GNP $288 bn (1987); $4,490 per head (1984)

chronology
1936-39 Civil war; General Francisco Franco became head of state and government; fascist party Falange declared only legal political organization.
1947 General Franco announced restoration of the monarchy after his death, with Prince Juan Carlos as his successor.
1975 Franco died; succeeded as head of state by King Juan Carlos I.
1978 New constitution adopted with Adolfo Suárez, leader of the Democratic Centre Party, as prime minister.
1981 Suárez resigned; succeeded by Leopoldo Calvo Sotelo. Attempted military coup thwarted.
1982 Socialist Workers' Party (PSOE), led by Felipe González, won a sweeping electoral victory. Basque separatist organization (ETA) stepped up its guerrilla campaign.
1985 ETA's campaign spread to holiday resorts.
1986 Referendum confirmed NATO membership. Spain joined the European Economic Community.
1988 Spain joined the Western European Union.
1989 PSOE lost seats to hold only parity after general election. Talks between government and ETA collapsed and truce ended.

Sri Lanka (Democratic Socialist Republic of)
(Prajathanrika Samajawadi Janarajaya Sri Lanka) (until 1972 Ceylon)

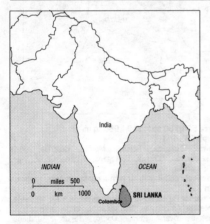

area 65,600 sq km/25,328 sq mi
capital and chief port Colombo
towns Kandy; ports Jaffna, Galle, Negombo, Trincomalee
physical flat in N and around the coast; hills and mountains in S and central interior
features Adam's Peak (2,243 m/7,538 ft); ruined cities of Anuradhapura, Polonnaruwa
head of state Ranasinghe Premadasa from 1989
head of government Dingiri Banda Wijetunge from 1989
political system liberal democratic republic
political parties United National Party (UNP), right-of-centre; Sri Lanka Freedom Party (SLFP), left-of-centre; Democratic United National Front (DUNF), centre-left; Tamil United Liberation Front (TULF), Tamil autonomy; Eelam People's Revolutionary Liberation Front (EPLRF), Indian-backed Tamil-secessionist 'Tamil Tigers'
exports tea, rubber, coconut products, graphite, sapphires, rubies, other gemstones

currency Sri Lanka rupee (Rs 66.00 = £1 July 1991)
population (1990 est) 17,135,000 (Sinhalese 74%, Tamils 17%, Moors 7%); growth rate 1.8% p.a.
life expectancy men 67, women 72 (1989)
languages Sinhala, Tamil, English
religion Buddhist 69%, Hindu 15%, Muslim 8%, Christian 7%
literacy 87% (1988)
GNP $7.2 bn; $400 per head (1988)

chronology
1802 Ceylon became a British colony.
1948 Ceylon achieved independence from Britain within the Commonwealth.
1956 Sinhala established as the official language.
1959 Prime Minister Solomon Bandaranaike assassinated.
1972 Socialist Republic of Sri Lanka proclaimed.
1978 Presidential constitution adopted by new Jayawardene government.
1983 Tamil guerrilla violence escalated; state of emergency imposed.
1987 President Jayawardene and Indian prime minister Rajiv Gandhi signed Colombo Accord. Violence continued despite cease-fire policed by Indian troops.
1988 Left-wing guerrillas campaigned against Indo-Sri Lankan peace pact. Prime Minister Ranasinghe Premadasa elected president.
1989 Premadasa became president; D B Wijetunge, prime minister. Leaders of the TULF and terrorist People's Liberation Front assassinated.
1990 Indian peacekeeping force withdrawn. Violence continued.
1991 March: defence minister, Ranjan Wijeratne, assassinated. March: Sri Lankan army killed 2,552 Tamil Tigers at Elephant Pass. Oct: impeachment motion against President Premadasa failed. Dec: New party, the Democratic United National Front, formed by former members of UNP.

Sudan (Democratic Republic of)
(Jamhuryat es-Sudan)

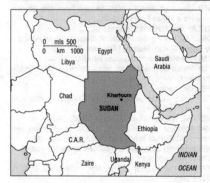

area 2,505,800 sq km/967,489 sq mi
capital Khartoum
towns Omdurman, Juba, Wadi Medani, al-Obeid, Kassala, Atbara, al-Qadarif, Kosti; chief port Port Sudan
physical fertile valley of river Nile separates Libyan Desert in W from high rocky Nubian Desert in E
environment the building of the Jonglei Canal to supply water to N Sudan and Egypt threatens the grasslands of S Sudan
features Sudd swamp; largest country in Africa
head of state and government General Omar Hassan Ahmed el-Bashir from 1989
political system military republic
political parties New National Umma Party (NNUP), Islamic, nationalist; Democratic Unionist Party (DUP),

moderate, nationalist; National Islamic Front, Islamic, nationalist
exports cotton, gum arabic, sesame seed, peanuts, sorghum
currency Sudanese pound (S7.31 official rate, 18.60 financial rate = £1 July 1991)
population (1990 est) 25,164,000; growth rate 2.9% p.a.
life expectancy men 51, women 55 (1989)
languages Arabic 51% (official), local languages
religion Sunni Muslim 73%, animist 18%, Christian 9% (in south)
literacy 30% (1986)
GNP $8.5 bn (1988); $330 per head (1988)

chronology
1820 Sudan ruled by Egypt.
1885 Revolt led to capture of Khartoum by self-proclaimed Mahdi.
1896-98 Anglo-Egyptian offensive led by Lord Kitchener subdued revolt.
1899 Sudan administered as an Anglo-Egyptian condominium.
1955 Civil war between Muslim north and non-Muslim south broke out.
1956 Sudan achieved independence from Britain and Egypt as a republic.
1958 Military coup replaced civilian government with Supreme Council of the Armed Forces.
1964 Civilian rule reinstated.
1969 Coup led by Col Gaafar Mohammed Nimeri established Revolutionary Command Council (RCC); name changed to Democratic Republic of Sudan.
1970 Union with Egypt agreed in principle.
1971 New constitution adopted; Nimeri confirmed as president; Sudanese Socialist Union (SSU) declared only legal party.
1972 Proposed Federation of Arab Republics, comprising Sudan, Egypt, and Syria, abandoned. Addis Ababa conference proposed autonomy for southern provinces.
1974 National assembly established.
1983 Nimeri re-elected. *Shari'a* (Islamic law) introduced.
1985 Nimeri deposed in a bloodless coup led by General Swar al-Dahab; transitional military council set up. State of emergency declared.
1986 More than 40 political parties fought general election; coalition government formed.
1987 Virtual civil war with Sudan People's Liberation Movement (SPLM).
1988 Al-Mahdi formed a new coalition. Another flare-up of civil war between north and south created tens of thousands of refugees. Floods made 1.5 million people homeless. Peace pact signed with SPLM.
1989 Sadiq al-Mahdi overthrown in coup led by General Omar Hassan Ahmed el-Bashir.
1990 Civil war continued with new SPLM offensive.
1991 Federal system introduced, with division of country into nine states.

Surinam (Republic of)
(Republiek Suriname)

area 163,820 sq km/63,243 sq mi
capital Paramaribo
towns Nieuw Nickerie, Brokopondo, Nieuw Amsterdam
physical hilly and forested, with flat and narrow coastal plain
features Suriname River
head of state and government Ronald Venetiaan from 1991
political system emergent democratic republic
political parties Party for National Unity and Solidarity (KTPI)*, Indonesian, left-of-centre; Surinam National Party (NPS)*, Creole, left-of-centre; Progressive Reform

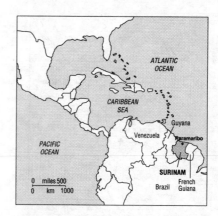

Party (VHP)*, Indian, left-of-centre; New Front For Democracy and Development (FDD)
*members of Front for Democracy and Development (FDD)
exports alumina, aluminium, bauxite, rice, timber
currency Surinam guilder (2.90 = £1 July 1991)
population (1990 est) 408,000 (Hindu 37%, Creole 31%, Javanese 15%); growth rate 1.1% p.a.
life expectancy men 66, women 71 (1989)
languages Dutch (official), Sranan (creole), English, others
religion Christian 30%, Hindu 27%, Muslim 20%
literacy 65% (1989)
GNP $1.1 bn (1987); $2,920 per head (1985)

chronology
1667 Became a Dutch colony.
1954 Achieved internal self-government as Dutch Guiana.
1975 Independence achieved from the Netherlands, with Dr Johan Ferrier as president and Henck Arron as prime minister; 40% of the population emigrated to the Netherlands.
1980 Arron's government overthrown in army coup; Ferrier refused to recognize military regime; appointed Dr Henk Chin A Sen to lead civilian administration. Army replaced Ferrier with Dr Chin A Sen.
1982 Army, led by Lt-Col Desi Bouterse, seized power, setting up a Revolutionary People's Front.
1985 Ban on political activities lifted.
1986 Antigovernment rebels brought economic chaos to Surinam.
1987 New constitution approved.
1988 Ramsewak Shankar elected president.
1989 Bouterse rejected peace accord reached by President Shankar with guerrilla insurgents, vowed to continue fighting.
1990 Shankar deposed in army coup.
1991 Johan Kraag became interim president. New Front for Democracy and Development won assembly majority. Ronald Venetiaan elected president.

Swaziland (Kingdom of)
(Umbuso weSwatini)

area 17,400 sq km/6,716 sq mi
capital Mbabane
towns Manzini, Big Bend
physical central valley; mountains in W (Highveld); plateau in E (Lowveld and Lubombo plateau)
features landlocked enclave between South Africa and Mozambique
head of state and government King Mswati III from 1986
political system near-absolute monarchy

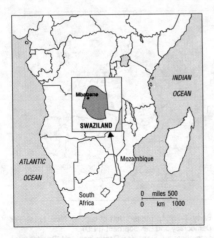

political party Imbokodvo National Movement (INM), nationalistic monarchist
exports sugar, canned fruit, wood pulp, asbestos
currency lilangeni (4.68 = £1 July 1991)
population (1990 est) 779,000; growth rate 3% p.a.
life expectancy men 47, women 54 (1989)
languages Swazi 90%, English (both official)
religion Christian 57%, animist
literacy men 70%, women 66% (1985 est)
GNP $539 million; $750 per head (1987)

chronology
1903 Swaziland became a special High Commission territory.
1967 Achieved internal self-government.
1968 Independence achieved from Britain, within the Commonwealth, as the Kingdom of Swaziland, with King Sobhuza II as head of state.
1973 The king suspended the constitution and assumed absolute powers.
1978 New constitution adopted.
1982 King Sobhuza died; his place was taken by one of his wives, Dzeliwe, until his son, Prince Makhosetive, reached the age of 21.
1983 Queen Dzeliwe ousted by another wife, Ntombi.
1984 After royal power struggle, it was announced that the crown prince would become king at 18.
1986 Crown prince formally invested as King Mswati III.
1987 Power struggle developed between advisory council Liqoqo and Queen Ntombi over accession of king. Mswati dissolved parliament; new government elected with Sotsha Dlamini as prime minister.
1991 Calls for democratic reform.

Sweden (Kingdom of)
(Konungariket Sverige)

---

area 450,000 sq km/173,745 sq mi
capital Stockholm
towns Göteborg, Malmö, Uppsala, Norrköping, Västerås
physical mountains in W; plains in S; thickly forested; more than 20,000 islands off the Stockholm coast
environment of the country's 90,000 lakes, 20,000 are affected by acid rain; 4,000 are so severely acidified that no fish are thought to survive in them
features lakes, including Vänern, Vättern, Mälaren, Hjälmaren; islands of Öland and Gotland; wild elk
head of state King Carl XVI Gustaf from 1973
head of government Carl Bildt from 1991
political system constitutional monarchy
political parties Social Democratic Labour party (SAP),

moderate, left-of-centre; Moderate Party, right-of-centre; Liberal Party, centre-left; Centre Party, centrist; Christian Democratic Party, Christian, centrist; Left (Communist) Party, European, Marxist; Green, ecological
exports aircraft, vehicles, ballbearings, drills, missiles, electronics, petrochemicals, textiles, furnishings, ornamental glass, paper, iron and steel
currency krona (10.58 = £1 July 1991)
population (1990 est) 8,407,000 (including 17,000 Saami (Lapps) and 1.2 million postwar immigrants from Finland, Turkey, Yugoslavia, Greece, Iran, other Nordic countries); growth rate 0.1% p.a.
life expectancy men 74, women 81 (1989)
languages Swedish; there are Finnish- and Saami-speaking minorities
religion Lutheran (official) 95%
literacy 99% (1989)
GNP $179 bn; $11,783 per head (1989)

chronology
12th century United as an independent nation.
1397-1520 Under Danish rule.
1914-45 Neutral in both world wars.
1951-76 Social Democratic Labour Party (SAP) in power.
1969 Olof Palme became SAP leader and prime minister.
1971 Constitution amended, creating a single-chamber Riksdag, the governing body.
1975 Monarch's last constitutional powers removed.
1976 Thorbjörn Fälldin, leader of the Centre Party, became prime minister, heading centre-right coalition.
1982 SAP, led by Palme, returned to power.
1985 SAP formed minority government, with Communist support.
1986 Olof Palme murdered. Ingvar Carlsson became prime minister and SAP party leader.
1988 SAP re-elected with reduced majority; Green Party gained representation in Riksdag.
1990 SAP government resigned. Sweden to apply for European Community (EC) membership.
1991 Formal application for EC membership submitted. Election defeat for SAP; coalition government formed; Carl Bildt became new prime minister.

Switzerland (Swiss Confederation)
(German Schweiz, French Suisse, Romansch Svizzera)

---

area 41,300 sq km/15,946 sq mi
capital Bern
towns Zürich, Geneva, Lausanne; river port Basel (on the Rhine)
physical most mountainous country in Europe (Alps and Jura mountains); highest peak Dufourspitze 4,634 m/15,203 ft in Apennines
environment an estimated 43% of coniferous trees,

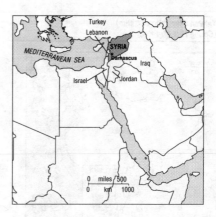

particularly in the central alpine region, have been killed by acid rain, 90% of which comes from other countries. Over 50% of bird species are classified as threatened

features winter sports area of the upper valley of the river Inn (Engadine); lakes Maggiore, Lucerne, Geneva, Constance

head of state and government René Felber from 1992

government federal democratic republic

political parties Radical Democratic Party (FDP), radical, centre-left; Social Democratic Party (SPS), moderate, left-of-centre; Christian Democratic Party (PDC), Christian, moderate, centrist; People's Party (SVP), centre-left; Liberal Party (PLS), federalist, centre-left; Green Party, ecological

exports electrical goods, chemicals, pharmaceuticals, watches, precision instruments, confectionery

currency Swiss franc (2.53 = £1 July 1991)

population (1990 est) 6,628,000; growth rate 0.2% p.a.

life expectancy men 74, women 82 (1989)

languages German 65%, French 18%, Italian 12%, Romansch 1% (all official)

religion Roman Catholic 50%, Protestant 48%

literacy 99% (1989)

GNP $111 bn (1988); $26,309 per head (1987)

chronology

1648 Became independent of the Holy Roman Empire.

1798-1815 Helvetic Republic established by French revolutionary armies.

1847 Civil war resulted in greater centralization.

1874 Principle of the referendum introduced.

1971 Women given the vote in federal elections.

1984 First female cabinet minister appointed.

1986 Referendum rejected proposal for membership of United Nations.

1989 Referendum supported abolition of citizen army and military service requirements.

1991 18-year-olds allowed to vote for first time in national elections. Four-party coalition remained in power.

1992 René Felber elected president with Adolf Ogi as vice president. Decision to apply for full EC membership.

Syria (Syrian Arab Republic)
(al-Jamhuriya al-Arabya as-Suriya)

---

area 185,200 sq km/71,506 sq mi

capital Damascus

towns Aleppo, Homs, Hama; chief port Latakia

physical mountains alternate with fertile plains and desert areas; Euphrates River

features Mount Hermon, Golan Heights; crusader castles (including Krak des Chevaliers); Phoenician city sites (Ugarit), ruins of ancient Palmyra

head of state and government Hafez al-Assad from 1971

political system socialist republic

political parties National Progressive Front (NPF), pro-Arab, socialist; Communist Action Party, socialist

exports cotton, cereals, oil, phosphates, tobacco

currency Syrian pound (Syr 34.12 = £1 July 1991)

population (1990 est) 12,471,000; growth rate 3.5% p.a.

life expectancy men 67, women 69 (1989)

languages Arabic 89% (official), Kurdish 6%, Armenian 3%

religion Sunni Muslim 74%; ruling minority Alawite, and other Islamic sects 16%; Christian 10%

literacy men 76%, women 43% (1985 est)

GNP $17 bn (1986); $702 per head

chronology

1946 Achieved full independence from France.

1958 Merged with Egypt to form the United Arab Republic (UAR).

1961 UAR disintegrated.

1967 Six-Day War resulted in the loss of territory to Israel.

1970-71 Syria supported Palestinian guerrillas against Jordanian troops.

1971 Following a bloodless coup, Hafez al-Assad became president.

1973 Israel consolidated its control of the Golan Heights after the Yom Kippur War.

1976 Substantial numbers of troops committed to the civil war in Lebanon.

1978 Assad re-elected.

1981-82 Further military engagements in Lebanon.

1982 Islamic militant uprising suppressed; 5,000 dead.

1984 Presidents Assad and Gemayel approved plans for government of national unity in Lebanon.

1985 Assad secured the release of 39 US hostages held in an aircraft hijacked by extremist Shi'ite group, Hezbollah. Assad re-elected.

1987 Improved relations with USA and attempts to secure the release of Western hostages in Lebanon.

1989 Diplomatic relations with Morocco restored. Continued fighting in Lebanon; Syrian forces reinforced in Lebanon; diplomatic relations with Egypt restored.

1990 Diplomatic relations with Britain restored.

1991 Syria fought against Iraq in Gulf War. President Assad agreed to US Middle East peace plan. Assad re-elected as president.

Taiwan (Republic of China)
(*Chung Hua Min Kuo*)

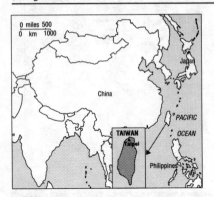

area 36,179 sq km/13,965 sq mi
capital Taipei
towns ports Kaohsiung, Keelung
physical island (formerly Formosa) off People's Republic of China; mountainous, with lowlands in W
environment industrialization has taken its toll: an estimated 30% of the annual rice crop is dangerously contaminated with mercury, cadmium, and other heavy metals
features Penghu (Pescadores), Jinmen (Quemoy), Mazu (Matsu) islands
head of state Lee Teng-hui from 1988
head of government Hau Pei-tsun from 1990
political system emergent democracy
political parties Nationalist Party of China (Kuomintang: KMT), anticommunist, Chinese nationalist; Democratic Progressive Party (DPP), centrist-pluralist, pro-self-determination grouping; Workers' Party (Kuntang), left-of-centre
exports textiles, steel, plastics, electronics, foodstuffs
currency New Taiwan dollar (NT$44.12 = £1 July 1991)
population (1990) 20,454,000 (84% Taiwanese, 14% mainlanders); growth rate 1.4% p.a.
life expectancy 70 men, 75 women (1986)
language Mandarin Chinese (official); Taiwan, Hakka dialects
religion officially atheist; Taoist, Confucian, Buddhist, Christian
literacy 90% (1988)
GNP $119.1 bn; $6,200 per head (1988)

chronology
1683 Taiwan (Formosa) annexed by China.
1895 Ceded to Japan.
1945 Recovered by China.
1949 Flight of Nationalist government to Taiwan after Chinese communist revolution.
1954 US-Taiwanese mutual defence treaty.
1971 Expulsion from United Nations.
1972 Commencement of legislature elections.
1975 President Chiang Kai-shek died; replaced as Kuomintang leader by his son, Chiang Ching-kuo.
1979 USA severed diplomatic relations and annulled 1954 security pact.
1986 Democratic Progressive Party (DPP) formed as opposition to the nationalist Kuomintang.
1987 Martial law lifted; opposition parties legalized; press restrictions lifted.
1988 President Chiang Ching-kuo died; replaced by Taiwanese-born Lee Teng-hui.
1989 Kuomintang (KMT) won assembly elections.
1990 Formal move towards normalization of relations with China. Hau Pei-tsun became prime minister.

1991 President Lee Teng-hui declared end to state of civil war with China. Constitution amended. DPP announced pro-independence campaign. KMT won landslide victory in new assembly elections, following resignation of remaining mainland-elected 'life representatives'.

Tajikistan (Republic of)

area 143,100 sq km/55,251 sq mi
capital Dushanbe
towns Khodzhent (formerly Leninabad), Kurgan-Tyube, Kulyab
physical mountainous, more than half of its territory lying above 3,000 m/10,000 ft; huge mountain glaciers which are the source of many rapid rivers
features Pik Kommuniza (Communism Peak); health resorts and mineral springs
head of state Rakhman Nabiyev from 1991
head of government Akbar Mizoyev
political system socialist pluralist
political parties Socialist (formerly Communist) Party of Tajikistan (SPT); Democratic Party; Islamic Revival Party
products fruit, cereals, cotton, cattle, sheep, silks, carpets, coal, lead, zinc, chemicals, oil, gas
population (1990) 5,300,000 (63% Tajik, 24% Uzbek, 8% Russian, 1% Tatar, 1% Kyrgyz, 1% Ukrainian)
language Tajik, similar to Farsi (Persian)
religion Sunni Muslim

chronology
1921 Part of Turkestan Soviet Socialist Autonomous Republic.
1929 Became a constituent republic of USSR.
1990 Ethnic Tajik/Armenian conflict in Dushanbe resulted in rioting against Communist Party; state of emergency and curfew imposed.
1991 Jan: curfew lifted in Dushanbe. March: republic endorsed maintenance of Union in USSR referendum. Aug: President Makhkamov initially supported anti-Gorbachev coup, but later forced to resign; Tajik Communist Party broke with CPSU. Sept: declared independence from the Soviet Union; Nabiyev elected president; Communist Party of Tajikistan (TCP) renamed Socialist Party of Tajikistan (SPT); state of emergency declared. Oct: Nabiyev resigned but was re-elected a month later. Dec: joined new Commonwealth of Independent States (CIS); independence acknowledged by USA but diplomatic recognition withheld.
1992 Jan: admitted into CSCE. Nabiyev temporarily ousted after 20 demonstrators killed in Dushanbe but returned at head of coalition; state of emergency lifted.

Tanzania (United Republic of)
(Jamhuri ya Muungano wa Tanzania)

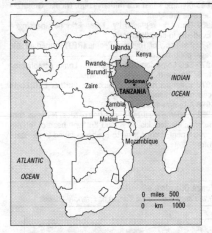

area 945,000 sq km/364,865 sq mi
capital Dodoma (since 1983)
towns Zanzibar Town, Mwanza; chief port and former capital Dar es Salaam
physical central plateau; lakes in N and W; coastal plains; lakes Victoria, Tanganyika, and Niasa
environment the black rhino faces extinction as a result of poaching
features comprises islands of Zanzibar and Pemba; Mount Kilimanjaro, 5,895 m/19,340 ft, the highest peak in Africa; Serengeti National Park, Olduvai Gorge; Ngorongoro Crater, 14.5 km/9 mi across, 762 m/2,500 ft deep
head of state and government Ali Hassan Mwinyi from 1985
political system one-party socialist republic
political party Revolutionary Party of Tanzania (CCM), African, socialist
exports coffee, cotton, sisal, cloves, tea, tobacco, cashew nuts, diamonds
currency Tanzanian shilling (371.64 = £1 July 1991)
population (1990 est) 26,070,000; growth rate 3.5% p.a.
life expectancy men 49, women 54 (1989)
languages Kiswahili, English (both official)
religion Muslim 35%, Christian 35%, traditional 30%
literacy 85% (1987)
GNP $4.9 bn; $258 per head (1987)

chronology
16th–17th centuries Zanzibar under Portuguese control.
1890-1963 Zanzibar became a British protectorate.
1920-46 Tanganyika administered as a British League of Nations mandate.
1946-62 Tanganyika came under United Nations (UN) trusteeship.
1961 Tanganyika achieved independence from Britain, within the Commonwealth, with Julius Nyerere as prime minister.
1962 Tanganyika became a republic with Nyerere as president.
1964 Tanganyika and Zanzibar became the United Republic of Tanzania with Nyerere as president.
1967 East African Community (EAC) formed. Arusha Declaration.
1977 Revolutionary Party of Tanzania (CCM) proclaimed the only legal party. EAC dissolved.
1978 Ugandan forces repulsed after crossing into Tanzania.

1979 Tanzanian troops sent to Uganda to help overthrow the president, Idi Amin.
1985 Nyerere retired from presidency but stayed on as CCM leader; Ali Hassan Mwinyi became president.
1990 Nyerere surrendered CCM leadership; replaced by President Mwinyi.
1992 CCM agreed to abolish one-party rule. East African cooperation pact with Kenya and Uganda to be reestablished.

Thailand (Kingdom of)
(Prathet Thai or Muang-Thai)

area 513,115 sq km/198,108 sq mi
capital and chief port Bangkok
towns Chiangmai, Nakhon Sawan river port
physical mountainous, semi-arid plateau in NE, fertile central region, tropical isthmus in S
environment tropical rainforest was reduced to 18% of the land area 1988 (from 93% in 1961); logging was banned by the government 1988
features rivers Chao Phraya, Mekong, Salween; ancient ruins of Sukhothai and Ayurrhaya
head of state King Bhumibol Adulyadej from 1946
head of government Anand Panyarachun from 1992
political system military-controlled emergent democracy
political parties New Aspiration Party; Samakkhi Tham (Justice and Unity) Party, right-of-centre, airforce-linked; Palang Dharma, anti-corruption; Social Action Party (Kij Sangkhom), right-of-centre; Thai Nation (Chart Thai), conservative, pro-business; Liberal Democratic Party
exports rice, textiles, rubber, tin, rubies, sapphires, maize, tapioca
currency baht (41.00 = £1 July 1991)
population (1990 est) 54,890,000 (Thai 75%, Chinese 14%); growth rate 2% p.a.
life expectancy men 62, women 68 (1989)
languages Thai and Chinese (both official); regional dialects
religion Buddhist 95%, Muslim 4%
literacy 89% (1988)
GNP $52 bn (1988); $771 per head (1988)

chronology
1782 Siam absolutist dynasty commenced.
1896 Anglo-French agreement recognized Siam as independent buffer state.
1932 Constitutional monarchy established.
1939 Name of Thailand adopted.
1941-44 Japanese occupation.
1947 Military seized power in coup.
1972 Withdrawal of Thai troops from South Vietnam.
1973 Military government overthrown.

1976 Military reassumed control.
1980 General Prem Tinsulanonda assumed power.
1983 Civilian government formed; martial law maintained.
1988 Prime Minister Prem resigned; replaced by Chatichai Choonhavan.
1989 Thai pirates continued to murder, pillage, and kidnap Vietnamese 'boat people' at sea.
1991 Military seized power in coup. Interim civilian government formed under Anand Panyarachun. 50,000 demonstrated against new military-orientated constitution.
1992 General election produced five-party coalition. Appointment of General Suchinda Kraprayoon as premier provoked widespread riots. Krapayoon fled the country after army shooting of 100 demonstrators in May; Somboon Rahong nominated to succeed him. Nomination rejected by King Abulyadej; Panyarachun restored as prime minister.

1960 French Togoland achieved independence from France as the Republic of Togo with Sylvanus Olympio as head of state.
1963 Olympio killed in a military coup. Nicolas Grunitzky became president.
1967 Grunitzky replaced by Lt-Gen Etienne Gnassingbé Eyadéma in bloodless coup.
1973 Assembly of Togolese People (RPT) formed as sole legal political party.
1975 EEC Lomé convention signed in Lomé, establishing trade links with developing countries.
1979 Eyadéma returned in election. Further EEC Lomé convention signed.
1986 Attempted coup failed.
1991 Eyadéma legalized opposition parties. National conference elected Joseph Kokou Koffigoh head of interim government; troops loyal to Eyadema failed to reinstate him.

Togo (Republic of)
(République Togolaise)

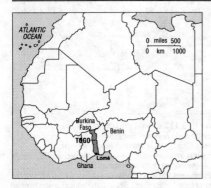

area 56,800 sq km/21,930 sq mi
capital Lomé
towns Sokodé, Kpalimé
physical two savanna plains, divided by range of hills NE–SW; coastal lagoons and marsh
environment the homes of thousands of people in Keto were destroyed by coastal erosion as a result of the building of the Volta dam
features Mono Tableland, Oti Plateau, Oti River
head of state President Eyadéma
head of government Jospeh Kokou Koffigoh from 1991
political system transitional
political parties Rally of the Togolese People (RPT), centrist nationalist; Alliance of Togolese Democrats (ADT), left-of-centre; Togolese Movement for Democracy (MDT), left-of-centre
exports phosphates, cocoa, coffee, coconuts
currency franc CFA (498.25 = £1 July 1991)
population (1990 est) 3,566,000; growth rate 3% p.a.
life expectancy men 53, women 57 (1989)
languages French (official), Ewe, Kabre
religion animist 46%, Catholic 28%, Muslim 17%, Protestant 9%
literacy men 53%, women 28% (1985 est)
GNP $1.3 bn (1987);   per head (1985)

chronology
1885-1914 Togoland was a German protectorate until captured by Anglo-French forces.
1922 Divided between Britain and France under League of Nations mandate.
1946 Continued under United Nations trusteeship.
1956 British Togoland integrated with Ghana.

Tonga (Kingdom of)
(Pule'anga Fakatu'i 'o Tonga) or *Friendly Islands*

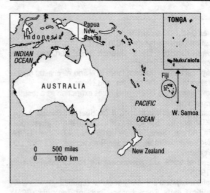

area 750 sq km/290 sq mi
capital Nuku'alofa (on Tongatapu island)
towns Pangai, Neiafu
physical three groups of islands in SW Pacific, mostly coral formations, but actively volcanic in W
features of 170 islands in the Tonga group, 36 are inhabited
head of state King Taufa'ahau Tupou IV from 1965
head of government Baron Vaea from 1991
political system constitutional monarchy
political parties none
currency Tongan dollar or pa'anga (T$2.11 = £1 July 1991)
population (1988) 95,000; growth rate 2.4% p.a.
life expectancy men 69, women 74 (1989)
languages Tongan (official), English
religion Wesleyan 47%, Roman Catholic 14%, Free Church of Tonga 14%, Mormon 9%, Church of Tonga 9%
literacy 93% (1988)
GNP $65 million (1987); $430 per head

chronology
1831 Tongan dynasty founded by Prince Taufa'ahau Tupou.
1900 Became a British protectorate.
1965 Queen Salote died; succeeded by her son, King Taufa'ahau Tupou IV.
1970 Independence achieved from Britain within the Commonwealth.
1990 Three prodemocracy candidates elected. Calls for reform of absolutist power.

Trinidad and Tobago (Republic of)

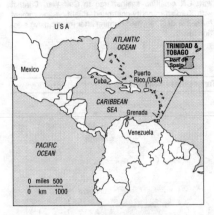

area Trinidad 4,828 sq km/1,864 sq mi and Tobago 300 sq km/116 sq mi
capital Port-of-Spain
towns San Fernando, Arima, Scarborough (Tobago)
physical comprises two main islands and some smaller ones; coastal swamps and hills E–W
features Pitch Lake, a self-renewing source of asphalt used by 16th-century explorer Walter Raleigh to repair his ships
head of state Noor Hassanali from 1987
head of government Patrick Manning from 1991
political system democratic republic
political parties National Alliance for Reconstruction (NAR), nationalistic, left-of-centre; People's National Movement (PNM), nationalistic, moderate, centrist
exports oil, petroleum products, chemicals, sugar, cocoa
currency Trinidad and Tobago dollar (TT$6.90 = £1 July 1991)
population (1990 est) 1,270,000 (40% African descent, 40% Indian, 16% European, Chinese and others 2%), 1.2 million on Trinidad; growth rate 1.6% p.a.
life expectancy men 68, women 72 (1989)
languages English (official), Hindi, French, Spanish
media freedom of press guaranteed by constitution and upheld by government; there are two independent morning newspapers and several weekly tabloids
religion Roman Catholic 32%, Protestant 29%, Hindu 25%, Muslim 6%
literacy 97% (1988)
GNP $4.5 bn; $3,731 per head (1987)

chronology
1888 Trinidad and Tobago united as a British colony.
1956 People's National Movement (PNM) founded.
1959 Achieved internal self-government, with PNM leader Eric Williams as chief minister.
1962 Independence achieved from Britain, within the Commonwealth, with Williams as prime minister.
1976 Became a republic, with Ellis Clarke as president and Williams as prime minister.
1981 Williams died and was succeeded by George Chambers, with Arthur Robinson as opposition leader.
1986 National Alliance for Reconstruction (NAR), headed by Arthur Robinson, won general election.
1987 Noor Hassanali became president.
1990 Attempted antigovernment coup defeated.
1991 General election saw victory for PNM, with Patrick Manning as prime minister.

Tunisia (Tunisian Republic)
(al-Jumhuriya at-Tunisiya)

area 164,150 sq km/63,378 sq mi
capital and chief port Tunis
towns ports Sfax, Sousse, Bizerta
physical arable and forested land in N graduates towards desert in S
features fertile island of Jerba, linked to mainland by causeway (identified with island of lotus-eaters); Shott el Jerid salt lakes; holy city of Kairouan, ruins of Carthage
head of state and government Zine el-Abidine Ben Ali from 1987
political system emergent democratic republic
political parties Constitutional Democratic Rally (RCD), nationalist, moderate, socialist
exports oil, phosphates, chemicals, textiles, food, olive oil
currency dinar (1.61 = £1 July 1991)
population (1990 est) 8,094,000; growth rate 2% p.a.
life expectancy men 68, women 71 (1989)
languages Arabic (official), French
media publications must be authorized; the offence of defamation is used to protect members of the government from criticism
religion Sunni Muslim 95%; Jewish, Christian
literacy men 68%, women 41% (1985 est)
GNP $9.6 bn (1987); $1,163 per head (1986)

chronology
1883 Became a French protectorate.
1955 Granted internal self-government.
1956 Independence achieved from France as a monarchy, with Habib Bourguiba as prime minister.
1957 Became a republic with Bourguiba as president.
1975 Bourguiba made president for life.
1985 Diplomatic relations with Libya severed.
1987 Bourguiba removed Prime Minister Rashed Sfar and appointed Zine el-Abidine Ben Ali. Ben Ali declared Bourguiba incompetent and seized power.
1988 Constitutional changes towards democracy announced. Diplomatic relations with Libya restored.
1989 Government party, RDC, won all assembly seats in general election.
1991 Crackdown on religious fundamentalists.

Turkey (Republic of)
(Türkiye Cumhuriyeti)

area 779,500 sq km/300,965 sq mi
capital Ankara
towns ports Istanbul and Izmir
physical central plateau surrounded by mountains

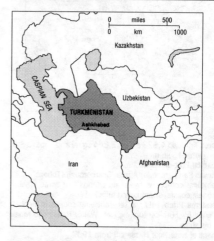

1989 Turgut Özal elected president; Yildirim Akbulut became prime minister. Application to join EC rejected.
1991 Mesut Yilmaz became prime minister. Turkey sided with UN coalition against Iraq in Gulf War. Conflict with Kurdish minority continued. Coalition government formed under Suleyman Demirel after inconclusive election result.

Turkmenistan (Republic of)

area 488,100 sq km/188,406 sq mi
capital Ashkhabad
towns Chardzhov, Mary (Merv), Nebit-Dag, Krasnovodsk
physical some 90% of land is desert including the Kara Kum 'Black Sands' desert (area 310,800 sq km/120,000 sq mi)
features on the edge of the Kara Kum desert is the Altyn Depe, 'golden hill', site of a ruined city with a ziggurat, or stepped pyramid; river Amu Darya; rich deposits of petroleum, natural gas, sulphur, and other industrial raw materials
head of state Saparmurad Niyazov from 1991
head of government Khan Akhmedov from 1989
political system socialist pluralist
products silk, karakul, sheep, astrakhan fur, carpets, chemicals, rich deposits of petroleum, natural gas, sulphur, and other industrial raw materials
population (1990) 3,600,000 (72% Turkmen, 10% Russian, 9% Uzbek, Kazakh 3%, Ukrainian 1%)
language West Turkic, closely related to Turkish
religion Sunni Muslim

environment only 0.3% of the country is protected by national parks and reserves compared with a global average of 7% per country
features Bosporus and Dardanelles; Mount Ararat; Taurus Mountains in SW (highest peak Kaldi Dağ, 3,734 m/12,255 ft); sources of rivers Euphrates and Tigris in E; archaeological sites include Çatal Hüyük, Ephesus, and Troy; rock villages of Cappadocia; historic towns (Antioch, Iskenderun, Tarsus)
head of state Turgut Özal from 1989
head of government Suleyman Demirel from 1991
political system democratic republic
political parties Motherland Party (ANAP), Islamic, nationalist, right-of-centre; Social Democratic Populist Party (SDPP), moderate, left-of-centre; True Path Party (TPP), centre-right
exports cotton, yarn, hazelnuts, citrus, tobacco, dried fruit, chromium ores
currency Turkish lira (7,027.94 = £1 July 1991)
population (1990 est) 56,549,000 (85% Turkish, 12% Kurdish); growth rate 2.1% p.a.
life expectancy men 63, women 66 (1989)
languages Turkish (official), Kurdish, Arabic
religion Sunni Muslim 98%
literacy men 86%, women 62% (1985)
GNP $62 bn (1987); $1,160 per head (1986)

chronology
1919-22 Turkish War of Independence provoked by Greek occupation of Izmir. Mustafa Kemal (Atatürk), leader of nationalist congress, defeated Italian, French, and Greek forces.
1923 Treaty of Lausanne established Turkey as independent republic under Kemal. Westernization began.
1950 First free elections; Adnan Menderes became prime minister.
1960 Menderes executed after military coup by General Cemal Gürsel.
1965 Suleyman Demirel became prime minister.
1971 Army forced Demirel to resign.
1973 Civilian rule returned under Bulent Ecevit.
1974 Turkish troops sent to protect Turkish community in Cyprus.
1975 Demirel returned to head of a right-wing coalition.
1978 Ecevit returned, as head of coalition, in the face of economic difficulties and factional violence.
1979 Demeril returned. Violence grew.
1980 Army took over, and Bulent Ulusu became prime minister. Harsh repression of political activists attracted international criticism.
1982 New constitution adopted.
1983 Ban on political activity lifted. Turgut Özal became prime minister.
1987 Özal maintained majority in general election.
1988 Improved relations and talks with Greece.

chronology
1921 Part of Turkestan Soviet Socialist Autonomous Republic.
1925 Became a constituent republic of USSR.
1990 Aug: economic and political sovereignty declared.
1991 Jan: After supreme soviet elections, Communist Party leader Niyazov became state president. March: endorsed maintenance of the Union in USSR referendum. Aug: President Niyazov initially supported anti-Gorbachev attempted Moscow coup; democratic activists arrested. Oct: independence declared after overwhelming approval in referendum. Dec: joined new Commonwealth of Independent States (CIS); independence acknowledged by USA but diplomatic recognition withheld.
1992 Jan: admitted into CSCE. May: new constitution adopted.

Tuvalu (South West Pacific State of)
(formerly *Ellice Islands*)

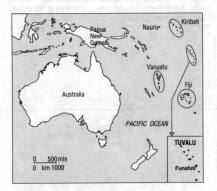

area 25 sq km/9.5 sq mi
capital Funafuti
physical nine low coral atolls forming a chain of 579 km/650 mi in the SW Pacific
features maximum height above sea level 6 m/20 ft; coconut palms are main vegetation
head of state Elizabeth II from 1978 represented by governor general
head of government Bikenibeu Paeniu from 1989
political system liberal democracy
political parties none; members are elected to parliament as independents
exports copra, handicrafts, stamps
currency Australian dollar (2.11 = £1 July 1991)
population (1990 est) 9,000 (Polynesian 96%); growth rate 3.4% p.a.
life expectancy 60 men, 63 women (1989)
languages Tuvaluan, English
religion Christian (Protestant)
literacy 96% (1985)
GDP (1983) $711 per head

chronology
1892 Became a British protectorate forming part of the Gilbert and Ellice Islands group.
1916 The islands acquired colonial status.
1975 The Ellice Islands were separated from the Gilbert Islands.
1978 Independence achieved from Britain within the Commonwealth with Toaripi Lauti as prime minister.
1981 Dr Tomasi Puapua replaced Lauti as premier.
1986 Islanders rejected proposal for republican status.
1989 Bikenibeu Paeniu elected new prime minister.

Uganda (Republic of)

area 236,600 sq km/91,351 sq mi
capital Kampala
towns Jinja, M'Bale, Entebbe, Masaka
physical plateau with mountains in W; forest and grassland; arid in NE
features Ruwenzori Range (Mount Margherita, 5,110 m/16,765 ft); national parks with wildlife (chimpanzees, crocodiles, Nile perch to 70 kg/160 lb); Owen Falls on White Nile where it leaves Lake Victoria; Lake Albert in W
head of state and government Yoweri Museveni from 1986
political system emergent democratic republic
political parties National Resistance Movement (NRM), left-of-centre; Democratic Party (DP), centre-left; Conservative Party (CP), centre-right; Uganda People's Congress (UPC), left-of-centre; Uganda Freedom Movement (UFM), left-of-centre
exports coffee, cotton, tea, copper
currency Uganda new shilling (1,136.59 = £1 July 1991)
population (1990 est) 17,593,000 (largely the Baganda, from whom the country is named; also Langi and Acholi, some surviving Pygmies); growth rate 3.3% p.a.
life expectancy men 49, women 51 (1989)
languages English (official), Kiswahili, Luganda, and other African languages
religion Roman Catholic 33%, Protestant 33%, Muslim 16%, animist
literacy men 70%, women 45% (1985 est)
GNP $3.6 bn (1987); $220 per head

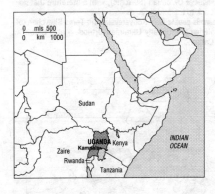

chronology
1962 Independence achieved from Britain within the Commonwealth with Milton Obote as prime minister.
1963 Proclaimed a federal republic with King Mutesa II as president.
1966 King Mutesa ousted in coup led by Obote, who ended the federal status and became executive president.
1969 All opposition parties banned after assassination attempt on Obote.
1971 Obote overthrown in army coup led by Maj-Gen Idi Amin Dada; ruthlessly dictatorial regime established; nearly 49,000 Ugandan Asians expelled; over 300,000 opponents of regime killed.
1978 Amin forced to leave country by opponents backed by Tanzanian troops. Provisional government set up with Yusuf Lule as president. Lule replaced by Godfrey Binaisa.
1978-79 Fighting broke out against Tanzanian troops.
1980 Binaisa overthrown by army. Elections held and Milton Obote returned to power.
1985 After opposition by National Resistance Army (NRA), and indiscipline in army, Obote ousted by Brig Tito Okello; power-sharing agreement entered into with NRA leader Yoweri Museveni.
1986 Agreement ended; Museveni became president, heading broad-based coalition government.
1992 East African cooperation pact with Kenya and Tanzania to be reestablished.

Ukraine

area 603,700 sq km/233,089 sq mi
capital Kiev
towns Kharkov, Donetsk, Odessa, Dnepropetrovsk, Lugansk (Voroshilovgrad), Lviv (Lvov), Mariupol (Zhdanov), Krivoi Rog, Zaporozhye

physical Russian plain: Carpathian and Crimean Mountains; rivers: Dnieper (with the Dnieper dam 1932), Donetz, Bug
features Askaniya-Nova Nature Reserve (established 1921); health spas with mineral springs
head of state Leonid Kravchuk from 1990
head of government Vitold Fokin from 1990
political system emergent democracy
political party Ukrainian People's Movement (Rukh), umbrella nationalist grouping, with three leaders
products grain, coal, oil, various minerals
currency grivna
population (1990) 51,800,000 (73% Ukrainian, 22% Russian, 1% Byelorussian, 1% Russian-speaking Jews; some 1.5 million have emigrated to the USA, 750,000 to Canada)
language Ukrainian (Slavonic), with a literature that goes back to the Middle Ages
famous people Ivan Kotlyarevsky and Taras Shevchenko
religion traditionally Ukrainian Orthodox; also Ukrainian Catholic

chronology
1918 Independent People's Republic proclaimed.
1920 Conquered by Soviet Red Army.
1921 Poland alloted charge of W Ukraine.
1932-33 Famine caused the deaths of more than 7.5 million people.
1939 W Ukraine occupied by Red Army.
1941-44 Under Nazi control; Jews massacred at Babi Yar; more than five million Ukrainians and Ukrainian Jews deported and exterminated.
1944 Soviet control re-established.
1945 Became a founder member of the United Nations.
1946 Ukrainian Uniate Church proscribed and forcibly merged with Russian Orthodox Church.
1986 April: Chernobyl nuclear disaster.
1989 Feb: Ukrainian People's Movement (Rukh) established. Ban on Ukrainian Uniate Church lifted.
1990 July: voted to proclaim sovereignty; Leonid Kravchuk indirectly elected as president; sovereignty declared.
1991 Aug: rallies and demonstrations against the abortive anti-Gorbachev coup; independence declared, pending referendum; Communist Party activities suspended. Oct: voted to create independent army. Dec: Kravchuk popularly elected president; independence overwhelmingly endorsed in referendum; joined new Commonwealth of Independent States (CIS); independence acknowledged by USA and EC.
1992 Jan: admitted into CSCE; pipeline deal with Iran to end dependence on Russian oil; prices freed. Feb: prices 'temporarily' re-regulated.

United Arab Emirates (UAE)

(*Ittihad al-Imarat al-Arabiyah*) federation of the emirates of Abu Dhabi, Ajman, Dubai, Fujairah, Ras al Khaimah, Sharjah, Umm al Qaiwain

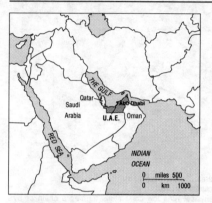

total area 83,657 sq km/32,292 sq mi
capital Abu Dhabi
towns chief port Dubai
physical desert and flat coastal plain; mountains in E
features linked by dependence on oil revenues
head of state and of government Sheikh Sultan Zayed bin al-Nahayan of Abu Dhabi from 1971
political system absolutism
political parties none
exports oil, natural gas, fish, dates
currency UAE dirham (5.95 = £1 July 1991)
population (1990 est) 2,250,000 (10% nomadic); growth rate 6.1% p.a.
life expectancy men 68, women 72 (1989)
languages Arabic (official), Farsi, Hindi, Urdu, English
religion Muslim 96%, Christian, Hindu
literacy 68% (1989)
GNP $22 bn (1987); $11,900 per head

chronology
1952 Trucial Council established.
1971 Federation of Arab Emirates formed; later dissolved. Six Trucial States formed United Arab Emirates, with ruler of Abu Dhabi, Sheik Zayed, as president.
1972 The seventh state joined.
1976 Sheik Zayed threatened to relinquish presidency unless progress towards centralization became more rapid.
1985 Diplomatic and economic links with USSR and China established.
1987 Diplomatic relations with Egypt restored.
1990-91 Iraqi invasion of Kuwait opposed; UAE fights with UN coalition.
1991 Bank of Commerce and Credit International controlled by Abu Dhabi's ruler collapses.

United Kingdom of Great Britain and Northern Ireland (UK)

area 244,100 sq km/94,247 sq mi
capital London
towns Birmingham, Glasgow, Leeds, Sheffield, Liverpool, Manchester, Edinburgh, Bradford, Bristol, Belfast, Newcastle-upon-Tyne, Cardiff
physical became separated from European continent about 6000 BC; rolling landscape, increasingly mountainous towards the N, with Grampian Mountains in Scotland, Pennines in N England, Cambrian Mountains in Wales; rivers include Thames, Severn, and Spey

territories Anguilla, Bermuda, British Antarctic Territory, British Indian Ocean Territory, British Virgin Islands, Cayman Islands, Falkland Islands, Gibraltar, Hong Kong (until 1997), Montserrat, Pitcairn Islands, St Helena and Dependencies (Ascension, Tristan da Cunha), Turks and Caicos Islands

environment an estimated 67% (the highest percentage in Europe) of forests have been damaged by acid rain

features milder climate than N Europe because of Gulf Stream; considerable rainfall. Nowhere more than 120 km/74.5 mi from sea; indented coastline, various small islands

head of state Elizabeth II from 1952

head of government John Major from 1990

political system liberal democracy

political parties Conservative and Unionist Party, right-of-centre; Labour Party, moderate, left-of-centre; Social and Liberal Democrats, centre-left; Scottish National Party (SNP), Scottish nationalist; Plaid Cymru (Welsh Nationalist Party), Welsh nationalist; Official Ulster Unionist Party (OUP), Northern Ireland moderate right-of-centre; Democratic Unionist Party (DUP), Northern Ireland, right-of-centre; Social Democratic Labour Party (SDLP), Northern Ireland, moderate, left-of-centre; Ulster People's Unionist Party (UPUP), Northern Ireland, militant right-of-centre; Sinn Féin, Northern Ireland, pro-united Ireland; Green Party, ecological

exports cereals, rape, sugar beet, potatoes, meat and meat products, poultry, dairy products, electronic and telecommunications equipment, engineering equipment and scientific instruments, oil and gas, petrochemicals, pharmaceuticals, fertilizers, film and television programmes, aircraft

currency pound sterling (£)

population (1990 est) 57,121,000 (81.5% English, 9.6% Scottish, 1.9% Welsh, 2.4% Irish, 1.8% Ulster); growth rate 0.1% p.a.

religion Christian (55% Protestant, 10% Roman Catholic); Muslim, Jewish, Hindu, Sikh

life expectancy men 72, women 78 (1989)

languages English, Welsh, Gaelic

literacy 99% (1989)

GNP $758 bn; $13,329 per head (1988)

chronology
1707 Act of Union between England and Scotland under Queen Anne.
1721 Robert Walpole unofficially first prime minister, under George I.
1783 Loss of North American colonies that form USA; Canada retained.
1801 Act of Ireland united Britain and Ireland.
1819 Peterloo massacre: cavalry charged a meeting of

supporters of parliamentary reform.
1832 Great Reform Bill became law, shifting political power from upper to middle class.
1838 Chartist working-class movement formed.
1846 Corn Laws repealed by Robert Peel.
1851 Great Exhibition in London.
1867 Second Reform Bill, extending the franchise, introduced by Disraeli and passed.
1906 Liberal victory; programme of social reform.
1911 Powers of House of Lords curbed.
1914 Irish Home Rule Bill introduced.
1914-18 World War I.
1916 Lloyd George became prime minister.
1920 Home Rule Act incorporated NE of Ireland (Ulster) into the United Kingdom of Great Britain and Northern Ireland.
1921 Ireland, except for Ulster, became a dominion (Irish Free State, later Eire, 1937).
1924 First Labour government led by Ramsay MacDonald.
1926 General Strike.
1931 Coalition government; unemployment reached 3 million.
1939 World War II began.
1940 Winston Churchill became head of coalition government.
1945 Labour government under Clement Attlee; welfare state established.
1951 Conservatives defeated Labour.
1956 Suez Crisis.
1964 Labour victory under Harold Wilson.
1970 Conservatives under Edward Heath defeated Labour.
1972 Parliament prorogued in Northern Ireland; direct rule from Westminster began.
1973 UK joined European Economic Community.
1974 Three-day week, coal strike; Wilson replaced Heath.
1976 James Callaghan replaced Wilson as prime minister.
1977 Liberal—Labour pact.
1979 Victory for Conservatives under Margaret Thatcher.
1981 Formation of Social Democratic Party (SDP). Riots occurred in inner cities.
1982 Unemployment over 3 million. Falklands War.
1983 Thatcher re-elected.
1984-85 Coal strike, the longest in British history.
1986 Abolition of metropolitan counties.
1987 Thatcher re-elected for third term.
1988 Liberals and most of SDP merged into the Social and Liberal Democrats, leaving a splinter SDP. Inflation and interest rates rose.
1989 The Green Party polled 2 million votes in the European elections.
1990 Riots as poll tax introduced in England. Troops sent to the Persian Gulf following Iraq's invasion of Kuwait. British hostages held in Iraq, later released. Britain joined European exchange-rate mechanism. Thatcher replaced by John Major as Conservative leader and prime minister.
1991 British troops took part in US-led war against Iraq under United Nations umbrella. Support was given to the USSR during the dissolution of communism and the restoration of independence to the republics. John Major visited Beijing to sign agreement with China on new Hong Kong airport. At home, Britain suffered severe economic recession and rising unemployment.
1992 Economic recession continued. Conservative Party, led by John Major, won fourth consecutive general election, but with reduced majority. Neil Kinnock resigned as Labour leader, succeeded by John Smith.

United States of America (USA)

---

area 9,368,900 sq km/3,618,770 sq mi
capital Washington DC
towns New York, Los Angeles, Chicago, Philadelphia,

Detroit, San Francisco, Washington, Dallas, San Diego, San Antonio, Houston, Boston, Baltimore, Phoenix, Indianapolis, Memphis, Honolulu, San José

physical topography and vegetation from tropical (Hawaii) to arctic (Alaska); mountain ranges parallel with E and W coasts; the Rocky Mountains separate rivers emptying into the Pacific from those flowing into the Gulf of Mexico; Great Lakes in N; rivers include Hudson, Mississippi, Missouri, Colorado, Columbia, Snake, Rio Grande, Ohio

environment the USA produces the world's largest quantity of municipal waste per person (850 kg/1,900 lb)

features see individual states

territories the commonwealths of Puerto Rico and Northern Marianas; the federated states of Micronesia; Guam, the US Virgin Islands, American Samoa, Wake Island, Midway Islands, Marshall Islands, Belau, and Johnston and Sand Islands

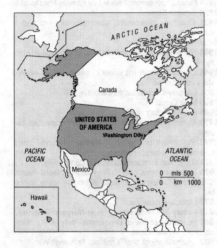

head of state and government George Bush from 1989
political system liberal democracy
political parties Democratic Party liberal, centre; Republican Party, centre-right
currency US dollar (US$1.61 = £1 July 1991)
population (1990 est) 250,372,000 (white 80%, black 12%, Asian/Pacific islander 3%, American Indian, Eskimo, and Aleut 1%, Hispanic (included in above percentages) 9%); growth rate 0.9% p.a.
life expectancy men 72, women 79 (1989)
languages English, Spanish
religion Christian 86.5% (Roman Catholic 26%, Baptist 19%, Methodist 8%, Lutheran 5%), Jewish 1.8%, Muslim 0.5%, Buddhist and Hindu less than 0.5%
literacy 99% (1989)
GNP $3,855 bn (1983); $13,451 per head

chronology
1776 Declaration of Independence.
1787 US constitution drawn up.
1789 Washington elected as first president.
1803 Louisiana Purchase.
1812-14 War with England, arising from commercial disputes caused by Britain's struggle with Napoleon.
1819 Florida purchased from Spain.
1836 The battle of the Alamo, Texas, won by Mexico.
1841 First wagon train left Missouri for California.
1846 Mormons, under Brigham Young, founded Salt Lake City, Utah.
1846-48 Mexican War resulted in cession to USA of Arizona, California, part of Colorado and Wyoming, Nevada, New Mexico, Texas, and Utah.

1848-49 California gold rush.
1860 Lincoln elected president.
1861-65 Civil War between North and South.
1865 Slavery abolished. Lincoln assassinated.
1867 Alaska bought from Russia.
1890 Battle of Wounded Knee, the last major battle between American Indians and US troops.
1898 War with Spain ended with the Spanish cession of Philippines, Puerto Rico, and Guam; it was agreed that Cuba be independent. Hawaii annexed.
1917-18 USA entered World War I.
1919-1921 Wilson's 14 Points became base for League of Nations.
1920 Women achieved the vote.
1924 American Indians made citizens by Congress.
1929 Wall Street stock-market crash.
1933 F D Roosevelt's New Deal to alleviate the Depression put into force.
1941-45 The Japanese attack on Pearl Harbor Dec 1941 precipitated US entry into World War II.
1945 USA ended war in the Pacific by dropping A-bombs on Hiroshima and Nagasaki, Japan.
1950-53 US involvement in Korean war. McCarthy anticommunist investigations (HUAC) became a 'witch hunt'.
1954 Civil Rights legislation began with segregation ended in public schools.
1957 Civil Rights bill on voting.
1958 First US satellite in orbit.
1961 Bay of Pigs abortive CIA-backed invasion of Cuba.
1963 President Kennedy assassinated; L B Johnson assumed the presidency.
1964-68 'Great Society' civil-rights and welfare measures in the Omnibus Civil Rights bill.
1964-75 US involvement in Vietnam War.
1965 US intervention in Dominican Republic.
1969 US astronaut Neil Armstrong was the first human on the Moon.
1973 OPEC oil embargo almost crippled US industry and consumers. Inflation began.
1973-74 Watergate scandal began in effort to re-elect Nixon and ended just before impeachment; Nixon resigned as president; replaced by Ford, who 'pardoned' Nixon.
1975 Final US withdrawal from Vietnam.
1979 US–Chinese diplomatic relations normalized.
1979-80 Iranian hostage crisis; relieved by Reagan concessions and released on his inauguration day Jan 1981.
1981 Space shuttle mission was successful.
1983 US invasion of Grenada.
1986 'Irangate' scandal over secret US government arms sales to Iran, with proceeds to antigovernment Contra guerrillas in Nicaragua.
1987 Reagan and Gorbachev (for USSR) signed intermediate-range nuclear forces treaty. Wall Street stock-market crash caused by programme trading.
1988 USA became world's largest debtor nation, owing $532 billion. George Bush elected president.
1989 Bush met Gorbachev at Malta, end to Cold War declared; high-level delegation sent to China amid severe criticism; large troop reductions and budget cuts announced for US military; USA invaded Panama, Noriega taken into custody.
1990 Bush and Gorbachev met again. Nelson Mandela freed in South Africa, toured USA. US troops sent to Middle East following Iraq's invasion of Kuwait.
1991 Jan-Feb: US-led assault drove Iraq from Kuwait in Gulf War. US support was given to the USSR during the dissolution of communism and the recognition of independence of the Baltic republics. July: Strategic Arms Reduction Treaty (START) signed at US–Soviet summit held in Moscow. Nov: Bush co-hosted Middle East peace conference in Spain.
1992 Bush's popularity slumped as economic recession continued. Widespread riots in Los Angeles.

Uruguay (Oriental Republic of)
(*República Oriental del Uruguay*)

area 176,200 sq km/68,031 sq mi
capital Montevideo
towns Salto, Paysandú
physical grassy plains (pampas) and low hills
features rivers Negro, Uruguay, Río de la Plata
head of state and government Luis Lacalle Herrera from 1989
political system democratic republic
political parties Colorado Party (PC), progressive, centre-left; National (Blanco) Party (PN), traditionalist, right-of-centre; Amplio Front (FA), moderate, left-wing
exports meat and meat products, leather, wool, textiles
currency nuevo peso (3,198.30 = £1 July 1991)
population (1990 est) 3,002,000 (Spanish, Italian; mestizo, mulatto, black); growth rate 0.7% p.a.
life expectancy men 68, women 75 (1989)
language Spanish
media the Ministry of Defence controls broadcasting licences
religion Roman Catholic 66%
literacy 96% (1984)
GNP $7.5 bn; $2,470 per head (1988)

chronology
1825 Independence declared from Brazil.
1836 Civil war.
1930 First constitution adopted.
1966 Blanco party in power, with Jorge Pacheco Areco as president.
1972 Colorado Party returned, with Juan Maria Bordaberry Arocena as president.
1976 Bordaberry deposed by army; Dr Méndez Manfredini became president.
1984 Violent antigovernment protests after ten years of repressive rule.
1985 Agreement reached between the army and political leaders for return to constitutional government. Colorado Party won general election; Dr Julio Maria Sanguinetti became president.
1986 Government of national accord established under President Sanguinetti's leadership.
1989 Luis Lacalle Herrera elected president.

Uzbekistan (Republic of)

area 447,400 sq km/172,741 sq mi
capital Tashkent
towns Samarkhand, Bukhara, Namangan
physical oases in the deserts; rivers Amu Darya, Syr Darya; Fergana Valley; rich in mineral deposits
features more than 20 hydroelectric plants; three natural gas pipelines
head of state Islam Karimov from 1990
head of government Abdul Hashim Mutalov from 1991
political system socialist pluralist
political parties Uzbekistan Socialist (formerly Communist) Party, reform-socialist; Democratic Party, tolerated opposition
products rice, dried fruit, vines (all grown by irrigation); cotton, silk
population (1990) 20,300,000 (71% Uzbek, 8% Russian, 5% Tajik, 4% Kazakh)
language Uzbek, a Turkic language
religion Sunni Muslim

chronology
1921 Part of Turkestan Soviet Socialist Autonomous Republic.
1925 Became constituent republic of the USSR.
1944 Some 160,000 Meskhetian Turks forcibly transported from their native Georgia to Uzbekistan by Stalin.
1989 June: Tashlak, Yaipan, and Ferghana were the scenes of riots in which Meskhetian Turks were attacked; 70 killed and 850 wounded.
1990 June: economic and political sovereignty declared.
1991 March: Uzbek supported 'renewed federation of equal sovereign republics' in USSR referendum. Aug: anti-Gorbachev coup in Moscow initially accepted by President Karimov; later, Karimov resigned from Soviet Communist Party (CPSU) Politburo; Uzbek Communist Party (UCP) broke with CPSU; pro-democracy rallies dispersed by militia; independence declared. Dec: joined new Commonwealth of Independent States (CIS); independence acknowledged by USA but diplomatic recognition withheld.
1992 Jan: admitted into CSCE; violent food riots in Tashkent.

Vanuatu (Republic of)
(*Ripablik Blong Vanuatu*)

area 14,800 sq km/5,714 sq mi
capital Vila (on Efate island)
towns Luganville (on Espíritu Santo)
physical comprises around 70 islands, including Espíritu Santo, Malekula, and Efate; densely forested, mountainous
features three active volcanoes
head of state Fred Timakata from 1989

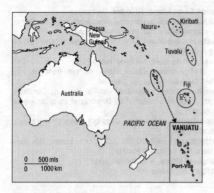

head of government Maxime Carlot from 1991
political system democratic republic
political parties Union of Moderate Parties (UMP),
Francophone centrist; Vanuatu National United Party
(VNUP), formed by Walter Lini; Vanua'aku Pati (VP), An-
glophone centrist; Melanesian Progressive Party (MPP),
Melanesian centrist; Fren Melanesian Party
exports copra, fish, coffee, cocoa
currency vatu (179.00 = £1 July 1991)
population (1989) 152,000 (90% Melanesian); growth
rate 3.3% p.a.
life expectancy men 67, women 71 (1989)
languages Bislama 82%, English, French, (all official)
literacy 53%
religion Presbyterian 40%, Roman Catholic 16%, Anglican 14%, animist 15%
GDP $125 million (1987); $927 per head

chronology
1906 Islands jointly administered by France and Britain.
1975 Representative assembly established.
1978 Government of national unity formed, with Father
Gerard Leymang as chief minister.
1980 Revolt on the island of Espíritu Santo delayed independence but it was achieved within the Commonwealth,
with George Kalkoa (adopted name Sokomanu) as president and Father Walter Lini as prime minister.
1988 Dismissal of Lini by Sokomanu led to Sokomanu's
arrest for treason. Lini reinstated.
1989 Sokomanu sentenced to six years' imprisonment;
succeeded as president by Fred Timakata.
1991 Lini voted out by party members; replaced by Donald
Kalpokas. General election produced UMP–VNUP coalition under Maxime Carlot.

Vatican City State
(*Stato della Città del Vaticano*)

area 0.4 sq km/109 acres
physical forms an enclave in the heart of Rome, Italy
features Vatican Palace, official residence of the pope;
basilica and square of St Peter's; churches in and near
Rome, the pope's summer villa at Castel Gandolfo; the
world's smallest state
head of state and government John Paul II from 1978
political system absolute Catholicism
currency Vatican City lira; Italian lira (2,187.00 ∞ £1 July
1991)
population (1985) 1,000
languages Latin (official), Italian
religion Roman Catholic

chronology
1929 Lateran Treaty recognized sovereignty of the pope.
1947 New Italian constitution confirmed the sovereignty

of the Vatican City State.
1978 John Paul II became the first non-Italian pope for
more than 400 years.
1985 New concordat signed under which Roman
Catholicism ceased to be the Italy's state religion.

Venezuela (Republic of)
(*República de Venezuela*)

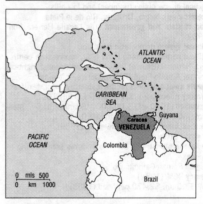

area 912,100 sq km/352,162 sq mi
capital Caracas
towns Barquisimeto, Valencia; port Maracaibo
physical Andes Mountains and Lake Maracaibo in NW;
central plains (llanos); delta of river Orinoco in E; Guiana
Highlands in SE
features Angel Falls, world's highest waterfall
head of state and of government Carlos Andrés Pérez
from 1988
government federal democratic republic
political parties Democratic Action Party (AD), moderate,
left-of-centre; Social Christian Party (COPEI), Christian
centre-right; Movement towards Socialism (MAS), left-
of-centre
exports coffee, timber, oil, aluminium, iron ore, petrochemicals
currency bolívar (Bs.88.90 = £1 July 1991)
population (1990 est) 19,753,000 (mestizos 70%, white
(Spanish, Portuguese, Italian) 20%, black 9%, amerindian 2%); growth rate 2.8% p.a.
life expectancy men 67, women 73 (1989)
religion Roman Catholic 96%, Protestant 2%
languages Spanish (official), Indian languages 2%
literacy 88% (1989)
GNP $47.3 bn (1988); $2,629 per head (1985)

chronology
1961 New constitution adopted, with Rómulo Betancourt as president.
1964 Dr Raúl Leoni became president.
1969 Dr Rafael Caldera became president.
1974 Carlos Andrés Pérez became president.
1979 Dr Luis Herrera became president.
1984 Dr Jaime Lusinchi became president; social pact established between government, trade unions, and business; national debt rescheduled.
1987 Widespread social unrest triggered by inflation; student demonstrators shot by police.
1988 Carlos Andrés Pérez elected president. Payments suspended on foreign debts (increase due to drop in oil prices).
1989 Economic austerity programme enforced by $4.3 billion loan from International Monetary Fund. Price increases triggered riots; 300 people killed. Feb: martial law declared. May: General strike. Elections boycotted by opposition groups.
1991 Protests against austerity programme continued.
1992 Attempted anti-government coups failed. Pérez promised constitutional changes.

Vietnam (Socialist Republic of)
(Công Hòa Xã Hôi Chu Nghĩa Viêt Nam)

area 329,600 sq km/127,259 sq mi
capital Hanoi
towns ports Ho Chi Minh City (formerly Saigon), Da Nang, Haiphong
physical Red River and Mekong deltas, centre of cultivation and population; tropical rainforest; mountainous in N and NW
environment during the Vietnam War an estimated 2.2 million hectares of forest were destroyed. The country's National Conservation Strategy is trying to replant 500 million trees each year
features Karst hills of Halong Bay, Cham Towers
head of state Vo Chi Cong from 1987
head of government Vo Van Kiet from 1991
political system communism
political party Communist Party
exports rice, rubber, coal, iron, apatite
currency dong (13,406.25 = £1 July 1991)
population (1990 est) 68,488,000 (750,000 refugees, majority ethnic Chinese left 1975-79, some settled in SW China, others fled by sea—the 'boat people'—to Hong Kong and elsewhere); growth rate 2.4% p.a.
life expectancy men 62, women 66 (1989)
languages Vietnamese (official), French, English, Khmer, Chinese, local
media independent newspapers prohibited by law 1989;

central government approval is required for appointment of editors
religion Buddhist, Taoist, Confucian, Christian
literacy 78% (1989)
GNP $12.6 bn; $180 per head (1987)

chronology
1945 Japanese removed from Vietnam at end of World War II.
1946 Commencement of Vietminh war against French.
1954 France defeated at Dien Bien Phu. Vietnam divided along 17th parallel.
1964 US troops entered Vietnam War.
1973 Paris cease-fire agreement.
1975 Saigon captured by North Vietnam.
1976 Socialist Republic of Vietnam proclaimed.
1978 Admission into Comecon. Vietnamese invasion of Cambodia.
1979 Sino-Vietnamese border war.
1986 Retirement of 'old guard' leaders.
1987-88 Over 10,000 political prisoners released.
1988-89 Troop withdrawals from Cambodia continued.
1989 'Boat people' leaving Vietnam murdered and robbed at sea by Thai pirates. Troop withdrawal from Cambodia completed. Hong Kong forcibly repatriated some Vietnamese refugees.
1991 Vo Van Kiet replaced Do Muoi as prime minister. Cambodia peace agreement signed. Relations with China normalized.

Yemen (Republic of)
(al Jamhuriya al Yamaniya)

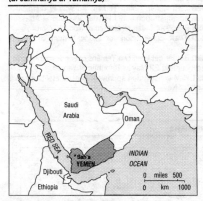

area 531,900 sq km/205,367 sq mi
capital Sana'a
towns Ta'iz; and chief port Aden
physical hot moist coastal plain, rising to plateau and desert.
features once known as *Arabia felix* because of its fertility, includes islands of Perim (in strait of Bab-el-Mandeb, at S entrance to Red Sea), Socotra, and Kamaran
head of state and of government Ali Abdullah Saleh from 1990
political system emergent democratic republic
political parties Yemen Socialist Party (YSP), Democratic Unionist Party, National Democratic Front, Yemen Reform Group
exports cotton, coffee, grapes, vegetables
currency rial (19.58 = £1 July 1991)
population (1990 est) 11,000,000; growth rate 2.7% p.a.
life expectancy men 47, women 50
language Arabic
religion Sunni Muslim 63%, Shi'ite Muslim 37%
literacy men 20%, women 3% (1985 est)
GNP $4.9 bn (1983); $520 per head

chronology
1918 Yemem became independent.
1962 North Yemen declared the Yemen Arab Republic (YAR), with Abdullah al-Sallal as president. Civil war broke out between royalists and republicans.
1967 Civil war ended with the republicans victorious. Sallal deposed and replaced by Republican Council. The People's Republic of South Yemen was formed.
1970 People's Republic of South Yemen renamed People's Democratic Republic of Yemen.
1971-72 War between South Yemen and the YAR; union agreement signed but not kept.
1974 Ibrahim al-Hamadi seized power in North Yemen and Military Command Council set up.
1977 Hamadi assassinated and replaced by Ahmed ibn Hussein al-Ghashmi.
1978 Constituent People's Assembly appointed in North Yemen and Military Command Council dissolved. Ghashmi killed by envoy from South Yemen; succeeded by Ali Abdullah Saleh. War broke out again between the two Yemens. South Yemen president deposed and Yemen Socialist Party (YSP) formed with Abdul Fattah Ismail as secretary general, later succeeded by Ali Nasser Muhammad .
1979 Cease-fire agreed with commitment to future union.
1983 Saleh elected president of North Yemen for a further five-year term.
1984 Joint committee on foreign policy for the two Yemens met in Aden.
1985 Ali Nasser Muhammad re-elected secretary general of the YSP in South Yemen; removed his opponents. Three bureau members killed.
1986 Civil war in South Yemen; Ali Nasser dismissed. New administration under Haydar Abu Bakr al-Attas.
1988 President Saleh re-elected in North Yemen.
1989 Draft constitution for single Yemen state published.
1990 Border between two Yemens opened; countries formally united 22 May as Republic of Yemen.
1991 New constitution approved; general election promised for Nov.

Yugoslavia

area 88,400 sq km/34,100 sq mi
capital Belgrade
towns Podgorica (Titograd), Kraljevo, Leskovac, Pristina, Novi Sad, Titograd
head of state to be elected
head of government Milan Panic from 1992
political system socialist pluralist republic

political parties Socialist Party of Serbia, ex-communist; Serbian Renaissance Movement, pro-monarchist; Democratic Party, Serbia-based, liberal, free-market; Montenegro League of Communists; Democratic Coalition of Muslims; Alliance of Reform Forces, Montenegro-based; Internal Macedonian Revolutionary Organization-Democratic Party for Macedonian National Unity (VMRO-DMPNE), Macedonian nationalist; Macedonian League of Communists
exports machinery, electrical goods, chemicals, clothing, tobacco
currency dinar (38.11 = £1 July 1991)
population (1990) 12,420,000 (53% Serb, 15% Albanian, 11% Macedonian, 5% Montenegrin, 3% Muslim, 2% Croat)
life expectancy men 69, women 75 (1989)
languages Serbian variant of Serbo-Croatian, Macedonian
religion Serbian Orthodox, with Muslim majority in Kosovo
literacy 90% (1989)
GNP $154.1 bn; $6,540 per head (1988)

chronology
1918 Creation of Kingdom of the Serbs, Croats, and Slovenes.
1929 Name of Yugoslavia adopted.
1941 Invaded by Germany.
1945 Yugoslav Federal Republic formed under leadership of Tito; communist constitution introduced.
1948 Split with USSR.
1953 Self-management principle enshrined in constitution.
1961 Nonaligned movement formed under Yugoslavia's leadership.
1974 New constitution adopted.
1980 Tito died; collective leadership assumed power.
1987 Threatened use of army to curb unrest.
1988 Economic difficulties: 1,800 strikes, inflation at 250%, 20% unemployment. Ethnic unrest in Montenegro and Vojvodina; party reshuffled and government resigned.
1989 Reformist Croatian Ante Marković became prime minister. 29 died in ethnic riots in Kosovo province, protesting against Serbian attempt to end autonomous status of Kosovo and Vojvodina; state of emergency imposed. May: inflation rose to 490%; tensions with ethnic Albanians rose.
1990 Multiparty systems established in Serbia and Croatia.
1991 Several republics called for secession. State president resigned; Stipe Mesic of Croatia became head of state. Clashes between Serbs and Croats in Croatia. Slovenia and Croatia declared independence; Serb-dominated federal army intervened. Slovenia accepted EC-sponsored peace pact. Fighting continued in Croatia, with thousands killed and many thousands more homeless. Repeated calls for cease-fires failed. Bosnia-Herzegovina and Macedonia declared sovereignty; Croatia, Slovenia, Bosnia-Herzegovina, and Macedonia severed formal ties with Yugoslavia.
1992 Jan: Serbia-Croatia cease-fire established; USA and EC recognized Slovenia's and Croatia's independence. Bosnia-Herzegovina and Macedonia declared independence. April: Bosnia-Herzegovina recognized as independent by EC and USA amidst increasing Serb/Croat/Muslim ethnic hostility; bloody civil war ensued. May: Western ambassadors left Belgrade.

Zaire (Republic of)
(République du Zaïre) (formerly Congo)

area 2,344,900 sq km/905,366 sq mi
capital Kinshasa
towns Lubumbashi, Kananga, Kisangani; ports Matadi, Boma
physical Zaïre River basin has tropical rainforest and sa-

vanna; mountains in E and W
features lakes Tanganyika, Mobutu Sese Seko, Edward; Ruwenzori mountains
head of state Mobutu Sese Seko Kuku Ngbendu wa Zabanga from 1965
head of government Jean Nguza Karl-i-Bond from 1991
political system socialist pluralist republic
political parties Popular Movement of the Revolution (MPR), African socialist; numerous new parties registered 1991
exports coffee, copper, cobalt (80% of world output), industrial diamonds, palm oil
currency zaïre (7,564.00 = £1 July 1991)
population (1990 est) 35,330,000; growth rate 2.9% p.a.

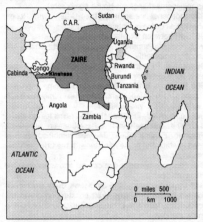

life expectancy men 51, women 54 (1989)
languages French (official), Swahili, Lingala, other African languages; over 300 dialects
religion Christian 70%, Muslim 10%
literacy men 79%, women 45% (1985 est)
GNP $5 bn (1987); $127 per head

chronology
1908 Congo Free State annexed to Belgium.
1960 Independence achieved from Belgium as Republic of the Congo. Civil war broke out between central government and Katanga province.
1963 Katanga war ended.
1967 New constitution adopted.
1970 Col Mobutu elected president.
1971 Country became the Republic of Zaire.
1972 The Popular Movement of the Revolution (MPR) became the only legal political party. Katanga province renamed Shaba.
1974 Foreign-owned businesses and plantations seized by Mobutu and given in political patronage.
1977 Original owners of confiscated properties invited back. Mobutu re-elected; Zairians invaded Shaba province from Angola, repulsed by Belgian paratroopers.
1978 Second unsuccessful invasion from Angola.
1988 Potential rift with Belgium avoided.
1990 Mobutu announced end of ban on multiparty politics, following internal dissent.
1991 Multiparty elections planned for 1992. After antigovernment riots, Mobutu agreed to share power with opposition. Mobutu vowed to remain as president beyond his seven-year term.

Zambia (Republic of)

area 752,600 sq km/290,579 sq mi
capital Lusaka

towns Kitwe, Ndola, Kabwe, Chipata, Livingstone
physical forested plateau cut through by rivers
features Zambezi River, Victoria Falls, Kariba Dam
head of state and government Frederick Chiluba from 1991
political system socialist pluralist republic
political parties United National Independence Party (UNIP), African socialist; Movement for Multiparty Democracy (MMD); National Democratic Alliance (Nada)
exports copper, cobalt, zinc, emeralds, tobacco
currency kwacha (103.76 = £1 July 1991)
population (1990 est) 8,119,000; growth rate 3.3% p.a.
life expectancy men 54, women 57 (1989)
language English (official); Bantu dialects
religion Christian 66%, animist, Hindu, Muslim
literacy 54% (1988)
GNP $2.1 bn (1987); $304 per head (1986)

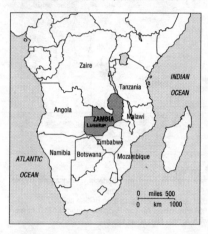

chronology
1899-1924 As Northern Rhodesia, under administration of the British South Africa Company.
1924 Became a British protectorate.
1964 Independence achieved from Britain, within the Commonwealth, as the Republic of Zambia with Kenneth Kaunda as president.
1972 United National Independence Party (UNIP) declared the only legal party.
1976 Support for the Patriotic Front in Rhodesia declared.
1980 Unsuccessful coup against President Kaunda.
1985 Kaunda elected chair of the African Front Line States.
1987 Kaunda elected chair of the Organization of African Unity (OAU).
1988 Kaunda re-elected unopposed for sixth term.
1990 Multiparty system announced for 1991.
1991 Movement for Multiparty Democracy won landslide election victory; Frederick Chiluba became president.

Zimbabwe (Republic of)

area 390,300 sq km/150,695 sq mi
capital Harare
towns Bulawayo, Gweru, Kwekwe, Mutare, Hwange
physical high plateau with central high veld and mountains in E; rivers Zambezi, Limpopo
features Hwange National Park, part of Kalahari Desert; ruins of Great Zimbabwe
head of state and government Robert Mugabe from 1987
political system effectively one-party socialist republic
political party Zimbabwe African National Union—Patriotic Front (ZANU—PF), African socialist

exports tobacco, asbestos, cotton, coffee, gold, silver, copper

currency Zimbabwe dollar (Z$5.22 = £1 July 1991)

population (1990 est) 10,205,000 (Shona 80%, Ndbele 19%; about 100,000 whites); growth rate 3.5% p.a.

life expectancy men 59, women 63 (1989)

languages English (official), Shona, Sindebele

religion Christian, Muslim, Hindu, animist

literacy men 81%, women 67% (1985 est)

GNP $5.5 bn (1988); $275 per head (1986)

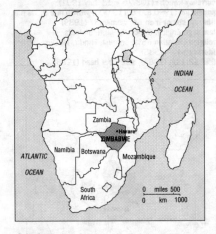

chronology

1889-1923 As Southern Rhodesia, under administration of British South Africa Company.

1923 Became a self-governing British colony.

1961 Zimbabwe African People's Union (ZAPU) formed, with Joshua Nkomo as leader.

1962 ZAPU declared illegal.

1963 Zimbabwe African National Union (ZANU) formed, with Robert Mugabe as secretary general.

1964 Ian Smith became prime minister. ZANU banned. Nkomo and Mugabe imprisoned.

1965 Smith declared unilateral independence.

1966-68 Abortive talks between Smith and UK prime minister Harold Wilson.

1974 Nkomo and Mugabe released.

1975 Geneva conference set date for constitutional independence.

1979 Smith produced new constitution and established a government with Bishop Abel Muzorewa as prime minister. New government denounced by Nkomo and Mugabe. Conference in London agreed independence arrangements (Lancaster House Agreement).

1980 Independence achieved from Britain, with Robert Mugabe as prime minister.

1981 Rift between Mugabe and Nkomo.

1982 Nkomo dismissed from the cabinet, leaving the country temporarily.

1984 ZANU—PF party congress agreed to create a one-party state in future.

1985 Relations between Mugabe and Nkomo improved. Troops sent to Matabeleland to suppress rumoured insurrection; 5,000 civilians killed.

1986 Joint ZANU—PF rally held amid plans for merger.

1987 White-roll seats in the assembly were abolished. President Banana retired; Mugabe combined posts of head of state and prime minister with the title executive president.

1988 Nkomo returned to the cabinet and was appointed vice president.

1989 Opposition party, the Zimbabwe Unity Movement, formed by Edgar Tekere; draft constitution drawn up, renouncing Marxism—Leninism; ZANU and ZAPU formally merged.

1990 ZANU—PF re-elected. State of emergency ended. Opposition to creation of one-party state.

MISCELLANEOUS

ABBREVIATIONS, SYMBOLS, AND ACRONYMS

A in physics, symbol for *ampere*, a unit of electrical current.

A1 abbreviation for *first class* (of ships).

AA abbreviation for the British *Automobile Association*.

abb abbreviation for *abbreviation*.

ab init abbreviation for *ab initio* (Latin 'from the beginning').

ABM abbreviation for *anti-ballistic missile*.

a/c abbreviation for *account*.

AC in physics, abbreviation for *alternating current*.

ACAS abbreviation for *Advisory, Conciliation and Arbitration Service*.

ACT abbreviation for *Australian Capital Territory*.

AD in the Christian calender, abbreviation for *Anno Domini* (Latin 'in the year of the Lord'); used with dates.

ADB abbreviation for *Asian Development Bank*.

ADC in electronics, abbreviation for analogue-to-digital converter.

ADH abbreviation for *antidiuretic hormone*, part of the system maintaining a correct salt/water balance in vertebrates.

adj in grammar, abbreviation for *adjective*.

ADP abbreviation for *adenosine diphosphate*, a raw material in the manufacture of ATP, the molecule used by all cells to drive their chemical reactions.

adv abbreviation for *adverb*.

aet abbreviation for *aetatis* (Latin 'of the age').

AEW abbreviation for *airborne early warning*, a military surveillance system.

AFD abbreviation for *accelerated freeze drying*, a common method of food preservation. See food technology.

AFL-CIO abbreviation for *American Federation of Labor and Congress of Industrial Organizations*.

AG abbreviation for *Aktiengesellschaft* (German 'limited company').

AH with reference to the Muslim calendar, abbreviation for *anno hegirae* (Latin 'year of the flight'—of Muhammad, from Mecca to Medina).

AIDS abbreviation for *acquired immune deficiency syndrome*, the newest and gravest of sexually transmitted diseases or STDs.

AK abbreviation for *Alaska*.

AL abbreviation for *Alabama*.

ALADI abbreviation for *Asociacion Latino-Americana de Integration* or Latin American Integration Association, organization promoting trade in the region.

AM in physics, abbreviation for amplitude modulation, one way in which radio waves are altered for the transmission of broadcasting signals.

am or **A.M.** abbreviation for *ante meridiem* (Latin 'before noon').

AMF abbreviation of *Arab Monetary Fund*.

amp in physics, abbreviation for *ampere*, a unit of electrical current.

ANC abbreviation for *African National Congress*; South African nationalist organization.

ANZUS acronym for *Australia, New Zealand, and the United States* (Pacific Security Treaty), a military alliance established 1951. It was replaced 1954 by the Southeast Asia Treaty Organization , (SEATO).

ap in physics, abbreviation for *atmospheric pressure*.

APC abbreviation for *armoured personnel carrier*, a battlefield vehicle.

approx abbreviation for *approximately*.

AR abbreviation for *Arkansas*.

ASA abbreviation for *Association of South East Asia* (1961–67), replaced by ASEAN, *Association of Southeast Asian Nations*.

a.s.a.p abbreviation for *as soon as possible*.

ASAT acronym for *antisatellite weapon*.

ASPAC abbreviation of *Asian and Pacific Council*.

ASSR abbreviation for *Autonomous Soviet Socialist Republic*.

AWACS acronym for *Airborne Warning and Control System*. The system incorporates a long-range surveillance and detection radar mounted on a Boeing E-3 sentry aircraft. It was used with great success in the 1991 Gulf War.

AZ abbreviation for *Arizona*.

BA in education, abbreviation for *Bachelor of Arts* degree.

BAFTA abbreviation for *British Academy of Film and Television Arts*.

BBC abbreviation for *British Broadcasting Corporation*.

BC in the Christian calendar, abbreviation for *before Christ*; used with dates.

BCE abbreviation for *before the Common Era*; used with dates (instead of BC) particularly by non-Christians, and some theologians in recognition of the multiplicity of belief worldwide.

BCG abbreviation for *bacillus of Calmette and Guérin*, used as a vaccine to confer active immunity to tuberculosis (TB).

Beds abbreviation for *Bedfordshire*.

Berks abbreviation for *Berkshire*.

BFI abbreviation for the *British Film Institute*.

BFPO abbreviation for *British Forces Post Office*.

bhp abbreviation for *brake horsepower*.

biog abbreviation for *biography*.

BIS abbreviation for *Bank for International Settlements* based in Basel, Switzerland.

BMA abbreviation for *British Medical Association*.

BNF abbreviation for *British Nuclear Fuels*.

BOT abbreviation for *Board of Trade*, former UK government organization, merged in the Department of Trade and Industry from 1970.

BP abbreviation for *British Pharmacopoeia*; also *British Petroleum*.

BR abbreviation for *British Rail*.

BSc abbreviation for *Bachelor of Science* degree. The US abbreviation is *B.S.*.

BST abbreviation for *British Summer Time*; *bovine somatotropin*.

BT abbreviation for *British Telecom*.

Btu symbol for *British thermal unit*.

Bucks abbreviation for *Buckinghamshire*.

c abbreviation for *circa* (Latin 'about'); used with dates that are uncertain.

C abbreviation for *centum* (Latin 'hundred'); *century; centigrade; Celsius*.

°C symbol for degrees Celsius (temperature scale).

CA abbreviation for *California* (USA).

CACM abbreviation for *Central American Common Market*.

CAD abbreviation for *computer-aided design*.

cal symbol for *calorie*.

CAM abbreviation for *computer-aided manufacture*.

Cambs abbreviation for *Cambridgeshire*.

Cantab abbreviation for *Cantabrigiensis* (Latin 'of Cambridge').

cap abbreviation for *capital*.

CAP abbreviation for *Common Agricultural Policy*.

CARICOM abbreviation for *Caribbean Community* and Common Market.

CAD abbreviation for *computer-aided design*.

CB abbreviation for *citizens' band* (radio).

CBI abbreviation for *Confederation of British Industry*.

CC abbreviation for *county council; cricket club*.

cc symbol for *cubic centimetre*; abbreviation for *carbon copy/copies*.

CCASG abbreviation of *Cooperative Council for the Arab States of the Gulf*.

CD abbreviation for *Corps Diplomatique* (French 'Diplomatic Corps'); *compact disc; certificate of deposit*.

CDU abbreviation for the centre-right *Christian Democratic Union* in the Federal Republic of Germany.

CE abbreviation for *Common Era; Church of England* (often *C of E*).

CEGB abbreviation for the former (until 1990) *Central Electricity Generating Board*.

CentCom abbreviation for US *Central Command*, a military strikeforce.

CENTO abbreviation for *Central Treaty Organization*.

CET abbreviation for *Central European Time*.

cf abbreviation for *confer* (Latin 'compare').

CFC abbreviation for *chlorofluorocarbon*.

CFE abbreviation for *conventional forces in Europe*.

Ches abbreviation for Cheshire.

CIA abbreviation for the US *Central Intelligence Agency*.

CID abbreviation for *Criminal Investigation Department*.

cif in economics, abbreviation for *cost, insurance, and freight* or *charged in full*.

cm symbol for *centimetre*.

CND abbreviation for *Campaign for Nuclear Disarmament*.

c/o abbreviation for *care of*.

co abbreviation for *company*.

CO abbreviation for *Commanding Officer*.

CO abbreviation for *Colorado* (USA).

COD abbreviation for *cash on delivery*.

COI abbreviation for *Central Office of Information*.

COIN acronym for *counter insurgency*, the suppression by a state's armed forces of uprisings against the state.

Comintern acronym for *Communist International*.

CPP abbreviation for *current purchasing power*.

CPVE abbreviation for *Certificate of Pre-Vocational Education* in the UK, educational qualification introduced 1986 for students over 16 in schools and colleges who want a one-year course of preparation for work or further vocational study.

CRT abbreviation for *cathode-ray tube*.

CSCE abbreviation for *Conference on Security and Cooperation in Europe*, popularly known as the Helsinki Conference.

CSE abbreviation for *Certificate of Secondary Education* in the UK, the examinations taken by the majority of secondary school pupils who were not regarded as academically capable of GCE O level, until the introduction of the common secondary examination system, GCSE, 1988.

CT abbreviation for *Connecticut* (USA).

cu abbreviation for *cubic* (measure).

CV abbreviation for *curriculum vitae*.

cwo abbreviation for *cash with order*.

cwt symbol for *hundredweight*, a unit of weight equal to 112 pounds (50.802 kg).

cwt symbol for *hundredweight*, a unit of weight equal to 100 lb (45.36 kg) in the US and 112 lb (50.8 kg) in the UK and Canada.

d abbreviation for *day; diameter; died*; in the UK, d was the sign for a *penny* (Latin *denarius)* until decimalization of the currency in 1971.

D abbreviation for *500* in the Roman numeral system.

DA abbreviation for *district attorney*.

DBE abbreviation for *Dame (Commander of the Order) of the British Empire*.

DC in music, abbreviation for *da capo* (Italian 'from the beginning'); in physics, for *direct current* (electricity); *the District of Columbia*.

DD abbreviation for *Doctor of Divinity*.

DE abbreviation for *Delaware* (USA).

DES abbreviation for *Department of Education and Science*.

DHSS abbreviation for *Department of Health and Social Security*, UK government department until divided 1988.

diag abbreviation for *diagram*.

DM abbreviation for *Deutschmark*, the unit of currency in Germany.

DMus abbreviation for *Doctor of Music*.

DNA abbreviation for *deoxyribonucleic acid*.

do abbreviation for *ditto*.

DPhil abbreviation for *Doctor of Philosophy*.

DPP abbreviation for *Director of Public Prosecutions*.

DSO abbreviation for *Distinguished Service Order*, British military medal.

DTI abbreviation for *Department of Trade and Industry*, UK government department.

E abbreviation for *east*.

EC abbreviation for *European Community*.

ECM abbreviation for *electronic countermeasures*, military jargon for disrupting telecom-

£munications.

ECOWAS acronym for *Economic Community of West African States*.

ECSC abbreviation for *European Coal and Steel Community*.

ECT abbreviation for *electroconvulsive therapy*.

ECTU abbreviation for *European Confederation of Trade Unions*.

ECU abbreviation for *European Currency Unit*, official monetary unit of the EC. It is based on the value of the different currencies used in the European Monetary System.

EEC abbreviation for *European Economic Community*.

EFTA acronym for *European Free Trade Association*.

EFTPOS abbreviation of *electronic funds transfer at point of sale* the transfer of funds from one bank account to another by electronic means.

eg abbreviation for *exempli gratia* (Latin 'for the sake of example').

emf in physics, abbreviation for *electromotive force*.

EMS abbreviation for *European Monetary System*.

ENT in medicine, abbreviation for *ear, nose, and throat*. It is usually applied to a specialist clinic or hospital department.

E & O E abbreviation for *errors and omissions excepted*.

EOKA acronym for *Ethnikí Organósis Kipriakóu Agónos* (National Organization of Cypriot Struggle) an underground organization formed by General George Grivas 1955 to fight for the independence of Cyprus from Britain and ultimately its union (*enosis*) with Greece.

EPLF abbreviation for *Eritrean People's Liberation Front*.

EPNS abbreviation for *electroplated nickel silver*.

ERM abbreviation for *Exchange Rate Mechanism*.

ERNIE acronym for *electronic random number indicator equipment*, machine designed and produced by the UK Post Office Research Station to select a series of random 9-figure numbers to indicate prizewinners in the government's national lottery.

ESA abbreviation for *European Space Agency*.

est abbreviation for *estimate(d)*.

et al abbreviation for *et alii* (Latin 'and others'); used in bibliography.

etc abbreviation for *et cetera* (Latin 'and the rest').

Euratom acronym for *European Atomic Energy Commission*, forming part of the European Community organization.

Eutelsat acronym for *European Telecommunications Satellite Organization*.

ex lib abbreviation for *ex libris* (Latin 'from the library of').

°F symbol for degrees *Fahrenheit*.

FA abbreviation for *Football Association*.

fao abbreviation for *for the attention of*.

FAO abbreviation for *Food and Agriculture Organization*.

FBI abbreviation for *Federal Bureau of Investi-*

gation, agency of the US Department of Justice.

FDN abbreviation for *Nicaraguan Democratic Front*.

fem in grammar, abbreviation for *feminine*.

ff abbreviation for *folios*; and *the following*; used in reference citation and bibliography.

fig abbreviation for *figure*.

fl abbreviation for *floruit* (Latin 'he/she flourished').

FL abbreviation for *Florida* (USA).

FM in physics, abbreviation for *frequency modulation*. Used in radio, FM is constant in amplitude and varies the frequency of the carrier wave.

FNLA abbreviation for *Front National de Libération de l'Angola* (French 'National Front for the Liberation of Angola').

FO abbreviation for *Foreign Office*, British government department.

FRS abbreviation for *Fellow of the Royal Society*.

ft abbreviation for *foot*, a measure of distance.

FTC abbreviation for *Federal Trade Commission*, US anti-monopoly organization.

g symbol for *gram*.

GA abbreviation for *Georgia* (USA).

gal symbol for *gallon*.

GATT acronym for *General Agreement on Tariffs and Trade*.

GCC abbreviation for *Gulf Cooperation Council*.

GCE abbreviation for *General Certificate of Education*, in the UK, the public examination formerly taken at the age of 16 at Ordinary level (O level) and at 18 at Advanced level (A level).

GCHQ abbreviation for *Government Communications Headquarters* (UK).

GCSE abbreviation for *General Certificate of Secondary Education* in the UK, from 1988, examination for 16-year old pupils, superseding both GCE O level and CSE, and offering qualifications for up to 60% of school leavers in any particular subject.

GDP abbreviation for *Gross Domestic Product*.

GDR abbreviation for *German Democratic Republic* (former East Germany).

gen in grammar, abbreviation for *genitive*.

ger in grammar, abbreviation for *gerund*.

GHQ abbreviation for *general headquarters*.

GI abbreviation for *government issue*; hence (in the USA) a common soldier.

Glos abbreviation for *Gloucestershire*, county in SW England.

GmbH abbreviation for *Gesellshaft mit beschrankter Haftung* (German 'limited liability company').

GNP abbreviation for *Gross National Product*.

GP in medicine, abbreviation for *general practitioner*.

GPU former name (1922–23) for KGB, the Soviet security service.

GRP abbreviation for *glass-reinforced plastic*, a plastic material strengthened by glass fibres, usually erroneously known as fibreglass.

GU abbreviation for *Guam*.

ha symbol for *hectare*.

Hants abbreviation for *Hampshire*.

Herts abbreviation for *Hertfordshire*.
HF in physics, abbreviation for *high frequency*.
HGV abbreviation for *heavy goods vehicle*.
HI abbreviation for *Hawaii* (USA).
HMSO abbreviation for *His/Her Majesty's Stationery Office*.
Hon abbreviation for *Honourable*.
hp symbol for *horsepower*.
HQ abbreviation for *headquarters*.
HRH abbreviation for *His/Her Royal Highness*.
ht abbreviation for *height*.
HWM abbreviation for *high water mark*.
Hz in physics, symbol for *hertz*.
IA abbreviation for *Iowa* (USA).
IADB abbreviation for *Inter-American Development Bank*.
IAEA abbreviation for *International Atomic Energy Agency*.
IBA abbreviation for *Independent Broadcasting Authority*, former name of the Independent Television Commission, UK regulatory body for commercial television and radio.
ibid abbreviation for *ibidem* (Latin 'in the same place'); used in reference citation.
ICBM abbreviation for *intercontinental ballistic missile*.
id abbreviation for *idem* (Latin 'the same'); used in reference citation.
ID abbreviation for *Idaho* (USA).
IDA abbreviation for *International Development Association*.
ie abbreviation for *id est* (Latin 'that is').
IEEE abbreviation for *Institute of Electrical and Electronic Engineers*, which sets technical standards for electrical equipment and computer data exchange.
IKBS abbreviation for *intelligent knowledge-based system*; in computing, an alternative name for the more usual KBS, knowledge-based system.
ILEA abbreviation for *Inner London Education Authority*, former UK educational body which administered education in London. It was abolished 1990 and replaced by smaller borough-based education authorities.
IL abbreviation for *Illinois* (USA).
IMF abbreviation for *International Monetary Fund*.
in abbreviation for *inch*, a measure of distance.
IN abbreviation for *Indiana* (USA).
Inc abbreviation for *Incorporated*.
INF abbreviation for *intermediate nuclear forces*, as in the Intermediate Nuclear Forces Treaty.
IOM abbreviation for *Isle of Man*.
IOW abbreviation for *Isle of Wight*.
ir in physics, abbreviation for *infrared*.
IRCAM abbreviation for the French *Institut de Recherche et de Coordination Acoustique-Musique*, organization in Paris for research into electronic music and synthesizers, founded 1976.
ISBN abbreviation for *International Standard Book Number*, used for ordering or classifying book titles.
ITU abbreviation for *intensive therapy unit*, a high-technology facility for treating the critically ill or injured; in the USA *ICU*, for *intensive care unit*.

IUCN abbreviation for *International Union for the Conservation of Nature*.
IUPAC abbreviation for *International Union of Pure and Applied Chemistry*.
IWW abbreviation for *Industrial Workers of the World*.
J in physics, symbol for *joule*, SI unit of energy.
jnr, jr abbreviation for *junior*.
JP abbreviation for *justice of the peace*.
KBE abbreviation for *Knight (Commander of the Order) of the British Empire*.
KC abbreviation for *King's Counsel*.
kcal symbol for *kilocalorie*.
Kcal abbreviation for *kilocalorie*.
kg abbreviation for *kilogram*.
KG abbreviation for *Knight of the Order of the Garter*.
KGB abbreviation for *Komitet Gosudarstvennoye Bezhopaznosti* (Russian 'Committee of State Security').
km symbol for *kilometre*.
kph or **km/h** symbol for *kilometres per hour*.
KS abbreviation for *Kansas* (USA).
kW abbreviation for *kilowatt*.
KY abbreviation for *Kentucky* (USA).
L Roman numeral for 50.
l symbol for *litre*, a measure of liquid volume.
LA abbreviation for *Louisiana* (USA); *Los Angeles*.
Lab abbreviation for *Labour* or *Labrador*, Canada.
Lancs abbreviation for *Lancashire*.
lat abbreviation for *latitude*.
lb symbol for *pound* (weight).
lbw abbreviation for *leg before wicket* (cricket).
lc in typography, abbreviation for *lower case*, or 'small' letters, as opposed to capitals.
LCD abbreviation for *liquid crystal display*.
LDR abbreviation for *light-dependent resistor*.
LEA in the UK, abbreviation for *local education authority*.
Leics abbreviation for *Leicestershire*.
LF in physics, abbreviation for *low frequency*.
Lib abbreviation for *Liberal*.
LIFFE acronym for *London International Financial Futures Exchange*, one of the exchanges in London where futures contracts are traded.
LDR abbreviation for light-dependent resistor, component of electronic circuits whose resistance varies with the level of illumination on its surface.
Lincs abbreviation for *Lincolnshire*.
loc cit abbreviation for *loco citato* (Latin 'at the place cited'); used in reference citation.
log in mathematics, abbreviation for *logarithm*.
long abbreviation for *longitude*.
Ltd abbreviation for *Limited*.
LW abbreviation for *long wave*, a radio wave with a wavelength of over 1,000 m/3,300 ft; one of the main wavebands into which radio frequency transmissions are divided.
LWM abbreviation for *low water mark*.
m symbol for *metre*.
M Roman numeral for *1,000*.
MA abbreviation for *Master of Arts* degree of education; the state of *Massachusetts* (USA).
MAD abbreviation for *mutual assured destruction*; the basis of the theory of deterrence by possession of nuclear weapons.

MAFF abbreviation for *Ministry of Agriculture, Fisheries and Food.*

Man abbreviation for *Manitoba*, Canadian province.

masc in grammar, abbreviation for *masculine.*

max abbreviation for *maximum.*

MBE abbreviation for *Member (of the Order) of the British Empire.*

MCC abbreviation for *Marylebone Cricket Club.*

MD abbreviation for *Doctor of Medicine*; the state of *Maryland* (USA).

ME abbreviation for *Maine* (USA).

ME abbreviation for *Middle English*, the period of the English language from 1050 to 1550.

MEP abbreviation for *Member of the European Parliament.*

Messrs abbreviation for *messieurs* (French 'sirs' or 'gentlemen') used in formal writing to address an organization or group of people.

MFA abbreviation for *Multi-Fibre Arrangement.*

mg symbol for *milligram.*

Mgr abbreviation for *manager*; in the Roman Catholic Church, abbreviation for *Monsignor.*

MHz symbol for *megahertz.*

mi symbol for *mile.*

MI abbreviation for *Michigan* (USA).

MICV abbreviation for *mechanized infantry combat vehicle.*

Middx abbreviation for *Middlesex*, former county of England.

MIDI abbreviation for *Musical Instrument Digital Interface*, a manufacturer's standard allowing different pieces of digital music equipment used in composing and recording to be freely connected.

min abbreviation for *minute* (time); *minimum.*

MIRV abbreviation for *multiple independently targeted re-entry vehicle*, used in nuclear warfare.

ml symbol for *millilitre.*

MLR abbreviation for *minimum lending rate.*

mm symbol for *millimetre.*

mmHg symbol for *millimetre of mercury.*

MN abbreviation for *Minnesota* (USA).

MO abbreviation for *Missouri* (USA).

MOD abbreviation for *Ministry of Defence.*

MOH abbreviation for *Medical Officer of Health.*

mp in chemistry, abbreviation for *melting point.*

MP abbreviation for *member of Parliament.*

mpg abbreviation for *miles per gallon.*

mph abbreviation for *miles per hour.*

MPhil in education, abbreviation for *Master of Philosophy* degree.

Mr abbreviation for *mister*, title used before a name to show that the person is male.

MRBM abbreviation for *medium-range ballistic missile.*

Mrs title used before a name to show that the person is married and female; partly superseded by Ms, which does not indicate marital status. Mrs was originally an abbreviation for *mistress.*

Ms title used before a woman's name; pronounced 'miz'. Unlike Miss or Mrs, it can be used by married or unmarried women, and was introduced by the women's movement in the 1970s to parallel Mr, which also does not distinguish marital status.

MS abbreviation for *Mississippi* (USA).

MSc in education, abbreviation for *Master of Science* degree. The US abbreviation is *MS.*

MSC abbreviation for *Manpower Services Commission.*

MS(S) abbreviation for *manuscript(s).*

MT abbreviation for *Montana* (USA).

MU in economics, abbreviation for *monetary unit.*

n abbreviation for *noun.*

N abbreviation for *north, newton*, and the chemical symbol for *nitrogen.*

NASA acronym for *National Aeronautics and Space Administration*, US government agency for spaceflight and aeronautical research.

NATO acronym for *N*orth *A*tlantic *T*reaty *Or*ganization.

NB abbreviation for *New Brunswick*; *nota bene* (Latin 'note well'), used in references and citations.

NBS abbreviation for *National Bureau of Standards*, the US federal standards organization, on whose technical standards all US weights and measures are based.

NC abbreviation for *North Carolina* (USA).

ND abbreviation for *North Dakota* (USA).

NE abbreviation for *Nebraska* (USA).

NEDC abbreviation for *National Economic Development Council.*

nem con abbreviation for *nemine contradicente* (Latin 'with no one opposing').

nem diss abbreviation for *nemine dissentiente* (Latin 'with no one dissenting').

NERC abbreviation for *Natural Environment Research Council.*

NF abbreviation for *Newfoundland* (Canada).

NH abbreviation for *New Hampshire* (USA).

NHS abbreviation for *National Health Service*, the UK state-financed health service.

NIEO abbreviation for *New International Economic Order.*

NJ abbreviation for *New Jersey* (USA).

NKVD the Soviet secret police 1934–38, replaced by the KGB. The NKVD was reponsible for Stalin's infamous purges.

NM abbreviation for *New Mexico* (USA).

n o abbreviation for *not out* (cricket).

no or *No* abbreviation for *number.*

nom in grammar, abbreviation for *nominative.*

Northants abbreviation for *Northamptonshire.*

Northd abbreviation for *Northumberland.*

Notts abbreviation for *Nottinghamshire.*

NPA abbreviation for *New People's Army* (Philippines).

NS abbreviation for *Nova Scotia* (Canada).

NSW abbreviation for *New South Wales* (Australia).

NT abbreviation for *Northern Territory* (Australia).

NTP abbreviation for *normal temperature and pressure*, former name for STP (standard temperature and pressure).

NV abbreviation for *Nevada* (USA).

NY abbreviation for *New York* (USA).

NZ abbreviation for *New Zealand.*

o/a abbreviation for *on account.*

OAPEC abbreviation for *Organization of Arab Petroleum Exporting Countries.*

ob abbreviation for *obiit* (Latin 'he/she died').

OBE abbreviation for *Officer (of the Order) of the British Empire*.

OCAM acronym for *Organisation Commune Africaine et Mauricienne*, body for economic cooperation in Africa.

ODA abbreviation for *Overseas Development Administration*.

OE abbreviation for *Old English*, the period of the English language from the 5th century to *c*. AD 1100.

OGPU former name 1923–34 of the Soviet secret police, now the KGB.

OH abbreviation for *Ohio* (USA).

OHMS abbreviation for *On Her (His) Majesty's Service*.

OIC abbreviation for *Organization of the Islamic Conference*, international Muslim solidarity association.

OK abbreviation for *Oklahoma* (USA).

o n abbreviation for *or near(est) offer*.

Ont abbreviation for *Ontario* (Canada).

op cit abbreviation for *opere citato* (Latin 'in the work cited'), used in reference citation.

OPEC abbreviation for *Organization of Petroleum-Exporting Countries*.

OR abbreviation for *Oregon* (USA).

OT abbreviation for *Old Testament*.

OU abbreviation for *Open University*.

OXFAM abbreviation for *Oxford Committee for Famine Relief*.

Oxon abbreviation for *Oxoniensis* (Latin 'of Oxford').

oz symbol for *ounce*.

p in music, abbreviation for *piano* (Italian 'softly').

p(p) abbreviation for *page(s)*.

pa abbreviation for *per annum* (Latin 'yearly').

PA abbreviation for *Pennsylvania* (USA).

part in grammar, abbreviation for *participle*.

PAYE abbreviation for *pay as you earn*.

PC abbreviation for *police constable*; *Privy Councillor*; *personal computer*.

PCB abbreviation for *polychlorinated biphenyl*; *printed circuit board*.

PCM abbreviation for *pulse-code modulation*.

PEN abbreviation for *Poets, Playwrights, Editors, Essayists, Novelists*, literary association established 1921 by C A ('Sappho') Dawson Scott, to promote international understanding among writers.

per pro abbreviation for *per procurationem* (Latin 'by the agency of').

PhD abbreviation for *Doctor of Philosophy* degree.

plc abbreviation for *public limited company*.

PLO abbreviation for *Palestine Liberation Organization*.

plur in grammar, abbreviation for *plural*.

PM abbreviation for *prime minister*.

pm or *PM* abbreviation for *post meridiem* (Latin 'after noon').

PO abbreviation for *Post Office*.

pp abbreviation for *per procurationem* (Latin 'by proxy').

ppm abbreviation for *parts per million*. An alternative (but numerically equivalent) unit used in chemistry is milligrams per litre (mg l⁻¹).

PR abbreviation for *public relations*; *proportional representation*.

PR abbreviation for *Puerto Rico*.

pref in grammar, abbreviation for *prefix*.

pro tem abbreviation for *pro tempore* (Latin 'for the time being').

PS abbreviation for *post scriptum* (Latin 'after writing').

pt abbreviation for *pint*.

PTO abbreviation for *please turn over*.

PX abbreviation for *Post Exchange*, a US organization that provides shopping and canteen facilities for armed forces at home and abroad. The British equivalent is the NAAFI.

QB abbreviation for *Queen's Bench*.

QC abbreviation for *Queen's Counsel*.

QED abbreviation for *quod erat demonstrandum* (Latin 'which was to be proved').

Qld abbreviation for *Queensland* (Australia).

quant suff abbreviation for *quantum sufficit* (Latin 'as much as suffices').

Que abbreviation for *Québec* (Canada).

qv abbreviation for *quod vide* (Latin 'which see').

RA abbreviation for *Royal Academy of Art*, London, founded 1768.

RAC abbreviation for the UK *Royal Automobile Club*.

RAF abbreviation for *Royal Air Force*.

RC abbreviation for *Red Cross*; *Roman Catholic*.

re abbreviation for Latin *'with regard to'*.

RI abbreviation for *Rhode Island* (USA).

RIBA abbreviation for *Royal Institute of British Architects*.

RIP abbreviation for *requiescat in pace* (Latin 'may he/she rest in peace').

RN abbreviation for *Royal Navy*.

RNLI abbreviation for *Royal National Lifeboat Institution*.

RPI abbreviation for *retail price index*.

rpm abbreviation for *revolutions per minute*.

RPV abbreviation for *remotely piloted vehicle*, a flying TV camera for military use.

RSFSR abbreviation for *Russian Soviet Federal Socialist Republic*, popularly known as the Russian Federation, the largest constituent republic of the USSR.

RSPB abbreviation for *Royal Society for the Protection of Birds*.

RSPCA abbreviation for *Royal Society for the Prevention of Cruelty to Animals*.

RSV abbreviation for *Revised Standard Version* of the Bible.

RSVP abbreviation for *répondez s'il vous plaît* (French 'please reply').

Rt Hon abbreviation for *Right Honourable*, the title of British members of Parliament.

S abbreviation for *south*.

SA abbreviation for *South Africa*; *South Australia*.

SAARC abbreviation for *South Asian Association for Regional Cooperation*.

SADCC abbreviation for *Southern African Development Coordination Conference*.

sae abbreviation for *stamped addressed envelope*.

SALT acronym for *Strategic Arms Limitation Talks*, a series of US-Soviet negotiations 1969–79.

SAS abbreviation for *Special Air Service*; also for

Scandinavian Airlines System.

Sask abbreviation for *Saskatchewan* (Canada).

SBS abbreviation for *Special Boat Service*, the British Royal Navy's equivalent of the Special Air Service.

sc abbreviation for *scilicet* (Latin 'let it be understood').

SC abbreviation for *South Carolina* (USA).

SD abbreviation for *South Dakota* (USA).

SDI abbreviation for *Strategic Defense Initiative.*

SDLP abbreviation for *Social Democratic and Labour Party* (Northern Ireland).

SDP abbreviation for *Social Democratic Party* (UK).

SDR abbreviation for *special drawing right.*

SEATO abbreviation for *Southeast Asia Treaty Organization.*

sec or *s* abbreviation for *second*, a unit of time.

SELA abbreviation for *Sistema Economico Latino-Americana* or Latin American Economic System.

seq abbreviation for *sequentes* (Latin 'the following').

SERC abbreviation for *Science and Engineering Research Council.*

SERPS abbreviation for *State Earnings-Related Pension Schemes*, the UK state pension scheme.

SFSR abbreviation for *Soviet Federal Socialist Republic.*

SHAPE abbreviation for *Supreme Headquarters Allied Powers Europe*, situated near Mons, Belgium, and the headquarters of NATO's Supreme Allied Commander Europe (SACEUR).

SHF in physics, abbreviation for *superhigh frequency.*

SI abbreviation for *Système International [d'Unités]* (French 'International System [of Metric Units]').

SIB abbreviation for *Securities and Investments Board*, UK regulating body.

sing abbreviation for *singular.*

SIS abbreviation for *Special Intelligence Service.*

SJ abbreviation for *Society of Jesus.*

SLBM abbreviation for *submarine-launched ballistic missile.*

SLD abbreviation for *Social and Liberal Democrats.*

SLR abbreviation for *single-lens reflex*, a type of camera in which the image can be seen through the lens before a picture is taken.

SOS internationally recognized distress signal, using letters of the Morse code (... – ...).

SPF abbreviation for *South Pacific Forum*, organization of countries in the region.

SPQR abbreviation for *Senatus Populusque Romanus.* (Latin 'the Senate and the Roman People').

sq abbreviation for *square* (measure).

Sr abbreviation for *senior*, also for *señor.*

SSR abbreviation for *Soviet Socialist Republic.*

Staffs abbreviation for *Staffordshire.*

START acronym for *Strategic Arms Reduction Talks.*

suff in grammar, abbreviation for *suffix.*

t symbol for *ton* or *tonne.*

tal qual abbreviation for *talis qualis* (Latin 'just as they come').

Tas abbreviation for *Tasmania.*

TASM abbreviation for *tactical air-to-surface missile.*

Tass acronym for the Soviet news agency *Telegrafnoye Agentstvo Sovyetskovo Soyuza.*

TB abbreviation for the infectious disease *tuberculosis.*

TD abbreviation for *Teachta Dála* (Irish 'a member of the Irish parliament').

temp abbreviation for *temperature; temporary.*

TIR abbreviation for *Transports Internationaux Routiers* (French 'International Road Transport').

TM abbreviation for *transcendental meditation.*

TN abbreviation for *Tennessee* (USA).

TT abbreviation for *Tourist Trophy; teetotal; tuberculin tested.*

TTL abbreviation for *transistor-transistor logic*, a family of integrated circuits with fast switching speeds commonly used in building electronic devices.

TUC abbreviation for *Trades Union Congress.*

TX abbreviation for *Texas* (USA).

UDC abbreviation for *urban district council.*

UFO abbreviation for *unidentified flying object.*

UHT abbreviation for *ultra heat treated.*

UK abbreviation for the *United Kingdom.*

UKAEA abbreviation for *United Kingdom Atomic Energy Authority.*

UN abbreviation for the *United Nations.*

UNCTAD acronym for *United Nations Commission on Trade and Development.*

UNEP acronym for *United Nations Environmental Programme.*

UNHCR abbreviation for *United Nations High Commission for Refugees.*

UNICEF acronym for *United Nations International Children's Emergency Fund.*

UNITA acronym for *National Union for the Total Independence of Angola.*

US abbreviation for the *United States of America* (popular and most frequent name used by speakers of American English for the nation).

USA abbreviation (official) for the *United States of America; US Army.*

USDA abbreviation for the *US Department of Agriculture.*

USGS abbreviation for the *US Geological Survey*, part of the Department of the Interior.

USIA abbreviation for *US Information Agency.*

USO abbreviation for *United Service Organizations.*

USS abbreviation for *US Ship.*

USSR abbreviation for the *Union of Soviet Socialist Republics.*

UV in physics, abbreviation for *ultraviolet.*

V Roman numeral for *five*; in physics, symbol for *volt.*

v in physics, symbol for *velocity.*

VAT abbreviation for *value-added tax.*

vb in grammar, abbreviation for *verb.*

VDU (abbreviation for *visual display terminal*) an electronic output device for displaying the data processed by a computer on a screen.

vi in grammar, abbreviation for *verb intransitive.*

VI abbreviation for *Virgin Islands*; *Vancouver Island* (Canada).

VIP abbreviation for *very important person*.

viz abbreviation for *videlicet* (Latin 'that is to say', 'namely').

VLF in physics, abbreviation for *very low frequency*.

voc in grammar, abbreviation for *vocative*.

vol abbreviation for *volume*.

VR abbreviation for *velocity ratio*.

VSTOL abbreviation for *vertical/short takeoff and landing*.

vt in grammar, abbreviation for *verb transitive*.

VT abbreviation for *Vermont* (USA).

W abbreviation for *west*; in physics, symbol for *watt*.

WA abbreviation for *Washington* (state) (USA); *Western Australia*.

wc abbreviation for *water closet*, another name for a toilet.

WCC abbreviation for *World Council of Churches*.

WHO acronym for *World Health Organization*.

WI abbreviation for *West Indies*; *Wisconsin* (USA).

Wilts abbreviation for *Wiltshire*.

Worcs abbreviation for *Worcestershire*.

wpm abbreviation for *words per minute*.

wt abbreviation for *weight*.

WV abbreviation for *West Virginia* (USA).

WWF abbreviation for *World Wide Fund for Nature* (formerly World Wildlife Fund).

WY abbreviation for *Wyoming* (USA).

X Roman numeral *ten*; a person or thing unknown.

x in mathematics, an unknown quantity.

yd abbreviation for *yard*.

YHA abbreviation for *Youth Hostels Association*.

YMCA abbreviation for *Young Men's Christian Association*.

Yorks abbreviation for *Yorkshire*.

YWCA abbreviation for *Young Women's Christian Association*.

Z in physics, the symbol for *impedance* (electricity and magnetism).

zB abbreviation for *zum Beispiel* (German 'for example').

ZST abbreviation for *zone standard time*.

FOREIGN WORDS AND PHRASES

Abbé (French 'abbot') a title of respect used to address any clergyman.

addendum (Latin) something to be added, usually in writing, which qualifies a foregoing thesis or statement.

ad infinitum (Latin) to infinity, endlessly.

ad lib(itum) (Latin) 'freely' interpreted.

ad nauseam (Latin) to the point of disgust.

aide-de-camp (French) officer who acts as private secretary to a general and would normally accompany the general on any duty.

al fresco (Italian 'in the cool') in the open air.

avant-garde (from French) in the arts, those artists or works that are in the forefront of new developments in their media.

ballet blanc (French 'white ballet') a ballet, such as *Giselle*, in which the female dancers wear calf-length white dresses.

belles lettres (French 'fine letters') literature that is appreciated more for its aesthetic qualities than for its content.

bête noire (French 'black beast') something particularly disliked.

Bildungsroman (German 'education novel') novel that deals with the psychological and emotional development of its protagonist, tracing his or her life from inexperienced youth to maturity. The first example of the type is generally considered to be Wieland's *Agathon* 1765–66.

billabong (Australian Aboriginal *billa bung* 'dead river') a stagnant pond.

billet doux (French 'sweet note') a letter to or from one's lover.

Blitzkrieg (German 'lightning war') swift military campaign, as used by Germany at the beginning of World War II 1939–41. The abbreviated form Blitz was applied to the German air raids on London 1940–41.

bloc (French) a group, generally used to describe politically allied countries, as in 'the Soviet bloc'.

bona vacantia (Latin 'empty goods') in law, the property of a person who dies without making a will and without relatives or dependants who would be entitled or might reasonably expect to inherit.

bon marché (French) cheap.

bon mot (French) a witty remark.

bonsai (Japanese) the art of producing miniature trees by selective pruning.

bon ton (French 'good tone') fashionable manners.

bon voyage (French) have a good journey.

bourgeois (French) a member of the middle class, implying that a person is unimaginative, conservative, and materialistic.

bric-à-brac (French) odds and ends, usually old, ornamental, less valuable than antiques.

cahier (French 'notebook') usually the working notes or drawings of a writer or artist.

caïque (French, from Turkish) long, narrow, light rowing boat.

canaille (French) the mob, rabble.

carpe diem (Latin 'seize the day') live for the present.

carte blanche (French 'white paper') no instructions, complete freedom to do as one wishes.

casus belli (Latin) a justification for war, grounds for a dispute.

caveat emptor (Latin) dictum that professes the buyer is responsible for checking the quality of nonwarrantied goods purchased.

cave canem (Latin) beware of the dog.

céad míle fáilte (Irish 'a hundred thousand welcomes') a conventional form of greeting.

c'est la vie (French) that's life.

chacun à son goût (French) each to their own taste.

chambré (French) (of wine) at room temperature, as opposed to chilled.

chef d'oeuvre (French) a masterpiece.

cicisbeo (Italian) 18th-century term for an aristocratic married woman's lover, similar to *cavaliere servente*.

cogito, ergo sum (Latin) 'I think, therefore I am'; quotation from French philosopher René Descartes.

comme il faut (French 'as it should be') socially correct and acceptable.

compos mentis (Latin) of sound mind.

conquistador (Spanish for 'conqueror'), applied to such explorers and adventurers in the Americas as Cortés (Mexico) and Pizarro (Peru).

corrigendum (Latin) something to be corrected.

coup d'état or *coup* (French literally 'stroke of state') forcible takeover of the government of a country by elements from within that country, generally carried out by violent or illegal means.

coûte que coûte (French) whatever the cost.

crème de la crème (French 'the cream of the cream') the elite, the very best.

cri de coeur (French) a cry from the heart.

cuius regio, eius religio (Latin) those who live in a country should adopt the religon of its ruler.

cul-de-sac (French, literally 'bottom of the bag') a street closed off at one end; an inescapable situation.

curriculum vitae or *CV* (Latin, literally 'the course of one's life') an account of a person's education and previous employment, attached to a job application.

de bene esse (Latin 'of wellbeing') in law, doing what is the best possible in the circumstances; the term usually relates to evidence.

decree nisi (Latin) conditional order of divorce. A *decree absolute* is normally granted six weeks after the decree nisi, and from the date of the decree absolute the parties cease to be husband and wife.

de die in diem (Latin) day after day.

de facto (Latin) in fact.

de gustibus non est disputandum (Latin) there is no accounting for taste.

Dei gratia (Latin) by the grace of God.

déjà vu (French 'already seen') the feeling that something encountered for the first time has in fact been seen before.

de jure (Latin) according to law; legally.

de novo (Latin) from the beginning; anew.

Deo (ad)juvante (Latin) with God's help.

Deo gratias (Latin) thanks to God.

Deo volente (Latin) God willing.

de profundis (Latin 'from the depths') a cry from the depths of misery. From the Bible, Psalm 130: *De profundis clamavi ad te*; 'Out of the depths have I cried to thee'.

de rigueur (French 'of strictness') demanded by the rules of etiquette.

détente (French) a reduction of political tension and the easing of strained relations between nations; for example, the ending of the Cold War 1989–90.

de trop (French 'of too much') not wanted, in the way.

deus ex machina (Latin 'a god from a machine') a far-fetched or unlikely event that resolves an intractable difficulty.

Dieu et mon droit (French 'God and my right') motto of the royal arms of UK.

doppelgänger (German 'double-goer') a ghostly apparition identical to a living person; a twin soul.

double entendre (French 'double meaning') an ambiguous word or phrase, usually one that is coarse or impolite.

dramatis personae (Latin) the characters in a play.

dulce et decorum est pro patria mori (Latin 'it is sweet and noble to die for one's country') quotation from Horace's *Odes*, also used by English poet Wilfred Owen as the title for his poem denouncing World War I.

Ecce Homo (Latin 'behold the man') the words of Pontius Pilate to the accusers of Jesus; the title of paintings showing Jesus crowned with thorns, presented to the people (John 19:5).

emeritus (Latin) someone who has retired from an official position but retains their title on an honorary basis, for example a *professor emeritus*.

éminence grise (French, literally 'grey eminence') a power behind a throne; that is, a manipulator of power without immediate responsibility. The nickname was originally applied (because of his grey cloak) to the French monk François Leclerc du Tremblay (1577–1638), also known as Père Joseph, who in 1612 became the close friend and behind-the-scenes adviser of Cardinal Richelieu.

enfant terrible (French 'terrible child') one whose rash and unconventional behaviour shocks and embarrasses others.

en masse (French) as a group, in a body, all together.

enosis (Greek) the movement, developed from 1930, for the union of Cyprus with Greece, which took place 1974.

en plein air (French) in the open air.

en route (French) on the way.

entente cordiale (French 'cordial understanding'), specifically, the agreement reached by Britain and France 1904 recognizing British interests in Egypt and French interests in Morocco. It formed the basis for Anglo-French cooperation before the outbreak of World War I 1914.

ergo (Latin) therefore; hence.

erratum (Latin) an error.

ersatz (German) artificial, substitute, inferior.

espadrille (French) a type of shoe made with a canvas upper and a rope sole.

et in arcadia ego (Latin 'I also in Arcadia') death exists even in Arcadia (a fabled land).

ex cathedra (Latin, literally 'from the chair') term describing a statement by the pope, taken to be indisputably true, and which must be accepted by Catholics.

exeunt (Latin 'they go out') a stage direction.

exit (Latin 'he/she goes out') a stage direction.

ex parte (Latin 'on the part of one side only') in law, term indicating that an order has been made after hearing only the party that made the application; for example, an ex parte injunction.

factotum (Latin 'do everything') someone employed to do all types of work.

fait accompli (French 'accomplished fact') something that has been done and cannot be undone.

faute de mieux (French) for want of better.

faux pas (French 'false step') a social blunder.

fellah (Arabic, plural **fellahin**) in Arab countries, a peasant farmer or farm labourer. In Egypt, approximately 60% of the fellah population live in rural areas, often in villages of 1,000–5,000 inhabitants.

fin de siècle (French 'end of century') the art and literature of the 1890s; decadent.

force majeure (French 'superior force') in politics, the use of force rather than the seeking of a political or diplomatic solution to a problem.

Gesellschaft (German 'society') a group whose concerns are of a formal and practical nature.

glasnost (Russian 'speaking aloud') Soviet leader Mikhail Gorbachev's policy of liberalizing various aspects of Soviet life, such as introducing greater freedom of expression and information and opening up relations with Western countries.

Götterdämmerung (German 'twilight of the gods') in Scandinavian mythology, the end of the world.

gulag (Russian) term for the system of prisons and labour camps used to silence dissidents and opponents of the Soviet regime.

hic jacet (Latin 'here lies') an epitaph.

honi soit qui mal y pense (French 'shamed be he who thinks evil of it') the motto of England's Order of the Garter.

hors de combat (French) out of action.

incunabula (Latin, originally from swaddling clothes) the birthplace, or early stages of anything; printed books produced before 1500, when printing was in its infancy.

in loco parentis (Latin) in a parental capacity.

in situ (Latin) in place, on the spot, without moving from position.

inter alia (Latin) among other things.

ipso facto (Latin) by that very fact.

j'adoube (French 'I adjust') used in chess to show that a player is touching a piece in order to correct its position rather than to move it.

je ne sais quoi (French 'I don't know what') a certain indescribable quality.

joie de vivre (French) finding pleasure in simply being alive.

kindergarten (German) another term for nursery school.

kohl (Arabic) powdered antimony sulphide, used in Asia and the Middle East to darken the area around the eyes.

Kyrie eleison (Greek 'Lord have mercy') the words spoken or sung at the beginning of the mass in the Catholic, Orthodox, and Anglican churches.

laissez faire (French) theory that the state should not intervene in economic affairs, except to break up a monopoly. The phrase originated with the Physiocrats, 18th-century French economists whose maxim was *laissez faire et*

laissez passer, (leave the individual alone and let commodities circulate freely).

lakh or *lac* or *lak* (from Hindi) in India or Pakistan, the sum of 100,000 (rupees).

Land (German; plural *Länder*) federal state of Germany or Austria.

Landtag (German) legislature of each of the *Länder* (states) that form the federal republics of Germany and Austria.

Lebensphilosophie (German) philosophy of life.

Lebensraum (German 'living space') theory developed by Hitler for the expansion of Germany into E Europe, and in the 1930s used by the Nazis to justify their annexation of neighbouring states on the grounds that Germany was overpopulated.

lingua franca (Italian, literally 'Frankish tongue') any language that is used as a means of communication by groups who do not themselves normally speak that language; for example, English is a lingua franca used by Japanese doing business in Finland, or by Swedes in Saudi Arabia.

locus standi (Latin 'a place to stand') in law, the right to bring an action.

Lumpenproletariat (German 'ragged proletariat') the poorest of the poor: beggars, tramps, and criminals (according to Karl Marx).

Machtpolitik (German) power politics.

magnum opus (Latin) a great work of art or literature.

Mardi Gras (French 'fat Tuesday' from the custom of using up all the fat in the household before the beginning of Lent) Shrove Tuesday. A festival was traditionally held on this day in Paris, and there are carnivals in many parts of the world, including New Orleans, Louisiana, Italy, and Brazil.

mare nostrum (Latin 'our sea') Roman name for the Mediterranean.

matzo or *matzoh* (from Hebrew) unleavened bread eaten during the Passover.

mea culpa (Latin 'my fault') an admission of guilt.

memento mori (Latin) a reminder of death.

menhir (Breton 'long stone') a prehistoric standing stone.

mens sana in corpore sano (Latin) a healthy mind in a healthy body.

Messrs abbreviation for *messieurs* (French 'sirs' or 'gentlemen') used in formal writing to address an organization or group of people.

mise en scène (French 'stage setting') in cinema, the composition and content of the frame in terms of background scenery, actors, costumes, props, and lighting.

modus operandi (Latin) a method of operating.

modus vivendi (Latin 'way of living') a compromise between opposing points of view.

mores (Latin) the customs and manners of a society.

mot juste (French) the right word, just the word to suit the occasion.

muezzin (Arabic) a person whose job is to perform the call to prayer five times a day from the minaret of a Muslim mosque.

née (French 'born') followed by a surname, indicates the name of a woman before marriage.

nemo me impune lacessit (Latin 'no one injures me with impunity') the motto of Scotland.

nil desperandum (Latin) never despair.

noblesse oblige (French) the aristocracy ought to behave honourably. The phrase is often used sarcastically to point out how removed this idea is from reality.

nom de plume (French 'pen name') a writer's pseudonym.

non sequitur (Latin 'it does not follow') a statement that has little or no relevance to the one that preceded it.

nuit blanche (French 'white night') a night without sleep.

nulli secundus (Latin) second to none.

obiit (Latin 'he/she died') found, for example, in inscriptions on tombstones, followed by a date.

ombudsman (from Swedish 'commissioner') official who acts on behalf of the private citizen in investigating complaints against the government. The post is of Scandinavian origin; it was introduced in Sweden 1809, Denmark 1954, and Norway 1962, and spread to other countries from the 1960s.

onus (Latin) a burden or responsibility.

outré (French) extreme, beyond the bounds of acceptability.

pace (Latin) with deference to, followed by a name, used to acknowledge contradiction of the person named.

padre (Italian 'father') a priest.

parvenu (French 'arrived') a social upstart.

passé (French) out of date.

passim (Latin 'in many places') indicates that a reference occurs repeatedly throughout the cited work.

perestroika (Russian 'radical restructuring') in Soviet politics, the wide-ranging economic and political reforms initiated during Mikhail Gorbachev's leadership of the Soviet state.

per se (Latin) in itself.

pièce de résistance (French) the most outstanding item in a collection; the main dish of a meal.

pied-à-terre (French 'foot on the ground') a convenient second home, usually small and in a town or city.

pique (French) a feeling of slight irritation or resentment.

plus ça change, plus c'est la même chose (French) the more things change, the more they stay the same.

poste restante (French) a system whereby mail is sent to a certain post office and kept there until collected by the addressee.

post hoc, ergo propter hoc (Latin) after this, therefore on account of this.

postmortem (Latin) dissection of a dead body to determine the cause of death. It is also known as an *autopsy*.

post scriptum (abbreviation PS; Latin) something written below the signature on a letter.

prêt-à-porter (French) ready-to-wear clothes.

prima facie (Latin) at first sight.

pro rata (Latin) in proportion.

pro tem(pore) (Latin) for the time being.

putsch (Swiss German) term for a violent seizure of political power, such as the abortive attempt by the Soviet 'Gang of Eight' to wrest power from President Gorbachev Aug 1991

quasi (Latin 'as if') apparently but not actually.

quid pro quo (Latin 'something for something') an exchange of one thing in return for another.

quod erat demonstrandum (abbreviation QED; Latin 'which was to be proved') added at the end of a geometry proof.

quod vide (abbreviation qv; Latin 'which see') indicates a cross-reference.

quo vadis? (Latin) where are you going?

raison d'être (French) a reason for existence.

réchauffé (French 're-heated') warmed up (as of leftover food); old, stale.

recherché (French 'sought after') rare.

revenons à nos moutons (French 'let us return to our sheep') let us get back to the subject.

ruat coelum (Latin 'though the heavens may fall') whatever happens.

rus in urbe (Latin) urban retreat where one could imagine oneself in the countryside.

Sachlichkeit (German) objectivity, matter-of-factness.

samovar (Russian) urn, heated by charcoal, used for making tea.

sang-froid (French 'cold blood') coolness, composure.

sans souci (French) without cares or worries.

savoir-faire (French) knowing what to do, how to behave.

Schadenfreude (German) malicious enjoyment at the misfortunes of others.

scilicet (Latin) namely, that is.

secrétaire (French) a small writing desk.

sic (Latin 'thus', 'so') sometimes found in brackets within a printed quotation to show that an apparent error is in the original.

si monumentum requiris, circumspice (Latin 'if you seek his monument, look about you') the epitaph of Christopher Wren in St Paul's Cathedral, London.

sine die (Latin 'without a day being appointed') indefinitely.

sine qua non (Latin 'without which not') absolutely essential.

soupçon (French 'suspicion') a very small amount, a dash.

sovkhoz (Russian) state-owned farm in the USSR where the workers are state employees. The sovkhoz differs from the *kolkhoz* where the farm is run by a collective.

status quo (Latin 'the state in which') the current situation, without change.

Sturm und Drang (German, literally 'storm and stress') German early Romantic movement in literature and music, from about 1775, concerned with the depiction of extravagant passions. Writers associated with the movement include Herder, Goethe, and Schiller.

sub judice (Latin) not yet decided by a court of law.

Sûreté (French) the criminal investigation department of the French police.

tabula rasa (Latin 'scraped tablet', from the Romans' use of wax-covered tablets which could be written on with a pointed stick and cleared by smoothing over the surface) a mind without any preconceived ideas.

tant mieux (French) so much the better.

tant pis (French) so much the worse.

tempus fugit (Latin) time flies.

terra firma (Latin) dry land; solid earth.

terra incognita (Latin) an unknown region.

terza rima (Italian 'third line') poetical metre used in Dante's *Divine Comedy*, consisting of three-line stanzas in which the second line rhymes with the first and third of the following stanza.

tête-à-tête (French'-to-head') private meeting between two people.

texte intégral (French 'the complete text') unabridged.

tour de force (French 'feat of strength') a remarkable accomplishment.

tout de suite (French) immediately.

tout ensemble (French 'all together') the overall effect.

trahison des clercs (French 'the treason of the intellectuals') the involvement of intellectuals in active politics.

tricoteuse (French 'knitter') in the French Revolution, one of the women who sat knitting in the National Convention and near the guillotine.

ultra (Latin) extreme.

uomo universale (Italian 'universal man'), someone who is at home in all spheres of knowledge; one of the ideals of the Renaissance.

urbi et orbi (Latin 'to the city and to the world') a papal proclamation.

ut pictura poesis (Latin) a poem is as a picture.

vade mecum (Latin 'go with me') a useful handbook carried about for reference.

veni, vidi, vici (Latin 'I came, I saw, I conquered') Julius Caesar's description of his victory over King Pharnaces II (63–47 BC) at Zela in 47 BC.

vérité (French 'realism'), as in *cinéma vérité*, used to describe a realistic or documentary style.

versus (abbreviation vs; Latin) against.

vice versa (Latin) the other way around.

vis-à-vis (French 'face-to-face') with regard to.

viva voce (Latin 'with living voice') an oral examination.

Völkerwanderung (German 'nations wandering') the migration of peoples, usually with reference to the Slavic and Germanic movement in Europe 2nd–11th centuries AD.

Weltanschauung (German 'worldview') a philosophy of life.

yeti (Tibetan) another term for the abominable snowman.

Zeitgeist (German 'time spirit') spirit of the age.

zenana (Hindi) the part of a house used by the female members of the household.

Zugzwang (German) a position in chess from which it is impossible to move without worsening one's situation.

Exchange Rates

World Exchange Rates (as of 1 July 1992)

country	currency	sterling
Afghanistan	afgháni	2231.42
Albania	lek	211.15
Algeria	dinar	39.64
Andorra	French franc	9.59
	Spanish peseta	181.03
Angola	kwanza	1055.73
Antigua	East Caribbean dollar	5.18
Argentina	peso	1.90
Aruba	florin	3.44
Australia	Australian dollar	2.58
Austria	schilling	19.98
Azores	port escudo	239.94
Bahamas	Bahamian dollar	1.92
Bahrain	dinar	0.72
Balearic Islands	Spanish peseta	181.03
Bangladesh	taka	74.28
Barbados	Barbados dollar	3.86
Belgium	Belgian franc	58.49
Belize	Belize dollar	3.84
Benin	CFA franc	479.49
Bermuda	Bermudian dollar	1.92
Bhutan	ngultrum	54.48
Bolivia	boliviano	7.52
Botswana	pula	3.99
Brazil	cruzeiro	7983.39
Brunei	Brunei dollar	3.10
Bulgaria	lev	43.65
Burkina Faso	CFA franc	479.49
Burma	kyat	11.29
Burundi	Burundi franc	391.59
Cambodia	riel	n.a.
Cameroon	CFA franc	479.49
Canada	Canadian dollar	2.27
Canary Islands	Spanish peseta	181.03
Cape Verde	Cape Verde escudo	122.52
Cayman Islands	Cayman Island dollar	1.63
Central African Republic	CFA franc	479.49
Chad	CFA franc	479.49
Chile	Chilean peso	700.89
China	Renminbi yuan	10.40
Colombia	Colombian peso	1472.06
Comoros	CFA franc	479.49
Congo	CFA franc	479.49
Costa Rica	colón	259.13
Côte d'Ivoire	CFA franc	479.49
Cuba	Cuban peso	2.53
Cyprus	Cyprus pound	1.22
Czechoslovakia	koruna	52.90
Denmark	Danish kroner	10.92
Djibouti Republic	Djibouti franc	341.13
Dominica	East Caribbean dollar	5.18
Dominican Republic	Dominican peso	25.19
Ecuador	sucre	2772.33
		2985.78
Egypt	Egyptian pound	6.36
El Salvador	colón	16.30
Equatorial Guinea	CFA franc	479.49
Estonia	kroon	n.a.
Ethiopia	Ethiopian birr	3.97
Falkland Islands	Falkland pound	1.00
Faroe Islands	Danish kroner	10.92
Fiji Islands	Fiji dollar	2.81
Finland	markka	7.78
France	franc	9.59
French Community/ Africa	CFA franc	479.49
French Guiana	local franc	9.95
French Pacific Islands	CFP franc	174.36
Gabon	CFA franc	479.49
Gambia	dalasi	17.34
Germany	Deutschmark	2.84
Ghana	cedi	806.19
Gibraltar	Gibraltar pound	1.00
Greece	drachma	348.64
Greenland	Danish krone	10.92
Grenada	East Caribbean dollar	5.18
Guadaloupe	local franc	9.59
Guam	US dollar	1.92
Guatemala	quetzal	9.89
Guinea	franc	1559.19
Guinea-Bissau	peso	9597.50
Guyana	Guyanese dollar	237.25
Haiti	goude	9.60
Honduras	lempira	10.86
Hong Kong	Hong Kong dollar	14.85
Hungary	forint	148.61
Iceland	Icelandic krona	105.17
India	Indian rupee	54.48
Indonesia	rupiah	3902.34
Iran	rial	2758.32
Iraq	Iraqi dinar	0.60
Irish Republic	punt	0.94
Israel	shekel	4.71
Italy	lira	2148.40
Jamaica	Jamaican dollar	43.28
Japan	yen	244.22
Jordan	Jordanian dinar	1.09
Kenya	Kenyan shilling	58.87
Kiribati	Australian dollar	2.58
Korea, North	won	4.13
Korea, South	won	1512.76
Kuwait	Kuwaiti dinar	0.56
Laos	new kip	1372.44
Latvia	Latvian rouble	n.a.
Lebanon	Lebanese pound	4155.72
Lesotho	maluti	5.31
Liberia	Liberian dollar	1.92
Libya	Libyan dinar	0.51
Liechtenstein	Swiss franc	2.53
Lithuania	Lithuanian rouble	n.a.
Luxembourg	Luxembourg franc	58.49
Macao	pataca	15.34
Madagascar	Malagasy franc	3459.99
Madeira	port escudo	239.94
Malawi	kwacha	7.56
Malaysia	ringgit	4.80
Maldive Islands	rufiya	19.73
Mali Republic	CFA franc	479.49
Malta	Maltese pound	1.74
Martinique	local franc	9.59
Mauritania	ougiya	155.27

Mauritius	Mauritian rupee	28.47		Turkey	lira	13746.54
Mexico	Mexican peso	5945.65		Turks and Caicos		
Miquelon	local franc	9.59		Islands	US dollar	1.92
Monaco	French franc	9.59		Tuvalu	Australian dollar	2.58
Mongolia	tugrik	76.78		Uganda	new shilling	2257.43
Montserrat	East Caribbean dollar	5.18		United Arab		
Morocco	dirham	14.97		Emirates	dirham	7.05
Mozambique	metical	4879.96		United Kingdom	pound sterling	1.00
Namibia	South African Rand	5.31		United States	US dollar	1.92
Nauru Island	Australian dollar	2.58		Uruguay	peso	5983.08
Nepal	Nepalese rupee	89.51		Vanuatu	vatu	201.55
Netherlands	guilder	3.20		Vatican City State	lira	2148.40
Netherland Antilles	Antillian guilder	3.44		Venezuela	bolivar	129.37
New Zealand	New Zealand dollar	3.52		Vietnam	dong	21229.67
Nicaragua	gold cordoba	9.60		Virgin Islands,		
Niger Republic	CFA franc	478.92		British	US dollar	1.92
Nigeria	naira	35.40		Virgin Islands, US	US dollar	1.92
Norway	Norwegian krone	11.16		Western Samoa	taia	4.73
Oman	Omani rial	0.74		Yemen, North	rial	n.a.
Pakistan	Pakistani rupee	48.18		Yemen, South	dinar	n.a.
Panama	balboa	1.92		Yugoslavia	dinar	383.90
Papua New Guinea	kina	1.84		Zaïre Republic	zaïre	1263363.10
Paraguay	guarani	2840.86		Zambia	kwacha	326.66
Peru	new sol	2.36		Zimbabwe	dollár	9.47
Philippines	peso	47.81				
Pitcairn Islands	pound sterling	1.00				

n.a. = not available. Data supplied by Bank of America, Economics Department, London Trading Centre.

	New Zealand dollar	3.52
Poland	zloty	26139.75
Portugal	escudo	239.94
Puerto Rico	US dollars	1.92
Qatar	riyal	7.37
Réunion Islands	French franc	9.59
Romania	leu	700.62
Russian Federation	rouble	n.a.
Rwanda	franc	267.26
St Christopher	East Caribbean dollar	5.18
St Helena	pound sterling	1.00
St Lucia	East Caribbean dollar	5.18
St Pierre	French franc	9.59`
St Vincent	East Caribbean dollar	5.18
San Marino	Italian lira	2148.40
São Tomé e Principe	dobra	460.68
Saudi Arabia	riyal	7.20
Senegal	CFA franc	479.49
Seychelles	rupee	9.60
Sierra Leone	leone	815.79
Singapore	dollar	3.10
Solomon Islands	dollar	5.57
Somali Republic	shilling	5029.09
South Africa	rand	5.31
Spain	peseta	181.03
Sri Lanka	rupee	84.25
Sudan Republic	Sudanese pound	191.95
Suriname	guilder	3.43
Swaziland	lilangeni	5.35
Sweden	krona	10.31
Switzerland	Swiss franc	2.53
Syria	Syrian pound	38.87
Taiwan	dollar	47.85
Tanzania	shilling	623.47
Thailand	baht	48.58
Togo Republic	CFA franc	479.49
Tonga Islands	pa'anga	2.58
Trinidad and Tobago	dollar	8.16
Tunisia	dinar	1.57

WEIGHTS AND MEASURES

Imperial, with Metric Equivalents

Linear Measure

1 inch (in)	= 25.4 millimetres
1 foot (ft) = 12 inches	= 0.3048 metre
1 yard (yd) = 3 feet	= 0.9144 metre
1 (statute) mile = 1,760 yards	= 1.609 kilometres

Square Measure

1 square inch (in² or sq in)	= 6.45 sq centimetres
1 square foot (ft²) = 144 sq in	= 9.29 sq decimetres
1 square yard (yd² = 9 sq ft	= 0.836 sq metre
1 acre = 4,840 sq yd	= 0.405 hectare
1 square mile (mile²) = 640 acres	= 259 hectares

Cubic Measure

1 cubic inch (in³ or cu in)	= 16.4 cu centimetres
1 cubic foot (ft³) = 1,728 cu in	= 0.0283 cu metre
1 cubic yard (yd³) = 27 cu ft	= 0.765 cu metre

Capacity Measure British

1 pint (pt) = 20 fluid oz = 34.68 cu in	= 0.568 litre
1 quart = 2 pints	= 1.136 litres
1 gallon (gal) = 4 quarts	= 4.546 litres
1 peck = 2 gallons	= 9.092 litres
1 bushel = 4 pecks	= 36.4 litres
1 quarter = 8 bushels	= 2.91 hectolitres

American dry

1 pint = 33.60 cu in	= 0.550 litre
1 quart = 2 pints	= 1.101 litres
1 peck = 8 quarts	= 8.81 litres
1 bushel = 4 pecks	= 35.3 litres

American liquid

1 pint = 16 fluid oz = 28.88 cu in	= 0.473 litre
1 quart = 2 pints	= 0.946 litre
1 gallon = 4 quarts	= 3.785 litres

Avoirdupois Weight

1 grain	= 0.065 gram
1 dram	= 1.772 grams
1 ounce (oz) = 16 drams	= 28.35 grams
1 pound (lb) = 16 ounces = 7,000 grains	= 0.4536 kilogram
1 stone (st) = 14 pounds	= 6.35 kilograms
1 quarter = 2 stones	= 12.70 kilograms
1 hundredweight (cwt) 4 quarters	= 50.80 kilograms
1 (long) ton = 20 hundredweight	= 1.016 tonnes
1 short ton = 2,000 pounds	= 0.907 tonne

Metric, with Imperial (British) Equivalents

Linear Measure

1 millimetre (mm) = 0.039 inch	
1 centimetre (cm) = 10 mm	= 0.394 inch
1 decimetre (dm) = 10 cm	= 3.94 inches
1 metre (m) = 10 dm	= 1.094 yards
1 decametre (dam) = 10 m	= 10.94 yards
1 hectometre (hm) = 100 m	= 109.4 yards
1 kilometre (km) = 1,000 m	= 0.6214 mile

Square Measure

1 square centimetre (cm² or sq cm) = 0.155 sq in	
1 square metre (m²)	= 1.196 sq yards
1 are = 100 sq metres	= 119.6 sq yards
1 hectare (ha) = 100 ares	= 2.471 acres
1 square kilometre (km²)	= 0.386 sq mile

Cubic Measure

1 millilitre (ml)	= 0.002 pint (British)
1 centilitre (cl) = 10 ml	= 0.018 pint
1 decilitre (dl) = 10 cl	= 0.176 pint
1 litre (l) = 10 dl	= 1.76 pints
1 decalitre (dal) = 10 l	= 2.20 gallons
1 hectolitre (hl) = 100 l	= 2.75 bushels
1 kilolitre (kl) = 1,000 l	= 3.44 quarters

Weight

1 milligram (mg) = 0.015 grain	
1 centigram (cg) = 10 mg	= 0.154 grain
1 decigram (dg) = 10 cg	= 1.543 grain
1 gram (g) = 10 dg	= 15.43 grain
1 decagram (dag) = 10 g	= 5.64 drams
1 hectogram (hg) = 100 g	= 3.527 ounces
1 kilogram (kg) = 1,000 g	= 2.205 pounds
1 tonne (metric ton) = 1,000 kg	= 0.984 (long) ton

Temperature

Fahrenheit: water boils (under standard conditions) at 212° and freezes at 32°

Celsius or Centigrade: water boils at 100° and freezes at 0°.

Kelvin: water boils at 373.15 and freezes at 273.15.

°C = 5/9(°F-32)

°F = (9/5°C) + 32

K = °C = 273.15

Wedding Anniversaries

In many Western countries, different wedding anniversaries have become associated with gifts of different materials. There is variation between countries.

anniversary	material
1st	cotton
2nd	paper
3rd	leather
4th	fruit, flowers
5th	wood
6th	sugar
7th	copper, wool
8th	bronze, pottery
9th	pottery, willow
10th	tin
11th	steel
12th	silk, linen
13th	lace
14th	ivory
15th	crystal
20th	china
25th	silver
30th	pearl
35th	coral
40th	ruby
45th	sapphire
50th	gold
55th	emerald
60th	diamond
70th	platinum

Major Holidays 1993

New Year	1 Jan
Ramadan begins	23 Feb
St Patrick's Day	17 March
First day of Passover (Pesach)	6 April
Good Friday	9 April
Easter Day	11 April
Easter Monday	12 April
May Day Holiday	3 May
Feast of Weeks (Shavuot)	26 May
Bank Holiday	31 May
Muslim New Year 1414	21 June
Bank Holiday	30 Aug
Jewish New Year 5754 (Rosh Hashanah)	16 Sept
Day of Atonement (Yom Kippur)	25 Sept
Christmas Day	25 Dec
Boxing Day	26 Dec
Bank Holiday	28 Dec
New Year's Eve	31 Dec

Birthstones

month	stone	quality
January	garnet	constancy
February	amethyst	sincerity
March	bloodstone	courage
April	diamond	innocence and lasting love
May	emerald	success and hope
June	pearl	health and purity
July	ruby	love and contentment
August	agate	married happiness
September	sapphire	wisdom
October	opal	hope
November	topaz	fidelity
December	turquoise	harmony

INDEX